THE OXFORD HANDBOOK

METHODIST
STUDIES

THE OXFORD HANDBOOK OF

METHODIST STUDIES

Edited by

WILLIAM J. ABRAHAM

and

JAMES E. KIRBY

OXFORD
UNIVERSITY PRESS

OXFORD

UNIVERSITY PRESS

Great Clarendon Street, Oxford OX2 6DP

Oxford University Press is a department of the University of Oxford.
It furthers the University's objective of excellence in research, scholarship,
and education by publishing worldwide in

Oxford New York

Auckland Cape Town Dar es Salaam Hong Kong Karachi
Kuala Lumpur Madrid Melbourne Mexico City Nairobi
New Delhi Shanghai Taipei Toronto

With offices in

Argentina Austria Brazil Chile Czech Republic France Greece
Guatemala Hungary Italy Japan Poland Portugal Singapore
South Korea Switzerland Thailand Turkey Ukraine Vietnam

Oxford is a registered trade mark of Oxford University Press
in the UK and in certain other countries

Published in the United States
by Oxford University Press Inc., New York

British Library Cataloguing in Publication Data
Data available

Library of Congress Cataloging in Publication Data
Data available

Library of Congress Control Number: 2009926748

Typeset by SPI Publisher Services, Pondicherry, India
Printed in Great Britain
on acid-free paper by
Ashford Colour Press Ltd.

ISBN 978–0–19–921299–6 (Hbk.)
978–0–19–969611–6 (Pbk.)

1 3 5 7 9 10 8 6 4 2

To Frank Baker, Franz Hildebrandt, Albert Outler, and
David Shipley, pioneer scholars in Methodist Studies

PREFACE

WILLIAM J. ABRAHAM

JAMES E. KIRBY

Methodist Studies emerged as a fresh academic venture in the 1950s with the decision to provide a proper edition of the works of John Wesley. A network of scholars in Britain and the university-related Methodist seminaries in the USA led by Albert Outler of Southern Methodist University, and by Robert Cushman, and Frank Baker at Duke University set about creating what became the *Bicentennial Edition of the Works of John Wesley.* This as yet incomplete effort will furnish the essential tools for future work. This pioneering endeavour has already become the fountainhead of various streams of investigation that have flowed unceasingly without coordination since then. A new generation of students and scholars is now firmly in place, and they are producing a steady stream of texts, university courses, seminars, and conferences watering the field.

Much of the early work has been historical in nature. However, given Albert Outler's ecumenical and broader theological interests, it was clear from the outset that the agenda was as much theological as historical, as much prescriptive as descriptive. Thus, in addition to the historians, there is now a lively, interdisciplinary band of scholars who are at work explaining and mining the history of Methodist ecclesial bodies and movements. Initially such activity was fed by a desire on the part of Methodists to explain themselves to other Christian bodies; more recently it is being motivated by the need for Methodists to find a new identity. The danger of internal schism and a lively debate about the nature of the tradition as a whole has increased the urgency of the enterprise.

Scholarly work on Methodism finds regular outlets in the Oxford Institute of Methodist Theological Studies, the Wesleyan Theological Society, the American Academy of Religion, and a host of ad hoc conferences related to various institutions and celebrations. It spills over into labour on the origins and nature of Pentecostalism and it reaches backwards into exploration of the sources that fed John Wesley and the Methodist Movement as a whole. The work is genuinely ecumenical in nature. There is a spirited interest in Wesley within mainline

Christianity, within Evangelicalism, and within those Wesleyan groups that broke with the mainline in the nineteenth and early twentieth centuries. While much of the scholarship has been carried out by scholars who are rooted in the Methodist traditions, non-Methodist scholars in college and university history departments are making a significant contribution as well. Historians are taking the impact of the Methodists seriously in their increasing interest in the society as a whole and its development.

Given the diversity of work being done and the variety of persons at work, summary statements are risky. However, it is fair to say that four features have marked the work as a whole. First, there has been a determined effort to provide a critical analysis of the life and work of John Wesley. There is also great interest in Charles Wesley and in some other early Methodist leaders, such as Fletcher of Madeley. Significant new biographies of Charles Wesley are now available. The primary interest has been in recovering the historical Wesleys over the hagiographical understanding of the brothers.

Second, considerable attention has focused on the Wesleyan contribution to the problem of authority, most notably on the so-called Wesleyan Quadrilateral of scripture, tradition, reason, and experience. While a few have challenged this notion both as a historical account of Wesley and as a prescriptive option in the epistemology of theology, the Quadrilateral continues to serve as an important legacy of the last generation.

Third, there has been great interest in the relation between Wesley and contemporary forms of liberation theology. This interest stems from Wesley's concern for the poor and from his wider commitment to reforming society; it has received extensive attention over the last thirty years in the Oxford Institute of Methodist Theological Studies.

Fourth, of late there has been a serious endeavour to explore the institutional configurations of Methodism. Methodists were very intentional about their structures and practices; these have naturally evolved over time; hence they are an obvious site of scholarly investigation. Duke Divinity School led a lengthy study that resulted in an important, five-volume set of texts.

It is now time to gather up the extensive work that has been done in the past half-century, to provide a map of the field as a whole, and to offer vistas for fresh work. *The Oxford Handbook of Methodist Studies* was created with these goals in mind. It is our hope that it will evoke a lively discussion on the nature and future of Methodist Studies. While the historical side of the work is very important, we have asked our contributors to move beyond it to develop fresh insights, hypotheses, and perspectives. Each has been invited to speak out of his or her experience and to develop his or her own best judgements about the subject in hand. Many have been selected as representatives of the people called Methodists across the world and to represent in their work the global nature of Methodism today.

We have chosen to use the term 'Methodist Studies' over against, say, 'Wesley Studies' or 'Wesleyan Studies'. The term 'Methodist' was the preferred designation of Wesley and of the movement that he initiated. Hence it has deep historical precedent. Second, while the term 'Wesleyan' has been widely used, it tends to signify a more evangelical and conservative view of the tradition. While we readily acknowledge that this branch of the tradition is extremely important, we prefer a term that will be recognized by everyone but without partisan connotations. Moreover, we wish to signal the fresh departure in the field as a whole. Nothing is set in stone in terms of current designation, but the term 'Methodist' can both reach back into the history and reach forward into new perspectives.

The objectives of this *Handbook* we hope are clear. We sought first to locate the centre of Methodist gravity in John Wesley and the accomplishments of his movement in the history of the church; hence it is crucial to set the tone and direction of the work as a whole by determining how best to characterize his life and work. We are convinced that Wesley belongs first and foremost in the history of piety and holy living in the Protestant tradition. The primary categories that capture what Wesley was and did are those of evangelist, spiritual director, revivalist, and renewalist. This is clearly visible in a host of ways. It shows up in a theology that concentrates on the *via salutis*. It is visible in the plethora of practices, from field preaching to conferencing, that he utilized. It is manifest in his vision of the mission of the church as summed up in his passion to save souls. This vision of Wesley represents a fresh departure from accounts of him that focus on his work as a folk theologian, church reformer, social activist, proto-liberationist, ingenious organizer, and the like.

We attempted, in the second place, to develop an appropriate set of categories sufficient to permit a fruitful and coherent mapping of Methodist Studies as a whole in the present. There is a vast array of study in play, so it is important to provide an illuminating framework that will permit the maximizing of diversity with a minimum of confusion. Our judgement is that Wesley launched a spiritual movement within Western Christianity that continues to express itself along a network of specific channels. What started as a surprising accident in the eighteenth century expressed itself in ecclesial, theological, moral, and political commitments over space and time. Our assumption is that what started as a spiritual experience in Wesley and other early Methodists both evoked and coloured a complex and multifaceted experiment within Western Christianity. Thus Methodism spawned its own characteristic ecclesial forms, spiritual experiences, forms of liturgy and worship, hymnody, theological themes and configurations, evangelistic practices, moral ethos and convictions, social and political impulses, educational institutions, and missionary activities.

Such expressions of the Christian faith are available both as historical precedents and as issues of contemporary decision and debate and are expressed in the chapters of this book. We believe they accurately chart the field of Methodist

Studies in terms of these discrete areas of inquiry. Our aim is both to do justice to current trends and to create space for new trends in the future. Methodism remains a living, dynamic tradition with both a contested record and an unidentified future; we aim to make room for both in the internal organization deployed.

Finally, we sought to recognize and address the reality that Methodism has become a global expression of the Christian faith. While Methodism originated in eighteenth-century England, it spread rapidly in North America and elsewhere. David Hempton, one of our authors, has recently captured this dimension of Methodism as an 'Empire of the Spirit'. While we acknowledge that the primary motivation and resources for Methodist Studies has been strongest in Britain and in the USA, Methodism came to be a worldwide phenomenon that cannot be confined to Anglo-American realities. Today it is constituted by a family of churches with over 75 million members and adherents across the world. To reflect this reality we have drawn heavily on the scholarly expertise both of scholars in North America and the United Kingdom, and of the international representatives of Methodism. We have shied away from superficial surveys and turned to more in-depth studies of Methodism outside Britain and the USA. We are convinced that drilling deep gives a more interesting and illuminating profile of the terrain.

We have sought in each case to match the best scholars in the field with the subject matter in hand. Within these parameters we have taken into account the fact that scholarship has changed over the last generation and now includes a variety of voices that once were muted or ignored. Our desire was to develop a volume that will encourage the full range of talent and interests as scholars seek to unpack and develop the resources of Methodism.

Acknowledgements

We extend our hearty thanks to Jeremy Nagorski for his splendid work in helping us edit this volume, and to Duane Harbin for his assistance with computing. A very special word of thanks goes to Mary Ann Marshall. From the beginning her work on this project has been nothing less than extraordinary. We thank her for her initial advice on organizing the work, for her patience throughout, and most especially for her meticulous attention to detail in the final phase of the operation. We are grateful to Perkins School of Theology, Southern Methodist University, for the many resources furnished to us as scholars in Methodist Studies.

Contents

PART II ECCLESIAL FORMS AND STRUCTURES

PART III WORSHIP: SACRAMENTS, LITURGY, HYMNODY, PREACHING

PART IV SPIRITUAL EXPERIENCES, EVANGELISM, MISSION, ECUMENISM

PART V THEOLOGY

PART VI ETHICS AND POLITICS

List of Contributors

William J. Abraham is Albert Cook Outler Professor of Wesley Studies and Altshuler Distinguished Teaching Professor in Perkins School of Theology at Southern Methodist University, Dallas, Texas.

Thomas R. Albin is Dean of the Upper Room Chapel in Nashville, Tennessee.

Pablo R. Andiñach is President and Professor of Old Testament at Instituto Universitario ISEDET in Buenos Aires, Argentina.

David W. Bebbington is Professor of History at the University of Stirling, Scotland.

Gennifer Benjamin Brooks is Styberg Associate Professor of Homiletics and holds the Ernest and Bernice Styberg Chair of Preaching at Garrett-Evangelical Theological Seminary, Evanston, Illinois.

Barry E. Bryant is Associate Professor of United Methodist and Wesleyan Studies at Garrett-Evangelical Theological Seminary, Evanston, Illinois.

Dennis M. Campbell is Headmaster at Woodberry Forest School, Woodberry Forest, Virginia.

Ted A. Campbell is Associate Professor of Church History in Perkins School of Theology at Southern Methodist University, Dallas, Texas.

David M. Chapman is a Circuit Minister at Horsham, West Sussex, Great Britain.

J. C. D. Clark is Hall Distinguished Professor of British History at the University of Kansas in Lawrence, Kansas.

Kenneth J. Collins is Professor of Historical Theology and Wesley Studies at Asbury Theological Seminary, Wilmore, Kentucky.

Elmer M. Colyer is Professor of Historical Theology and Stanley Professor of Wesley Studies at the University of Dubuque Theological Seminary, Dubuque, Iowa.

Jane Craske is a Circuit Minister in Leeds, Great Britain.

D. Lyle Dabney is Associate Professor of Theology in the Department of Theology of the College of Arts and Sciences at Marquette University, Milwaukee, Wisconsin.

Donald W. Dayton is a retired independent scholar living in Pasadena, California who continues an international ministry of teaching and lecturing.

Thomas Edward Frank is University Professor at Wake Forest University, Winston Salem, North Carolina.

William B. Gravely is Professor Emeritus of Religious Studies, University of Denver, Colorado.

Stanley Hauerwas is Gilbert T. Rowe Professor of Theological Ethics at Duke University Divinity School, Durham, North Carolina.

Elaine A. Heath is McCreless Associate Professor of Evangelism in Perkins School of Theology at Southern Methodist University, Dallas, Texas.

Richard P. Heitzenrater is William Kellon Quick Professor Emeritus of Church History and Wesley Studies at Duke University Divinity School, Durham, North Carolina.

David Hempton is Alonzo L. McDonald Family Professor of Evangelical Theological Studies at Harvard Divinity School, Cambridge, Massachusetts.

Simeon O. Ilesanmi is Washington M. Wingate Professor of Religion at Wake Forest University, Winston Salem, North Carolina.

James E. Kirby is Professor Emeritus of Church History in Perkins School of Theology at Southern Methodist University, Dallas, Texas.

Sarah Heaner Lancaster is Professor of Theology in the Bishop Hazen G. Werner Chair of Theology at Methodist Theological School in Ohio, Delaware, Ohio.

Swee Hong Lim is Assistant Professor of Church Music at Baylor University, Texas.

D. Stephen Long is Professor of Systematic Theology at Marquette University, Milwaukee, Wisconsin.

Robin W. Lovin is Cary M. Maguire University Professor of Ethics at Southern Methodist University, Dallas, Texas.

Manfred Marquardt is Professor Emeritus of Theology, United Methodist Theological Seminary, Reutlingen, Germany.

Philip R. Meadows is Director of Postgraduate Studies at Cliff College, Derbyshire, Great Britain.

Sergei V. Nikolaev is President of the Seminary and E. Stanley Jones Professor of Evangelism at the Russia United Methodist Theological Seminary, Moscow, Russia.

J. Steven O'Malley is John T. Seamands Professor of Methodist Holiness History at Asbury Theological Seminary, Wilmore, Kentucky.

Harold J. Recinos is Professor of Church and Society in Perkins School of Theology at Southern Methodist University, Dallas, Texas.

Russell E. Richey is William R. Cannon Distinguished Professor of Church History in Candler School of Theology at Emory University, Atlanta, Georgia.

Dana L. Robert is Truman Collins Professor of World Christianity and History of Mission and Co-Director of the Center for Global Christianity and Mission at Boston University School of Theology, Massachusetts.

Lester Ruth is Research Professor of Christian Worship at Duke University Divinity School, Durham, North Carolina.

Lamin Sanneh is D. Willis James Professor of Missions and World Christianity and Professor of History at Yale Divinity School, New Haven, Connecticut.

Marjorie Suchocki is Professor of Theology Emerita and co-director of the Center for Process Studies at Claremont School of Theology, California.

Douglas D. Tzan is a Ph.D. student in the History of Christianity at Boston University School of Theology, Massachusetts.

Jason E. Vickers is Associate Professor of Theology and Wesleyan Studies and Director of the Center for Evangelical United Brethren Heritage at United Theological Seminary, Dayton, Ohio.

Geoffrey Wainwright is Robert Earl Cushman Professor of Theology at Duke University Divinity School, Durham, North Carolina.

Jerry L. Walls is Visiting Scholar in the Center for Philosophy of Religion at the University of Notre Dame.

Martin Wellings is Superintendent Minister of the Oxford Methodist Circuit in Oxfordshire, Great Britain and President of the World Methodist Historical Society.

Karen B. Westerfield Tucker is Professor of Worship at Boston University School of Theology in Boston, Massachusetts.

John H. Wigger is Professor of History at the University of Missouri, Columbia, Missouri.

PART I

HISTORY OF METHODISM

CHAPTER 1

THE EIGHTEENTH-CENTURY CONTEXT

J. C. D. CLARK

CHANGES IN THE RECEIVED MODEL OF THE EIGHTEENTH CENTURY

MUCH has changed since 1965, when Sir Herbert Butterfield, introducing an official *History of the Methodist Church*, placed early Methodism in the context of a historical interpretation of its age (Butterfield 1965: 3–33). Then it seemed natural that the fragile experiment of eighteenth-century Methodism should be confidently presented in the light of the self-image, or myth of origins, established by Methodism's numerical explosion and denominational separation in the nineteenth. It seemed equally natural that Methodism should be interpreted against the eighteenth-century context constructed by a yet-unchallenged modernist historiography.

This historiography characterized eighteenth-century Britain in terms of growing secularism and self-interest in society; latitudinarianism and lukewarmness in the church; urbanization, industrialization, and alienation in the economy; the rise of class and of the 'working-class movement' in politics. Such assumptions, prevalent in 1965, differed little from those of the earlier official *History* of 1909 (Townsend 1909a: 77–133, 1909b: 335–78). As late as 1965 Methodist history was the preserve of present-day Methodists: it focused on the inner life of the denomination, with little serious comparison against surrounding religion; it was dominated by a personality cult of John Wesley; and it was often written normatively, to celebrate the presumed action of the Holy Spirit (even Rupp 1986: 453), rather than analytically, to determine the historically accessible role of human agency in Methodism's rise and later decline.

Since 1965, our understanding of eighteenth-century Britain has greatly developed. Then, England was allowed to stand proxy for Wales, Scotland, and Ireland; now, historians explore the contrasts between those societies. By 1909, Methodism looked like a massive international movement, and its followers wished to explain its spread as the ubiquitous success of a consistent formula: the preaching of free grace and the new birth. Yet in the eighteenth century the Welsh, Irish, and Scottish experience showed Wesleyan Methodism to be highly culturally specific, an English formulation that had difficulty in establishing itself beyond the borders of Anglicanism, and showed Whitefield's Methodism to be most successful in colonial North America.

Anglicanism itself has been reassessed in its pastoral and intellectual effectiveness, and Methodism therefore increasingly appears as evidence of the Church's vitality rather than of its somnolence. Modernist historiography blocked an appreciation that the critical reaction of the eighteenth-century church to Methodism had been well-informed, insightful, and sophisticated, but this exclusion is now problematic. It has been shown that the eighteenth century did not see the rise of religious indifference, but of lasting religious conflict, partly between denominations, partly within them, as assertions of natural religion clashed with a still-vital Trinitarian religiosity. It is also clearer that the eighteenth century is not to be labelled 'the Age of Reason'. 'The Enlightenment' was a late nineteenth-century term, imposed retrospectively for reasons that initially had much to do with the attempts of nineteenth-century agnosticism to secure parity of esteem with the church. John Wesley never noticed or commented on any process of secularization at work in his society. On the contrary, he believed in, and saw evidence of, the mass conversion of sinners: this implied a popular psychology eager for religious experience, not indifferent to it. There is today a growing disbelief in the idea of a nascent secular society in which the church was increasingly irrelevant to the state. Of this older world, early Methodism was a part, not a negation.

Politics, too, has been reassessed. As historians have become more aware of the politicization of religion in the long eighteenth century, Wesleyan Methodism's suspected early association with Jacobitism, its opposition to the American Revolution, and its loyalism during the French Revolution now appear as evidence of its intrinsic churchmanship rather than as aberrations from which Methodism's later links with the Liberal and Labour Parties redeemed it. Historians often now downplay the sense in which the Revolution of 1688 marked a break with monarchical rule, signalled the arrival of the 'modern state', or heralded the advent of parliamentary government. There has been a growing acceptance that wars of religion did not cease with the seventeenth century, and that 1688 did not signal any 'rise' of a 'middle class' which, in association with a 'scientific revolution', broke the intellectual hegemony of classical antiquity, of an aristocratic elite, or of hierarchical churches.

Economic historians have scaled down earlier estimates of the overall rate of economic growth; there is a growing acceptance that the 'Industrial Revolution' was another term of historiographical art retrospectively imposed on the eighteenth century in the late nineteenth. It is now appreciated that urbanization, with some exceptions, was not as extensive or as rapid in Wesley's lifetime as was once assumed, and that the age of the great industrial conurbation waited until the 1880s. There was, then, no clear transition to a new world in the eighteenth century; rather, 'modernity' was itself a late nineteenth-century project, retrospectively imposed on the eighteenth. No longer can it be in any broad sense assumed that eighteenth-century Methodism was aided by economic change while its rivals were not.

What this means for our understanding of Methodism has yet to be fully worked out. John Wesley's lifetime was a time of change (like all lifetimes), but not of change on a scale that transformed English society. He did not perceive an 'industrial revolution': although he preached regularly in such growing towns as Birmingham, Doncaster, Glasgow, Leeds, Liverpool, Manchester, Newcastle, Rotherham, Sheffield, Warrington, and Wigan, he drew no connection between industry or urban growth and vital religion. When he commented in his *Journal* of 1 May 1776 that trade had 'amazingly increased' in 'these two last years', he referred by name to counties in the south and south-west of England, as well as to ones in the north associated with manufactures, and offered a non-industrial explanation echoing the perceptions of the 1720s and 1730s: 'such is the fruit of the entire civil and religious liberty which all England now enjoys!' Population increase, too, he recorded, was evident 'not only in every city and large town but in every village and hamlet' (John Wesley 1975– : xxiii. 11–12).

Wesley, like the commercial society of the old order, was not romantic about '*rural life*'. He satirized the Horatian idyll of rural self-sufficiency: 'Our eyes and ears may convince us, that there is not a less happy body of men in all England than the country farmers. In general their life is supremely dull, and it is usually unhappy, too. For of all people in the kingdom, they are most discontented, seldom satisfied either with God or man' (John Wesley 1975– : *Journal*, 5 November 1766, xxii. 66–7). Wesley's mission was often to towns, but not because he saw in towns the face of the future. Indeed his social views, like his politics, came from an older world only now being properly understood. In 1772 Wesley expressed early eighteenth-century attitudes in blaming high prices of foodstuffs on luxury, gin drinking, and 'the enormous taxes' needed to service 'the national debt' (Tyerman 1870–1: iii. 130–4); he did not attribute high prices to burgeoning consumer demand. John Wesley and George Whitefield, to take even the most original characters of early

Methodism, were more children of their age than has been appreciated. In their lifetimes England remained a politico-ecclesiastical society, church and state intimately associated both in high theory and in daily practice; even Wesley's ordination of Methodist preachers was not a thoughtless or merely pragmatic step, but came after long reading in, and debate over, the questions of ecclesiology that still exercised his fellow clergy.

It has been an unexplored paradox that the young John Wesley, although an Arminian, perceived the religious temper of his age in Calvinist or Puritan terms as profoundly corrupt, immoral, and impious. His stance is, however, explicable when compared to his political condemnation of Walpole and George II. As he wrote of Whig and Tory:

How violent soever the conduct of either party seemed to be, yet their animosities were founded upon religion. It was now said, by the Tories, that impiety and heresy were daily gaining ground under a Whig administration. It was said, that the doctrines of the true religion, were left exposed on every side, and open to the attacks of the dissenters and Socinians on one part, and of the catholics on the other. The lower orders of clergy sided with the people in these complaints; while the ministry not only refused to punish the delinquents, but silenced the clergy themselves, and forbade their future disputations on such topics. This injunction answered the immediate purpose of the ministry; it put a stop to the clamours of the populace, but it produced a worse disorder; it produced a negligence in all religious concerns.   (John Wesley 1776: iv. 112, 156–7, 160–1)

It was a perception derived from his parents, but John also echoed their tension between Hanoverian Toryism and Jacobite Toryism. There is still much that we do not know about the early Wesley. His 'new birth' at a religious society in Aldersgate Street, London, on 24 May 1738 is familiar, but little is known about that society. It was evidently formed by James Hutton, bookseller, soon better known as a Moravian; but Hutton was the son of a Nonjuring clergyman, John Hutton; what relation the son's religious society had to the Nonjuring congregation in Aldersgate Street served by John Lindsay remains a question, for Wesley's early spiritual experience has instead been reconstructed in relation to the Moravians (Podmore 1998: 34–6, 42). Wesley was also not alone in having a political past. The young Whitefield was patronized by the Philipps family, baronets and Welsh MPs, finally a Jacobite dynasty into the 1750s; the Stuart loyalties of the earl and countess of Huntingdon were dangerously overt (Schlenther 1997: 27–31). Political allegiances were often fluid, but early Methodism and its social constituencies had closer links to a still-widespread Jacobitism than has yet been appreciated. By the rising of 1745 Whitefield and the Wesleys openly professed loyalty to the Hanoverian monarch, but this did not wholly erase their earlier political predispositions. Early Methodism was not the spiritual arm of Jacobitism; but Methodism and Jacobitism both stemmed from a profound antecedent rejection of the Whig order in ways that scholarship has hardly yet recovered. The nature of threatened revolution in the 1740s, 1770s, and 1790s was very different.

CHANGING MODELS OF METHODISM

Just as historians' views of Methodism's context have developed over time, so too have accounts of Methodism itself, each embodying some truth, each challenged by recent research. First was John Wesley's own image of Methodism as an unplanned development of 'what was afterwards called a *Society*' (John Wesley 1749: 256), its participants 'all zealous members of the Church of England', even when the breach with George Whitefield over the latter's Calvinism produced 'two sorts of Methodists' (John Wesley 1765: 368, 370); the movement being directed by 'many providential incidents', 'a strange chain of providences' (John Wesley 1781: 428, 437). This image was arguably at odds with John Wesley's practice, which involved both planning and an early implicit separation from the church.

Methodism was later explained within the context of an 'evangelical revival' in the English-speaking world, triggered in the late 1730s when 'a small group of men returned to the primitive faith of Christianity and evoked a fervent response in a largely unconverted population' (Kent 2002: 23–5). John Wesley's self-image of Methodism as representing a revival of 'real' or 'vital' religion in protest against the merely 'formal' religion of the church undoubtedly spread to constitute the vision of recent historians who knew little of either. It makes a difference to our analysis of Methodism's role if there was no such revival, but if that revival's alleged features were instead recurrent characteristics of a prevalent religiosity that underpinned Methodism and much else. Even the notion of 'new birth' was not unique to Wesley: the Presbyterian minister Samuel Wright's *A Treatise of Being Born Again: without which no man can be saved*, first appearing in 1715, had reached its sixteenth edition by 1738. Nor was John Wesley the first Methodist to have a conversion experience. His younger brother Charles, Whitefield, and Benjamin Ingham preceded him.

Methodism (and, later, Evangelicalism) may have retrospectively rewritten its own history by its doctrine of instantaneous spiritual justification and assurance. Yet Wesley himself had felt like that before his 'new birth' of 1738. On reading Law's *Serious Call* in 1729, he wrote: 'The light flowed in so mightily upon my soul that everything appeared in a new view' (John Wesley 1975– : xviii. 244). Wesley often later expressed doubts about his religious state: the symptoms of religious rebirth need historical interpretation. And it supports the view that an evangelical revival has been wrongly identified, that Old Dissent (Presbyterians, Congregationalists, Baptists) did not expand in numbers, but contracted substantially, in *c*.1700–1750: Nonconformity was not carried forward by an evangelical tide.

The phenomena of violent conversion, 'strange fits' as Wesley described them (ibid. xix. 54), were not confined to the Methodists: they were present at 'revivals' in Northampton, New England in 1735 (of which Jonathan Edwards wrote); in Scotland at Cambuslang and Kilsyth in 1741, as a result of the preaching of Church of Scotland ministers; and elsewhere in the Church of England, for example at

Everton, where the minister, John Berridge, presided over a revival (ibid. xxi. 195–200, May 1759). They had already been seen in Wales. This disposition to emotional collapse in the face of preaching on sin was evidently widespread in Protestant culture for reasons yet to be fully ascertained.

Present-day historians often contend that they have superseded the model of Methodism as a providential deliverance of English religiosity by internationalizing Methodism, turning it into a particular case of an international evangelical revival (Bebbington 1989; Ward 1992; Noll, Bebbington, and Rawlyk 1994; Ditchfield 1998). It may be, however, that by internationalizing it they have provided a wider setting for an older scenario rather than answering the harder question: why simultaneously in such widely separated cultures? Perhaps 'vital religion' was not 'revived' because it had not previously declined. Whitefield began open-air preaching near Bristol on 17 February 1739. But how could thousands of people be assembled to hear him, and then to hear John Wesley on 2 April? It cannot have been that the church failed to reach the masses: it was ubiquitous, Methodists in the eighteenth century were few. The Wesleys' early ministry in Bristol and elsewhere could reach large numbers because it engaged with an already-existing religious infrastructure including the 'religious societies', flourishing from their foundation in late seventeenth-century high churchmanship. There were many ways in which Methodism drew strength from a prevalent Anglicanism; and John Walsh has argued that Whitefield had a particular role in revitalizing Old Dissent.

Over time, there developed an additional set of explanatory models of Methodism that partly became self-validating as life was drawn to imitate art. The second of these, in the early nineteenth century, was the early historiography of what Methodism had now become: an independent denomination, fuelled by Evangelicalism. This self-image was, however, at odds with earlier experience. There is little evidence that Wesley intended to found a widespread religious movement until after the breach in July 1740 in the religious society meeting at Fetter Lane; and the cause of this breach was a difference over theology, not ecclesiology. Only from the Conference of 1744 did John Wesley begin to regulate the discipline of those in what he now saw as his 'connexion', but the groups that he began to assemble into a network were the result of local initiatives by clergy and Anglican evangelicals, not just the Wesleys (Rack 2002: 213–22). Only from the covenantal agreement of 1752, annually renewed, did the signatories pledge allegiance to each other.

Third was the self-image of Methodism as a reaction to the phenomena of urbanization and industrialization (Townsend 1909b: 340–1). This self-image, too, was not present at the outset. By the Conference of 1791, when Methodist members (narrowly defined) were reported to number 72,476, and when Methodism clearly flourished most in 'the manufacturing and trading Towns', observers such as Joseph Benson, who wrote from Manchester, did not distinguish between the old phenomenon of trade and the new one of manufactures (Benson 1793a: 42). By 1937, however, it seemed self-evident that 'Methodism, on the human side, can be regarded as the child of the Industrial Revolution...Its growth was slow in the decades when industrial endeavour was still sleepy and sluggish. Its expansion increased as the use of machinery extended' (Wearmouth 1947: 1). Methodism, as later historians expressed the same point, was a response to alienation, an attempt to construct order and belonging in a new, insecure, and changing world.

Yet this model did not square with the very diverse occupational make-up of early Methodists, who spanned the range of occupations of a long-established and complex commercial economy with its great numbers of artisans, craftsmen, miners, fishermen, and suchlike: Methodism developed within commerce, and did not wait for manufactures. Methodism was often described by historians in the twentieth century as offering something especially needed by people in a period of profound social and economic change. But no sense of any such function is revealed by John Wesley's or George Whitefield's *Journals*; these men treated the human condition as timeless, and more recent historians have questioned for how many people economic development in the eighteenth century changed life experiences. These two strands of history—the denominational and the economic—have not yet been brought together.

Fourth was the self-image of Methodism as a vehicle for working-class self-consciousness. Despite the continued official expressions of loyalty by Conference for the monarchy, and its keeping clear of party politics, grassroots evidence from the 1790s suggests a changing local reality: Methodist organization promoted democracy while its leaders condemned it. In 1831, William Lovett's National Union of the Working Classes copied its internal structure of class meetings direct from the Methodists; so did Chartism. Later, Methodists (especially Primitive Methodists) were prominent in the formation of non-revolutionary trade unions (Wearmouth 1947: 36–52, 92–3, 126–8, 139–57, 179–222; Moore 1974; Scotland 1981). Yet if 'class' as an idea emerged only in the 1820s and 1830s (Clark 2000: 164–200), it is not clear that the Methodism of the Wesleys and Whitefield had any necessary connection with it.

Fifth was the self-image of Methodism as a vehicle for individual protest. Its authorized history, in 1909, had presented Methodism in Hegelian terms as the embodiment of a 'primary *Idea*', namely 'its emphasis of experience', stemming from a view of the Reformation as 'the protest of individualism' (Workman 1909: 6–7). This developed by the 1960s into Gordon Rupp's formulation 'It *is* among rebel minds and minority groups that we find emerging values' (Davies, George, and Rupp (eds.) 1965–88: i. p. xv), and a characterization of Methodism as 'a concern for the souls and bodies of the disenfranchised' (Heitzenrater 1995: 1). Yet this image of individualism contrasted with the highly communal and coercive quality of the organization that John Wesley devised. Even conversion, which was presented as highly individual, followed highly stereotyped forms.

These historiographical models tended to persist over time, each overlaid but not erased by the next. E. P. Thompson, although famously critical of Methodism's psychological impact on its followers, nevertheless accepted most of the structural analysis within which Methodism had by then been embedded (Thompson 1963). Since then, both elements, the nature of eighteenth-century society and the nature of Methodism within it, have been subject to revision. Especially, Methodism can now be seen as part of a movement occurring simultaneously across Europe and North America; it cannot be explained in English terms alone (Ward 2006).

Methodism, then, was successively redescribed in the light of a series of partly overlapping myths of origin, eventually united around the cult of John Wesley. It is currently in a phase of reassessment as these myths are identified and revised by historical research; as the handful of leading Methodists are reassessed in the context of larger numbers of evangelicals; as Methodism is compared with the church; and as English religion is replaced in an international context.

FOUNDERS AND BOUNDARIES

The historical analysis of Methodism depends on what is included under that label. As John Wesley conceded, by the 1760s the term 'Methodist' was applied to many people: to his followers and to seceders from him such as Thomas Maxfield; to followers of Whitefield and to antinomian seceders from Whitefield such as William Cudworth and James Relly; to evangelicals within the church such as Henry Venn, William Romaine, Martin Madan, and John Berridge; and to some Dissenters of evangelical tone ([John Wesley] 1765: 370–1). Yet their differences were great. Even Wesley and Whitefield differed over 'perfection, irresistible grace, the perseverance of the saints, imputed righteousness, and election and reprobation' (Nightingale 1807: 444–5). The 'movement' at the outset had lacked a clear founding moment and clear boundaries (Heitzenrater 1989). By 1749, however, Whitefield complained that John Wesley was 'monopolising the name Methodist to himself only' (Benyon 1960: 229), and this increasingly became the norm. John Wesley wrote the history of Methodism, and Whitefield was airbrushed out. Yet this was not hard, for Whitefield's legacy was revolution in the 1770s, not organization in the 1740s. Whitefield's own history of the operation of divine grace did not depict an organized movement and omitted the term 'Methodism' (Whitefield 1747).

Methodism had lacked a single founder. According to Charles Wesley, it was he who began the movement at Oxford, and was first called a Methodist; his brother John joined the society six months later (Charles Wesley to Dr. Thomas Bradbury Chandler, 28 April 1785, in Davies, George, and Rupp (eds.), 1965–88: iv. 204). Wesleyanism's history was determined by John's supplanting of Charles. Perhaps John Wesley really emerged as the archetypal English Methodist only with Whitefield's absences in America in 1739–41 and 1744–8; by 1763 even Whitefield was writing of John Wesley as 'that famed leader of the Methodists' (Whitefield 1763: 34).

Yet John Wesley, despite his later personality cult, was not the first instance of a phenomenon that both preceded him and was international. There were earlier such phenomena in German-speaking central Europe, known as Pietism; their relation to Methodism is still being explored. Revivals that did not obviously trigger early English Methodism occurred in Britain's New England colonies (Ward 1992). Wales saw autonomous 'revivals' led by such men as Griffith Jones (1684–1761), Howel Harris (1714–73), and Daniel Rowland (1711?–90); Harris and Rowland both experienced spiritual rebirth in 1735, as did Whitefield; Charles and then John Wesley followed in 1738. A longer continuity has been proposed with similar 'revivals' extending back to early seventeenth-century Scotland (Schmidt 2001: 49, 215), of which the events at Cambuslang and Kilsyth in 1741 were only the latest. The larger question for historians, not yet fully answered, is why a shared religious experience was observed nearly simultaneously in some areas of Protestantism but not in others. This suggests that the commonalities between 'Protestant' churches have been exaggerated, but historians have seldom yet explored this possibility.

Even within England, many other evangelists were the catalysts for the emergence of religious societies, and built up connexions around themselves. One such group was served by Benjamin Ingham (1712–72), influenced by the Wesleys at Oxford, ordained in 1735 but pursuing an independent ministry as an itinerant evangelist in Yorkshire and the north from 1739. By 1756 he claimed six preachers serving some thousand members; in that year, although only in deacon's orders in the Church of England, he even ordained two preachers himself. John Wesley resisted his overtures for reunion (Baker 1970: 130; Charles Wesley 1849: ii. 122). John Cennick (1718–55), expelled by John Wesley from the connexion in 1741 for his Calvinism, responded with a preaching tour of his own that led to the formation of the Wiltshire Association, a Calvinist network, and another network in Ulster from 1746 (Lewis 1995). There were many more, and their experience of 'new birth' was normally independent, not owed to the influence of what came to be called Methodism.

Whitefield's followers also had a prominent role, overlapping with Lady Huntingdon's Connexion and the Welsh Calvinistic Methodists. Whitefield had a small scattering of chapels. The countess of Huntingdon had eight formally associated with her by her death in 1791, but between fifty-five and eighty that were informally associated and often later became Congregationalist. That Wesley's following eventually became far larger may be explained partly in terms of Whitefield's unstable character, bad judgement, and conflicts with potential allies: in 1748 he recorded that the thousands that flocked to hear him preach in the 1730s had dwindled to a hundred (Schlenther 2004); by the 1760s he had become a target of satire for the London stage and for William Hogarth, as he already had for the novelist Henry Fielding. A comparison of John Wesley and Whitefield emphasizes how very mixed the fortunes of early Methodism were.

The greater historical problem is not the founding of Methodism in the 1730s, for many similar initiatives can be traced at that time, but the emergence of Wesley's connexion in the 1770s and 1780s as the paradigm case (the group to which the title 'Methodist' was often confined) and its later numerical growth. Despite John Wesley's outspoken loyalism during the American Revolution, it may be that this emerging prominence for his connexion had something to do with the rise of extra-parliamentary popular political activity from the 1760s, recently recovered by other historians but hardly yet integrated into Methodist history.

THE RECEPTION OF METHODISM

A historical appraisal of Methodism demands a serious comparison with the church; this has almost never been done (see, however, Baker 1970; Hempton 1996). Historians tended instead to identify Anglicanism with patriarchy and deference, to argue that these were in decline, and to treat Methodism as an agent of that decline. Yet it is now clear that most people continued in the church, despite other forms of religion on offer; that early industrial ventures were often patriarchal, but in a new way; and that early Methodism throve most within Anglicanism, whether in England, Ireland, or North America, extending Anglican religiosity more than negating it. Methodism's message was probably handicapped in its appeal within a predominant Anglicanism by its doctrines, widely regarded as implausible, of immediate conversion, Christian perfection, and (in Whitefield's case) final perseverance. That Methodist 'hearers' outnumbered 'members' by at least four to one is usually interpreted as a mark of Methodist strength; it might better be interpreted as a sign of the wide unacceptability of Methodism's peculiar doctrines and the disciplinary structure of band and class meetings, even among those impressed by Methodists' sincerity and piety. This ratio might be evidence that people shared Sydney Smith's complaint that Methodism coarsened and overfamiliarized the sacred truths of a shared faith (Smith 1808), or Sir Walter Scott's attitude in 1826: that Methodism was good because 'it introduces morality among people who would never practice it unless it came recommended by a faith which addresses itself to the passions. But [it] seems to [be] an awful priestcraft concern' (Scott 1932–7: ix. 400–2).

Methodism was indeed difficult to assess, then and later. Together with the dedication and the devotion went mass hysteria and, sometimes, fraud: on 5 August 1740 Charles Wesley reproved a girl, Jenny Deschamps, 'who confessed that her fits and cryings out (above thirty of them) were all feigned, that Mr Wesley might take notice of her' (Charles Wesley 2008: i. 276). Methodism, like Old Dissent, was also an implicit challenge to social hierarchy. The Wesleys were respectable, but those caught up in the wider movement were very varied: one Wesleyan Methodist in c.1758–9, in Dover and Sandwich (and possibly in London in 1766–7) was evidently Thomas Paine (Keane 1995: 46–9, 61–2, 501, 544). Even John Wesley himself could arouse mixed reactions. On 26 April 1738, the month before his 'new birth', the trustees of the Georgia colony accepted his implicit resignation as their clergyman there, as Lord Egmont recorded 'with great pleasure, he appearing to us to be a very odd mixture of a man, an enthusiast and at the same time a hypocrite, wholly distasteful to the greater part of the inhabitants, and an incendiary of the people against the magistracy' (Egmont 1920–3: iii. 481).

In 1965, Gordon Rupp, writing of the sermons of John Wesley and George Whitefield, phrased the central problem as it then appeared: 'Why should a set of ideas, none of them original, which had long been inert and dormant, be able to strike deeply into the minds of many thousands of men and women?' (Davies, George, and Rupp 1965–88: i. p. xviii). Today historians doubt whether those ideas had in fact been so 'inert and dormant' in the decades before Whitefield and Wesley. On the contrary, Methodism may be analysed as evidence of the strength of English popular religiosity rather than of a spiritual vacuum (Sommerville 1977; Jacob 1996). If so, it may be that in such a setting Methodism's special doctrines were more of a hindrance than a help.

A proper historical appraisal of Methodism would therefore need to give a balanced attention to the writings of Methodism's supporters and its critics (Green 1902; Lyles 1960; Roberts 1988; Field 1991); but this is almost never done. Opposition to Methodism has seldom been reconstructed from original sources, and so has often been parodied: the self-interest of corrupt churchmen, snobbery, a fear of levelling tendencies, or (inconsistently) an early fear of Jacobite associations. Yet although these themes might have appeared in mob passions, they seldom found their way into anti-Methodist writings. Nor were churchmen alone, for Old Dissent was equally critical: Richard Price, Nonconformist minister and Arian, deplored how 'the lower orders of people...are sinking into a barbarism in religion lately revived by Methodism, and mistaking, as the world has generally done, the service acceptable to God for a system of faith souring the temper, and a service of forms supplanting morality' (Price 1789: 16).

Methodism is also generally assessed with the benefit of hindsight, in the light of its later course as a respectable mass movement. But Whitefield's and Wesley's contemporaries reacted instead against a tiny minority taking extreme positions: a growing populist and anticlerical dismissal of the existing clergy, established and Dissenting, as ungodly; a denial that existing members of the church were really Christians at all; a latent promise, or threat, of social transformation; even what might seem to be a claim to work miracles. Parishioners often reacted with indignation to the implication, or the rhetorically heightened allegation, that they were Godless, or that their good works were valueless. Methodist accounts of their own religious experience (for example, the knowable attainment of Christian perfection) might often have seemed implausible, and were sometimes rejected as hypocritical. If the church refused institutionally to adapt to Methodism, there were good reasons for not doing so. If parishioners rejected Methodism, they might soon find many of its more acceptable components within the Church in a burgeoning Evangelicalism whose moderate Calvinism may have set powerful limits to the expansion of Wesleyanism (Kent 2002: 140–86).

The critical reaction to John Wesley and George Whitefield in their lifetimes heavily outweighed the approval; and early criticisms came from an impressive array of scholars including Samuel Hallifax, Thomas Herring, George Horne, Thomas Randolph, Thomas Rutherforth, Richard Smalbroke, Henry Stebbing, Augustus Toplady, and Daniel Waterland. The seven volumes of Whitefield's *Journals* published between 1738 and 1741 gave his opponents ample ammunition. They made public what Whitefield had asserted in America: 'he took the Bishop of *London* [Edmund Gibson] to be no better a Judge, or knew more of Christianity, than *Mahomet*, or an Infidel; and that he was now proving him to be such'; that one of Gibson's books 'was sufficient to send Thousands to Hell; as also Archbishop *Tillotson*, and the Author of the *Whole Duty of Man*' (Stephens 1742: ii. 307–8). Charles Wesley recorded that his advice that Whitefield's journal not be published was 'overruled' (Charles Wesley 1849: i. 126). John Wesley followed suit, with two volumes of his *Journal* appearing in 1740, and more volumes in 1742, 1744, 1749, 1753, 1754, 1756, 1759, and later (John Wesley 1975– : xviii. 120, 217; xix. 1, 115, 225; xx. 1, 149, 291, 404). Only six months after ordination as a priest, Whitefield was claiming that 'the whole world is now my parish', defying the church's requirement for a call to a particular living. The open avowal of direct divine intervention in the world, and of diabolical intervention, ran counter to developing ideas on the nature of miracle and providence. To unpersuaded readers, these journals could be evidence of remarkable egotism and of implausible claims to direct divine commission that some churchmen, such as Joseph Trapp, even termed blasphemous.

Methodism can be analysed in several ways, but it seems less plausible to treat it as a challenge by reawakened faith to somnolence; increasingly it seems to have had elements of sectarian challenge to rational religion. Early Methodist religiosity may have been closer to the sectarian religion of the 1640s than it later appeared. In such a setting, often-quoted Anglican reactions become more intelligible. Joseph Butler, bishop of Bristol, who interviewed John Wesley three times in August 1739, cited Whitefield's published *Journal*, and (during lengthy and careful conversations) commented: 'Sir, the pretending to extraordinary revelations and gifts of the Holy Ghost is a horrid thing, a very horrid thing.' Wesley replied that Whitefield must answer for himself, and only countered that he, Wesley, did not pretend to such revelations or gifts 'but what every Christian may receive'. Where the bishop complained that Wesley was not authorized to preach in Butler's diocese, Wesley replied that, having been ordained on the title of his Oxford fellowship, he had 'an indeterminate commission' to preach anywhere; again, this did not apply to Whitefield or to others. We have only Wesley's account of these meetings (John Wesley 1975– : xix. 471–4); but even there Butler, perhaps the most able Anglican theologian of his age, did not speak rashly.

Although Butler did not reply in print, his chaplain, Josiah Tucker, whom Wesley remarkably charged with holding that 'there needs no atonement for original sin', did so. Tucker's sophisticated analysis traced the problem to the contradictory borrowings from both Calvinism and Arminianism in William Law, Whitefield's and Wesley's common 'master', a theological confusion that they both failed to understand (Tucker 1742). Tucker's claim deserves historical investigation: that the schism between Wesley and Whitefield, immensely damaging as it was to the Methodist cause, was due not to a conflict between Arminianism and Calvinism but to a confusion over the content of those systems.

Butler had gone at once to what Anglicans meant by 'enthusiasm'. Samuel Johnson had a similarly insightful objection.

Speaking of the *inward light*, to which some methodists pretended, he said, it was a principle utterly incompatible with social or civil security. 'If a man (said he,) pretends to a principle of action of which I can know nothing, nay, not so much as that he has it, but only that he pretends to it; how can I tell what that person may be prompted to do? When a person professes to be governed by a written ascertained law, I can then know where to find him'. (Boswell 1791: sub 1770, Dr. Maxwell's report)

An unknown churchman put the same point in a remarkably perceptive analysis, framed as anonymous private letters to Wesley in 1745–8. 'John Smith' showed how Wesley had given 'an evasive answer' to his critics and engaged in a 'shifting of the question'. Wesley's general response was indignantly to disclaim responsibility for Whitefield's teaching, and to complain that he was damned by association with others, also called Methodists; so that when a critic 'has linked them together by one *nickname* he may hang either instead of the other!' Smith replied that he had distinguished between Wesley and 'so weak and empty a person as Mr. Whitefield'. He pointed out that although Wesley claimed to have no 'singularities' in doctrine, Methodists in fact did, notably 'unconditional predestination, perceptible inspiration, and sinless perfection'; even Wesley denied the first. Yet, in debate, 'you distinguished away all that sounded peculiar, and pleaded that you maintained no singular doctrines at all'. As to instantaneous rebirth, Smith replied: 'the experience of mankind, the general tenor of the Word of God, and the nature of the thing, all in my opinion make evidently and flatly against you'. Wesley's position on 'perceptible inspiration' and salvation by faith, Smith argued, rested on the premise that the inner working of 'the divine Spirit on the human spirit' could be as clearly known as the outward fruits of such influence; Smith contended: 'I maintain that it is a work so slow and gentle as to be altogether imperceptible.' To those who agreed, the claims of Methodists about the working of God in them might seem to be unprovable claims to special revelation (John Wesley 1975– : ii. 138–46, 153–61, 164–72, 175–90, 197–207, 209–15, 229–37, 238–42, 244–52, 258–61, 287–94, at 141, 170, 181, 183, 188, 213).

The writings of churchmen on the Methodist question were extensive, sophisticated, and continued for decades. One key pamphlet, attributed to Edmund Gibson, Bishop of London, took a legalistic approach, censuring Methodist preachers for not qualifying themselves under the Toleration Act; it warned of 'that Spirit, which had caused so much Confusion in the Kingdom' before the Restoration thanks to the 'unbounded Licentiousness in holding Assemblies for Divine Worship'. Field preaching was specifically forbidden by the Act of 22 Car. II, c. 1; the Toleration Act itself applied only to those who previously notified their fixed places of worship to the bishop, archdeacon, or JP. The Methodists' 'exalted' idea of religion would put it beyond reach of many, and negate 'a careful and sincere Observance of *Moral Duties*'. Regular religious observance was a better form of devotion than 'those sudden Agonies, Roarings and Screamings, Tremblings, Droppings-down, Ravings and Madnesses' referred to in Wesley's and Whitefield's *Journals*. The doctrine of perfection would only lead to 'a *Contempt*' of those who were 'gradually *working out*' their Salvation', and leading 'the Inferiors' to 'a Disesteem of their Superiors' who were 'regular Attendants on the Ordinances of Religion'. Was 'a *sudden* and *instantaneous*' accession of grace really reliable? Were unlicensed itinerants, leading to 'a *Disesteem*' of parish clergy, in the best interests of religion? Was Whitefield right to call the clergy 'those blind Leaders of the Blind…no better than Wolves in Sheeps-cloathing', urge the burning of Archbishop Tillotson's works, and claim that 'Thousands' had been 'miserably deceived' by *The Whole Duty of Man*? Methodism was promoted by 'a few young Heads' who 'set up their own Schemes, as the great Standard of Christianity', persuading those who had lived 'from their Infancy under a Gospel Ministry' that they had not 'been instructed in the true Way of Salvation before'. Did Methodists not make '*extraordinary Pretences* of God directing and assisting them'? Were they not attempting 'to erect a new Church-Constitution, upon a *foreign* Plan'? An anthology of effusive and extravagant language, quoted from leading Methodist authors, provided impressive chapter and verse ([Gibson] 1744: 3–4, 9–13).

This pamphlet was anonymous, but Gibson had criticized Whitefield in a pastoral letter of 1739, and similar criticisms would appear in his *Charge* of 1746–7 (Gibson 1739, 1747). Wesley suspected Gibson to be the author of the pamphlet of 1744, and his reply was a careful response, item by item, in which he denied that the *Observations* had produced evidence to substantiate its claims. This was often true (the pamphlet was a brief one), but did not establish that such evidence did not exist. Wesley's other responses were more revealing. He insisted that he urged his followers to attend church, obey its ordinances, and receive 'the sacrament' there;

but his account of such 'attendance' was that he himself had practised it for many years, yet 'during that whole time I had no more of the love of God than a stone'. Wesley, indeed, had no real doctrine of the church. The extreme symptoms of his congregations he attributed to God's pleasure; 'I cannot hinder it.' The '*sudden* and *instantaneous* change' of the new birth can be 'distinguished from fancy and imagination' easily, 'Just as easily as light from darkness.'

On such key points, Wesley's position was a flat assertion, clarified and made plausible only by splitting the charges against him into their smallest components. Similarly Wesley defended himself against the allegation of 'enthusiasm', by which men meant 'a sort of religious madness; a *false imagination* of being inspired by God; and by an enthusiast, one that *fancies* himself under the influence of the Holy Ghost, when in fact he is not' by the bald statement: 'Let him prove me guilty of this who can.' Yet in defending the present-day operation of the Holy Ghost, Wesley only contended: 'I do not mean that Christians now receive the Holy Ghost in order to work miracles', as the apostles did at Pentecost; but he did not explain why not (John Wesley 1744–5: 121–2, 127, 170–2). John Wesley's own cast of mind was often coolly rational, but this was not a conclusive argument even in his case, let alone in the cases of undisciplined and emotional members of the wider movement. Indeed, Wesley struggled to purge his connexion of just such followers. But when he heard one such layman, Thomas Maxfield, preach, Wesley changed his mind, and accepted that laymen might be called of God to do just that.

In defending the movement as a whole, Wesley was on weaker ground. Smal-broke charged that Wesley and Whitefield disagreed; Wesley replied that in 'our fundamental doctrines…we do and have agreed for several years', ignoring the rending controversies that were lastingly to split Methodism and leave a large part of the evangelical movement within the church. Without any profound theological understanding of the nature of the church, Wesley insisted, in legalistic language, that his followers did not dissent from it, and so had no need of the Toleration Act, and, since they did not intend sedition, were not covered by 22 Car. II, c. 1. As to the effects of his teaching, Wesley stressed the political loyalty of Methodism and its effect in promoting respectable manners, but appealed explicitly to the subversive example of the apostles. Such were 'these "floods of ungodliness" that are still continually pouring in' that any conduct by Methodists, Wesley implied, was justified. As to doctrine, he insisted that it mattered not what his followers believed: 'Whether they embrace this religious opinion or that is no more concern to me than whether they embrace this or that system of astronomy.' But this was hardly the case, as his continued campaigns against Calvinist predestination showed (John Wesley 1744–5: 172–3, 180, 186–7, 318, 323).

Wesley's similarly passive-aggressive reply to Gibson of 1747 by implication shifted most of the blame for the excesses of Methodism onto Whitefield, and seemed to use refinements to avoid the allegation that he, Wesley, taught the possibility of sinless perfection. Wesley's defence was that he personally was not guilty as charged, but he did not deny that the wider movement had the general features often attributed to it. He defended himself and his brother effectively against the allegation that their irregular ministry was for their own financial gain, but he omitted to mention his dubious fellow-labourer (John Wesley 1747: 336, 339, 344–5, 348). Once again, Whitefield, whose financial dealings were questioned, and nameless local Methodist preachers, were Wesley's great embarrassments.

Gibson's 'foreign Plan' was made explicit by George Lavington, bishop of Exeter, in a best-selling work to which John Wesley felt obliged to write three replies (John Wesley 1975– : xi. 359, 377, 431). Lavington drew a comparison between the 'wild and pernicious Enthusiasms', the claims to 'Extraordinary Revelations' and 'Extraordinary Assistance' made by Methodists and 'Papists', thereby drawing on English memories of both Reformation and Civil War to argue that 'this new dispensation is a Composition of Enthusiasm, Superstition, and Imposture'. Methodists were evasive: sometimes 'they seem to disclaim Miracles', at other times 'they seem to retain them' ([Lavington] 1749–51: i. pp. iii, 58, 79; ii. 50). Lavington's lengthy comparison with 'Popery' seems, to present-day readers, laboured and protracted; in its time, it spoke effectively to still-powerful anti-Catholicism, a prejudice that John Wesley fully shared, and to anti-sectarianism.

This charge continued: the degree of authoritarian organization of Methodists was such, wrote another observer in 1830, that it could only be compared with the Jesuits ([Aspland] 1831: 3–4; Methodism 1779: 3; Douglas 1814: 5–6). The church's historical sense was well developed: one commentator in 1752 placed Methodism within a history of 'Enthusiasts' that included the Family of Love, the Covenanters, the sects of the 1640s, the New England persecutors of witches, Quakers, Cameronians, and Fifth Monarchy Men (Evans 1752: p. v). In 1820, another edition of Lavington appeared with a 312-page introduction in which the editor fitted Methodism into the history of Puritanism from the reign of Elizabeth I. But his assessment was not wholly negative: the main effect of Methodism, according to Richard Polwhele, an Anglican priest, had been to stimulate a rallying to the church and a reassertion of its doctrine (Polwhele 1820: pp. i–xxv, cxv–cxvi). This thesis deserves exploration.

William Warburton, an aggressive satirist, by then bishop of Gloucester, pursued similar themes in 1763. He rehearsed some familiar points against Methodists in the central section of a treatise on the operation of grace, equally an attack on free-thinkers such as Conyers Middleton and on enthusiasts, primarily Wesley. Wesley, he claimed, pretended to 'some extraordinary measure of the Spirit', although such gifts had ceased with the early church (he thereby associated Wesley with contemporary 'Popery'); 'the features of modern Fanaticism' could be seen in 'the famed Leader of the Methodists, Mr. John Wesley... this extraordinary man hath, in fact, laid claim to almost every Apostolic gift and grace'. Wesley's 'Enthusiasm consists in believing those benefits' received by his followers 'to be miraculously conferred, thro' a change in the established course of Nature'. Wesley went through the texts Warburton cited from his Journal, and replied: 'But what does all this prove? Not that I claim any gift above other men; but only that I believe God now hears and answers prayer, even beyond the ordinary course of nature' but did not deal with the central point of the persistence to the present of direct divine and diabolical intervention in human affairs. Warburton complained of 'a *fanatic manner* of preaching', so that Wesley's sermons were 'attended with tumults and disorders'; Wesley only replied, without evidence, that field preaching 'has no such effect', and did not discuss the preaching of other Methodists. Warburton drew an analogy between Methodism and the Puritans and Independents of the seventeenth century, notably the testimony of the regicides on the eve of execution 'upon the subjects of Faith, Grace, Redemption, Regeneration, Justification, &c.'; Wesley refused to enter into historical analysis. Warburton put his finger on Wesley's passive-aggressive stance: 'He wanted to be persecuted', and was frustrated to live in a land of toleration (Warburton 1762: 116–17, 119, 169, 181, 186–7, 229; John Wesley 1763: 468, 474, 482, 484). In dialectical skill, the Oxford don had the better of his autodidact opponent; in point of substance, Methodism was neither fairly charged nor fully exonerated.

George Whitefield, whom Warburton termed 'much the madder of the two' (Warburton 1762: 250), also replied, not dealing with Warburton's arguments and only asserting, with loose rhetoric, that the bishop 'denies and ridicules the standing and unalterable operations of the Holy Ghost' in the present day (Whitefield 1763: 8, 31). Whitefield was wholly unable to deal with the formidable theological objections against Methodism. Only John Wesley, among early Methodists, had the intellectual calibre to do so, and his acute but sometimes evasive publications probably established his personal integrity more than they persuaded the intelligentsia of the truth of his theology. Far more typical was the repeated insistence by churchmen that 'sudden Conversion . . . is not the ordinary Method of God's Proceedings with those that have been regenerated by Baptism . . . the Purification of the Heart is a gradual work' (Tottie 1766: 19).

The reaction of Anglican theologians is understandable. But why did so many ordinary people react so violently against early Methodism? If the mobs that attacked Methodist preachers were sometimes encouraged to do so by gentry, clergy, or their agents, why did so many people answer that prompting? As we now appreciate, the claim of access to an inner light provided a discourse of social empowerment in the 1740s as much as in the 1640s, and this would be clearly understood by those who sided with custom as well as by those who sided with reason in opposing 'enthusiasm'. Increasingly, historians see Hanoverian Britain not as a somnolent and stable oligarchy, but as an unstable and divided society, keenly debating and seeking to solidify its grounds for stability; in such a setting Methodists would be resented by more than embraced their message. If Methodism was seen as the enemy within, this does not necessarily signal unthinking religious indifference.

When local populations turned violently on Methodist preachers, was this always the result of spiritual blindness or of violence (as the preachers memorably depicted it, and as it sometimes was) or sometimes of a realistic insight by those who were part of a churchmanship that had already taken on the nature of a folk religion? Did they rightly see that Methodists were the disruptive force they claimed not to be? The riots were written up by Methodist itinerants as crude, unthinking violence; but the reassessment of popular action pioneered by historians in the 1960s and 1970s now calls these early accounts in question. It may be as noteworthy that mobs could be mobilized so easily against the Methodists as that Methodist preachers could assemble open-air congregations of thousands (Walsh 1972; Snape 1998).

We still lack studies of the response to Methodism by the church and by 'Old Dissent'. Although the Wesleys and the Whitefields had a high sense of their own importance, it is remarkable that Methodism still apparently attracted little attention from an efficient and industrious clergyman such as Thomas Secker, bishop of Bristol 1735–7 and of Oxford 1737–58, archbishop of Canterbury 1758–68. He did urge his clergy 'We have in Fact lost many of our People to Sectaries by not preaching in a Manner sufficiently evangelical', but did not name the Methodists (Secker 1766: 299; cf. id. 1988, 1991; Ingram 2007). Not until the 1790s did this clerical indifference change. Yet if the church failed to deal with Methodism, Methodists equally failed to deal with Anglican objections. It remains for historians to ask whether these objections were effective in limiting Methodist growth until the early nineteenth century. Even by that stage, doctrinal differences were held to be decisive. As a Methodist wrote in 1834, their doctrine required 'that *present* and *entire* sanctification of soul, which is absolutely necessary to our ultimate admission into the Kingdom of Heaven. The difference is so great that—unless the Clergy, as a body, are prepared to embrace the doctrinal views of the Methodists, on these essential points of Christian doctrine—there *can be no union*' (Vevers 1834: 13).

Historians have debated the arguments for Methodism's pastoral success without examining their major premise; but how successful was it? It is easy in retrospect to trace an exponential growth in Methodist numbers and to assume its inevitability, like figures for increasing cotton output. It may be asked whether this inevitability has been historically demonstrated. The first figures for overall Methodist membership numbers were given to the Conference of 1766. Although the Canterbury, Devon, London, and Oxfordshire circuits had failed to forward returns, the rest of England managed only 19,267 members. With the missing figures, the total for England was reported in 1767 as 25,211, Wales as 232, and Scotland as 468. Even by 1783, the figures were: England 38,932; Wales 487; Scotland 523; Ireland 6,053 (Kent 2002: 68). These were not impressive numbers for a movement whose starting point is conventionally set in 1738. Moreover, visitation returns sent to bishops of the established church often treated the early Methodist presence in the countryside tolerantly, describing it, where it existed, as small, under-resourced, and unimportant (ibid. 69).

It was initially unclear what Methodists' aims ultimately were: to reform the established church from within, or to create new alternative structures for Christian practice? Numerically, in the eighteenth century, Wesley's gains looked impressive only because his starting point was so low. It was Evangelicalism within the church, by addressing the elite (which Wesley repudiated) that exercised the larger influence in England into the early nineteenth century (Brown 1961; Hilton 1988). Methodism's greatest numerical gains came after Wesley's death, and the greatest gains of all were overseas, especially in the new United States. But that cultural context was so different, and the American variant so distinctive, that it may not be historically justifiable to treat world 'Methodism' by c.1900 as being essentially the same phenomenon as that which John Wesley shaped in the 1740s in Bristol and London. The name remained; the reality changed.

METHODISM AND REVOLUTION

Was Methodism's immediate political impact to avert revolution in the 1790s? This issue was familiar at the time. As a Methodist addressed a bishop in 1834,

Your lordship cannot have forgotten the awful state of things in this country, at the period of the French Revolution, when the sentiments and maxims of the infidel writers of that country, were imbibed with voracious avidity by the peasantry of Great Britain; and when such was the excitement which pervaded the nation, that 'One part of the kingdom looked on the other with the stern and relentless glance of keepers, who are restraining madmen; while the others bent on them the furious glare of madmen conspiring revenge on the keepers' (Sir Walter Scott). At this crisis, my Lord, how did the successors of the patriotic Wesley act?

Their loyalty was apparent in the Conferences of 1792, 1793, 1798, 1812, 1817, and 1818 (Vevers 1834: 27–9).

In 1878, Lecky was clear about the role of Methodism in averting revolution, but argued that 'The Methodist movement was a purely religious one.' His explanations for it were wholly biographical, and that Methodism constituted 'an extraordinary revival of the grossest superstition', conducted by an 'appalling system of religious terrorism'. Nevertheless, Lecky considered that among the 'many causes' why 'England . . . escaped the contagion' of the 'revolutionary spirit' sweeping Europe 'a prominent place' must be given to 'the new and vehement religious enthusiasm', both within the church and in Methodism (Lecky 1878–90: ii. 598, 633, 637–7, 642, 691–2). Elie Halévy later attached his name to the same thesis (Halévy 1906, 1912, 1924, 1949: 424–5, 427–8; id. 1971; Olsen, 1990). He interpreted Methodism as a reassertion of the Puritanism that he believed to constitute the English national character, and he believed that the new industrial proletariat, susceptible to Methodism, was incapable of independent action. It needed leadership; the Methodists provided it. But Halévy offered only a few suggestions, with no worked-out argument, no mass of evidence, no appreciation of religion as religion. His case was set out briefly, on the basis of almost no academic research into the local phenomena.

Without this research, historians usually agreed. But Bishop George Horne thought otherwise, arguing in 1800 that English Jacobins, deterred from open irreligion, were adopting a different strategy: 'to affect a great zeal for orthodoxy; to make great pretensions to an extraordinary measure of the Holy Spirit's influence; to alienate the minds of the people from the Established Clergy, by representing them as sordid worldlings'; meanwhile 'the real Methodist . . . is kept in utter ignorance' of this design (Horsley 1800: 19–20). Others wrote against Methodists in extreme terms (Walsh 1965: 303–4). If Methodists respected John Wesley's injunction to avoid politics, that did not make them active loyalists, like John Reeves's Association for the Preservation of Liberty and Property against Republicans and Levellers; it made them quietists (Taylor 1935: 12). 'We endeavour to "lead a quiet and peaceable life in all godliness and honesty"' (Bradburn 1794: 26). At most, they preached the acceptance of inequalities of property, even poverty, as a providential dispensation that made possible the practice of virtue; that the Methodists were the virtuous remnant in the nation who averted the wrath of God (Walsh 1965: 304–6). But this was not enough to shield Methodists from criticism in the 1790s. The *Anti-Jacobin* attacked them, as did many zealous friends of the established order; Methodists responded in kind, demanding religious liberty and invoking the rights of man. Alexander Kilham (1762–98), campaigning for democratic egalitarian reform within Methodism, argued that 'We all have an equal right to vote in these [denominational] matters'; the government of Methodism 'is not so perfect as it ought to be, and therefore must have a few more revolutions before it is fully established' (Kilham 1795: 36, 60).

There was a latent threat even within Wesleyan Methodism: its professions of loyalty to church and king in the 1790s could easily seem intended to disarm criticism rather than to meet the point that its critiques of the established clergy for enjoying '*affluence, ease* and *honour*' but not performing their duties (Benson 1793*a*: 33, 41, 55, 58) were not intended to reform the church but to redefine its relation to the state and even to deny the 'validity' of the ordination of at least one of its clergy compared with that of Methodist preachers. As Joseph Benson addressed the curate of Pershore, 'You know not yet what Christianity is!' (Benson 1793*b*: 62–4, 67, 71, 84). It is not clear that Methodism was the bulwark against revolution that Halévy depicted. In recent decades it has become apparent that the main bulwark against revolution was the church itself, and that a main engine of revolution in the English-speaking world remained denominational conflict.

If the Methodism of the 1740s is to be understood in part as an Anglican enterprise in social control, the evolution of Methodism in the direction of Dissent may have limited the movement's ability to provide an underpinning for society. Despite the formal loyalty of many of the leaders into the age of Jabez Bunting, many Methodists on the ground increasingly stood aside from the Anglican ascendancy and eventually became more hostile to it than was Old Dissent. Early Methodists often attended their parish church with more regularity, but by 1781 it was objected that Methodists show 'an ill-placed, uncharitable severity and censoriousness . . . chiefly directed against the regular Clergy' (Mainwaring 1781: 16). By 1820, after John Wesley's restraining influence was no more, an Anglican vicar in Cornwall, a stronghold of Methodism, drew a comparison between Methodists and Cromwellians: 'We see the same levelling spirit, the same indifference to rank or station, the same insolent contempt of authority, the same disposition to riot and rebellion' (Polwhele 1820: p. cxcvi).

Historians of this question have focused too narrowly on the 1790s, and on Wesley. Whitefield's impact was quite different, but in the colonies: as early as in 1764 he had announced influentially in New England that 'My heart bleeds for *America*. . . There is a deep laid plot against both your civil and religious liberties, and they will be lost' (Gordon 1788: i. 143–4). He continued to denounce the policy of the metropolitan government, and from the 1740s he 'dominated American evangelical networks' (Andrews 2000: 31) until his death in Massachusetts in 1770. Whitefield, published by Benjamin Franklin, had a leading role in unifying a discourse of colonial revivalism, hitherto fragmented in widely separated colonies, and in giving anti-Anglican religious fervour a political application. He did so, moreover, on an interdenominational basis, laying a key foundation for cooperation between colonies in the Revolution (Mahaffey 2007). 'More than anyone else, Whitefield popularized the evangelical tradition that provided a moral framework and vocabulary permitting thousands of ordinary men and women to conceptualize and discuss revolutionary events.' Whitefield thereby achieved symbolic status. In the Revolution, soldiers from the Continental Army on one occasion entered his crypt, cut off pieces of his clothing, and carried into battle 'amulets taken from the body of one whose life and ministry had become a symbol of hope and salvation' (Lambert 1994: 198–225). Thomas Paine, formerly a Methodist, also acted as a political catalyst among colonists who were themselves neither Methodists nor freethinkers. Through such catalysis, the tyranny of sin was transmuted into the tyranny of kings and bishops; the spiritually empowered individual was given a politically redemptive role; the Thirteen Colonies experienced a collective 'new birth' to become a 'redeemer nation'. Nor did Irish Methodism avert an attempted revolution there in 1798. Methodism was a diverse phenomenon: its varieties both discouraged revolution and promoted it.

It is too soon to attempt a summing up of Methodism in general. William Law showed an early insight: the Methodists 'may be a Means of reforming a vicious World; and may rejoice in the Good they have done, perhaps *Half a Century* after most of their *Social* opponents, the gay Scoffers of the present Generation, are laid low, and forgotten, as if they had never been' ([Law] 1733: 20). Methodism, it was boasted in 1834, 'has already done more for the moral education of Great Britain, Ireland, and the West Indies, than any other system whose energies have been brought to bear upon the ignorance and misery of man' (Vevers 1834: 40). But against this we may set the prediction of John Wesley's insightful clerical opponent 'John Smith', describing in 1746 the ill effects of itinerant lay preachers: 'The very irregularity of their impetuous zeal awakens some to seriousness, but at the same time it opens a door in the long run to the hurt of many more; and if we cast up the account at a hundred years' end we shall find the loss exceed the profit.' Wesley only replied: 'I am not careful for what may be a hundred years hence' (John Wesley 1975– : xxvi. 212, 235).

John Wesley tried to run Methodism as a proprietorial 'religious society', not an independent denomination, but its very growth gave it a developing life of its own. After his death in 1791, the nature of the movement was found to be, in important ways, undefined by its most famous founder (Bradburn 1792: 19); the early nineteenth century was to see Methodism fall into schism again and again, gravely weakening its effectiveness. Methodists disagreed on what 'Methodism' meant. Yet much of the historiography still depends implicitly on a normative view of the movement's outcomes, called in question by recent scholarship. Was Methodism really a success? Did it fail in its first purpose, to revitalize the church from within? Or did it provoke just such a revitalization, but itself disintegrate into a conflicting series of Nonconformist sects? Today, such historical questions can once again be asked.

Suggested Reading

Gibson, William (2001). *The Church of England 1688–1832: Unity and Accord*. London: Routledge.

—— and Ingram, Robert G. (eds.) (2005). *Religious Identities in Britain, 1660–1832*. Aldershot: Ashgate.

Harding, Alan (2003). *The Countess of Huntingdon's Connexion. A Sect in Action in Eighteenth-Century England*. Oxford: Oxford University Press.

Hindmarsh, D. Bruce (1996). *John Newton and the English Evangelical Tradition between the Conversions of Wesley and Wilberforce*. Oxford: Clarendon.

Lovegrove, Derek (1988). *Established Church, Sectarian People: Itinerancy and the Transformation of English Dissent, 1780–1830*. Cambridge: Cambridge University Press.

Nockles, Peter (1994). *The Oxford Movement in Context: Anglican High Churchmanship, 1760–1857*. Cambridge: Cambridge University Press.

Rupp, Ernest Gordon (1986). *Religion in England 1688–1791*. Oxford: Clarendon.

Walsh, John, Haydon, Colin, and Taylor, Stephen (eds.) (1993). *The Church of England, c. 1689–c. 1833: From Toleration to Tractarianism*. Cambridge: Cambridge University Press.

References

Andrews, Dee E. (2000). *The Methodists and Revolutionary America, 1760–1800: The Shaping of an Evangelical Culture*. Princeton: Princeton University Press.

[Aspland, R. Brook] (1831). *The Rise, Progress and Present Influence of Wesleyan Methodism*. London: British and Foreign Unitarian Association.

BAKER, FRANK (1970). *John Wesley and the Church of England.* London: Epworth.

BEBBINGTON, DAVID W. (1989). *Evangelicalism in Modern Britain: A History from the 1730s to the 1980s.* London: Unwin Hyman.

BENSON, JOSEPH (1793a). *A Defence of the Methodists, in Five Letters, addressed to the Rev. Dr. Tatham.* London: G. Paramore for G. Whitfield.

BENSON, JOSEPH (1793b). *A Farther Defence of the Methodists, in Letters, addressed to the Rev. W. Russel, Curate of Pershore.* London: G. Paramore for G. Whitfield.

BENYON, TOM (1960). *Howel Harris's Visits to London.* Aberystwyth: Cambrian News Press.

BOSWELL, JAMES (1791). *The Life of Samuel Johnson LL.D.* 2 vols. London: Henry Baldwin for Charles Dilly.

BRADBURN, SAMUEL (1792). *The Question, Are the Methodists Dissenters? Fairly Examined.* ?Liverpool: n.p.

—— (?1794). *Equality. A Sermon on 2 Cor. VIII. 14 Preached at the Methodist-Chapel, Broad-Mead, Bristol, February 28, 1794.* Bristol: Lancaster & Edwards.

BROWN, FORD K. (1961). *Fathers of the Victorians: The Age of Wilberforce.* Cambridge: Cambridge University Press.

BUTTERFIELD, SIR HERBERT (1965). 'England in the Eighteenth Century'. In Davies, George, and Rupp (eds.) (1965–88), i. 3–33.

CLARK, J. C. D. (2000). *English Society 1660–1832.* Cambridge: Cambridge University Press.

DAVIES, RUPERT, GEORGE, A. RAYMOND, and RUPP, GORDON (eds.) (1965–88). *A History of the Methodist Church in Great Britain.* 4 vols. London: Epworth.

DITCHFIELD, GRAYSON (1998). *The Evangelical Revival.* London: Routledge.

DOUGLAS, JAMES (1814). *Methodism Condemned; or, Priestcraft Detected.* Newcastle on Tyne: for the author.

EGMONT (1920–3). *Historical Manuscripts Commission. Manuscripts of the Earl of Egmont. Diary of the First Earl of Egmont (Viscount Percival).* 3 vols. London: His Majesty's Stationery Office.

EVANS, THEOPHILUS (1752). *The History of Modern Enthusiasm, from the Reformation to the Present Times.* London: W. Owen, and W. Clarke.

FIELD, CLIVE D. (1991). 'Anti-Methodist Publications of the Eighteenth Century: a revised bibliography'. *Bulletin of the John Rylands University Library of Manchester* 73/2: 159–280.

GIBSON, EDMUND (1739). *The Bishop of London's Pastoral Letter to the People of his Diocese... By way of Caution, against Lukewarmness on one hand, and Enthusiasm on the other.* London: S. Buckley.

[——] (1744). *Observations upon the Conduct and Behaviour of A Certain Sect, Usually distinguished by the Name of Methodists.* ?London: E. Owen.

—— (1747). *The Charge of the Right Reverend Father in God, Edmund, Lord Bishop of London, at the visitation of his diocese in the years 1746 and 1747.* ?London: n.p.

GORDON, WILLIAM (1788). *The History of the Rise, Progress, and Establishment, of the Independence of the United States of America.* 4 vols. London: for the author, for Charles Dilly, and James Buckland.

GREEN, RICHARD (1902). *Anti-Methodist Publications Issued during the Eighteenth Century.* London: C. H. Kelly.

HALÉVY, E. (August 1906). 'La naissance du Méthodisme en Angleterre'. *La Revue de Paris* 519–39, 841–67.

HALÉVY, E. (1912–28). *Histoire du peuple anglais au XIXe siècle.* Paris: Hachette.

—— (1924). *England in 1815,* trans. E. I. Watkin and D. A. Barker. 2nd edn. 1949. London: Fisher Unwin.

—— (1971). *The Birth of Methodism in England,* trans. Bernard Semmel. Chicago: University of Chicago Press.

HEITZENRATER, RICHARD P. (1989). 'What's in a name? The meaning of "Methodist"'. In *Mirror and Memory.* Nashville: Kingswood Books, 13–32.

—— (1995). *Wesley and the People called Methodists.* Nashville: Abingdon.

HEMPTON, DAVID (1996). *The Religion of the People: Methodism and Popular Religion, c. 1750–1900.* London: Routledge.

HILTON, BOYD (1988). *The Age of Atonement: The Influence of Evangelicalism on Social and Economic Thought, 1795–1865.* Oxford: Clarendon.

HORSLEY, SAMUEL (1800). *The Charge of Samuel Lord Bishop of Rochester, to the Clergy of his Diocese, delivered at his second general visitation, in the year 1800.* London: Nichols & Son, for James Robson.

INGRAM, ROBERT G. (2007). *Religion, Reform and Modernity in the Eighteenth Century: Thomas Secker and the Church of England.* Woodbridge: Boydell.

JACOB, W. M. (1996). *Lay People and Religion in the Early Eighteenth Century.* Cambridge: Cambridge University Press.

KEANE, JOHN (1995). *Tom Paine: A Political Life.* London: Bloomsbury.

KENT, JOHN (2002). *Wesley and the Wesleyans.* Cambridge: Cambridge University Press.

KILHAM, ALEXANDER (1795). *The Progress of Liberty, Amongst the People called Methodists. To which is added, The Out-Lines of a Constitution Humbly recommended to the serious consideration of the preachers and people, late in connection with Mr. Wesley.* Alnwick: J. Catnach.

LAMBERT, FRANK (1994). *'Pedlar in Divinity': George Whitefield and the Transatlantic Revivals, 1737–1770.* Princeton: Princeton University Press.

[LAVINGTON, GEORGE] (1749–51). *The Enthusiasm of Methodists and Papists, Compar'd* (three parts). London: J. and P. Knapton. Reprinted in a collected edition in 1754 and in an abridged form as *The Popery of Methodism* (Leeds, 1839).

[LAW, WILLIAM] (1733). *The Oxford Methodists: Being some Account of a Society of Young Gentlemen in that City, so denominated.* London: J. Roberts.

LECKY, WILLIAM EDWARD HARTPOLE (1878–90). *A History of England in the Eighteenth Century.* 8 vols. London: Longmans.

LEWIS, DONALD M. (ed.) (1995). *The Blackwell Dictionary of Evangelical Biography 1730–1860.* 2 vols. Oxford: Blackwell.

LYLES, ALBERT M. (1960). *Methodism Mocked: The Satiric Reaction to Methodism in the Eighteenth Century.* London: Epworth.

MAHAFFEY, JEROME DEAN (2007). *Preaching Politics: The Religious Rhetoric of George Whitefield and the Founding of a New Nation.* Waco: Baylor University Press.

[MAINWARING, JOHN] (1781). *An Essay on the Character of Methodism.* Cambridge: J. Archdeacon.

METHODISM (1779). *Methodism and Popery Dissected and Compared.* London: Fielding & Walker.

MOORE, ROBERT (1974). *Pit-Men, Preachers & Politics: The Effects of Methodism in a Durham Mining Community.* Cambridge: Cambridge University Press.

NIGHTINGALE, JOSEPH (1807). *A Portraiture of Methodism*. London: C. Stower for Longman, Hurst, Rees & Orme.

NOLL, MARK A., BEBBINGTON, DAVID W., and RAWLYK, GEORGE A. (eds.) (1994). *Evangelicalism: Comparative Studies in Popular Protestantism in North America, the British Isles, and Beyond, 1700–1900*. Oxford: Oxford University Press.

OLSEN, GERALD WAYNE (ed.) (1990). *Religion and Revolution in Early-Industrial England: The Halévy Thesis and Its Critics*. Lanham, Md.: University Press of America.

PODMORE, COLIN (1998). *The Moravian Church in England, 1728–1760*. Oxford: Clarendon.

POLWHELE, R. (ed.) (1820). *The Enthusiasm of Methodists and Papists Considered*. London: A. J. Valpy for G. & W. B. Whittaker. A second edition followed in 1833.

PRICE, RICHARD (1789). *A Discourse on the Love of Our Country*. London: George Stafford for T. Cadell.

RACK, HENRY D. (2002). *Reasonable Enthusiast: John Wesley and the Rise of Methodism*. 3rd edn. London: Epworth.

ROBERTS, RICHARD OWEN (1988). *Whitefield in Print: A Bibliographic Record of Works by, for, and against George Whitefield*. Wheaton, Ill.: R. O. Roberts.

RUPP, ERNEST GORDON (1986). *Religion in England 1688–1791*. Oxford: Clarendon.

SCHLENTHER, BOYD STANLEY (1997). *Queen of the Methodists: The Countess of Huntingdon and the Eighteenth-Century Crisis of Faith and Society*. South Church: Durham Academic Press.

—— (2004). 'George Whitefield'. *Oxford Dictionary of National Biography*. Oxford: Oxford University Press.

SCHMIDT, LEIGH ERIC (2001). *Holy Fairs: Scotland and the Making of American Revivalism*. 2nd edn. Grand Rapids: Eerdmans.

SCOTLAND, NIGEL (1981). *Methodism and the Revolt of the Field: A Study of the Methodist Contribution to Agricultural Trade Unionism in East Anglia 1872–96*. Gloucester: Sutton.

SCOTT (1932–7). *The Letters of Sir Walter Scott*, ed. H. J. C. Grierson. 12 vols. London: Constable.

SECKER, THOMAS (1766). 'A Charge delivered to the Clergy of the Diocese of Canterbury, In the Year 1766'. In Thomas Secker, *Eight Charges Delivered to the Clergy of the Dioceses of Oxford and Canterbury*. London: John and Francis Rivington, and Benjamin White, 1769.

—— (1988). *The Autobiography of Thomas Secker Archbishop of Canterbury*, ed. John S. Macauley and R. W. Greaves. Lawrence: University of Kansas Libraries.

—— (1991). *The Correspondence of Thomas Secker, Bishop of Oxford 1737–58*, ed. A. P. Jenkins. Oxford: Oxfordshire Record Society.

SMITH, SYDNEY (1808). Review of R. A. Ingram, *The Cause of the Increase of Methodism and Dissension* (1807). In *The Edinburgh Review*, Davies, George, and Rupp (eds.) (1965–88), iv. 323–6.

SNAPE, MICHAEL FRANCIS (1998). 'Anti-Methodism in Eighteenth-Century England: The Pendle Forest Riots of 1748'. *Journal of Ecclesiastical History* 49: 257–81.

SOMMERVILLE, C. JOHN (1977). *Popular Religion in Restoration England*. Gainesville: University Presses of Florida.

STEPHENS, WILLIAM (1742). *A Journal of the Proceedings in Georgia, beginning October 20, 1737*. 3 vols. London: W. Meadows.

TAYLOR, E. R. (1935). *Methodism and Politics*. Cambridge: Cambridge University Press.

THOMPSON, E. P. (1963). *The Making of the English Working Class*. London: Gollancz.

TOTTIE, JOHN (1766). *Two Charges Delivered to the Clergy of the Diocese of Worcester in the Years 1763 and 1766*. Oxford: at the Theatre.

TOWNSEND, W. J. (1909*a*). 'The Times and Conditions'. In Townsend, Workman, and Eayrs, i. 77–133.

—— (1909*b*). 'English Life and Society, and the Condition of Methodism at the Death of Wesley'. In Townsend, Workman, and Eayrs, i. 335–78.

—— WORKMAN, H. B., and Eayrs, George (1909). *A New History of Methodism*. 2 vols. London: Hodder & Stoughton.

TUCKER, JOSIAH (1742). *A Brief History of the Principles of Methodism*. Oxford: James Fletcher.

TYERMAN, LUKE (1870–1). *The Life and Times of the Rev. John Wesley, M.A., Founder of the Methodists*. 3 vols. London: Hodder & Stoughton.

[VEVERS, WILLIAM] (1834). *Reasons for Methodism*. London: Hamilton, Adams.

WALSH, JOHN (1965). 'Methodism at the End of the Eighteenth Century'. In Davies, George, and Rupp (1965–88), i. 277–315.

—— (1972). 'Methodism and the Mob in the Eighteenth Century'. *Studies in Church History* 8: 213–27.

WARBURTON, WILLIAM (1762). *The Doctrine of Grace: Or, the Office and Operations of the Holy Spirit Vindicated from The Insults of Infidelity, and The Abuses of Fanaticism*. 2 vols. London '1763' for 1762: A. Millar, and J. and R. Tonson.

WARD, W. R. (1992). *The Protestant Evangelical Awakening*. Cambridge: Cambridge University Press.

—— (2006). *Early Evangelicalism: A Global Intellectual History, 1670–1789*. Cambridge: Cambridge University Press.

WESLEY, CHARLES (1849). *Journal of the Rev. Charles Wesley*. 2 vols. ed. Thomas Jackson. London: Wesleyan Book Room.

—— (2008). *The Manuscript Journal of the Reverend Charles Wesley, M.A.*, ed. S. T. Kimbrough Jr. and Kenneth G. C. Newport. 2 vols. Nashville: Kingswood Books.

WESLEY, JOHN (1975–). *The Works of John Wesley*. 34 vols. projected. Oxford: Clarendon; Nashville: Abingdon.

—— (1744–5). *A Farther Appeal to Men of Reason and Religion*. London: W. Strahan. In Wesley, John 1975– : xi. 95–325.

—— (1747). *A Letter To the Right Reverend the Lord Bishop of London: Occasioned by his Lordship's Late Charge to his Clergy*. London: W. Strahan. In Wesley, John 1975– : xi. 333–51.

—— (1749). *A Plain Account of the People called Methodists. In a Letter to the Revd. Mr. Perronet. Vicar of Shoreham in Kent*. Bristol: Felix Farley. In Wesley, John 1975– : ix. 253–80.

—— (1763). *A Letter to the Right Reverend The Lord Bishop of Gloucester*. London: at the Foundery. In Wesley, John 1975– : xi. 465–538.

[——] (1765). *A Short History of Methodism*. London: at the Foundery. In Wesley, John 1975– : ix. 367–72.

—— (1776). *A Concise History of England*. 4 vols. London: R. Hawes.

—— (1781). 'A Short History of the People Called Methodists'. In Wesley, John 1975– : ix. 425–503.

WEARMOUTH, ROBERT F. (1947). *Methodism and the Working-Class Movements of England 1800–1850*. 2nd edn. London: Epworth.

WHITEFIELD, GEORGE (1747). *The Christian History: Or, a General Account of the Progress of the Gospel, In England, Wales, Scotland, and America: So far as The Rev. Mr. Whitefield, his Fellow-Labourers, and Assistants are concerned.* London: John Lewis.

—— (1763). *Observations on Some Fatal Mistakes, In a Book lately published, and intitled, The Doctrine of Grace.* London: E. Dilly et al.

WORKMAN, H. B. (1909). 'The Place of Methodism in the Life and Thought of the Christian Church'. In Townsend, Workman, and Eayrs, i. 3–73.

CHAPTER 2

....

THE FOUNDING
BROTHERS

....

RICHARD P. HEITZENRATER

To write the history of early Methodism entails more than simply retelling the stories about the origin of the Wesleyan movement. It entails attention to several frequently ignored principles:

1. The Methodist movement developed and grew through the leadership of John Wesley, who envisioned the goal, synthesized suggestions, and drew together factions.
2. Brother Charles's involvement (even if indirectly) in the leadership of the movement helped shape the Wesleyan heritage.
3. The relationship between the brothers was one of love and respect, in spite of their differences, but was marked by Charles being the younger brother.
4. Methodism is more than the lengthened shadow of one man: it is a lay movement built around 'the people called Methodists'.
5. The attacks of the Wesleys' opponents should neither be accepted necessarily at face value nor be dismissed summarily as irrelevant polemics.
6. The Wesleys themselves were not reliable historians: their stories about early Methodism gave rise to many myths and legends.

Interpretations of early Wesleyan Methodism have varied over the last two centuries. The story told here will attempt to dispel the myths with information gleaned from the most recent research and create a picture that makes sense both internally and in its eighteenth-century context. The movement unfolds from year to year without a previously conceived master plan, as Wesley would say, under the watchful providence of God.

A number of factors shaped the Methodist movement, including the attempts by John and Charles Wesley to renew the Church of England to be a more vital means of promoting holy living in society. Although the brothers shared many goals, their methods and emphases often brought them into conflict—sometimes in public, but more often behind the scenes. The role and influence of these two brothers, and their continuing relationship to each other and to the Methodist movement, however, have resulted in a variety of differing interpretations.

CHILDHOOD, YOUTH, AND EARLY EDUCATION

As rector of Epworth, Samuel Wesley senior served a remote parish of somewhat primitive country people. His parishioners often did not appreciate his interests in philosophy, theology, politics, and literature. His wife, Susanna, did her best to protect their offspring from the crudities of the neighbouring children by limiting their outdoor playtime and teaching them strict rules of conduct. Unfortunately, two rectory fires forced Susanna to send some of her children to stay with neighbours, resulting in a subsequent need to reform the children's manners and language.

As the fifteenth child in the Wesley family, John (b. 1703) was four and a half years older than Charles (b. 1707). When Charles was beginning to read at age 5, John was about a year from leaving for school in London. They had little time together, then, as young siblings to become close. John was nearer in age to two of his sisters, Anne (b. 1702) and Martha ('Patty', b. 1706), for whom he developed a lasting fondness (Heitzenrater 2003: 41–6).

Although Susanna provided her children's basic education, Samuel was also influential in shaping their religious and theological perspectives. All the children, including the girls, learned the three Rs in weekly tutorial sessions with Susanna, but they also heard their father's sermons on Sunday mornings. Samuel's personal library also provided resources for shaping their religious and intellectual interests. More careful study of the theology of Samuel and Susanna would contribute to a fuller understanding of the Wesleyan heritage.

John and Charles both attended school in London, John at Charterhouse School (1713–20), and Charles several miles away at Westminster School (1716–26). No evidence suggests that they spent much time together while at school. John seems to have broadened his religious perspective from his strict Anglican upbringing to include more knowledge of the Continental reformed traditions and may have developed some musical tastes from the tune books of John Patrick, former preacher of Charterhouse, whose tune books were presumably still in use at the school. Charles studied biblical languages at Westminster with his older brother, Samuel, who was an Usher (teacher) at that school. Very little evidence has survived from this formative period in both brothers' lives, and little Methodist attention has focused on the nature of education at those two eighteenth-century institutions.

OXFORD, THE FIRST RISE OF METHODISM

John matriculated at Christ Church, Oxford, and had finished his baccalaureate degree (1724) and had been elected Fellow of Lincoln College (1726) by the time Charles arrived as a student. Eight months later, John earned his master's degree (1727) and soon moved north to become curate for his father in the Epworth living, which then included the parish of Wroot. At that time, Charles seems to have looked upon his older brother as a model student and Christian, and frequently appealed to him for advice.

John Wesley became more serious spiritually when he decided, after receiving his baccalaureate degree, to continue at Oxford as a tutor, necessitating that he become an ordained clergyman. This daunting prospect led John by early 1725 to focus upon his manner of Christian living, following the advice of his parents and several authors in the holy living tradition, especially Thomas à Kempis and Jeremy Taylor. His attempts to implement his new vision of Christian living, aided now by keeping a diary, included trying to convince friends to follow suit, usually without success. When Charles came to the University, he was not inclined to pursue this same manner of serious religion.

While John was in Epworth as curate, the University officials began to encourage tutors to enforce the school's statutes, which expected study of the Scriptures and classic divinity, as well as practical implementation of religion in the students' lives. In that context, Charles had a 'religious reformation' that he described in a letter to John early in 1729, asking for advice on how to proceed: what to read, what to do, and how to keep a diary. When Charles noted in May that he was trying to adopt this new programme and had convinced a classmate to study and attend Sunday services with him, John became excited enough to leave the north country for a summer visit to Oxford.

No organized activities developed during the summer before the brothers went north for the holidays in August. Certainly, no contemporary evidence exists that Charles started a group that was identifiable or regular, as is often claimed (Heitzenrater 1989: 68–9 and n.). But when the brothers returned to Oxford in the late autumn, a pattern of activities begins to develop that takes a recognizable shape by the following spring (1730). The Wesleys and two or three others begin to meet as a study group, rotating among their rooms, reading and discussing the typical Oxford curriculum: classics on three evenings during the week and works of divinity on Sunday evening. They were neither the first nor the only group at that time to have such an agenda at Oxford. During the autumn and early winter of that year, one of the group, William Morgan, convinced them to assist him in visiting the prisoners at the city jail and county prison, as well as to help him teach some orphans and to supply several poor widows and children with food, clothes, and other necessities. During that year, the small band of friends, under John's leadership, had begun to take on a recognizable identity (Heitzenrater 1995: 39–43). A careful study of their reading programme might help unfold the development of Wesleyan theology during this period.

The organizational structure of Oxford Methodism was similar to the religious society pattern of the time: the centrality of a small group around their leader, John Wesley, with peripheral groups formed around individuals from the central group. The network of cell groups derived its rules and patterns of activity from the leading group: lists of questions, ciphers for diary entries, books for study, and schedules for visiting needy people. Several of these Wesleyan groups seem to have existed around the University and in the city in the months after mid-1732 (Heitzenrater 1995: 6–14).

The group's social outreach gained it additional public notice, and its name shifted briefly from 'Sacramentarians' (due to their regular church attendance) to 'Holy Club' (because of their assistance to the needy). According to John, this name (which he especially disliked because of the implications of being a social 'club') was superseded within six months by 'Godly Club', 'Supererogation Men', 'Bible Moths'—epithets that caricatured their various attempts at holy living. By 1732, they were called 'Methodists' by an observer at Christ Church, who may have noticed that the theology in John's sermons exhibited an Arminian flavour typical of the 'New Methodists' of the previous generation (Heitzenrater 1989: 13–32).

The theology of these Wesleyans has often been mistakenly described as semi-pelagian—trying to earn salvation by doing good works. John's sermons during this period clearly diffuse such criticism, especially his 1733 sermon before the University, 'The Circumcision of the Heart'. The inward focus, indicated by both his title and text (Rom. 2: 29), displayed a meditative piety oriented on a virtue ethic. The Methodists' interest was not earning salvation by doing good things, but rather allowing God's grace to help them become like Christ, filling them with Christlike virtues that would free them from sinfulness and allow them to have the mind of their Saviour and walk as he walked (Phil. 2: 15). Their reliance on God's prevenient grace as the starting point of this process betrays Wesley's lifetime theological stance against the predeterminism of the Calvinists and the semi-pelagian moral rectitude of some Anglicans.

Oxford Methodism manifested a double focus on loving God and neighbour, the sum of what the Wesleys always considered to be the purpose of the Christian life, the mark of a genuine Methodist, and the promise of the New Testament—Christian perfection. The importance of both Christian fellowship ('social holiness') and outreach ('social concern') demonstrated the Methodist double emphasis on works of piety and mercy. Their broad range of activities with the sick and poor, young and old, imprisoned and needy, followed the pattern of their Master, who 'went about doing good'. Members of the groups suggested many of the specific activities to Wesley, and not every group followed the same pattern. But they all followed the Wesleyan scheme of testing their actions by the Scriptures and trying to implement holy living in the academy, the church, and the community.

GEORGIA, THE SECOND RISE OF METHODISM

The death of Samuel Wesley senior in early 1735 was a life-changing event for John and Charles. Samuel had wanted to become a missionary to America, and his sons soon took the endeavour upon themselves. John was not certain that this mission was providential—even the recommendation of his mother did not end his round of enquiries to friends. But once convinced, he exerted every effort to persuade Charles to accompany him. A contemporary observed that Charles always held John in deference, and in this case Charles succumbed, over his oldest brother's (Samuel's) objections (Heitzenrater 2003: 235).

The Georgia mission is often portrayed as a total failure for the Wesleys. Some evidence supports that view—the brothers' unfortunate encounters with designing women, their clash with the colonial authorities in Savannah, Charles's poor health and early return to England, John's failed romance with Sophy Hopkey, and the indictment of John (by a 'packed jury') on ten counts of maladministration and malfeasance. However, one should not overlook the importance of this period for the Wesleys' development and the shaping of Methodism.

While the Wesleys' contact with the Moravians during this period and John's interview with August Spangenberg have gained biographical notoriety, as has Wesley's contact with the slaves in South Carolina, other signs also indicate that the Wesleyan mindset was expanding. Charles encountered the duties of parish ministry, including preaching (on shipboard in both directions, he copied many of John's sermons for his own use (Heitzenrater 2003: 153)), and began exercising a latent talent for writing poetry. John refined his own perspectives on theology and mission. Attendance at public worship in Savannah grew under John's leadership, the American church gained its first printed book of *Psalms and Hymns* (published by John in Charleston in 1737), and the new settlement in Frederica experienced the first 'Methodist' meeting in America in June 1737 (Heitzenrater 1995: 62–4). Additionally, John's linguistic abilities expanded into German, French, Spanish, and Italian, and his private writings began to exhibit (at Charles's suggestion) his use of Byrom's shorthand as a method of 'covered' correspondence.

In the midst of colonial turmoil, the brothers' support of each other drew them closer together in new ways. For weeks in Georgia, they travelled together, helped and defended each other, and confided in each other. Nevertheless, Charles left the colony after less than half a year, discouraged and in weak health. John left at the end of 1737 under threat of a trial. The reflections of despair in John's journal for January 1738 questioning his state of salvation, however, are subsequent insertions (when he edited the material for publication two years later) and demonstrate a viewpoint more typical of the influence of Peter Boehler, a post-Georgia friend. His Moravian perspective refracted Wesley's own view of his life up to that point and has thus skewed the interpretations of Methodist historians for generations.

LONDON, THE THIRD RISE OF METHODISM

John Wesley's contemporary ambivalence towards his time spent in America emerges while he is still on his docked ship in the arrival port in Portsmouth. Discovering that George Whitefield was about to sail for America on another ship in the same harbour, John sent him a note to dissuade him. Whitefield was not diverted from his intentions to assume the Wesleys' mission in Georgia and proceeded on the first of his seven trips to America. However, neither of the Wesleys ever returned to the New World.

The German pietists in Georgia, especially Spangenberg, had turned John Wesley's attention to the need for personal appropriation of the scriptural truths that were at the heart of Anglican soteriology. Now in England, Boehler continued to press the need for a personal faith that would dispense any doubt, fear, and sin. When Wesley despaired of ever having that level of faith, Boehler encouraged him to continue preaching faith until he actually received an assurance of it within himself, which the Moravians claimed would be accompanied by complete love, peace, and joy.

At this point, both Wesley brothers, under the spiritual tutelage of the Moravians, were active in the religious societies of London. This disparate network of small groups consisted of various evangelicals associated with a diverse group of leaders, including George Whitefield, James Hutton, Peter Boehler, and some former Oxford Methodists, many of whom were Anglicans. On 1 May 1738, Boehler began a small fellowship at Hutton's house that became the Fetter Lane Society. John Wesley, visiting Hutton that evening, attended the meeting. Boehler soon left town, however, and Wesley began to exercise more leadership in the society, though never as its primary leader. Nevertheless, he later viewed the establishment of this society as the 'third rise' of Methodism.

Wesley's relationship with this group was rocky at best. Besides noting theological differences, the Moravian leadership also expressed some concern that the Wesley brothers' attraction to women in the group (and vice versa) was a divisive distraction. At the same time, John challenged their growing emphasis on 'quietism', which countered his emphasis on constant use of the various means of grace through works of piety and mercy—opportunities for persons to open themselves to the presence and power of God in their lives. His growing disenchantment with that society led Wesley to separate from them, followed by a small clutch of friends, and form a new society in November 1739 at the Foundery, the site that became the primary home of Methodism in London.

The Moravians also played an important role in the Wesleys' spiritual development. On Pentecost Sunday 1738, Charles experienced the 'assurance of salvation' that Boehler had been prescribing for weeks, sensing a 'strange palpitation of heart' that signalled his acceptance by God as a child of faith. Three days later on 24 May, John experienced a similar sense of assurance of faith during a society meeting on Aldersgate Street. John's descriptive language similarly reflected the Moravian heart theology—'my heart was strangely warmed'. The Wesleys had both experienced a personal appropriation of the faith they had been preaching. John saw now beyond the theological affirmation that Christ had died for the sins of the world, which was the truth that he could affirm to Spangenberg in Georgia. Now he realized that Christ had died 'for *me*' and had taken away '*my* sins'. Although the Wesleys continued to have theological disputes with the Moravians, continued to refine their understanding of faith, maintained their emphasis on the necessity of being active in doing good, and eventually discarded much of the Moravian theology, these spiritual experiences in May 1738 were a crucial step for each of them in his spiritual pilgrimage towards becoming a mature Christian (Heitzenrater 1989: 126–39).

This period also witnessed the beginning of Charles's poetical endeavours. He finished writing a hymn on 22 May in response to his spiritual experience and even left some blank space in his manuscript journal to enter the verses. But he never entered the hymn or indicated which one it was (probably either 'And Can It Be' or 'Where Shall my Wondering Soul Begin'). In any case, rhyming lines began to pour out of Charles's heart as he began to exercise his talent for expressing in poetry the spiritual core of the Methodist message.

During the remaining fifty years of his life, Charles produced verse at an amazing rate. The total has been estimated as high as 9,000 poems, although that number seems to include duplicates that appeared in different publications (Kimbrough 1990: i. 17–18). Hundreds of these poems have been put to music, old and new, and sung in religious services for generations. The list of well-known Wesleyan hymns is long, typified by such favourites as 'Hark, the Herald Angels Sing', 'O For a Thousand Tongues to Sing', 'Love Divine, All Loves Excelling', and 'Christ the Lord is Risen Today'.

John and Charles had differences of opinion on what constituted appropriate wording for Methodist hymnody. John was the final editor of most of the hymn publications and on occasion either changed or omitted some of Charles's work. John did not allow 'Jesus, Lover of My Soul' into the main collection of 1780 and changed such phrases as 'Dear Saviour' because they echoed the sentimental language and 'coarse expressions' typical of the Moravian hymns. At times, Charles published small hymn tracts on his own, such as the 'Hymns on God's Everlasting Love' (1741). At stake was not only a certain sensitivity to language but also a concern for theological expression. Despite the more recent opinion that the hymns were the primary vehicle of Wesleyan theology during the revival, one must recognize that poetry is not an ideal form by which to express the carefully nuanced theological concepts that John was constantly forced to define and refine.

Music presented another issue regarding the Wesleyan hymnody. Charles was not a musician—he neither composed tunes nor played the organ or harpsichord. A few hundred of his poems became sung hymns, and the music that accompanied them was largely taken from the repertoire of contemporary hymn tunes. A few were composed for his words by popular composers of the day, such as George Frederick Handel and John Frederick Lampe. Some were adapted from popular tunes by earlier composers such as Henry Purcell. The current idea that some of the music came from tavern songs perhaps results from a misunderstanding of the concept of the 'bar form' of some songs, which refers to the repetition of melodic patterns, not to drunken ditties.

The poetic work of John and Charles Wesley not only contributed significantly to the development of hymnody in the eighteenth century but also provided a lasting expression of and contribution to the vital spiritual experiences of millions of people in denominations across the wide spread of Christianity.

THE EARLY METHODIST REVIVAL

The Methodist movement had become visible on the British scene by 1740. However, the most noticeable 'Methodist' in London until halfway through that decade was George Whitefield. When various people wrote tracts and pamphlets attacking the Methodists, more often than not they aimed their barbs at Whitefield. He was the most notable orator of the time, he was the most notorious rabble-rouser among the religious societies, and he was most likely to get the attention of both the curious public and the church leadership. Calvinism became his cause, and he carried on an extensive public battle with John Wesley, his personal friend and former mentor. Their meeting houses, the Wesleys' Foundery and Whitefield's Tabernacle, were on the same street north of Moorfields in Greater London.

The close association between Whitefield and the Wesleys began at Oxford, where George had first become acquainted with Charles and then came to know John about the time the Wesleys were leaving Oxford. Whitefield also considered himself as successor to the Wesleys' work, first at Oxford and then in Georgia, where he followed Charles's advice and started an orphanage, called Bethesda. In 1739, when they were all back in England, Whitefield convinced John Wesley to take over his work with two of the religious societies in Bristol (Baldwin Street and Tabernacle Street Societies). Wesley soon built a 'New Room', or preaching house, for the combined groups, which he then called the 'United Societies'. Whitefield suggested that Wesley take sole proprietorship of the building, so as not to fall prey to the doctrinal and missional demands of financiers (J. Wesley 1975– (1990), xix. 56). Whitefield also turned over to the Wesleys his work in a school among the mining families at nearby Kingswood.

This working relationship was sorely tested when Wesley preached 'Free Grace' in Bristol, which directly attacked the Calvinism that Whitefield supported. Wesley's publication of the sermon brought on a heated controversy that followed Whitefield to America again. Whitefield's counterblast, 'Free Grace, Indeed!' argued that free grace meant that God was free to choose the elect, not that humankind was free to choose God's salvation. Several attempts at compromise between the Wesleys and Whitefield, sometimes including other evangelical leaders, failed to resolve the basic tensions between the general Arminianism of the Wesleyans and the Calvinism of Whitefield and his supporters. At one such meeting, the participants agreed not to attack each other in public and not to use inflammatory terms (such as 'sinless perfection' or 'predestination')—an agreement that Charles soon ignored in some of his poetry (J. Wesley 1975– (1991), xx. 295).

The organization of Methodism developed in response to needs rather than from a preconceived plan. Wesley was convinced that God had raised up the Methodist preachers to spread scriptural holiness across the land. The singularity with which he pressed the fulfilment of this goal—holy living, love of God and neighbour, having the mind of Christ and walking as he walked—gives an impression of the implementation of a general design. But the particulars of the organization and mission arose in response to practical circumstances that required a timely solution, which Wesley usually provided in consultation with Scripture, his friends, and eventually his preachers. During the early years of these developments, Charles remained largely in the background, still functioning as the younger brother and trusted (though subordinate) colleague. John seemed to be very self-confident but at the same time appeared to rely on his brother's support.

John had developed a network of friends at Oxford that continued to provide a matrix for his pattern of activities even after his return from Georgia. The network grew as his acquaintances broadened and his activities widened throughout England. In 1739, one gathering of these friends resulted in a resolution to meet every three months to encourage each other, with an annual meeting in the summer in London. No evidence confirms whether these conferences ever happened during the next three years. But the pattern was eventually implemented within the developing movement. The first instance of a subsequent meeting of this sort occurred in 1743, when John sent word to Charles to make his way quickly from Cornwall to London for a conference among the Wesley brothers, Whitefield, Spangenberg, and John Nelson. The intent was to have a theological conversation to work out some of the differences between the Wesleyan, Moravian, and Calvinist perspectives of the participants. This attempt failed to materialize fully when the Moravians discouraged Spangenberg from attending and Whitefield failed to appear (C. Wesley 2008: 369–70). The conversation between the remaining three has never been viewed as an official conference—apparently no minutes were kept and no major decisions were recorded by the participants. But it did provide the pattern and rationale for succeeding conferences, which began to meet annually at Wesley's behest the following summer.

Spread and Organization of Methodist Movement

This period of 'evangelical revival' in the eighteenth century witnessed a series of spiritual awakenings in many parts of the world. In the British Isles, many local revivals blossomed. The leadership of these small movements ranged across the religious spectrum, from established church to radical Dissenters. Several of these local revivals were led by persons who knew Wesley, either by previous association (especially at Oxford) or by reputation, as Wesley's notoriety grew.

There was no 'wildfire' spread of Methodism, as is often claimed, but the movement did spread throughout the three kingdoms during the 1740s, as some of these local revivals came into association with the Wesleys. This amalgamation of revivals contributed to the growth of the Wesleyan movement to over 20,000 members by the 1760s, at which point Methodists started keeping careful records. That is a relatively small number, considering that the population of England then was nearly ten million and compared with the numbers that purportedly attended Methodist outdoor preaching occasions at the time—often reported to be 20,000–30,000 people on some weekends. Curiosity seekers often attended the Societies then, but could only visit three times without joining the group.

The relatively slow growth also resulted from the membership process. The only requirement for joining the United Societies of People Called Methodists was 'a desire to flee from the wrath to come and be saved from your sins'. But the requirements for retaining a membership card (class ticket) included an examination every three months that tested a continuing desire for salvation—were members still following the three 'General Rules': do all the good you can, avoid evil of every kind, and attend to the ordinances of God (use the means of grace). These rules entailed specific examples of 'good' and 'evil' behaviour and a list of the means of grace, including religious conversation, the Lord's Supper, fasting, praying, and Scripture reading. On some occasions, these examinations resulted in the expulsion of a large proportion of a local society, who either left the movement or were required to join a 'penitential band' (similar to the 'probationary band', an initial requirement for each new member) for at least three months. This tight discipline resulted in a membership limited to those who were serious about Christian living and were able to demonstrate that concern in specific ways (Heitzenrater 1995: 138–9).

The local Methodist societies were composed of and led by laypeople who were committed to the Wesleys' vision of holy living. Similar to the earlier religious societies, they benefited from the strengths of the small group concept. Each local society was divided into 'classes' or neighbourhood groups of about a dozen people, each with a leader (layperson) who was responsible for nurturing the spiritual well-being of the members. The 'bands' however, were voluntary groups that furthered more intimate spiritual nurture by their homogenous composition, determined by gender, age, and marital status—single young men, married older women, and the like. Laity also held other positions in each society, such as 'stewards' to handle the money, 'trustees' to manage the property, and 'visitors' to care for the sick (Heitzenrater 1995: 117–19). Even the preachers who led these societies were laypeople, picked and 'set apart' by the Wesleys as 'helpers' and 'assistants'. Preaching was the regular feature of the society meeting, held in buildings known as 'preaching houses'. The meetings also included special events such as watch nights, love feasts, and letter days (when they read personal descriptions of religious experiences that exemplified holy living and holy dying). As the connexion developed 'circuits' within regions—groups of societies within a geographic region that could be served by a group of preachers who circulated around the circuit—the term 'Assistant' came to designate the supervising preacher on a circuit.

Besides leading exemplary lives, the members were also expected to contribute to the local and connectional programmes of the society, which came to include the establishment of educational institutions, medical clinics, housing subsidies, loan funds, and other forms of assistance designed primarily for the members, many of whom were poor. The Methodists were representative of the general population in that two-thirds of them could be classified as 'poor' by government standards since their annual worth was less than £30. At the same time, Wesley's movement had attracted approximately twice the proportion from the top 2 per cent on the economic ladder. It was these 'rich' persons to whom Wesley looked for funding of programmes to assist the poor. When he went 'begging' through the streets of London, he was not standing on a street corner with a tin cup, but was knocking on the doors of people that he felt would provide aid for specific needs (J. Wesley 1975– (2003), xiv. 2–3). On one occasion, he raised only a disappointing £200 in a week, but that amount converted into today's currency would top £12,000.

While this ministry to the rich on behalf of the poor was an essential part of the programme, Wesley's principle of philanthropy, or Christian charity, extended across the economic spectrum. Any persons who had more than the 'necessities' of life were expected to contribute of their 'superfluities' to those who were in need. As the economic level of the Methodists improved throughout the century, 'necessities' were fleshed out adjectivally by somewhat generous terms as 'decent' clothing, 'suitable' housing, and 'nutritious' food. A few people in England may have lived on the rock-bottom level of 'extremities'—everyone else was expected to help those who were worse off than they were. The biblical story of the widow's mite was Wesley's model for this principle, which he universalized to all levels of society. Some of Charles's most powerful lines describe not only Christ as the 'sinner's friend' but also 'the poor as Jesus' bosom-friends' (Kimbrough 1990: 2, 404).

Preaching and Publications

The printed word became as important as the preached and sung word among the Methodists. Both of the Wesleys kept cryptic notes in daily diaries, from which they developed narrative accounts in manuscript journals. They wrote each other journal letters, which were narratives of their own and others' experiences. These were often read on 'letter days' in the society meetings. The Wesleys later abridged these documents into the more familiar journals associated with each. They also collected prayers, poetry, various contemporary religious writings, and historical classics in divinity. John Wesley published dozens of these abridged and 'collected' works, many of which he had prepared in the 1720s and 30s while at Oxford. Not only did he publish these works singly, often anonymously, but he also included many, along with his own writings, in a multi-volume edition of 'Wesley's Tracts' sold in the mid-1740s. He placed many in his 50-volume *Christian Library* in the mid-1750s, and even included several in the publication of his 32-volume collected *Works* in the 1770s. Some of them he also published in his monthly journal,

The Arminian Magazine, begun in the late 1770s. Wesley considered these published materials collected from other writings as part of his own works and every bit as important for his people as the sermons and treatises that he himself had composed. His primary intent was to spread scriptural holiness across the land, which seems to have included making a great variety of religious literature, past and present, available to people at a reasonable price.

One of the staple items in the Wesleyan corpus is the published sermons. Preaching was a hallmark of the Methodist revival. Whitefield was often seen as the epitome of the Methodist preacher, though his theology was not fully Wesleyan. John on the other hand was not known as a dynamic speaker—eyewitnesses report that his voice was clear and his message was pointed, but his method was not remarkable. One woman reported that if Wesley had not occasionally reached up and turned the page of his manuscript, one would have thought he was a 'speaking marble statue' (Heitzenrater 1989: 162–73). Nevertheless, the message affected the hearers powerfully, which was also the intent of the published works.

The published sermons were primarily intended to help the preachers and people understand the principles of the Christian life as seen in Scripture. The first volume, written during the height of the field-preaching revivals of the mid-1740s, focused on themes related to conversion—salvation, faith, and justification. The preachers at the earliest conferences asked Wesley to publish some sermons, which he did in 1746. But soon the Wesleys decided to focus on the establishment of societies rather than on field-preaching, and the second volume in 1748 shifts towards the principles of the Christian life, such as Christian perfection and themes from Christ's Sermon on the Mount. In 1750, John completed his original design to produce three volumes of sermons. This design not only expanded to include a fourth volume in 1760, but within thirty years, Wesley had written a hundred more sermons and produced an eight-volume set of these homiletical treatises.

These *Sermons on Several Occasions*, however, were not the sermons he preached daily. His favourite preaching texts are not represented in the published collection, and a large percentage of the published sermons were apparently never preached— they were written treatises elucidating the scriptural principles that undergird the Christian life (Heitzenrater 1989: 179–82). His anecdotal oral style contrasted remarkably with the written sermons, according to first-hand accounts (J. Wesley 1975– (1987), iv. 515–16).

Preaching was the hallmark of the Methodist movement, both out of doors and in society meetings. The gathering places were called 'preaching houses', as distinguished from the consecrated 'chapels' of the Church of England and the registered 'meeting houses' of the Dissenters. The great numbers of people who attended these occasions, a notable feature of the movement, became a matter of contention. Charles betrays some scepticism in 1739 concerning the 'innumerable multitude' that reportedly gathered in Moorfields to hear Whitefield, and also mistrusted the more specific number that came to hear his brother John—'above ten thousand (as was supposed)', he records in his journal. But when Charles decided to enter the ranks of field preachers a week later, he noted (with tongue in cheek) that he 'found ten thousand helpless sinners waiting for the word in Moorfields' (C. Wesley 2008: 179–80).

Sometimes the numbers raise serious questions. How would the 34,000 people whom John recorded at Gwennap Pit have fit into the topography of the area? Where would that many people have come from in rural Cornwall? How would that many people have travelled to such a remote area? How were they accommodated for food and lodging? And where were that many horses kept?

Nevertheless, Wesley was indeed concerned about numbers. Beginning in 1770, the membership list in the annual *Minutes* has an asterisk beside those societies that decreased in size, usually about a quarter of the four or five dozen groups in the British Isles. As the percentage of asterisks increased, the method switched in 1781 to a more positive approach, indicating those societies that increased in size during the year—often less than half of them. By 1785, the asterisks had been dropped completely from the membership records. By 1791, nevertheless, the British Methodist movement had 72,476 members, an average annual increase of about 2,000 members during the previous twenty years (more rapid growth than during the first thirty years).

The various connectional funds had also increased proportionally: the annual Kingswood School Collection from about £200 to over £1,000; the Preachers' (pension) Fund from under £50 to over £700; and the contributions for Yearly Expenses (for building debt reduction and active preachers' support) nearly tripled to over £1,200. These funds alone represent a contribution of nearly a shilling per member every year, which (according to Wesley's personal financial records) was equivalent to the cost of a cloak, a pair of children's shoes, a good book, or two bottles of ink.

Although the membership in the Methodist societies did not grow exponentially, the need for preachers in the movement outstripped the supply of ordained Anglicans interested in associating with Methodists. The question of using lay preachers arose early: Charles declared against it as early as 1739. John succumbed to the need for such assistance when convinced that their work bore spiritual fruit. The tension between the brothers on this issue (and several others) presented a continuing source of friction. Charles worried that John would take some action that would result in separation from the church. The pressure from the lay preachers for ordination and permission to administer the sacraments presented a threat in that direction, as did the scheduling of society meetings at 11 a.m. on Sunday mornings, conflicting with the local parish church services (which the Wesleys hoped Methodists would attend). Charles was a 'Church Methodist' and was much more willing to abandon Methodism before he would separate from the church. John worried about having enough leaders among the societies, however, and was less concerned than Charles about their talents and theological sophistication. He generally opposed separation, but felt there were only two ways that such a cleavage would happen: if the hierarchy of the church kicked them out, or if they declared themselves Dissenters and left—neither of which he thought would happen.

ECCLESIOLOGY AND MINISTRY

John Fletcher, one of the Wesleys' trusted allies among the ranks of Anglican clergy, and Joseph Benson, one of the Wesleyan preachers, presented a compromise plan in the mid-1770s. They proposed the creation of Methodism as a 'daughter church' of the Church of England, with the doctrinal standards altered to reflect the Wesleyan emphases—the Articles of Faith 'rectified' by Scripture, and the Book of Common Prayer and Homilies likewise receiving 'needful alterations'. Wesley rejected the plan, although a decade later he provided American Methodists with a similar set of standards for their new denomination (Heitzenrater 1995: 256–7).

Methodist women's call to preach tested Wesley's attempts to correlate principle and practicality. He consistently held the principle that 'Methodists admit of no women preachers'. This view was necessary to prevent separation from the Church of England, which had a strong bias against having women in leadership positions, especially ordained ministry. But he also recognized that some women were adept at speaking to the societies and felt a strong call to do so. Mary Bosanquet convinced him that such an 'extraordinary call' was not unlike that of the male lay preachers in the connexion. Wesley therefore allowed selected women to lead services in the societies, within strict limits—they were not to 'preach' on a text or speak continually for twenty minutes, but were simply to hold Bible studies or exhort their listeners, interspersing their discourse with occasional prayers. These women were not 'set apart' as members of the Conference, but were simply given the personal permission of Wesley to provide assistance in the societies. In only one instance was a woman (Sarah Mallet) actually granted written permission to preach in her circuit, under a 1787 provision that required non-connexional preachers to be approved by Wesley and the Conference (Heitzenrater 1995: 298).

A leadership crisis arose in the early 1750s when some of the preachers demonstrated a lack of both competence and basic morality. Charges of adultery against one preacher resulted in his claiming that other preachers were likewise complicit. John recognized an opportunity for Charles to become more involved in the guidance of the connexion and thus asked Charles to examine the preachers and determine which ones should be dismissed. Charles's journal letters to John during the visitations of 1751 exhibit him exercising independent judgement and contain some ebullient references to his own travail among the societies. Such a view of his own importance in the movement provided undergirding for Charles's continuing struggles with John over their different emphases on 'gifts' or 'grace'. By the end of the year, the brothers submitted some of their differences to arbitration (the third party was Mr Perronet), and the covenants that they drew up attempted to move towards personal agreement on key issues as well as to promote a supportive covenant relationship among the preachers (Newport 2007: 502–4). Charles's attempts to control John—such as expecting to have equal say in who was accepted or dismissed from the ranks of preachers—was not matched by a willingness to participate equally in the ongoing daily administration of the connexion. John's occasional pleas for a show of unity between the brothers were not heeded; Charles even stopped attending the annual conference. In 1785, John recognized that he could have benefited from a closer partnership with Charles: 'Perhaps if you had kept close to me, I might have done better. However, with or without help, I creep on.'

The ordination problem heightened when the American colonies became a separate nation after their Revolutionary War. Wesley never fully understood the New World, given his limited, off-putting experience in Georgia. His ambiguous attitude towards their cause became explicit in his *Calm Address to Our American Colonies*, a plagiarized version of Samuel Johnson's pamphlet supporting British taxation of the colonies to help pay for their military protection. When hostilities broke out and the Anglican clergy returned to England, the Methodists were left without access to the sacraments. John Wesley, who had denied the requests of English Methodist preachers for ordination, saw this as a 'case of necessity' that required exceptional action, against the advice of his brother and other advisers in the Methodist Conference in England. His was a definitive, though not hasty, reaction to the need, and the setting apart of Thomas Coke and Francis Asbury as 'general superintendents' for America provided the core of an ecclesiological framework for a new denomination in the new country. That Wesley 'ordained' Coke to his episcopal office, as Wesley recorded in his diary, is in keeping with the Anglican view of three orders of ministry: deacon, priest, and bishop (J. Wesley 1975– (1995), xxiii. 497). That Wesley reacted against the Americans adopting the term 'bishop' is in keeping with his own view that the Methodists there were still under his own leadership.

Wesley's actions with regard to American political and ecclesiastical freedom demonstrate a continuing tendency on his part towards synthetic and reactive leadership. He was a master of analysing a situation, perceiving needs, putting together solutions, and guiding the momentum in a direction that he felt was productive, if not providential. His action is often precipitated by the insistence of those more directly involved, and his positions are often expressed in terms of those who have dealt with the problem more thoroughly. But he realized that by adding the weight of his reputation at crucial moments on the side of what was 'right', he might be able to sway both public opinion and official action, as in the case of his opposition to the slave trade in England and America. Although his views are certainly in keeping with many of the social causes of the present day, his own position should not be extended beyond the boundaries of the somewhat limited social consciousness of the eighteenth century.

THEOLOGY AND SOTERIOLOGY

The precise meaning and limits of eighteenth-century language and concepts must be carefully considered when Wesley's views are appropriated in the present. Wesley often uses the term 'conversion', for instance, in the sense of assurance rather than the specific initial soteriological transformation from heathen to Christian. When he first claims that he was 'converted' on 24 May 1738, in Aldersgate Street, a close examination of the text of his explanation reveals a discussion of the meaning and place of 'assurance' and 'faith' in the Christian life. Any assumption that he was describing an initial experience of justification (being 'saved') causes confusion when in the following months he feels that he is not really a Christian any longer. The picture that emerges from this period, then, is not of a watershed event on a particular day but the beginning of a decade-long process of crises and developments that unfold the meaning and significance of his pneumatological epistemology relative to justification, sanctification, faith, and assurance (Heitzenrater 1989: 146–9).

Similarly, his mention of 'converting ordinance' should be understood in the context of his opposition to Moravian 'quietism'—the extreme view that prior to receiving full assurance of salvation, one is not a Christian and should not use prayer, Bible reading, church attendance, and other such opportunities for spiritual improvement. Wesley illustrates his contrary position by explaining that his mother had experienced assurance of salvation while attending the Eucharist—that it was thus a converting ordinance. He was not claiming that she had never before been a Christian. In fact, to understand this example of conversion in terms of transformation from heathen to Christian would have Wesley referring to his mother Susanna Wesley as being a non-Christian until shortly before her death. No one would suggest that John and Charles were raised, taught, nurtured, and supported by a heathen mother. Similarly, in Wesleyan terms, one should not suggest that assurance of salvation is necessarily equivalent to becoming a Christian or initial justification, which Wesley felt could be coincident with infant baptism. An appreciation of the terminology of the eighteenth century and its specific usage by Wesley and others is crucial to a full understanding of their various theological positions.

The key to understanding Wesley's soteriology is his use of the concepts of prevenient grace and of backsliding. Wesley agrees with the traditional Christian view that humanity is tainted by sin and has the tendency towards sin. The gospel of salvation explains how a person can overcome that situation. The idea that God's presence and power precede any human effort towards salvation is a crucial element of Wesley's answer to the Calvinist position called predestination—the idea that God's sovereignty requires that God decrees who shall be elect or damned. Wesley affirms that God indeed takes the first action, but disagrees with the idea of divine fiat. He holds, rather, that the precedent divine action illuminates the human mind concerning good and evil and gives the person the freedom to choose.

Thus, a free human response to God's preceding action is crucial to salvation from sin. The relationship of this Wesleyan view to the larger framework of the Arminian–Calvinist theological controversies is a matter of continuing discussion and nuanced work.

In many instances, Wesley appears to understand the history of and implications behind the various positions that he adopts, such as atonement or anthropology. But his main concern in working with the Methodists is to raise up the scriptural implications for holy Christian living—how a particular theological issue relates to the Great Commandment to love God and love neighbour, to have the mind that was in Christ and walk as he walked.

Wesley insisted that assurance is a daily framework for understanding one's salvation. Assurance is never a conviction or guarantee of final perseverance or a place in heaven. The central concern is a daily evaluation of one's relationship to God—assurance is a conviction that one is presently a child of God, responding in faith to God's direction. This condition is always susceptible to backsliding, however—falling from grace, not responding in faith, slacking in one's attempts to be loving (Maddox 1994: 164). This inherent tension in the Wesleyan view, which necessitates a disciplined life that daily demonstrates a desire for salvation, gives vitality rather than size to the movement. Wesley was always concerned that Methodism should maintain the power as well as the form of religion, lest it become a dead sect.

This central operating principle, putting Scripture into practice, rests behind the 'practical divinity', the heart of a distinctive Wesleyan theology. Wesley felt that God raised up the Methodist preachers 'to reform the nation, especially the Church, and spread scriptural holiness across the land'. For Wesley, holiness is simply pure love—love of God and neighbour. Theologically, he uses terms such as sanctification, entire sanctification, and Christian perfection to explicate the centrality of this position, but those terms all come back to the same thing—love.

Wesley felt that this distinctive idea, though foundational to the character of a Methodist, was not uniquely Methodist but simply the mark of a genuine Christian. While very particular in his explanation of the central Christian doctrines, Wesley was open to the variety of expressions of Christian thought and practice evident within the ecumenical church. Although not part of his vocabulary, he would agree with the motto of the Dissenters who desired unity in essentials, liberty in non-essentials, and charity in all things. The crucial question in such instances, however, is the matter of distinguishing between essentials and non-essentials, between matters of doctrine to be held fast and matters of opinion that are indifferent. Wesley would certainly place the 'three grand doctrines' of Methodism—repentance, faith (justification), and holiness (sanctification)—in the first category, along with others such as the Trinity, original sin, and the new birth. At the same time, his 'catholic spirit' would allow for some differences of opinion between denominations on modes of baptism, forms of worship, and other secondary matters (Heitzenrater 1995: 219–24). Obviously, not every group (such as the Baptists) would agree with this particular distinction, which is why Wesley could sound so tolerant on the one hand and be so firm on the other.

END OF THE CENTURY

Well into old age, Wesley celebrated his birthdays by reflecting upon the goodness of God's providence in preserving his health and strength. Some of his journal comments on those occasions seem hyperbolic—his health has never been better, his eyesight is as good as ever (J. Wesley 1975– (1995), xxiii. 369). Charles's recapitulations on such occasions were quite different—how is it that I am still alive, having suffered so many trials and tribulations? (C. Wesley 2008: 484; 586). Thus, in 1788 when John received word that his younger brother was sick in bed yet again, he replied that good exercise would do more good than staying in bed. In this instance, however, John miscalculated the seriousness of the illness. The next letter broke the bad news that Charles had died. The depth of their relationship, in spite of the continuing tensions and outward conflicts, emerged in the next service that day, when John was lining out the hymn for the people to sing (Charles's 'Come, Thou Traveller Unknown'). He valiantly proceeded halfway through the first verse to the lines, 'My company before is gone, and I am left alone with thee', before he broke down crying, unable to continue. Charles's death had little other impact at the time on the continuing political development of the Methodist connexion. But his hymns have had a lasting impact, not only upon the Methodists but also upon worldwide Christianity.

John knew that his own end was approaching. He did everything necessary to prepare for the continuation of the movement—organizing the Conference as an official body through the Deed of Declaration, registered at the Public Records Office in Chancery Lane; providing for continued leadership through selected ordinations; designating in his will special committees to carry out tasks relating to the publishing concerns and his own books and manuscripts. Anticipating that some preachers would become Dissenters and some others might become Church of England priests, he also tried to entice some to remain faithful to Methodism by promising that any preacher who remained in the connexion for at least six months after Wesley's death should receive a copy of the eight-volume collection of his sermons (Heitzenrater 2003: 208).

The anticipated divisions and controversies at his death, though causing numerable debates and hard feelings, brought only one major split in the first decade. And even the turmoil caused by that division did not prevent an acceleration in the growth of membership in the Wesleyan body, which passed 100,000 well before the turn of the century (Heitzenrater 1995: 264). The Plan of Pacification in 1795 acknowledged that the Methodist movement was indeed a separate body from the Church of England. It would take another two generations to work out the implications of that development, but by that time Methodism was a growing influence in the society of Great Britain, developing a self-understanding that began to move beyond its eighteenth-century roots.

The strength of the Wesleyan heritage has been the close interaction of its theology, organization, and mission. The spiritual quest of the Wesley brothers provides the central image of the spiritual pilgrimage at the heart of the movement—a quest to discover how the disciple of Christ can best love God and neighbour. The Wesleyan focus has always been on practice rather than theory, and practical divinity manifests itself primarily in vital Christian living. The implicit ecclesiology underlying such an approach has been elusive, if not ignored. The mission of Methodism has grown out of an attempt to relate faith and works as equally important means of grace—opportunities for experiencing the presence and power of God in human life. To understand the implications of this theological emphasis is to catch the significance of the impulse that motivated the Wesley brothers to renew the church.

SUGGESTED READING

BAKER, FRANK (1970). *John Wesley and the Church of England*. Nashville: Abingdon.

DAVIES, RUPERT, et al. (1965–88). *History of the Methodist Church in Great Britain*. 4 vols. London: Epworth.

HEITZENRATER, RICHARD P. (2001). *The Poor and the People Called Methodists*. Nashville: Kingswood.

JARBOE, BETTY (1987). *John and Charles Wesley: A Bibliography*. Metuchen, N.J.: Scarecrow.

LLOYD, GARETH (2007). *Charles Wesley and the Formation of Methodism*. Oxford: Oxford University Press.

RACK, HENRY (2003). *Rational Enthusiast*. 3rd edn. Peterborough: Epworth.

VICKERS, JOHN (2000). *A Dictionary of Methodism in Britain and Ireland*. Peterborough: Epworth.

WATSON, DAVID (1985). *The Early Methodist Class Meeting*. Nashville: Discipleship Resources.

REFERENCES

HEITZENRATER, RICHARD P. (1989). *Mirror and Memory*. Nashville: Kingswood.

—— (1995). *Wesley and the People Called Methodists*. Nashville: Abingdon.

—— (2003). *The Elusive Mr. Wesley*. 2nd edn. Nashville: Abingdon.

KIMBROUGH, S. T., JR. (ed.) (1990). *The Unpublished Poetry of Charles Wesley*. 3 vols. Nashville: Kingswood.

MADDOX, RANDY (1994). *Responsible Grace*. Abingdon: Kingswood.

NEWPORT, KENNETH G. C., and CAMPBELL, Ted A. (2007). *Charles Wesley: Life, Literature, & Legacy*. Peterborough: Epworth.

WESLEY, CHARLES (2008). *The Manuscript Journal of Charles Wesley*. Nashville: Kingswood.

WESLEY, JOHN (1975–) *The Bicentennial Edition of the Works of John Wesley*. 34 vols. Nashville: Abingdon.

CHAPTER 3

....

FRANCIS ASBURY AND AMERICAN METHODISM

....

JOHN H. WIGGER

FRANCIS ASBURY came to America in 1771 with high hopes, and by the end of 1776 there was much that he could feel good about. A revival in the South had swept thousands of new believers into the fold, offsetting the challenges that the impending revolution would undoubtedly present. 'God is at work in this part of the country; and my soul catches the holy fire already', he wrote (F. Asbury 1958: i. 166) when he first entered the Brunswick circuit, the heart of the revival in southern Virginia and North Carolina, in October 1775. By January 1776 he could write that 'Virginia pleases me in preference to all other places where I have been' (ibid. 178). Despite its raucous emotionalism, the revival was exactly what he had been praying and working for since his arrival in America.

Others were not so sure. Thomas Rankin, Wesley's senior preacher in America since 1773, had joined with Asbury to enforce the discipline of the class meeting and love feast and extend circuit preaching beyond the cities. Yet when Rankin journeyed through Virginia during the summer of 1776 he was dismayed by the emotionalism of southern worship. At a conference of the preachers soon afterward, Rankin launched into a tirade against 'the spirit of the Americans', criticizing the preachers for allowing 'noise' and 'wild enthusiasm' in their meetings and for becoming 'infected with it' themselves. As he listened, Asbury 'became alarmed, and deemed it absolutely necessary that a stop should be put to the debate', according to Thomas Ware, who witnessed the event. Jumping up, Asbury pointed across the room and said, 'I thought,—I thought,—I thought', to which Rankin asked, 'pray...what did you thought?' [sic] 'I thought I saw a mouse!' exclaimed Asbury. This joke 'electrified' the preachers, and in the ensuing laughter Rankin realized that he had lost. The result was 'alike gratifying to the preachers generally, and mortifying to the person concerned [Rankin]', according to Ware (Ware 1832: 102; 1840: 252–3). Asbury's timing must have been prefect to get such a big laugh from 'I thought I saw a mouse!' But the deeper significance of this story has to do with his understanding of the intersection of faith and culture.

UPBRINGING AND EARLY CAREER

Francis Asbury was born about 20 August 1745 in a cottage in the parish of Handsworth, Staffordshire, about four miles outside Birmingham. His parents were Joseph Asbury and Elizabeth Rogers Asbury, known as Eliza. Joseph was a farm labourer and gardener employed by two wealthy families in the parish. While Francis was still quite young the family moved to a cottage in nearby Great Barr, which at the time was attached to a brewery and is still standing. In all likelihood Joseph worked for the brewery and the cottage was part of his compensation (Hallam 2003: 2–4). By age 6 Asbury could read the Bible, and he attended a charity school at Sneal's Green, about a quarter of a mile from the family's cottage. But, as Asbury later remembered, the schoolmaster was 'a great churl, and used to beat me cruelly' (F. Asbury 1958: i. 721). His severity filled Asbury 'with such horrible dread, that with me anything was preferable to going to school'. So he left school at about age 13 and was soon apprenticed to a local metalworker, slipping into the rapidly expanding metalworking industry that made Birmingham an early centre of the industrial revolution. As a metalworker's apprentice and the son of a gardener, Asbury understood the lives of working people, which later enabled him to forge a bond with American Methodists, most of whom came from the lower and middle ranks of society. This was particularly true of the American preachers, almost all of whom came from artisan and farming backgrounds with little formal education. They accepted Asbury so easily because he was one of them.

The death of Asbury's sister Sarah in May 1749 at the age of 6 was a severe blow to Elizabeth Asbury, but also the root of her spiritual awakening. According to Asbury his mother sank 'into deep distress at the loss of a darling child, from which she was not relieved for many years' (ibid.). The tragedy of Sarah's death drove Elizabeth to search for deeper spiritual meaning in life. Elizabeth soon gained a reputation for seeking out almost anyone with evangelical inclinations, including local

Methodists. Asbury's religious convictions grew along with his mother's, who directed him to Methodist meetings in nearby West Bromwich and Wednesbury. Asbury was impressed by the zeal of the preachers and their audience. After an intense search for the assurance of salvation, he experienced conversion at about age 15 and sanctification, or something close to it, a year or so later.

Asbury soon joined a class meeting and a band, and at about age 17 he began to exhort and then preach in public. At 21 he took the place of the travelling preacher assigned to the Staffordshire circuit. In August 1767 he was admitted on trial (a probationary period for new itinerant preachers) and assigned to the Bedfordshire circuit. In August 1768 he was admitted into full connexion and over the next three years rode the Colchester, Bedfordshire, and Wiltshire circuits, none of which were particularly easy. Nevertheless Asbury stuck with it, demonstrating a resiliency that characterized his entire career. At the Bristol Annual Conference in August 1771 he answered Wesley's call for volunteers to go to America.

Under Asbury's leadership Methodism in America grew at an unprecedented rate, rising from a few hundred members in 1771 to more than 200,000 in 1816, the year of his death (Methodist Episcopal Church 1840: 5. 282). Methodism was the largest and most dynamic popular religious movement in America between the Revolution and the Civil War. In 1775, fewer than one out of every 800 Americans was a Methodist; by 1812 Methodists numbered one out of every 36 Americans. These figures are even more impressive given the movement's wider influence. Many more Americans attended Methodist gatherings than actually joined the church, particularly during this early, volatile period of growth.

As the movement's leader Asbury had a hand in shaping the religious lives of more people than probably any other American of his generation. Yet his dedication to the ministry cost him dearly, requiring that he set aside more worldly desires. During his forty-five-year career in America he never married, and never owned a home or much more than he could carry on horseback. He travelled at least 130,000 miles by horse and crossed the Allegheny Mountains some sixty times. He was more widely recognized face to face than any person of his generation, including such national figures as Thomas Jefferson and George Washington. Landlords and tavern keepers, not to mention ordinary Methodists, knew him on sight in every region.

ASBURY'S METHOD

Asbury communicated his vision for Methodism in four enduring ways that came to define much of evangelical culture in America. The first was through his legendary piety and perseverance, rooted in a classically evangelical conversion experience. No other Methodist, perhaps few other Americans, maintained as spiritually disciplined a life over such a long period of time as did Asbury. Where most Methodists, even most preachers, settled for a serviceable faith, he strove for a life of extraordinary devotion. Despite a gruelling schedule, he usually rose at 4 or 5 a.m. to pray for an hour in the morning stillness. During his forty-five years in America he essentially lived as a houseguest in thousands of other people's homes across the land. This manner of life 'exposed him, continually, to public or private observation and inspection, and subjected him to a constant and critical review; and that from day to day, and from year to year', wrote Ezekiel Cooper (1819: 21), who knew Asbury for more than thirty years. He had no private life beyond the confines of his mind.

Asbury's spiritual purity produced a 'confidence in the uprightness of his intentions and wisdom of his plans, which gave him such a control over both preachers and people as enabled him to discharge the high trusts confided to him, with so much facility and to such general satisfaction', observed one contemporary (Bangs 1839: ii. 401). Perseverance counted for much among evangelicals, and on this score Asbury had few equals. He relentlessly pushed himself to the breaking point of his health, seldom asking more of other Methodists than he was willing to do. From 1793 on he suffered from progressively worsening congestive heart failure, probably brought on by bouts of streptococcal pharyngitis (strep throat) and rheumatic fever that damaged his heart valves. As a result, he suffered from oedema in his feet made worse by endless hours on horseback with his feet dangling until they were too swollen to fit in the stirrups. Towards the end of his life he often had to be carried from his horse to his preaching appointments because he could not bear the pain of walking, which must have been an inspiring, if bizarre, sight. It left one observer who saw him preach in this condition in 'breathless awe and silent astonishment' (ibid. 364). Asbury's piety brought him respect, even renown, based on sacrifice rather than accumulation of buildings, money, or other trappings of power. 'It was almost impossible to approach, and converse with him, without feeling the strong influence of his spirit and presence.... There was something, in the remarkable fact, almost inexplicable, and indescribable', wrote Ezekiel Cooper (1819: 25–6) shortly after Asbury's death. Even James O'Kelly (1801: 61), who, in 1792, led the most bitter schism from the Methodist church in Asbury's lifetime, and acknowledged his 'cogent zeal, and unwearied diligence, in spite of every disappointment'. One lesson of Asbury's life is that mass religious movements are built on the backs of those who are willing to sacrifice body and soul to 'the work', as early Methodists would have said.

The second way that Asbury communicated his vision was through his ability to connect with ordinary people. 'Connexion' was an important word for early Methodists, and Asbury embodied its meaning better than anyone. As he criss-crossed the nation from year to year he conversed with countless thousands, demonstrating a gift for building relationships face to face or in small groups.

It is remarkable how many of those he met became permanent friends, even after a single conversation. Asbury often chided himself for talking too much and too freely, especially late at night. He considered this love of close, often lighthearted, conversation a drain on his piety. In reality it was one of his greatest strengths, allowing him to build deep and lasting relationships and to feel closely the pulse of the church and the nation. Henry Boehm (1866: 443), who travelled some 25,000 miles with Asbury from 1808 to 1813, recalled that 'in private circles he would unbend, and relate amusing incidents and laugh most heartily'. Asbury once told the Ohio preacher James Quinn, 'if I were not sometimes to be gay with my friends, I should have died in gloom long ago'. Quinn also remembered that in frontier cabins, 'the good Bishop always made himself pleasant and cheerful with the families, so that they soon forgot all embarrassment' (Wright 1851: 164, 245). In these settings Asbury felt most at home. 'His conversational powers were great. He was full of interesting anecdotes, and could entertain people for hours', Boehm (1866: 447) remembered. 'As a road-companion, no man could be more agreeable; he was cheerful almost to gaiety; his conversation was sprightly, and sufficiently seasoned with wit and anecdote', wrote Nicholas Snethen (1816: 9), who was Asbury's travelling companion for several years beginning in 1800. People found him approachable and willing to listen to their concerns more than they found him full of inspiring ideas. 'He was charitable, almost to excess, of the experience of others', remembered Snethen (ibid. 4).

Many recognized Asbury's ability to connect with people on a personal level, though few found it easy to explain. The dissident Methodist preacher Jeremiah Minter (1814: 7, 10, 11) concluded that Asbury must have been a 'sorcerer', 'in league with the devil' to have 'enchanted [and] deceived' so many who 'thought him a good man'. Asbury's only equal in this regard, Minter believed, was the famous evangelist Lorenzo Dow. 'With their *sorcery* and enchantments', Asbury and Dow had 'bewitched multitudes, who take them to be, as it were, the great power of God', Minter wrote in 1814, two years before Asbury's death. Few would have agreed with Minter's analysis, but many would have recognized what it was about Asbury that so annoyed Minter. Even James O'Kelly (1801: 61) confessed a 'disagreeable jealousy' over Asbury's ability to influence those closest to him.

The third conduit of Asbury's vision was the way that he understood and used popular culture. John Wesley and Asbury were alike in their willingness to negotiate between competing religious and cultural worlds. In his biography of Wesley, Henry Rack (1989: 352) argues persuasively that Wesley acted as a 'cultural middleman' between Methodists on the one hand and clergymen and educated gentlemen in England on the other. If so, then Asbury acted as a mediator between Wesley and common Americans. Wesley and Asbury came from significantly different backgrounds, but they shared a realization that the dominant religious institutions of their day were failing to reach most common people. The great question they both addressed was how to make the gospel socially and culturally relevant in their time and place. The audience was never far from their minds. This led Asbury to do things in America that he would not have done in England, some of which Wesley disapproved. Asbury, for example, accepted the emotionalism of southern worship in the 1770s, promoted camp meetings in the early 1800s, and reluctantly acquiesced to southern Methodists holding slaves. This mediating impulse, transmitted from Wesley through Asbury, became a trademark of American Methodism.

Yet Asbury did not accept American culture without reservation and never simply identified the mission of Methodism with that of America. He grew dismayed at the presence of slavery in the church, a reality that he tacitly accepted, but which haunted him for the last thirty years of his life. Furthermore, cultural adaptation is never a static thing, since both the church and the broader culture are constantly changing. Asbury was remarkably well informed (the product of his travels and love of conversation) and flexible in keeping up with these changes, but everyone has their limits. Though the American Revolution led to a good deal of persecution of American Methodists, Asbury fretted that its end would produce too much prosperity and thereby dampen Methodist zeal. Later he worried that the availability of cheap land in the West would have the same effect, drawing people's attention from spiritual concerns to the cares of this world. As long as they were poor, most Methodists agreed with Asbury that wealth was a snare. But as Methodists became generally more prosperous they became less concerned about the dangers of wealth, much to Asbury's dismay. By the end of his career he was largely out of step with the church that he was so instrumental in creating. This, in the end, seemed to him a great tragedy.

The fourth way that Asbury communicated his message was through his organization of the Methodist church. He was a brilliant administrator, and a keen judge of human motivations. He had a 'superior talent to read men', as Peter Cartwright ([1856]: 155) put it. As Asbury crisscrossed the nation year in and year out, he attended to countless details of doctrine, finance, discipline, and staffing. Yet he never lost sight of the people involved. The system he crafted made it possible to keep tabs on thousands of preachers and lay workers. By 1812 Asbury had nearly 700 itinerant preachers under his supervision (Methodist Episcopal Church 1840: 211).

At the centre of Asbury's system was the itinerant connexion. Asbury learned the itinerant system in England under John Wesley, bringing it to America where it worked even better than it had in England. Methodist itinerant preachers, or circuit riders, did not serve a single congregation or parish, but rather ministered to a number of congregations spread out along a circuit that the preacher continually rode. Under Asbury, the typical American itinerant rode a predominantly rural circuit 200 to 600 miles in circumference, typically with twenty-five to thirty preaching appointments per round. He completed the circuit every two to six weeks, with the standard being a four weeks' circuit of 400 miles. This meant that circuit riders had to travel and preach nearly every day, with only a few days for rest each month. Often they were assigned a partner, but even so, they usually started at opposite ends of the circuit instead of travelling together (Wigger 1998; 2001: 56–62). The itinerant system worked well for reaching post-revolutionary America's rapidly expanding population. In 1795, 95 per cent of Americans lived in places with fewer than 2,500 inhabitants; by 1830 this proportion was still 91 per cent. While Methodism retained a stronghold in the seaports of the middle states, Asbury hammered its organization into one that had a distinctly rural orientation adept at expanding into newly populated areas. 'We must draw resources from the centre to the circumference', he wrote in 1797 (F. Asbury 1958: iii. 332).

Despite its success, keeping the itinerant system intact proved the greatest challenge of Asbury's career. From the beginning he faced opposition from those unhappy with its demands and constraints. Some, like Joseph Pilmore, wanted to focus Methodist resources more on the cities of the Atlantic seaboard, where they believed it was important for Methodism to build a base of influence and social respectability. Others, like James O'Kelly, wanted to make Methodist polity more congregational, allowing preachers who had built up a local following to remain on the same circuit indefinitely. Asbury believed that all such proposals would ultimately limit the movement's ability to reach the most people with the gospel. He maintained that sending preachers where they would have the most telling impact, rather than leaving them where they were most comfortable, was crucial to the success of the Methodist system. For the most part Asbury succeeded in defending the itinerant system until the last decade of his life. By then a new generation of Methodists, one accustomed to a higher social status than their parents had enjoyed, had begun to chip away at his cherished itinerant connexion. For all its usefulness, the itinerant system was rooted in a particular place and time, something that Asbury couldn't fully understand.

There was another, less obvious but equally important, component of Asbury's system that went to the heart of what it meant to be a Methodist: to practise a method; the necessity of a culture of discipline. As individuals and communities, believers had to take it upon themselves to regulate their spiritual lives. Neither Asbury nor his preachers could be everywhere at once. This is why, from his first days in America, he insisted on upholding the requirement that all members attend class meetings, and that love feasts be limited to active members, creating an atmosphere of mutual trust and support. He delegated authority to others, recognizing that a voluntary system would not work if it relied on coercion from above. It needed to become a central component of people's world-view. Though there were plenty of disagreements along the way, Methodists succeeded where other religious groups failed in large measure because they were more disciplined. This culture of discipline nonetheless changed over time, much to Asbury's chagrin, as the church itself became more respectable and less countercultural (Wigger 1998; 2001: 173–90).

For all his focus on a single goal, Asbury remained a complex figure. At the core of his personality was a fear of rejection that at times made him seem aloof or severe in settings he found intimidating. He tended to hold others at arm's length until he could be sure of their intentions. John Wesley Bond ([1817]) remembered that Asbury himself believed 'that by nature he was suspicious'. Henry Boehm recalled that at a distance Asbury often seemed 'rough, unfeeling, harsh, and stoical'. While rarely mean-spirited, he feared being taken for a fool. 'I grant he had a rather rough exterior, that he was sometimes stern; but under that roughness and sternness of manner beat a heart as feeling as ever dwelt in human bosom', Boehm (1866: 451) asserted. Nicholas Snethen, who often opposed Asbury's policies after 1812 and later left the Methodist Episcopal Church, was not as forgiving as Boehm. Snethen believed that Asbury's 'suspicious disposition' stemmed 'from his well known irritability, his faculty of obtaining the most secret information, and the quickness and penetration of his genius'. Yet even Snethen did not believe that Asbury's 'ambition' flowed from 'a criminal nature'. Like nearly everyone who knew Asbury well, Snethen acknowledged his ability to assess human motivations, or, as he said, to judge 'human nature'. 'In what related to ecclesiastical men, and things, he was all eye, and ear; and what he saw and heard he never forgot. The tenacity of his memory was surprising. His knowledge of human nature was penetrating and extensive', wrote Snethen (1816: 6, 9). Asbury was a keen observer of the human heart, and it often left him melancholy.

For all his insight, Asbury was not a good preacher. His sermons were often disjointed and nearly impossible to follow. 'This excessive delicacy of feeling, which shuts my mouth so often, may appear strange to those who do not know me', he wrote in August 1806, and it did (F. Asbury 1958: ii. 515). Nathan Bangs heard him for the first time in New York in June 1804. 'His preaching was quite discursive, if not disconnected, a fact attributed to his many cares and unintermitted travels, which admitted of little or no study... He slid from one subject to another without system. He abounded in illustrations and anecdotes', remembered Bangs (Stevens 1863: 128). This was more or less what everyone said about Asbury's preaching.

Asbury's inability to speak clearly in formal settings led him to work through proxies. He was the quintessential backroom negotiator, perhaps his least admirable trait. 'In a judicial or legislative capacity he seemed not to excel, and hence he did not often appear to the best advantage in the chair of conferences', recalled Snethen, who observed Asbury at many conferences from 1794 to 1814. 'He knew also the art of governing, and seldom trusted to the naked force of authority. Indeed, the majesty of command, was almost wholly concealed, or superceded by that wonderful faculty, which belongs to this class of human geniuses, and which enables them to inspire their own disposition for action, into the breasts of others', concluded Snethen (1816: 6).

Wesleyan perfectionism—his belief that it was the duty of all believers to seek perfection in this life—also coloured Asbury's personality. It heightened his resolve but also his insecurities. His failings instilled in him a genuine humility. By the end of his career any number of churches had been named for him, but 'he did not approve of this, and called it folly', according to Boehm (1866: 446). He did not expect great rewards in this life because he did not believe he deserved them.

Yet Wesleyan perfectionism was not a theology of despair. With diligence, holiness was attainable in this life, if only for brief periods. Ultimately, believers could be confident of God's grace if their resolve did not waver. Guiding the church towards this goal became an all-consuming passion for Asbury. 'His patience in bearing disappointments was equal if not superior to that of any man I ever knew', remembered Bond ([1817]). According to Bond, Asbury rarely allowed himself to 'repine' or 'brood' over past difficulties, instead he turned them over in his mind, thinking 'How shall I mend it:—How can things be made better?'. In fact, Asbury did brood and fret, but it did not define him. He could sink deep within himself when concentrating on a problem, but this was not the same thing. 'At times he appeared unsociable, for his mind was engrossed with his work', recalled Boehm (1866: 448). Or, as Bond ([1817]) put it, Asbury 'thrust himself into every part of his charge; lest something might be wrong—lest some part of the cause of God might suffer'. Asbury had a thorough and even subtle mind, but he was often slow in formulating his ideas. He could work his way through thorny problems, but it took time. The long hours he spent on horseback gave him the space for reflection, prayer, and meditation he needed. Those who did not know him sometimes mistook his preoccupation for severity.

Coupled with Asbury's fear of rejection was a genuine compassion for others, especially the downtrodden. He believed that true religion embraced the suffering of the poor and did all that was possible to alleviate it. Resources should be channelled to those most in need, not squandered on luxuries, he believed. This is why he allowed himself few comforts. His clothes were cheap and plain, though he took some care to appear presentable. He often said 'that the equipment of a Methodist minister consisted of a horse, saddle and bridle, one suit of clothes, a watch, a pocket Bible, and a hymn book. Anything else would be an encumbrance' (Boehm 1866: 445; Smith 1848: 34). Indeed, Asbury rarely owned much more than this. At the same time, he gave away nearly all the money that came his way. Both Boehm and Bond kept track of Asbury's funds while travelling with him as assistants. 'He would divide his last dollar with a Methodist preacher', Boehm (1866: 454–5) recalled. 'He was restless till it was gone, so anxious was he to do good with it.' Once, in Ohio, Asbury and Boehm came across a widow whose only cow was about to be sold for debt. Determining that 'It must not be', Asbury gave what he had and solicited enough from bystanders to pay the woman's bills. 'His charity knew no bounds but the limits of its resources; nor did I ever know him let an object of charity pass without contributing something for their relief', wrote Bond ([1817]). He recalled that Asbury often gave money to strangers he met on the road whose circumstances seemed dire, especially widows. He had his share of failings, but the love of money wasn't one of them. This won him a great deal of respect from almost everyone who knew him.

LEGACY

After Asbury's death in 1816 admirers and critics sought to define his legacy. The former pointed to his intense spirituality and perseverance, his ability to connect with people and his administrative finesse as the defining qualities of his career. The latter decried his lack of democratic sensibilities and what they saw as apostolic pretensions. What neither Asbury's admirers, including Ezekiel Cooper (1819), Nathan Bangs (1839), Abel Stevens (1867), John Emory ([1827]), Frederick Briggs (1890) and Ezra S. Tipple (1916), or his critics, Edward Drinkhouse (1899), Alexander M'Caine (1850), and Nicholas Snethen (1816), for example, doubted was that he was important. Yet by the Civil War Asbury had begun to lose his salience in popular culture. 'There is a man, not even named in our leading histories, who yet has wrought more deeply into American life in its social, moral, and religious facts than any other who lived and acted his part in our more formative period', began an 1866 article in *Harper's New Monthly Magazine* ('Francis Asbury', 1866). What follows is a brief laudatory biography of Asbury that assumes, clearly enough, that readers know little about him. In the fifty years following his death Asbury had failed to become an American hero. 'The names of Ethan Allen and Anthony Wayne have been more familiar to the popular ear of America than that of Asbury; yet how trivial their influence compared to his!' concluded the anonymous author in *Harper's*.

Methodists themselves were largely responsible for Asbury's fall from popular grace. Upwardly mobile Methodists were glad to be shot of ministers 'who preached dreary out-of-date sermons, and who lacked even the most rudimentary sense of social distinctions', as Harold Frederic put it in his popular novel, *The Damnation of Theron Ware* (1896, 1960). Asbury meant little to Methodists who were generally happy to see the church's rise in wealth and social status.

By the twentieth century most Methodists saw themselves as part of the Protestant mainstream. From this vantage point Asbury looked different than he had in the nineteenth century. Much of this new historical perspective was shaped by William Warren Sweet (1881–1959), the dean of Methodist studies in the first half of the twentieth century. Sweet grew up in Baldwin City, Kansas, before attending college at Ohio Wesleyan University and seminary at Drew University, followed by a doctorate at the University of Pennsylvania. He then taught at Ohio Wesleyan and Depauw University before becoming Professor of American Christianity at the University of Chicago. He was, according to his biographer, 'the first trained, professional, American historian who specialized in religion' (Ash, 1982: p. xiv).

Sweet was shaped by his background in the church (he had planned to become a minister before his doctorate) and the academy. As was typical of historians of the early twentieth century, he believed that history could be pursued as an objective science, free of personal bias, in which the facts spoke for themselves. He was also deeply influenced by Frederick Jackson Turner's frontier thesis, which hypothesized that the availability of 'free' frontier land had made possible the development of American democracy and individualism. Sweet's contribution was to find a role for the church (by which he mostly meant the Methodists, Baptists, Presbyterians, and Congregationalists) in this scheme, arguing that organized religion's greatest contribution to American life was in bringing civilization to the frontier. 'On every American frontier life was crude, and ignorance and lawlessness were everywhere in evidence. The great majority of the people were indifferent to the prevailing conditions and accepted them as a matter of course', Sweet (1952: 161–2) writes in one of his later books. Fortunately, all was not lost. 'There was in every considerable community a little company of people, the majority of them constituting the membership and the ministry of the frontier churches, who believed that conditions could be changed; that life on every frontier could be raised to a higher level, and thus through them the seeds of culture were planted in the west', writes Sweet (ibid. 161).

Within this framework Asbury is presented as a 'benevolent despot' and an agent of order and control (ibid. 115). In regard to the 'religious frenzy' often associated with frontier revivals, Sweet assures his readers that it is 'an entire misconception' that Asbury and his preachers did anything to promote such 'extravagances'. 'Asbury, like Wesley, believed that everything should be done decently and in order. Indeed, order was his passion and this he communicated to his preachers' (Sweet 1933: 159). Sweet's scholarship was voluminous (he published twenty-five books, beginning in 1912) and he did more than anyone to make primary sources readily available. Nonetheless his interpretation of Asbury has done as much to obscure as illuminate. In Sweet's hands Asbury became the patron saint of decency and decorum.

These views were reflected in what remained of Asbury's image in the broader culture. As the US Army Band played 'The Star-Spangled Banner' on a 'perfect' October day in 1924, with 'not a fleck of cloud in the sky', an imposing bronze statue of Asbury on horseback was unveiled in Washington, DC, at the intersection of Sixteenth and Mount Pleasant streets (Carroll 1925: 13). Celebrated amidst much fanfare in front of a distinguished audience—President Calvin Coolidge gave the keynote address—the unveiling marked a high-water mark for Methodist influence in American society, and perhaps for all mainstream Protestantism. The Scopes monkey trial took place the next summer in Dayton, Tennessee. It is significant that the church selected Asbury to represent them, though it was a carefully crafted image of Asbury that the clergy and politicians chose to remember. To them Asbury was first and foremost a patriotic American. 'On the foundation of a religious civilization which he sought to build our country has enjoyed greater blessings of liberty and prosperity than were ever before the lot of man', Coolidge declared amid cries of 'Hear! Hear!' and vigorous applause. 'Asbury must be called great, because he laid the foundation of the great Christian empire, of the increase of whose ministry and peace there shall be no end', added Methodist Bishop J. W. Hamilton (ibid. 31, 33). Granted, public celebrations of this nature are generally not the place to raise a controversy, but the effect was to obscure Asbury behind a haze of patriotic consensus, to make him seem no different from any of the generals memorialized in bronze throughout the city, only perhaps less well armed.

The most sensational biography of Asbury is Herbert Asbury's *A Methodist Saint: The Life of Bishop Asbury*, published by Alfred A. Knopf in 1927. Having turned his back on his strictly religious upbringing in a small town in south-eastern Missouri, Herbert Asbury intended to expose Francis Asbury as the demagogue of a fanatical religion that promised 'spiritual loot' to simple country folk (H. Asbury 1927: 53). In an earlier book, *Up From Methodism* (he later wrote *Gangs of New York*), Asbury describes growing up among Methodists on his father's side (he claims that Francis Asbury was the half-brother of his great-great-grandfather, but this is unlikely) and Baptists on his mother's side. The more devout the relative, the more repressive and sadistic the religion. 'Among all my relatives I do not recall one whose home was not oppressed, and whose life was not made miserable and fretful, by the terrible fear of a relentless God whose principal occupation seemed to be snooping about searching for someone to punish', writes Herbert Asbury (1926: 98). 'I find myself full of contempt for the Church, and disgust for the forms of religion. To me such things are silly; I cannot understand how grown people can believe in them, or how they can repress their giggles as they listen to the ministerial platitudes and perform such mummeries as are the rule in all churches', concludes Asbury (ibid. 168). No unbiased observer, this Herbert Asbury.

Asbury (1927: 1) begins *Methodist Saint* by informing his readers that while Elizabeth Asbury 'was pregnant God appeared to her in a vision and told her that her child would be a boy and that the lad was destined to become a great religious leader and spread the Gospel among the heathen, although He did not specify the Americans'. We are also told that Elizabeth was 'ambitious' for Francis 'to become Archbishop of Canterbury', and that her 'favourite scriptural readings were the bloody horrors of the Old Testament, and those portions of the gospels which describe the agonies of Christ bleeding on the cross', which she dinned into Francis even during his infancy. And this is all on the first page! Later, Herbert tells us that at the time Francis came to America 'the people generally were not only weary of wresting a living from the wilderness, but had become alarmed and frightened by the clamours and excitements of the impending Revolution, and had reached that pitch of emotional insanity and instability which has always been essential to the success of Methodism' (ibid. 51–2).

In a chapter entitled 'The Father of Prohibition', Herbert tells us that Francis was 'the real father of prohibition in the United States', who did more than anyone else to frighten good folk away from the enjoyment of a refreshing beverage (ibid. 137). In making such a claim he either ignored or was ignorant of the fact that Asbury drank alcohol in moderation. With evident glee Herbert (ibid. 249) describes the 'jerking, barking, jumping, hopping, dancing, prancing, screeching, howling, writhing in fits and convulsions, falling in cataleptic trances' and other 'holy antics' that attended camp meetings. 'One child was considered especially blessed because she barked hoarsely, like a mastiff, while the best the others could do was to imitate spaniels or other small dogs,' he informs us, though without citing a source (ibid. 258). 'Francis Asbury regarded camp-meetings with great favour; to him the spectacle of thousands of men and women and little children writhing in torment was a glorious visitation of the Lord, and he loved to hear a score of howling prophets belabouring the wicked', he writes (ibid. 248). One has to admire the audacity of an author who, when faced with a lull in his narrative, simply makes something up, the more outrageous the better. In the end, Herbert's main complaint against Francis was that he did not drink, smoke, or chase women enough. Instead, Francis's 'whole life is a record of fearful grovelling before the Almighty' (ibid. 264). *Methodist Saint* is a fun read, but only if one does not take it too seriously.

But many did. It is a testimony to just how little the reading public knew about Francis Asbury or early Methodism that Herbert Asbury could publish *Methodist Saint* with a leading commercial press to generally favourable reviews. A review in the *New York Times* touted the book as 'impressively documented' and 'damaging to Methodism' in the way that it exposed the church's early fanaticism and 'grotesque personalities' ('Bishop Asbury' 1927). This kind of reception helps explain why William Warren Sweet and the Asbury monument backers were anxious to make their founding figure seem so rational and respectable. They can perhaps be forgiven for seeing in Asbury only what seemed most pertinent to their needs at the moment. They were willing to admit that he could be heavy-handed, but they insisted that he was also a calmly rational man who would have felt perfectly at home in modern America.

More recent analyses of early Methodism and biographies of Asbury have done better at identifying the importance of Methodism in America's religious landscape and Asbury's role in formulating the church. While Methodism is declining in membership in the US today, some of its offshoots, including much of Pentecostalism, are thriving, as is evangelical culture in general, which Methodism did much to create. The cultural and religious patterns that Asbury helped to create are a big reason why. Asbury is a model of a new kind of religious leader, defined by a sincere practice of piety, an ability to connect with ordinary people, a considerable degree of cultural sensitivity, and an ability to organize effectively. This model has proved remarkably resilient across the American religious landscape.

SUGGESTED READING

The two most recent biographies of Francis Asbury are Darius Salter's *America's Bishop* (2003) and L. C. Rudolph's *Francis Asbury* (1966). A number of recent works have integrated Asbury into the larger story of early American Methodism and the rise of new religious movements between the American Revolution and the Civil War. These include Dee Andrews's *The Methodists and Revolutionary America, 1760–1800* (2000), Nathan Hatch's *The Democratization of American Christianity* (1989), David Hempton's *Methodism: Empire of the Spirit* (2005), Christine Leigh Heyrman's *Southern Cross* (1997), Cynthia Lynn Lyerly's *Methodism and the Southern Mind, 1770–1810* (1998), Mark Noll's *America's God* (2002), and Russell Richey's *Early American Methodism* (1991).

REFERENCES

ANDREWS, DEE E. (2000). *The Methodists and Revolutionary America, 1760–1800: The Shaping of an Evangelical Culture.* Princeton: Princeton University Press.

ASBURY, FRANCIS (1958). *The Journals and Letters of Francis Asbury*, ed. E. T. Clark, J. M. Potts, and J. S. Payton. 3 vols. London: Epworth.

ASBURY, HERBERT (1927). *A Methodist Saint: The Life of Bishop Asbury.* New York: Alfred A. Knopf.

—— (1926). *Up From Methodism.* New York: Alfred A. Knopf.

ASH, J. L. (1982). *Protestantism and the American University: An Intellectual Biography of William Warren Sweet.* Dallas: Southern Methodist University Press.

BANGS, NATHAN (1839). *A History of the Methodist Episcopal Church.* 2 vols. New York: T. Mason & G. Lane.

'Bishop Asbury as the Devil's Foe: Methodism's Founder in America Sought to Build Up a "Poor Man's Religion"' (3 April 1927). *New York Times*, ProQuest Historical Newspapers (1851–2003).

BOEHM, HENRY (1866). *Reminiscences, Historical and Biographical, of Sixty-Four Years in the Ministry.* New York: Carlton & Porter.

BOND, J. W. ([1817]) 'Anecdotes of Bishop Asbury'. Madison, N.J.: Drew University Library.

BRIGGS, F. W. (1890). *Bishop Asbury: A Biographical Study for Christian Workers.* 3rd edn. London: Wesleyan Conference Office.

CARROLL, H. K. (ed.) (1925). *The Francis Asbury Monument in the National Capital.* Francis Asbury Memorial Association Press of the Methodist Book Concern. (n.p.).

CARTWRIGHT, PETER ([1856]). *Autobiography of Peter Cartwright: The Backwoods Preacher*, ed. W. P. Strickland. Cincinnati: Cranston & Curts.

COOPER, EZEKIEL (1819). *The Substance of a Funeral Discourse, Delivered at the Request of the Annual Conference, on Tuesday, the 23d of April, 1816, in St. George's Church, Philadelphia: on the Death of the Rev. Francis Asbury, Superintendent, or Senior Bishop, of the Methodist Episcopal Church.* Philadelphia: Jonathan Pounder.

DRINKHOUSE, E. J. (1899). *History of Methodist Reform.* Baltimore: Methodist Protestant Church, i.

EMORY, JOHN ([1827]). *A Defence of 'Our Fathers', and of the Original Organization of the Methodist Episcopal Church, Against the Rev. Alexander M'Caine and Others.* New York: Phillips & Hunt.

'FRANCIS ASBURY' (July 1866). In *Harper's New Monthly Magazine* 33/194: 210–21.

FREDERIC, HAROLD (1896, 1960). *The Damnation of Theron Ware*, ed Everett Carter. Cambridge, Mass.: Harvard University Press.

HALLAM, D. J. A. (2003). *Eliza Asbury: Her Cottage and Her Son*. Studley, Warks.: Brewin Books.

HATCH, NATHAN O. (1989). *The Democratization of American Christianity*. New Haven: Yale University Press.

HEMPTON, DAVID (2005). *Methodism: Empire of the Spirit*. New Haven: Yale University Press.

HEYRMAN, CHRISTINE LEIGH (1997). *Southern Cross: The Beginnings of the Bible Belt*. Chapel Hill: University of North Carolina Press.

LYERLY, CYNTHIA LYNN (1998). *Methodism and the Southern Mind, 1770–1810*. New York: Oxford University Press.

M'CAINE, ALEXANDER (1850). *Letters on the Organization and Early History of the Methodist Episcopal Church*. Boston: Thomas F. Norris.

Methodist Episcopal Church (1840). *Minutes of the Annual Conferences of the Methodist Episcopal Church for the Years 1773–1828*, New York: T. Mason & G. Lane.

MINTER, JEREMIAH (1814). *Scripture Proofs of Sorcery, and Warning Against Sorcerers*. Richmond, Va.: Ritchie & Trueheart.

NOLL, MARK A. (2002). *America's God: From Jonathan Edwards to Abraham Lincoln*. New York: Oxford University Press.

O'KELLY, JAMES (1801). *Vindication of the Author's Apology, With Reflections on the Reply and a Few Remarks on Bishop Asbury's Annotations on His Book of Discipline*. Raleigh, N.C.: Joseph Gates.

RACK, HENRY (1989). *Reasonable Enthusiast: John Wesley and the Rise of Methodism*. London: Epworth.

RICHEY, RUSSELL E. (1991). *Early American Methodism*. Bloomington: Indiana University Press.

RUDOLPH, L. C. (1966). *Francis Asbury*. Nashville: Abingdon.

SALTER, DARIUS L. (2003). *America's Bishop: The Life of Francis Asbury*. Nappanee, Ind.: Evangel Publishing House.

SMITH, THOMAS (1848). *Experience and Ministerial Labors of Rev. Thomas Smith, Late an Itinerant Preacher of the Gospel in the Methodist Episcopal Church. Compiled Chiefly From His Journal*, ed. David Dailey. New York: Lane & Tippett.

SNETHEN, NICHOLAS (1816). *A Discourse on the Death of the Reverend Francis Asbury*. Baltimore: John J. Harrod.

STEVENS, ABEL (1867). *History of the Methodist Episcopal Church in the United States of America*. 4 vols. New York: Carlton & Porter.

—— (1863). *Life and Times of Nathan Bangs, D. D*. New York: Carlton & Porter.

TIPPLE, E. S. (1916). *Francis Asbury: The Prophet of the Long Road*. New York: Methodist Book Concern.

SWEET, W. W. (1933). *Methodism in American History*. New York: Methodist Book Concern.

—— (1952). *Religion in the Development of American Culture, 1765–1840*. New York: Charles Scribner's Sons.

WARE, THOMAS (1832). 'The Christmas Conference of 1784'. *The Methodist Magazine and Quarterly Review* 14/1: 96–104.

—— (1840). *Sketches of the Life and Travels of Rev. Thomas Ware*. New York: T. Mason and G. Lane.

WIGGER, J. H. (1998, 2001). *Taking Heaven by Storm: Methodism and the Rise of Popular Christianity in America.* New York: Oxford University Press; Urbana: University of Illinois Press.

WRIGHT, J. F. (1851). *Sketches of the Life and Labors of James Quinn.* Cincinnati: Methodist Book Concern.

CHAPTER 4

THE PEOPLE CALLED METHODISTS

TRANSITIONS IN BRITAIN AND NORTH AMERICA

DAVID HEMPTON

THE four most important insights on the rise of Methodism in the north Atlantic world to emerge in the last quarter of a century are: that Methodism, although originating in England in the 1730s, was a genuinely international religious movement with roots in European intellectual culture in the age of Enlightenment; that Methodism developed organizational and spiritual characteristics enabling it to thrive in symbiosis with the rise of modernity including the growth of individualism, markets, and democracy; that Methodism, although led largely by men, was in its rank-and-file predominantly a women's movement; and that in terms of understanding the 'lived religion' of the Methodist faithful in all its rich diversity the task of historical reconstruction has barely just begun.

The contrast between these four observations and the state of scholarship on the rise of English and American Methodism a quarter of a century ago could hardly be starker, and is revealing of the trajectory of Methodist historical studies since the middle of the twentieth century. When I first became interested in English

Methodism in the 1970s, for example, most of the important scholarship operated around four major questions arising directly out of the English historiographical tradition. What was the relationship between Methodism, proto-industrialization, and the rise of factory production? To what extent did Methodism contribute to English political stability in the era of the French Revolution? How far was Methodism an important contributor to the rise of the English liberal tradition? And lastly, to what extent did Methodism advance the cause of the English labor movement through the inculcation of organizing and speaking skills? The most well-known scholars to address these questions were respectively E. P. Thompson, Elie Halévy, Bernard Semmel, and Robert Wearmouth. Together they helped integrate Methodism into the English historical narrative, which was no mean achievement, but in so doing they helped perpetuate a 'little Englander' approach to the Methodist movement. Similar approaches, albeit asking different questions pertinent to their own national traditions, characterized the work of historians on Irish, Welsh, Canadian, American, and Australasian Methodism. In the United States, for example, where Methodism achieved its most resounding numerical success, scholars were interested primarily in assessing the relationship between Methodism and the rise of a market economy, the democratization of religious and political culture, and the civilizing of the fast-moving Western frontier. All these questions were determined not so much by attempts to get to the heart of Methodism as a transnational religious movement, but rather to investigate how its rise related to the established discourses of American history. In short, until around the mid 1970s most of the scholarship on Methodism in the British Isles and North America was occasioned more by the pre-existing discourses of national historical traditions than by any attempt to come to terms with Methodism as a popular religious movement that helped shape the lives and religious beliefs and practices of hundreds of thousands of people. That picture has changed considerably in the last thirty years. In the light of that change the aim of this chapter is to sketch in the state of scholarship on the four important issues mentioned in the opening paragraph and to make some suggestions about how they might be developed even further in the future.

The first point, namely the idea that Methodism was an international religious movement with roots in European intellectual culture in the age of Enlightenment, has been amplified in several important books by W. R. Ward. In his magisterial book *The Protestant Evangelical Awakening* Ward (1992) locates the seeds of the eighteenth-century Great Awakening among the anxieties of European Protestants in the aftermath of the Thirty Years War. A combination of low morale, fear of persecution, confessional conflict, heightened eschatological expectation, and pious devotion characterized the Protestant communities of central Europe at a time of religious and political instability. The religious life of Europe was quite simply breaking free from state-imposed confessional control at precisely the time when such control was pursued with renewed vigour. As a result the pietism of

Halle and Herrnhut was fanned into revivals in various Protestant corners of the Habsburg Empire and was then carried to the British Isles and North America by sweeping population movements and by a remarkable collection of revivalists who knew of each other's labours, believed themselves to be part of a worldwide movement of grace, and corresponded vigorously with one another. In addition to the mountain of evangelical correspondence, both the Moravians and the Methodists frequently gathered for 'letter days' on which letters were read aloud about the progress of religious revivals. The aim was to spread news, stimulate prayer, and persuade the faithful that they were part of a worldwide movement of grace transforming the world in their own lifetimes. Not only were letters and print circulating at remarkable speed, but also revival groups borrowed from one another's liturgical forms, organizational structures, and discipling techniques. In short, the revived saw themselves as an expanding, communicating, and connecting movement not confined to a particular locale or country.

As letters circulated so too did the people who wrote them. A combination of confessional cleansing, imperial expansion, cultural fascination with the peripheries of empire, religious revivalism, the rise of global trade (including the execrable but flourishing slave trade), and the movement of armies all combined to produce a remarkably mobile population of popular Protestants in the eighteenth century. Historians more interested in structural changes than personal narratives often ignore individual stories of migration, partly because they were later embellished for pious consumption and hagiographical purpose, but that is a mistake, for they are deeply revealing of Methodism as an international movement. A few examples may serve to make the point. Barbara Ruckle was part of a colony of German refugees from the Palatinate given land grants in Ireland in the wake of Louis XIV's successive devastations of the Palatinate. Ruckle, her husband Paul Heck, and her cousin Philip Embury, like many other European Protestant refugees in eighteenth-century Ireland, were revived by John Wesley before moving to New York where they were instrumental in setting up a Methodist society and building the first Methodist chapel in America. But the story does not end there. Forming Methodist societies along the way, the Hecks later migrated up the Hudson Valley and then, as Empire Loyalists, on up into Montreal and later to Augusta township in Upper Canada. Their story of how a European pietist minority, displaced and persecuted as a result of confessional cleansing, came into contact with a new kind of enthusiastic Protestantism in Britain and Ireland, which was then exported to America and Canada, is powerfully emblematic of the awakenings of the eighteenth century.

There are yet further dimensions to how this worked. Methodism thrived, for example, among soldiers in barracks and garrisons. A combination of a dangerous occupation and mutual dependence, whether in mines, seaports, or armies, was always good for Methodist recruitment. But armies were particularly useful as a means of transmission, because they moved, conquered, and demobilized. Michael Snape has shown that Methodism was particularly strong among the ranks of

British soldiers in the eighteenth century, including some remarkable instances of Methodist-inspired revivalism in Flanders in 1745. In the same year John Wesley preached to Dutch, Swiss, and German troops on station in the north of England to suppress the Jacobite Rebellion. Snape (2005: 57) concludes from all this that although the international dimension of Methodism has been emphasized in recent years 'its military dimensions have been largely ignored, notwithstanding the fact that the wars of the mid-eighteenth century helped to displace tens of thousands of Protestants in northern Europe, the British Isles and North America and bring them into much closer contact with one another'. For example, Thomas Webb, an English military veteran of the Seven Years War, demobilized, and then organized Methodist societies with military efficiency in the middle Atlantic colonies in the 1760s. Indeed, wherever one looks at the spread of Methodism in its pioneering phase, soldiers patrolling the empire were often key figures in its transmission. The earliest Methodist societies in South Africa (1806) and Tasmania (1820), for example, were directly the result of military mobility.

Early Methodist preachers (some of whom were soldiers) were similarly mobile. It is a striking feature of the biographies of early Methodist itinerant and local preachers throughout the English-speaking world how many of them were born in one country and ministered in several others. The first Wesleyan preacher to travel in America, Robert Williams, grew up in Wales and ministered in Ireland before fetching up in America. Similarly, John Newland Maffitt, who had the rare honour of preaching before the United States Senate and House of Representatives in 1842, was born in Dublin in 1794, migrated to New York in his twenties, then moved to New England before following the general westward and southern drift of American Methodism and helping to establish important Methodist publishing ventures in Cincinnati and Nashville. In this way the symbiosis of a Methodist structure that was built for mobility and an international order of unprecedented population movement was a particularly important factor in the rise of Methodism from an English sect to an international movement. From the sugar plantations of the Caribbean Islands to the trading routes of the East India Company, and from the south-western migrations of American slaves to the convict ships bound for Australasia, Methodists exploited the mobile margins of trade and empire establishing societies as they travelled. Equipped with a flexible ecclesiology that easily facilitated expansion and armed with a sense of being part of a growing international movement, Methodism was highly mobile. The Methodist laity, identified by their ubiquitous class membership tickets, which acted as both religious currency and abbreviated letters of recommendation, could change their location without changing their religious tradition.

International movement and migration are only part of the story however, for in Ward's most recent book on *Early Evangelicalism* he shows how the rise of Methodism needs to be located in the global intellectual culture of the late seventeenth and early eighteenth centuries. According to Ward (2006: 4) early evangelicals, though sometimes bitterly divided over both belief and practice, nevertheless constructed a global fraternity around at least six important themes: 'the close association with mysticism, the small-group religion, the deferred eschatology, the experimental approach to conversion, anti-Aristotelianism and hostility to theological system, and the attempt to reinforce religious vitality by setting it in the context of a vitalist understanding of nature'. These themes 'formed a sort of evangelical hexagon lasting until the original evangelical cohesion began to fail'.

Ward locates John Wesley and early Methodism within this evangelical hexagon. Although Wesley brought Puritan precisionism into his mysticism, and although he denounced the mysticism of the Moravians, he nevertheless displayed some mystical traits beyond his conversion and included his favourite mystics in his *Christian Library* for the benefit of his followers. Ward's sharp observation is that Wesley's favourite mystics were the energetic activists such as De Renty and Lopez rather than the exotic visionaries such as Madame Guyon. Moving on around the hexagon Wesley promoted experiential conversion and heart religion, used Bengel's eschatology to ensure that Methodism did not become a millennial sect, employed small group religion and a mild version of the priesthood of all believers at the heart of his organizational system, held the line against Aristotelian theological systems especially in his fierce opposition to Calvinism, and flirted with the paranormal in any number of guises (including belief in poltergeists) in his own highly distinctive vitalization of nature. Here in a six-point nutshell are many of the most important components of early Methodism.

What then does an international perspective reveal about what was distinctive about Methodism as a religious movement? I attempted to answer that question at some length in my book, *Methodism: Empire of the Spirit* (Hempton 2005), but some of the points bear reiteration. It is clear, for example, that in its early spread across the North Atlantic region Methodism thrived most in those areas settled by Anglicans and European pietists. From Welsh valleys to the border counties of southern Ulster, and from Antigua to the Delmarva Peninsula, Methodism operated initially as a more enthusiastic form of Anglicanism. Another fruitful line of enquiry would be to compare the detailed micro histories of Methodist expansion in both the British Isles and North America which make the point that Methodism expanded along the arteries of emerging transportation systems, and therefore expanded with the growth of market economies. Such studies also make clear that Methodism thrived in areas where paternalistic social control was either absent or under attack, and in areas where Calvinist theological ideas and their cultural consequences were resented or repudiated. In social contexts experiencing the anxiety of rapid transformation, Methodism with its harsh disciplines and tender pieties offered a powerful blend of discipline and ecstasy. Almost all of these features show up in the different parts of the world into which Methodism expanded in the first hundred years of its existence, and none of them is quite as sharply focused when analysis is confined only to one location or national tradition. Taken together and pursued rigorously, these shared components have the capacity to revolutionize future historical writing on the Methodist movement. By interpreting Methodism as an international movement rather than as a product of a particular national tradition, historians will not only have a better grasp of what was distinctively Methodist about Methodism, but also acquire a wider range of analytical tools and comparative devices for investigating the effects of Methodism in a particular locality, region, or country.

Perhaps the most difficult question framed around Methodism as an international movement, and one that needs urgent attention is this: is it possible to identify within the Methodist diaspora a single compelling idea at the heart and centre of the Methodist component of the international Great Awakening? Is there a meme of Methodism, and if so, what is it? One contender for the central idea of Methodism is a strong belief in the achievability of personal and social holiness on earth as in heaven. In that respect Methodism, by propagating religion as a means and a way to a better life for individuals and communities was a kind of popular Protestant parallel to the Enlightenment. Crucial to the holiness experiment was the notion that pure religion was a self-adopted choice, not a state-sponsored obligation. The deceptively simple idea propagated in word and song by John and Charles Wesley was that notwithstanding the political corruption and pastoral lethargy of Hanoverian England it was possible through divine initiative, human cooperation, and the empowerment of the Spirit to promote personal and social holiness of such quality that it dared hope for perfection in the life of the believer and purification of the wider society. Sometimes in writing about Methodism the concepts of Arminian theology and entire sanctification are used with almost forensic theological detachment to describe the kind of religious animal Methodism was. But these are concepts worth pausing over, for they describe a movement that was constructed on the outrageous propositions (at least for early moderns) that human beings could cooperate with divine intentions and that holiness or wholeness was possible both within the human heart and the social order. Not only was personal and social holiness possible, it was deemed essential as a welcoming gift to the returning Christ. It was this millennial optimism about the imminence of the kingdom of God and the transformation of the human condition that helped fuel Methodist expansion throughout the North Atlantic region and beyond in the eighteenth and nineteenth centuries.

There are still other distinctive aspects of Methodist expansion across the north Atlantic region in the eighteenth and nineteenth centuries that shed light on the nature of the Methodist movement. Compare for example the fate of Methodist expansion among Native Americans and African Americans. The Methodist mission to Native Americans in the nineteenth century was by no means a total failure, but neither could it be described as a conspicuous success. It limped along with enough success stories to swell the annual reports of the Missionary Society, but with insufficient éclat or dynamism to attract energetic enthusiasts from without or a vital leadership from within. Methodists believed that the power of the gospel would 'convert the savage hearts' and then 'the light of civilization' would change their habits. This tidy vision of Native Americans converting to Christianity, forsaking nomadic customs, opting for a settled and domesticated lifestyle, and becoming a generation of good citizens, pious Christians, and industrious farmers proved to be incapable of mass realization. Unlike other kinds of Methodist migrants, Native Americans did not choose to move in search of self-improvement or to avoid religious persecution, but were victims of draconian removals perpetrated by the very civilization the Methodists represented. This mismatch between what Methodism offered and what Native Americans wanted or needed was too stark for Methodism ever to achieve a substantial presence among them. In short, Methodism's symbiosis with modernity failed to resonate with those who were among modernity's most conspicuous victims.

This analysis can be deepened further by comparing the relative failure of the Methodist mission to Native Americans with its much greater success among African American slaves, who were also spatially disrupted and brutally treated. The Methodist mission to African slaves in the Caribbean Islands and in the American South benefited from early Methodism's opposition to slavery, the religious congruity of some aspects of African tribal religions with those of popular evangelicalism, the appeal of biblical deliverance narratives to those in bondage, and the ability of African Americans to adapt Methodism's oral and singing traditions to their own cultural traditions. In addition, African American slaves, though badly treated, were nevertheless growing numerically and expanding geographically, neither of which was true of Native Americans. Methodism, along with the Baptists, reaped a rich harvest among African slaves, and for a time was organized as a biracial religious movement, but inexorably throughout the nineteenth century black Methodists withdrew to found their own Methodist traditions in which they could offer leadership and experience worship without suffering from white control and discrimination. In the last few decades there has been significant progress made in our understanding of the growth and characteristics of black Methodism, but much more remains to be done, especially in coming to grips with how it was that populist forms of white evangelical Protestantism made such an impact on black religious culture. In particular, the role of black agency of both women and men in how that story unfolded is only now beginning to be told.

If Methodism largely failed to bring its modernizing message to the Native Americans, a population defined by culture and ethnicity, it failed equally to make much impact among a much larger population defined by religion and tradition, the Roman Catholics. In the annual reports of the Methodist missionary societies on both sides of the Atlantic, anti-Catholicism is ubiquitous. So too is a Methodist self-image of a predominantly Anglo-American movement providentially selected by God to redeem the world. The growth and progress of the British Empire and the

United States, of science and enlightenment, of trade and industry, of freedom and democracy, and of evangelical Protestantism and the English language were all thought to be linked in a great divine plan in which the Methodists were destined to play a central role. Wherever Methodists encountered strong, established traditions of Roman Catholicism, whether in Ireland, France, Mexico, or the growing migrant populations of American cities, the same old stories of anti-Catholic polemic and lack of evangelistic success show up in the archives. As Methodism spread across the north Atlantic region in the eighteenth and nineteenth centuries, it bumped up against, but rarely infiltrated, communities built around Roman Catholic traditions, symbols, and liturgies. Only by viewing Methodism through a transnational lens does it become clear that Methodism and Roman Catholicism were largely antithetical religious systems whose mutual suspicion was based not merely on the historical contingencies and political power structures of a particular place.

What then of the second of the issues posed in our opening paragraph, namely how did Methodist expansion in Britain and North America relate to other changes in cultural sensibilities associated with modernity? One creative way into that discussion is through Methodist conversion narratives and what they reveal about changing notions of the self in the early modern period. In an important recent book Bruce Hindmarsh (2005: 32) suggests that evangelical conversion narratives appeared along with new conceptions of the self at what he calls 'the trailing edge of Christendom and the leading edge of modernity'. According to Hindmarsh the Renaissance made people more aware of themselves as individuals while Reformation Protestantism made them more aware of themselves as sinners. Penitential traditions of Christianity with their emphases on anxiety, awareness of sin, and guilt were thus brought into contact with modern conceptions of the self arising from commercial individualism and Lockean empiricism. The result of this encounter was to produce modern selves with increased awareness of sin and guilt to which the evangelical message brought new possibilities of release, reformation, and refashioning. This is complicated stuff, for different traditions of evangelicalism—Methodist, Moravian, Calvinist, Dissenting, and Anglican—have different taxonomies of religious conversion depending on their theological and ecclesial traditions. For example, Moravian conversion narratives, as befitted the roots of the tradition in late medieval piety, are more quietist and less agonistic, more preoccupied with the bodily suffering of Christ, and more shaped by liturgical rhythms than those of the other branches of evangelicalism. Methodist conversions by contrast are more characterized by charismatic joy and spontaneous ecstasy, and are often recorded again and again as the Methodist faithful sought entire sanctification and the peace that came with holy dying, which was the ultimate demonstration of the durability of the new birth. Calvinist conversions were recorded within a framework of biblical and catechetical literacy, reformed covenanting theology, and Presbyterian ministerial oversight which sometimes edited out unpresbyterian experiences such as dreams and visions.

To emphasize ecclesial variety, however, is only to scratch the surface of the complexity of conversion narratives. Further levels of analysis are required to show the differences between personal descriptions in private journals and those published for public consumption which inevitably represent important time lags between experience and recorded experience. Similarly, one has to explore the gender dynamics at work in a movement led by and edited by men, but that almost always had a majority of women. Gender, memory, power, consumption, convention, and expression are all unstable variables within which early-modern conversion narratives need to be interrogated. But when all is said and done there remains the stubborn reality that very large numbers of women and men, slave and free, and black and white across the north Atlantic region in the eighteenth and nineteenth centuries claimed they had experienced a new birth as a gateway to a new life. The joy of the experience and the compulsion to tell it to others was at the heart of both Methodist experience and Methodist expansion.

The invitation to receive Christ and experience religious conversion was but the entry point to a life of faith and service of others. But how was that faith to be nourished and experienced? More particularly, what did early Methodist spirituality look like? In their efforts to mark out a distinctive spirituality and communal loyalty for their followers early evangelical leaders, including the Wesley brothers, went to extraordinary lengths to condense, edit, filter, reproduce, and disseminate spiritual classics of the Christian tradition. Within only a few years of the birth of Methodism, John Wesley had issued over forty abridged and inexpensive editions of spiritual classics. What is remarkable about Wesley's list is its eclecticism. Among the authors represented in his reprints are the Roman Catholic mystics Thomas à Kempis and Gaston de Renty, the English Puritan John Bunyan, the Hallesian Pietist August Hermann Francke, the Moravian founder Count Nicolaus Ludwig von Zinzendorf, the Scottish episcopalist Henry Scougall, the Anglican High Churchman William Law, and the American Congregationalist Jonathan Edwards. A decade later Wesley completed his massive collection of texts in fifty volumes issued as *A Christian Library: Consisting of Extracts from the Abridgements of the Choicest Pieces of Practical Divinity which have been publish'd in the English Tongue* (1749–55). To the list of authors already mentioned Wesley added the apostolic church fathers, Jeremy Taylor, Richard Baxter, Blaise Pascal, and many others. If one were to fast forward to the inventory of Wesley's book warehouse taken just after his death in 1791, the eclecticism of the Christian traditions represented is even more remarkable, including even the founder of the Jesuits, Ignatius of Loyola. The point of all this was not merely to supply elite texts for the educated Methodist cognoscenti, but to issue affordable and well-thumbed little pocketbooks of devotion for the people called Methodists. Of course all sorts of caveats need to be issued about this material. It was issued partly out of self-interest and competitive advantage to control a voluntary movement and guarantee its survival. *He* who controlled the tradition controlled everything. Moreover he was he, because the ratio of men to women in the exemplary lives issued by John Wesley was 5:1 whereas the sex ratio in eighteenth-century Methodism was 3:2 in favour of women. This powerful asymmetry of male power and prescription and female following has been one of the most enduring, and one has to say, disagreeable features of the Methodist tradition. However appropriate are the criticisms that need to be offered about Methodist attempts to connect the eighteenth-century revivals with the past, it was nevertheless a remarkable exercise in earthing a new movement in a surprisingly inclusive history of Christianity. Methodist spirituality, with its roots in conversion, the Bible, the cross, and the Christian tradition, and with its characteristic emphases on discipline, testing, discernment, sanctification, and mission, was a powerful instrument of character formation for ordinary people. In the words of one recent writer, Methodists employed spiritual discipline as an instrument of self-fashioning, freedom, and modernity (Mack 2008). They employed spiritual discipline not as an instrument of self-repression, as Marxist historians such as E. P. Thompson once alleged, but rather as a way of producing the necessary self-control within which personal agency could work more effec- tively. Far from being an oxymoron, therefore, Methodist spirituality drew from a surprisingly eclectic range of Christian sources and served as a means and a way to a better life for those who subjected themselves to its tender mercies and severe disciplines. But how was that spirituality to be transmitted to ordinary people?

It has long been recognized that the most distinctive, characteristic, and ubiqui- tous feature of the Methodist message, indeed of the entire evangelical revival, was its transmission by means of hymns and hymn singing. If one were to choose one single artefact of eighteenth-century Methodism to lock in a canister for posterity that would somehow capture its essence, one defensible choice would be the 1780 *Collection of Hymns for the Use of the People called Methodists*. For a movement that has attracted far more abuse than praise from scholars, the *Collection of Hymns* has commanded almost universal admiration. John Wesley was an inveterate collector and publisher of hymns beginning with *A Collection of Psalms and Hymns*, pub- lished in 1737 for the use of the infant Anglican colony in Georgia. It was the first Methodist hymnbook, the first Anglican hymnbook, and probably the first hymn- book published in America for use in public worship. The Wesley brothers issued over thirty hymnbooks: some with tunes, some without; some intended for special occasions, some for more general consumption; some intended for all 'real Chris- tians', some only for Methodists. John was the selector, organizer, editor, and publisher; Charles was the prolific poet, writer, and lyricist. It is estimated that he composed some 9,000 hymns and sacred poems, some of which are classics of devotional literature, many of which are truly dreadful and easily forgettable. The point is that well before the 1780 *Collection of Hymns* Methodism was a movement distinguished by its devotion to sacred songs.

Why then was there such a mania for singing? What was sung? Where were hymns sung and by whom? How were they sung and what effects did they have on the singers? The 1780 *Collection of Hymns* offers a way in to answering these questions. John Wesley's Preface is instructive. After carefully delineating the market objectives for the new volume ('a collection neither too large, that it may be cheap and portable, nor too small, that it may contain a sufficient variety for all ordinary occasions'), Wesley stated that the volume contained

all the important truths of our most holy religion, whether speculative or practical; yea to illustrate them all, and to prove them both by Scripture and reason. And this is done in a regular order. The hymns are not carelessly jumbled together, but carefully ranged under proper heads according to the experience of real Christians. So that this book is in effect a little body of experimental and practical divinity.

In Wesley's words poetry was to be 'the handmaid of piety' in quickening devotion, confirming faith, enlivening hope, and kindling or increasing the Christian's love of God and humankind. What is striking about the hymns as a body is their relative absence of systematic doctrine and their concentration instead on the Christian life as a pilgrimage, a journey from earthly despair to heavenly blessing. They are filled with personal pronouns, active verbs, and intense struggles. They aim to persuade, to convince, and to plead. They are more winning than threatening, more appealing than damning.

Hymns were sung not only on public occasions, they were sung privately or memorized. Wherever one looks in Methodist archives, from the recorded experiences of itinerant preachers to the diaries of the Methodist faithful, hymns are used for expression, consolation, anticipation, and interpretation. Methodists absorbed their faith through the words of their hymns and sacred verse. Hymns transmitted complex theological ideas in accessible language; they reached deep into the will and the emotions of believers through metre, rhyme, and melody; they made connections with the wider culture through the appropriation of popular tunes; they were easily memorized (more so than the biblical verses that inspired them) and used by individual believers in the crisis moments of their lives; they helped build communal solidarity and collective devotion; they enlivened meetings of all kinds that otherwise would have run into the ground of emotional sterility; they inspired the imagination, mediated biblical metaphors, and helped build a system of symbols; they defined for Methodism a religious content and style of a more vibrant and populist kind than was available through confessions of faith or chanted liturgies; in short, they supplied a poetic music of the heart for a religion of the heart. The medium and the message were in perfect harmony.

If Methodism helped embrace modernity through its conceptions of self and its accessible spirituality, it also spread rapidly in the United States in symbiosis with the new Republic's embrace of free markets and democratization of culture and politics. Mark Noll (1992: 153) states that 'the Protestant churches that flourished most decisively in the first half of the nineteenth century were the Baptists and the

Methodists, the two bodies that succeeded in joining most efficiently a democratic appeal with effective leadership'. Similarly, Nathan Hatch (1989: 9) calls this period of Methodist expansion the democratization of American Christianity which 'has less to do with the specifics of polity and governance and more to do with the incarnation of the church into popular culture'. The popular religious movements of the early republic, in their refusal to defer to the clergy and learned theologians and in their willingness to take the religious experiences of ordinary people at face value, articulated a profoundly democratic spirit. The rise of a popular religious culture of print, the place of origin of which shifted from eastern seaboard cities to west of the Alleghenies, together with the widespread dissemination of personal stories of transforming religious experience, further contributed to the notion that the religion of the people no longer depended upon clerical mediation. The style of religious communication and worship also changed. There was a move away from refined sermons of doctrinal exposition to populist addresses employing humour, sarcasm, and popular wisdom. Similarly, the content and expression of religious hymns, ballads, and verse became more accessible to popular taste. According to Nathan Hatch (ibid. 227) 'better than any other source, popular poems and songs capture the force of the early republic's populism, they translate theological concepts into language of the marketplace, personalize theological abstractions, deflate the pretension of privileged church leaders, and instill hope and confidence in popular collective action'. Their most common themes are anticlericalism, anti-Calvinism, anti-formalism, anti-confessionalism, and anti-elitism. Empowerment was from God, knowledge was from the Scriptures, salvation was available to all, and the Spirit was manifested, not in structures and ecclesiastical order, but in freedom and heart religion. There were, of course, raw edges to populist religious enthusiasm. Frenetic revivalism, apocalypticism, and sectarian fragmentation were all in evidence as an energetic lay leadership of both men and women struggled free from the control of traditional religious structures. Methodism, with a relatively coherent Wesleyan theology and with its distinctive combination of ecclesiastical authoritarianism and connexional discipline, was in a good position to accommodate popular enthusiasm without capitulating to its most bizarre manifestations. The paradox at the heart of Methodism in the United States in this period is of the creation of an authoritarian religious structure empowered by the authority of the people—an egalitarian spiritual message that did not result in democratic ecclesiastical structures. Methodism in the United States after the Revolution was therefore a form of popular religion that successfully attacked social, ecclesiastical, and professional elites rather than a genuine movement of political or ecclesiastical democracy. So good was the fit between Methodism and the infant Republic's defining characteristics that on the eve of the Civil War Methodism was the largest Protestant denomination in the United States.

The third feature of Methodism mentioned in the introductory paragraph that is beginning to receive the attention it merits is the fact that Methodism, although mostly led by men, was nevertheless a predominantly female movement. This is true of virtually any geographical region in the rise of Methodism in the eighteenth and nineteenth centuries. Indeed there is much to be said for Ronald Knox's (1950: 30) assertion that 'the history of enthusiasm is largely a history of female emancipation'. As with many other popular religious traditions, the history of Methodism is really a history of female preponderance. Surveys of class member- ship on both sides of the Atlantic consistently show that women comprised a majority of the membership. Clive Field's (1994: 153–69) extensive survey of English Methodist membership lists before 1830 has shown a female mean of 57.7 per cent. Comparable figures, though based on significantly smaller samples, are available for early Methodism in the United States. Dee Andrews's (2000: 247–8) figures for the eastern seaboard cities of New York, Philadelphia, and Baltimore in the years 1786–1801 show a preponderance of women ranging from 59 to 66 per cent depending on location and year. In Boston the proportion of women members in the 1790s varied from 61 to 71 per cent. Single or widowed women consistently accounted for over a third of the total membership.

What is true of the gender proportions within Methodism is probably largely the case for many other religious denominations. As has been pointed out by Ann Braude (1997: 87–107) and others, a sober recognition of the preponderance of women in American religious history would make a dramatic difference to the conceptual frameworks within which that history has been reconstructed. That insight is even more important for an understanding of Methodism. Quite simply, as purveyors of hospitality, deaconesses, visitors, evangelists, prayers, exhorters, testifiers, class members and leaders, and preachers, women helped define the character of the Methodist movement. There were, of course, constraining factors to the emergence of women as full participants in the Methodist project in both Britain and America including contemporary notions of social propriety and female modesty, strained relations with the Church of England or with the estab- lished colonial denominations, the sometimes vigorous opposition of male itiner- ant preachers, conventionally understood biblical injunctions against women leaders, fear of unflattering parallels being drawn between the Methodists and the Quakers, and the damaging impact of anti-Methodist publications that delighted in emphasizing its alleged appeal to 'emotional' women. But in the context of undeniable female successes, Wesley adopted an increasingly pragmatic view of women's public role culminating in his characteristic invention of the device of 'the extraordinary call', which was a way of allowing him to hold on to a conventional Pauline hermeneutic while acknowledging that women's abilities could be successfully harnessed to the mission of the church. By the 1770s there was a critical mass of women preachers within Methodism that could not easily be ignored. The law once enunciated by Joan Thirsk that women could make their most substantial gains in the early stages of movements before male controls were reimposed had come into operation. Indeed it was almost inevitable in a movement that emphasized experience, empiricism, spiritual egalitarianism, enthusiasm, and direct empowerment from God.

A similar pattern emerged in American Methodism. Thousands of women shared testimonies and exhortations during church services, camp meetings, love feasts, and class meetings which were Methodism's most distinctive social occasions. As the movement grew women were encouraged to 'speak' in ever-widening spheres so that the rise of public female discourse within Methodism preceded its acceptability in other social spheres by almost half a century. Methodist emphases on liberty, orality, and communalism facilitated women. There was also a degree of gender blurring in early Methodist discourse. According to Diane Lobody (1993: 127–44) Methodism was a 'women's church because it spoke a woman's language . . . over and over again, with almost ritual intonation, we hear the language of tender and uncontrollable emotionalism' as Methodists felt, wept, trembled, groaned, melted, softened, and sank into God.

As women's voices became more ubiquitous and significant in the popular evangelical sects that grew prolifically in early Republican America, so too did their broader contribution to religious movements such as the Methodists, the Free will Baptists, and the Disciples of Christ. Within Methodism Brekus has shown how women benefited from the political, economic, and social instability of the early Republic to carve out important positions as prayers, exhorters, and preachers. Although women thrived in a religious environment characterized by the lack of ordained clergy and the new emphasis on female piety and virtue, they also encountered limits. Their public voice was greater in the north than in the south; they were not ordained nor permitted to administer the sacraments; and they were kept out of positions in ecclesiastical governance. It would be a mistake however to underplay the significance of what was being achieved by female agency: 'Given the failure of the American Revolution to extend true equality to either women or blacks, the decision to allow them into the sacred space of the pulpit was radical indeed' (Brekus 1998: 158). By dressing and speaking plainly, by sustaining 'islands of holiness' in an otherwise raucous environment, and by building a grander Christian family out of their manifold and diverse families, women not only reshaped the American denominational order, but also made a remarkable contribution to the shaping of the American Republic.

There is one further twist to the story of women, Methodism, and nation-building. Schneider has persuasively shown how Methodism was instrumental in ushering in a distinctive kind of evangelical domesticity in which the 'idea of the family as belonging to a private sphere of affection and moral discipline that was to be set over against a public sphere of competition and self-interest' was conveyed. In this interpretation Methodism not only helped undermine an eighteenth-century American cultural ethos based upon patriarchal sovereignty and honour codes, but helped establish a new domestic ethic in which mutual affection and self-denial were inculcated, first in class meetings and love feasts, and then in homes. 'The way of the cross' so assiduously cultivated by the Methodists in building a new religious family of fathers and mothers, brothers and sisters, came to be applied to actual families. In these secluded spaces women, men, and children sought to replicate 'relationships within the family of God'. In this way the Victorian cult of domesticity was at least in part a Methodist creation. The consequences both for women and the church were mixed. Over time actual family units undermined and then subverted the familial mechanisms of the church, most notably its class meetings and love feasts. Families came to monopolize domestic piety while voluntary reform movements and political parties helped organize Methodism's public face. What was left for the church, in Schneider's words (1993: pp. xvi–xxviii), was to become 'a nascent bureaucracy made up of specialized agencies and programs designed for denominational self-propagation'. The balance sheet for women was similarly ambiguous. While they gained as instruments of the middle-class domestic piety that shaped great tracts of American culture in the nineteenth century, they also lost as public agents of the religious movement that helped domesticate them. As in Britain the prescribed religious behaviour of American women subtly began to change. Before 1810 female domesticity on the whole was not paraded as a model in Methodist publications; women were admired rather for their religious experience, progress in holiness, and contribution to the religious and social mission of the church. Yet by 1850, women came to be admired more for their pious domesticity than for their public contribution to the work of mission.

If the language of Methodism supplied a vocabulary and a grammatical structure that allowed women to articulate their religious experience without alienating men, the same was true of their pursuit of sanctification, which brought with it the possibility of a dramatic subversion of traditional hierarchies at least within the Methodist spiritual economy. For sanctification was no respecter of conventional boundaries. If women, even African-American slave women, could aspire to entire sanctification (and most of the credible claims were made by women), then here was an aspect of life, and for Methodists the most important aspect of human life, in which gender was not a disadvantage. Indeed the most influential popularizer of a modified version of John Wesley's perfectionism was the Methodist lay revivalist, Phoebe Palmer, whose 'altar theology' helped reduce the old Wesleyan pursuit of sanctification to three simple steps: consecration of one's life fully to God; belief in God's promise to sanctify; and bearing witness to what God has done. Palmer's theology and revivalist energy made an important contribution not only to the rise of the Holiness traditions, such as the Church of the Nazarene in the United States and the Keswick Movement in Britain, but also to the later emergence of Pentecostal and charismatic movements.

There is widespread agreement that within Methodism there were few *concerted* attempts to challenge established gender boundaries either within the denomination or within the wider society. On both sides of the Atlantic there were few demands for ordination, few were involved in women's rights movements, few refused to submit to male authority, and most female preachers were single or widowed thereby avoiding opprobrium as deserters of domestic responsibility. Moreover, as time went on women's sphere of activity and influence first expanded and then was reined in and diminished as Methodism settled into denominational mode. So much is relatively well known, but there is a need to probe even deeper. In what sense was Methodism really a women's movement, and not just a movement in which a few especially talented women could attain important roles in the public ministry of the church? How did all this work out in practice, not among the female preachers who were exceptional, but among the many thousands of women who were not? Did gender matter to Methodist women, not in the obvious sense of understanding their place within the overwheiming maleness of institutional power in Methodism, but more importantly in any distinctively 'religious' sense, however that is to be defined? For example, in the early divisions among religious societies between Calvinists and Wesleyans more women were attracted to the 'softer' Arminianism of the Wesley brothers than the perceived harsher Calvinism of George Whitefield and Howell Harris. I have tried to offer some other answers to these questions in *Empire of the Spirit*, but in truth the great task of reconstructing the first hundred years of Methodist history as a religious movement with a preponderance of women has a long way to go. Dee Andrews (2006: 328–30) has observed that in most treatments of evangelical history that are not expressly about gender women are not entirely absent, but they are not entirely present either. In that sense the writing of the history of Methodism still inhabits a liminal zone in which women's numerical preponderance is acknowledged, but its consequences for historical reconstruction remain unaddressed. The same could be said for children and young adults. Of course the availability of sources for this kind of work will always be inadequate, but the fundamental problem lies not with the surviving evidence but with structures of power—past and present—and the limitations of the historical imagination.

That observation brings us back to the introductory paragraph of this chapter. Since the 1970s the scholarship on the rise of Methodism in the British Isles and the United States has made considerable progress in viewing Methodism as an international movement, a movement with symbiotic connections to the Enlightenment and the rise of modernity, and a movement with a clear majority of women in its ranks. In taking these issues seriously better answers have been supplied to the fourth area of inquiry identified in the introductory paragraph, namely the nature of the 'lived religion' of all kinds of Methodists, not just adult white male elites. But there is still much to be done. Not only does the social history of Methodism need to be treated as seriously as its historical theology, but new kinds of social and cultural history emphasizing the agency of children, women, and different ethnicities will need to be imagined. What is being advocated here is not merely an emphasis on diversity for its own sake, or even worse a kind of wooden political correctness, but rather more sophisticated ways of explaining how it was that hundreds of thousands of people across the North Atlantic world in the eighteenth and nineteenth centuries gave their allegiance to a new religious movement that affected how they thought of themselves, their relationships, their families, their political allegiances, and their work. Just as the questions that have interested historians over the past quarter of a century have differed markedly from those that were in the ascendancy in a previous period, a handbook of Methodist studies published in another quarter of a century will inevitably look very different from this one.

SUGGESTED READING

ANDREWS (2000).
HEMPTON (2005).
MACK (2008).
RICHEY, RUSSELL E., ROWE, KENNETH E., and SCHMIDT, JEAN MILLER (eds.) (1993). *Perspectives on American Methodism: Interpretive Essays.* Nashville: Kingswood.
WARD (1992).
WIGGER, JOHN H., and HATCH, NATHAN O. (eds.) (2001). *Methodism and the Shaping of American Culture.* Nashville: Abingdon.

REFERENCES

ANDREWS, DEE (2000). *The Methodists and Revolutionary America, 1760–1800: The Shaping of an Evangelical Culture.* Princeton: Princeton University Press.
—— (2006). Book review in *Journal of the Early Republic* 26/2.
BRAUDE, ANN (1997). 'Women's History *is* American Religious History'. In Thomas A. Tweed (ed.), *Retelling U.S. Religious History.* Berkeley: University of California Press.
BREKUS, CATHERINE A. (1998). *Strangers & Pilgrims: Female Preaching in America, 1740–1845.* Chapel Hill: University of North Carolina Press.
FIELD, CLIVE D. (1994). 'The Social Composition of English Methodism to 1830: a Membership Analysis'. *Bulletin of the John Rylands University of Manchester* 76/1.
HATCH, NATHAN O. (1989). *The Democratization of American Christianity.* New Haven: Yale University Press.
HEMPTON, DAVID (2005). *Methodism: Empire of the Spirit.* New Haven: Yale University Press.
HINDMARSH, D. BRUCE (2005). *The Evangelical Conversion Narrative: Spiritual Autobiography in Early Modern England.* Oxford: Oxford University Press.
KNOX, R. A. (1950). *Enthusiasm: A Chapter in the History of Religion.* Oxford: Clarendon.
LOBODY, DIANE H. (1993). '"That Language Might Be Given Me": Women's Experience in Early Methodism'. In Russell E. Richey, Kenneth E. Rowe, and Jean Miller Schmidt (eds.), *Perspectives on American Methodism: Interpretive Essays.* Nashville: Abingdon.

MACK, PHYLLIS (2008). *Heart Religion in the British Enlightenment: Gender and Emotion in Early Methodism*. Cambridge: Cambridge University Press.

NOLL, MARK A. (1992). *A History of Christianity in the United States and Canada*. Grand Rapids: Eerdmans.

SCHNEIDER, A. GREGORY (1993). *The Way of the Cross Leads Home: The Domestication of American Methodism*. Bloomington: Indiana University Press.

SNAPE, MICHAEL F. (2005). *The Redcoat and Religion: The Forgotten History of the British Soldier from the Age of Marlborough to the Eve of the First World War*. London: Routledge.

WARD, W. R. (1992). *The Protestant Evangelical Awakening*. Cambridge: Cambridge University Press.

—— (2006). *Early Evangelicalism: A Global Intellectual History, 1670–1789*. Cambridge: Cambridge University Press.

CHAPTER 5

METHODISM IN THE NINETEENTH AND TWENTIETH CENTURIES

MANFRED MARQUARDT

THE two centuries ensuing the decease of John Wesley saw spread, splits, and reunions of the Methodist movement, its development from a tiny group of devoted believers into a family of Christian churches all over the inhabited world. They were a time both of Methodist promulgation within and beyond the Anglo-American world and also of great challenges from within and without. They saw Methodists striving to guard what had been entrusted to them as well as following Christ's lead to new places. This chapter will not give a comprehensive survey of two centuries of worldwide Methodist history; it is rather an attempt to identify different strands and to sketch major developments.

DISSEMINATION AND DIVERSITY
OF METHODISM

Methodists viewing their denomination sometimes seem to presume that their particular perspective is true for Methodism in general. But Methodism is much more and often more diverse than what can be overlooked from the top of one's own church spire.

Britain

By the time of John Wesley's death (1791) Methodism had spread into English-speaking areas on both sides of the Atlantic Ocean. In 1784, the Methodist Episcopal Church in North America had been founded; Methodism in England rapidly developed into a church.

During the nineteenth and twentieth centuries, two currents can be recognized: There were strong revival movements, partly fuelled by American camp meetings, spreading quickly to other parts of the country. Their leaders began to introduce decentralized connexional structures. The Wesleyan Conference decided not to integrate these movements into their evangelistic activities and to exclude its leaders, who in turn formed the Primitive Methodists (1811), claiming to be true guardians of the original, or primitive, form of Wesley's Methodism. Their major emphases beyond evangelism were a stronger lay participation in church government, as well as simplicity in their chapels and worship services.

On the other side, there was a development within the Methodist Connexion holding a high doctrine of the pastoral office, and constructing more stylish church buildings. More pastors received a better education, started settling down and getting married, serving more affluent and influential urban congregations; itinerancy was reduced, and people outside the societal boundaries of the church were hardly being reached any longer. Alienation from democratically oriented lay members led to opposition and to break-aways like the Methodist Protestants (1828), the Wesleyan Association, and the Wesleyan Reformers (1849), forming the United Methodist Free Churches in 1857.

Wesleyan and Methodist Churches grew rapidly, especially in the expanding industrial areas with workers, who had to endure economic hardships, which their faith helped them to cope with by living simply and relying on a supportive community. Wesleyan Methodism became a middle-class connexion, whose membership had risen to 450,000 by the end of the nineteenth century. Eventually (1932), Wesleyans, Primitive Methodists, and United Methodists came together to form the present Methodist Church in Great Britain.

Methodism in Wales was in part the result of a Calvinistic revival, linked with George Whitefield and Lady Selina, the countess of Huntingdon, and sharing their predestinarian understanding of God's grace. Considerable persecutions and the rapid growth of their societies led to the demand for a separate organization with its own ministers. In 1811, eight lay preachers were ordained. These Calvinistic Methodists eventually developed into the Presbyterian Church in Wales.

Wesleyan Methodism in Wales was born as a part of the movement in Britain. A Mission to Welsh-speaking people was launched in 1800 under the authority of the annual conference, while English and Welsh language congregations were administered as separate. The connexion grew to be one of the most influential forces in the Welsh nation, playing an important role in the religious and social life. In the early twentieth century, a decline in the iron and steel and manufacturing industries as well as the disappearance of the coal industry reduced the numbers, attendance, and commitment of members significantly. In 1974, a Council for Methodism in Wales was created, covering both the English and Welsh Districts.

Methodism in Ireland was one of the first-fruits of John Wesley's visits beginning in 1747, where some preachers had already gathered a society in Dublin. The development into a separate church brought about two distinct bodies: the Primitive Wesleyan Methodist Connexion (within the Church of Ireland) and the Wesleyan Methodists; after sixty years of separation, the two groups formed the Methodist Church in Ireland (1878). The Irish Methodist Church has made large contributions to the people, through both education and social action, and also to the peace process in Northern Ireland.

Methodism in Scotland is a part of the Methodist Church in Great Britain. It had begun with Wesley's visits and the work of pioneer preachers in the late eighteenth century. Rent by a series of schisms in the early nineteenth century, Methodism settled down in the second half, and a period of steady expansion began. In the last decade of the twentieth century it became involved in the Scottish Church Initiative for Union with the Church of Scotland, the Episcopal Church, and the United Reformed Church.

North America

American Methodism became an independent institution at an early stage of its history. In a country lacking any form of established church and with 'passion for expansion and a zeal for religious reconstruction' (Cracknell 2005: 45), Methodism was growing quickly and yet keeping its Wesleyan legacy: evangelistic zeal, social concern, ethical life style, itinerant preachers, classes, and the conference system. By 1828, some 2,500 itinerant preachers were serving the Methodist societies and moving with the settlers to new places. Their extraordinary mobility enabled them to keep up with the fluctuation, to make connections with people of all kinds of origin, status, or religious orientation and to minister to their ecclesial needs.

New forms of religious gatherings emerged; the American camp meetings, the first being held in 1800 in Kentucky, were the most typical for the nineteenth century. They met the needs of those who, in their frontier homes, often lived far away from their neighbours. They came together by hundreds and sometimes by thousands from up to thirty or forty miles away to spend several days together praying and singing, listening to testimonies and fiery sermons, enjoying Christian fellowship with sudden conversions and emotional uplifting that sometimes led to excesses of dancing, shouting, and unusual bodily movements. But many started a new life putting aside their undisciplined ways of living and becoming responsible citizens. After the Second Great Awakening (1800–1830s) their significance decreased, along with the frontier society. The growing cities needed pastors remaining in their places for a longer time. Larger and more beautiful church buildings replaced plain meeting houses, richer worship services and a better-educated clergy seemed to be more suitable for a 'respectable' constituency. The number of churches grew within four decades from 2,700 in 1820 to 19,883 in 1861. 'Earlier generations had followed Americans from East to West, from urban to frontier, and from lower to middle and upper-middle classes. But success led to staying with practices . . . increasingly less effective' (Weems 2007). Since Methodists have been convinced that no person is beyond the reach of God's love, the question remained central, what kind of mobility was needed to reach *all*.

By the end of the nineteenth century, there were more than twenty Methodist denominations. One of the oldest is the African Methodist Episcopal Church. African Americans finding themselves considered 'a nuisance in the house of worship' among their white sisters and brothers, started to build their own meeting places. Methodist Episcopal Church (MEC) Bishop Asbury consecrated their first chapel in Philadelphia, ordained Richard Allen and, in 1816, consecrated him bishop. The second largest body of black Methodists is the African Methodist Episcopal Zion Church, which began in New York by providing themselves with a separate building. The Coloured Methodist Episcopal Church (1870) was organized by black members of the MEC (South), who had left the church after the Civil War. In 1956, the name was changed into Christian Methodist Episcopal Church. Other African-American Methodists remained in the MEC, yet often within separate congregations and even conferences: the Central Jurisdiction was formed for all African-American members in 1939—the only one shaped by race, with segregated structures, a lack of resources, and a large geographical area. It was dissolved and integrated into the United Methodist Church (UMC) (1968); the wounding experiences, however, are still being felt, healing has only begun.

Methodism in Canada began in different places during the last third of the eighteenth century. Part of the work fell under the supervision of the British Wesleyans and, in 1855, became the Wesleyan Methodist Conference of Eastern British America, another part had formed the Wesleyan Methodist Church (1833), a third group the

Methodist Episcopal Church of Canada (1834). The two Wesleyan churches merged in 1874 to become the Methodist Church of Canada. Ten years later they joined with the MEC in Canada, the Bible Christian Church, and the Primitive Methodist Church in Canada; the new Methodist Church included all Canadian Methodists except a few small groups. In 1925, with 418,352 members in 4,797 congregations, it united with the Congregational Union and the majority of the Presbyterian Church to form the United Church of Canada, the first union of churches to cross denominational lines, and the largest Protestant denomination in Canada.

In the beginning of the nineteenth century, a Methodist work among Native Americans was begun by itinerant preachers visiting with them. Missionary stations were built in Ohio and Upper Canada around 1820, with other states following, Oregon was reached in 1834. Day schools and manual labour training schools were organized. An 'Indian Mission Conference' was established 1844. The ongoing political and economic measurements, including relocations, did not improve the living conditions of these nations. More impressive is the number of 18,000 known native people in the UMC today (2006). Native people can be found in all areas of church ministry and their churches throughout the whole continent. In 1992, the UMC General Conference adopted a *Confession to Native Americans*, confessing that 'the Christian churches, including The United Methodist Church and its predecessors, have participated in the destruction of Native American people, culture and religious practices' and postulates new measures to be taken on all church and state levels (*Book of Resolutions* 2004: 361–2).

The largest non-English language group within Methodism until the 1920s were German and Swiss immigrants and their offspring. Immigrants from Germany formed such churches as the United Brethren in Christ (1800) and the Evangelical Association (1807) with a pietistic-Methodist emphasis on personal experience and ecumenical openness. After 1830, with a new wave of immigration, the Methodist Episcopal Church began German missions, which—within forty years—developed into three German conferences with 700 itinerant preachers and 63,000 members (1874). At the time of the First World War and the years after, anti-German emotions and a push for Americanization led to the demise of German Methodism within the MEC. The two autonomous churches survived after having assimilated to the American culture. In 1946, they became the Evangelical United Brethren Church (EUB).

Scandinavian Methodists in America also formed churches and conferences of their own. Preaching started on a ship in New York harbour (1845), and a Swedish Methodist congregation was founded the same year. By 1893, there were three Swedish conferences, followed by two more in 1901 and 1908. After 1924, the 208 churches with 20,600 members and 177 preachers were transferred step by step into English-speaking conferences until 1942. Norwegian Methodism built its first church in 1852. Four years later, a district was organized and joined with Danish churches in 1870; a Norwegian–Danish conference was established after ten more years. In 1939, all these congregations merged with the Methodist Church.

METHODIST MISSIONS IN
OTHER COUNTRIES

Mission by being faithful and serving in love, and mission done by intentional planning, preparing, and starting a mission initiative were the two main channels by which Methodism spread.

Mission in English-Speaking Countries

Mission initiatives starting from Britain and North America were moving in the tracks of Anglo-American colonization and civilization. The first areas where Methodist missions took root were the West Indies, then Gibraltar and Sierra Leone; Australia and South Africa following in the early nineteenth century. Methodist emigrants to other countries found a new place in their mostly non-Methodist environment to share with their new neighbours what faith in Christ and a life in his Spirit meant to them, inviting them into their homes and starting a bible reading group or a class.

In many African countries, one can find Methodist churches from different strands of Methodism, reflecting the mission history of the last centuries. In Sierra Leone, a group of freed slaves, after having arrived in 1792, started to organize a congregation; British Methodist preachers joined them in 1811 to build the Methodist Church Sierra Leone. The United Brethren in Christ started their Sierra Leone mission in 1855. Today, they are part of the West Africa Central Conference of the UMC which also includes Liberia (1816) and Nigeria. The African Methodist Episcopal Church, going back to a mission in 1820, now encompasses conferences in Sierra Leone, Liberia, Ghana, Nigeria, and the Ivory Coast, and is part of the global African Methodist Episcopal Church. The Africa Central Conference of the United Methodist Church includes annual conferences in Eastern and Western Angola (established in 1885), East Africa (Burundi, 1984, a merger of different predecessors), Mozambique (1890), and Zimbabwe (1897); other Methodist churches deriving from American Methodist mission work include the Congo Central Conference and denominations in Southern Africa.

Missions in Southern Africa began with the arrival of Methodist soldiers at the very beginning of the nineteenth century; the first Methodist missionaries landed in Cape Town (1816) and spread throughout Southern Africa, forming the Methodist Church and several independent African churches. Smaller churches such as the Bible Christians, the Primitive Methodists, the Methodist New Connexion, and the Free Methodist Church entered unions, no longer using their original names. Most of the black Methodists, like other Christians of colour in Africa, have undergone painful treatment by their white 'superiors' and an often bloody process of liberation. Methodists were engaged in the process of bringing forth a new Africa and a closer community of the Christian churches on the black continent. The Methodist Church in South Africa rejected the apartheid ideology from the beginning and was a vocal critic of government policy. The end of apartheid and the process of reconciliation have demonstrated the strength and wisdom of African people of faith and their churches.

United Methodist churches in the North of Africa (Algeria, Tunisia), since 1972 a part of the Protestant Church of Algeria, belong to the Central Conference of Southern and Central Europe. In Egypt, the Holiness Movement Church started in 1899 and united with the Free Methodist Church in 1959, serving churches and missions in a number of African states and in the Middle East. New UMC mission initiatives have been started in Senegal (1989) and Cameroon (2005).

African Methodist churches have always and everywhere been strong in educational and social work. Supported by Methodist churches and mission societies in America, Europe, Australia, and Latin America they have become partners in mission. Since the late twentieth century they have been blessed with the fastest growth of churches in the world.

Methodism in Australia, New Zealand, and Oceania was born during the early decades of the nineteenth century. In Australia, two Methodist schoolteachers had begun by establishing class meetings. In 1815, their request for support was fulfilled, the first circuit was founded in Sidney, and the mission extended to neighbouring places and to the islands in the South Pacific. During the course of time, other Methodist denominations followed, most of them uniting in 1904 to become the Methodist Church of Australasia. In 1913 the Methodist Church of New Zealand formed its own conference together with the New Zealand Church and the Primitive Methodist Church. At a very early stage of its history, Methodism took a stand in favour of the aborigines to improve their legal, social, and economic situation and opened its churches for the ministry to their indigenous neighbours. In 1977 the Uniting Church in Australia was started together with Congregationalists and Presbyterians with a constituency of over a million people. The Wesleyan Methodist Church of Australia, which began its work after the Second World War as a Holiness church, did not take part in the merger negotiations.

Methodism in Asia and the Pacific

Methodism's way to the Indian subcontinent will always be connected with the commemoration of Thomas Coke, its first great pioneer missionary, who died on the journey to India. A former soldier, who had formed a Methodist society in Madras, welcomed the missionaries on Sri Lankan shores in 1783. A British missionary to India arrived in 1817. The Methodist Episcopal Church followed by sending a missionary (1856) and in 1870 the MEC Women's Foreign Mission

Society sent the first two women, an educator and a medical doctor, to India. Education, health ministry, and evangelism have become the main activities in this large subcontinent with its mainly Hindu, Muslim, and Buddhist population. The ministry of the Methodists was devoted especially to the lower-caste people. Within fifty years the constituency of the MEC had grown to about 200,000. While the Methodist Churches of British and Australian origin joined the two great unions of 1947 (Church of South India) and 1970 (Church of North India), the Methodist (Episcopal) Church refrained and, in 1981, was inaugurated as Methodist Church in India (MCI), autonomous, yet affiliated with the UMC.

Since 1984, there is also a small Methodist Church in Bangladesh, connected with Korean Methodists, and the Church of Pakistan, formed in 1970 of the Anglican, Methodist, Presbyterian, and Lutheran churches. They offer an unusually large number of educational and medical programmes in the overwhelmingly Muslim environment of the two countries.

There are two Methodist churches in Myanmar (Burma), the Methodist Church of Upper Myanmar in the north (British origin, established in 1887), and the Methodist Church of Lower Myanmar in the south (MEC origin, established 1870). When Burma became independent in 1964, all mission schools and hospitals were nationalized, all missionaries left the country, and the Methodist Churches received autonomy. Their ministry is being pursued in one of the least-developed countries with a 90 per cent Buddhist majority, and confined within its borders.

The Methodist Church in Singapore received British missionaries from South India in 1884 and during the following years Americans arrived from Burma; churches were organized by the main language groups. Today, one of the three annual conferences is English speaking, one Chinese, and one Tamil. Malaysia and Indonesia also received Methodism from neighbouring countries: Malaysia in 1885 from India and in 1901 from China, Indonesia from Malaysia and America in 1904–5. In 1950, the new South East Asia Central Conference included Burma, Malaysia, Singapore, and Indonesia; the denominations became autonomous in 1964. All are active in educational, social, and evangelistic ministries.

The Philippines, a 94 per cent Christian, mostly Roman Catholic, country, has three major churches with Methodist roots: the United Methodist Church, the Evangelical Methodist Church, and the United Church of Christ. When religious freedom was granted to non-Catholics in 1899, Methodist work began with missionaries from the United States, the new governing power over the Philippines. The UMC has eighteen annual conferences in six episcopal areas now; it takes a clear stand for human rights and justice and a lead in ecumenical activities. The Evangelical Methodist Church seceded from the MEC in 1909 to obtain freedom from alien control. The United Church of Christ has a constituency of more than 10 per cent of the 65 million Filipinos.

Tonga, Samoa, and Fiji have a strong Methodist heritage since the second third of the nineteenth century. In 1826, a third attempt at starting a mission received a favourable response after two Haitians had prepared the way, and by the end of 1834 a breakthrough led to quick growth of the Methodist Church and Christianity in general. In 1977, the Free Wesleyan Church of Tonga, encompassing the majority of the population as well as the royal family, gained autonomy from Australia, keeping relationship with the new Uniting Church there. The Samoa Methodist Church began with a Samoan chief who had been converted in Tonga and returned to his country in 1828. A British Methodist mission eventually developed into the Congregational Church in Samoa. In 1962, Western Samoa declared independence; autonomy of the Methodist Church came in 1964. Most Samoan villages have a Methodist church, and the denomination keeps strong connections with Samoan Methodist churches in the Pacific region. In 1835, Australian Methodist missionaries began to found schools and to preach in Fiji. In 1892, an Indian mission became active among Indian labourers. The autonomous Methodist Church of Fiji and Rotuma was established in 1964 as a multiracial and multicultural community; it is the largest Christian denomination in Fiji, with a constituency of one-third of the population.

Methodism was introduced into China in 1847 by missionaries of the MEC and the MEC (South), and in 1851 British missionaries arrived in Hong Kong; the True God Church was established in Foochow in 1856. In 1946, all missionary workers had to leave, but 78,000 Methodists from British and 190,000 from American traditions remained as faithful believers under the Communist regime. They were forced by the government of the People's Republic to become the Three-Self Church, i.e. self-governing, self-supporting, and self-propagating, and survived the Cultural Revolution with no contacts with the free world. Since the renewal of religious freedom, thousands of Protestant churches are open again, but still no foreign mission work is allowed, whereas contact with Methodist churches outside China is alive. In 1949, the Methodist Church in the Republic of China moved to Taiwan, and in 1972 became autonomous. Hong Kong is hosting two larger denominations of the Methodist family. The Methodist Church in Hong Kong was founded in 1975 as a union of The Chinese Methodist Church, Hong Kong District (commenced in 1884, British origin) and The Methodist Church, Hong Kong (1953, American origin). Also a united church body is The Hong Kong Council of the Church of Christ in China, brought together in 1918 as an indigenous effort from Presbyterian, Congregational, and Methodist traditions.

The first independent Methodist Church in Asia was in Japan, which until 1853 was closed to Western influence. Methodist missionaries had arrived from the MEC and the Canadian MC in 1873, from the Evangelical Association in 1875, and from the United Brethren in 1898, followed by Methodist Protestants, Free Methodist, and MEC (South) missionaries. In the year 1907 the Japan Methodist Church was established. The Evangelical Church and the United Brethren, together with other Protestant churches formed the Kyodan, the Church of Christ in Japan (1941). Besides social and medical services, educational work became an outstanding achievement of these denominations.

The Korean Methodist Church became a self-governing body in 1930, after Methodist (MEC and MECS) missionary work had started in 1884. The church was divided again after the Second World War, but reunited in 1949. Education, especially for women, was as important from the beginning as medical service and missionary work. During the Korean War the church suffered through the loss of leaders and the destruction of buildings, but since then has grown rapidly to a membership of more than 1.5 million believers. Bible studies (especially in weekly class meetings) and evangelism, work for social justice and peace in the divided country and in the world are major emphases of the (South) Korean Methodist Church.

Since the latter years of the twentieth century, there is a United Methodist Church of Central Asia, comprising new Methodist churches in Kazakhstan, Kyrgyzstan, Tajikistan, and Uzbekistan. They form a district in the Eurasia Episcopal Area which shows a steady process of building new and growing churches. New mission initiatives have also been started in Cambodia (1989), Nepal, Thailand, Vietnam, and Mongolia.

Methodism in Continental Europe

Methodist churches in continental Europe mostly started with emigrants, returning to their home countries and sharing their life-changing experience with relatives and neighbours. In nineteenth century Europe, most countries had coinciding borderlines of state and church: Roman Catholic (e.g. Italy, Spain, Poland), Orthodox (e.g. Greece, Russia, Bulgaria), Lutheran (e.g. the Scandinavian and many German states), and Reformed (Switzerland). In those countries, the dominant church had a privileged status as the (quasi-)state church over against small and often disadvantaged religious minorities; only foreigners were permitted to establish a local church for their own purposes. The modern process of enforcing de facto freedom of religion has been successful in many places, though not yet accomplished everywhere.

During and after the Second World War, about 30 million Europeans were expelled from their homes or relocated in foreign places. Homes and churches were destroyed, large cities lay in ruins. The horrors of enmity, warfare, and criminal killing became familiar to all. On the other hand, former enemies had met in prison camps and learned to know each other personally. Questions of reconciliation and of building peaceful relationships arose, relief supplies were sent to the needy from overseas, churches in Germany and other countries confessed not having been courageous and strong enough in faith, prayer, and resistance against evil. The Methodist Churches in Europe renewed their relationships and remained connected even after the iron curtain separated East and West. The connexional character of Methodism, put to the test, proved to be a reliable foundation for Christian fellowship and personal associations.

Most of the Methodist Churches in continental Europe are small. Some, such as those of Portugal and Italy (of British origin), are independent, the majority belonging to the worldwide United Methodist Church; all are members of the European Methodist Council. There are three central conferences: Northern Europe (Denmark, Estonia, Finland, Latvia, Lithuania, Norway, Sweden, and the Eurasia Area diocese including Russia), Central and Southern Europe (Albania, Austria, Bulgaria, Croatia, Czech Republic, France, Hungary, Macedonia, North Africa, Poland, Serbia, Slovak Republic, and Switzerland), and Germany.

The Wesleyan Missionary Society started missionary work in Italy, Portugal, and Spain during the second half of the nineteenth century. In Italy, the Wesleyan Methodist Church (1861) and the Episcopal Methodist Church in Italy (1871) united in 1946 to form the Evangelical Methodist Church of Italy, achieving independence in 1962. Since 1979 they live in a Federation with the Waldensians. Two English laymen brought Methodism to Portugal in 1854/64 by initiating prayer and bible study groups, the first church being built in 1868. During the period of the Salazar dictatorship (1932–68), the Portuguese Evangelical Methodist Church was forced to close its schools, but its ecclesial and social work continued successfully. Independence from the British Conference was granted in 1996. Missionary work was done in Spain at the beginning of the nineteenth century, but had to be discontinued because of the Spanish inquisition. A second attempt under a new regime led to the first church in Barcelona (1869), a limited work was possible in a few places, freedom of religion was not established before the end of the Franco dictatorship (1936–75). In 1955 the Methodist Church joined the Spanish Evangelical Church (with Congregationalists, Lutherans, Presbyterians).

The Scandinavian Methodist Churches have their beginning in the middle of the nineteenth century, when Scandinavians returned home after having been converted on the Bethel ship in New York harbour, a mission place for Scandinavian immigrants and sailors. A young Norwegian started preaching in Norway in 1853; the first Methodist Church in Norway was established in 1856. In 1858, a Dane started evangelizing in the whole of Scandinavia. In Copenhagen the first Danish congregation was established in 1859. In the 1850s, preaching in Sweden led to the setting-up of the Methodist Church (1868). Methodist preaching began in Finland in 1859; the first Swedish-speaking congregation was established in 1881 and a Finnish-speaking one six years later. Finland suffered heavily under Soviet occupation.

In Estonia, Methodism began in 1907; the first congregation was organized in 1910. Estonian churches survived the occupation period better than their two neighbours. The Evangelical Association from Königsberg (Kaliningrad) started evangelistic work in Latvia in 1908, the first church being built in Riga in 1912, developing rapidly. Methodism in Lithuania had begun in a German-speaking community on the outset of the twentieth century, a Lithuanian-speaking congregation followed in 1923. The United Methodist Churches in Estonia, Latvia, and Lithuania suffered under the ravages of wars and Soviet rule; almost all Methodist activities were stopped until 1991, apart from Estonia. For nearly fifty years, Methodists had been denied their places of worship and existence. In 1991 the UMC of Latvia was started anew. When, in 1994, a mission team launched an initiative to renew Methodism in Lithuania, three former Methodist parsonages, two Methodist church buildings, and three surviving Methodists were found; Methodist services started anew in 1995 in Kaunas and were followed by nine congregations until 2000.

In 1889, a mission to Russia was established from Finland, meetings held in St Petersburg and other places with approval by the Tsar (1909). The Bolshevik Revolution in 1917 put a stop to all church work. After the dismantling of the Soviet Union and a fifty-five-year absence, Methodism appeared again in Russia in 1990. An extensive outreach was initiated by the UMC Mission Board; congregations were founded within Russia and the Ukraine. Groups of Methodists arose in several places all over Eurasia which, in 1992, was made an independent Episcopal Area within the Northern Europe Central Conference, and the Russia United Methodist Church became a provisional annual conference in 1996. In 2001 Eurasia comprised four annual conferences: Central Russia, North West Russia, South Russia–Ukraine–Moldova, and East Russia–Kazakhstan with a total of 106 congregations and officially recognized Bible groups and 105 ordained ministers.

The Wesleyan Methodist Association in Germany came into being when, in 1831, an emigrant returned home from England; he started prayer and class meetings in his neighbourhood and an awakening began to spread. The very first deaconesses' work was started with the participation of two young women from this community.

In 1897 the Wesleyan Association joined the Methodist Episcopal Church, which had sent a German-born American to start a Methodist church in Germany (1849); others followed and a great work began to grow. The Evangelical Association (later a part of the EUB Church) started missionary work in German-speaking Europe in 1851, fourteen years later the first annual conference was convened and the work expanded through Germany, Switzerland, Hungary, and parts of the Austrian Empire. The United Brethren followed in 1869 when a homecoming preacher started evangelizing in Eastern Germany; they joined the MEC in early twentieth century. Because of strict limitations on religions the Methodist churches concentrated on building congregations, classes, and Sunday schools, publishing periodicals and books, educating pastors, and setting up diaconal services on different levels.

Similar beginnings are reported from Switzerland (1840, first church in Lausanne) and Austria (Vienna 1870) with Wesleyans from southern Germany, followed by the MEC in 1856; the Switzerland Annual Conference being formed in 1887. The Evangelical Association's first church was built in Berne (1866) and the first annual conference met in 1879. The different strands of Methodism were united in 1968 with the formation of the UMC. Switzerland originated missionary work on other continents and at home for people from other countries seeking shelter and living.

British Methodist missionaries to France arrived in 1791, establishing a French Wesleyan Conference in 1850. Before the Second World War, sixteen congregations joined the French Reformed Church; six abstained, forming the autonomous Evangelical Methodist Churches in France (EMF). In 1868, the Evangelical Association started founding churches in Strasbourg and its environment. After the merger of 1968, the links between the United Methodist Church and the EMF were strengthened, and eventually, the EMF was incorporated into the UMC (UEEMF).

In Austria the Wesleyan Methodist Association joined the MEC around the turn of the nineteenth century. A first mission conference included churches from Hungary and Serbia. With the end of the First World War, the Austro-Hungarian Empire collapsed. Religious freedom was enhanced and the church expanded in spite of Fascist and Nazi oppression. In its special position at a junction of different nations, it started serving refugees from mostly south-eastern countries; until today it stands as a bridgehead for Methodism in the Balkans and Eastern Europe.

Methodist missionaries went to Hungary from Germany and Austria in 1898. The respectable constituency of the Hungarian churches was severely diminished, when, at the end of the First World War, the country lost two thirds of its territory; after the Second World War the German-speaking population was deported and all church institutions confiscated. After 1989, a time of renewal and growth began under better conditions.

Methodism reached Bulgaria, then a part of the Osman Empire, in the middle of the nineteenth century; the first worship service was held in 1859. New churches were planted in often turbulent times. The one outstanding contribution to the Bulgarian people was the translation of the Bible into modern Bulgarian by Dr Albert Long, an American missionary. Under the Communist regime, a terrible persecution of the churches began: pastors were beaten, imprisoned, and even killed, church buildings taken, and all international ties forbidden. In 1989 a new era of recovery and growth allowed evangelism and social activities with international support.

The countries of the former Yugoslavia had to suffer from similar oppression, though not as hard as in Bulgaria. The Methodist work in Serbia and Macedonia survived the totalitarian period under difficult conditions. The work in Macedonia had begun in 1873 through missionaries from America. In the Vojvodina (Serbia), German immigrants started preaching and offered the first worship service in 1898. After the Second World War, most pastors and members had to leave the country and charitable and educational work was forbidden, but new congregations were founded. 'Bible women' travelled to remote regions, giving out Bibles, teaching women to read, and offering sewing and nursing courses. The Methodists serve the ethnic minorities and help to create friendly relationships between the different faith groups (Orthodox, Protestant, Catholic, and Muslim). There is one annual conference serving both politically independent countries.

Croatia saw Methodist attempts to build congregations in the early 1920s but they failed to continue. In 1995, a German pastor of Croatian parentage and his wife followed the call to start a new work in this mostly Roman Catholic country, where, as in other Eastern European countries, UMCOR was very active.

A small congregation was founded in Split; evangelism, children's work, and the production of Christian literature are their major tools for spreading the gospel.

Albania saw a short period of Methodist work (schools, especially for girls) in the nineteenth century. An oppressive atheistic communist regime then banned any Christian activity. After 1991, a German Methodist congregation started to support the process of reconstruction, rebuilding schools in mountain villages. Charity work and evangelization were going hand in hand. In 1998, the first twenty-four people were baptized.

Methodist work in Belgium, Czechoslovakia, and Poland was begun by the MEC (South) after the First World War. In Belgium, a promising development was interrupted by the Second World War. In 1952 the Belgium Conference with its twenty-five churches was integrated into the newly formed Central and Southern Europe Central Conference. Two unions among Protestant churches (1969 and 1978) led the Methodist Church into the United Protestant Church of Belgium. The work in Czechoslovakia was initiated in 1920, growing rapidly until a difficult time of suffering and oppression under totalitarian regimes (Nazis, Communists) brought a painful setback. In Poland, the Methodist Church was formed in 1921, remaining under American leadership until the Second World War, after which Poland lost one-third of its Eastern territory to the Soviet Union, millions of people were relocated in the West (formerly German East). The immeasurable destruction in these areas was affecting most Methodist church buildings and congregations. When, in 1989, new opportunities were offered, the Methodist churches in Czechoslovakia, Poland, and Eastern Germany recovered, building new churches, evangelizing, and offering social services. The churches in former communist countries continue to develop with great commitment and the support of the European Fund of Mission as well as other UMC churches and boards.

Methodism in Latin America

The history of Methodism in the Caribbean goes back to the eighteenth century, when the first Methodist congregation was established in 1759 on the island of Antigua. In 1809, work started in Trinidad and in 1817 in Tobago. In 1967, the Methodist Church in the Caribbean and the Americas (MCCA) with eight districts, was formed, bringing autonomy from the British Conference. In 1997, the MCCA changed some of its structure and was renamed the Connexional Conference.

Missionaries from the United States (MEC, MEC (South), EUBC) started their ministries in Latin America, beginning in the 1830s in Brazil, Argentina, and Uruguay. In 1836, the first churches were founded in Rio de Janeiro and Buenos Aires. During the nineteenth century, Methodist congregations came into being in almost all Latin American countries. Roman Catholic dominance as well as political and economic colonialism limited the freedom of their ministry. The mission focus on Central America began after the foundation of a new republic in Mexico (1857), and, in 1885, the Mexico Conference of the MEC was organized. In 1892, a South America Conference was established, covering Argentina, Uruguay, Paraguay, Brazil, Chile, Peru, and Bolivia, and in 1920 South America, Central America, and Mexico were connected to be the Central Conference of Latin America, with two Episcopal sees, in Buenos Aires and Mexico City. Social and political changes made the Methodists in Latin America conclude that their witness might be compromised by their historical and organic relationship to North American Methodism. In 1930, Brazil and Mexico started to become autonomous. The new UM General Conference (1968) voted favourably to the requests for autonomy, which then occurred in twenty-eight of the countries with UMC mission work. The (British) Methodist Church in the Caribbean and the Americas and the Methodist Church of Puerto Rico were recognized as Concordat Churches, granting them representation at the General Conference.

The newly formed Council of Evangelical Methodist Churches of Latin America and the Caribbean (CIEMAL) is providing a way to cooperate with other ecumenical churches and with the UMC as a whole. CIEMAL is affirming the rich heritage of the past and the creative new connections with partners throughout the world. New initiatives of witness and mission are emerging for more than 1,400,000 of the 'people called Methodist' of Latin America.

METHODISM ON THE ROAD

The rise of Methodism was the beginning of a movement within a Christianized society. This movement's character was not limited to itinerancy as a means of mission, but was inherent to the self-understanding of Methodists as witnesses of God's gracious presence in all places and with all people and pioneers of vital communities and worship life in multiple social, cultural, national, and religious contexts. This mutual correspondence of Methodist faith and spirituality on the one hand and Methodist mission and polity on the other has been one of the strongest incitements behind its astounding spread and enculturation around the globe.

Developments, Divisions, and (Re-)Unions of Methodist Churches

The nascence of Methodist congregations is owed to various causes and motives. But there were also, especially during the nineteenth century, quite a number of

Methodist break-aways or splits of existing churches because of intractable or insoluble conflicts about doctrine, ethics, polity, or the personal conduct of leaders. Wesleyan and Calvinist Methodists (doctrine), Primitive Methodists and Bible Christians (style of worship or evangelism), Methodist Protestant Church (lay representation), Wesleyan Methodist Connection (episcopacy), Independent Methodist Church (local autonomy), Methodist Episcopal Church and MEC (South) (slaveholding), Free Methodists (Holiness) are only a few outstanding consequences of those conflicts. In most cases, an ensemble of reasons were working together to exclude certain parts of a Methodist church or to cause people to leave the denomination in order to form their own. By the end of the century, there were around thirty Methodist denominations on the Christian map of North America. Stating this does not entail judging the honesty, devotedness, or seriousness of those believers, all of whom claimed to be good Methodists. However, there were a number of less respectable causes for separation than the preservation of the noble legacy of fathers and mothers, and the question whether or not, and to what extent, the will of Christ had been disregarded and disobeyed. Both the reference to common grounds in confessional and doctrinal tradition and the high esteem of personal experience and individual freedom were bearing very different fruit: vital Christianity and broken fellowship, strong leaders and a sectarian spirit. There was need of a new spirit to overcome divisions, to heal dogmatism and transgressions and overcome arrogance and exclusivism.

The movement of reuniting Methodist communities began about the turn of the twentieth century. In 1907, the Methodist New Connexion, the Bible Christians, and the United Methodist Free Churches joined to form the United Methodist Church. In 1932, the United Methodist Church, the Wesleyan Methodist Church, and the Primitive Methodist Church formed the Methodist Church. In the North American tradition, the Methodist Episcopal Church, the Methodist Episcopal Church (South), and the Methodist Protestant Church united and brought into being the Methodist Church in 1939, with effect for their international branches. The result of the first union of churches to cross denominational lines in modern times was the United Church of Canada in 1925. A second wave of unifications of both types—inter-Methodist and Methodists with other Protestant churches similar to those in India and Australia—followed after the Second World War, among them the unification of the Methodist Church and the Evangelical United Brethren Church in 1968 on a global level (*Book of Resolutions* 1992). Models of closer cooperation of Methodist and non-Methodist churches below the level of union can be found in Italy (with the Waldensians), in Britain (with the Church of England and the United Reformed Churches), and other countries. Again, the reasons for these unification and cooperation are manifold, the decline of membership and shortage of resources being a major factor in many cases.

The Ecumenical Movement

Before these achievements were obtained, the Ecumenical Methodist Conference had been created in Wesley's Chapel, London, in 1881, by delegates from thirty Methodist bodies around the world, one of the first Christian World Communions to be organized. In 1951, the original name was changed to World Methodist Council; it met at five-year intervals with delegates of seventy-five member Churches from more than 132 countries. Recent unification has reduced the number of churches while adding united and new member churches representing about 75 million members, thus making Methodists one of the largest Protestant church families in the world (*Handbook* 2007).

The awareness of being a part of the One, Holy, Catholic, and Apostolic Church of Christ and believing 'that the Lord of the church is calling Christians everywhere to strive toward unity' (*Book of Discipline* 2004: Constitution, Article V. 23) has been an essential element of Methodist faith and spirituality. Thus, it is no surprise to see Methodists at the forefront of the modern Ecumenical Movement. Methodists were founding members of the Evangelical Alliance (1846), the World Student Christian Federation (1895), the World Missionary Conference (1910), and the World Council of Churches (1948), the latter three being connected with the Methodist layman John R. Mott (1865–1955), who received the Nobel Prize in 1946, as well as international, national, and regional councils of Christian churches. They have been bridge-builders across traditional rifts and facilitators of mutual understanding and cooperation until this day. Moreover, 'Methodist influence and effectiveness has never been limited to…the planting and growth of specifically Methodist churches…it has always been a fertilizer of common ground of Christian mission' (Klaiber 2005: 264).

The Ecumenical Movement has created a special type of global community. Wesley's 'Catholic Spirit' and his differentiation between essentials and opinions are more than ever important basics for this community among Christian churches and denominations. The more religion is becoming a commodity, or a source of fundamentalist enmity, the more Christianity needs the spirit of Christ, who encourages his followers to be witnesses of God's love and to relate to people of other faiths in self-critical and honest dialogue.

Social Responsibility

'Social engagement is a lasting characteristic of Methodism' (Wainwright 2003: 506). The ways of engagement vary depending on the needs of the society in which this responsibility is taken. Unfinished tasks are the eradication of hunger, the provision of medical care and of education—especially for women—and the abolition of slavery. Racial and gender discrimination are still strong even in developed societies. The decay of social structures and moral standards is generating challenges mostly in the so-called first world. Worsening economics and social injustices are a by-product of a kind of globalization that cannot be approved.

The rediscovery and revitalization of early Methodist mobility and hospitality seem crucial for the credibility and distinctiveness of its witness and ministry. Methodist itinerancy must receive a new identity by seeking out those who are becoming lost in an economized society with no respect for the uncompetitive. 'Methodists on the road' has always entailed moving mentally, spiritually, and physically in the direction that the love of God, which encompasses both neighbours and enemies, is leading. Being Methodist has always necessitated creating and being a caring community beyond borders.

SUGGESTED READING

CASE, RILEY (2004). *Evangelical and Methodist. A Popular History.* Nashville: Abingdon.

DAVIES, RUPERT E., RAYMOND, GEORGE, and RUPP, GORDON (eds.) (1965–88). *A History of the Methodist Church in Great Britain.* 4 vols. London: Epworth.

GUILLERMO, ARTEMIO R. (ed.) (1991). *Churches Aflame. Asian Americans and United Methodism.* Nashville: Abingdon.

HARMON, NOLAN B. (ed.) (1974). *The Encyclopedia of World Methodism.* 2 vols. Nashville: United Methodist Publishing House.

KIRBY, JAMES E., RICHEY, RUSSELL E., and ROWE, KENNETH E. (1996). *The Methodists.* Westport, Conn.: Greenwood Press.

NOLEY, HOMER (1991). *First White Frost. Native Americans and United Methodism.* Nashville: Abingdon.

RICHEY, RUSSELL E., CAMPBELL, DENNIS M., and LAWRENCE, WILLIAM B. (eds.) (1997–2005). *United Methodism and American Culture.* 5 vols. Nashville: Abingdon.

ROWE, KENNETH E., YRIGOYEN, CHARLES, MASER, FREDERICK, and McELLHENNEY, JOHN (eds.) (1992). *United Methodism in America. A Compact History.* Nashville: Abingdon.

SHOCKLEY, GRANT S. (ed.) (1991). *Heritage and Hope. The African American Presence in United Methodism.* Nashville: Abingdon.

STREIFF, PATRICK (2003). *Der Methodismus in Europa im 19. und 20. Jahrhundert.* Stuttgart: Medienwerk der EmK. English version available through the Baltic Methodist Theological Seminary, Tallinn, Estonia, www.emkts.ee.

REFERENCES

The Book of Discipline of The United Methodist Church (2004). Nashville: United Methodist Publishing House.

The Book of Resolutions of The United Methodist Church (1992). Nashville: United Methodist Publishing House.

—— (2004). Nashville: United Methodist Publishing House.

GONZALEZ, JUSTO L. (ed.) (1991). *Each in Our Own Tongue. A History of Hispanic United Methodism*. Nashville: Abingdon.

Handbook of Information of the WMC (2007). Waynesville, N.C.: Cornerstone.

KLAIBER, WALTER (2005). *Methodist Identity and Ecumenical Perspective*. Stuttgart: Medienwerk der EmK.

WAINWRIGHT, GEOFFREY (2003). *Methodism*. In *The Encyclopedia of Christianity*. Grand Rapids: Eerdmans.

WEEMS, LOVETT H., JR. (2007). 'Ten Provocative Questions for the United Methodist Church', An address to the Council of Bishops of the United Methodist Church, 5 November 2007. Lake Junaluska, N.C.

CHAPTER 6

....

THE EVANGELICAL UNITED BRETHREN CHURCH

A HISTORY

....

J. STEVEN O'MALLEY

THIS denomination is popularly classified as a German-American version of
Methodism, which, as this chapter will indicate, is a partially valid generalization
but deficient in historical accuracy. The Evangelical United Brethren (EUB) existed
as a distinct denomination only between 1946 and 1968, when they and the
Methodist Church voted to unite, thereby forming the United Methodist Church.
However, the EUB were themselves the result of a 1946 denominational merger,
formed by the union of the Church of the United Brethren in Christ (1800–1946)
with the Evangelical Church (1816–1946). The origins of the two latter denominations may be traced even earlier, to 1767 and 1800 respectively. Each of these church
bodies will be treated separately, as foundational to the EUB, following their
historical succession.

CONTINENTAL INFLUENCES

The Church of the United Brethren in Christ traced its origin to a 'big meeting' (*grosse Versammlung*) which convened at the Isaac Long barn in Lancaster, Pennsylvania, on Pentecost Sunday 1767. These were forerunners of later camp meetings, but were usually held in large barns and in the 'bush'. They were four-day revival meetings, consummating in a 'sacramental service' on Sunday morning, that attracted seekers from a diversity of Pennsylvania-German sects, as well as the non-churched. This noteworthy meeting, which by some estimates numbered as many as one thousand persons, was attended by a prominent pastor from the 'Evangelical' Reformed Church of Baltimore, Philip William Otterbein (d. 1813), who was drawn to the message of the 'new birth' preached by a Mennonite lay bishop, Martin Boehm (d. 1812). Following Boehm's sermon, Otterbein went forward and embraced the preacher with the fervent declaration, 'we are brethren' (*wir sind Brüder*).

This event has been considered the inception of the Otterbein-Boehm movement, which developed into the United Brethren in Christ. These revivalists were not seeking to form a new religious denomination but to manifest a 'higher unity' in Jesus Christ that would transcend their formal ties to historical church bodies. Their sense was that God was moving to complete the plan for salvation history by bringing together awakened believers in a movement of Pentecost that would usher in what Otterbein called a 'more glorious state of the church' than ever has been. Both men intended to remain in the ministry of their home churches, while prizing their association with a growing and ever-widening circle of 'awakened' Christians, from multiple German traditions, who would provide support and encouragement for the travelling preachers associated with the blossoming revival among the descendants of German immigrants to colonial America.

These persons were concentrated in south-eastern Pennsylvania, and also in Maryland and the Shenandoah Valley of Virginia. They had initially been touched by the itinerant revival fanned by George Whitefield in the 1740s. It is thought that Boehm was converted by the preaching of 'New Light' ministers in Virginia. His successive field preaching among Mennonites in Pennsylvania resulted in the formation of not only the United Brethren, but also the River Brethren, now known as the Brethren in Christ, who reflected a convergence of Anabaptist and revivalist impulses. Boehm eventually was excluded from the office of bishop in his local Mennonite congregation for his advocacy of 'Pietist' measures, featuring his emphasis on the new birth as a conscious experience of salvation apart from the administration of ecclesial baptism. As a movement, Pietism sought to counteract the formal, non-personal systems of Protestant scholastic theology that emerged in defence of Protestant orthodoxy and its confessions within Germany in the era following the Protestant Reformation. It is largely associated with the Lutheran pastor, Philip Jacob Spener (d. 1705).

For his part, Otterbein's predilection to identify with the message preached by Boehm can be traced to his education in the leading school of Pietist persuasion within the Reformed Church of Germany. The Herborn Academy (established 1584) was long known as the centre for a non-scholastic, 'life-centred' approach to salvation, based on the irenic Reformed teachings of the *Heidelberg Catechism* (1563), This document had become not only a doctrinal teaching manual for laity, but also the chief confessional symbol of the Reformed churches in Germany. In tenor, it represented a 'low' Calvinist theology. This entailed a de-emphasis on unconditional predestination by advocating an infralapsarian view of God's ordering of human redemption in Christ in view of the fallen condition of humanity. Its main focus rests upon the existential question, 'What is your only comfort in life and in death?' The answer, 'that I belong to my faithful Savior Jesus Christ', was explicated with a threefold emphasis on a sense of one's misery apart from Christ, one's redemption in Christ, and one's vocation to live in thankfulness for this salvation by serving one's neighbours (*Heidelberg Catechism* 1963). As read by Pietists, the affirmation found in that question was not a foreordained conclusion for those who gave a perfunctory confession of its message; rather, it was the outcome of a mature life of godliness, in which the reborn believer is fitted to be a pilgrim, rescued from the turmoil of this world, and headed for the peace and light found through the reconciliation of a new humanity in the kingdom of Christ.

Herborn had become a centre first of two forms of Pietism: there was the 'normative' kind, which was committed to the revitalization of Christendom as it was then constituted in Europe, and there was also the radical option, advocated by those who looked towards a total displacement of the old historical order by a new age of the Spirit. Each of these versions of Pietism exerted specific influence upon the founders of the United Brethren and the Evangelicals, and upon their literary documents.

First, the church Pietists: the anti-scholastic tradition of interpreting the Heidelberg Catechism that was inherent to the theological tradition at Herborn made it receptive to embracing Pietist writers and texts. This reflected a circular movement: Olevianus (1536–87), a co-author of the Catechism, was the first theological professor there, and pioneered the development of a theology of covenant that would be definitive for the Christian life. Students of Olevianus in the early seventeenth century became teachers of Johannes Cocceius (d. 1669) at the Reformed university of Bremen (Germany). Cocceius, in turn, became the celebrated founder of the 'federal' or covenant school of Reformed theology, while professor of theology at Leiden. He succeeded in displacing the popularity of Aristotle as the preferred philosophical framer for Protestant Orthodoxy, and he did so by grounding the Protestant confessions in the biblical motifs of covenant and kingdom. Salvation history (*Heilsgeschichte*), not deductive logic, now becomes the framework for interpreting doctrine and the course of history.

The next step was for Cocceius' Pietist students to make the unfolding of salvation become the basis for the ordering of salvation (*Heilsordnung*) in the personal practice of piety.

This line was developed by the great pastoral theologian of the German Reformed church in the eighteenth century, Friedrich Adolf Lampe (d. 1729) at Bremen, whose work formed the basis for a theological compendium in use at Herborn in the days of Otterbein. Sections from Lampe's *Geheimnis des Gnadenbundes* (Mystery of the Covenant of Grace) were joined with those from the Cocceian biblical scholar, Campegius Vitringa (d. 1722), to form the theological compendium in use at Herborn in the mid-eighteenth century. Otterbein graduated from this academy in 1752. Lampe's commentary on the Catechism, the *Milk of Truth* (*Milch der Wahrheit*) also provided Otterbein and his brothers in ministry with a template for their extensive work in catechizing the youth of their parishes according to the *praxis pietatis*. Otterbein would acknowledge to Methodist Bishop Francis Asbury that he had come into a state of saving grace 'by degrees' while serving at Lancaster. This response reflects the Herborn Pietist legacy, whereby the 129 questions and answers of the Heidelberg Catechism are viewed as an ascending order of salvation, whose steps must be climbed by every believer-pilgrim as a *scala paradesis*. Full salvation is attained only by completing this ascent, so that one may confess with personal assurance the answer to question 1.

When Philip William Otterbein, as a young pastor at Ockersdorf, Germany, experienced resistance for his introduction of Pietist 'measures' (e.g. revival preaching and conventicles that included stated prayer meetings), his mother suggested to him that he seek service elsewhere, since 'this place is too narrow for you'. Opportunity soon appeared when Michael Schlatter came to Herborn to recruit missionaries for America, under the authority of the classis of Amsterdam. These recruits were deployed to focus upon the considerable population of Reformed émigrés from Germany who had settled in Pennsylvania and Maryland. Otterbein soon became the leader of the Pietist wing of that communion in those colonies. It was during his pastoral service, which was consummated in his long tenure at his semi-autonomous Reformed congregation in Baltimore (1774–1813) that he reached beyond his parish borders to seek the salvation of all who had not embraced the new birth. All such 'lost' persons were sternly rebuked for their godlessness and were then warmly invited to embrace the gift of free grace in Christ, available as God's justifying and sanctifying grace, to be taken to heart and lived out in a progressive pilgrimage of faith. It was in this quest for souls that he encountered Martin Boehm. This event occurred before the advent of Methodist preaching or organization in America. From a different perspective, it may be regarded as the successor to Count Zinzendorf's unsuccessful effort to effect a unitive 'Congregation of God in the Spirit' among the Pennsylvania sects in 1742–3. Both efforts, that of Zinzendorf and of Otterbein, reflected influence from radical Pietist Philadelphian sources.

Second, German radical Pietism may be traced to spiritual and theosophical streams identified with visionaries such as those popularized by the cobbler Jakob Boehme (d. 1624). These ideas found appeal among disaffected nobility, notably women, and an assortment of literate urban entrepreneurs and craftsmen, who became disenchanted with state-church Christendom and looked towards a coming apocalyptic day of judgement, anticipated for the end of the turbulent seventeenth century. That age, marked by horrendous religious warfare among the landed classes, had devastated the Holy Roman Empire, and became a nurturing ground for chiliastic visionaries of many varieties. The main line of development can be traced to the translation of Boehme into English, influencing the rise of the English Philadelphians, under the influence of Jane Leade (d. 1704). Her symbolic-prophetic and allegorical reading of Revelation 2–3 envisioned a coming remnant church of brotherly love, the church of Philadelphia, that, as the true bride of Christ, would be the agency for renewing the lost, an (androgenous) image of God within humanity. It would supplant the adulterous bride that Christendom as then constituted represented.

Philadelphian thinking soon won a following in Germany through many advocates, including Heinrich Horch, a Herborn professor who linked its themes with Cocceius' schema for salvation history. Horch would produce a new translation of the Bible, known as the Symbolic and Prophetic Bible, or simply the Marburg Bible. Before Otterbein's arrival there, Horch was dismissed from its faculty because of his calls for separation from the 'godless' state-church bodies. The chief voice of these emerging radicals was the former Lutheran historian Gottfried Arnold (d. 1714). In such works as *Die Erste Liebe* (*The First Love*) and *Die Unparteiische Kirche und Ketzer Historie* (*The Unpartisan History of the Church and Heresy*), he traced the authentic remnant of the bride of Christ through history as those mystical believers whose first love for their Bridegroom led them to dissociate from partisan religious conflicts on the grounds of their 'unpartisan' love. The latter volume appeared in that fateful year, 1699, which was on the eve of the expected eschaton.

However, when that apocalyptic crisis did not appear in 1700, radical thinkers in Germany began to shift to revivalist themes. The Philadelphians were in some measure reconstituted and also supplanted by the New Prophets, known also as the Society of the Inspired. Originating in the Camissard revolt against the anti-Huguenot Bourbon kings in France during the seventeenth century, their successors now launched an aggressive mission throughout Germany. They heralded a coming Age of the Spirit, a renewed Pentecost, in which God's elect would be identified with those nominal Christians now baptized in the Holy Spirit, and marked by lives of holiness and spiritual empowerment. This would be a unitive movement, bringing together all genuine, or mystical, believers in an unpartisan fellowship.

Philadelphian and Inspirationist themes are reflected in two monumental works produced by radical authors in the small German principality of Wittgenstein

(Germany). One was the massive *Berleburger Bibel*, a six-volume translation and commentary, and the other was an encyclopedic journal, *Die Geistliche Fama* (*The News of the Spirit*), which traced the progress of the world revitalization movement then in progress under the direction of the Spirit. Both of these works would be influential among early United Brethren and Evangelicals in North America. For example, in his only extant sermon, published in Lancaster (Pennsylvania) in 1760, Otterbein develops his text (from Hebrews 2: 14–15) by appealing to the lampstands of the seven churches. This was an allusion to the Philadelphian reading of the seven churches of Revelation 2–3, which were given a symbolic-prophetic rendition in the *Berleburger Bibel* (O'Malley 1995: 19–41).

During the Revolutionary War era, Otterbein conducted meetings with like-minded Reformed pastors in these colonies, spearheading a revitalization network within their communion. Soon the web extended to embrace work with representatives of other German church bodies, particularly Boehm's 'pietistic' Mennonites. Formal organization began to take shape, based at Otterbein's parish in Baltimore, where a conference was held in 1789 that embraced their first confession of faith, composed by Otterbein. Better documentation exists regarding the first organization of the 'United Brotherhood of Christ Jesus' in 1800. Otterbein and Boehm were selected by the brethren assembled as 'elders' who functioned as superintendents. They called themselves an 'unpartisan' (*unparteiisch*) fellowship, thereby adopting the language of the German radical Pietists, notably Gottfried Arnold (d. 1714). The themes of Arnold were mediated to Otterbein via the *Berleburger Bibel*, which early United Brethren historians noted was owned and read by Otterbein at Baltimore. In that spirit, Otterbein declared in the Protocol of the United Brethren that the chief sin was a 'party spirit', which meant partisan bickering that threatened to rend asunder the unity of the brethren. Also, early United Brethren societies were known by the name of the local house leader, such as *Lichtes Leute* (Light's People), reflecting the pattern of the early Philadelphians, as described by their chronicler, the Marsay de Renty.

DISTINCTIVES OF THE UNITED BRETHREN IN CHRIST

It was in 1815, two years after Otterbein's death, that the first general conference of the United Brethren convened and adopted a constitution and confession of faith, which turned them from being an awakening movement among multiple church groups to following the road to denominational organization. However, they

eschewed referring to themselves as a church (*Kirche*), which reflected their negative experience with state churches in Europe, preferring instead the title, 'United
Brotherhood in Christ Jesus'. This reflected their unitive, Philadelphian roots as
embodied in the reconciliation of a state church Reformed pastor with an Anabaptist preacher at the 'big meeting' on Pentecost 1767.

While Otterbein had maintained a dual relationship with the Reformed classis
and also the emerging United Brethren, he gave impetus for the rise of the latter by
consenting near the end of his life to ordain two brethren for ministry in the 'West'
(Ohio). One of those, Christian Newcomer (d. 1830), would emerge as the great
missionary bishop of the United Brethren. He introduced the United Brethren
message and planted congregations in such far-flung areas as Maryland, Ohio,
Indiana, and Kentucky in the first two decades of the nineteenth century. Newcomer also left a journal that documents his work. He planted the United Brethren
in the Miami Valley of Western Ohio in the first decade of the nineteenth century,
and then in the Cumberland Valley of Kentucky, traversing those regions contemporary with the itinerancy of Methodist Bishop Francis Asbury. Asbury had called
on Otterbein, his spiritual mentor at Baltimore, to share in his ordination as first
Methodist bishop at the Methodist Christmas Conference (1784), which established
the Methodist Episcopal Church.

Although Asbury encouraged the older Otterbein to adopt Methodist polity for
the work being done among the Germans, the fact is that Otterbein and Boehm
reflected Reformed and Mennonite distinctives that put them at odds with the
Methodists. For example, the United Brethren constitution called for a single order
of ministry (elder), rather than a two-stage progression from deacon to elder, as in
Episcopal polity. And, in deference to Mennonite practice, lay preachers were
granted ordination as well as membership in the conference of preachers. As
with Otterbein at Baltimore, United Brethren preachers held membership in
local congregations, which were their base for evangelistic mission. Bishops were
elected for four-year terms. They also were not permitted to make unilateral
decisions about appointment of preachers, as that was a corporate function for
the preachers in conference. Superintendents, who came to preside over annual
conferences, were also elected by the preachers in that conference.

The United Brethren sense of being an 'unpartisan' brotherhood led them by
mid-century in some instances to license women preachers, beginning with Charity
Opheral in the White River Conference (Indiana) in 1847. They were born on
Pentecost, 1767, and saw themselves as being called to manifest the prophetic
unity of the people of God, in accordance with the prophecy of Joel 2: 28, which
indicated that the Spirit was imparted to humanity, male and female. This unitive
thinking also influenced their early (1821) rejection of slaveholding among members, and to their early advocacy of liberation of slaves both in North America and
in West Africa. In brief, their symbolic prophetic reading of Scripture positioned
the United Brethren to take a proactive stand with regard to issues of social

justice throughout the nineteenth century. This outlook also contributed to their reticence to admit as members those who belonged to fraternities governed by secret rites, such as the Masons, since such rites were regarded as impediments to full brotherhood in Christ, which they were to share with one another without reservation. In brief, their egalitarian outlook led them to prize democratic values, in distinction from the more hierarchical pattern of Methodist Episcopal polity. Their early historians liked to point out their American identity, and claimed they were the first denomination born in America, using the Long's barn event as their point of origin. As a case in point, there was the narrative that Francis Scott Key was a song leader in Otterbein's Baltimore congregation, prior to his composition of 'The Star-Spangled Banner' during the War of 1812. The United Brethren also shed their preference for German language worship in the early decades of the nineteenth century, as they were working with third- and fourth-generation immigrant families who had assimilated to rural American culture. They would become the most rural of major American denominations, with the great majority of their members and congregations in open country or villages with fewer than 2,500 inhabitants. They were slow to enter cities, reflecting some level of disdain for urban life and religion. When they did plant urban missions, they were often characterized by rural mores and idiosyncrasies, which may have distinguished them from their upscale Protestant counterparts as much as did any theological emphases.

In searching for theological issues that engaged United Brethren in the nineteenth century, first attention is to be given to their terse Confession of Faith, written by Otterbein, probably for the 1789 Conference, but adopted in 1815 at their organizing general conference. By comparison with the Methodist Articles of Religion, the Confession speaks more of God's activity in history than of God's ontological being, in the language of the Nicene Creed. Emphasis is given to God's providential and redemptive ordering of creation and humanity. This priority is especially noted in the portrayal of the Holy Spirit's work, especially in completing the sanctification of the believer. Christ is a universal Saviour of humanity with reference to his atoning work, and his saving work is efficacious only for those who choose to accept his invitation. On both of these points, Otterbein laid aside the Calvinist confession to which he had subscribed at the time of his commissioning as a missionary by the classis of Amsterdam. The Bible is not described so much in terms of its plenary inspiration, although this is assumed; what the Confession emphasizes, though, is that it is essentially a guide for the pilgrim on her faith journey: it is called the 'way to holiness' and also the 'guide' (*Richtschnur*) to be followed 'under the influence of the Spirit of God' (Drury 1895: parts 2, 3).

Otterbein's *ordo salutis* essentially reflects the Reformed *ordo* of the Heidelberg Catechism: repentance, faith, forgiveness, and discipleship (*Nachfolge Christi*) (O'Malley 1987: 51–64). This *ordo* is identified as the heart of the Christian mission to the world. Revisions to the confession were frequent in the 1810s, particularly in the strengthening of the discussion of ordinances, which are now sacraments. However, all further revisions were prohibited after 1841, perhaps due to the pressure of conservatives not to relax the prohibitions against secret societies, which would increasingly become a divisive issue for United Brethren. Perhaps the major doctrinal dispute to shake the general conference in the 1840s concerned a debate over original sin, which was part of an effort to avoid implications of Pelagian tendencies in the early affirmation that one could be saved by Christ 'if one wills'.

ORIGIN AND CHARACTER OF THE EVANGELICAL ASSOCIATION

There is a second tradition that runs somewhat parallel to the United Brethren. In the last decade of the eighteenth century, we meet a Pennsylvania-born farmer and tilemaker and Revolutionary War veteran named Jacob Albright (d. 1808). He had come to a crisis of conscience leading to a profound experience of new birth, which is recorded in a biography written by an early associate, George Miller (Miller 1811). Albright had experienced the death of several children, and a soul struggle that thrust him into the kind of existential despair that is reminiscent of that of Luther. He had been baptized and reared, at least nominally, in a local Lutheran parish, but it was a United Brethren lay preacher who was instrumental in directing Albright to the new birth. He also attended a Methodist class meeting briefly, though his membership lapsed when he turned his attention to ministering to his German-speaking neighbours, whom he perceived were lost without the new birth. Albright embarked upon this calling when he found that his fervent petitions for God to send a messenger of salvation to the German people went unheeded, and he perceived that, despite his lack of formal training, God was calling him to that awesome task. After a period of intense fasting and prayer, he began his ministry, without the assistance of a church body to support or sustain him.

Albright preached a fervent message of salvation and new birth in Christ, marked by a call to holiness and entire sanctification. He respected all places of worship, yet urged members of the different German churches to look solely to Christ for the new birth, rather than relying on the 'external' traditions that they professed. He appealed to his hearers not to rely on external marks of religiosity, but solely on the merits of Christ and the witness of his Spirit. His audience represented mostly nominal adherents of the 'church' Deutsch (Lutherans and Reformed) and the 'plain' Deutsch (Mennonites and Dunkers). The guardians of those communities regarded Albright as an intruder and religious fanatic, and the preacher received much ridicule and physical abuse. However, many hungry hearts were filled with the love of God through the winsome message of this preacher, and reports spread of Albright's 'radiant', even transfigured countenance as he spoke tenderly to his hearers.

With appreciation for Methodist polity and discipline, which he had encountered in the class meeting of Isaac Davies, in 1800 Albright set about organizing his converts in classes. It is instructive to note that, in the first decade of his ministry, his assemblies were called 'Pentecostal' meetings, referencing the cataclysmic baptism in the Spirit that many of his hearers manifested. This theme emphasized the instantaneous and transformative message of sanctifying grace that accompanied or followed the new birth, which was the forming of 'Christ in us', as opposed to the traditional Lutheran emphasis on the 'Christ for us'. Similarly, Otterbein had counselled, if there is no Christ 'in' you then there can be no Christ 'for' you—a reversal of the *ordo salutis* characteristic of the theology of the Protestant Reformers. As with the Methodists, Albright gave greater attention of 'classing' his converts, with strict structures of accountability to the class leader. This was also a feature of the radical German Pietists, particularly the Inspirationists, who had also characterized their assemblies as 'Pentecost' meetings. An important feature of Albright and those 'assistants' who preached with him was their tenacity in pursuing seekers, like the hounds of heaven, until they gave in to the anointed message for hardened sinners to surrender and abandon themselves to the Christ who sought to live in their broken hearts, and to transform them by the baptism of his Spirit. In this message, he replicated the evangelistic appeal not only of Pietist theologians such as Lampe but especially that of the radical preachers, particularly Ernst Hochmann von Hochenau and Gerhard Tersteegen in Germany. In 1806, Albright's leading converts and co-labourers in the gospel acclaimed him to be a 'truly evangelical' preacher who had been God's instrument to convey to them the apostolic message of salvation in Christ. They proceeded to lay hands upon him, ordaining him to that office, even though they themselves were non-ordained laymen. He functioned then not only as a preacher but as the de facto episcopal head of the movement. This action contradicted the pattern followed in the Anglican and Continental magisterial tradition of Reformation, consisting of apostolic succession conveyed by clergy ordained by legally constituted church bodies. However, it may be seen as having precedent in the apostolic Christian community, where bishops were named and consecrated by popular acclamation of the congregation, as in the case of Ambrose.

Albright preached like a meteor that rose high but was soon extinguished. His calling was to ignite a movement, which attracted gifted converts to Christ who complemented one another in their capacities to equip the nascent association of the so-called 'Albright people'. These persons included Johannes Walter (d. 1818), a powerful young preacher who was particularly gifted in hymn composition. He published the first hymnal used by the Albright people in 1811. His hymns included some of the best-known and most beloved Pennsylvania-German 'bush meeting' choruses, some of which were inspired by the hymnody of Gerhard Tersteegen (d. 1769), the most renowned Pietist revivalist and poet from Muhlheim/Ruhr.

Another convert was George Miller (d. 1816), the literary voice of the early Albright people, whose works included his biography of Albright, transcribed from the narrative given by the founder himself, a volume of practical theology, *Practical Christianity* first printed in 1814, and, most important, the first *Book of Doctrine and Discipline* (1809). Miller was commissioned to complete the latter after the untimely death of Albright in 1808. His work was modelled after the Methodist Episcopal Discipline and Articles of Religion, which had first been translated into German by a physician, Dr Ignatius Römer. Miller adapted the Articles to become the *Glaubenslehre* (Articles of Faith), which included an article on the last judgement, taken from the Lutheran Augsburg Confession, and an extended article on 'Christian Perfection and Entire Sanctification', which reflected Wesleyan themes but now being cast in the manner of the German Inspirationists, echoed the language of Pentecost. This German Discipline was adopted by the conference of 1809, meeting after the death of the founder, when the name 'Newly Formed Methodist Conference' was adopted for the new movement.

In the years after Albright's death, no one was elected in conference to succeed Albright as bishop, although the Discipline provided for such an office. Instead, a presiding elder, John Dreisbach (d. 1871), served several decades as de facto episcopal head of the denomination. He too was a convert under Albright's ministry, although, unlike his peers, he lived to an advanced old age. It was in 1816, under his tenure of leadership, that the first general conference changed the name to the Evangelical Association (*die Evangelische Gemeinschaft*). As with the United Brethren, this name signified an avoidance of the word 'church', laden as it was with oppressive connotations in the German state church context, and signified instead that these were members of a living community of newborn believers, who were expressions of God's imminent kingdom, which is the age of the Spirit.

The two decades following the first general conference of the Evangelicals was a time of struggle and small growth. With strict membership standards, enforced in view of the requirements of entire sanctification, there were many expulsions of members and preachers, even while intense revivals were breaking out in 'bush' settings. One occurred at Orwigsburg, Pennsylvania, in 1823 under the leading of a zealous hound of heaven, a young preacher named John Seybert (d. 1860).

The impact of this particular revival was felt throughout the nascent denomination. Seybert left an engaging journal of his incessant itinerant travels, which, after his election as the first constitutional bishop of the Evangelical Association, took him from his native Pennsylvania through the Great Lake states and even northward into Ontario and westward beyond the Mississippi into Iowa. He was then the sole bishop for the entire denomination. In all, he travelled some 250,000 miles, seeking the lost among the numerous Germans on these frontiers. Preaching and visiting seekers almost daily, he also transported by buckboard loads of Bibles, hymnals, and devotional works put out by the denomination's little press at New Berlin, Pennsylvania. Records of his achievements are found in his unpublished journals and were also reported on a monthly basis in the *Christliche Botschafter* (English edn.: 'The Evangelical Messenger'), which became the longest-running German-American religious periodical in American history (1836–1946). In his written accounts, his promotion of holiness of heart and life was described in the language of Pentecost, and services of baptism were characterized as authentic if accompanied by the 'baptism in the Spirit' (O'Malley 2008). A veritable St Francis of the American wilderness, Seybert was primarily responsible for shifting the centre of Evangelical work from its base in Pennsylvania to the upper Midwest. By the time of his death on the eve of the Civil War, the denomination had multiplied from a few hundred to over 40,000 members.

Like the United Brethren, Evangelicals took a strong stand against slaveholding and trading among members, as well as opposing liquor and immorality. Like their Methodist counterparts, they were a highly disciplined and often socially prophetic voice in the communities where they served. Evangelicals differed from the United Brethren in two major respects. They had a more highly centralized episcopal polity. They also retained the use of German in services and literature into the twentieth century, having found ample justification with the massive German immigration into the United States that occurred throughout the nineteenth century.

MATURING AS WORLD BODIES

United Brethren expansion tended to be in the lower Midwest, and continuing into the lower Plains states, whereas Evangelicals concentrated on the upper Midwest and Canada, with both extending their work to the West coast by 1900. With their staunch antislavery positions, both denominations made little headway in the South, with the exception of western Virginia and east Tennessee, which contained pockets of antislavery sentiment. By 1906, United Brethren had grown to become the ninth largest religious body in North America, with over 300,000 members, and Evangelicals were not far behind (*Census 1906* (1910): 22, 27). Both denominations were originally rural bodies, and the United Brethren in particular retained that identity into the twentieth century. Preachers were educated through a conference course of study, under the guidance of clergy. By the 1840s, sentiment began to favour 'Christian higher education', with the United Brethren starting one of the earliest co-educational colleges (Otterbein University in Ohio, 1847). Soon both denominations were planting colleges and, by the 1870s, seminaries for educating the ministry of the church. These ventures were launched as schools of the prophets, seen as extensions of the ministry of the denominations. However, many continued to receive training through the conference study programmes, and neither denomination would require a seminary education for entry into ordained ministry.

By the mid-nineteenth century, both United Brethren and Evangelicals also launched plans for overseas missions. Before that time, all ministry activity was regarded as mission. United Brethren began with a mission to plant a colony in British-controlled Oregon in 1853.

In 1848, Evangelicals, under Bishop Seybert's leadership, organized a Missionary Society which made a return to the German 'Fatherland' its first and primary non-American mission. By 1865, a Germany conference was organized, based in Württemberg in south Germany, but extending by the end of the century to dozens of German cities and hundreds of villages, with three annual conferences, plus one in Switzerland. That mission would extend before the First World War into Alsace (France), present-day Poland, East Prussia, and Latvia. Before schools for theological education were begun in the American church, Evangelicals in Germany, operating as a 'free church' without the legal governmental protection or sanction, opened a theological seminary in Reutlingen (1877). Soon several hospitals, staffed by a new order of deaconesses, were opened in Germany, Switzerland, and France, which extended the ministry of this often persecuted free church to provide medical aid for the larger society. Missions abroad gave new impetus to the mother church in North America, and the Mission Society next turned to the Orient, establishing a mission in Japan (1872) and later China (1890s) and Nigeria (1920s). The latter mission operated in a comity plan with the Sudan Interior Mission. Home missions were launched to reach minority groups in North America in the early twentieth century, including Italians in Wisconsin cities and Kentucky in Appalachia.

The United Brethren commitment to breaking through barriers of religious exclusivism, race, and gender was expressed in their unitive emphasis and their opposition to slavery, as well as their practice of licensing, then ordaining, women for pastoral ministry, which began in 1847. All of these features were expressions of their quest for an 'unpartisan' brotherhood in Christ. This same outlook guided their choice in overseas missions. In 1852, their newly organized Home, Frontier, and Foreign Missionary Society decided to launch their first overseas mission in what had been the epicentre of the eighteenth century slave trade, later the site of the British colony of Sierra Leone. They were the first to reach into the tribal communities of the interior of that colony. Their success was based on the recruitment of an effective African-American missionary couple, Joseph and Mary Gomer, who extended the United Brethren vision for reconciling estranged and hostile peoples to a mission that, despite tragic setbacks, successfully addressed the issues of tribal warfare in that colony and resulted in a strong indigenous church. United Brethren worked through their Women's Missionary Society to plant work in South China in the 1880s. Here, as well as in Japan, the Philippines, and Puerto Rico, United Brethren operated under the principle of surrendering their denominational identity and establishing a united, indigenous church, working in cooperation with other Protestant mission boards, and allowing autonomy for these younger churches within the framework of the larger 'brother-hood' of the denomination (O'Malley 2003: 5–9).

In addition to these overseas fields, United Brethren established home mission work among the Native Americans of New Mexico and in the Latino community of Tampa, Florida.

An Era of Turbulence

As these two denominations developed after the Civil War, internal tensions surfaced that resulted in divisions within each before the end of the nineteenth century.

With its growth and entry into more urban settings, the United Brethren began to attract as members persons who belonged to Masonic orders. To conservatives in the denomination such as Bishop Milton Wright, this practice violated the original constitution and confession of faith, which prescribed that there be no internal partisanship within the brotherhood. Wright was the father of Wilbur and Orville, of aviation fame, who actively supported their father's position on this issue. Debate on this issue led in 1889 to the acceptance of a revised constitution and confession of faith by General Conference, with the result that the conservatives, known as radicals, seceded and reorganized as the Church of the United Brethren in Christ, Old Constitution, with headquarters and a college at Huntington, Indiana. The majority body, known as the liberals, constituted the great majority of members and churches, and they were now known as the Church of the United Brethren in Christ, having prefixed the term 'church' to their title. This schism was never healed. United Brethren began a programme of theological education for clergy with the establishment of the Bonebrake School of Theology (later United Theological Seminary) at Dayton, Ohio, in the 1870s.

The division in the Evangelical Association reflected a more complex set of factors. It may be traced to a dispute over the constitutional doctrine of 'Christian perfection and entire sanctification', which was publicly challenged by a presiding elder in Pennsylvania in the 1850s, Solomon Neitz. His opponent was William W. Orwig, a church editor and later bishop, who defended the official doctrine and called for the censure of Neitz. The controversy continued with the election of John J. Esher to the episcopacy, who became the most zealous protagonist of the official position. In addition to the doctrinal dispute, there was the contention over language. The western conferences, concentrated in Illinois and the upper Midwest, favoured the continued use of German, since church growth in this region was linked to the rapid influx of new German immigration, which totalled over 7 million persons in the nineteenth century, making the Germans the largest American ethnic group. Esher represented that contingent as well, as opposed to those eastern conferences that had largely been assimilated to an English-speaking culture.

A third factor concerned the authority of the episcopal office. Esher, known for accentuating the office of bishop, found himself in personal controversy in the church press with Rudolph Dubs, a fellow bishop from Pennsylvania, who objected to Esher's leadership style. Laity soon became involved in these volatile issues, as well. The sides polarized to the point where two rival general conferences were convened simultaneously in 1891, one meeting in Indianapolis and the other in Philadelphia. The result was the division of the denomination into the Evangelical Association, the original body, representing three-fifths of the membership and concentrated in the western region, and the United Evangelical Church, concentrated in the eastern region. The latter body was more progressive, in introducing lay delegation to church conferences, and adopting new Articles of Faith based on the writings of Methodist theologian Milton Terrey, which placed much emphasis on world mission. United Evangelicals took the forefront in opening a Protestant mission in the central China province of Hunan. They also placed restrictions on episcopal authority and looked more favourably on English-language worship.

The era of the First World War did much to discourage continued use of German-language worship among Evangelicals, and also brought to the fore a new generation of leadership that began to look towards reunion of the divided denomination. That goal was reached in 1922, when the general conferences of the two bodies met in a union conference. The name for the reunited denomination was now changed from the Evangelical Association to the Evangelical Church, a body with over 250,000 members worldwide. A minority group from the United Evangelicals, numbering more than 20,000 members, chose not to join the new body. They reorganized themselves as the Evangelical Congregational Church, which was now based at Myerstown, Pennsylvania. This new ecumenical trend among Evangelicals was also reflected in the election of an Evangelical bishop, John S. Stamm, as president of the Federal Council of Churches in the United States.

THE EVANGELICAL UNITED BRETHREN

From the earliest days of both denominations there had been free exchanges of pulpits and clergy, and Methodists were often included in that fraternal swapping. However, efforts to achieve formal church union, which were attempted through many different configurations (and, in the twentieth century, involving discussions with other denominations to participate in that process), ultimately bore no fruit. This ecumenical impulse can be traced to the unitive emphasis of the early United Brethren, and the later participation of Evangelicals in that circle of conversation. At last, the two denominations organized serious discussions that eventuated in a highly successful church union, which was consummated at a uniting general conference in Johnstown, Pennsylvania, in 1946. The formation of the Evangelical United Brethren Church, with more than 720,000 members and almost 5,000 congregations in North America, was the largest church merger in America occurring without the loss of a single congregation. There were also seven colleges and three theological seminaries in the United States. Both churches were of comparative size, ethnic heritage, and theological commitment. In the three states where they overlapped in greatest strength (Pennsylvania, Ohio, and Indiana), the resulting union produced a presence that gave them a critical mass in the religious make-up of the population. The work of the united church was represented in forty states and in seventeen nations.

As a denomination, the Evangelical United Brethren were largely lower middle class and rural in demographics, with a higher percentage of church attendance and financial giving per family than in most Protestant denominations. They thrived in an era when strong family life was prized, and, indeed, the denomination as a whole was imbued with a pronounced 'family' spirit, which was known for extending hospitality to one other, and to visitors, in ways appropriate to a people grounded in the warmth of a Pietist religious ethos. Congregations and conferences were designed to be governed by a spirit of consensus, with major authority placed not in the board of bishops but in a general council of administration and in local church councils of administration, involving laity and clergy. The Board of Missions was granted authority in planting and nurturing missions, both at home and overseas, and it consecrated missionaries for that service apart from the authority of the board of bishops. Bishops tended to function as leaders of the brotherhood, elected for four-year terms by all clergy represented at the general conference. As with the United Brethren, conference superintendents continued to exercise much influence in appointing pastors, and were themselves elected by the clergy members of their conference. There was a continuation of the United Brethren practice of pastors holding membership in the local church(es) to which they were appointed, as well as in the annual conference. Church property was held in trust by the local church for the denomination.

EUB membership reached its peak in 1963, with 763,000 members in North America, and approximately another 200,000 in the larger constituency of the several indigenous and annual conference organized mission fields around the world. The latter figure reflects the largest constituency attained in each of those fields, although these numbers were reached at different times in different fields, and in several of them, declines occurred due to adverse political circumstances. The latter included (1) the defeat of Germany in the two world wars, resulting in the loss of many German-language congregations in areas lost to German governmental control; (2) the loss of extensive united church work on the Chinese mainland in the era of the Maoist revolution following the Second World War; and (3) decline in the membership of the Kyodan, the state-supported united Protestant church in Japan, in which Evangelicals and United Brethren had been constitutive members, as a result of Japanese defeat in the Second World War.

The EUB discipline upheld high moral standards, including a disdain for affluent lifestyles and a commitment to sharing resources with those in need. Indeed, despite their modest resources, EUB were among the leaders in providing material aid to victims of the Second World War and assisting in rebuilding communities devastated by that conflict. There was a greater emphasis on diversity in liturgical practice, with various modes of baptism being acknowledged, for example. This reflects the earlier Pietist emphasis on the centrality of the new birth as the basic qualifying factor for Christian and church identity. For this reason, the language of confirmation was not used, and, in its place, children and youth were catechized and then accepted into church membership when the experience of conversion was overtly manifested. There were exceptional congregations that adopted a more formal liturgical practice, along the lines developed by twentieth-century Methodism, but these tended to be in the minority.

The Board of Missions in the united church continued to nurture the long-standing mission projects that had been launched by the predecessor churches, and whose ministries had been bequeathed by church union to the new church. In addition, new missions were organized during the EUB period in these areas: Brazil and Ecuador in South America, and in Indonesia. EUB also took leadership in ecumenical affairs, with one of their bishops, Reuben H. Mueller, being elected president of the successor body to the Federal Council of Churches, the National Council of Churches of Christ, in the 1960s. Mueller also took leadership in the successful effort to achieve union with Methodism in 1968.

The united church had a life of twenty-two years before it surrendered its autonomy on behalf of another union, in this case with Methodism, forming the United Methodist Church in the uniting conference of 1968. This union was narrowly approved by EUB, who expressed concern regarding the numerical disparity between the two denominations. Together they represented the largest Protestant denomination in North America at the time of union.

SUGGESTED READING

ALBRIGHT, RAYMOND W. (1956). *A History of the Evangelical Church*. Harrisburg, Pa.: Evangelical Press.

BEHNEY, J. BRUCE, and ELLER, PAUL H. (1979). *The History of the Evangelical United Brethren Church*. Nashville: Abingdon.

O'MALLEY, J. STEVEN (1973). *Pilgrimage of Faith: The Legacy of the Otterbeins*. Metuchen, N.J.: Scarecrow.

REFERENCES

CENSUS 1906 (1910). US Department of Commerce and Labor, *Special Reports, Religious Bodies*, Part I.

The Discipline of the Evangelical United Brethren Church (1959). Harrisburg and Dayton: Board of Publication, The Evangelical United Brethren Church.

DRURY, A. W. (1895). 'Die Lehre der Vereinigten Brüder in Christo'. In *Disciples of the United Brethren in Christ*, Art. 4. Dayton: United Brethren Publishing House.

—— (1924). *History of the Church of the United Brethren in Christ*. Dayton: Otterbein.

The Heidelberg Catechism (1963). Philadelphia: United Church Press.

MILLER, GEORGE (1811). *Kurze Beschreibung der würdenden Gnade Gottes bei dem Jakob Albrecht*. Reading: n.p.

—— (1959). *Jacob Albright: The First Biography of the Founder of the Evangelical Association*, trans. George Edward Epp. Dayton: Historical Society of the Evangelical United Brethren Church.

O'MALLEY, J. STEVEN (1987). 'A Distinctive German-American Credo: The United Brethren Confession of Faith'. *Asbury Theological Journal*. (Spring): 51–64.

—— (1995). *Early German-American Evangelicalism; Pietist Sources on Discipleship and Sanctification*. Lanham, Md.: Scarecrow.

—— (2003). *On the Journey Home: The History of Mission of the Evangelical United Brethren Church, 1946–1968*. New York: General Board of Global Ministries.

—— (2008). *Bishop John Seybert and the Evangelical Heritage*. Lexington, Ky.: Emeth.

OTTERBEIN, PHILIP WILLIAM (n.d). 'Letter concerning the millennium'. In Arthur Core (ed.), *Philip William Otterbein: Pastor, Ecumenist* (1968). Dayton: EUB Board of Publication, 102–3.

CHAPTER 7

AFRICAN-AMERICAN METHODISM

WILLIAM B. GRAVELY

As John Wesley discovered in colonial Georgia and South Carolina, in the world where Methodism arose, slaveholding was virtually an unchallenged practice. Nothing per se in the logic of free market capitalism grounded in a slavery-based agricultural economy necessarily led to abolition. Wesley's prohibition against slave trading in his early general rule was therefore distinctive. There were as yet no anti-slavery societies. In the same century American Quakers courageously purged slave-owners from their ranks, but success came with a price—a small sectarian constituency. There were eighteenth century voices of conscience, including Wesley's, but neither Catholic nor Protestant doctrine contained explicit theological and ethical condemnation of racism—modern slavery's foundation. In contrast, biblical pro-slavery arguments preceded Christian abolitionist counterattacks. In the United States the first and strongest intellectual defences of slavery originated not in the South but in the Northeast. The law of African slavery defined the status of a child by the status of the mother. If the mother was free, so was the child. If she was a slave, so was the child.

The eighteenth-century evangelical revival in the American colonies gave Africans settings to claim some free space in their lives. Evangelists were delighted that their converts responded so powerfully to the Christian gospel. Such a reaction confirmed their capacity for spiritual experience and contradicted the racist cynics who denied that Africans had souls. It mattered to the slaves to have a 'good' owner and to be treated well and it was important that some Christians cared about their spiritual welfare, but nothing substituted for emancipation. Most Africans were neither Christian nor free, but among those who converted some coveted the chance to preach and teach those around them.

Africans in North America became active participants in the Methodist system as members and leaders of classes. They earned tickets to love feasts, welcomed the itinerants on their rounds, and contributed to support the preachers. When quarterly conferences came around they attended in large numbers, despite the practice of racial separation during services. When the camp meeting movement spread, Methodists easily integrated it into its evangelistic outreach and their black constituency benefited from its success. In time the English and native ministers began to license black preachers and exhorters, but they were cautious about ordaining even the most talented. The numbers of black Methodists, nonetheless, grew to 20 per cent of the total American membership by 1820.

Over the next two centuries people of colour with ancestral roots in Africa were a constant presence in the global movement spawned by the brothers Wesley. By that constancy and by their own initiatives, black Methodists grew their own institutions, none of which were more important than their independent churches. Their Christian faith helped them maintain integrity in the face of harsh difficulties. They belonged to the abolitionist minority in the US in challenging the domestic slave trade and the extension of slaveholding and they dissented from the religious arguments intended to justify their enslavement and mistreatment. 'African Methodism', a self-designated phrase popular especially in the nineteenth century, began to make its presence known in international settings. As early as 1846 the African Methodist Episcopal (AME) Church sent a fraternal message and a delegate to the convocation of the Evangelical Alliance in Edinburgh. Later in the century representatives from black Methodism routinely attended national and international gatherings, even the World's Parliament of Religions in 1893. Some conventions supported Sunday Schools. Others sponsored foreign missions or formed interfaith councils promoting a social gospel to address urbanization, immigration, and industrial capitalism.

No global meetings were more important than the series of Ecumenical Methodist Conferences beginning in 1881 and continued after 1951 as World Methodist Conferences. In them black Methodists claimed their distinct place and confronted Anglo-American white Methodists about the harsh realities of modern racism. Gradually its representatives built a theological ethic that fostered social transformation not only in the US but in conjunction with other Christian agencies also in South Africa. The final four decades of the twentieth century saw Jim Crow segregation (though not all legacies of racism) and South African apartheid end.

Of the 15 million Methodists among peoples of black African descent today, more than 5 1/2 million are in the US. The AME Church has 3 million members and the African Methodist Episcopal, Zion (AMEZ) denomination about half that number. Membership in the Christian (formerly Colored) Methodist Episcopal (CME) Church ranges around 430,000 while in the United Methodist Church (UMC) more than 300,000 members are African Americans. The World Methodist Council (WMC) embraces these communions, along with the Union AME Church (dating back to 1813) and two smaller bodies that seceded from the AME Church (Ledbetter and Wyatt 2003: 254–67; Payne 1991: 80–1, 88–90, 105, 110).

Black Methodist denominationalism first took shape between 1813 and 1822. After Peter Spencer led black members out of Ezion ME Church in Wilmington, Delaware, the African Union Church became the first to separate but its base remained regional. Unlike Spencer's movement, the AME Church, which retained bishops, combined in 1816 Philadelphia's Bethel church under Richard Allen and Daniel Coker's congregation in Baltimore. Up to 1822 its largest local church was in Charleston, South Carolina before white authorities disbanded it in reaction to the Denmark Vesey insurrection. Over the next twenty years future bishop William Paul Quinn led AME missions into the Midwestern states and Canada. To meet increased demand to serve refugees from slavery and from hostile northern mobs, the British Methodist Episcopal Church, formed first as an AME conference, became a separate black Canadian denomination.

When the Methodist Episcopal Church (MEC) would not assist the creation of an independent AMEZ organization (1822) in New York City, William Stillwell, a congregational Methodist, had to perform their ordinations. The Zion communion soon split over polity and naming the denomination but healed the rift by 1860. Not until 1880 were its general superintendents called bishops or given lifetime appointments. Like the AME Church following the Civil War its headquarters moved to the South, where churches multiplied dramatically.

Following emancipation the black members within the Methodist Episcopal Church South, (MECS) declined to join the AME, AMEZ, or missions of the ME churches. Instead they formed the CME Church in 1870. All its bishops until the early twentieth century were born in slavery. By their concession to the MECS that prevented churches being used for political purposes, the early CME leadership strategically retained buildings that they, during slavery, had helped construct. Their departure from the MECS left it with an exclusively white membership and ministry. As their price for union with the MEC and the Methodist Protestants in 1939 the Southern church, which had spread nationally, insisted on keeping racially separate conferences organized into a national race-based jurisdiction.

Despite their marginality until the mid-twentieth century, African Americans within the MEC retained their historic place in the denomination. Into the 1840s their churches, like the Zionites, were also called African Methodist Episcopal. By the 1850s white bishops presided over informal conferences of black local deacons and elders which were in 1864 turned into regular 'coloured' conferences with ordained clergy and finally by 1920 with black bishops. In 1876, the MEC General Conference, despite protests, made racially separate annual conferences into policy. The description of the MEC as Northern Methodist is misleading since after 1865 missions to both the freed people and southern whites made it also national. For another century, loyal African Americans in the MEC—and its successors the Methodist Church (MC 1939–68) and the UMC (1968–present)—advocated a church without 'caste'—the earlier term for racism. Eliminating the Central Jurisdiction beginning in 1968 realized, in part, that goal.

'African Methodism' in Methodist Studies and Black Church Research

Over the past generation an impressive range of African-American studies research, teaching, and publishing has significantly impacted several academic fields including theological school curricula. Scholars can now access previously obscure sources for invigorating black Methodist history. Refuting the old stereotype that they did not exist, there are church records in multiple locations. Literary scholars in black studies have drawn new attention to Methodist conversion accounts, fugitive slave narratives, and autobiographies. Little-known biblical and theological works by 'African Methodists' have also been recovered. Local, regional, and national newspapers of 'the Negro press' and denominational publications detail the religious life of black communities. Manuscript and material culture resources are in federal institutions such as the Smithsonian and the National Archives, in public libraries such as New York City's Schomburg Center and at state libraries, archives, and historical societies. Major universities and historically black colleges and denominational and missionary research centres house important special collections. All have African-American Methodist relevance. Documentary compilations such as the African-American religious history project at Amherst College and Princeton University begun in 1987 and the completed Black Abolitionist Papers microfilm and book-publishing programme contain a treasure of Methodist authors, subjects, and institutions (Conser and Twiss 1997: 52–71; Ripley 1985–92).

Beyond expanded sources, there have been methodological shifts in the study of black religion. They cross traditional disciplinary boundaries and represent new lines of enquiry. Social history and popular culture studies illuminate valuable dimensions of lived religion. Focusing on the vital ways people experience their faith these approaches illustrate how human need encounters divine response. From the spirituals to modern gospel songs, musicologists show that biblical images and stories combine with African rhythms and musical scales in black Christian music. Cultural anthropologists analyse generational transmission of myths and rituals from West African societies and carry out ethnographic studies of congregations. Theologians concerned with liberation themes find rich evidence in African-American history.

In his imaginative book on global Methodism David Hempton (2005) also brings together fresh interdisciplinary perspectives. He employs sociology's attention to race, class, and gender, situates economic history's relevance for how successful religious movements adapt to competition, and attends to communication theory in considering the sounds of preaching, prayer, and song. Such scholarship moves church history from internally focused surveys to the consideration of Methodism as a social movement. In the same vein surveys of American Methodism, including documentary sourcebooks, volumes from the Duke Divinity School project with the Lilly Foundation, and Methodist representation in general African-American religious studies literature, flesh out teaching materials and identify new topics for research.

Since future Methodist history won't be written narrowly from the angle of Anglo-American triumphalism, black Methodist studies can most fruitfully proceed from W. E. B. DuBois's formulation of a 'double-consciousness' in African-American identity. The dialectic for Methodism affirms racial separation in autonomous African-American churches on the one hand but incorporates black–white interaction and interdependence on the other. This approach manages the tension between two interpretative strands accounting for separate black churches—white proscription and African-American autonomy. The stories of offensive caste distinctions in Methodism are numerous. At the same time, separate churches became essential institutions in the infrastructure of black community life. Both factors interacted. Given the racist corruption of nineteenth-century Christianity as in the Hamite myth and given the pervasive ideology of scientific racism into the early twentieth century, what is not always fully appreciated is how African-American converts salvaged the gospel. The exodus from biracial to independent churches confirmed an experiential basis of knowing Jesus as neither created nor controlled by white Christians. Here lay the foundation for a theology and an ethic of anti-racism (Fulop and Raboteau 1997: 133–52).

On the separatist side of the dialectic, there are important monographs on the rise of independent black Methodist churches, critically recognized biographies of formative figures, and illuminating analyses of 'African Methodism' from particular eras. New and reprinted older denominational histories and autobiographies detail not only institutional developments and internal conflicts typical of Methodists but also feature the life histories of the men and women who contributed to civic life and service to society.

The other dimension of the dialectic, black and white interaction in religion, has become a new hermeneutic in the study of American Christianity. Featuring creative cross-racial exchanges, Sylvia Frey and Betty Wood illustrate it in their informative exploration of African-American Protestantism in the Caribbean and American South up to 1830. They consider this development to be 'perhaps *the*, defining moment in African American history' (Frey and Wood 1998: p. xi). Often paradoxical in nature, interchange between white Americans and African Americans demonstrates how each collectively shaped and has been shaped by the other. Tracing 'African Methodism' in its interplay with European Americans and how it has engaged the growing Methodist communions of Africa, Asia, and South America will be an ongoing interpretative challenge for future historians.

A well-known example shows both patterns. At Old St George's, MEC, when white trustees forced Allen and others to move to a gallery, black members walked out. The 'gallery incident' was frequently retold, even before the World's Anti-slavery Convention in London in 1843 (Ripley 1985–92: i. 110). It came to be a paradigm, symbolizing other clashes between white and black Methodists around styles of worship, about burial grounds, over white pastors refusing to hold black infants at baptism, over black communicants being served last at the Eucharist, and, especially in the South, over state laws prohibiting separate worship unless white persons were present.

The gallery story, however, should not be read as if black–white interdependency ended. In June 1794 MEC Bishop Francis Asbury preached the dedicatory sermon for Allen's Bethel AME church building. Allen remained for seventeen years an MEC local deacon to which role Asbury ordained him in 1799. During that period Allen and his wife regularly provided room and board for white preachers such as William Colbert when they came to Philadelphia. In 1798 in a biracial revival Allen even had sufficient grace to work with Henry Manly, one of the trustees who offended him at St. George's. Though the walkout clearly symbolized black self-determination, it did not end black–white interchange.

Assessing African-American Methodism in a global context is part of Hempton's agenda. At the outset he notes that there were more black Methodists in the US at the end of the nineteenth century, when his book concludes, than the entire Methodist population of Europe. Grounded in a particular kind of Christian experience, spread by the labours of women as much as of men, and extended globally, 'African Methodism' from North America conforms to Hempton's most general definition of the shared traits of Methodism. One could take his creative dialectical pairings to probe how boundaries and margins, mapping and mission, and the like have functioned in the black Methodist past. A more fruitful procedure would be to examine two of his concepts in relation to the African-American story—'host environment' and the claim that 'Methodism at its heart and center had always been a profoundly countercultural movement' (Hempton 2005: pp. x, 201).

'AFRICAN METHODIST' COUNTERCULTURE, 1786–1881

After numerous attempts to keep the two goals together, Francis Asbury's fateful compromise in 1809, when he made the hard choice that the salvation of the souls of the slaves was finally more important than emancipation, shaped the pattern of evangelization without liberation. His decision haunted Methodism and no one recognized it more clearly than African-American church folk who were always there to witness what was taking place. Asbury's choice harmonized with an ecclesiology of the 'spiritual Church' whose ultimate result came in 1858 when the MECS deleted all mention of slavery from its *Discipline*, even Wesley's original general rule. The action, prefigured by issuing, for slaveholding areas, *Disciplines* in 1804 and 1808 without the chapter on slavery, proceeded from the logic of a sectarian withdrawal from worldly matters. But there was no such withdrawal and Methodism was not a sect like the Quakers, but a denomination with increasing cultural and political power. By the 1850 census, for instance, thirty-four of the forty-seven southern delegates to the general conference of the MEC in 1844, which split the denomination, were slaveholders. Their spiritual mission to the slaves replaced condemnation of slavery and they thereby exempted the institution from normative judgement.

Black Methodist congregations and denominations arose in these host environments of the MEC and MECS. Because there were slaveholding members in their border conferences after 1844, and because the Wesleyan Methodists took their most active abolitionists into their denomination, the battle in the MEC over slavery would be repeated over the next two decades. But the full context for these issues in the churches cannot be fathomed apart from the larger social and political world surrounding all black people.

The secular host environment contained several interconnected features. To begin with, though slavery ended through state legislation, court decisions, and constitutional provisions in the First Emancipation, beginning in 1780, gradual manumission schemes did not spread to Delaware, Maryland, and further south. By 1860 there were 4 million slaves. In the same year not quite 500,000 African Americans were free people, split about evenly between the two sections. While slavery had ended in the North, free African Americans regularly faced segregation and exclusion there.

In the second place, though absent from the Constitution and Declaration of Independence, the colour codes of race first appeared in the Naturalization Act of 1790 by which all persons of European descent were termed 'white'. The legislation remained in effect until 1952 and 'white' remains the only unchanged category in the US Census. Slavery was a racially based institution. If any trace of African descent was present, the person could not be classified as white. Thirdly, the civil rights of free black Americans diminished between the Revolution and the end of slavery, so that proportionately fewer voted in 1860 than in 1780. Pennsylvania in 1839 withdrew the right to vote for black men, leaving impartial male suffrage only in five Northeastern states and New York. That fact alone means that Reconstruction was not merely an attempt at democratizing a defeated South, but was a valiant though short-lived national effort to create a biracial republic as relevant in Connecticut, which rejected black suffrage three times after 1865, as in Mississippi. The push for post Civil War sectional reunion after 1876 coincided with the defeat of Reconstruction to make the US into a predominantly white Christian republic.

To turn to the counter-cultural norm that Hempton assigns to Wesley's movement, African Methodists actively participated both in the black abolitionist and in the white-led biracial anti-slavery movements. Their abolitionism linked the end of slavery to full civil and political citizenship, rejected colonization schemes and denied compensation to slave-owners. AME preachers Daniel Coker, William Paul Quinn, and M. M. Clark and AMEZ author Hosea Easton wrote anti-slavery narratives and celebrative race histories. Future AMEZ bishop Jermain Loguen and Josiah 'Uncle Tom' Henson, also a Methodist, published their stories of escape on the underground railroad. So did Harriet Tubman and Frederick Douglass who belonged to the Zion Methodists. Both Sojourner Truth as an itinerant speaker and the writer David Walker depended on the African Methodist church network to carry out their distinctive callings. After his early years in the Carolinas, Walker kept up Methodist connections in Boston through former slave 'Father' Samuel Snowden and with Allen's denomination. His important *Appeal* (1829) promoted black communal unity, opposed pro-slavery Christianity, exposed the ill-treatment of slaves, and countered the psychological damage to black people caused by white racist ideology and practice (Hinks 1997).

Carol George's phrase 'practical abolitionism' captures a less ideological abolitionist orientation of representative northern black clergymen including several Methodists, but she underestimates the black church's anti-slavery resistance and defence of civil rights (Fulop and Raboteau 1997: 153–76). In New York leaders in the Mother Zion Church sponsored the first of several freedom celebrations marking the end of the foreign slave trade on 1 January 1808 and afterwards. Around the abolition of slavery in New York State, 5 July 1827 and beyond, and especially when emancipation dawned in the British Empire, black freedom celebrations on 1 August with regular Methodist involvement spread across thirteen states and moved abroad. African Methodists knew and recounted the stories of the slaves in the Indies who turned the Wesleyan watchnight service on 31 July 1834 into a vigil for freedom. At midnight they shouted and sang what became a freedom anthem, Charles Wesley's hymn, 'Blow Ye The Trumpet Blow' (Hackett 2003: 121–38).

Assisting fugitive slaves to get to Canada, organizing Vigilance Committees to publicize openly their successful work, forming intra-communal associations to train race leaders, and raising money to buy slaves to reunite families, African-American Methodists demonstrated practical activism that addressed concrete needs. But these leaders also operated in state and regional networks, first in the multi-state coloured convention movement from 1830 to 1836 initially organized by Bishop Allen. Between 1846 and 1865 the concept expanded to more than fifty black conventions across nineteen states. Black Methodist churches hosted at least 40 per cent of them (Foner and Walker 1979, 1980). Much of the training that northern free blacks including many Methodists brought to politics during Reconstruction originated from these gatherings. Given the powerful influence of pro-slavery Christianity in both the North and the South, given the obscene forms of anti-black ideology in popular culture, given the need to refute the charge that free blacks were incompetent to manage their own affairs, the institutional success of African-American Methodism over its first century was a potent expression of protest against slavery and racism.

HOST ENVIRONMENTS AND COUNTER-RACISM ON A WORLD METHODIST STAGE, 1881–1931

Hempton's *Methodism* concludes with the post-Reconstruction period in the US. A brutal era in race relations from 1880 to 1930 followed. The hopes for a revolution in terms of race began to be defeated as early as 1870 when southern white terrorists called 'redeemers' violently seized power state by state. Thereafter, the secular environment for black Methodism was the coercive world of white supremacy expressed through disfranchisement, intimidation of successful farmers and teachers, increasingly barbaric lynchings, and the removal of black officeholders. These practices were the most obvious in the former Confederacy, but they also occurred elsewhere. They could not have succeeded apart from compliant northern whites, including Methodists.

On the world stage of the Ecumenical Methodist Conferences held every ten years between 1881 and 1931 African-American Methodists addressed their dire situation. At these forums delegates commemorated their origins, gave statistical evidence of their institutional success, and articulated commonalities shared with white Methodists. They claimed a distinct appropriation of Wesley's heritage while testifying about their ongoing confrontations with racism throughout segregated America.

At each conference African-American representatives presided over sessions, led devotions and Bible study, and preached and lectured on a wide range of topics generic to all Methodists. There were repeated attempts to define Methodist essentials. Former Reconstruction politician, AMEZ bishop and denominational historian J. H. Hood in 1881 testified about how his enjoyment of sanctification made him more useful in the church (EMC 1881: 155). In London in 1901, Zion Methodist Bishop and civil rights activist Alexander Walters wanted 'to indulge in an old-fashioned Methodist shout', as he looked over the throng coming from all over the world to 'the shrine' of John Wesley (EMC 1901: 41). Former slave and CME Bishop L. H. Holsey articulated the distinctive Methodist mandate 'to love souls because they are what they are—made in the image of God'. At the same time Holsey emphasized the social reform side of the tradition, saying that when all the means of outreach 'are employed for a noble purpose—the amelioration of man', the result was 'wonderful and glorious' (EMC 1881: 78–9).

To venerate Wesley, black Methodists traced their lineage to him. Ex-slave and AMEZ Bishop Joseph P. Thompson told the first conference, 'I want to say to these dear brethren that I am one of the grandsons of our father, John Wesley, born in 1832, by the Spirit of God' (ibid. 392). Ten years later Zion Bishop J. H. Jones used a similar family image but drew it on into American Methodism. 'We believe in Methodism pure and simple; we believe in it as John Wesley did; and while we are a daughter of the grand old Methodist Episcopal Church', he declared, 'we think that we are in full line with John Wesley' (EMC 1891: 106). Holsey claimed his denomination's succession: 'I hail from the Southern Methodist Church,—that is, we were organized by that Church; she is our mother, and I love her' (EMC 1881: 315). Another CME preacher added, 'We are Methodists from top to bottom' (EMC 1911: 306).

The affirmation of lineage also involved ensuring that the majority white delegates acknowledged black Methodism. Ohio state politician and AME Bishop B. W. Arnett warned against neglecting the African Methodist contingent from the eighteenth century on, remarking, 'When they were looking for first things yesterday I wondered if there was any left for me.' He took the omission, however, as a challenge, stating 'I must prove to you, if possible, that we have a mother, and it is a very difficult matter sometimes for a mother even to recognize her own children' (EMC 1891: 99). A similar counsel came from AME Bishop Henry B. Parks in 1911 when he explained the separatism of African Methodism in terms of 'the ultimate result of a resistless necessity' (EMC 1911: 25).

Black links to the family tree of the movement came to be familiar in recitations of Protestant or Methodist saints by always adding, as did one AME preacher, someone like Richard Allen to his list of Huss, Luther, and Wesley (ibid.). In his litany Walters started with British Methodists from Wesley on, then moved to eminent white American Methodists after Asbury and finally concluded with Allen, AMEZ founder James Varick, and CME Bishop W. H. Miles (EMC 1901: 43).

Forty years apart Arnett and AMEZ Bishop W. J. Walls made sure everyone knew that 'Betty the African servant' in New York and Aunt Annie Switzer in Maryland were members of the first Methodist societies. The sharp-tongued Arnett put the matter bluntly, 'you see we are connected with the British and American Methodisms. No matter where they find their source, we are there and . . . we are going to stay there. So whatever belongs to you belongs to us.' Bishop Jones sounded a similar note, 'Methodism has given us everything it has given you—all but one thing. We have not our civil rights' (EMC 1891: 99, 106; 1931: 52).

To press their fellow delegates to come to terms with racial problems, African Methodist speakers celebrated Wesley's abolitionism, affirmed themselves as—as AME pastor P. A. Hubbard put it in 1901—'one of the products of American slavery' and attacked 'color prejudice', 'the colour line', 'racialism', and 'caste' (EMC 1881: 230, 293; 1901: 41, 64, 88–9, 106, 234–5; 1911: 531–2; 1931: 40, 53, 423–4). Grounding opposition to racism theologically in the doctrine of creation, Holsey quoted Scripture, 'God made of one blood' (EMC 1881: 315–16). Three decades later CME minister J. A. Bray objected to delegates using the phrase 'inferior race' while in 1921 the physician Dr C. H. Phillips, Jr. of the same church testified to the resiliency of African-American faith 'though lynched and disfranchised, jim-crowed and segregated' (EMC 1911: 723; 1921: 61–2).

To confront the racial assumptions of white Methodists was no simple task. Speakers at the 1911 Conference in Toronto especially exalted Anglo-Saxon cultural superiority (EMC 1911: 59–60, 118, 745). Early on MECS Bishop E. E. Hoss lifted up 'the White Christ' as the saviour of Anglo-Saxons. Later white MEC preacher George Elliott feared foreign immigration to the US which threatened 'the last standing ground of the white man in his Western march'. Southern Methodist H. M. DuBose deemed blacks as 'an alien race, a race from practical barbarism' which 'we in the United States have been able to shape and develop'. These sentiments resounded a decade later in London when a British Wesleyan missionary condemned interracial marriage and advocated 'the science of eugenics' (EMC 1911: 28, 56, 62; 1921: 154–5).

Further efforts to control the dialogue about race came from leaders of the MECS. After instructing his audience in 1881 that his denomination, as the second largest communion present, 'too represents Christianity in earnest', minister J. W. Tucker objected to 'the frequent references on this floor, to the fact that these, my coloured brethren, were not always free men'. Calling such comments 'not germane', 'productive of *no* good', and originating in 'an *unwholesome* senti-ment', Tucker demanded, 'Let them cease now, here, elsewhere, and forever more' (EMC 1881: 579). The theology of the spiritual church, silent and aloof from controversies over race, was still powerful in post-Reconstruction America.

After black ME executive of the Freedmen's Aid Society, M. C. B. Mason reminded the conference that 'quite often the black man accused of crime has no jury at all', tempers flared (EMC 1911: 55, 106–7). Later when the conference secretary H. K. Carroll introduced a resolution condemning 'mob violence' against 'foreigners or any class or classes of any community', MECS Bishop Collins Denny jumped up to insist that the motion refer to 'some features, or acts, that cause mob violence'. Invoking rape hysteria to justify lynching, which a decade before Bishop Walters had factually undercut (EMC 1901: 42–3), Denny appealed for a woman's right 'to an unterrified existence'. Calling the move 'a partisan action', the bishop succeeded in deflecting the thrust of the protest. It was consistent with his earlier defence of Southern Methodism's 'spiritual church' policy as he proudly admitted 'that we do not infringe upon the province of the State, that we are not a political party, but a Church of Jesus Christ, whose fundamental purposes are the conversion of sinners' (EMC 1911: 303–4, 717–19).

Such forms of intimidation reified racial domination but African Methodists did not go silent. To answer Denny, a CME pastor first concurred with the bishop in saying 'every negro Methodist in the Southland condemns mob violence' and 'those things which lead up to it'. Then I. S. Pierson stood his ground and condemned lynching, whose causes, he insisted, were 'not the destroying of the sacredness of the home' in most cases, but simply that 'petty little differences' often led a white mob to go after someone. 'We are sorry to see our men murdered', Pierson exclaimed. 'We are sorry to see them led to the stake and burned. We are sorry to see them put to death in any way. But for God's sake let the Methodist Church stand up for their life until you prove them guilty' (MC 1911: 718–19).

In 1921 CME pastor N. C. Cleaves warned that Christians could not have Christ and racial prejudice, and named segregation a sin. When three African-American speakers, CME Bishop Charles H. Phillips, AME Professor A. S. Jackson, and AME layman Oscar W. Adams seconded his remarks, the president of the British Conference, J. Alfred Sharp rebuked them. They touched, he charged, a 'grave and far-reaching matter' in an 'atmosphere of declamation and denunciation', and in criticizing 'the white man's religion' they were 'slanging' the churches. Halting the discussion, Sharp patronizingly lectured 'his coloured brethren to remember that the rights and liberties they possessed' resulted from the church's 'great message'. Black delegates still refused to be intimidated. Segregated seating in 'modern revival services', AME Bishop L. J. Coppin declared, violated 'the cosmopolitan aspect' of the original Pentecost. In a farewell speech his AME colleague Bishop A. J. Carey applauded people of colour for the fight for freedom and justice and ironically observed that this conference had given 'a great opportunity to the Anglo-Saxon people to-day to go forth re-christianized and rebaptized with power from on high' (EMC 1921: 157–8, 309, 356).

The most systematic formulation of a counter-racist ethic also came in 1911 with Dr R. R. Wright's masterful talk on the church and social morality, prepared, he reassured his audience, 'in the spirit of science and the spirit of a Christian seeking the truth only—the truth that can make us free'. Pleading that the subject should not be lumped together with issues such as ignorance, poverty, and crime, the future AME bishop went to the heart of the matter. 'It is principally in the attitude of whites toward negroes' that a 'negro has no rights that a white man is *bound* to respect', he said, and that 'social' and 'psychological attitude' created 'a dual standard of social morality'. After illustrating these double standards, Wright faced squarely the 'feeble effort' of the churches to suppress the barbarism of lynching—the taking of 'the life of a human being, to riddle him with bullets, burn him at the stake, and sell his bones on the streets as souvenirs of white supremacy' (ibid. 379–81).

Wright next took on spiritual church theology and its private ethic. Very much as Christian abolitionists in the nineteenth century conceded that slaveholders might be virtuous in their private character but would not assume social responsibility to end human bondage, Wright acknowledged that thousands of whites never did personal wrongs to black individuals, were kind and considerate, supportive of black churches and schools, and helpful in need. 'They think they are Christians', the preacher-professor proceeded. 'They deplore conditions, but profess they cannot change them.' Drawing analogies from MECS Bishop James Cannon's tirade against liquor in a preceding speech, Wright exclaimed, 'We cannot hide behind individualism. This is a social age, and we are all responsible for our own acts and co-responsible for society's.' The Ph.D. graduate of the University of Pennsylvania ended his remarks by advocating free speech in place of letting racist demagogues control the dialogue about race, cooperative investigation to uncover facts and use them 'to fight lynching as we did liquor', and pulpit instruction on social morality (ibid. 381–3).

At the final pre-Second World War world meeting in 1931 in Atlanta, Bishop Walls introduced the executive for the Council for Interracial Cooperation by designating MECS minister Will Alexander 'a prophet of brotherhood' whose labour was 'demonstrating the American proposition of two races diverse in color and historical background, but with common hopes living side by side'. In a poignant reminiscence about growing up surrounded by Methodist institutions in the white South, Alexander confessed that he never heard 'any voice of the Church [give] a clear and deliberate intimation that my religion had anything to do with my attitude to people of other races'. His family members were Democrats and Southern Methodists, but it did not 'seem inconsistent to be at the same time a Christian and a member of the Ku Klux Klan'. Alexander cogently framed the legacy of the spiritual church doctrine of antebellum Protestantism. His change of perspective came from the missionary movement's contribution to racial under-standing despite its many biases, from the drawing together of humankind into closer intimacy, and from the new interest, from the universities to Mahatma Gandhi, in the life, teaching, and attitudes of Jesus whose 'revolutionary doctrine' marks 'as deadly sin all contempt based on race' (EMC 1931: 51, 421–2).

AFRICAN-AMERICAN METHODISTS, CIVIL RIGHTS, AND SOUTH AFRICAN APARTHEID

Meeting every five years after 1947 and gradually moving outside the orbit of Europe and the US the World Methodist Conferences retained many of the constants from the earlier gatherings. As the number of delegates increased the format changed to working groups and seminars. There was increased need for a theology of liberation and an anti-racist ethic to confront and overcome Jim Crow in the US and apartheid in South Africa. With no racial barriers in accommodation, the sessions at Lake Junaluska, NC in 1956 highlighted Mexican seminary Professor G. Baez-Carmago's brilliant lecture on Christianity and Race Relations. Like Dr Wright in 1911 he combined social science and theological argument (WMC 1956: 168–80). Ten years later AMEZ Professor John Satterwhite drew on the work of George Kelsey, a black Baptist, former teacher of Martin Luther King, Jr., and Drew Theological School ethicist. Kelsey took a different tack by characterizing racism as a faith, a false but powerful expression of ultimate value that had deep ideological roots in Europe and America (WMC 1966: 134–42).

Within the 1947, 1951, and 1956 delegations there were two leaders who had served on Harry Truman's ground-breaking President's Committee on Civil Rights beginning in 1946—CME representative Channing Tobias and AME attorney Sadie Alexander (EMC 1947: pp. xxxix, 236–40; 1951: 8; WMC 1956: 33). By 1961 in Oslo the new phases of civil rights activism prompted white MC Bishop James K. Matthews to explain its new terminology—sit-ins, kneel-ins, freedom rides. Then AME Dr Archibald Carey showed that at local levels black Methodists were fully engaged in these struggles. Oliver Brown from Topeka, Kansas was a black minister whose lawsuit for school desegregation in 1954 contained his name—*Brown* v. *Board of Education*. Rosa Parks, famous in the Montgomery bus boycott, belonged to St Paul's AME Church there. Co-founder of the Congress for Racial Equality, James L. Farmer was an African-American Methodist minister, as was the father of Roy Wilkins of the National Association for the Advancement of Colored People. Among others non-violent Methodist activist James Lawson and African-American MC minister Joseph Lowery would give their social action leadership later. To empathize how long the struggle had taken, Carey recounted Bishop Walls's refusal for seven hours in 1934 to leave the Union Station restaurant in Washington, D.C. until he was served (WMC 1961: 121–3, 177–83).

At the Honolulu international gathering in 1981 AME Professor James Cone joined Argentine Methodist José Míguez Bonino in extending black liberation theology to third-world settings. It was, however, the South African freedom struggle that preoccupied global Methodist concerns. The black activist preacher from there, Abel Hendricks, received the World Methodist Peace Award. His moving testimony described the struggle over how to pray for the supporters of apartheid—who crucified Christ on the cross again and again. The delegates formally condemned South Africa's leadership and racism worldwide including the backlash occurring in the US (WMC 1981: 34–9, 75–6, 101–4, 234).

Even though the political transfer in South Africa was still eight years ahead, World Methodists meeting in Nairobi in 1986 with more than 250 African-American representatives present pronounced apartheid dead. The conference was a continuous celebration of faith and hope—from Bible studies to Sir Alan Walker's advocacy of non-violent resistance to racial oppression and war, from UMC Bishop Leontine Kelly's vibrant preaching 'Called to Make a Difference' to AMEZ leader Cecil Bishop testifying that 'the same God who moved for us is moving around the world'. As guest preacher Archbishop Desmond Tutu owned that Methodists christened him and that he once belonged to the AME Church in South Africa. The conference included, he pointed out, seven delegates who had recently been in prison for opposing apartheid (WMC 1986: 66–7, 121, 128–33, 160–9).

The white activist Peter Storey preached, as Will Alexander had done in 1931, about his need for 'two testimonies', a need he insisted shared by every white South African to see anew 'out of eyes blinded by 300 years of privilege'. Storey praised the Jesus who breaks down walls and summarized what he himself was able to do while chaplain for the inmates on Robben Island. They included Nelson Mandela, also a product of Methodism. The future bishop shouted, 'Celebrate with me: *That Apartheid is doomed*', and then appealed to President Botha for no more sacrifice of blood on its altar (WMC 1986: 173–7).

Perhaps moved by Storey's witness, the host for the conference Kenyan Bishop Lawi Imathiu in his closing address told a story about his wife having a blood transfusion. When white friends volunteered to donate, he thought, 'But I was not sure of white blood in a black person's body, how it will work.' He began to wonder if their children yet to be born would have a different colour. Race-based fear, he recognized, had crept into his own consciousness. 'It is not only the white that is prejudiced of color,' declared the future recipient of the World Methodist Peace Award, 'but also the black. . . . It is both sides. So when we are accusing each other, we must know it is our problem, not their problem' (WMC 1986: 216).

Global black Methodism's grand climax at Nairobi came two centuries after Richard Allen organized his first coloured class in Philadelphia. The peoples who survived slavery, lynching, segregation, colonialism, and apartheid had come together in a truly international black Methodist movement. They would have understood the words of AME theologian and Bishop Benjamin Tanner back in 1901 that 'we have seen people rejoice in truths crushed to earth, and we have seen these truths rise without any human personality behind them—only God' (EMC 1901: 180–1).

When in Seoul in 2006 former prisoner Bishop Mvume Dandala told stories from South Africa's Truth and Reconciliation Commission, delegates recognized how his narratives coincided with their conference theme—God was in Christ reconciling. Later CME Professor Evelyn Parker gave an account of a black welfare mother who lost her son in a Klan killing. Two arrests and convictions led to one execution. Then a civil suit against the Klan succeeded. The survivor got a life sentence and Beulah Mae Donald's forgiveness. Simply she said, 'From Day One, I turned the situation over to God' (WMC 2006: 113–19, 142). Her testimony, combining accountability and reconciliation, came out of powerful reservoirs in African-American Christianity from which Methodism had drawn and to which it contributed.

SUGGESTED READING

Earlier denominational histories remain useful alongside more recent work by David Bradley, Sr. and W. J. Walls for the AMEZ story, George Singleton and Howard D. Gregg for AME history, and Othal H. Lakey for the CME Church. Grant Shockley, *Heritage and Hope* (1991), details the African-American presence in the UMC as does J. Gordon Melton, *A Will to Choose* (2007). Lewis Baldwin (1983) rescued the African Union Church's history from invisibility. Among recent biographies Stephen W. Angell's book on Bishop Henry M. Turner (1992) models critical scholarship. James T. Campbell, *Songs of Zion* (1996), treats the AME Church in the US and South Africa with sharp insight. Lawrence Little, *Disciples of Liberty* (2000), and Clarence Walker, *A Rock in a Weary Land* (1982), are superb studies of the AMEC in two different eras. Raymond R. Somerville, Jr. dispels the stereotype of the CME Church as apolitical in *An Ex-Colored Church* (2004).

REFERENCES

CONSER, WALTER H. JR., and TWISS, SUMNER B. (eds.) (1997). *Religious Diversity and American Religious History*. Athens: University of Georgia Press.

Ecumenical Methodist Conference (EMC 1881). *Proceedings of the Ecumenical Methodist Conference.... London September, 1881*. London: Wesleyan Conference Office.

—— (1891). *Proceedings... Washington, October, 1891*. New York: Hunt & Eaton.

—— (1901). *Proceedings... London September, 1901*. New York: Eaton & Mains.

—— (1911). *Proceedings... Toronto October 4–17, 1911*. Cincinnati: Jennings & Graham.

—— (1921). *Proceedings... London, September 6–16, 1921*. New York: Methodist Book Concern.

—— (1931). *Proceedings... Atlanta, October 16–25, 1931*. New York: Methodist Book Concern.

—— (1947). *Proceedings... Springfield, Massachusetts, September 24–October 2, 1947*. Nashville: Methodist Publishing House.

—— (1951). *Proceedings... Oxford 28th August–7th September 1951*. London: Epworth.

FONER, PHILIP S., and WALKER, GEORGE E. (eds.) (1979, 1980). *Proceedings of the Black State Conventions*. 2 vols. Philadelphia: Temple University Press.

FREY, SYLVIA R., and WOOD, BETTY (1998). *Come Shouting to Zion: African-American Protestantism in the American South and British Caribbean to 1830*. Chapel Hill: University of North Carolina Press.

FULOP, TIMOTHY E., and RABOTEAU, ALBERT J. (eds.) (1997). *African-American Religion: Interpretive Essays in History and Culture*. New York: Routledge.

HACKETT, DAVID (ed.) (2003). *Religion and American Culture: A Reader*. 2nd edn. New York: Routledge.

HEMPTON, DAVID (2005). *Methodism: Empire of the Spirit*. New Haven: Yale University Press.

HINKS, PETER P. (1997). *To Awaken My Afflicted Brethren: David Walker and the Problem of Antebellum Slave Resistance*. University Park: Pennsylvania State University Press.

LEDBETTER, ANNA, and WYATT, ROMA (eds.) (2003). *World Methodist Council Handbook of Information*. Lake Junaluska, N.C.: World Methodist Council.

PAYNE, WARDELL J. (ed.) (1991). *Directory of African American Religious Bodies: A Compendium by the Howard University School of Divinity*. Washington: Howard University Press.

RIPLEY, C. PETER (ed.) and associates (1985–92). *The Black Abolitionist Papers*. 5 vols. Chapel Hill: University of North Carolina Press.

World Methodist Conference (WMC, 1956). *Proceedings of the Ninth World Methodist Conference, Lake Junaluska, North Carolina, August 27–September 12, 1956*. Nashville: Methodist Publishing House.

—— (1961). *Proceedings… Oslo, Norway, 17th-25th August 1961*. London: Epworth.

—— (1966). *Proceedings… (London)*. London: Epworth.

—— (1981). *Proceedings… Honolulu, Hawaii, July 21–28, 1981*. Asheville, N.C.: Biltmore.

—— (1986). *Proceedings… Nairobi, Kenya, July 23–29, 1986*. Waynesville: Mountaineer Graphics.

—— (2006). *Proceedings… Seoul, Korea, 2006*. Waynesville: Cornerstone Printing and Design.

CHAPTER 8

METHODISM IN LATIN AMERICA

PABLO R. ANDIÑACH

INTRODUCTION

THE arrival of Methodism to Latin America coincides with the arrival of other Protestant churches. Originally, this was due more to the natural movement of population as the result of commerce and wars than to an explicit missionary outreach. The first Protestants of which we have news in Latin America—including some Methodists—arrived in 1806 when England tried to take the city of Buenos Aires, which at the time was the capital of the River Plate viceroyalty. The British military forces occupied the city for only a few months before being expelled by the local forces; by this time, however, some English officers had married the daughters of Argentine families and decided to stay in the country. It is from this group that thirty years later the first Methodist Church was organized in Latin America. In 1836 Revd Fountain E. Pitts arrived from the USA with the intention of organizing such a Church, bringing with him, among other documents, a letter of recommendation signed by the president of the United States of America. When he reached Buenos Aires the local government authorized him to preach and develop his pastoral charge, but only among people who spoke English. This restriction expressed on the one hand the Catholic fear of Protestant churches, and on the other the feeling that Protestants were foreigners and should be treated as such. His report to the annual conference in Cincinnati that year moved them to send two more missionaries to strengthen the work. Since 1836 until the present much has changed in Latin American Methodism but much has been maintained. This chapter will seek to show in an abbreviated form that development and its significance for our time, pointing out what still remains to be written on the history of Methodism in Latin America from the many national histories that have developed and certain monographic articles. I would like this chapter to be a contribution towards what others can do in this area.

CHARACTERISTICS OF METHODISM
IN LATIN AMERICA

There are three elements that characterize Methodism in Latin America. In the first place Methodist growth in the continent goes hand in hand with the arrival of other churches such as Presbyterian and Baptist. We point to these affinities because they place Latin American Methodism together with the 'missionary' churches, which differentiate from the 'transplant' churches because of their vocation from the very beginning to influence and take root in the national culture. The difference between missionary and transplant churches refers to the fact that the former address the local population using their language and seek to adopt their cultural features, while the latter respond to the foreign communities that imported from Europe both language and church, seeking to preserve their particular characteristics, and establishing a certain distance from the national population. Lalive D'Epinay (1968) has described these various forms. Methodism—except for a few exceptions—did not arrive following migration currents seeking to attend to the religious needs, but as a new ecclesial force that expected to change the religious and ethical foundations of national society. The current vacuum in the history of Methodism in Latin America can be partly filled by tracing the history of Protestantism in general in the continent. The main theological differences between Presbyterians and Baptists do not hinder the presence of common conceptual elements that allow unification criteria and achieve a common figure in various aspects. Hostility against Roman Catholicism, for example, forged many common elements of 'defence' (liturgy, hymnology, temple architecture, etc.) which in one way unified theologies and minimized differences.

In the second place it is necessary to take into account that Latin America was not considered by European Protestantism as mission territory in the classical understanding. This was clearly evident in the World Missionary Conference in Edinburgh 1910, which not only did not consider Latin America as part of its agenda, but also denied recognition to the missionaries who came from that part of the world. For Europeans Latin America was considered Christian land and Roman

Catholic. This attitude of the European churches was not shared by the delegation from the United States of America, who six years later organized in Panama what came to be known as the First Missionary Conference with continental reach for Latin America. All were invited to attend, but the European delegation was small, mainly because their countries were suffering the effects of the First World War. They did, however, express their concern about legitimizing mission in the region. The fact that most of the representatives were Methodists, Presbyterians, and Disciples of Christ provided a clear missionary nuance to this meeting. At the same time what might be understood as a secondary piece of information turned into a sign of something much deeper in the missionary context for the Protestants in general and the Methodists in particular. The conference had to be held in the recently created Canal Zone due to the hostility of the Roman Catholic bishop of the area who refused to allow a Protestant conference to be held in any part of his jurisdiction.

At the beginning of the nineteenth century Roman Catholics made up the vast majority of the population. Even near the end of the century there were only small Protestant communities, and they continually had to convince their mother churches of the justification for the missionary task. This placed the Methodists in the particularly difficult situation of having to work in a religiously and culturally hostile society, while at the same time convincing their Methodist brothers in the north that their efforts were legitimate and had some future.

Thirdly, it is important to note that Methodism arrived in Latin America in the heat of the introduction of political and economic liberalism and the social institutions that represent these ideals. In the second half of the nineteenth century, Latin America saw the triumph of economic liberalism and societies open in different degrees according to the new cultural winds. The old oligarchies related to the provincial economies were transformed by the new owners of the land who sought to offer their agricultural products for sale in Europe and begin to be influenced by and attracted to the civil liberties, free thinking, and the possibilities of enjoying the benefits that industry provided in exchange for raw materials. This economic opening collides with the religious world of a conservative Catholic reality crystallized in 1870 with the First Vatican Council, which, if it did not cause a rupture between church and state in many countries, at least led to conflict between the Roman Catholic church and many liberal leaders, who when they reach power favoured a more open-minded attitude towards other religious traditions who had established themselves in the region. This relationship between social, political, and economic liberalism influenced Methodism for good and for bad. Anyway, the transition in Latin America from a traditional society to a more modern one, was not linear or without contradictions, but for the Methodist Church—as with other Protestant churches—these were elements that accelerated the process (Míguez Bonino 1983: 21 *passim*).

The Development of
Methodist Mission Work

It is not easy to summarize in a few pages the richness of such a history, so we focus on central pieces of information that characterize the churches in the different countries, sometimes grouping them together when their history allows for it. In this summary I am grateful for the help provided by Bishop Aldo Etchegoyen and his work. It is inevitable to fall into the dryness of names and dates, finding consolation in the fact that without these it is impossible to organize a posteriori a more analytical history. Only in passing will we mention the creation of schools and hospitals and other works of service that have been and continue to be important to the Methodist mission. Other ecumenical institutions were very close to the Methodist Church in all its development and were in some cases pillars on which this mission was supported. Among these are the Bible Society, the YMCA, and many university student movements. Another case, though different, is the attachment of many Methodist ministers and leaders who were Masons, but its history exceeds the limits of this chapter.

Avoiding these subjects—practically in their totality—I am aware that I leave out a good part of what was the backbone of the mission and hope readers will be able to infer from the basic information provided the larger dimension this still has today. I leave matters of evaluation and integration to the end of this study.

Argentina and Uruguay

We have already referred to Fountain Pitt's recommendation to begin a missionary outreach in Argentina. As a result of his efforts, towards the end of 1836 John Dempster reached these shores as a missionary, receiving governmental authorization limiting him to 'working only with foreigners and . . . his pastoral duties were to be carried out in English'. A board of three local Methodists, chaired by lay preacher Guillermo Junior, examined Dempster on doctrine before he was accepted. Under Dempster's leadership the mission strengthened and grew; the first Methodist Sunday School in Latin America began in 1837 and the first infant baptism was that of Guillermo Juan Dempster Junior, celebrated 24 September 1837. William H. Norris was Dempster's successor and had the honour of dedicating the first Methodist church in South America, 4 January 1843.

Dempster visited Montevideo (capital of Uruguay) in 1838 and gathered Methodist lay leaders who had been around since 1836. They were mainly people dedicated to commerce and employees of British firms. As a result of this visit the call for a missionary was made, and was answered with the arrival of William

Norris in 1839. His boat trip took seventy-seven days and he found Montevideo under siege by Argentine military troops. His work drew together a small group who purchased a house in the neighbourhood, and on Sunday afternoons he would preach on the boats anchored in port. The political situation was very fragile and internal conflicts put the lives of the missionaries at risk to such an extent that the Missionary Society called them to return to the USA in 1841. As a result the work in Uruguay was suspended, but not in Buenos Aires, as Dempster decided to stay on. One of Dempster's most outstanding successors was Dr William Goodfellow who arrived in 1856 and was in charge of the mission until 1869.

Missionary work continued in Argentina and in 1860 Andrew Milne, an agent for the American Bible Society, invited John F. Thompson in Buenos Aires to visit Montevideo to reactivate the mission. Thompson's personality and ability summoned large groups. His preaching was aimed at breaking the absolutism established by the Roman Catholic Church and it attracted a generation of young intellectuals. In 1878 Milne was replaced by Thomas Woods who dedicated his efforts towards organizing the church. In this year the first Methodist Church in Montevideo was established, that today is the Central Methodist Church located in the centre of the city. Wood's vision was that to best implement mission there was a need for local ministers. That is why he took the initiative to form, together with the Waldensian Church, the first institute for the training of ministers. Two years later this institute was transferred to Buenos Aires and continued its work under the name of the Evangelical Faculty of Theology. With successive name changes but with a clear institutional continuity that small school founded by Wood has now become the University Institute ISEDET (Instituto Superior Evangélico De Estudios Teológicos), consolidated as the oldest theological training institution in Latin America. In 1910 Argentina and Uruguay joined to form the Annual Conference of East South America.

Brazil

In 1836, Justin Spaulding arrived in Rio de Janeiro, and Daniel P. Kidder, with his wife, arrived a year later. Shortly after their arrival she died, aged 22, possibly a victim of smallpox. Kidder returned to the USA taking their only child, and the Methodist work in Brazil came to a halt for about twenty years. Later, in 1867, Junios E. Newman picked up the mission and tried to begin an independent Protestant church bringing together Methodists, Baptists, and Presbyterians. His efforts failed when the other denominations opened their own churches. He later dedicated his efforts to consolidating the Methodist mission and in 1876 the MECS sent its first missionary, J. J. Ranson, a member of the Tennessee Conference, who is recognized as the organizer of the church in Brazil. He became fluent in Portuguese and remained in the country until 1886.

The first bishop to visit the mission was John C. Granbery in 1886. In September he organized the Mission Annual Conference with three ordained missionary preachers,

J. L. Kennedy, J. W. Tarboux, and H. C. Tucker. There were seven congregations, six local preachers, 211 members, forty-two probationers, six Sunday schools, and a girl's school with seventy students. It is said it was the smallest annual conference ever organized in the history of Methodism. Fifty years had elapsed since the visit of Fountain E. Pitts and only now with new missionaries did the mission begin preaching in Portuguese—the language of the country—and English. The mission established by the MEC in the city of Rio Grande do Sul joined the mission of the MECS in 1900.

Paraguay

Methodist presence in Paraguay goes back to 1879, and until 1916 it was the first Protestant Church with several congregations and two schools. During the Panama Missionary Conference of 1916 it was decided that the Methodist mission would be transferred, for economic and strategic reasons, to the Church of the Disciples of Christ. This mission prospered and is currently a consolidated church. But in 1988 due to the initiative of missionaries from Brazil, a Methodist mission was begun and soon extended throughout the country, constituting of twenty congregations in the five departments of the country. What is particular to this church is that it preaches in four very diverse languages: Guarani and Toba (two of the country's aboriginal languages); Korean, due to the immigrant communities; and Spanish, introduced by the *conquistadores*.

Peru

The Pacific coast of South America received its first missionary in 1859 when the first Methodist, James Swaney, arrived. He preached first in English to the foreign residents living in Lima and the port city of El Callao. The following year he organized a congregation and thus began the Methodist mission in Peru. The legendary William Taylor arrived in 1877, but his ministry was interrupted by lack of funds and disruptions caused by the Pacific war between Peru, Bolivia, and Chile. Soon afterwards Francisco Penzotti, from Argentina, visited Peru; he was a traveller for the American Bible Society, and took up the evangelization task, which reached its peak in July 1888 with the first formal service. A short time later, in January 1889, Penzotti founded the first MEC in El Callao, the first Protestant congregation in the country. These were hard times, and Penzotti was imprisoned for evangelizing. In 1890 the first quarterly conference of the Methodist Church in El Callao was held, chaired by Charles W. Drees. In 1891, Thomas Wood arrived from Montevideo as a missionary. As he had done there, he began an important educational enterprise. A year later the First Methodist Church in Lima was founded, and in following years the pastoral and educational task in the whole country began to grow.

Mexico

In Mexico the missionary efforts of the Methodists from both the north and the south of the United States converge. This entailed that for over fifty years there were two representatives of Methodism acting in independent ways. Happily, towards 1930 steps were taken to unify the work and so provide testimony to all Methodists that the importance of mission should overcome internal differences.

The mission was initiated by the MEC in the USA, who sponsored the visit of Bishop Gilbert Haven in 1872. He was passenger on the first rail journey from Veracruz to Mexico City. He returned to the USA in 1873, pointing out in his report that the opportunity for work was exciting. As a result William Butler, who had planted the MEC mission in India, arrived in Mexico City in February 1873 as a missionary, and purchased the current building in Gante Street. The building had belonged to the Franciscans and it is estimated that its construction was begun in the 1500s. To begin his task Butler contacted a number of people who were Protestants, among whom were some former Roman Catholic priests. With them he began the mission of the Methodist Church, which soon extended to the cities of Puebla, Pachuca, Orizaba, Querétaro, Guanajuato, and Oaxaca. One of the greatest problems faced was the explicit rejection and hostility of the Roman Catholic Church, which led to assaults on ministers and lay people, and in some cases the loss of human lives.

The MECS also sent Bishop John C. Keener, and he too reached Mexico City in 1873. At the same time on the northern frontier of the country Alexander H. Southerland and William M. Patterson began evangelization into the central areas. The work extended and consolidated in the cities of Toluca, el Oro, Guadalajara, San Luis Potosí, Monterrey, Saltillo, Nuevo Laredo, Torreon, Chihuahua, Juarez, and Durango. In 1885 the first annual conference of the MEC was held in Mexico City with Bishop William Harris presiding. The same year the annual conference of the MECS, presided over by Bishop Holand N. McTyeire, also met.

It was only in 1923 that the two branches of Methodism began seriously to consider becoming one ecclesial body, and in 1925 Bishop George A. Miller of the MEC developed a scheme to unite them. In this project Bishop William B. Beauchamp of the MECS played an active role. Both approved the plan in principle, and in 1930 the process was confirmed and formal agreements were reached to enable reunification. The *Discipline* reads: 'By the Grace of God in the city of Mexico on 16 September 1930 in the Church of the Holy Trinity, the first General Conference of the Methodist Church of Mexico meets, and legislates and regulates its first Discipline, formulates work plans, elects and consecrates its first Bishop, Rev. Juan Nicanor Pascoe.' The Methodist Church of Mexico was born, the first autonomous church in relation to its mother church in the USA. It is significant that the autonomy meant the full unity of the two branches into which Methodism in the USA was divided.

Chile

It was also due to William Taylor, a man of missionary spirit who had developed his ministry in Australia, Africa, and India, that missionary work began in Chile. Due to financial difficulties in the Board of Missions he decided to begin work by organizing schools that Methodist traders and businessmen of Chile and Peru were willing to finance to educate their children. The teachers were also preachers and in 1877 seventeen missionaries had begun work. The mission faced many difficulties, though schools were founded in Tacna, Iquique, Antofagasta, Copiapó, Coquimbo, Santiago, and Concepción that functioned also as bases for evangelization and leadership training. Concepción and Coquimbo were, however, the only two of the fourteen stations in which the work went on continuously. In 1888, Goddsel F. Arms and his wife, Ida Taggard, reached Chile. The work was consolidated and evangelization took place in the south of the country. In 1897 the first annual conference took place.

Costa Rica and Panama

The first Methodist presence dates back to 1881 with the visit of the tireless William Taylor. Beginning in this year, and each year thereafter, the Methodist colporteur Francisco Penzotti, who worked for the American Bible Society, visited the region. In 1920 the Missionary Conference, which included Costa Rica and Panama, was created. The centre for the work was located in Alajuela, and in 1921 a missionary by the name of Louis Fiske organized a day school in the city of San José, the capital of the country. Between 1922 and 1927 a number of important evangelization efforts were carried out and the mission expanded. The first missionaries to arrive in Panama were John Elkins and his wife, sent by the Foreign Missionary Board of the MEC in New York. Other documents mention that the first missionary to arrive was D. Thomas Wood. Wood arrived in 1804 as a missionary employed by the United States government to serve personnel constructing the Panama Canal. Once there he extended his ministry to the entire Panama isthmus. Wood thought El Malecón would be the ideal spot to build a church and a school, and asked the Mission Board to carry out a feasibility study. As a result, the Board sent Elkins to Panama, where he received approval for the building of the church. During this time Clara Peña, from Colombia, a member of the Presbyterian Church, accepted the post of teacher. As in many other places in Latin America, the same building was used for worship, Sunday School, and the various service programmes that took place. During the next few years the Methodist Church extended and consolidated its pastoral and teaching mission.

Cuba

In 1873, the General Conference of the MECS appointed Carlos A. Fulwood as minister of Stone Church in Key West, Florida. Together with the colporteur Francisco Diaz he began his evangelization mission among the Cuban people who already lived in the area. In November 1873 José E. A. Vanduzer was named for the Cuban mission in Key West, but he lived only two years before succumbing to yellow fever in 1875.

In 1883 the preachers in the Florida Annual Conference gathered enough funds to enable Enrique Benito Someillán and Aurelio Silveira to go to Havana and set up a chapel in a borrowed hall and establish a small Methodist community. In 1889 the General Mission Board sent J. J. Ramson and in 1890 Clemente Moya, who developed an important teaching ministry. In 1898 newly elected Bishop Warren A. Candler of the MECS, W. R. Lambuth, presiding elder of the Tampa District of the Florida Conference, visited various Cuban cities, including La Havana, Cien Fuegos, Sagua la Grande, Caibarién, Santa Clara, Manzanillo, Santiago de Cuba, Cárdenas, and Matanzas. The Bishop also invited David W. Carter, a missionary in Mexico and editor of 'El Evangelista Mexicano', to examine the possibilities of mission on the island. He reported in 1899: 'If we had dedicated men who spoke Spanish, we could, without delay begin congregations in all towns.' As a response to this challenge the Florida Annual Conference, presided over by Bishop Candler, decided to create the Cayo Hueso Missionary District on the island of Cuba and proceeded to name ministers for La Habana, Matanzas, Cárdenas and Cibarién, Cienfuegos, Santiago de Cuba, and Manzanillo. Baker was named as Secretary for Mission of Cuba.

Puerto Rico

In 1899 two representatives of the Missionary Society visited the island to explore the possibilities for beginning missionary work. The visitors were Bishop William Xavier Ninde and Leonard. They presented a report that resulted in the arrival of Charles W. Drees in Puerto Rico the following year, as missionary of the MEC. Drees had previously worked in Argentina and in four years he established the church in San Juan, Guayama, Arecibo, Vieques, Ponce, and other places. He also achieved the appointment of various missionaries such as John Volver, T. M. Harwood, Samuel Culpeper, Manuel Andújar, Aquiles H. Lambert, and Meter van Fleet. In 1903 he organized the publishing of El Defensor Cristiano. His concern for the preparation of local leaders led to the training and appointment of three Puerto Rican ministers: Juan Vázquez, Genaro Cotto, and Enrique Cuervos.

In 1905 Drees was replaced by Benjamin S. Haywood, who served nine years as Superintendent of the Church. During his term there were about thirty-two congregations, seven missionaries, twenty-five Puerto Rican ministers, ten new buildings, two orphanages, and over twenty-five rural chapels. In 1913 it constituted itself as a missionary conference of the MEC. In 1941 it became a provisional annual conference and in 1968 it was recognized as an annual conference of the United Methodist Church (UMC). It became an affiliated autonomous church in 1992 and in 1993 it was constituted as the Methodist Church of Puerto Rico.

Bolivia

In 1906 Francis Marion Harrington and his wife reached La Paz, and their arrival coincided with the approval by Parliament of religious freedom in Bolivia. Soon after this Harrington proposed to the government the creation of a Methodist education institute. As a result the American Institute of La Paz began and developed its ministry among the higher classes of society. Harrington died of tuberculosis two years later. In 1912 the Methodist missionaries John E. Washburn and his wife founded the American Institute of Cochabamba. The educational and pastoral task in Bolivia developed both among the white population and the aboriginal people of the Altiplano. At the end of the twentieth century it is still a church of aboriginal majority.

Dominican Republic

During the 1920s the Methodists, Presbyterians, and United Brethren united their efforts and begin missionary work on the island. As a result in 1922 the Evangelical Church of the Dominican Republic was born. In 1932 the Wesleyan Methodists, who already worked in the Dominican Republic, joined the effort and in 1960 the Moravian Church, that had been present on the island since the beginning of the century, joined. All these churches together exercised mission in four areas: religion, health, social action, and education. The Evangelical Church pioneered work in literacy programmes for adults, church schools, recreation, and human development. Over the last few years it has been modifying its organization to constitute a Methodist Church in the country.

Guatemala

The result of the missionary work of an independent Methodist church of the USA, the church was recognized by the government in 1938. This church developed a mission bringing together educational and congregational activities. Over time it developed ties with the aboriginal population, particularly the Quiché. Towards

1980 the congregations had a clear aboriginal identity and were constituted under the name of Primitive National Evangelical Methodist Church of Guatemala, adopting a presidential structure of government.

Ecuador

The beginnings of the church go back to the early years of the twentieth century with the creation of schools. Years later (1946) the Andean Indigenous Mission was created, related to the Methodist Church of the USA, and in 1964 was integrated into the United Evangelical Church together with Presbyterians, Disciples of Christ, and United Brethren. In 1988 the General Assembly began a process to adopt a Methodist identity which ended in 2002, when it was constituted as the United Evangelical Methodist Church of Ecuador.

Colombia

In 1981 Bishops Armando Rodriguez of Cuba and Joel Mora of the Episcopal Conference of Northern Mexico joined in Colombia with Gustavo Tibasosa Quiroga to begin the work of the Methodist Church. This initiative came from the Latin American Council of Evangelical Methodist Churches (CIEMAL in its Spanish initials) but faced the obstacles of internal conflicts which led to a time of stagnation until 1987 when contacts were resumed by Luis Castiblanco. In 1995 a leadership training course led by Bishop Isaías Gutierrez of Chile took place and focused the mission in areas of social action and health. The work extended to the whole country with the support of the General Board of Global Ministries of the UMC. In its organization it adopted the episcopal form of government, and Bishop Juan Alberto Cardona was the first elected bishop.

Emerging Churches

Towards the end of the twentieth century and as the result of a combination of local initiatives and the efforts of CIEMAL, work began in four countries where there were no Methodist churches. These were called 'emerging churches', a name that will die away as they consolidate into communities.

Nicaragua and Venezuela

Due to the efforts of CIEMAL with the support of the General Board of Global Ministries and the Council of Bishops of the UMC, in Managua—capital of Nicaragua—the First Episcopal Meeting for peace was held in 1989.

The Meeting led to important contacts in the country and in 1991 Professor Rubén Pack, an Argentine Methodist living in Managua, was called to lead this work. The efforts were consolidated in Managua with growth of congregations and an effective social-educational work. A document prepared by the Nicaraguan leadership says, 'from the very beginning our walk has been accompanied and supported—in the first place by CIEMAL, who formally began work in Nicaragua, and by the Board of Global Ministries and the Women's Division of the USA'.

Methodist presence in Venezuela dates to the beginning of the 1990s when Bishop Paulo Lockman of Brazil was contacted by Francisco Mendoza, who led a group of believers. An official visit by the CIEMAL's bishop Clory Trindade de Oliveira and general secretary Prof. Mercio Meneguetti followed in October 1991.

After this Bishop Isaías Gutierrez was entrusted with the pastoral oversight of the beginnings of the Methodist Christian Community that had the recognition of CIEMAL as an emerging church. It worked mainly in the poorest of neighbourhoods on the outskirts of Maracaibo, in San Carlos island, and in Carolita and Barinas in the interior of the country.

El Salvador and Honduras

In El Salvador work began in the city of Ahuachapan, a town near the Guatemala border. Juan F Mayorga contacted the General Board of Global Ministries and received the support of CIEMAL. In 1994 pastoral work began and the following year a training workshop took place in Cuba where two leaders of this new church participated. The work later reached the capital of the country.

In 1996, owing to the initiative of the General Board of Global Ministries of the UMC, preparations for work to establish the Methodist Church of Honduras began. Bishop Armando Rodriguez and his wife, Alida E. Rodriguez, were commissioned as missionaries. In a report they presented in March 1999 they said 'the development of religious work continues to affirm and develop adequately. Colonia Loas Alps is where there has been most growth.' The Methodist Church of Puerto Rico has helped by contributing pastoral and financial support. CIEMAL was present with the visits of its president Bishop Isaías Gutierrez and of the general secretaries.

EVALUATION AND PROJECTION

Autonomy and CIEMAL

A key date in the history of Latin American Methodism was the year 1969. In this and the following year two important, related events took place, with a third following in 1971. The first was the recognition of the autonomy of the Methodist churches in Latin America in relation to the UMC; the second was the creation of CIEMAL. These two events went hand in hand and should be understood as the culmination of a long process, the convergence of different lines of action in which theological, political, and missionary issues were intertwined. The third event was the agreement of Latin American Methodists to develop a political theology that provided answers to the needs and demands of the continent. This will be expressed in different countries where the churches adhere to the theology of liberation, even contributing some of their best exponents (cf. Míguez Bonino 1975: Arias 1973). Hand in hand with that awareness was the participation of Latin American Methodists in the wider ecumenical movement, to which they offered a committed leadership. Since 1960 there has been a significant Latin American Methodist participation in the ecumenical movement. Emilio Castro, a minister from Uruguay, became general secretary of the World Council of Churches (1985–92), and Argentine Bishop Federico Pagura, together with two other bishops, was co-founder and first president of the Latin American Council of Churches (1978–95). I will attempt a summary.

With the exception of the churches in Mexico and Brazil that were autonomous from 1930, the other Methodist churches in Latin America were declared autonomous in 1969. This began as a process that was called for by the Latin Americans due to their growing maturity and the endeavour to strengthen the culture in each country. It was also driven by the need of these churches to gain some distance from all that proceeded from the USA, which at the time suffered loss of prestige due to the Vietnam War, the evidence of painful internal situations made manifest by the struggles led by Martin Luther King, and the impact of the Cuban Revolution (1959) on the ideology of the poor countries of Latin America. At the same time, a form of Methodism linked to the USA could not be sustained given that bishops would be designated from that country and that local pastoral leadership would continue to depend on missionaries. In this context Latin American Methodists sought a more flexible relation with the mother church and the UMC made a unilateral decision declaring the Latin American churches to be autonomous. Even though it was a hasty decision and it was probable that not all Latin American Methodism had sufficient human or theological resources to carry out the totality of ecclesial responsibilities, in actual fact autonomy was a catalytic that enabled the identification of Methodists with the struggles and hopes of each country and of the continent. As a result they began to walk in the direction of liturgical, theological, and pastoral forms much more in accordance with the realities of the continent. This was strongly supported with the creation on CIEMAL, the Council that grouped together Methodist churches and provided continental cohesion through common projects and its Council of Bishops. On the other hand it is interesting to note that after nearly four decades of the practically forced autonomy, both sides (Latin American Methodism through CIEMAL and the UMC) have engaged in a round of dialogue with the intention of evaluating and revising the concept of autonomy and the search to re-establish an ecclesial relationship that goes beyond the financial contributions that the church in the north may make to the churches in the south. Elaine Robinson (2007) has written one of the few studies that analyse the consequences of Methodist autonomy in the region. Latin American Methodism of the twenty-first century has first-rate theologians, with a long experience in missionary matters, who have been involved in the defence of human rights, social struggles, and evangelization, and can make an important contribution to the dynamics of the life of the UMC in particular and Methodism in general. In these rounds of dialogue, one of the central issues to evaluate is the way Methodist connectionalism relates to the concept of an autonomous church. Another issue is the meaning of being Methodist and belonging to this church which is part of the 'church universal' when the churches in Latin America are defined through their national identity (i.e. Peru, Uruguay, etc.) and declare autonomy from the rest of the body. In Latin American churches there is a feeling that though autonomy did have its valuable fruits, it also left the churches with a sense of being orphaned from the rest of the Methodist body, a deprivation that was only partially corrected by participation in the World Methodist Council, an organization that seems to be more a series of fraternal meetings of sister churches than a unique body that celebrates faith within a common tradition. This is evident in its inability to decide on doctrinal questions that have to do with the common identity. These are ecclesiological issues that need rapid answers. In 2007 representatives of both bodies (CIEMAL and UMC) met in Panamá and agreed to continue conversations towards strengthening connexional bonds in programmatic and missionary issues. The next few years will probably show a closer arrangement and a new way to reconstitute the international Methodist community based on firmer links than those implied in the expression 'autonomous churches'.

New Liturgical Forms and Ecumenism

After about two centuries of Methodism in Latin America it can be said that only during the last fifty years have there been liturgical changes that express the character of national churches. In the musical/song area the majority of churches have incorporated to the classical Protestant and Methodist hymns popular melodies and lyrics that pick up the local ethos, and this way try to overcome the clearly foreign character of the hymns that the missionaries bought with them during the first century and a half. This evolution first crystallized in the successive editions of the *Cancionero Abierto,* an ecumenical product from the very beginning composed by a group of people with an important Methodist presence. The book was a landmark in Latin American hymnology since it included songs with popular rhythms and lyrics that reflected the new theological trends in the continent. Many such songs have become classics of popular Protestant song, and have been translated into various languages and incorporated into congregational singing around the world. Changes in song were accompanied at the same time by changes in liturgy, in searching of a language that would interpret Latin American ways and styles. Thus 'Methodist' liturgy gained in spontaneity and made a closer connection with the spirit of the various people among whom the church developed its mission. The *Book of Worship* translated from English gave way to *Festejemos juntos al Señor*, prepared by CIEMAL (1989) and distributed throughout the continent. Similarly with worship: it began with traditional Methodist forms but developed its own pattern, adopting elements from other traditions and, recently, including elements from other Protestant expressions in Latin America, in what might be called a transversal ecumenism that extends to other areas including mission. Such absorption is the result of a shared evangelical culture and not necessarily of a conscious choice to adopt one form or another. Such a process can be evaluated both as a blessing and a warning to be alert: a blessing because it has developed the capacity to create a language that is particular to Methodism in Latin America, in harmony with other religious expressions, and because with the evolution of time it has ended the image of the churches as foreign to the continent, which was not something they cultivated but which the context imposed on them. It must be asked where the boundaries to these new liturgical, hymnological, and pastoral forms lie, beyond which belonging to the Methodist family begins to blur, and what it is that actually makes a community of believers Methodist. There is no easy answer to this in Latin America, where Methodism has adopted different forms, according to the region in which it developed, that range from Pentecostal to what could be called 'social gospel', and include the defence of human rights; an ecumenical spirituality in dialogue with other expressions of faith; a blend of popular songs with traditional Wesleyan hymns; and the search for a particular missionary attitude which has led to exploration of new forms of relationship with people who are mostly Roman Catholics. It is probable that Latin American Methodist identity will be in combination with several of these elements together with the recognition of the theological and pastoral inheritance received from their elders. But what has become evident in the last few years is that Methodism in Latin America must find a common doctrinal and missionary base that expresses its identity and its belonging to universal Methodism or it is at risk of losing some of the basic elements that are essential to its being. The desire to learn and revise the Methodist heritage was greatly aided by the Spanish language publication of the *Works of Wesley*, directed by Professor Justo L. Gonzalez. When in 2006 the General Assembly of the Methodist Church of Brazil voted to withdraw from all ecumenical organizations in which the Roman Catholic Church participated, many Methodists in Latin America asked themselves if this denial of dialogue with a sister Christian church did not lead to losing one of the marks of Methodism. In the same sense the question arose when the Cuban Methodist Church decided to withdraw from the

Matanzas Theological Seminary, where for years its ministers had been trained together with the Presbyterians and Anglicans. Are not these the symptoms of the loss of Methodist identity that raise the question of how to reconstruct that identity outside of the parameters that had marked Latin American Methodism since the beginnings of the century.

At the beginning of twenty-first century Methodism in Latin America has been able to absorb the richness of cultural diversity of the continent, and at the same time it faces the challenge of finding a common language that creates bonds and unity with the rest of the worldwide Methodist community. This search is no different from the one faced by the early Christians who began with a faith built on Semitic Scripture but were soon confronted with the Roman culture. They found the words to proclaim the gospel to a different world while preserving the essence of the message. Methodism in Latin America faces a similar task.

Suggested Reading

To continue the study of Methodism in Latin America we recommend the following: Jean-Pierre Bastian, *Historia del protestantismo en América Latina* (Mexico: CUPSA, 1990); José Duque (ed.), *La tradición protestante en la teología latinoamericana. Primer intento: la tradición metodista* (San José: DEI, 1983); Sidney Rooy, 'La evangelización protestante en América Latina, una evaluación', *Cuadernos de Teología* 13/1 (1993): 43–7.

There are various local writings, among which we would like to point out those of Daniel P. Monti, *Ubicación del Metodismo en el Río de la Plata* (Buenos Aires: La Aurora, 1976); Claudio Ribeiro et al., 'Caminhos do Metodismo no Brasil'. *75 Anos de Autonomia* (São Paulo: Facultade de Teologia, 2005); J. Piquinela, *Protestantismo en el Uruguay 1808–1880* (Montevideo: Methodist Church of Uruguay, 2007); Alejandro Calle Mamani, 'Primer Centenario de la Iglesia Metodista en Bolivia (1906–2006)', *Revista Evangélica de Historia* 3–4 (2005–6), 9–36.

References

Arias, Mortimer (1973). *Salvación es liberación*. Buenos Aires: La Aurora.

Lalive D'epinay, Christian (1968). *El refugio de las masas: estudio sociológico del Protestantismo chileno*. Santiago de Chile: Pacífico.

Míguez Bonino, José (1975). *Doing Theology in a Revolutionary Situation*. Philadelphia: Fortress.

—— (1983). *Protestantismo y liberalismo en América Latina*. San José: DEI.

Robinson, Elaine (2007). 'El exilio del metodismo argentino'. In *Cuadernos de Teología* 26: 160–79.

CHAPTER 9

BRITISH METHODISM AND EVANGELICALISM

MARTIN WELLINGS

No informed observer of contemporary culture could fail to be impressed by the resurgence and global expansion of evangelicalism in the second half of the twentieth century. Writing in 1994, the British Baptist scholar Derek Tidball discerned 'the ascendancy of evangelicalism' in many parts of the World Church, from Korea to Brazil and from sub-Saharan Africa to the USA. Even in the United Kingdom, where processes of secularization were apparently eviscerating traditional patterns of church attendance and Christian adherence, evangelicals seemed to be bucking the trends, registering significant numerical growth, gaining new respect in the corridors of power, and attracting bemused, admiring, or apprehensive comments from the media (Tidball 1994: 10–11). In his appreciative foreword to Tidball's study, Clive Calver, General Director of the UK Evangelical Alliance, quoted an unnamed secular commentator: 'Whatever one may think of them... tomorrow belongs to the evangelicals' (ibid. p. x).

This late twentieth-century resurgence in evangelical numbers, confidence, and influence was accompanied by a renaissance in the study of evangelical history. In the hands of such scholars as W. R. Ward, David Bebbington, Mark Noll, and Bruce Hindmarsh a sophisticated analysis of the origins and development of evangelicalism emerged, respecting the complexity and diversity of a phenomenon that comprises overlapping movements and which therefore defies neat categorization.

The 'great spate of historical enquiry' identified by Ward generated a plethora of specialist studies, but also works designed for the general reader. It is a striking feature of this popular historiography that while the Wesleys' Methodism often occupies a central place in the early history of evangelicalism, Methodists progressively move to the margins of the picture as the story advances into the nineteenth century, and by the twentieth century they have all but disappeared (Ward 2006: 1; Bebbington 2005: jacket). The thesis argued in this chapter is that for much of its history British Methodism has been part of the family of evangelical movements, and that Methodist responses to the challenges and vicissitudes of British cultural and social developments from the mid-eighteenth to the mid-twentieth centuries have been recognizably evangelical.

Mapping the relationship over time between British Methodism and evangelicalism is no easy task, involving as it does the interpretation of two complex and evolving entities. An early twenty-first century perspective may serve to introduce and to illustrate some of the issues.

The legal foundation of the British Methodist Church, the 1932 Deed of Union, incorporates a doctrinal clause to which Methodist ministers give annual assent as a matter of discipline and which operates as a benchmark for Methodist preaching and teaching. The clause expresses Methodism's continuing commitment to 'the evangelical faith', and it might therefore be assumed that Methodists may confidently be located within the broad constituency of evangelical Christians. The 2005 English Church Census, however, showed that only 32 per cent of Methodist churches chose to describe themselves as 'evangelical', while a recently published survey of more than 1,300 British Methodist ministers revealed a wide range of opinions on some key statements in the Creeds and on 'conservative-evangelical' and 'charismatic' emphases. Significantly, 77 per cent of the respondents thought that theological pluralism was a positive feature of the contemporary Methodist Church (Brierley 2007: table 5.14; Haley and Francis 2006: 105, 112, 118, 162). Given this situation it is not surprising that for more than half a century confessing conservative evangelicals have formed sectional associations for mutual support within the British Methodist Church (Wellings 2005: 36–7). The presence of self-selected 'evangelical' groups within an officially 'evangelical' denomination makes the point that definitions and identities are in some confusion, if not in dispute. The qualifying adjective 'conservative' used by or about particular evangelical groups is also telling. The account that follows will seek to show how the Methodist movement grew within an evangelical framework, gradually developing into a denomination that could simultaneously cherish its evangelical heritage, tolerate an autonomous evangelical organization within its structures, and also prize theological pluralism.

The origins and effects of the eighteenth-century evangelical revival continue to exercise historians. For Alister McGrath, the family history of evangelicalism begins with the sixteenth-century European Renaissance and especially with the

Reformation. For W. R. Ward, the thought-world, intellectual debates, and Pietist movements of Central Europe are crucial. In his discussion of 'antecedents and stirrings' Mark Noll synthesizes Puritanism, Pietism, and the High Church spirituality of the Church of England, while John Kent provocatively deflates the whole movement by referring to 'the myth of the so-called evangelical revival' (McGrath 1993: 11–18; Ward 2006; Noll 2004: 43–63; Kent 2002: 1). Methodist hagiography has sometimes collapsed the entire phenomenon into John Wesley's autobiography, so there is a need to recognize the multifarious roots of the revival in the Reformation, in the different strands of European Pietism, and in the traditions of English and North American Puritanism, among others. It remains the case, however, that the Wesley brothers and the movement that developed 'in connexion with' them was hugely significant within the wider context of the revival. Regardless of the debates about the nuances of evangelical origins, John and Charles Wesley were part of the nexus of leaders propagating the evangelical gospel of justification by grace through faith and the evangelical experience of conversion, by preaching, by example, by correspondence, and by publication. They were intimately involved in the network of relationships disseminating accounts of the work of God in personal letters and in journals and magazines. They expressed the evangelical experience in sermons and especially in hymns. They gave shape and structure to the movement through the growing network of societies, bound by a common rule and linked by the itinerancy of the Methodist preachers.

Many attempts have been made to define the essence of evangelicalism. The most influential formulation, now widely accepted by historians, was crafted by David Bebbington. In his seminal study *Evangelicalism in Modern Britain*, Bebbington identified four 'special marks of evangelical religion': '*conversionism*, the belief that lives need to be changed; *activism*, the expression of the gospel in effort; *biblicism*, a particular regard for the Bible; and … *crucicentrism*, a stress on the sacrifice of Christ on the cross' (Bebbington 1989: 3–4). Built on meticulous and wide-ranging research, the so-called 'Bebbington quadrilateral' has proved persuasive because it not only accounts for the 'family resemblance' that unites otherwise disparate evangelicals, but also allows for diversity and development. Evangelicals might agree in placing the cross at the centre of their theology, for example, without necessarily subscribing to identical theories of the atonement.

The Wesleys' Methodism may be located firmly within the matrix of emphases identified by Bebbington and endorsed by other historians as definitive of evangelicalism. Charles Wesley's hymns were soaked in Scripture, and John Wesley famously described himself as 'a man of one book'. Conversion was central to the experience and the message of the first Methodists, as evidenced by the biographies that John Wesley solicited, edited, and then published in his *Arminian Magazine* (Hindmarsh 2005: 226–7). Although the Methodists did not dwell on the 'blood and wounds' of Christ in the way the Moravians did, the sense of forgiveness through the atoning love of God was characteristic of the early movement. John

Wesley's account of his Aldersgate Street experience makes the point: 'I felt I did trust in Christ, Christ alone for salvation and an assurance was given me that he had taken away *my* sins, even *mine*, and saved *me* from the law of sin and death.' Methodist activism was legendary, and was expressed in the first of the 'Twelve Rules' drawn up by John Wesley for his 'helpers' in 1753: 'Be diligent. Never be unemployed. Never be triflingly employed. Never while away time...' (Ward and Heitzenrater 1988: 250; *CPD* 1988: 77).

Early Methodism, however, while characteristically evangelical, was also distinctive in several significant ways. First, it put a premium on experience, emphasizing that saving faith was 'not barely a speculative, rational thing, a cold, lifeless assent, a train of ideas in the head; but also a disposition of the heart'. In this the Wesleys stood with those evangelicals who were more concerned with preaching Christ and encouraging holy living than with the articulation of doctrine and the enforcement of orthodoxy. Although they were not indifferent to doctrine, their principal concerns were conversion and sanctification. John Wesley was impatient of those who got bogged down in disputes about what he called 'opinions', and advocated a 'catholic spirit' and 'union in affection' among all who love God (Wesley 1984: 120; 1985: 81–95).

This generous orthodoxy was not always consistently applied, because, second, the Wesleys' Methodism was passionately Arminian at a time when many fellow evangelicals tended towards moderate Calvinism. As early as 1740, John Wesley and George Whitefield clashed publicly over the question of free grace. Wesley preached on the issue in April 1739, subsequently publishing a sermon in which he called predestination 'a doctrine full of blasphemy' (Wesley 1986: 554) and appending his brother's thirty-six-stanza hymn, 'Universal Redemption'. Controversy broke out again in the 1770s, and the *Arminian Magazine* was launched in 1778 explicitly to counter what Wesley called the 'poison' of Calvinism (Hindmarsh 2005: 229–30; McGonigle 2001).

Third, the Wesleys' emphasis on assurance and their teaching on holiness were not shared by other evangelicals. Both aspects clearly differentiated Wesleyans from evangelicals in the Reformed tradition, who taught election rather than assurance and who found John Wesley's doctrine of entire sanctification unbiblical and bizarre. For Wesley, however, the assurance of salvation—the work of the Holy Spirit bearing witness with the spirit of the believer that he or she was a child of God—was the normal experience of Christian people, while the possibility of Christian perfection was the very raison d'être of the movement, the 'grand depositum' lodged with the people called Methodists.

Fourth, the Wesleys' Methodism was distinguished by the rhetoric and the reality of connexionalism. Other evangelicals, such as Whitefield and the countess of Huntingdon, used the language of 'connexion' to describe the networks of groups and individuals over which they exercised influence and leadership, but the Wesleys perfected this method of organization and made of it a structure of discipline and accountability, as well as an instrument of mission. Individual Methodists were assigned to a class, one of the small groups into which every local society was divided, and were required to meet weekly under the direction of a leader. The societies were not autonomous: they belonged to the 'united societies' which together formed the Wesleys' 'connexion', under the authority of the Annual Conference. Methodist discipline was embodied in the 'Rules of the Society' (1743) and in the Minutes of the Conference, codified and published in successive editions of the 'Large Minutes' from 1753 onwards. Methodist preachers, stationed annually by the Conference to supervise the societies in a given area, were those who laboured 'in connexion with' Wesley; later, in the 1790s and early 1800s, reception into full connexion with the Conference became the Methodists' 'virtual ordin-ation'. As Methodism acquired property, it was placed on John Wesley's 'model trust' of 1763, firmly linking it to the preachers appointed by Wesley and to the doctrines taught in his *Sermons* and *Notes on the New Testament*. The 1784 Deed of Declaration bequeathed Wesley's rights and powers in his connexion to the Con-ference, thereby ensuring institutional continuity and the maintenance of central control: Conference became 'the living Wesley' (Lawson 1965; Baker 1965). Thus by a combination of pioneer evangelism, the successful absorption of the work of others, an attention to the detail of organization, a blend of charm and charisma and a streak of ruthless autocracy, the Wesleys created a tight-knit movement with an effective structure, a strong internal sense of discipline and a longevity beyond their own lives. Not only did the Wesleyan polity endure, but the eighteenth-century terminology took root in Methodism, shaping the movement's subsequent identity and sense of itself as a connexion of united societies, walking by rule. All this gave a particular identity to Methodist evangelicalism.

The century after John Wesley's death in 1791 witnessed remarkable expansion in the evangelical movements in Great Britain. The denominations most affected by the eighteenth century revival—Baptists, Congregationalists, and Methodists—experienced great numerical growth. An evangelical school of thought developed in the Church of England, and began to secure both a measure of recognition and a degree of representation among the bishops and senior clergy. As evangelical theology and spirituality became increasingly prevalent in the British churches, so evangelical influence was felt in public life and wider society. Evangelicals from different denominational and theological traditions banded together in a whole range of devotional, missionary, and philanthropic enterprises. Evangelicals who had learned to work together against the slave trade in the 1780s combined to produce and circulate Christian literature in the Religious Tract Society (1799) and the British and Foreign Bible Society (1804), to promote overseas missions in the Missionary Society (1795), to encourage Sunday schools through the Sunday School Society (1785) and the Sunday School Union (1803), and to campaign for social purity in the Society for the Suppression of Vice (1802). Evangelical philan-thropy reached into the prisons, the factories, and the homes of the poor, working for humanitarian reform and the alleviation of need. It may be argued, moreover, that evangelical influences helped to mould the seriousness and high-mindedness which became characteristic of Victorian Britain (Bradley 1976; Prochaska 2006).

Methodists played a full part in all these initiatives. John Wesley's last letter, written less than a fortnight before his death, was sent to encourage William Wilberforce in his Parliamentary campaign against the slave trade. Wesley looked forward to the destruction of the 'execrable villainy' of slavery itself, and Methodists contributed substantially to the petitioning campaigns of 1791–2 and 1832–3. The growth of Wesleyan missions in the West Indies encouraged this involvement: the missionary W. J. Shrewsbury was forced to flee for his life from Barbados in 1824 because of his opposition to slavery, and Richard Watson called for emancipation at the Wesleyan Methodist Missionary Society annual meeting in 1830 (Wesley 1931: 265; Vickers 2000: 317; Hempton 1987: 208–9; Brendlinger 2006: 165, 169). Adam Clarke, Methodism's outstanding biblical scholar, was deeply engaged with the work of the Bible Society and was explicitly (and unusually, given the general reluctance to allow a minister to leave pastoral work or to stay in one location longer than three years) designated by the Conference to this role (Stevenson 1884: 231). Jabez Bunting, the dominant force in Wesleyan Methodism in the first half of the nineteenth century, supported the Bible Society and the Anti-Slavery Society, and even took the chair at the meeting that established the pan-evangelical periodical the *Eclectic Review* in 1804 (Bunting and Rowe 1887: 208–13). Over forty years later, Bunting also played a prominent part in the founding conference of the Evangelical Alliance. Between a fifth and a quarter of the 900 people who attended the conference, held in London in August 1846, were Methodists, and Methodists were well represented among the Alliance's officers and donors (Wellings 2005: 18–19).

Bunting's biographers told the story of his brief involvement with the *Eclectic Review* as a cautionary tale: sadly, the *Review* 'ceased to be catholic, when it impugned the principles of Evangelical Arminianism', and from this experience Bunting learned that 'denominational methods' were generally to be preferred to non-specific initiatives: 'he dreaded lest what were intended as manifestations of union should prove occasions of discord; and he thought that the parts separately would accomplish more than could the whole combined' (Bunting and Rowe 1887: 211–13). While remaining recognizably evangelical in doctrine and ethos in this period, therefore, Methodists were inclined to devote their energies to their own denominational agencies, rather than to pan-evangelical endeavours. They were not unique in this: the non-denominational Missionary Society saw the Baptists and the evangelical Anglicans, as well as the Wesleyans, establish their own separate organizations between 1792 and 1818, and regretfully adopted the less grandiose title 'London Missionary Society' in the latter year.

The preference for denominational work was driven partly by a felt need to exercise greater control over burgeoning activities at a time of rapid expansion: in the 1820s, for example, the Wesleyan Conference took steps to bring previously free-standing Sunday schools under ministerial supervision and to associate the schools firmly with societies, circuits, and a formal Connexional structure. The imposition of discipline, which provoked many of the divisions in Methodism in the first half of the nineteenth century, also proved inimical to interdenominational collaboration and non-denominational enterprises. As Bunting recognized, more-over, pan-evangelical cooperation could founder in the face of real differences of doctrine and ecclesiology. The Arminian/Calvinist divide that turned Bunting against the *Eclectic Review* also made Dr Coke suspicious of the LMS (Martin 1983: 64–8). Later in the century Wesleyans were incensed by the sympathy and support shown by some Baptists and Congregationalists towards seceders from the 'old Connexion' in the bitter conflicts of 1834–5 and 1849–57. Meanwhile Wesleyans in particular were uncomfortable with the open hostility shown by evangelicals in the older Nonconformist or Dissenting traditions towards the Church of England, but were also increasingly suspicious of a national church in which High Church influences seemed to be reviving with the Oxford Movement of the 1830s. Reluctant to join the Nonconformist campaign for the disestablishment of the Church of England, but fearful of the 'Romeward drift' of the national church, Methodists practised their evangelicalism largely within their own Connexions. Again, it should be noted that the congregational polity of Old Dissent made Baptists and Congregationalists critical of Wesleyan connexionalism in the 'Wesleyan Reform' agitation of the mid-nineteenth century, while evangelicals in the Church of England, keen to prove their respectability as loyal Churchmen, could be very dismissive or patronizing towards Methodists.

In many respects Methodism simply reflected, in its own milieu, general evangelical responses to contemporary theology and culture. In others it gave evangelical concerns a distinctive Methodist twist, so that holiness teaching, for example, followed a trajectory emphasizing the traditional Wesleyan emphasis on full sanctification, rather than the 'rest of faith' taught by the leaders of the Keswick school or the strenuous discipline of the Reformed tradition. Despite these nuances, Methodists in this period remained recognizably evangelical, examples of what Bebbington describes as the mid-nineteenth century 'dominance of evangelicalism' (Bebbington 2000, 2005).

From the 1880s, however, the theological and cultural assumptions of evangelicalism were challenged from several directions. New critical scholarship, defined as 'higher criticism', questioned or rejected traditional beliefs about the history and authorship, if not the inspiration and authority, of the Bible. Darwinian biology posed uncomfortable questions not only about the relationship between Genesis and geology but also about the entire biblical scheme of creation, fall, and redemption. A swelling chorus of voices challenged the cross-centred theology of traditional evangelicalism, repudiated substitutionary theories of the atonement, and rejected the doctrine of the eternal punishment of the impenitent. Evangelical taboos and ethics also came under scrutiny as the churches struggled to respond to a growing and now predominantly urban population and to the craze for sports and leisure among the young. The limits of orthodox belief and the boundaries of acceptable behaviour were tested in all the churches, and evangelical denominations, groups, and agencies faced a struggle for integrity and identity, and sometimes even for survival (Wellings 2005: 24–6).

From the perspective of a resurgent late twentieth-century conservative evangelicalism, the years between 1880 and 1930 witnessed a cleavage between those evangelicals who stayed faithfully in the 'old paths' and those who lost their footing and slid inexorably into theological liberalism or modernism. This case has been made repeatedly in histories of student Christianity, describing how a growing accommodation on the part of the Student Christian Movement to broader theologies and a wider range of ecclesial loyalties (including Anglo-Catholicism) provoked a secession by conservatives that eventually led to the formation of the rival Inter-Varsity Fellowship (Barclay and Horn 2002: 59–78). Some contemporaries took a similar view of developments, famously summed up in the polemics against 'down-grade' theology published in C. H. Spurgeon's *The Sword and the Trowel* from late 1889 and less famously in the splenetic *Journal of the Wesley Bible Union* in the 1910s and 1920s.

It may be argued, however, that the stark division between liberals and conservatives proposed by this reading of evangelical history and the impression of a substantial section of the evangelical movement evaporating into modernist apostasy do not accord with reality. Evangelicalism in the late nineteenth and early twentieth centuries was flexible and diverse enough to accommodate a range of responses to 'modern thought'. If the spectrum began with hardline conservatives and shaded off into those who abandoned evangelical theology and spirituality for a species of modernism, it also included many varieties of 'central' or 'liberal' evangelicals. Typically, they remained loyal to the Bible, while accepting much mainstream biblical criticism. They emphasized the preaching of the cross, while reinterpreting the atonement in terms other than penal substitution. They advocated conversion, while also seeking a renewal of spiritual and sacramental life to overcome a perceived shallowness or staleness in conventional evangelical spirituality. They encouraged activism, but re-evaluated some traditional evangelical shibboleths, priorities, and prohibitions, endorsing church-sponsored leisure programmes, embracing culture, and engaging with the reforming politics of the Liberals and even the emerging Socialists. Evangelicalism remained a complex coalition of movements, a matrix of beliefs, emphases, and experiences within which groups and individuals evolved their own responses to the challenges and opportunities of the times (Wellings 2003a: 318–21).

Methodism in its various forms found a place within this world. Many of its developments reflected the broadening of evangelicalism. In controversies from the late 1870s to the early 1900s the Wesleyans maintained a consistently conservative position on eternal punishment: advocates of the 'larger hope' were expelled from the ministry and even the cautious speculations of J. A. Beet attracted official censure. Higher criticism, however, was given mild endorsement by a London Wesleyan audience including such conservative grandees as J. H. Rigg as early as 1891, while the Primitive Methodists entrusted the theological education of their student ministers after 1892 to A. S. Peake, one of the most gifted of the younger generation of critical scholars and an influential exponent of the new theories in the denominational press. An attempt to block the appointment of another advocate of 'modern thought', George Jackson, to a chair at the Wesleyans' Didsbury College in 1913 ended in the humiliating rout of the ultra-conservatives. In systematic theology J. S. Lidgett developed an emphasis on the incarnation and on the fatherhood of God to complement traditional theologies of the atonement, while Russell Maltby challenged expiatory theories of the cross and advocated a view of Christ's saving work as an identification with fallen humanity. The creation of the Wesley Guild in 1896 marked a constructive engagement with the aspirations of young people by providing a blend of devotional, literary, and social activities. In the Fellowship of the Kingdom, founded in 1919, Maltby and Newton Flew offered ministers a new style of spirituality and intellectual adventure, and this was complemented by the Free Church Catholicism of Henry Lunn, J. E. Rattenbury, and A. E. Whitham. In its advocacy of a 'New Evangelicalism' committed to social reform, the Wesleyan Methodist Union for Social Service brought together Rattenbury and Lidgett, W. B. Fitzgerald, founder of the Wesley Guild, the Christian Socialist Samuel Keeble, and Frank Ballard, *bête noir* equally of the fundamentalists and the secularists (Carter 1998; Wellings 2002; Bebbington 1989: 14–15, 202; Keeble 1906). Methodism in this period, then, found its evangelicalism transposed into a broadly liberal evangelical key.

Given the divisiveness of the issues surrounding 'modern thought' in such evangelical bastions as the Baptist Union, the Church Missionary Society, and the SCM, it may be asked why Methodism largely escaped a 'fundamentalist' controversy in the early twentieth century. Several answers may be given. The new scholarship quickly won the intellectual arguments with the rising generation of college tutors and ministerial students, and there was no effective or credible conservative response. New views were commended in cautious terms by scholars and leaders whose known orthodoxy and personal evangelical experience were trusted: Peake, for example, was both a biblical scholar of international renown and an earnest preacher of a Christ-centred gospel, who won and retained the respect and loyalty of those who disagreed with his views on higher criticism, while Jackson and Ballard were known for their work as evangelists and apologists (Wellings 2003*b*: 512–14; A. Jackson 1949: 15–25).

It may be argued, further, that the ethos and structures of Methodism were conducive to this evolution. Methodist evangelicalism had always been activist and experiential, rather than intellectual. Writing in 1903 about the Methodist emphasis on the witness of the Spirit, George Jackson offered this insight into the theological awareness and priorities of contemporary Wesleyans: 'Our people are not, as a rule, quickly sensitive to differing shades of theological thought, and on some subjects it might be possible for a preacher to teach questionable doctrine without exciting any general alarm among his hearers; but a false note in the pulpit on this subject would be detected and resented at once' (G. Jackson 1903: 43). Methodist suspicions were more likely to be aroused by a failure of experience than by a shift of doctrine. This experientialist ethos was complemented by a connexional polity which promoted unity, discouraged party groupings, and made congregational separatism very difficult. Candidates for the ministry were selected and trained connexionally; the stationing of ministers was a connexional responsibility; the three-year itinerancy kept ministers moving; and the circuit system acted against single-church pastorates and ensured that the deployment of preachers and the filling of pulpits was under the control of the circuit, not the local society. The rhetoric of connexionalism remained strong too: when the conservatives of the Wesley Bible Union attempted to use the disciplinary procedures of the Wesleyan connexion against Jackson, Ballard, and other liberal evangelicals in the 1910s they were subjected to a telling counter-charge of 'unbrotherly conduct' (Wellings 2002: 166).

Although liberal evangelicalism had a great deal going for it in the early twentieth century, it did not win universal approval in Methodism. First, there was a small but vocal backlash at connexional level against higher criticism and 'modernist' theology, provoked by Jackson's appointment to Didsbury in 1913. The outraged conservatives whose campaign to reverse the appointment failed so spectacularly in the Wesleyan Conference drew together in the Wesley Bible Union, and spent the next decade and a half fomenting a series of minor fundamentalist controversies in Methodism. A combination of tactical ineptitude, weak argument, and sheer ill-temper ensured that the WBU's efforts served only to rally majority support for persecuted liberals, to discredit the conservative cause for at least a generation, and to induce the Conference to redefine the Connexion's doctrinal standards to prevent the use of John Wesley's *Sermons* and *Notes* as a weapon against biblical criticism. By the early 1920s the WBU was a laughing-stock and was drifting towards non-denominational evangelical groups such as the Protestant Truth Society. The further apparent dilution of Wesleyan doctrinal standards in the negotiations for Methodist union led the WBU finally to cut its connections with Methodism and to change its name to the British Bible Union in 1932. It seems unlikely that this departure caused much distress in the Connexion (ibid. 157–68).

Much more significant than the tiny band of ultra-conservatives in the WBU was the survival of what might be termed a 'constructive conservative' position, occupying ground between the emerging liberal evangelical consensus and the militant fundamentalists. This outlook was illustrated by such ministers as Samuel

Chadwick (1860–1932), Dinsdale Young (1861–1938), W. H. Heap (1869–1953), J. A. Broadbelt (1878–1962), and C. H. Hulbert (1878–1957). Chadwick, Heap, Broadbelt, and Hulbert were linked by ties of friendship. They shared ministerial experience in the great northern preaching centres of Methodism, and were variously involved in the evangelical networks emanating from Cliff College, the institution for the training of lay evangelists taken into connexional ownership in 1903: Chadwick and Broadbelt were the second and third principals of the college. Cliff was intertwined with the weekly newspaper *Joyful News*, edited by Chadwick and then by Heap, and a further contact came through the annual Southport Holiness Convention. Chadwick, Heap, Broadbelt, and Hulbert exemplified a traditional Wesleyan commitment to evangelism and scriptural holiness, and, while doctrinally conservative, they stood apart from the WBU and its polemics. Theirs, moreover, was a largely Methodist evangelicalism, in the sense that they were principally or exclusively active in Methodist networks (Vickers 2000: 44, 58, 169; Lazell 2005). In outlook and affiliation Dinsdale Young came closer to fundamentalism. An admirer of the Puritan divines, he was interested in the British-Israelite theory and supported conservative evangelical or quasi-fundamentalist initiatives such as the Advent Testimony Movement and the Bible Testimony Fellowship. Despite initial expressions of sympathy, however, he still escaped the clutches of the WBU and his death in 1938 drew forth a frank assessment from Scott Lidgett: 'The unsettlement of the age did not touch him. In so far as he conceived that current teachings were incompatible with the Gospel as he believed and preached it, he either passed them by or dismissed them with a hearty, yet genial, anathema' (Murray 1938; *Methodist Recorder* 27 January 1938: 4). Not dissimilar was the outlook of the Primitive Methodist Thomas Jackson (1850–1932), pioneer of the Whitechapel Mission in the East End of London. Jackson, too, stuck to a simple gospel: 'Modernism does not trouble him, and he is not versed in the Higher Criticism. Far from disdaining these things, and while cherishing the friendliest feelings for their exponents, his time has been occupied with weightier matters' (Potter 1929: 167). The absence of party loyalties in Methodism is emphasized when it is realized that Jackson's work was supported by the Primitive Methodist plutocrat Sir William Hartley, who also paid Peake's salary and enabled ministerial students to spend two years at the Manchester college. On the Wesleyan side, Heap and Hulbert were protégés of Chadwick's friend Samuel Collier, founder of the Manchester Mission, and Collier's friend and biographer was none other than George Jackson. Theological differences in Methodism existed within a close-knit family.

The constructive conservatives in early twentieth-century Methodism emphasized evangelism and evangelical experience, and tended to avoid polemics. At a time when liberal evangelical influences were growing in the colleges, and among younger ministers, it may be seen that there was a real possibility that the conservative case might go by default and traditional Methodist evangelicalism wither. That this did not happen was due to three principal causes.

First, the 'New Evangelicalism' of the colleges and the denominational publications percolated only slowly into the local circuits and societies of Methodism. It should not be forgotten that the majority of services in British Methodist churches in the twentieth century (as in the nineteenth) were conducted by Local (lay) Preachers, and not by ministers.

Although voluntary schemes of training for Local Preachers were introduced in the 1890s, connexional courses of biblical and theological study became compulsory only after Methodist Union in 1932 (Milburn and Batty 1995: 76–82, 98–103). Many Sunday services were therefore led by preachers effectively trained under an apprenticeship model and examined viva-voce in the circuit Local Preachers' meeting on their Christian experience and knowledge of Wesley's *Sermons*. While this in no way prevented the acquisition of considerable erudition by Local Preachers, it did mean that the systematic diffusion of the latest scholarship was very difficult. It was possible for circuits and societies to remain largely unaware of the debates of the early twentieth century and to be surprised—and dismayed—when confronted by the 'assured results' of modern scholarship. It should not be forgotten, moreover, that the staple ingredient of Methodist worship in this period was hymnody, and that successive British hymnals contained a substantial number of Charles Wesley's hymns (Pratt 2004: 49–53). In this way, Methodist congregations were fed a steady diet of evangelical and experiential theology through exposure to the Wesley hymns.

Second, this innate conservatism was nurtured, or made more explicit and articulate, by a range of conservative networks. Some were distinctively Methodist, like the readership of *Joyful News*, or the churches visited by students from Cliff College on their summer vacation evangelistic 'treks', or the individuals who supported the Southport Convention. Others were non-denominational, such as the beach missions organized in seaside resorts by the Children's Special Service Mission, the regional Bible conventions that drew on local evangelical churches for audiences, conservative evangelical newspapers, magazines, and periodicals, and pan-evangelical missionary societies. The latter influences might draw conservatively inclined evangelicals out of Methodism, or they might make an evangelical Methodist more definitely conservative. Thus Fred Mitchell, a Bradford chemist who became Home Director of the China Inland Mission in 1942, was converted as a teenager and became a Wesleyan Local Preacher at 17, and remained a Methodist until his death in an aeroplane accident in India in 1953. Mitchell's growing interest in China in the 1920s, however, took him into unusual circles for a Methodist: first, support for CIM, and then involvement with the Keswick movement (Thompson 1954: 17, 24, 42–3, 71–4, 84–93, 114).

Third, from the 1930s and especially after the Second World War, conservative evangelicalism in Britain moved beyond mere survival to experience a significant renaissance. The IVF, formed in 1927, was a key element, coordinating conservative groups in the universities. Fed by recruits from the CSSM and from increasingly effective work in the public schools, the small and somewhat beleaguered 'Evangelical Unions' of the 1920s grew in numbers and influence, and nurtured a new generation of conservative evangelical scholars and church leaders. Youth for Christ developed programmes in British towns and cities during and after the war. British evangelists such as Tom Rees proved able to fill large venues for evangelistic rallies. The Billy Graham crusades of 1954–5 gave evangelism a new impetus, and conservative evangelicalism a new confidence and higher public profile. The National Evangelical Anglican Congress at Keele University in 1967 marked the recovery of the conservative strand within the evangelical school in the Church of England, and by this time charismatic renewal was beginning to influence the traditional denominations and to create new churches and alliances. These developments took place against a backdrop of liberal evangelical decline in the face of social change and the challenge of theological pluralism. By the last quarter of the twentieth century conservative evangelicalism had become a powerful force in British Christianity. It represented an increasingly diverse and sometimes fractious coalition of groups: older denominations and 'new churches'; Free Church and Anglican; liturgical traditionalists, 'emerging' churches, and 'fresh expressions'; Reformed and Arminian; spiritually reflective and exuberantly charismatic. The sinews of the movement included festivals of worship and teaching, such as Spring Harvest, networks such as the Evangelical Alliance, CARE, and TEAR Fund, and the burgeoning print and electronic media. The theology of the movement remained conservative, but its style, language, and appeal were contemporary. Evangelicalism had always had global and transatlantic dimensions, but these influences increased in the late twentieth century as multi-ethnic Britain witnessed the growth of black-led churches and as the communications revolution brought North American trends to bear ever more powerfully on British evangelical life (Bebbington 1989: 249–70).

These broader evangelical changes and developments were reflected in Methodism. Liberal evangelical theology, married to social concern and a commitment to evangelism, remained dominant through the 1930s and 1940s, and was represented by Colin Roberts's innovative 'Christian Commando Campaigns' during the Second World War. The liberal evangelical hegemony, although challenged by more aggressively liberal and even radical voices, as well as by resurgent conservatism during the 1950s, held up through the era of the Graham crusades, hoping for a revival which always seemed to be just around the next corner. In the 1960s, however, this consensus came under pressure from all directions. A catastrophic decline in membership, the collapse of the Sunday schools, and a dramatic drop in candidates for the ministry brought home the structural weaknesses of the Connexion and, for many, dealt a death blow to confidence in traditional styles of evangelism. The old guard of college tutors and theologians seemed unable to cope with the new theology of Bultmann and Bonhoeffer, popularized by John Robinson in *Honest to God* (1963). The nadir was reached when the laborious process of the

Anglican–Methodist 'Conversations' issued in the rejection of Methodism by the Church of England—twice—in 1969 and 1972 (Hastings 1991: 548–9; Bebbington 2003: 200–5). The post-war Methodist project of reconstruction, outreach, and ecumenism seemed to have failed at all points. The subsequent quests for new theologies, new models of church life, and new approaches to mission generated diversity, experimentation, and pluralism, in which liberal evangelicalism was eclipsed both by more radical and more conservative options.

It has already been seen that traditionalism and a range of denominational and non-denominational networks kept conservative evangelicalism alive in Methodism after the departure of the WBU. It was not until after the Second World War, however, that the conservatively inclined felt confident enough to form an organization. The Revival Fellowship, constituted in 1952, grew from existing Methodist evangelicalism, but also drew on IVF contacts and benefited from the conservative and charismatic renaissance of the 1960s. The Fellowship, officially named the Methodist Revival Fellowship in 1955, weathered the storms of debate over the 'Conversations' and charismatic renewal, survived several high-profile secessions, and entered the 1970s as an established dialogue partner in a pluralist church. In 1971 it proved possible to create another body, Conservative Evangelicals in Methodism, with a brief for theological study and reflection. The following year the magazine *Dunamis* was launched to cater for Methodists involved with charismatic renewal. In 1987 MRF and CEIM came together to form Headway, 'a movement of Methodists committed to prayer for revival and witness to the evangelical faith'. Eight years later the *Dunamis* network dissolved into Headway, which by 2007, when it was rebranded 'Methodist Evangelicals Together', claimed a membership of 2,000, including 400 ministers. MRF, CEIM, and Headway leaders were linked to Cliff College and to the Southport Convention, but also to non-Methodist evangelical groups, such as the Evangelical Alliance, the Keswick Convention, Youth for Christ, and the faith missions. The weakening of denominational loyalties and the flourishing of new expressions of evangelicalism through the 1980s and 1990s meant that Methodist evangelicals were drawn to use worship and study resources, attend conferences and celebratory events, and support campaigning groups from across the whole evangelical spectrum. In some ways this enriched Methodism, but in others it diminished Methodist distinctiveness and promoted an evangelical homogeneity divorced from any explicitly Methodist/Wesleyan roots. Telling in this regard were the widespread replacement of traditional Methodist hymns with modern worship songs, looser denominational affiliations, and the development of a congregationalist rather than a connexional mindset (Wellings 2005: 36–7).

British Methodism was born in the evangelical revival, and it contributed significantly to the shaping and success of the phenomenon of evangelicalism. Although always occupying a particular place within the evangelical family as an Arminian holiness movement and an often self-sufficient denomination, Methodist history for more than two centuries marched in step with the interaction of a wider evangelicalism with developments in British thought, society, and sensibility. In the first half of the twentieth century many Methodists accompanied their fellow evangelicals into an accommodation with 'modern thought'. The erosion of liberal evangelicalism from the 1960s cut liberal Methodists loose from their evangelical origins, while the conservative evangelical revival drew its chief inspiration from sources other than the Wesleyan/Methodist tradition. Conservative evangelicals in Methodism have an assured place in a denomination that now prizes pluralism, but it remains to be seen whether they will retain, or regain, the ability to express and transmit their evangelicalism in a distinctive and recognizably Methodist idiom.

References

BAKER, FRANK (1965). 'The People called Methodists: 3. Polity'. In Rupert Davies and Gordon Rupp (eds.), *A History of the Methodist Church in Great Britain*. London: Epworth, i.

BARCLAY, OLIVER R., and HORN, ROBERT M. (2002). *From Cambridge to the World*. Leicester: IVP.

BEBBINGTON, DAVID W. (1989). *Evangelicalism in Modern Britain. A History from the 1730s to the 1980s*. London: Unwin Hyman.

—— (2000). *Holiness in Nineteenth Century England*. Carlisle: Paternoster.

—— (2003). 'Evangelism and Spirituality in Twentieth Century Protestant Nonconformity'. In Alan P. F. Sell and Anthony R. Cross (eds.), *Protestant Nonconformity in the Twentieth Century*. Carlisle: Paternoster.

—— (2005). *The Dominance of Evangelicalism. The Age of Spurgeon and Moody*. Downers Grove, Ill.: IVP.

BRADLEY, IAN (1976). *The Call to Seriousness*. London: Jonathan Cape.

BRENDLINGER, IRV A. (2006). *Social Justice through the Eyes of Wesley*. Ontario: Joshua.

BRIERLEY, PETER (ed.) (2007). *Religious Trends 6*. London: Christian Research.

BUNTING, T. P., and ROWE, G. STRINGER (1887). *The Life of Jabez Bunting, D.D.* London: T. Woolmer.

CARTER, DAVID (1998). 'Joseph Agar Beet and the Eschatological Crisis'. In *Proceedings of the Wesley Historical Society*. Birmingham: Westpoint.

CPD (1988). *Constitutional Practice and Discipline of the Methodist Church*. Peterborough: Methodist Publishing House, i.

HALEY, JOHN, and FRANCIS, LESLIE J. (2006). *British Methodism: What Circuit Ministers Really Think*. Peterborough: Epworth.

HASTINGS, ADRIAN (1991). *A History of English Christianity 1920–1990*. London: SCM.

HEMPTON, DAVID (1987). *Methodism and Politics in British Society 1750–1850*. London: Hutchinson.

HINDMARSH, D. BRUCE (2005). *The Evangelical Conversion Narrative. Spiritual Autobiography in Early Modern England*. Oxford: Oxford University Press.

JACKSON, ANNIE (1949). *George Jackson. A Commemorative Volume*. London: Epworth.

JACKSON, GEORGE (1903). *The Old Methodism and the New*. London: Hodder & Stoughton.

KEEBLE, SAMUEL (1906). *The Citizen of Tomorrow. A Handbook on Social Questions.* London: C. H. Kelly.

KENT, JOHN (2002). *Wesley and the Wesleyans.* Cambridge: Cambridge University Press.

LAWSON, JOHN (1965). 'The People called Methodists: 2. "Our Discipline" '. In Rupert Davies and Gordon Rupp (eds.), *A History of the Methodist Church in Great Britain.* London: Epworth, i.

LAZELL, DAVID (2005). *Harry Heap's Joyful News.* Loughborough: David Lazell.

McGONIGLE, HERBERT BOYD (2001). *Sufficient Saving Grace. John Wesley's Evangelical Arminianism.* Carlisle: Paternoster.

McGRATH, ALISTER (1993). *Evangelicalism and the Future of Christianity.* London: Hodder & Stoughton.

MARTIN, ROGER H. (1983). *Evangelicals United: Ecumenical Stirrings in Pre-Victorian Britain: 1795–1830.* Metuchen: Scarecrow.

MILBURN, GEOFFREY, and BATTY, MARGARET (1995). *Workaday Preachers: The Story of Methodist Local Preaching.* Peterborough: Methodist Publishing House.

MURRAY, HAROLD (1938). *Dinsdale Young, the Preacher.* London: Marshall, Morgan & Scott.

NOLL, MARK A. (2004). *The Rise of Evangelicalism.* Leicester: IVP.

POTTER, WILLIAM (1929). *Thomas Jackson of Whitechapel.* London: C. Tinling.

PRATT, ANDREW (2004). *O for a thousand tongues: The 1933 Methodist Hymn Book in Context.* Peterborough: Epworth.

PROCHASKA, FRANK (2006). *Christianity and Social Service in Modern Britain.* Oxford: Oxford University Press.

STEVENSON, GEORGE J. (1884). *Methodist Worthies.* London: Thomas C. Jack.

THOMPSON, PHYLLIS (1954). *Climbing on Track: A Biography of Fred Mitchell.* London: China Inland Mission.

TIDBALL, DEREK J. (1994). *Who Are the Evangelicals? Tracing the Roots of Today's Movements.* London: Marshall Pickering.

VICKERS, JOHN A. (ed.) (2000). *A Dictionary of Methodism in Great Britain and Ireland.* Peterborough: Epworth.

WARD, W. R. (2006). *Early Evangelicalism: A Global Intellectual History, 1670–1789.* Cambridge: Cambridge University Press.

—— and HEITZENRATER, RICHARD P. (eds.) (1988). *The Works of John Wesley: Journals and Diaries I, 1735–1738.* Nashville: Abingdon.

WELLINGS, MARTIN (2002). 'The Wesley Bible Union'. In *Proceedings of the Wesley Historical Society.* Birmingham: Westpoint.

—— (2003a). *Evangelicals Embattled: Responses of Evangelicals in the Church of England to Ritualism, Darwinism and Theological Liberalism, 1890–1930.* Carlisle: Paternoster.

—— (2003b). 'Peake, Arthur Samuel'. In Timothy Larsen (ed.), *Biographical Dictionary of Evangelicals.* Leicester: IVP.

—— (2005). *Evangelicals in Methodism: Mainstream, Marginalized or Misunderstood?* Ilkeston: Moorley's.

WESLEY, JOHN (1931). *The Letters of John Wesley,* ed. John Telford. London: Epworth.

—— (1984). *Works: Sermons I, 1–33.* Nashville: Abingdon.

—— (1985). *Works: Sermons II, 34–70.* Nashville: Abingdon.

—— (1986). *Works: Sermons III, 71–114.* Nashville: Abingdon.

CHAPTER 10

METHODISM AND PENTECOSTALISM

DONALD W. DAYTON

INTRODUCTION

IT will surprise some to find this topic in a book on Methodism. Many Methodists will be unhappy with the conjunction in the title, and many Pentecostals will be surprised by it. Yet the 'and' is appropriate. Pentecostalism cannot be understood apart from its deep roots in the Methodism experience. And Methodism similarly cannot be understood entirely without acknowledgement of this paternity—though for sociological and theological reasons, this relationship has often been suppressed in official historiography.

After a quarter of a century of involvement in the ecumenical movement (both nationally and globally), I have noticed that participants in such dialogue generally prefer to look 'up' the social ladder and 'backwards' in history for partners that will give them prestige and underline their own importance in such dialogue. Rarely does one look 'down' and 'forwards' for such partners. This may be particularly true of Methodism, which has always been haunted by a sort of ecclesiastical 'inferiority complex', in part a product of the nineteenth-century struggle for recognition in the face of Presbyterian and Episcopalian condescension (Methodists don't know how to 'do theology'—the Presbyterian critique—or how to 'do church'—the Episcopalian critique).

I remember a couple of decades ago sitting in a meeting of the Faith and Order Commission of the National Council of Churches of Christ (USA) where the topic of discussion was the importance of opening up dialogue with Pentecostalism. We were being led by commissioner Mel Robeck, somewhat oxymoronically an Assemblies of God clergyman serving as Professor of Ecumenism and Church History at Fuller Theological Seminary—the iconic seminary of the 'neo-evangelical' renaissance often defined by its opposition to 'ecumenism'. I was sitting next to a United Methodist representative who seemed to break out in a cold sweat at the very idea and kept trying to change the subject to the importance of Christian/Buddhist dialogue.

Similarly I have been in Pentecostal circles where Methodism was often used as the paradigmatic illustration of the bourgeois and domesticated church life that many Pentecostals understood themselves to be fighting. Some Pentecostal church historians, on their own trajectory towards acceptance by a more 'reformed' (i.e. Calvinist) form of evangelicalism, have violently opposed any suggestion of roots in the Methodist revival. They have also often resented my suggestion that the best clues about the future of Pentecostalism are to be found in the history of Methodism—that Pentecostalism in its upward social mobility, founding of universities, and increasing openness to ecumenism is following the patterns of Methodism, only a century later in its cycle.

The Methodist Roots of Pentecostalism

It is notoriously difficult to define Pentecostalism. Early efforts gave prominence to the practice of 'speaking in tongues' (an early Lutheran critique spoke of *The Tongue Speaking Movement*). This often led to sociological and anthropological interpretations in terms of various 'deprivation' theories, whether economic or psychological. The practice is also not specifically Christian and appears in many religions around the world. My University of Chicago dissertation published as *Theological Roots of Pentecostalism* was one of the first outsider attempts to offer a full-orbed theological analysis in terms of the 'foursquare gospel', most sharply articulated by Aimee Semple McPherson, founder of the International Church of the Foursquare Gospel. She spoke regularly of Jesus as Saviour, Baptizer with the Holy Spirit, Healer, and Coming King, and embedded these themes in the hymnody, literature, iconography, flags, and architecture of Angelus Temple in Los Angeles.

A minimalist definition of Pentecostalism might be something like that branch of Christianity that teaches that individuals must experience a 'personal Pentecost' along the lines of the book of Acts—and that this event is evidenced by the practice of speaking in tongues (though not all Pentecostals accept this 'evidence' doctrine). This involves the claim that the separation of the giving of the Spirit at Pentecost from becoming a disciple of Jesus is not an accident of the history of the early church but a normative pattern for the lives of all Christians. This involves a distinctive way of reading the Bible (the priority of the Luke-Acts material as the hermeneutical key based on a 'restorationist' reading that takes seriously the peculiarities of the New Testament narrative—rather than, as in most of the classical traditions, claiming that since Pentecost Christians receive the Holy Spirit in conversion). It is this move that gave the movement its most distinctive name: Pentecostalism.

There are intimations of this position in various Christian traditions. Advocates have pointed to the Puritan doctrines of the Holy Spirit, especially a 'sealing of the Spirit' as taught by Thomas Goodwin. Interestingly, the book of Acts is often read similarly by paedobaptist churches with a doctrine of confirmation that associates the reception of the Spirit with a second experience accompanied by the 'laying on of hands'. But the clearest source of these teachings is to be found in Methodism, from which we can trace very precisely the path to Pentecostal theology and its distinctive pattern of reading the Bible.

John Wesley is also notoriously difficult to interpret. All sorts of theological agenda have found justification in his complex and fertile mind. Donald Durnbaugh in *The Believer's Church* expands the sect/church typology of Ernst Troeltsch into a triangular diagram that attempts to place the range of Christian traditions in relationship to each other based on a trinitarian analysis. In the centre he places Methodism and Pietism and suggests that these traditions are the most unstable of all and are inclined to move quickly towards a greater stability at one of the points of the triangle—back towards Catholicism and the cathedral, towards classical Protestantism and the preaching chapel, and even towards pneumatological 'enthusiasm' and the meeting house. Each of these moves has produced its own interpretation of Wesley and the historiography of Methodism. And all such readings have struggled with where to place Wesley's distinctive doctrine of 'perfect love' or 'entire sanctification'.

Debates will continue about Wesley's doctrine of 'Christian perfection' and the shape of Christian experience it has engendered. Characteristic of Wesley's position was an emphasis on a complex process of 'salvation' that looked forward to a goal, possibly achieved before death, of victory over intentional sin that manifested itself in fulfilment of the twofold love commandment of Jesus (towards God and neighbour). In Wesley this teaching was very Christologically defined. To be entirely sanctified was to 'walk in the way Jesus walked' or to 'have the mind of Christ in you'.

Key changes in the articulation of this doctrine and experience may be associated with the 'Calvinistic controversy' of the early 1770s. It has been suggested that Wesley had become more focused on the 'event' or 'crisis' of 'entire sanctification' in the decade or so before this controversy. (It may be worth noting that this development illustrates, according to the Wesleyan Quadrilateral, the extent to which experience played a role in Wesley's articulation of doctrine—in this case the experience of his followers who in testimonies began to witness to the importance of a 'second blessing'.) This shift from 'process' to 'crisis' was a key factor in what followed.

These developments were centred in Trevecca, the college in Wales that was under the patronage of the countess of Huntingdon and thus a centre of the Calvinistic wing of the Methodist movement. There the emphasis on divine sovereignty (rather than the synergistic models of the Arminian wing of Methodism) provided a congenial location for the rise of a doctrine of the 'baptism of the Holy Spirit'. This apparently took place in the thought of president John Fletcher, Wesley's 'designated successor', who failed to take Wesley's place because he died before Wesley, and headmaster Joseph Benson, Fletcher's editor and first biographer. Both figures left Trevecca in the 'Calvinistic controversy' (Benson was dismissed for his Arminianism, and Fletcher resigned in sympathy). Benson and Fletcher began to speak of the 'event' of 'entire sanctification' as a 'baptism of the Holy Spirit' and moved to interpret 'Pentecost' as a moment of 'entire sanctification'.

The interpretation of these questions has become a subject of major controversy, especially in the circles of the Holiness Movement where this development has its greatest influence. Literally dozens of articles on the subject have been published in the *Wesleyan Theological Journal*. Some, especially Larry Wood of Asbury Theological Seminary, have seen in this development the fulfilment of Wesleyan theology. Others, myself and such scholars as Randy Maddox, have seen it as a development that Wesley did not embrace. I have debated the issues involved with Larry Wood in a series of exchanges in the pages of *Pneuma*, the journal of the Society for Pentecostal Studies.

As I see it, this development set in motion a trajectory that would result in Pentecostalism, though the process would take over a century and the full implications of Fletcher's doctrine of 'Pentecostal sanctification' would not be immediately clear. It involved, first of all, a shift in exegetical foundations—from the predominantly Johannine sources of Wesley's doctrine to the Lukan (especially the book of Acts) character of Fletcher's thought—and a shift to a basically narrative text. The book of Acts is less congenial to Wesleyan themes (there is only the single reference to 'purifying their hearts by faith' in chapter 15). More characteristic of the Lukan pneumatology is an emphasis on 'power' for prophecy, healing, and even the speaking in tongues in the account of Pentecost and its subsequent outworking in a variety of contexts. One might even argue that Fletcher's orientation set up an intra-canonical struggle within Methodism that finally broke out in Pentecostalism to give a more natural reading of the Lukan texts than the efforts to preach Wesleyan theology through the book of Acts.

Fletcher's doctrine of 'Pentecostal sanctification' had other implications as well. It underlined the 'event' character of 'entire sanctification'; 'Pentecost' is after all an 'event' or a moment in time and the image has much less place for the 'process' dimensions of Wesley's teaching. It also contributed to a shift from the 'teleological' character of 'Christian Perfection' in Wesley to a more 'inaugural' status in

Fletcher. That is, Wesley struggled with how much of what other traditions postponed to a 'glorification' after death might be experienced in this life as a sort of 'realized eschatology'. For Wesley 'Perfect Love' was the goal of the Christian life that might be anticipated before death. 'Pentecostal sanctification' tends to move the experience to an 'inaugural' position—so that a century later in the camp meeting culture many believers would testify along the line of 'I was saved and sanctified (or baptized in the Spirit) and then...'

The move of Fletcher also had profound implications for the shape of eschatological themes that would find their fulfilment in Pentecostalism. First of all, Fletcher developed a doctrine of 'dispensations'—three in number based on the persons of the Trinity: the dispensation of the Father (roughly the Old Testament era), the dispensation of the Son (the life of Jesus), and the dispensation of the Spirit (the church age since Pentecost). These stages in the history of the race were to be replicated in the life of each believer—yielding what might be called, as above, the 'Pentecostal hermeneutic'. Wesley preferred more classical patterns and tended to speak of history as divided into two periods, the covenant of 'works' and the covenant of 'grace'—or occasionally as the 'Jewish dispensation' and the 'Christian dispensation', retaining a twofold pattern.

This Fletcherian pattern of dispensations was not the same as the seven dispensations of the technical 'dispensationalism' that developed early in the next century under the influence of John Nelson Darby (as was enshrined in the Scofield Bible and more recently in the 'Left Behind' novels)—but it did earn Fletcher a place in the history of dispensationalism as one who anticipated some of its patterns of thought. There is a big debate about whether Pentecostalism is essentially 'dispensationalist' in the technical sense. I am among those who would argue that it is not, in spite of the fact that in the North American context it is often so assimilated into the fundamentalist culture as to be indistinguishable from it on this point. It is striking, however, that some forms of Pentecostalism, that of Aimee Semple McPherson for example, preserve the Trinitarian pattern of Fletcher's doctrine of dispensations.

Wesley was apparently receptive to Fletcher's doctrine of dispensations. Some, Larry Wood for example, have argued that this approval should be extended to the whole reconstruction of Fletcher. As I read the sources, however, Wesley was attracted to the idea of dispensational stages on the personal level because it gave him a way of describing his more complex soteriology. Wesley was not inclined to speak, as Baptists often do, of two categories of human beings, the 'saved' and the 'unsaved'. Wesley was more inclined to speak of three categories: the 'natural man' (Kierkegaard's Don Juan or the professor, with their fears of commitment to a single woman or intellectual framework), the 'legal man' (Kierkegaard's Judge Williams, who in a sort of Kantian way commits to the universal law), and the 'evangelical man' who has come to understand that Christian faith calls one beyond the expectations of the 'decent citizen' or 'person of good will'. (Similarities between Søren Kierkegaard and John Wesley in their analysis of Christian experience are evident in Wesley's sermon, 'On the Spirit of Bondage and the Spirit of Adoption'.) Wesley used various biological metaphors of growth (the bud, the flower, etc., or the baby, the young person, the adult) to expound his understanding of Christian experience—and Fletcher's doctrine of 'dispensations' gave him another means of speaking of these 'stages on life's way'.

There is another way in which Fletcher's reformulation recast Wesleyan eschatology in the direction of Pentecostalism. Wesley is again on this point difficult to interpret and he has been claimed by advocates of a number of positions. I remember being asked once in Israel why the Methodist tradition has had so little interest in 'prophecy' and its interpretation. Like other evangelists and pietists, Wesley was so soteriologically oriented that he did not develop a systematic articulation of eschatology or the 'last things'. One must tease out his eschatological position. I am among those who think that Wesley should be interpreted in the line of the 'post-millennialism' that gained force in the next century, in part under his influence. This natural social or cosmic correlation of his doctrine of 'Christian perfection' emphasized a dimension of 'victory' over sin in history that would result in a millennial experience that would be followed by the physical return of Christ in a final consummation in which God's righteousness would cover the earth. In this scheme one does not look forward to an imminent return of Christ in one's own lifetime.

Partly as a result of this position, Wesley's eschatology stood most naturally in the Puritan tradition of 'holy living and holy dying'. In Wesley one struggled more with one's own fate, the going to heaven, and the transformation of 'holiness without which one will not see the Lord'. Fletcher's articulation shifted attention to the 'blessed hope' of the personal return of Christ. Fletcher argued that every dispensation included a promise towards which the era yearned. In the 'dispensation of the Father' (the Old Testament) one looked forward to the coming of the Messiah. In the era of the New Testament one looked forward to the 'promise of the Father' or the coming of the Spirit at Pentecost. And in the church age (age of the Spirit) one yearned for the return of Christ. In this way Fletcher's exposition contributed to a heightened emphasis on the visible return of Christ.

I am convinced that Fletcher's formulation helped prepare the way for the reception of 'dispensational premillennialism' in many contexts. Often in the nineteenth century the adoption of this position was predated by about a decade by the doctrine of 'Pentecostal sanctification'—though, again, Fletcher cannot be blamed for all the features of this new eschatology. But his thought did tend in this direction. To use sociological language there was an 'elective affinity' between 'premillennialism' and 'Pentecostal sanctification'. Both shared a more 'tarry and wait' orientation that undercut the more synergistic style of Wesley's thought. Indeed in the mid-nineteenth century, Daniel Steele, president of Syracuse University, and other more classical Methodists, would denounce the influence of dispensational premillennialism in Methodism as 'antinomianism revived' and essentially a form of Calvinist theology. One might also argue that there is a shift here from 'prophetic' categories of thought, in which there is an appeal to human action and response in 'bringing in the Kingdom' to more apocalyptic modes of thinking, in which the 'kingdom comes' without or in opposition to human action. Again, Fletcher himself did not move in this direction (he was, after all, the great Methodist critic of Calvinism) but his position helped prepare the way in some circles for the acceptance of dispensationalism—essentially a theological position that uses the 'apocalyptic' texts in the Bible (notably Daniel and the book of Revelation) as the hermeneutical key for a 'prophetic' interpretation of the whole.

But all this is to jump ahead of our story. These fissures were not immediately obvious in the eighteenth century. Fletcher's premature death robbed his thought of some impetus and Wesley tended to be dominant, with some pockets of Fletcher's influence in his own circles and in such works as the spiritual autobiography of Hester Ann Rogers. Some have tried to suggest that there was no tension between Wesley and Fletcher, but their correspondence indicates that they were both clear on their differences over the doctrine of 'Pentecostal sanctification'.

In a letter to Fletcher dated 22 March 1775, Wesley described their differences in these words:

It seems our views on Christian Perfection are a little different, though not opposite. It is certain that every babe in Christ has received the Holy Ghost, and the Spirit witnesses with his spirit that he is a child of God. But he has not obtained Christian Perfection.

And three years later, on 7 March 1778, Fletcher would write to his future wife, Mary Bosanquet along the same lines:

You will find my views of this matter in Mr. Wesley's sermons on Christian Perfection and on Scriptural Christianity; with this difference, that I would distinguish more exactly between the believer baptized with the Pentecostal power of the Holy Ghost, and the believer who, like the Apostles after our Lord's ascension, is not yet filled with that power.

But the greater divergence of these positions is a story that took place on the American scene, and it is to North America that we must now turn.

North America and the Rise of the Holiness Movement

The Wesleyan movement may have been born in England, but there is a sense that it found its destiny in North America. At the time of the Revolution, Methodism was an unorganized movement on the margins of American culture. By 1840 it had overtaken the burgeoning Baptists by a ratio of ten to six and by a similar ratio the total membership combined of the Presbyterian, Congregational, Episcopal, Lutheran, and Reformed churches. Methodism also set the tone for other denominations, contributing to the emergence of the 'evangelical' wing of Episcopalianism and 'New School' or revivalist Presbyterianism. Illustrative of the latter is the development of 'Oberlin Perfectionism' in Presbyterian and Congregationalist circles. In the late 1830s at Ohio's Oberlin College president Asa Mahan and evangelist Charles Grandison Finney, professor of theology, under the influence of reading Wesley and Fletcher, began to advocate a doctrine of 'Christian perfection' very similar to Methodism. It is not too much to say that for a century Methodism was the dominant Protestant Influence in North America, so much so that the nineteenth century through the First World War (and beyond!) has often been called, even by non-Methodists, the 'Methodist Age in American History'.

It was also in the 1830s that we find currents that would culminate in what we now call the Holiness Movement, the middle term between Methodism and Pentecostalism. Debates continue about the shape of antebellum Methodism and the extent to which one finds the motifs of 'Christian perfection' in the preaching of the era. There is a sociological sense in which the preaching of a deeper Christian experience prospers in later generations of a movement when the power of 'conversion' has dimmed for those raised as Christians. On the other hand, the boundless optimism of the young nation provided a context for the proliferation of varieties of 'perfectionism' and social and utopian experimentation. But, for whatever reason, from the 1830s we can trace an increased interest in the theme of 'entire sanctification' both within and beyond the boundaries of Methodism.

An early harbinger of this movement was the publication of *The Christian's Manual; A Treatise on Christian Perfection, with Directions for Achieving that State* (1825) by Timothy Merritt of Boston and published by the Methodist Episcopal Church. This miniature volume consisted of selections mainly from Wesley but also from Fletcher. In 1839 Merritt founded *The Guide to Christian Perfection,* a periodical that was later edited by Phoebe Palmer in New York City as *The Guide to Holiness.* There it served to promote the theme of 'entire sanctification' that was being cultivated in Palmer's parlour 'Tuesday Meeting for the Promotion of Holiness'. Both the meeting and the periodical had numerous imitators throughout the nineteenth century across the continent.

Historian Mel Dieter has suggested that the Holiness Movement is best understood as the confluence of Finneyite revivalism and the populist side of Methodism protesting the antebellum *embourgeoisement* of the church. This is somewhat negatively confirmed by a mantra of the Tuesday Meeting that claimed that it was not Wesley and Fletcher nor Finney and Mahan but the Bible only that was studied in their gatherings. This conjunction is also revealed in the shape of Palmer's teaching. The theologies of Jonathan Edwards and Charles Grandison Finney are often contrasted with the comment that Edwards prayed for an 'awakening' that would be bestowed in God's own time according to the inscrutable sovereign will, while Finney set to work to produce a 'revival' that could be brought about by the utilization of the 'appropriate means' because God was always ready to visit those who turned to the divine. There is a similar contrast between Wesley and Palmer. For Wesley, 'entire sanctification' was the culmination of the Christian life. Palmer's 'shorter way' bypassed the complexity of this process in her 'altar theology', which suggested that God would be faithful in bestowing the 'blessing' on those who asked for it. (Interestingly, in light of the later caricatures of the movement, this theology was a response to those who felt no 'emotion' in the experience; they were encouraged to believe in the faithfulness of God and trust that they had received the 'blessing' even when this was not accompanied by feeling.)

The Holiness Movement moved west with the frontier, often in an increasingly radical form. In addition to innumerable periodicals and parlour meetings, the major instrument of propagation was founded in 1867 as the National Camp Meeting Association, which held regular encampments starting in New Jersey and moving west through Pennsylvania and beyond. Many regional, state, and local 'holiness associations' were founded along with literally hundreds of camp meetings. (Some Methodist historiography ignores this stream, suggesting that the camp meeting had a substantial influence in antebellum Methodism but died out about the time of the Civil War, when actually the later nineteenth century was the period of its greatest cultural influence.) With the western expansion the influence of the more 'conservative' east (that is, the more traditionally Methodist wing of the movement) was diluted by the rise of a more radical stream that picked up themes of divine healing and dispensational eschatology in spite of the leadership of the National Camp Meeting Association which forbade the discussion of such topics at officially sanctioned camps.

By the end of the nineteenth century a complex movement had been formed. This included major pockets of continuing influence within Methodism, especially those centred in independent camp meetings around the country (Indian Springs in Georgia, Camp Sychar in Ohio, Redlands in California, etc.) and colleges founded by the movement (such as Taylor University, the Asbury institutions in Wilmore, Kentucky, and so on). The Black Methodist churches showed profound influence from these themes. Some Methodist splits, especially the Abolitionist Wesleyan and Free Methodist churches, were swept into the movement. Some independent Holiness churches, most notably the Church of God (Anderson, Indiana) were formed. The Salvation Army was founded in England out of more radical forms of Methodism and under the influence of American Holiness figures—and in North America confirmed and extended its commitment to the Holiness Movement, culminating in membership in the Christian Holiness Association (CHA). The fragments of the Holiness Movement began to coalesce by an agglutinative process into more traditional denominational forms (the Church of the Nazarene, perhaps the archetypal Holiness church, the Pilgrim Holiness Church, and others often rooted in the interdenominational overflow of the

Holiness Movement into Congregational, Presbyterian, Baptist, and Quaker circles). Various smaller groups of Quakers (several yearly meetings that later called themselves the Evangelical Friends Alliance) and Anabaptist-like groups (the Brethren in Christ, various tributaries of the United Missionary Church, and so forth) fell deeply under the influence of the Holiness Movement, some to the point of joining the CHA. Many key figures of what became the evangelical movement were essentially Holiness in orientation (Presbyterian A. B. Simpson of the Christian and Missionary Alliance, Baptist A. J. Gordon behind Gordon College and Seminary outside Boston, and so forth). The evangelical world was deeply influenced by a moderate form of the holiness teaching associated with the town of Keswick in the Lake District of England. In fact, like the charismatic movement of our own time, the spirit of the Holiness Movement became a determinative influence in late nineteenth century North America.

The Holiness Movement has been neglected in American, Methodist, and evangelical historiography—so much so that many things (among them the ministry of women, the 'social gospel', and other currents) are not yet well understood. This is also true demographically. The United Methodist Church has now just under 9 million members, but on a given Sunday only about a third of these are in church. Holiness churches often have attendance figures larger than membership (thus the extremely high statistics of per capita giving reported in the National Council of Churches *Yearbook*). Taken together there may be more persons in distinctly Holiness churches on a given Sunday than in United Methodist Churches in the United States. The grandchildren and the great-grandchildren of Wesley are certainly more numerous than his children in the faith.

Robert Anderson, in the original Columbia University dissertation that became *The Vision of the Disinherited*, has commented that when the Holiness Movement and Pentecostalism are fully incorporated into fundamentalist and evangelical historiography, the results will be revolutionary and the whole will have to be redone. As things stand now, the divisions within Protestantism (producing what Martin Marty has called the 'two-party system' reflected by the National Council of Churches and the National Association of Evangelicals) are usually interpreted through the experience of Baptists and Presbyterians in the fundamentalist/modernist controversy in the 1920s resulting in a 'conservative/liberal paradigm'. This construction is not useful for the interpretation of the Holiness Movement and its radicalization into Pentecostalism. In many ways the Holiness Movement is not so much a conservative form of Methodism as a more radical form. Most of the Holiness churches were founded in struggles over social issues (abolitionism, the ministry to the poor in the style of the Salvation Army, the ministry of women, etc.) in which mainstream Methodism was the 'conservative' party. When the Methodist experience is properly used as the lens for the interpretation of the nineteenth-century America, the formation of the Holiness Movement will become the paradigm for the interpretation of the larger 'evangelical' movement. Attention will be shifted away from the twentieth century (and the formation of the Ortho-dox Presbyterian Church within the Presbyterian tradition) to the late nineteenth century and the Holiness Movements (and within Presbyterianism to the Christian and Missionary Alliance).

This will require radical reorientations in thinking. Such issues as millennialism and the 'higher Christian life' will be restored to central defining themes. The coalition of the NAE (three quarters Holiness and Pentecostal in denominational membership) will make more sense. 'Evangelicalism' will be better interpreted through a 'Pentecostal' historiography that recognizes that evangelicalism is a small minority of a much larger current shaped by the monumental growth of Pentecostalism in the twentieth century. And it will become clear that Pentecos-talism is a very natural outgrowth of the currents that took shape in the late nineteenth century under the influence of the Holiness Movement.

THE EMERGENCE OF PENTECOSTALISM

We now return to the conflicts between Wesley and Fletcher at the end of the eighteenth century in England. When Methodism came to America, it was defined by both Wesley and Fletcher, though the conflicts remained largely subliminal. The works of Fletcher were printed in America early in the nineteenth century. *The Christian's Manual*, perhaps the founding document of the Holiness Movement, included texts from both Wesley and Fletcher.

Supported by the optimism of the antebellum era, the language of perfection remained dominant—and Wesley was perhaps misread in terms of a more exclusive emphasis on 'perfection'. Most sermons on the theme included an excruciating list of denials—that the topic did not imply absolute, Adamic, angelic, Edenic (and so on) but 'Christian' perfection. The early writings of the Oberlin theology, typified by Asa Mahan's *Scripture Doctrine of Christian Perfection* (1839), used this language—though pneumatological language and hints of a doctrine of the 'baptism of the Holy Spirit' occasionally surfaced, as they also sometimes did within Methodism.

By mid-century the weight was beginning to shift towards Fletcher and motifs rooted in the images of Pentecost. In 1856 Irish Methodist and Conference President William Arthur published *The Tongue of Fire* which climaxed in a prayer:

And now, adorable Spirit, proceeding from the Father and the Son, descend upon all the Churches, renew the Pentecost in this our age, and Baptize thy people generally—O, baptize them yet again with tongues of fire! Crown this nineteenth century with a revival of 'pure and undefiled religion' greater than that of the last century, greater than that of the first, greater than any 'demonstration of the Spirit' ever yet vouchsafed to men.

This book, published in the USA by Harper Brothers, became immensely popular, requiring seventeen editions before the end of the decade (a publishing record that continued into the twentieth century where it was kept in print by the publishing houses of both Northern and Southern Methodism, various Holiness publishers, and under the imprint of independent Holiness and Methodist evangelists). It was a favourite of Walter Rauschenbusch of the 'social gospel' movement who reviewed it and gave copies to friends. Arthur was correcting the proofs of the book on an American tour in 1855—and no doubt preaching along the same line.

Phoebe Palmer turned to Pentecostal imagery in her large volume, *The Promise of the Father* (1859), simultaneously a defence of the ministry of women and an articulation of the doctrine of 'Pentecostal sanctification'—under the subtitle 'a neglected specialty of the latter days'. Her preaching during a tour of England reported in *Four Years in the Old World* (1866) reveals similar patterns. And in 1870 Asa Mahan of Oberlin, now at Methodist Adrian College (jointly sponsored by the Wesleyan Methodists and the Methodist Protestants), published some of his chapel addresses during the preceding decade as *The Baptism of the Holy Ghost*, teaching the doctrine of 'entire sanctification' in a 'form old and yet new'. Significantly, this book was published by the Palmers, giving it the apparent endorsement of the Methodistic side of the Movement. In England it was published with an appendix containing a lecture by evangelist Finney on the theme. These editions circulated around the world with a number of publishers and translations, resulting in one of the most influential books of the period.

By February of 1874, Daniel Steele, two years after leaving the presidency of Syracuse University, would testify in Phoebe Palmer's *The Guide to Holiness* to his own experience of 'entire sanctification' as a 'baptism of the Holy Spirit'. He advised Methodists to 'cease to discuss the subtleties and endless questions arising from entire sanctification or Christian perfection'. He urged all to 'cry mightily to God for the Baptism of the Holy Spirit ... promised to all believers in Jesus'.

Such tendencies and rhetoric snowballed through the rest of the century and contributed to growing tensions within Methodism. Many Methodists were beginning to critique the doctrine of 'entire sanctification', especially in the more reductionist form preached in the camp meetings. The holiness emphasis was increasingly seen there as a hobby or speciality that would draw Methodism into too narrow a focus. In the South Methodists began to pass legislation that allowed the superintendents and bishops to curtail Holiness meetings by independent evangelists. Such practices led eventually to the formation of new distinctly Holiness denominations. In these passionate Holiness circles Fletcher's doctrine of 'Pentecostal sanctification' prospered. The Holiness Movement became fixated on 'Pentecostal' rhetoric, so much so that in January 1897 *The Guide to Holiness* changed its subtitle from 'and revival miscellany' to 'and the Pentecostal life', and claimed 'that the "Pentecostal idea" is pervading Christian thought and life more than ever before'. Sermons were published in a column entitled the 'Pentecostal

Pulpit', testimonies as 'Pentecostal Testimonies', and reports of women's activities under the rubric 'Pentecostal Womanhood'.

As the doctrine of 'entire sanctification' declined in mainstream Methodism, the doctrine of the 'baptism of the Holy Spirit' grew in influence in Holiness Movement and also in the wider revivalistic culture. In the Holiness Movement Pentecost was seen as a moment of 'entire sanctification', the doctrine of 'Pentecostal sanctification'. But this was not without its strains. There was an increasing awareness that the Lukan texts taught more the theme of 'power' than 'purity'. The topic was tackled by A. M. Hills, an Oberlin-oriented Congregationalist who became the first theologian of the Church of the Nazarene, in *Holiness and Power* (1897), a veritable catalogue of the late nineteenth-century's views on the question. Many Holiness advocates solved this problem by speaking of a negative side (sanctification) and a positive side (empowerment), the 'cleansing' that was required before the 'filling'.

This resolution of the problem did not always work. On the experiential level, some seemed to have 'purity' but not 'power'—and vice versa. Some handled the question by breaking down 'Pentecostal sanctification' into two experiences, resulting in what came to be known in Holiness circles as 'the three-blessing heresy'. This was advocated by B. H. Irwin in the Midwest (especially Kansas) and R. C. Horner in Canada who contributed to the founding of three denominations there. Both were associated with the cultivation of 'physical manifestations'. Irwin published an attack (also issued as a pamphlet) on the 'pyrophobia' of the more traditional Holiness Movement. Horner was more literate and wrote articulately about the history of the doctrine of 'Pentecostal sanctification' with full awareness that Wesley did not approve of this development.

But the doctrine of the 'baptism of the Holy Spirit' also found wide acceptance outside the Holiness Movement, especially in the tradition of 'modern revivalism' with its roots in the work of Charles Grandison Finney, who late in his life explicitly taught the doctrine with an emphasis on the 'empowerment' of the experience. The revivalist tradition generally suppressed the elements of 'purity' in favour of 'power'. In this form the doctrine appears as a minor theme in the ministry of D. L. Moody, but was brought to the fore by R. A. Torrey, his assistant and superintendent of Moody Bible Institute in Chicago (and later of the Bible Institute of Los Angeles— the antecedent of today's Biola University). Torrey considered the teaching, along with an emphasis on biblical authority, as key to Moody's success. His book on *The Baptism with the Holy Spirit* (1895) described a number of biblical synonyms for the experience ('filled', 'gift', 'empowered', etc.) and argued for the definiteness of the experience (one would know whether one had received it), its subsequence (i.e. distinct from conversion), but its character as 'empowerment for witness and service' (rather than 'sanctification'). Interestingly, Torrey was a Yale classmate of A. M. Hills—intimate to the point of being involved in weddings and ordination services of each other, and their conflict over this question is a key illustration of the break of the revivalist tradition into a fundamentalist and a holiness wing.

This theme, often in a more moderate form of being 'filled with the Spirit', has continued to be characteristic of the revivalist tradition and descendants in the 'neo-evangelical' movement of the mid-twentieth century. It is not often noticed that Campus Crusade for Christ, the international organization of the late Bill Bright, was known for passing out two little pamphlets, not only the better-known 'Four Spiritual Laws' but also one on 'How to be Filled with the Spirit'. Such phenomena are clear evidence of the roots of neo-evangelicalism in the Holiness Movement and its continuing affinity with Pentecostalism and the 'Pentecostal hermeneutic'. Such facts reveal the usefulness, again, of reading the evangelical movement through the prism of the Holiness and Pentecostal Movements.

But the basic point is that the late nineteenth-century revivalist tradition was suffused by several understandings of a 'baptism with the Holy Spirit'. These ranged from the Holiness equation of the experience with 'entire sanctification' through the 'three-blessing' teaching to the more moderate revivalist understanding of 'empowerment for service'. One needs only to add the practice of 'speaking in tongues' to have full-blown Pentecostalism, whose fissures and theological struggles reveal the problems inherited by this diversity.

The formal emergence of Pentecostalism took place at the turn of the twentieth century in Topeka, Kansas, at a bible school founded by Charles Parham, an independent Methodist evangelist in the Holiness tradition. As he reported, 'In December of 1900 we had our examination upon the subject of repentance, conversion, consecration, sanctification, healing, and the soon coming of the Lord.' Parham was about to leave the school for revival meetings. He noted that 'we had reached in our studies a problem. What about the second chapter of Acts?' He left the students with an assignment: to study 'the bible evidence of the baptism of the Holy Ghost'. When posed in this way, the question admitted of only one answer. The students concluded that it was 'speaking in tongues', and Agnes Ozman had the experience, thereby initiating the Pentecostal Movement that would overwhelm the Christian world in the twentieth century, claiming as much as a quarter of the Christian population (perhaps as much as half a billion).

Vinson Synan, historian from the Pentecostal Holiness Church (the original denomination of Oral Roberts before he joined the United Methodist Church), claims that for the first decade, the Pentecostal Movement remained clearly Holiness in character, largely in the 'three-blessing' Holiness stream of Pentecostalism that has prospered in the South. This was certainly true at the Azusa Street Revival that launched the Pentecostal Movement into a global movement. W. J. Seymour, an African American who had circulated through other streams of the Holiness Movement (the Church of God, Anderson, Indiana, and probably God's Bible School in Cincinnati), studied with Parham at another bible college in Houston (though prevented by segregationist 'Jim Crow' laws from actually sitting in the classroom) before migrating to Los Angeles to become the major force behind Azusa Street.

It is no accident that the Azusa Street revival took place in Los Angeles. The city is often interpreted through its Spanish/Mexican Catholic heritage, but in the early years of the twentieth century, it was a hotbed of the Holiness currents that prospered at the time. Even Hollywood was founded as something of a communal movement by temperance (and probably Holiness) Methodists. What is now downtown Los Angeles had within a few blocks Black Holiness churches, a Baptist Holiness congregation, the 'glory barn' (the mother church of the Church of the Nazarene), the location of an extended tent revival of the Church of God (Anderson, Indiana), the Peniel Mission (and other rescue missions in the Holiness tradition), and so on. Half way to Pasadena on the Arroyo Seco was a community of Free Methodists on the east side, a camp ground in the park along the arroyo, and on the west side a community founded by a Methodist doctor from Denver who eventually joined the Pentecostal movement. Adjacent to the site of Azusa Street is now the Japanese Union Church associated with the family that founded the Japanese Holiness Church. And the region had a strong community of Holiness Quakers (the spiritual home of Richard Nixon).

When Seymour came to Los Angeles, he went first to the Holiness churches, but was locked out of the church that he thought he was called to pastor when the congregation heard his message of tongues. He floated around Los Angeles, especially on Bonnie Brae Street (which now ends a few blocks away on Glendale Avenue at the site of the 5,000-seat Angelus Temple that Aimee Semple McPherson would construct fifteen years later) and eventually settled in a stable on Azusa Street that had once served as a Black Methodist Church, now under the plaza of the Japanese/American Cultural Center.

The experience of 'speaking in tongues' split the Holiness churches and resulted in intense struggles over turf. Theological polemics broke out. The Pentecostal Church of the Nazarene would drop the term 'Pentecostal' and struggle to disassociate itself from the new movement. 'Churches of God' would add the headquarters to their names to make the distinction (Anderson, Indiana, to indicate strictly Holiness; Cleveland, Tennessee, to indicate Holiness Pentecostal, for example). But the Holiness culture would persist in the Pentecostal Movement. Almost all the Black Holiness churches went Pentecostal so that in the African-American tradition a 'sanctified' church is Pentecostal, and the large Church of God in Christ and the smaller United Holy Church of America (the spiritual home of James Forbes, recently retired pastor of New York's Riverside Church) reveal Holiness origins. In the white holiness community, fewer churches went Pentecostal, resulting in a continuing Holiness Movement that ranks in the top ten statistically of streams of Christianity around the world. Only recently has the hostility between the Holiness Movement and Pentecostalism begun to wane, at least on the academic level (the Wesleyan Theological Society and the Society for Pentecostal Studies now hold a joint meeting every five years).

The most influential Pentecostal Church in North America is the Assemblies of God, which claims a 'Reformed' identity (in part a product of efforts to assimilate into evangelical culture and move beyond Holiness behavioural and dress legalisms). Its historians minimize the roots of the denomination in the Holiness Movement, claiming to be followers of William Durham, the pastor of a Pentecostal mission in Chicago, who taught a 'finished work' doctrine of sanctification. They interpret Durham as an evangelical, teaching a gradual sanctification after conversion. I am convinced this is mistaken. Durham's 'finished work' theology is more like that of Moravian Count Zinzendorf in his conflicts with Wesley. Durham taught that all God promised was bestowed in conversion, including 'entire sanctification'. The 'fundamental truths' of the Assemblies of God contained an article on 'entire sanctification'. I am told that this statement was something of a compromise. Nearly all affirmed 'entire sanctification'; the difference was over the method by which it was received, some teaching the Wesleyan/Holiness 'second blessing' while others taught the 'finished work' that all was received in 'conversion'. This article was modified in several steps in the twentieth century to approximate the evangelical position, but it remains a testimony to the Wesleyan/Holiness roots of even this more 'Reformed' wing of Pentecostalism.

In recent years the growing theological awareness of third-world Pentecostalism has resulted in a 'post-colonial' theory of Pentecostal origins that argues for a simultaneous polygenesis of the movement around the world. I am sympathetic to this tendency. My own analysis of the way in which the global Holiness Movement prepared the way for Pentecostalism helps explain how this can be so. The advocates of 'polygenesis' are, however, not able to detach Pentecostalism from Holiness antecedents.

In Chile, for example, Pentecostalism is intensely Methodist in character, though it is often offered as an illustration of an 'indigenous' (i.e. not missionary) Pentecostalism. Chilean Methodism has its roots in the work of William Taylor, a maverick Methodist Missionary Bishop identified with the Holiness Movement. Taylor tended to found self-supporting and self-governing churches around the world (including India and Africa—he was the American 'bishop of Africa'). The Methodist mission board tended to follow him around the world, bringing these congregations back under North American control. It has been suggested that the outbreak of Pentecostalism under the ministry of North American doctor W. C. Hoover in the Methodist church of Valparaiso outside Santiago masked an effort to reassert the independence that Taylor had encouraged. In Chile over 90 per cent of Protestantism is Pentecostal, and the Roman Catholic Church is increasingly nervous about the fact that on a given Sunday there may be as many Pentecostals in church as Catholics. Another interesting Chilean Pentecostal church is the *Iglesia Wesleyana*, founded by Victor Mora in the mining district and named to honour Wesley's work among miners in Northern England. Newspapers marvel over members who don't smoke or drink, speak in tongues, and vote socialist. Victor Mora was a member of the 'junta' of Allende's socialist party in Chile.

Another major illustration of polygenesis sometimes offered is the Pune Revival in India under Pandita Ramabai, founder of a community for widows and prostitutes. Advocates of the independence of this movement sometimes slight the fact that her assistant was Minnie Abrams, a Holiness Methodist figure who had been a classmate of Mrs Hoover and continued to correspond with her. Interpreters of Pandita Ramabai often neglect her Holiness connections. She was, for example, a friend of founder B. T. Roberts of the Free Methodist Church and sent her daughter to study at what is now Roberts Wesleyan College in upstate New York. Similar analyses can be made of the Holiness and Methodist roots of other Pentecostal outbreaks that were not a direct product of the influence of Azusa Street.

CONCLUSION

I hope that I have demonstrated what I suggested at the beginning of this chapter: that neither Methodism nor Pentecostalism can be fully understood without reference to the other. Historically, they are like 'Siamese twins' bound to each other while fighting for their own identities. Free Methodist Howard Snyder has argued in *The Divided Flame* that the two movements need each other—that purity and power must be rejoined. He may be right; in some places Methodism has lost its 'power' and recent scandals in Pentecostalism may reveal a lack of 'purity'. But whatever one makes of this constructive proposal, the historical connections are clear and ought to be acknowledged on both sides.

SUGGESTED READING

ANDERSON, ROBERT MAPES (1979). *Vision of the Disinherited: The Making of American Pentecostalism*. New York: Oxford University Press.

ARTHUR, WILLIAM (1920). *The Tongue of Fire: The True Power of Christianity*. Nashville, Tenn.: Publishing House of the M.E. Church, South.

DAYTON, DONALD (1987). *The Theological Roots of Pentecostalism*. Grand Rapids, Mich.: Francis Asbury Press.

DIETER, MELVIN EASTERDAY (1996). *The Holiness Revival of the Nineteenth Century*. Lanhan, Md.: Scarecrow Press.

SNYDER, HOWARD A. (1986). *The Divided Flame: Wesleyans and the Charismatic Renewal*. Grand Rapids, Mich.: Francis Asbury Press.

WOOD, LAWRENCE W. (1980). *Pentecostal Grace*. Wilmore, Ky.: Francis Asbury Press.

CHAPTER 11

'THE WORLD IS MY PARISH'

METHODISM AND THE ROOTS OF WORLD CHRISTIAN AWAKENING

LAMIN SANNEH

OLD WORLD ORDER

METHODISM's roots in the Great Awakening dovetailed with great consequence with other contemporary historical movements to set the long-term course of Christianity's rise in its current post-Western phase. The Protestant Reformation restricted Christianity to Europe's prickly scruples, as Hilaire Belloc indicated with his assertion that 'Europe is the faith', and, in its mission, that the faith was Europe. Christianity's domestication in Europe was compounded by its colonial captivity abroad, and that double jeopardy hampered the religion for much of the period up to the end of the colonial empires. In the long, bleak centuries before the founding of Christian settlements among littoral populations, European missions focused on the conversion of rulers, chiefs, princes, and members of the nobility as the basis of church planting and European expansion because it was a similar structural model that accounted for the conversion of Europe. In that era wealthy dukes, princes, and the nobility endowed churches, monasteries, and other religious foundations to spread Christianity, thereby enabling the religion to rise by political sponsorship.

An early example of this process was the rule of Charlemagne (d. 814), who, crowned as Holy Roman Emperor on Christmas Day, AD 800, baptized the Saxons by 'platoons'. Understanding himself as the Christian 'caliph' who would replicate in the West the imperial religious establishment of his Abbásid Muslim peers in the East, Charlemagne took Christianity out of the sacristy and made it a monarchical theocracy as 'Christendom', as territorial prescription under a single divinely sanctioned prince (Rahner 1992; see also Pirenne 1968). (Theodosius created a Christian orthodox state but stopped short of divine kingship, as Ambrose's successful challenge to his authority demonstrated.) In that scheme the political ruler was God's appointed agent, the herald and instrument of God's earthly mission, like Bertha, queen of Kent, who, according to the guide for visitors, kept 'the flame of Christianity burning in pagan times'. Political affairs and religious matters were intertwined, with the political strand laying down the pattern of conformity for religion. In this arrangement state authority had precedence over ecclesiastical authority, with political orthodoxy the boundary marker for ecclesiastical jurisdiction.

Eventually the great religious orders consolidated Christianity in the empire, integrating aspects of primitive folk religion, Roman and Gallic practices, and ancient ideas of the ties between the living and the dead with the new Christian teachings. As Christopher Dawson (1950, 1994) argues, Europe owed its identity to the legacy of the Roman Empire, the Classical heritage, and the Catholic Church. This working synthesis was promptly carried to West Africa in the three centuries between 1470 and 1785 and attempted in the old kingdoms of Elmina, Warri, Benin, and the Kongo, among others, but without success. Feudal or dynastic, Africa's political development had not advanced to the same degree or even along comparable lines to allow it to follow Europe into the faith. The colonial empires that arrived on the heels of the Atlantic slave trade were at best a mixed blessing for mission. Thus the drive to export establishment Christianity failed, and whatever achievements remained of those pioneer centuries were absorbed and reconstituted in the new phase.

NEW WORLD ORDER

This new phase had as one of its formative influences the eighteenth-century evangelical awakening whose coalescence with anti-slavery and other social movements produced a profound shift in moral sentiments and ignited a Transatlantic campaign against the slave trade. As far back as the seventeenth century anti-slavery sentiments circulated freely in religious and humanitarian circles. Thus did the American Jesuit, Alonso de Sandoval, denounce slavery in 1610 as a violation of the God-given right of human freedom. Slavery, he contended, was rife with everything that degraded human beings, and, as such, stood condemned in God's law (Williams 1969: 44). Similarly, the exertions in the 1680s of Lourenço da Silva de Mendouça, an Afro-Brazilian, on behalf of his fellow blacks held in slavery in Brazil and Lisbon made a deep impact on the Papal Curia, leading it to issue a strong condemnation of slavery and the slave trade (Gray 1990: 11–27).

Though significant on their own terms, these anti-slavery exertions, however, had little effect because they never attained social scale, and so they never broke surface to fashion a historical movement. That happened only from the mid-eighteenth century when throngs of Africans, slave and free, flocked to revival religion and imbibed the message of itinerant Methodist or Methodist-inspired preachers and lay leaders. The coming of the American Revolution handed these blacks the welcome opportunity of combining religion with freedom, and thus with the Transatlantic anti-slavery efforts then gathering momentum, particularly in England. The new language of religion was seeded with sentiments of the moral elevation of those held in bondage and captivity, a view very different from Old World notions of society and religion in which, as David Brion Davis (2006) has argued, slavery and bondage were accorded a respectable place. In that old order few questioned the place of slavery in the workings of civilized society, and it was that settled consensus and its supporting Christian frame that the evangelical movement and its humanitarian allies disrupted once and for all. Various strategies designed to resist anti-slavery and to preserve the Christian status quo availed little.

This explains the appeal of evangelical religion to slaves, captives, and free blacks, among others, and, thanks to the work of John and Charles Wesley, popular evangelical piety soon possessed a growing corpus of hymns and songs, with the music and movement to go with them, which was the most substantial yet in any modern language and that, for the first time, connected Christianity to slaves and captives' yearning for physical and spiritual deliverance. The free-floating sentiment about poor suffering Africans and the flickering impulse of its amelioration hardened into a robust organized religious and humanitarian response. The work of the Wesleys met this rising need with lucid force and steady focus. Their newly minted hymns and songs did not rely on learning or high culture for the ability to understand them, while the music made their memorization virtually a routine of regular usage and habit.

GIFT OF TONGUES

As a northern European language, English soon acquired in diaspora communities the force of a vernacular idiom as pidgin English, Krio, Gullah, and other dialects and variants. What the Wesleys did was to crystallize with lyrical brilliance the imperishable and homebred vernacular of the faith and devotion of common people by establishing religion in hymn and song in the living habits and practices of worshippers, to the scandal of establishment society. Accordingly, John Wesley claimed popular hymnody as the original contribution of Methodism. On the occasion in 1779 of commissioning a new hymnal, 'one comprised in so moderate a compass, as to be neither cumbersome nor expensive', he affirmed, 'As but a small part of these hymns is of my own composing, I do not think it inconsistent with modesty to declare, that I am persuaded no such hymn-book as this has yet been published in the English language.' In piety and poetry, to amend Wesley's own language, evangelical Methodism gave English Christianity unprecedented popular access and cross-cultural range and effect, including interdenominational appeal. As John Wesley put it, the original design of the Methodists was 'not to be a distinct party, but to stir up all parties, to worship God in spirit and in truth. With this view I have uniformly gone on for fifty years, never varying from the doctrine of the Church [of England] at all; nor from her discipline, of choice, but of necessity.' Roman Catholicism, however, remained a stumbling block for evangelical religion, though in the slave diaspora the doctrinal hackles were considerably blunted. In mitigation mention may be made, too, of a sermon John Wesley preached on 'Catholic Spirit', based on the text of 2 Kings 10: 15:

And when he was departed thence, he lighted on Jehonadab the son of Rechab coming to meet him, and he saluted him, and said to him, Is thine heart right, as my heart is with thy heart? And Jehonadab answered: It is. If it be, give me thine hand.

In that sermon Wesley roundly rejected latitudinarianism, declaring 'that a catholic spirit is not speculative latitudinarianism', and dwelled at length on the importance of ecumenical solidarity with Christians of other churches.

At any rate, having come under the influence of Granville Sharp and Anthony Benezet, John Wesley wrote an anti-slavery tract in 1774 called *Thoughts Upon Slavery* where he advanced arguments based on natural justice and natural law, quite apart from any religious reasons, to condemn slavery. Such was the appeal of the tract that it went into four editions within a year, being disseminated to Methodist society groups in every part of Britain. In a piece he wrote in 1775, *Calm Address to Our American Colonies*, Wesley turned his attention to the American colonies, saying the Americans' struggle for political freedom was an open contradiction of their continuing enslavement of Africans. In that view, enslavement was a moral offence more grave than colonial rule.

Now that he had raised the anti-slavery issue, Wesley recognized that his earlier remonstrations against Methodist involvement in political affairs must be set aside. In 1776 he followed up with a pamphlet entitled *A Seasonal Address to the More Serious Part of the Inhabitants of Great Britain* where he called the slave trade 'a trade of blood, [which] has stained our land with blood!' He returned to the subject in 1778 with a *Serious Address to the People of England with Regard to the State of the Nation* in which he described slavery as the greatest national reproach. When the Society for the Abolition of the Slave Trade was formed in 1787, anti-slavery was given renewed impetus after a hiatus of several years. By the time of John Wesley's death in 1791 Methodism had become an intercontinental anti-slavery powerhouse, and few things epitomized the new spirit better than the republication in 1788 of Hannah Moore's poem against slavery in the *Arminian Magazine*. The sentiments of Moore's poem ran like a fault line in the hard crust of establishment resistance to abolition. Charles Wesley followed in Moore's footsteps and published a similar poem in the *Arminian Magazine* that became a mouthpiece of the cause.

The authorities attacked evangelical religion as tending to social insubordination, i.e. as a sop to notions of racial equality. Thus did an Anglican clergyman of Salem, Massachusetts, deride the Great Awakening as pandering to blacks and other social rejects:

So great has been the enthusiasm created by [John] Wesley and [George] Whitefield and [Gilbert] Tennent, that people talk of nothing but, 'renovating, regeneration, conviction and conversion'. Even children 8–13 assemble in bodies preaching and praying, nay the very Servants and Slaves pretend to extraordinary inspiration, and under the veil thereof cherish their idle dispositions and in lieu of dutifully minding their respective businesses run rambling about to utter enthusiastic nonsense.   (Raboteau 1978: 129)

That highbrow putdown is echoed in another prickly dismissal of the Protestant Reformation itself. The Reformation's reliance on the Scripture in the vernacular gave the Bible an explosive and disintegrating effect by placing the book 'into the hands of the commonality and interpreted no longer by the well-conditioned learned, but by the faith and delusion, the common sense and uncommon nonsense, of all sorts of men' (Elton 1964: 52). Luther's completed translation of the Bible was not published until 1534. A contrasting and more lenient view is offered by the Oxford historian, Christopher Hill, to the effect that the translated Bible appealed to the revolutionary social principle of instituting 'the vulgar tongue' of the people as the common standard of faith and worship. Consequently, 'the availability of the Bible in English was a great stimulus to learning to read...It was a cultural revolution of unprecedented proportions, whose consequences are difficult to over-estimate' (Hill 1994: 11).

CUMULATIVE IMPETUS

It cannot be denied that the progressive anti-slavery views of the Methodist leaders had undoubtedly a pragmatic basis in society: the alliance with the new urban classes and with the emerging mobile middle class; the use of tracts and pamphlets as propaganda assets; plugging into the network of society meetings as transfer points; aligning with the new forces of industrial and urban innovation; harnessing habits of sobriety, frugality, and discipline for maximum social effect; making strategic use of lay agency; and capitalizing on the increasingly active role of women in society—Lady Selina Hastings, the Countess of Huntingdon, Hannah Moore, Dorothy Ripley, Phyllis Wheatley—all these had been instrumental in giving shape and substance to the movement and to the larger society.

Yet faith and moral leadership were equally important, and together caused a shift in moral attitudes, demonstrating the persuasive power of moral discourse about human nature and the obligations of a common humanity. Equality was given an ethical superstructure, and justice a common point of reference, and that made robust moral intervention against wrong and injustice necessary and justified.

The disdain of polite society for evangelical religion is longstanding, as is evident in an article in the *Edinburgh Review* of 1808. 'The wise and rational part of the Christian ministry', it asserted, 'find they have enough to do at home. But if a tinker is a devout man, he infallibly sets off for the East', William Carey being the intended butt of that remark. Such eastbound missionaries were considered 'little detachments of maniacs, benefiting us much more by their absence, than the Hindus by their beliefs' (Smith 1859: 136–7). Yet the pious display that so offends elite sensibility was the very thing that slaves utilized to create new forms of community. As Mary Kingsley observed, 'conscience, when conditioned by Christianity, is an exceedingly difficult thing for a [slave] trader to manage successfully to himself' (1964: 128). The trade persisted despite the huge toll it took because the reservoir of polite virtue and of the profit motive was too domesticated to spark a backlash. In this sphere the rules of expedience and natural advantage could not set the bounds of moral responsibility or defy establishment interests. Evangelical religion, on the other hand, was the victims' historic second chance.

REDEEMING LANGUAGE

The language of sin and redemption that suffuse so much of the Wesley hymns became emblematic of the spirit of the new age and offered a sharply defined anti-slavery idiom, one that shaped abolitionist argument. Slaves, for example, could identify with a Jesus who came 'Me from this evil world to free, To purge my sins, and loose my bands'. One of the hymns speaks directly to the condition of bondage and captivity, as follows: 'Long my imprisoned spirit lay | Fast bound in sin and nature's night; | Thine eye diffused a quickening ray, | I woke, the dungeon flamed with light; | My chains fell off, my heart was free, | I rose, went forth, and followed thee.' The sentiment resounds, for example, in these hymns of Charles Wesley:

> In want my plentiful supply,
>   In weakness my almighty power,
> In bonds my perfect liberty.
>
> Thou, O Christ, art all I want,
>   More than all in Thee I find.
> Raise the fallen, cheer the faint,
>   Heal the sick, and lead the blind.
>
> By Thine agonizing pain
>   And sweat of blood, we pray,
> By Thy dying love to man,
>   Take all our sins away:
> Burst our bonds. And set us free.
>
> Come, Thou long-expected Jesus,
>   Born to set Thy people free,
> From our fears and sins release us,
>   Let us find our rest in Thee.
> Born Thy people to deliver,
>   Born a child and yet a king,
> Born to reign in us for ever,
>   Now Thy gracious kingdom bring.

God's kingdom was transposed into the realm of freedom and deliverance from enslavement, and that idea captured in a provocative way the situation of the Africans held in bondage. At the 1780 Baltimore Conference, the Methodists adopted a resolution requiring itinerant white preachers who held slaves to promise to free them because 'slavery is contrary to the laws of God, man, and nature[is] hurtful to society; [is] contrary to the dictates of conscience and pure religion, and [is] doing that which we would not others should do to us and ours' (Raboteau 1978: 143). It is apparent that the sentiment failed to carry the object in view for we find Conference feeling the need to repeat the call in 1783 and again in 1784 when a motion was tabled appealing to Methodists 'to extirpate this abomination from among us'. Those failing to comply within twelve months were threatened with expulsion from the ranks of Methodists, while slaveholders were to be admitted to membership only after they signed an undertaking to emancipate their slaves.

Because of 'their peculiar circumstances' Virginia slaveholders were given a special dispensation of two years to comply, an indication that emancipation was a passage too difficult to pull off all at once. In the end, as both Thomas Coke and Francis Asbury admitted, slavery was too entrenched for Methodist teaching, still 'in too infantile a state', as Coke expressed it, to inveigh against. Asbury expressed a sense of mounting frustration about having to concede the reality of slavery while proclaiming the Methodist teaching that condemned it in plain terms. No wonder Asbury confessed that it was painful to have to admit to himself that he was indeed shackled to slaveholders in spite of the fact that he was born free. As long as that remained the case he was a slave to his circumstances. His Methodist scruples conflicting with his public responsibility left him more than simply a distracted Christian leader.

More than a matter of personal consistency, Asbury implied that Methodism's very raison d'être was here at stake. Along with other mainline Protestant denominations, the Methodist denomination, Asbury bemoaned, was becoming too identified with anti-slavery to be viable in white society. The price for viability, he reasoned, was for the Methodists to relent and to exchange amelioration for emancipation, in effect, to forego Methodism's anti-slavery principles in favour of the prevailing status quo. Although the leaders of the evangelical awakening were too reluctant to admit it, this retreat into the lap of moral acquiescence amounted to a desertion of the cause of New World Africans in deference to Southern interests. Still, the historic ferment of sizeable numbers of Africans flocking to revival religion for the first time was too potent to reverse. For one thing, the language of redemption and of breaking the fetters of sin was too deeply inscribed into evangelical preaching to remove by the expedience of cultural respectability, while, for another, the social scale of the African response to evangelical religion was too great to ignore. Accordingly, even when it was in contravention of civil and ecclesiastical ordinance, black preachers were licensed as lay exhorters and dispatched on itinerant tours among their fellow blacks. They acted the part of evangelists, ministers, and community organizers to their people in spite of the legal prohibition against black ordination, and that work in effect carried the revival flame into slave camps and among slave families and did far more than any other institution to create a distinctive New World black Christian culture. Historians have noted the salient fact that slave rebellions virtually ceased for much of the second half of the nineteenth century, a curious fact that may not be unconnected to the dynamics of community building and the forging of a new historical role for blacks.

As de Tocqueville analysed it, the dilemma of slavery in America was clear:

The South could, at a pinch, abolish slavery, but how could it dispose of the blacks? The North rids itself of slavery and of the slaves in one move. In the South there is no hope of attaining this double result at the same time . . . So by abolishing slavery the southerners could not succeed, as their brothers in the North have done, in advancing the Negroes gradually toward freedom; they would not be able to diminish the numbers of the blacks appreciably, and they would be left alone to keep them in check. In the course of a few years one would have a large free Negro population among an approximately equal white population.   (de Tocqueville 1969: 353, 355)

Tocqueville reasoned that as long as America remained committed to democratic freedom while upholding slavery, so long would it have to segregate itself from its black population to whom it denied freedom and equality. In that case, the full measure of democratic freedom would be diminished by continuing slavery, and in both cases America would not find the tranquillity it desired. Because evangelical religion addressed this discrepancy well, in the hands of black preachers it offered their community a viable, if a no less challenging, alternative course between the repressive disadvantages of slave rebellion and the frustrated prospects of full integration. Religion gave New World black identity a public moral standing for the first time, however often contested.

TRANSATLANTIC CHALLENGE

An equally urgent challenge confronted Christianity in West Africa, the source of much of the Transatlantic slave trade, and of the failed centuries-long Christian mission. The very values of personal salvation, moral sobriety, civic responsibility, an industrious, productive lifestyle, and an upright, ethical conduct identified with 'the society of the people called Methodists' belonged as much with the demand end of Transatlantic slavery in Europe and North America as they did with the supply end in West Africa, and in both cases they constituted a challenge to establishment interests. The evangelical awakening was, therefore, faced with a double imperative, the need for a home mission and for a corresponding foreign mission, the kind of unified missionary impulse that the Protestant Reformation succeeded too well in stifling. The resulting national churches made missionary outreach superfluous, and that contributed to the fact that Christianity was unable to avert, or even to subvert, the extensive slave exploitation of Africans and others. As such, West Africa continued within range of the European slave trade without the ameliorating intervention of the gospel. As a consequence the slave trade boomed at the time of the evangelical awakening, and it was a matter of time before attention was drawn to it at the supply end.

The ground was laid with John Wesley's own critical reflections on the obligation to carry the gospel beyond the traditional heartlands in Europe even if that included Abyssinia and China. It was an ironic observation given the fact that Abyssinia and China were both ancient Christian strongholds long before England ever was. 'If you ask on what principle I acted', Wesley explained,

it was this: 'A desire to be a Christian; and a conviction that whatever I judge conducive thereto that I am bound to do; wherever I judge I can best answer this end, thither it is my duty to go'. On this principle I set out for America; on this I visited the Moravian church;

and on the same am I ready now (God being my helper) to go to Abyssinia or China, or whithersoever it shall please God, by this conviction, to call me.   (Wesley 1980: 67)

He continued:

I look upon all the world as my parish; thus far I mean, that, in whatever part of it I am, I judge it meet, right, and my bounden duty to declare unto all that are willing to hear, the glad tidings of salvation. This is the work which I know God has called me to; and sure I am that His blessing attends it.   (*idem*)

The inauguration of what was called 'a Christian experiment' in Sierra Leone, haltingly in 1787 and more purposefully in 1792, offered the opportunity for mission abroad and outreach into the hinterland regions of West Africa. The new Sierra Leone settlement provided the basis for demonstrating the primary, special religious view of history. Its explicit evangelical matrix was Methodist in nature, with the stress on lay piety and social responsibility steeped in notions of individual liberty, personal industry, social discipline, civic activism, and moral reform of society. The practical expression of redemption and holiness was the cultivation of the associated and corroborative social habits (Miller and Johnson 1963: i. 1–79).

The central core of this view was very simple: the individual, redeemed by God, was the root and branch of society, politics, and law. The congregation as the body of the gathered saints, what the Puritans called 'the visible elect', inspired the open town meeting to which the Methodist society meeting can trace its roots. The society meeting was a governance structure within the connexional system John Wesley established for Methodism. The habit of regular church attendance and lay responsibility that the society meeting encouraged was a model for a social covenant binding the brethren. Furthermore, the language of open, personal access to God supplied the basis of equal participation in the fellowship and in society at large. People who had a notion of their equal standing before God should not establish a normative caste system among themselves, however strong the case or urge for social differentiation in other spheres of life. And since the litmus test of human welfare was one's being persuaded of God's gracious and unconditional acceptance, then a religious community worthy of the name would enshrine a free and awakened conscience as the mark of the fellowship. Thus began that decisive shift of understanding in which the end of human felicity was a matter supremely of God's prerogative, which ultimately produced the novel and productive view that redemption of human sin belonged with the rehabilitation of society (Tawney 1966: 272; Walzer 1965: 114, 118). There is nothing in this of the idea that the state had any business in the believer's relationship with God except, that is, to give public validation to the evidence of personal faith and ethical conduct (Pennington 1849: 12).

Many studies of the Methodist movement have approached the subject from a number of vantage points without necessarily showing how Methodism marked a break with Old World ideas about church, state, and society, and especially about how the Methodist phase of eighteenth-century popular, lay evangelism made a pivotal connection with the first modern mass movement into Christianity by a non-Western population, namely, the mass conversion of New World Africans. When we view the Methodist story from that point of view we gain a new perspective on Christianity's intercontinental range and effect. It was the merit of early Methodism that non-European people were being attracted to the gospel in conditions utterly unlike anything accompanying the rise of Christianity in the West. The hymns of the two Wesley brothers gave eloquent voice to the new moral sensibility that was troubling the waters beyond the West.

The fact that the Methodist awakening was contemporaneous with the anti-slavery agitation meant that Methodism's message of groaning in sin and being freed from bondage resonated powerfully with the plight of slaves and captives whose freedom was a tangible achievement of the gospel. It was for such as these that Christ came. The Methodist movement had found a destination almost as soon as it was born. Streaming through the gates the Methodist revival opened for them, Africans shared none of the sense of cultural entitlement and inhibition of Christian Europeans, while their historical circumstances of suffering, poverty, and injustice rendered them particularly prone to receive Methodist teaching about God's favour resting on the maimed and lame, both of body and spirit.

The eagerness with which Africans responded to Methodist preaching showed their affinity with the peculiar temper of Christianity's call for personal rehabilitation and social renewal. Both areas were in utter ruin, with personal lives and whole societies ravaged by the violence and exploitation slavery fostered. A second chance for these victims could only come by way of supernatural aid, and Methodism was the appointed agency. Few can survey the landscape of the Transatlantic and trans-Saharan global slave trade without a sense of the staggering scope and depth of the injury inflicted on a maligned portion of the human race, and without a sense, too, of the scale of the moral change necessary to end it. That second chance Methodism offered in its strong and peculiar teaching. It was a historic turning point for the human dignity of the Africans and for the moral restoration of their abusers.

AGENCY OF VICTIMS

Methodist teaching gave a role for former slaves and ex-captives to assume control of the direction of their lives and to lead others in the cause. Nothing of that order had existed in any branch of Christianity before, certainly not on the same scale. Whatever their preconceived ideas about Methodism, other Christian bodies could not now ignore the challenge before them: emancipated Africans had a role in designing the church's mission and in taking responsibility for their societies. From the vantage point of the gospel, Europeans stood in a relation of equality with Africans, however long it might take for the world to recognize that fact.

This spirit penetrated the ranks of former slaves and former captives, as the example of Paul Cuffee makes clear. Freed by his conscience-stricken Quaker master in New England, Paul Cuffee embraced the cause of Transatlantic anti-slavery and mission in whose name he made representation to what he called 'enlightened Methodists', challenging them to say how they could fail to see the evil of making merchandise of a brother. He took the message to the New York Methodist Conference. The theme had been set forth in the *Epistle of the Society of Sierra Leone*, which demanded that the saints held in bondage be liberated, that blacks should be freed of 'the galding [galling] chain of slavery, that they may be liberated and enjoy liberty that God has granted unto all his faithful Saints' (Sherwood 1923: 189; Wiggins 1996: 116–17). Among the signatories in Freetown were James Wise, Moses Wilkinson, Joseph Brown, and John Ellis.

A study of his letter sent to William Allen in London shows that Cuffee was thinking very much in the language of the new society. He spoke about the place religion occupied in Freetown, pointing out that four meetings are held on Sunday and two on other days. He said there were two Methodist churches, one Baptist, and one without denominational affiliation that was run by 'an old woman, Mila Baxton who keeps at her dwelling house' (Sherwood 1923: 190). He described the measures taken for poor relief: an organization convening for the purpose once every month, and people appointed to take responsibility for those needing care. A general meeting was held every six months.

Cuffee then went into detail about the necessity of a sober life, and how the habit of regular meetings would promote 'all good and laudable institutions...and increase your temporal and spiritual welfare'. He harped on the theme of sobriety, steadfastness, and faithfulness, so that the community may be served by good examples in all things, 'doing justly, loving mercy, and walking humbly' (ibid. 192 (Micah 6–8)). He admonished against 'following bad company and drinking of spiritous liquors', to keep 'out of idleness, and [be] encouraged to be industrious, for this is good to cultivate the mind, and may you be good examples therein yourselves'. Those who work and serve should be 'brought up to industry; may their minds be cultivated for the redemption of the good seed, which is promised to all who seek after it' (ibid.; Wiggins 1996: 234). He returned to an address he gave to free people of colour at Philadelphia in 1796. 'They are advised to attend to religion, to get an elementary education, teach their children useful trades, use no spiritous liquors, avoid frolicking and idleness, have marriage legally performed, lay up their earnings, and to be honest and to behave themselves' (Sherwood 1923: 192). Idleness was the great Puritan vice, and so it remained for Cuffee and the brethren. This point of setting useful, industrious example was remarked on by a travelling Quaker minister, Stephen Grellett, who reported from Liverpool at the time of Cuffee's visit there whom he described as, a black man, owner and master of a vessel . . . He is a member of our Society . . . The whole of his crew is black also. This together with the cleanliness of his vessel, and the excellent order prevailing onboard, has excited very general attention. It has, I believe, opened the minds of many in tender feelings toward the poor suffering Africans who, they see, are men like themselves, capable of becoming like Paul Cuffee, valuable and useful members of both civil and religious Society.   (Wiggins 1996: 128)

For the blacks, idleness was not just a personal vice, the mark of fallen man, but the symptom of social ill. For remedy, it called for social enterprise. Evangelical religion construed the affairs of organized society as the public face of the signs of the redeemed and sanctified life. John Wesley was tempted to offer a rather narrow justification of the evangelical vocation of personal and social reform when he declared:

Permit me to speak plainly. If by catholic principles you mean any other than scriptural, they weigh nothing with me; I allow no other rule, whether of faith or practice, than the holy Scriptures. But on scriptural principles, I do not think it hard to justify whatever I do. God in Scripture commands me, according to my power, to instruct the ignorant, reform the wicked, confirm the virtuous.   (Wesley 1980: 67)

What did weigh heavily with the Methodists were transformation of personal lives and reconstruction of society. Religion was about character building in society, not ultimately about implacable doctrines and blinding creeds.

At a meeting of the Wesleyan Methodist Missionary Society in London in 1834, Thomas Fowell Buxton, Wilberforce's anti-slavery successor in Parliament, appealed for missionaries for Africa, saying Methodists should remember the wrongs done to Africa, and suggested religious instruction as suitable compensation. Speaking in the year following the Parliamentary act ending slavery in the British Empire, Buxton was appealing to the idea that religious instruction would inculcate the faith, habits, and values that are capable of raising a new generation of Africans weaned of the slave trade and its deleterious social consequences.

Methodism thus gave the impetus for the missionary movement to proceed as a shared intercontinental endeavour among brothers and sisters as spiritual kin of the tribe Jesus wrought by his work of atonement. It cut against the grain, offending sensibilities of race, breeding, and rank. Methodists laboured under the debilitating suspicion of antinomianism and social pretentiousness. Yet a new direction was set, with no turning back.

The Methodist connexion was extended through the work of Lady Selina, the Countess of Huntingdon, who was a colleague of John Wesley, whose influence shaped her own vocation. Olauda Equiano (1969: i. preface) lists John Wesley as a subscriber in the cause of abolition. The countess was no stranger to matters in America. In 1770 after the death of George Whitefield at Newburyport, Mass., she took charge of the Orphan House at Bethesda, Georgia, which Whitefield bequeathed to her. Whitefield had laid elaborate plans for Bethesda as 'The Princeton' of the South, but failed in his efforts to get the necessary backing for it. There is no indication in his plans that Whitefield saw Bethesda as in any way allied with the cause of abolition. He himself owned slaves (Stout 1991: 257ff.). After the meeting of the first Philadelphia Congress in 1774, the countess received reports from her brother in America warning of impending war. In July 1775, reports spoke of the countess attempting to write what was called 'a Plan of Government for the Americans', in which she supported the cause of the colonies (Welch 1995: 146–7) In fact she and her family supported the Americans: she wrote to her daughter in those terms, and was allied for the purpose with her son, a Whig and a member of the Leicestershire Revolution Club. One of her preachers, Cradock Glascott, preached a sermon in London in support of the American struggle. In deference to her pro-American sympathies and her ideal of local autonomy, she arranged to have Bethesda transferred to American control (ibid. 147).

Lady Selina was the contact for John Marrant who was indirectly responsible for bringing the Countess of Huntingdon's Connexion to Sierra Leone. Marrant was born of free black parents in New York in 1755, and moved with his mother to St Augustine, Florida, where he went to school. After a year and a half he moved to Georgia and eventually came to Charlestown, South Carolina. He describes how he met George Whitefield, the revival leader, whose message fell on him like a thunderclap and knocked him out of his senses. Converted thus at Whitefield's hands, Marrant went in search of a missionary cause, running away from hostility at home and 'travelling on for nine days, feeding upon grass, and not knowing whither I was going', except that the hymns of evangelical religion sustained him, he testified. He found himself among the Cherokee Indians to whom he preached. 'I prayed in English a considerable time, and about the middle of my prayer, the Lord impressed a strong desire upon my mind to turn into their language, and pray in their tongue. I did so, and with remarkable liberty', a performance that impressed the people enough to cause them to rescind the sentence of death and spare his life (Marrant 1785: 23–4). Marrant was in Charlestown when the town came under siege and was evacuated to New York from where he was pressed into service with the British navy. He was discharged in London 'where I lived with a respectable and pious merchant three years ... During this time I saw my call to the ministry fuller and clearer; had a feeling concern for the salvation of my countrymen' (ibid. 38–9). Marrant received a letter from his brother in Nova Scotia asking for a pastor to minister to the growing body of black Christians and asking Marrant to introduce himself to the community in Bath. Marrant approached Lady Selina with the request.

Lady Selina ordained Marrant at Bath in 1785 as a minister of the Connexion and sent him to Nova Scotia to found a congregation at Birchtown before leaving again for London where he died in 1791. He had, meanwhile, passed the torch to Cato Perkins, also a Charlestonian, who, with William Ash, another Charlestonian, established the Connexion in Freetown. Perkins was a companion of David George when the two visited London in 1793, during which visit Perkins met Lady Anne Erskine, an associate and a successor of Lady Selina who had died in 1791. Lady Erskine extended help to Cato Perkins.

Another associate of Lady Selina was Revd Thomas Haweis, whom Perkins met. Haweis was an Oxford-educated son of a Cornish lawyer who happened to have cluttered himself with the coarse remnants of a long-running dispute about simony in Aldwinkle, a Northamptonshire village. In any case the meeting with Perkins inspired Haweis to contemplate a mission to Africa. Failing that, he became a founder of the London Missionary Society. At any rate Lady Selina's flock prospered greatly in Sierra Leone, and Cato Perkins's successors presided over a branch of the church that now outstripped its parent. An official report of the Connexion described how the Sierra Leone church first came to their attention in 1825 by means of a letter sent by John Ellis, a minister, through a settler woman. Nothing further was heard until 1839 when two blacks from Sierra Leone showed up in church, saying they had come to England on business, and were taking the opportunity to make personal representation for the Connexion in Sierra Leone. Thus was established the relationship long sought by the settlers, though London was careful to note that the policy of association was based not on 'control ... but rather to advise, to inspire, and to help. In the matter of money', the statement continued, 'what has been sent from England has been only a part of that required for the work. The larger portion of the expenditures has been met by the contributions of the people themselves' (Bainton n.d.: 7).

Perkins died in 1805, to be succeeded by John Ellis, who presided over the work of the Connexion without any further contact with the London branch. Then Anthony Elliott took over the leadership following Ellis's death in 1839, and under his leadership contacts with London were renewed, as we saw. Elliott was born in Dartmouth, Nova Scotia, and was 15 or 16 when he arrived in Sierra Leone. He was licensed as a pilot to bring ships into Freetown harbour, but on New Year's Eve, 1813, he experienced a conversion and subsequently turned preacher.

Elliott led the church in its expansive missionary phase, promoting the cause among the recaptives in the colony villages on the Peninsula. By 1835 he had established congregations at Goderich and Waterloo, and the following year groups were assembling in Campbell Town and Rokel. In the 1840s new meetings were being held in Ibo Town, Tombo, and Hastings, with others set up in other parts of Freetown colony. Thomas Ellis, a Maroon timber trader, opened a mission at Mabang, on the Ribi, and Bai Yinka, a chief of the Small Scarcies River, allowed Joseph Easton, a Huntingdonian preacher, to build a chapel and school at Rokonta. No wonder that Easton could boast about how the work was prospering without European agency. 'All hearts were glad', he wrote, 'to see the Gospel carried by black men to black men, for the first time without any European being present' (Fyfe 1962: 260). There were eleven chapels, forty-eight preachers, and eighty-nine class leaders. In 1852, Scipio Wright, a local preacher, was brought to England and ordained into the ministry of the Connexion.

The Waterloo church of the Connexion, St Mark's, was under the care of Henry Steady, a disbanded African soldier who was in the employment of the Church

Missionary Society as a teacher in Waterloo. After he was dismissed by the CMS, he continued to live in Waterloo, working as a carpenter. Until 1843 when the CMS opened a mission in Waterloo, goaded into action by the launch of the 1841 Niger Mission, which was inspired, among others, by Samuel Ajayi Crowther, religious life was under the care of the settlers and recaptive lay leaders, both men and women.

INDIGENOUS POTENTIAL

Recaptive Methodists played a leading role in the community. One such was John Ezzidio, a Nupe from Nigeria rescued in his teens from a Brazilian slave ship and resettled in Freetown in 1827. Ezzidio was apprenticed to a French shopkeeper under whom he learned the ways of trade and business. A self-taught man, he succeeded in becoming manager of a European shop and was able to carry out his own personal and business correspondence. With the profits from his expanding business in the import–export sector he purchased plots of land, which he developed into successful commercial ventures. In 1844 the governor of the colony, Dr Fergusson, a West Indian army doctor, appointed Ezzidio alderman, and in 1845 mayor of Freetown. From that position Ezzidio was elected by his mercantile associates to sit on the Legislative Council, an example of such rapid African advancement that the Colonial Office in London baulked. Ezzidio was the last such appointment as a result. Henceforth governors acquired the authority for such appointments.

While he remained in the Legislative Council Ezzidio carried his lay Methodist credentials into the corridors of power. Modest, diligent, generous, honest, and impartial, Ezzidio won the admiration even of his critics and political enemies. 'He was no demagogue seeking public glory in fiery speeches, nor did he misuse his position for personal advantage; often the minutes record only that he was present at a meeting' (Fyfe 1955: 220).

Ezzidio embraced his role as a leader accountable to his people. He referred to himself as 'an oracle' of the people, meaning his voice was theirs, and they in turn addressed him in more earthy terms as 'the dancing bear' on account of his physical energy and bulk. He kept open house, welcoming friends and visitors, who returned his respect amply. Unemployed labourers gathered at his house sitting on his veranda to which people gave the nickname 'unofficial labour exchange'. He gave generously and unstintingly to civic and religious causes, raising money among his English business contacts for the purpose. He devoted time and energy to Methodist mission and outreach efforts. He joined the

Methodist Church in 1835 and quickly rose to positions of trust and responsibility. He ran a Sunday school, was a chapel trustee, and served as preacher and class leader. At the Jubilee celebration of the Wesleyan Missionary Society in 1864 he gave the largest single cash contribution to the jubilee fund. He raised money to build a grand Wesley Church to rival in architectural prominence the colony's Anglican cathedral. Yet, to show that Ezzidio was no partisan hack, he joined other Africans in supporting the work of the CMS, the Anglican missionary society. As a member of the Legislative Council Ezzidio voted in 1863 to grant the CMS funds for its work, enthusiastically backing another vote in 1867 which raised the amount substantially.

The testimony of Charles Marke, a fellow Nupe receptive, about Ezzidio's character is to the point, all the more poignant for coming from someone with similar background. Marke reported on Ezzidio's religious conversion, saying Ezzidio exhibited 'a heart strangely warmed' in familiar Wesleyan language, with proof of spiritual regeneration evident in Ezzidio's gifts as preacher and devotional leader. From his own personal acquaintance with Ezzidio, Marke testified that Ezzidio commonly withdrew from his shop during business hours for prayer and devotion. 'At the family altar, and also at the class and prayer-meetings, his prayer was generally characterized by earnestness, fervency, and reverence...his house was open to all' (Marke 1913: 59).

At a meeting in Freetown of the Anti-Slavery Society in 1870 shortly before his death, Ezzidio gave an address in characteristically modest laconic terms. 'This neck which you see wearing a tie to-day', he said in self-deprecation, 'was invested at one time with a chain' (Fyfe 1955: 223).

It was by now clear that the leading agents of the missionary engagement with Africa were the Africans themselves who had been enslaved, or were likely to be, not the chiefs and rulers who enslaved them for gain, and even for ritual slaughter. Equiano wrote:

When a trader wants slaves, he applies to a chief for them, and tempts him with his wares. It is not extraordinary, if on this occasion he yields to the temptation with as little firmness, and accepts the price of his fellow creatures liberty with as little reluctance as the enlightened merchant. Accordingly he falls on his neighbor, and a desperate battle ensues. If he prevails and takes prisoners, he gratifies his avarice by selling them.   (Equiano i. 24)

For it was these chiefs, for example, who, when they died, brought up the sanguinary rule that as many slaves be killed as befitted the deceased chief's rank and power, and buried with him. Slaves were thus as good as funeral fodder. The Methodist missionary Piggott reports on the death in 1826 of old King George shortly after visiting him. He said at his funeral the old King's wish to forgo the custom of killing slaves to accompany his soul was honoured. It 'evidently showed there was something good in him', Piggott testified. The practice was widespread as is reported in accounts of Ethiopia (Baldick 1997: 36–7).

CHURCH AND STATE

Anti-slavery spawned in Sierra Leone a new society with a premium on personal industry and civic virtue. The new design for society placed emancipated and industrious Africans at the heart of the enterprise. By their cumulative example of hard work, a sober lifestyle, honesty, social activism, self-denial, public benevolence, and public service, these Africans tried to establish a new kind of society based on equality, the rule of law, and individual enterprise. Shortly after arriving in Freetown, for example, Clarkson lost no time in moving to establish standards of respect and the rule of law. He ordered three European sailors flogged for being offensive to the Nova Scotians and for disobeying orders. Simon Proof, a Nova Scotian ex-serviceman, carried out the flogging in public (Fyfe 1962: 39). The directors of the Sierra Leone Company, for example, reported that the Nova Scotians agitated to have a jury system established when the governor and council dismissed one of them for showing disrespect to his superiors. On that occasion they 'applied to have a law established, that no Nova Scotian working for the Company should in future be turned off, unless after a verdict by a jury of his peers' (Report 2, 68). Burton derided Freetown juries as stacked with 'half-reclaimed barbarians clad in dishclouts [sic] and palm oil', and 'cankered' with tribal malice. He deemed mission in Sierra Leone a setback for 'the ruling race' and for progress (Burton 1991: i. 217).

In a detailed memorandum on social conditions in the settlement, Robert Hogan, the Chief Justice, wrote in 1816 that he spared no effort to

inculcate with the most anxious and unaffected earnestness in the minds of the [settlers] that they are all equally free, all entitled to the same encouragement and protection: all possessed of the same right, without distinctions, as well as liable to the same penalties for infringing [the rights] of others, and all alike objects of the paternal care and constant solicitude of the common government. A steady adherence to this principle, and the undeviating application of it to practice promise the most salutary effect, and with the aid of the measures which Governor McCarthy [sic] has already adopted and is preparing to put in execution for the good government and prosperity of this colony bid fair to prove for his administration here, the enviable honour of being ranked among the most useful of the investments employed by providence for the benefit of mankind.

(Chief Justice Robert Hogan, Letter 25 May 1816: 267/43)

In paying tribute to the achievement of the Nova Scotian and receptive lay leadership in Sierra Leone, Christopher Fyfe underlined the role, among other influences, of evangelical Methodism in bringing about personal change and social transformation. The recaptives, he said, found in Sierra Leone economic opportunities of a kind they never knew in their homeland. Yet equally significant was the fact that they found a new religion to sustain them. Missionaries of the Church and Wesleyan Missionary Societies, or independent churches—Methodist, Baptist, and

Huntingdonian—run by Nova Scotian and Maroon inhabitants, gave the recaptives a gospel that took no account of their abused circumstances, and addressed them as persons with dignity.

With its emphasis on personal conversion and social responsibility, evangelical religion was an effective prescription for the dislocated Africans who landed in Freetown. The 'Methodist church government (which even the C.M.S. partly adopted in Sierra Leone), where laymen play so large a part, offered the newly-rich trader a chance of social leadership not only by commercial success but with office as a local preacher, supplementing the work of missionary or pastor, or as a class-leader responsible for the moral welfare of a small group within the congregation' (Fyfe 1955: 216). The use of lay agency allowed the churches to spread their influence in the community far more effectively than missionaries could ever have done, and it provides a link with the forces of the post-Western Christian awakening of the twentieth century. In the Ivory Coast and Ghana, for example, the Methodists made the opportune and decisive partnership with the mass conversion movement of the charismatic Prophet William Wade Harris between 1916 and 1918 to launch their mission on a new basis. That charismatic theme was the crucible of slave conversion from the eighteenth century, and became a critical force in the rise of World Christianity later.

REFERENCES:

ANON (1968). *Five Slave Narratives: A Compendium.* New York: Arno and New York Times.

BAINTON, JOSEPH, and MANLY, T. (n.d.). *The Sierra Leone Mission Supported by the Churches of the Countess of Huntingdon's Connexion and the Free Church of England.* Tunbridge Wells: n.p.

BALDICK, JULIAN (1997). *Black God: The Afroasiatic Roots of the Jewish, Christian and Muslim Religions.* London: I. B. Tauris.

BURTON, RICHARD F. (1991). *Wanderings in West Africa.* 2 vols. London: Tinsley Brothers.

COWPER, WILLIAM (1855). 'The Task: The Winter Morning Walk'. London: James Nisbet.

—— (1950). *Religion and the Rise of Western Culture.* London: Sheed & Ward.

DAVIS, DAVID BRION (2006). *The Rise and Fall of Slavery in the New World.* New York: Oxford University Press.

DAWSON, CHRISTOPHER (1994). *The Making of Europe: An Introduction to the History of European Unity.* New York: Barnes & Noble.

ELTON, G. R. (1964). *Reformation in Europe, 1517–1559.* Cleveland: World Publishing Co./Meridan Books.

EQUIANO, OLAUDAH (1969). *The Life of Olaudah Equiano, or Guistavus Vassa, the African: 1789.* 2 vols. London: Dawsons of Pall Mall.

FYFE, CHRISTOPHER (1955). 'The Life and Times of John Ezzidio'. *Sierra Leone Studies* 4 (June): 213–33.

—— (1962). *Short History of Sierra Leone.* London: Longmans.

GRAY, RICHARD (1990). *Black Christians and White Missionaries*. New Haven: Yale University Press.

HILL, CHRISTOPHER (1994). *The English Bible and the Seventeenth Century Revolution*. London: Penguin.

HOGAN, ROBERT [Chief Justice] (1816). Letter 25 May 1816. Public Record Office, London.

KINGSLEY, MARY (1964). *West African Studies*. London: Frank Cass.

MARKE, CHARLES (1913). *Origin of Wesleyan Methodism in Sierra Leone and History of Its Missions*. London: Charles H. Kelly.

MARRANT, JOHN (1785). *A Narrative of the Lord's Wonderful Dealings with John Marrant, a Black*. London: Gilbert & Plummer.

MILLER, PERRY, and JOHNSON, THOMAS H. (eds.) (1963). *The Puritans: A Sourcebook of their Writings*. 2 vols. New York: Harper Torchbooks.

PIRENNE, HENRI (1968). *Mohammed and Charlemagne*. London: Unwin University Books.

RABOTEAU, ALBERT J. (1978). *Slave Religion*. New York: Oxford University Press.

RAHNER, HUGO (1992). *Church and State in Early Christianity*, trans. Leo Donald Davis. San Francisco: St Ignatius.

SHERWOOD, HENRY NOBLE (1923). 'Paul Cuffe'. *Journal of Negro History* 8 (April).

SMITH, SYDNEY (1859). *The Works of the Reverend Sydney Smith*. London: Longman, Brown, Green.

STOUT, HARRY S. (1991). *The Divine Dramatist: George Whitefield and the Rise of Modern Evangelism*. Grand Rapids: Eerdmans.

TAWNEY, R. H. (1966). *Religion and the Rise of Capitalism: A Historical Study*. Harmondsworth: Penguin.

DE TOCQUEVILLE, ALEXIS (1969). *Democracy in America*, ed. J. P. Mayer, trans. George Lawrence. New York: Harper Perennial.

WADSTRÖM, CARL B. (1794). *Essay on Colonization, particularly applied to the Western Coast of Africa with some Free Thoughts on Cultivation and Commerce; also Brief Descriptions of the Colonies already formed, or attempted, in Africa, including those of Sierra Leone and Bulama*. 2 vols. London: Darton & Harvey.

WALZER, MICHAEL (1965). *The Revolution of the Saints*. Cambridge, Mass.: Harvard University Press.

WELCH, EDWIN (1995). *Spiritual Pilgrim: A Reassessment of the Life of the Countess of Huntingdon*. Cardiff: University of Wales Press.

WESLEY, JOHN (1980). *Works*, XIX. *Journals and Diaries*, ed. W. Reginald Ward and Richard P. Heitzenvater. Nashville: Abingdon.

WIGGINS, ROSALIND COBB (ed.) (1996). *Captain Paul Cuffe's Logs and Letters: 1808–1817: A Black Quaker's 'Voice from Within the Veil'*. Washington, D.C.: Howard University Press.

WILLIAMS, ERIC E. (1969). *From Columbus to Castro: The History of the Caribbean 1492–1969*. New York: Harper & Row.

PART II

ECCLESIAL FORMS AND STRUCTURES

CHAPTER 12

CONNECTION AND CONNECTIONALISM

RUSSELL E. RICHEY

In June 1773, the Methodist preachers in the American colonies gathered in Philadelphia for what is counted the first annual conference. They recorded their proceedings in accordance with the designation standard across the Atlantic: 'Minutes of Some Conversations between the Preachers in Connection with the Rev. Mr. John Wesley' (*Minutes*/MEC 1773).

Commenting on the import of the terminology 'in Connection with', the great constitutional historian John Tigert observed:

Thus from the beginning in both England and America, Methodism has been a 'Connection'. The term is technical, and characteristic of the denomination. Connectionalism is of the essence of the system, equally opposed to congregationalism in the churches and to individualism in the preachers. Mr. Wesley, in America no less than in England, was, at the first, the center of union. Connection with him was the living bond which held incipient American Methodism together. He was the foundation of authority, acknowledged by all as rightful, original, and supreme. Through him a closer organic union subsisted between the Methodism of America, recognized at home as scarcely more than a needy but promising and fruitful mission-field, and that of England, than between the colonies, now on the eve of revolt, and the mother country. Mr. Wesley was the patriarch and apostle, the founder and creator, of Ecumenical Methodism. (Tigert 1908: 58–9)

From the beginning, connection and connectionalism have had multiple, complex, interlacing, changing meanings. The terms designate Methodism's origins; relationships that existed among the preachers and peoples and between them and Mr Wesley; ordained ministerial status and conference membership; conference structures that governed; whatever the actions or measures or processes that held the movement together, i.e. that connected; the evolving movement as institution or polity; a theology or specifically an ecclesiology, often more implicit than explicit; an organizational classification; the consequent presumption that Methodism and Methodists would adhere or connect; and therefore a denominational self-understanding.

In exploring these complex meanings, we look at connectionalism as

- commitment;
- competing connectional principles, specifically those of work, authority, and power;
- adhesive or connective mechanisms—what actually connected period-to-period;
- denominational classification;
- Christian conferencing as practice and ecclesiology.

CONNECTIONALISM: A FORM OF COMMITMENT

Incipient, implicit, assumed, potential, the meanings to connectionalism have emerged, devolved, changed, re-emerged over time. Today's Methodists, at least United Methodists, may emphasize the church's connectionalism and connectional nature more than their predecessors. That emphasis reflects and reacts to the atrophying of connectional tissue, strong counter-currents of localism, quasi-independence of tall steeple congregations, declining value put on denomination in American society, erosion of the old Protestant mainline, culture war divisions within the church, and the attraction of other modes of spirituality and community. To counter the deconnecting tendencies, Methodist leadership puts a rhetorical premium on and issues exhortations to connectionalism.

The salience of connectionalism today represents a recovery of the initial self-understanding, one eroded in the decades after American Methodist independence in 1784. Early in the denomination's life, the new Methodist Episcopal Church (MEC) downplayed the connection with Wesley and with British Methodism so as to achieve full independence. Its initial commitment to Wesley, made in the *Book of Discipline* crafted at the organizing Christmas Conference of 1784 was truly remarkable, conceding plenary authority:

During the life of Rev. Mr. Wesley, we acknowledge ourselves his Sons in the Gospel, ready in Matters belonging to Church-Government, to obey his Commands. And we do engage after his Death, to do every Thing that we judge consistent with the Cause of Religion in America and the political Interests of these States, to preserve and promote our Union with the Methodists in Europe.   (Richey, Rowe, and Schmidt 2000: 82)

The new MEC expressed that loyalty, indeed obedience, in a variety of ways. It took over the constitution-like 'Large Minutes' of Wesley's gatherings to constitute its *Book of Discipline*, adding and deleting as appropriate for a church functioning in a new nation. Thereby it committed itself to defining Wesleyan practices—itinerancy; a superintending authority (later episcopacy); the organizational structure of class, society, circuit, quarterly conference, and conference; a social ethic and individual moral code; expectations of discipline; practices of piety (testimony, hymn-singing, fasting); forms of worship (love feast, watch night); and the hallmark Wesleyan purposes 'to reform the Continent, and to spread scriptural Holiness over these Lands' (Richey, Rowe, and Schmidt 2000: 82). Wesley had selected the new superintendents (bishops) of the church, Thomas Coke, whom he personally ordained and Francis Asbury, whom Coke was to ordain. In accord with clear intimations in his transmittal directive 'To Dr. Coke, Mr. Asbury, and our Brethren in North America' (ibid. 71–2), the new church adopted an ordering of ministry derived from Wesley's church, the Church of England, the threefold ministry of superintendents (bishops), elders, and deacons. The new church also accepted Wesley's adaptation, editing, and pruning of the Anglican Articles of Religion and its liturgy (BCP). The MEC continued to sing Charles Wesley's hymns. It adhered to Wesley's disciplinary expectations, guidelines for admission into society, and rules for the exercise of ministries. And it sustained signature Wesleyan commitments— the prohibition of 'Ministers or Travelling-Preachers' drinking 'spirituous Liquors' and courageous and extensive legislation against slavery.

Complicating American Methodist compliance with the deferential connection with Mr. Wesley, with his continuing exercise of authority and his vision of a global connection, were the behaviour and actions of his deputy and their superintendent, Thomas Coke. By prior understanding, Coke returned to Britain after the 1785 American conferences. He would be back in the United States in 1787, 1789, and 1791, punctuating his American visits with presidential or oversight roles on Wesley's behalf in Ireland, the West Indies, and British North America. Coke returned to the US in 1787 with explicit, written directions from Wesley to 'appoint a General Conference of all our preachers in the United States, to meet at Baltimore on 1st May 1787' and further that 'Mr. Richard Whatcoat may be appointed Superintendent with Asbury'. Wesley had proposed, in addition, that Freeborn Garrettson be superintendent for British North America. Such directives accorded with the 1784 'binding minute'. They hardly accorded with American sensitivities.

Of Wesley's several directives through Coke, the Americans honoured only the most inconsequential. They met on 1 May in Baltimore rather than as they had themselves appointed at Abingdon, Maryland, on 24 July. They did not, at that point, elect Whatcoat to the episcopacy, some fearing that his elevation might produce the recall of Asbury, nor carry out the comparable elevation of Garrettson. More pointedly, they circumscribed Coke's episcopal authority, stipulating in the Annual Minutes to the first question 'Who are the superintendents?' the answer 'Thomas

Coke, (when present in the States), and Francis Asbury'. And they extracted from Coke a certificate promising not to exercise superintending authority when absent and limiting it, when present, to ordaining, presiding, and travelling, that is, to ceremonial and homiletical duties, not the key role of making appointments. Dramatically, they also rescinded the binding minute of loyalty to Wesley from the Discipline, sometimes described as dropping Wesley's name from the Minutes (*Minutes*/MEC 1787 [1813]: 62–8).

In 'Connection with the Rev. Mr. John Wesley', meaning compliant commitment to him within a global church under his command, would not do for American Methodism. If anything American Methodism cohered 'in connection with Mr. Asbury'. As Wesley's assistant in the colonies, Asbury had earned the respect, admiration, and support of the Americans by sticking with them during the Revolution when other Wesley appointees had fled. With remarkable prescience and no small degree of strategic self-interest, he had in 1784 laid the foundation for consensual governance and America-specific connectionalism, created the pattern of American Methodist episcopacy, and established his own authority by insisting on conference election of the superintendents (bishops), not merely Wesley's appointment. Over time Asbury came to behave, not as Wesley's appointee, but as Wesley's American counterpart. He deferred to the highly educated Dr Coke in certain public settings but was 'the' American bishop. Until he died, Asbury travelled tirelessly across the expanding Methodist movement, connecting it through his appoint-making and assisting it to set in place other connectional practices, structures, and offices.

Francis Asbury died en route to the 1816 General Conference, a gathering shadowed by his departure from them. On the last day of its tense, future-oriented legislative activity, anxiously envisioning a church lacking the Asbury connection, after sitting for three full weeks, and amidst the reports concerning the Book Concern and instructing the editors on various publishing tasks (authorizing a magazine, for instance), an unexplained motion came from the floor. 'William Phoebus moved, that the word "connection" be expunged from our Discipline, and the words "Church", "community", and "itinerancy" be inserted, as the grammatical construction may require. Carried' (*JGC*/MEC 1816: i. 173).

That nomenclature change deserved no mention from historian Nathan Bangs, a very active member of that general conference, maker of the motion concerning a magazine, and soon-to-be editor himself, who devoted over twenty pages specifically to its work and import (Bangs 1860: iii. 33–54) and dedicated himself unreservedly to the spirit of that legislative initiative—namely getting Methodism and Methodists to recognize their standing as a church properly so called. 'Church' the 1816 General Conference decided the MEC would be, and it took various actions to provide churchly infrastructure and resources. Nevertheless, the word 'connection' remained a vitally important and frequently used part of the Methodist lexicon, indeed, a mandated item in every annual conference's sitting. Third in the mandated questions that governed conference business was, 'Who are admitted into full connection?' That status for preachers—part of the travelling connection and gained after probation or trial—made them members of an annual conference, conferences being composed of those admitted or to be admitted into full connection. Only those in conference connection legislated, governed, directed, and disciplined—increasingly a concern, even a grievance—for those outside this ministerial aristocracy. The exclusion from conference membership, from this privileged connection, of laity and other leaders (local preachers, exhorters, stewards, class leaders) would lead to division, notably that of the Methodist Protestants in 1830.

Notwithstanding the 1816 action, then, Methodists continued to speak amongst themselves of their church as a connection. But Phoebus's simple motion might well symbolize Methodists' inability and/or lack of desire adequately to draw out the rich implications of their connectionalism either for themselves or for the larger Christian community. What they lacked in theory they more than provided for in connectional practices, policies, and structures, these institutionalizations an outworking of inherited Wesleyan patterns, invigorated or informed when necessary by a look back to Mr Wesley's myriad connecting activities.

COMPETING CONNECTIONAL PRINCIPLES

Other chapters in this *Handbook* detail fully John Wesley's roles at the heart of and constitutive of the Methodist connection. The connectional background for the Evangelical and United Brethren is complex, showing some indebtedness to Wesley; having deeper roots in the Magisterial Reformation (Lutheran and Reformed respectively); but betraying as well the critiques mounted by Pietism and Anabaptism. Here we highlight three dimensions of his connectional authority and power that have proved important, albeit competitive, in American Methodism: first, his exercise of the superintending, directive, or episcopal role; second, his gathering of preachers into a deliberative conference; and third, his oversight of the movement's work, services, and infrastructure.

The first of Wesley's roles was nicely summarized by bishops Thomas Coke and Francis Asbury in their 1798 annotations of *The Doctrines and Disciplines of the Methodist Episcopal Church, in America* and in defence of their own office and conduct therein (Richey, Rowe, and Schmidt 2000: 123):

[W]e must observe that nothing has been introduced into Methodism by the present episcopal form of government, which was not before fully exercised by Mr. Wesley. He presided in the conferences; fixed the appointments of the preachers for their several circuits; changed, received, or suspended preachers, wherever he judged that necessity required it; travelled through the European connection at large; superintended the spiritual and temporal business; and consecrated . . . bishops . . . besides ordaining elders and deacons.

Asbury and Coke's high doctrine of superintendency had already generated vehement opposition and a connection-dividing schism, that of the Republican Methodists led by James O'Kelly, against whom their apologetic was directed. The autocratic power of the superintendency (episcopacy) continued to generate criticism and produced several subsequent schisms, including that of the Methodist Protestants. And the contest over slavery and a slave-holding bishop, which divided episcopal Methodism north and south, hinged on and reinforced differing views of the relative authority of bishops and general conference. To a high view of episcopacy, an Asburian conception, a commitment to superintendency, and conference as coordinate branches of government, the Methodist Episcopal Church (South) (MECS) thereafter dedicated itself (Kirby 2000: 127–72; Ch. 23 below).

Second, although Wesley gathered his preachers into a deliberative conference, they came to confer with him who remained the decision-maker, a point nicely stated by historian and Bishop Thomas Neely (1892: 9–10), 'But let it not be supposed that the Conferences which Mr. Wesley called had any governing power. The members discussed, but Mr. Wesley decided. They debated, but he determined. Mr. Wesley was the government; and, though he invited the preachers to confer with him, he did not propose to abandon any of his original power. They had a voice by his permission, but he reserved the right to direct.' Could/would Americans live with such autocratic rule, on the part of Wesley or his American deputy? At one point, they came close. During the Revolution, American Methodist preachers embraced a conferring role for themselves and conceded to Francis Asbury a Wesley-like determining authority. A manuscript version of the 1779 Conference minutes—the bolded phrasing in Asbury's hand, the subsequently published wording represented by the numbered entries—detailed this concession (*Minutes*/Leesburg 1977 (1775–93): 20–2):

Ought not Br. Asbury to Act as General Assistant in America whilst he shall Continue therein Under Present Circumstances.

A. He Ought because Originally Appointed by Mr. Wesley to Act Jointly therein with Mr. Rankin & Mr. Shadford.

Quest. 12 Ought not brother Asbury to act as General Assistant in America?

Ans. He ought: 1st, on account of his age; 2d, because originally appointed by Mr. Wesley; 3d being joined with Messrs. Rankin and Shadford, by express order from Mr. Wesley.

How far shall this Power Extend

A. To the Hearing Each Preacher in Conference for or Against any Matter—to offer his Reasons—& then the Right of Determination to Lay in his breast—to Act According to the Printed Minutes of Conference & in his Absence the Committee to Act in Like Manner.

Quest. 13 How far shall his power extend?

A. On hearing every preacher for and against what is in debate, the right of determination shall rest with him according to the Minutes.

From this high watermark (or low, depending on one's perspective) of a Wesley-like conferring, gradually American Methodists developed what Neely termed the 'governing conference' (1892). The lodging of an authoritative voice and of denominational decision-making in conference came via stages:

in a single conference which kept a record of its actions;
in multiple annual conferences that consolidated their commitments into one set of minutes;
in the organizing Christmas Conference that legislated a new church into being;
in conference practice of making motions, debating and voting;
through the experiment with a Council;
with the convening of a general conference in 1792;
and to the establishment of the constitutional 'Restrictive Rules' and the principle of representation or delegation. (*Handbook*; Richey 1996)

And both the Methodist Protestants in their organization in 1830 and the MEC after the division of 1844 sustained commitment to the plenary authority of general conference.

Third, Wesley personified the connection, oversaw its organizational activity, and administered its key support or infrastructure functions. He served as the movement's publisher, expanding from the printing of his own writing and his brother's hymns into a range of materials for both preachers and people, and establishing printed works as the criteria for Methodist orthodoxy. He directed the work and mission of the movement, oversaw its acquisition of property, dealt with conflicts and controversy, envisioned and provisioned its expansion. He served as the connection's primary fund-raiser—initially adapting the class meeting as a money-raising gathering to pay for a Methodist property (the New Room), finding ways to support other chapels and the school, seeking resources to care for those in need. He constituted the faculty for the preachers, though delegating that role for lower schools to others. By personal contact, travel, correspondence, and publications he held the connection together. In short, he directed the organizational life and work of Methodism.

To the gradual emergence of offices and structures that institutionalized this dimension of Wesley's connectional authority we turn in the section below. Suffice it to say here that American Methodism gradually structured these Wesley organizational activities into yet a third system, that of corporate boards.

Today's Methodism institutionalizes those three dimensions of Wesley's connectional office into three competing power centres or structures, each with considerable authority: superintending and appointment-making in bishops, legislative decision-making authority in conference, and organizational work in agencies. So, for instance, in United Methodism bishops continue Wesley's appoint-making in their respective conferences, and through a general Council of Bishops sustain something of Wesley's teaching office. The only body that speaks authoritatively for United Methodism and exercises 'full legislative power over all matters distinctly connectional', however, is the General Conference which meets quadrennially, revising the *Discipline*, authorizing changes to liturgy, hymnody, policy, and practice, and issuing resolutions on matters of ethical and political interest. And between the quadrennial meetings of General Conference, general boards, commissions, and councils carry on the work of the church, their names giving some sense of their work:

General Commission on Archives and History
General Commission on Communication
General Commission on Christian Unity and Interreligious Concerns
United Methodist Publishing House
General Commission on Religion and Race
General Council on Finance and Administration
General Board of Higher Education and Ministry
General Board of Discipleship
General Commission on United Methodist Men
General Board of Global Ministries
General Board of Pensions and Health Benefits
General Board of Church and Society
General Commission on Status and Role of Women

How did authority, power and work—so tightly knit when preachers were in connection with the Revd Mr John Wesley—become distributed into three competitive systems?

THE EVOLUTION OF CONNECTION

In Britain, Wesley could and did effect the connecting—the movement's day-to-day communication, transmission, exchange, production, direction. That centred functionality and connectivity gradually eroded in the expanding American movement. One conference gave way to multiple. Asbury kept on the move. Experiments with decision-making culminating in the Baltimore Conference and then through a Council of presiding elders proved unacceptable. A general conference solved the decision-making problem but sat for only a few weeks every four years. Multiple bishops provided the requisite superintending and appoint-making but did well to coordinate those tasks. They struggled with the increasing regionalism, tensions, and conflicts in the expanding denomination. And the bishops were not individually or collectively capable of managing the growing and maturing church's infrastructural needs for schools; magazines, papers, and books; regularized finance; and missionary outreach (Kirby 2000: 72–85; Richey, Campbell, and Lawrence 1997: 1–20).

How would American Methodists handle Mr Wesley's roles of publishing, missions oversight, education, and fund-raising? They began conventionally with Asbury (and to a lesser extent Coke) attempting Wesley's oversight. For instance, Asbury appointed John Dickins as publisher in or around 1783, moved him from North Carolina to New York so as better to undertake the church's publishing, relocated him later to Philadelphia, and kept in regular touch with Dickins until he died in 1798 (Pilkington 1968: 43–116). And one of the important initiatives coming out of the Christmas Conference of 1784 and of Coke's initial visit was his and Asbury's effort to create a school for American Methodism. Modelled after Wesley's Kingswood School and immodestly named for themselves, Cokesbury did not prosper.

When in 1789 and 1790 Asbury gathered the presiding elders as a Council, a central authority to coordinate and streamline decision-making, it made publishing and education its main business (*Proceedings* 1789: 3–7; *Minutes*/MEC 1790: 3–8). Its 1789 session adopted an eight-point 'Constitution', half of which governed procedure, the other half of which pertained to these organizational initiatives. It deemed itself constituted:

1. To direct and manage all the Printings which may be done, from Time to Time, for the Use and Benefit of the Methodist Church in *America*.
2. To conduct the Plan of Education and manage all Matters which may, from Time to Time, pertain to any College or Houses built, or about to be built, as the Property of the Methodist Connection.
3. To remove, or receive, and appoint the Salary of any Tutors, from Time to Time, employed in any Seminary of Learning belonging to the said Connection.
4. In the Intervals of the Council, the Bishop shall have Power to act in all contingent Occurrences relative to the Printing Business, or the Education and Economy of the College.

In its second and last (1790) session, the Council claimed itself 'invested with *full* power to act *decisively* in all temporal matters'. It devoted much of its attention again to publishing and education (Cokesbury) but added missions as a concern as well. Consistent with its presumption of plenary authority, it established a committee of advisers for the book business and imagined itself actually do the staffing:

Any Preacher, being recommended by the presiding Elder and Conference of a district, as a proper person to act in such business, shall be appointed by the Council, when sitting; and, in the intervals of the Council, by the Bishops.
Quest. Who shall form such a Committee?
Ans. Richard Whatcoat, Henry Willis, Thomas Haskins, and John Dickins, or any two of them.

After 1792 General Conference assumed the plenary oversight roles that the Council had presumed for itself but as a quadrennially meeting body could hardly provide day-to-day supervision.

Building on the precedent set with the Council, General Conference began what might be termed a double delegation of ongoing oversight for key connectional functions. First with publishing, later with the missionary enterprise, and eventually with Sunday schools, tracts, and other activities, General Conference elected the head of the operation from among the travelling connection (i.e. a preacher and typically also a delegate to General Conference). It then assigned oversight to the specific annual conference of which he was a member. The annual conference, in turn, further delegated that to a local committee, increasingly either in Philadelphia or New York. With most of these enterprises (other than publishing), the Missionary Society (1819), the Sunday School Union (1827), and the Tract Society (1852), Methodism adopted the organizational principle then regnant across American Protestantism, that of the voluntary society. Methodists belonged to the local, conference, and national Missionary Society, for instance, by paying the annual dues or buying a life membership. That membership entitled them to participation in the annual meeting at which a board would be constituted, reports heard, and business done. Effectively that gave the governance of key connectional business to the local (i.e. headquarters) Methodists who turned out for the Philadelphia or New York meeting and then elected a board typically also of leaders from that locale. Missional, purposive, flexible, adaptive, expansive, pluraform, and decentralized, the societies and society principle effectively energized, indeed *connected* Methodism and Methodists around its key organizational tasks.

With multiple and itinerating bishops, a general conference that met only every four years, and numerous annual conferences, episcopal Methodism found itself indeed connected through much of the nineteenth century by its organizational work—by the editors who at the helm of the *Christian Advocate*, one of the regional *Advocates* or the *Methodist Quarterly Review* quite literally spoke regularly to and for the entire connection and by the corresponding (general) secretaries of the several societies who organized, boosted, and implemented both outreach and infrastructural activities. By the end of the Civil War, first the MEC, then the MECS and other Methodist bodies, realized that these vital services needed greater denominational accountability. In 1872 MEC General Conference heard from its Special Committee on the Relation of Benevolent Institutions of the Church to the General Conference (*JGC/MEC* 1827: i. 295–9; Richey, Rowe, and Schmidt 2000: 371).

The management and disposition of the affairs and property of the corporation known as 'The Missionary Society of the Methodist Episcopal Church' are by its charter vested in a Board of Managers to be annually elected at a meeting of the Society, to be called for that purpose, and held in the City of New York at such time and on such notice as the Board of Managers, for the time being, shall previously prescribe.

The members of the Board are elected by members of the Society, and the members of the Society are those persons who become such by the payment of twenty dollars or more to its fund.

The General Conference has no legal connection with the Society, except only that by the charter it is provided that the Corresponding Secretaries of said Society shall be elected by the General Conference; and shall hold their offices for four years, and until their successors are elected, and that in case of vacancy the Bishops shall elect their successors to hold till the ensuing General Conference.

In 1872 the MEC and in 1874 the MECS reincorporated and transformed these Methodist voluntary societies into denominational boards accountable to General Conference, giving the church a corporate structure and preserving the principle of mirroring boards or committees at conference and congregational levels. Thus a bureaucratized Methodism connected itself, top to bottom. Over the first half of the twentieth century, the board system prospered. New expectations of systematic, per-member financing, a centralized treasurer, a district superintendency functioning as regional corporate offices, professionally trained staff, new means of production and communication, efficiencies of scale, and the inclusion of laity (men and women) into governance and employment kept programmes flowing downwards and money flowing upwards. The boards and their leadership had the trust of the connection, a significant token of which was the regular election of the corresponding (general) secretaries to yet a higher connectional office, that of the episcopacy.

What elevated the boards fully into the position of a third connectional power centre, eviscerated much of the actual connective effectiveness of bishops and General Conference, and at times made it seem as though boards were the denomination, was the union of 1939. Unification brought back together the Methodist Protestants, the MEC, and the MECS. It did so by dividing the United States into five regional and one all-Black jurisdiction, a principled segregation and precondition for MECS participation. To jurisdictions was given what had been General Conference's authority to elect bishops and to select the directors or board members of the several agencies (*Doctrines and Discipline* 1940: 277–8, 291, etc.). Taken from General Conference as well was its authority to elect general secretaries. The agencies were then empowered to select their own heads, a move undertaken in the interest of achieving greater professionalism in leadership and in the belief that a board close to an agency's work could act more responsibly in selections. A new judicial council assumed the prerogative of ruling on the constitutionality of general conference legislation, actions, and rulings by bishops and conference initiatives, prerogatives enjoyed previously by an MEC committee and the MECS board of bishops.

The 1872/4 reincorporations had replaced local and conference oversight of agencies with that of General Conference, a loss doubtless of some real ongoing and day-to-day supervision in favour of accountability at the highest level. The 1939 changes effectively severed that accountability as well. And the interposition of jurisdictions between annual conferences and General Conference regionalized both the church and the episcopacy, leaving the now largely independent boards as the truly connectional entities but bound only programmatically and by trust to the Methodist people and their congregations. Several delegates to the 1939 Uniting Conference perceived the damage to connectionalism from removing from General Conference the authority to staff general agencies themselves and the jurisdictions to effect these key personnel decisions, radical changes even as means to achieve higher levels of staff professionalism (*Daily Christian Advocate*/MEC 1939: 179, 181, 182). J. M. M. Gray (Detroit) insisted,

[I]n some fashion we must combat effectively the disintegrating influence of Jurisdictional lines upon our general connectional influence. And when we elect all our secretaries by boards and elect all our boards by Jurisdictions we have flung away the last of the great influences that have bound us together as a connection.

I am in favor of the election of the Secretary by the General Conference.

Agreeing, Harold Paul Sloan (New Jersey) spoke against the tendency to 'ensmall' the church and of the divisive potential of elections by the boards of their staff,

I feel there is grave danger of breaking our great American Methodism up into a lot of small groups, each Board will be a group, each Jurisdiction will be a group, and the large interests of the Church instead of coming into focus in the great United General Conference, will never come to focus at all, but will be in expression in these small groups.

[T]he responsibility in most instances with these executive leaders is a responsibility in which they can commend themselves to the Church as a whole. A man who has not made an impression upon the Church as a whole as an effective leader for a Board ought not to be elected to that place.

To be sure, 1939 created new connectional institutions, in addition to the Judicial Council, a Council of Bishops (COB). However, the latter's capacity to speak, teach, and lead connectionally has only recently emerged. For several decades little needed to be said about the COB (Harmon 1962: 74–7) and it functioned best in creating bonds between and among the bishops. And over that period, perhaps to the union of the Methodists with the Evangelical United Brethren (EUB) in 1968, the boards did seem to be the denomination, connecting Methodists around programme and mission, and so constituting the connection.

The new 'The United Methodist Church' (UMC) came into being in a period when denominations generally were undergoing massive restructuring at the connectional level, undertaken in the interest of efficiency and effectiveness but a portent of trouble ahead. United Methodists pulled separate agencies into superboards and adopted what had been an EUB programme and coordinating structure, a Council of Ministries, to bring into common focus the competitive entities. That Council, abolished in 2004 after its own self-studies in the face of a hostile campaign over several quadrennia, came to symbolize the eroding of denominational belief in, loyalty to, and acceptance of agency connectional leadership. It is hard to separate cause and effect in the destruction of the one key bond, the remaining operative connection, between the boards and agencies and the UMC people's and congregations' trust.

Loss of trust in national, corporate, governmental, social, and religious structures occurred through the social-political turmoil of the 1960s and 1970s, first on the socio-political left and thereafter on the right (Mickey and Wilson 1977). And the UMC brought that turmoil within, having committed itself as part of the 1968 deal with the EUB to ending the scandal and closing down the segregated Central Jurisdiction. At roughly the same time, racial, ethnic, gender, and cause-specific caucuses emerged, in Methodism as elsewhere in American society. Moreover, mainline Protestants began to awake to the realization that their hegemony in American society and politics had ended and to witness the growing strength of fundamentalist, evangelical, and pentecostal bodies. Cause and identity heightened interest in representation on boards and in jurisdictional and general conference delegations and in the selection of leaders. In the decades before and after the turn of the twenty-first century, caucuses and struggle groups, while connecting persons around their own causes, balkanized denominations, turning board meetings and conferences into contentious and demoralizing rather than unifying and galvanizing experiences. Some of the caucuses align themselves into two broad coalitions, liberal and conservative, within and indeed beyond denominational, even religious, boundaries and creating parties that threatened to divide, perhaps even destroy, denominations.

All this conflict, posturing, identity-politics, and social turmoil interposed itself between connectional entities—including the boards—and the people whom they sought to serve. Distrust replaced trust and the boards as the on-going, day-to-day connectional entities came to symbolize a denomination out of touch with its constituency. Too liberal, too bureaucratic, too absorbed in identity-politics, too professionalized, too clerical, too oriented to justice-issues, too self-absorbed, too mired in structural change (ibid.), the boards seemed to some the cause not the symptom of the ills in the denomination, including its massive numerical losses. And with the dawning of the digital age and its new media, local churches, particularly the larger ones, found they no longer needed agencies as they could generate their own programmatic materials or shop for them anywhere. Denominational loyalty, at least among former mainline denominations, atrophied. Individuals, congregations, and regional judicatories began protesting decisions, priorities, inefficiencies, waste, monetary claims, and the onerous burden of the bureaucratic board and agency structure that seemed the cohesive but oppressive principle in denominations. Agencies responded with the new organizational techniques and theories of the day, resorting to new measures of influence regulation, grant-making, franchising, consulting, credentialing tactics that permitted them to make individual 'sales' of their programmes.

Increasingly, the agencies faced the question, 'Whom do we serve?' and the denomination the query, 'Who are we?' A Methodism haemorrhaging and hardly 'United' in North America, found itself growing in its central conferences, especially those in Africa and the South Pacific. The numbers from Central Conferences increased in General Conference, on the boards, and in the COB. Was the UMC truly a global connection? General Conference found itself to be. The COB has thought so. And the agencies increasingly have followed suit, though much of their programming and services have been and remain oriented to North America and central conferences and have largely depended on their own resources or otherwise coped.

The body that has most effectively moved into the connectional vacuum is the COB. It has done so by reclaiming, to the extent possible and constitutional, the three dimensions of Wesley's connecting activity. It has found ways as a corporate body of giving leadership to the denomination in its temporal and spiritual business. Especially vital have been study commissions and policy-guiding publications, notably *In Defense of Creation* (1986), treating the threat of nuclear war, and *Vital Congregations—Faithful Disciples* (1990), exhorting the church to spiritual renewal. Since then the COB has dealt with children and poverty and the children of Africa. Their self-consciousness in this exercise of the episcopal teaching office in a 600-page publication, *Vision and Supervision* (Mathews and Oden 2003). The COB's behaviour as a conference has to be witnessed. The bishops have taken 'Christian conferencing' to heart, placed themselves in small covenant groups, committed themselves to spiritual disciplines, undertaken Wesleyan works of mercy and of piety, and reshaped their meetings to prioritize the means of grace, particularly the sacrament and Christian conversation (what Wesley meant by Christian conference). Valuing what Christian conferencing has done for their own 'connection', they endeavour to lead their individual conferences towards similar priorities, commitments, and lifestyle. Through both their teaching and their leading, the COB has edged towards engagement with the 'work' of the denomination that goes beyond the chairing role they play in general and annual conferences and in the agencies. Their aspirations to guide policy and legislation, in ways that Asbury as well as Wesley did, is represented in early twenty-first-century proposals to establish a set-aside and permanent president so as to bulk up the staffing for the COB.

The actual adhesive or connective mechanisms of Methodism have changed, evolved, and differed from period to period. Through those transformations Methodism has actually lived out and practised connectionalism in rich and interesting ways. Its development and elaboration of its connectional fabric has also aligned Methodism with connectional churches.

A DENOMINATIONAL CLASSIfiCATION

Commentators on the American scene sometimes speak of churches as connectional. With that term they differentiate denominations with strong corporate, centralized, or hierarchical polities from those with systems that function self-consciously or operationally as congregational, independent, or free church (Kauffman 1967). Although the word lacks precision, it differentiates episcopal and presbyterian from congregational bodies. So connectional churches include Roman Catholics, Lutherans, Episcopalians, Presbyterians, and Methodists; non-connectional, the Baptist, Congregational (UCC), Restorationist, and Mennonite churches.

While accepting the fact that exceptions, complexities, and mixed patterns come easily to mind (the UCC, though congregational in polity, enjoyed established status in New England and the Southern Baptist Convention is controlling and connectional), connectional communions, if Protestant, by and large derive from the Magisterial Reformation and often have enjoyed privileged status as state or established churches. By contrast, many, though not all, of the non-connectional churches have roots or affinities with the Radical or Anabaptist Reformation and a free church ecclesiology. The latter fit comfortably within American social and legal patterns, where voluntarism, separation of church and state, localism, and individualism hold sway. The former have clashed with the courts from time to time. Connectional churches also struggle with the press and with popular opinion that presumes churches to be local bodies 'owned' by members or trustees. To a public, and even a membership, that 'knows' religion to be voluntary, connectional churches have had to explain themselves. This burden has been borne most heavily by the Roman Catholics but virtually all connectional churches can recall some moment of conflict around connectionalism. And this angularity of connectionalism with respect to American values and practice that puts it forth as a term for distinction also occasionally binds these churches together. Connectional churches, Methodist included, have recognized their common interest and joined in *amicus* filings in important liability, authority, and property cases. Methodism's 'trust clause', Wesley's innovation for protecting connectional interests through the deeding of property to the annual conference, has been tested time and again, especially as disaffected congregations have attempted to exit with the church building(s).

Describing Methodism's connectional nature, one would list the trust clause among a number of bonding factors—a centralized treasurer; apportionments; general, incorporated boards; connectional support for theological education and other causes; a general conference, judicial council, and council of bishops; a connectional brand, logo, and website; and so forth. But these substantive factors of property-holding and organizational fabric do not exhaust connectionalism's meaning for Methodists. Nor does our connectionalism derive from the Magisterial Reformation or privileged status as a state church. While United Methodism and other episcopal Methodisms owe much to Anglicanism, the Wesleys, John and Charles, pre-eminently John, defined our connectionalism. To be sure, Americans enriched Wesley's connectionalism by borrowing Anglican ecclesiology and practice and by defining their place in American society alongside other connectional denominations. For some, these later accretions epitomize connectionalism, accretions such as apportionments and corporate bureaucratic boards that spend the apportionments. And when Methodists attempt to reform the church or reshape it following merger, these later accretions tend to preoccupy the architects of the new order. However, the term has a very special meaning for Methodists, an ecclesiological significance lacking in other communions.

CONNECTION AND CHRISTIAN CONFERENCING AS ECCLESIOLOGY

Elsewhere I elaborate connectional meanings but here I mention a Wesleyan precept, a covenantal commitment, an ethic of equity and proportionality, a missional principle, a tactical stratagem, an elastic and evolving standard, a theology in praxis, an ecclesial vision (Richey, Campbell, and Lawrence 1997: 1–20). The fountain from which these meanings flow is that with which we began, namely gathering in conference. Wesley's precept might be seen as twofold, namely his calling of preachers to confer and his identification of Christian conference as one of the instituted means of grace, along with prayer, searching the Scriptures, the Lord's Supper, and fasting. By Christian conference he meant the prayer-guided, gracious, heart-to-heart engagement in conversation that shaped disciplined and faithful discipleship. This precept from the 'Large Minutes' carried over into the American *Discipline* in the section 'Of the Duty of Preachers to God, themselves, and one another'. As such, Christian conversation constituted the expectation and ideal of conferences, indeed of the movement as a whole. Methodism might be seen as a sequence of such Christian conversations—in class, society, quarterly conference, annual conference, and general conference. And at least in early Methodism these gatherings, even the largest, possessed great spiritual intensity, producing conversions and revivals (Richey 1996). Each of these Christian conversations, each conference level, functioned with its own covenantal commitment, measured on entry through the relation of (conversion) experience and in every meeting thereafter with the review of character, both producing powerful bonding among members. Walking or travelling in covenant with one another meant adopting an ethic of equity and proportionality. Early Methodism symbolized that ethic with a common salary (among bishops, presiding elders, preachers), the shared adversity of travelling (for itinerants), holding one another to a disciplined life. Today's Methodism symbolizes that ethic with apportionments. Methodism defined its purpose, missionally, 'to reform the continent and spread scriptural holiness over these lands' and 'to raise a holy people'. That prefatory Disciplinary missional principle oriented people and preachers to witnessing, to concern for the neighbour, to anti-slavery, to an inclusive fellowship, to evangelism, to revival, to reform, to expansion. As missionally guided, as we have seen, Methodists felt empowered to adapt new mechanisms for outreach, communication, and formation—papers, magazines, missionary societies, Sunday schools, colleges, boards. Such purposive connectionalism, a tactical stratagem, at its best reflected not simply pragmatism but the Wesley-like confidence in the guidance of providence, the Spirit's ongoing leading of the church. At moments the Spirit seemed to have departed, as evidenced in conflict and divisions, struggles to be fully inclusive, and especially in its early retreat from anti-slavery and later embrace of segregation. In its better and more 'inspired' moments, new strategies and structures for mission gave Methodism and Methodist connectionalism an elastic and evolving standard. Each period altered the connectional fabric, often adding, sometimes (as we have seen) tearing a bit, occasionally renewing and reweaving, making for now a rich tapestry. Although never formally and officially enunciated as such, connectionalism has enacted an understanding of the church. The connectional theology in praxis, an ecclesial vision, perhaps best still captured by 'Christian conferencing' provides the church universal a distinctive view and yet one that remains faithful to tradition and Scripture.

SUGGESTED READING

FRANK, THOMAS EDWARD (2006). *Polity, Practice, and the Mission of The United Methodist Church*. Nashville: Abingdon.

KIRBY, JAMES E. (2000). *The Episcopacy in American Methodism*. Nashville: Kingswood Books/Abingdon.

MULLIN, ROBERT BRUCE, and RICHEY, RUSSELL E. (eds.) (1994). *Reimagining Denominationalism: Interpretative Essays*. New York: Oxford University Press.

RICHEY (1996). The Methodist Conference in America: A History. Nashville: Kingswood Books. Abingdon.

REFERENCES

BANGS, NATHAN (1860). *A History of the Methodist Episcopal Church*. 12th edn. 4 vols. New York: Carlton & Porter.

The [Daily] Christian Advocate/MEC (1939).

Doctrines and Discipline of The Methodist Church (1940).

HARMON, NOLAN B. (1962). *The Organization of The Methodist Church*. 2nd rev. edn. Nashville: The Methodist Publishing House.

JGC/MEC (*1796–1856*) refers to the *Journals of the General Conference of the Methodist Episcopal Church*. 3 vols. New York: Carlton & Phillips.

KAUFFMAN, DONALD T. (1967). *The Dictionary of Religious Terms*. Westwood, N.J.: Fleming H. Revell.

'The Leesburg Minutes of the Methodist Connection, 1775–1783'. *Virginia United Methodist Heritage* 5 (Autumn 1977).

MATHEWS, JAMES K., and ODEN, WILLIAM B. (2003). *Vision and Supervision: A Sourcebook of Significant Documents of the Council of Bishops of The United Methodist Church, 1968–2002*. Nashville: Abingdon.

MEC/*Minutes of the Annual Conferences of the Methodist Episcopal Church for the Years 1773–1828* (1840). New York: T. Mason & G. Lane.

MICKEY, PAUL A., and WILSON, ROBERT L. (1977). *What New Creation? The Agony of Church Restructure*. Nashville: Abingdon.

Minutes: Taken at a Council of the Bishop and Delegated Elders of the 'Methodist-Episcopal Church' *held in Baltimore in the State of Maryland, December 1, 1790* (1790). Baltimore.

NEELY, THOMAS B. (1892). *A History of the Origin and Development of the Governing Conference in Methodism*. Cincinnati: Curts & Jennings.

PILKINGTON, JAMES P. (1968). *The Methodist Publishing House*. 2 vols. Nashville: Abingdon, i.

Proceedings of the Bishop and Presiding Elders of the Methodist-Episcopal Church, in Council Assembled, at Baltimore, on the First Day of December, 1789 (Baltimore, 1789), 3–7.

RICHEY, RUSSELL E. (1996). *The Methodist Conference in America: A History*. Nashville: Kingswood Books/Abingdon.

—— and CAMPBELL, DENNIS M., (2005). *Marks of Methodism*. United Methodism and American Culture 5. Nashville: Abingdon.

—— —— and LAWRENCE, WILLIAM B. (eds.) (1997). *Connectionalism: Ecclesiology, Mission, and Identity*. United Methodism and American Culture 1. Nashville: Abingdon.

—— ROWE, KENNETH E., and SCHMIDT, JEAN MILLER (eds.) (2000). *The Methodist Experience in America: A Sourcebook*. 2 vols. Nashville: Abingdon, ii.

TIGERT, JNO. J. (1908). *A Constitutional History of American Episcopal Methodism*. 3rd edn. Nashville: Publishing House of the Methodist Episcopal Church (South).

CHAPTER 13

METHODIST EPISCOPACY

JAMES E. KIRBY

At the end of the American Revolution, it was clear to Wesley that the old plan of associating Methodists in America with the Church of England was impossible. Even if Asbury and those who followed him had desired to continue to receive the sacraments in the parishes of the Church of England it was no longer possible. The Church of England in the former colonies was largely in disarray. Many parishes were without priests or had closed entirely; where they remained, church property had been damaged or destroyed during the war. There was no bishop in America to ordain new ones. As a result, many Methodists on the frontier had not received the sacraments in years. Asbury had unsuccessfully pleaded their cause with Wesley and urged him to provide them with an ordained clergy. In 1779 Asbury managed to suppress a movement that would have separated a large number of Methodists in Virginia and North Carolina from the Wesleyan connexion and formed them into a presbytery.

By 1784, however, the reality of the situation had impressed itself on Wesley sufficiently for him to realize he had either to provide the means for the Americans to become an independent church or to lose them entirely. Since they already had two of the classic marks of the church—the preaching of the word and faithful disciples, the only thing lacking was the due and proper administration of the sacraments. Since Wesley considered himself 'a high churchman, the son of a high churchman', he favoured the creation of an episcopal organization in America. The problem was that despite the fact that he was acknowledged as its overseer, and had the pledge of the Americans to follow him in matters of church government, he had no authority to create it. Wesley belonged to a church that functioned with a three-order ministry, deacons, priests, and bishops. Wesley had been ordained only as deacon and priest and lacked the power to ordain others. In ecclesiastical polity, ordination confers power and jurisdiction on the ordinand. Only the bishop has power to ordain others, and John Wesley was not a bishop. He was clearly an 'overseer' (*episcopē*) or 'superintendent' of the Methodists in Great Britain and America, but he was not their bishop. Wesley's problem was to formulate a theologically legitimate rationale for doing what he knew had to be done. He had been tempted to ordain persons for England in 1756 in a situation much like the one he faced in America in 1779, but did not do it, in part because his brother Charles was fiercely opposed to the move, seeing it as separation from the Church of England.

The justification he was seeking came from the past. Wesley explained in a letter written to James Clark on 3 July 1856, that he had long been convinced 'the Episcopal form of government to be both scriptural and apostolical'. But he goes on in the same letter to say that reading Edward Stillingfleet's *Irenicum* [*sic*] had persuaded him that no one form of church government was 'prescribed in Scripture' (Wesley 1931: iii. 182). And in other places he confesses he does not believe in an historic, literal episcopate. In the letter sent with Coke in 1784 to 'Our Brethren in America', written almost forty years after the one to Clark, he recounts that reading Lord Peter King's *Account of the Primitive Church* in January, 1846 'convinced me . . . that bishops and presbyters are the same order and consequently have the same right to ordain' (ibid. vii. 238). Frank Baker in his *John Wesley and the Church of England* adds that Wesley's study of the early church in Alexandria had taught him that 'the presbyters . . . had ordained as bishop one of themselves rather than dilute their ecclesiastical purity by seeking aid from a foreign bishop' (Baker 1970: 263). Baker concludes:

Wesley . . . was not only a presbyter with a presbyter's inherent right to perform the office of the Presiding presbyter or bishop; by his extraordinary call to found and rule the Methodist societies it had been demonstrated that in function he was the equivalent of a scriptural bishop. . . . Both in *ordine* and *gradus* he was a scriptural *episcopos*.   (ibid.)

Wesley's recent biographer, Henry Rack, is not persuaded by Baker's conclusion and says that Wesley used recognized authorities such as King and Stillingfleet to fortify and justify a position he wished to hold for other reasons. He observes that reading them had not persuaded him to ordain in either the 1740s or 1750s, in 1784 he decided to use King and Stillingfleet 'for apologetic purposes . . . to support actions he had decided to take for practical and not theological reasons' (Rack 1992: 292).

There is no doubt that Wesley himself should appropriately be described as an *episcopē* (overseer), but in no ordinary meaning of the word can he be understood to have been an *episcopos* (bishop) since the Church of England regards that as a third order of ministry to which Mr Wesley had not been elevated. Nor was he a member of any organized presbytery that corresponded in any way to the one in Alexandria that he cites as an example. Despite his claim to have been convinced of his authority to ordain for some forty years prior to actually doing it, what he did both for Methodists in America, and later in England, was inconsistent and irregular. To say the least, Mr. Wesley did not have the executive nor ecclesial power understood in the Church of England as necessary to authorize him to ordain persons for ministry. Nor did he act in accord with some other well-formulated understandings of church order in England or America. Tigert (1913: 190–1) astutely observes that 'it seems inexplicable that the Methodist Episcopal Church in America entered on its great career with an ordained ministry but without a General Conference, and that English Methodism, on the death of Wesley, began with a fully organized Conference government, but without an ordained ministry'. Coke's ordination paper, written by Wesley, clearly states that he 'set apart' Coke 'as a superintendent by the imposition of my hands, and prayer (being assisted by other ordained ministers)' (ibid. 174). This implies that Coke, a presbyter, was 'consecrated' or 'designated' to be a superintendent rather than ordained a bishop. Wesley, as the recognized overseer of the people called Methodists in Europe and America, had full authority to do that. He had earlier designated Thomas Rankin and later Francis Asbury to be the 'General Superintendent' for America. But Wesley instructed Coke to 'ordain' Francis Asbury, a local preacher with the title of General Assistant in America, 'deacon, elder and superintendent'. Wesley also devised a modified version of the Prayer Book for use in America that contained, along with the Sunday Service, his revision of the Thirty-Nine Articles, and the liturgies of the Church of England for the 'ordination' of deacons, elders, and bishops. Furthermore, he recorded in his private diary for 1 September 1784 that he had 'ordained' for America. Nor was this his last ordination. Alexander Mathew was ordained deacon, elder, and superintendent by Wesley and appointed to superintend all the Methodist work in England.

The letter to 'Our Brethren in America' (10 September 1784) described what Wesley had done as 'appointing Dr. Coke and Mr. Francis Asbury to be Joint Superintendents over our brethren in North America'. This might be construed simply as Wesley's increasing the size of their jurisdiction by making them 'overseers of the whole'. It is not difficult to understand why Wesley thought it necessary to ordain Asbury deacon and elder since he was, indeed, a lay person, but it does not appear that his authority as the General Assistant for America would have been enhanced by ordaining him a General Superintendent. If anything, it simply brought Coke administratively to Asbury's level of authority. American Methodism's first historian, Jesse Lee, used the word 'ordain' to describe what Coke did for Asbury, but Coke's account of the event in his Journal says that he 'set apart' by the 'imposition of my hands' Asbury as a deacon, elder, and superintendent. This may imply that in his mind consecration and ordination were the same, but it seems more likely that an Oxford Doctor of Civil Laws and a presbyter in the Church of England would clearly recognize the difference. Asbury did not, however, see it that way. He records in his diary that after being elected to the superintendency 'my ordination followed, after being previously ordained deacon and elder' (Asbury 1958: i. 47).

Charles Wesley considered the action taken by his brother both to be ordination and the final link in a long chain of events leading to final separation of the Methodists from the Church of England. He was bitterly disappointed by John's decision, angry and frustrated because he was not consulted or informed beforehand. Writing to Dr Chandler, an Anglican priest, shortly after the ordinations, he said:

I can scarcely yet believe it, that, in his eighty-second year my brother, my old intimate friend and companion, should have assumed the Episcopal character, ordained Elders, consecrated a Bishop and sent him to ordain our lay-Preachers in America! I was then in Bristol, at his elbow; yet he never gave me the least hint of his intention.

(Jackson 1841: 391)

Although John had consulted with a small group of preachers at the Bristol Conference, there was little reason for him to have spoken to Charles for he already knew what he thought. Charles accused him of having acted impulsively and John defended himself by claiming, 'I do nothing rashly. It is not likely I should. . . . If you will go hand in hand with me do. But do not hinder me, if you will not help. Perhaps if you had kept close to me I might have done better' (Wesley 1931: vii. 285). The dispute between the two continued and on 13 September 1785 John wrote what appears to be his final word on the subject. 'I can see no use of you and me disputing together; for neither of us is likely to convince the other. You say I separate from the Church; I say I do not. Then let it stand' (ibid. 288).

To Wesley's credit, he had consistently maintained his societies were created by an extraordinary call of God to mission within the Church of England. He did not understand them to be a separate church despite his numerous acts done to ensure their organization and continuance. Shortly after Wesley's death in 1791, the president of conference, John Pawson, affirmed yet again 'that we have no design or desire of making our Societies *separate churches*' (his italics; British Conference i. 278–82). And with this understanding, it may be possible to argue that Wesley's ordinations for America were missional in nature and intended to ensure the faithful continuation of God's extraordinary call to the people called Methodists.

The Methodist Episcopal Church in America was formed in Baltimore in December, 1784. Among the actions taken was to prepare a definition of the office of a 'superintendent'. They were given responsibility 'to ordain superintendents, elders, and deacons, to preside as a moderator in our Conferences; to fix the appointments of the preachers for the several circuits; and in the intervals of the

Conference, to change, receive or suspend preachers, as necessity may require; and to receive Appeals from preachers and people, and decide them' (*Minutes* 1785: 11–12). In addition they stipulated that 'No persons shall be ordained a superintendent, elder or deacon without the consent of the majority of the Conference and the consent and imposition of the hands of a superintendent.' They also made their superintendents accountable to the Conference and declared them ineligible for any ministerial office in the church should they for any reason cease to travel without the consent of the Conference. Itinerancy was the keystone of oversight.

A few years later in the annotated *Discipline* of 1789, the conference answered a question concerning the nature and polity of the newly formed church as being a government of 'moderate episcopacy'. That grew out of an action taken in 1787 when, without the knowledge of Wesley or the American preachers, Asbury, John Dickens, and Coke changed the name of America's 'overseers' in the *Discipline* from 'superintendent' to 'bishop'. Wesley objected strenuously to the change by telling Asbury in a now famous letter, 'Men may call me a knave or a fool, a rascal, a scoundrel, and I am content; but they shall never by my consent call me Bishop' (Wesley 1931: viii. 91). Asbury argued that the terms were synonymous, but bishop was more commonly found in Scripture. The majority of the preachers agreed to the change 'seeing that it was a scripture name, and the meaning of the word *Bishop,* was the same with that of *Superintendent*' (Lee 1928: 125). It is clear that by changing the title given to him earlier by Wesley, neither Asbury nor his brothers in the ministry intended to establish a three-order ministry, for they did not understand their bishops to be a higher order. Near the end of his life Asbury wrote to Joseph Benson in England: 'With us a bishop is a plain man, altogether like his brethren, wearing no marks of distinction advanced in age and by virtue of his office can sit as president in all the solemn assemblies of the ministers of the gospel; raised to a small degree of constituted and elective authority above all his brethren' (Asbury 1958: iii. 544–5). The 'moderate' form of episcopacy created in the newly organized Methodist Episcopal Church in America is a two-order ministry that denies the validity of a historic episcopate, as Wesley himself did, but functions in practice as *episcopē* by *episcopoi*. In his 'Last Will and Testament' (6 June 1813) Asbury described himself as 'Superintendent and Bishop of the Methodist Church in America' (ibid. 472). When he spoke for the last time to the conference of 1816, he described himself as the 'Senior Superintendent', and his colleague William McKendree as the 'Junior Bishop' (ibid. 533). Despite Asbury's preference for a distinction between junior and senior superintendents, the conference in 1800 had rejected this idea in favour of giving all the bishops legal parity (Lee 1928: 267).

Asbury, who in 1784 had little knowledge of bishops, and in all likelihood had never even seen one, became, nevertheless, Methodism's model for 'itinerant, general superintendency'. To give proper oversight was to do what Asbury did, and his place in the history of American Methodism is unique. He became in America what John Wesley was to Methodists in Great Britain. Coming to America in 1771, he never returned to England, never owned a home, nor married. In the exercise of his office, he sometimes travelled as much as 5,000 miles in a year, making him one of the most familiar figures in the nation. There was no part of the connexion that he failed to reach at one time or another. John Wigger writes in Chapter 3 of this volume that Asbury crossed the Allegheny Mountains some sixty times, and under his leadership Methodism grew from a few hundred members in 1771 to more than 200,000 in 1816. From 1784 until his death in 1816, there were few years in which Asbury did not appoint every Methodist preacher in America. In the truest meaning of the word, Asbury was a missionary bishop and itinerancy was the most essential aspect of his understanding of the office to which he had been elected and ordained.

The extensive personal power and authority exercised by Asbury notwithstanding, neither he nor the conference ever lost sight of the fact that the ultimate power in the American connexion resided in the body of preachers. It was conveyed to them when Asbury refused to receive Wesley's ordination from Coke without first being elected to the office by the preachers who would serve under his authority. This was something that neither Coke nor Wesley had anticipated and is arguably the most significant event in the history of early American Methodism. From the beginning, the bishops have been amenable to the conference for their life and administration. And this requirement became in 1844 one of the major points in the debate that divided the connexion North and South. The preachers in conference were and are the gateway to the ministry at all levels. No bishop can refuse to ordain a person who has been voted into membership or orders by the conference. Today the preachers exercise their authority through a delegated body called the General Conference, but it has not been surrendered.

A second hallmark of episcopacy is the itinerant system. The earliest regulations passed in 1784 said that if, for any reason, a superintendent ceased to 'travel' without the consent of conference, he would be declared ineligible for any ministerial office in the church. Properly to 'oversee' the superintendent must preside in the conferences, appoint the preachers to their stations, and discipline them when the occasion demands. If these requirements cannot be met, the superintendent has no place in the connexion.

And when the Methodist Episcopal Church in 1808 adopted a constitution that provided for the delegated General Conference, it contained six restrictions that limited its powers. The third of these 'Restrictive Rules' provides that the Conference cannot 'change or alter any part or rule of our government, so as to do away episcopacy or to destroy the plan of our itinerant general superintendency' (*Journals* 1856: i. 82–3). But between that time and the present significant changes in the nature of episcopacy have been made. The Rule was amended in 1856 to permit the MEC to create a new order of bishops who were allowed to function only in overseas assignments. They were not general superintendents. With the notable exception of British Methodism, related groups that now constitute global

Methodism have adopted episcopacy but in a variety of forms. The Rule was specifically enacted to guard and ensure the Asburian form and understanding of the office. And even in the United Methodist Church, the episcopal areas have been reduced in size sufficiently to call into question whether, in fact, the denomination still continues an 'itinerant general superintendency' at all. The claim must be based on the fact that United Methodist Bishops are required once a quadrennium to make an overseas visit and that the Council of Bishops is represented at every jurisdictional conference.

Despite Wesley's early ordinations for England and Scotland, British Methodists did not ordain preachers by laying on hands until 1836, and they have never adopted the office of superintendent. Since the death of Wesley, they have understood *episcopē* to be a shared responsibility of conference, circuits, and the local churches, and the districts under the leadership of a chairperson. Disregarding or ignoring the decision he made with regard to the governance of American Methodism, Wesley conveyed his authority in Great Britain to the conference. In the same year he ordained for America he prepared a 'Deed of Declaration' that created a legally defined group of one hundred preachers (the Legal Hundred) and at Wesley's death they, through the conference, assumed the authority and powers he exercised. It, in turn, elected a largely symbolic and ceremonial president who serves a term of one year. The conference directs and leads the church, establishes its structure (e.g. districts and circuits), and approves and ordains its ministry.

Since 1955, British Methodism has been engaged in on and off conversation with the Church of England designed to explore the uniting of the two bodies. In these conversations, a major obstacle has been the requirement imposed on the Methodists to accept the historic episcopate claimed by the Anglicans, and the resistance of the Church of England to the ordination of women to the episcopacy demanded by the Methodists. In Chapter 26 of this volume, Methodism and the Future of Ecumenism, David Chapman has written, 'Questions relating to the mutual recognition of ministries remain the most sensitive aspects of relations between Methodists and Anglicans.' Despite good intentions and serious efforts to reach a suitable agreement, the process has so far been unsuccessful. Methodists have been unwilling to accept any requirement that implies their present ministry has for any reason been flawed or invalid. They have also been insistent that any form of episcopacy they might adopt must not reject their commitment to a collegial form of oversight. A report adopted at the 1998 Conference surveyed the discussions from 1937 forward and concluded that 'while British Methodism does not regard episcopacy as being an essential element of Church order, the Conference has expressed its willingness to embrace the historic episcopate in order to further the cause of Christian unity' ('Episcopé and Episcopacy' 2007: 96). The Committee on Faith and Order at the same time reaffirmed its conviction that 'it would be helpful for the Conference to affirm its willingness to embrace episcopacy in the context of a unity scheme or as a significant step to bring the unity of the church closer'. But it went on to discourage the conference from seeking to 'develop its own form of episcopacy outside that context' (ibid. 100). The charge to the conference at its meeting in 2007 was to agree on a form of episcopacy but it was unable to reach agreement and the issue is yet to be settled.

The Faith and Order Committee was fully aware that there are many forms of episcopacy in the Methodist family. German-speaking groups associated with Methodists adopted the episcopal form of church government when they organized in 1800. 'They elected William Otterbein and Martin Boehm as superintendents or bishops' (Behney and Eller 1979: 98). They were elected to serve for life. Both these individuals had been closely associated with Asbury for many years; Otterbein participated in the laying on of hands when Coke ordained Asbury superintendent. The German word for superintendents, *Eldesten*, literally translated means 'elders'. When Boehm died in 1812, Christian Newcomer was chosen to replace him but was granted a term of only one year. The following year the conference extended his term by three years and a pattern of four-year term episcopacy was established (ibid. 101). In 1825, the practice of consecrating bishops among United Brethren by laying on hands was discontinued, being judged unscriptural and unnecessary.

A related group led by Jacob Albright formed the Evangelical Association in 1803; Albright, a licensed Methodist 'exhorter', was elected to lead them and given the title 'elder preacher'. He was an *episcopē* without the title of bishop. Methodists had in 1792 designated its supervising preachers in the circuits as 'presiding elders'. Four years later, however, Albright was given the title of bishop. Upon his death, his successors were not given that title, but the Methodist title of 'presiding elder'. Their duties, however, were not the same. Methodist presiding elders were considered a local extension of episcopacy, chosen to serve at the pleasure of the bishop for a limited term. In 1830, the *Discipline* of the Evangelical Association was revised to provide for term episcopacy and to limit the service of any bishop to two four-year terms. As a result, the first 'bishop' to follow Albright was John Seybert who was elected in 1839.

The Evangelical Association and the United Brethren in Christ merged in 1946 and formed the Evangelical United Brethren. The new church continued the practice of term episcopacy but did not limit the number of terms any bishop might serve. In the twenty-two years of its independent existence before uniting with the Methodist Church in 1968, it never failed to re-elect a sitting bishop. The episcopal office was considered administrative in nature and its ecclesial functions were limited. Its holders also function as the judicial council for the denomination that gave them a certain veto power over actions taken in the general conference.

Traditional African-American Methodists also opted for episcopal polity, but have exercised far greater authority than their EUB counterparts. The earliest bishop elected was Richard Allen who was ordained deacon by Francis Asbury.

After a dispute with the leaders of the congregation in St George's Church in Philadelphia, he and Absalom Jones in 1787 organized the Free African Society. It became in 1815 the African Methodist Episcopal Church. The African Methodist Episcopal, Zion, was organized in 1821 in New York; the third major group, the Christian (originally Colored) Methodist Episcopal Church, was organized following the Civil War by the leaders of the Methodist Episcopal Church (South). All these bodies have maintained forms of life tenure in episcopacy until the present.

The Asburian pattern of episcopacy in America was seriously challenged even while he was alive. James O'Kelly urged the 1792 Conference to allow the preachers to appeal their appointments from the bishop to the conference. When it was determined that a new bishop would be elected in 1800, Ezekiel Cooper proposed that a bishop should be elected for each of the seven annual conferences. Had this been adopted, Methodism would have embraced diocesan episcopacy. Attempts to elect presiding elders, rather than have them appointed by the bishops, continued until 1828. And even though general superintendency was reaffirmed as the form of episcopacy and all bishops declared 'equal', the last truly 'itinerant general superintendent' in American Methodism was William McKendree. McKendree, whose election on 6 May 1808 was noted by Asbury in his journal as 'the electing [of] dear brother M'Kendree assistant bishop', was a man of the frontier with a mind of his own. At the first session of the newly formed general conference he gave the first 'episcopal address'. Asbury had not been told he planned to do it and rose to protest it as 'doing a new thing'. McKendree stood, faced the venerable bishop and replied, 'You are our *father*, we are your sons; you never had need of it. I am only a *brother*, and have need of it' (Paine 1872: i. 264). It has been given on the opening day of every general conference since. It was also McKendree who organized the presiding elders into a cabinet and utilized them in the making of appointments. Once again Asbury protested, but that practice has also continued.

The greatest change associated with McKendree was not one he favoured. When Asbury died in 1816, Robert Roberts and Enoch George were elected to fill out the ranks of the episcopacy. Roberts was the first bishop to be married at the time of his election. In 1824 two more bishops were elected, Joshua Soule and Elijah Hedding, both of whom were from the north-east. By this time there were seventeen annual conferences to be served by five bishops. McKendree, the senior bishop, decided to form his colleagues into a council whose duty it would be to decide how best to divide the work in the conferences. Roberts and Soule assumed responsibility for the southern conferences of the church and Hedding and George took the ones in the north and east. McKendree, who was in poor health, was given no specific assignment but was left to work when and wherever he was able. Over the opposition of Bishop George, they agreed that at the beginning of the third year of the quadrennium the conferences would be exchanged. But the exchange never took place and the connexion was effectively divided into two parts.

This arrangement lasted twenty years. During that time Hedding made one trip into the southern conferences and Soule made one into the north in 1831. The practice was begun in the interest of efficiency and convenience, but the results were that all the bishops with the exception of McKendree ceased 'to itinerate throughout the connection' and in so doing ceased in the real sense to be 'itinerant general superintendents'. The 1832 General Conference sanctioned the basic concept of the change by allowing the annual conferences to determine whether it was 'conducive to the general good . . . whether it be or be not expedient for each of the bishops, in the course of four years to visit each of the Annual Conferences' (Tigert 1913: 411). An even more ominous aspect of this change was that it demonstrated the reality and power of sectionalism that was destined to divide the church and plunge the nation into civil war.

This was but the most glaring early example of the manner in which practice was to change the shape of episcopacy in the Methodist Episcopal Church. American Methodists have been 'doers' more than they have been 'thinkers', and unexpected results have often been accepted without question as 'the way it is done'. Today United Methodist bishops are more properly understood as diocesan officers than as itinerant general superintendents. The office has begun in many ways to function like an order. The number of annual conferences has been consistently reduced so that most UMC bishops today preside over only one. Long before the formal separation in the 1840s a dispute had arisen in the MEC about the nature of episcopacy itself. The conferences in the southern part of the church generally accepted the idea that the bishops were a co-equal branch of church government with the general conference. They argued that Methodism had bishops before there was a general conference. Asbury remained their model despite the modifications that had taken place in the operation of episcopal oversight. The Methodist Protestant Church was formed in 1830 to empower laypersons and to protest what they regarded as the excessive authority of the bishops. Groups within the denomination looked for ways by which their power could be limited rather than enhanced or acknowledged. In parts of the church that favoured the abolition of slavery, attempts were made to override the bishop's power to set the agenda of the annual conference.

The conflict came with all its fury into the General Conference of 1844. The major issue before the delegates was whether the institution of slavery would be allowed into the episcopacy, and it was focused on a southern bishop named James O. Andrew who had come into the possession of slaves after his election to the episcopacy in 1832. The issue was whether a bishop who was associated with slavery could continue in his office, and who had the power to decide. The circumstances by which Andrew had come to own slaves and the fact that he had never been charged with any offence in the twelve years of his episcopal service complicated the discussion. The southern delegates to the conference argued that the episcopacy was protected by the Third Restrictive Rule of the Constitution of 1808 that

Jon Tigert described as 'the constitutional charter of the episcopacy' (Tigert 1913: 485). Andrew, they argued, was protected by the rule and either it had to be changed or he had to be charged and convicted of maladministration or moral failure. Without that, the general conference had no power to remove him.

The northern conferences, on the other hand, insisted that bishops were officers elected by the general conference, and if they could be elected by that body, they could certainly be removed by it 'for the good of the church'. The theory behind this argument was articulated during the debates by a delegate from Ohio, Leonidas L. Hamline. At the time he was the editor of *The Ladies' Repository*. In what is known as the Croton River Speech, Hamline argued that the general conference is supreme in its legislative, judicial, and executive authority. It, he said, is 'the sun of our system', from which all parts of the connexion receive light and power. Rather than being a co-equal branch of church government, the episcopacy is 'an abstraction' that can be worked 'into a concrete form in any hundred or more ways we may be able to invent'. Just as bishops have the power to remove preachers or preachers have the authority to remove church officials 'for the good of the church', so also the supreme body in the church enjoys that same privilege ('Debates 1844': 128–34). Hamline's theory carried the day and the delegates voted that Andrew should 'desist in the exercise of his office' so long as he was associated with slavery. Moreover, it is the theory that has to a large degree informed Methodist ideas of episcopacy ever since.

Despite the fact that the Third Restrictive Rule has been amended only twice, once in 1856 to allow the creation of a new episcopal office in the Methodist Episcopal Church, that of Missionary Bishop, the episcopacy has been in an almost constant state of change and adjustment to meet the needs it has faced.

Missionary Bishops were created in response to the repeated calls for episcopal supervision from overseas missions. Francis Burns, both the first African-American and Missionary Bishop, was elected and assigned to Liberia in 1858. Missionary Bishops were elected by the general conference in the United States, but limited to service as bishops only in the mission field to which assigned. They were bishops who had full powers in their areas, but limited jurisdiction. They could not serve as general superintendents in the US unless elected to that office. Upon the completion of their missionary service, they returned to their annual conferences as elders. Once again there were unforeseen consequences. In no sense were they general superintendents, nor were they equal to their colleagues who were. The situation became even more complex when in 1920 Matthew Wesley Clair, Sr. and Robert Elijah Jones, both African Americans, were elected general superintendents. They, like Missionary Bishops, were limited in their jurisdiction and could serve only in African-American Conferences in the US, but they were general superintendents. Their colleagues with the same title could serve anywhere in the connexion. The Methodist Episcopal Church (South) avoided all these complications by assigning their general superintendents overseas.

By 1924 the Methodist Episcopal Church had organized all its overseas missions into central conferences and the 1928 General Conference empowered them to elect their own bishops, creating yet another variation in the office. The resolution was a distinction made between two kinds of episcopal service, General Superintendency and Limited Superintendency. General superintendents, with the exception of the African Americans, were constitutional bishops protected by the Third Restrictive Rule. Limited superintendency, on the other hand, was subject to limitations imposed by legislation (Committee on Judiciary 1932: 632). The ruling was prompted by a decision in the central conference to impose term limits on their bishops. The era of Missionary Bishops closed in 1932 and today central conferences affiliated with the United Methodist Church are organized into areas, each of which is presided over by a bishop. Some of these bishops are restricted to a term of office, others are not.

The most sweeping change in the episcopacy, again without modification of the Third Rule, came in 1939 when the Methodist Protestants, Methodist Episcopal, and Methodist Episcopal Church (South) united to form the Methodist Church. The key to reunion was the creation of five geographic and one racial jurisdiction. Bishop John M. Moore observed that the church had reunited by 'reorganizing'. The election of bishops was moved from the general to the jurisdictional conferences, and bishops were restricted to service in the jurisdiction in which elected. A provision to allow the transfer of a bishop across jurisdictional lines has existed from the beginning but has never been utilized in either the Methodist Church or the United Methodist Church. The process of localizing episcopacy that began in 1826 was complete when the jurisdictional structure was put into place. Electing persons in the jurisdictions increased the number of bishops and changed the type of person who could be elected. Following Asbury's advice, early Methodism kept the number of bishops small and persons were elected who were widely known for their work as editors of church publications, leaders of missionary societies, college presidents, and heads of boards or agencies. The Methodist Church, by contrast, almost exclusively elected persons who were appointed to large congregations, and in the United Methodist Church the emphasis was more clearly focused on the local congregation. Rarely have United Methodist bishops lived or served for any significant period of time outside the bounds of their jurisdictions, and almost without exception they have attended college and seminary there, too. Their theological training has usually been in seminaries in proximity to their homes. Going away to school is no longer a viable choice. Seminaries have become regional, too. Candidates for election have a better chance for success if they have been nominated by an annual conference (it helps to lead the delegation), do well in the series of interviews with delegations from the various conferences prior to the jurisdictional conference, and have an episcopal area that agrees in advance to accept them if they are elected.

Moreover, once elected they must cope with the reality that the powers of their office have been significantly limited. The enactment of a mandatory retirement age has given the church a de facto system of term episcopacy. Persons elected usually have only two or three quadrenniums to serve. Some central conferences have formally adopted term episcopacy. Since 1976 bishops have been limited to eight years of service in an episcopal area unless missional priorities require an additional four years. The authority to station the preachers has also been systematically reduced by procedures outlined in the *Disciple*. Deacons who are conference members are appointed by bishops only in the sense that they ratify their positions in secular or ecclesial settings. Staff appointments in larger congregations are generally negotiated by senior pastors. Clergy in large churches are generally chosen by them and are rarely moved. Any ruling made by a bishop about a law of the church that is challenged will be reviewed by the Judicial Council. Boards and agencies on which bishops serve often limit their authority by electing them as presidents thus limiting their participation. Some bishops have complained they are expected merely to be messengers from the boards and agencies to the Council of Bishops. They preside but are not members of either the general or jurisdictional conferences.

The Plan of Union adopted in 1939 created the Council of Bishops and the Judicial Council. This gave the Methodist Church two constitutional entities, a Judicial Council elected by the general conference and a Council of Bishops elected by the jurisdictional conferences. Bishops do not serve on the Judicial Council. All bishops, active and retired, in the church, are members of the Council of Bishops and the College, its jurisdictional counterpart. Retired bishops have the privilege to speak but may not vote. The Constitution prohibits active bishops from meeting in separate sessions. In its early years seniority determined leadership in the Council; it was later reorganized into a committee structure, but since its creation it has been customary for the Council to operate by consensus. Currently there are fifty active bishops, nineteen bishops from central conference and ninety-three retired. Minority reports are not adopted so it is difficult for topics of disagreement to be publicly acknowledged. In 1996 fifteen members of the Council went public with their opposition to the church's stand on homosexuality. Their action was not welcomed by most other members of the Council. The president of the Council serves a term of two years; an executive secretary, who is a retired bishop, serves for four. The Council also has an Ecumenical Officer who may be either active or retired who also serves a four-year term. The president of the Council is empowered to speak publicly for the denomination only 'when consonant with the position of the General Conference and (2) according to processes established by the Council' (Bylaws 2004: 5). Attempts to create an office of Presiding Bishop with a four-year term and significant powers have either been defeated or ruled unconstitutional. While the Council cannot speak for the church, it can address the church and has done so by means of 'Pastoral Letters' or 'Position Papers' on a variety of topics such as the ministry, evangelism, nuclear disarmament, racism, terrorism, AIDS, etc.

(Mathews and Oden 2003). Such pronouncements, however, have only the weight of their logic and concern. The general conference alone makes policy for the United Methodist Church.

United Methodist bishops are charged today, as they have been in the past, with the 'oversight' of the entire church, and their parish now truly is the world. At the meeting of the general conference in 2004 there were more delegates from the Congo than from the Western Jurisdiction of the United States. Even more overseas delegates were present in 2008. At the 2004 conference yet another commission was appointed to study the episcopacy. It suggested a revision to the mission statement of the church, urged better and more consistent standards of evaluation, recommended raising the age of mandatory retirement to 72, and reluctantly agreed at the urging of the General Commission on Finance and Administration to recommend the number of active bishops in the United States be reduced by four (*Daily Christian Advocate* 2008: 1113–15). The Episcopal Fund regularly runs a deficit. The 2008 conference accepted their recommendation to raise the mandatory retirement age thus enabling a few bishops facing retirement at their upcoming jurisdictional conferences to serve another quadrennium. The total number of active bishops were reduced by four through attrition. The Southeastern Jurisdiction was exempted from the requirement.

The questions all Methodists face today are 'What kind of leadership does a global church require?' and 'Is it possible with our current organization and practices to identify and provide such leaders?' British Methodists and all those united with them across the world in the practice of *episcopē* must finally settle their relation to the Church of England by deciding in the near future whether to accept the historic episcopate it claims. United Methodists must begin their deliberations by accepting the fact that they at best have a limited itinerant general superintendency that bears little resemblance even to the 'moderate episcopacy' of early Methodism that is assumed and protected by the Third Restrictive Rule of the Constitution. The episcopal areas of United Methodism now more closely resemble those of diocesan episcopacy. Secondly, the jurisdictional system that dictates to a large degree the kind of person who is elected to the episcopal office is outmoded and expensive. Its primary responsibility is electing the bishops and other more efficient and less expensive ways are available to accomplish that task. Only the Southeastern Jurisdiction maintains any significant programming or structure. Overseas Methodists have no similar organization. Bishops could be elected by the delegates to the general conference during its regular meetings. A simple transition to this change could be made by maintaining the boundaries of the present jurisdictions for the purpose of electing bishops and allowing their delegates to vote as jurisdictions. Persons elected in this manner, however, could be assigned by the Committee on Episcopacy of the General Conference to the areas to which their gifts and graces are best suited without regard to jurisdictional boundaries.

Likewise, the Council of Bishops must streamline its operation. Changes are already in process and old patterns are being modified. Two large classes of new bishops have joined the council in the past eight years. A smaller council would be more efficient and this reduction might be possible by limiting the membership of retired bishops equal to their years of active service. The council needs the strong leadership a presiding bishop could provide. It needs, in addition, to acknowledge and encourage the presence of differences of opinion among its members and express them forthrightly in order to encourage the church as a whole to do the same. The issues faced today in a global church are far too complex to be aired only in closed meetings where real differences are not expressed and debated. The church of the twenty-first century whose diversity is already a transforming reality must be led by persons who value its free expression. While notable progress is obvious in that arena, by no means has an acceptable level been achieved in either organization or practice. The Episcopal Address was given by a woman only for the second time in 2008.

The umbrella that claims to represent world Methodism is the World Methodist Council. It is a powerless body based in the mountains of North Carolina that is not empowered to speak for any of its members, has no adequate financial base for support, and cannot in any true sense claim to be the organization of world Methodism. The reality, however, is that if such a body did not exist we would probably have to invent it. The challenge is to strengthen it to represent the rich variety of Methodists across the world and give it adequate powers to implement its actions. The General Conference of United Methodism continues to be dominated by American Methodists. But it, too, is being transformed as at each session the number of delegates from central conferences increases dramatically and will in the near future be in the majority. The general conference for now, however, remains the voice of the United Methodist Church in the United States. And for the first time, it is in real danger of schism in the church. The connexional system as it exists today no longer has the power to bind it together. Real and tangible differences have overcome our common heritage. Today's Methodists have learned the value and effectiveness of caucus politics. Bishops, who in spite of their disciplinary mandate to 'oversee the church' lack the power to stem that tide. Many of them are, in fact, products of it. Methodism needs a new kind of leader who has the vision, power, and courage to lead a church that is both global and fragmented; and in order to provide such leadership a new method must be devised for identifying and choosing it.

Perhaps it is a gift that the concept of Methodist episcopacy as 'an abstraction that can be formed in any one of a hundred ways' has prevailed today. And our hope is that leaders as suited to the time, tasks, and setting of our day as those sturdy followers of Wesley in the midlands of England and Asbury on the American frontier in the eighteenth century can shape it to speak the Word as clearly in the twenty-first.

REFERENCES

ASBURY, FRANCIS (1958). *The Journals and Letters of Francis Asbury*, ed. E. T. Clark, J. M. Potts, and J. S. Payton. 3 vols. London: Epworth.

BAKER, FRANK (1970). *John Wesley and the Church of England*. Nashville: Abingdon.

BEHNEY, J. BRUCE, and ELLER, PAUL H. (1979). *The History of the Evangelical United Brethren Church*. Nashville: Abingdon.

British Conference (1791). *Minutes of the Methodist Conferences from the First Held in London by the Late Reverend John Wesley, A. M. in the Year 1744 (1791–1836)*. London: Thomas.

'Bylaws of the Council of Bishops' (2004). United Methodist Church. Unpublished.

Committee on Judiciary (1932). 'Report of the Committee on Judiciary'. *Journal of the Thirty-First Delegated General Conference of the Methodist Episcopal Church*, ed. John M Arters. New York: The Methodist Book Concern.

Daily Christian Advocate (2008). Advance Edition. 'Report to 2008 General Conference from the Task Force to Study the Episcopacy'. Nashville: The United Publishing House.

'Debates in the General Conference, 1844' (1932). In *Journal of the General Conference of the Methodist Episcopal Church*. 3 vols. New York: Carlton & Phillips.

'Episkopé and Episcopacy' (2007). A report from the Faith and Order Committee to the Methodist Conference of Great Britain.

JACKSON, THOMAS (1841). *The Life of the Rev. Charles Wesley, M.A.* London: John Mason.

Journals of the General Conference of the Methodist Episcopal Church 1796–1856 (1856). 3 vols. New York: Carlton & Phillips.

LEE, JESSE (1928). *A Short History of the Methodists in the United States of America*. Baltimore: Magill & Clime.

MATHEWS, JAMES K., and ODEN, WILLIAM B. (eds.) (2003). *Vision and Supervision: A Sourcebook of Significant Documents of the Council of Bishops of the United Methodist Church 1968–2002*. Nashville: Abingdon.

Minutes of Several Conversations between the Rev. Thomas Coke, LL.D., the Rev. Francis Asbury and others, at a Conference, Begun in Baltimore in the State of Maryland on Monday, the 27th of December, in the year 1784. Composing a Form of Discipline for the Ministers Preachers and other Members of the Methodist Episcopal Church in America (1785). Philadelphia: Charles Cist.

PAINE, ROBERT (1872). *Life and Times of William M'Kendree*. 2 vols. Nashville: Publishing House of the Methodist Episcopal Church South.

RACK, HENRY D. (1992). *Reasonable Enthusiast*. Nashville: Abingdon.

TIGERT, JNO. J. (1913). *Constitutional History of American Episcopal Methodism*. Rev. and enlarged edn. Nashville: Publishing House of the Methodist Episcopal Church, South.

WESLEY, JOHN (1931). *Letters*, ed. John Telford. 8 vols. London: Epworth.

CHAPTER 14

DISCIPLINE

THOMAS EDWARD FRANK

THE most notable feature of discipline as a topic of Methodist Studies is the dearth of scholarship addressing discipline per se in the Methodist traditions. 'Discipline' is a term embracing many of Methodism's arguably most signature practices. Many of them are explored under other topics in this *Handbook*, such as conference, episcopacy, ministry, means of grace, holiness, missions, and ecumenism.

One might well ask, then, what is left to discuss under the separate heading of discipline. This question is an accurate reflection of the sparse literature on the subject. Books that explore Methodist discipline as a whole, seeking to name its constitutive elements and core practices and the way those elements and practices combine to generate Methodism's unique character as a movement, have numbered three or less in most every generation—at least of American Methodism. Discipline in particular understood as the published covenants inclusive of church order and governance of the far-flung branches of Methodism is a subject largely left to the political activities of governing bodies themselves.

Thus a broad and fertile field of scholarly interest, largely untouched over the last century, awaits any who would venture into its unexplored and intriguing questions. What is distinctive about the contexts within which Methodist discipline arose and has been practised? What elements give Methodist discipline its unique character? What does the Methodist heritage of order and governance offer to critical and constructive conversations with contemporary organizational and political practices, within the churches as well as in civil government, business corporations, and non-profit agencies? A new generation of scholarship must explore this heritage and clarify its distinctiveness in order to make its wisdom available to church and society.

Methodist discipline has sustained a purpose, style, and tone distinct among Protestant traditions. Other Protestants, particularly churches grounded in the Reformed tradition, would term church law about membership, local church organization, and ministry, matters of church order. Reformed books of church law are typically titled 'The Book of Order'. The term 'discipline' in many Protestant traditions is confined to standards and expectations of church members and refers especially to descriptions of practices or behaviours that, exercised by individuals or by congregations, are sufficient to provoke procedures such as inquiry, trial, and if necessary, some form of censure, recompense, or expulsion (Frank 2003; Long 2001).

Methodism as a whole has held a far broader and more irenic view of discipline. Only on occasion in Methodist history has discipline functioned primarily as an instrument of censure or exclusion. Indeed, the books of church law embracing all aspects of church life across Methodism are most often titled *The Book of Discipline*.

Methodism's distinctive understanding of what discipline is in the life of the Christian community has evolved in eight phases of Methodist development. Each of the eight contributes a feature of Methodist discipline that remains an active element in the chemistry of contemporary Methodism. Each is deserving of study in its own right.

The originative phase of Methodism in eighteenth-century England profoundly shaped the character of the movement and its discipline. This first definitive phase of discipline as *common rule of life* had its roots in the fascination of John Wesley and his companions at Oxford with traditions of Christian spirituality and holy living across the centuries. Wesley became convinced that Christian practices—popularly associated with monastic communities in which such practices comprised the daily lives of participants—could also be formative for Christians living the everyday life of work and home in ordinary towns and villages. Wesley saw no reason why all Christians could not live disciplined lives that would enable them to grow in the knowledge and love of God.

Thus when Methodist societies began to form, the document central to their common life—and certainly the originative document of all Methodist discipline—was the General Rules. Here Wesley laid out in simple and abbreviated form a paragraph explaining why Methodist societies had been formed, a short section on the organization of class meetings and the responsibilities of class leaders, and then three sections that comprised a framework for Christian life and practice to be shared by all who joined Methodist societies. First was an admonition to do no harm, 'by avoiding evil of every kind', followed by a list of behaviours and outlooks that would not 'evidence [a] desire of salvation'. Second was an admonition to do good, 'by being in every kind merciful', followed by a list of actions to be encouraged especially in building up all those who shared this covenant. Third was a brief schedule of Christian practices that Wesley termed 'the ordinances of God' because they were patterns of action through which God had promised grace to the participant: worship, reading the Word of God, the Lord's Supper, prayer, 'searching the Scriptures', and fasting.

Wesley asserted that the General Rules were grounded in Scripture, 'the only rule, and the sufficient rule, both of our faith and practice'. In the context of his own study of Christian traditions and his ministry, he had composed a rule of life that he believed to derive from the earliest practices of Christian communities. Like a monastic community, Methodist societies were to be guided by a basic pattern shaping the everyday lives of participants in ways that would enable them to grow more fully in the knowledge and love of God.

The gradual displacement of the General Rules from their generative role in the movement, and the widespread contemporary amnesia about their power to constitute Methodism as Methodism, is a remarkable feature in the eventual development of Methodism. The General Rules are still published in Methodist books of discipline; for example, they are specifically protected from facile alteration and are printed with other doctrinal standards in the United Methodist *Book of Discipline* (2008: §§21, 103). Yet they are little studied and are largely unknown to contemporary Methodists.

In part this ignorance derives from the same gross misunderstanding of discipline that typified Wesley's theological critics. The 'rules' are heard as 'laws' or 'prohibitions', the basis for throwing people out or censuring them for ungodly behaviour. Wesley on the contrary understood the rules as an invitation open to all who evidence 'a desire to flee from the wrath to come, and to be saved from their sins'. Joining a Methodist society brought an obligation to follow the rule of life, to be sure, accompanied by mutual bonds of fellowship in helping 'each other to work out their salvation'. The Methodist covenant was both an open invitation and a definite commitment. But it was far more a commitment to finding the way forward together than a sworn allegiance to a creed or defined set of righteous behaviours.

While a few of the items listed under 'doing no harm' or 'doing good' were specific—drunkenness, slave-holding, or avoiding customs duties under the former heading, for example—most were matters of judgement. 'Singing those songs, or reading those books, which do not tend to the knowledge or love of God' was listed; but how would one know which was which? Conversely, the rules admonished followers to give food to the hungry and clothing to the naked; but how and to what extent and under what circumstances is one called to do this? The General Rules were an argument that one could not know in solitary, that the only holiness was 'social holiness' sought in company with others, together with whom one could continue to grow and deepen in good and faithful judgement of how to live as a Christian in a complex world.

The logic of the General Rules is central to how Methodism has characteristically understood discipline. This logic is grounded on an assumption of invitation into a way of life, structured by practices of studying and conversing in community to find the most useful ways to do good, avoid evil, and grow in the knowledge and love of God, and given substance by the divine ordinances through which God's grace is present. As scholars who have studied the Rules and their inherent theology have noted, their intent was to nurture 'an ongoing relationship with God...as a continual growth in love', in Henry Knight's words (1992: 36–7). Adherence to the rule of life was 'first and foremost a response to God's grace, and not a striving for virtue, nor yet an expectation of instant salvation', as David Watson put it. Rather, life under such a rule was the Methodist's disciplined acceptance of the obligations inherent in responding to grace, the disciple's participation in the journey of salvation—going on to perfection in love (Watson 1985: 87).

This invitational, relational, developmental logic of the Christian life is essential Methodism. How odd, then, that the foundational document in which the logic is embedded is so little acknowledged in contemporary Methodist bodies. A polity scholar of an earlier generation, Nolan B. Harmon (1977), was surely right to devote a major section of his book on *Understanding The United Methodist Church* to discussion of the General Rules. Yet the implications for organizing the entire church law of a tradition around a rule of life—that is, grounding church order on the common rule of a people in covenant to grow together in the Christian life—have yet to be fully explicated. Certainly Methodism's foundation in the General Rules has profoundly shaped the other seven phases of Methodist disciplinary development and is central to Methodism's characteristic tension over continuing as a movement parallel to a monastic order or more fully developing the marks and forms of church.

The second feature of Methodist discipline that originated early on was its nature as a *connexional conversation*. As Wesley attracted and sent out increasing numbers of preachers, he sustained a deeply personal and rigorous 'connexion' with them through energetic and persistent correspondence and regular visits to their preaching places. More significantly for the development of Methodist discipline, though, was Wesley's calling together of his preachers in conference. Through these connexional practices, Wesley could ensure that a theology of God's grace and human growth in the Christian life was thoroughly shared among the preachers. He could also help them identify the challenges and possibilities of the societies across England—and increasingly in other nations—and lead them towards mutually agreed approaches to ministry and mission.

Wesley believed, as was evident in Methodist class meetings, that Christian conversation was a means of grace, of drawing people into closer relationship with God. He listed conference or conversation under the 'Instituted' means of grace: '(5.) Christian conference: Are you convinced how important and how difficult it is to "order your conversation right?" Is it "always in grace? seasoned with salt? meet to minister grace to the hearers?" Do not you converse too long at a time?' (Large Minutes, 1872: Q. 48). He sought to make the conversations in conference like a class meeting writ large, that is, as searching as possible.

He pushed the preachers to think more constructively about the most effective means of preaching, the most responsible way to handle funds, the most appropriate way to address conflicts with other theological views. Conference was not for the faint of heart.

What was notable about conference in the early development of a distinctively Methodist form of church discipline, though, was that the Methodists did not follow their meetings by issuing doctrinal statements or church laws. Wesley certainly produced his share of tracts and pamphlets. But these were not the public face of conference itself. Rather, the Methodists published a record of their conversations as such, in that very form.

The 'Minutes of several conversations' among John Wesley and Methodist preachers were published regularly following the initial conference in 1744. Later known as the 'Large Minutes', they were organized in a question and answer format, as if to serve as a verbatim record of an actual conversation. Questions ranged from poignant examinations of accountability ('Why is it that the people under our care are no better? Why are we not more holy?') to mundane ('How many circuits are there now?'), and from general ('What is faith?') to specific ('What is the office of a Helper?'). Wesley edited them, of course, and the questions obviously were managed. The 'Minutes' were not really a verbatim record.

Yet Methodists chose to keep them in this form as the public report of their activities. When Methodist preachers began to meet in the new United States, for example, they first published in 1785 *Minutes of several conversations between Coke, Asbury and others composing a form of Discipline for the ministers, preachers and other members of the Methodist Episcopal Church in America*. Soon the book's title was formalized and in the several Methodist denominations in the US took the wording *Doctrines and Discipline of the* [variously] *Methodist Episcopal Church in America, African Methodist Episcopal Church*, and so on. Yet the question and answer format (printed with sequentially numbered Q and A), including many of the topics and much of the content of the Large Minutes, persisted through the nineteenth century and in some branches into the twentieth century.

Here again, little scholarship has pursued the implications of the conversational format for Methodism's character, or the consequences of replacing it in recent generations with more formal discursive statements of church law. In United Methodism, for example, the only remnant of the Q and A format remains in the reports of boards of ordained ministry to their respective annual conferences ('Who is elected probationary member? Who is elected elder?' and so on). What is gained or lost by the diminishing of this tradition?

Much has been made of 'conversation' in contemporary politics, universities, and organizations of all types. Conversation has replaced 'discussion' or 'debate' in many contexts, the latter replete with assumptions of clash and confrontation. 'Dialogue' suggests only two partners, when contemporary organizations must include a wide variety of voices. It seems that Methodists stopped defining themselves through 'conversation' at just about the time the rest of society needed to know how to construct it and make the most of it.

What 'conversation' contributes to a uniquely Methodist sense of discipline is the character of openness and flexibility. A conversation is dynamic, not static as in closely worded and formally adopted pronouncements of church law. A conversation may take many turns, responsive to a change of question, a newly arisen need, or a fresh insight. A conversation may widen its circle, so that growing numbers of voices can participate. And the report of a conversation teaches the reader how a certain conclusion was reached, what alternative possibilities were considered, and in short, how to think—in the terms of United Methodism's statement of 'Our Theological Task' (*Book of Discipline* 2008: §104)—critically and constructively, individually and communally, contextually and incarnationally, and above all, practically, about Christian life and work.

As in the logic of the General Rules, a conversation is foremost a relationship and interaction among persons seeking God together, and thus an apprehension of divine grace. If a person is to grow in the knowledge and love of God, s/he must grow in judgement of what is conducive to relationship with God. If a connexion is to grow in effectiveness of ministry, it must grow in judgement of what will exhibit the gospel. This growth, whether personal or connexional, occurs through conversation. So Methodist discipline has taught.

Contemporary books of discipline are written in a style more closely conforming to church or canon law. Yet their conversational character is not entirely lost. The United Methodist bishops stated in their 'Episcopal Greetings' introducing the 2008 *Book of Discipline*, for example, that the book 'is not sacrosanct or infallible, but . . . a document suitable to our heritage. It is the most current statement of how United Methodists agree to live their lives together' (2008: p. v). These are the words of a community in conversation together, not the pronouncements of a churchly *magisterium*.

The conversational character of Methodist discipline, normally flexible, inclusive, and loath to discourage or exclude anyone who comes seeking the Christian life, is maddening to Christians of other traditions who need to know who is in and who is out, where exactly the church stands, or who has the authority to make a final decision. Conversations can also be aimless and unproductive, and Methodists have participated in plenty of that sort. Would Methodism be better served by proposals to move the tradition towards a more rigorous legal form of church discipline with clearer lines of authority and doctrine? Or by scholarly and focused attention on how to deepen appreciation and understanding of the conversational form and ways to improve its practice, including a more vivid realization of what contribution Methodism's conversational heritage can make to practices in other associations and organizations? This, too, is fertile ground for Methodist studies—and conversation.

A third, *constitutional* phase of Methodist discipline came naturally at the conclusion of the Wesley era, at the points where Methodism needed to constitute itself as a church with a continuing organization independent of the founding generation. In the United States, for example, the Methodist preachers continued to meet under the superintendency of Francis Asbury for nearly twenty-five years after the organizing conference of Christmas 1784, largely following the traditions of the Large Minutes adapted to a new land. Methodist preachers met in general conference annually at first, then every four years after 1792. Each general conference successively exercised more authority over the growing annual conferences, but without any restraints whatsoever on its powers. A particular general conference could have decided to reform or abolish almost any aspect of Methodist practice. This would have produced schism, no doubt, but nothing prevented the conversations of Methodist preachers from taking such a turn.

In 1808, however, following various disputes over the authority of Asbury and the powers of the preachers and laity, the general conference adopted new rules protecting essential elements of Methodism from meddling by any later general conference. These 'Restrictive Rules' formed in effect the first constitution of the Methodist Episcopal Church in America. The General Conference was now to be formally constituted as a delegated body (at first one travelling elder elected for every five). And to General Conference was conferred by the whole body of elders in the American connexion the power to legislate for the connexion as a whole, with certain definite restrictions. The Articles of Religion as adapted for the US church by Wesley, as well as the General Rules, were protected from revocation, alteration, or change. The support of clergy benefits through income from Methodism's publishing house was perpetually assured, as well as the right of clergy and laity to a church trial. General Conference could not 'do away with episcopacy or destroy the plan of our itinerant general superintendency', a provision that protected the whole system of itinerant, sent ministry (*Book of Discipline* 2008: §§17–22, 27).

With these rules the Methodist Episcopal Church (MEC) protected the elements that constituted Methodism—elements and practices that brought Methodism into being, made it what it is, and gave it its distinct identity. If these elements were taken away, what remained would not be Methodism as such any more—at least as the MEC understood the tradition.

When various Methodist bodies sought unification in 1939 and the Methodist Church and the Evangelical United Brethren Church united in 1968, the respective general conferences and uniting conferences mandated an extensive constitution that functioned to constitute or bring into being the new church and name its constitutive or most fundamental elements. Thus the current United Methodist Church (UMC) constitution, adopted in 1968 and subsequently amended, begins by naming the church and its fundamental character as an ecumenical and inclusive church body. Three divisions follow, prescribing the membership, powers, and duties of the various conferences, the episcopacy, and the judiciary.

As United Methodism reached its fortieth anniversary in 2008, coincidentally the 200th anniversary of the Restrictive Rules, another notable lacuna in Methodist

Studies became glaringly apparent. Despite the frequency of churches composing and revising constitutional documents through various ecumenical conversations and negotiations for church unions, no constitutional history of Methodism in twentieth-century America had appeared. James M. Buckley (1912) published his *Constitutional and Parliamentary History of the Methodist Episcopal Church* from the 'northern' viewpoint, John J. Tigert's (1916) account of *A Constitutional History of American Episcopal Methodism* from the 'southern' view went through multiple editions early in the century. But no scholar followed his line of enquiry directly, though constitutional matters certainly were addressed as a topic in polity textbooks and denominational histories (Frank 2006; Harmon 1962; Tuell 2005; Washburn 1984; Wilson and Harper 1988).

The lack of scholarly or ecclesial discussion of what constitutes Methodism has had dire consequences for the churches of the tradition, particularly its largest branch, United Methodism. Few delegates to a general conference appear to know exactly what is in the constitution, or to grasp the impact of amending it. More significantly, as United Methodism anticipates the possibility of structuring itself into a more global connexion, adapting to the rapid growth of the UMC in Africa and the Philippines and perhaps in union with other branches of Methodism outside the US, participants in the conversations must be able to name and discuss intelligently the elements that should constitute such a church. But they will have few sources to which to turn to inform themselves and the church about what is essential and what is at stake in their deliberations.

For example, an originative constitutional principle of United Methodism—as well as Methodism more broadly—is conference: that the powers and duties of legislative governance belong to delegated assemblies of clergy and laity. No executive body or agency is empowered to write church laws, issue statements of church teaching, initiate major programmes, or raise and expend funds beyond what a conference has authorized. This contrasts sharply with the dominant model of organizations in global capitalism and some global Christian organizations in which chief executive officers and boards of directors exercise command and control through pyramidal, hierarchical structures.

Some advocates of a global connexion could very well propose an executive body to make policy between sessions of a seemingly unwieldy general conference. Many US annual conferences have already attempted to install central councils with executive powers over programmes and budgets, accompanied by slogans and campaigns strikingly similar to corporate advertising. The lack of constitutional research and knowledge within Methodist Studies only makes such initiatives more likely and responses to them less substantive.

A fourth, *legal* phase of Methodist disciplinary development, following on its constitutional foundations, reflected the expansion of Methodist mission and the maturing of ministries. In many branches of Methodism the turn towards church law also marked an abandonment of the question and answer conversational form of discipline. Church law clarified policy in areas once left to habitual practice or cultural assumptions. *Books of Discipline* became progressively longer and weightier as legislation was added authorizing the proliferating initiatives and agencies of ministry and mission.

Church law expanded in several key areas. The work of a local society of Methodist people for years was described in the simple terms of a class meeting, but by the end of the twentieth century a separate chapter on the 'local church' elaborated all matters of church membership and local organization for ministry. The policies and procedures for ordained ministry gradually became more detailed and elaborate. The testing of a call to ministry in the Large Minutes, while still printed in the procedural paragraphs, began to seem quaintly naive: '(1.) Do they know God as a pardoning God? ... (2.) Have they gifts (as well as grace) for the work? ... (3.) Have they fruit?' (Large Minutes, 1872: Q. 50). These tests, relying on the judgement of more experienced preachers, were increasingly supplemented by new procedures addressing everything from entry qualifications to leave and retirement policies to a complaint process. In part these elaborations expressed a desire to enhance the quality of ordained ministry, and in part they responded to institutional crises such as the multiplication of complaints of clergy misconduct. Clear policies would help the church with its internal processes, while at the same time protecting the church from unwonted civil inquiries. The 'Administrative Order' section of the UMC *Discipline* also expanded greatly across the twentieth century. This reflected the full absorption of connexional agencies, most founded in the nineteenth century as independent voluntary associations with their own constitutions, into the administrative structure of the Methodist Church and then the UMC under authority of the general conference.

The physical alterations to Methodist *Disciplines* across the twentieth century are a telling symbol of their changing role in church life. Even well into the century, a *Book of Discipline* of any Methodist body could be slipped easily into the pocket of a jacket or a handbag. The book retained the gentle flow of the originally adapted Large Minutes and read something like a catechism of Methodist teachings and work. By mid-century the book was sized for a bookshelf, with sequentially numbered paragraphs, discursive statements of church law, and extensive provisions not only for regular church work but also for many exceptional situations that might arise. The UM bishops still appealed, as they had since Asbury, for the book 'to be found in libraries of local churches...as well as in the homes of ordained, diaconal, and licensed ministers and lay members' (*Book of Discipline* 2008: p. vi). But this seemed increasingly unlikely given the weightiness and density of the tome.

This remarkable growth in church law has received little scholarly attention. It has not gone without notice, but it has received almost no critical analysis from the standpoint of Methodist heritage or identity. Many polity questions would be fertile ground for more extensive scholarship. What has been the effect of creating a 'local church' chapter in the *Book of Discipline*, localizing church membership and separating the quarterly conference from the other conferences—thus turning charge conference into a kind of annual meeting similar to those of self-constituted congregations with independent polities? What is the significance in church and civil law of the trust clause governing ownership of church property? No area of the *Discipline* demonstrates more clearly the connexion in which United Methodists (and other Methodist bodies) are bound, and Methodist people need to be able to articulate this and show how it is a substantive alternative to hierarchical and congregational models of property ownership (Topolewski 1998; Tuell 2005: 147–56; Everett and Frank 1997).

Inquiry is long overdue on the impact of the Judicial Council of the UMC on both constitutional and legislative church law. The Council was instituted in the Methodist Episcopal Church (South) in 1934, and became a constitutional body of the MC in 1939 and then the UMC in 1968. The constitution empowers it with final say over the constitutionality of church laws and practices. Over those years the Council has issued well over a thousand opinions on decisions of law by bishops and on constitutional interpretations of the *Discipline*. No critical account of this growing legal heritage has been published. Is a 'supreme court' an appropriate way to resolve disputes in 'Christian conversation?' Or does it inflame the contentiousness of differing church parties in already divided and litigious societies? Such questions merit scholarly attention and interpretation.

Discipline in Methodism, in a fifth dimension, has always been *political*. Politics are endemic to any human society or organization, simply as the name for practices through which people seek justice and work together towards the common good. Polity is the term for structures of authority and forms of governance in a collective body, through which its political practices are ordered. Early Methodist conversations certainly were charged politically. Wesley and his preachers had continually to explain that they were not dissenters, for example, and not seeking to divide the Church of England. They also took on many heated social issues of the day, such as the plight of children among the poor, the use of tariffs to control production and trade, and the perpetuation of human slavery.

The General Rules explicitly opposed slavery and certainly implied that Methodist people were to wrestle in their conversations with issues of economic and social justice and their own role in ameliorating unjust practices. Methodists were not to charge 'unlawful interest', for example, to put on 'gold or costly apparel', or to purchase 'goods without a probability of paying for them'. These were personal behaviours, to be sure, but representative of larger social issues of the exploitation of the poor and the temptation of businesses to cater more to the rich than to those of modest or negligible means.

Methodists in the US found themselves with a more powerful social sway than Methodists had enjoyed in England. Less than 1 per cent of the English joined a Methodist society; in the US by 1850 a third of all church members were

Methodist. With that social prominence came increasing pressure to give voice to Christian conscience on current issues. By 1908 the MEC had a Social Creed, and when the UMC was created in 1968 participants in the former Methodist and Evangelical United Brethren Churches agreed that the new denomination must make a public statement of its Social Principles. The current Principles encompass the whole range of human life and address an astonishing number of issues from air pollution to sexual abuse to genetic research to human rights. The document is framed as 'a call to faithfulness . . . intended to be instructive and persuasive in the best of the prophetic spirit . . . [and] a call to all members . . . to a prayerful, studied dialogue of faith and practice' (*Book of Discipline* 2008: 97).

The Social Principles and their heritage have also been little studied, in sharp contrast, for example, to the considerable scholarship devoted to Catholic social teachings. Only one recent scholar, Darryl Stephens, investigated the thorough-going Americanness of the document—from its Preamble beginning 'We, the people called United Methodists' to its assumption of an open society in which human rights can be freely discussed—as well as its varied and often inconsistent moral logic. He also examined the adaptation and use of the Principles in nations other than the US, concluding that on this score (and many others) United Methodists do not know what each other is teaching or doing across conference and national boundaries (Stephens 2005).

The Social Principles can be viewed as an appropriate heir of concern for the social polity in the General Rules. Yet stark differences must also be noted. The General Rules clearly functioned (or were intended) as a rule of life shared by a community. The Social Principles by contrast read like position papers—thoughtful and usually well researched—whose audience is ambiguous. Are they for UMC members, that is, are UMC members in covenant to live by these Principles and assent to these teachings? Or are they intended as public statements of a denomination seeking to have influence on economic and social policy? Or all of the above? These questions deserve much more consideration by Methodist scholars.

Tensions over the Social Principles and their American character are only one mark of the emerging dynamics of global Methodism. The UMC and other Methodist bodies today constitute a worldwide mission reaching into most nations of the world and thus comprise one of the largest Protestant communions. This *missional* phase of the discipline of Methodism gained momentum across the nineteenth century as English and American Methodist bodies planted Methodist societies and agencies in Asia, Africa, and Latin America. By the mid-twentieth century many Methodist churches sought more indigenous leadership and autonomy from governing and funding arms of their original English and American sponsors. This led to the fragmentation of shared polity as churches constituted themselves autonomous bodies. Yet the trend also unquestionably enhanced the sense of a fellowship of peers in such gatherings as the World Methodist Conference.

Similar dynamics were present even within the UMC, comprising jurisdictional and central conferences with churches in over fifty nations of Africa, the Philippines, Europe, and America. The UMC had one quadrennial general conference, one council of bishops, one general board of global ministries, and one *Book of Discipline*. Yet the question persisted of whether a common discipline of life and work could really be articulated and practised in a worldwide church. This is a critical challenge to thoughtful scholarship, particularly to name and explain both historically and theologically the practices that constitute these culturally diverse churches as one connexion.

Actually not one *Discipline* but many *Disciplines* guide the life of United Methodists. While one English-language book, published in the US, is officially altered and authorized by General Conference, the same book is translated into various languages by conferences in other nations. Central conferences are empowered 'to make such changes and adaptations of the *Book of Discipline* as the special conditions and the mission of the church in the area require...*provided* that no action shall be taken that is contrary to the Constitution and General Rules' (*Book of Discipline* 2008: §543. 7). They have leeway particularly to adopt procedures for church membership, conduct of conferences, investigations and trials, and rituals and ceremonies that more closely fit the local culture. Stephens discovered in the course of his investigations that no person or office of the UMC actually holds current copies of all the *Disciplines* across the UMC. No one is charged with examining whether disciplinary adaptations are consistent or constitutional.

The *Discipline*'s appeal to the General Rules as a basis for judgement of adaptations becomes all the more poignant. Does any common rule of life provide a framework for United Methodism across nations and cultures? What really are the essential, constitutive elements of the UM connexional covenant? By extension, the same questions should be posed to the Methodist communion more broadly. Is there a common discipline in the dimensions adumbrated in this chapter, and if so, how is it practised?

Methodism's implicit response to these questions is not a turn towards the grounds of church law and polity, but rather an appeal once more to mission. Twenty-first-century Methodism, both within the UMC and within the broader communion of Methodist bodies, insists in word and action that what bridges differences in polity, ritual, or practices of discipline is the common mission of the church. The UMC adopted a concise statement of that mission in 1996: 'to make disciples of Jesus Christ' (*Book of Discipline* 2008: §121). The church's disciple-making mission is then restated at the beginning of most every chapter of the *Discipline*, emphasizing its all-embracing directive for every aspect of the church's ministries. The mission statement thus functions as the common discipline, and allegiance to it as the shared practice.

This statement has rightly provoked some lively scholarly debate. Many have argued that a slogan of 'making disciples' does not have specific roots in Wesleyanism;

that it is borrowed from an evangelicalism expressed mainly by independent, non-connexional churches lacking Methodism's heritage; that it is a brand associated with popular small-group or cell formats in which Methodism long since developed greater wisdom and theological balance; and that it is impoverished theologically both by privileging one biblical text to the exclusion of many others of equal or greater significance (such as, say, 'Love one another') and by supplanting God's grace with human action and production ('*We make* disciples', *Book of Discipline* 2008: §122, ital. mine). The language itself contrasts sharply with the General Rules or the Large Minutes, which rely on terms such as the 'means of grace' or 'scriptural holiness' to signal the origin and ground of Christian faith and life in the unnameable graciousness, holiness, and mystery of God.

What might be explored in greater depth is the significance of a church adopting a mission statement in the first place. This is a common practice in global business corporations and other enterprises. Can a mission statement serve as a common rule of life and shared discipline for a connexion of Methodists? Was it adopted because no such rule of life guides the tradition any more? Or are these questions stirring up a froth for no reason, because the mission statement is simply a rewording of how the Large Minutes (1872: Q. 3) expressed 'God's design' for the Methodists: 'to reform the nation, particularly the Church; and to spread scriptural holiness over the land'?

However the mission statement is understood, it is one sign of what might be called a fresh *pentecostal* phase of Methodist discipline. In many dimensions of Methodist life—rituals, songs, prayers, as well as forms of authority and governance established through the connexion over generations of common work— traditional practices have given way to a fresh spirit of innovation. Distinctions among Christian traditions hold less weight as Methodist people borrow, adapt, and mix and match practices from many different Christian groups in a spirit of doing whatever works to achieve the mission.

In 1996, for example, United Methodism threw off much of the connexional model that had mandated parallel structures for ministry and mission for every conference of the church—charge, district, annual, or general. For instance, the model advanced themes of racial justice throughout the connexion by mandating that an officer or commission focused on 'religion and race' be elected in every local church or charge as well as in the district and annual conference, to be linked to and provided resources by a general commission of that name. This was an astonishing and ambitious effort to make racial reconciliation central to the ministry of every unit of United Methodism, regardless of locally held opinions on race.

The reforms of 1996 opened the way for local churches and annual conferences to organize their ministry and mission in any form, as long as basic administration of money, personnel, and property is properly tended. This has resulted in a wide array of organizational models and terminology unique to various charge and annual conferences, as well as widespread borrowing from models of other Christian groups (particularly large, independent congregations) and business corporations. The appeal to the Spirit in organizing for mission has been accompanied in many conferences by a rejection of older forms of conducting the gathered conference itself. Rules of organization and order grounded in the procedures of Robert's *Rules of Order* have given way to models of consensus-building. Innovating and borrowing has its consequences; for instance, lines of authority adopted in the earlier polity to ensure separation and balance of powers in the church, such as authorizing distinct bodies for approving programme initiatives and for raising and managing money, have often been blurred or ignored. Some reforms promising participation and responsiveness have resulted in the more centralized power typical of command-and-control hierarchies.

New scholarship is needed today to uncover the roots and contexts of these changes and to interpret their accord with Methodist heritage. The churches would benefit from research on what structures have actually evolved in the last generation, and how practices of conference have affected the church's ministries. The balance of structure and Spirit is as much a continuing question in Methodism as in any tradition. To what extent can a connexion have coherence around an appeal to the Spirit's movement? A critical perspective on these pentecostal changes might note that what passes for the work of the Spirit usually has a pattern and language of its own (such as 'spontaneous' prayers that sound very much alike, or the jargon of 'team' and 'team leader' to replace 'committee' and 'chairperson'). So does Methodism really have new forms of common work, or is it actually just borrowing facilely and uncritically from other church traditions, business corporations, or cultural fads?

Finally, Methodist discipline has entered into a new phase that is unfolding too quickly for ready appraisal. Methodist conversation is increasingly *virtual*, multiplying across the Internet in ways inconceivable even late in the twentieth century. Web sites, blogs, and networks for conversing with fellow Methodists combine with instant access to resources for ministry and mission to create a 'just in time' connexionalism infinitely adaptable to changing needs and circumstances.

The impact of the Internet on traditional forms of polity is hotly debated in all organizations, since central control of information (accompanied by deference to exclusive knowledge) has long been a source of authority. Now the same information is available to everyone, at least everyone with web access (itself a new justice issue). Books of discipline are a source of income for publishing houses and are not usually freely available on the Web. Much could be said for making them available, though, as a way of being sure that the *Discipline* is a presence in every home. Of course, nothing prevents paraphrases or discussions of disciplinary content from being posted on denominational or local church websites. The UMC home page, for example, posts extensive descriptions of UM history, theology, and discipline, along with paragraphs from the published *Discipline*. Is this site becoming a source of UM polity, and should it also be controlled by the authorized body, the General Conference? Should local church web sites be expected to define congregational mission and organization for ministry using specifically Methodist terminology?

Or is Methodism living in a pentecostal, informational age of immediacy and adaptability in which the church should open itself to infinite malleable possibilities? If so, what would be the core practices that Methodist people now hold in common that constitute them as Methodist? These questions are worthy of Methodist scholarship.

Each of the eight phases of Methodist discipline has had a formative impact on the substance and practice of Methodism's common life. Over two hundred and fifty years of change, surprising lines of continuity—from eagerness for wise and searching conversation to the attraction of disciplined growth in the Christian life—mark the development of Methodist discipline. Each phase offers a continuously active element in Methodist polity, creating a synthesis with inherent tensions and unique possibilities that is evident in contemporary books of discipline and conversations about the church's ministries. Separately and collectively the eight phases merit fuller exploration and interpretation in Methodist Studies, to redress the perennially underdeveloped field of Methodist discipline.

Suggested Reading

Methodist discipline and polity in the tradition of the Methodist Episcopal, Methodist, and United Methodist churches have been explored in several works across the past century, from Buckley (1912) to Tigert (1916) to Harmon (1977) to Tuell (2005) to Frank (2006). Elements that historically have been essential to Methodism are interpreted in Russell E. Richey et al. (2005), *Marks of Methodism: Theology in Ecclesial Practice* (Nashville: Abingdon). On the uniquely Methodist form of episcopacy, see Richey and Frank (2004). For Evangelical United Brethren polity discussed as part of the story of that tradition, see I. Bruce Behney and Paul H. Eller (1979), *The History of the Evangelical United Brethren Church*, ed. Kenneth W. Krueger (Nashville: Abingdon) and Washburn (1984). For a provocative glossary of United Methodist terminology, see Alan K. Waltz (1991), *A Dictionary for United Methodists* (Nashville: Abingdon). Everett and Frank (1997) discussed Methodist discipline in the context of US polity and governance. On the impact of discipline on local church congregations, see Thomas Edward Frank, 'What is the Common Discipline for Local Churches?' (1999), in Russell E. Richey et al. (eds.), *Questions for the 21st Century Church* (Nashville: Abingdon). For discussion of polity as a practice in continuity with Wesley's methods in British Methodism, see Angela Shier-Jones (2004), 'Being

Methodical: Theology within Church Structures', in Clive Marsh et al. (eds.), *Unmasking Methodist Theology* (London: Continuum). For a classic interpretation of Methodist discipline in the African-American tradition, see Henry McNeal Turner (1885), *The Genius and Theory of Methodist Polity, or The Machinery of Methodism* (Philadelphia: African Methodist Episcopal Church).

REFERENCES

The Book of Discipline of The United Methodist Church 2008. Nashville: United Methodist Publishing House.

BUCKLEY, JAMES M. (1912). *Constitutional and Parliamentary History of the Methodist Episcopal Church*. New York: Methodist Book Concern.

EVERETT, WILLIAM J., and FRANK, THOMAS EDWARD (1997). 'Constitutional Order in United Methodism and American Culture'. In Russell Richey et al. (eds.), *Connectionalism: Ecclesiology, Mission, and Identity*. Nashville: Abingdon.

FRANK, THOMAS EDWARD (2003). 'Polity'. In Hans J. Hillerbrand (ed.), *Encyclopedia of Protestantism*. New York: Routledge.

—— (2006). *Polity, Practice, and the Mission of The United Methodist Church*. Nashville: Abingdon.

HARMON, NOLAN B. (1962), *The Organization of The Methodist Church*. 2nd rev. edn. Nashville: Abingdon.

—— (1977). *Understanding The United Methodist Church*. Nashville: Abingdon.

KNIGHT, HENRY H., III (1992). *The Presence of God in the Christian Life: John Wesley and the Means of Grace*. Metuchen, N.J.: Scarecrow.

Large Minutes, *see* 'Minutes of several conversations' below.

LONG, EDWARD LeROY (2001). *Patterns of Polity: Varieties of Church Governance*. Cleveland, Ohio: Pilgrim.

'Minutes of several conversations between the Rev. Mr. Wesley and others from the year 1744 to the year 1789' (Large Minutes) (1872). *The Works of John Wesley*, ed. Thomas Jackson. Reprint edn. Grand Rapids: Zondervan, viii.

RICHEY, RUSSELL E., and FRANK, THOMAS EDWARD (2004). *Episcopacy in the Methodist Tradition: Perspectives and Proposals*. Nashville: Abingdon.

STEPHENS, DARRYL W. (2005). 'Face of Unity or Mask over Difference?: The Social Principles in the Central Conferences of The United Methodist Church'. *Thinking About Religion* 5 (2005), <http://organizations.uncfsu.edu/ncrsa/journal/v05/stephens_face.htm>, accessed 12 January 2009.

TIGERT, JOHN J. (1916). *A Constitutional History of American Methodism*. 6th edn. Nashville: ME Church South.

TOPOLEWSKI, JOHN LEO (1998). 'Mr. Wesley's Trust Clause: Methodism in the Vernacular'. Unpublished paper on-line at <www.gcfa.org>.

TUELL, JACK M. (2005). *The Organization of The United Methodist Church*. Nashville: Abingdon.

WASHBURN, PAUL (1984). *An Unfinished Church: A Brief History of the Union of the Evangelical United Brethren Church and The Methodist Church*. Nashville: Abingdon.

WATSON, DAVID LOWES (1985). *The Early Methodist Class Meeting: Its Origin and Significance*. Nashville: Discipleship Resources.

WILSON, ROBERT L., and HARPER, STEVE (1988). *Faith and Form: A Uniting of Theology and Polity in the United Methodist Tradition*. Grand Rapids: Francis Asbury Press.

CHAPTER 15

MINISTRY AND ITINERANCY IN METHODISM

DENNIS M. CAMPBELL

MINISTRY in Methodism has always been characterized more by emphasis on practicality and results than by theology and tradition. This does not mean that Methodism has lacked a theology of ministry, but that its theology of ministry has been based on practice rather than theory. Over the course of more than two hundred years, there has been perpetual tension within Methodism in regard to the meaning of ordination, orders of ministry, education for ministry, relationships between ordained members and lay members, and the normative significance of tradition. The theological idea of itinerancy is a hallmark of official ministry in Methodism; but its meaning and practice has evolved through the years as practical matters of polity, shaped by social, demographic, economic, and institutional realities have prevailed. An understanding of the historical origins of Methodist conceptions of ministry illuminates the reasons for the confusion that accompanies an effort to systematize ministry and itinerancy within the Methodist tradition and the various churches that make up the worldwide Methodist family.

HISTORICAL OVERVIEW OF METHODIST MINISTRY IN ENGLAND

Methodism had its origin within the Anglican Church in the eighteenth century in England. The English Reformation that produced the Anglican Church was significantly different from the Reformation in continental Europe because it was an act of state. The English church separated from Rome for reasons rooted in conflict over state power and national identity, including cultural distinctions, more than theological and ecclesiastical issues. While there were early reformers prior to the separation of the church in England from Rome, primary theological arguments and justifications followed after the break (cf. Dickens 1964; Rupp 1965). The Lutheran and Calvinist reform movements, on the other hand, were characterized by strong theological views of both Scripture and ministry. Sharply differentiating themselves from Roman Catholic understandings of Scripture and authority in ministry, the Continental Reformers set forth theological claims about the nature of ordained and lay ministry that later characterized the churches in the Lutheran, presbyterian, and congregational traditions. Because their break with Roman Catholicism was theologically and biblically informed, ministry, in a variety of forms, came to be viewed as systematically related to a larger ecclesiology.

The Anglican Church, perhaps because its origin was less theological than practical, essentially retained and adopted the Catholic form and conception of ordained ministry even as it separated from the Roman Church in regard to matters of papal authority. Gradually there arose differences of style, practice, and structure, but these were the result of setting and culture rather than theological construct. The English Reformers maintained that Anglican orders derived directly from Catholic orders. The authority for ordination, therefore, came from the claim of an unbroken line of ordained ministry reaching back to the earliest apostolic ministry within Christianity, an idea known as apostolic succession. The fact of separation from the Roman Catholic Church cannot, however, be denied; and while Roman theology understands Anglican ministry to have efficacy, it does not recognize Anglican orders as identical to those of its priests. Roman Catholic theology and teaching posits a distinction between its orders and those of other Christian traditions, including Anglicanism (cf. Dix 1948).

Anglicanism continued the form of ministerial orders inherited from the classical Catholic tradition, including various lay orders and the three ordained orders of deacon, priest, and bishop (Sykes 1995). It was into this understanding of clerical orders that the Methodist movement was born, because John Wesley, the founder and father of Methodism, was the son of an Anglican priest and himself an Anglican priest throughout his life, as was his famous brother, Charles, the poet and hymn writer.

Born in 1703, John Wesley was raised in an Anglican rectory and greatly influenced not only by his father, Samuel, but especially by his pious and rigorous mother, Susanna. The Wesleys were 'high church' Anglicans, meaning that they believed the church and its clergy rightly deserved high status and influence in the social and political order of the English nation. John Wesley became a student at Christ Church, Oxford University. While in Oxford, he and his brother Charles became central in a group of students resolved to practise their Christian life in a meticulous manner. Wesley's Oxford diaries demonstrate extraordinary attention to a disciplined life of Christian prayer, Scripture reading, and regular attendance at occasions for worship, including sacramental observance. This group of serious-minded Christian students was initiated not only to provide communal support and encouragement, but also discipline and accountability in all aspects of the Christian life. John and Charles Wesley were recognized in Oxford as motivators of a particularly methodical brand of the Anglican Christian life. Sophisticated Oxford students and faculty ridiculed the earnestness of this group, and used terms like 'holy club' and 'methodists' to describe them. Wesley's conviction was that there were practical methods by which it was possible to live a rigorously disciplined life in order to grow in grace. The theme of practice thus emerged very early in the history of Methodism (Heitzenrater 1985: 1–47).

John Wesley was ordained a deacon in 1725 and a priest in 1728 by John Potter, the bishop of Oxford. Though he never served an Anglican parish as a priest-in-charge, he functioned as a clergyman all his life. His active leadership of the Methodist movement sometimes put him at odds with the established Anglican Church, but Wesley never renounced his Anglican orders, and he assumed and accepted the rightness of the Anglican conception of ordained offices of ministry (deacon, priest, and bishop) that had been retained by Anglicanism at the time of the Reformation. He did, however, early come to the conviction that in the primitive church the offices of presbyter (priest) and bishop were the same order, and he thought this view should carry normative authority for understanding these roles (Wesley 1938: iii. 232, 20 January 1746).

In its early days, the evangelical revival movement led by Wesley was not intended to be a separate church, but to exist within the Church of England. His image was of groups of disciplined lay Christians within the parish structure of the Church being ministered to by ordained Anglican clergy for purposes of the sacramental ministries. Wesley's strong evangelical gospel message called men and women to repentance and new life in Jesus Christ. Even though there was always an evangelical tradition in Anglicanism, his approach to preaching, and the content of his witness, set him apart from the dominant form of church life in eighteenth-century England. He was accused of 'enthusiasm' by much of the established church and charged with upsetting the conventional order of both church and society in England. Increasingly, his was a ministry to the poor and marginalized in a society experiencing rapid social and economic change. The

Methodist revival targeted men, women, and children who were not being reached by the traditional parish church system.

Although there were Anglican clergy who were sympathetic to, and active in, the Methodist revival, lay people, most of them not previously participant in the church, characterized the movement. Wesley, reluctantly at first, began to recognize the uncommon effectiveness of some lay leadership, and appointed lay leaders for Methodist groups in the various communities. Wesley supervised what became an increasingly elaborate system of classes and bands; and he developed a group of leaders within the movement to help him to provide supervision. Some Anglican clergy took on this role; but significantly, he broadened the leadership by including lay persons. Early Methodism is a study in brilliant leadership, organization, and administration for growth. Wesley's approach was to observe those methods that were effective, and to implement what worked well, bringing the results he wanted. He believed that God expected and blessed hard work and persistent effort. The strong practical and experiential commitments that characterized Wesley's leadership throughout his life allowed him to recognize the gifts and graces for ministry on the part of some of his lay leaders, including some of the women in the movement. Wesley gradually authorized selected lay preachers, because he witnessed the reality of their Christian faith commitment and the power of their witness. The recognition of lay preachers as having legitimate gifts for preaching ministry set Wesley apart from his Church.

While many in the established Anglican Church leadership objected to the evangelical character of Wesley's theology and ministry, they were troubled especially by two aspects of the movement. One was the fact that Wesley, and other Methodist leaders, led revival ministries throughout the country without regard to settled parish boundaries. Indeed, when most parishes were closed to him, because of the perceived threat his ministry and message represented to the Anglican parish ministry system, Wesley held outdoor revivals and meetings, travelling constantly to communicate with his own followers and to make new disciples for Christ. The second was the willingness of the Methodists to recognize the legitimacy of lay preaching to serve and advance the work of the movement. These two realities, extra-parochial ministry and the recognition of an official lay ministry, became fundamental to what would increasingly be a Methodist understanding of ministry and itinerancy (Hempton 2005).

Throughout his long life (he died in 1791), John Wesley maintained that he was an Anglican priest in good standing, and that his Methodist movement was within the Anglican Church. In fact, despite the fact that it included numerous Anglican clergy as part of the movement, Methodism in England became increasingly a parallel structure, and perhaps in practice gradually separate from the Church of England, by its creation of 'chapels' throughout the land served by lay leaders and preachers, and by its institution of a system for providing leadership and organization for the movement. While the actual formation of a separate Methodist

Church in England did not occur until after Wesley's death, for many the act that seemed to point towards a separation was his 'ordination' of ministers for the Methodist societies in America.

THE INITIATION OF METHODIST MINISTERIAL ORDERS FOR AMERICA

Wesley was modestly familiar with America because of his service as an Anglican clergyman and missionary in Georgia when he was a young man. He later encouraged the planting of Methodist societies in America, which grew rapidly and became a formidable presence in colonial America, especially in the mid-Atlantic areas, and, after the Revolution, throughout the early Republic. When most of the Anglican clergy in America went back to England at the time of the Revolution, Methodist leaders, notably Francis Asbury, remained in America. Ironically because of its separateness from the Anglican Church in the colonies, Methodism was able to prosper after the Revolution by not being identified with the official established church of the mother country and former colonial power. At first, Wesley envisioned American Methodists as having the same kind of relationship to Anglican ministries in America for sacramental purposes as Methodists in England. After most Anglican clergy left the colonies at the time of the Revolution, Methodists were left largely without ordained ministers for sacramental observance. It is interesting that neither the American Methodists nor Wesley simply went ahead and 'ordained' some of their leaders. They looked to Wesley, and Anglicanism, for their understanding of the meaning of 'official' ministers of the sacraments. Wesley clearly recognized the need for ordained ministers for American Methodists, and sought to get an Anglican bishop to ordain one or more of his preachers, but he was unable to achieve this aim. He then took things literally into his own hands.

In 1784, John Wesley ordained Thomas Coke, who was already an elder (priest) of the Church of England, as a 'superintendent' for America. He directed Coke, in turn, to ordain Francis Asbury, a lay preacher, whom Wesley had sent to the colonies in 1771, and who was already Wesley's main 'assistant' in America, a deacon, elder, and superintendent (cf. Baker 1976). This act became known as the 'controversial ordinations', and it has been the root of confusion concerning the authority and authenticity of Methodist orders ever since (Campbell 1988: 59–68).

In the same way that John Wesley claimed 'extraordinary' authority to preach without regard to parish boundaries, to allow and encourage lay ministries, and to establish what was, in fact, a movement parallel to, if not completely outside, the established Anglican Church, so he appropriated to himself episcopal powers to ordain for America (Outler 1964: 21). He justified this act by arguing that, although he had not been ordained a bishop of the Church of England, yet he functioned as a bishop, in the theological, spiritual, and practical sense of the historic concept of episcopacy, among the Methodists. Evidence from Wesley's writings indicates that, as a result of his careful study of scholarly accounts of ministry in primitive Christianity, he had long questioned the theological reality of episcopacy as a separate order of ministry. Thus American Methodist clerical orders, and indeed all episcopal Methodist orders, derive from the laying on of hands by an Anglican priest, an 'elder' of the church, who 'functioned' as a bishop for what he viewed as purposes of necessity. He claimed to be a *scriptural episkopos*. In a letter to his brother, Charles, he said 'I firmly believe I am a scriptural episkopos as much as any man in England or in Europe' (Wesley 1931: vii. 284).

THEOLOGICAL AND PRACTICAL CONSIDERATION OF METHODIST MINISTERIAL ORDERS

The interpretation of Wesley's ordinations for Methodists in America characterizes and defines all subsequent views of Methodist clerical orders. On the one hand it can be argued that, from a theological point of view, Wesley was in fact a *scriptural episkopos*. The argument that in the early church bishops were presbyters serving in a designated role convinced Wesley that, in his ministry, he was acting as a bishop, exercising teaching authority and ecclesiastical leadership. In this view, Wesley had legitimate scriptural and theological authority to provide necessary ordained leadership for the American church. Wesley made it clear that the reason this could be justified was that it was for the American Methodists, in a new and separate country, and that therefore the Church of England order and structure did not necessarily apply and, most significantly, did not have to bind, and therefore impede, the growth of Methodism. Indeed, Methodism was to be a new church in a new country, neither of which was bound any longer by the English church or nation.

On the other hand, Wesley was obviously not a bishop in the conventional traditional ecclesiastical sense of the word. He was a priest, who took it upon himself to exercise episcopal powers. Methodist orders thus derive from a view of ordained ministry more like that of non-Anglican Protestant churches, more presbyteral than episcopal.

This debate has continued throughout the history of Methodism and has resulted in two forms of church order and structure, episcopal Methodism and non-episcopal Methodism. Episcopal Methodism is the dominant form of American Methodism, and includes the United Methodist Church and the major African-American Methodist churches. Through its missionary efforts, especially in the late nineteenth and early twentieth centuries, American episcopal Methodism spread throughout the world, and episcopal Methodist churches are present in many nations, especially on the continents of Europe, Asia, Africa, and South America; but episcopal Methodism has its roots in North America. English Methodism, on the other hand, because of its initial ambiguous relationship to the established church, and then its gradual separation from Anglicanism, has always been non-episcopal, with one order of official ordained ministry corresponding to the order variously referred to as priest, presbyter, or elder depending on various church traditions. English Methodism also engaged in missionary activity, and planted non-episcopal Methodist churches around the world, but especially in parts of Africa, Asia, and other former British colonial areas.

American episcopal Methodism owes its creation largely to Francis Asbury. It was he who began to use the title 'bishop' after his ordination by Thomas Coke and appointment by John Wesley to be a superintendent. The ordinal by which he was ordained was sent to America by John Wesley. It was a modest modification of the ordination services in the Anglican Book of Common Prayer (Outler 1970: 113). Wesley maintained three offices of ministry: deacon, elder, and bishop, with the title of the latter changed to 'superintendent'. American Methodists, led by Asbury, found the designation 'superintendent' awkward, and perhaps confusing, and since the office had the function of a bishop, therefore determined the title to be appropriate, despite Wesley's objections. Perhaps Asbury simply wanted the grander title; but it was a new church in a new nation, and therefore not subject to the complex history and meaning of episcopacy in England. Asbury became a quintessential 'new American' and considered himself free to 'do his own thing' in the best interests of the new church and nation. Asbury, like Wesley, was committed to practicality and effectiveness, and so determined that the episcopal office would serve Methodism well. Through his indefatigable service to the Methodist Church, and his advocacy of a strong episcopal office, he created the Methodist episcopacy by his aggressive implementation of the role. He assumed the authority of the office, and exercised it in such a way that it set a permanent standard for the church.

The office of bishop in episcopal Methodism is itself a complex and technical reality. Episcopal Methodism has taught that there are two orders of ordained ministry, deacon and elder, and three offices, deacon, elder, and bishop. This is a distinction that through the years was designated in the ordination liturgy in such a way that deacons were ordained, elders were ordained, and bishops were consecrated. In all cases, regardless of the office, it was necessary for a bishop to lay on hands for the ordination or consecration to be official. On the one hand, the church has taught that a bishop is an elder who has been consecrated to a particular office and set apart to serve. Despite this understanding, the church has *treated* the episcopal office as a separate order. The evidence for this is not difficult to see. A bishop is elected for life, and even after retirement from active service is a member of the Council of Bishops and partakes of all the rights, privileges, and perquisites of the episcopal office. A bishop is authentically consecrated only by the laying on of hands by other bishops (although it is often the case that other elders also are invited to lay on hands during the service) (cf. Short 1976, 1985; Mathews 1985).

One of the more notable characteristics of Methodism is the appointment power of the bishop. In this sense, the Methodist episcopacy is among the strongest clerical supervisory offices in Christianity, more like the episcopal office in the Roman Catholic Church than in other Protestant churches, including the Episcopal Church. Methodist ministers are not members of any local congregation, but their membership is in an annual conference (a regional body of church order). Full clergy members of the annual conference are officially 'travelling elders' to designate that they are itinerant and not local. This strong affirmation of the non-local character of the ministry is further demonstrated by the fact that ministers are appointed annually to specific ministries by the bishop who is responsible for the conference.

At various times in the history of the United Methodist Church there have been challenges to the idea of life tenure for bishops. These efforts have sought to democratize the ministry. Episcopal Methodism is by structure and practice a strongly hierarchical church. A bishop cannot be removed from office unless there are serious moral and ethical charges brought against him or her, and a bishop's appointment power in regard to the clergy is final. In the late nineteenth century, and through the middle of the twentieth century, Methodism was a major player in American social and political culture. The influence of the Methodist bishops, even in the larger society, therefore, was great and significantly recognized. In the late twentieth century and into the twenty-first, the cultural role and power of Methodism declined, but the structures of the church's ordained ministry have remained essentially the same, with one major change. By general conference action the office of deacon as a stepping-stone on the way to the order of elder was eliminated. The permanent diaconate is now an order designed for those persons formerly denominated 'consecrated lay workers'. These persons are not ordained for word and sacrament and are not appointed in the same way as are the travelling elders. United Methodism, then, has one order of ordained clergy who are full members of an annual conference.

The Nature of Authority for Methodist Ministerial Orders

The debate about orders of ministry and the place of lay offices, and the subsequent changes brought about by the general conference in regard to ministerial orders, is worthy of some reflection, because it provides a specific case study of Methodist polity and theology in regard to ministry. There has always been a tension in Methodism between ordained ministers and 'official lay ministers'. This is made more complicated and confusing because the church has also had several categories of official lay ministers. One group is referred to as 'lay preachers'. The idea of the lay preacher is as old as Methodism itself, as we saw in our brief historical overview. The place of lay preachers in the church has always been important because they have served in areas of significant need, but where fully ordained preachers were unable or unwilling to serve. Lay preachers are appointed by the bishop, but are not full members of the annual conference, do not have a guaranteed appointment and often are more local, even if their ministry is full-time. As time went on, a further distinction came about because of educational requirements.

Traditionally Methodist preachers were not necessarily required to have advanced education leading to a college or seminary degree. Many early Methodists were aggressively anti-intellectual, arguing that too much education was a detriment to the power of the Holy Spirit in preaching and ministry. Through the years Methodism developed an official course of study required of its preachers, organized and administered by the bishops and their designated representatives. As the denomination grew in size, power, and status, however, there was a movement towards greater educational attainment. Methodism has always been aggressive about founding colleges, and college degrees became common among even the early preachers who achieved leadership in the church. Graduate theological education came more gradually as the church, and some of its institutions of higher education, began to establish seminaries and divinity schools. A graduate theological degree was viewed by some as negative; they argued that too much education dampened the spirit. Others saw such advanced education as positive, because the needs of the church for an educated clergy were perceived to be growing as the laity increased in knowledge and influence. As some congregations grew wealthy, and included in their membership business, political, and social leaders, they wanted preachers of whom they could be proud, and who could be recognized as worthy in comparison to the clergy in the leading congregations of other denominations, especially Episcopal, Congregational, and Presbyterian churches of influence and distinction.

Because it was large and diverse, however, Methodism needed and encouraged lay preachers who would serve in settings that could not command fully ordained ministers, or where fully ordained ministers might be less effective. The social and economic diversity in Methodism was significant, requiring a diversity of ministerial styles. Eventually the educational requirements for a fully ordained elder became more stringent, generally requiring a graduate theological degree. This further distinguished the lay pastors, who were required to do the course of study, from the ordained clergy, who needed undergraduate and graduate degrees. Once it was established by most annual conferences that elders in full connexion should have a graduate, professional theological degree, the question then became which institutions would qualify as worthy to grant a degree that would be recognized by boards of ordained ministry. This was complicated by the reality that different schools of theology within the Methodist tradition, in other Christian traditions, and in ecumenical settings, represented different approaches to theology and ministry.

The debate about the nature of requirements for ordination, the make-up of the annual conference, and the role and place of lay pastors is likely to be with Methodism forever. One of the generally unspoken reasons for this is that small, and or poor, congregations, both rural and urban, cannot afford salary and benefits for fully ordained clergy, yet want, and need, ministers. Because Methodism historically has been a 'popular' denomination, meaning inclusive of diverse social, economic, and educational levels, the church is likely to continue to need lay preachers. An example of this, for instance, is among Methodist ministries to growing Hispanic communities in the United States. The course of study, as an alternative to seminary, still exists, now administered by the general board of ministry rather than the bishops.

The other official lay ministry group was made up of lay persons serving as parish educators, musicians, and sometimes church administrators. Persons in these roles generally have served large urban or suburban congregations that are rich enough to afford multiple staff. Such congregations often have one or more appointed ordained clergy and then one or more Christian educators and sometimes full-time organists and choral musicians. These professional persons were lay persons serving in staff positions in local churches. Sometimes they gained influence and power in the congregations because they often served for many years in the same local church while the clergy moved according to episcopal appointment. The larger denomination, because Methodism has always been prone to bureaucracy, recognized that it might be useful to regularize educational requirements, policies, procedures, and benefits for lay professionals serving in these specialized ministries, usually in congregations, but sometimes at the conference level.

Not entirely unlike lay pastors, these lay professionals found themselves in a curious position between lay members and clergy. There was a move for status, recognition, and security. The first step was the designation of a consecrated lay worker status granted and regularized by the annual conference. This office was often misunderstood as a kind of 'super lay person' and resulted in special status in the annual conference, and much confusion about just what the office meant theologically, let alone in terms of church polity.

Historically in Christianity the clergy were set apart for purposes of sacramental and teaching ministry. Theologically, clergy were not to be thought of as 'better than', 'more holy than', 'more ethical than', or 'more important than' any other Christian. They were set apart for service of a particular kind. The development of various lay orders was a theological confusion not unique to Methodism, but Methodist structures and Methodist tensions between the theological and the practical led to confusion. This was especially clear when the general conference voted to change the historic structure of ministry in Methodism to recognize one order of ordained ministry, the elder, for full membership in the annual conference, as travelling elders under appointment, and to use the diaconate (permanent deacon) for what previously was a lay office of consecrated lay worker (Moede 1978).

What is particularly interesting and significant about this shift is what it says about the theological authority for ministry in Methodism. On the one hand it can be looked at as simply a political accommodation to the desires of professional lay workers for status, recognition, and benefits. On the other, it can be understood as indicating that the theological foundation for ministry in Methodism derives from the conviction that God's gift of ministry is constantly evolving and changing through the work of the Holy Spirit, and that no historical structure carries permanent efficacy. The United Methodist Church dropped John Wesley's three-fold office structure in favour of a ministerial structure more like that of English Methodism, or of other Protestant churches that have one order of ordained ministry. If this theological conception is correct, then the Methodist episcopacy, too, is subject to the same understanding and interpretation. That is, Methodist episcopacy is an office of practical convenience for church order and governance, and could, in theory, be changed for theological and practical reasons, just as the diaconate was changed. In fact, the episcopacy is protected by a restrictive rule that prohibits the general conference from abolishing it. However, it must be understood that this is a governmental restriction, not a theological one. Article III states that 'the General Conference shall not change or alter any part or rule of our government so as to do away with episcopacy or destroy the plan of our itinerant general superintendency' (*Book of Discipline* 2004: §19. 27). Perhaps that is why early bishops insisted on such a restrictive rule, so that a general conference would not vote to restructure the church in such a way as to eliminate the episcopal office as it was conceived.

Another example of evolution in the understanding of ordained ministry in Methodism is the role of women. John Wesley himself acknowledged that women could be effective teachers and leaders. Just as he gradually recognized lay preachers as having a legitimate role in the movement, so did he come to recognize gifts and graces for ministry on the part of women. In both of these cases Wesley was out of step with the Anglican Church in the eighteenth century. Though they played significant roles in teaching and other leadership, women were not permitted to be ordained in most Methodist traditions until after the middle of the twentieth century. Arguments for the ordination of women were characterized by biblical, theological, and practical considerations, and the general conference eventually voted to open the door to full status for women in ordained ministry in 1956. Once this change occurred, women rapidly became a vital part of the ordained ministry, including the episcopacy. The first woman bishop was elected in 1980. Percentages of women in pursuing theological education for ordination increased dramatically in the last thirty years of the twentieth century.

CONTINUITIES IN UNDERSTANDING AND PRACTICE IN METHODIST MINISTRY

Throughout all of the changes that have characterized the structures of Methodist ministry through the years, several continuities can be identified. These have shaped a Methodist understanding of ministry from the earliest days of the movement up to the present time. There has always been an insistence in Methodism that the ordained elder is an essential ministerial office that incorporates a number of functions. The first of these is the *sacramental ministry*, the second is the *preaching and teaching ministry*, the third is the *ordering of the life of the church*, and the fourth is *ministry to the larger community*, often characterized by commitment to social justice and social action of various kinds.

From its earliest day, Methodist theology and practice has related sacramental ministry to ordination. There was never debate about the necessity for ordination for celebration of the sacraments of the church even in the days when lay preachers were prevalent. The circuit-riding, itinerant, ordained, travelling elders were expected to celebrate the sacrament when they were present in the community. They also were expected to provide educational leadership for both lay members and lay preachers. The teaching and preaching ministry incorporated oversight of biblical interpretation and theological exploration within the congregations. Methodists were committed to education for the outside community, as well, and a commitment to education for church and society has always characterized Methodist ministry. The elder was also appointed to 'order' the life of the church. The use of the term 'charge' to refer to a minister's appointment carries the idea of responsibility for seeing to it that the congregation is properly 'ordered' for ministry and service according to the *Discipline* of the church set by the general conference. Methodism has always had a commitment to the larger community, and clergy have often led the way in ministries of social justice in their communities. Methodists have a tradition of seeking to influence the life of their respective nations through advocacy of political and social programmes viewed as compatible with Christian teaching, as well as through cooperative work with other churches in ecumenical initiatives and agencies.

THE THEOLOGICAL MEANING AND PRACTICAL REALITY OF ITINERANCY

One of the particular characteristics of the Methodist ministry is the concept of itinerancy. Itinerancy refers to the practice of moving ministers, through appointment, to specific places where their services are needed and can best be used. In the earliest days of English Methodism, John Wesley travelled constantly. He covered much of the nation every year preaching and visiting his preachers and people. Historians have suggested that Wesley was perhaps seen and heard by more people in England than any other person including the king. Early Methodist preachers in England were assigned to circuits of communities where Methodists were gathered with the intention of ministering, educating, and evangelizing. Unlike the Anglican parish system, where clergy were settled, often for life, early Methodist ministry was characterized by perpetual movement. The same insistence upon itinerancy that characterized Wesley was emphasized perhaps even more aggressively by Bishop Francis Asbury in America. Asbury railed against what he called 'locality', and pressed his preachers to be constantly on the move to spread the gospel and expand the Methodist movement (Campbell, Lawrence, and Richey 1997: 23–38).

Methodist preachers in America were sometimes simply appointed to a geographical territory, rather than a specific congregation or community, and directed to move about within the territory establishing Methodist meetings, classes, and congregations. There are many anecdotal stories of Methodist preachers being among the first to show up in the most remote settlements on the American frontier. Gradually, as these gatherings of lay Methodists grew into identifiable congregations, they were placed on circuits to be served variously by lay preachers and ordained travelling elders. Lay preachers would care for the needs of the congregation and do the preaching. Periodically the travelling elder would come to preach, celebrate Holy Communion, and supervise the ministry. This became regularized as at least a 'quarterly conference' in each area; and this is the reason that early Methodists got used to quarterly, rather than weekly, celebrations of Holy Communion. The sacrament was celebrated when the ordained elder was present.

The image of the Methodist preacher as circuit rider became part of popular American frontier tradition. American Methodism experienced explosive growth during the early nineteenth century. Its rapid expansion was the result of the extraordinary, tireless work of the circuit riders, who sought out settlers in the most remote areas of the new nation. Unlike the ordained ministry of the Episcopal and Presbyterian Churches, where more education and a tradition of a 'settled' parish ministry prevailed, the itinerant Methodist ministry was perfectly suited to the young nation with an ever-expanding frontier. The circuit riders were usually young, highly disciplined, and accountable to the bishops, who were also constantly travelling across the connexion.

The term 'connexion' is also fundamental to Methodism. It suggests that the ministry of the church is never whole in any one locality, but is, in fact, a dynamic community connected by commitment and service. Early Methodists did not refer to 'local churches' or 'parishes'; rather, they talked about circuits, appointments, and charges. A 'charge' was the appointment a preacher was given; and he became the 'minister in charge' in the sense of responsibility and accountability for teaching and administration of the people called Methodists in that place and time. The church was bigger than any locality, always transcending the particularity of any specific place. Indeed the early bishops traversed the whole nation, and were not assigned specific geographical territories. Only gradually did growth dictate the development of what would later be called 'local churches', geographical conferences, and ultimately episcopal areas. Local churches were generally on a circuit with the preachers serving several congregations. Even after the development of what came to be called 'station' churches, stand-alone congregations, the preachers were moved regularly by the bishops to different charges. To this day all appointments of Methodist ministers are annual. Well into the twentieth century, preachers and their families would not know where they would be living and working until the bishop read the appointments at the end of the annual conference. Then they would pack up and move to the next place of service. Similarly, congregations would not know who their preacher would be until the same moment.

The Methodist parsonage system, in which each charge has a parsonage for the minister and family, was developed to facilitate the movement of the preachers from charge to charge. In many conferences the parsonages were fully furnished, so that the family could move right in. The tradition of moving every two or four years was deeply ingrained in the preachers, their families, and the churches.

In the mid-twentieth century, this began to change as social, economic, educational, and practical factors forced the church to adjust some of its earlier practices. Even as more consultation with congregations and ministers took place, however, the expectation of itinerancy prevailed, though in a modified version. The Methodist 'system', which had always been a method of deploying clergy, became more structured and procedural. Every denomination must have some system to match clergy with congregations, and the Methodist system of appointments made by bishops following consultation by district superintendents with both congregations and clergy continues to be effective. In the case of non-episcopal Methodism, the appointments are generally done by an appointments committee, sometimes made up of both clergy and lay persons.

Originally Methodist bishops were not assigned territories, but were genuine itinerant general superintendents. Through the years this changed as the church grew and transportation required that a bishop serve several specific annual conferences rather than the whole denomination. This has continued in such a way that bishops generally are now resident in one annual conference, and therefore are not really visible leaders of the whole church. While bishops are not permanently limited to one geographical area, this trend toward greater 'locality' has changed the nature of the episcopal office in significant ways.

Perhaps the biggest change for Methodism has been in the length of service in any one charge on the part of ministers. The length of the average appointment has increased, in part due to changed expectations of both laity and clergy, and congregational studies that suggest that clergy effectiveness is greater with appointments that are at least seven years, and probably not more than fourteen or fifteen years. This has produced some occasional unhappiness among the clergy when the big, or so-called 'high steeple', churches keep their clergy for many years, and thus block the process of upward movement. This comment is itself controversial because it implies that there is a career path for the clergy involving early years in small churches and steady movement upwards in size of congregations and salary, with concomitant increase in status. While this is not always a welcome image, it is not untrue; and longer pastorates in the really large churches definitely have an impact on the reality of itinerancy. It is harder to claim an itinerant ministry when some of the clergy are in one appointment for fifteen, twenty, or more years. This is one of the realities that Methodism faces in the changing dynamics of church life in the twenty-first century. Clergy demands for their own family life and security are surely a part of this; and some churches (and annual conferences) have even started allowing ministers to buy their own homes and to receive a housing allowance. This practice is decidedly non-Methodist and is a real threat to itinerancy because it represents a 'settled' clergy.

There is no question that itinerancy is a practical system. It has developed through the history of both episcopal and non-episcopal Methodism as an effective means of appointing clergy to their work. But it would be a mistake to miss the fact that itinerancy in the Methodist tradition is really a theological concept, and not just an administrative tool for deployment. John Wesley constantly emphasized the dynamic character of Christian faith. His notion of 'going on to perfection' is best and rightly understood to mean that the Christian life is lived in procession with movement toward the goal of fulfilment in Christ. The Christian is never static, but always moving forward. This same image characterizes ministry in Methodism. Ministry is not a settled professional activity, but a dynamic reality bringing together leadership and people for service to God.

MINISTRY AND ITINERANCY AS
THEOLOGICAL REALITIES IN METHODISM

Consideration of ministry in Methodism illustrates not only the complex forms and orders by which the movement and the churches emerged and developed, and by which they structured their lives, but also the underlying theology that informs Methodist thinking and action (Campbell, Lawrence, and Richey 1997). Methodism has placed great emphasis on the immediate power and work of the Holy Spirit to enliven human forms of life and ministry. This has meant that, although Methodists have been prone to structure the church in a clear manner through the *Discipline*, those structures are understood to emerge from prayerful reception of guidance from the Holy Spirit. While it is certainly the case that the *Discipline* is the product of a delegated general conference, made up of clergy and lay members, and thus a very human political process, it is the conviction of the church that the Spirit works through this process, even if that conviction is often unstated. The Methodist general conference is a political body subject to all the shortcomings of any human institution. At the same time, the church has witnessed to the reality of the Holy Spirit working through the political process to advance its earthly life and work. The Methodist churches are dependent upon the collective wisdom of what has sometimes been called 'holy conferencing' to establish the forms and directions of the church. This includes the various forms and orders of the ministries of the church.

The tension between theology and tradition, on the one hand, and practical need and expediency on the other has thus always existed in Methodism. This has produced an uncommon symbiotic relationship between the church and its social and cultural setting. On the one hand, the church has been influenced by the culture in which it is found, on the other, it has influenced the culture. In Methodism, there are no absolutes of ecclesiological authority to resist changes influenced by culture, but the witness of biblical authority and church tradition act to balance contemporary reality. The church has in turn helped to shape the culture by the changes it has made in practice. The delicate balance between biblical authority, church tradition, and contemporary experience that characterizes Methodism, has meant that ministry in Methodism has always been shaped profoundly by its responsiveness to the needs of the people in any time and place. It is thus the case that its ministry will always be shaped by Methodism's practical theology more than by ecclesiological authority and theological tradition.

SUGGESTED READING

BOWMER, JOHN C. (1975). *Pastor and People: A Study of Church and Ministry in Wesleyan Methodism from the Death of John Wesley (1791) to the Death of Jabez Bunting (1858)*. London: Epworth.

CAMPBELL, DENNIS M. (1988). *The Yoke of Obedience: The Meaning of Ordination in Methodism*. Nashville: Abingdon.

CANNON, WILLIAM RAGSDALE (1969). 'The Meaning of the Ministry in Methodism'. *Methodist History* 8/1 (October): 3–19.

LAWSON, A. B. (1963). *John Wesley and the Christian Ministry: The Sources and Development of His Opinions and Practices*. London: SPCK.

OUTLER, ALBERT C. (1970). 'The Ordinal'. In William F. Dunkle, Jr. and Joseph D. Quillian, Jr. (eds.), *Companion to the Book of Worship*. Nashville: Abingdon.

RAYMOND GEORGE, A. (1951). 'Ordination in Methodism'. *London Quarterly and Holborn Review* 176 (April): 156–69.

RICHEY, RUSSELL E. (1983). 'Evolving Patterns of Methodist Ministry'. *Methodist History* 22 (October): 25–37.

THOMPSON, EDGAR W. (1957). *Wesley: Apostolic Man: Some Reflections on Wesley's Consecration of Dr. Thomas Coke*. London: Epworth.

REFERENCES

BAKER, FRANK (1976). *From Wesley to Asbury: Studies in Early American Methodism*. Durham: Duke University Press.

The Book of Discipline of The United Methodist Church (2004). Nashville: United Methodist Publishing House.

CAMPBELL, DENNIS (1988). *The Yoke of Obedience: The Meaning of Ordination in Methodism*. Nashville: Abingdon.

—— LAWRENCE, WILLIAM B., and RICHEY, RUSSELL E. (eds.) (1999). *Doctrines and Discipline*, iii. *United Methodism and American Culture*. Nashville: Abingdon.

DICKENS, A. G. (1964). *The English Reformation*. New York: Schocken Books.

DIX, GREGORY (1948). *The Question of Anglican Orders*. London: Dacre.

HEITZENRATER, RICHARD (1985). 'Introduction'. *Diary of an Oxford Methodist: Benjamin Ingham, 1733–1734*. Durham, N.C.: Duke University Press.

HEMPTON, DAVID (2005). *Methodism: Empire of the Spirit*. New Haven: Yale University Press.

MATHEWS, JAMES K. (1985). *Set Apart to Serve: The Role of Episcopacy in the Wesleyan Tradition*. Nashville: Abingdon.

MOEDE, GERALD F. (1978). *A Renewed Diaconate in The United Methodist Church?* Nashville: United Methodist Publishing House.

OUTLER, ALBERT C. (ed.) (1964). *John Wesley*. New York: Oxford University Press.

—— (1970). 'The Ordinal'. In William F. Dunkle, Jr. and Joseph D. Quillian, Jr. (eds.), *Companion to the Book of Worship*. Nashville: Abingdon.

Rupp, E. G. (1965). *Studies in the Making of the English Protestant Tradition.* Cambridge: Cambridge University Press.

Short, Roy H. (1976). *Chosen to Be Consecrated.* Lake Junaluska: Commission on Archives and History of The United Methodist Church.

—— (1985). *The Episcopal Leadership Role in United Methodism.* Nashville: Abingdon.

Sykes, Stephen (1995). *Unashamed Anglicanism.* London: Darton, Longman, & Todd.

Wesley, John (1931). *The Letters of the Rev. John Wesley, A.M.,* ed. John Telford. 8 vols. London: Epworth.

—— (1938). *The Journal of the Rev. John Wesley, A.M.,* ed. Nehemiah Curnock. 8 vols. London: Epworth.

CHAPTER 16

MEANS OF GRACE AND FORMS OF PIETY

TED A. CAMPBELL

THE concept and practice of the 'means of grace' have been central to Methodist spirituality and theology since the earliest years of the evangelical revival under the leadership of John and Charles Wesley. Methodist or Wesleyan spirituality is sometimes described as a distinctive combination of evangelical and sacramental spiritual practices (Campbell 2001: 160–1) and for this reason the means of grace play a central role as historic forms of piety in the spirituality of historic Wesleyan and Methodist communities.

John Wesley's sermon on 'The Means of Grace' defines 'means of grace' as denoting '*means ordained* of God, as the usual channels of his grace', or more specifically as 'outward signs, words, or actions, ordained of God, and appointed for this end, to be the ordinary channels whereby he might convey to men, preventing, justifying, or sanctifying grace' (Wesley 1984–7: i. 378, 381). A closely related term for John Wesley was 'ordinances': on one occasion, in fact, Wesley defined 'means of grace' as 'outward ordinances, whereby the inward grace of God is ordinarily conveyed to man' (Wesley 1873: i. 248), and the specific 'ordinances of God' that he named in the 'General Rules' overlap his lists of 'means of grace'. Considered in the light of broader Christian spiritual and ecclesial traditions, we might say that 'means of grace' and 'ordinances' embrace a variety of Christian practices that have been either explicitly authorized in Christian tradition and

Scripture or have been found helpful for Christians as means by which they experience divine grace. Thus, the categories of 'means of grace' and 'ordinances' in Wesleyan practice and thought can be understood as a somewhat larger and more inclusive category than that of 'sacraments' (in Western churches, a term Wesley also utilized) or 'mysteries' (in Eastern churches).

The expression 'means of grace' had been utilized prior to the rise of Methodism. The General Thanksgiving in Book of Common Prayer (1662), for example, offered thanks to God 'for the means of grace, and for the hope of glory' (*Book of Common Prayer* 1999: 105) and John Wesley cited this prayer in his sermon on 'The Means of Grace'. The catechism of the Book of Common Prayer defined a 'sacrament' as involving an 'outward and visible sign' instituted by Christ which is a 'means' of receiving an inward and spiritual grace (ibid. 189), and Wesley also cited this definition of sacrament in the same sermon.

John Wesley's conflict with a particular group of London Moravians prompted him to define his understanding of the means of grace. In response to this controversy he wrote the sermon entitled 'The Means of Grace' sometime between 1739 and 1741 (Wesley 1984–7: i. 379–80). It is very important to note that the views of this London group have been regarded by subsequent Moravians as highly eccentric, and in fact it came at the beginning of a very problematic period in the development of the renewed Unity of Brethren, a period that Moravians call 'the sifting time'. Wesleyan and Methodist scholars, then, should not report the views of this group as representing (in Outler's phrase) 'the Moravian position' (ibid. 376). Wesley's concern at this point was to refute the view that those who have not received the full assurance of justification (i.e. consciousness of the pardon of their sins) should abstain from outward means, especially the Lord's Supper. In his sermon on 'The Means of Grace', Wesley asked if there were any means ordained by God within the new covenant, and he offered scriptural evidence for prayer, 'searching the Scriptures', and the Lord's Supper as such means. Wesley was clear in this sermon that the means of grace could be abused, for example, when Christians relied on outward signs or actions only as evidence that they had received divine grace.

Just a few years after the sermon on 'The Means of Grace', John and Charles Wesley clarified expectations of members of Methodist societies in the General Rules (1743). In this set of rules, which functioned as the original covenant for Wesleyan societies, 'attending upon the ordinances of God' is a third general category after avoiding evil of all kinds and doing good of all kinds. The practice of each of the three 'means of grace' defended in the earlier sermon on 'The Means of Grace' appeared as requirements for continuation of members in Wesleyan societies in the General Rules, and a few more items were added, so the full list of 'ordinances of God' required in the General Rules (Wesley 1873: viii. 271) is as follows:

the public worship of God
the ministry of the word, either read or expounded

the supper of the Lord
family and private prayer
searching the Scriptures
fasting, or abstinence.

The list of ordinances given in the General Rules thus includes all of the means specified in the earlier sermon on 'The Means of Grace' (prayer, the Lord's Supper, and 'searching the Scriptures') and adds public worship, the ministry of the Word, and fasting (or abstinence). Although the list of 'ordinances of God' is larger than the earlier list of 'means of grace', each of the ordinances listed here was understood by Wesley to involve a means of divine grace.

John Wesley expanded his understanding of means of grace in the document historically called the Large Minutes, where he made a distinction between 'instituted' and 'prudential' means of grace (Large Minutes, qu. 48, Wesley 1873: viii. 322–4). The 'instituted' means included prayer, 'searching the Scriptures', the Lord's Supper, fasting, and 'Christian conference', by which Wesley meant carefully guarded conversation with other Christians (see the following for further comment on each of these items). The 'prudential' means included rules that individual Christians might make to be kept with the help of their societies, attending class and band meetings, occasions on which preachers could meet with society or class members, and even more specific items such as abstaining from meat or late meals, drinking water, and temperance in the use of wine and ale.

Although the Large Minutes did not elaborate on Wesley's terms, it seems clear enough that the 'instituted' means were practices instituted in Scripture, from the beginning of the Christian community, and thus Wesley understood them to be binding on the church at all times and in all places (cf. for example Wesley's argument about these practices in the sermon on 'The Means of Grace', Wesley 1984–7: i. 379–80). The 'prudential' means, by contrast, included all the specifically and distinctively Methodist practices, that is, practices that were not instituted in Scripture but which were simply found to be prudentially helpful by Methodist people. The distinction John Wesley drew between instituted and prudential means of grace, then, seems to follow the pattern in his thought by which he distinguished what is commonly Christian from those things that marked the distinctive mission of the Methodist movement. In other words, Wesley identifies the Methodist people as a distinct religious movement whose prudential practices supplemented those of the broader Christian community.

Prayer is consistently held to be a divinely appointed means of grace in the Wesleyan tradition. John Wesley defended prayer as a means of grace in his sermon on 'The Means of Grace' (late 1730s), he included 'family and private prayer' among the 'ordinances of God' to which Methodists were held accountable in the General Rules (1743), and he included prayer among the 'instituted means' of grace in the Large Minutes (probably late 1740s). The latter account is expanded in a manner that gives some of the content of his understanding of daily prayer as a spiritual practice:

(1.) Prayer; private, family, public; consisting of deprecation, petition, intercession, and thanksgiving. Do you use each of these? Do you use private prayer every morning and evening? if you can, at five in the evening; and the hour before or after morning preaching? Do you forecast daily, wherever you are, how to secure these hours? Do you avow it everywhere?   (Wesley 1873: viii. 322–3)

Wesley's reference to 'private, family, [and] public' prayer indicates a conjunction of private and communal practices of prayer, and each of these should involve the four movements of 'deprecation' (penitence), petition, intercession, and thanksgiving. Earlier in the same document, Wesley had referred to the same pattern of 'deprecation, petition, intercession, and thanksgiving' as the consistent parts of Anglican worship, compared to which Methodist occasional services were 'defective' since the latter usually lacked the full structure of these four elements (ibid. 321–2). This comment, then, implies that John Wesley took the form of prayer he knew from the Book of Common Prayer to be a complete pattern of Christian daily prayer.

John and Charles Wesley were formed as Christians by daily family prayer utilizing the services for Morning and Evening Prayer in the Book of Common Prayer. Methodists came to be known even within the Wesleys' lifetime for extempore prayer (as Wesley (ibid. 321) himself put it, 'we frequently use extempore prayer'), although John Wesley's introduction to his 1784 revision of the Prayer Book urged Methodist elders to celebrate the Lord's Supper every Sunday, to use the prescribed forms for daily Morning and Evening Prayer on Sundays, to use the Litany of his revised Prayer Book on Wednesdays, and to pray extempore on other days (Wesley 1984: p. ii). This suggests that a balance of practices of extempore prayer and set forms of prayers from the Prayer Book tradition characterized the Methodist movement in the Wesleys' lifetimes and beyond. In the nineteenth and twentieth centuries Methodist publishing houses would offer a variety of publications offering forms of prayer.

Methodist people have often used hymns as part of their private as well as family and congregational devotional life, and Methodist hymnals often include prayers, psalms, and other resources that can be used for prayer and personal devotion in addition to hymns. *The United Methodist Hymnal* of 1989, for instance, includes forms for morning and evening prayer for the use of small groups, families, or individuals (*United Methodist Hymnal* 1989: 876).

An evolution of the Methodist prayer tradition in the United States can be seen in *The Upper Room*, a devotional guide that originated under the auspices of the Methodist Episcopal Church (South) in 1935, and which came to have an international readership within a few decades. Within thirty years (by 1963) the publication was available in thirty-five languages. Utilizing a small, single-page format and published monthly, *The Upper Room* offers for every day of the month a Scripture passage, a devotional reflection (often involving personal testimony) offered by a very wide range of contributors from throughout the world, and a brief prayer.

A second means of grace consistently inculcated by John Wesley was what he termed 'searching the Scriptures', and what today we might refer to as the spiritual practice of devotional biblical study. This practice was defended as a means of grace in John Wesley's sermon on 'The Means of Grace', it was included in the 'ordinances of God' expected of Methodists in the General Rules, and explicitly named as an 'instituted' means of grace in the Large Minutes (Wesley 1984–7: i. 386–9; Wesley 1873: viii. 271, 323). The latter offers an expanded comment that allows us to understand what Wesley meant by this spiritual practice:

(2.) Searching the scriptures by,

(i.) Reading: Constantly, some part of every day; regularly, all the Bible in order; carefully, with the Notes; seriously, with prayer before and after; fruitfully, immediately practising what you learn there?
(ii.) Meditating: At set times? by any rule?
(iii.) Hearing: Every morning? carefully; with prayer before, at, after; immediately putting into practice? Have you a New Testament always about you?

The same general pattern of reading, meditating, and hearing had appeared in the sermon on 'The Means of Grace', where Wesley stated that 'under the general term of searching the Scriptures, both hearing, reading, and meditating are contained' (Wesley 1984–7: i. 387). In fact, in the latter account Wesley gave priority to the hearing of Scripture as the usual means by which faith is engendered in Christians: 'faith came . . . by hearing' (cf. Romans 10: 17), so that reading the Scriptures served to confirm the truth first apprehended in hearing the Scriptures.

The distinction that John Wesley drew between 'hearing' and 'reading' the Scriptures implies the same conjunction noted with respect to prayer above, namely the conjunction of private devotional practice (in this case 'reading' the Scriptures) and communal practice ('hearing' the Scriptures). This distinction also appears in the General Rules, where John and Charles Wesley included both 'searching the Scriptures' and 'the ministry of the word, either read or expounded' ('General Rules', Wesley 1873: viii. 271). 'Hearing' the Scriptures in a community would have been possible for Methodists in the Wesleys' era on a daily basis where Methodist early morning preaching was scheduled and in Anglican parishes where the service for Morning Prayer (including the reading of the Scriptures in the daily lectionary) was recited. However, Wesley's reference to reading 'all the Bible in order' implies a preference for the Reformed practice of strictly sequential biblical study in contrast to the Anglican use of the daily lectionary of the Prayer Book, which was arranged in a pattern that involved sequential reading of some books, but was also tied to the annual liturgical calendar.

Despite John Wesley's consistent distinction of prayer and searching the Scriptures, his comments imply that the two practices were closely linked: he suggested that Methodists should engage in prayer in 'the hour before or after morning preaching', and the practice of searching the Scriptures should be accompanied by prayer (ibid. 322–3). This was consistent with the long Christian tradition of daily prayer accompanied by Scripture reading represented in the Book of Common Prayer and its own roots in older traditions of daily prayer and *lectio divina* that reached back to the early Middle Ages.

Methodist churches after the time of the Wesleys made available a variety of resources for devotional biblical study. Wesley referred to his own *Explanatory Notes upon the New Testament* in the passage cited above from the Large Minutes, a work that he had prepared for the use of Methodist people and that has served as a doctrinal standard in Methodist churches. Wesley's *Notes*, however, were supplanted by Adam Clarke's *Commentary* (1825) early in the nineteenth century. Clarke's *Commentary* remained a Methodist standard for almost a century, replaced in the twentieth century by *Peake's Commentary* (1920) in the United Kingdom and the *Abingdon Bible Commentary* (1929) in the United States, and Methodists continued to utilize these two commentaries through the later decades of the twentieth century. As noted above, daily biblical passages are set in such Methodist devotional literature as *The Upper Room*.

A third means of grace consistently taught by the Wesleys was the Lord's Supper, defended as such in the sermon on the 'Means of Grace', attendance at which was expected of Methodists according to the General Rules, and which was listed among the instituted means of grace in the Large Minutes (Wesley 1984–7: i. 389–90; Wesley 1873: viii. 271, 323). In the latter document, Wesley asked Methodists about the Lord's Supper, 'Do you use this at every opportunity? with solemn prayer before; with earnest and deliberate self-devotion?' Frequent communion had been the Wesleys' own practice since their time in Oxford (cf. Heitzenrater 1985: 13), and their emphasis on receiving the sacrament 'at every opportunity' is consistent with John Wesley's exhortations in a sermon on 'The Duty of Constant Communion', originally written in 1732 and then released again in 1787 with a notice, 'But I thank God I have not yet seen cause to alter my sentiments in any point which is therein delivered' (Wesley 1984–7: 3, 428). John Wesley's 1784 revision of the Prayer Book, similarly, asserted that ordained elders in the newly established American Methodist church should celebrate the Lord's Supper every Sunday (Wesley 1984: p. ii).

John Wesley's sermon on 'The Duty of Constant Communion' makes very clear his consistent conviction that the sacrament of the Lord's Supper conveys divine grace, the grace of forgiveness of sins committed after the new birth and the grace of sanctification, 'that we may obtain holiness on earth and everlasting glory in heaven' (II: 5, Wesley 1984–7: iii. 432). Anticipating the objection that some would refuse communion because they considered themselves to be unworthy of the sacrament, John Wesley wrote, 'And what then? You are unworthy to receive any mercy from God. But is that a reason for refusing all mercy? God offers you a pardon for all your sins' (II: 7, ibid. 433). John and Charles Wesley made this sense of the present power of divine grace eminently clear in their rich collection of *Hymns on the Lord's Supper* (1745; in Rattenbury 1948: 195–249, 204–24, esp. section II, 'As it is a Sign and a Means of Grace'), although very few of these hymns made it into the *Hymnal* of 1780, which served as the first standard Methodist hymnal for many decades or into subsequent Methodist hymnals until the late twentieth century.

The lack of ordained clergy authorized to celebrate the sacrament of the Lord's Supper was a strong factor that led to John Wesley's authorization of an American Methodist church (subsequently named the Methodist Episcopal Church) in 1784, and the celebration of the Lord's Supper was a consistent mark of Methodist life, even in the periods when Methodists were best known for vigorous evangelistic activity. Camp meetings, for example, had grown out of the Scots and Scots–Irish Presbyterian sacramental (eucharistic) celebrations as these were imported to North America (Westerkamp 1988: *passim*; Schmidt 1989: 50–68), and American Methodist camp meetings often culminated in the celebration of the sacrament (see the examples in Ruth 2005: 214–16). Consistent with this development, hymns originally designated for eucharistic celebration (such as Charles Wesley's 'Come, Sinners, to the Gospel Feast') have often been utilized interchangeably as hymns for the 'altar call' or invitation to Christian discipleship at the conclusion of Methodist evangelistic meetings (see the two variations of this hymn in *The United Methodist Hymnal* 1989: 339, 616). Celebration of the sacrament also consistently marked the spirituality of black congregations in Methodist denominations and in the historically African-American Methodist denominations, the AME, AME Zion, and CME Churches (see, for example, the discussion of the sacrament in Turner 1885: 181–2). Even such a work as the *Cokesbury Worship Hymnal* (1938), which offered a selection of popular gospel hymns for the use of Southern Methodists in the US, was printed in numerous editions containing the ritual for the celebration of the Lord's Supper (*ibid.* 347; though the ritual for Holy Communion does not appear in all editions of this hymnal).

The 'ordinances of God' listed in the General Rules (1743) included 'the public worship of God' in addition to 'the ministry of the word, either read or expounded' and 'the supper of the Lord' ('General Rules', Wesley 1873: viii. 271). Public worship did not appear as a separate item in lists of the means of grace, either in 'The Means of Grace' or in the instituted and prudential means listed in the Large Minutes, although it was discussed in the Large Minutes, which insisted that Methodists were expected to participate in Anglican services as well as preaching and other services offered by Methodists (ibid. 321–2). The category of 'public worship' could denote Methodist preaching services and Anglican celebrations of Morning and Evening Prayer and the Lord's Supper in the Wesleys' time, and thus overlaps other items identified as 'means of grace', including the hearing of the Scriptures (read and expounded) and public prayer.

The Large Minutes identify fasting or abstinence as an instituted means of grace, and John Wesley's sole question on this point was not whether Methodists fasted on Fridays but 'How do you fast every Friday?' (ibid. 323). Similarly, John Wesley's

'Directions Given to the Band-Societies' (1744) asked participants 'To observe, as days of fasting or abstinence, all Fridays in the year' (ibid. 274). This custom followed not only the Prayer Book prescription of fasting on Fridays (*Book of Common Prayer* 1999: 58), but it also reflects John Wesley's knowledge of early Christian practice by way of Tertullian's treatise *De Ieiunio* ('On Fasting'), which had prescribed fasting on every Wednesday and Friday from morning through the ninth hour of the day, and John Wesley often observed both Wednesday and Friday fasts from sun-up until he took tea in the afternoon (Campbell 1991: 98–9). John Wesley's seventh sermon in his series on the Sermon on the Mount discusses fasting at some length, including various degrees of fasting or abstinence, weekly fasts and the annual Lenten fast, and the significance of fasting as a spiritual exercise (Wesley 1984–7: i. 592–611).

Fasting continued to be observed as a spiritual exercise by Methodist people beyond the time of the Wesleys, although the specific observation of the Friday fast seems to have fallen out of use among Methodists in the early nineteenth century. British Methodist theologian William Burt Pope's *Compendium of Christian Theology* (1880) devoted at least a short section to fasting (iii. 210), and AME Bishop Henry McNeal Turner's classic work on *Methodist Polity* (1885), a work approved as a whole by the 1888 General Conference of the AME Church, dealt with fasting and abstinence as normative expectations of Christians (186–7).

A fifth means of grace listed among the instituted means in the Large Minutes (and only there) is identified as 'Christian conference'. Wesley's questions following the identification of this means of grace illuminate his understanding of it:

Are you convinced how important and how difficult it is to 'order our conversation right?' Is it 'always in grace? seasoned with salt? meet to minister grace to the hearers?' Do not you converse too long at a time? Is not an hour commonly enough? Would it not be well always to have a determinate end in view; and to pray before and after it?

(Wesley 1873: viii. 323)

When Wesley spoke of 'Christian conference' in this context, then, he denoted what we might call 'Christian conversation'. If this seems an odd item to lay alongside fasting, prayer, devotional Bible study, and the sacrament of the Lord's Supper as means of grace instituted in Scripture and binding upon the universal Christian community, it is worth noting that many of Jesus' words had to do with speech, and the subject of proper conversation among Christians had long been a topic in Christian spirituality, especially with the development of cenobitic (monastic) communities in the fourth century. John Wesley devoted a sermon to 'The Cure of Evil Speaking', which he defined as 'speaking evil of an absent person' (Wesley 1984–7: ii. 252–65; quotation on 252). Thus, although 'Christian conference' was not explicitly mentioned among the 'ordinances of God' in the General Rules, this document did rule out 'the using many words in buying or selling' and 'uncharitable or unprofitable conversation, particularly speaking evil of Magistrates or of Ministers' (Wesley

1873: viii. 270). John Wesley himself had been accustomed in his Oxford years and beyond to note in his private diaries when he conversed with others and whether his conversations were 'religious' and 'necessary' (see the example given in Heitzenrater 2003: 60–1). Although 'conference' became a central Methodist term (where it denoted quarterly, annual, and eventually quadrennial meetings), the later uses of the term did not retain this earlier sense of the importance of holy conversation.

Beyond the instituted means of grace considered here, the Large Minutes identified a number of 'prudential' means of grace clustered under activities of 'common Christians', of Methodists, of preachers, and of 'assistants' (Wesley 1873: viii. 323). As noted above, the prudential means indicated customs or activities not instituted in Scripture, but were simply found to be prudentially helpful. Most of them beyond the first category given are distinctive of the Methodist movement, for example, attending classes and bands, meeting with societies (on the part of preachers), and conscientiously executing the office of a Methodist 'assistant'. The category of 'prudential' means, then, signals that the means of grace could be in a sense creatively discovered, as believers and communities found certain practices to be useful or fruitful in the Christian life.

The category of the 'means of grace' was a staple of Methodist theological reflection and catechesis and remained so in Methodist churches and in the broader Wesleyan community through the nineteenth and twentieth centuries. A 1905 *Junior Catechism* developed jointly by the ME and ME (South) Churches in the US and still in use in the CME Church describes the means of grace as the Word of God, prayer, the Church, and the sacraments (*Junior Catechism* 1905: qu. 76, p. 15; n.d.: qu. 76, p. 17). Nazarene theologian H. Orton Wiley, writing in 1943, elaborated on these same four means, dividing them into two broad categories: the 'universal' means (the Word of God and prayer), and the 'economic' means (the fellowship of the saints and the sacraments; Wiley 1943: iii. 150–1 and following). The current (2004) *Doctrines and Discipline* of the AME Church gives the full list of instituted and prudential means of grace (following the Large Minutes) in a section describing the 'Personal Life of a Pastor' (*Doctrines and Discipline of the African Methodist Episcopal Church* 2004: 109). Older Methodist institutions such as classes and class leaders have been maintained in some global Methodist churches such as the AME and AME Zion churches, some African-American United Methodist congregations, and Caribbean Methodist churches as well. Korean Methodist churches in the twentieth century began organizing congregations into small groups, following both the earlier Wesleyan/Methodist pattern and patterns they had learned from Korean Presbyterian groups.

In contemporary Wesleyan and Methodist life, the category of 'means of grace' has proved to be a rich concept for contemporary Christian spiritual and theological renewal. Henry H. Knight's 1992 study, *The Presence of God in the Christian Life: John Wesley and the Means of Grace*, makes the case for a contemporary Wesleyan theology and spirituality in which the means of grace serve to balance the more evangelical aspects of Christian theology and spirituality, allowing for a distinctive ethos that values orthodoxy, orthopraxis, and (utilizing a term from Theodore Runyon) 'orthopathy', thus, appropriate belief, appropriate practice, and appropriate affections. In the words of Don Saliers' introduction to Knight's book, the Wesleyan emphasis on the means of grace yields a vision of Christian faith and life that is 'remarkably relevant to a range of questions facing those who yearn to hold catholicity and evangelical faith together' (Saliers in Knight 1992: p. xiii).

Methodists and other Wesleyan Christians have explored a number of forms of piety in contemporary Christian experience, some directly related to their roots in early Methodist spirituality and others that are expressions of trends in Christian spirituality in the broader ecumenical community. Methodists throughout the world became involved in the Charismatic movement in the 1970s, and this led to some historical scholarship demonstrating the connections between the earlier Wesleyan movement and its evolution into the Holiness and Pentecostal movements that lay in the background of the Charismatic movement of the second half of the twentieth century ('Guidelines: The United Methodist Church and the Charismatic Movement' 1987; cf. Dayton 1987).

A notable instance of the renewal of particular forms of early Methodist spirituality has been the movement for Covenant Discipleship which has been spearheaded by Dr. David Lowes Watson. Watson's approach is grounded in his Duke Ph.D. dissertation, a critical historical examination of the class meeting in the time of John Wesley, subsequently published as *The Early Methodist Class Meeting* (Watson 1985). Watson encouraged Christians to join together in small groups that would develop a contemporary covenant to which members of the group would commit themselves for a specified period of six months or more (Watson 1984). The group would meet weekly to hold members accountable for their fidelity to this covenant. Watson has expanded this concept with a series of resources that provided training for class leaders utilizing the format of covenant discipleship (Watson 1991*a*, *b*).

The Walk to Emmaus represents another contemporary Wesleyan approach to Christian spirituality, growing initially out of a Catholic spiritual movement that was given a distinctively Wesleyan expression. The Catholic *Cursillo* movement originated among Spanish Catholics in 1944 as a 'brief course' (*cursillo*) in basic Christianity, involving an intensive weekend retreat. Methodist leaders became familiar with *Cursillo* from the early 1970s, and the Upper Room in Nashville began to sponsor *Cursillo* retreats (Wood 2001: 5–19). Eventually a decision was made to develop a Methodist expression of this spiritual tradition apart from Catholic leadership (ibid. 19–22). When this Methodist expression was developed, the theological lectures in the retreat were focused on central elements of the Wesleyan understanding of the 'Way of Salvation', including prevenient grace, justifying grace, and sanctifying grace. A further lecture deals explicitly with the topic of means of grace (ibid. 22–9). In this way, the Walk to Emmaus retreat involves key elements of Wesleyan spiritual traditions, and in many cases these lectures are offered even when the Walk to Emmaus occurs in the context of other Protestant traditions such as Presbyterian churches. The Walk to Emmaus retreats encourage participants to form reunion groups that are modelled after early Methodist class and band meetings.

The flourishing of varied historic forms of Christian spirituality since the 1980s has led many Wesleyan Christians to recover older spiritual traditions and to connect these to the Wesleyan tradition. Thus Roberta Bondi of Emory University has written on the spiritual practices of the monks of the Egyptian desert (Bondi 1987a, 1991, and others), and also on the specific connections between John Wesley's spirituality and the spirituality of early Christian monasticism (Bondi 1987b: 171–84). Bondi and other Wesleyan and Benedictine scholars participated in a 1994 gathering in Italy on the topic of 'Sanctification in the Benedictine and Methodist Traditions' (Bondi 1995/6: 27–33; Campbell 1995: 5–6 and this issue of the *Asbury Theological Journal* in general). Similarly, she and other Methodist and Wesleyan scholars also participated in a series of four international ecumenical gatherings considering Orthodox and Wesleyan Spirituality (the results of the first three of these were published in Kimbrough 2002, 2005, 2007).

REFERENCES

BONDI, ROBERTA C. (1987a). *To Love as God Loves: Conversations with the Early Church*. Philadelphia: Fortress.

—— (1987b). 'The Meeting of Oriental Orthodoxy and United Methodism'. In Paul Fries and Tiran Nersoyan (eds.), *Christ in East and West*. Macon, Ga.: Mercer University Press.

—— (1991). *To Pray and to Love: Conversations on Prayer with the Early Church*. Minneapolis: Fortress.

—— (1995/6). 'Sanctification in the Tradition of the Fathers: A Methodist Perspective'. *Asbury Theological Journal* 50/2 and 51/1 (together, Autumn 1995 and Spring 1996).

The Book of Common Prayer: 1662 Version (1999). Everyman's Library 241. London: David Campbell.

CAMPBELL, TED (1991). *John Wesley and Christian Antiquity: Religious Vision and Cultural Change*. Nashville: Kingswood Books.

—— (1995). 'Introduction' to a series of papers on 'Sanctification in Benedictine and Methodist Traditions'. *Asbury Theological Journal* 50/2 and 51/1 (together, Autumn 1995 and Spring 1996).

—— (2001). 'Conversion and Baptism in Wesleyan Spirituality'. In *Conversion in the Wesleyan Tradition*, ed. Kenneth J. Collins and John H. Tyson. Nashville: Abingdon.

Cokesbury Worship Hymnal (1938). Nashville: Methodist Publishing House.

DAYTON, DONALD W. (1987). *Theological Roots of Pentecostalism*. Grand Rapids: Francis Asbury Press.

Doctrines and Discipline of the African Methodist Episcopal Church (2004). Nashville: AMEC Sunday School Union.

'Guidelines: The United Methodist Church and the Charismatic Movement' (1976). A statement adopted by the 1976 General Conference of the United Methodist Church. Nashville: Discipleship Resources.

HEITZENRATER, RICHARD P. (ed.) (1985). *Diary of an Oxford Methodist: Benjamin Ingham, 1733–1734*. Durham, N.C.: Duke University Press.

—— (2003). *The Elusive Mr. Wesley*. 2nd rev. edn. Nashville: Abingdon.

Junior Catechism (1905). Methodist Episcopal Church and Methodist Episcopal Church South. New York: Methodist Book Concern.

—— (n.d.). Christian Methodist Episcopal Church. Memphis: CME Publishing House.

KIMBROUGH, S. T., JR. (ed.) (2002). *Orthodox and Wesleyan Spirituality*. Crestwood, N.Y.: St Vladimir's Press.

—— (ed.) (2005). *Orthodox and Wesleyan Scriptural Understanding and Practice*. Crestwood, N.Y.: St Vladimir's Press.

—— (ed.) (2007). *Orthodox and Wesleyan Ecclesiology*. Crestwood, N.Y.: St Vladimir's Press.

KNIGHT, HENRY (1992). *The Presence of God in the Christian Life: John Wesley and the Means of Grace*. Metuchen, N.J.: London: Scarecrow.

POPE, WILLIAM BURT (1880). *Compendium of Christian Theology*. 3 vols. London: Wesleyan Conference Office.

RATTENBURY, J. ERNEST (1948). *The Eucharistic Hymns of John and Charles Wesley*. London: Epworth.

RUTH, LESTER (ed.) (2005). *Early Methodist Life and Spirituality: A Reader*. Nashville: Kingswood Books.

SCHMIDT, LEIGH ERIC (1989). *Holy Fairs: Scottish Communions and American Revivals in the Early Modern Period*. Princeton: Princeton University Press.

TURNER, HENRY MCNEAL (1885). *The Genius and Theory of Methodist Polity, or The Machinery of Methodism*. Repr. edn. (1986). Nashville: AMEC Sunday School Union.

The United Methodist Hymnal: Book of United Methodist Worship (1989). Nashville: United Methodist Publishing House.

WATSON, DAVID LOWES (1984). *Accountable Discipleship: A Handbook for Covenant Discipleship Groups in the Congregation*. Nashville: Discipleship Resources.

—— (1985). *The Early Methodist Class Meeting: Its Meaning and Significance*. Nashville: Discipleship Resources.

—— (1991*a*). *Class Leaders: Recovering a Tradition*. Nashville: Discipleship Resources.

—— (1991*b*). *Forming Christian Disciples: The Role of Covenant Discipleship and Class Leaders in the Congregation*. Nashville: Discipleship Resources.

WESLEY, JOHN (1873). *Works*, ed. Thomas Jackson. Repr. edn. London: Wesleyan Conference Office.

—— (1984). *John Wesley's Sunday Service of the Methodists in North America*. Special edn. of *Quarterly Review*. Introduction by James F. White. Repr. edn. Nashville: United Methodist Publishing House and General Board of Higher Education and Ministry of the United Methodist Church.

—— (1984–7). *Sermons*. Bicentennial Edition of the Works of John Wesley, ed. Albert C. Outler. Nashville: Abingdon.

WESTERKAMP, MARILYN (1988). *Triumph of the Laity: Scots–Irish Piety and the Great Awakening, 1625–1760*. New York: Oxford University Press.

WILEY, H. ORTON (1943). *Christian Theology*. 3 vols. Kansas City: Beacon Hill.

WOOD, ROBERT (2001). *The Early History of the Walk to Emmaus*. Nashville: Upper Room Books.

PART III

WORSHIP: SACRAMENTS, LITURGY, HYMNODY, PREACHING

CHAPTER 17

MAINSTREAM LITURGICAL DEVELOPMENTS

KAREN B. WESTERFIELD TUCKER

IN a letter dated 9 September 1784, John Wesley stated his conviction that the Book of Common Prayer (1662) of the Church of England exceeded all other liturgies, ancient or modern, in its expression of a 'solid, scriptural, rational piety'. Despite such an affirmation, Wesley acknowledged the imperfections and deficiencies in the Prayer Book when measured against what he perceived to be the ideal worship found in scriptural and apostolic Christianity. He exhibited a restrained liberty in adjusting the established Anglican texts, rubrics, and canons while also taking up additional practices deemed expedient for spreading the gospel. Thus we find within Mr Wesley himself a pattern and tension that would persist among later generations of Methodists in various places and times: the desire for clearly defined liturgical forms; the freedom within reason to depart from, emend, or supplement those forms; and reliance upon the witness of scripture and Christian antiquity to support both approaches.

Early Methodist Liturgical Practices and the Book of Common Prayer

Because of its origin as a movement or 'society' within the Church of England, Methodism from its inception was linked with the English liturgical mainstream by means of the rites and ceremonies of the Book of Common Prayer. John Wesley, who throughout his life claimed to resist separation from the Church of England, expected the people called Methodist to attend Lord's day worship in the local parish church and thus imbibe the Prayer Book's liturgies, which for Sunday morning consisted usually of Morning Prayer, the Litany, and the first part of the Order for Holy Communion inclusive of the sermon or homily (the 'ante-communion') that was prior to the sacramental section. To encourage—or at least not inhibit—such participation, Methodist 'preaching' services consisting principally of Scripture reading, preaching and/or exhortation, prayer, and song were to be held outside 'church hours' on Sundays, typically very early in the morning and late in the afternoon; these Methodist gatherings were ideally to be a complement to, and not a replacement of, parish worship. With the legal requirement that the documentation of both births and marriages be kept at the parish church, many Anglican-Methodists who were lukewarm to the established church nonetheless also experienced the liturgies of the Prayer Book at baptisms and weddings. Even persons affiliated with Methodism who were not communicants in the Church of England (e.g. Congregationalists, Baptists, Quakers, and Moravians) would have been exposed to selected liturgical material of the Prayer Book via the Methodist gatherings. Methodist preachers of Anglican background quoted or paraphrased material from the Prayer Book in their sermons, and snippets from the collects and other formal prayers would probably have appeared in some extemporaneous prayers because such prayer language was familiar to both ear and heart. Many of Charles Wesley's hymns contain direct quotations from or allusions to the contents of the Prayer Book liturgy—at a time when the use of recently composed hymnody was not permitted during Anglican worship proper. For example, a hymn with the heading 'Therefore with Angels and Arch-Angels, &c.' from *Hymns and Sacred Poems* (1739), which reappears in the collection of *Hymns on the Lord's Supper* (1745) as Hymn 161, draws directly upon the Sanctus and its introduction from the communion rite:

> Lord and God of heavenly powers,
> Theirs—yet oh! benignly ours;
> Glorious King, let earth proclaim,
> Worms attempt to chant thy name.

> Thee to laud in songs divine,
> Angels and archangels join;
> We with them our voices raise,
> Echoing thy eternal praise.
>
> Holy, Holy, Holy Lord,
> Live by heaven and earth adored!
> Full of thee, they ever cry,
> Glory be to God most High!

Another hymn, originally published in the second part of *Hymns and Sacred Poems* (1742), repeats from the Order for the Burial of the Dead the long-controversial phrase that committed every deceased person to the ground in 'sure and certain hope of resurrection to eternal life'. Charles Wesley's hymn subtly addressed the concerns the Puritan wing and others had for the phrase by expressly identifying the departed as a professing believer:

> Come, let us who in Christ believe
> With saints and angels join,
> Glory, and praise, and blessing give,
> And thanks, to love divine.
>
> Our friend in sure and certain hope
> Hath laid his body down;
> He knew that Christ shall raise him up,
> And give the starry crown.
>
> To all who his appearing love
> He opens paradise;
> And we shall join the hosts above,
> And we shall grasp the prize.
>
> Then let us wait to see the day,
> To hear the joyful word,
> To answer, Lo! we come away,
> We die to meet our Lord.

The Church's liturgical year also found hymnic expression in Charles's repertoire with both single texts and special collections that addressed Advent/Christmas, Epiphany, Good Friday (Crucifixion), Easter, Ascension, Whitsunday (Pentecost), and Trinity.

Even though the Book of Common Prayer constituted England's liturgical mainstream, the Methodists turned to little-observed instructions in the book to justify a few of their liturgical 'innovations'. The Methodist watch night, an extended service of praise, thanksgiving, and prayer typically held on Friday nights nearest a full moon, was, in addition to apostolic precedent and Moravian custom, inspired by the Prayer Book's direction for 'vigils' as indicated by 'A table of the vigils, fasts, and days of abstinence to be observed in the year'. Anglicans who complained about the inappropriateness of Methodist midnight gatherings were reminded of their own Prayer Book's provision. The Wesleys' desire for Methodists to participate regularly in the eucharist, each week if possible, was invited by Scripture (cf. Matthew 6: 11; Acts 2: 46), early Christian praxis, and a rubric near the conclusion of the Order for the Administration of the Lord's Supper that allowed for weekly reception of the sacrament at cathedral and collegiate churches.

While the Wesleys and other early Methodist leaders remained connected with the Prayer Book and its resources, they also mined the liturgical riches of the early church for practices not found in Anglicanism that could stoke spiritual fires in hearts grown cold. In recovering selected practices, the Methodists employed the three-pronged strategy of classical Anglican theology utilizing the norms of Scripture, Tradition, and Reason, to which was added another: a pragmatism determined by spiritual efficacy in both the individual and the community. Yet their efforts to reclaim aspects of Christian antiquity associated them with the stream of Prayer Book dissent and unofficial liturgical revisions that looked to recover material from earlier versions of the Prayer Book (especially 1549) and from texts believed to originate during the apostolic and Nicene periods (especially the *Apostolic Constitutions*). The Wesleys were familiar with some of these liturgical experiments from their own century and the previous one, and had acquaintance with such revisers as the Arian William Whiston (*The Liturgy of the Church of England, Reduc'd Nearer to the Primitive Standard*, 1713), the Non-Juror Thomas Deacon (*A Compleat Collection of Devotions*, 1734), and the Unitarian Theophilus Lindsey (*The Book of Common Prayer Reformed According to the Plan of the Late Dr. Samuel Clarke*, 1774). Even though the Wesleys distanced themselves from such sometimes theologically suspicious work, John in particular was sympathetic to certain of their conclusions, for example, that the Athanasian Creed with its so-called 'damnatory clauses' might not be appropriate for liturgical use. Among the dozens of Prayer Book revisions or substitutes produced during the century and a half, the Methodist adoption of the love feast (the primitive *agapē*) was apparently unique, although it was a practice shared with minority communities of Separatists, Baptists, Anabaptists, and Moravians.

THE SUNDAY SERVICE OF THE METHODISTS

Perhaps the greatest evidence of the Book of Common Prayer's significance to John Wesley was his use of it for the creation in 1784 of a collection of services for the Methodists in North America. Rather than abandon the Prayer Book as some of his contemporaries had done, Wesley instead abridged it, and in so doing addressed both long-standing complaints against the book made by various factions within and outside the Church (especially the concern about the inclusion of 'unscriptural' material) and what he perceived to be the liturgical need of the Methodist communities in the newly emancipated American colonies.

Wesley's revisionary spirit was first displayed as a priest in Georgia when, according to his diary dated 5 March 1736, he made unspecified alterations to the Prayer Book and the Psalter. Almost twenty years later, in 1755, he revealed in the essay 'Ought We to Separate from the Church of England?' some of the substance of his editorial inclinations. In that essay he declared theologically and scripturally indefensible the Prayer Book's inclusion of the Athanasian Creed, sponsors in baptism, the office of confirmation, the absolution in the visitation of the sick, the thanksgiving in the burial office, and the assumption of an 'essential difference' between bishops and presbyters. All these matters he dealt with directly in 1784 in what he termed an edition of the Prayer Book: they simply were deleted; and bishops became 'superintendants' [sic], though the issue of the 'essential difference' was left unresolved by Wesley's choice to have them 'ordained' to that office. Wesley's editorial hand did not stop there, however. Operating principally by a method of excision, Wesley removed full rites—private baptism, the visitation of the sick (but leaving the communion of the sick), the churching of women, the commination, and prayers to be used at sea and for observing the accession of the reigning monarch—and also such components as sung liturgical texts, readings from the Apocrypha (sparing only a reading from Tobit in the communion office), various statements from the two baptismal rites, and the giving of both bride and ring in the marriage rite. The sanctoral calendar along with certain liturgical seasons and holy days disappeared. Instructions and tables not deleted were substantially truncated. Psalms and portions of Psalms deemed inappropriate for Christian lips, such as the so-called 'cursing' psalms, were excised from the Psalter. So also were selected passages that referred to musical instruments played during worship—e.g. Psalm 149 disappears and verses 3–5 of Psalm 150 are dropped—a move consistent with Wesley's preference for unaccompanied congregational singing; inexplicably, however, Psalm 147: 7 survives. Probably to avoid redundancy and to answer complaints regarding the length of the Sunday liturgy (with or without the eucharist), the Nicene Creed was removed from the order for communion since that office was generally preceded by Morning Prayer which contained the Apostles' Creed. Even though Wesley's pruning substantially reduced the Book of Common Prayer, his dependency upon that liturgical source is unmistakable in the prayers and services that remained: Morning and Evening Prayer; certain collects and stipulated Scripture readings for particular days; the Litany; rites for the Lord's Supper, baptism of infants and those of 'riper years', matrimony, communion of the sick, and burial of the dead; and ordination rites for deacon, elder (presbyter), and 'superintendant'.

The trimmed Prayer Book text received few additions from Wesley, with perhaps the most significant being an instruction for the option of extempore prayer at the conclusion of the communion office. Surprisingly no similar rubric appears in the other services (including Morning Prayer and Evening Prayer, where it might be expected) despite Wesley's own willingness to interject extempore prayer when using the Prayer Book and the strong preference of many Methodists to pray without a written text. Equally bewildering is the absence of rubrics sanctioning congregational singing even though such participation would have been common—even encouraged—before, during, and after Methodist occasions of worship.

At Wesley's direction, copies of the *Sunday Service of the Methodists in North America. With other Occasional Services* were sent across the Atlantic in the company of Richard Whatcoat, Thomas Vasey, and Dr. Thomas Coke, all three of whom Wesley had recently set apart for pastoral leadership. Also accompanying the three were copies of *A Collection of Psalms and Hymns for the Lord's Day* (a revision of the 1741 *Collection of Psalms and Hymns*), and a letter that, along with the rubrics in the newly minted *Sunday Service*, stated Wesley's (perhaps unreasonable) expectations for the book's use and for Methodist liturgical practice in general. Although he provided no instructions on how the two orders were to be fused (and thus avoid multiple recitations of the same text, e.g. the Lord's Prayer), Wesley specified that Morning Prayer and the Order for the Administration of the Lord's Supper were to be celebrated every Lord's day—an expectation considerably more generous than the Church of England's canon. Evening Prayer was also to be said each Sunday, but, like Morning Prayer, was for use only on that day; extempore prayer was designated for all other days. The Litany's Sunday rehearsal was eliminated, though it was still to be said on Wednesdays and Fridays.

The *Sunday Service* was sent loose-leaf to America out of haste or from a desire to avoid the duty on bound books, and this circumstance would contribute to questions regarding Wesley's intentions for the performance of the Lord's Supper and infant baptism. Extant copies of the 1784 *Sunday Service* exist in two versions: one includes rubrics for the manual acts (the celebrant's gestures) during the prayer of consecration in the communion rite and for the post-baptismal signing of the cross in the infant baptismal rite; the other omits both. It is uncertain which actions reflect Wesley's original plan and which may have been the preference of Dr. Coke, who Wesley claimed had altered material without his knowledge. The survival of the manual acts and the absence of signation in the infant rite in later editions of the *Sunday Service* only contribute to the puzzle.

In 1786, Wesley (probably with the assistance of Coke) brought out a revision of the 1784 book, with the principal changes made in the baptismal services (including the removal of references and allusions to baptismal regeneration). Two versions were produced, one for the 'United-States of America', and the other intended for the British context since references to royalty in rubrics and prayers, deleted in the 1784 version, were restored. This British version came under two titles: *The Sunday Service of the Methodists* was almost certainly meant for use in Britain itself; and the other, with the added referent of '*His Majesty's Dominions*', was intended for Methodist mission areas such as Antigua, Nova Scotia, and Newfoundland. Subsequent editions published in England with Wesley's oversight had only minor alterations mostly related to the exclusion or inclusion of royal language. A 1788 edition apparently destined for Methodists in all locations included *A Collection of Psalms and Hymns for the Lord's Day* as had the 1786 edition, but now for the first time in continuous pagination with the liturgical texts. Although designated for the United States, a 1790 version oddly contained prayers for the King in the daily office and communion liturgies. No location was specified on the title page of a 1792 edition, published the year after Wesley's death, but the contents indicate the recipients were to be Methodists in Britain and the 'British Dominions'.

METHODIST RECEPTION OF THE
SUNDAY SERVICE

In the United States

The Methodist preachers attending the Baltimore Christmas Conference of 1784 agreed, in Richard Whatcoat's words, 'to form a Methodist Episcopal Church, *in which the Liturgy* (as presented by the Rev. John Wesley) *should be read*, sacraments to be administered by a superintendent, elders, and deacons, who shall be ordained by a presbytery, using the episcopal form, as prescribed in the Rev. Mr. Wesley's prayer book' (Sandford 1843: 363). The *Sunday Service* was not the first source to provide a structured ordering of worship for some Methodists in the 'New World': persons with even a marginal relationship to the Anglican parish church would have been acquainted with particular liturgies from the Book of Common Prayer; and a few Methodists in the South probably experienced the liturgical patterns for the administration of the sacraments drawn up at the controversial Fluvanna Conference of 1779, in which the Lord's Supper according to the 'Church order' was proceeded by singing, prayer, and exhortation (Connor 1970: 107–8). The adoption of 'Mr Wesley's prayer book' may have been motivated principally out of duty to their 'venerable Father', but the expediency of such a resource would also have been recognized by many of the preachers who themselves came from an Anglican background. Nevertheless, certain Methodists were reluctant to accept any directives from England so soon after the struggle for independence, and some found prohibitive both the expense of the books and the necessity of transporting them into remote areas. In addition, stipulated orders for worship along with printed prayers were alien to many Methodists (especially rural and lower-class) who had no direct Anglican affiliations, who valued freedom of expression in worship, and whose piety gravitated towards a more extempore and informal style—even though, in America as in England, prayer, hymns, and the reading and interpretation of Scripture constituted the repeated and stable liturgical core of all Methodist gatherings.

The publication of multiple editions of the *Sunday Service* allocated for the US during John Wesley's lifetime, and comments recorded principally in diaries and journals of the clergy, indicate that the book received some usage. Reflecting on the years immediately after the Christmas Conference, Methodist elder and historian Jesse Lee noted that 'in the large towns, and in some country places, our preachers read prayers on the Lord's day: and in some cases the preachers read part of the morning service on Wednesdays and Fridays' (Lee 1810: 107). By 'preachers' Lee would have meant the ordained clergy, since approved legislation did not allow lay preachers to 'read our liturgy'—that is Morning and Evening Prayer and Litany—without written permission of the elder or superintendent/bishop. Lee's observation is silent about the realization of Wesley's instruction regarding the Lord's Supper every Lord's day; only elders and superintendents/bishops were authorized to perform the sacrament, and while these men might experience weekly eucharist as they presided in various locations, not all the far-flung Methodist communities would have the same opportunity. However, despite this limitation, Methodists valued the sacrament and arranged to receive it whenever possible, often at the quarterly meeting. Where the Lord's Supper was celebrated, it might be preceded or followed by observance of the love feast, which though it lacked a formal ritual text, had the characteristic components of hymn singing, prayers, the sharing of bread and water, a collection of alms, testimonies, and addresses or exhortations (Ruth 2000: 103–55, 214–15).

The reality that only a minority of leaders were authorized to 'read our liturgy', coupled with the majority's preference for worship not taken from a book, contributed to the laying aside of Wesley's plans for Lord's day worship. Even so, some standard contents for Methodist worship were expected. Jesse Lee notes that the short-lived Council, concerned for uniformity in Lord's day worship, in 1789 made recommendations for both the time of worship (with 10 o'clock preferred) and its form ('singing, prayer, and reading the Holy Scriptures, with exhortation or reading a sermon in the absence of a preacher') (Lee 1810: 152–3). This truncated form for Sunday morning was authorized at the general conference convened in 1792 (the year after John Wesley's death), when the Morning and Evening Prayer services, the Litany, the Psalter, the abbreviated lectionary, and the propers were replaced by a set of rubrics in the section 'Of Public Worship' in the *Doctrines and Discipline of the Methodist Episcopal Church*:

Quest. What directions shall be given for the establishment of uniformity in public worship amongst us, on the Lord's-day?

Answ. 1. Let the morning-service consist of singing, prayer, the reading of a chapter out of the Old Testament, and another out of the New, and preaching.

2. Let the afternoon-service consist of singing, prayer, the reading of one chapter out of the Bible, and preaching.

3. Let the evening-service consist of singing, prayer, and preaching.

4. But on the days of administering the Lord's Supper, the two chapters in the morning-service may be omitted.

The conference also voted that Wesley's rites of baptism, Lord's Supper, marriage, burial, and ordination be abbreviated, altered, and placed into a thirty-seven page section of 'Sacramental Services, &c'. in the *Discipline*. With the action of 1792, American Methodists lost a prayer book per se; yet the collection of sacramental and occasional services (later known as the 'Ritual') preserved much of Wesley's revision, though in subsequent years all the texts underwent significant adjustments in the different Methodist/Wesleyan denominations.

Wesley's services for the Lord's day received renewed attention in the second half of the nineteenth century and throughout the twentieth (Westerfield Tucker 2001: 16–23). For example, the Methodist Episcopal Church (South), in 1866, approved the printing of *The Sunday Service of the Methodist Episcopal Church, South* (1867) which restored for optional use, with some alterations, the Sunday-related and festal material that had been jettisoned in 1792 and affixed it to that body's currently approved sacramental and occasional services. Almost fifteen years later, the African Methodist Episcopal Church in 1880 took a similar approach to reintroducing 'Wesley's Prayer Book'. The 1965 *Book of Worship* of the Methodist Church reproduced 1784 Morning Prayer in a section of 'Services in the Methodist Tradition'. The revision of that book, the *United Methodist Book of Worship* (1992), included orders for daily prayer, but neither drew directly from the 1784 texts nor expected the morning office to be observed on the Lord's day. In the early twenty-first century, only a few fragments from the *Sunday Service* remain in the official liturgical texts of Methodists in the US, with the most preserved by the African Methodist Episcopal Church's *Book of Worship* (1984).

In Great Britain

Although in 1786 John Wesley prepared an edition of the *Sunday Service* for use in Britain, no direct mention of its existence—or the existence of the 1788 and 1792 versions—appears in the Minutes of the conferences for the span of those years. Two items preserved in the Minutes during that time, however, give hints to the liturgical situation in the last years of Wesley's life. First, Wesley advised that preachers 'read the Psalms and Lessons, with part of the Church prayers', in circumstances where Methodist services during church hours were warranted, as a means of 'endear[ing] the Church Service to our brethren, who probably would be prejudiced against it, if they heard none but extemporary prayer' (*Minutes* 1786: 191). Second, regarding the question 'What further directions may be given concerning the Prayers of the Church of England', the answer stated that the assistants, on non-eucharistic Sundays in the parish church and with agreement from the local society, could read the 'prayer book' in Methodist preaching houses on Sunday mornings (*ibid.* 1788: 208). While these recommendations might reference the *Sunday Service*, they more likely speak to Methodist use of the 1662 Prayer Book for Lord's day morning worship, supplemented by the informal preaching service on Sunday afternoons and evenings and on other days of the week. But there is evidence that the *Sunday Service* quickly found a place in a few Methodist places of worship—and that Wesley himself, perhaps conforming to canonical requirements, in practice preferred the 1662 liturgy to his own abridgement—if Methodist preacher Samuel Bradburn's report is accurate:

Mr. Wesley abridged the 'Book of Common Prayer', first for the Americans; and afterwards, with some variations, published it for the Methodists at large. I found this in use at Snowsfields and Wapping Preaching-Houses, when I was appointed for London in the year 1786. I used it a few times, 'till Mr. Wesley came to Town. I then said many things against continuing to do so, and he gave me leave to do as I pleased; I accordingly laid it aside. My reason for this, was not that I believed it wrong to use it, or that any thing in it was injured by Mr. Wesley; but because he and his curates continued to use the old one [the Prayer Book]. I saw no propriety in this conduct, and therefore bore my testimony against it. But many people who called themselves strict church-folks, had other reasons for not using it. When they saw that all the Saints' Days, the Athanasian and Nicene Creeds, several of the Articles of Religion, and many of the Psalms, were left out, they rejected it with disdain, and it is not used yet but in a very few towns in England.

(Bradburn 1792: 13–14)

Questions had long been raised about the administration of the Lord's Supper in Methodist chapels and societies, and after Wesley's death, debates on sacramental celebration as well as the topic of services during church hours intensified as Methodists struggled to define their relationship with the Church of England. To stave off division, 'Articles of Agreement for General Pacification' were approved in 1795 that dealt substantially with liturgical matters, including leadership for baptism and the burial of the dead (*Minutes* 1795: 322–6). Persons authorized by the conference were permitted to administer the Lord's Supper on Sunday evenings when it had not been made available in the morning at the parish church; some exceptions were allowed for church hours. The Prayer Book liturgy for Holy Communion (not Wesley's revision) was always to be used in England, but with the addition of hymns, extempore prayer, and exhortation. For places where non-eucharistic worship was approved during church hours, it was stipulated that the officiant read 'either the Service of the Established Church, our venerable father's Abridgement [i.e. the 1792 version], or at least, the Lessons appointed by the Calendar', with preference given to the first two. This meant, ideally, Morning Prayer and Litany, though following Anglican custom, the sermon from the ante-communion would have been included. Hymns, exhortation, and extempore prayer would probably have found a place as well. The phrase 'or at least, the Lessons appointed by the Calendar' is revealing, for such a minimum recognized that in many places neither the Prayer Book nor Wesley's revision would find a home. The Minutes recorded after 1795 indicate that enforcement of the Articles was an ongoing problem.

Although apparently the *Sunday Service* was used minimally for British Methodist worship since preference was given either to the Prayer Book or to the preaching service according to local custom (with the common components of Scripture readings, four or more hymns, extempore prayers, and a sermon), it survived as a separate publication into the first decade of the twentieth century as a liturgical resource for what became the Wesleyan Methodist Connexion. From 1816 (the next edition after 1792) to 1910, at least twenty-eight versions of the book were published under the title *The Sunday Service of the Methodists*, though not always with the same ritual contents and the same wording in the texts. Two short-lived variants are notable: a truncated version sold as *The Sunday Morning Service of the Methodists* (1812), which contained texts from *Sunday Service* permitted under the Articles, with some alterations, and an incomplete daily New Testament lectionary; and *Selections from the Sunday Service of the Methodists; Designed for the use of Sunday-Scholars on the Morning of the Lord's Day* (1838, 1842), which included Morning Prayer, the Litany, collects, Wesley's Select Psalms, and the Order of Holy Communion to the end of the collects for the monarch. In addition, separate books were published between 1839 and 1881 containing the sacramental texts from the *Sunday Service*, to which after 1848 the rites of marriage, burial, and ordination were added (Swift 1957–8: 112–18, 133–43).

British Methodists after 1784 thus faced three competing liturgical approaches—the authorized Prayer Book, Wesley's revision, and the preaching and prayer services developed locally—whereas their kin in the US principally dealt with only two. Mr Wesley himself was able to hold these liturgical complexities together, perhaps because of his early and ongoing exposure to the Prayer Book, to the liturgical life of the parish church, and to regular informal and extemporaneous worship in the home and in small groups. Although formal, elaborate services with a printed text and informal, simple services with spontaneous expression were equally part of the Methodist/Wesleyan liturgical inheritance, Wesley's spiritual descendants on both sides of the Atlantic—and later around the globe—frequently placed them at odds. However, all Methodists agreed that two resources were essential to worship: a Bible and a collection of hymns.

ONGOING TENSIONS: SIMPLICITY
AND COMPLEXITY

Prior to 1800, Methodists in both Britain and the US faced divisions, demonstrating a tendency towards fissiparousness that would continue well into the next century. Fractures resulted from disagreements concerning the authority of the leadership, the role of the laity, methods of evangelism, issues of race, class, and geography, and—though often not the primary precipitating issue—practices of worship. Leaders who, with or without denominational legislation to support them, strove to obtain some uniformity in worship in order to present a clear denominational identity both liturgically and theologically, were routinely charged with an 'un-Wesleyan' limitation of God-given liberties and advocacy of spiritless formalism and 'ritualism'. Nevertheless, the majority of denominations—even if they were constituted in part over objection to printed liturgical rites and prayers or other liturgical issues—in the end (officially or unofficially) published their own resources for worship for optional use, even though the texts may have been little used. Methodists in Britain, influenced by a prayer-book culture, tended to publish discrete books of worship, while Methodists in the US and their mission communities abroad embedded liturgical texts alongside other conference-approved items in their books or manuals of *Discipline*.

The preaching service that was Methodism's principal paraliturgical expression within the Church of England continued to be its defining liturgical event even as new and distinct Methodist denominations emerged in the years after Wesley's death. The so-called 'free' style of worship was reinforced in Britain as branches of Methodism came to associate themselves with Nonconformist groups or with the conversion-oriented worship practices of the camp-meeting and revival. The evangelistic pragmatism of Methodists in the US, along with the legislated rubrics for the contents of Lord's day public worship (singing, prayer, Scripture reading, preaching) that were typically kept as new denominations emerged, ensured the perpetuation of the locally adaptable preaching service. Inevitably the 'free' style carried over into the observance of baptism and the Lord's Supper, despite the presence in some denominations of authorized (though not mandated) ritual forms and explicit legislation forbidding improvisation.

The service of Morning Prayer was used on the Lord's day throughout the nineteenth century in a minority of congregations in Britain, among them prominent chapels in the Wesleyan Connexion. The practice was also found in the denomination's theological colleges, and was then exported to Methodist mission areas by new graduates appointed abroad (George 1996: 34).

In general during the first part of the nineteenth century, published ritual texts for baptism, the Lord's Supper, marriage, and burial used by Methodists on both sides of the Atlantic were drawn directly from the Book of Common Prayer, from Wesley's abridgement of it, or from a revision undertaken of Wesley's work. Only minor adjustments were made to these rites at this time (with the baptism rites receiving the most attention) as denominations focused instead on organizational development and numerical growth, although new denominations might at the time of their creation engage in a more radical pruning of their liturgical inheritance. Textual changes tended to reflect shifts in theology (e.g. variations in the relation seen between baptism and the spiritual experience of regeneration), integration of dominant cultural practices (e.g. the restoration of the ring in marriage despite Wesley's removal of it), and new civil legislation (e.g. replacement of the banns with legal declarations stipulated by the British Marriage Act of 1836).

The second half of the century, however, saw substantial revisions to the printed sacramental and occasional rites as Methodism came to draw more substantially on the middle class for its membership, more Methodist clergy received formal theological educations, the results of the Oxford Movement were particularly felt in the largest of the Methodist denominations (positively and negatively), and new theological perspectives and societal developments arose. In the United States, attention to revision was also coupled with episcopal Methodism's emergence as a 'national' church, made visible by the construction of architecturally beautiful and socially prominent houses of worship. Of course, there was internal and external dismay about the emerging liturgical modifications—concerns about departing from the ritual course that Wesley had charted; and (especially from the Holiness branches, but not exclusively), worry about increasing ritualism and cultural accommodation ('worldliness') and their perceived partner, spiritual dryness. Signs of the loss of Methodist simplicity and spiritual fervour were believed by some to be evident by the decline of the Methodist 'great festivals': the love feast, the watch night, and in the United States especially, the service of renewing the covenant with God that had been a Methodist practice at least since 1755.

For Wesleyan Methodists in Britain, the years 1874–82 constituted a liturgical crisis. Not only were there calls to consolidate the multiple editions or impressions of the *Sunday Service* and the various books in circulation containing orders for the administration of sacramental and occasional services, but questions were also raised about the appropriateness of the Prayer Book and even the *Sunday Service* in Methodist chapels by those who feared a move by Anglicanism in a Roman Catholic direction. The Wesleyan Conference in 1874 set out to revise its liturgical resources with an eye to eliminating anything contrary to evangelical Protestantism. Yet for some this purging did not go far enough:

[I]f the history of Methodism in its life, power, and progress is associated with extempore prayers; if the general condition of Methodism calls more for a baptism of the Holy Spirit than for read prayers; if our ministry is being so much more educated to qualify them for extempore prayers, in a literary point of view; if read prayers are attended with such dangers to the vigour, freedom, and blessedness of public worship as their history shows them to be;

why, in the name of thousands upon thousands of Methodists, and of the highest weal of Methodism now and hereafter, should the question even be mooted of making a liturgical service for use in our congregations? Is the Spirit of God in this, or the spirit of the Devil? Let this be well considered.   (Bate 1880: 14)

In the end, the conference published the *Book of Public Prayers and Services* (1882) and a shorter version as the *Order of Administration of the Sacraments and other Services*, which shows reliance upon both the 1662 Prayer Book and Wesley's *Sunday Service*. Morning Prayer was kept with few changes, and most of the rites received only a few alterations, the exception being the baptismal offices. Yet the conference continued to give congregations the option of using any liturgical forms previously approved, which explains why the *Sunday Service* went through additional printings after 1882.

Nowhere are liturgical changes at this time more evident than in the adjustments made to Lord's day worship in some of the churches in the US. Specified orders of worship in outline start to be produced in the last quarter of the nineteenth century, many with liturgical components not seen officially since the conference of 1792: the Lord's Prayer, responsive readings, doxologies, psalmody, the collection of money, and benedictions. The Apostles' Creed appeared in the Methodist Episcopal Church's worship order of 1896, the first time the creed was designated for regular Sunday worship since Wesley's Morning Prayer was replaced with rubrics. Also in the 1890s, the African Methodist Episcopal Church restored the Decalogue (part of Wesley's ante-communion dropped in 1792), placing it as the last reading before the sermon. Despite fierce battles to keep choirs out of Methodist worship for fear they would supplant congregational singing, choir anthems or voluntaries began to be listed in worship outlines.

Of course, throughout this time, the simple and variable preaching service remained the normative Sunday morning practice in many Methodist congregations around the world, though there was an increasing tendency in some places towards elaboration and greater complexity.

ECUMENICAL ENGAGEMENT AND LITURGICAL RENEWAL

The ecumenical conversations across the borders of denominations and world communions that began in earnest at the end of the nineteenth century and continued into the twentieth had the added result of creating a greater awareness of the worship practices—and printed worship resources—of different Christian communities. Methodists sometimes borrowed prayers or portions of liturgical texts for transplantation, introducing turns of phrase or more substantial sections into their own proliferating printed liturgical resources, both those denominationally authorized and those produced by individuals or by ecumenical teams. International pan-Methodist dialogues provided an opportunity for Wesley's descendants to share their liturgical inheritances as well as to explore the variations that had emerged from Wesley's *Urtext* and from new developments.

The creation in Britain and in the US of two new denominations during the 1930s—each called the Methodist Church—from a reunion of separated Methodist bodies, was marked with the production of revised worship materials which, in both cases, carried the strong liturgical stamp of the largest group entering merger. In 1936 the Methodist Church in Britain brought out from its publishing house *The Book of Offices, being the Orders of Service authorized for Use in the Methodist Church, together with The Order for Morning Prayer,* which, in addition to the long-standing sacramental and occasional rites, included such services as the Thanksgiving of Mothers (a Methodist version of the Anglican 'churching' rite) and the Dedication of Sunday School Teachers. In keeping with the ecumenical thrusts of the time, the Preface to the volume explains that '[t]he wealth of liturgical devotion which is the noble heritage of the universal Church has been largely used, and forms of worship belonging to the East and the West, to ancient times and to more modern days, have all been explored to enrich these pages'. Yet sensitive to ongoing worries about ritual forms and the reality that the preaching service with extemporaneous prayer was alive and well (now routinely including five hymns, children's addresses, and musical offerings by choir and organist), the Preface also notes that the new book is not an attempt to 'disparage the practice of free prayer': 'There is no real conflict between free prayer and liturgical prayer, for the most fervent and the most helpful prayers that ever came from the inspiration of the moment will be found to owe much in their expression to the remembrance of the language of the Bible, of the great liturgies, and of the hymns of Methodism'. Similar language expressing a design inclusive of ecumenical and historical breadth, plus the need to be both 'liturgical and free', is found in the *Book of Worship for Church and Home* (1945) of the Methodist Church in the United States. The collection was the first separately published worship book with official standing in American Methodism since *Sunday Service* was laid aside—although its use was indicated to be 'optional and voluntary' and its contents (as indicated by the title) included aids for domestic worship. The *Book of Worship* also showed attention to particular days and seasons of the Christian year, expanding significantly beyond what had been found in some authorized hymnals, namely, seasonal subject headings for hymn organization and, as in the 1905 *Methodist Hymnal,* responsive readings for a few special days.

In the 1930s and 1940s, the Methodist Sacramental Fellowship in Britain and the Brotherhood (later Order) of St Luke in the US were born, conceived for the encouragement of informed and frequent eucharistic reception and for the cultivation of interest in the liturgical renewal grounded in ancient Christian practices that was sweeping through other churches. Yet the first textual revision taking into consideration this renewal came neither from Britain nor the US, but from a new denomination created in 1947 from the merger of several traditions, including the Methodist of British origin. The pioneering eucharistic liturgy produced by the Church of South India in 1950 in many ways anticipated the liturgical developments of the Second Vatican Council by its attention to the normativity of word and sacrament on the Lord's day (cf. Luke 24: 13–35; Justin Martyr, 1 Apology 67), the doxological aspect of the eucharist, the active participation of the faithful, and the need for inculturating liturgical language and symbols in the idioms of the people.

Given the momentum of earlier years, it was to be expected that the Methodist Church in Britain and the Methodist Church in the US—after merger in 1968 with the Evangelical United Brethren, the United Methodist Church—would introduce plans for liturgical revision that took into account the major liturgical shifts generated by Vatican II, not only for Sunday morning, but also for baptism (including restoration of the adult catechumenate), weddings, and funerals. In the *Methodist Service Book* (1975) of the British church, Morning Prayer disappeared, though it would be restored, but as part of a daily office, in the *Methodist Worship Book* (1999). Along with a reprinting of the 1936 Sunday liturgy, a new Sunday liturgy of word and sacrament ('The Sunday Service') was supplied in the 1975 book that proceeded according to a structure reminiscent of the familiar Anglican/Wesleyan Order for Holy Communion, but with a eucharistic prayer patterned upon historic West Syrian/Antiochene models. Although the General Directions for the Sunday Service asserted the normativity of word and sacrament, nevertheless textual provision was made in a separate section for a service of the word without the sacrament. The United Methodist Church similarly developed a Sunday 'basic pattern' of word and sacrament using an Antiochene structure for its eucharistic prayers, but not relying directly upon the Prayer Book tradition for its ordering of the word section. A peculiarity of the *United Methodist Book of Worship* (1992) was the inclusion of full eucharistic prayers ('Great Thanksgivings') composed according to liturgical season or occasion.

EMERGING DEVELOPMENTS

At the beginning of the twenty-first century, interest continues in the liturgical renewal generated by Vatican II and by the World Council of Churches' convergence document *Baptism, Eucharist and Ministry* (1982), particularly in the churches outside Europe and the United States that were planted by Methodist missionaries. Many of these churches are now developing their own unique liturgical resources, informed by the best of Wesleyan and ecumenical liturgical scholarship, and attentive to the need for inculturated forms. The *Korean Methodist New Book of Worship* (2002) of the Korean Methodist Church is one such example.

Other churches, particularly those in multicultural contexts, continue to devise forms inclusive of a range of styles and voices. Experiments are underway in some places to establish an essential 'core' for services of communion, baptism, matrimony, and burial that might allow for local variety while adhering to a commonly held frame. 'Contemporary' and charismatic worship and 'emerging church' movements have engaged Methodists in different parts of the world. Yet the preaching service that eighteenth-century Methodists might recognize remains a staple for many.

Thus the dual pattern combining liturgical forms and freedom of expression that John Wesley bequeathed many generations ago remains his enduring legacy.

SUGGESTED READING

CHAPMAN, DAVID M. (2006). *Born in Song: Methodist Worship in Britain*. Warrington: Church in the Market Place Publications.
FELTON, GAYLE C. (1992). *This Gift of Water: The Practice and Theology of Baptism among Methodists in America*. Nashville: Abingdon.
WESTERFIELD TUCKER, KAREN B. (1996).
—— (2001).

REFERENCES

BATE, JOHN (1880). *The Desire for a Methodist Liturgy; (A Protest)*. London: E. Stock.
BRADBURN, SAMUEL (1792). *The Question, 'Are the Methodists Dissenters?' Fairly Examined: Designed to Remove Prejudice, Prevent Bigotry, and Promote Brotherly Love*. [Liverpool]: n.p.
CONNOR, ELIZABETH (1970). *Methodist Trail Blazer: Philip Gatch, 1751–1834*. Rutland, Vt.: Academy Books.
GEORGE, A. RAYMOND (1996). 'From *The Sunday Service* to "The Sunday Service"'. In Karen B. Westerfield Tucker (ed.), *The Sunday Service of the Methodists: Twentieth-Century Worship in Worldwide Methodism*. Nashville: Kingswood, 31–52.
LEE, JESSE (1810). *A Short History of the Methodists in the United States of America; beginning in 1766, and continued till 1809*. Baltimore: Magill & Clime.
Minutes of the Methodist Conferences, from the First, Held in London, by the Late Rev. John Wesley, A.M. in the Year 1744 (1812). London: Printed in the Conference Office by Thomas Cordeux, i.
RUTH, LESTER (2000). *A Little Heaven Below: Worship at Early Methodist Quarterly Meetings*. Nashville: Kingswood.

SANDFORD, P. P. (1843), *Memoirs of Mr. Wesley's Missionaries to America*. New York: G. Lane & P. P. Sandford.

SWIFT, WESLEY F. '"The Sunday Service of the Methodists": A Study of Nineteenth-Century Liturgy'. *The Proceedings of the Wesley Historical Society* 31 (1957–8): 112–18, 133–43.

WESTERFIELD TUCKER, KAREN B. (1996), *The Sunday Service of the Methodists: Twentieth-Century Worship in Worldwide Methodism*. Nashville: Kingswood.

—— (2001). *American Methodist Worship*. New York: Oxford University Press.

CHAPTER 18

LITURGICAL REVOLUTIONS

LESTER RUTH

WITH respect to Methodist worship, what John Wesley intended was not what he got. Although Wesley desired for Methodist worship to supplement the worship of the Church of England, which he wanted Methodists to attend, instead he sparked a movement whose members preferred their own Methodist practices and kept a tenuous connection to Anglicanism.

The tension appeared early, even while Wesley was insistent that Methodists were faithful Anglicans. However, a divergence was clear. For example, at the 1766 Annual Conference, to a question of whether Methodists were Dissenters (those who separated themselves legally from the Church of England), Wesley's aggressive response that they were not highlighted his sensitivity on the matter while revealing, nonetheless, Methodists' contrary tendency. Worship was at the centre of the clash. Wesley defended attending Anglican worship, stating that it was not sinful to do so (the legal position of a Dissenter) and insisting that the preachers schedule their Methodist services so that they could attend Anglican worship at least twice a month.

After commanding that preachers 'never make light of going to church either by word or deed', Wesley sought to encourage attending Anglican worship by shaming the Methodists with an anecdote featuring a Roman Catholic hero! Wesley's message was clear: attend Anglican worship from duty, if not from desire. Of course, when viable alternatives were available, desire sought to be fulfilled and cold duty was cast to the side.

And Methodist worship did provide a viable alternative. Indeed, it was a rich spread of worship that John Wesley had cultivated in the Methodist movement with Charles Wesley's hymns instilling a passion for God throughout it all. It was an intoxicating mix, much more satisfying to the typical Methodist than what she or he experienced in the parish church. John Wesley himself recognized this quality and identified Methodist services as 'prudential means of grace', that is, God's special provision for the vitality of Methodism (Knight 1992: 3, 5).

His specific reply to the insistence that 'our own service is public worship' (the Methodists' response to Wesley's defence of Anglican worship) was instructive for seeing how Wesley saw the relationship between Anglican and Methodist worship. To the notion that Methodist worship alone was satisfactory, Wesley insisted that he never designed it to replace Anglican worship. Wesley argued that Methodist worship presupposed Anglican and was 'essentially defective' without it. He noted two precise 'defects': it seldom had a sufficient breadth of prayer (Wesley noted deprecation (i.e. confession), petition, intercession, and thanksgiving) and it did not conclude with the Lord's Supper.

Wesley ended his reply to the original question by exhorting all Methodists to 'attend the service of the Church, at least, every Lord's Day'. As the eighteenth century unfolded, his exhortation fell on deaf ears. The dream of Methodists living in two complementary liturgical worlds went largely unfulfilled.

Wesley never quite gave up his dream. Indeed, as separation from the established church grew more apparent towards the end of his life, Wesley felt the need to encourage British preachers who conducted Methodist services at the same time as the Anglican parish—it appears that his earlier exhortations were ineffective—to use the Anglican liturgy to endear it to the Methodists 'who probably would be prejudiced against it, if they heard none but extemporary prayer' (*Minutes* (1862) for 1786: i. 193). However, by then, it was a fight already largely lost.

Wesley's vision of Methodists living in two liturgical worlds was about drawing upon the riches of a longstanding liturgical tradition (Anglicanism) and infusing it with the power of Pietism that animated Methodist life. And the vision reflected a complexity in Wesley's liturgical thought in holding things together in tension. Methodists have often sought to resolve these tensions, usually in a way that cut the connection to their Anglican roots and sometimes unintentionally impoverishing their own worship eventually.

The worship of early Methodists helped shape the future of English-speaking Protestant worship, especially in America. Looking at Methodist worship in that region is useful as a case study to see how Methodists worshipped when free from the immediate oversight of John Wesley, free from a pervasive backdrop of an established church, and in contact with a non-European ethnic group (i.e. African Americans). References to Methodists below will refer to American Methodists unless otherwise noted. As the first independent Methodist church (the Methodist Episcopal Church was organized in 1784)—and a hugely successful one at that (Methodists expanded from 2 per cent of the total church population in 1775 to 34 per cent in 1850) (Wigger 1998: 3)—American Methodism brought many practices to the mainstream of English-speaking Protestantism.

ANGLICAN AND METHODIST WORSHIP PRACTICES COMPARED

The Anglican worship that Methodists shunned was a text-based liturgy. Sunday morning included three services from the Book of Common Prayer: Morning Prayer, the Litany, and ante-communion (i.e. the early parts of the communion service). It culminated with a sermon (Hatchett 1976: 369–85; Spinks 2006: 492–533). The result was a lengthy period filled with the reading of Psalms, other biblical texts, prayers, and other prescribed acts of worship, and punctuated with the occasional singing of metrical Psalms. Evening Prayer rounded out Sunday.

The dominant architectural feature, a multi-decked pulpit, reinforced the text-centredness. The lowest part was a desk for a clerk, who led the congregation in their responses and singing. Behind and above was the reading desk for the minister. Here he read the services and the appointed Scripture lessons, using his Bible, Prayer Book, and metrical Psalter. Above that desk was the pulpit from which the sermon was read. Anglican worship thus consisted of a dialogue between these leaders and the congregation, each constituency reciting their parts.

Anglican worship had to contend with the levelling dynamic of group reading. Anyone familiar with worship that involves extended reading by congregations soon realizes the measured monotone that corporate reading can produce. Variety in pace and tone are lost as the congregation finds its common reading voice. Where worshippers were illiterate (universal literacy had yet to come), parishioners would have known the service by heart; but equally the memorization would have restricted innovation and encouraged a monotonous style.

Anglican worship was not all dreariness, however. In some parishes music was led by the parish band, which might include a variety of instruments. Some affluent city parishes had an organ. A choir could support the singing and sometimes contributed chant. In some congregations the psalms and other songs were sung to popular folk tunes.

Even in these 'livelier' settings, however, the basic ethos of worship did not change. Anglican worship was a text-based approach that engaged the ear in hearing by using the eye in reading. Regular weekly rhythms, punctuated by the classic feasts and seasons, provided orderliness over time. The Church of England's liturgy breathed a piety that was, as John Wesley himself described it, 'solid, scriptural, and rational' (White 1984).

But Methodists preferred worship that left them breathless, overwhelmed by a sense of God's presence that was explosive (not just solid), Scripture-experiencing (not just infused with Scripture texts), and emotional (not just rational). And Methodism was a complex liturgical world involving many kinds of services in a dizzying array of rhythms (Ruth 2000; Westerfield Tucker 2001). The foundation was the preaching service involving prayer, songs, Scripture, and sermon (and sometimes an exhortation), concluded by a closing prayer and song. The service was very flexible, allowing adaptation for indoors or outdoors and could be either spontaneous or scheduled (the original meaning for a preacher's 'appointment'). There were no prescribed texts to read. Scheduled services at any one appointment on a circuit tended to occur every two weeks, on any day of the week, as the itinerants travelled through. In cities, which had a higher concentration of preachers (and less distance to travel), any single congregation would have two to three preaching services every Sunday.

Various prayer services were another staple. Methodist families were expected to hold their own prayer sessions. In addition, congregations had prayer meetings. In cities, these could be scheduled on a weekly basis. Finally, occasional times of prayer, such as Friday fasting and intercessions, were held. Like preaching services, the emphasis was on extemporaneity since there were no prescribed prayer texts. Prayer services followed a simple order: a sequence of several extemporaneous prayers by different people (including women or children) often with hymns interspersed. Occasionally sermons or exhortations slipped into the mix.

Methodists included many of these same elements in classes, the small groups required for Methodist membership. They were a kind of training ground for Methodist practices. On a weekly basis, members experienced and practised the capacity to sing passionately, pray from the heart fervently, and testify of their experience of God dramatically.

These dynamics often exploded in those occasional services that Methodists limited to members and those with special permission. Love feasts, the most important, involved the sharing of bread and water, testimonies, an offering for the poor, and signs of mutual love. Watch-night services were preaching services lasting several hours. Themes of repentance, eschatological judgement, and providing an alternative witness to the world's sinful ways were common. To accentuate personal dedication to God Methodists also held covenant renewal services. In them Methodists uttered all or nothing commitments to God. The rhythms for holding these services was more occasional, some on quarterly and some on yearly patterns (e.g. covenant renewal done during a New Year's Eve watch night).

American Methodists excelled in clustering worship services together over several days. They had several versions of such liturgical festivals in which the range of services was held. Quarterly meetings, originally just the business meeting for a circuit, developed into one of the most frequent. Eventually these shorter forms developed into full-blown camp meetings after the start of the nineteenth century.

THE DIFFERING ETHOS

The difference between Anglican and Methodist worship went deeper than varying practices. The core character, what liturgical scholar James White has called the 'central ethos' (White 1989: 23) for each, was poles apart. Even though Methodism was a movement derived from Anglicanism, the character of its worship largely existed outside that root. Indeed, at many points, it was more similar to parallel heart-religion movements than it was to its Anglican origins. These parallel movements included Continental Pietists, some Baptists and Presbyterians, and even some Quakers. The defining principle for this alternative world was 'experimental religion' (to use the eighteenth-century phrase). The hallmark was an emphasis upon an inwardly perceived experiencing of God's grace, especially as it dealt with salvation. This ethos defined the core character of Methodist worship and showed the points at which it differed from Anglicanism.

Two critical differences for the Methodist ethos were the object of liturgical adoration and the nature of that adoration. Their worship expressions reflected a fixation on Jesus Christ, conveyed with the strongest affection, and on pilgrimage to heaven. With concerns like these, Methodists did not find overtly disagreeable material in the Anglican liturgy; they just found the worship blasé. The studied, balanced content of Anglican worship did not match the things that captivated the Methodist heart.

Consider hymn collections that early American Methodists assembled in the late eighteenth and early nineteenth centuries, whether published (Allen 1801) or unpublished. When they chose the hymns they wanted to preserve or distribute, approximately 90 per cent focused on Jesus Christ and named him expressly. Hymns that focused on the other two Persons of the Trinity or spoke of God generically were less common. That was not surprising, considering the nature of early Methodists' spirituality. As in similar contemporaneous movements, a focus on salvation led to concentrating on the Saviour (Marini 2002: 287–95). The other dominant theme, mentioned in a large majority of the hymns, was safe pilgrimage to heaven through Christ. This heavenly motif gave a strong eschatological character to Methodist worship, much more than the typical Anglican liturgy.

Anglican liturgical texts did not talk about the things Methodists wanted to, or, if they did, the expression was not intense enough. The measured language of Anglican services, dutifully read, could not replicate what was on the Methodist heart. Methodist contemplation of Jesus Christ and heaven was more passionate than the texts from the Book of Common Prayer. Thus Henry Bradford loved to sing:

> The Lord into his garden comes
> The spices yield a sweet perfume.
> The lily grows and thrives.

> Refreshing showers of grace divine
> From Jesus flow on every vine
> And make the dead alive.
> But when we come to reign above,
> And all around the throne of love,
> We'll drink a fresh supply.
> Jesus will lead his armies forth
> To a living fountain pure and fresh
> That never will run dry.   (Bradford n.d.: 10)

Methodist devotion could even be erotic sometimes. For Sarah Jones, for example, Christ was a heavenly lover:

How overwhelmed I am in the sea of Jesus' love. I really do not feel as I can bear much more without bursting my chains and hurling them aside and seeing Jesus as he is. A river of God's untold love from bank to bank has flowed over my soul. How do you think Christ's breathing is as he pronounces you his fair one and kisses you with the kisses of his mouth? His love, I see, is so kingly he will not abide a rival but must have a throne all alone in the soul.   (Jones 1792–3)

A heart enflamed with such devotion would have been bored in the steady reading that characterized Anglican worship.

To early Methodists, Anglican worship would have seemed to lack a 'plot' in that it did not lead to dramatic experience. In contrast to the order prescribed by the Book of Common Prayer, Methodist worship paralleled the inward experience of grace, another critical aspect of its liturgical ethos. Methodists grew to expect that, whatever spiritual condition they arrived with, they could have a deeper experience of God's saving grace; so they anticipated a 'plot' for their worship that involved a dramatic resolution. In contrast, Anglican worship would have seemed to be about an amorphous 'sometime', not *now*, as the day of salvation (2 Cor. 6: 2).

Dramatic scenes of conversion in American Methodist worship were common, crossing geographical and racial lines. Consider the spectacle of worship in rural Virginia in the late 1780s:

In many places in this circuit, as soon as the preacher begins to speak, the power of God appears to be present, which is attended with trembling among the people, and falling down. Some lie void of motion or breath, others are in strong convulsions. And thus they continue, till the Lord raises them up, which is attended with emotions of joy and rapture. When one gets happy, it spreads like a flame so that, one after another, they arise to join in the praises of their loving Redeemer.

But the greatest work in many parts of this circuit is among the Blacks...A few nights past we held a night-meeting for the Negroes in the Isle of Wight County. Soon after preaching began, there arose a cry among the poor slaves (of which there was a great number present) which in a short time drowned the preaching. A number was on the floor crying for mercy, but soon one and another arose praising God. Those who were happy [i.e. joyful in salvation] would surround those who were careless with such alarming exhortations as appeared sufficient to soften the hardest hearts. If they could get them to hang down their heads, they would begin to shout and praise God, and the others would soon begin to tremble and sink. I saw a number (some who at first appeared to be most stubborn) brought to the floor and there lie crying till most of them got happy.   (Bruce 1790: 563–4)

This episode reflected a quite different dynamic from that in the typical Anglican parish. The ethos of its Prayer Book worship centred in the doing: the steady rhythm of set services over the course of a week and year slowly formed the worshiper in the scriptural Christianity that was implicit in the liturgies. For Methodists, this process was much too slow and non-experiential. Thus they spoke repeatedly of the danger of formalism in Anglican worship, that is, worshipers mistakenly using the prescribed forms of worship as their own end, rather than seeking the saving power of God about which they spoke. In contrast to Anglicanism, the ethos of Methodist worship focused on the outcome, which was the creation of experience. For Methodists, inwardly experiencing grace was the critical matter. Their formula was simple: no experience, no salvation. Thus they worshipped in a way that resulted in heart-warming experiences. For non-Methodists, this focus hinted of enthusiasm, the dreaded danger of claiming direct, unmediated experiences of God (Knight 1992: 29–49).

Another difference in the Methodist liturgical ethos as compared to Anglicanism dealt with the propriety of reading. Early Methodists strongly preferred spontaneously composed prayer. The starting point for Methodist prayer was not a written text but the heart. That was the place to find the words to address to God. When they wanted to pray, Methodists opened their hearts, not a book.

While the impulse for praying extemporaneously was not unique to Methodists—and had not originated with them—it was one of their liturgical standards. This contribution to the Methodist liturgical ethos came from John Wesley, who himself had noted that extemporaneous prayer was a distinguishing mark of Methodist worship. Wesley himself admitted that he constantly added extempore prayer, even in leading Anglican worship (Westerfield Tucker 1996: 18). But the way that Wesley phrased it in terms of *adding* extempore prayer revealed a difference between him and other early Methodists, who shifted the weight to extemporaneity.

Methodists found several things in extempore prayer that matched their fiery devotion. One aspect was the intensity that it allowed. Extemporaneity permitted Methodists to vent the heights and depths of what they felt in their hearts. Pace, pitch, tone, and pathos could vary with spontaneity better than with reading, leading to praying that resonated with greater fidelity with their inward experience. Extemporaneity also facilitated increased volume, meaning that Methodists could indulge their pinnacle of worship: shouting praise.

Extemporaneity also entailed liberty, a critical word to describe the essence of their liturgical ethos. The freedom to speak easily from the heart, whether in preaching or in praying, was an important standard to assess whether one was under the Holy Spirit's inspiration. Freedom in praying manifested itself in several ways. The most straightforward was in an individual feeling the liberty to pray in a manner that suited the spirit of the moment. This liberty also allowed someone to pray when she or he felt led.

Extemporaneity's freedom allowed several people to pray at the same time, even speaking different prayers. Portrayals of early Methodist worship show that this situation was often the case, especially when the services had become the most exuberant. From corner to corner worshippers would assault the gates of heaven in prayer. Gatherings around 'mourners' under the conviction of sin were special arenas for intense praying. In this exuberance, there was often a levelling of worship leadership roles as people often marginalized in society (women, children, blacks, and the poor) were at the head of this symphony of prayer.

Extemporaneous praying matched Methodist spirituality, too, because it facilitated ecstasy. Accounts of Methodist worship spoke of participants so caught up in emotion that they were able to utter only one or two words repeatedly: 'Glory, glory, glory!' one might pray while the next worshipper might be saying, 'Dear Jesus, dear Jesus, dear Jesus'. Indeed, such times could get so intense that some American Methodists themselves disapproved. John Fanning Watson, reflecting on what he observed in Philadelphia Methodism, for instance, complained that some of his fellow Methodists showed an 'indecent familiarity' in prayer or used excessively intimate 'fondling words' when addressing the divine. In particular, he thought Methodists used the word 'dear' too much (Watson 1819: 121).

Notwithstanding Watson's 'minority report', most Methodists appreciated extempore prayer's ability to disclose their hearts. That they did not have to handle a book also contributed to ecstasy and its physical expressiveness. With nothing to hold, Methodist hands were free to be lifted or clapped, eyes were free to be lifted heavenward, and feet were free to dance. In Methodists' estimation, written prayers too easily inhibited the joy that sought to rush out of hearts renewed in God's love through a prayer's whole body. Extemporaneity, on the other hand, allowed the flood to flow.

Indeed, so close was the link between extemporaneous praying and Methodist identity that the ability to pray from the heart was seen as a mark of authentic spiritual experience. Echoing a perspective that reached back at least to the Puritans, Methodists recognized that even the unregenerate could pray from a written page but that the new birth opened up the heart to address God authentically (Watters 1806: 19).

Methodists' preference for extempore prayer also reflected their social placement. As Rhys Isaac has pointed out, the reading of services from the Book of Common Prayer in Anglican parishes was part of a web of relationships which emphasized a gentry-centred social order (Isaac 1982: 63–5, 260–4). Thus to prefer extemporaneity—and to view it as spiritually superior—was a way to attack the values of the gentry, which was a favourite Methodist activity. In addition, extemporaneous praying had the advantage of not requiring worshippers' literacy, a helpful convenience as Methodism spread among slaves and lower levels of white society.

The ecstatic dimension was another key difference in Methodism's liturgical ethos. Methodists exhibited several overlapping types of worship-related ecstasy. The basic level was getting 'happy', which involved a deep sense of joy in knowing God's grace. Shouting praise was also common. The overflow could also be demonstrated by exhorting those around or by praying exuberantly or by rotating between shouting, exhorting, and praying in a continual loop. Physical demonstrations were frequent as Methodists clapped, jumped, convulsed, and danced. Ecstasy could also have the opposite effect of dissociative states. At worship Methodists sometimes fell, lost the ability to move or speak, or lay in a stupor. Such phenomena sometimes involved visions during worship. At one love feast, for instance, James Horton was caught up in a vision of worship in heaven. Coming to, he found himself standing on his chair, hands raised. Looking around, his fellow Methodists looked like the heavenly host whose company he had just left (Horton 1839: 85–6). It is hard to imagine any scene in contemporary Anglican worship that could have approached it, although it was present in British Methodism (Rack 1992: 193) and elsewhere in contemporaneous heart-driven movements.

Indeed, ecstasy in worship was so rampant that some American Methodists eventually grew concerned about its extent, particularly its standardization. Their complaints showed how entrenched the phenomenon was. One preacher, for example, protested in 1807 about those who formed jumping, dancing, and shouting 'into a system' (Taves 1999: 78). Probably showing a similar divide, the Annapolis, Maryland, society had separated into two parties by 1809: the shouters and the 'anti-shouters' (Smith 1848: 257).

Notwithstanding some objection, there was an ecstatic quality in much of early American Methodist worship. Several interrelated factors account for this general exuberance. For one thing, although the propensity for liturgical liveliness was latent on both sides of the Atlantic, the church–state forces that helped keep this desire on the margin in England were not nearly as strong in America (Wigger 1998: 105, 111; Andrews 2000: 6, 80). American exuberance was enhanced, too, by not having to live under the shadow of the controversy that had rocked London Methodists in the 1760s with extreme teachings and an excitational form of worship. Memories of such excesses dwelt long among British Methodists, perhaps causing many to shy away from exuberant worship (Lloyd 2001/2).

The influence of a large African-American presence in American Methodism was also a contributing factor. As Dee Andrews notes, early black Methodists were able to translate forms of ritualized ecstasy from African roots into comparable Methodist forms (Andrews 2000: 81; Taves 1999: 78–9). The presence of so many African Americans in Methodist worship took what was latent in Methodism and pushed it to a higher level, particularly in the aspects of institutionalization and ritualization. Ecstasy thus became a corporately learned behaviour that was triggered by certain practices such as musical repetition, improvisation, preacher/congregation inter-action through call-and-response, and bodily movement during music, especially in the use of the body to provide percussion (Taves 1993: 213).

ESSENTIAL METHODIST PRACTICES

This list of triggers of liturgical ecstasy suggests two essential practices that would have been key points of distinction from Anglican worship. Just as extemporaneous praying contributed to the ethos of Methodist worship, so did Methodist preaching and music serve as cornerstones of its worship.

With respect to who preached and how they preached, Methodist and Anglican services differed greatly. Methodist required neither ordination nor formal educa-tion to preach. With neither requirement, very little time often passed between a preacher's conversion and first sermons. That was no problem since Methodist listeners expected the power of one's experience to shine through the sermon. Methodist sermons sought to penetrate the heart, usually in an exposition of the doctrine of salvation. To achieve this end, Methodist preachers used small portions of Scripture (sometimes a single word), preaching extemporaneously, guided at most by outlines. The sermons sometimes came in overwhelming waves as Meth-odist preacher followed Methodist preacher. Exhortations by yet other speakers served as interludes to make sure the worshippers had heard the offer of salvation and exploit their readiness to experience it.

The difference in Methodist preaching also included content. Consider the contrasts that Freeborn Garrettson, who grew up Anglican but later became a Methodist, highlighted in his reminiscing (Ruth 2005: 74–80). What he remembered hearing in his upbringing were 'moral sermons' read. In his later appraisal, this meant that there was no gospel preached. In particular, the new birth (i.e. regener-ation) was not spoken of or heard. (Anglicans would have assumed that the entire congregation was already regenerate by virtue of being baptized as infants. Why speak about what one already presumes is true for the people?) In contrast, Methodist preachers sought to proclaim an experiential gospel powerfully or, in the words of Methodist bishop Francis Asbury, they were to 'feel for the power' (Wigger 1998: 77). If Methodists thought Anglicans preached 'moral sermons', in contrast they sought to proclaim a 'saving knowledge of Christ' and a 'spiritual and experimental [i.e. experiential] knowledge of repentance, faith, regeneration, and sanctification' (Asbury 1958: 2. 597).

The focus on experience was likewise shown in the importance of testifying in Methodist worship. Whether on a spontaneous basis or in services largely devoted to testimonies (the love feast), Methodists were quick to testify of their experience of God's saving grace. Testifying was not limited to ministers since all Methodists were expected to be able to name what God had done for them. Whenever a Methodist acknowledged that Christ had died 'for me' and spoke of when she or he had felt the inward witness of the Spirit, it meant the gospel was neither remote nor theoretical.

The second of the essential Methodist practices in worship was hymn singing. Methodist proclivity for hymn singing is well-documented. Thus a thorough review will not be attempted but only a review of those aspects that distinguished the Methodist worship ethos. The first dimension was the role of the hymns to reinforce the immediate and personal possibilities in the drama of salvation. Indeed, the ability to take this cosmic drama ('for all') and personalize it ('for me') was a recurring aspect in early Methodist hymnody.

The second dimension was what little role the Psalms, whether sung or spoken, played in Methodist worship. The rhythms of Anglican Morning and Evening Prayer assumed a steady progression through the Psalms every month. In addition, metrical Psalms were the mainstay in singing. Methodists, on the other hand, made little use of Psalms at all. Their musical texts were more specific and intense than the typical Psalm. Gradually working through a schedule of Psalms could have seemed like an imposition.

The last dimension was the use of hymn singing as part of more complex rituals to create dramatic conversion experiences. One such ritual was the ring shout. Probably beginning in the simple practice of gathering around mourners to pray, the ring shout eventually developed into a form of circular singing, dancing, praying, and shouting (Taves 1999: 99–101). The ring shout was stylized musical ritual used to evoke religious experience.

Anglicans in America realized the competition of Methodist hymn singing and sometimes sought to respond by introducing Methodist hymns into parish worship (Cameron 1985: 17). Others went a step further, putting together the first *official* Anglican hymnal ever in response to the Methodists (Marshall 2004: 155). Whether such attempts provided much of a deterrent to the exodus to the Methodist churches is not known. However, given the rapid growth of Methodism, it was unlikely.

THE SOURCES OF AND THE TENSIONS IN THE METHODIST WORSHIP ETHOS

The irony in the Methodist liturgical ethos was that much of it could be linked to John Wesley, at least in its genesis as he crafted most of the services (e.g. love feasts and Covenant services) that distinguished Methodism as a parachurch movement. He was an inveterate borrower in this process, adapting from wherever he found something useful, whether Patristic, Puritan, or Continental Pietist sources. John also shaped Methodism as a movement of lay preachers. Other deviations from standard Anglicanism he introduced included the use of outdoor or unconsecrated space to hold preaching services and the use of extemporaneous praying. Indeed, John was so adept at finding useful liturgical practices from the past that historian James White has identified Wesley as a 'pragmatic traditionalist' (White 1989: 151). Even Charles Wesley, who generally was more conservative than his brother, contributed to the wayward tilt of early Methodist worship so much so that he has been called 'the paradoxical Anglican' (Lloyd 2007: 64–87). He, of course, was the writer of the bulk of hymns used by Methodists. But Charles had an even more radical side, for example, showing a surprising willingness for women to play an active role in Methodist affairs. Of course, both men were ardent advocates of the experienced-based spirituality that Methodists called 'experimental religion'. This piety was the touchstone for the Methodist liturgical ethos.

But the Wesleys were not the only advocates of 'experimental religion'. Thus, while most of Methodism's liturgical ethos found its genesis with them, not all of it did. Other strands of eighteenth-century Pietism influenced American Methodism as David Hempton (2005: 81) has noted: American Methodists' 'real language of common spiritual discourse was more radically pietist [i.e. of European Pietism] than its British antecedents'.

Such influence of a more radical pietism highlighted the tension between the Anglican-inclined character of John Wesley and the spirituality of American Methodists. Specifically, while the Americans shared a common core of piety and practices with the Wesleys, they did not have the same theological breadth, which is what allowed John Wesley to hold together in worship being both an Anglican and a proponent of 'experimental religion'. Without the same span of thought, and with a different nuancing of pietism, Methodists by and large could not balance the same tensions that Wesley could, sometimes perhaps to the detriment of Methodism.

There are several reasons why the Wesleys had a breadth that other Methodists did not. The first was the difference in basic attitudes towards the Church of England. The Wesleys embraced it while typical Methodists distrusted it. To them the Church of England held the ever-lurking danger of formalism, that spiritual condition where one substitutes regular use of the forms of worship for true religion. The local Anglican parish and its priest often reminded Methodists of 2 Timothy 3: 5, 'having a form of godliness, but denying the power thereof'. Indeed, Methodists sometimes tied the validity of Anglican worship to the holiness of its ministers. They used their perception of the ungodliness of priests as a reason for not attending worship.

Additional factors contributed to a different attitude towards the Church of England. For one thing, Methodism tended to be strongest in areas where

Anglicanism had been weak, in keeping up with population shifts and British expansion (Hempton 2005: 19). In other words, Methodists had not always been much exposed to Anglicanism. Moreover, an increasing number of Methodists were brought in from non-Anglican or Dissenting backgrounds, with a consequent prejudice against the Church of England, a condition about which John Wesley complained (Wesley 1986: 466). This fact was true for Americans, especially as Methodism expanded into New England and into new western territories. Finally, Methodists attended non-Anglican or Dissenting worship, against which Wesley had similarly complained (Wesley 1987: 82). In America there was ample evidence of cross-over church attendance.

Even those Methodists who came from an Anglican background did not necessarily have fond memories of it in contrast to Wesley where commitment to the Church was a matter of family principle. A different family experience was another reason why Wesley's Anglicanism was not found among Methodists.

Consider the example of Ezekiel Cooper, an important American preacher. He was born in Maryland in 1763 to parents who were dutiful members of the local parish. Cooper and all his siblings were baptized in this church as infants. The Cooper family probably appeared as solid Anglican worshippers. But Cooper's appraisal was much harsher. Despite appearances, Cooper believed that 'we were all too great strangers to anything truly spiritual' (Phoebus 1887: 12). Cooper's critique extended to his neighbours: 'Religion in those days, in our parts, appeared to be universally neglected. It was almost a miracle to find a man of real piety. The land truly mourned by reason of wickedness and the neglect of religion.... but we were all members of the Church'. In contrast to Wesley's family experience, Cooper sounded a note of impoverishment and even a sense of betrayal by the Church. Whenever shared by other Methodists, it could lead to a suspicion of worship that reminded them of a disappointing Anglican upbringing.

Early Methodists did not have John Wesley's breadth of perspective. The lack created a trajectory that sought to resolve the liturgical tensions that he could hold together. On the whole, it was easier for the first several generations to drift from, not towards, Anglican sensibilities in worship.

AMERICAN METHODIST WORSHIP AS A CHURCH

Wesley's original desire for Methodists to worship in Anglican ways had not changed when he took steps in 1784 to provide ordination for the American Methodists, and thus for their existence as an independent church. At that time he undertook a conservative revision of the 1662 Book of Common Prayer, praised it highly in a cover letter, and sent it to America under the title *The Sunday Service of the Methodists in North America*. In the revision, he removed things about which he had qualms, eliminated a few Psalms he thought inappropriate for Christians to use, deleted references to royalty (an obvious need for America), and changed things having obvious reference to Anglican parishes (e.g. mentions of choirs, which Methodists rarely had). He also sought to reduce the length of the combined Sunday morning services. But the basic ethos implicit in this text-based approach to worship remained the same. It therefore represented a continuation of Wesley's intention that Methodist worship complement Anglican, not replace it.

Wesley's desire fell flat in America. Indeed, even the title of his revision showed a serious flaw in his understanding of what he had spawned in American Methodism. Its name, *The Sunday Service*, was out of sync with an itinerant system constantly moving and where preachers led worship on nearly every day of the week. Only in a few large cities, where worship more closely followed a Sunday-based rhythm, could Wesley's directions have a chance of melding into already-established practices.

Given all the dynamics of the Methodist ethos for worship that had become well ingrained prior to 1784, it is understandable that *The Sunday Service* did not find a place at the centre of worship after then. Methodism's original ethos and practices were not to be displaced. Indeed, perhaps as surprising was how many preachers made an honest attempt to use the new resource.

Itinerant Thomas Haskins's attempts were probably typical of those who tried to use it. After *The Sunday Service*'s introduction, he led worship by reading prayers. He continued for a month but then quit, noting, 'Altho' this [the service from *The Sunday Service*] is most excellent in itself, yet I scarcely think it will be of much use among us, as a people' (Haskins 1785).

His story was common. Jesse Lee, another Methodist preacher and its first American historian, looking back in 1810 at the failed introduction of *The Sunday Service* into Methodist worship, highlighted its demise:

At this time the prayer book, as revised by Mr. Wesley, was introduced among us; and in the large towns, and in some country places, our preachers read prayers on the Lord's day: and in some cases the preachers read part of the morning service on Wednesday and Fridays. But some of the preachers who had been long accustomed to pray extempore, were unwilling to adopt this new plan. Being fully satisfied that they could pray better, and with more devotion while their eyes were shut, than they could with their eyes open. After a few years the prayer book was laid aside, and has never been used since in public worship.   (Lee 1974: 107)

Even the more Anglican of the Methodists could be ambivalent about the new text. Thus Bishop Thomas Coke's 1786 statement to Freeborn Garrettson urged cautiousness in spreading *The Sunday Service*: 'I would have you introduce the Prayer-book everywhere, so far as you possibly can without giving great offense: but I would not give great offense to precious souls even for the best of forms' (Coke 1786).

Coke needed not worry. Great offence to the early Methodist people was largely avoided. Editions of *The Sunday Service* soon stopped being printed. In 1792 the parts that Methodists had found useful (the sacramental services, the pastoral rites, ordination materials, and the doctrinal statements in the Articles of Religion) were amended and appended to the *Discipline*, the Church's book of polity. It was a practical step to becoming a church in its own right. The year 1784 and the introduction of *The Sunday Service* had not shifted the basic character of American Methodist worship.

But some things were perhaps lost in not successfully incorporating *The Sunday Service* more fully, things that Wesley's breadth in being both Methodist and Anglican in worship allowed him to appreciate. In so being he had a certain balance in worship that arose by keeping together several liturgical tensions. By marginalizing the Anglican dimension, Methodists have often tried to resolve the tensions in one direction or another. This sway towards resolution began in early Methodism and has continued, particularly in denominational spin-offs in the nineteenth and twentieth centuries.

One area of breadth that Wesley had was the diet of Scripture that he expected in worship. The immediately inspired choices of Methodist preaching were balanced and expanded by the Anglican monthly rotation of Psalms and other Scriptures in Morning and Evening Prayer as well as texts appropriate for yearly feasts. Together the two methods would have provided immediacy, relevance, and a regularity of scriptural coverage. American Methodists, however, relied almost entirely on immediate inspiration. There was no lectionary in early Methodism. Even though the 1792 General Conference provided for whole chapters to be read from the Old and New Testaments, there is scant evidence that many followed the requirements. Some of Wesley's descendants today still consider suspect prescribed lists of Scriptures for worship.

Another area of breadth that Wesley held together was the diet of prayer that he could achieve by both praying extemporaneously and praying Anglicanism's set forms. Extemporaneity provided the authenticity of speaking from the heart while the set forms provided, as Wesley called it, the 'grand parts of public prayer' (i.e., a range of types and functions of prayer). Indeed, Wesley had complained how Methodist worship alone often failed to have sufficient breadth in praying, a condition still found sometimes today.

Wesley's complex approach likewise maintained an important tension with sacraments. He had ways to affirm Anglicanism's positive statements about sacramental efficacy yet maintain an emphasis from 'experimental religion' about affective experiences of grace. This combination meant that Wesley kept contact with the larger Western tradition of sacramental theology, emphasizing God's activity in the sacraments, while also holding a gospel that sought to touch people's hearts (Campbell 2001: 160–74). The latter was easier for Methodists to keep, however, than the former. The domination of feelings and experience in Methodism's ethos meant that the tradition about God's activity in the sacraments was harder to maintain. Because Methodist convictions about God's presence in the sacraments was more experiential than thoughtfully theological, the convictions could evaporate as worship experiences faltered.

The danger applied to both sacraments. Although early American Methodists had a strong attachment to the Lord's Supper (in continuity with Wesley), this vitality of piety was lost somewhere since the eighteenth century. Baptism had a more tenuous hold on Methodists. One can see this especially in the issue of baptismal regeneration. Because of their conviction that new birth was an inwardly known experience, Methodists have had a hard time conceiving of God bringing about regeneration through baptism, especially for infants, despite Wesley's statements to this effect.

Methodists also shifted the balance Wesley had in liturgical tradition and pragmatism, resolving the tension towards the pragmatic side. Wesley's approach could be called 'pragmatic traditionalism', meaning that, if gaps in current liturgical practice were found, then the 'universal tradition' would be searched 'for practices that have worked in similar situations' (White 1989: 152). American Methodists, on the other hand, imbibed more fully than Wesley from democratic cultural currents that saw validation in numbers, not in a person's or thing's pedigree. Therefore they tended to resolve this tension by becoming traditional pragmatists. In other words, they helped instigate an approach to worship in America that has continually sought to find the ever-new method for reaching people through worship. The quest itself became the new tradition and worship was often conducted not as directed primarily towards God but towards people as a means of evangelizing them.

The clearest example of the rise of liturgical pragmatism in early American Methodism is the development of camp meetings at the rise of the Second Great Awakening in the nineteenth century. Methodists went from never having heard the term at the start of the century to holding 400 to 500 camp meetings by that name annually, from Canada to Mississippi, with an estimated one million in annual attendance by 1811 (Wigger 1998: 97; Hatch 1989: 257 n. 1). The process by which camp meetings emerged and were promoted has been repeated countless times in a never-ending series of American worship innovations.

Wesley would not always recognize what American Methodists helped unleash in worship. For example, as Methodism became mainstream in the nineteenth century, it helped establish a devotional focus on Christ in worship content. Indeed, later evangelical worship has often been so focused on Christ that some have begun to ask 'Whatever happened to the Father?' and others have wondered if the current state is not functional Unitarianism (Torrance 1996: 20; Parry 2005: 2; Witvliet 2005: 9).

He also probably would not recognize the standardized role that liturgical ecstasy has achieved in some churches. Although the concern for respectability often led to worshippers in the Methodist Episcopal Church marginalizing exuberance, it was never eliminated, particularly in Wesleyan branch movements and churches. Moreover, expectations that emotions should run hot, that the heart must be engaged, and that intense crisis experiences in worship were normative have characterized much American Protestantism, including the recent rise of Pentecostalism. Even here, however, Methodist influence was present through one of Pentecostalism's main streams of origin, the Holiness Movement, which thought it was preserving the best of what had characterized early Methodism.

Whether or not the Movement—or other spiritual descendants of Wesley—did depends on whether Methodist worship is defined by looking at Wesley or at those in the movement he spawned. For what Wesley intended in Methodist worship was not what Wesley got. The worship-related influence of the movement he generated was revolutionary, nonetheless.

REFERENCES

ALLEN, RICHARD (1801). *A Collection of Hymns and Spiritual Songs.* Philadelphia: T. L. Plowman.

ANDREWS, DEE E. (2000). *The Methodists and Revolutionary America, 1760–1800: The Shaping of an Evangelical Culture.* Princeton: Princeton University Press.

ASBURY, FRANCIS (1958). *The Journal and Letters of Francis Asbury.* Nashville: Abingdon.

BRADFORD, HENRY (n.d.). *Hymnbook.* Chapel Hill, Miss.: Southern Historical Collection, Wilson Library, University of North Carolina.

BRUCE, PHILIP (1790). 'An extract of a letter from Philip Bruce, elder of the Methodist Episcopal church, to Bishop Coke, dated Portsmouth, Virginia, March 25, 1788'. *The Arminian Magazine.*

CAMERON, KENNETH WALTER (1985). *Connecticut's First Diocesan.* Hartford, Conn.: Transcendental Books.

CAMPBELL, TED A. (2001). 'Conversion and Baptism in Wesleyan Spirituality'. In Kenneth J. Collins and John H. Tyson (eds.), *Conversion in the Wesleyan Tradition.* Nashville: Abingdon.

COKE, THOMAS (1786). 'Thomas Coke to Free Garrettson, n.d.'. MS, John Wesley Papers, United Methodist Church Archives-GCAH. Madison, N.J. Coke's letter is on the reverse side of Wesley's letter to Garrettson, dated 25 February 1786.

HASKINS, THOMAS (1785). Journal, MS, 23 January 1785. Manuscripts Division. Library of Congress, Washington, D.C.

HATCH, NATHAN (1989). *The Democratization of American Christianity.* New Haven: Yale University Press.

HATCHETT, MARION J. (1976). 'A Sunday Service in 1776 or Thereabouts'. *Historical Magazine of the Protestant Episcopal Church* 45/4.

HEMPTON, DAVID (2005). *Methodism: Empire of the Spirit.* New Haven: Yale University Press.

HORTON, JAMES P. (1839). *A Narrative of the Early Life, Remarkable Conversion, and Spiritual Labours of James P. Horton, Who has been a Member of the Methodist Episcopal Church Upward of Forty Years.* n.p.: Printed for the author.

Isaac, Rhys (1982). *The Transformation of Virginia 1740–1790.* Chapel Hill: University of North Carolina Press.

Jones, Sarah Anderson (1792–3). Diary. MS. Manuscript and Rare Books Department, Swem Library, College of William and Mary, Williamsburg, Va.

Knight, Henry H., III (1992). *The Presence of God in the Christian Life: John Wesley and the Means of Grace.* Metuchen: Scarecrow.

Lee, Jesse (1974). *A Short History of the Methodists, in the United States of America; Beginning in 1766, and Continued till 1809.* Rutland, Vt.: Academy Books.

Lloyd, Gareth (2001/2). '"A Cloud of Perfect Witnesses": John Wesley and the London Disturbances 1760–1763'. *The Asbury Theological Journal* 56/2 (Autumn) and 57/1 (Spring): 117–36.

—— (2007). *Charles Wesley and the Struggle for Methodist Identity.* New York: Oxford University Press.

Marini, Stephen (2002). 'Hymnody as History: Early Evangelical Hymns and the Recovery of American Popular Religion'. *Church History* (June): 287–95.

Marshall, Paul Victor (2004). *One, Catholic and Apostolic: Samuel Seabury and the Early Episcopal Church.* New York: Church Publishing.

Minutes of the Methodist Conferences, From the First, Held in London, by the Late Rev. John Wesley, A.M., in the Year 1744 (1862). London: John Mason.

Parry, Robin (2005). *Worshipping Trinity: Coming Back to the Heart of Worship.* Milton Keynes: Paternoster.

Phoebus, George A. (1887). *Beams of Light on Early Methodism in America.* New York: Phillips & Hunt; Cincinnati: Cranston & Stowe.

Rack, Henry D. (1992). *Reasonable Enthusiast: John Wesley and the Rise of Methodism.* 2nd edn. Nashville: Abingdon.

Ruth, Lester (2000). *A Little Heaven Below: Worship at Early Methodist Quarterly Meetings.* Nashville: Kingswood.

—— (2005). *Early Methodist Life and Spirituality, A Reader.* Nashville: Kingswood.

Smith, Henry (1848). *Recollections and Reflections of an Old Itinerant.* New York: Lane & Tippett.

Spinks, Bryan D. (2006). 'Anglican and Dissenters'. In Geoffrey Wainwright and Karen B. Westerfield Tucker (eds.), *The Oxford History of Christian Worship.* Oxford: Oxford University Press.

Taves, Ann (1993). 'Knowing through the Body: Dissociative Religious Experience in the African- and British-American Methodist Traditions'. *The Journal of Religion* 73.

—— (1999). *Fits, Trances, & Visions: Experiencing Religion and Explaining Experience from Wesley to James.* Princeton: Princeton University Press.

Torrance, James B. (1996). *Worship, Community & The Triune God of Grace.* Downers Grove, Ill.: InterVarsity Press.

Watson, John Fanning (1819). *Methodist Error; Or, Friendly, Christian Advice, To those Methodists, Who indulge in extravagant emotions and bodily exercises.* 2nd edn. Trenton, N.J.: D. & E. Fenton.

Watters, William (1806). *A Short Account of the Christian Experience, and Ministerial Labours, of William Watters.* Alexandria: S. Snowden.

Wesley, John (1986). *Works,* ed. Albert C. Outler. 4 vols. Nashville: Abingdon, iii.

—— (1987). *Works,* ed. Albert C. Outler. 4 vols. Nashville: Abingdon, iv.

WESTERFIELD TUCKER, KAREN B. (1996). 'Form and Freedom: John Wesley's Legacy for Methodist Worship'. In Karen B. Westerfield Tucker (ed.), *The Sunday Service of the Methodists: Twentieth-Century Worship in Worldwide Methodism.* Nashville: Kingswood.

—— (2001). *American Methodist Worship.* New York: Oxford University Press.

WHITE, JAMES F. (ed.) (1984). *John Wesley's Sunday Service of the Methodists in North America.* Nashville: The United Methodist Publishing House.

—— (1989). *Protestant Worship: Traditions in Transition.* Louisville, Ky.: Westminster John Knox.

WIGGER, JOHN H. (1998). *Taking Heaven by Storm: Methodism and the Rise of Popular Christianity in America.* New York: Oxford University Press.

WITVLIET, JOHN (2005). 'The Opening of Worship—Trinity'. In Leanne Van Dyk (ed.), *A More Profound Alleluia: Theology and Worship in Harmony.* Grand Rapids: Eerdmans.

CHAPTER 19

MUSIC AND HYMNODY

SWEE HONG LIM

It is the hymns, repeated over and over again, which form the container of much of our faith...They are probably in our age the only confessional documents which we learn by heart. As such, they have taken the place of our catechisms. Tell me what you sing, and I'll tell you who you are!

(Heuvel 1966: 6)

INTRODUCTION

MUSIC, in particular congregational song, is an important component of Methodist worship. In the life of Methodism, its founders John and Charles Wesley, much like Martin Luther, were adamant in getting congregational songs into the hands of their congregants. This is clearly evident by the brothers' effort in hymn writing that gave rise to various Methodist hymnals such as *A Collection of Psalms and Hymns* (1737, new hymnal albeit same title in 1741), *Hymns and Spiritual Songs* (1753), *Hymns and Sacred Poems* (1739, new hymnal albeit same title in 1740, and again in 1742), and in 1780, an abridged version of *A Collection of Psalms and Hymns*

(1741) became *A Collection of Hymns for the Use of the People Called Methodists.* Indeed as noted Methodist scholar S. T. Kimbrough, Jr. observed, 'The hymns of the church are theology. They are theological statements: the church's lyrical, theological commentaries on Scripture, liturgy, faith, action, and hosts of other subjects which call the reader and singer to faith, life, and Christian practice' (Kimbrough 1985: 59). This musical phenomenon is important for global Methodism even as Philip Jenkins's *The Next Christendom* (2002) points towards the rapid growth of Christianity outside Western Europe and North America. A quick survey of the various Methodist Churches around the globe by Westerfield Tucker in *The Sunday Service of the Methodists: Twentieth-Century Worship in World-Wide Methodism* (1996) is a testament of this impending shift of influence from the West to the non-West. In so doing, what is the implication for music and hymnody?

This brief chapter will look specifically at the practice of music and hymnody in various Asian contexts that are not necessarily Methodist but significant in affording us a glimpse of the general state of music and hymnody in Asia. At the same time, this chapter seeks to offer some thoughts on the contextualization of church music that can elucidate current development in music and hymnody. It is crucial that 'hymnody', in this chapter, is not taken in its strictest hymnological sense, i.e. strophic verses set to music. Rather, it needs to be defined as pieces of music sung by the congregation in Christian worship. Hymnody needs to encompass strophic, composed, and short repetitive song types. In this chapter, 'hymns' and 'congregational songs' are used interchangeably.

In his preface for the hymnal companion, *Sound the Bamboo: Asian Hymns in Their Cultural and Liturgical Contexts* (Loh forthcoming), C. Michael Hawn challenges us to rethink our concept of the hymn as merely a musical genre. He writes, 'This is a matter of identity both as a Christian and as a human being from a particular cultural context. Understanding the nature of Asian hymns is a window into understanding how Asian Christians pray and how they understand God's work in the world'. Equally significant is the juxtaposition of this thought to the function of hymnody in Methodism as Westerfield Tucker (2001: 156) tells us, 'Public worship, as well as private, family, and social worship, would not have been considered Methodist unless accompanied with song. What prayer books were for some Christians, the hymn books were for generations of Methodists'. Thus, not surprisingly, Methodist missionaries who ventured into Asia and other parts of the world took with them hymnals that ultimately shaped those to whom they sought to minister. In time to come, these missionaries would translate the hymn texts for the locals who became Christians, and they would then be sung using the same Western tunes. In most Asian countries, this nineteenth-century effort continues to dominate much hymnody to the present. In fact, the revised *Hymnal of Universal Praise* (Tam 2005), expected to be widely used by Mandarin-speaking congregations throughout Asia in this decade and beyond, maintains this tradition of translated hymns. It contains a majority of hymns with some contemporary praise and worship songs as the latter are gaining broader use in Asia. The basis for which they are included is that they must be 'representative and mature works that carry solid biblical and theological content with logical structure and sequence' (ibid. 12). One organization that actively supports the translation of Western hymnody (and to a lesser extent, the praise and worship songs) is the World Association of Chinese Church Music (WACCM).

Though translated works still dominate the congregational song landscape of Asia, attempts to write new congregational songs in various genres are also emerging. Some continue to use the form of strophic hymn type, others turn towards the praise and worship song genre. Samples of this mixture can be found in the *Hymnal of Universal Praise* as well as the *Hymns of United Worship* (Chan and Gan 1997). In most instances, these hymns continue to imitate Western musical nuances in terms of harmony and melody construction. Also, there have been some efforts to juxtapose Western and Asian musical characteristics and to a lesser yet significant extent, to create works that are localized in their musical approach. This effort seems more obvious in Asian countries with a strong in situ tradition such as India, Indonesia, China, Cambodia, Thailand, Philippines, etc. Even so, the preponderance of translated Western hymnody throughout Asia is obvious.

The earliest attempt to explore non-Western musical approaches in hymnody can be traced to D. T. Niles's (1963) *East Asian Christian Conference* (*EACC*) hymnal. This work was rather popular and saw several reprints. In 1990, I-to Loh created the *Sound the Bamboo* hymnal that was subsequently revised a decade later. This hymnal is distinctive in that one of its guiding principles is to put into print emerging congregational songs in various unique Asian styles. Unlike Niles's work that combined various Asian melodies with Western harmony, Loh literally transcribed many of the hymns as they were sung and audio-recorded by him in their local contexts. Hence, musically speaking, the *Sound the Bamboo* hymnal had a significant edge in terms of being stylistically accurate with regard to diverse musical styles found in Asia. Indeed, the impact of Loh's creative effort in *Sound the Bamboo* is quite dramatic. Asian hymns no longer look nor sound similar to each other across different geographical regions. In addition, there is a newfound sense of depth and integrity in the music. Moreover, it has been much welcomed as an important hymnological resource for the world church, in particular the West, even as it showcased the diverse musical styles within Asia. In fact, GIA publishing company has licensed the rights to publish this work for the North American region from the Christian Conference of Asia (CCA) and it will publish the companion to this hymnal in the near future.

Somewhere in between the *Sound the Bamboo* hymnal with its pan-Asian repertoire and *Hymns of Universal Praise* with its translated Western hymnody are the hymnological efforts of local organizations such as Yamuger (Indonesian Institute for Sacred Music). Through its hymnal, *Kidung Jemaat*, this organization is widely known for its stance on the contextualization of church music in

Indonesia. Its ministries include the collection and publication of indigenous hymns and the training of church musicians. Its primary purpose is to promote and nurture the use of local congregational song in Indonesia. Equally remarkable is the Protestant Christian Church in Bali, Indonesia with its strong emphasis on building a Christian identity 'in solidarity with the Balinese community and culture' (see <http://www.christianchurchbali.org>, accessed 2 January 2009). This objective is highly significant given the fact that Hinduism is integral to Balinese life and culture and it requires much decisive theological articulation on the part of the Protestant Christian Church to create a pathway through the religio-cultural syncretism. A glimpse of the unique localized musical approach of the denomination can be seen in the publication, *Kristus Sundaring Bali* (Loh 1988).

Such emerging efforts of contextual hymnody can also be found in other parts of Asia. One instance is the Thai Covenant Church, a local evangelical-strand Christian denomination which has done much to nurture the growth of indigenous Thai hymnody, in particular the north-east Udon Thani area, since the 1970s (Lim 2006: 219–22). Not surprising, their hymnological effort has also been documented by I-to Loh in a 1989 songbook entitled, *Rak Phra Jao, Rao Pen Thai*. At present, its Non-Governmental Organization (NGO) affiliate, Thai Faith and Music Foundation (TFMF) established by Inchai and Ruth Srisuwan, has brought this significant effort of contextual Christian congregational song to the Thai capital of Bangkok (http://www.thaicov.org/tfmf.html, accessed 2 January 2009). This work has been particularly successful for many reasons, one of which is the particularity of the Thai language. Typical hymnological processes of matching translated text to existing Western hymn tunes do not work well due to the inherent tonal inflection of the language. Similar limitations apply to Mandarin, Burmese, Vietnamese, and Khmen. Furthermore, Udon Thani, the rice bowl of Thailand, where this process of innovation first began in the 1970s, has limited access to Western instruments. Enlightened missionaries who had initiated the work in Udon Thani were equally adamant that no Western instruments should be introduced into Christian worship so that Christianity would be strongly rooted in Thai culture. This became a guiding philosophy for subsequent work throughout Thailand as embodied in the ministry of the Srisuwans. In Cambodia, collaboration by the World Federation of Chinese Methodist Churches and Methodist Churches in South Korea, Singapore, Switzerland, and the United States culminated in the establishment of the Methodist Church in Cambodia. As part of the process of formation, a hymnal, *The Christian Hymn and Worship Book* (Kimbrough 2001), was created for this new Methodist conference. The distinctive feature of this hymnal is that 57 per cent of its corpus of 194 hymns are regionally composed with the remaining works coming from the rest of the world, including traditional Western hymns that were translated into the Khmer language.

South Asia is a long-time stalwart of contextual hymnody, though like most regions in Asia its urban centres tend to be more influenced by unadulterated

Western hymnody due to its long history of being a British colony; nevertheless its nationalistic temperament coupled with utter poverty in rural areas have been a stronghold for indigenous hymnody. The formation of the unitive Church of South India in the late 1960s further fuelled the development of local hymnody. Theological institutions in Tamil Nadu and Bangalore have done much to nurture this growth. In my view, indigenous South Asian hymnody is by far the most localized and least affected by Western influences at the present time.

Diametrically different from such contextual hymnody is the music of churches that continue to depend solely on Western hymnological materials without translation. Most of these are situated in urban centres where English is widely used. Take for example the local churches of the English-speaking Trinity Annual Conference of the Methodist Church in Singapore. Given its brief history as an autonomous conference, the lack of a local denominational hymnal, and other limiting factors, a majority of its local churches arbitrarily make use of the United Methodist hymnal (Young 1989) for worship use even though it does not serve as the official hymnal of this conference. In the same predicament is the English-speaking Trinity Annual Conference of the Methodist Church in Malaysia that continues to use the Methodist Hymnal (Young 1964). Not surprisingly, these churches also draw on the praise and worship song resources coming from producers of contemporary Christian music such as Integrity Music and Vineyard of the United States and Hillsongs of Australia. Predictably, with an increasing number of congregations exclusively adopting such non-Methodist congregational song resources, there are voices within the Methodist Church raising questions regarding the long-term formation of Methodist identity in relation to the congregational songs sung in churches. The Methodist School of Music (MSM), known before 1997 as the Council on Worship and Music, was established as an agency of the General Conference of the Methodist Church in Singapore in 1997 and has taken preliminary steps to offer alternatives to local churches through its annual Church Music Encounters training programme, more recently launching a publication series, the MSM Choral Anthem Series, that promotes the creation of new Asian choral works. Its first fruit, the Aldersgate Hymn Festival (2007), featured seven emerging Asian Methodist composers providing ten new settings to Charles Wesley's texts in commemoration of his 300th anniversary. A year earlier, MSM entered into a partnership with a local ecumenical seminary, Trinity Theological College, to train church musicians through a formal graduate degree programme in the field of worship, liturgy, and church music marked by a deliberate Asian emphasis.

In the Philippines, where the arts richly thrive, the Asian Institute for Liturgy and Music (AILM) in Manila has had more than two decades of history in nurturing the development of local Asian hymnody since its inception in 1980. Among the graduates of this institution are several Methodists, such as Lu Chen Tiong (Malaysia), Daud Kosasih (Indonesia), Joy Nilo (Philippines), and Lim Swee

Hong (Singapore) who are beginning to make a mark for themselves in church music in their respective home countries. Aside from its academic endeavours of training church musicians, AILM in particular through the contribution of I-to Loh in the mid-1980s to the early 1990s had championed the promotion of indigenous Asian hymnody through its publication series, the AILM Church Music Collection (Lim 2006: 247–9). These works documented the practice of indigenous church music previously unavailable for English language readers and became an unique avenue for such musical praxis to be disseminated beyond its local setting. Another important tertiary institution that had been actively promoting the local adaptation of worship and church music is Tainan Theological College and Seminary, Taiwan. Between 1996 and 2002 when I-to Loh served as president of this institution, he launched a graduate church music programme that sought to redirect Taiwanese churches' fascination with translated Western hymnody, providing it with a viable alternative in the form of global congregational songs, locally composed hymns, and locally inspired liturgical expressions. Even though Loh has since retired from the Taiwanese seminary, the significance of this programme continues to reverberate throughout the island and beyond.

Equally important is Loh's paradigm for the contextualization of Asian church music. Prior to his groundbreaking work in 1984, there was not much theological thought given to the praxis of church music in Asian churches even though, from the above discussion, we can clearly observe that there are several strands of congregational song—Western, translated Western, and contextual. The underlying motivation for Loh's formulation of a paradigm for the contextualization of church music is to provide a possible path in which congregational song can move from its Western hymnodic heritage to an incarnational hymnodic expression that better reflects the local context and enables meaningful participation. This paradigm was presented at the faculty seminar of Tainan Theological College and Seminary and subsequently published as an article entitled 'Toward Contextualization of Church Music in Asia' in the *Asian Journal of Theology* (Loh 1990: 293–315). Loh's initial paradigm was conceived as a five-stage process in which musical style moves from its beginning practice of imitative Western hymn style, by way of developing a sense of local culture, followed by attempts at rediscovering self-identity, and moving towards syncretism before attaining a matured contextualized standard (see Table 19.1).

In 2004, Loh revised the paradigm in which he examined the role of human agency in the process of contextualization. Essentially, he sees that there are four types of people—the younger generation, the intelligentsia, the protectors/preservers of indigenous music, and the general public (see Table 19.2). Here, Loh submits that the process of contextualization can be implemented by means of understanding the various people in church and their concerns.

Loh further explicated his paradigm in late 2005. In an unpublished article, 'Clarification of the Four Stages of Development of Contextualized Compositions',

Table 19.1. A summary of Loh's five-stage process of contextualization (Loh 1990)

Stage	Process of contextualization	Distinctive features
1	Imitation of Western gospel hymn style	• Imitation of a musical style familiar to composers (typically Western gospel hymn) • Musical works either totally ignore native cultures or incorporate certain ornaments or glides that echo native singing styles • Lyrics may feature cleverly inserted superficial cultural expressions
2	Awareness of one's own culture	• Texture of western style prevails • Some attempt to integrate nostalgic native elements and idioms
3	Rediscovery of identity	• Actual adaptation of folk or native melodies readily identified by both native church circle and outside • Use of native instrumentation that emphasizes original tradition • Harmony may still be in Western style
4	Syncretism	• New composition in native style using traditional or contemporary Western harmonic idiom • Not adaptation of folk music but the integration of the elements and idioms that capture the spirit of the culture • Melody may be native but harmony remains Western with both components syncretized
5	The mature contextualized work	• Mature control of technical skills • Lyrics exhibit sound theology infused with poetic beauty that reflects the need and concern of the culture • Composition derived from native ways is melodically and harmonically (if used) innovative • Musical style is neither native nor Western, but both at once, a new tradition

Source: Loh 1990.

he spelled it out by way of compositional techniques (Lim 2006: 291). He sees the process of contextual composition going through a series of phases, from imitation via adaptation and motivic development to innovation (see Table 19.3), a postulation that follows the course of the various streams of hymnody in Asia remarkably closely.

However, Loh's paradigm, even through significant adjustments, assumes that there is an in situ traditional culture that can reliably be a source for innovation. It further presupposes that churches are fully intent on using their inherent folk tradition for Christian worship. While this model may speak effectively to homogenous cultures or in countries where the dominant ethnic group has overwhelming influence in the given society, such as China, Thailand, Vietnam, Cambodia, Philippines, Indonesia, Taiwan, Japan, and Korea, it offers a limited solution to

Table 19.2. Loh's description of the congregation and approaches to contextualization

Types	Profile of congregation	Approaches to contextualization
1	General younger generation—followers of Western pop-oriented mass culture	• Compose in contemporary Western popular style with the possibility of incorporating certain native and traditional musical idioms and instruments to link the past to the present, the local with the Western • Give small doses of other musical styles to broaden their musical world
2	Intelligentsia—highly educated and typically subscribed to Western value systems with very little or no interest in either pop or traditional folk music	• Re-educate theologically and aesthetically, helping them understand and accept traditional music as a gift from God • Adopt traditional musical motifs or folk melodies that do not carry other religious or negative connotations and set them to Christian texts • Traditional Western harmony or innovative harmonic idioms may be used
3	Protectors/preservers of native traditional music—minority group who are interested to learn, preserve, and promote ancient national musical tradition	• Adapt certain traditional instrumental pieces for worship, especially those without particular religious associations • Compose new works for liturgical use, which can be in one particular traditional style, a combination of various traditional styles, or musical hybrids of both East and West
4	Majority of general public—not strongly opinionated—open to guidance and education	• Simple hymns with folk idioms may be introduced by a trusted leader • New syncretic works utilizing folk motifs or imitating folk styles may be arranged or harmonized innovatively or in non-Western styles

Source: Loh 2005: 450–74.

immigrant societies that are multi-religious or have an obvious lack of in situ traditions that can be used to formulate localized Christian expressions.

In this instance, a broader and all-encompassing version of Loh's paradigm is called for. To that end, Lim Swee Hong offered a three-stage cyclical approach for the contextualization of church music in Asia (ibid. 190–219). This proposal sees contextualization as a fluid process without *terminus a quo* or *terminus ad quem*. Unlike Loh's approach, that focused on the efforts of the producers and creators of musical works, Lim's approach weighs heavily on the interplay of sociocultural

Table 19.3. Clarification on the four stages of development of contextualized compositions

Stage	Process of contextualization	Distinctive features
1	Imitation of Western gospel song styles	• Melodies and harmonies are in traditional Western gospel song style
2	Adaptation of native folk or traditional songs	• Adaptation of existing folk songs or traditional melodies for newly written Christian text • Use of traditional (19th century) Western harmony
3	Motivic development	• Adaptation of folk or native elements of motifs to develop new compositions • Use of a combination of Western and native styles of harmony
4	Innovative Asian styles	• Utilization of native elements or folk melodies with native or innovative harmonic treatment • Result being neither native nor Western but a combination of native, Asian, pan-Asian, and contemporary

contexts, the chronological relationship between past and present, and the hermeneutical process of theological reflection that gives rise to the need and desire for meaning and relevance in Christian musicmaking process for the crucial formation of Christian identity in any given society. According to Lim, 'the degree of hybridity in any contextualizing efforts is ultimately dependent on the parameters' (ibid. 217). He thus asserts that several models can be extrapolated from this approach.

Lim's approach sees the process of contextualization as consisting of three phases that are determined by the need for the Christian faith to relate meaningfully to the sociocultural context. Through the phases of emulation, juxtaposition, and innovation, Lim maintains a sense of progression that is the hallmark of Loh's paradigm. However, Lim's postulation does not see one phase as being less valued than the others. Rather, the stages are seen as equally valued, essential, a natural process of forming Christian identity through congregational song (see Table 19.4).

In this approach, Western hymnody is not seen as a precursor or as inferior to hymnody that draws its resources from in situ musical nuances. Rather, it is seen as a living entity that breathes and shapes congregations and is in turn shaped by the sociocultural context and theological consciousness of the congregation. In essence, hymnody takes on the spirit of *lex cantandi, lex credendi* (Yardley 2002).

In such a process of church music contextualization there will always be a season of imitating the predominant musical praxis. In most Asian countries, the immediate result would be the imitation of Western hymnody and its varied manifestations. Therefore rather than merely adopting Western hymnody or using translated Western hymns, churches would begin to create their own expressions in this same manner. For the most part, their preliminary efforts would be in character through strophic hymn or praise and worship songs. Congregations that

Table 19.4. Lim's proposed approach to the contextualization for church music

Phase of contextualization	Distinctive features
Emulation	• Imitation of styles that are acceptable to the community • Minimal regard for sociocultural context
Juxtaposition	• Creative efforts, performance practices, and receptivity reflect growing awareness of local milieu • Sociocultural consciousness dictates the need for meaning and relevance, which in turn gives rise to efforts of assimilation
Innovation	• The process of assimilation continues • Hybrid and heterogeneity expressions dominate as differentiation of intra-cultural exchanges becomes less significant

value their missional heritage would readily accept such efforts. When the local church gains confidence in itself and develops a sense of self-awareness in terms of cultural heritage and tradition, it would not be uncommon to witness a period of juxtaposition. This is the effort of balancing what has been received from the missionaries as an imparted 'gift of tradition' with the newfound sense of cultural identity that can be incorporated into Christian worship. With maturity and self-confidence, local churches would be willing to incorporate local cultural nuances and create innovative Christian worship and musical expressions that have much meaning for their congregations.

With this in mind, one can see that Asian hymnody is not static and will change through time. At present, even though Western and translated Western hymnody seems to dominate the Asian landscape, it is possible to catch a glimpse of the change that is coming even in a highly Westernized society such as Singapore. For instance, the few megachurches in Singapore, such as City Harvest Church, Lighthouse Evangelism Church, and Cornerstone Community Church, have members who are writing congregational songs that are used in their worship services. Even with brief acquaintance with these works, it is fairly obvious that they come under the 'emulation' category. On the other hand, there are also Singaporean works such as 'Still for Thy Loving Kindness', 'In Whom We Live', and 'Blest Be the Dear Uniting Love' clearly exhibiting innovative characteristics that are used by some Chinese-speaking Methodist churches (Chan 1997: 248 ff.). Therefore, if we see multi-ethnic, multi-cultural, multi-religious Singapore as a microcosmic reality of Asia, one can state with much confidence that contextual hymnody is alive and well in Asia. Such hymnody, however, may not necessarily be an adaptation of any in situ folk traditions but is ultimately innovative in nature, stemming from the desire to find meaningful expression for Christian worship in order to root Christian identity in a given sociocultural context.

Finally, it remains the task of the church to be mindful of its history, legacy, and cultural traditions. The Asian church in particular needs 'to look beyond its

western missiological heritage and to challenge itself in allowing the incarnational work of God to engage its cultural settings and transform its worship
expressions' (Lim 2006: 239). It bodes well for the Asian church to remember the
words of one of its own, well-known Methodist theologians D. T. Niles, when he
observed,

The Gospel is like a seed and you have to sow it. When you sow the seed of the Gospel in
Palestine, a plant that can be called Palestinian Christianity grows. When you sow it in
Rome, a plant of Roman Christianity grows. You sow the Gospel in Great Britain and you
get British Christianity. The seed of the Gospel is later brought to America and a plant
grows of American Christianity. Now when missionaries came to our lands they brought
not only the seed of the Gospel, but their own plant of Christianity, flower pot included! So,
what we have to do is to break the flower pot, take out the seed of the Gospel, sow it in our
own cultural soil, and let our own version of Christianity grow.

(Chandler 1997: 16; Hawn 2003: 32)

SUGGESTED READING

Hawn (2003).

Jenkins (2002).

Khmer hymnal. <http://gbgmumc.org/global_news/pr.cfm?articleid=453&CFID+46424438
&CFTOKEN=52993029>, accessed 20 August 2007.

Kimbrough, S. T., Jr. (1985). 'Hymns are Theology'. *Theology Today* 42.

—— (1994). 'Lyrical Theology'. *Journal of Theology* 98.

—— (2001). *Christian Hymn and Worship Book*. Phnom Penh: Cambodia Christian Methodist Association.

—— (2006a). 'Lyrical Theology: Theology in Hymns'. *Theology Today* 63.

—— (2006b). *Music and Mission: Toward a Theology and Practice of Global Song*. New York:
General Board of Global Ministries.

Kroeker, Charlotte (2005). *Music in Christian Worship*. Collegeville, Minn.: Liturgical
Press.

Lim, Swee Hong (1998). 'A Brief Survey of Asian Indigenous Hymnody'. In K. L. Forman
(ed.), *The New Century Hymnal Companion: A Guide to the Hymns*. Cleveland:
Pilgrim.

—— (2006).

Loh, I-to (ed.) (1989). *Rak Phra Jao, Rao Pen Thai* (The Love of God Sets Us Free). Manila:
Asian Institute for Liturgy and Music.

—— (2008).

Westerfield Tucker (1996).

Wicker, Vernon (ed.) (1991). *The Hymnology Annual*. Berrien Springs, Mich.: Vere.

Wren, Brian (2000). *Praying Twice: The Music and Words of Congregational Song*.
Louisville, Ky.: Westminster John Knox.

Yardley (2002).

REFERENCES

CHAN, HUNG DA, and GAN, MARY Y. T. (1997). *Hymns of United Worship*. Hong Kong: Chinese Christian Literature Council.

CHANDLER, PAUL-GORDON (1997). *God's Global Music: What We Can Learn From Christians Around the World*. Downers Grove, Ill.: InterVarsity Press.

HAWN, C. MICHAEL (2003). *Gather into One: Singing and Praying Globally*. Grand Rapids: Eerdmans.

HEUVEL, ALBERT VAN DEN (1966). *New Hymns for a New Day*. Geneva: World Council of Churches.

JENKINS, PHILIP (2002). *The Next Christendom: The Coming of Global Christianity*. New York: Oxford University Press.

LIM, SWEE HONG (2006). 'Giving Voice to Asian Christians: Assessing the Pioneering Work of I-to Loh in the Area of Congregational Song'. Ph.D. dissertation, Drew University.

LOH, I-TO (ed.) (1988). *Kristus Sundaring Bali* (Christ is the Light to Bali). Manila: Asian Institute for Liturgy and Music.

—— (1990). 'Toward Contextualization of Church Music in Asia'. *Asian Journal of Theology* 4.

—— (2005). 'Revisiting Ways of Contextualization of Church Music in Asia'. In Theology and the Church 30, *Theological Journal of Tainan Theological College and Seminary*.

—— (forthcoming). *Sound the Bamboo: Asian Hymns in Their Cultural and Liturgical Contexts*. Grand Rapids: Eerdmans.

NILES, DANIEL T. (ed.) (1963). *E. A. C. C. Hymnal*. Tokyo: East Asian Christian Conference.

TAM, ANGELA (ed.) (2005). *Hymns of Universal Praise. New Revised Edition*. Hong Kong: Chinese Christian Literature Council.

WESTERFIELD TUCKER, KAREN B. (ed.) (1996). *The Sunday Service of the Methodists: Twentieth-Century Worship in World-Wide Methodism*. Nashville: Abingdon.

—— (2001). *American Methodist Worship*. Oxford: Oxford University Press.

YARDLEY, ANNE B. (2002). 'Lex Cantandi, Lex Credendi: The Theology of Music in Methodist Worship'. Paper, North America Academy of Liturgy.

YOUNG, CARLTON R. (1964). *The Book of Hymns: Official Hymnal of the United Methodist Church*. Nashville: United Methodist Publishing House.

—— (ed.) (1989). *United Methodist Hymnal*. Nashville: United Methodist Publishing House.

CHAPTER 20

THE SACRAMENTS

GEOFFREY WAINWRIGHT

THE SOTERIOLOGICAL AND ECCLESIOLOGICAL SCOPE

As a priest of the Church of England, John Wesley was canonically committed to the definition of the sacraments in the Articles of Religion and printed with the 1662 Book of Common Prayer. Article XXV, 'Of the Sacraments', reads:

Sacraments ordained of Christ be not only badges or tokens of Christian men's profession, but rather they be certain sure witnesses, and effectual signs of grace, and God's good will towards us, by the which he doth work invisibly in us, and doth not only quicken, but also strengthen and confirm our Faith in him.

There are two Sacraments ordained of Christ our Lord in the Gospel, that is to say, Baptism, and the Supper of the Lord.

Specifically, baptism (according to Article XXVII) is 'a sign of Regeneration or new Birth, whereby, as by an instrument, they that receive Baptism rightly are grafted into the Church: the promises of forgiveness of sin, and of our adoption to be sons of God by the Holy Ghost, are visibly signed and sealed'; and the Lord's Supper (according to Article XXVIII) is 'not only a sign of the love that Christians ought to have among themselves one to another; but rather is a Sacrament of our Redemption by Christ's death: insomuch that to such as rightly, worthily, and with faith, receive the same, the Bread which we break is a partaking of the Body of Christ; and likewise the Cup of Blessing is a partaking of the Blood of Christ'. These same points are put in more pedagogical form in the Church of England's Catechism, which John Wesley often quoted (and notably in the sermon precisely on 'The Means of Grace') for its fundamental definition of a sacrament as 'an outward and visible sign of an inward and spiritual grace given unto us, ordained by Christ himself, as a means whereby we receive the same, and a pledge to assure us thereof'.

The Articles themselves bear marks of the initial controversies between Catholics and Reformers and of the continuing tensions within Protestantism. Among those who, in connection with the sacraments, retain both the primacy of grace and the need for responsible reception, debates surround—from the divine side—the nuances of 'sign', 'instrument', 'means', 'pledge'; and the requirements on the human side are spelled out thus in the Catechism:

Q. What is required of persons to be baptized?
A. Repentance, whereby they forsake sin: and Faith, whereby they stedfastly believe the promises of God made to them in that Sacrament.
Q. Why then are Infants baptized, when by reason of their tender age they cannot perform them?
A. Because they promise them both by their Sureties; which promise, when they come of age, themselves are bound to perform.
Q. What is required of them who come to the Lord's Supper?
A. To examine themselves, whether they repent them truly of their former sins, stedfastly purposing to lead a new life; have a lively faith in God's mercy through Christ, with a thankful remembrance of his death; and be in charity with all men.

The thrust of these Articles and the Catechism is *soteriological*, concerning the conveyance and acceptance of salvation; and, precisely for that reason, they carry *ecclesiological* implications, concerning the nature, function, and location of the church. The ways in which the sacramental principles are interpreted and practised will be influenced by ecclesial circumstances and will in turn contribute to the shaping of the doctrine and life of the church. To gain a historical, systematic, and prospective picture of the sacraments in Methodism, we shall need to look successively—and perhaps kaleidoscopically—at three stages in the story: (1) the origins of Methodism in eighteenth-century Anglicanism; (2) the subsequent autonomous existence of Methodism as a 'denomination' (or family of denominations) claiming a part and place in 'the Church Universal as the Body of Christ'; (3) the ecumenical commitment of Methodism to the cause of Christian unity.

In the nature of the ecclesial case, our exposition of the sacraments in Methodism will bear a problematic cast; but we shall also try to highlight those features that carry promise for the recovery of Christian unity. Our 'third phase', in fact, will extend to the turn into the twenty-first century, where we shall look for the sacramental results of Methodist participation in the twentieth-century liturgical movement across the churches as well as in ecumenical dialogues with their attention to baptism and eucharist. As with every church, it will be important—though always difficult—to distinguish in 'real-existing Methodism' between official doctrine, theological opinions, pastoral practice, and popular perceptions. And in the interplay between the *lex orandi* and the *lex credendi* it must be remembered that, in Methodism, official service books are typically 'authorized', though not 'mandated'.

WESLEYAN METHODISM

John Wesley was convinced that God had raised up Methodism in order to 'spread scriptural holiness'—not only 'over the land' (of England) or over the continent (of North America) but over the face of the earth (as we discover in his sermon on 'The General Spread of the Gospel'), including countries that were nominally Christian (whether Protestant, Catholic, or Orthodox) as well as parts of the world that were historically unevangelized. Crucial to the preacher's project was to mediate the *assurance* of faith (in God's work of justification for the forgiveness of sins) and the *experience* of 'new birth' (as God's initial work of sanctification for the start of growth in holiness). Thereby the question of baptism—as traditionally the sacrament of entry into the Christian life and into the church—was inevitably brought into play. Not far behind came the Lord's Supper, and the question of what, by its nature and institution, were its proper functions in relation to the various stages in the Christian life and to membership in the Body of Christ.

John Wesley's most formal teaching on baptism occurs in the abridged version of his father Samuel's 'Short Discourse of Baptism' (1700) that he published in a section of his own *Preservative against Unsettled Notions in Religion* (1758). Rather naughtily, one might wonder whether those 'unsettled notions' might have been due, at least in part, to what Wesley himself had been preaching since the early 1740s concerning 'the new birth', for which we have evidence in the published sermons: 'The Marks of the New Birth', on John 3: 8 (1748), 'The Great Privilege of those that are Born of God', on 1 John 3: 9 (1748), and 'The New Birth', on John 3: 7 (1760). If part of the divine design was 'to reform the nation, particularly the Church', then Wesley's preachers had to confront not only the dissolute among those who had received baptism at the hands of the established church but even those who displayed the 'form of godliness', but not its 'power'. The scriptural 'marks' of being 'born of God' are, first, a 'true, living, Christian *faith*' (or, quoting the words of the Anglican Homily 'Of Salvation', a believer's 'sure trust and confidence in God that through the merits of Christ his sins are forgiven, and he reconciled to the favour of God'), and (Wesley himself goes on) its 'immediate and constant fruit' of 'power over sin' (which Wesley will affirm as 'the *great* privilege' in the following sermon), and a 'peace which all the powers of earth and hell are unable to take from' the believer. The second 'mark' is 'so to *hope* in God through the Son of his love as to have not only the "testimony of a good conscience," but also "the Spirit of God bearing witness with your spirits that ye are children of God"'. And the third 'mark' is 'so to *love* God, who hath thus loved you . . . that ye are constrained to love all men as yourselves, with a love not only ever burning in your hearts, but flaming out in all your actions and conversations, and making your whole life one "labour of love"'. Now Wesley had begun his sermon on the 'marks' by asserting that 'these privileges, by the free mercy of God, are ordinarily annexed to baptism (which is thence termed by our Lord . . . the being "born of water and the Spirit")'. Then the homiletical crunch comes only after the 'marks' have been listed:

Lean no more on the staff of that broken reed, that ye *were* born again in baptism. Who denies that ye *were* born again in baptism? Who denies that ye were then made 'children of God, heirs of the kingdom of heaven' [quoting again from the Anglican Homily 'Of Salvation']? But notwithstanding this, ye are now children of the devil; therefore ye must be born again. . . . Ye have heard what are the marks of the children of God; all ye who have them not on your souls, baptized or unbaptized, must needs receive them, or without doubt ye will perish everlastingly. And if you have been baptized, your only hope is this: that those who were made the children of God by baptism, but are now the children of the devil, may yet again receive 'power to become the sons of God'; that they may receive again what they have lost, even the 'Spirit of adoption, crying in their hearts, Abba, Father!'

Albert Outler (1964: 318) judged that the 'obvious purpose' of John's publishing the 'extract' from Samuel's treatise was 'to re-enforce the wavering convictions of some of the Methodist people as to the validity of infant baptism and to re-emphasize the objectivity of divine grace in this sacrament'. After naming 'an episcopal administrator' as 'essential to Christian baptism' (a sideswipe at 'the Anabaptists') and allowing for any of the three modes—'washing', 'dipping', 'sprinkling'—for baptism 'in the Name of the Father, Son and Holy Ghost', Wesley *père et fils* set out the 'benefits' of this 'initiatory sacrament' that Christ 'designed to remain always in his Church' as 'a sign, seal, pledge and means of grace, perpetually obligatory on all Christians'. It is a 'free gift' for 'washing away the guilt of original sin by the application of the merits of Christ's death', and 'the ordinary instrument of our justification'. The 'regeneration which our Church in so many places ascribes to baptism is more than barely being admitted into the Church' (although it is certainly that, since the baptized are 'made members of Christ its Head'), for 'in consequence of our being made [thereby] children of God, we are heirs of the kingdom of heaven'. All this is ascribed not 'to the *outward* washing, but to the *inward grace* which, added thereto, makes it a sacrament': 'Herein a principle of grace is infused which will not be wholly taken away unless we quench the Holy Spirit of God by long-continued wickedness. . . . *Baptism doth save us now* if we live answerable thereto—if we repent, believe, and obey the gospel—supposing this, as it admits us into the Church here, so into glory hereafter.'

Then comes 'the grand question': 'Who are the proper subjects of baptism? Grown persons only, or infants only?' In that they die, infants prove themselves to belong to 'the whole race of mankind' that is liable 'both to the guilt and punishment of Adam's transgression'. That provides the first of 'the grounds of infant baptism', which are to be 'taken from Scripture, reason and primitive universal practice': '*Infants* need to be washed from original sin; therefore they are proper subjects of baptism.' The second ground resides in the nature of a covenant. Already 'the custom of nations and common reason prove that infants may enter into a covenant and may be obliged by compacts made by others in their name and receive advantage by them'. That was the case with the children of Abraham, who were admitted to the covenant of promise by the sign of circumcision. Although the sign has changed, the infants of Christian believers remain 'under the evangelical covenant. Therefore, they have a right to baptism, which is now the entering seal thereof.' Third, infants can 'come to Christ' (Matthew 14: 13–14), at least by being 'brought' (Luke 18: 5). Fourth, apostolic precedent is claimed for the inclusion of 'whole families', including infants, in fulfilment of the command to 'disciple' by way of baptism. Lastly, it is 'in conformity to the uninterrupted practice of the whole Church of Christ from the earliest ages, to consecrate our children to God by baptism' (at least such was 'never opposed till the last century but one by some not very holy men in Germany'!).

In the 'New Birth' sermon of 1760, Wesley returns to the question of baptism. He declares quite bluntly:

Baptism is not the new birth: they are not one and the same thing. . . . For what can be more plain than that the one is an external, the other an internal work? That the one is a visible, the other an invisible thing, and therefore wholly different from each other; the one being an act of man, purifying the body, the other a change wrought by God in the soul. So that the former is just as distinguishable from the latter as the soul from the body, or water from the Holy Ghost.

In making such radically sharp distinctions, Wesley gave hostages to fortune among sacramentally disinclined Methodists, who like to quote only the distinctions, not the positive relation between the outward and the inward. The point about a sacrament is precisely that it is *ordinarily* the *means* for conveying and accepting the promised grace. In the treatise on baptism, Wesley had, of course, affirmed the traditional principle that God himself 'is not bound by his sacraments' (in the sense that his action is not limited to them: 'where [baptism] cannot be had, the case is different, but extraordinary cases do not make void a standing rule'); but when they are performed and received in accordance with Christ's institution, their effect is sure. In 'New Birth', however, he noticeably omits from his quotation of 'the Church Catechism' the phrase about a sacrament as a 'means' of receiving grace. Wesley indeed allows that 'our Church supposes that all who are baptized in their infancy are at the same time born again. . . . Nor is it an objection of any weight against this that we cannot comprehend how this work can be wrought in infants: for neither can we comprehend *how* it is wrought in a person of riper years.'

Wesley's argument is rather that 'it is sure that all of riper years who are baptized are not at the same time born again'. Wesley puts the matter in terms of 'fruits': 'Divers of those who were children of the devil before they were baptized continue the same after baptism...without any pretence either to inward or outward holiness.' The omission of regenerative efficacy from the order of infant baptism in (some printings of) *The Sunday Service* that John Wesley first sent to the Methodists in the newly independent United States in 1784 may not be Wesley's own doing, but it is noteworthy that in the accompanying abridged version of the Articles of Religion, 'Of Baptism' (now XVII) is much abbreviated, and while the sacrament is still 'a sign of regeneration, or the new birth', the language of 'instrument' is dropped.

A hint towards Wesley's conception of the proper relation between the sacramental and the experiential/ethical may perhaps be found in what he published in 1780—with deep indebtedness to English Puritan traditions of the seventeenth century—as *Directions for Renewing Our Covenant with God*. The initial entrance into the covenant occurs 'visibly' in baptism through the receiving of 'the seal'. To that then corresponds an inward 'engagement' or 'closure' that can be expressed in word and gesture by a 'solemn vow or promise' that is 'aptly accommodated to all the substantials of our baptismal covenant'. On God's side, the covenant 'stands firm'. On the human side, the covenant can be renewed as needed, and Wesley provided regular occasions for such renewals within the gatherings of the Methodist societies, often with a link to the holy communion (Tripp 1969).

For the other dominical sacrament, the principal Wesleyan teaching comes in *Hymns on the Lord's Supper*, a collection of 166 texts published in 1745 under the joint names of John and Charles. Written both for instructional and meditational purposes, they were also sung during the distribution of communion in the large gatherings that characterized the Methodist revival. Their principal literary inspiration was a treatise by the Anglican Dean Daniel Brevint (1616–95), *On the Christian Sacrament and Sacrifice* (1673), which was 'extracted' in order to form a preface to the *Hymns*. Adapting somewhat Brevint's structure, the Wesleys maintained the threefold temporal reference of the Supper to the past (hymns 1–27: 'A Memorial of the Sufferings and Death of Christ'), the present (hymns 28–92: 'A Sign and a Means of Grace'), and the future (hymns 93–115: 'A Pledge of Heaven'), and thus matched the teaching of St Thomas Aquinas, in the *Summa Theologiae* III q. 60 a. 3, of the eucharist as a *signum rememorativum*, a *signum demonstrativum*, and a *signum prognosticum*, which is more picturesquely put in an antiphon for the medieval western feast of Corpus Christi: 'O sacred banquet, in which Christ is received, the memory of his passion celebrated, the heart filled with grace, and the pledge of future glory given us.' Against perceived Roman Catholic teaching, the Wesleyan hymns reject the notion of a 'local Deity' (63) and, while invoking the Holy Spirit (16; 72), refuse to speculate on '*how* the means transmit the power' (57–9). The all-sufficiency of the one sacrifice on Calvary is constantly affirmed, even while the church's rite 'shows' it to the Father as Christ himself now pleads it in heaven (116–27); by faith, our offering of praise and thanksgiving and our self-oblation are responsively 'joined' to Christ's own sacrifice, who 'bears' us into the Father's presence (128–57). Contained within the *Hymns*, too, is anti-Calvinist sentiment against a limited atonement and any depreciation of the earthly ritual action.

These last matters form part of the background to another controversial question in the Wesleyan revival: the gift and appropriation of justification, and here the sacramental focus is, perhaps surprisingly, not baptism as was the case with regeneration, but rather the Lord's Supper, and who may and should partake of it; and the occasion was the dispute with Moravian quietism in the early 1740s. Whereas the Moravians held that earnest seekers should abstain from all the 'means of grace' until God had favoured them out of the blue, Wesley held that those with some degree of repentance and faith should partake of the Lord's Supper. When, in the *Journal* for 27–8 June 1740, Wesley affirms that 'the Lord's Supper was ordained by God to be a means of conveying to men either preventing, or justifying, or sanctifying grace, according to their several necessities', the triple formula is explicated by the ensuing declaration that 'the persons for whom it was ordained are all those who know and feel that they want the grace of God, either to restrain them from sin, or to show their sins forgiven, or to renew their souls in the image of God'. *All* that is required—but it *is* required—is 'a sense of our state, of our utter sinfulness and helplessness' and 'a desire to receive whatsoever [God] pleases to give'. Once the beginnings of conviction are there (which, for Wesley, includes 'a willingness to know and do the whole will of God', an 'earnest desire for universal holiness', as he states in the letter of 17 June 1746 to Thomas Church entitled 'The Principles of a Methodist Farther Explained'), it is appropriate for a person to come expectantly to the Lord's Table. When, in the anti-Moravian sermon on 'The Means of Grace' (1746), Wesley encourages 'unbelievers' (a designation he uses for the original disciples before Pentecost) to receive communion, he has in mind people who do not yet have *full assurance* of faith. He recognized that there were 'degrees of faith' that might precede assurance. In a later letter, of 25 July 1755 to Richard Tompson, Wesley wrote that 'a man who is not assured that his sins are forgiven may yet have a kind or degree of faith, which distinguishes him not only from a devil but also from a heathen, and on which I may admit him to the Lord's Supper'.

The benefits of appropriate participation at the Lord's Table are detailed in Wesley's sermon 'The Duty of Constant Communion', written in 1732 (for his pupils at Oxford) and published in 1787 (perhaps because, as Outler (1964: 334) suggests, by then 'many Methodists were adopting the Puritan notions of infrequent celebration' and 'excuses for nonattendance at parish Communions were gaining the force of conscientious objection'). The benefits are 'the forgiveness of our past sins, the present strengthening and refreshing of our souls':

As our bodies are strengthened by bread and wine, so are our souls by these tokens of the body and blood of Christ. This is the food of our souls: this gives strength to perform our duty and leads us on to perfection. If, therefore, we have any regard for the plain command of Christ, if we desire the pardon of our sins, if we wish for strength to believe, to love and obey God, then we should neglect no opportunity of receiving the Lord's Supper.

Not just 'frequent', but 'constant' communion matches this 'command of God' and 'mercy to man'. To plead that one is 'unworthy' is to compound one's disobedience. To the objection that constant communion 'abates our reverence for the sacrament', Wesley retorts that the 'true religious reverence' shown in obeying the Lord's command will rather be confirmed and increased. To any who claim they have 'not found the benefit' they expected from communion, Wesley replies that they will 'find benefit sooner or later, perhaps insensibly'.

When, in September 1784, Wesley appointed Coke, Whatcoat, and Vasey to the newly independent United States, a main reason was avowedly to provide for the Lord's Supper. In his letter to 'Our Brethren in America', he 'advise[d] the elders to administer the Supper of the Lord on every Lord's Day'. The Article 'Of the Lord's Supper' (now XVIII) is retained in its entirety in *The Sunday Service* and remained so in the Methodist Episcopal Church's *Discipline* of 1808, when the first Restrictive Rule took effect.

DENOMINATIONAL METHODISM

In point of fact, the eucharistic thrust of Wesleyan Methodism was largely lost, on both sides of the Atlantic, in the denominational Methodism of the nineteenth century. In the United States this may be attributed in part to the shortage of ordained elders, particularly in 'frontier' conditions. In England, the desire of Methodists to have the sacrament administered by their own preachers was a major factor in the separation with the established church; but the subsequent decline in observance may in fact precisely reflect the fact that 'frequent' (let us not say 'constant') communion had never really caught on in the great majority of parish churches in the eighteenth century; and when the Oxford Movement started to become influential in the 1830s and 1840s, the resultant 'Anglo-Catholicism' raised fears of a Romeward drift, and Methodism aligned itself more and more with the 'free churches' as the century went on.

Karen Westerfield Tucker (2001: 155) summarizes the American history thus:

Methodism arguably became a separate denomination in response to the strong desire of the Methodist societies to receive the sacraments. Yet within a century, the Lord's Supper was largely perceived as a respected but occasional interruption to the Sunday morning preaching service. Ironically, while Methodists were beginning to understand themselves more confidently as church rather than as religious society, enthusiasm for both administration and reception generally waned. Each *Discipline* continued to describe the Eucharist in sacramental terms as a divinely initiated and effective means of grace, and as an instrument for the upbuilding of the community of saints. With some exceptions, the contents of the approved Lord's Supper rite remained relatively close to Wesley's original. But the prevailing Enlightenment rationality that permeated society and church—when added to Methodism's evangelical accent on inward holiness and the validity of individual experience—encouraged the reasonable explanation that the Supper was a simple memorial meal observed in obedience to Christ's command whereby each person (perhaps fearfully) confronted God and was inspired for moral living. Emphasis upon the welfare and faith of the individual and a diminished sense of the faith of the community was reinforced by the decline in references to the body of Christ in liturgical texts.

Among nineteenth-century theologians, honourable exceptions are to be found in Samuel Luckey's *The Lord's Supper* (1859) and Thomas O. Summers's *Systematic Theology* (posthumously, 1888); and, in England, William Burt Pope's *Compendium of Christian Theology* (2nd edn. 1880; esp. iii. 299–334). The theological and practical situation hardly improved in the first half of the twentieth century. Whereas selections from the *Hymns on the Lord's Supper* (*HLS*) had been included in official American Methodist hymnals throughout the previous century (and continued to be so in Britain), the 1905 joint *Hymnal* of the Methodist Episcopal Church and the Methodist Episcopal Church (South) hid just two in other sections of the book, and the 1935 *Hymnal* took away even what its immediate predecessor had left. The 1966 *Hymnal* of the Methodist Church climbed from zero to four (*HLS* 40, 57, 96, 165), but the 1989 *Hymnal* of the United Methodist Church sank back to two (*HLS* 29, 57). Meanwhile, the beginnings of revival in eucharistic interest can be detected in the creation of the Methodist Sacramental Fellowship in Britain (1935) and the Brotherhood of St Luke in the United States (1946; Order, from 1948). These precursors belong, in fact, to our next phase: Ecumenical Methodism.

ECUMENICAL METHODISM

Methodist scholars—notably James F. White in North America and A. Raymond George in Great Britain—were among the leaders in the 'liturgical movement' that swept through much of Western Christendom, both Catholic and Protestant, in the second half of the twentieth century. The main documentary evidence is found in two rounds of revised or entirely new service books.

As to the eucharist, the British *Methodist Service Book* of 1975 declared, as the first general direction under 'The Sunday Service', that 'the worship of the Church is the offering of praise and prayer in which God's Word is read and preached, and in its fullness it includes the Lord's Supper, or Holy Communion'. The first order for the Lord's Supper is retained from the 1936 *Book of Offices* (which was basically that of the Book of Common Prayer of 1662), for 'where people are attached to the older forms, they should not be deprived of them'. However, the new book offers in first place a new order for the full service, where the ritual restructuring is more important than shifts in style and vocabulary: the 'Ministry of the Word' includes Old Testament Lesson, Epistle, and Gospel, the Sermon, and Intercessions; 'The Lord's Supper' includes the Peace, the Nicene Creed, the Setting of the Table, the Thanksgiving, the Breaking of the Bread, the Sharing of the Bread and Wine. Clearly, the intention was to reach back behind the Reformation and the Middle Ages to the Patristic Period and 'the undivided Church'. The most important feature of all was the recovery of the Great Thanksgiving or Eucharistic Prayer—past, present and future in reference—with its rehearsal of God's work in creation and redemption, the *anamnesis* of Christ's death and resurrection, the *epiclesis* of the Holy Spirit (that 'we who receive your gifts of bread and wine may share in the body and blood of Christ'), the offering of 'our sacrifice of praise and thanksgiving' and of 'ourselves to be a living sacrifice', and prayer to 'bring us with the whole creation to your heavenly kingdom' (the holy communion being 'a foretaste of the heavenly banquet prepared for all mankind'). The basic pattern was retained in the *Methodist Worship Book* of 1999, with several seasonal variants in theme for the entire eucharist.

A similar trajectory was followed in the United Methodist Church. The 1972 'alternate text' for the Lord's Supper followed 'liturgical movement' lines; and a pattern of 'Word and Table' became established through the 1970s and 1980s until its incorporation in *The United Methodist Hymnal* (1989) and *The United Methodist Book of Worship* (1992). Again, the latter half of the Great Thanksgiving—picking up from the recital of the institution by Christ at the Last Supper—is particularly important for eucharistic theology, and its formulation—in Wesleyan mode—of the joining of our sacrifice and Christ's is (as we shall see) of ecumenical significance:

> And so,
> in remembrance of these your mighty acts in Jesus Christ,
> we offer ourselves in praise and thanksgiving
> as a holy and living sacrifice,
> in union with Christ's offering for us,
> as we proclaim the mystery of faith:
> *Christ has died; Christ is risen; Christ will come again.*

Proceeding interactively with liturgical revision was the doctrinal convergence among the churches that was registered in *Baptism, Eucharist and Ministry* (*BEM*), a text finalized by the WCC Faith and Order Commission at Lima, Peru, in 1982. Of the official responses made by almost 200 member churches, that of the council of bishops of the United Methodist Church (Thurian 1986: 177–99) was among the most thorough and most positive, particularly with regard to 'Eucharist'. In the eucharist, the bishops declared, 'God's effectual word is revealed, proclaimed, heard, seen, and tasted'. With gratitude to 'concentrated liturgical scholarship and ecumenical dialogue', the response endorses 'E' in these terms:

In terms of the congregation's appropriation of the reality of Christ's presence, the *anamnesis* (memorial, remembrance, representation) means that past, present and future coincide in the sacramental event. All that Jesus Christ means in his person and redemptive work is brought forth from history to our present experience, which is also a foretaste of the future fulfilment of God's unobstructed reign. And this presence is made to be a reality for us by the working of God's Spirit, whom we 'call down' (*epiklesis*) by invocation, both upon the gifts and upon the people. All this we find explicitly taught by John and Charles Wesley, who knew and respected the apostolic, patristic and reformed faith of the Church.

The bishops undertook to 'urge our congregations to a more frequent, regular observance of the sacrament'. Much remains to be done in the areas of instruction and practice, however. A four-year church-wide study produced the report *This Holy Mystery: A United Methodist Understanding of Holy Communion*, which was 'approved' overwhelmingly by the General Conference of the UMC in 2004. The document speaks even-handedly of 'a strong sense of the importance of Holy Communion in the life of individual Christians and of the church' and 'at least an equally strong sense of the absence of any meaningful understanding of Eucharistic theology and practice'. The UMC report aims at the 'better education of pastors in sacramental theology and practice' and a greater discipline in the 'accountability' of ministers to bishops, superintendents, and conferences; it provides guidance in the 'principles' and 'practices' of celebration; and a study edition has been assembled by Gayle Carlton Felton and published by the UMC's 'Discipleship Resources' (2005).

The British Methodist Church was distinctly cooler in its response to *BEM* (Thurian 1986: 210–29). It noted that 'the history and structure of Methodism make weekly celebrations in all our churches all but impossible'; consequently, Methodists have learned to nourish themselves on preaching services without communion, and 'many would not now wish to see the balance altered in favour of more frequent communion. They would argue that it is not now a matter of administrative necessity, but rather that the infrequency of celebration actually heightens the sense of the eucharist's importance.' Nevertheless, Methodism had made 'great gains in both experience and understanding of the holy communion in the last two or three decades' and had been 'glad to be involved' in the 'liturgical reform [that had] been the most striking example of convergence between the churches'. By the time of a denomination-wide study in 2003, the British reported that a 2001 survey of around 10 per cent of people worshipping in Methodist churches in England on the day of the national census 'revealed, perhaps surprisingly, that Holy Communion was valued more highly than preaching'; nevertheless, 'within our church there is a wide diversity of practice and a whole range of ways in which Holy Communion is valued'. The 2003 study itself—*His Presence Makes the Feast: Holy Communion in the Methodist Church*—was intended as a 'tool for learning'. It showed Methodist theologians to have profited from twentieth-century work in liturgics and sacramentology regarding 'performative words', 'sign-acts', 'dynamic gestures', the 'communicative' character of 'physical realities' and thus the roles of both word and sacrament in forming the ecclesial body of Christ (*His Presence* 137–46; cf. 9, 123–4). Interestingly, the British attitude towards *BEM* seems to have mellowed. In a relatively lengthy exposition of 'nine key themes in the theology of Holy Communion, drawn from the Bible and Christian Tradition', *His Presence Makes the Feast* includes (though in a different sequence) all those found in the central section of *BEM* on 'The Meaning of the Eucharist', and adds to each heading a phrase from the Scriptures or Methodist liturgical texts:

> Thanksgiving (Eucharist): 'He gave thanks'
> Life in Unity (Koinonia): 'We are one body'
> Remembering (Anamnesis): 'Do this in remembrance of me'
> Sacrifice: 'For you'
> Presence: 'His presence makes the feast'
> The Work of the Spirit (Epiclesis): 'Pour out your Spirit'
> Anticipation (Eschatology): 'A foretaste of the heavenly banquet'
> Mission and Justice: 'To live and work to God's praise and glory'
> Personal Devotion: 'Bread to pilgrims given'.

An attractively illustrated booklet published in 2006—with an endorsement by the Archbishop of Canterbury—testifies to the hope of the British Conference that these themes and this pattern will make their way more deeply and more widely in popular Methodist awareness: *Share This Feast: Reflecting on Holy Communion*.

Helped greatly by J. Ernest Rattenbury's *The Eucharistic Hymns of John and Charles Wesley* (1948), the second half of the twentieth century saw revivals of interest in the *Hymns on the Lord's Supper* at least *as texts* (the extent of their actual use in the Methodist *lex orandi* remains an open question in *His Presence Makes the Feast* and in *This Holy Mystery*). This occurred as part of a modest recovery in Wesleyan roots but also under ecumenical interests. The first report from the dialogue between the World Methodist Council and the Roman Catholic Church ('Denver 1971') noted that the Wesleyan hymns found 'echoes and recognition' among Catholics: they were seen as 'giving a basis and hope for discussion of doctrinal differences about the nature of the real presence and the sense of the sacrificial character of the Eucharist' (9). The passage quoted above from the Great Thanksgiving comes close to what the Catholic Church desired in its response to *BEM*: 'The description of the Church's activity in the Eucharist as thanksgiving and intercession needs to be filled out by some reference to the self-offering of the participants of the Eucharist, made in union with the eternal "self-offering" of Christ.' While most Methodist responses were content to endorse *BEM's* general affirmation that 'the Church confesses Christ's real, living and active presence in the eucharist', they were wary about calling the mode of Christ's eucharistic presence 'unique'. The Roman teaching of 'transubstantiation' remains a bugbear, harking back to Anglican Article XXVIII (Methodist XVIII) which rejects it as 'overthrowing the nature of a sacrament'; but there may be hope in a mutual approach to such points of difference in light of 'our best ecumenical insights and judgment', such as Albert Outler secured for the United Methodist attitude to the 'anti-Roman' Articles through a 'resolution of intent' at the General Conference of 1970. Clearly, a considerable measure of doctrinal agreement will be necessary to the attainment of the goal of 'full communion in faith, mission and sacramental life' set by the dialogue between the World Methodist Council and the Roman Catholic Church.

Existing ecclesial bodies continue to differ as to whether 'eucharistic communion' may properly be practised between them at some stage on the way to full unity or comes only as the seal of such unity. But it ought surely to be agreed—as Pope John Paul II forcefully declared in his encyclical of 2003, *Ecclesia de Eucharistia vivit*—that important questions of doctrine need to be settled before it can be affirmed that different churches are engaging *in the same event* when they respectively 'celebrate the eucharist'.

In the area of baptism, tensions remain within Methodism. In the 1960s, Methodists on both sides of the Atlantic started to use the name 'confirmation' for what was, in effect, the successor to 'admission into (full) membership' dating from Methodism's 'societary' origins but now seen as relating to the church universal. Baptism continued, as always, to be by intention a sacrament of the church universal.

From the 1960s and on through the 1990s the United Methodist Church moved towards a reinvigoration of baptism. The report *By Water and the Spirit*, adopted by the General Conference in 1996, set the historical context for the sacrament's decline thus:

On the American frontier where human ability and action were stressed, the revivalistic call for individual decision-making, though important, was subject to exaggeration. . . . Later toward the end of the nineteenth century, the theological views of much of Methodism were influenced by a new set of ideas which had become dominant in American culture. These ideas included optimism about the progressive improvement of humankind and confidence in the social benefits of scientific discovery, technology and education. Assumptions of original sin gave way before the assertion that human nature was essentially unspoiled. In this intellectual milieu, the old evangelical insistence upon conversion and spiritual rebirth seemed quaint and unnecessary.

Needed now—in a benevolent interpretation of the baptismal teaching of Methodism's principal founder—was a restoration of 'the Wesleyan blend of sacramental and evangelical aspects', 'the creative Wesleyan synthesis of sacramentalism and evangelicalism'. The report of 1996 then expounds 'the baptismal covenant' in terms of the services in *The United Methodist Hymnal* (1989; repeated in *The United Methodist Book of Worship* of 1992):

In baptism the Church declares that it is bound in covenant to God; through baptism new persons are initiated into that covenant. The covenant connects God, the community of faith, and the person being baptized; all three are essential to the fulfillment of the baptismal covenant. The faithful grace of God initiates the covenant relationship and enables the community and the person to respond with faith.

The report places the efforts of United Methodism within the 'ecumenical convergence' that seeks to 'reach the core of the meaning and practice of baptism' by a journey 'back through the life of the Church to the Apostolic Age'. Where *BEM* declared that 'baptism is both God's gift and our human response to that gift' (B 8), the United Methodist study declares that 'faith is both a gift of God and a human response to God'; and it may be remembered that for St Augustine, baptism was precisely the *sacramentum fidei*. *BEM* also saw baptism as 'related not only to momentary experience, but to life-long growth into Christ' (B 9), and the United Methodists claim for Wesley the view that 'baptism ... was a part of the lifelong process of salvation'.

In the British *Methodist Worship Book* of 1999, a strong emphasis is placed upon the prevenience of God's comprehensive love (or, in traditional Wesleyan–Arminian terms, the universal sufficiency of Christ's redemptive work and a restoration of human freedom adequate for response to the preaching of the gospel):

Baptism shows the love of God for all people, displayed supremely in the self-giving of Jesus Christ, and demonstrates all that Christ has won for us through his death and resurrection. Baptism makes plain that, before and without any response on our part, Christ died for us. ... Water, the central symbol of Baptism, speaks to us ... of being washed clean and of making a new beginning. God's offer of new life in Christ invites us to respond, challenges us to discipleship and calls us to the life of faith in the Church and in the world. Such discipleship is possible only with the help of God's Holy Spirit.

Baptism is presented as 'a rite of initiation, the ritual beginning of a journey of faith'. Confirmation 'marks a significant point along the journey of faith which starts with Baptism':

Confirmation reminds us that we are baptized and that God continues to be at work in our lives: we respond by affirming that we belong to Christ and to the whole people of God. At a Service of Confirmation, baptized Christians are also received into membership of the Methodist Church and take their place as such in a local congregation.

It must be hoped that the rather 'declaratory' tone of these expositions carries with it an intention also to 'effect'. As to the baptism of young children as yet 'not able to answer for themselves', the promises called for from the parents or godparents to raise the children in the Christian faith are now located only after the baptism, whereas in the 1975 *Methodist Service Book* they figured before the water act on the grounds that the sacrament was administered to infants on the parents' 'promise so to do'.

On the ecumenical front, a paradox exists when, in a state of division among Christians and their communities, the reception of baptism (and confirmation) in a particular ecclesial community—claiming to be (part of) the One Church of Christ—*excludes* one from participation in any or all activities of another ecclesial community. Progress towards the overcoming of that paradox has been made by moves in favour of the mutual recognition of baptism. Where happily achieved, such mutual recognitions of baptism do not yet settle the unavoidable question of ecclesiology: what is the church, what is the church for, and where is the church concretely to be found? What, ecumenically, are the necessary and sufficient conditions of its unity? What is the proper form of that unity? A 'study report' of 2004/5 from the Joint Working Group (JWG) between the Roman Catholic Church and the World Council of Churches is entitled 'Ecclesiological and Ecumenical Implications of a Common Baptism'. Especially in connection with divergences over infant baptism—but the areas of dispute are wider—the report recognizes among the issues needing resolution 'the questions of the nature and purposes of the Church and its role in the economy of salvation' (para. 57); and notes soberly that 'the mutual recognition of baptism implies an acknowledgment of each other's baptism, but in itself is only a step toward full recognition of the apostolicity of the church involved' (para. 98). The question must be put in any constellation of presently divided 'churches' among which mutual recognition of baptism exists: what more do you require of the partners—and of yourself—before you can discern 'church'? Meanwhile, the JWG report offers a solemn admonition that Methodists—perhaps especially in the United States—need to hear:

Through the ecumenical movement, separated Christians have come to acknowledge a significant degree of *koinonia*. In light of this we ask churches not to allow practices to develop, which threaten the unity they now share in respect of the *ordo*, theology and administration of baptism. One example is the replacement of the traditional Trinitarian baptismal formula (Father, Son, Holy Spirit) with alternative wording. Another example is the admission of persons to the eucharist before baptism.   (109)

Programmatic admission of the unbaptized to the Lord's table in fact downplays the ecclesiological significance of both sacraments. The practice of an 'open table' in American Methodism—not in an ecumenical but in a putatively evangelistic sense—dates from the late nineteenth century and may not be unconnected with 'the ideals of democracy' and 'concerns about psychological damage rendered to people by their exclusion from the table' (Westerfield Tucker 2001: 147). *The United Methodist Book of Worship* is inaccurate in declaring that 'we have no tradition of refusing any who present themselves desiring to receive': earlier Methodism had, in fact, a considerable discipline of communion (see the entire section on 'admission to the table', ibid. 143–8). The British Methodist Church is constitutionally committed to the sacraments of baptism and the Lord's Supper—in that order —as 'of divine appointment and of perpetual obligation'; and an ecumenically more responsible position than undisciplined access to the table is that currently stated in the British *Methodist Worship Book* (114):

One of the keynotes of the Methodist revival was John Wesley's emphasis on 'The Duty of Constant Communion' and it is still a duty and privilege of members of the Methodist Church to share in this sacrament. The Methodist Conference has encouraged local churches to admit baptized children to communion. Those who are communicants and belong to other Churches whose discipline so permits are also welcome as communicants in the Methodist Church.

Ecumenical dialogue entails, as Pope John Paul II recognized in his encyclical *Ut Unum Sint* (1995), not only 'an exchange of ideas' but also 'an exchange of gifts'; and this became a major theme in the Seoul Report of 2006 from the Joint Commission between the World Methodist Council and the Roman Catholic Church, *The Grace Given You in Christ: Catholics and Methodists Reflect Further on the Church*. As that dialogue has progressed, it has clearly become the most important venue for continuing work on the sacraments in both their soteriological and their ecclesiological dimensions.

SUGGESTED READING

BORGEN, OLE E. (1972). *John Wesley on the Sacraments*. Zurich: Publishing House of the United Methodist Church.

CHAPMAN, DAVID M. (2006). *Born in Song—Methodist Worship in Britain*. Warrington: Church in the Market Place Publications.

LOCK-NAH KHOO, LORNA (2005). *Wesleyan Eucharistic Spirituality—Its Nature, Sources, and Future*. Adelaide: ATF.

RATTENBURY, J. ERNEST (1948). *The Eucharistic Hymns of John and Charles Wesley*. London: Epworth.

SMYTH, C. RYDER (1927). *The Sacramental Society*. London: Epworth.

STEVICK, DANIEL B. (2004). *The Altar's Fire*. Peterborough: Epworth.

WAINWRIGHT, GEOFFREY (1995). 'Introduction'. In *Hymns on the Lord's Supper*. Madison, N.J.: Charles Wesley Society.

—— *Methodists in Dialogue*. Nashville: Abingdon/Kingswood.

WESTERFIELD TUCKER, KAREN B. (2001). *American Methodist Worship*. New York: Oxford University Press.

—— (ed.) (1996). *The Sunday Service of the Methodists—Twentieth-Century Worship in Worldwide Methodism*. Nashville: Kingswood, 305–22.

References

'Ecclesiological and Ecumenical Implications of a Common Baptism' (1999–2005). In *Joint Working Group between the Roman Catholic Church and the World Council of Churches: Eighth Report 1999–2005*. Geneva: WCC Publications; and in *Pontifical Council for Promoting Christian Unity Information Service* 117. (2004/iv): 188–204.

OUTLER, ALBERT C. (ed.) (1964). *John Wesley*. New York: Oxford University Press.

THURIAN, MAX (ed.) (1986). *Churches Respond to BEM: Official Responses to the 'Baptism, Eucharist and Ministry'*. Geneva: World Council of Churches, ii.

TRIPP, DAVID (1969). *The Renewal of the Covenant in the Methodist Tradition*. London: Epworth.

WESTERFIELD TUCKER, KAREN B. (2001). *American Methodist Worship*. New York: Oxford University Press.

CHAPTER 21

PREACHING

GENNIFER BENJAMIN BROOKS

INTRODUCTION

PREACHING is an act of the church. It is the proclamation of the gospel to the gathered community. It gives voice to the message of good news that is the foundation on which the church stands. However, the necessity for preaching good news depends on a perceived need—that those to whom one preaches need such good news in order to live fully as disciples of Jesus Christ. In addition, as can be recognized in the stated definitions of preaching offered by many homileticians, preachers, and church members at large, there is an additional element that most consider a requirement of the preaching of the church. Although they acknowledge the necessity for offering good news, they also consider that calling hearers to definitive acts that are considered Christian is essential to Christian discipleship. Such definitions give expression to the need for the preaching act to impact directly the formation of Christians as disciples of Jesus Christ. John Wesley's understanding of preaching was in accord with this type of definition. And as the acknowledged founder of Methodism, his instructions on preaching were specific in directing the Methodist preachers of his day to ensure that their sermons met the criteria of both offering good news and forming Christian disciples.

Wesley turned to Scripture for both the good news and the directives on Christian discipleship. In the Preface to all his published sermons he explained his method and purpose of delving into Scripture for determining the content of each sermon: 'I sit down alone: only God is here. In his presence I open, I read his book; for this end, to find the way to heaven' (Wesley 1975– : i. 105–6). His sermons

were inherently scriptural and he directed the preachers of the Methodist movement to look to Scripture as the only source of their sermonic material. He
instructed them to focus the content of their sermons on what he called the three
grand scriptural doctrines—original sin, justification by faith, and inward and
outward holiness. In other words the content of Methodist sermons delivered by
all preachers, like Wesley's own sermons, was to be taken from Scripture.

As one considers the state of Methodist preaching and the content of too many
present-day sermons, it gives rise not only to the question of what Wesley would say
to many preachers across Methodism, but also to how many twenty-first century
preachers would respond to Wesley's instructions to the preachers of his day:

> I think, the right method of preaching is this: At our first beginning to preach at any place,
> after a general declaration of the love of God to sinners, and his willingness that they should
> be saved, to preach to law, in the strongest, the closest, the most searching manner possible;
> only intermixing the gospel here and there, and showing it, as it were, afar off. After more
> and more persons are convinced of sin, we may mix more and more of the gospel in order
> to 'beget faith'.   (Wesley 1872: xi. 486–7)

In too many places and too many sermons across Methodism there is a dearth of
good news and even less of Scripture. The idea of salvation as a necessity for
Christian discipleship falters on the unwillingness of many to admit the presence of
sin in human life, and the love of God is too often identified as synonymous with
earthly gain and financial prosperity. In many places, good preaching has been
characterized by good storytelling, whether or not the stories have any basis or
grounding in Scripture. This practice is so far removed from the Wesley's guidelines
that it seems necessary in a study of Methodist preaching to unearth the roots and
retrace the legacy that should inform the content and purpose of Methodist
preaching even in the twenty-first century.

A LEGACY OF THE CHURCH

The legacy of which Methodist preaching is a beneficiary may be traced most
directly to the roots of Methodism's founder, John Wesley. Both his understanding
and his method of preaching represent an intersection of his ecclesiological and his
familial roots. On one hand his Anglican roots taught him that preaching was the
responsibility of the clerical office, and that church's doctrines impressed on him the
essential element of Scripture as foundational to the development of sermons. In
addition, at the time of Wesley's arrival on the scene as a priest of the Church of
England, the *Book of Homilies* produced earlier by Thomas Cranmer 'for the
purpose, he announced, of preventing ignorant preachers from spreading their

errors' (Booty 1981: 85) was the source of all sermons, since priests were mandated, by both royal and ecclesiastical decree, to read them in parish churches each Sunday.

On the other hand, Wesley was the beneficiary of a preaching inheritance that originated from both sides of his family tree. Three paternal generations of preachers—his father, Samuel Wesley, his grandfather, John Wesley, and his great-grandfather Bartholomew Wesley, had been ordained in the Church of England. His maternal grandfather, Dr Samuel Annesley, a Nonconformist greatly admired by Wesley, was known for his gifted preaching.

From his ecclesiological roots, Wesley inherited both the doctrinal undergirding of sermons of the Church of England and the influence of the Puritans and their exuberant style of preaching. In the reformed Church of England of Wesley's day, where formerly liturgy had almost completely overshadowed it, preaching began to assume an important role in both the academy and the church. Included in that new development was the establishment of weekly sermons at the major universities, and the study of Scriptures in the original languages for the specific purpose of sermonic exposition. For Anglican preachers, it was important to demonstrate their knowledge and learning. Sermons were erudite, well written, and well read, but often dull and heavy, noted more for literary distinction than for scriptural content or inspiring delivery. Often, emphasis focused on the style and language of the sermon, rather than on the gospel truth it should contain, and by the time of Wesley's entrance on the scene, Anglican sermons had been reduced generally to rational discourses or essays with little of prophecy or theological wisdom. Similar to many heard in the church today, morality was a favoured theme, and preaching was generally perfunctory and uninspiring (Davies 1996b: 67–9).

Puritans, on the other hand, gave exceptional importance to preaching, and considered the sermon 'the climax of divine service' (Davies 1996a: 294). The preacher's task was to present Scripture with definitive life and power as the Word of God, and with a view to empowering, enlivening, and inspiring the hearers in a way that moved them to glorify God and to be transformed in heart and life (Lloyd-Jones 1977: 92). Puritan preachers considered the Scriptures as the primary source for preaching and for developing individual Christian discipleship.

Puritans believed that preaching was the means chosen by God for illuminating the minds, mollifying the hearts, sensitizing the consciences, strengthening the faith, quelling the doubts, and saving the souls of mankind. To that end the Puritan brethren dedicated their chief energies to preaching clearly, faithfully, sincerely, and movingly, trusting that the Holy Spirit would take their human words and make them the 'lively oracles of God' to their congregations.   (Monk 1999: 301)

The Puritan sermon was simple, designed to avoid distracting the hearer from the message of the Scripture text. Although focused specifically on the biblical text, preachers often used their sermons to address current situations and to offer spiritual direction to the hearers and to the church at large. In fact, 'much of the theological teaching of the Puritans was given in the form of preaching and sermons' (Lloyd-Jones 1977: 94). These two ecclesiological streams directed Wesley such that he accorded a central place to the act of preaching in shaping the church, even as he recognized its role as instructive for Christian living.

WESLEY AND THE CONSTRUCTION OF METHODIST PREACHING

Wesley attracted persons to his preaching not through the delivery of his message but because of its contents. Using the whole of Scripture as his text he offered his hearers a vision of the Christian life that was framed by the good news of salvation by faith in Jesus Christ. His scriptural message reached the hearts of those who had been denied a place in the established church, and 'opened the door of hope for men and women who had been crowded off into the margins of society' (Wesley 1975– : i. 17). Throughout his preaching he stressed the need for justification and directed his hearers to strive for inward holiness in order to reach the goal of Christian perfection. His focus on the several means of grace was meant to provide assurance of the facility of the way of salvation. He preached that the goal of Christian perfection and eternal salvation were to be realized by adherence to the commandments of God to love God and neighbour, and the substance of his message came directly from Scripture. This was his understanding of the task of preaching—an exposition of Scripture, and not simply a testimony of one's experience or even an exhortation of one's hopes.

Wesley violated defined parish boundaries and preached in fields in order to reach the masses with his message of salvation by faith. His aim in preaching was 'that every sermon proclaim the essential gospel as if for that time only' (Wesley 1975– : i. 15–16), and that message came directly from Scripture. His sermons were replete with Scripture, using texts to exegete other texts with the stated purpose of proclaiming the gospel in a way that would invite hearers to experience a change of heart and life. His preaching was aimed as much at individuals as at the church, and he called for holy living individually and corporately. Above all Wesley preached by the power of the Holy Spirit. In the creation as well as in the delivery of sermons, Wesley depended on the power of God to transform the words of Scripture into the living Word of God. He directed his preaching to the church in its identity as the body of Christ and although his evangelistic fervour was aimed at conversion of his hearers, as Methodism became established in the societies, he understood and responded through his preaching to the spiritual needs of those who had become part of the movement. In fact, his published sermons were aimed at such nurturing of the members as well as a method of providing guided direction to less-trained Methodist preachers. Unlike the directive that forced Anglican priests to read the *Homilies* to their congregations, Wesley's sermons were to be used as teaching tools for Methodist preachers and by them in the preparation and content of sermons. By following his teaching, Methodist preachers could guide believers to continue on the path to perfection through holy living in the same way that Wesley did.

As the movement spread and flourished, concerned for the content, structure, and delivery of sermons to the people called Methodist, Wesley began to gather the Methodist preachers annually under his direct leadership. The first issue he addressed in the conference in 1745 was what they were to preach. This initial conference, held at the height of the movement, provided the forum for Wesley to express and address his concern about the content of sermons particularly as it related to preaching to the converted. Because the societies had been in place for some time, Wesley addressed sustainability of membership through the content of the preached word. It was an issue that he considered of major importance because many in the societies who had come to faith from the position of unbelievers, and had already experienced conversion, needed to be strengthened in their faith. He felt that 'there was more need to exhort those in the society "in whom the foundation is already laid" to go on to perfection' (Heitzenrater 1995: 152).

Wesley's primary intention in his conference gathering was clearly to guide those who were part of the preaching ministry of the movement to follow the sermonic pattern that he set and specifically to maintain a style of preaching that was, above all, scriptural in nature and content. Not only did Wesley direct his preachers with respect to their sermons, he also provided directives for their personal lives. His *1746 Examination of Preachers* investigated their personal faith walk and included questions that were specific to their preaching:

1. Do they know in whom they have believed?

   Have they the love of God in their hearts?
   Do they desire and seek nothing but God?
   And are they holy in all manner of conversation?

2. Have they gifts (as well as grace) for the work?

   Have they (in some tolerable degree) a clear, sound understanding?
   Have they a right judgment in the things of God?
   Have they a just conception of salvation by faith?
   And has God given them any degree of utterance?
   Do they speak justly, readily, clearly?

3. Have they success?

   Do they not only so speak as generally either to convince or affect the hearers?
   But have any received remission of sins by their preaching?
   A clear and lasting sense of the love of God?

As long as these three marks undeniably concur in any, we allow [i.e. acknowledge] him to be called of God to preach. These we receive as sufficient reasonable evidence, that he is moved therein by the Holy Ghost.   (*Minutes* 1745: 30–1)

At the 1747 annual meeting, Wesley went a step further in directing Methodist preachers, and provided *Rules for Preaching*:

1. Be sure to begin and end precisely at the time appointed.
2. Sing no hymns of your own composing.
3. Endeavour to be serious, weighty, and solemn in your whole deportment before the congregation.
4. Choose the plainest texts you can.
5. Take care not to ramble from your text, but to keep close to it, and make out what you undertake.
6. Always suit your subject to your audience.
7. Beware of allegorizing or spiritualizing too much.
8. Take care of anything awkward or affected, either in your gesture or pronunciation.
9. Tell each other, if you observe anything of this kind. (*Minutes* 1747: 38)

Wesley was so intentional about providing direction to his preachers that one could readily formulate a definition of Methodist preaching, including both the content and delivery of sermons, based on his stated directives as well as his own preaching. This, combined with Wesley's ecclesiology that disavowed boundaries for the preaching of the gospel, offered Methodism a new blueprint for effective preaching.

Wesley's understanding of the church and of preaching enabled him to overcome prejudices of place, allowing him to preach in the open air; of ordination, approving lay preachers; and of gender, ultimately permitting women access to the pulpit. His preaching to the church was, he felt, 'the true, the scriptural, experimental religion' (Wesley 1975– : i. 106), and both his preaching techniques and his expansion of the preaching role in the church helped to transform 'the function of the pulpit and also the religious life of England and North America' (Davies 1996*b*: 143). In his own words, his sermons offered 'plain truth for plain people' (Wesley 1975– : i. 104), enabling his hearers to understand the meaning of his sermons and more importantly, to accept the words of Scripture for themselves and thus advance the life and work of the church.

The church that developed from the societies despite Wesley's objections, and the church that developed in the Americas under the aegis of Methodism, was thus constrained under Wesley's directive with respect to preaching. The preacher, representative of the leadership of the church, was charged with presenting the words of Scripture with clarity and with zeal so that the body of Christ could be nurtured and strengthened for service in the world. Wesley had learned the prevailing lecture style of Anglican preaching and he directed the preachers of

Methodism away from that model. He was concerned about gospel preachers who tended to neglect the law in their preaching, considering it irrelevant to salvation in Jesus Christ, and he charged his churchmen to preach the whole Bible, both law and gospel, as essential to the development of faith. He considered neglect in preaching the law as a subversion of the gospel and harmful to the development of both Christian perfection in individuals and social holiness in the gathered community. Preaching in the Methodist societies, whether by duly ordained priests, by lay persons, or women was not seen 'as a right to be seized. Rather, it was a gift of God to an exceptional few to be exercised with a profound sense of responsibility' (Chilcote 1993: 61–2).

PREACHING: AN ACT OF THE CHURCH

'Preaching is not a distinctive practice but is a part of the practice of worship' (Allen 1997: 12) for which the church gathers. Preaching is an interpretation of the presence of God active in the church; it is a gift of God's grace; it is empowered by the Holy Spirit. 'The preaching event is an aspect of the broader work of the Spirit to nurture, empower and guide the church in order that it may serve the Kingdom of God in the power of the Spirit' (Forbes 1989: 19). When the church engages the divine gift, the words of Scripture are contextualized for the community, the preacher looks to God for the interpretative, transforming word, and the preaching of the church becomes transformative in the life of the hearers. The preacher, the sermon, and the hearers are key elements of preaching. In the act of preaching the text has a direct relationship with each of these elements and it also connects the elements each with the other.

Scripture provides the text that the preacher engages to discern its relevance as the Word of God for the people in a particular time and place. Having faithfully delved into the text and unearthed its meaning for preaching, the preacher becomes the vessel by which the gospel is proclaimed, and the words of the sermon are the medium through which the Word of God is delivered to the people. Homileticians and preachers in general have accepted that only through divine mystery can the text from the lips of the preacher be transposed into the Word of God, and only as the Word of God can the words of the sermon be effective in transforming the minds and hearts of the hearers. 'Preaching the sermon is a *task*; proclaiming the Word is the hoped-for *goal*' (Lowry 1997: 37). The evocation, as Lowry calls the bridge between the task of preaching the sermon and the goal of proclaiming the Word, transforms the words of the preacher into the Word of God, and enables the transformation of lives through the effectuation of that divine word.

Preaching as an act of the church is both performed by the church and directed to the church. The church as the gathered community is called out by Christ to live in faithful fellowship with one another and work together for the transformation of the world. In order to do this effectively, the church must be committed to the task of proclamation of the gospel. Wesley and the Methodists understood Scripture as the source of the good news on which they anchored their preaching. Although Wesley resisted the creation of a new denomination, he understood the societies he formed to be the church, with its corporate identity as the Body of Christ. He understood the called-out nature of that fellowship of believers, and that the preached word was directed to this body even as it was aimed at encouraging the transformation of individuals and ultimately of society. The membership of the Methodist societies was the church; the 'body of people united together in the service of God' (Wesley 1975– : iii. 46). They were 'those whom God had "called out" of the world' (ibid. 47), united as one body, under one Spirit, having 'one faith, one baptism, one God and Father of all, who is above all and through all and in you all' (ibid. 50). As such, within the societies the act of preaching was important for directing individual and corporate spiritual life.

The church as the location of preaching brings together both preacher and people, and through the divine presence operating in the words of the sermon, the people of God are encouraged in their faith even as the preached sermon constructs 'in consciousness a "faith-world" related to God' (Buttrick 1987: 11). Not only is God present and basic to the words of preaching, but both preacher and people, gathered together in the place of initiation and in sight of the table, where the grace of God is evident in both the cleansing water of baptism, and the nurturing food of communion, can live into the unique fellowship as Christ's body. This fellowship is the true forum for the feast that is the Word of God, and that is offered in the act of preaching. It is the church at its best, the only place of preaching, and worthy of receiving only a preached word that is scriptural in content and divinely inspired in presentation.

In *Homiletics*, Karl Barth offers these two descriptive statements about preaching that he identifies as 'An Attempt at a New Definition':

1. Preaching is the Word of God which he himself speaks, claiming for the purpose the exposition of a biblical text in free human words that are relevant to contemporaries by those who are called to do this in the church that is obedient to its commission.
2. Preaching is the attempt enjoined upon the church to serve God's own Word, through one who is called thereto, by expounding a biblical text in human words and making it relevant to contemporaries in intimation of what they have to hear from God himself. (Barth 1991: 44)

These definitions speak directly to the understanding of the connection between preaching and the church. In both statements, the Word of God is offered to the people of God in their time and place and in their identity as the church.

As a cleric, ordained to the work of a preacher, Wesley understood his responsibility to spread scriptural holiness for the sake of the church and the world, and this he felt gave him the authority to preach the Word of God at any time and in any place. The challenge to do so within the prevailing church doctrines led to a reshaping of Wesley's ecclesiology that had great significance for the societies and ultimately for the shaping of Methodism and Methodist doctrines. 'John Wesley was convinced that strict church order and evangelical efficacy did not always make an ideal couple' (Barth 1991: 44), and the position he took in preaching the Word of God often put him at odds with his Anglican Church. The substance of his preaching and his commissioning and teaching of Methodist preachers evidenced a different understanding of the church than he had held previously. According to this revised definition the church was still the place where the pure Word of God is preached, as he had learned through Anglican doctrine, but that place became more fully aligned with its identity as the fellowship of the gathered community.

Using Wesley's reframed meaning of 'church', one can come to a clearer understanding of preaching as an act of the church, intrinsic to its identity and purpose and to recognize authentic preaching as 'simply the creative and faithful act of a person living out the faith as a community. In other words, no authentic preaching occurs apart from the Eucharistic community, which is itself constantly being formed by the presence of God in Christ as known in Word and Sacrament' (Rice 1991: 25). Preaching is thus *of* the church, originating from the church in its nature as the body of Christ, and not simply *for* the church, as a creative act that brings into being the church's identity as the beloved community of Christian believers. The preacher emerges from within the body of Christ and stands with the people even as he or she delivers the Word of God revealed in Scripture for the particular time and place.

AMERICAN METHODISM DEVELOPS A NEW PREACHING STYLE

In the Preface to all his published sermons Wesley explained the method by which he developed his sermons:

I sit down alone: only God is here. In his presence I open, I read his book; for this end, to find the way to heaven. Is there a doubt concerning the meaning of what I read? Does anything appear dark or intricate? I lift up my heart to the Father of lights: 'Lord, is it not thy Word, "If any man lack wisdom, let him ask of God"? Thou "givest liberally and upbraidest not". Thou hast said, "If any be willing to do thy will, he shall know". I am willing to do, let me know, thy will'. I then search after and consider parallel passages of Scripture, 'comparing spiritual things with spiritual'. I meditate thereon, with all the attention and earnestness of which my mind is capable. If any doubt still remains, I consult those who are experienced in the things of God, and then the writings whereby, being dead, they yet speak. And what I thus learn, that I teach.   (Wesley 1975– : i. 105–6)

His intention was that Methodist preachers would follow his example and give the same type of attention to the development of their own sermons. However this formula for the preparation of sermons modelled by Methodism's founder was also time-consuming and required discipline and due diligence. Whether this process was emulated by the preachers in the societies cannot be determined. However, as Methodism crossed the ocean to America, the conditions faced by the settlers, the lack of ordained clergy, and situations of their preaching combined to ensure that Methodist preachers had little opportunity to engage Wesley's process of sermon development.

No longer were preachers assigned to specific societies or congregations, instead they itinerated over large stretches of rugged territory called circuits. They travelled on horseback and were forced to endure great hardship in their task as preachers. Held to the same strictures as Wesley's early preachers, many of these Circuit riders had little experience in preaching but they tried to follow the dictates of Methodism's founder. The message was still 'salvation by faith' and preachers were focused more on content than delivery of the sermon. Circuit riders developed societies and would pay regular visits during which they would preach and administer the business of the society. In their absence, class leaders and local preachers would guide the fellowship of the society. However as the population grew and societies increased in membership, the lack of clergy caused home-grown preachers to emerge in settled areas. Not only were these preachers faced with the tasks of forging a new life in a new world, they were untrained in biblical exposition and insufficiently educated for the depth of research Wesley's model required. O. C. Edwards records the experience of one such preacher, Peter Cartwright, the self-named 'Backwoods Preacher', who established a preaching circuit for himself and engaged the task of soul-winning through his preaching (Edwards 2004: 502–4).

The greatest change to Methodist preaching came with the institution of the camp meeting. Families travelled miles to attend such meetings that could last from a weekend to two weeks or even longer. Camp meetings involved much exuberant singing and preaching, however there was a marked difference in the content of sermons from that preached in the societies. The preacher offered 'an extensive sermon; it was good, sound doctrine and, although Methodism, it was Methodism of the mildest tone and divested of the bitterness of denunciation, as, indeed, is generally the case with Methodism in America' (Luccock and Hutchinson 1954: 255). This seems to mark a watershed moment for American Methodism that would change the tenor of its preaching to a more palatable gospel that bypassed the recognition of human sinfulness and focused on the love of God; that simply affirmed the human condition without requiring any type of redemption or action that would lead to Christian perfection.

Circuit riders were committed to the cause of evangelistic preaching that included the naming of sin and the need for repentance and salvation. Ardent in fervour, and fuelled in their preaching by the same zeal that drove them to take on the harrowing ministry of the circuit rider, these Methodist preachers followed in the preaching path set by Wesley and later by Francis Asbury. Methodist preachers at camp meetings, competing for a listening audience with other preachers, who preached at the same time in different areas of the camp, were often less inclined to be forceful in naming sin and its consequences and calling for repentance. The exuberance of the camp meeting was exemplified in the performance of the many preachers, and sermons were delivered extemporaneously. In fact, 'not only was an inability to preach without a manuscript regarded as an indication of practical incompetence, it was also taken as prima facie evidence that the preacher was unconverted: the Spirit would tell the truly called what they should say' (Edwards 2004: 506).

Preaching at camp meetings was noteworthy more for the delivery than the content. Preachers were loud in order to be heard over the crowds and extremely expressive in order to move the emotions of the hearers. Despite the fact that 'there was considerable variety in the homiletical diet of a camp meeting' (ibid. 507), Cartwright noted a change in Methodist preaching during this period. He writes that it was 'overtaken by the sort of refinement that made Presbyterians so ill-adapted to following settlers west. More store was set by the education and good taste of clergy than their passion for souls. This was not the spirit that had won a million souls in sixty years' (ibid. 504). Perhaps this period, considered to have democratized American religion (ibid. 507), is the time stamp that marks the change in Methodist preaching that has resulted in the fragmented and often uninspiring state of much of today's preaching. Although it does not follow that a learned clergy should lead automatically to uninspired preaching, the fervour of Methodist preaching has waned significantly even as the clergy have become more educated. In a real sense much preaching in Methodist Churches in the United States is reminiscent of the preaching in the Church of England of Wesley's day.

A WESLEYAN RESPONSE TO METHODIST PREACHING

The creation and development of the societies was a visible sign of Wesley's 'burning desire to revitalize the church, or at least to conduct the experiment of building a model of Christian community in one Anglican parish' (Baker 2000: 52). His venture into extemporaneous and open-air preaching was a departure from the doctrines and mores of the Church of England, but it was the scriptural content of his preaching that impacted the lives of his hearers. He understood the conditions of the persons who flocked to hear his sermons and could recognize in the hearers their hopeful expectancy to receive the Word of God for their lives and to experience the revelation of God for the salvation of their souls. Wesley's response came by means of the proclamation of the gospel through the preached word. The lesson that his preaching offers to the church is one that should not be lost to preachers or that has been bypassed by the church as it engages its ministry of the proclamation of the Word of God.

Several characteristics noted by homileticians in today's sermons are readily recognizable in Methodist preaching. Many preachers in Methodism focus on offering the grace of God, but they do so without connecting it in any way to the Christian need for salvation from sin. In fact, sin is never named from many pulpits, and hearers are not apprised of the way of salvation nor the need for either justification or sanctification. The need for faith is also not given the emphasis that Wesley would demand nor is the critical nature of faith in living a Christian life expounded. Faith as a gift of divine grace, offered freely to all, but necessitating a decision by the believer, was an essential element of Methodist preaching that spoke to the heart of Methodist doctrine of salvation by faith. Wesley included this element of Christian discipleship in a majority of his sermons and stressed its critical nature to the members of the societies and to his preachers. Unfortunately, little emphasis seems to be attached to the need for faith, except in dire situations. Preachers seem to have devalued this gift of God's grace. While preaching cannot carry all the blame for this loss of the faith element, as a key ingredient in calling Christians to faith in Christ, the preaching of the church must bear some responsibility for fact that it is often found wanting.

There is also an absence of Scripture from many sermons. According to the doctrine of the Church of England, Wesley believed and passed down his definition of the church as the place where the pure Word of God is preached. This pure Word he understood as Scripture. In order for Methodism to be faithful in its identity as the church, its preaching requires the substantive words of Scripture. What does the preacher offer the hearers without the definitive Word of God? How can the preaching of the Methodist church have significance for those who gather as a manifestation of Christ's body without offering the pure Word of God? If Scripture contains the witness of the eternal grace of God, and gives testimony to the redemptive love of God, how can hearers hope to gain the knowledge they need to seek God's grace for themselves, if the preacher neglects to pass it on through scriptural preaching?

In The United Methodist Church, the most widespread branch of Methodism, lay and clergy members alike have decried the state of preaching. Observations and objections run the gamut of content and delivery. Preachers are criticized for the level of exegesis, exposition, and application of the preached word to the context of their lives. Some sermons have been critiqued and dismissed for lack of clarity and the absence of structure. Unfortunately, the issue of a lack of scriptural foundation is often overlooked or is given second place to the narration of appropriate stories even as the act of preaching is devalued or relegated to a subordinate place in the hierarchy of church ministries or clergy responsibilities. For Wesley, preaching was essential to the life of the church and it did not exist without Scripture. It was the bedrock of every sermon he wrote or preached; it was the Word of God that he exposed and interpreted and applied to the lives of his hearers and his readers. And any effort that is launched to recapture the power of preaching in advancing the work of Christ in the church requires first and foremost recognition of scripture as the foundation of the semon and a return of the act of preaching to a primary place in the ministry of the church.

In describing his process of sermon preparation, Wesley stated clearly that his purpose in this endeavour was to find the way to heaven. His was a methodology that required him to be in close communication with God throughout the process of sermon development and delivery. The Preface provides a description of an orderly, systematic process engaged by the founder of Methodism, and those who have continued on the preaching path that he set would be greatly helped to follow his lead. Wesley refused to be hindered in his desire to take the good news to those that he considered needed it most. His goal was to offer all who heard him a path to salvation not to start a new church. Despite serious opposition from many established church leaders, the preaching of the gospel advanced within the societies, and the Methodist movement grew and flourished to become a new church.

CONCLUSION

Wesley did not present his scriptural messages from a position of superiority. His delving into Scripture was first for his own edification and then to be shared with the people. As he described it: 'And what I thus learn, that I teach' (Wesley 1976–: i. 106). His style of preaching was problematic for those in positions of authority in the Church of England, but it connected at the grass-roots level with those who needed a word from God; who needed the hope of the gospel; who were looking for a way to live in a world that had rejected them. Wesley considered all Scripture to be the Word of God and therefore a directive that pointed the way to heaven. Salvation by faith was above all the message that he wished to impart and Scripture contained the full substance of everything that the message required. Preaching was his way of life and his preparation for preaching took him to Scripture above everything else.

Unlike many preachers whose sermons are written to offer palliatives to the people or who do not wish to disturb the hearts of their hearers, Wesley offered the fullness of Scripture—both law and gospel. For Wesley, salvation by faith in Jesus Christ did not mean a rejection of the law; rather the law prescribed the gospel. He saw the whole Bible as a testimonial to the redemptive grace of God in Jesus Christ and stepped out boldly on the basis of that foundation to offer the good news of Jesus Christ found in all Scripture to the Christian people called Methodist. In *Preaching the Whole Bible as Christian Scripture* Graeme Goldsworthy addresses this issue that many preachers find problematic: 'The problem we face as preachers is not a new one. Throughout the ages Christian preachers have struggled with the question of the centrality of Christ and how this affects the way we handle the text of the Bible' (2000: 2). Perhaps this problem of finding Christ and redemption in the whole Bible may in part account for the absence of Scripture from so many sermons. And perhaps because of this missing link, preachers are fearful to introduce the problem of sin lest they are unable to provide the mitigating response to sin. Even when it becomes a struggle, preachers must offer Christ through an authentic interpretation of Old Testament scripture even as they recognize the requirement of adherence to the law that is present also in the New Testament scriptures.

The crisis in preaching that exists in United Methodism 'is aided and abetted in some situations by the persistence of a preaching service in which Scripture is minimally in evidence' (ibid.). Not only does Scripture not always show up in sermons, in many instances it is absent in recognizable form from the entire service. Some preachers in their concern for the length of the service bypass the reading of Scripture and launch precipitously into a message that does not have the necessary biblical foundation. Wesley used Scripture liberally in his sermons in a way that was authoritative for those understanding the message of Christ and for human salvation. As one studies preaching in Methodism, Wesley's example as a preacher of the gospel as well as the biblical nature of his sermons are critical models for the church in the twenty-first century. Methodist preachers can play an important role in the future of Methodism by ensuring that their preaching offers the pure Word of God to the people of God.

SUGGESTED READING

BURDON, ADRIAN (1991). *The Preaching Service—The Story of the Methodists: A Study of the Piety, Ethos and Development of the Methodist Preaching Service.* Bramcote: Grove.

CHILCOTE, PAUL WESLEY (1991). *John Wesley and the Women Preachers of Early Methodism.* Metuchen, N.J.: Scarecrow.

HEITZENRATER, RICHARD P. (1997). 'John Wesley's Principles and Practice of Preaching'. In *Beyond the Boundaries: Preaching in the Wesleyan Tradition*, ed. Richard Sykes. Oxford: Applied Theology Press, 12–40.

JONES, SCOTT J. (1995). *John Wesley's Conception and Use of Scripture*. Nashville: Kingswood.

LENTON, JOHN H. (2000). *My Sons in the Gospel: An Analysis of Wesley's Itinerant Preachers*. Loughborough: Wesley Historical Society.

RACK, HENRY D. (2002). *Reasonable Enthusiast: John Wesley and the Rise of Methodism*. London: Epworth.

REFERENCES

ALLEN, RONALD J. (1997). *Interpreting the Gospel: An Introduction to Preaching*. St Louis: Chalice.

BAKER, FRANK (2000). *John Wesley and the Church of England*. 2nd edn. London: Epworth.

BARTH, KARL (1991). *Homiletics*. David G. Buttrick (foreword). Louisville, Ky.: Westminster John Knox.

BOOTY, JOHN E. (1981). 'Introduction: The Basic Theme'. In id. (ed.), *The Godly Kingdom of Tudor England: Great Books of the English Reformation*. Wilton, Conn.: Morehouse-Barlow.

BUTTRICK, DAVID (1987). *Homiletic: Moves and Structures*. Philadelphia: Fortress.

CHILCOTE, PAUL W. (1993). *She Offered Them Christ: The Legacy of Women Preachers in Early Methodism*. Nashville: Abingdon.

DAVIES, HORTON (1996a). *Worship and Theology in England, Book 1*. Grand Rapids: Eerdmans.

—— (1996b). *Worship and Theology in England, Book 2*. Grand Rapids: Eerdmans.

EDWARDS, O. C., JR. (2004). *A History of Preaching*. Nashville: Abingdon.

FORBES, JAMES (1989). *The Holy Spirit & Preaching*. Nashville: Abingdon.

GOLDSWORTHY, GRAEME (2000). *Preaching the Whole Bible as Christian Scripture: The Application of Biblical Theology to Expository Preaching*. Grand Rapids: Eerdmans.

HEITZENRATER, RICHARD P. (1995). *Wesley and the People Called Methodists*. Nashville: Abingdon.

LLOYD-JONES, D. MARTYN (1977). 'Preaching'. In *Anglican and Puritan Thinking*. Cambridge: The Westminster Conference.

LOWRY, EUGENE L. (1997). *The Sermon: Dancing the Edge of Mystery*. Nashville: Abingdon.

LUCCOCK, HALFORD E., and HUTCHINSON, PAUL (1954). *The Story of Methodism*. New York: The Methodist Book Concern.

MONK, ROBERT C. (1999). *John Wesley: His Puritan Heritage*, 2nd edn. Nashville: Abingdon.

RICE, CHARLES (1991). *The Embodied Word*. Minneapolis: Augsburg Fortress.

WESLEY, JOHN (1872). 'Of Preaching Christ'. In *Works*, ed. Thomas Jackson. 3rd edn. London: Wesleyan Conference Office, xi. 486–92.

—— (1975–). *The Works of John Wesley*. Nashville: Abingdon.

PART IV

SPIRITUAL EXPERIENCES, EVANGELISM, MISSION, ECUMENISM

CHAPTER 22

....

EXPERIENCE
OF GOD

....

THOMAS R. ALBIN

THE key to the Methodist passion and mission of John and Charles Wesley is to be found in their personal encounter with God, by grace, through faith in Jesus Christ. The transformation that comes through this experience of God is both gift and response, a mystery and an expected outcome of obedience to the 'drawings of the Father' in and through the Holy Spirit. Therefore, all experience of God is meditated experience.

The early twenty-first century is clearly engaged in an active dialogue concerning the appropriate ways to understand and interpret accounts of spiritual experiences inherent in the major world religions (Boeve and Hemming 2004; Coolman 2004; Gellman 2001; Hick 2006; Schlitt 2007); including the experience of God, the transcendent, or a 'transpersonal Reality', as John Hick suggests. Within the Christian tradition, Kevin Hart and Barbara Wall (2005) provide a postmodern response to the discussion of *The Experience of God* (James 1929). Within the scientific community, Jensine Andresen (2001: 1) describes the birth of 'a new field and a new approach to understanding religion' involving scholars from varied disciplines 'willing to tackle... cognitive theories of religion in general and the neural bases of religion in specific' resulting in the emergence of a coherent area of research and writing she refers to as a 'cognitive science of religion'.

The basic grammar and definition of terms for this chapter will be drawn from Jerome I. Gellman's chapter on 'Mysticism and Religious Experience' in *The Oxford Handbook of Philosophy of Religion* (Wainwright 2005: 138–63). Mystical experiences are narrowly understood as 'A (purportedly) super sense-perceptual or sub sense-perceptual *unitive* experience granting acquaintance of realities or states of affairs that are of a kind not accessible by way of sense-perception, somatosensory modalities, or standard introspection.' Religious experiences are normally more broadly understood, including religious visions, auditions, feeling of religious awe, sublimity, and Friedrich Schleiermacher's sense of 'absolute dependence'. Religious experiences can be numinous in the sense identified by Rudolph Otto as an encounter with one who is 'wholly other' than the subject, producing a sense of dread and fascination before an incomprehensible mystery. However, numinous experiences are not restricted to this definition (note the critique of feminist philosophers, ibid. 162–3).

When an experience includes sense perception, Gellman calls it an *extrovertive* experience. When an experience is wholly non-sensory, it is *introvertive*. Union with God 'signifies a rich family of experiences rather than a single experience, it involves a falling away of the separation between the person and God, short of identity. When mystics speak as though they have a consciousness of being identical with God, this is beyond the Christian tradition' (ibid. 141–3).

THE EXPERIENCE OF GOD IN THE EARLY METHODIST TRADITION

The Methodist understandings and experiences of God were, for the most part, religious, extrovertive, transformational, and tending towards a deeper union with God. While one must acknowledge the inadequacy of any attempt of a finite human being to describe or understand an encounter with an infinite, transcendent being—God—one can argue the probability of God's existence and the rational possibility of divine revelation in which the acts of God are apprehended because of the divine illumination of the human mind itself (Wiebe 2004: 195–220).

THE WESLEY FAMILY AND THE EIGHTEENTH-CENTURY CONTEXT

The Methodist movement that emerged in the lives and the ministries of John and Charles Wesley must be understood within the larger context of the Christian heritage of England (Heitzenrater 1995: 1–95), the widespread sources of the evangelical revival independent of any contact with the Wesleys (Walsh 1966; Ward 1992), and the family home in Epworth (Davies and Rupp 1965: 1–79, 115–44). The theological and spiritual environment of the Wesley home was both High Church and Puritan. It was a spiritual theology based on the 'love of God' rather than the 'faith in Christ' of Continental Protestantism. There was a genuine concern for 'inward religion' as represented by Henry Scougal's *The Life of God in the Soul of Man*, *The Spiritual Combat* of the Italian Scupoli, the *Pensées* of Blaise Pascal, *The Imitation of Christ* by Thomas à Kempis, and *The Life of Monsieur de Renty*.

OXFORD METHODISM, 1725–1735

When John Wesley (1703–91) made the decision to enter Holy Orders in 1725 and 'make religion the business of his life', he found insight and the inward experience of 'much sensible comfort . . . such as I was an utter stranger to before', in Thomas à Kempis, *The Imitation of Christ*. By it John was convinced 'that true religion was seated in the heart, and that God's law extended to all our thoughts as well as our words and actions' (Wesley 1975– : xviii. 243–4). Jeremy Taylor's *Rules for Holy Living and Dying* reinforced this message and led him to keep a daily record of his spiritual experiences. William Law's *Serious Call to a Devout and Holy Life*, and *Christian Perfection*, strengthened John's commitment to 'purity of intention' (to do the will of God) and 'simplicity of affection' (love for God and neighbour).

REASON AND REVELATION

John Wesley's letter of 22 November 1725 documented the outcome of an extended discussion of the nature of Christian faith with his parents, moving the 22-year-old away from the prevailing rationalism of Oxford and re-establishing the primacy of divine revelation. 'I am, therefore, at length come over entirely to your opinion, that saving faith (including practice) is an assent to what God has revealed because He has revealed it and not because the truth of it may be evinced by reason' (Wesley 1975– : xxv. 188). This adjustment in the normative authority of revelation over reason separated John Wesley from the dominant philosophy of the Enlightenment and grounded Methodism in Holy Scripture as the primary locus of divine authority and revelation (Jones 1995: 17–61). 'The law and the testimony' (Isaiah 8: 20) became a favourite phrase of John Wesley to represent the Old and New Testaments as the absolute standard by which any experience of God was to be evaluated. At the same time, the Wesley brothers continued to value reason and conscience because these faculties of the human soul were gifts from God.

Human reason, according to John and Charles Wesley, functioned in three ways: (1) sense perception—simply taking in information, (2) judgement—evaluating the information received, and (3) discourse—comparing this information to other information and experiences (Wesley 1975– : ii. 590; see Matthews 1986: 125–56). The human conscience was 'that faculty of the soul which, by the assistance of the grace of God, sees at one and the same time, (1) our own tempers and lives, the real nature and quality of our thoughts, words and actions; (2) the rule whereby we are to be directed, and (3) the agreement or disagreement therewith' (Wesley 1975– : iii. 485).

UNDERSTANDING AND EXPERIENCE

The human capacity to understand and experience God is explained in John Wesley's first University Sermon, preached at St. Mary's in Oxford (15 November 1730). Simply put, the Creator endowed Adam and Eve with all the qualities needed for an authentic relationship (ibid. iv. 293–5). They were created spiritual beings in the image and likeness of God (*imago Dei*). Even though their free choice resulted in the fall into sin, the defacement of the divine image, and the brokenness of divine–human relationship, this relationship was not totally destroyed because of God's free choice to continue by grace what was no longer possible by nature.

During the period 1725–35, John Wesley read more books by John Norris than any other author listed among the 684 different works identified in his private Oxford diaries (Heitzenrater 1972: 493–525). Norris wove together the strands of moralism, mysticism, and rationalism in a theology of holiness and happiness that the Wesleys found philosophically and existentially attractive. Along with Thomas à Kempis, Jeremy Taylor, Robert Nelson, and William Law—John Norris reflected and reinforced many of the core values of the Wesley family. In contrast to William Law's *Serious Call to a Devout and Holy Life*, which appealed directly to the human will and reason, convicting the reader of the need to change, Norris appealed to the heart and provided spiritual motivation for his reader to live a holy life. Norris affirmed 'the Design of the Christian Dispensation is to perfect Holiness, to advance the interest of the Divine Life, to elevate us in the utmost Degree of Moral Perfection our Nature is here capable of, and, as far as possible, to make us

Partakers of the Divine' (Norris 1707: i. 10). Therefore, a prudent Christian would pray for temporal things conditionally, and for spiritual things 'such as pardon of sin, and grace to leave it' knowing 'that God *would have all men to be saved*, to attain the happiness for which he made them' (John Wesley's extract from Norris, *Christian Prudence*, cited here from the Pine edition of the *Works* (Wesley 1771–4: viii. 165–6)).

It is reasonable to claim that Charles Wesley and the other forty-three members of the Oxford Methodist movement shared this understanding of humankind because Norris's works were required reading for the Oxford Methodists and later these extracts were published for the use of Holy Club members (Heitzenrater 1972: 332–81). These early Methodists were confident that it was possible to experience God because God was capable of communicating with his creation in 'several Ways, and in several Manners, and by several Instruments'. Norris provided the theological, philosophical, and spiritual foundation for eighteenth-century Methodist openness to a variety of religious experiences. They believed that God speaks *within* (through reason, the light of inward truth, and the secret whispers of his Spirit) and *without* (through all of creation)—and most directly—through the Holy Scriptures (Norris 1707: iii. 237–44). God can speak through all and be experienced in all; however, the normal means for a Christian to experience God is through the means of grace.

THE MEANS OF GRACE

During the Oxford years, there is a clear sense that it is the duty of humankind to cooperate with the grace of God and participate in all the 'means of grace': worship, prayer, searching the Scriptures, fasting, Christian conversation, and regular participation in the Lord's Supper. Prayer is the first means of grace identified by the Wesley brothers and their first publication was a book of *Prayers for Every Day of the Week*. Prayer helps focus one's thoughts on God, stirs up awareness of the human need for God, quickens the desire for the prayer to be answered, and maintains the religious passion. The spiritual life would soon be extinct without the breathings of prayer to inspire and give it motion.

The prudent Christian gives attention to the reading or hearing of Scripture because it enlightens the understanding and composes the mind into a religious temper. The aim in reading is not curiosity or speculation, but with a clear design to learn and do the will of God. In a similar manner, one is to attend carefully, humbly, expectantly to the Word preached—waiting for the grace of God in obedience to the ordinances of God.

The Methodists understood that 'works of mercy' and 'works of piety' were essential to develop the 'dispositions of soul which constitute real Christianity' (Wesley 1975– : i. 572–91). Works of charity or mercy include everything that would be of benefit to the body or soul of the neighbour, be it words of spiritual advice, instruction, or reproof; or, the actions of giving alms, feeding the hungry, clothing the naked, visiting the sick or imprisoned. These actions are means of grace; and, when done with purity of intention, allow one to experience God. Works of piety included prayer, worship, searching the Scriptures, fasting, Christian conference, and the Lord's Supper; rightly understood, they were means 'to commune with God' (ibid. 575).

UNION WITH GOD

The aim of the Christian life was union with God. This understanding 'that the Perfection of the Soul is her Union with God' was common to John Norris and other writers that appeared in the required reading list for the Oxford Methodists and in *The Christian Library* published for the lay leaders and travelling preachers (fifty volumes published 1749–55). The connection between affection, attention, and union was absolute: 'Whatever we love, we unite our selves to, and the more we love, the more we are so United' (Norris 1707: iii. 166–99). John Wesley's sermon before the University in 1733 made it clear that participation in the divine life is the essence of Christian existence: 'One thing shall ye desire for its own sake—the fruition of him that is all in all. One happiness shall ye propose to your souls, even an union with him that made them, the having "fellowship with the Father and the Son".... One design ye are to pursue to the end of time—the enjoyment of God in time and in eternity' (Wesley 1975– : i. 408; see also Newport 2001: 96 ff.).

This suggestion that union with God might include fellowship with the individual members of the Trinity was a reality for some of the early Methodist people in the later part of the century. In a letter of spiritual guidance to Lady Maxwell (1742–1810), John Wesley disclosed: 'Mr. Charles Perronet was the first person I was acquainted with who was favored with the same experience as the Marquis de Renty, with regard to the ever-blessed Trinity; Miss Ritchie was the second; Miss Roe (now Mrs. Rogers) the third. I have as yet found but a few instances; so that this is not, as I was at first apt to suppose, the common privilege of all that are "perfect in love"' (Wesley 1831: xii. 403). De Renty's experience demonstrated that a Christian might 'carry about with you an experimental verity, and a fullness of the presence of the ever-blessed Trinity' which empowered a love for neighbour that found expression in concrete actions envisioned in Matthew 25: 32–44.

THE STRUGGLE WITH MYSTICISM

Through William Law, the Wesley brothers were introduced to the *Theologica Germanica* and the *Sermons* of Eckhart Tauler (Wesley 1975– : xviii. 245 n.). Over the years, John Wesley abridged and published their works and the accounts of nine Roman Catholic mystics: Macarius, de Renty, Fénelon, Brother Lawrence, Pascal, Madame Borignon, Juan D'Avila, Molinos, Lopez, and Madame Guyon. Robert G. Tuttle, Jr., argued that Wesley continued to admire the ascetic or extravertive mystics because of their attention to the inner journey towards union with God in love; and, the outward journey of obedience to the ethical and moral instruction to love one's neighbour, feed the hungry, and proclaim good news to the poor (Tuttle 1989). It was the quietistic or more introvertive mystics that John Wesley found to be speculative, antinomian, and near-pantheistic—those who denied the means of grace almost destroyed Wesley's own faith in the period 1735–8 (Davies and Rupp 1965: 45).

THE MISSION TO NORTH AMERICA, 1735–1738

The journey to North America brought the Wesley brothers into contact with a variety of different people, cultures, and theologies; none more important than the Moravian Brethren who were spiritual descendants of John Huss and the Bohemian Brethren (Podmore 1998). The contrast of the religious experience of the Wesley brothers in relation to their Moravian friends was striking. The progressive process of salvation envisioned by the Wesleys at this time did not produce the same feeling of assurance offered by the Moravian experience of instant, perceptible salvation by grace through faith alone. Contact with the Moravian Brethren in Georgia also afforded the Wesleys important insights into new forms of spiritual practice (including the singing of hymns) and structures for the spiritual formation (organizing men, women, and children into small groups).

THE POWER OF MUSIC

Onboard the ship to Georgia, the Wesley brothers were deeply impressed with the Moravian practice of singing hymns. They observed firsthand the power of music to open the way to a different dimension of spiritual experience. Before Charles returned to England he took the first Methodist *Collection of Psalms and Hymns* to be published in Charlestown by Lewis Timothy; the first of many books of hymns and spiritual songs the Wesleys would publish for their followers. The spiritual power of these hymns and sacred poems helped reinforce the content of Methodist preaching and publications.

THE INFLUENCE OF MORAVIAN THEOLOGY AND THE EXPERIENCE

After John and Charles Wesley returned to England in the spring of 1738 they met Peter Böhler, who persuaded them that 'true faith in Christ . . . had those two fruits inseparably attending it, "dominion over sin, and constant peace from a sense of forgiveness"' (Wesley 1975– : xviii. 247–8). This theological conversion was followed by an inward evangelical experience of the new birth; first Charles on Pentecost Sunday, 21 May; then John on Wednesday, 24 May. Charles described his inner transformation as 'a strange palpitation of heart' (Kimbrough and Newport 2008: 106); John's description was more detailed: 'I felt my heart strangely warmed. I felt I did trust in Christ and Christ alone for salvation, and an assurance was given me that he had taken away *my* sins, even *mine*, and saved *me* from the law of sin and death' (ibid. 250; Maddox 1990).

THE EMERGENCE OF WESLEYAN METHODISM

Following their experiences of the new birth, John and Charles entered the most formative decade of their lives. The period 1738–48 was marked by intense theological conflict with Moravian Quietism, Calvinistic Predestination, Anglican Antinomianism, and the excessive behaviour of some Huguenot prophets and prophetesses. Different segments of the Church of England accused the Wesleys of teaching works righteousness, rank enthusiasm, and popery. Rapid expansion was hindered by separation from the Moravians, the Calvinistic Methodists, and some Church of England evangelicals.

For the Wesleys, understanding and experiencing God were refined in the crucible of the evangelical experience. Within days of their respective conversions, they were faced with unexpected spiritual struggles; Charles dreamed of fighting two devils on 22 May 1738 (Kimbrough and Newport 2008: 108) and John's experience of the new birth did not match his expectation of absolute assurance of salvation and uninterrupted joy. John's empirical orientation forced him to modify his teaching and allow for greater variety than did his Moravian mentors. John and Charles Wesley's commitment to the centrality of faith in Christ and the authority of Scripture did not change from this point onward; however, the Methodist understanding and interpretation of experience continued to be refined (Wesley 1975– : xviii. 250–1).

The Moravian expectation was that the power of the Holy Spirit and the gift of saving faith was to be received in a moment—and that moment was *now*. By the early months of 1739 ordinary people, young and old, male and female, lay and clergy, experienced the power of God to awaken, convince, convert, and sanctify. Preaching, prayer, Christian conversation, Holy Scripture, and participation in the Lord's table were transformed from 'confirming ordinances' to assist the Christian on the gradual journey of spiritual growth into 'converting ordinances' and occasions for an immediate, life-changing encounter with God (ibid. xix. 158–9).

From 1738 to 1748 the Wesley brothers struggled to reconcile the Moravian theology of saving faith with their own understanding and experience of God; to say nothing of the variety of experiences of their followers (Hindmarsh 2005: 130–92). John's letter to his brother Charles in 1748 marks the conclusion of the struggle to distinguish between the feeling of assurance and the reality of justifying faith. 'Is justifying faith a sense of pardon? *Negatur*—it is denied' (Wesley 1975– : xxvi. 254).

After 1748 the Wesleys modified their distinction between the faith of a 'servant' and that of a 'son' or child of God and affirmed that both of these degrees of faith were sufficient for salvation. The faith of a servant was understood to be 'such a divine conviction of God and of the things of God as even in its infant state enables every one that possesses it to "fear God and work righteousness"'. The servant who continues to seek faith will one day 'receive the faith of the children of God by his *revealing* his only-begotten Son in their hearts' so that the servant may enjoy the spiritual assurance and privileges of those who have been adopted as children of God. In the 1788 sermon 'On Faith' John confirmed this move away from their earlier position. Faith is 'a divine evidence and conviction of things not seen' (Hebrews 11: 1) that included 'every species of faith, from the lowest to the highest'. He lamented the fact that Methodist preachers in the early years 'were not sufficiently apprised of the difference between a servant and a child of God' condemning any who did not have an absolute assurance of salvation (ibid. iii. 497).

STRUCTURES AND SPIRITUAL GUIDANCE

Central to the experience of God in Wesleyan Methodism were the small group structures that emerged to support people on the journey to spiritual maturity and scriptural holiness. John and Charles knew the spiritual benefits of Oxford Methodism and the Moravians expanded their understanding to include different groups for people at different stages of their spiritual maturity and readiness to engage in spiritual practices. The Wesley brothers developed three distinct types of small groups called 'band meetings', 'select bands', and 'class meetings'.

The Methodist band meetings were for those who had experienced justifying grace—like the Moravian choirs, these groups were separated on the basis of gender and marital status. Unlike the Moravian structures, the Methodist bands had only four to eight members with one person designated as the leader with the additional responsibility to attend the leaders meeting (Albin 2001: 45–8).

The Methodist select band or select society was a unique structure that emerged in 1741 to help those who had experienced the sanctifying grace of God and to help support those who sincerely desired it. It was also a place for the spiritual care of the movement's leaders, including the Wesleys (Wesley 1975–: ix. 270). Unlike the male and female bands for new believers, the select band included everyone actively engaged in this stage of the spiritual journey; men and women, married and single—all met together.

The Methodist class meeting emerged as a uniquely Methodist phenomenon. In February of 1742, Captain Foye recommended that the Bristol Society be subdivided into local neighbourhood units or 'classes' of about twelve families in each in order to facilitate a weekly collection of a penny per week per family to pay the builders of the New Room. The unintended consequence was that the physical and spiritual state of each family was immediately known. If the family was in financial need, the class leader sought help from the Society stewards; and, if the family was living in chaos or sin, the leader became an instrument of 'correction, reproof and instruction in righteousness' (Watson 1985).

Membership in the class meeting included people of all ages and without regard to gender or marital status. The required religious experience was a sincere desire for God (convincing grace) and the willingness to actively engage in the spiritual journey. Within the class participants learned the basic principles of Christian faith, behaviour, and affections or tempers necessary for Christian transformation. Research into the remaining records indicated that nearly half the early Methodist people came to saving faith *after* they were admitted to the class meeting (Albin 1985: 275–80).

The health and growth of the class meeting was directly related to the quality and character of the local class leaders. Selected personally by John or Charles Wesley, a leader was responsible for determining the time and place of the weekly meeting, choosing the hymns that were sung, leading the meeting, providing spiritual and scriptural advice for the members, and offering prayers appropriate to each member's expressed need.

The United Society was the structure that emerged in 1743 to provide spiritual guidance and oversight to the Methodist members and to support the development of local spiritual leaders. Each person desiring admission had a sponsor; someone who was already a member and willing to attest to the readiness of the prospective member to keep the General Rules. These rules were read to the prospective member and explained so that he or she could understand the Methodist way of life embodied in the three rules: (1) do no harm, (2) do good to the bodies and souls of others, and (3) participate in all the means of grace that were identified as 'the ordinances of God' (Wesley 1975– : ix. 68–73). Those who agreed were placed in a trial band for eight to twelve weeks to determine the level of their sincerity and commitment to living the Methodist doctrine, discipline, and way of life. Those who successfully completed the trial period were then admitted as members of the Methodist Society and assigned to a class or band meeting based on their personal experience of grace. As they progressed in their spiritual journey, the small groups provided the context for regular instruction, shared experiences, mutual support, and accountability for their life in grace: prevenient grace (field preaching and the trial band), convincing grace (the class meeting), justifying grace (the band meeting), and sanctifying grace (the select band) (Albin 2001: 33–52, 52–66).

SPIRITUAL GUIDANCE FOR LOCAL LEADERS THROUGH THE TRAVELLING PREACHERS

The United Society provided a system that allowed the local leaders of the classes, bands, stewards, and trustees to meet with the Wesleys and their appointed assistants. The Leaders Meeting and later the Quarterly Meeting provided occasions for spiritual guidance, instruction, prayer, and leadership development. The itinerant system of travelling preachers and assistants made it possible for local leaders to receive teaching and spiritual guidance from a variety of different personalities and perspectives. This, in turn, enhanced the spiritual growth and maturity of local leaders, both male and female. The increasing numbers of lay leaders provided the necessary human resources for the continued growth and spread of the Methodist movement.

TESTING AND INTERPRETING THE EXPERIENCE OF GOD

In her 1727 letter of spiritual advice to her son, Susanna wrote: 'The tree is known by its fruit, but not always by its *blossoms*; what blooms beautifully sometimes bears bitter fruit' (Wesley 1975– : xxv. 210). The phrase appeared repeatedly in John Wesley's letters and journal; for example, 20 February 1758, at Maldon in Essex,

John noted with approval the large congregation at five in the morning and observed, 'Fair blossoms! But which of these will bring forth fruit?' (ibid. xxi. 136, 265).

For the Wesleys, the first test of a purported experience of God was the fruit of a transformed life. 'I have seen (as far as a thing of this kind can be seen) very many persons changed in a moment from the spirit of fear, horror, despair, to the spirit of love, joy, and peace; and from sinful desires till then reigning over them to a pure desire of doing the will of God....' These transformed lives 'are my living arguments for what I assert, viz. that God *does now, as aforetime, give remission of sins and the gift of the Holy Ghost, even to us and to our children*' (ibid. xix. 60).

As the dramatic physical responses to the presence and power of God increased in 1739, the Wesleys were clear that all experiences were to be evaluated in light of the Scripture. Christians 'were not to judge of the Spirit whereby anyone spoke, either by appearances, or by common report, or by their own inward feelings. No, nor by any dreams, visions, or revelations supposed to be made to their souls, any more than by their tears, or any involuntary effects wrought upon their bodies.' John Wesley warned them 'all these were in themselves of a doubtful, disputable nature: they might be from God and they might not, and were therefore not simply to be relied on (any more than simply to be condemned) but to be tried by a farther rule, to be brought to the only certain test, "the law and the testimony"' (ibid. 73).

In addition to the test of Scripture and fruit, John and Charles Wesley applied the test of time to any supposed religious experience. John would visit those who had experienced strong physical manifestations of the supposed work of the Holy Spirit repeatedly, beginning the day after the event took place and then each time he was in that same location to see if the work begun was bearing the fruit of the Spirit in righteousness and true holiness of heart and life (ibid. 32 n.).

Spiritual Senses and Perceptible Inspiration

Because human beings were given, by grace, spiritual senses, it was possible for them to experience the 'inward witness' Samuel Wesley identified as the strongest proof of Christianity in 1735. The Methodist appeal to the 'spiritual senses' drew upon a tradition within the Christian church that can be traced back to Origen, Pseudo-Marcarius, and Bonaventure. This tradition extended through Puritan authors such as Richard Baxter, William Perkins, John Owen, and Richard Sibbes. All of these writers employed the analogy of sense perception in describing the work of grace. Rex Matthews is correct in pointing to Henry Scougal's devotional classic, *The Life of God in the Soul of Man*, as the most likely source for the Wesley brothers joining the New Testament Hebrews text with the concept of spiritual sensation made possible only in those who believe (Matthews 1986: 232–46; see Wesley 1975– : xi. 46). John Wesley wrote to John Bennet stating succinctly, 'Faith is seeing God; love is feeling God' (Wesley 1975– : xxvi. 108).

The 'Witness of the Spirit' was the subject of two sermons by John Wesley written and published in 1746 and 1767. The *objective witness of the Spirit* was a result of the work of God perceived by the soul in a manner similar to the way human knowledge was the result of sense experience perceived by the mind. The *subjective witness of one's own spirit* and conscience came in response the initiative of the Holy Spirit. On the one hand, ' "we love God, because he first loved us," and for his sake we "love our brothers also" '; and, on the other 'It is hard to find words in the language of men to explain "the deep things of God". Indeed there are none that will adequately express what the children of God experience' (ibid. i. 274–5).

DIVERSITY OF RELIGIOUS EXPERIENCE AFFIRMED

By 1765, it is clear that John Wesley had come to accept the limits of religious language in relation to Christian experience. He argued that 'true believers do not all speak alike' and 'it is not to be expected that they should' for there are 'a thousand circumstances that may cause them to vary from each other' including education, religious tradition, natural abilities, and time. Wesley was willing to allow that 'Men may differ from us in their opinions as well as their expressions. . . . 'Tis possible they may not have a *distinct apprehension* of the very blessing which they enjoy. Their *ideas* may not be so *clear*, and yet their experience may be as sound as ours' (ibid. 454–6). At the close of his life John affirmed 'whatever change is wrought in men, whether in their hearts or lives' must be of God even if these persons have no clear understanding of 'those capital doctrines, the fall of man, justification by faith, and of the atonement made by the death of Christ, and of his righteousness transferred to them. . . . I believe the merciful God regards the lives and tempers of men more than their ideas. . . . "Without holiness," I own, "no man shall see the Lord;" but I dare not add, "or clear ideas" ' (ibid. iv. 175).

METHODISM IN THE NINETEENTH CENTURY

With the death of Charles Wesley in 1788 and John in 1791, the Methodist movement was left without a leadership structure sufficient to maintain the diverse theology, structure, and practice that had emerged. The spiritual desire for union with God and practical implications for the love of neighbour were too complex for the 'Legal Hundred' and the annual conference to manage without the classical and theological education of the Wesley brothers. The substance of the select band was quickly supplanted by the emotion of the prayer meeting; and, the North American camp meeting soon overshadowed the field preaching of ordinary local pastors. The movement began to fragment over the issues related to church government (e.g. Methodist New Connexion) and regional revivals (e.g. Primitive Methodism in Staffordshire, 1811, and the Bible Christian Movement in south-west England, 1815).

Methodism in Great Britain and the United States achieved recognition as a distinct Christian denomination; however, they failed to keep their power as a movement composed of diverse types of small groups to assist people at various stages of the spiritual journey. The complex structures of the Wesleyan movement designed to nurture leaders capable of sustaining the expansion of the movement gave way to the organizational structures needed to care for the institution.

The last fifty years of the nineteenth century was the era of great preachers, and Methodist spirituality was undoubtedly influenced by the 'cult of the pulpit' (Wakefield 1999: 51). The Holiness Movement focused on the Methodist teaching about the need for sanctification and a second work of God that would eradicate inbred sin. The centre for this movement in Great Britain was Cliff College in the Derbyshire Peak District and Samuel Chadwick (d. 1932) became one of the key leaders.

METHODISM IN THE TWENTIETH CENTURY

At the turn of the century William James's (1842–1910) pivotal works, *Principles of Psychology* (1890) and *The Varieties of Religious Experience* (1902), provided a foundation for intellectual conversation about religious experience of the Wesleyan Christians and gave rise to the wider conversation about religious experience in other world religions (Proudfoot 2004). Sydney Dimand extended the conversation with the Wesleyan tradition with his work on *The Psychology of the Methodist Revival: An Empirical and Descriptive Study* (1934). However, Dimand made no attempt to relate his work to the needs of the contemporary mission of the Methodist churches and it was, for the most part, neglected.

Samuel Chadwick helped to found the Southport Convention to bring spiritual renewal and scriptural holiness. To some extent, Southport stood for the doctrine of the eradication of inbred sin and imparted holiness, as against the Keswick teaching of repression of sin and imputed righteousness.

In North America the fundamental faith of the Holiness tradition encountered the Pentecostal movement that began in the Bible College founded in 1900 by Charles Parham. The Pentecostal Holiness movement resulted from the union of these two revival movements.

The British reaction to revivalism and the various strands of the Holiness tradition can be seen in the works of Newton Flew, W. R. Maltby, J. Alexander Findlay, and Leslie Weatherhead. These more liberal clergy drew their spirituality from the synoptic gospels and the cross. According to Findlay, 'The only Pentecost which can really turn the world upside down is the Pentecost that shall follow a new vision of Calvary' (Wakefield 1999: 65).

During the 1960s many Methodists lost confidence in orthodox Christianity and traditional methods of spirituality resulting in more radical expressions of theology and experience. Those inclined towards mysticism moved in the direction of Eastern religions or the New Age movement. Those inclined towards activism joined the 'Jesus People' movement or into Christian communities dedicated to mission and evangelism. Those inclined to philosophy found the work of Albert North Whitehead (1861–1947) and Process Theology of value; e.g. Charles Hartshorne, Schubert M. Ogden, John B. Cobb, Jr., and W. Norman Pittenger. Those inclined to ecumenism moved towards the work of the Consultation on Common Texts to develop versions of key liturgical texts (Gloria, Creed, Lord's Prayer, etc.); however, this work was soon taken up by an international body which became known as the International Consultation on English Texts (ICET). Those who preferred forms of worship that were more historic and high church moved in the direction of the liturgical renewal.

In the final decades of the twentieth century, postmodern philosophy and theology in the northern and western hemispheres made room for renewed conversation about the Christian experience of God; for example, Morton Kelsey's work, *Encounter with God: A Theology of Christian Experience*, and Kenneth Leech, *Experiencing God: Theology as Spirituality*. There was also a growing interest in world religions and the possibility of a more universal experience of God.

METHODISM IN THE TWENTY-FIRST CENTURY

Reflecting on the Methodist movement of the past two centuries, John Kent has speculated that in every generation there are some who need the experience of 'primary religion... with its basic belief in intrusive supernatural power'. He argued that this form of religion 'survives at all times and... at all social levels'. The success of Wesleyan Methodism of the eighteenth century was precisely because it met this basic human need (Kent 2002: 7–8). Perhaps this insight is helpful as many Methodists and mainline Christians struggle to understand the rise of global Pentecostalism in the twenty-first century.

The weakness of many Methodist and Wesleyan movements of the nineteenth and twentieth centuries had to do with their focus on the past glories of revival and renewal. The impact of the early Methodists were often idealized and exaggerated, creating an inappropriate standard to evaluate the work of God's Spirit in the present day and obscuring the need for innovation and change in order to live faithfully into the future.

Where Christian theologians and religious leaders have accepted the modernist antipathy towards the supernatural and mystical, the spiritual needs of the people go unmet. Where the supernatural and mystical experiences are not guided and nurtured by Scripture, tradition, and reason—fanaticism and superstition may cause confusion and discredit those experiences of God that are authentic.

Perhaps what is needed by those in the Methodist traditions today is the willingness to hold theological formulations carefully, with humility and grace, acknowledging that no tradition has the ability to comprehend the fullness of God's counsel; reclamation of the appropriate structures and practices to assist people on their spiritual journey of grace; and, engagement in the mission to spread 'scriptural holiness' across the land with the understanding that Christianity has never taken philosophy, natural science, or any metaphysical scheme as its starting point. The human experience of God began with the activity of God in creation, it became clear in the incarnation and self-revelation of Jesus, and it continues through the intimate, transforming power of the Holy Spirit.

CONCLUSION

The Methodist understanding and experience of God is grounded in the Judaeo-Christian Scripture and developed in the context of the eighteenth-century Enlightenment. Through the leadership of John and Charles Wesley, Methodism was able to bring together a dynamic understanding of reason and revelation based on the biblical teaching that humankind is created in the image and likeness of God. Therefore, human beings are capable of an authentic relationship with their creator. The direct experience of God described in the early chapters of Genesis was disrupted by human disobedience and sin; however, it was not destroyed because God chose to continue by grace what was no longer possible by nature. The provision of the law, the prophets, and the Messiah were all understood to be a part of God's plan of redemption. In Christ, God took on human flesh and lived in relationship with those who were willing to follow him. By the Holy Spirit, the first disciples became living examples of the new life made possible in Christ.

All experience of God, for the Wesleys, was a gift of grace, to be received by faith. The only adequate response was faith, love, and obedience. The wide diversity of Christian experiences within the Methodist movement were nurtured to maturity through a complex system of spiritual guidance involving: (1) a spiritual mentor or sponsor, (2) a small-group leader of the class or band, (3) a variety of larger settings for spiritual instruction and practice; e.g. the meeting of the united society, the watch-night, the love feast, and the covenant renewal service; (4) literature for the spiritual instruction of those who could read; and (5) leadership training, and opportunities for service that included both laymen and laywomen. In addition to the local leaders, travelling preachers in connexion with the Wesleys were available to assist in the more difficult matters of spiritual guidance, theology, or practice.

Susanna Wesley's insight served her sons well and remains relevant: 'Fair blossoms, but which will bring forth fruit?'

SUGGESTED READING

ELLENS, J. HAROLD (2008). *Understanding Religious Experiences: What the Bible Says about Spirituality*. Westport, Conn.: Praeger.

GELLMAN, JEROME (2001). *Mystical Experience of God: A Philosophical Inquiry*. Burlington, Vt.: Ashgate.

HART, KEVIN, and WALL, BARBARA (2005). *The Experience of God: A Postmodern Response*. New York: Fordham University Press.

HEITZENRATER, RICHARD P. (1995). *Wesley and the People Called Methodists*. Nashville: Abingdon.

HEMPTON, DAVID (2005). *Methodism: Empire of the Spirit*. New Haven: Yale University Press.

MADDOX, RANDY L. (1994). *Responsible Grace: John Wesley's Practical Theology*. Nashville: Kingswood.

WIEBE, PHILLIP H. (2004). *God and Other Spirits: Intimations of Transcendence in Christian Experience*. Oxford: Oxford University Press.

REFERENCES

ALBIN, THOMAS R. (1985). 'An Empirical Study of Early Methodist Spirituality'. In Theodore Runyon (ed.), *Wesleyan Theology Today: A Bicentennial Theological Consultation*. Nashville: Kingswood.

ALBIN, THOMAS R. (2001). 'Inwardly Persuaded: Religion of the Heart in Early British Methodism'. In Richard B. Steele (ed.), *'Heart Religion' in the Methodist Tradition and Related Movements*. Lanham, Md.: Scarecrow Press.

ANDRESEN, JENSINE (2001). *Cognitive Perspectives Ritual, and Experience*. Cambridge: Cambridge University Press.

BOEVE, LEIVEN, and HEMING, LAURENCE P. (2004). *Divinising Experience: Essays in the History of Religious Experience from Origen to Ricoeur*. Dudley: Peeters.

COOLMAN, BOYD TAYLOR (2004). *Knowing God by Experience: The Spiritual Senses in the Theology of William of Auxerre*. Washington, D.C.: Catholic University of America Press.

DAVIES, RUPERT, and RUPP, GORDON (1965). *A History of the Methodist Church in Great Britain*. 4 vols. London: Epworth, i.

DIMAND, SYDNEY G. (1934). *The Psychology of the Methodist Revival: An Empirical and Descriptive Study*. Oxford: Oxford University Press.

GELLMAN, JEROME I. (2001). *Mystical Experience of God: A Philosophical Inquiry*. Burlington, Vt.: Ashgate.

HART, KEVIN, and WALL, BARBARA (2005). *The Experience of God: A Postmodern Response*. New York: Fordham University Press.

HEITZENRATER, RICHARD P. (1972). 'John Wesley and the Oxford Methodists, 1725–1735'. Ph.D. Dissertation. Duke University.

—— (1995). *Wesley and the People Called Methodists*. Nashville: Abingdon.

HICK, JOHN (2006). *The New Frontier of Religion and Science: Religious Experience, Neuroscience and the Transcendent*. New York: Palgrave MacMillan.

HINDMARSH, D. BRUCE (2005). *The Evangelical Conversion Narrative: Spiritual Autobiography in Early Modern England*. Oxford: Oxford University Press.

JAMES, WILLIAM (1929). *The Varieties of Religious Experience*. London: Longmans.

JONES, SCOTT J. (1995). *John Wesley's Conception and Use of Scripture*. Nashville: Kingswood.

KENT, JOHN (2002). *Wesley and the Wesleyans*. Cambridge: Cambridge University Press.

KIMBROUGH, S. T., JR., and NEWPORT, KENNETH G. C. (2008). *The Manuscript Journal of the Reverend Charles Wesley, M.A.* 2 vols. Nashville: Kingswood.

MADDOX, RANDY L. (1990). *Aldersgate Reconsidered*. Nashville: Kingswood.

MATTHEWS, REX (1986). 'Religion and Reason Joined'. Th.D. dissertation. Harvard University.

NEWPORT, KENNETH G. C. (2001). *The Sermons of Charles Wesley*. Oxford: Oxford University Press.

NORRIS, JOHN (1707). *Practical Discourses on Several Divine Subjects*. 4 vols. London.

ODEN, THOMAS C. (1984). *Care of Souls in the Classic Tradition*. Philadelphia: Fortress.

PODMORE, COLIN (1998). *The Moravian Church in England, 1728–1760*. Oxford: Oxford University Press.

PROUDFOOT, WAYNE (ed.) (2004). *William James and a Science of Religions: Reexperiencing Varieties of Religious Experience*. New York: Columbia University Press.

SCHLITT, DALE M. (2007). *Experience and Spirit: A Post-Hegelian Philosophical Theology*. New York: Peter Lang.

TUTTLE, ROBERT G., JR. (1989). *Mysticism in the Wesleyan Traditon*. Grand Rapids: Francis Asbury Press.

WAINWRIGHT, WILLIAM J. (2005). *The Oxford Handbook of Philosophy of Religion*. Oxford: Oxford University Press.

WAKEFIELD, GORDON S. (1999). *Methodist Spirituality*. London: Epworth.

WALSH, JOHN (1966). 'Origins of the Evangelical Revival'. In *Essays in Modern English Church History*. New York: Oxford University Press.

WARD, W. R. (1992). *The Protestant Evangelical Awakening*. Cambridge: Cambridge University Press.

WATSON, DAVID LOWES (1985). *The Early Methodist Class Meeting*. Nashville: Discipleship Resources.

WESLEY, JOHN (1771–4). *The Works of the Rev. John Wesley, M.A.*, ed. W. Pine. 32 vols. Bristol.

—— (1831). *The Works of John Wesley*, ed. Thomas Jackson. 14 vols. London: John Mason.

—— (1975–) *The Bicentennial Edition of the Works of John Wesley*. 34 vols. ed. Frank Baker and Richard P. Heitzenrater. Nashville: Abingdon.

WIEBE, PHILLIP H. (2004). *God and Other Spirits: Intimations of Transcendence in Christian Experience*. Oxford: Oxford University Press.

CHAPTER 23

THE QUEST FOR HOLINESS

ELAINE A. HEATH

PHOEBE Worrall Palmer (1807–74) was one of the greatest spiritual leaders of the nineteenth century, and in the entire history of Methodism (Raser 1987; White 1986; Wheatley 1984). Palmer was a revival preacher, evangelist, and lay theologian who led over 25,000 people to a deep faith in Christ (Westerfield Tucker and Liefeld 1987: 263). As part of her holistic evangelism Palmer was a humanitarian who helped found the first immigrant settlement house in Manhattan, Five Points Mission. A prolific writer, Palmer authored eighteen books and many articles, and edited the widely read periodical *Guide to Holiness* (1864–74). Her most popular book was her spiritual autobiography, *The Way of Holiness*, which became a best-seller, undergoing numerous printings and being translated into several foreign languages. Palmer's seminal *Promise of the Father* offered a strong defence of women's right to public ministry based on Palmer's pentecostal pneumatology. Over a dozen new denominations were formed by Christians who were influenced by Palmer's holiness teaching. Those who came to her for spiritual guidance included bishops, theologians, and clergy. For these and other reasons, Palmer came to be known as the mother of the Holiness Movement. A classical Christian mystic, Palmer's extraordinary spiritual vision and power originated in her transformative encounters with God that took place in her quest for holiness. To be utterly given to God was the central theme of Palmer's life and thought.

Through most of the twentieth century Palmer has been marginalized for her sanctification theology, which she called 'The Shorter Way'. Palmer's critics have caricatured her as having distorted John Wesley's sanctification theology, taking it in directions that were alien to Wesley's intent. What Palmer's detractors have failed to understand is her fundamentally apophatic mysticism and its missional power, and her location within the long history of Christian mystics. They have also failed to distinguish between Palmer's theology and the skewed interpretations of it offered by subsequent holiness preachers.

What Palmer provides for Methodism is a distinctly Methodist, mystical theology of kenosis, an apophatic theology that was undeveloped in Wesley. Like so many mystics of the church, Palmer has been sidelined, caricatured, trivialized, and muffled by the dominant church of her tradition. Yet today as the Methodist Church faces the staggering loss of missional vitality, it has never been more in need of Palmer's wisdom.

THE APOPHATIC PATH

Apophatic mysticism is a spiritual path that is marked with a de-emphasis on affective religious experience, or the relativization of experience. In apophatic spirituality the emphasis is on God being so much more than our experience of God. The apophatic path is also the way of kenosis, or self-emptying. It is about surrender to God, especially in the face of not knowing just what the consequences will be. The result of genuine apophatic Christian mysticism is increasing inward freedom and outward transformation, an ever-deepening love of God and neighbour.

Experience, emotion, affectivity are all part of incarnational faith, thus it is to be expected that a genuine Christian faith journey will also include kataphatic spirituality, that is, it will also be marked with affective religious experience, and will be embodied in ordinary life. Because Christianity is incarnational, it must include both apophatic and kataphatic expressions. Neither of these two paths is sufficient on its own. Among the Christian mystics, however, there is a tendency to be more oriented towards either apophatic or kataphatic spirituality. The overall trajectory both in this discussion and in Palmer's writing is her general de-emphasis on affective experience along with her focus on kenosis in her quest for holiness.

NAKED FAITH IN THE NAKED PROMISE

The first indicator of Palmer's apophatic mysticism came in her early years as she struggled for assurance of sanctification. Having grown up in a devout Methodist household, Palmer was exposed to Methodist revivalism from childhood. Revival preachers stressed the need for a second work of grace subsequent to salvation, through which the believer is sanctified for a life of holiness. Methodist revivalists preached a kataphatic message in that the second work of grace was to be affectively marked by an 'inner witness of the Spirit', testifying within oneself that sanctification had taken place.

Palmer, who had experienced salvation at age 4, struggled mightily through her teen years to experience a second work of grace marked by a changed 'feeling', yet the feelings would not come. Like many who make authentic faith commitments as young children, Palmer could not remember *not* walking with God. Yet the sense of a divine call to deeper holiness persisted, and with it the feeling of condemnation (Palmer 1867: 49–53). Palmer describes finally reaching a crisis point in which she felt she either had to experience the 'second work' or lose her salvation:

Others may act upon the principle that it is optional with themselves whether they will remain in a state of justification, or go on to a state of entire sanctification, but, with me, the command was absolute, 'Go on to perfection'—'be ye holy;' and, if I had not obeyed, how could I have been in a state of condemnation and in a state of justification at the same time?
(Palmer 1979: 26)

For Palmer 'entire sanctification' meant utterly giving over to God everything she was, everything she had, all her relationships, dreams, hopes, and especially her will. It meant putting herself on the altar to be a living sacrifice, an 'eternal surrender of life, reputation, and friends dearer than life' (ibid. 27). Thus the life of kenosis was, for Palmer, 'the way of holiness'.

The crux of Palmer's struggle was her lack of kataphatic experience, which produced great anxiety in the young seeker of holiness. No amount of good works, prayer, anxiety, or thought could produce the desired affective awareness that she was one with God, given over to live in one accord with God's will. Again and again as she wrestled with absence of feeling, she felt Satan tempting her with the accusation that she was presumptuous for even thinking she could be holy (Palmer 1867: 82).

In this struggle Palmer was experiencing the affective 'nothingness' or emptiness that is part of apophatic mysticism. She felt intense and unremitting desire (*erōs*) for oneness with the God who seemed to have become affectively absent. Palmer was, in the schema of contemplative theologians Francis Nemeck and Marie Coombs, passing through one of seven critical thresholds along the way to the mature spiritual development of a contemplative (Nemeck and Coombs 1987: 48). A 'critical threshold' is a major spiritual change in which the contemplative is permanently transformed at a deeper level, never going back to the way he or she 'used to be'. The thresholds are progressive over the course of the contemplative's lifetime (ibid. 33–4). To use language from the great mystic-apostle St. Paul, the thresholds are the process of being transformed 'from glory to glory' while living in a posture of adoration towards God (2 Corinthians 3: 18).

Spiritual thresholds are often precipitated by personal trauma such as serious illness, or the death of a loved one (ibid. 35). Grief over the deaths of three of her children, particularly Eliza who died exactly one year before her experience of sanctification, led Palmer to conclude she had loved her family idolatrously (Palmer 1979: 145–6; 1867: 151–2). Because of this she felt a divine imperative to detach from an 'idolatrous' clinging to her family. This process of detachment from one's family is part of kenosis and is well described in the lives and writings of many Christian mystics, especially St Ignatius of Loyola (Egan 1978: 399–426). It is best understood as detaching from a possessive grip rather than a cessation of relationship.

The definitive breakthrough came for Palmer on 26 July 1837, which she called the 'Day of Days' when she made her irrevocable 'altar covenant' with God (Palmer 1988: 114). Her breakthrough came as a result of the realization that holiness was promised to her by God's Word and that promise was true regardless of her emotions. Palmer came to view her previous demand for an emotional 'proof' of sanctification as being like the sinful demand of the Pharisees for Jesus to produce ever more 'signs and wonders' before they would believe his words. At the same time, Palmer was seized with a deepened conviction that she must give her husband and children to God rather than cling fearfully to them.

So it was that as Palmer kenotically relinquished to God both the demand for affective proof of sanctification and her attachment to her family, she finally experienced sanctification—the state of simple, undivided rest in God, the absolute commitment to God—for which she had longed (ibid. 114–22). Though she went on to have many kataphatic mystical experiences afterwards, including dreams and visions in which she experienced her call to public ministry, throughout her life and teaching Palmer was essentially an apophatic mystic (Heath 2006: 87–111). Her message was one of kenosis.

THE SHORTER WAY

Palmer's shorter way of sanctification involves three steps, each of which has its own assumptions about Scripture, faith, and the nature of salvation. These steps are entire consecration, faith, and testimony. Palmer's three steps are best understood as events that take place both at the beginning of sanctification, as literal steps, and also as a simultaneous threefold process that is to characterize the journey of a sanctified believer for the rest of his or her life. Because of the latter meaning, the labelling of these three elements of Palmer's altar theology as 'steps' has in some ways contributed to skewed interpretations of the shorter way.

Palmer understands human holiness to be the experience of entire devotion to God, of being a living sacrifice on the altar of Christ, of being continuously 'washed, cleansed, and renewed after the image of God' as one is ceaselessly presented to God (Palmer 1988: 189). Romans 12: 1–2 is a critical text for Palmer and as such, illustrates her affirmation of the process of sanctification.

The Apostle's phrase 'living sacrifice' implies a dynamic, ongoing, organic process involving daily choice. Living sacrifices must choose daily whether to 'stay on the altar'. The transformation that is expected of sanctified believers is a journey that takes time as the mind is gradually and increasingly 'renewed'. Sanctification is a 'way' of holiness, writes Palmer, another image that implies movement, process, time, growth, and journey. The very language of Scripture is both/and in terms of sanctification as an event and a process. Hebrews, the biblical book with Palmer's premier texts on holiness, applies a typological hermeneutic to the Exodus event to teach Christians that one cannot simply enter the promised land, one must increasingly 'possess' it through ongoing obedience to God.

Palmer's use of the term, 'shorter way' does not then imply absence of process or journey in sanctification. Nor does the phrase necessarily imply instantaneousness over process. Rather, the word 'shorter' underscores the potential for entering the way of holiness sooner rather than later, and gives a method for entering the way of holiness. For Palmer, sanctification is the beginning, not the end of the journey of holiness. The sooner one enters the way of holiness the sooner one will be empowered for lifelong service and purity of heart, with which to love God and neighbour. For Palmer, holiness is missional, the union of the Christian and the church with the *missio Dei*.

Palmer cites numerous texts from the Bible in which God's people are commanded to be holy. Of these texts, Hebrews 12: 14 is most prominent: 'Pursue peace with everyone, and holiness, without which no one will see the Lord' (NRSV). Other commands to holiness include Leviticus 11: 45 and 2 Corinthians 7: 1. These passages when taken in context, which Palmer was careful to do, also imply the importance of daily choice in remaining in the way of holiness.

At times Palmer seems to go so far as to give the impression that a professing Christian could actually miss out on heaven if he or she has not entered the way of holiness, since 'without holiness, no man will see the Lord'. In this respect she seems to edge toward near-Pelagianism, and it is this element of her altar theology that may have partially contributed to a works righteousness tendency in later holiness theology. At the same time it must be said that Palmer's emphasis on grace as the divine energy that makes holiness possible, serves to balance her occasionally semi-Pelagian statements.

The only way for a sanctified believer to stay holy, according to Palmer, is to keep everything 'on the altar'. True to her Wesleyan, Arminian theological heritage, she believes that the Christian never loses his or her free will, with which continuous decisions are made about keeping on or removing from the altar, that which has previously been consecrated. The warning passages of Hebrews 4: 1–11, 6: 4–6, 10: 26–39, and 12: 14–29 carry sombre messages of judgement for those who have once walked in the way of holiness, then lost their way through disobedience. Putting all on the altar is an ongoing choice with serious ramifications. At the same time, because the altar, Christ, sanctifies the gifts in Palmer's theology, sanctification takes place in a dynamic relationship between divine grace and human cooperation.

Though many of Palmer's theological progeny have focused on the instantaneous side of the shorter way (having a personal 'day of days', so to speak, to which one could point as the day of one's sanctification), it is clear that a daily process of surrender is involved, one which requires all three 'steps' on an ongoing basis. Palmer issues repeated admonitions against losing one's holiness, and the need to walk faithfully day by day in order to retain a state of sanctification.

Palmer's altar theology, the foundation of her shorter way of sanctification, centres on two concepts: first that the altar sanctifies the gift, and second that Christ himself is the altar. As always, these convictions are based upon Scripture. Palmer's understanding that the altar sanctifies the gift is based upon texts from Exodus and Matthew, among others (Palmer 1867: 43–4).

Palmer's citations from Exodus 29 are part of a lengthy section giving instructions for the consecration of priests. Her use of this text is doubly significant in that Palmer's theological thrust in sanctification is towards preparedness of the church for holy, priestly service in the world. Not only is she making a statement about the altar sanctifying the gift, she is subtly reinforcing her missional focus, which is sanctification as empowerment for mission. The promise of the Father is given so that the gospel may be proclaimed everywhere, not just through professional clergy, but through every Spirit-baptized son and daughter of God. Sanctification is much more concerned with taking the gospel to 'Jerusalem, Judaea, Samaria, and the uttermost parts of the earth' (Acts 1: 8), than with individual piety or asceticism.

Throughout the cultus regulations of Exodus 29 the emphasis is on the 'set-apartness' of holiness. Whatever is sanctified or consecrated is completely set apart for God. The many offerings, cleansing rituals, priestly garments, anointing procedures, and explicit times for each ritual detailed in Exodus 29 are all meant to underscore the solemnity of the covenant. Once consecrated, the priests will belong wholly to God. They will no longer be like other Israelites and will not live according to other tribes' standards.

The 'otherness' of the Levites is especially pronounced in the prohibition against their owning land. According to Numbers 18: 20–1, the only inheritance the Levites will have is the tithe of the rest of the Israelites. The Levites are to understand that they are not their own but are actually God's gift to the rest of the Israelites (Numbers 18: 5–6). The consecrated priests are to mediate God's presence to the rest of Israel. Israel, in turn, is to mediate God's presence to the whole world. That holy task is to become their singular, guiding vision. They do not have other options that are acceptable to God.

In Palmer's theology similar expectations are placed upon sanctified believers who have placed all upon the altar of Christ. Once sanctified, they will be 'the Lord's *property*', writes Palmer. Unlike other people who might cling to material wealth, status, and other accoutrements of success, sanctified Christians are on a missional journey, their lives utterly given over to God's purposes. The testimony of those who are sanctified becomes the contemporary version of taking the gospel to Jerusalem, Judaea, Samaria, and the uttermost parts of the earth. Sanctified believers are the priestly mediators of God's saving love to a world in desperate need.

Those who are sanctified cannot claim holiness based upon personal effort. As Palmer stresses so often, it is the altar that sanctifies the gift. At the centre of Exodus 29 and its various rites of consecration is the altar upon which the offerings are made. Before the priests could be consecrated the altar itself had first to be sanctified. Once the altar was 'atoned for', (that is cleansed and set apart exclusively for God according to Exodus 29: 37), it became holy, therefore anything that touched it was also made holy. The gifts offered there were not intrinsically holy. Rather the altar of sacrifice was what sanctified the gifts.

Under the new covenant, argues Palmer, Christ is the altar: 'The altar, thus provided by the conjoint testimony of the Father, Son, and Holy Spirit, is Christ. His sacrificial death and sufferings are the sinner's plea; the immutable promises of the Lord Jehovah the ground of claim' (ibid. 43).

Palmer's understanding of Christ as the altar is based upon an interpretation of Hebrews 13: 10 in which believers are assured: 'We have an altar from which those who officiate in the tent have no right to eat.' Following Adam Clarke and others, Palmer understands the altar in this passage and the rest of Hebrews to be Christ. In Hebrews Christ is all three: the sacrifice, the priest, and the altar. This interpretation of 'altar' as a metonym for Christ the perfect and final sacrifice, is consistent not only with Clarke but also with much of Church tradition since antiquity and is well-supported in contemporary scholarship (Lane 1991: 538–9; Attridge 1989: 391).

In citing Jesus as the altar according to Hebrews 13: 10, by extension Palmer also references the subsequent instructions for those who would place themselves on the altar. Sanctified believers, following the instructions of verses 13–16, express their sanctification in several ways. First, they are willing to bear whatever disgrace or persecution the world might heap upon them, for they are identified with Jesus' interests 'outside the camp' (Hebrews 13: 13). The desire for human approval, in other words, no longer has power over the sanctified Christian. Moreover, the set apart ones are on pilgrimage, detached from this world and its seductions (Hebrews 13: 14). The true destination, the true home lies ahead in eternity. Therefore the sanctified are in this world as sojourners rather than citizens. The sacrifices that are to be offered by the priestly, sanctified believers are living sacrifices of praise, and lips confessing the name of Jesus (Hebrews 13: 15).

Palmer's sanctification theology is deeply rooted in her biblical theology of kenosis, with special attention to passages having to do with priestly consecration, the role of Jesus as the altar, and the expectations of those who would walk in the way of holiness.

THE WHOLE OFFERING

Understanding, then, the foundation of her altar theology, let us consider the three parts of the shorter way of sanctification. The first step of the shorter way is the step of entire consecration, in which the individual takes inventory of every part of his or her life, wilfully and with irrevocable commitment placing everything on the 'altar' that is Christ himself. Nothing is held back. Romans 12: 1–2, in which Paul exhorts believers to present themselves as living sacrifices is the scriptural command for this step. As part of this step the believer also implores God to reveal if there is anything that has not been surrendered. If anything is held back, whether it is a relationship, possessions, or even the sin of doubt, one cannot expect to receive the full blessing of sanctification (White 1986: 136–7).

For Palmer, this inventory and prayer has the nature of a legal document such as a last will and testament. In her book *Entire Devotion to God* Palmer includes a representative covenant prayer that can be personalized (ibid. 247). Notably, Palmer's covenantal approach is consonant with the biblical commandments for preparing and giving to God the *olah*, the whole burnt offering. Palmer's preference for the theological model of Leviticus is in keeping with Jesus and the early church in their understanding of the meaning of Jesus' sacrificial death (Wenham 1979: 36–7). To plumb more deeply Palmer's intent in using the sacrificial language and image of *olah* to explain sanctification, let us return to Leviticus.

While Leviticus treats of both God's and humanity's actions in sanctification, clearly teaching that only God can sanctify people, the emphasis of the book lies in humanity's part in making things holy (ibid. 22–3). Holiness is as much about completeness and wholeness as about correct moral choices (ibid. 24). Old Testament laws forbidding the interbreeding of animals, mixing of different crops in the field, and so on are symbolic of the core value of wholeness, completeness, and purity (Leviticus 19). At the deepest level these laws and concepts of holiness all signify the importance of God's people avoiding syncretism. Throughout the prohibitions and commandments of Leviticus rings the refrain: 'I am the Lord.' There is only one God, Yahweh. Human holiness is about complete surrender of self to God, more than anything else.

God's holiness is intrinsic to God's being, and is not particularly about God's morality. Beyond God's judgement of sin there is little in the Pentateuch that defines

God's holiness in terms of morality. The commandment to 'be holy, for I am holy' is therefore a commandment to be fully set aside for God's purposes, to be whole and complete, to obey the law, and to be one who does not profane the name of the Lord.

These kinds of expectation are all found in Palmer's understanding of holiness. The sanctified believer is one who is fully set aside for God's purposes, one who lives according to God's word in the Bible, one who does not profane the name of the Lord, and one who is made complete in Christ. Romans 12: 1–2 describes this person as a living sacrifice, referring to the *olah*, the whole burnt offering of Leviticus 18.

The first requirement for a whole offering in Leviticus 18 is that the offering be ritually clean, for only clean animals can become holy. As Wenham notes, cleanness is more than purity, it 'approximates to our notion of normality' (ibid. 20). Specific kinds of animals are designated as acceptable for the whole offering: sheep, goats, cattle, and birds. In order to qualify for the whole offering these animals have to be without blemish. One of Malachi's indictments against Israel was their 'contempt-ible' practice of profaning God's name in using diseased, crippled, and blind animals for the whole offering (Malachi 1: 7–8).

The Old Testament requirement of sacrificial animals that were 'clean' and 'without blemish' takes on a new meaning in the light of the New Testament. In Palmer's Wesleyan theology the believer who seeks sanctification is already jus-tified. He or she, in other words, has already been made 'clean' by the grace of justification. Imputed cleanness has made the person a candidate for becoming a living sacrifice, a whole offering on the altar of Christ. The second work of grace, sanctification, is the imparted grace that will make the person holy. Thus the justified believer is the 'clean' and acceptable candidate for a living sacrifice.

The most distinguishing feature of the whole offering was that the entire animal except its skin (or crop if a bird) was burned on the altar (Leviticus 1: 8, 16). Unlike other offerings, none of the whole offering was given to the priests. It was all given to God. Wenham (ibid. 51) observes that in an agrarian culture for which meat was a rare and expensive luxury, the sacrifice of a lamb or bull was very costly.

The whole offering thus underscores the costliness of sin, for the whole offering was given to atone for human sin (Leviticus 1: 4). The purification offering described in Leviticus 4 and the guilt offering in Leviticus 5 are also designated to atone for sin, but the whole offering is an atonement for sin in a somewhat different way (ibid. 57). The whole offering makes fellowship between God and humanity possible again after sin has caused a separation. The restoration of relationship provided by the burnt offering is suggested in Leviticus 14: 20 and 16: 24, as well as numerous other passages in the Old Testament.

The whole offering meant more than atonement for sin, however. It was also at times an act of worship, obedience, faith, or thanksgiving for deliverance (Exodus 18: 11–12; 24: 3–8; Numbers 6: 14; 15: 3; Psalms 50; 66: 13–15). In addition to these applications, the whole offering may be understood as a 'ransom' paid by the worshipper.

Ransom, however, is the premier meaning of atonement in Leviticus 17: 11, in which Yahweh says: 'I have given the blood to make atonement for your lives, for the blood makes atonement at the price of a life' (ibid. 60–1). This is the dominant meaning of all whole offerings, according to Wenham: 'God in his mercy allowed sinful man to offer a ransom payment for sins, so that he escaped the death penalty that his iniquities merit' (ibid. 61).

The ransom aspect of the whole offering is especially evident in the instructions for the worshipper to lay hands upon or lean on the animal during the prayer. The laying on of hands coupled with sincere prayer from the heart are the human actions that make the sacrifice acceptable (Leviticus 1: 4; 3: 2, 8, 13; 4: 4, 15, 24; 16: 21).

How does all this translate into Palmer's sanctification theology? There is no question that Palmer sees Christ as the ultimate sacrifice for sin. The atonement and ransom aspects of the whole offering apply to Christ, not to those seeking salvation and sanctification. That is, Christ is the perfect sacrifice once and for all. Christ has atoned for the sins of the world. Christ has ransomed the world, paying a debt the sinful world could not pay. Palmer has a clear and unambiguous grasp on the reality of salvation by grace and not by works. Thus the atonement aspect of the whole offering is not what she has in mind in equating the whole offering with putting oneself on the altar.

According to Romans 12: 1, Christians are to offer themselves as whole offerings as a grateful and reasonable response to God's mercy. Worship is the motivating factor for those who would truly seek sanctification. This is in keeping with the whole offering of the Old Testament as an act of worship, obedience, faith, and thanksgiving for deliverance from sin. The costliness of the whole offering also figures into Palmer's theology, in her insistence that the seeker put *all* on the altar.

From a standpoint of Palmer's apophatic spirituality, giving oneself as a whole offering is a supremely negating, self-surrendering act of worship. The one who is on the altar is there utterly for God. No longer having a self-life apart from God, no longer having a will of his or her own, the Palmerian *olah* is one whose life is continuously ascending to God in the fire of kenotic adoration. To make the choice daily, even hourly, to keep all on the altar, is an ongoing expression of apophatic spirituality. Just as in Leviticus the fragrance of the *olah* was a 'soothing aroma' to God, the 'aroma' of the living whole offering is a sweet and most precious fragrance to God (2 Corinthians 2: 14–16; Ephesians 5: 1–2).

FAITH IN GOD'S PROMISE

The second step of the shorter way is the exercise of faith: wilfully trusting the promise of God in Scripture concerning sanctification, regardless of outward signs, emotions, or religious manifestations. This step requires 'naked faith in the naked word of God'.

Before considering what Palmer does mean by 'naked faith' in this context, it must be emphasized that Palmer does not mean passivity. Palmer (1979: 76) expects a holy lifestyle to manifest itself in those who claim to be sanctified. Even though one might claim to be sanctified upon making a full surrender to God, prior to having had time to see the fruit of sanctification, Palmer expects fruit to follow such claims. In Palmer's eyes, the way of holiness is an eminently practical way of life that is marked by virtuous behaviour and holy action. While these acts of piety do not bring about sanctification, true sanctification always results in a life of piety. This is an important point when exploring the apophatic dimension of her spirituality. It is evident from Palmer's expectations of incarnational holiness, that she does not embrace an excessive apophaticism that diminishes creation or the incarnation.

Palmer also believes that perfection (e.g. sanctification) is not an exhaustive possession of all spiritual wisdom or knowledge, but a fullness of capacity to love. In other words, the 'perfected' (sanctified) Christian has the capacity to love God and neighbour wholeheartedly (Palmer 1867: 60–1). In this doctrine she reflects Wesley's understanding of perfection as the teleological fullness of love of God and neighbour. The fullness of love grows deeper as the sanctified believer continues to mature spiritually. There is a dynamic quality to the experience and expression of such love.

Thus the lived experience of Christian sanctification is neither one devoid of human error, nor is it a static way of life that does not continue to mature. These two qualifiers concerning the role of works and the presence of ongoing human frailty in sanctified believers are necessary in order to understand what Palmer means by the second step of faith in God's promise. If one ignores Palmer's understanding of the presence of works and the presence of human frailty and simply plucks out of context her statements about naked faith in the naked word of God, one could present a skewed version of her theology. She could be accused of promoting a new kind of quietism in which experience is irrelevant to faith. When Palmer describes the second step as faith in God's promise regardless of outward signs or manifestations, she is therefore not rejecting or ignoring religious activity. Rather, she attributes holy activity to the effect rather than cause of sanctification.

Palmer's apophatic mysticism is particularly evident in her approach to religious emotion and its role in the sanctified believer as she articulates the second step of the shorter way. Palmer has learned over the course of many years to accept 'consolations and desolations' (to borrow the language of many Catholic mystics) as part of the journey, while allowing neither to determine her level of commitment to God. If anything, the more desolate she feels emotionally, the harder she clings to the naked word of God.

Palmer's journey included many seasons in the dark, many bouts of emotional desolation and absence of spiritual assurance, for reasons known only to God. For Palmer these seasons of naked faith were experienced as a kind of testing, not unlike the testing of Jesus in the wilderness, whose sustenance was the naked word of God (Luke 4: 1–13). This kind of spiritual struggle marked Palmer's spiritual journey throughout her lifetime. It is not surprising, then, that in describing the second step of the shorter way, Palmer lists emotional manifestations and emotional assurance as phenomena that may or may not accompany the initial experience of sanctification.

As is the case with religious activity, Palmer is not denying the validity or even desirability of emotional experience as part of sanctification. Palmer's journal entries and autobiographic material reflect that after her 'Day of Days' she experienced profound emotional encounters with God, and throughout her life she enjoyed deep and loving relationships with her husband, family, and friends. What Palmer wants to make clear is the contingency of emotional experience. She wants those who seek sanctification to know that sanctification is not a guarantee of a particular set of emotional experiences, nor should Christians base their testimony of God's sanctifying grace on emotional experiences. She does not want people to think they have lost sanctification because of shifting emotions.

Palmer's emphasis on this point was powerful in bringing stability and needed rest to those who, like herself, had worn themselves out seeking a preconceived emotional experience in order to believe that God had accepted them as living sacrifices. According to Palmer, once believers have taken genuine inventory and have offered everything on the altar of Christ, they may be certain that God will sanctify the gift.

Since God promises to receive all who fully consecrate themselves (2 Corinthians 6: 16–7: 1), the believer has no reason to fear being rejected by God. Even if the one seeking holiness is not sure about having confessed all sin and consecrated everything to God, there is no reason to doubt because Philippians 3: 15 promises that if the Christian thinks incorrectly about something but is still open to God, God will surely reveal and correct the incorrect thinking (ibid. 137–8). The entire thrust of Old and New Testament sacrificial theology is that God longs for people to pray precisely this kind of prayer: a heartfelt and adoring surrender. Because of the overwhelming teaching of the Bible on God's posture towards sincere seekers, no one who prays in this way need fear that God will reject him or her.

Not only should seekers put aside fear of rejection, they should also put aside doubt, argues Palmer. To doubt that one is sanctified after having fully consecrated oneself is to doubt God's word, which is sinful according to Palmer (White 1986: 139; Palmer 1979: 47–9). This kind of doubt can actually prevent sanctification from taking place, since one must believe the promise of God in order to receive the promise (Palmer 1979: 177–9).

Telling Others

The third and final step of the shorter way is that of testimony. Indeed if this step is omitted, argues Palmer, sanctification cannot be retained. John Fletcher, who in some ways influenced Palmer more than Wesley did, reports that he lost the blessing of holiness five times because of failing to testify about it. Palmer (1979: 60) begins the section of *Full Salvation* entitled 'Publish It, Tell It' with Fletcher's experience, then goes on to describe the power of the Holy Spirit that came upon a camp meeting when a certain minister there finally began to testify to having been sanctified. Several others present who had 'lost the blessing' regained it as this man testified to the baptism of the Holy Spirit (ibid. 61–2). Citing Romans 10: 9–10, Palmer urges those who have believed in their hearts to also 'testify with their mouths' to the truth of what God has done. Palmer follows Wesley in this step, for he also urged Christians to tell others what God has done for them (White 1986: 139).

Testimony is necessary because the goal of sanctification is complete love of God and neighbour, and central to the expression of that love is the sharing of what God has done. The good news of the gospel, including the news of sanctification, is to be given away, not selfishly kept as a private blessing. No experience of God is meant simply as a private gift. Everything in the believer's life is to have a larger impact upon the world. 'God's gifts must be *diffused* or lost', declares Palmer. 'And no one enjoying the grace but will testify to the truth of this. A light put under a bushel goes out, and then it neither enlightens ourselves nor others' (Palmer 1979: 71). Testimony, like the other two steps of the shorter way, is an ongoing requirement, a spiritual discipline for the rest of one's life.

Though Palmer does not explicitly say this, there is also a psychological dimension to testifying to sanctification. Each time the sanctified believer tells others of his or her experience, the reality of his or her own sanctification is reinforced and the new paradigm of Christian life as the vow to be a living *olah* is reaffirmed.

In some ways the phenomenon of 'testifying to sanctification' is a bit like wedding anniversaries. As couples celebrate their anniversary they remember their wedding vows, recall the love that first drew them together, and celebrate the many shared experiences of their journey thus far. In a similar way, the sanctified believer who gives a testimony about sanctification, remembers the love with which God drew him or her, recalls the personal 'vow of *olah*', and reflects upon the consecrated life that has followed upon that commitment to being a living sacrifice.

As is the case with the first and second steps of the shorter way, the third step of testimony holds the potential for a skewed interpretation. If taken at a surface level, it could be argued that Palmer teaches magical thinking. That is, one could say she believed that all one has to do is utter the right words and regardless of heart condition or life condition, rest assured of sanctification. This criticism is uncon-vincing in the light of the overall trajectory of Palmer's writing and the holiness of her own life. Yet this is the sharpest criticism directed against Palmer's shorter way, both in her day and now. To critics both then and now, Palmer's shorter way seems like what Bonhoeffer called 'cheap grace' (Bonhoeffer 1963: 45). It seems that Palmer is making it far too easy for sinful, spiritually fruitless believers to claim a spiritual perfection they do not possess. As already demonstrated however, such criticisms do not take into account the full corpus of Palmer's teaching and the testimony of her own life.

Despite Palmer's repeated words about holiness of life and her warnings against Christian 'professors' who failed to live as Christ in the world, despite her expo-sitions on the meaning of 'naked faith in the naked word of God', within a short time of her death Palmer's theology underwent a significant interpretative shift. In no small part because of the theological shift, Palmerian theology moved away from its apophatic underpinnings, losing much of its original power.

CONCLUSION

Phoebe Palmer's quest for holiness began early in childhood when she gave herself to Jesus at the age of 4. Throughout her life the central question that drove her teaching, preaching, writing, and humanitarian work was the issue of holiness, that is, of belonging unreservedly to God. Palmer's altar theology was based upon her careful and thorough reading of the Bible, much of which she had memorized, and her Wesleyan vision for mission. Her theology of the 'Shorter Way' arose from her own apophatic journey of kenosis. Out of that journey Palmer articulated for Methodists in her own day and into the future, a distinctly Wesleyan form of apophatic spirituality, one that calls the church back to its missional vocation.

REFERENCES

ATTRIDGE, HAROLD (1989). *Hebrews*. Hermeneia. Philadelphia: Fortress.

BONHOEFFER, DIETRICH (1963). *The Cost of Discipleship*. New York: Macmillan.

EGAN, HARVEY (1978). 'Christian Apophatic and Kataphatic Mysticisms'. *Theological Studies* 39: 399–426.

HEATH, ELAINE (2006). 'The Via Negativa in the Life and Thought of Phoebe Palmer'. *Wesleyan Theological Journal* (Autumn): 87–111.

LANE, WILLIAM (1991). *Hebrews 9–13*. Word Biblical Commentary 48. Dallas: World Books.

NEMECK, FRANCIS, and COOMBS, MARIE (1987). *The Spiritual Journey.* Collegeville, Minn.: Liturgical Press.

PALMER, PHOEBE (1867). *The Way of Holiness, with Notes by the Way.* Salem, Ohio: Schmul.

—— (1979). *Full Salvation: Its Doctrine and Duties.* Salem, Ohio: Schmul.

—— (1988). *Selected Writings.* Sources of American Spirituality. New York: Paulist.

RASER, HAROLD (1987). *Phoebe Palmer: Her Life and Thought.* Lewiston, N.Y.: Edwin Mellen.

WENHAM, GORDON (1979). *The Book of Leviticus.* New International Commentary on the Old Testament. Grand Rapids: Eerdmans.

WESTERFIELD TUCKER, RUTH, and LIEFELD, WALTER (1987). *Daughters of the Church.* Grand Rapids: Academie.

WHEATLEY, RICHARD (1984). *The Life and Letters of Mrs. Phoebe Palmer.* New York: Garland.

WHITE, CHARLES (1986). *The Beauty of Holiness: Phoebe Palmer as Theologian, Revivalist, Feminist, and Humanitarian.* Grand Rapids: Francis Asbury Press.

CHAPTER 24

THE JOURNEY OF EVANGELISM

PHILIP R. MEADOWS

INTRODUCTION

MUCH of the current debate in the theology of evangelism can be framed by a common set of themes. First, it is clear that 'evangel-ism' is primarily concerned with the *evangel*, the gospel, or the good news we bear in the world. How we understand the nature of the gospel is of fundamental importance. Second, the *telos*, end or goal of evangelism is properly determined by the nature of the gospel itself. Contemplating this goal is a complex matter, however, because evangelism is a human activity that bears a promise that only God can fulfil. Any theology of evangelism must, therefore, carefully distinguish between that which can be accomplished through the means of our own striving, and that which results from the gracious activity of God alone. Third, the *ethos*, character or purpose of our practice is shaped by the goal of evangelism and must be understood in terms of 'working together with God' for the spread of the gospel.

The broad evangelical tradition has preserved what may be called a 'soteriological paradigm' of evangelism, rooted in the *evangel* of personal salvation. The centre of its concern is the *telos* of conversion: a life-transforming experience that brings the assurance of sins forgiven, new birth into a personal relationship with God, and the promise of eternal life. This goal is typically understood as a radical change that takes place in a moment of time, emphasizing the initiative of God's unconditional grace. The *ethos* of evangelism is proclamation, having the character of announcement, call, and response, with the purpose of bringing people to a point of spiritual awakening, crisis, and decision-making. The practice of evangelism is the means through which God brings conviction of sin, a spirit of repentance, and receptivity to the gift of faith. Evangelists are those gifted or trained individuals who lead unbelievers into this experience of personal salvation through a variety of means, from field preaching to faith sharing. In this paradigm, the Christian community may be the origin and the end of evangelistic outreach, but evangelism itself is usually thought of as an 'extraordinary' activity of building bridges to those beyond its borders.

Contemporary scholarship has tended to look upon this paradigm with suspicion (Abraham 1989: 40–69). First, there is often an individualism at work in the idea of personal salvation that reduces the gospel to a form of private spirituality. This neglects the social and material dimensions of the gospel, and renders ecclesial life merely incidental to the business of evangelism itself. In this way, conversion is easily sundered from discipleship. Second, it runs the risk of anthropocentrism in so far as the goal of conversion can become exclusively identified with datable moments of decision-making or certain patterns of emotional experience. The danger is that anthropocentric goals can be attained with or without the cooperation of God, or made available for consumption with or without the summons to costly discipleship. Third, pursuing such a diminished goal is often accompanied by a pragmatic inclination to calculate the effectiveness of evangelistic practices as the means of making converts (Stone 2007: 18, 29–53). In other words, there can be a mechanistic illusion that they have inherent power to produce conversion, and the assumption that any means is justified by this end. Evangelism that succumbs to these temptations also makes little demands on the faithful witness of Christian community itself.

This challenge to the soteriological paradigm also coincides with a 'missiological turn' in the theology of evangelism (Arias 1984). A new paradigm is emerging that recasts our understanding of the *evangel* in terms of Jesus' own teaching on the eschatological kingdom of God and the cosmic scope of the *missio Dei* to renew all creation. The gospel cannot be reduced to personal salvation, since the social and material reality of Christian community, whose life together is a sign, foretaste, and herald of the kingdom, is both the means and end of authentic evangelism. The logic of this paradigm exchanges the *telos* of conversion for that of discipleship as the proper response to the gospel, and the way in which kingdom life is embodied. Although it may be anticipated that unbelievers will eventually come to an experience of conversion, the purpose of evangelism is to facilitate a journey, not solicit responses as such. Indeed, conversion tends to be redefined as a life-transforming process rather than a radically transformative moment. The fundamental decision required of those being evangelized is to become a disciple; or, to seek entry into the kingdom of God through a complex process of spiritual, moral, and intellectual catechesis often compared to that of the pre-Constantinian church (Abraham 1989). The *ethos* of evangelism, then, is that of initiation into the kingdom of God, conceived as a clearly theocentric and ecclesial activity, rooted in the 'ordinary' practices of discipleship

(Jones 2003). Unbelievers are evangelized through an encounter with, and participation in, a community that bears faithful witness to the gospel, so that they may come to share in the new life of the kingdom for themselves. The task of the evangelist may be apostolic in nature, but it is also to ensure this ecclesial witness is intact, and properly coupled to intentional practices of inclusion and catechesis.

By embracing this 'missiological paradigm', however, care must be taken not to throw the baby out with the soteriological bathwater. Affirming the social reality of the gospel must not cause us to neglect the full range of experience associated with evangelical conversion. The soteriological paradigm cautions us that conversion cannot be reduced to one 'aspect' among many in a process of initiation, but is a gift of spiritual power that makes the new life of the kingdom possible, and without which both discipleship and fellowship slide into the mere form of religion. There is also an important distinction to be made between witness and evangelism. Witness may be the gospel made audible, visible, and tangible in the lives of Christians, but evangelism signifies the means by which unbelievers engage with that witness in the first place, and embrace the life-transforming reality of the gospel for themselves. The very idea of evangelism as a particular charism is in danger of becoming meaningless when defined so broadly as faithful witness in an unbelieving world, or as the implicit character of any ecclesial practice.

The benefit of laying out these issues paradigmatically is that it can help clarify the internal logic of two broad directions in the theology of evangelism (see Table 24.1). The danger, however, is that the distinctions between them may become overdrawn and the paradigms seen as closed alternatives rather than mutually correcting perspectives. The argument presented here is that the history of early Methodism and the tradition of Wesleyan theology can provide a resource for a more holistic undertaking. On the one hand, the roots of the soteriological paradigm can be traced back to the very soil of evangelical revival in which the early Methodist movement was grown (Skevington Wood 1967; Coleman 1994). Wesley can easily be taken as a champion of personal salvation with its logic of proclamation and conversion. On the other hand, he claimed that the movement was raised up to spread scriptural holiness, not merely to make converts. In this way, early Methodism can also be interpreted in terms of the missiological paradigm, as a faithful witness to the kingdom of God, with the logic of initiation and

Table 24.1 Paradigms of evangelism

Soteriological paradigm	Missiological paradigm	A Wesleyan paradigm
evangel of personal salvation	*evangel* of the eschatological kingdom	*evangel* of holy love
telos of conversion	*telos* of discipleship	*telos* of communion with God
ethos of proclamation	*ethos* of initiation	*ethos* of spiritual direction

discipleship. Indeed, Wesley came to see the similarity between the evangelistic function of Methodist fellowship and the early church practice of catechesis for those who responded to apostolic preaching (Wesley 1958: iii. 518–19).

Assuming that the example of early Methodism does not simply place us on the horns of a dilemma, the question is how these different emphases were held together in a coherent way, and what this might contribute to contemporary thinking about evangelism. The hypothesis explored here is that Wesley does not make conversion or discipleship the ultimate end of evangelism but communion with the triune God, and that this reality can integrate and transform insights from both the soteriological and missiological paradigms.

The Evangel: The Gospel of Communion with God

It has been claimed that the 'catholic substance' of Wesley's theology is the theme of 'participation' in God (Wesley 1984: 99; Allchin 1988: 24–47; Karkainen 2004: 72–81). The tradition has used the theological language of 'participation', 'union', and 'communion' as more or less synonymous references to the mutual indwelling of the Christian life with the triune God (Wesley 1779: 199 ff.; WMM 1849: 801–944; Flew 1934: 313–41; Matthaei 2000: 55 ff.).

Wesley's understanding of communion with God is deeply eschatological; rooted in a vision of the new creation when the crowning glory of humanity will be 'an intimate, an uninterrupted union with God; a constant communion with the Father and his Son Jesus Christ, through the Spirit; a continual enjoyment of the Three One God, and of all creatures in him' (Wesley 1984: ii. 510). The end of Christ's coming is that the communion with God known by Adam might be restored: who was 'unspeakably happy; dwelling in God, and God in him; having an uninterrupted fellowship with the Father and the Son, through the eternal Spirit' (ibid. 475–6). A life shaped by communion with God is the present experience or foretaste of this eschatological future, begun in conversion and deepened through a life of growth in grace towards perfect love. The kingdom of God is present within and among those who seek the perfect love of God and neighbour in their lives.

For Wesley, the whole way of salvation is encompassed by this communion of love with the triune God. The ultimate goal of evangelism and discipleship is that people may receive the gift of 'that deep communion with the Father and the Son, whereby they are enabled to give him their whole heart; to love every man as their own soul, and to walk as Christ also walked' (Wesley 1958: iii. 342).

For Wesley, the gospel is first and foremost the good news of holy love (Wynkoop 1972; Collins 2007; Jones 2003), and is a summons to that divine embrace in which the experience of evangelical conversion and growth in discipleship are held together.

Because God is love, to be loved by God is to be offered the gift of God's own self. It is only as God's love is shed abroad in our hearts, that we are able to love God in return, and love our neighbour as God has loved us. It is a mutual participation in which we find our life caught up and renewed in God; while God's own life is poured out and reproduced in us. Wesley describes this participation in the divine life with the mystical language of 'spiritual respiration'. It is

the continual inspiration of God's Holy Spirit; God's breathing into the soul, and the soul's breathing back what it first receives from God . . . an unceasing presence of God, the loving, pardoning God, manifested to the heart, and perceived by faith; and an unceasing return of love, praise, and prayer, offering up all the thoughts of our hearts, all the words of our tongues, all the works of our hands, all our body, soul, and spirit, to be a holy sacrifice, acceptable unto God in Christ Jesus.   (Wesley 1984: i. 434, 442)

The goal of evangelism is that persons may enter into communion with God (conversion), and journey deeper into the divine embrace (discipleship). Drawing upon the tradition of Wesleyan theology, I suggest it is helpful to think of communion with God as having four distinct but mutually conditioning aspects. The first two terms, *fellowship* and *holiness*, roughly correspond to the relationship between justification and sanctification as the two 'grand branches' of salvation. The second two terms, *vision* and *witness*, correspond to the relationship between faith as 'supernatural intercourse' with divine reality, and the 'beauty of holiness' that lights up the world.

FELLOWSHIP

Entering communion begins a life of fellowship with God, by which we receive what God has done *for us* in Christ: the grace of pardoning love, by which we are freed from the guilt of sin, adopted into the family of heaven, and restored to the favour of God. This justifying grace, which effects a 'relative change', is marked by the personal conviction of benefiting from the merits of Christ, an assurance of sins forgiven, and the witness of the Spirit. Communion as fellowship emphasizes the loving union of the soul with God, or the participation of *our life in God*. It is a life of repentance from attachment to worldly ends and sinful desires; a life of resignation in which all we are and do is offered up to God as a living sacrifice; a life of abiding and delighting in God, in whose hands our past, present, and future is held.

This fellowship is marked by ceaseless prayer that catches up every moment into the life of the triune God; joyful prayer that always celebrates the gifts of past, present, and future salvation; and thankful prayer that is stayed on God's providential care over every area of daily life.

HOLINESS

Entering communion begins a life of holiness, by which we receive what God does *in us* by the Holy Spirit: the grace of transforming power in which we are brought to new birth, freed from the bondage of sin, and restored to the image of God. This sanctifying grace, which effects a 'real change', is marked by the personal experience of victory in Christ over the power of sin, the gifts and fruit of the Spirit, and loving obedience to God. The emphasis of communion as holiness is on 'partaking of the divine nature', or the participation of *God's life in us*. It is a life of 'mortification' in which our attachment to worldly ends is cut off and sinful desires are reordered by holy love; a life of hungering and thirsting after the healing power of the indwelling Spirit; a life of being perfected in love towards God and neighbour, which is the renewal of heart and life in the likeness of Christ. Holiness is marked by a purity of heart in which worldly affections are replaced by godly virtues; a singularity of intention that aims at pleasing God in all things; and a constancy of obedience that is devoted to the glory of God in loving service of others.

VISION

Entering communion involves a life-transforming vision of God, as the Spirit brings us into a fellowship of holiness with the Father who is both love and light, through the Son whose love lights up the world. Communion as vision emphasizes the engagement of our 'spiritual senses', by which we are awakened *to perceive God*. It is a life of joyful thanksgiving in which the providence and grace of God are seen in all the vagaries of daily existence. To see God is to be in communion with God, and be renewed in mind, heart, and life. Beholding the glory of God is to be changed from glory to glory. Looking unto Jesus, as the Author and Perfecter of our faith, is to be filled with the mind of Christ and to walk as Christ walked. We become what we see because our lives are filled with that which we fix our attention upon. Faith is exercised by practising the presence of God, to set God always before us, to cultivate a 'single eye' for the triune God so that our whole body may be full of light, and we might walk in the light. 'Seeing him that is invisible', being sensible of 'the presence of the ever blessed Trinity', and developing an 'uninterrupted sense of the presence of God' in the midst of daily life is the perfecting of our faith.

WITNESS

Entering communion involves a visible witness to God, as we are caught up by the Spirit, into the mission of the Son, sent by the Father, to be the light of the world. Communion as witness emphasizes the uncontainable nature of divine love and light that fills and transforms us in order *to make God visible* in the world. A life that embodies the 'beauty of holiness' is a sign, foretaste, and herald of the kingdom. Communion with God makes us 'transcripts of the Trinity', by which we become living invitations to share in the reign of holy love. The Spirit shines in our hearts so that the knowledge of the glory of God in the face of Jesus Christ might be made visible in the transfigured weakness of our mortal flesh. To be the light of the world is to embrace the apostolic vocation of communion with God for the sake of sharing it with those who walk in darkness. To participate in God is to participate in the *missio Dei*. Communion with God is the means and the end of evangelism.

THE EVANGELIZED: MADE FOR COMMUNION WITH GOD

Any theology of evangelism in the Wesleyan mode is likely to build upon certain basic theological convictions about the human condition (Outler 1996: 32–3).

Human beings are created in the divine image, which means having the capacity for personal relationship with God, so that the likeness of God may be reproduced in their lives. The image of God can only subsist in this communion of love, and is marred by sin through the brokenness of that relationship. The ability to know, desire, and choose a life of communion with God is dissipated by the sinful nature and its attachment to false ends. This corruption of the divine image lies at the root of human unhappiness, and is manifest in a general state of dissatisfaction and restlessness. Wesley follows in the spirit of Augustine, by arguing that we are made for a communion of love with God, and our hearts are restless until they find their rest in him.

This restlessness is actually God's own longing for us before it is our longing for God. The mission of holy love reaches out and embraces a fallen world in the form of prevenient grace. Notwithstanding the damage of sin, there is no one in a state of 'mere nature', for everyone is graced by the life-transforming presence and power of God, whose desire to save is fundamentally irresistible (Collins 2007: 80–1). The effect of prevenient grace is an incipient participation in God that turns every human being into a 'seeker' after that happiness which can only be found in the renewal of the divine image.

Prevenient grace is both love and light. Through the indwelling Spirit, the light of Christ preveniently enlightens everyone who comes into the world, so that they might be drawn to the Father. Our ability to perceive divine reality is rooted in the possession of 'spiritual senses' that represent the capacity to both see and seek God. (For the spiritual senses tradition, see Rahner 1979: 81–134; Von Balthasar 1982: 367 ff.). The sinful nature, however, lies like a veil over them and reduces us to a state of spiritual sleep. Rather than training our natural senses to enjoy creation in so far as it leads us to the Creator, they are occluded by an idolatrous sensuality that attends to worldly pleasure as an end in itself. Nevertheless, the enlightening gift of prevenient grace imparts within all people a rudimentary state of spiritual sensitivity that is at the root of our restlessness.

Wesley notes this spiritual sensitivity is commonly referred to as 'natural conscience'. He complains, however, that this is a vulgar and misleading expression because conscience is not inherent to the sinful nature. Rather, it is a fruit of prevenient grace that carries the promise of communion with God. It is the initiative of holy love that makes it possible to be addressed by God, in Word and Spirit, and led along the way of salvation. It is a preparation for the gospel, and the basis of our confidence in evangelism.

The idea of spiritual 'awakening' is central to a Wesleyan understanding of evangelism. Being confronted with the gospel of holy love is to have the givenness of one's life and perceptions of reality challenged all the way down. Sinful attachments to false ends become exposed for what they are, leading to the conviction of sin. If prevenient grace works on the spiritual senses to open up the perception of divine reality, then convincing grace works to involve us imaginatively in the truth of it, so that we might begin to see ourselves in the light of the gospel and respond to the summons of God's future.

Awakening to the reality of a world that exists in the hands of God is like giving sight to the blind! When the spiritual senses are fully opened through the gift of faith, there is an awakening like a new-born child into a 'new world' where nothing remains the same as it was:

he that before had ears, but heard not, is now made capable of hearing. He hears the voice that raiseth the dead... At the same time, he receives the other spiritual senses, capable of discerning spiritual good and evil. He is enabled to taste, as well as see, how gracious the Lord is. He enters into the holiest by the blood of Jesus, and tastes the powers of the world to come...   (Wesley 1984: iv. 172–3)

Only by the vision of faith, in the experience of new birth, do the natural senses fulfil their design: enabling us to understand, desire, and live in a world made for communion with God. As the sinful nature is reordered, and the 'veil of the flesh' is rendered transparent to the reality of God, the eschatological kingdom of heaven is opened up within and around us.

Evangelism is a means of prevenient grace through which God simultaneously stirs up and addresses the spiritual longings of the human soul. It is also a means of convincing grace in so far as the soul is turned to God in a spirit of repentance, and seeks after the transforming power of the divine embrace.

EVANGELISM: JOURNEYING INTO COMMUNION WITH GOD

Although it was George Whitefield who first persuaded Wesley to preach in the fields, there arose a famous distinction between their respective methods of evangelism. Like other so-called 'gospel preachers' (Wesley 1958: xi. 486 ff.), who offered the benefits of free grace without the requirement of costly disciple-ship, Whitefield's manner of revival preaching aimed at the immediate fruit of evangelical conversion, with little concern for the organization of his converts into religious societies. Whitefield was later to observe, however, that 'Wesley acted wisely. The souls that were awakened under his ministry he joined in societies, and thus preserved the fruit of his labour. This I neglected, and my people are a rope of sand' (cited in Ayling 1979: 201; also Logan 2005: 25–47). Wesleyan theology retains the instinct that 'conversion is never more than the bare threshold of authentic and comprehensive evangelism... The scope of evangelism was never less than the fullness of Christian experience', or holiness in heart and life (Outler 1996: 21).

Wesley insisted that his preachers must offer the unconditional love of Christ along with the summons of Christ to a life of loving obedience. Indeed, he even recommended that an emphasis should be placed on proclaiming the law of Christ, as command and promise, in order to show that evangelical conversion is not an end in itself, but the foundation upon which a life of holiness is to be built. Advising his preachers to begin with a general announcement of God's love and desire to save, they should keep the gospel 'afar off' to ensure that it was received only by those who were convinced of sin and yearned for holiness. He notes that 'it is only in private converse with a thoroughly convinced sinner', or in the context of disciplined Christian fellowship, 'that we should preach nothing but the gospel' (Wesley 1958: xi. 487).

For Wesley, the most important fruit of evangelistic preaching and proclamation was not conversion as such, but the awakening of sinners to the need of salvation. Those who responded to the promises of the gospel were initiated into a Methodist society; or, if needed, a new society was planted for the purpose. Awakened seekers were incorporated into class meetings as the basic unit of society membership, and the primary means by which they made the journey into communion with God. Research has shown that it could take up to two years of participation in Methodist society before evangelical conversion was experienced (Albin 2003).

A good account of the journey into communion with God can be found in Wesley's *Collection of Hymns* (Wesley 1989). The wide range of hymns and spiritual songs in the *Collection* was sufficient to accompany every step on the way of salvation. Singing through the first few sections inscribed seekers into a prayerful journey of awakening and conversion: from turning towards God, to finally proving the truth of holy love and saving grace in their own experience. The newly awakened seeker is one that senses the promises of God through a veil of sin and unbelief. They are blind but long to *see* God face to face; deaf but long to *hear* the word which raises the dead; hard of heart but long to *feel* the embrace of forgiving love and *taste* the goodness of God (Wesley 1989: hymns 1, 2, 75, 81, 83, 85, 109, 113, 118, 122, 124, 133). The prayer that courses through these hymns is to have the veil of sin taken away, so that one may enter the holy place of communion with God, whose 'mystic name' is Love. This prayer expresses a longing to be 'lost in the ocean of God', to have that 'mystic fellowship of love' shed abroad in the heart, and receive the 'mystic power' of life-transforming union with God that conquers sin and imparts holiness (ibid. hymns 9, 18, 27, 78, 96, 98, 144, 145).

In these hymns, the journey of awakening and entering into communion with God is marked by two attitudes. First, awakening implies a conviction of sin. It is a 'double grace' by which conscience is reproved in order to make way for the gift of repentance; the 'wound' of divine conviction to be healed by the 'balm of pardoning love' (ibid. hymns 84, 89, 105, 106). Second, awakening brings a sense of spiritual struggle in which one labours under the oppression of sin while wrestling for the gift of salvation. On the one hand, a deep sense of 'displacence' and restlessness arises among the *poor in spirit* who seek the kingdom of God. They are held captive to the promises of the gospel as 'prisoners' of faith, hope, and love (ibid. hymns 105, 123, 144, 150). On the other hand, there is a deep appetite for communion with God in the prayerful soul that groans and 'gasps' for the breath of life; that *mourns* and cries for the comforting witness of sins forgiven; that *hungers* and *thirsts* for the righteousness of new birth (ibid. hymns 99, 100, 101, 110, 119, 121,

134, 137, 147). This language deliberately draws upon the Beatitudes, describing those who seek the happiness that comes from entering the kingdom of God.

The hymns frequently draw upon the biblical imagery of the Emmaus road to describe the journey of awakening and conversion: travelling in the company of One we barely recognize but whose presence and word enchant our souls, instils a restless longing to know more, makes our hearts and homes hospitable to the truth, and finally blesses us with the vision of faith. When the seeker is struggling for vision, God is frequently addressed as the One who sees before being seen, and must not withhold the grace of divine self-revelation (ibid. hymns 101, 106, 117, 130, 135). The account of Jacob wrestling the 'angel' at Jabbok becomes a celebrated pattern for this spiritual journey. The importunate spirit of a seeker that wrestles with God for the blessing of salvation turns out to be God's own way of loving us back to himself (ibid. hymn 140; also 151, 155, 156).

In the Methodist society, the desire for salvation was evidenced in a willingness to abide by the General Rules. This was not merely a test of sincerity, but an immersion in the means of grace, by which one enters the divine embrace. It was through them that seekers took hold of the One who had preveniently taken hold of them, and 'waited' upon the One who had been waiting for them.

For Wesley, the language of convincing, justifying, and sanctifying grace is a way of describing the manner in which God works within people according to their spiritual need. Apart from field preaching, he did not identify a specialized set of practices associated with evangelizing seekers, and another for saints pursuing holiness. Rather, the same means of grace—prayer, searching the Scriptures, participating in the Lord's Supper, and works of mercy when suffused by these ordinary means—were the common practices by which people journeyed through the whole way of salvation together (Meadows 2001: 223–39).

Joining a Methodist society was more like taking on a new way of life shaped by the means of grace; a scriptural form of life capable of being filled with the loving presence and power of God. In that sense, works of piety and mercy cannot be reduced to spiritual techniques because they are meant to constitute a pattern of whole-life discipleship fit for the kingdom of God. Nor can such discipleship be finally interiorized or privatized because this new life is essentially social in character. In Wesley's words, 'there is no holiness but social holiness'. The life of communion with God is inseparable from a life of communion with neighbour: first in the friendship of those sharing a common spiritual journey; and, second, in the faithful witness of a community whose life together is shaped by the reign of holy love (Wesley 1958: xiv. 437; 1984: i. 533–49).

A Wesleyan approach to evangelism means inviting seekers on a journey into communion with God as they participate in Christian fellowship: clothing themselves in a form of life that encourages spiritual awakening, repentance, and wrestling with God; and engaging in the means of grace through which the experience of entering communion with God can be anticipated.

EVANGELISTS: SHARING OUR COMMUNION WITH GOD

Evangelists are those who lead people into the divine embrace so that they may embark on the journey into communion with God. One way to interpret the complex process of evangelizing the seeker in early Methodism is through the lens of 'spiritual direction'.

Although spiritual direction is typically identified with a relationship between two people, it can refer to any relational practice that helps a person 'hear, see, and respond to God' (Bakke 2000: 18). As a form of spiritual direction, evangelism does not aim at producing decisions, or patterns of experience, or making converts as such. Rather, it is a process of 'seeking God, seeking fuller communion with the Holy Spirit, and seeking to trust God for and in whatever unfolds'. As a theocentric practice, the essence of spiritual direction is a 'deepening love and communion with God' which involves attending to, waiting on, and pursuing a personal relationship with God in the anticipation that grace may abound (ibid. 35). As such, evangelism may be thought of as 'initial spiritual direction' (Johnson 1991); which, from a Wesleyan perspective, aims at introducing seekers to the means of grace by which God may be sought and found.

EVANGELISM AS SPIRITUAL DIRECTION

Although God may act sovereignly to awaken sinners, Wesley notes that there is an 'ordinary' pattern of experience in the spiritual journey. The seeker 'is going on his own way, not having God in all his thoughts, when God comes upon him unawares, perhaps by an awakening sermon or conversation'. The awakened seeker then 'begins searching the scriptures' and praying to God with other believers; 'thus he continues in God's way, in hearing, reading, meditating, praying, and partaking of the Lord's supper, till God, in the manner that pleases Him, speaks to his heart' (Wesley 1984: i. 393–4).

A Wesleyan approach to evangelism as initial spiritual direction would have three inseparable dimensions. First, there is the dimension of *proclaiming* the gospel, which broadly characterizes any activity having the form of call and response. Obviously, this is the case for evangelistic preaching, whether in the fields or in the great congregation; but it may also include the instruction of moral and intellectual catechesis, the mutual exhortation of small-group ministry, or sharing testimony in personal conversation (Klaiber 1997: 193–208). What matters is that the gospel of holy love is communicated as a means of convincing grace; an invitation to participate in the truth of the triune God for oneself.

Second, evangelism as initial spiritual direction involves *equipping* seekers with the means of grace, both works of piety and mercy. It is the role of the evangelist to discern and recommend these means according to the particular need of the seeker. Evangelists must 'work together with God', to 'second the motions of the blessed Spirit', and thereby lead the seeker 'step by step, through all the means which God has ordained; not according to our own will, but just as the providence and the Spirit of God go before and open the way' (Wesley 1984: i. 394–5). Wesley commends a form of spiritual direction, artful in its response to the needs of the seeker, and prudential in the application of particular disciplines for the journey: 'the means into which different men are led, and in which they find the blessing of God, are varied, transposed, and combined together, a thousand different ways... for who knows in which God will meet thee with the grace that bringeth salvation?' (ibid. 395).

Third, evangelism as spiritual direction involves *journeying* alongside the seeker as those sharing the common goal of entering and deepening communion with God. Evangelists do not lead seekers into their own private spiritual experience, but invite them to share in Christian fellowship, as brothers and sisters in the family of God, and fellow participants in the kingdom of heaven. Evangelism is, therefore, an ecclesial activity in so far as the divine embrace does not come apart from the embrace of the body of Christ, gathered and filled by the Spirit.

EVANGELISM AS FAITH SHARING

In early Methodism, evangelism as initial spiritual direction was both a personal and social practice. Faith sharing as a personal practice was essentially a work of mercy; a relational activity in which people were led into communion with God through specific attention to the needs of both body and soul (Wesley 1984: ii. 166). Faith sharing, therefore, involved a holistic approach, where one might say the soul was the centre if not the circumference of the evangelistic concern: 'Having shown that you have a regard for their bodies, you may proceed to inquire concerning their souls. And here you have a large field before you; you have scope for exercising all the talents which God has given you... Ask of God, and he will open your mouth' (ibid. iii. 391).

In an important sense, all faith sharing is personal in so far as each person must enter into communion with God. To have a personal relationship with God, however, is not to have a private, individual relationship with God. The truth of social holiness implies a responsibility towards all those with whom one is joined in

Christian fellowship, as travellers together on the journey (Swanson and Clement 1996; Knight and Powe 2006). Faith sharing as a social practice could be found in the evangelistic matrix of mutual accountability in early Methodist societies and class meetings: watching over one another in love; reproving, encouraging, and exhorting one another to grow in grace and good works; striving with one another to enter and deepen their communion with God.

EVANGELISM AS PRUDENTIAL PRACTICE

The early Methodists also took up and adapted a whole range of practices with evangelistic potential in response to their unfolding missionary context (Hong 2006: 147–62). Much to the chagrin of institutionalized sensibilities, and in defence of Methodist innovations, Wesley claimed that 'the end of all ecclesiastical order' was the salvation of souls (Wesley 1958: xii. 80–1). Today, we would say that the church is essentially missionary or evangelistic in nature. In other words, the actual shape of the church's life must be determined by the goal of salvation that, for Wesley, meant both evangelical conversion and the pursuit of holiness. This did not make him a pragmatist, but it did reveal the exercise of prudential wisdom. He had the ability to discern and respond to divine providence by adapting ancient and modern practices as prudential means of grace for the evangelistic needs of the moment. The development of the class meeting is one such example. Others include field preaching, love feasts, and the covenant service, each of which contributed to the awakening and spiritual direction of seekers on their journey into communion with God.

The quasi-sacramental nature of the love feast was important in building up Christian fellowship, but it was the evangelistic use of personal testimony that Wesley often described in detail. The covenant service, however, marked the need for decision-making. Entering and affirming one's covenant with God was done personally, but also face-to-face among those who were resolved to help each other follow Christ; whether a seeker wrestling for conversion or a saint pursuing holiness.

CONCLUSION

The Wesleyan paradigm of evangelism proposed here has sought to integrate themes from both the soteriological and missiological approaches through the logic of communion with God. It is rooted in the gospel of holy love. The triune

God who is love, loves the world into being and, when that communion is broken, graciously loves it back into a reconciling and re-creating communion of love once again. The gospel of salvation is that God has made a way of communion in which we are set free from sin and death, and filled with holy love. The kingdom of God is nothing other than a threefold cord of love that binds each person to God and their neighbour. It is really present in the Christian community, but awaiting fulfilment in the eschatological reunion of heaven and earth.

The goal of evangelism is that humanity may enter this communion with God, which is at once intensely personal and inescapably social. It is a life-transforming intimacy with God taking flesh in a life of loving fellowship with neighbour. The experience of conversion is to have the love of God shed abroad in the heart, overflowing in a life of holy love towards others, and thus returned to God in joyful obedience. Entering the reign of God, and the new life of the kingdom, means taking up a life of discipleship that is nothing less than a participation in God's saving embrace of the world: a missionary movement of grace in which the love of God flows out to every person, overflows from one to another, and returns to God in the communion of a new creation.

Understood this way, I have suggested that the general ethos of evangelism is best described as initial spiritual direction; or leading people into communion with God. Evangelism has the character of initiation in so far as the promise of communion is sought by participation in a community of disciples, and by taking up the life of discipleship as a means of grace. It also has the character of proclamation in so far as the unbeliever is continually urged to seek God through these means, and to anticipate the gift of new life along the way. Evangelism as initial spiritual direction, then, may be understood theologically as a human endeavour in and through which the work of the Spirit is discerned, drawing others to Christ, who is the way to the Father.

Facilitating the journey of awakening and seeking communion with God, however, presents us with particular challenges in contemporary Western culture. In the eighteenth century, the early Methodists addressed a culture on the cusp of modernity and in the midst of Christendom. At the beginning of the twenty-first century, we find ourselves in an emerging post-modern and post-Christendom culture in which there is both widespread ignorance of the gospel story, and a general suspicion of any claims to truth and reality. Under these conditions, however, the idea of evangelism as a journey, in the form of spiritual direction and in the context of Christian fellowship, has undergone a revival in recent years.

The Wesleyan emphasis on prevenient grace, spiritual sensitivity, and the initial stages of evangelism as a journey of awakening can provide a much-needed theological resource for the theology of evangelism in what some are calling an increasingly 'spiritual age' (Croft 2005). It would seem that the postmodern condition is accompanied by a new openness to the re-enchantment of everyday life in the aftermath of modernity. From a Wesleyan perspective, one might conclude that the 'veil' of practical atheism inherent in the modern world-view has worn thin in places, making it possible for dormant spiritual senses to penetrate the tightly woven fabric of techno-scientific culture and imagine what lies within and beyond. This is not merely a renewed fascination with the super-natural, but a response to the missionary initiative of holy love in the hearts of those who have been made for communion with God.

Postmodern culture, however, has no resources in itself to direct the spiritual seeker, except perhaps for offering fragments of ancient religious traditions as useful fictions for individual consumption. At the end of modernity, the challenge of evangelism is how to connect the gospel story—as one story among many—with the reality of God as its Author and End. The Wesleyan tradition presses us to consider how the church's life of communion with God can become a 'hermeneutic of the gospel' that reunites the truth we *proclaim* about God with the *reality* of God's life-transforming presence and power. Evangelism, therefore, presupposes a community of 'real' or 'authentic' Christians whose life together makes visible the truth of its communion with God.

It may seem ironic to suggest that early Methodism can inspire a form of evangelism suited to life after Christendom. Nevertheless, Wesley would probably have sided with the Anabaptists rather than the 'magisterial' Reformers in the debate about Constantine. For him, the 'Christendom synthesis' marked the fall of the church and a fatal compromise of its vocation as a holy witness in the world. It is frequently argued that Christendom has resulted in the interiorization, privat-ization, and marginalization of the church's life and faith. Fellowship with God is reduced to an individualistic 'personal relationship'; holiness is reduced to a therapeutic sense of emotional well-being; the vision of God is reduced to a post-mortem state of heavenly bliss; and witness is reduced to various forms of chaplaincy, seconded by the world to help people get through in the meantime.

Evangelism in a post-Christendom culture will emphasize the calling of the church to be a faithful, visible, and costly witness in a world of unbelief. It must embody the social and material reality of the gospel so that the world may come into contact with the truth, beauty, and goodness of God (Outler 1996: 22 ff., 57 ff.; Stone 2007: 277 ff.). Wesley insisted that the biggest stumbling block to the spread of the gospel was the lives of Christians (Wesley 1984: ii. 495), but he was also wary of striving for an outward form of life—either personal or social—apart from the inward power of renewed hearts. The church must not exchange Christendom for fresh expressions of nominal Christianity.

The challenge facing Methodist evangelism in a postmodern and post-Christendom age lies in cultivating an authentic embodiment of the holy love that arises from a genuine communion with God. The need is for communities of disciples whose *fellowship* with God is embodied in hospitable, reconciling, and peaceable relationships; whose *holiness* is embodied in a disciplined life of piety and mercy; whose *vision* of God is embodied by an imaginative participation in the *missio Dei*; and whose *witness* is embodied by a fellowship of holiness that makes the eschatological kingdom both visible and tangible as a living invitation to the world. From a Wesleyan perspective, this is why evangelism and renewal must always coexist. The kind of Christian life that awakens seekers and facilitates the journey of evangelism arises only among those who participate in the real presence and power of the triune God.

References

ABRAHAM, WILLIAM J. (1989). *The Logic of Evangelism: A Significant Contribution to the Theory and Practice of Evangelism.* London: Hodder & Stoughton.

ALBIN, THOMAS (2003). 'Finding God in Small Groups'. *Christianity Today* 47/8.

ALLCHIN, A. M. (1988). *Participation in God: A Forgotten Strand in Anglican Tradition.* Wilton, Conn.: Morehouse-Barlow.

ARIAS, MORTIMER (1984). *Announcing the Reign of God: Evangelization and the Subversive Memory of Jesus.* Lima, Ohio: Academic Renewal Press.

AYLING, STANLEY (1979). *John Wesley.* Nashville: Abingdon.

BAKKE, JEANNETTE A. (2000). *Holy Invitations: Exploring Spiritual Direction.* Grand Rapids: Baker.

COLEMAN, ROBERT E. (1994). *Nothing to Do but Save Souls: John Wesley's Charge to His Preachers.* Napanee, Ind.: Evangel.

COLLINS, KENNETH J. (2007). *The Theology of John Wesley: Holy Love and the Shape of Grace.* Nashville: Abingdon.

CROFT, STEVEN, et al. (2005). *Evangelism in a Spiritual Age: Communicating the Faith in a Changing Culture.* London: Church House.

FLEW, R. NEWTON (1934). *The Idea of Perfection in Christian Theology: An Historical Study of the Christian Ideal for the Present Life.* London: Oxford University Press.

HONG, JOHN SUNGSCHUL (2006). *John Wesley the Evangelist.* Lexington, Ky.: Emeth.

JOHNSON, BEN CAMPBELL (1991). *Speaking of God: Evangelism as Initial Spiritual Guidance.* Louisville, Ky.: Westminster John Knox.

JONES, SCOTT J. (2003). *The Evangelistic Love of God and Neighbor: A Theology of Witness and Discipleship.* Nashville: Abingdon.

KARKAINEN, VELI-MATTI (2004). *One With God: Salvation as Deification and Justification.* Collegeville, Minn.: Liturgical Press.

KLAIBER, WALTER (1997). *Call & Response: Biblical Foundations for a Theology of Evangelism.* Nashville: Abingdon.

KNIGHT, HENRY H., III, POWE, F. DOUGLAS (2006). *Transforming Evangelism: The Wesleyan Way of Sharing Faith.* Nashville: Discipleship Resources.

LOGAN, JAMES C. (2005). *How Great a Flame: Contemporary Lessons from the Wesleyan Revival.* Nashville: Discipleship Resources.

MATTHAEI, SONDRA HIGGINS (2000). *Making Disciples: Faith Formation in the Wesleyan Tradition.* Nashville: Abingdon.

MEADOWS, PHILIP R. (2001). 'Embodying Conversion'. In Kenneth J. Collins and John R. Tyson (eds.), *Conversion in the Wesleyan Tradition*. Nashville: Abingdon.

OUTLER, ALBERT C. (1996). *Evangelism & Theology in the Wesleyan Spirit*. Nashville: Discipleship Resources.

RAHNER, KARL (1979). *Theological Investigations*. Vol. XVI. New York: Seabury.

SKEVINGTON WOOD, ARTHUR (1967). *The Burning Heart: John Wesley, Evangelist*. Exeter: Paternoster.

STONE, BRYAN (2007). *Evangelism after Christendom: The Theology and Practice of Christian Witness*. Grand Rapids: Brazos.

SWANSON, ROGER K., and CLEMENT, SHIRLEY F. (1996). *The Faith-Sharing Congregation*. Nashville: Discipleship Resources.

VON BALTHASAR, HANS URS (1982). *The Glory of the Lord*. Vol. I. New York: Crossroad.

WESLEY, JOHN (1779). 'Communion with the Father and the Son in Grace and Glory'. *Arminian Magazine* 2.

—— (1958). *The Works of John Wesley*, ed. Thomas Jackson. 14 vols. Grand Rapids: Zondervan.

—— (1984). *The Works of John Wesley, Sermons*, ed. Albert C. Outler. 4 vols. Nashville: Abingdon.

—— (1989). *The Works of John Wesley*, vii. *A Collection of Hymns for the Use of the People Called Methodists*, ed. Franz Hilderbrandt and Oliver A. Beckerlegge. Nashville: Abingdon.

WMM (1849). Letter to the Editor. 'Spiritual Communion with the Tri-Une God'. *Wesleyan Methodist Magazine* 5.

WYNKOOP, MILDRED BANGS (1972). *A Theology of Love: The Dynamic of Wesleyanism*. Kansas City: Beacon Hill.

CHAPTER 25

....

TRADITIONS AND TRANSITIONS IN MISSION THOUGHT

....

DANA L. ROBERT

DOUGLAS D. TZAN

I look upon all the world as my parish.

JOHN WESLEY wrote these defiant words in response to being denied use of a pulpit on grounds that he violated church order. He consequently moved into the fields where he could reach those who lacked a church home. 'The world is my parish' is the title of numerous books, articles, sermons, and plays. It is inscribed at the foot of the famous Wesley statue at his chapel in London. Like Martin Luther's 'Here I stand', the motto connects a founder with the essence of his contribution to the formation of a distinct Christian tradition.

Methodists have frequently invoked Wesley's words as the quintessential statement of Methodism's identity as a mission movement. 'The world is my parish' is the most widely used metaphor for Methodist mission. Thus it is used to forward different definitions of the tradition in different times and places, and to claim that these definitions are consistent with the vision of John Wesley.

The positive view of human capabilities that characterized Methodism's Arminian theology, faith in democracy, and sense of destiny contributed to its striking achievement as the most successful nineteenth-century missionary movement in North America. By 1850, one-third of all churchgoers in the United States were Methodists, and Methodism's missionary vision turned abroad. Stated Stephen Baldwin, an early Methodist missionary in China, 'With an ambition like Alexander's, only that it is holy and unselfish, it [Methodism] is ever longing for "more worlds to conquer"' (Barclay 1957: 157). The optimism, activism, and Western chauvinism of American Methodism in the early twentieth century reflected its self-confidence as the largest cluster of Protestant denominations in North America, with the largest mission force.

An expansionistic interpretation of Wesley's metaphor was especially common in the early twentieth century. American Methodists saw their movement as God's agent for 'progress' and 'conquest' in the spread of Christianity. In 1919, American Methodist denominations used it as the slogan for a vast missionary exhibition in Columbus, Ohio, that celebrated the hundredth anniversary of the Methodist Missionary Society. There were over a million visitors to exhibits that showcased pageants of 'native' ways of life, and demonstrated how Methodist missionaries were working to evangelize and transform the world.

In addition to geographic expansionism, 'the world is my parish' underscores Methodism's character as an evangelistic movement, marked by sharing the message of salvation through Jesus Christ. Wesley's decision to become 'more vile' to reach the working classes reflected belief in unlimited atonement—that God's salvation is available to all, without exception. This message of free grace is a missionary theology. The outward movement of the Trinity, and the incarnation— God becoming human—are profound missionary truths that show the loving nature of God, who is committed to the salvation of humankind. Theologian William Ury (1996), states: 'That is the core of Methodist missions: free salvation for all sinners, and full salvation from all sin.'

In 1990, nearly two thousand 'evangelical' Methodists held an important convocation entitled 'The World Forever Our Parish', on the continued need for United Methodists to engage in world evangelization. Speakers including bishops, pastors, missionaries, and scholars stressed what George Hunter, Dean of the E. Stanley Jones School of World Mission at Asbury Theological Seminary, called Methodism's tradition of 'apostolicity'—emulation of the early apostles in spreading the gospel (Hunter 1991: 142). Leading churchmen and scholars called upon the United Methodist Church to recommit to its Wesleyan heritage of active concern for the salvation of the world. The paraphrase of Wesley's words in the name of the convocation linked United Methodism's Wesleyan theological heritage with its determination to remain an outward-looking mission movement rather than be a 'chaplain' overseeing numerical decline in the United States.

Another major interpretation of Wesley's phrase was promoted in the late twentieth century by 'progressive' Methodists who emphasized that the distinctive contribution of Methodist mission in the world was social outreach. Wesley's concern for the whole world, rather than a small corner of Christendom, represented a holistic theology of care for human needs. President Emeritus of Iliff Seminary, and author of a book on contemporary images in mission, Don Messer noted that even conservative columnist George Will invoked John Wesley's compassionate care for the sick as exemplar for an age of global epidemics. Wrote Messer (2002: 2),

The precedent of Wesley, following the pattern of Jesus, going everywhere to preach, teach and heal the sick has been a powerful motif for Methodists over the centuries. Why hasn't our slogan, 'the world is my parish', translated into an aggressive and compassionate program against global AIDS? Involvement in the problems of the world is the hallmark of Methodist mission, emphasizing the 'healing power of love for body and soul'.

Care for the whole person is such a compelling interpretation of 'the world is my parish' that it is cited outside Methodism as a classic statement of holistic mission. The *Fraternidad Teológica Latinoamericana*, a major association of Latin American Protestant theologians, promotes the idea of *missión integral*, or holistic mission with a 'particular concern for the poor, the outcast, and the marginalized people of the world' (Cordingly 2004: 9). In a volume on missional ecclesiology, Anabaptist theologian Nancy Bedford (2004: 110) suggests that apostolicity is an essential mark of integral mission, reflecting God's concern for all life, expressed by Wesley's phrase 'the world is my parish'. She notes that it 'is not some colonialist or imperialist motto, but a recognition of the profound inter-relatedness of the whole of life on this planet and its involvement in God's redemptive dynamic, in which all of us may participate'.

The social context of globalization in the twenty-first century led Argentinean Methodist theologian José Míguez Bonino to use Wesley's phrase to compare contemporary globalization with that of Wesley's period. Noting Methodism's dual role as both a contributor to the beginnings of globalization in the early eighteenth century, and a bearer of Wesley's concern for the poor and opposition to slavery, Míguez Bonino proposed that the 'world parish' be read as the desire for a new form of relationship built by love, the source of justice and peace, in which all may find a place (Míguez Bonino 2003: 93–103).

As these examples demonstrate, despite its limitations, 'the world is my parish' continues to resonate among Methodists around the world. But what do the diverse interpretations of these words reveal about the meaning of Methodist mission in the twenty-first century? The continuous use of Wesley's phrase over the past hundred years indicates that Methodists think of themselves as a people actively in mission, proclaiming a core message of salvation for all. Being in mission is essential to Methodist identity. Born as a movement to reform the church and to spread 'scriptural holiness' across the land, the tradition of Methodism is to move outwards into the world with a message of free grace and social concern. Methodists never argue over whether theirs is a mission movement: they only argue over the nature of the mission.

The creativity of 'the world is my parish' is its pragmatic flexibility. But a self-identity as a missional community is not the same as a fully developed mission theology. One danger in thinking of oneself as a mission movement is that since everything is mission, nothing is mission: complacency about the church's missional nature can lead to a failure to nurture essential aspects of outreach such as missionaries, mission scholarship, and voluntarism. Another danger lies in an undeveloped ecclesiology that takes an instrumentalist view of the church, thus opening the way towards activism with little reflection on the nature of the church as a community sent by the Triune God. A third danger of a missional self-understanding is that fighting over the corporate identity of Methodism—as seen in the multiple uses of Wesley's phrase—often takes place over competing definitions of mission.

The remainder of this chapter will analyse the core tradition of twentieth-century Methodist mission thought against a basic framework for a holistic theology of mission. It will then reflect on selected contemporary contributions by Methodists to the field of missiology. While this article is not limited to discussions of North American Methodism, the knowledge base of the authors biases them in that direction, in particular towards the United Methodist Church.

EVANGELISM, CHURCH, AND KINGDOM

Mission anthropologist Paul G. Hiebert developed a conceptual framework that serves as one way to analyse and critique Methodist missiology. He argued that mission thought has historically been divided into three distinct emphases—evangelism, church, or kingdom of God. Although he noted that occasionally mission thinkers have attempted to integrate two or all of these foci, contemporary missiology has typically prioritized only one at a time.

A missional concern for evangelism has inspired countless missionaries to go to remote areas and to give their lives to sharing the gospel. The church today is largely a result of their pioneering efforts. Those who promote evangelism as a missional priority point to the presence of churches and manifestations of the reign of God in the world as the result of their work. A missiological paradigm prioritizing only evangelism, however, frequently leads to minimal follow-up with new converts who turn back to their old faith or practise 'a shallow Christianity plagued by syncretism'. Such a prioritization also suffers from a flawed ecclesiology in which little attention is given to building church communities and which defines salvation in modern individualistic terms (Hiebert 1999: 153–5).

A second reductionist approach makes the church the priority of mission. Under this rubric, mission emphasizes building churches, organizing congregations, training leaders, and educating children in faith. Although concern with worship, Christian community, and spiritual growth can be strengths of this approach, it also suffers from two dangers. The church can become ingrown and self-serving, and, using its resources for itself, lose a passion for evangelism. A second danger of ecclesiocentric mission is that it highlights human efforts at building 'the church by planning, programs, and activities'. Little space is left for God to act (ibid. 155–6).

A third reductionist missiology prioritizes the kingdom of God as the major theme of mission. This approach emphasizes the social demands of the gospel. Evangelism and the church are merely means of proclaiming the kingdom. Jesus himself preached the inbreaking reign of God. The central task of his followers was to proclaim justice and peace in the world and to bring the good news of the gospel to places of oppression and violence here and now. The strength of this approach is 'its concern for righteousness on earth and its encompassing view of the mission of the church'. Mission is incomplete without the fullness of God's reign. This view, however, is marred by tendencies to overlook the human need for Christ and to make the church a political agent. Christianity can become a civil religion justifying 'democracy, capitalism, individual rights, and western civilization' (ibid. 157–8).

Hiebert argued that a full missiology requires the interpenetration of evangelism, church, and kingdom. Such an integrated missiological paradigm, however, has not been easily attained. He lamented, '[W]e find it hard to keep a balance between three centers. Either evangelism, or the church, or the Kingdom is neglected in the implementation. We are unable to keep a burning commitment to all three' (ibid. 158). All three, however, are vital if a missiology is to avoid reduction or truncation.

Ultimately, Christian mission must be understood as rooted in the nature of God. This concept, called the *missio Dei* (mission of God), emerged in the twentieth century and found broad acceptance among Christians of differing theological perspectives. Going against many popular definitions that considered mission to be a programme or project of the church, mission was now viewed as flowing from the Trinity. As David Bosch (1991: 390) wrote, 'The classical doctrine on the *missio Dei* as God the Father sending the Son, and God the Father and the Son sending the Spirit was expanded to include yet another "movement": Father, Son, and Holy Spirit sending the church into the world.' Thus mission does not flow from ecclesial activism, but from the nature of God.

THE METHODIST MISSION PARADIGM

At key moments in the twentieth century, Methodists tried to integrate understandings of evangelism, church, and kingdom into a holistic missiology. For the most part, however, Methodism has lived in the tension between its tradition as a mission movement, and ecclesiocentrism. Mission movements work the margins of society. Churches, however, concern themselves with structures, discipline, and continuity. The history of Methodism, therefore, is a cycle of successful mission movements followed by institutionalization, followed by rebellions against institutionalization in the name of renewing the mission. Methodism provided the matrix from which major revival movements and indigenous forms of Christianity around the world have emerged over the past century.

Given the tendency of church structures to rigidify over time, it is no surprise that the major mission paradigm of Methodism subordinated ecclesiology to a synthesis of the missional priorities of evangelism and kingdom. In melding missional emphases of evangelism and kingdom, the concern was not the establishment of churches and church institutions, but the dual proclamation of Christ and the transformation of society. While this Methodist mission paradigm was not fully holistic according to Hiebert's scheme, it was extremely effective in an era of expansion and cross-cultural outreach. E. Stanley Jones (d. 1973), called by *Time* magazine 'the world's greatest Christian missionary' ('Religion' 1938: 47), exemplified this approach in early to mid-twentieth-century Methodist missions.

As an evangelist, Jones sought to strip the Christian message of all but Christ and to present him in an Indian context. Sharply critical of missionary approaches that were only concerned with saving souls or promoting democracy, Western civilization, or 'a blocked-off, rigid, ecclesiastical and theological system', Jones asserted that Christ could be transplanted to India because, he 'appeals to the universal heart'. The missionary task was to offer Christ to Indians, and then allow Indians to interpret him as they saw fit (Jones 1925: 35–40). As the title of his most famous book implied, Christ must be at home on 'the Indian Road'. In a story that served as the book's keynote, Jones wrote of a friend's conversation with a Brahman who disliked the Christ presented in creeds and churches but who could 'love and follow' the Christ

dressed in Sadhus' garments, seated by the wayside with the crowds about him, healing blind men who felt their way to him, putting his hands upon the heads of poor, unclean lepers who fell at his feet, announcing the good tidings of the Kingdom to stricken folks, staggering up a lone hill with a broken heart and dying upon a wayside cross for men, but rising triumphantly and walking on that road again.   (ibid. 32)

Here in his early book, Jones tied the missiological foci of evangelism and kingdom together in a belief that Christ offered freedom from India's social ills.

The kingdom of God was a recurring theme in Jones's mission thought that developed over the course of his career from early, individualistic conceptualizations to later visions of a comprehensive restructuring of society influenced by his encounter with Russian Marxism (Bundy 1988). In his fullest understanding of the kingdom of God, Jones called for its rediscovery as a 'total life plan to be practiced now, both in individual and collective life' (Jones 1972: 69). Setting forth a forty-three point description of the kingdom, he stressed that entrance into it was through the individual's 'new birth'. But the kingdom itself was social, encompassing the whole of life (ibid. 81). The 'manifesto' of Jesus' Nazareth sermon and the Sermon on the Mount both described life in the kingdom 'applied to life here and now' (ibid. 115, 275).

For Jones, the church was neither a necessary conduit for the message of Christ nor a necessary outcome of its reception, as he believed that Christ was being conveyed to India through the 'irregular' channel of Gandhi (ibid. 73–86). In his own practice, Jones left converts to decide if they thought it necessary to be baptized and join a church (ibid. 94–5). Above all, Jones believed the church needed reformation. He argued that the message of the kingdom had been lost by identifying the church itself as the kingdom (ibid. 72).

The classic Methodist mission paradigm of evangelism/kingdom was also evident in the mission thought of world YMCA president and Nobel Peace Prize laureate John R. Mott (d. 1955) and in women's mission work. Mott saw himself as an evangelist who believed that the gospel of Jesus Christ brought salvation to both individuals and society. Since laywomen were central to Methodist mission work throughout the twentieth century, their missiological assumptions shaped Methodism around the world. Restricted from formal responsibility for ecclesial structures, the mission work of women focused on personal evangelism, social services, and human rights issues for women and girls (Robert 1996: 409–18). Belle Bennett, the great southern Methodist mission leader, summarized the goals of women's mission work as 'Eternal life for the individual, the kingdom of God for humanity' (Im 2008: 80).

TRANSITIONS IN MISSION THEORY

The productive tension between personal evangelism and social transformation evident in the missiology of Jones, Mott, and Methodist women's work lost its focus from the 1960s through the 1980s. Reasons for this are complex and cannot be fully explored in a brief chapter; but a few broad trends must be mentioned. First, the mainline missionary movement had come of age. A generation of highly educated and influential national church leaders emerged after the Second World War. Their calls for the decolonization of mission structures and theologies shaped the missiological agenda for several decades. Second, Western churches were plagued with self-doubt and guilt about their complicity with colonialism, imperialism, and racism. This loss of confidence in Western Christianity resulted in a collapse of missiology in mainline seminaries, dramatic reductions in the number of missionaries, denominational numerical decline, and conflict over the continued relevance and meaning of Christian mission in an age of religious pluralism. Third, multiple movements towards church unity sucked off energy formerly directed towards outreach, and in denominational circles mission was subsumed under ecclesiastical agendas. While attention to ecclesiology is an important aspect of a holistic missiology, the reduction of mission to controlling church structures (and economic resources) made the newly founded United Methodist Church into a battleground between evangelism and kingdom interpretations of mission.

Fragmentation and competition characterized Methodist mission thought during this period. And yet, even in an era of controversy, individual Methodists exercised major leadership in ecumenical mission organizations as the conversation over mission theory moved from captivity to Western culture into a global arena. Contextual theologies emerged from the struggle to decolonize mission thought and practice. Paradigmatic of the transition from old to new was the leadership of Sri Lankan Methodist D. T. Niles, chairman of the World Student Christian Federation, member of the Presidium of the World Council of Churches, and founder of the East Asia Christian Conference. In 1962, Niles produced the first major study of mission theology written in English by a non-Western Protestant. *Upon the Earth* demonstrated Niles's Methodist background in his advocacy of both witness to Jesus Christ as crucial for the individual, and the promise of God's kingdom as foundational for world mission. And yet, the Church remained captive to 'the westernity of the base': it was predominantly Western, addressed Western issues, was controlled by Western money, and was trapped in maintaining Western structures (Niles 1962: 194–220). The church of the future needed to develop its 'Easternity'. Mission should be to and from churches everywhere rather than be a unidirectional form of Western paternalism.

Decolonization, Liberation, and the Recovery of Evangelism

The merger of the International Missionary Council into the World Council of Churches in 1961 was an attempt to put global mission concerns at the heart of interdenominational unity. It is fascinating to speculate why Methodists were disproportionately involved in ecumenical unity movements in this period, particularly on the 'mission' rather than 'faith and order' side of the ecumenical equation. Possibly the 'catholic' tendencies of Methodist connexionalism, combined with cross-cultural relationships and the innate activism of 'the world is my parish' predisposed Methodists toward ecumenism. Another possibility is that the strong Methodist focus on higher education and campus ministry had nurtured effective leaders ready to take charge in a new era. For whatever reason, the history of mission ecumenism after mid-century reads like a 'who's who' of global Methodist leadership. In addition to Niles, other notable Methodist mission ecumenists included

West Indian Philip Potter, Uruguayan Emilio Castro, missionary Eugene Stockwell, and Ghanaian Mercy Amba Oduyoye. Under Potter, Castro, and Stockwell—all heads of the Commission on World Mission and Evangelism of the WCC—ecumenical mission thought moved strongly towards a kingdom-centric mission theology that focused on global issues of social justice and political liberation.

The move towards kingdom-type mission theories in the 1960s and 1970s was partly a response to the problem of 'Westernity', articulated by Niles. The emergence of new nations from under European imperial control and anti-colonial critiques that linked Christian missions with imperialism led to calls for a moratorium on Western missionaries. Methodists such as Emerito Nacpil in South-East Asia and José Míguez Bonino in Latin America were prominent leaders in the moratorium debates. Much of the strongest support for kingdom-type mission theologies also came from missionaries themselves, who by the 1960s were widely involved in nationalist movements, anti-racism movements, and criticisms of America's Cold War foreign policy. For example, in 1961 almost all the thirty-three indigenous Methodist pastors in colonial Angola were sent into exile, imprisoned, or murdered, and five American missionaries arrested and deported for opposing the colonial government. The missionaries asserted that all humans were equal children of God and that Christians were called to work for the coming of the kingdom of God on earth (Gesling 2005: 219–22). Similarly, missionaries who opposed racism in Rhodesia, such as Bishop Ralph Dodge and Norman Thomas, were deported (Dodge 1986). In South Korea, missionary George Ogle was arrested and deported for demanding justice for men killed by the military dictatorship (Ogle 1977).

The North American context also contributed towards the shift to a kingdom-centred missiology as the first organizational meeting of the new United Methodist Board of Missions in 1968 coincided with social upheavals taking place in American cities, university campuses, and around the world. In 1969, a youth taskforce presented a major position paper to the Board that accused the church of being complicit with 'the forces of colonialism, racism, and oppression'. The North American church had become identified 'with the nature, assumptions, goals, and values of the American society', leading to the theological corruption of its 'nature, message, and mission... and the misdirection of its resources towards its own self-perpetuation, power, and aggrandizement instead of towards the service of the poor, the weak, and the oppressed'. The youth report challenged the 'supremacist assumptions' of the missionary movement and their effect on other religions and cultures (quoted in Harman 2005: 15–17). Though particularly strident, this critique was generally representative of the broader missiological concerns of the period.

Latin-American Methodists expressed well-developed, kingdom-centred mission theories influenced by the emergence of Liberation Theology in the late 1960s. These missiologies placed God's kingdom as the foundation for further reflection on Christian mission. José Míguez Bonino (1975: 33) sought to describe a 'new way' of being Christian emerging within the Latin American context. God's kingdom was to be built within human history, in response to which humans acted 'in the concrete arena of history with economic, political, ideological options' (ibid. 138). Emilio Castro also wrote of mission from the perspective of the kingdom. Building on the centrality of the kingdom in Jesus' preaching, Castro (1985: 16) described it as the 'horizon' within which Christians, led by the Holy Spirit, were free to act in mission. The kingdom was a 'theological symbol' that could overcome divisions among Christians because the kingdom 'embraces the whole of reality' (ibid. 36, 76).

Tarnished by its perceived association with paternalistic missions and American imperialism, the word 'evangelism' virtually disappeared from mainline North American mission discourse during the late 1960s and 1970s. Even as Latin-American Methodists and former missionaries articulated kingdom missiologies that focused on 'humanization', or social and economic liberation, they also led the recovery of the word 'evangelism'. At the WCC Assembly in Nairobi in 1975, Bolivian Methodist bishop Mortimer Arias gave a plenary address advocating a 'holistic or integral' evangelism that combined word and deed, that dealt with the whole person, and that sought Christian unity so that 'the world may believe' (Arias 1976: 17–18). In the WCC, mission theologians in the late 1970s worked to end the divisive rhetoric and chasm between kingdom and evangelism definitions of mission. The landmark consensus document of 1982 formulated under Emilio Castro's leadership, *Mission and Evangelism: An Ecumenical Affirmation*, reconciled liberationist and personal understandings of salvation and received wide support from member churches (World Council of Churches 1982).

Despite progress in the WCC, in the United Methodist Church the struggle to restore evangelism as a missional priority continued. In 1983, James Robb wrote a scathing exposé of the General Board of Global Ministries (GBGM), accusing it of supporting radical political causes, overspending on administrative overheads, and steadily shrinking support for missions and missionaries: the denomination was supporting only 453 career missionaries, down from 1,500 in 1965 (Robb 1983). Also in 1983, former missionary and distinguished missiologist Gerald Anderson gave an important speech calling for the founding of a new missionary society to restore Methodism's emphasis on reaching the unreached with the gospel. To restore the primacy of evangelistic mission, the E. Stanley Jones School of Mission was founded at Asbury Theological Seminary in 1983, and in 1984 the independent Mission Society for United Methodists. Some of the most famous names in Methodist missions supported the new society. But other missionaries, working within the structures of the GBGM, opposed the new society as 'illegal' and as a cover for racism by evangelicals who had lost power over the resources of the denomination. Radical division over mission theology and practice continued in the UMC throughout the 1980s.

Church-Centred Mission

The 1960s and 1970s also gave rise to ecclesiocentric mission theories that further fragmented Methodist mission thought. Methodists justified their participation in multiple denominational and congregational merger movements as missional acts. In addition, with the founding of the United Methodist Church, the local congregation emerged as a new locus for mission. Whereas an earlier view considered mission to be done principally by itinerant preachers or select individuals supported by the wider membership of the church, the 1968 *Discipline* contained a new paragraph asserting: 'The Church of Jesus Christ exists in and for the world. It is primarily at the level of the local church that the Church encounters the world. The local church is a strategic base from which Christians move out to the structures of society' (*Book of Discipline* 1968: 67). This paragraph was expanded in subsequent years as the missionary task of the local church described in the *Discipline* grew to include helping people to confess Jesus Christ, live holy lives, minister to the community, cooperate ecumenically, defend creation, and participate 'in the worldwide mission of the church' (*Book of Discipline* 2004: 127–8).

In subsequent versions of the *Book of Discipline*, mission was increasingly folded into the functions of the local church, with the language of mission used both to describe the purpose of the church and in the narrower sense of 'outreach'. The purpose of the church was 'to make disciples of Jesus Christ', (ibid. 87) while the principal responsibility for outreach was assigned to the GBGM (Robinson 2005: 41). According to this formulation, the mission of disciple-making was to occur principally within the context of the local church (ibid. 45–6). At the level of formal church policy, the primacy of the local church ultimately resulted in a fundamental inversion of the connexional Methodist mission tradition, and the reductionism about which Hiebert warned in his description of church-centred missiology.

THE RENEWAL OF METHODIST MISSIOLOGY

After several decades of conflict and fragmentation in mission thought, the early 1990s saw a renewal of missiological reflection. Although in American Methodism arguments continued between evangelicals and social justice liberals, release of a major theological statement, 'Grace Upon Grace' (United Methodist Church 1990) grounded missional outreach firmly in the nature of the loving God, and identified Methodism's distinctive mission tradition as a response to waves of God's grace. In addition to theological progress, bridges were built between different factions. For example, denominational officials had ignored professors of mission and missiologists since the late 1960s. In 1991, Methodist professors of mission initiated annual meetings with staff members from the Board of Global Ministries. In response to criticisms that the church had spent decades on social programmes rather than evangelizing the unreached, the GBGM opened the office of Mission Evangelism around 1990, and held a significant academic consultation on missiology in 1995. After the collapse of the Soviet Union opened new possibilities for the re-establishment of Methodism in Russia, the GBGM in 1991 launched the Russia Initiative as a more transparent, entrepreneurial, and collaborative approach towards opening new 'mission fields' than had been the case since the founding of the UMC.

By the 1990s, mission scholars—following the lead of Scottish Methodist historian Andrew Walls—were finally succeeding in spreading the word that Christianity was becoming a largely non-Western religion, and that mission theology and practice needed to reflect these new realities. The rapid growth of Methodism in Africa and Asia, led primarily by indigenous people, required flexible patterns of collaboration across national boundaries. The commitment of thousands of short-term mission volunteers also created grassroots partnerships for cross-cultural outreach, even as the number of full-time denominational missionaries continued to decline. In retrospect, it appears that the changes in mission structures from the 1990s onwards reflected the effects of globalization, with a multivalent, networking model beginning to replace the centralized corporate structures and carefully regulated bilateral partnerships of the mid-twentieth century.

'Mission' was rediscovered as a topic for church-based reflection in a way it had not been since the 1960s. Don Messer's 1992 book on images in mission started with an acknowledgement that he had completely ignored 'apostolic' ministry in his previous books (Messer 1992: 16–18). Several major 'schools of thought' can be discerned among Methodist mission scholars from the 1990s onward. Although these groups made little attempt to integrate themselves into a formal Methodist missiology, their approaches reveal a common grounding in Methodist distinctives, a shared 'DNA' of concern for both individuals and social structures such as that personified by E. Stanley Jones.

Holistic Evangelism and Church Growth

One major body of Methodist mission thought in the late twentieth century focused on world evangelization. While most of the literature on evangelism emphasized a domestic agenda of church growth in North America, creative reflection on its global context occurred at the E. Stanley Jones School of Mission at Asbury Theological Seminary, under the leadership of George Hunter and Darrell Whiteman. The ESJ School collected the largest group of Methodist mission scholars in one place. Working from a pan-Methodist perspective, scholars such as Hunter, Whiteman, Matt Zahnhiser, Bob Tuttle, Howard Snyder, and others pursued inter-disciplinary scholarship in support of world evangelization, in combination with a graduate training programme in missiology. Their scholarship was marked by commitment to Wesleyan holism and dialogue with missiologists from other traditions.

The ESJ scholars assumed that the gospel concerned the whole of life. Hunter rooted his work on church growth in the theology and practices of Wesley and Asbury, for example, thereby maintaining kingdom concerns within an evangelistic framework. A former GBGM missionary in Oceania, Whiteman applied cultural anthropology to the cross-cultural communication of the gospel. In addition to his writings, including editorship of the journal *Missiology*, Whiteman conducted cultural training for in-service missionaries from multiple denominations and ethnicities. In 2004 he served as president of the International Association of Mission Studies, and in 2005 became resident missiologist of The Mission Society.

Latin-American Kingdom Theology

In his classic text on models of the reign of God, former Free Methodist missionary to Brazil Howard Snyder commented on the great breadth of kingdom-based theologies that emerged from the 1980s onwards, in liberal, evangelical, and pentecostal circles. Snyder (1991: 12) attributed the explosion of reflection on the kingdom to the context of globalization, and the growing internationalization of the church. Snyder's own interest in a kingdom-based missiology reflected his Wesleyan holism, experience in Latin America, and distinct continuity with E. Stanley Jones.

In many respects, the missiologists of the late twentieth century who most closely mirrored the classic Methodist mission paradigm combining evangelism and kingdom were Latin-American Methodist mission theologians, including missionaries such as Snyder. Theologians José Míguez Bonino, Emilio Castro, and Mortimer Arias promoted a kingdom missiology of prophetic social justice and liberation that nevertheless took personal commitment to Jesus Christ seriously, thus playing a crucial bridging role between liberation theology and individual commitment required of Jesus' followers. Míguez Bonino (1988: 13), for example, argued for a redefinition of Wesley's ideas on conversion and sanctification beyond focus on the individual lest evangelization become 'a mere instrument for the reproduction and sacralization of the dehumanizing conditions in which people live'.

Mission History

Non-Methodists frequently cite Wesley and E. Stanley Jones as models for activistic evangelism/kingdom paradigms of mission thought, but Methodist missiology in the late twentieth century lacked a systematician on par with Reformed theologians David Bosch and Darrell Guder, or Catholicism's Steve Bevans and Robert Schreiter. Yet some of the most important historians of missions and world Christianity were Methodists. Reasons for the missiological focus on history instead of doctrine may relate to the essentially narrative theology characteristic of Methodist spirituality, starting with the necessity of being able to account for God's work of grace in one's own life and an optimistic view of God's action in the world. History becomes the arena for God's works of grace, both for the individual and for society. The evangelism/kingdom paradigm characteristic of Methodist mission theology is also compatible with historical and praxis-based methodologies.

Andrew Walls was the pre-eminent historian of mission whose analyses of Christianity as a cross-cultural movement brought new awareness of the global nature of Christianity. As a narrative theologian and former missionary to Sierra Leone, Walls's historical work flowed from his oft-stated faith in the multicultural nature of the Revelation vision (Walls 1996). Former Methodist Lamin Sanneh's numerous important studies challenged the monolithic interpretation of mission as a tool of Western colonialism. As a major African scholar, Sanneh's voice re-energized the subject of mission history by focusing on indigenous contributions to mission. The third leading Methodist mission historian who shaped the broader field of missiology in the late twentieth century was Gerald Anderson, former missionary to the Philippines, who edited some of the most important collections of mission thought, conceptualized and edited the *Biographical Dictionary of Christian Missions*, and edited the *International Bulletin of Missionary Research*. Anderson was the first president of the American Society of Missiology, and first American president of the International Association of Mission Studies.

Other Methodist scholars who made significant contributions to historical understandings of mission included former Zimbabwe missionary Norman Thomas, editor of the massive *International Mission Bibliography* and a major document collection. In his histories of Christianity and of Latin-American missions, Cuban Justo González charted a path towards reading the history of Christianity from a multicultural lens. Kenneth Cracknell, former missionary to Nigeria and Methodist tutor at Cambridge University, addressed the history of attitudes towards world religions and interreligious dialogue, as well as co-authored an overview of global Methodism. Dana L. Robert introduced the contributions of women into the analytical framework for mission theory and history, and chaired the UMC mission professors. In addition to the work of individual denominationally based scholars such as S. T. Kimbrough, Jr., the United Methodist Church launched a new multi-volume history of missions in the denomination and its predecessors. By the early twenty-first century, through historical scholarship, awareness of its strong missionary tradition and linkage with global Christianity was flowing back into the Methodist movement.

Contextual Theologians

The emergence of contextual theologies in the 1970s was closely related to missiology and grew from deliberate reflection on the meaning of the gospel in concrete situations (Bevans 2002; Schreiter 1985). Both missiology and contextual theologies employ cultural hermeneutics for understanding the nature of the gospel in particular contexts, emphasize liberation theologies, and extend post-colonial critiques of Western missions. Methodist theologians from multiple cultures began to ground theologies in specific cultural and political contexts, and historical experiences of oppression. Often they built on missiological foundations while criticizing Western missions as inherently imperialistic. While the range of contextual theologians is impossible to treat in this chapter, it is important to mention the work of Mercy Oduyoye, daughter of a mission pastor in Ghana, student movement leader, ecumenist, feminist, and founder of the Circle of Concerned Women Theologians. While working at the WCC, Oduyoye organized African women theologians to write about their own realities, including critiquing women's oppression under both Western colonialism and traditional cultural patriarchal systems. Unlike those by many male theologians, writings by women in the Circle apply a cultural hermeneutic that reveals women's experiences under male-dominated systems, and thus do not romanticize traditional practices like polygamy. Oduyoye's definition of contextualization thus encompasses themes of both liberation and cultural analysis, and her influence has been wide-ranging and profound.

CONCLUSION

As the much-touted phrase 'the world is my parish' indicates, Methodism was born as a mission movement. But church structures rigidify over time, and as George Hunter quips, the parish becomes the world. The cycle begins anew, of reclaiming the mission heritage by seeking renewal both within church structures and by starting new movements. While mission represents the outward movement of God toward the margins of human need and alienation, the calcification of structures represents an inward-looking movement towards self-satisfied complacency. The reclamation of mission language becomes necessary to remind people of their core commitments. Although its meaning is contested widely among many stakeholders, the energy around reinterpreting 'the world is my parish' serves as something of a bellwether for Methodist missional vitality.

As one of the most vigorous cross-cultural mission movements in the first half of the twentieth century, Methodism bridged many cultures and generated prayer meetings, revivals, churches, schools, clinics, community centres, and national leaders around the world. The operative missiology on the ground was exemplified by E. Stanley Jones, who linked personal salvation through Jesus Christ with faith in the inbreaking kingdom of God, represented by attention to social justice and meeting human needs. The dialectic between evangelism and kingdom resulted in a highly activistic mission paradigm whose success relied on an optimistic view of human capabilities under the graceful guidance of a loving God. The combination of personal commitment and social holiness is a powerful mission theology that not only has attracted people to Methodism, but has also given rise to related movements, including pentecostalism and numerous campaigns for social justice.

In the United Methodist Church, the general conference of 2008 endorsed as the denominational motto 'making disciples of Jesus Christ for the transformation of the world'. The paradigm of evangelism-kingdom once again became the summary sound bite for popular understandings of mission. While this slogan was eagerly embraced as a return to the classic Methodist dialectic between evangelism and social justice, it did not integrate the nature of the church into a full missiology. It represented an essentially pietistic and activistic definition of mission that neither grounded mission in the *missio Dei*, nor addressed the nature of the church, nor provided a cultural hermeneutic. With the local church the de facto locus of mission in the *Book of Discipline*, United Methodism still lacked a fully missional ecclesiology to justify its historic connexionalism and its recent claim to be a global church.

As in the past, the future of Methodism lies not in the perfection of its doctrinal formulations, but in the commitment of its people to answer God's call to mission. As Methodism continues to grow in Africa and Asia, no doubt the 'world is my parish' will take on deeper meaning than ever before.

REFERENCES

ARIAS, MORTIMER (1976). 'That the World May Believe'. *International Review of Mission* 65/ 257: 13–46.

BARCLAY, WADE CRAWFORD (1957). *The Methodist Episcopal Church, 1845–1939: Widening Horizons, 1845–95*. History of Methodist Missions 3. New York: Board of Missions of the Methodist Church.

BEDFORD, NANCY (2004). 'The Theology of Integral Mission and Community Discernment'. In Tetsunao Yamamori and C. René Padilla (eds.), *The Local Church, Agent of Transformation: An Ecclesiology for Integral Mission*. Buenos Aires: Ediciones Kairós.

BEVANS, STEPHEN B. (2002). *Models of Contextual Theology*. Rev. and exp. edn. Faith and Cultures. Maryknoll: Orbis.

The Book of Discipline of The United Methodist Church, 1968. Nashville: Methodist Publishing House.

—— *2004*. Nashville: Methodist Publishing House.

Bosch, David Jacobus (1991). *Transforming Mission: Paradigm Shifts in Theology of Mission*. American Society of Missiology. Maryknoll: Orbis.

Bundy, David (1988). 'The Theology of the Kingdom of God in E. Stanley Jones'. *Wesleyan Theological Journal* 23/1–2.

Castro, Emilio (1985). *Freedom in Mission: The Perspective of the Kingdom of God: An Ecumenical Inquiry*. Geneva: WCC.

Cordingly, Brian (2004). 'Translator's Preface'. In Tetsunao Yamamori and C. René Padilla (eds.), *The Local Church, Agent of Transformation: An Ecclesiology for Integral Mission*. Buenos Aires: Ediciones Kairós.

Dodge, Ralph E. (1986). *The Revolutionary Bishop: Who Saw God at Work in Africa: An Autobiography*. Pasadena: William Carey Library.

Gesling, Linda (2005). *Mirror and Beacon: The History of Mission of the Methodist Church, 1939–1968*. United Methodist Church History of Mission 3. New York: General Board of Global Ministries, United Methodist Church.

Harman, Robert J. (2005). *From Missions to Mission: The History of Mission of The United Methodist Church, 1968–2000*. United Methodist Church History of Mission 5. New York: General Board of Global Ministries, United Methodist Church.

Hiebert, Paul G. (1999). 'Evangelism, Church, and Kingdom'. In Charles Van Engen, Dean S. Gilliland, and Paul Pierson (eds.), *The Good News of the Kingdom: Mission Theology for the Third Millennium*. Eugene, Ore.: Wipf Stock.

Hunter, George G. (1991). 'Is the World Still Our Parish'. In Dean S. Gilliland (ed.), *The World Forever Our Parish*. Lexington, Ky.: Bristol Books.

Im, Mi-Soon (2008). 'Role of Single Women Missionaries of the Methodist Episcopal Church, South, in Korea 1897–1940'. Th.D. dissertation, Boston University.

Jones, E. Stanley (1925). *The Christ of the Indian Road*. New York: Abingdon.

—— (1972). *The Unshakable Kingdom and the Unchanging Person*. Nashville: Abingdon.

Messer, Donald (1992). *A Conspiracy of Goodness: Contemporary Images of Christian Mission*. Nashville: Abingdon.

—— (2002). 'Commentary: What would Wesley do about global AIDS?' Available at <http://www.ncm.org/pdf/Donald_Messer_article.pdf>, accessed 8 January 2009.

Míguez Boníno José (1975). *Doing Theology in a Revolutionary Situation*. Confrontation Books. Philadelphia: Fortress.

Míguez Bonino (1988). 'Conversion: A Latin American Reading'. In Dow Kirkpatrick (ed.), *Faith Born in the Struggle for Life: A Re-reading of Protestant Faith in Latin America Today*. Grand Rapids: Eerdmans.

—— (2003). ' "El Mundo Entero es mi Parroquia": Misión y Oikoumene en el Contexto Global Metodismo y Globalización a Comienzos del Siglo XVIII'. *Cuadernos de teología* 22: 93–103.

Niles, Daniel Thambyrajah (1962). *Upon the Earth: The Mission of God and the Missionary Enterprise of the Churches*. Foundations of the Christian Mission, Studies in the Gospel and the World. New York: McGraw-Hill.

Ogle, George E. (1977). *Liberty to the Captives: The Struggle against Oppression in South Korea*. Atlanta: John Knox.

'Religion' (1938). *Time* 32: 24, 47.

Robb, James S. (1983). 'Missions Derailed: A Special Report on the UM General Board of Global Ministries'. Available at <http://www.goodnewsmag.org/renewal/mission_derailed.htm>, accessed 8 January 2009.

ROBERT, DANA L. (1996). *American Women in Mission: A Social History of Their Thought and Practice.* Macon, Ga.: Mercer University.

ROBINSON, ELAINE A. (2005). 'The Global Mission of The United Methodist Church'. In Elaine A. Robinson and W. Stephen Gunter (eds.), *Considering the Great Commission: Evangelism and Mission in the Wesleyan Spirit.* Nashville: Abingdon.

SCHREITER, ROBERT J. (1985). *Constructing Local Theologies.* Maryknoll: Orbis.

SNYDER, HOWARD A. (1991). *Models of the Kingdom.* Nashville: Abingdon.

United Methodist Church (1990). *Grace upon Grace: The Mission Statement of The United Methodist Church.* Nashville: Graded Press.

URY, WILLIAM (1996). 'The World is Still Our Parish'. *Good News Magazine.* Available at <http://www.goodnewsmag.org/library/articles/ury-nd96.htm>, accessed 8 January 2009.

WALLS, ANDREW F. (1996). *The Missionary Movement in Christian History: Studies in Transmission of Faith.* Maryknoll: Orbis.

World Council of Churches (1982). *Mission and Evangelism: An Ecumenical Affirmation.* Geneva: Commission on World Mission and Evangelism, World Council of Churches.

CHAPTER 26

....

METHODISM AND THE FUTURE OF ECUMENISM

....

DAVID M. CHAPMAN

METHODISTS have been at the forefront of the modern ecumenical movement since its inception, which is usually traced to the Edinburgh Conference on World Mission (1910). Its chairman was an American Methodist layman, John R. Mott, whose outstanding passion for evangelism inspired a similar commitment to the cause of Christian unity, earning him the distinction of being invited to preach at the inaugural meeting of the World Council of Churches (WCC) in 1948. Besides the spirited contribution of individuals such as Mott, institutionally Methodism has been a longstanding participant in ecumenical instruments, dialogues, and unity schemes. But what of Methodism's continuing contribution in what has sometimes been described as the current winter of ecumenism? This chapter will consider the question under five headings: 'catholic spirit'; ecumenical relations; theological dialogue; obstacles to unity; and future priorities.

CATHOLIC SPIRIT

The earliest attempt by Methodists at ecumenism was the famous 'Letter to a Roman Catholic' (1749) in which John Wesley pleads for mutual respect and forbearance between the two communities. The same theme is developed in his sermon on 'catholic spirit'. According to Wesley, catholic or universal love 'embraces with strong and cordial affection neighbours and strangers, friends and enemies'. Those possessed of catholic love manifest 'catholic spirit', which adheres to the 'essentials' of Christian doctrine whilst tolerating diverse theological 'opinions'. Committed to membership of a particular church ('congregation'), those possessed of catholic spirit

[love] as friends, as brethren in the Lord, as members of Christ and children of God, as joint partakers now of the present kingdom of God, and fellow-heirs of his eternal Kingdom, all of whatever opinion or worship or congregation who believe in the Lord Jesus Christ; who love God and man; who, rejoicing to please and fearing to offend God, are careful to abstain from evil and zealous of good works.   (Sermon 39, Wesley 1984: ii. 94)

Whilst it would be anachronistic to turn Wesley into the forerunner of the modern ecumenical movement as some have tried to do, nevertheless he was deeply concerned that Christians should manifest a spiritual unity based on catholic spirit. At the same time, he recognized the importance of 'outward ties of Christian fellowship' and accepted that some theological differences may constitute an impediment to visible unity.

Wesley's emphasis on catholic spirit provides theological underpinning for Methodism's characteristic openness towards Christians of other traditions. In 1820 the Wesleyan Conference in Britain declared that 'Methodists are the friends of all and the enemies of none', though it would be another 150 years before that sentiment could with reasonable confidence be said to apply in the case of Roman Catholics. In the United States catholic spirit in Methodism was similarly marred by hostility towards Roman Catholics. *The Sunday Service of the Methodists in North America* (1784), one of the foundation documents of American Methodism, contains an abridged version of the Thirty-nine Articles perpetuating the anti-Catholicism of the seventeenth-century Church of England. Embarrassed by such outdated sentiments, in 1970 the General Conference of the United Methodist Church adopted a 'Resolution of Intent', promising to interpret Methodism's historic texts in the light of the best insights of the modern ecumenical movement.

In the early years of the twentieth century Methodists began to reflect theologically on their status as a Protestant denomination. According to the British Methodist Deed of Union (1932), 'The Methodist Church claims and cherishes its place in the Holy Catholic Church which is the Body of Christ.' But how were Methodists to understand their ecclesial location in relation to other churches?

Led by Robert Newton Flew, John Scott Lidgett (Great Britain), and Albert Outler (United States), in the middle years of the twentieth century Methodist theologians devoted considerable energy to studying the place of Methodism in the Holy Catholic Church. In a seminal essay on 'Methodism and the Catholic Tradition' Flew (1933: 515–30) argued that the defining characteristics of Methodism, especially its emphasis on holiness, were authentic features of apostolic Christianity. A further characteristic of Methodism was its Catholic doctrine inherited from the Church of England. In his sermons and writings Wesley was not aware that he had substantially departed from Catholic doctrine as the Church of England had received it from the apostles. What was more, Methodism had introduced no new doctrines, though it had perhaps contributed a fresh emphasis on the work of the Holy Spirit.

Flew made no attempt to justify Methodism's separation from the Church of England which he regarded as an accident of history. Nevertheless, the break had occurred and Methodism now existed de facto as a church, its fruitfulness a sign of an effective contribution to Christian mission. Methodists could be 'content in all humility to let the facts of our tradition, our history, our present experience, speak for us, while at the same time we recognise gratefully our growing debt to the other communions of the Catholic Church'.

Building on the foundation laid by Flew and others, *The Nature of the Christian Church* (1937) (Methodist Church of Great Britain 1983) locates Methodism in the ecclesial ground between Roman Catholicism and Protestantism. According to this first official statement of Methodist ecclesiology, Roman Catholic and Protestant formularies did not adequately reflect the nature of the Christian church. The 'conception of the Church' had been 'over-estimated in Catholicism and often under-estimated in Protestantism'. Methodists wanted to avoid 'exaggerating the place of the Church, and clothing it, as Rome has done, with attributes that are properly predicable only of God himself'. Equally, Methodists disapproved of the Protestant tendency to transpose the church into a 'remote and ideal realm'. Instead Methodists recognized the decisive element in the New Testament understanding of the church to be the presence of the living Christ in its midst. Created by God, the church was the instrument of God's divine purpose, not an association of individuals but the Body of Christ. For historical reasons Methodism had been compelled to become a separate community raised up by God to spread scriptural holiness. Methodists now accepted, however, that it was their duty with fellow Christians 'to make common cause in the search for the perfect expression of that unity and holiness which in Christ are already theirs'. Significantly, the statement includes the Roman Catholic Church among those churches that could 'humbly claim to belong to the Body of Christ'; though none could claim to be 'the whole of the Catholic Church on earth' (*Nature of the Christian Church* §3) (Methodist Church of Great Britain 1983).

As a result of this reappropriation of the catholic spirit in Methodism, outdated attitudes towards Roman Catholics gradually disappeared during the twentieth century as Methodists came to recognize that the presence and providential guidance of the Holy Spirit could not be identified exclusively with Protestantism. As an official Methodist observer at the Second Vatican Council, Outler tirelessly encouraged Methodists to develop better relations with Roman Catholics.

Nowadays United Methodists retain a Lutheran definition of the church as 'a community of all true believers under the Lordship of Christ. It is the redeemed and redeeming fellowship in which the Word of God is preached by persons divinely called, and the sacraments are duly administered according to Christ's own appointment' (*Book of Discipline* 2004: 21). The latest British Methodist statement on the church, *Called to Love and Praise* (Methodist Church 1999), proposes an alternative, less tightly drawn criterion for identifying the church: 'wherever people join together to respond to Christ as Lord—there is the Church' (§2.4.9). Visible margins are not unimportant in these inclusive definitions of the church, though it would be a mistake to describe in too precise detail its boundaries.

Emerging from Methodist reflection on the nature of the church in recent years is an approach to ecumenism that reflects Methodism's distinctive history as a holiness movement that combines elements of both Catholic and Protestant doctrine and spirituality. Methodists increasingly value what they have inherited from pre- and post-Reformation sources and continue actively to seek closer relations with Christians of all traditions. As a consequence of their ecclesiology, Methodists are reluctant to 'unchurch' other Christians, believing that a common experience of the Holy Spirit may lead to very different expressions of ecclesial life. Appealing to catholic spirit, Methodists place few theological obstacles in the way of unity with other Christians whose understanding of the nature and identity of the church is compatible with their own.

ECUMENICAL RELATIONS

In the nineteenth century British Methodism was racked by internal schism driven by the fissiparous tendencies inherent in renewal movements. In the United States the Methodist Episcopal Church was similarly beset by domestic disputes, exacerbated by interracial tensions, which eventually led to the formation of several Methodist denominations. Thus in Britain and in America rival brands of Methodism competed for members at home and increasingly overseas. For this reason early attempts by Methodists at ecumenism were often directed towards internal reunification. Following a series of mergers British Methodism was finally reunited in 1932, and in the United States major reunions took place in 1939 and 1968 to form the present United Methodist Church.

In several countries Methodists have been enthusiastic participants in local unity schemes, relinquishing their ecclesial independence in order to join united or uniting churches, such as in Canada (1925), South India (1947), Zambia (1965), Pakistan (1970), and Australia (1977). In territories where Methodists maintain their ecclesial independence relations with other Christians are generally good; though in South and Central America and Eastern Europe there are sectarian tensions with Catholic and Orthodox. In Western Europe ecumenical relations are well advanced. In 1996 seven European Methodist churches signed a Joint Declaration of Church Fellowship establishing intercommunion with the Community of Protestant Churches in Europe, formerly the Leuenberg Church Fellowship.

In Great Britain failed unity schemes in 1972 and 1982 involving Methodists and the Church of England triggered a crisis of confidence in ecumenism at an institutional level, leaving both parties wary of investing time and energy in future proposals. However, a burgeoning number of Local Ecumenical Partnerships involving Anglicans and Methodists provided a fresh stimulus for rapprochement. Encouraged by repositioning on both sides (Anglicans ordaining women and Methodists signalling their willingness to embrace episcopacy), in 2003 the Methodist Church of Great Britain and the Church of England entered into a formal covenant in which both parties committed themselves 'to work to overcome the remaining obstacles to the organic unity of our two churches' (§194). Significantly, the common statement declares: 'We affirm one another's churches as true churches belonging to the One, Holy, Catholic and Apostolic Church of Jesus Christ and as truly participating in the apostolic mission of the whole people of God' (§194).

Now the biblical concept of 'covenant' is central to the way Methodists understand ecclesial relations and the sacraments. For Methodists the new covenant in Christ signifies a solemn and binding relationship among and between Christians and their Lord. At the annual covenant service Methodists recommit themselves to discipleship described in covenantal terms. Since Anglicans tend not to attach the same significance to covenantal language, the two churches might usefully have engaged in a joint study of the subject before entering into a covenant relationship. As it is, twice jilted at the altar, British Methodism appears to regard the mutual obligations implied by the covenant with more serious intent as a sign of betrothal than does its partner. Yet it would be naive for Methodists to imagine that even the most binding commitment to overcome the remaining impediments to their solemn nuptials would be sufficient to guarantee success. Methodists tend to underestimate the difficulties that Anglicans and others have with certain features of Methodism.

American Methodism, in its very different ecclesial context, has no particular affinity with the Anglican Communion and therefore has not felt inhibited in seeking other ecumenical partners, notably the Evangelical Lutheran Church of

America and Lutheran churches in Europe. As a result of the common statement agreed by the international Methodist–Lutheran dialogue in 1984 (see below), formal relations involving intercommunion between United Methodists and Lutherans have now been established in Germany (1990), Austria (1991), Sweden (1993), and Norway (1997). In the United States relations between United Methodists and Lutherans entered a new phase in 2008 as the result of proposals for 'full communion' between the two churches (see below).

At a global level, Methodists are involved in ecumenism under the auspices of the World Methodist Council (WMC). At the instigation of American Methodists, an Oecumenical Methodist Conference first met in London in 1881 to foster closer links between Methodist denominations around the world. Thereafter the Conference met every ten years until 1931. Since 1951 the WMC (and Conference) has met every five years, most recently in Seoul, where attendees represented seventy-six member churches in 132 countries and a global community of 75 million people, approximately equal in size to the Anglican Communion. Although its influence on internal reunification has been limited, the WMC establishes an official Methodist presence at the level of world communions, thereby providing an opportunity for participation in international ecumenical dialogues.

A notable recent achievement of the WMC has been to associate Methodists with the Joint Declaration on the Doctrine of Justification (JDDJ) between the Roman Catholic Church and the Lutheran World Federation (1999). Following consultations among member churches of the WMC, all three parties signed the Official Common Affirmation of the Methodist Statement of Association with the JDDJ at the WMC in Seoul (World Methodist Council 2006). As a result, Methodists, Roman Catholics, and Lutherans affirm together their fundamental doctrinal agreement with the teaching expressed in the JDDJ, thereby committing themselves to strive to deepen their common understanding of justification in theological teaching, study, and preaching as a step towards common mission and eventual full communion. The signatories also affirm that any outstanding differences among them concerning justification are not to be considered sufficient cause for their continuing separation.

From Methodism's inception, Methodist churches have been among the most committed contributors to the WCC, providing three general secretaries: Emilio Castro (1985–92); Philip Potter (1972–84); and Samuel Kobia (2004–). Since the inter-war years when Robert Newton Flew was a major figure in the Faith and Order Movement, Methodists have been particularly active in this aspect of the WCC. Geoffrey Wainwright, world Methodism's leading ecumenist, served on the WCC Faith and Order Commission from 1977 to 1991 and was principal editor at Lima, Peru, of the landmark convergence statement *Baptism, Eucharist and Ministry* (World Council of Churches 1982).

SURVEY OF THEOLOGICAL DIALOGUES

Methodists are, or have been, involved in bilateral conversations sponsored jointly by the WMC and the following world communions: the Roman Catholic Church (1967–); Lutheran World Federation (1977–84); World Alliance of Reformed Churches (1985–7); Anglican Communion (1992–6); Orthodoxy (1992–5); and the Salvation Army (Report to the WMC 2006: 206).

Theologically the most mature of Methodism's bilateral conversations is the dialogue with Roman Catholics, co-chaired by Geoffrey Wainwright since 1986. Established in the immediate aftermath of the Second Vatican Council, this dialogue so far has produced eight reports, conveniently known by the name of the city in which the WMC was meeting when they were presented.

Briefly, the *Denver Report* (Joint International Commission 1971) and *Growth in Understanding* (Dublin: ibid. 1976) are essentially exploratory, establishing broad areas of convergence and identifying topics requiring further discussion. *Towards an Agreed Statement on the Holy Spirit* (Honolulu: ibid. 1981) is a more substantial report that registers considerable agreement about the person and work of the Holy Spirit. It further identifies the doctrine of the Trinity as the most promising theological framework for resolving outstanding differences between Roman Catholics and Methodists concerning the nature of the church.

Following the lead of BEM and ARCIC I *The Final Report* (1981), *Towards a Statement on the Church* (Nairobi: Joint International Commission 1986) introduces *koinonia* language into Methodist–Roman Catholic dialogue, believing this to be the most valuable 'model' for understanding the nature of the church (§23). The church is described in terms of *koinonia*: 'Because God so loved the world, he sent his Son and the Holy Spirit to draw us into communion with himself. This sharing in God's life, which resulted from the mission of the Son and the Holy Spirit, found expression in a visible *koinonia* of Christ's disciples, the Church' (§1). A rich definition of *koinonia* is offered:

For believers [*koinonia*] involves both communion and community. It includes participation in God through Christ in the Spirit by which believers become adopted children of the same Father and members of the one body of Christ sharing in the same Spirit. And it includes deep fellowship among participants, a fellowship which is both visible and invisible, finding expression in faith and order, in prayer and sacrament, in mission and service.   (§23)

For the first time the goal of Methodist–Roman Catholic dialogue is set as 'full communion in faith, mission and sacramental life' (§20).

The Apostolic Tradition (Singapore: ibid. 1991) explores how both communities understand their continuity with the apostles. *The Word of Life* (Rio de Janeiro: ibid. 1996) investigates the nature of revelation and faith. *Speaking the Truth in Love*

(Brighton: ibid. 2001) considers teaching authority among Methodists and Roman Catholics, each side describing their own tradition and posing a number of pertinent questions to the other (Meyer and Vischer 1984; Gros, Meyer, and Rusch 2000; Gros, Best, and Fuchs 2007).

Recently the dialogue has returned to ecclesiology. Building on foundations secured in previous reports, *The Grace Given you in Christ* (Seoul: Joint International Commission 2006) identifies those ecclesial elements and endowments that Methodists and Roman Catholics can recognize in each other as being truly of the church. The Seoul report proposes an exchange of gifts in the shape of ecclesial elements and sets out some general principles for developing relations between Methodists and Roman Catholics.

The large measure of theological agreement between Methodists and Roman Catholics so carefully established in the course of forty years of bilateral dialogue is impressive. Nevertheless, substantial differences remain that are not easily resolved. Despite the fact that relations between the two communities continue to improve in many parts of the world, unity remains some way over the horizon. Besides theological agreement, full communion between Methodists and Roman Catholics 'will also depend upon a fresh creative act of reconciliation which acknowledges the manifold yet unified activity of the Holy Spirit throughout the ages. It will involve a joint act of obedience to the sovereign Word of God' (*The Apostolic Tradition*) (Joint International Commission 1991: §117).

Regrettably, notwithstanding its achievements, the international dialogue between Methodists and Roman Catholics is also characterized by the problem of reception that besets ecumenism. As a consultative body, the WMC has no executive authority amongst member churches which therefore makes it difficult to disseminate the results of ecumenical dialogue. Reports issued by dialogue commissions have no status in member churches of the WMC unless autonomous conferences formally receive them. Yet as recently as 2003 the Methodist Church of Great Britain became the first member church of the WMC to ask its Faith and Order Committee to evaluate the reports emanating from the international Methodist–Roman Catholic dialogue. As a result of this failure in reception at the level of Methodist conferences and Catholic bishops' conferences, many Methodists and Roman Catholics remain unaware that their communions are in bilateral conversations, and some continue to hold outdated views of the other. Only when the problem of reception is overcome will Methodists and Roman Catholics be able to live out the fullest possible degree of communion based on existing bilateral agreements.

On other ecumenical fronts involving Methodists there has been impressive progress towards unity, though here, too, reception remains a problem. Conversations between the WMC and the Lutheran World Federation have produced a common statement on *The Church: A Community of Grace* (Lutheran–Methodist

International Dialogue 1984). Behind the different theological expressions and forms of Christian life represented by Methodism and by Lutheranism, the conversations discovered shared basic convictions and sufficient agreement about (1) the authority of the Scriptures, (2) salvation by grace through faith, (3) the church, (4) means of grace, and (5) the mission of the church, to be able to recommend that 'our churches take steps to declare and establish full fellowship of word and sacrament' (§91). Unresolved issues meriting further discussion were identified as 'providence and two kingdoms, aspects of anthropology, and forms of unity' (§88). It is on the basis of this common statement that American Methodism has been able to enter into the agreements of intercommunion with Lutheran churches noted above.

Dialogue between the WMC and the World Alliance of Reformed Churches produced a short statement, *Together in God's Grace* (Reformed–Methodist 1987). Noting substantial agreement between Methodists and Reformed across a range of theological topics, the statement considers five areas of dispute (the Tradition and traditions, grace, the church as covenant community, church and state, and perfect salvation), before concluding that 'Historic differences of theological perspective and practice still maintain their influence, but are not of sufficient weight to divide us' (Gros, Meyer, and Rusch 2000: 270). In particular, differences between Wesley and Calvin concerning freedom and grace have usually been perceived as constituting a fundamental division between Methodists and Reformed. In Calvinist understanding it is the elect who come to faith and therefore receive saving grace, whereas in Arminian Methodism it is those who in freedom will to be saved. Nevertheless, 'that Wesley and Calvin advocated conflicting ways of holding together what they affirm in common should not constitute a barrier between our traditions' (ibid. 272). In general, 'the classical doctrinal issues [...] ought not to be seen as obstacles to unity between Methodists and Reformed' (ibid. 274). In view of this significant theological agreement, the final recommendations are surprisingly tentative—merely inviting Methodists and Reformed to consider closer cooperation and whether there are countries in which union negotiations might be initiated. The question remains whether continuing soteriological differences will permit Methodists and Reformed to develop a common understanding of missiology.

Dialogue between Methodists and Anglicans internationally began at the initiative of the 1988 Lambeth Conference, quickly focusing on the ministry as the main point of contention between the two communions. Acknowledging the considerable agreement between Anglicans and Methodists concerning faith and doctrine, and believing there to be sufficient convergence in understanding ministry and mission, *Sharing in the Apostolic Communion* (Anglican–Methodist Dialogue 1996) invited the WMC and the Lambeth Conference to recognize and affirm that:

- 'Both Anglicans and Methodists belong to the one, holy, catholic and apostolic church of Jesus Christ and participate in the apostolic mission of the whole people of God;
- In the churches of our two communions the word of God is authentically preached and the sacraments instituted by Christ are duly administered;
- Our churches share in the common confession and heritage of the apostolic faith' (§95).

A second resolution called for the establishment of a joint working group to prepare guidelines for procedures whereby national and regional authorities would be able to implement the mutual recognition of members, eucharistic communion extending beyond mutual hospitality, the mutual recognition and interchangeability of ministries and rites, and structures of common decision-making.

Not for the first time, however, difficulties relating to the ministry were underestimated. Whereas the WMC meeting in 1996 unanimously adopted the key resolutions, the 1998 Lambeth Conference declined to adopt them in the form presented. Instead member churches of the Anglican Communion were invited to study the report and, where appropriate, to develop local 'agreements of acknowledgement'—less theologically loaded a proposition than *recognition*. Moreover, the Lambeth Conference cautiously envisaged the role of the joint working group as preparing 'guidelines for moving beyond acknowledgement to the reconciliation of churches and, within that, the reconciliation of ordained ministries and structures for common decision-making'. Reference to the *reconciliation* of ministries signals that, as things presently stand, Anglicans are unable formally to *recognize* Methodist ordination as such. Although this outcome was disappointing for Methodists, the substance of the first resolution was eventually enshrined in the mutual affirmations contained in the Anglican–Methodist Covenant in Great Britain whereby both partners recognize each other as true churches (*Anglican–Methodist Covenant* 2001). Questions relating to the mutual recognition of ministries remain the most sensitive aspect of relations between Methodists and Anglicans.

John and Charles Wesley were strongly influenced by the early church fathers, and via its founders Methodism has absorbed some of the theological riches of the Eastern church. A joint preparatory commission appointed by the WMC and the Ecumenical Patriarchate of Constantinople unanimously agreed to recommend the inauguration of an international Orthodox–Methodist dialogue. *Orthodox and Methodists* (1995) is a short 'brochure' produced by the commission containing a self-description by both partners, an appreciation by each tradition of the principal features of the other, and suggestions concerning the aims, benefits, and possible topics for future conversations. Unfortunately, Orthodox have yet to accept the commission's recommendation to begin formal dialogue with Methodists. A particular challenge for this dialogue will be how to develop a methodology that takes account of the very different historical, theological, and liturgical contexts of Methodism and Orthodoxy.

The Methodist origins of the Salvation Army make the two communions natural dialogue partners, though until recently relations have often been strained by historical tensions. Formal conversations between the two communions finally began in 2003, the intention being 'to explore our common heritage as Wesleyan Christians, examining the historical/doctrinal moorings of the Salvation Army and "Methodist essentials"' (Report to the WMC 2006: 206). Subsequent conversations have focused on how Methodists and Salvationists each understand the church. An important discovery has been that Methodists can benefit from a renewed understanding of the church as mission, articulated so clearly by Salvationists, who in turn can benefit from the apostolic and sacramental vision of the church in Methodism. For Methodists, the dialogue with Salvationists fulfils the aims of the first Oecumenical Methodist Conference in bringing together Christians with a common Wesleyan heritage.

Supplementing these international conversations are several national dialogue commissions involving Methodists. Bilateral conversations between Methodists and Roman Catholics in Great Britain and in the United States have produced a number of convergence statements, notably on Mary and on the nature of the church (British Methodist–Roman Catholic Committee 1995; United Methodist Church 2005). In New Zealand dialogue between Methodists and Roman Catholics began in the 1980s and is still at an early stage. In Australia Methodist–Roman Catholic conversations began in the early 1970s, focusing on common beliefs and pastoral concerns relating to baptism. Since 1977 the Uniting Church in Australia (a member of the WMC) has extended the dialogue with Roman Catholics into areas of common pastoral concern. The most recent report to emerge from this dialogue, *Interchurch Marriages: Their Ecumenical Challenge and Significance for our Churches* (1999), deserves attention beyond Australia.

In the United States Methodist–Lutheran dialogue has reached an advanced stage after preliminary conversations covering baptism (1977–9), episcopacy (1985–7), and eucharistic sharing (2001–4). In 2004 proposals for eucharistic sharing were adopted by both communities as an interim measure in anticipation of further convergence. *Confessing our Faith Together* (United Methodist–Lutheran Dialogue Commission 2005) is a common statement intended as the basis for full communion between the United Methodist Church and the Evangelical Lutheran Church of America. As envisaged in the statement, full communion will comprise: (1) a common confessing of the Christian faith; (2) mutual recognition of baptism and sharing of the eucharist; (3) mutual recognition of ordained ministries; (4) common commitment to evangelism, witness, and service; and (5) 'a means of common decision making on critical common issues of faith and life'. In 2008 the UMC General Conference and the Lutheran Assembly approved proposals to implement 'full communion' between the two churches based on *Confessing Our Faith Together*.

OBSTACLES TO UNITY

Following rapid progress in ecumenism during the past forty years, the remaining obstacles to reuniting the church appear formidable. Christians even disagree about what constitutes unity. Some prefer to think of unity in terms of 'reconciled diversity', whereby denominations maintain an independent ecclesial existence in a state of 'full communion'. The fundamental weakness of this description of unity is that by perpetuating separate ecclesial structures it tolerates visible *disunity*. To characterize this state of affairs as 'full communion' is therefore misleading. In fact, it would be more accurate to describe such a relationship between canonically independent churches as intercommunion.

Identifying the goal of Methodist–Roman Catholic dialogue as 'full communion in faith, mission and sacramental life' is therefore quite subtle. Full communion in sacramental life necessarily involves the reconciliation of ministries (and therefore ecclesial structures) in a way that may legitimately be described as *visible* unity, even if it suggests that Methodists may retain their own ecclesial identity as such. From this vantage point, the 'full communion' soon to be established between Methodists and Lutherans in the United States appears more like an interim stage on the way to visible unity.

To illustrate from a Methodist perspective how some of the remaining theological obstacles to unity may eventually be overcome, we shall draw on aspects of the WCC (1982) convergence statement *Baptism, Eucharist and Ministry (BEM)* beginning with the section on ministry.

According to *BEM*, the traditional threefold pattern of ministry (bishop, presbyter, and deacon) may serve as an expression and means of achieving Christian unity (*BEM* Ministry §22). Churches that do not have this pattern are urged to consider whether it has a powerful claim to be accepted (§25). Methodists need not resist this proposal. Since 1784 American Methodism has appointed certain presbyters to the office of bishop, albeit without constituting a separate order of ministry. British Methodism has more than once signalled its willingness to 'take episcopacy into our system', though internal attempts to do so have failed for various reasons that include a lingering suspicion of clerical hierarchy. In 2007 British Methodists gave a lukewarm response to yet another internal discussion document entitled *What Sort of Bishops?* (Methodist Church 2007).

Some would argue that it is more appropriate for Methodist churches that lack bishops to receive episcopal orders from an ecumenical partner. However, the degree of ecclesial convergence required before another church would be willing to confer episcopal orders on Methodist ministers makes this a remote eventuality. Indeed, the prospects for such convergence appear slim without the influence of a distinct order of Methodist bishops constituted along traditional lines. Establishing a threefold pattern of ministry within Methodism has the potential to become a fruitful aspect of future ecumenical strategy, not least because reconciling episcopal orders is likely to be less problematic than attempts to unify episcopal and non-episcopal ministries, which give rise to correspondingly divergent forms of ecclesial life.

The ministry of oversight or *episkopē* in Methodism raises a number of related issues that have yet to be fully addressed in conversations with ecumenical partners. *BEM* (Ministry §26) suggests that 'The ordained ministry should be exercised in a personal, collegial and communal way.' However, *episkopē* in Methodism has mostly been exercised communally, even in those Methodist churches endowed with bishops. Whilst nowadays Methodists are more committed than ever before to the exercise of *episkopē* in communal, collegial, and personal ways, they have yet to work out satisfactorily the theological relationship between these elements. Only after this will it be possible to achieve an appropriate balance in Methodism's instruments of authority. As things currently stand, Methodists have barely begun to reflect on the implications for the church's ministry of the fact that the Holy Spirit bestows gifts upon individuals for the building up of the body (1 Corinthians 12). For reasons that derive from their experience in the eighteenth century, as well as from the influence of democratic movements in the early nineteenth century, Methodists favour a corporate and distributed form of authority that is representative of those communities over which it is set. Methodists are often well versed in the weaknesses inherent in investing authority in individuals. They need to show greater awareness of the weaknesses of communal forms of authority, which may be no less susceptible to impeding the Holy Spirit than individuals.

The priestly nature of the church and the ordained ministry is another source of dispute that stems from the Reformation. Methodists have tended to interpret the royal priesthood of the people of God either individualistically or else corporately. Either way, there has been fierce resistance to associating the ordained ministry with any form of priesthood that does not properly belong to all Christians. Responding to *BEM*, British Methodists suggested that their Deed of Union precluded conceiving the ordained ministry as having a priestly character of its own (Thurian 1986: 210–29).

Mature reflection on the nature of ecclesial being suggests that such a stance is no longer necessary since the royal priesthood of the church need not be regarded as incompatible with an ordained ministry that has a priestly nature. The only priesthood in the church is that of Christ himself. Deriving from his priesthood, the priesthood of the church may be thought of as belonging to Christ's corporate body and to its individual members in ways proper to their *ordo* within the church. Underpinning this perspective is a relational understanding of ecclesial being in which the primary ontological distinction is between the baptized and the non-baptized (rather than between lay and ordained). The precise details would have to be worked out so as to avoid the royal priesthood of the church and the priesthood of its ordained ministry eclipsing each other.

Besides issues relating to ministry, differences concerning baptism also constitute obstacles to Christian unity. Methodists have always been energetic proponents of infant baptism, even though they have often failed to give sufficient
attention to the grace conferred by the sacrament. This, coupled with a strong
'connexional' (as against a congregational) polity, means that Methodists have not
found congenial dialogue partners in Baptists and others that adhere to believers'
baptism as the sole means of entry into the church. Indeed, Baptists are the only
major Western tradition with which Methodists have no history of international
conversations.

In recent years, however, there has been increasing recognition across the
ecclesial spectrum that the baptism of adults is normative in Christian mission,
though in company with the majority of Christians Methodists maintain that
infant baptism is a concession permissible in appropriate circumstances. *BEM*
(Commentary §12) invites infant-baptist and believer-baptist traditions to consider
whether they can 'regard as equivalent alternatives for entry into the Church both a
pattern whereby baptism in infancy is followed by later profession of faith and a
pattern whereby believers' baptism follows upon a presentation and blessing in
infancy'. Recent Anglican–Baptist dialogue in Britain adopts a similar approach to
Christian initiation, and Methodists should be able to endorse both patterns
without weakening their commitment to infant baptism (Church of England
2005: esp. 73–5).

A related issue concerns what constitutes 'appropriate circumstances' for infant
baptism. Particularly in Europe, where Christianity is fast becoming a residual
religious feature of society, there is a danger of infant baptism becoming little more
than a folk ritual divorced from entry into the church. A priority for churches that
practise infant baptism is to develop an ecumenical strategy that safeguards its
integrity and strengthens its sacramental character.

Elsewhere in this volume (Ch. 20) Geoffrey Wainwright shows how eucharistic
theology and liturgy in the mainstream Christian traditions have converged in
recent years. Dialogue between Methodists and Roman Catholics has achieved
considerable agreement in teaching on the eucharist but theological differences
remain, notably concerning the real presence and eucharistic sacrifice. Reflecting
their origins in the comprehensiveness of the eighteenth-century Church of
England, Methodists have been content to affirm that the presence of Christ at
the eucharist is true, real, and substantial without speculating on its precise mode
and how it relates to the other ways in which Scripture tells us the Lord makes
himself present to his people. Reformation disputes about transubstantiation
need not feature prominently in continuing theological dialogue since Aristotelian metaphysics no longer holds sway as the principal philosophical means of
construing reality. Nevertheless, describing the presence of Christ at the eucharist
in relation to other forms of his presence remains a challenge for ecumenical
dialogue.

The sacrificial nature of the eucharist, hotly disputed at the time of the Reformation, remains an obvious difference in eucharistic rites. The principal sources of Methodist liturgy are John Wesley's Abridgement of the 1662 Book of Common Prayer and the modern liturgical movement, neither of which (for different reasons) places much emphasis on the eucharist as sacrifice. As a result, Methodist eucharistic rites do not describe the eucharistic sacrifice in a way that Roman Catholics are able to recognize as being consistent with their own teaching. Yet Charles Wesley's *Hymns on the Lord's Supper* (1745) contain powerful references to eucharistic sacrifice. Further dialogue in this area offers the prospect of substantial agreement.

Use of the consecrated elements outside the eucharist is a further source of dispute between Roman Catholics and Protestants. In recent times Methodists in the United States and in Britain have developed rites of 'extended communion' for the sick that are forms of reserved sacrament in all but name. Presumably, a strong doctrine of the enduring presence of Christ is required to legitimate use of the consecrated elements in this way, though Methodist theology has yet to catch up with the implications of this development in eucharistic practice. Since Roman Catholics and Methodists agree that preserving the eucharistic species is intended primarily for the communion of the sick (Joint International Commission 1976: Dublin §61), further dialogue may establish that secondary uses (such as for veneration) need not be regarded as sufficient cause for continuing separation.

FUTURE PRIORITIES

The plethora of ecumenical agreements, instruments, and dialogues in which Methodists currently participate, internationally and nationally, presents a variety of possibilities for the future. Just as earlier separations occurred in a ragged way, unity seems most likely to be achieved in a similarly untidy fashion. Their pragmatic concern for mission, allied with a high degree of autonomy, enables Methodists to pursue national and regional opportunities for ecumenism as these present themselves.

Internal tensions among Methodists will no doubt continue to influence ecumenical strategy. Whereas American Methodists set great store by the WMC as a means of achieving greater unity within global Methodism, British Methodists attach greater importance to local ecumenical initiatives. Despite such differences, however, one guiding principle is commonly accepted. Methodist ecclesiology reflects the origins of Methodism as a renewal movement. Raised up by God to spread scriptural holiness, Methodism adopts a practical perspective on the nature and identity of the church. Methodists would not be true to their original inspiration if they failed to stress the soteriological and missiological horizon of all theological reflection on the church.

Yet Methodists are also open to fresh insights into the nature of the church. Recently, Methodism's 'connexional' principle has been brought into fruitful dialogue with koinonia ecclesiology. Likewise Methodists are willing to describe the church as a 'communion of communions' and even refer to it as 'the sacrament of God's love for the world and the sacrament of Christ's continuing presence in the world' (United Methodist Church 2005 §58; Methodist Church of Great Britain 1999 §3). Sacramental language has considerable potential in Methodist–Roman Catholic dialogue since it holds together the church's visible dimension (a Roman Catholic emphasis) and its invisible dimension (a Methodist emphasis).

In the present crisis of authority in the church as a whole it is questionable whether current instruments of discernment within Methodism are sufficiently robust to maintain unity in the face of potent challenges to Christian doctrine. Following John Wesley's lead, hitherto Methodists have mostly assumed that there is a core of essential doctrine to which all Christians can subscribe. However, various contemporary controversies that transcend denominational boundaries, coinciding with a widespread failure in catechesis, mean that this assumption may no longer be tenable. In the face of complex and divisive issues relating to faith and morals, instruments of discernment may be needed in Methodism beyond the level of autonomous conferences. Indeed, if they are serious about ecumenism, Methodists must consider how the counsels of Christians of other traditions might enhance their own practice of Christian conference.

Postmodernity raises a cluster of challenges that hitherto ecumenism has largely failed to address. In one way or another these relate to the relativity of all forms of human culture. One of the insights of recent studies in this field is the growing awareness that there was never a time when the apostolic tradition was culture-free since the incarnation occurred in a particular time and place. As a result, the transmission of the apostolic tradition involves a dialogue between cultures— biblical, apostolic, patristic, medieval, Protestant, Counter-Reformation, and contemporary. Inculturation of the gospel cannot simply mean embedding a supposedly culture-free tradition in a contemporary setting. Postmodernity encourages Christians to be more aware of the hidden dynamics involved in such processes, especially how power is exercised in the inevitable clash between cultures.

So far as ecumenism is concerned, in transmitting the apostolic tradition each Christian community privileges certain cultures that are important in its particular history. Greater awareness of the cultural setting of doctrine within a community may help uncover a basic convergence between apparently divergent traditions. Even the cultural setting of ecumenism itself needs to be taken into account. International dialogues tend to involve participants mainly from North America and Europe. The present volume includes Methodist voices from a variety of cultures that deserve to be heard in ecumenism as much as in other fields of study. More generally, the study of ecumenical hermeneutics is still at an early stage and requires further work.

For the foreseeable future the dialogue with Roman Catholics remains the most challenging but potentially the most rewarding of Methodism's bilateral conversations since it seeks to bridge the deep fissures in the Western church caused by the Reformation. Whilst there can be no shortcuts, painstaking endeavour has yielded substantial convergence and the prospect of deepening relations. Promisingly, the fresh approach proposed in the most recent round of dialogue seeks to relocate the centre of encounter away from theological dialogue between small numbers of professionals towards mutual engagement in an ecclesial setting and at various levels. Only as ecumenism is thus absorbed into the bloodstream of the local church will it be able to shape an ecclesial context in which reconciliation is increasingly recognized as a gospel imperative.

Whilst the onset of an ecumenical spring might seem a remote prospect at the present time, the future of ecumenism is far from bleak so far as Methodists are concerned. Despite the obstacles to be overcome, the catholic spirit in Methodism is sufficiently resilient not to be discouraged in the long haul towards Christian unity. Methodists may disagree among themselves about the final destination and the best route to follow, but their strong sense of the priority of Christian mission compels them to seek greater unity with fellow Christians.

John Wesley did not fear that Methodism would one day cease to exist but he did fear that it would continue only as a dead letter. If, in the divine providence, God raised up Methodism to spread scriptural holiness, then Methodists may one day come to recognize a point when their extraordinary commission can without loss be subsumed into the mission of a reunited church. Hopefully, at that juncture the catholic spirit will lead Methodists to relinquish their independent ecclesial existence in favour of full visible unity with fellow Christians.

Suggested Reading

An Anglican–Methodist Covenant (2001).

Chapman, David M. (2004). *In Search of the Catholic Spirit: Methodists and Roman Catholics in Dialogue.* Peterborough: Epworth.

Outler, Albert C. (1975). 'Discovery: An Olive Branch to the Romans, 1970s-style: United Methodist Initiative, Roman Catholic Response'. *Methodist History* 13: 52–6.

Rouse, Ruth, and Neill, Stephen Charles (1954). *A History of the Ecumenical Movement 1517–1948.* London: SPCK.

United Methodist Church (2001). *Methodist–Catholic Dialogues: Thirty Years of Mission and Witness.* US Catholic Bishops' Conference/United Methodist Church.

Wainwright, Geoffrey (1983). *The Ecumenical Moment: Crisis and Opportunity for the Church*. Grand Rapids: Eerdmans.

—— (1995). *Methodists in Dialogue*. Nashville: Abingdon.

References

An Anglican–Methodist Covenant (2001). *An Anglican–Methodist Covenant: Common Statement of the Formal Conversations between the Methodist Church of Great Britain and the Church of England*. Peterborough: Methodist Publishing House.

Anglican–Methodist International Dialogue (1996). *Sharing in the Apostolic Communion*.

Anglican–Roman Catholic International Commission (ARCIC) (1982). *The Final Report*. London: CTS/SPCK.

The Book of Discipline of the United Methodist Church (2004). Nashville: United Methodist Publishing House.

British Methodist–Roman Catholic Committee (1995). *Mary, Mother of the Lord, Sign of Grace, Faith and Holiness: Towards a Shared Understanding*. London: CTS/Methodist Publishing House.

Church of England (2005). *Pushing at the Boundaries of Unity: Anglicans and Baptists in Conversation*. London: Church House.

Flew, R. Newton (1933). 'Methodism and the Catholic Tradition'. In N. P. Williams and Charles Harris (eds.), *Northern Catholicism*. London: SPCK, 515–30.

Gros, Jeffrey, Meyer, Harding, and Rusch, William G. (eds.) (2000). *Growth in Agreement II: Reports and Agreed Statements of Ecumenical Conversations on a World Level, 1982–1998*. Grand Rapids: Eerdmans.

—— Best, Thomas F., and Fuchs, Lorelei F. (eds.) (2007). *Growth in Agreement III: International Dialogue Texts and Agreed Statements 1998–2005*. Grand Rapids: Eerdmans.

Interchurch Marriages: Their Ecumenical Challenge and Significance for our Churches (1999). Uniting Church of Australia–Roman Catholic Church in Australia.

Joint International Commission for Dialogue between the World Methodist Council and the Roman Catholic Church (1971). *Denver Report*.

—— (1976). *Growth in Understanding*. Dublin.

—— (1981). *Towards an Agreed Statement on the Holy Spirit*. Honolulu.

—— (1986). *Towards a Statement on the Church*. Nairobi.

—— (1991). *The Apostolic Tradition*. Singapore.

—— (1996). *The Word of Life: A Statement on Revelation and Faith*. Rio de Janeiro.

—— (2001). *Speaking the Truth in Love: Teaching Authority among Catholics and Methodists*. Brighton.

—— (2006). *The Grace Given You in Christ: Catholics and Methodists Reflect Further on the Church*. Seoul.

Lutheran–Methodist International Dialogue (1984). *The Church: Community of Grace*.

Methodist Church of Great Britain (1983). *Statements of the Methodist Church on Faith and Order 1933–1983*. London: Methodist Publishing House.

—— (1999). *Called to Love and Praise*. Peterborough: Methodist Publishing House.

—— (2007). *What Sort of Bishops?* Peterborough: Methodist Publishing House.

MEYER, HARDING, and VISCHER, LUKAS (eds.) (1984). *Growth in Agreement: Reports and Agreed Statements of Ecumenical Conversations on a World Level.* New York: Paulist.

Reformed–Methodist International Dialogue (1987). *Together in God's Grace.*

Report to the World Methodist Conference on the International Dialogue Between the Salvation Army and the World Methodist Council (2006). *Proceedings of the Nineteenth World Methodist Conference Seoul, Korea: God in Christ Reconciling.* Lake Junaluska: World Methodist Council.

Roman Catholic Church/Lutheran World Federation (1999). *Joint Declaration on the Doctrine of Justification.* Vatican/Lutheran World Federation.

THURIAN, MAX (ed.) (1986). *Churches Respond to BEM.* Geneva: WCC, ii.

United Methodist Church (2005). *Through Divine Love: The Church in Each Place and All Places.* United Methodist/Roman Catholic Dialogue Commission.

United Methodist–Lutheran Dialogue Commission (2005). *Confessing our Faith Together.*

WCC (World Council of Churches) (1982). *Baptism, Eucharist and Ministry.* Geneva: WCC.

WESLEY, JOHN (1984). *Works,* ed. Albert C. Outler. Nashville: Abingdon, ii.

World Methodist Council (2006). *Official Common Affirmation of the Methodist Statement of Association with the Joint Declaration on the Doctrine of Justification between the Roman Catholic Church and the Lutheran World Federation.* Lake Junaluska: World Methodist Council.

CHAPTER 27

THE ORTHODOX CHALLENGE TO METHODISM IN RUSSIA

SERGEI V. NIKOLAEV

EVEN prior to the 1905 Imperial Law on Freedom of Conscience there were Methodist Christians in Russia. From 1889 to the end of the 1930s and from the early 1990s until the present, the Methodist Church in Russia has existed side by side with the Russian Orthodox Church. This more than fifty-year history of Methodism in Russia is presently leading to the emergence of a particular Methodist identity—Russian Methodism, a form that raises questions in the fields of ecumenism, ecclesiology, and theology and about other aspects of Christian ecclesial life in Russia that also have bearing on the Christian community around the world. One of the unique characteristics of such an emerging Methodist identity is that it is being influenced by an Orthodox Church to a larger extent than any other form of Methodism around the world.

This chapter argues that applying a three-sided conceptualization of Methodist–Orthodox relations in Russia—the Russian Orthodox Church, American Methodism, and Russian Methodism—provides a more effective methodology for understanding the phenomenon of Russian Methodism than the simplistic, currently dominant two-sided concept of American Methodism and Russian Orthodoxy. The third part of this chapter attempts to go beyond politically based accusations of proselytism and engage the ecumenically oriented thought of the period between the two world wars of such Russian Orthodox theologians in exile as Sergii Bulgakov and Georges Florovsky. Before exploring questions of possible theological and ecclesiological engagement of the Russian United Methodist with the Russian Orthodox Church, this chapter highlights some contextual realities that characterize the Russian Orthodox conversation regarding Russian Methodism.

CONTEXTUAL REALITIES

The primary Russian Orthodox frame of reference in relation to Russian Methodists, even though stated anecdotally, is 'Methodists are good Christians, let them go back to America'. This statement presupposes a standard narrative that many Methodists have heard from Russian Orthodox officials of different levels versed in Russian Orthodox–United Methodist relations. The narrative begins with the golden age of such relations, i.e. the final period of Soviet history, when the United Methodist Church was sending significant financial contributions to the Russian Orthodox Church to support Christianity in Russia and to help people in Russia via the Russian Orthodox Church. The narrative then turns from this positively described period of cooperation to a less favourably described stage, in which the United Methodist Church began to help the Russian people directly (in partnership with the Russian Peace Foundation) during the late 1980s and early 1990s, which led to the emergence of some local United Methodist congregations in Russia. Next, an even more negative period is described, characterized by the assignment of a United Methodist bishop in 1992 to oversee the lives of existing United Methodist congregations in Russia. The entire narrative ends with direct or indirect accusations of United Methodists practising proselytism and encouragement for the United Methodist audience to return to the golden age of Russian Orthodox–United Methodist relations.

The same frame of reference is evoked by Russian Orthodox leaders in ecumenical forums of different levels. They characterize Methodism in Russia as the recent missionary activity of American Methodism, thus subtly, and sometimes not so subtly, accusing the United Methodist Church of treating Russia as a mission field and of disregarding and disrespecting the millennium-old history of the Russian Orthodox Church. This rhetoric permeates general discussion in the World Council of Churches to the degree that, in a typical interview, the former WCC general secretary Konrad Raiser in describing the situation in Russia refers to the Methodist presence in Russia as nothing less than 'intentional proselytism', from the perception of the Russian Orthodox Church (Simion 2003: 6). This standing of the Russian Orthodox ecumenists resulted in pressure even on the ecumenically minded representatives of the United Methodist Church, particularly related to the General Commission on Christian Unity and Interreligious Concerns, the ecumenical agency of the United Methodist Church. When asked why on their visits to Russia on ecumenical business GCCUIC members rarely visit units of the Russia United Methodist Church, they reply that they simply want to remain 'faithful to their ecumenical partners'.

In addition, the term 'proselytism' is typically used in a specific non-theological meaning. It is often used by Orthodox non-theological researchers as conversion to any religion, even including conversion from atheism or agnosticism, as opposed to the more nuanced evangelical distinction, where proselytism means a purposeful activity aimed at luring Christians belonging to a particular Christian church or denomination to another Christian church or denomination. The ministry of the church aimed at acquainting non-Christian individuals, for the first time, to life in Christ would typically be called evangelization. Not willing to distinguish between the two, Orthodox Christians tend to mean by proselytism the conversion of any individual in Russia to non-Orthodox Christianity (Prodromou 2006).

These typical themes raised in discussion of the Methodist presence in Russia that are pursued by Russian Orthodox leaders while outside Russia or with non-Russian audiences have additional components in terms of Orthodoxy vs. sect or Orthodoxy vs. heterodoxy in the discussions within Russia or with a Russian audience. Whereas on the parish-life level Russian Orthodox priests are not so quick to brand Russian Baptists or Pentecostals as a sect, more often than not, in explaining who the Methodists are, they qualify the Methodist Church as a sect.

One factor among others contributing to the resolute Russian Orthodox qualification of Methodism in Russia as a sect is a gap in the historically significant presence of Methodism in Russia proper after the death of the earlier Methodist leaders who perished in the GULAG prison camps in the 1930s and the re-emergence of United Methodist congregations in Russia in the 1990s. (Even between the 1930s and 1990s there survived Russian-speaking congregations in Estonia and Western Ukraine.) Another important factor is that even today there are only around one hundred United Methodist congregations in Russia with 5,000 members and a constituency of about 15,000 overall. In practice, such a miniscule presence in the Russian population of 140 million cannot claim high priority on the to-do list of the Russian Orthodox Church. Consequently, the reality of the existence of the Russia United Methodist Church in Russia is not addressed by the Russian Orthodox Church in any constructive way. Rather, in principle, the Russian Orthodox Church strives to interpret any Methodist presence in Russia as a variation of the American Methodist presence in Russia and would prefer to address this situation by appealing to the American representatives of the United Methodist Church, rather than to the Russian Methodist leaders.

On the other hand, local congregations of the United Methodist Church are recognized and have been registered by the Russian government from the early 1990s and the Russia United Methodist Church has been considered a Russian centralized religious organization from 1996. On 24 December 2007, one of the central TV channels informed Russian viewers, in a positive light, that this date is Christmas Eve for Roman Catholics, Lutherans, Baptists, Pentecostals, and some of the Methodists in Russia. At the same time, in reality, the attitude of government officials towards local United Methodist congregations depends significantly on the attitude of the local Russian Orthodox priest or hierarch: an open attitude results in local government officials relating positively towards United Methodists, whereas a negative attitude has the opposite effect. Nonetheless, the existence of Russian Methodists in Russia is an indisputable fact, supported both by the first stage of Methodist history in Russia before the 1930s and by the present development of the Russia United Methodist Church.

THE CASE FOR THE REALITY OF RUSSIAN METHODISM

Methodologically, I suggest that analysing the phenomenon of Russian Methodism in terms of a three-sided relationship (American Methodism, Russian Orthodoxy, and Russian Methodism) has potential for a deeper understanding of its reality than analysing it in terms of a two-sided relationship: Russian Orthodoxy and American Methodism. Russian Methodists have convergences and divergences with both Russian Orthodoxy and American Methodism. Whereas Russian Methodists share with the Russian Orthodox Church the same cultural heritage, but differ in significant elements of ecclesial life, Russian Methodists share with American Methodists an ecclesial context and life, but differ in the cultural dimension of life.

Of course, the reality of the Russian Methodist identity is more complex: there is a continuing important influence of European, especially Scandinavian, Methodism on Russian Methodism—they represent an older and more defined Methodist tradition on the central conference level of the United Methodist ecclesial governance. The Russia United Methodist Church, as well as the United Methodist Church in other former Soviet Republics, belongs to the Northern European Central Conference, which determines key polity matters for the United Methodist Church in Scandinavian countries and the former Soviet Republics, including election of the bishop for the Russia United Methodist Church. The growing interaction of Russian Methodism with Russian Protestant Churches also results in a growing influence of Russian Protestantism on the development of Russian Methodism. Additionally, there are Russian, American, and European secular influences on Russian Methodism. Nonetheless, this chapter will focus on the interaction between Russian Orthodoxy, American Methodism, and Russian Methodism as the dominant ecclesial interactions shaping the Russian Methodist identity today and throughout its early history.

EARLY HISTORY

In 1889 Methodists came to Russia as a mission of the Swedish Annual Conference of the Methodist Episcopal Church, receiving at the 1892 General Conference the status of the Finland and St Petersburg Mission Conference (Dunstan 1995: 54–69). For the first fifteen years, Methodists kept a low profile and did not have noticeable interaction with the Russian Orthodox Church (ibid. 57). Methodist ministry was primarily aimed at Swedish- and Finnish-born Russians. One reason for such a focus was that religious work with these ethnic minorities was tolerated in Russia even before 1905, while mission towards ethnic Russians was against the law.

The 1905 Edict of Religious Toleration made it possible, at least till 1910 (Simon 1973: 234–5; Dunstan 1995: 67), for each citizen of the Russian Empire to choose his or her religious adherence in accordance with personal convictions. This resulted in an increased growth of Methodism in Russia, particularly from 1907. In 1907 a Finnish-trained, Russian-born pastor, Hjalmar Salmi, obtained government permission to hold public meetings in St Petersburg province and, within a year, his ministry resulted in more than 150 conversions to Methodism in six Finnish–Russian villages (Dunstan 1995: 58). With the appointment of an American Methodist pastor George Simons as superintendent of the Finnish and St Petersburg Mission the same year, the first Russian Methodist quarterly magazine, *Methodism in Russia*, started to be published in 1908, though in English. The first Russian-language Methodist monthly *Khristianski Pobornik* (*Christian Advocate*) followed shortly, in 1909. This new active stage of development of early Methodism in Russia led to some confusion in the later Russian literature in placing the emergence of Russian Methodism at 1907 rather than 1889, when the first congregation was organized in St Petersburg (ibid. n. 61). The stronger and more visible to the public Russian Methodists became, the greater the attention the Methodist Church paid to the Russian Orthodox Church.

However, the first quarter of the twentieth century was a challenging time in the ecclesial life of the Russian Orthodox Church. By 1905 several different views on how to embody the life of the church in the twentieth century had formed. A group of liberal professors and priests were urging 'renovation' of the Russian Orthodox Church that would include such measures as lifting celibate restrictions of epis-copacy, discontinuing veneration of relics, and accepting the Gregorian calendar. A group of conservative monastic clergy were opposed to the ideas of the Renovators. After the February Revolution of 1917, this conservative group called for an All-Russian Ecclesial Council or *sobor*, where the institution of Patriarchate in the Russian Orthodox Church was re-established for the first time after its removal by Peter the Great at the beginning of the eighteenth century.

After the 1917 Bolshevik Revolution, the Bolshevik government entered into the internal church struggle between the Patriarchal Party and the 'Living Church' (as the Renovators called themselves later) within the Russian Orthodox Church. Whereas the newly elected Patriarch Tikhon and his supporters were opposed to the Bolsheviks and in favour of autocracy, the Living Church movement chose to support the Bolshevik government in the misguided hope that the Bolsheviks would support the progressive movement in the church. The Bolshevik govern-ment, unable to break the Patriarchal Party even through the imprisonment of Tikhon and severe persecution during the 1921 famine, reached a compromise with Tikhon. The Living Church movement leaders that compromised themselves by defrocking Patriarch Tikhon and seizing power during his imprisonment eventu-ally lost their ground. By 1924 new Living Church leaders joined the Patriarchal Party and formed the conciliatory Holy Synod of the Russian Orthodox Church.

The awkwardness of the early history of relations of Methodists in Russia with the Russian Orthodox Church is rooted in the fact that they cooperated primarily with the Renovators and the Living Church movement within the Russian Ortho-dox Church. During his visit to Russia in 1922 one of the European Methodist bishops, John Nuelsen, met with Archbishop Antonine of Moscow of the Living Church and discovered mutual interest in each other's churches. Bishop Nuelsen was interested in encouraging the development of the Russian church on a social-democratic basis, whereas Archbishop Antonine thought it helpful to learn from the experience of the Methodist establishment of a free church in the United States (Malone 1995: 45). Archbishop Antonine had previously received a copy of the *Discipline of the Methodist Episcopal Church*, and the American Social Creed of the Church was circulating in the Russian Orthodox Church.

On the invitation of the Living Church, Bishop Edgar Blake attended the All-Russia Church Council in 1923, where in his speech he emphasized church unity and pledged the support of the Methodist Episcopal Church to the Russian Orthodox Church. Within two years American Methodists collected thousands of dollars to send to Russia for reopening the Moscow and St Petersburg Theo-logical Academies, which had been closed after the Revolution. For those who could not attend these schools, Bishop Blake developed correspondence courses patterned after the Methodist course of study in the United States. Despite the early work of Methodists in Russia together with the controversial movement within the Russia Orthodox Church, Methodist help was recognized and appreciated even by the Holy Synod of the Russian Orthodox Church. At the death of Patriarch Tikhon in 1925, the head of the Holy Synod, in a letter to Bishop Nuelsen, affirmed his appreciation for the help of the American Methodists and other Christian friends, stating that it will 'go down in the history of the Orthodox Church as one of its brightest pages in that dark and trying time of the church' (Kimbrough 1995: 51).

Thus, in the early history of Methodism in Russia, the contacts of the Methodists with the Russian Orthodox Church, such as meetings of bishops on both sides, supply of Methodist literature, the experience in establishing a free church, and financial support, all engaged American Methodists, making Russian Methodists virtually invisible to the Russian Orthodox Church. This pattern was reinforced even further by Methodists in Russia themselves after 1914.

In this respect, the description of *Khristianski pobornik* throughout its publication in St Petersburg, 1909–1917, is quite revealing. From 1909 to 1913, it was described on the title page as *Russkii Organ Metodistskoi Episkopal'noi Tserkvi* (*Russian Publication of the Methodist Episcopal Church*). Apparent in this description is the desire to communicate the Russianness of the Methodist ministry in Russia. This pattern reached its summit when in 1913 *Khristianski pobornik* on its title page was described as *Ezhemesiachnii Vestnik Evangel'skikh Obshchin Metodistov* (*Monthly Herald of the Evangelical Congregations of Methodists*), dropping the American-styled *Episcopal Church* in favour of the then current Russian Protestant conceptual phrasing *Evangelical Congregations*. The First World War raised strong anti-German attitudes in Russia. Not surprisingly, *Khristianski pobornik* did its best to drop any allusions to the Protestant character of Methodism, which in Russia was linked first of all with Germany. Instead, both in its title-page description and content, *Khristianski pobornik* became the *Ezhemesiachnii Russko–angliiskii Religioznii Vestnik* (*Monthly Russian–English Religious Herald*). Simons, as publisher, conscientiously placed emphasis on the American side of Russian Methodism, minimizing its European components, sometimes even at the expense of its Russian side.

Accordingly, relationships among Russian Orthodox Christians, Russian Methodists, and American Methodists had a particular asymmetric pattern from the inception of Methodism in Russia in 1889 to the end of the 1920s. That is, American ecclesial officials on their visits to Russia developed relationships both with the Russian Orthodox leaders and with the Russian Methodists; both Russian Orthodox leaders and Russian Methodists responded and, in turn, developed their relationships with American Methodists. However, the interaction along the third side of the triangle, between the Russian Orthodox Church and Russian Methodists, seems to have been almost non-existent, although several Russian Orthodox institutions, including the Holy Synod and the Department of Foreign Relations, were subscribers to *Khristianskii pobornik*. Nonetheless, even its publisher and the superintendent of the Russian Mission, George Simons, was primarily considered as a representative of American Methodism in Russia, not of Russian Methodism, given his American birth and training.

In this light, the life and work of a Russian-born and American-trained Methodist pastor and scholar, Julius Hecker, is particularly interesting because it exemplifies the path that brought a Russian Methodist to prominence in the eyes of the Russian Orthodox Church on the level of American Methodists. Born in St Petersburg, Hecker attended the Methodist Church there. He received his Ph.D. in theology from Columbia University in 1916, serving as pastor of a Russian Methodist Episcopal Church in New York and publishing a Russian monthly *Prosveshchenie (Enlightenment)* while in the doctoral programme. Before coming to Russia after the Bolshevik Revolution, Hecker worked with Russian prisoners of war in Austria-Hungary on a commission from John Mott, general secretary of the Young Men's Christian Association.

With a specialization in Russian Sociology, Hecker started teaching at the faculty of the Moscow Theological Academy when it reopened at the end of 1923. Though Hecker was a Russian Methodist, the Russian Orthodox hierarchy respected him and included him in their typical letters of gratitude to the Methodist Episcopal Church leadership, such as in Metropolitan Eudokim's letter to the 1924 General Conference: 'Our Church will never forget the Samaritan service which Bishops Blake, Nuelsen, Doctors Hartman, Hecker and your whole church [have] unselfishly rendered to us' (Kimbrough 1995: 50). Yet, this exception underscores the rule, that there was no meaningful relationship between the Russian Orthodox Church and Russian Methodists in the early history of Methodism in Russia. In order for Hecker to have meaningful interaction with the Russian Orthodox Church, he had to earn an American graduate degree and achieve a prominent position on the American and international scene.

American Methodists were called out of Russia by the United States government in 1918 after the American intervention in Archangelsk. George Simons moved his headquarters to Riga and continued his Russian ministry until the end of the 1920s, at which time he returned to the US. In 1928 Russian Methodism counted 2,300 members and probationary members. With the inception of the Five-Year Plans, there began a systematic assault on religion in the Soviet Union. Julius Hecker died in one of the GULAG labour camps in the mid-1930s together with many Russian Orthodox believers and other Russian Christians.

CURRENT HISTORY

Though Methodism did not endure throughout the Soviet period in Russia proper, it survived in Estonia and Western Ukraine in a number of local congregations

(Elliott 1995: 151–67). When a Russian young man, Vladislav Spektorov, during his compulsory military service placement in Tallinn, Estonia in the late 1980s, was converted in a Russian-speaking Methodist Church, the historical circle of the Methodist journey in Russia was complete: the post-Revolution path that led Methodism from Russia to Estonia now brought it back from Estonia to Russia. Samara, Russia, to which Spektorov returned after his conversion with the desire to spread the gospel among Russian people, became one of the three centres of modern Russian Methodism in the 1990s.

Another centre of modern Russian Methodism emerged in Moscow also in the 1990s, where South Korean and American Korean diplomats and businessmen who lived and worked in Moscow, having started regular Bible study lessons for themselves, opened the meetings to Russian Koreans. Eventually they registered as the Russian–Korean–American Methodist Fellowship, led by Pastor Young Cheul Cho. This Methodist congregation gave birth to three other Methodist local churches in the early 1990s that were founded by the Russian Koreans but consisted predominantly of Russians.

The third centre of Russian Methodism emerged in Yekaterinburg as a result of the exchange of student visits at Ural State University. On several occasions in the early 1990s, American Methodist pastor Dwight Ramsey gave lectures on religion at Ural State University, after which a group of students and professors at the university decided to form a Methodist congregation in order to experience the way of life that Ramsey described. Ramsey's interpreter, Lydia Istomina, became the leader of the new First United Methodist Church of Yekaterinburg, which soon numbered around five hundred worshippers.

Thus, the re-emergence of Methodism in Russia in the early 1990s was not the result of planned mission activity of the United Methodist Church, but rather the result of natural social and cultural developments, such as travel within Soviet borders, international diplomatic and trade contacts, and international academic exchange made possible by the openness of Russian society in that historical period. There was no plan by American Methodists for systematic planting of Methodist churches in Russia.

When the leaders of the General Board of Global Ministries and the Council of Bishops of the United Methodist Church visited Russia in the early 1990s, they made plans to work with the Russian Peace Foundation and the Russian Orthodox Church to provide social and humanitarian support to the Russians, who were suffering from unfortunate economic conditions after the collapse of the Soviet Union. At the same time, American Methodists discovered on the institutional level that there existed local Methodist churches in Russia. By 1992 there existed eleven local Methodist Churches in Russia, and the general conference of the United Methodist Church, recognizing that these churches needed supervision, assigned Bishop Ruediger Minor, a former Methodist bishop from Eastern Germany and a former director of the Methodist Theological Seminary in Eastern Germany, to oversee the ecclesial life of the existing local Methodist churches in Russia.

Thus, by 1992, American Methodists restored the historical relationship pattern that existed in Russia in the beginning of the twentieth century: American Methodists had relationships both with the Russian Orthodox Church and with Russian Methodists. The key difference in that pattern was that in the beginning of the twentieth century the Russian Methodist Mission was directed by a superintendent-in-residence, with the Methodist bishop placed in Europe visiting several times a year, whereas at the end of the twentieth century, the Russian United Methodist Mission had a Methodist bishop-in-residence placed in Russia. Consequently, by the beginning of the twenty-first century, Russian Methodists were gaining stronger representation in the global United Methodist Church, and hence, taking an active role in making global United Methodist Church decisions, rather than being merely passive receivers of decisions made by others. This process will reach its visible summit with the election of the first Russian United Methodist bishop, which may happen as soon as 2013.

This new development affected the balance of the relationships in the Russian Orthodox, American Methodist, and Russian Methodist triangle in its different dimensions. Presently the top-rank American Methodists from the United States and other countries (with the exception of some representatives of the General Committee on Christian Unity and Interreligious Concerns of the United Methodist Church) visiting Russia primarily visit the United Methodist Episcopal headquarters in Moscow, thus forming their plans in partnership with Russian Christians, including financial support on the basis of the Russian United Methodist analysis of the situation in Russia. Russian United Methodists view American and other non-Russian United Methodists as a natural part of the global United Methodist Church, building full-fledged partnerships with the United Methodists from other countries in every aspect of their ecclesial existence, including common ministry, education, finances, polity, and governance on every level of the United Methodist ecclesial organization.

Without distinguishing between American Methodism and Russian Methodism, Russian Orthodox leaders have a difficult time coming to terms with the Methodist phenomenon in Russia. Accusations of proselytism that are raised against Methodists in Russia are primarily politically based and do not describe correctly the complex social and cultural processes that led to the re-emergence of Methodism in Russia in the 1990s. Further, accusations of proselytism in the case of Russian Methodism reduce real life to conceptual, politically based, defensive stereotypes, leading to impoverishment of the understanding of human life in Russia at the end of the twentieth and the beginning of the twenty-first century by attempting to place a protective conceptual shell of the stereotype of proselytism over the complex aspects of the human search for meaning in life and a religious component in it.

Still one aspect of the Methodist–Orthodox relations has not been properly developed or explored: the relationship between the Russian Orthodox Church and Russian Methodists. Among the many political and historical reasons mentioned above explaining the absence of relationships between the Russian Orthodox Church and Russian Methodists, the question of the maturity of Russian Methodism should be raised. Indeed, in order for an institution to make an impact on its surrounding environment or offer something that other institutions could be interested in, the first institution or some of its individuals must achieve a certain maturity of general self-reflection, and in particular within the surrounding environment and in relation to those institutions.

At the beginning of the twentieth century such Methodist self-reflection regarding Methodism in Russia and in relation to its surrounding environment and the Russian Orthodox Church was done primarily by American Methodists. Russian Methodist pastor and scholar Julius Hecker represented perhaps one of the very few exceptions. In the beginning of the twenty-first century this process of Methodist self-reflection, although still remaining heavily represented by American and European Methodists, is gaining a stronger Russian Methodist voice, one aspect of which inevitably consists of attempts to grasp obvious and subtle, present and future influences that the Russian Orthodox Church, simply by its dominant presence in Russia, exercises on the Russian Methodism.

THE ORTHODOX CHALLENGE TO RUSSIAN METHODISM

After spending some time reflecting on possible sites of Orthodox influences on Russian Methodism, one starts to recognize that there are some significant matters with which Russian Methodism has to come to terms in the light of the Christian way of life represented by the Russian Orthodox Church, if one can look past the defensive political and reductionist accusations of proselytism. In reflecting on past, present, and future possible influences, Russian Methodists could learn much from the history of the Russian Orthodox Church abroad between the two world wars (1918–40).

The period between the two world wars is one of the most fertile periods for studying Orthodox ecumenism in general, and Russian Orthodox ecumenism in particular. It is the formative period of modern Orthodox ecumenism in the context of the modern ecumenical movement. Crucial for understanding the developments that contributed to the unique ecumenical environment is to see that, after 1918, the Soviet government exiled hundreds of representatives of the Russian religious, academic, and cultural elite to Europe. For this group of Russian exiles with tremendous creative potential, their Russian Orthodoxy became one of the primary elements that ensured their physical and cultural survival in Europe. However, they believed that the Russian Orthodox theology and world-view must become seriously engaged with the Roman Catholic, Anglican, and Protestant theologies and world-views in order to be able to claim their own space in the European context. Due to its political and social position in the Russian Empire, the Russian Orthodox Church had generally not found it important to pursue serious ecumenical conversations with other Christian churches. The uniqueness of the conditions existing after 1918 lay in the new need to find an Orthodox position outside traditionally Orthodox lands. Russian Orthodox believers also found themselves in frequent contact with non-Orthodox Christians, which provided them with multifaceted first-hand impressions rather than academic stereotypes. Between the wars some influential Russian Orthodox believers outside Russia had serious intentions of being engaged in ecumenical conversations with non-Orthodox Christians because their survival was dependent on such interaction.

Western Christians recognized the urgent need that the Russian Orthodox believers faced in exile and many did contribute significantly to ensuring their survival. The prominent Methodist leader John Mott provided the primary money grant of $5,000 to help Russian Orthodox Christians in exile to acquire a property in Paris, France, for establishing an Orthodox Theological Institute for training Orthodox priests to serve Russians across Europe and for providing an environment for the Russian Orthodox theologians to pursue theological research (Lowrie 1954). St Sergius Orthodox Theological Institute in Paris became the leading Orthodox educational institution in the period between the wars and served as a home base for such important Orthodox thinkers as Sergii Bulgakov, Georges Florovsky, Nicolas Afanasiev, George Fedotov, Anton Kartashov, and others. The questions that these Russian Orthodox thinkers directed especially to Protestant churches in their quest to find a proper place for the Russian Orthodox tradition within the Western context can provide an invaluable source for Russian Methodists who would like to reflect on serious and open conversation with the Russian Orthodox tradition beyond mere political accusations (Nikolaev 2007).

Sergii Bulgakov's and George Florovsky's inter-war engagement with Protestant thought can be distilled into four fundamental questions. In looking at the Russian United Methodist–Russian Orthodox milieu, Russian Methodists are faced with four analogous questions: What is the nature of the church? In what way do United Methodists belong to the one church that Christ established on earth? What aspect of the understanding of the nature of God should influence Russian United Methodist–Russian Orthodox relations, and in what way? How should the nature of the Russian United Methodist–Russian Orthodox relations be understood? Mutually accepted understanding on these four questions could serve as a good foundation for establishing a relationship along the third side of the triangle: Russian Methodism–Russian Orthodoxy.

For both Bulgakov and Florovsky, the church is something that cannot be described as a concept because the reality of the its existence is beyond the grasp of the human mind. However, the church really exists and ecclesial life is the most tangible experience that any true member of the church has. It is the experience of meeting Christ and living with him. Bulgakov held that 'the Church is not an institution; it is *a new life with Christ and in Christ*, moved by the Holy Spirit' (Bulgakov 2003: 3). However, this spiritual experience and life is not given to a person individually, but *soborno* (in the sense of catholicity), as an ecclesial experience of a person within the church, where the church does not hinder the human in relation with God, but is the only way ordained by God for the human being to reach him (Bulgakov 1925: 66). The person becomes a part of the living, unchangeable, and uninterrupted ecclesial experience, a part of the Holy Tradition that Florovsky (1927: 128) described as 'a living sameness in communion overcoming time'.

It is most likely that Russian Methodists could accept Bulgakov's description of the church as their own. In a recent essay, leading Methodist historian Richard Heitzenrater (2007: 119–28) suggested that it could be argued that John Wesley understood the Church as a means of grace. Heitzenrater's description of the most basic element of John Wesley's ecclesiology, God's grace, is similar to Bulgakov's ecclesiological description. Heitzenrater describes Wesley's understanding of grace as 'God's relationship with us, grounded in his divine attributes, reflected in his attitude towards us, and manifest as his presence and power in our lives' (ibid. 125) or, in John Wesley's words, 'that power of God the Holy Ghost which "worketh in us both to will and to do of his good pleasure"' (ibid.).

However, there is more to Bulgakov's description that makes it particularly an Orthodox understanding of the Church. Bulgakov, as well as Florovsky, held that the Orthodox Church is the true Church of Christ on earth in its historical dimension (Bulgakov 2003: 3). Both Bulgakov and Florovsky maintained that the church has a spiritual, invisible, and divine nature and a material, visible, and human nature. These two natures are united in the reality of the church in the same way that they are united in the person of Christ: without mixing the two and without damaging either. Consequently, Bulgakov and Florovsky held that given the human–divine nature of the church, in history it can exist only as the church of tradition because it can be only something given or not given by God to people, preserved from that point on, and cannot just emerge at a point in time as a human organization, lacking direct access to the divine.

Christ gave this authority to his apostles, who passed it on, together with the entire tradition, to their followers, ensuring that the church of later times is self-identical to the church of the apostolic time. Tradition, being creatively preserved, developed, and fulfilled in the life of the church, gained sacred authority that will be kept to the end of the world. The central element of the tradition is the presence of the church hierarchy that is given authority from above to bring about the grace of the Holy Spirit as intermediaries between God and human beings. Further, according to Bulgakov and Florovsky, the Orthodox Church represents the fullness of the life of the church (Bulgakov 1925: 67).

It is particularly important to underscore the following aspects of the Russian Orthodox understanding of the church: the church is a divine–human organism. Tradition is indispensable for the existence of the church. The church of a later time is self-identical to the church of the apostolic time. The priesthood plays a principal role in the church. The Orthodox Church represents the fullness of everything that Christ left to his apostles. Some of these basic ecclesiological statements that Orthodox theologians hold to characterize the Orthodox Church as more the Church of Christ on earth than other churches are difficult for the Russian Methodists to accept. The Orthodox understanding of the church as a divine–human organism could provide common theological ground with the Methodist theology in the light of Heitzenrater's argument for the Methodist understanding of the church as a means of grace.

The two Orthodox statements on the indispensability of tradition and on the self-identity of the later church with the apostolic church pose difficulty to the Methodist mind in the light of its Reformation heritage. Yet, there might be ways in which Russian Methodists could entertain the idea of seeking understanding with the Orthodox Church on these issues within its own established identity. The question regarding the priesthood's role in maintaining tradition and being appointed by God as intermediaries of grace for regular people poses a much deeper challenge for the Russian Methodists and has to be addressed within the more general question of the nature of ordination in the Methodist Church.

The last question represents the most difficult challenge that the Russian Orthodox Church poses to the Russian Methodist Church. Whereas the Russian Methodist Church typically holds some variation of the 'branch theory' ecclesiology, advocating that Christianity is represented by three branches: Orthodox, Roman Catholic, and Protestant, Russian Orthodox theologians of all kinds staunchly reject the branch theory and insist that the Orthodox Church represents the Church of Christ on earth, the entire fullness of the church that Christ established. In claiming the fullness of the church, both Bulgakov and Florovsky argued that the Orthodox Church possesses the full truth that Christ brought on earth, including the fullness of doctrinal teachings, dogmas, and the entire ecclesial tradition, especially in the Word of God, sacraments, and total fullness of worshipping God (ibid. 69).

These questions are important because they lay the ground for understanding in what way the United Methodist Church belongs to the church that Christ established on earth from the Orthodox point of view. Both Bulgakov and Florovsky based their understanding on how non-Orthodox churches belong to the one church on the rationale provided by an influential Russian Orthodox lay theologian Alexei Khomiakov, who argued that the church 'acts and knows only within her own limits . . . the rest of mankind, whether alien from the Church, or united to her by ties which God has not willed to reveal to her, she leaves to the judgment of the great day' (Khomiakov 1953). Thus, both Bulgakov and Florovsky would agree that the United Methodist Church does not belong to the Church of Christ on earth as does the Orthodox Church.

Both Bulgakov and Florovsky classified non-Orthodox churches in terms of the degrees of their falling away from the fullness of the ecclesial existence that is presumably embodied by the Orthodox Church. On the other hand, they would not have claimed that Methodists have no connection to the church, because both of them held that baptism in the name of the Father, the Son, and the Holy Spirit is the outer limit within which everyone in some way belongs to church. Thus, following Bulgakov's and Florovsky's reasoning, Russian Methodists end up in that area of the ecclesial existence exemplified by two concentric circles, where the inner circle represents the canonical limits of the Orthodox Church and the outer circle includes all the baptized.

Both Bulgakov and Florovsky would agree in their Orthodox perception that the Methodist Church had fallen away from the fullness of the ecclesial existence in three stages. In terms of ecclesial forms these would be the three 'cessations' from the church: first, in 1054 as a result of the split of the Roman Catholic Church from the Eastern Orthodox Church; second, in the sixteenth century in the split of the Church of England from the Roman Catholic Church; and third, at the end of the eighteenth century, when the Methodist movement within the Church of England became a separate Methodist Church.

In terms of the content of ecclesial life, following Bulgakov's understanding of Protestant Christianity, Russian United Methodism would be classified as non-ecclesial Christianity that lost a significant part of Christian tradition and expresses its character in some dogmatic misconceptions (Bulgakov 2003: 129–30). Bulgakov held that Protestants' opposition of the invisible reality of the church to its visible reality damages the understanding of its totality and leads to confusion in the search for the proper foundations of the church. Orthodox theologians reject the Reformation practice of opposing Holy Scripture and Holy Tradition in order to discern what has primacy, and instead argue that this practice is a concern rooted in a sensibility foreign to the church. The Orthodox Church thinks that the Protestant search for primacy fails to comprehend that both Scripture and tradition belong to one and the same life of the church (ibid. 23–8).

Another deficiency of ecclesial life in Protestantism according to Orthodox theologians comes from rejecting the priesthood in the Reformation. Bulgakov believed that some congregations and entire nations depleted their ecclesial life and, in a certain sense, rejected the apostles and Christ from their midst, and to this day remain without sacraments and the grace of God communicated in them (ibid. 90–1). Bulgakov believed that not unrelated to this problem with Protestantism was the truncated number of sacraments in Protestantism, which do not function effectively in providing an objective divine foundation for a grace-filled life, allowing human subjectivism to rule with all its mistakes (ibid. 211). A particular characteristic of Bulgakov's criticism of Protestant churches is aimed at Protestantism's 'mysterious and incomprehensible insensibility toward the Mother of God' (ibid. 220). He believed that unwillingness to venerate the mother of God in life and dogma was the principal characteristic that removed Protestantism the furthest from ecclesial Christianity in both its Orthodox and Roman Catholic forms. This unwillingness was possible only at the expense of grasping the fullness and power of the incarnation of God.

Despite all the deficiencies of Protestantism, Bulgakov valued the fact that it has some dogma in common with what Bulgakov called ecclesial Christianity, such as the Christological dogma of the ecumenical councils in the full power of its realism, as well as the Trinitarian dogma (ibid. 193, 195). Among unique Protestant positive characteristics, Bulgakov underscored the important role of laity in the church, emphasizing the anointing of all people, expressed, for example, in wide participation of the laity in worship (ibid. 254). However, Bulgakov underscored that this participation does not justify rejection of hierarchy. Preaching becomes the centre of Protestant ministry and worship (ibid. 96, 253). However, Bulgakov believed that the art of preaching in a sense was developed to balance the paucity of worship (ibid. 254). In a unique way, Protestantism embodies moral honesty in everyday life and intellectual research, though it has led to the emergence of peculiar 'autonomous ethics' disconnected from religiosity (ibid. 243, 288).

Bulgakov believed that the crucial characteristic that brings Protestantism potentially closer to ecclesial Christianity, particularly to Orthodoxy, is its spirit of freedom in combination with the spirit of ecclesial unity, allowing Protestantism to grasp the Orthodox concept of *sobornost*. In its anarchical form, Protestantism does not recognize the ecclesial tradition contained in ecclesial *sobornost*; the ecclesial teaching for Protestantism fully coincides with a scholar's personal opinion or with the composition and certain degree of agreement among several separate opinions. This second Protestant understanding of ecclesial teaching is in fact a process of moving towards elucidating the objective *sobornyi* truth (cf. Gershenzon 1912: 14). Bulgakov went so far as to see in Protestant conferences and councils that drafted confessional formulas an analogy to ecclesial organs with tentatively infallible authority that is eventually finalized *soborno* by the church. He even believed that Protestant conferences, providing forums of ecclesial *soborovanie*, represented Protestantism's de facto entrance onto that path, though this reality had not yet been understood in dogmatic terms (Bulgakov 2003: 159–60, 357). Thus, United Methodism's ecclesial practice of discerning the mind of the church by means of conferences on many levels could provide a fertile area of convergence with the Russian Orthodox understanding of elucidating the *sobornyi* mind of the church.

Returning to Methodism's place between the canonical limits of the Orthodox Church and the circle of the baptized according to both Bulgakov's and Florovsky's understanding of the Protestant churches, there can be recognized differences within the Russian Orthodox views on how further relationships with the Protestants could be viewed.

Bulgakov's main premise was that the Orthodox Church is wider than its canonical limits. He believed that the time in which he lived was a new period in the history of the Orthodox Church, which was characterized by its recognition of the reality of sacraments beyond its canonical limits and realization that there is one undivided eucharist given to the church. This recognition was a part of the general Christian drawing to unity that Bulgakov believed could be understood from within the church only as an expression of an already existing unity. In the twentieth century even the Orthodox hierarchy was participating in prayer fellowship with non-Orthodox Christians, which had previously been prohibited by Orthodox canons. Though still holding that non-Orthodox Christianity had lost or distorted the fullness of life in the church to different degrees, Bulgakov believed that the Orthodox Church was called to open its arms to non-Orthodox churches within the framework of the universal church.

Florovsky's main premise is based on recognition that Christians in schisms and heresies (meaning non-Orthodox Christians) receive salvation, which for him meant that the church continues to act in schisms, not that schismatics are still in the church. The line between the church and schisms is not only canonical but also spiritual. Florovsky argued that in this age the church does not have enough information to discern the manner of God's work outside its canonical limits, or to decide whether it is called to work actively in that area. Rather, in this age the church leaves the question of Christianity beyond itself alone, letting it be addressed by God in the second coming of Christ.

Finally, their interpretations caused them to see the existing Christian unity in different lights. Bulgakov's interpretation allowed him to conceive of the existing Christian unity as an already existing unity between East and West that simply had to be realized. For him, the existing unity was an *already achieved* first stage on the further path to the general reunion of the church. Florovsky's interpretation made him conceive of the existing Christian unity as the *not yet fully disappeared* remnant of the unity that had existed in the past. It is not an indicator and a foundation of coming future reunion; it was a dead end that would not lead anywhere. It is insignificant for the work of reunion, which, for Florovsky, consisted of making non-Orthodox Christians recognize that they exist in schisms and heresies and need to repent and come to the fullness of Christian life, which is in the Orthodox Church.

Theologically, the difference in Bulgakov's and Florovsky's ecumenical positions becomes clear in the light of the question of whether or not the Orthodox Church, participating in the ecumenical movement, should take a step towards broken non-Orthodox traditions in order to help their healing. Bulgakov argued that out of ecclesial love and in response to the acts of the Holy Spirit in the ecumenical movement, it should do so. Florovsky, on the contrary, argued that it should not do so. According to him, the role of the Orthodox Church in the ecumenical movement should be to make clear to non-Orthodox Christians the fullness of Orthodoxy and the depravity of non-Orthodoxy, and, in that, the disloyalty of non-Orthodox Christians to Christ. Clarity on this issue would thus decrease the non-Orthodox Christians' will to dissension and bring about their repentance and their return to the fullness of Christian life in the Orthodox Church. In terms of drawing on particular elements of God's character in their ecumenical positions, the pattern of Bulgakov's position followed the logic of the self-humiliating God who emptied himself in order to save broken humanity. Florovsky's ecumenical logic emphasized rather Christ's teaching office in communicating to humanity the truth of life in God.

Conclusion

Russian Methodists who would try to go beyond political accusations of proselytism in Russia and to become engaged in serious conversations with Russian Orthodox theologians will have to address a host of issues that could prove enlightening and inspiring for understanding and developing their own identity as Russian Methodists. Some of these issues are the concept of canonical territory, the nature of the eucharist, veneration of icons and saints, and the understanding of the theology of the Mother of God, as well as the place of the church in the political and social life of the country. Some of the Russian Orthodox positions would be less constructive and applicable to the Russian Methodist ecclesial existence in Russia, some would be more promising and encouraging, but all of them will be challenging and will require engagement on a sophisticated theological level.

Suggested Reading

Avgustin, Archimandrite (Nikitin) (2001). *Metodizm i pravoslavie* (Methodists and Orthodoxy). St Petersburg: Svetoch.

Florovsky, Georges (1933). 'The Limits of the Church'. *Church Quarterly Review* 117.

Kimbrough, S. T., jr. (2007). *Orthodox and Wesleyan Ecclesiology*. Crestwood, N.Y.: St Vladimir's Seminary.

Wainwright, Geoffrey (1995). *Methodists in Dialogue*. Nashville: Kingswood.

REFERENCES

BULGAKOV, SERGII (1925). 'Ocherki ucheniia o Tserkvi I' (Essays on the Teaching on the Church I). *Put'* 1.

—— (1988). *The Orthodox Church.* Crestwood, N.Y.: St Vladimir's Seminary.

—— (2003). *Pravoslavie* (Orthodoxy). Moscow: AST.

DUNSTAN, JOHN (1995). 'George A. Simons and the Khristianski Pobornik: A Neglected Source on Methodism in St. Petersburg'. In S. T. Kimbrough, Jr. (ed.), *Methodism in Russia and the Baltic States: History and Renewal.* Nashville: Abingdon.

ELLIOTT, MARK (1995). 'Methodism in the Soviet Union Since World War II'. In S. T. Kimbrough, Jr. (ed.), *Methodism in Russia and the Baltic States: History and Renewal.* Nashville: Abingdon.

FLOROVSKY, GEORGES (1927). 'Kniga Moliera o tserkvi' (Möhler's Book on the Church). *Put'* 7.

GERSHENZON, MIKHAIL (1912). *Obrazi proshlogo* (*Images of the Past*). Moscow: Okto.

HEITZENRATER, RICHARD P. (2007). 'Wesleyan Ecclesiology: Methodism as a Means of Grace'. In S. T. Kimbrough, Jr. (ed.), *Orthodox and Wesleyan Ecclesiology.* Crestwood, N. Y.: St. Vladimir's Seminary.

KHOMIAKOV, ALEXEI STEPANOVICH (1953). *The Church is One.* New York: Archdiocese, Eastern Orthodox Catholic Church in America.

Khristianskii pobornik (*Christian Advocate*). 1909–17.

KIMBROUGH, S. T., JR. (ed.) (1995). *Methodism in Russia and the Baltic States: History and Renewal.* Nashville: Abingdon.

LOWRIE, DONALD A. (1954). *Saint Sergius in Paris.* London: SPCK.

MALONE, DONALD KARL (1995). 'A Methodist Venture in Bolshevik Russia'. In S. T. Kimbrough, Jr. (ed.), *Methodism in Russia and the Baltic States: History and Renewal.* Nashville: Abingdon.

NIKOLAEV, SERGEI V. (2007). 'Church and Reunion in the Theologies of Sergii Bulgakov and Georges Florovsky, 1918–1940'. Ph.D. dissertation (Southern Methodist University).

PRODROMOU, ELIZABETH (2006). 'Mission, Religious Freedom, and Global Christianity'. A paper presented at the Fourth Orthodox–Wesleyan Consultation 'One, Holy, Catholic, and Apostolic Church: Ecclesiology and the Gathered Community' at St Vladimir's Orthodox Theological Seminary, 8–13 January 2006.

SIMION, MARIAN GH. (2003). 'The World Council of Churches and the Future of Ecumenism: A Conversation with Konrad Raiser, WCC Secretary General'. *Bulletin of the Boston Theological Institute* 3.1.

SIMON, GERHARD (1973). 'Church, State, and Society'. In George Katkov et al. (eds.), *Russia Enters the Twentieth Century.* London: Methuen

PART V

THEOLOGY

CHAPTER 28

....

SCRIPTURE AND REVELATION

....

SARAH HEANER LANCASTER

WHAT do we know about God, and how do we know it? For Methodists, this question is not simply academic, even though academic resources may be brought to bear in answering it. Our tradition has understood that knowledge of God has powerful experiential effects, so we have long felt that something is at stake in the way we understand God's communication to us. Our claims about Scripture, and even our arguments among ourselves about those claims, are rooted in this deep commitment that Scripture reveals the life-giving Word of God. The Methodist mission to spread 'Scriptural holiness' assumes a connection between the Bible and a way of living that demonstrates the saving work of God. Revelation, then, even when it has been taken to be propositional (consisting of assertions to be believed) has been considered, not simply a matter of intellectual belief, but a matter of life-changing and life-shaping importance. If there is anything distinctive about a Methodist understanding of Scripture and revelation, it will be found in this connection between knowledge and life.

EARLY METHODIST DIRECTIONS

John Wesley

John Wesley never needed to provide a developed theological account of the connection between Scripture and revelation. Living in the same century as Johann Salomo Semler and Hermann Samuel Reimarus (who were opening the door for 'higher criticism' in Germany), Wesley undertook his ministry at the cusp of the change in biblical studies that would determine much of the discussion about this topic in the nineteenth century. While he certainly engaged Enlightenment ideas in England, he could also assume a long and still widely accepted understanding of Scripture as God's revelation to humankind. Wesley understood that knowledge of the original biblical languages was important, and in that sense he had become acquainted with certain critical translation questions, but he had not come to ask critical questions about authorship and the setting that may have produced biblical texts. For him, the author of the Bible was ultimately God, even though God worked through human authors, and he could borrow language that suggested dictation and accommodation from a doctrine of Scripture that had been developed by Protestants in earlier centuries. Although Wesley can talk about God's giving the very words of Scripture (notably in the book of Revelation), he can also allow more human involvement in the writing than a mechanical dictation theory would suggest. The important point seems to be that God ensures the Bible is without mistake, and that clear passages could be used to interpret obscure ones—the typical Protestant affirmation (Jones 1995: 18–31). In this way, he depended on an already existing theological account of Scripture rather than offering a new understanding of it. He was comfortable with the idea that God inspired human authors to write Scripture, so he believed it was a reliable source for knowledge of God.

Wesley's own concerns were less about the origin and production of Scripture than about its interpretation. The long religious conflicts in England before his birth, as well as the lively religious debates that occurred in his own lifetime, certainly bore witness to diverse understandings of what Scripture meant. Scripture was its own interpreter because the 'whole scope and tenor' of Scripture should guide interpretation of any part of it (Wesley 1986: iii. 554). Still, it was also necessary to confirm that a particular interpretation did in fact conform to the whole tenor of Scripture, and to this end he could appeal to the early interpretation of the church, to Anglican doctrines, to reason, and to the lived experience of believers (Gunter et al. 1997). These tests never led Wesley to question the reality of revelation in Scripture. Nor did Wesley use these tests in any systematic way, although his twentieth-century descendants extrapolated a method from his intuitive practice. It mattered to Wesley to be as clear as possible about how Scripture should be interpreted, but he also could allow to some extent for differences in opinion regarding matters of theology and practice. He never doubted that the essential points revealed in Scripture could be known; but on less essential matters, interpretation was something of an inexact science.

While Wesley devoted his skills in logic to clarifying matters of doctrine, another kind of understanding required a different kind of clarity. It was not only important to comprehend what the Bible was saying; it was also important to 'know' its truth in a deeply existential way. While his word for the latter is 'faith' rather than 'revelation', both are important for talking about knowledge of God. Wesley (1985: ii. 138) joined with other theologians of the past to say that 'even the devils believe' in the sense that they understand the truth of who God is and what Jesus Christ has done. Only when belief includes faith as trust and confidence in God (which 'the devils' lack) does it fulfil the condition for our justification. The *knowing* that makes faith *saving* could not be gained either through revealed propositions or correct interpretation. It arises as response to grace—the power and presence of God that displays God's love for us unmistakably. Both revelation and faith depended on God's action to make something known.

Because he believed that knowledge of God was both informational and experiential, Wesley had to defend Methodism on two fronts. On the one hand, he argued against those who overvalued reason that God did in fact reveal information that cannot be known otherwise. On the other hand, he denied the private revelations of enthusiasts (ibid. 587–9). In both cases, Scripture played a key role. Wesley pointed out that reason by itself could never prove life after death or produce faith, hope, and love that were promised in Scripture. When enthusiasts appealed to visions and dreams for knowing the will of God, Wesley insisted that Scripture gave sufficient guidance when read with reason, experience, and the ordinary assistance of the Holy Spirit (Wesley 1984: i. 54, 59). Any privately communicated information not ruled by Scripture was imaginary and dangerous. God's revelation in Scripture provided knowledge not available in another way, but it did so in a way that was available to all and was not simply a private matter.

Scripture and revelation, then, were intimately connected. Scripture alone gave us reliable and complete access to the knowledge of God that was necessary for salvation. It provided what we could not know otherwise, and the knowledge it provided did not need to be supplemented by further revelations. As the Articles of Religion held, Scripture was sufficient for salvation, though reason and experience also had their roles to play. Revelation aims not only to inform, but also to transform our lives. It cannot inform except through our rational faculties, and it cannot transform except through our faithful reception of grace. We need to grasp revelation on both levels, and Scripture is both vehicle and guide for this comprehension.

The Nineteenth Century

As Methodism moved into the nineteenth century, it faced a rapidly changing intellectual landscape that brought a number of issues to the forefront of reflection that had not previously demanded attention. The new century brought with it the establishment of historical criticism in biblical studies, scientific advances in geology and biology that challenged straightforward readings of the chronology of creation in the Bible, and increased encounters with other cultures and religions through expanded missionary activity. In the face of these developments, it became harder simply to assume connection between revelation and Scripture; instead, it needed to be defended. If revelation provided information, but if that information conflicted with information known through other sources or was difficult to reconcile internally, then the reliability of the knowledge God provides was at stake. This problem was not simply a Methodist problem. All Christians faced these challenges, and theological work through the nineteenth century was quite pre-occupied with them.

The theologians who produced the resources for training Methodist clergy (and thus shaped the thinking of Methodist leaders) in the nineteenth century tended to follow the basic orientation to revelation that had been established in the wider Christian world for many years, for instance that revelation conveyed knowledge that came directly from God, and that it provided humans with knowledge human reason could not provide. Within this basic orientation, some of the concerns shifted as the century progressed. Early on, Richard Watson placed reason quite clearly in a subordinate position to revelation. He argued that special revelation was needed because human reason was weak. He used the example of 'heathen' religions to show that humans cannot develop adequate moral systems simply with our own capacities. Reason may ascertain evidence for revelation (miracle, proph-ecy, doctrinal coherence), and when it is properly enlightened by revelation, it may also play a role in interpretation. The proper response for humans is to accept the authority of the truth revealed in Scripture (Watson n.d.: i. 18, 102–3).

Watson does not include any significant discussion of inspiration, but this particular topic became more important later in the century as the publication of Charles Darwin's *On the Origin of Species by Means of Natural Selection* (1859) and further advances in historical criticism of the Bible raised questions that needed to be addressed. Since the Reformation, the reliability and clarity of revealed knowledge in the Bible had been maintained for Protestants by a specific understanding of inspiration that could support Scripture's absolute authority. This view understood inspiration as a special process for producing the written words of Scripture without error. While initially, the need for this doctrine of inspiration was to counter the authority of the Catholic Church, it also clearly placed the authority of the Bible over reason. As many direct statements in the Bible seemed to defy the emerging historical and scientific understanding of the world, the idea that Scripture was without error came under severe challenge. Methodist theologians distanced themselves from this idea in order to allow a place for the new developments of their time while retaining the conviction that Scripture does provide knowledge of God that cannot be known simply through human effort.

W. B. Pope in England and John Miley in the United States both found ways of talking about inspiration as an operation by which the Holy Spirit enabled human agents to express the mind of God without insisting that the very words of Scripture were dictated. Protestant claims about the inerrancy of Scripture required particular attention. Pope argued more closely than Miley did along the lines of the standard Protestant position, including language about 'plenary inspiration' and holding that the Bible could not contain anything untrue. He explained, though, that the Holy Spirit inspired by suggestion rather than by dictation, and that the Bible's infallibility lies in matters of religious truth, not in exact historical records or scientific matters (Pope 1881: i. 170–4). Miley addressed more directly than Pope did problems raised by science. Miley discusses what we can and cannot know through nature by means of our natural faculties, and he argues for theology as a 'science' in the sense that it is a rational study that has grounds for certitude. Inspiration is the way that the Holy Spirit operates on the mind of a human agent to ensure that what is written truthfully expresses God's mind. That expression, though, does not depend on exact wording that comes directly from God (Miley 1892: i. 23; 1894: ii. 480–5). We find in both theologians a defence of the special nature of the Bible as the faithful record of knowledge revealed by God to which humans would otherwise have no access; but while that defence insists that the Bible is 'true', it does not insist that its truth depends on being without error of any sort.

While Pope and Miley approached the challenges to Scripture by accepting the basic structure of the Protestant doctrine of Scripture but modifying its notion of inspiration, Borden Parker Bowne is credited with having made a greater break with tradition, thereby preparing the way for the expansion of liberal theology among Methodists in the United States during the twentieth century (Chiles 1965: 64–5, and Abraham 1984). For Bowne, who was tried and acquitted for heresy in 1904, revelation does not reveal doctrinal statements but rather 'the righteousness and grace of God' (Bowne 1898: 9). He has moved from a standard propositional understanding of revelation, but in doing so he has not abandoned the notion that revelation has intellectual content. Scripture reveals an idea of God—that God is our friend, supporter, and guide—so that we may recognize a moral purpose for human beings in the world (ibid. 37–8). This idea is superior to anything that can be known about God through nature, which is ambiguous, incomplete, and cannot tell us about God's character. It is also superior to any revelation that may occur in other religions. Christian revelation in Scripture, then, is special rather than general and unique among special revelations.

Bowne maintains the view that the Bible is inspired, but not through dictation. While not identical to the very words, revelation is 'in' the Bible, which records God's self-revelation 'in history and in the thought and feeling of holy men'. Inspiration consists of influence, something like the way that a teacher inspires a student to learn. Though holy, the men who recorded the self-revelation of God were imperfect, and God's revelation was adapted to them and recorded by them in the light of their own historical understandings. As human understanding of God and God's purposes grew, God progressively revealed more until the knowledge God wanted to share was objectively completed in Jesus Christ. Our subjective understanding of revelation (which embraces not only reason, but also the affections and will) continues even now to improve as the spiritual meaning of the Bible and doctrines unfolds in light of our changed understanding of the world (ibid. 10, 106). The truth of Scripture is finally known and tested in living, not in an abstract doctrine of inerrancy (ibid. 56–8).

Unlike Wesley, Methodist theologians of the nineteenth century did have to provide a developed account of the connection between Scripture and revelation; and as the century progressed, the foremost question was whether revelation could withstand the scrutiny of reason. Pope and Miley both stress knowledge of God as intellectual content and defend the way the Bible delivers that content through its written statements. Revelation is not guaranteed by the truth of every individual sentence in the Bible, but it is propositional in the sense that it is concerned about the truth of assertions about God and about human life before God. Existential knowledge of God was not completely absent (Pope could talk about 'assurance' that personal knowledge of God brings), but theoretical questions about the credibility of the content of the Bible were paramount. Whatever else humans may know (Miley could affirm the place of natural theology as well as some restricted special revelation to other religions), Scripture provides superior intellectual understanding of God that cannot be gained in any other way.

Bowne, too, recognizes the intellectual content of Christian revelation. His approach, though, is not to defend the truth of what the Bible says in its own terms, but to seek the spiritual meaning behind its statements. He does not try to defend what the Bible says by defending the way the Bible says it; rather he attempts to give, in the light of the knowledge of his time, a reasonable account of how God communicates in and through the Bible to make known to us truth that may direct our lives. Both conservative and liberal approaches, then, tried to show how the Bible could provide unique understanding of God that mattered for human life, even if their approaches were different.

REVELATION AS PROPOSITION OR EXPERIENCE?

The Early Twentieth Century

In 1965, Robert E. Chiles traced the development of Methodism from Wesley's death to the early twentieth century. He understood the trajectory of Methodism in the

United States to be moving away from its roots and towards a regrettable accommodation to culture. One of the transitions he identifies is from revelation to reason. Although Watson and Miley play a role in that transition, the chief exemplar of the capitulation to reason is for him Bowne's student, Albert C. Knudson. Because he formulated his thesis at mid-century, and because he subsumed experience under reason, Chiles was not yet in a position to recognize another equally important development in theology, namely, the increasing significance of experience as a category for talking about knowledge of God. Methodists were involved in this transition also, and Knudson is a key figure for understanding what was happening.

Already, Bowne had introduced language of feeling and affection to the understanding of revelation. In doing so, he was manifesting a tendency in the nineteenth century to embrace intuition and feeling as a counterpoint to the rationalism of the previous century. For Bowne this move was not simply a reaction against reason; it was a way to show that Christian faith was indeed reasonable given the questions of the time. Liberal theology, following in the path set out by Schleiermacher, began to talk about revelation, not as the delivery of propositional truth that found expression in doctrine, but as consciousness of God. If doctrinal assertions were questionable and biblical accounts of events were not always believable, the truth of Christian faith could yet be embraced as an intuitive grasp of the divine. 'Experience' (which encompasses many ways of undergoing human life, such as emotions, events, relationships) began to find a place alongside 'reason' in theological discussion.

For Methodists, experience had a natural place in theology, and Knudson developed it as a category for knowing God. He tends to use the language of religious experience and faith instead of 'revelation' because that word had for so long been associated with a body of knowledge stated propositionally and imposed authoritatively. Despite the different language, he is talking about a way of knowing that is unique and that matters for life. Like Bowne before him, Knudson criticizes theories about revelation and inspiration that had been worked out apart from lived experience, so he looks to what we know in other ways to shed light on how we know God. He explains that even in secular disciplines, experience, reason, and faith are neither independent of nor opposed to one another, so religious experience is as valid as secular forms of knowing (Knudson 1924: 179, 185; 1950: 43). He also argues that religious experience is self-justifying, in the sense that it does not depend on any external authority. He does not thereby intend to cut off and protect Christian faith from scrutiny (1924: 183–6). Because the experiencing subject is always interpreting that which is being experienced, there is always the possibility of some kind of mistake. The potential fallibility of interpretation does not deny the objective ground of experience, nor does it mean that interpretation is wrong through and through, but it does indicate that testing and reflection are necessary even for religious knowledge. Knudson is offering an apologetic for Christian knowing that both attends to its uniqueness and shows its place in relation to other areas of human life so that it does not simply overrule what we know in other ways.

Knudson's theoretical work explains how the faith of religious people in a modern age could be justified. But what about Scripture? Is it possible to talk about 'revelation' to its writers that would be distinct from the kind of experience that other people have? For the most part, Knudson was concerned to argue against a dictation theory of inspiration rather than provide an alternative account of how Scripture was produced, but he does say a few things that suggest the approach he might take. The notion of inspiration as inerrant dictation, he says, is based in a notion of a particular experience of passive reception. Experience, though, always involves some kind of creative activity. He describes the inspiration of the prophets as 'moral and spiritual passion'—not mechanical, but ethical. They received insight from God that helped them infer profound truth from what they knew of human nature, and they expressed their understanding in ways that would prompt others to respond (ibid. 91–2; 1914: 45). These expressions of insight are not timeless truths but developed over time, reaching their culmination in the New Testament (Knudson 1918). Religious experience, then, provides the basis for the knowledge that is recorded in the Bible, and in that sense knowledge is revealed; but religious experience is always bound together with other kinds of life experiences, so the knowing that comes with it is never pure access to the mind of God. Because even the prophets recorded interpreted experience rather than some pure, immediate experience, what the Bible says is always subject to reasoned reflection.

From Liberal to Liberation Theology

Knudson shows the extent to which Methodism could use experience as a category for explaining revelation, but his views were not universally accepted. Indeed, the move to embrace experience in theology proved controversial, not simply for Methodists, but also in the wider Christian world. If human reason could threaten to rival the authority of revelation, human experience could also. Critics of liberal theology claimed that revelation was so reduced to human experience that it was not at all clear that any knowledge was coming to us from the outside at all. One reaction to liberal theology in the early twentieth century was fundamentalism, a movement that can be traced in the United States back to 1910 but which gained force in the 1920s. It reasserted the propositional content of revelation by insisting that belief in certain doctrines was essential to Christian faith, and even though the movement was led primarily by people with other denominational affiliations, some Methodists also took part. For instance, Harold Paul Sloan wrote a book during this time calling many Course of Study books of the Methodist Episcopal Church 'anti-Christian', and he lists fundamental doctrines that are denied in them. He includes more than the famous five fundamentals, and he believes all these truths were delivered supernaturally in a Bible that cannot be in error about them (Sloan 1922).

In the academic world, Karl Barth presented the counterpoint to liberal theology that set the terms of the discussion about revelation for a few decades. Barth's neo-orthodoxy vigorously defended God's revelation as *sui generis*. The point that God's revelation should stand on its own and not be subsumed under any human intellectual or cultural endeavour had particular poignancy after what had happened in Germany in the first decades of the century. Not all theologians, though, agreed with Barth's way of trying to address the relationship between revelation and other forms of human knowledge. Lively intellectual debate about the extent to which theology should draw from philosophy and other disciplines dominated theologians' attention. The major voices in this debate (among them, Paul Tillich, Rudolf Bultmann, and Emil Brunner) were not Methodist, but Methodist theologians learned from them. As happened also in the case of funda-mentalism, Methodists did not speak out of a distinctive tradition, but rather added their voices to a conversation that was crossing denominational boundaries.

One major consequence of the debate that took place at this time is that theologians who sought an alternative to identifying revelation with the words of Scripture or with doctrine could reclaim the language of revelation that Knudson had avoided. Many theologians began to work with the idea of revelation as God's disclosure of God's own self. With this approach, revelation could be deeply involved with experience but still have an objective ground. It could be connected to Scripture but not restricted to Scripture. Disclosure of self rather than disclosure of propositions allowed theologians the opportunity to explore how that disclosure might take place. Although as a whole, they did not produce many writings that were exclusively devoted to the topic, Methodists—even those such as Schubert M. Ogden (1966; 1986: 22–44), who has been seen as representing the liberal bent toward reason—did consider the question of revelation in their work.

In 1983, Roman Catholic theologian (and later Cardinal) Avery Dulles published *Models of Revelation*, which helpfully captured the options that were available at the time. He suggested five models (revelation as doctrine, as history, as inner experi-ence, as dialectical presence, and as new awareness) for how Christians explain the way in which God reveals. It was not the burden of his book to talk about the way that experience was affecting the understanding of revelation, but one can see in his models how important that issue was becoming. The first model asserts the propositional form of revelation. The other four all utilize some kind of experience as the basis of revelation, namely, experiencing God's acts in history, experiencing God directly in one's inner self, experiencing an encounter with a mysterious and transcendent God, and experiencing consciousness-raising. Each of these four models reflects different concerns, but all offer alternatives to an understanding that primarily involved intellectual understanding of and assent to propositions.

At the time that Dulles wrote the book, he acknowledged that the different forms of liberation theology emerging at that time might eventually lead to a different model altogether. These theologies did indeed have an effect on thinking about revelation. First, some forms of liberation theology called attention to obstacles for believing what the Bible said that were quite different from the ones that science or historical criticism had found. For instance, Scripture's passages about slavery and its generally patriarchal world-view also required a way of thinking about revelation that was not simply propositional. Second, these theologies, along with the heightened influence of postmodernism in the last quarter of the twentieth century, served to intensify attention to experience and to reshape understanding of it. The idea of universal human experience, and thus the potential for a common understanding of revelation, began to yield to the notion of particular experiences as more and more voices pointed out how purported 'universal' experience did not fit certain communities or even individuals. Liberation theologies themselves had to begin to examine the way that they had 'universalized' experience even for people in their communities of concern. Social location, then, began to be important for thinking about the way in which the Bible is revelatory.

The twentieth century opened up many options for thinking about revelation, and Methodists have taken places all along the spectrum. Church members, pastors, and theologians have occupied positions from fundamentalism to feminism. Even as the attention to experience has opened up options that have been attractive to some Methodists, others have reasserted a propositional view (Abraham 2006). Different ideas about revelation lead also to different understandings of Scripture. Methodists who have wanted to defend the truth of the Bible's assertions as supernaturally revealed and inspired have sometimes embraced its inerrancy, at least on matters of doctrine and practice (Merritt 1986; Grider 1984). Other Methodists deny that the Bible must be considered inerrant and infallible in order for it to witness faithfully (Wenham and Davies 1959). Still others argue that 'revelation' includes discerning the will of God for our time, so it should be thought of as ongoing and cannot be restricted to what Scripture has said (Shier-Jones 2004: 82–94). This variety of positions within Methodism provides the background for looking at the most distinctive Methodist development in the twentieth century—the Quadrilateral.

The Quadrilateral

The merger between the Methodist Church and the Evangelical United Brethren Church in the United States brought with it the need to decide about the place of their summary confessional statements—the Articles of Religion for the Methodists and the Confession of Faith for the EUBs—in the newly formed United Methodist Church. A commission was charged to study the problem, and it was given the freedom to write a new confession. Instead, it concluded that no single doctrinal summary would serve the church well. It embraced a certain degree of pluralism in theology (within the heritage and guidelines stated in the *Book of*

Discipline) and offered a way of reflecting on historic theological treasures in order to appropriate them for a new time (Outler 1991: 20–5). Scripture, tradition, reason, and experience were identified as distinct elements in this process of reflection.

Anglican theology had long used Scripture, tradition, and reason in doing theology, and the distinctive Methodist addition was experience. In the version of the *Book of Discipline*'s statement used from 1972 to 1984, this fourth category primarily meant 'Christian experience', that is, faith's reception of the truth in Scripture that brings 'new life in Christ'. Scripture was the 'constitutive witness to God's self-revelation', serving as a 'deposit of a unique testimony to God's self-disclosures'. Experience, then, did not chiefly serve to support a theory of revelation, but rather played the role of appropriating and enlivening for Christians the revelation recorded in Scripture (*Book of Discipline 1972* 1973: §70). The last sentence of the section on experience, though, does broaden this category by saying, 'All religious experience affects human experience; all human experience affects our understanding of religious experience.'

In 1984, the General Conference of the UMC authorized another group to rewrite the statement, and the revision was passed at the 1988 General Conference. Every element in the Quadrilateral received new attention, but changes in two sections especially represent the tension between propositions and experience that existed in the church. Many wanted to reinforce the primacy of Scripture in the Quadrilateral, and the new version stressed the unique origin and role of Scripture by saying that the authors of the Bible were 'illumined' and 'inspired' so the Bible bears 'authentic' and 'authoritative' witness to God's revelation. The section on experience, though, reflected how theology was coming to understand the deep shaping influences of the different kinds of experience people undergo in daily life, as well as the importance of communities for theological reflection. In the revision, the sentence that concluded the section on experience in earlier *Disciplines* was moved nearer the beginning of the section. Christian experience retained the confirming and illumining role it had before, but it was joined much more thoroughly with broader human experiences. The new statement, then, at the same time affirmed the normative nature of the revelation that occurred in the past and recognized how deeply our interpretation of that revelation depends on what we know through daily life (*Book of Discipline 1988*: §69).

Although it began as a statement for a singular event in the history of one form of Methodism, the Quadrilateral has resonated with other Methodists. What Methodists outside the UMC find important is the idea that Scripture, tradition, experience, and reason all have a place in theological reflection, not the specific description of their relationship that United Methodists have spelled out. As a result, this identifying feature of Methodism is not employed in the same way in every branch of Methodism. In fact, the Quadrilateral has been the subject of much academic examination, as well as popular debate. Enquiry about what Wesley might have meant when he used those terms stands alongside enquiry about what it means to employ these categories in theological reflection, given what we know about each of them today. Although the most basic idea of the Quadrilateral is that each should work together in some mutual clarification, it is common to hear conversations about controversial issues in which one party will claim to rely on Scripture and another on experience (or reason) to support divergent positions. Methodists do not regularly find consensus on any particular issue by using the Quadrilateral, but perhaps the amount of attention given to it shows just how much it reflects the issues that Methodists think are important.

DIRECTIONS FOR FUTURE REFLECTION

Methodists have joined other Christians in tending to choose between propositional and experiential understandings of revelation, but Methodists also have commitments that ought to work against those polarized options. The connection that Methodists have seen between knowledge and life ought to call us to make use of recent insights about cognition that are emerging in various fields as we talk about the way that Scripture is revelatory. Concepts expressed in propositions have a complicated relationship with experience. To state a proposition, one needs words, and to have words, one needs to be able to use a language. The ability to use a language depends on being involved in a social community that shares ways of describing events, physical items, emotions, and more. The language shared by the community both expresses experience and shapes experience, and the less tied a concept is to a concrete thing, the more language shapes what we know (Niebuhr 1989: 35–8). Cognition is about much more than assertions of truth because those assertions are embedded in a vast network of values, practices, relationships, expectations, etc. that may not be articulated in propositions but are 'known'.

Because articulation of any Christian belief is expressed in human language, it cannot escape the complex interactions that constitute cognition; and any approach to revelation will have to come to terms with them. Revelation is an act of communication, so it involves both God's initiative and human reception. Taking into account the processes through which human beings come to understanding does not subtract from God's activity; it simply shows what is involved for humans to grasp what God is disclosing. Methodists of all people should see the relevance of human participation in the activity of God, so the more we understand about human cognition, the better we can appreciate and participate in God's action for our salvation. This approach also allows us to talk about our participation in a variety of ways, for instance, we can examine how Scripture shapes our knowing through its full range of resources and uses (for instance, poetry, story, and liturgical reading). Many things contribute to Christian understanding.

Acknowledging this complexity will lead to rethinking how to approach traditional categories and problems in revelation. For instance, theologians have long distinguished between general and special revelation. General revelation was usually thought of as knowledge that God made available to all humans, and it implied that all humans would understand it alike. In contrast, special revelation indicated both a special act of God and a special understanding that humans gained through this act. If we think about the ways that our daily life experiences affect our cognition, then both these categories will be affected. No matter how 'general' God's activity may be, humans' reception will never be identical. It would not take a special act of God to produce unique understanding, but even if God does act occasionally in a special way, the understanding humans gain from God's act will still be shaped by the conceptual options that are available to them in their communities. One question raised by this line of reflection is whether the distinction between general and special is meaningful or helpful any longer, or at least how the distinction might be made in such a way as to be helpful and meaningful in the light of what we know about the diverse ways that human minds comprehend their experiences.

The tendency to talk about the 'locus' of revelation as either in the past (the written words of the Bible, the events lying behind the words in the Bible) or in the present (the experience of the believer) would also be open to rethinking. Whatever God was doing in the past was recorded so that it could be preserved and passed on. The record bears witness to God's disclosure, but because God's activity is preserved and passed on through human language, it also bears the marks of the social communities in which humans told about what God has done. As Christians in later times come to know the story that the Bible tells, their understanding is shaped to some extent by this linguistic record. Most Christians hear and read the Bible in a language other than that in which it was written, so there is another layer of social shaping that goes on through translation. People cannot come to a Christian understanding of God without participating in the linguistic tradition of telling about God, but that understanding will never be simply what it was in previous generations and cultures. Furthermore, for this understanding to come to life for a person so that it is life-shaping and life-transforming, God has to act in some illuminating way in the present. 'Revelation', then, has to encompass both the understanding we have received from the past and the understanding we gain in the present.

Another area for rethinking is the way theologians have discussed the relationship between revelation and reason. This issue has always been bedevilled by the different meanings of the word 'reason' (a human faculty, rules of logic, a body of knowledge), but usually the contrast has been between knowledge that has been gained by an action of God and knowledge that has been gained by human effort alone. Behind this contrast lies a concern about truth, whether one intends to safeguard the truth of revelation by showing it to be superior to reason or whether one intends to question information in the Bible by showing it does not conform to what we know of the world. This way of approaching the question of truth pits one against the other so that one must be wrong if the other is right. The Protestant doctrine of inspiration has been haunted by the problem of 'error' that is rooted in this dichotomous view. Recognizing the complex process of gaining comprehension, though, might allow theologians to reframe these problems in a different way. 'Reason' is not as clearly distinct from other aspects of human life as it has been treated in the past, and 'revelation' is also bound together with features of human life that give us understanding. The changed character of these categories will affect the way that theologians negotiate the question of how Christian faith may be held with integrity in the light of all that we know.

From the beginning, Methodism has relied on understandings of Scripture and revelation that came from larger conversations within the Christian community. As a specific tradition, we have given more attention to thinking through the way that Scripture interacts with human activities (the way we hand down faith, the way we reflect on faith, the way we undergo our lives as Christians and as humans) than we have to a theory of revelation. The almost intuitive grasp Methodists have had about Christian reflection, though, puts us in a good position to respond to the new insights about human understanding that are coming to light. It is not the specific description of the Quadrilateral that puts us in this position (indeed, the lines among the four categories get blurred for several reasons), but rather why the Quadrilateral resonates for so many, namely, our attentiveness to how features of human life matter for our understanding. Methodists have the resources, not simply to borrow from what others have done, but to contribute to Christian reflection about how Scripture may be vehicle and guide for knowing God that is based in our deeply held convictions that intellectual and existential understanding must go together.

Suggested Reading

Abraham, William J. (2002). *Canon and Criterion in Christian Theology: From the Fathers to Feminism*. New edn. Oxford: Oxford University Press.

Lancaster, Sarah Heaner (2002). *Women and the Authority of Scripture: A Narrative Approach*. Harrisburg, Pa.: Trinity Press International.

Tomasello, Michael (1999). *The Cultural Origins of Human Cognition*. Cambridge, Mass.: Harvard University Press.

Wood, Charles M. (2000). *The Formation of Christian Understanding: Theological Hermeneutics*. Repr. Eugene, Ore.: Wipf & Stock.

Young, Frances (2002). *Virtuoso Theology: The Bible and Interpretation*. Repr. Eugene, Ore.: Wipf & Stock.

Zull, James E. (2002). *The Art of Changing the Brain: Enriching the Practice of Teaching by Exploring the Biology of Learning*. Sterling, Va.: Stylus.

References

Abraham, William J. (1984). 'Inspiration, Revelation and Divine Action: A Study in Modern Methodist Theology'. *Wesleyan Theological Journal* 19: 38–51.

—— (2006). *Crossing the Threshold of Divine Revelation*. Grand Rapids: Eerdmans.

The Book of Discipline of The United Methodist Church 1972 (1973). Ed. Emory Stevens Bucke. Nashville: The United Methodist Publishing House.

—— *1988* (1988). Ed. Ronald Patterson. Nashville: The United Methodist Publishing House.

Bowne, Borden Parker (1898). *The Christian Revelation*. 2nd edn. Cincinnati: Curtis & Jennings.

Chiles, Robert E. (1965). *Theological Transition in American Methodism: 1790–1935*. Nashville: Abingdon.

Dulles, Avery, SJ (1983). *Models of Revelation*. 1st edn. Garden City, N.Y.: Doubleday.

Grider, J. Kenneth (1984). 'Wesleyanism and the Inerrancy Issue'. *Wesley Theological Journal* 19: 2–61.

Gunter, Stephan W. et al. (1997). *Wesley and the Quadrilateral: Renewing the Conversation*. Nashville: Abingdon.

Jones, Scott (1995). *John Wesley's Conception and Use of Scripture*. Nashville: Kingswood.

Knudson, Albert C. (1914). *The Beacon Lights of Prophecy*. New York: The Methodist Book Concern.

—— (1918). *The Religious Teaching of the Old Testament*. New York: Abingdon.

—— (1924). *Present Tendencies in Religious Thought*. New York: Abingdon.

—— (1950). *Basic Issues in Christian Thought*. New York: Abingdon.

Merritt, John G. (1986). 'Fellowship in Ferment: A History of the Wesley Theological Society, 1965–1984'. *Wesley Theological Journal* 21: 185–203.

Miley, John (1892 and 1894). *Systematic Theology*. 2 vols. Library of Biblical and Theological Literature. New York: Eaton & Mains.

Niebuhr, H. Richard (1989). *Faith on Earth: An Inquiry into the Structure of Human Faith*. New Haven: Yale University Press.

Ogden, Schubert M. (1966). *The Reality of God and Other Essays*. New York: Harper & Row.

—— (1986). 'On Revelation'. In *On Theology*. San Francisco: Harper & Row.

Outler, Albert C. (1991). 'Introduction to the Report of the 1968–1972 Theological Study Commission'. In Thomas A. Langford (ed.), *Doctrine and Theology in The United Methodist Church*. Nashville: Kingswood.

Pope, William Burt (1881). *A Compendium of Christian Theology: Being Analytical Outlines of a Course of Theological Study, Biblical, Dogmatic, Historical*. 3 vols. 2nd edn. New York: Phillips & Hunt; Cincinnati: Cranston & Stowe.

SHIER-JONES, ANGELA (2004). 'Conferring as Theological Method'. In Clive Marsh, Brian Beck, Angela Shier-Jones, and Helen Wareing (eds.), *Methodist Theology Today: A Way Forward*. New York: Continuum.

SLOAN, HAROLD PAUL (1922). *Historic Christianity and the New Theology*. Louisville, Ky.: Pentecostal.

WATSON, RICHARD (n.d.). *Theological Institutes: Or, a View of the Evidences, Doctrines, Morals, and Institutions of Christianity*. 2 vols. 29th edn. New York: Nelson & Phillips.

WENHAM, JOHN, and DAVIES, RUPERT E. (1959). *A Debate: Is the Bible Infallible?* London: Epworth.

WESLEY, JOHN (1984–7). *The Bicentennial Edition of the Works of John Wesley: Sermons*, ed. Albert C. Outler. 4 vols. Nashville: Abingdon.

CHAPTER 29

....

TRINITY

....

ELMER M. COLYER

INTRODUCTION

....

THE Trinity in early Methodism was not simply a doctrine affirmed, but *the* vibrant Divine Source, Agency, and Telos of all Christian faith, life, and practice, crucial to the vitality of the Methodist movement. We see this in John Wesley's reflections on the Trinity and the way he relates the Trinity to other aspects of Christian faith, in Charles Wesley's hymns on the Trinity, and in the way the Trinity informs other dimensions of early Methodism. The subsequent history of the Trinity in Methodism is one of affirmation but neglect, though there is recent resurgent interest in the Trinity and its integral relation to everything else Christian.

What follows is not a purely historical survey of the Trinity within Methodism. Rather it is a historical and theological argument for a particular understanding of the Trinity in relation to all Christian faith, life, and practice, with constructive implications concerning how to read the history of Methodism and concerning the direction Methodism in all its multiple dimensions should evolve.

THE TRINITY IN EARLY METHODISM

Wesley on the Trinity

John Wesley affirmed the doctrine of Trinity as essential to Christianity. The reason why Wesley was so adamant about the centrality of the *doctrine* of the Trinity is because he saw the *Reality* of the Trinity as crucial to all vital faith and practice: The Trinity 'enters into the very heart of Christianity' (Wesley 1985: 384). 'The thing which I here particularly mean is this: the knowledge of the Three-One God is interwoven with all true Christian faith, with all vital religion' (ibid. 385).

In his sermon, 'On the Trinity', Wesley describes coming to faith in explicit Trinitarian terms: 'I know not how anyone can be a Christian believer...till God the Holy Ghost witnesses that God the Father has accepted him through the merits of God the Son' and having this witness he honours the Son and the blessed Spirit "even as he honours the Father".' Wesley concludes: 'Therefore I do not see how it is possible for any to have vital religion who denies that these three are one' (ibid. 385–6).

For Wesley, it is impossible to be a Christian without at least tacit affirmation of the Trinity, for Christian faith is intrinsically Trinitarian: both the gospel itself and our participation in the gospel are aboriginally and inherently Trinitarian. Both are rooted in the patterned activity of the economic Trinity. God the Father reconciles us through the Incarnate Son and his life, death, and resurrection and realizes that reconciliation in our lives through the person and activity of the Holy Spirit.

Since the Trinity 'enters into the very heart of Christianity', throughout his publications Wesley provides brief capsule summaries of Christian faith manifesting this same Trinitarian pattern:

As soon as he is born of God there is a total change in all these particulars. He sees 'the light of the glory of God', his glorious love, 'in the face of Jesus Christ'. . . . He feels 'the love of God shed abroad in his heart by the Holy Ghost'. . . . And now he may be properly said *to live*: God having quickened him by his Spirit, he is alive to God through Jesus Christ. He lives a life . . . that 'is hid with Christ in God'. God is continually breathing, as it were, upon his soul, and his soul is breathing unto God. Grace is descending into his heart, and prayer and praise ascending to heaven. And by this intercourse between God and man, this fellowship with the Father and the Son, as by a kind of spiritual respiration, the life of God in the soul is sustained: and the child of God grows up, till he comes to 'the full measure of the stature of Christ'.   (Wesley 1985: 192–3)

When Wesley summarizes Christian faith it is most often in participatory Trinitarian terms. The love of God the Father flows to us through the grace of our Lord Jesus Christ in the communion of the Holy Sprit, awakening new life and faith in us so that in the communion of the Holy Spirit we cannot but breathe prayer and praise back to God through Christ. Justification, new birth, and assurance as are all Trinitarian.

The life of the Triune God is the wellspring of new life from which all Christian faith, life, and practice flow. This is the spiritual and theological centre around which everything else in early Methodism revolves, providing insight into Methodist forms of life, ministry, and polity designed to embody and mediate this Trinitarian vision of Christian faith that Wesley here summarizes.

In his 'Letter to a Roman Catholic', Wesley focuses on what Protestants and Catholics believe in common. He follows the Nicene Creed and repeats phrases from it, thus aligning himself with the most thoroughly Trinitarian Creed in the history of Christianity:

I believe that this one God is the Father of all things . . . that he is in a peculiar manner the Father of those whom he regenerates by his Spirit . . . but in a still higher sense, the Father of his only Son, whom he hath begotten from eternity. . . .

I believe that Jesus of Nazareth was the Saviour of the world, the Messiah so long foretold . . . I believe he is the proper, natural Son of God, God of God, very God of very God; and that he is the Lord of all . . . but more peculiarly *our* Lord. . . .

I believe the infinite and eternal Spirit of God, equal with the Father and the Son, to be . . . the immediate cause of all holiness in us: enlightening our understandings, rectifying our wills and affections, renewing our natures, uniting our persons to Christ, assuring us of the adoption. . . . purifying and sanctifying our souls and bodies to a full and eternal enjoyment of God.   (quoted in Outler 1964: 494–5)

Several points are noteworthy. Wesley is not afraid to make insightful statements about the Trinity *ad intra*, God's inner Trinitarian life as God. Jesus Christ is not only the Saviour, but the proper natural Son of God, very God of very God, begotten from all eternity. The Spirit, likewise, is infinite, coequal and coeternal with the Father and the Son. Most fascinating of all is Wesley's contention that in the highest sense God's Fatherhood has nothing to do with God's relation to creation or to us, but is rather an intra-Trinitarian relation to the Son, and of course, to the Spirit as well.

Second, Wesley indicates that God's Trinitarian activity extends throughout the *via salutis*, from prevenient grace (enlightening our understanding) to sanctifying and perfecting grace (purifying and sanctifying our souls). When Wesley says that the Spirit is the 'immediate cause' of all holiness he implies that the Father and the Son are also involved in their own unique ways.

Finally, when comparing the sermon 'On the Trinity' with this 'Letter to a Roman Catholic' it is noteworthy that while Wesley understands our basic participation in the gospel in thoroughly Trinitarian terms, when he discusses Trinitarian credal Christian faith, he does so in relation to soteriology, that same participation in the gospel. Wesley's concern is not with an abstract concept of God developed outside the purview of the gospel, but with the understanding of the Triune God that arises out of participation in the gospel. This is a defining characteristic of Wesley's doctrine of the Trinity and its relation to vital Christian faith.

A TRINITARIAN *VIA SALUTIS*?

From the discussion above it is clear that Wesley conceives of the central event of justification, new birth and assurance in relation to the Trinity. How about the beginning and the end of the *via salutis*? Does Wesley understand even prevenient grace and perfecting grace in Trinitarian terms?

In his sermon, 'The Scripture Way of Salvation', Wesley asserts that salvation includes everything that transpires in the human heart under what is usually

> termed 'natural conscience', but more properly, 'preventing grace'; all the 'drawings' of 'the father', the desires after God . . . all that 'light' wherewith the Son of God 'enlighteneth everyone that cometh into the world', *showing* every man 'to do justly, to love mercy, and to walk humbly with his God'; all the *convictions* which his Spirit from time to time works in every child of man.   (Wesley 1985: 156–7)

Prevenient grace is not some spiritual substance separable from God, but actually the Triune God, the Father, Son, and Holy Spirit, working together in a pattern of co-activity in which the respective dimensions of each Person's activity, the Father drawing, the Son enlightening, the Spirit convicting, co-inhere and interpenetrate the activities of the other two (Maddox 1994: 139). Wesley is very clear that 'Christ does not give life to the soul separate from, but in and with, himself. Hence his words are equally true of all people, in whatever state of grace they are. . . . We have this grace not from Christ but in him' (Outler 1964: 285–6).

We find the same pattern in Wesley's Trinitarian definition of Christian perfection: 'Constant communion with God the Father and Son *fills* their [Christians'] hearts with *humble love*. Now this is what I always did, and do now mean by [Christian] "perfection"' (Wesley 1992: 245). We already saw, in the 'Letter to the Roman Catholic', how Wesley says that the Holy Spirit is the *immediate cause* of this union and communion with the Son and the Father. So even Christian perfection is understood by Wesley in relation to the Trinity: in the communion of the Spirit we may enjoy constant communion with the Father and the Son, which fills our hearts with humble love for God and neighbour.

This is entirely consistent with Wesley's vision of humanity's Trinitarian eternal destiny: 'And to crown all, there will be a deep, an intimate, an uninterrupted union with God; a constant communion with the Father and his Son Jesus Christ, through the Spirit; a continual enjoyment of the Three-One God, and of all the creatures in him!' (Wesley 1985: 510). The forensic categories, such as justification and forgiveness, in Wesley's soteriology are in service of a participatory Trinitarian understanding of salvation: our destiny in this life and the next is union and communion with the Triune God and with one another, indeed with all creation.

Wesley, in various sermons, describes all aspects of the *via salutis* in relation to the Trinity along these same lines. Thus, Sandra Matthaei (2000: 32) argues persuasively for a description of the *via salutis* in terms of 'invitation to communion', 'deepening communion', and 'full communion', with the Three-One God and all creation. In the light of Wesley's Trinitarian reading of the *via salutis*, we can begin to understand why Charles Wesley wrote such lines as, 'And when we rise in love renew'd, our souls resemble Thee, an image of the Triune God, to all eternity' (Wesley, C. 1767: 58), and 'You whom he ordained to be Transcripts of the Trinity' (Wesley, J. 1983: 88).

Trinitarian Ecclesiology

In the light of Wesley's Trinitarian account of salvation, it is no surprise that Wesley's brief definition of ecclesiology in his 'Letter to a Roman Catholic' is not a 'functional' or 'practical' description of the church as a means of grace, but rather those 'who have fellowship with God the Father, Son and Holy Ghost' (Outler 1964: 495). This is entirely consistent with Wesley's more substantive discussions of the church in his sermons.

Wesley wrote 'Of the Church' in 1785, after his ordinations of Whatcoat and Vasey for the Methodist Episcopal Church in America, in response to a rumour that he was leaving the Anglican Church. In the introductory part of the sermon Wesley discusses points that the New Testament makes about the church. Wesley then moves to the two key questions: 'who are properly "the church of God"? [and] What is the true meaning of that term?' (Wesley 1986: 48). Wesley answers the questions with a fully Trinitarian understanding of his text in Ephesians 4: 1–16 and of the church. The church is 'the saints' or 'holy persons' who worship the Triune God, 'which the Apostle here considers as "one body"; comprehending not only... the Christians of one city, of one province or nation; but all the persons upon the face the earth who answer the character here given' (Wesley 1986: 48). Wesley then goes point by point through the list in that passage:

'There is one Spirit' who animates all these, all the living members of the church of God.... 'There is one Lord' who has now dominion over them...
'There is one faith,' which is the free gift of God... the faith which enables every true Christian to testify... 'The life I now live, I live by faith in the Son of God, who loved me and gave himself for me'....
'There is one God and Father of all' that have the Spirit of adoption, which crieth in their hearts, Abba, Father; which 'witnesseth' continually 'with their spirits' that they are children of God.... 'And in you all—in a peculiar manner living in you that are one body in one spirit:

Making your souls his abode,
The temples of indwelling God.

Here then is a clear, unexceptionable answer to the question, What is the church? (ibid. 49–50).

Wesley here defines the church in the very same participatory Trinitarian terms used in his sermon, 'On the Trinity'. The church is all those persons everywhere throughout the world animated by the Spirit of Christ who bear witness in their hearts that they are children of God the Father through Jesus Christ their Saviour. The church is constituted by its participatory encounter with the activity of all three Trinitarian Persons and lives its life in union and communion with the Triune God.

What is also noteworthy about Wesley's sermon, 'Of the Church', is that he even subsumes the Protestant marks of the church under his participatory Trinitarian understanding, stating that this account is 'exactly agreeable' with the nineteenth Article of the Church of England, which views the church as a congregation of the faithful where the pure Word of God is preached and the sacraments are rightly administered (Wesley 1986: 51).

This Trinitarian understanding of the essence of the church appears in other places in Wesley's writings. One of the most profound discussions is found in his sermon, 'Spiritual Worship'. The sermon is significant for it underscores the doxological dimension so essential to Wesley's doctrine of the Trinity and Trinitarian soteriology and ecclesiology.

Wesley defines spiritual worship in Trinitarian terms. He says that his text, 1 John, deals with 'the whole Christian church in all succeeding ages' and 'does not treat directly of faith...neither of inward or outward holiness...but with the foundation of all, the happy and holy communion which the faithful have with God the Father, Son and Holy Ghost' (ibid. 89–90). Here Wesley makes the participatory Trinitarian dimension the 'foundation', the most basic relations constitutive of the church.

Later in the sermon, Wesley summarizes the Epistle:

'...God *hath* given us', not only a title to but the real beginning of 'eternal life. And this life is' purchased by, and treasured up 'in his Son', who has all the springs and the fullness of it in himself, to communicate to his body, the church.

As our knowledge and our love of him increase by the same degrees...we 'grow up in all things into him who is our head'. And when we are...'complete in him'...more properly when we are 'filled with him'; when 'Christ in us, the hope of glory', is our God and all...when we dwell in Christ, and Christ in us, we are one with Christ, and Christ with us...then we live all 'the life that is hid with Christ in God'. Then, and not till then, we properly experience what that word meaneth, 'God is love; and whoever dwelleth in love, dwelleth in God, and God in him'.   (ibid. 96–7)

For Wesley, eternal life and the church as the Body of Christ are intimately related and inseparable. Eternal life refers to our communion in the Spirit with Christ and through Christ with the Father. The church refers to the reality of our being constituted members together in the Body of Christ, inseparably bound in the Spirit through Christ with God and with one another. The church as communion with the Triune God and one another is the actual form that eternal life takes both now in history and in the eschaton.

This, of course, is what it finally means to be 'transcripts of the Trinity'; we are united by the Spirit with Christ who *is* our eternal life, who lives his life through us, so that our life is hid with Christ in God. We live in communion with the Three–One God and one another, indeed with all redeemed creation, in overflowing praise to the Triune God who has loved us with the very love that God is.

It is no surprise that Wesley defines the sacraments and even schism (ibid. 61–8) along participatory Trinitarian lines. There are, of course, many areas that Wesley does not work out in relation to the Trinity, like his deeply problematic doctrine of providence. What is remarkable, however, is the sheer consistency of Wesley's doctrine of the Trinity interwoven with all Christian faith and the way he relates the Trinity to soteriology and ecclesiology.

EMBODIMENT OF WESLEY'S TRINITARIAN PERSPECTIVE

If Christian faith, salvation, and community are Trinitarian, constituted by the activity of the Trinitarian Persons, then the Trinity is inherently related to all aspects of Christian faith, life, and practice, and ought to inform and influence all their complex expressions. So we would expect that Wesley and the early Methodists did embody this kind of Trinitarian expression of Christian faith explicitly and implicitly in the multiple dimensions of the Methodist movement. Though this embodiment was neither systematic nor complete, the following examples illustrate how the Trinity did influence various dimensions of the Methodist experiment.

Charles Wesley published an entire collection of hymns in 1767 entitled, *Hymns on the Trinity*. The hymnal contains 136 hymns divided into four parts. Charles adds 52 'Hymns and Prayers to the Trinity' for a total of 188. Charles had previously published a collection of *Hymns to the Trinity* in 1746. Furthermore, in the 1780 *Collection of Hymns for the Use of the People Called Methodist*, the closest thing to an official hymnal in early Methodism, 25 per cent of the hymns are explicitly Trinitarian (Tripp 1994–5). This shows how deeply the Trinity is embedded in the worship of early Methodism, and reveals the close connection for the Wesley brothers between Trinitarian theology and Trinitarian doxology, a connection profoundly reinforced in the minds, hearts, and lives of the early Methodists by singing Charles's hymns.

The Trinity also finds its way into the liturgy of early Methodism. Here is one example from the Covenant Renewal Service used especially on New Year's day:

I take you, Father, Son, and Holy Spirit for my portion....
I will strive to order my whole life according to your direction.
Glory be to you, O God the Father...

Glory be to you, O God the Son...

Glory be to you, O God the Holy Spirit...

Almighty God, the Lord Omnipotent, Father, Son, and Holy Spirit, you have now become my covenant Friend. And I through your infinite grace, have become your covenant servant.

So be it. And may the covenant I have made on earth be ratified in heaven. Amen.

(*The United Methodist Book of Worship* 1992: 294)

Since the Trinity permeates the hymnody and liturgy of early Methodism, it is no coincidence that there are examples, particularly from 1770s on, of Methodist laity who understand and speak about their Christian faith and life in explicitly Trinitarian terms (Rack 1987–8). In his letters to various lay persons, John Wesley on occasion asks them if they have a clear sense of the presence of the ever-blessed Trinity.

Wesley gradually developed a highly evolved organization, 'connexion' as he called it, designed to nurture those awakened in this Trinitarian faith. Wesley conceives of early Methodist 'connexion' in the societies, classes, bands, and various conferences in participatory Trinitarian terms:

It is only when we are knit together that we 'have nourishment from Him [Christ]'... When they were strengthened a little, not by solitude, but by abiding with him and one another, he commanded them to 'wait', not separated, but 'being assembled together', for 'the promise of the Father'.... Express mention is made in the same chapter, that '... all that believed were together, and continued steadfastly' not only 'in the Apostles' doctrine', but also 'in fellowship and in breaking of bread', and in praying 'with one accord'. Agreeable to which is the account the great Apostle gives of the manner... 'for perfecting the saints, for edifying the body of Christ'... all who will ever come, in 'the unity of the faith, unto the perfect man, unto the measure of the stature of the fulness of Christ' must 'together grow up into Him: From whom the whole body fitly joined together and compacted' (or strengthened) 'by that which every joint supplieth, according to the effectual working in the measure of every part, maketh increase of the body unto the edifying itself in love'. (Wesley 1829: 333–4)

Wesley here provides his biblical/theological rationale for particular forms of life and ministry, a set of relationships, communal structures, and practices that he designates 'connexion'. Connexion, in Wesley's Trinitarian understanding of salvation and the church, is invitation to communion, deepening communion, and full communion with the Triune God and one another. The Triune God builds up Christ's followers towards full salvation within particular forms of community that manifest certain kinds of relations or 'connexion'. The small groups, the societies and the conferences that constitute early Methodist connexion were simultaneously an expression of communion with God and neighbour and also formation towards communion with God and neighbour. Note the tight relationship between connexion and discipline in the next three quotations.

Wesley's understanding of connexion becomes even clearer in his searching questions directed at the failure of the Anglican Church to embody this kind of Trinitarian communion with God and one other at the heart of his understanding of vital religion:

Who watched over them in love? Who marked their growth in grace? Who advised and exhorted them from time to time? Who prayed with them and for them, as they had need? This, and this alone is Christian fellowship. But alas! ... Name what parish you please. ... What Christian connexion is there between them? What intercourse in spiritual things? What watching over each other's souls? What bearing one another's burdens?

(Wesley 1989: 259)

The character of connexion is further clarified by the questions band members were required to ask each other: 'Have you forgiveness of sins? Have you peace with God through our Lord Jesus Christ? ... Is the Love of God shed abroad in your heart? ... Do you desire to be told all your faults, and that plain and home?' (ibid. 77–8).

We see the same pattern in Wesley's rationale for the select bands or societies. In his 'Plain Account of the People Called Methodists', Wesley tells of some Methodists who 'outran the greater part of their brethren, continually walking in the light of God, and having fellowship with the Father, and with his Son, Jesus Christ' (ibid. 269). Wesley says, 'My design was ... to direct them now to *press after perfection*; to exercise their every grace, and improve every talent they had received; and to incite them to love one another more, and to watch more carefully over each other. ... They had no need of being encumbered with many rules, having the best rule of all in their hearts [which, of course, is love]' (ibid. 269–70).

'Connexion', watching over one another in love in community, entails a set of communal relations and specific practices designed simultaneously to express communion with Triune God and neighbour and form communion with Triune God and neighbour. So Wesley understands connexion and its expressions in societies, classes, bands, and conferences in participatory terms in relation to the Trinity.

These are only some of the notable examples of how the early Methodists related the Trinity to various dimensions of the Methodist movement. This is not to say that this Trinitarian development was always self-conscious, but there is a coherent and comprehensive Trinitarian pattern evident in, and characteristic of, the fontal expression of Methodism.

THE TRINITY IN THE HISTORY OF METHODISM

The fate of the Trinity in the history of Methodism after Wesley until fairly recently is one of marginalization and neglect. It is not that Methodism stopped officially affirming the doctrine of the Trinity, but rather that the Trinity played little role in the creative and constructive intellectual history of Methodism and did not significantly influence other dimensions of the movement, as in early Methodism. This is part of a wider Methodist neglect of Wesley as a theological guide, even though he was revered as the founder of Methodism (Maddox 1999).

THE NEGLECT OF THE TRINITY

One major intellectual stream of Methodism after Wesley, particularly in North America, draws upon philosophy out of an apologetic intent first to defend Methodism from critique and then later to develop a credible theology in the face of Enlightenment criticism and produce a refurbished articulation of Christian faith that could speak to Modernity. The result of these theological moves is first systematic neglect of the Trinity and then reinterpretation of the Trinity in order to bring it into coherence with the various theological–philosophic syntheses that developed.

The initial occasion in the nineteenth century for Methodist appropriation of philosophical resources in theological construction was the debate with Calvinists concerning the sovereignty of God in relation to human sin and freedom. The ongoing appeal to a philosophically defined personality of God by Methodist theologians in their defence is a significant reason for the neglect of the Trinity. This 'personality' of the one God proved to be incoherent with any Trinitarian interpretation of personhood and created insuperable problems when trying to make sense of the Trinity (Powell 1983).

A result of this focus on the personality of the one God, with its neglect of the Trinity, is that both the *via salutis* and ecclesiology gradually lose their Trinitarian relation characteristic of Wesley and early Methodism. Soteriology and ecclesiology become connected to different theological deep-structures, which inevitably redefine salvation and the church. From Boston Personalism onwards, it is most often some form of panentheist God–world relation that replaces the Trinity as the deep-structure configuring other doctrines and dimensions of the faith.

Daniel Whedon, editor of the *Methodist Quarterly Review* from 1856 to 1884, illustrates these theological tendencies. In his monograph, *Freedom of the Will as a Basis of Human Responsibility and a Divine Government* (1864), Whedon argues that human moral consciousness (his philosophical anthropology) not only implies human freedom and immortality, but even a particular view of God as a 'person'. The God demanded is 'an infinitely free, excellent, meritorious Person', for 'the *necessary* CONDITION to the *possible existence of a true Divine Government is the Volitional* FREEDOM, *both of the infinite and the finite Person*' (Whedon 1864: 315–16, 436).

Whedon's philosophical interpretation of human nature as a fact of human experience becomes the point of departure for the theological construction of the other aspects in his theology. His book contains only two references to Wesley and there is not even a subsection of a chapter on the Trinity, even though chapters and subsections deal with God's existence, as well as God's attributes.

Whedon and this stream of Methodism do not reject the Trinity, the Trinity simply fades into the background, as the personality of the one God moves to the forefront in theological construction. Whedon represents both the culmination of previous tendencies, and also the point of departure for complete philosophical–Methodist syntheses by Methodist theologians right up to the present.

At the end of the nineteenth century Borden Parker Bowne developed Boston Personalism by synthesizing neo-Kantian idealism with his Methodist heritage. Personalism provided Bowne with an alternative to the naturalism and materialism of scientific and secular modern Western culture. His goal was to purge Methodism of mystical and ceremonial elements to make it credible in the Modern era.

Traditional doctrines, such as the Trinity, had to be altered or eliminated in the process. Thus there is no discussion of the Trinity in Bowne's (1905) book, *The Immanence of God*. The same is true of other Personalists, such as Edgar Brightman, whose monograph, *Is God a Person?* (1932) also contains no discussion of the Trinity, even though there is a chapter on 'The Place of Christ in the Interpretation of a Personal God'. Neglect of the Trinity is even more profound than in Whedon, since Bowne and Brightman systematically replace the Trinity as a deep-structure of Methodist theology with a Personalist God–world relation.

No one has thought out the theological implications of a particular panentheist God–world relation for Christian faith more systematically than United Methodist theologian John Cobb. Cobb finds in process philosophy the key to the nature of reality and the solution to the ultimate problems of philosophy and theology.

Cobb systematically reworks Christology in light of the central category of process thought: 'Creative Transformation...the immanence of God in the world...life itself, the life by which all that is alive lives' (Cobb 1988: 144.). While Cobb discusses the Trinity, he radically harmonizes it with the process world-view. He identifies the Logos with primordial nature of God and the Spirit with God's consequent nature (Cobb 1975: 70–7, 259–64; 1988: 152–3). In so doing, Cobb is finally compelled to assert, 'that it is God who is incarnate in Jesus and that this God is the Trinity in its totality' (1988: 153). Other Methodist theologians in this long tradition deal with the Trinity along lines similar to those found in Bowne and Cobb.

THE MARGINALIZATION OF THE TRINITY

Wesley never produced a systematic theology, so subsequent generations of Methodist theologians took up the task. However, instead of developing Wesley's insights regarding the Trinity and then creating an architectonic structure for theology that reflects Wesley's seminal perceptions, these systematicians borrow form, and at times content, from other traditions. This stream of Methodist theology discusses the Trinity, but in the end marginalizes the doctrine within the dogmatic structure of theology so that the Trinity does not play the formative role in relation to other aspects of theology.

Nowhere is this more evident than in British Methodist, Richard Watson, and his *Theological Institutes* (1906), the most influential systematic theology in Methodism from its publication in 1828 to near the end of the nineteenth century. It was the main theological text required in the course of study for over fifty years in American Methodism with tremendous influence on Methodist preachers and their congregations. Watson's borrowed model for theology is Protestant scholasticism.

The subtitle of the work is, 'A View of The Evidences, Doctrines, Morals, and Institutions of Christianity', and his *Institutes* begins with 150 pages of 'Evidences of the Divine Authority of the Holy Scriptures', a rationalist apologetic for the revelatory status of Scripture. Only 40 of the works 750 pages deal with the Trinity, and 30 of those try to deduce the doctrine from Scripture. This leaves only a couple of pages summarizing the Trinitarian content (Watson 1906).

It is not all that different in the works of other Methodist systematicians after Watson. John Miley's two-volume *Systematic Theology* (1892) covers the Trinity in 18 pages out of over 1,000, less space than he devotes to positivism and evolution. Thomas Summer's discussion of the Trinity in his *Systematic Theology* (1888) is 12 pages out of 1,100, most of which is devoted to scriptural proofs for the Trinity and discussion of inadequate views of it. British Methodist J. Scott Lidgett's *The Christian Religion* (1907) includes a chapter on the doctrine of God, but no subsection on the Trinity and only a few comments under headings such as 'the love of God' and 'the unity of the Godhead'.

Furthermore, the participatory evangelical and doxological approach found in Wesley's discussion of the Trinity is most often absent in these systematic theologies, though Wiley at least acknowledges that the Trinity is 'a central truth of the Gospel', closely bound up 'with all that is evangelical in Christian theology', and without which Christian faith 'falls away into a mere moral system' (Miley 1892: 271).

In Watson's *Theological Institutes*, Wesley's participatory approach is lost save for a single quotation from Dr. Waterland:

While we consider the doctrine of the trinity as interwoven with the very frame and texture of Christian religion, it appears to me natural to conceive that the whole scheme and economy of man's [*sic*] redemption was laid with a principal view of it ... Such a redemption was provided ... so that men [*sic*] might know that there are three Divine persons .. . and might accordingly be both instructed and inclined to love, honor, and adore them here, because that must be a considerable part of their employment and happiness hereafter.

(Watson 1906: 262)

Watson seems unaware that this quotation undermines his approach to the doctrine of the Trinity, indeed undermines the entire architectonic structure of his *Institutes*. If the doctrine of the Trinity is interwoven with the very fabric of Christian faith and is the Origin, Agency, and End of the whole scheme and economy of redemption, then this has to inform both the discussion of the Trinity and every other aspect of a systematic theology, including theology's very structure. The Trinity cannot be isolated in the dogmatic structure of theology, for this marginalizes it, prevents it from influencing the explication of other areas of theology, and encourages a corollary marginalization in the life, ministry, and polity of the church.

This is precisely what takes place both in the Watson's theology and in the life and ministry of Methodist preachers and their churches influenced by his work. The Trinity is still affirmed, but as one doctrine among others, and it plays little other role in theology or in Methodist churches throughout the nineteenth and twentieth centuries. The Trinity loses its connection to vital religion.

The various systematic theologies written by Methodists following Watson throughout the nineteenth and most of the twentieth century affirm the doctrine of the Trinity and include a section on it. But most often their discussions simply state the bare facts of the doctrine, attempt to show that it is not a contradiction, and maybe defend it from criticism or indicate its biblical roots. Nearly all uproot the doctrine of the Trinity from the soteriological and doxological matrix found in Wesley and isolate it in the structure of theology so that it does not influence the development of other loci of theology, particularly the *via salutis*, and thereby nearly all subvert the Trinitarian spiritual/theological dynamism of early Methodism.

The stream of twentieth-century Methodist theology where one might most expect the kind of Trinitarian theology found in early Methodism to find expression and development is the neo-Wesleyan movement. Yet despite a spate of recent articles on Wesley's doctrine of the Trinity, twentieth-century neo-Wesleyanism published little on the doctrine of the Trinity or the Trinitarian expression of Christian faith, thought, and practice. The neo-Wesleyan movement did, however, help pave the way for a Trinitarian renaissance within Methodism by again focusing attention on Wesley and early Methodism, and providing numerous primary and secondary resources to this end.

THE CONTEMPORARY SCENE

There is serious dialogue about the Trinity and Trinitarian expression of Christian faith, thought, and practice in Methodist circles today. This conversation has developed primarily through ecumenical encounters and the influence of Trinitarian theologies outside the Methodist tradition, especially those of Karl Barth and Karl Rahner and others who followed, rather than because of the influence of Wesley and early Methodism. Whatever the sources of this Trinitarian impulse, it is generating creative work on the part of a long list of Methodist scholars and leaders. What follows are examples that illustrate this new attention to the Trinity within Methodism.

British Methodist theologian Geoffrey Wainwright combines both streams of Trinitarian influence, ecumenical and resurgent interest in the Trinity via Barth and Rahner, along with an intimate knowledge of Wesley's work on the Trinity. Wainwright has written the most insightful essays on Wesley's doctrine of the Trinity to date. His own constructive work is thoroughly Trinitarian, as is evident in his one-volume theology, *Doxology: The Praise of God in Worship, Doctrine and Life* (1980). In this work, Wainwright reflects the profound doxological and participatory orientation characteristic of Wesley's theology in general and his doctrine of the Trinity in particular.

Theodore Runyon, an American Methodist also influenced by ecumenical encounter and the revival of Trinitarian theology, is another astute reader of Wesley's Trinitarian theology. His book, *The New Creation: John Wesley's Theology Today* (1998), emphasizes the Trinitarian character of Wesley's theology, including the atonement and the sacraments, and is especially sensitive to the participatory character of Trinitarian Christian faith, life, and practice.

Several Methodist bishops have written monographs that emphasize the importance of the Trinity. American, Scott J. Jones's work, *United Methodist Doctrine: The Extreme Center* (2002), devotes an entire chapter to the Trinity, including a section on Wesley's understanding of the Trinity. Other American United Methodist bishops, such as Timothy Whitaker and Will Willimon, are also part of this Trinitarian renaissance.

German bishop Walter Klaiber and his colleague Manfred Marquardt, in their theological monograph *Living Grace*, emphasize the Trinitarian character of the central Methodist affirmation that 'God is Love'. Love is not simply an attribute of God, but rather 'the basic definition of God's essence, whose dynamic is disclosed in the movement of the triune God' (Klaiber and Marquardt 2001: 55–6).

The ever-pugnacious Stanley Hauerwas provides a winsome example of the way in which the Trinity bears upon all aspects of Christian faith, life, and practice in his provocative article, 'A Trinitarian Theology of the Chief End of all Flesh'. Rooted in a Trinitarian account of creation, Hauerwas emphasizes the importance of 'living the way of the Trinity' in how Christians relate to other animals. Hauerwas calls for non-violence towards animals, even vegetarianism as a witness to the world concerning the Triune God's peaceable intent for all creation (Hauerwas 1995: 196).

Michael Pasquarello's *Christian Preaching* develops, as indicated by the subtitle, *A Trinitarian Theology of Proclamation* (2006), demonstrating the relevance of the

Trinity to yet another area of Christian faith. There are many other contemporary Methodists who are pursuing this renaissance of the Trinity and Trinitarian Christian faith within Methodism today.

Nevertheless, there is still no monograph on Wesley's doctrine of the Trinity, nor one developing a Methodist doctrine of the Trinity for today. Thus far Methodists have not developed a fully Trinitarian theology, nor a comprehensive Trinitarian expression of Christian faith, life, and practice along the lines begun by Wesley and early Methodism.

THE TRINITY IN THE FUTURE
OF METHODISM

If Methodism is to become fully Trinitarian, it will need to reappropriate, refine, and extend the Trinitarian insights of Wesley and early Methodism. This will require further work on Wesley's doctrine of the Trinity, on the Trinitarian character of various aspects of his theology, and on how the Trinity influenced multiple dimensions of the Methodist experiment, including ecclesial forms, liturgy, hymnody and worship, spirituality, discipleship, morality and social witness, and the rest. The same is true regarding the subsequent history of Methodism, though here we need to understand more precisely how and why the Trinity and the dynamic Trinitarian character of early Methodism were not effectively mediated to and exploited by later Methodists.

This historical work, important in itself to the self-understanding of Methodism, needs to serve the current renaissance of the Trinity taking place within Methodism and spill over into the wider Christian community. Methodism is in profound need of not only deeper and broader work on the Trinity, but also on the Trinitarian character of all Christian theology. While Methodism needs to retrieve Wesley's practical *form* of theological activity and produce rich and theologically sound materials for Christian formation, worship, and witness, Methodism also needs to develop its own rigorous form of Trinitarian theology.

Here Wesley is part of the problem, for he did not provide Methodism with a rigorous *Institutes* or *Summa*. The Wesleyan body of divinity, or world-view, which frames faith, life, and practice, ought to be given careful, comprehensive, and architectonically strong expression in a way that discloses its distinctive Trinitarian theological patterns as well as becoming a participatory activity in relation to and in praise of the Triune God, in keeping with the insights of Wesley and early Methodism.

What is clear is that if Methodism is to become a living, dynamic movement as it was at its inception, it will include much greater attention to the Trinity and the

Trinitarian character of all Christian faith, life, and practice than is evident throughout much of its history.

SUGGESTED READING

BRYANT, BARRY E. (1990). 'Trinity and Hymnody: The Doctrine of the Trinity in the Hymns of Charles Wesley'. *Wesleyan Theological Journal* 25/2: 64–73.

POWELL (1983).

VICKERS, JASON E. (2007). 'Charles Wesley and the Revival of the Doctrine of the Trinity: A Methodist Contribution to Modern Theology'. In Kenneth G. C. Newport and Ted A. Campbell (eds.), *Charles Wesley: Life, Literature and Legacy.* Peterborough: Epworth, 278–98.

WAINWRIGHT, GEOFFREY (1990). 'Why Wesley Was a Trinitarian'. *The Drew Gateway* 59/2: 26–43.

REFERENCES

BOWNE, BORDEN P. (1905). *The Immanence of God.* Boston: Houghton Mifflin.

BRIGHTMAN, EDGAR (1932). *Is God A Person?* New York: Association Press.

COBB, JOHN B. (1975). *Christ in a Pluralistic Age.* Philadelphia: Westminster.

—— (1988). 'Christ Beyond Creative Transformation'. In Stephen T. Davis (ed.), *Encountering Jesus: a Debate on Christology.* Atlanta: John Knox.

HAUERWAS, STANLEY (1995). *In Good Company: The Church as Polis.* Notre Dame, Ind.: University of Notre Dame Press.

JONES, SCOTT J. (2002). *United Methodist Doctrine: The Extreme Center.* Nashville: Abingdon.

KLAIBER, WALTER, and MARQUARDT, MANFRED (2001). *Living Grace: An Outline of United Methodist Theology,* trans. J. Steven O'Malley and Ulrike R. M. Guthrie. Nashville: Abingdon. (First published in 1993 as *Gelebte Gnade: Grundriss einer Theologie der Evangelisch-methodistischen Kirche.* Stuttgart: Christliches Verlagshaus.)

LIDGETT, J. SCOTT (1907). *The Christian Religion.* New York: Eaton & Mains.

MADDOX, RANDY (1994). *Responsible Grace: John Wesley's Practical Theology.* Nashville: Kingswood.

—— (1999). 'Respected Founder/Neglected Guide: The Role of Wesley in American Methodist Theology'. *Methodist History* 37/2: 71–88.

MATTHAEI, SONDRA HIGGINS (2000). *Making Disciples: Faith Formation in the Wesleyan Tradition.* Nashville: Abingdon.

MILEY, JOHN (1892; repr. 1984). *Systematic Theology.* 2 vols. New York: Eaton & Mains.

OUTLER, ALBERT C. (ed.) (1964). *John Wesley.* New York: Oxford University Press.

PASQUARELLO, MICHAEL, III (2006). *Christian Preaching: A Trinitarian Theology of Proclamation.* Grand Rapids: Baker.

POWELL, SAMUEL M. (1983). 'The Doctrine of the Trinity in 19th Century American Methodism 1850–1900'. *Wesleyan Theological Journal* 18: 33–46.

RACK, HENRY D. (1987–8). 'Early Methodist Visions of the Trinity'. In *Proceedings of the Wesley Historical Society* 46: 38–44, 57–69.

Runyon, Theodore (1998). *The New Creation: John Wesley's Theology Today.* Nashville: Abingdon.

Summer, Thomas (1888). *Systematic Theology.* 2 vols. Nashville: Methodist Episcopal Church South.

The United Methodist Book of Worship (1992). Nashville: Abingdon.

Tripp, David (1994–5). 'Methodism's Trinitarian Hymnody: A Sampling, 1780 and 1989, and Some Questions'. *Quarterly Review* 14/4: 359–85.

Wainwright, Geoffrey (1980). *Doxology: The Praise of God in Worship, Doctrine and Life.* New York: Oxford University Press.

Watson, Richard (1906). *Theological Institutes: or, A View of the Evidences, Doctrines, Morals and Institutions of Christianity.* Nashville: Methodist Episcopal Church South.

Wesley, Charles (1746). *Gloria Patri, &c. or, Hymns to the Trinity.* London: Strahan.

—— (1767). *Hymns on the Trinity.* Bristol: Pine.

Wesley, John (1829). *The Works of John Wesley,* ed. Thomas Jackson. 3rd edn. London: John Mason, xiv.

—— (1983). *The Works of John Wesley,* xii. *A Collection of Hymns for the Use of the People Called Methodist,* ed. Franz Hildebrandt and Oliver A. Beckerlegge. Oxford: Clarendon.

—— (1985). *Works,* ii. *Sermons,* ed. Albert C. Outler. Nashville: Abingdon.

—— (1986). *Works,* iii. *Sermons,* ed. Albert C. Outler. Nashville: Abingdon.

—— (1989). *Works,* ix. *The Methodist Societies,* ed. Rupert Davies. Nashville: Abingdon.

—— (1992). *Works,* xxi. *Letters I, 1721–1739.* ed. Frank Baker. Oxford: Clarendon.

Whedon, Daniel D. (1864). *Freedom of the Will as a Basis for Human Responsibility and a Divine Government.* New York: Carlton & Lanahan.

CHAPTER 30

ORIGINAL SIN

BARRY E. BRYANT

WHILE John Wesley may be best known for his emphasis on the doctrine of grace, it should also be acknowledged that he placed a great deal of importance on the doctrine of original sin. There are two theological coordinates one may use to get an immediate bearing on his understanding of it. Wesley was constantly pledging his support of and demonstrating his conformity to the Anglican Articles of Religion, one of which is Article IX on 'Original sin'. In Wesley's defence of his principles and practice, Article IX had been extracted in *A Farther Appeal to Men of Reason and Religion* (Wesley 1975: 112). It would be extracted yet again in his sermon, 'On Sin in Believers' (1763) and prefaced with the comment, 'And herein our own Church (as indeed in most points) exactly copies after the primitive...' (Wesley 1984: 317–18). So far as Wesley was concerned, this was not just a doctrine of the Church of England, but also of the early church, a theological authority that was perhaps second only to Scripture in his mind (Campbell 1991). Furthermore, this doctrine of the early church and the Church of England would also become a doctrine of American Methodism, as it would be extracted yet again and adapted as Article VII in the *Sunday Service of the Methodists* (Wesley 1784).

A careful comparison reveals that Article VII of the *Sunday Service* omits Article IX's references to linking original sin with 'concupiscence' and saying that it 'deserveth God's wrath and damnation'. This represented a significant theological development for Wesley. It indicates how Wesley tried to rethink the Augustinian teaching that associated original sin with concupiscence. Furthermore, by deleting the reference to damnation it also meant that Wesley had come to see original sin as a way of explaining the corruption of original sin without focusing on its guilt. While all the guilty are sinners, not all sinners are guilty. For example, Wesley would insist, 'no infant ever was or ever will be "sent to hell for the guilt of Adam's sin", seeing it is cancelled by the righteousness of Christ as soon as they are sent into the world' (Wesley 1931: vi. 239–40). That being the case, it must be asked, why and how did the doctrine of original sin come to occupy a place of such significance for Wesley? In answering these two questions a better understanding of Wesley's doctrine of original sin will be obtained.

The Doctrine of Original Sin

His controversies over quietism and Calvinism, along with the rigours of his preaching schedule obscured the doctrine's importance until 1757, when he published the largest of all his theological treatises, *The Doctrine of Original Sin, According to Scripture, Reason, and Experience*. It was his response to Dr John Taylor (1694–1761), and his publication of *The Scripture-Doctrine of Original Sin Proposed to Free and Candid Examination*. Succinctly put, Taylor's argument was that the 'Cause of Sin is the choice of our Wills, and not its proceeding from Adam's first Transgressions; seeing, upon the Supposition, it would not proceed from it' (Taylor 1740: 129). Original sin is reduced to being merely bad choices. To Wesley, when compared to the Article IX, Taylor's position was as problematic as it was Pelagian. But, Taylor's attack on original sin exposed a vulnerable point in Wesley's own theology where the doctrine of original sin was concerned. Given the nature of Wesley's Arminianism and the doctrine of free grace, which gave rise to free will, how could Wesley maintain both, original sin and free will?

To Wesley's chagrin, Taylor's neo-Pelagian views were being widely read and favourably received by a significant number of the clergy, who were already caught up in the Enlightenment atmosphere of deism, rationalism, and a limp moralism. Such an environment of optimism in the innate human condition eventually caused Wesley to write, 'it is now quite unfashionable to talk otherwise, to say anything to the disparagement of human nature' (Wesley 1985: 173). Wesley believed Taylor (and one could perhaps even argue the Enlightenment too for that matter) had done more harm to Christianity than either Islam or Deism (Wesley 1931: iv. 48; 1979: 9, 193). He concluded that Taylor's rejection of original sin ultimately

saps the very foundation of all revealed religion, whether Jewish or Christian. 'Indeed, my L—,' said an eminent man to a person of quality, 'I cannot see that we have much need of Jesus Christ'. And who might not say, upon this supposition, 'I cannot see that we have much need of Christianity'? Nay, not any at all; for 'they that are whole have no need of a Physician'; and the Christian Revelation speaks of nothing else but the great 'Physician' of our souls; nor can Christian Philosophy, whatever be thought of the Pagan, be more properly defined than in Plato's word: It [therapy of the soul] is, 'the only true method of healing a distempered soul'. But what need of this, if we are in perfect health? If we are not diseased, we do not want a cure. If we are not sick, why should we seek for a medicine to heal our sickness? What room is there to talk of our being renewed in 'knowledge' or 'holiness, after the image wherein we were created,' if we never have lost that image? if we are as knowing and holy now, nay, far more so, than Adam was immediately after his creation? If, therefore, we take away this foundation, that man is by nature foolish and sinful, 'fallen short of the glorious image of God', the Christian system falls at once; nor will it deserve so honourable an appellation, as that of a 'cunningly devised fable'.   (Wesley 1979: ix. 194)

Wesley's argument was rather simple. The doctrine of original sin was the theological presupposition to the 'scripture way of salvation' and with it the doctrines of prevenient, justifying, and sanctifying grace. For Wesley, grace had no meaning without original sin, and furthermore salvation was rendered unneces- sary. At least two things become clear from this. First, the doctrine of original sin was as constitutive to Wesley's theology as the doctrine of grace. Secondly, Wesley saw an intra-doctrinal relationship between this and other doctrines. If the doc- trine of original sin falls, other doctrines fall with it. It would be essential for Wesley to show how he maintains a doctrine of original sin on the one hand while maintaining a doctrine of free grace and free will on the other. To make this defence would require a theological method.

'... According to "Scripture, Reason, and Experience"'

When Wesley wrote his response to John Taylor, on the title page he indicated his defence would be according to 'Scripture, Reason, and Experience'. It was not uncommon for Wesley to use these three elements as constitutive sources for his theological method. But they go beyond methodological considerations. What Wesley seems to have been suggesting was that there are three ways in which one may have 'knowledge', or a theological 'understanding' of something, in this case original sin. In philosophical terms, Wesley attempted to establish an epistemology of original sin. Before using Scripture, reason, and experience as bases for a theological method to develop or articulate a doctrine of original sin, it would be helpful to understand how they function epistemologically. Such an understanding will determine how they are used methodologically (Gunter and Jones 1997).

One of the significant questions raised by epistemology is 'what are the most reliable sources of knowledge?' Wesley answered that question succinctly and surprisingly in *A Compendium of Logic*, his translation of *Artis logicae compendium* (1691), by Henry

Aldrich (d. 1710). Wesley would have studied this text while a student at Oxford, and used it while a tutor at Lincoln College and Moderator of Disputations at the college. In 1756 Wesley translated it from Latin into English and published it as *A Compendium of Logic* so it could be used at his Kingswood School. In composing *Artis logicae*, Aldrich relied heavily upon *Summulae logicales*, the work of Peter of Spain, a Thomist, a Dominican, a logician, and Pope (John XXI, d. 1277). The *Summulae* became a standard medieval textbook of logic, which went through some 166 reprinted editions. There was a shared logical tradition between Peter of Spain, Henry Aldrich, and John Wesley. The essential nature of the tradition was Thomistic and Aristotelian.

While most of the *Compendium* deals with the nature of logic, there is a section in which the issues of 'certainty' and 'evidence' are discussed. There, it is asserted that the certainty of things is confirmed by nature, reason, and divine revelation. This means the certainty of what we know or perceive is dependent on the reliability of the source of knowledge. On this basis one may construct a 'scale of assent' from the less certain to the most certain sources of knowledge. Human beings may both deceive and be deceived (experience). Reason and nature are not easily deceived and not as likely to deceive their followers (reason). God can neither deceive nor be deceived (Scripture) (Wesley 1756: 26). Consequently,

If therefore we were to make a Sort of *Scale of Assent*, it might consist of the following Steps: 1. *Human Faith*, an Assent to a doubtful Proposition: 2. *Opinion*, to a probable: 3. what we may term *Sentiment*, an Assent to a certain Proposition: 4. *Science*, to a certain and evident Conclusion: 5. *Intelligence*, to a Self-Evident Axiom: 6. *Divine Faith*, to a Divine Revelation.
(ibid. 27; 1979: xiv. 178)

All of this is to say, of the three sources of knowledge in Wesley's theological methodology, experience is reliable. Reason is more reliable. Scripture is most reliable. The 'scale of assent' was constituted of an epistemological hierarchy grounded in an Aristotelian tradition and used to defend the doctrine of original sin against the attacks of Taylor's enlightened rationalism. It was an assent from experience to metaphysics. In terms of the epistemology, Wesley favoured Aristotle and Aldrich over Locke (Wesley 1979: xiv. 456, 463; Long 2005: 62–5). Consequently the doctrine of original sin becomes a case study in how Wesley utilizes epistemology in his theological method.

As Wesley considered Taylor's version of an enlightenment doctrine of original sin, he considered it grossly inconsistent with the Biblical record.

But in the meantime, what must we do with our Bibles? For they will never agree with this. These accounts, however pleasing to flesh and blood, are utterly irreconcilable with the scriptural. The Scripture avers that 'by one man's disobedience all men were constituted sinners' [Romans 5: 19]; that 'in Adam all died' [1 Corinthians 15: 22], spiritually died, lost the life and the image of God; that fallen, sinful Adam then 'begat a son in his own likeness' [Genesis 5: 3]; nor was it possible he should beget him in any other, for 'who can bring a clean thing out of an unclean?' [Job 14: 4].   (Wesley 1985: 173)

Wesley could piece together passages that represented what he believed to be the Scriptural doctrine of original sin, but how is all of that to be interpreted? Had not Taylor done the same thing? What follows is a theological reconstruction of Wesley's doctrinal interpretation.

The Image of God in the Soul of Adam: Wesley's Speculative Anthropology

Wesley's doctrine of original sin included trying to postulate the state of Adam's original nature before the fall in order to surmise what was lost by it. He eventually had to confess that we cannot know the true difference between the state of humanity now and Adam's state then (Wesley 1777: i. 179). Whatever is said about Adam's nature is ultimately a speculative anthropology.

Wesley explored this through the concept of the image of God. As a result, it has as much to do with the doctrine of God as the doctrine of humanity. Implicit throughout the entire doctrine was something of an assumption about the nature of the God in whose image the first humans were created. To be human meant to share in some way something with the nature of God. The problem would be in determining which aspects of the divine nature humanity is able to share by way of the concept of 'image'.

The way Wesley most commonly talked about the image of God was that of the triune God consisting of a political (governing), natural (rational), and moral (relational) nature. This concept of the image of God is principally relational and is much better suited for the profoundly relational aspect of his doctrine of Christian perfection (Maddox 1994: 68–72).

The Political Image

Comparatively speaking, Wesley did not say much about the political image of God. First, it consisted of a governing trait, as Adam was made 'the governor of this lower world', which essentially spoke of the Adamic relationship with the remainder of creation beneath him in the chain of being (Wesley 1985: 188). Adam was given dominion over all creation (Wesley 1757: 362; 1979: ix. 381). In the *Doctrine of Original Sin* there is the concept of the 'political image' as the human vested with dominion over creation without using the phrase 'political image' to describe it (Wesley 1757:

325–6; 1979: ix. 400–1). The political image implied human beings acting as God's agents in the world (Weber 2001: 36). This dominion was seen as one of the blessings God gave to Adam because it resulted in peace and harmony with all creation (Wesley 1757: 362; 1979: ix. 381). Wesley's neglect of the political image has been seen as a missed opportunity to integrate his politics with the way of salvation, resulting in the lack of a political language in Wesley's theology (Weber 2001: 19, 36, 391–420).

THE NATURAL IMAGE

He did say considerably more about the natural image of God. He took it to be endued with understanding, will, and liberty, primarily rational concepts as seen in his early sermon, 'The Image of God' (1730). The basic concept of Adam's original righteousness as understanding, will, and liberty remained intact throughout his career, as a comparison of 'The Image of God' with his sermons, 'The General Deliverance' (1781), and, 'On the Fall of Man' (1782) reveals. However, there were some further developments.

First, in 'The General Deliverance' he added 'self-motion', which separated animate from inanimate objects such as 'machines, stocks and stones'. Secondly, 'liberty' was a bit more emphatic in 'The General Deliverance' (1781). Without liberty, or freedom of choice, Adam would not have been any different from 'a piece of marble'. This becomes an important part of what it means to be human (Wesley 1985: 438–9). As noted in the sermon, 'The New Birth' (1760), although Adam was made in the image of God, he was created to stand but liable to fall (ibid. 189). The natural image (as understanding, will, and liberty) is what enabled him to do one or the other, i.e. to keep the moral law, or to break it.

The concept of liberty had more than just abstract or speculative consequences. In spite of the fallen human nature, liberty had profound political consequences for Wesley. For example, he would use it as the basis for abolitionism.

Liberty is the right of every human creature, as soon as he breathes the vital air. And no human law can deprive him of that right, which he derives from the law of nature. If therefore you have any regard to Justice, (to say nothing of Mercy, nor of the revealed Law of GOD) render unto all their due. Give Liberty to whom Liberty is due, that is to every child of man, to every partaker of human nature ... Away with all whips, all chains, all compulsion! Be gentle towards all men. And see that you invariably do unto every one, as you would he should do unto *You*.   (Wesley 1774: 51–2; 1979: xi. 79; Benezet 1781: 8)

Here liberty is seen as a part of the law of nature. Given the part liberty also played in the image of God, Wesley implicitly linked the two together and strengthened the conclusion that slavery must be wrong (Smith 1986).

While he firmly believed slaves should be given their liberty, he drew a different conclusion where the American cries for liberty were concerned. He never sought to conceal his Toryism, which he defined as 'one that believes God, not the people, to be the origin of all civil power' (Wesley 1931: vii. 305–6). In defence of this position, Wesley (1776) wrote *Some Observations on Liberty: Occasioned by a Late Tract*. In it, Wesley would not talk about moral and physical liberty as some of his contemporaries had. He argued for religious and civil liberty instead, of which Wesley thought the Americans had plenty (Wesley 1776: 3–5; 1979: xi. 90–118). In *Thoughts upon Liberty* Wesley argued that every human being has an 'indefeasible' right to choose his or her own religion and to worship God according to his or her own conscience (Wesley 1772*b*: 9; 1979: xi. 37–8). This was rather close to seeing religious liberty as a human right (Weber 2001: 303). Civil liberty, on the other hand, consisted of a 'liberty to enjoy our lives and fortunes in our own way; to use our property, whatever is legally our own, according to our own choice' (Wesley 1772*b*: 15; 1979: xi. 41; Weber 2001: 303–52). His argument was that Americans had both religious and civil liberties already. What they really wanted was not liberty, but independence (Wesley 1776: 5). To Wesley, the desire for independence was a fault of devils, not a virtue of saints (Wesley 1986: 606–7).

The greatest objection was what he saw as the 'indefensible' republican notion that power had its origin in the people. To him, 'There is no power but of God' (Wesley 1772*a*: 5; 1979: xi. 52–3). He was convinced that instead of independence the Americans should long for *real* liberty from sin, oppression, and violence, while maintaining a liberty to enjoy life and even property (Wesley 1986: 607).

For Wesley, the image of liberty suggested certain rights as a human being. But to press a political theory with a definition of liberty that saw people, not God, as the origin of power went beyond liberty and sought to usurp the power of God. This was not a liberty in the image of God, but the image of Satan, the essence of original sin itself. The positive side of Wesley's concept of liberty was that it was to be used to maintain a right relationship with God as creator, and with other human beings, as God's creation in the Divine image.

THE MORAL IMAGE

The third area in which Adam was created in the image of God was in a moral image, endued with knowledge, righteousness, and true holiness. It also entailed knowledge of God, God's will, and God's law (Wesley 1985: 475). This is the most relational of all the aspects—and Wesley would insist to Taylor that this was the most important part—of the image of God (Wesley 1757: 284; 1979: ix. 341). In short, the moral image of God was knowledge of God's moral law, to which God required perfect obedience (Wesley 1985: 410–11, 475). As a result of keeping the moral law Adam offered to God perfect love, which is true holiness of heart (Wesley 1984: 184; 1979: ix. 354). Love was the essence of Adam's original righteousness (Wesley 1757: 289; 1979: ix. 344). This was not just 'negative righteousness', or even an imputed righteousness, but a positive and dynamic righteousness and holiness, experienced and maintained by Adam's obedience to the moral law before the fall. Because he was righteous and holy he was also happy. In holiness was the fullness of love, and happiness was the enjoyment of that love (Wesley 1984: 185; 1985: 452). The lost moral image is what will ultimately be recovered through entire sanctification, or Christian perfection, in the 'way of salvation'.

In all, before the fall, Adam's political, natural, and moral image of God resulted in the supreme perfection of what it meant to be human—morally, physically, spiritually, and intellectually (Wesley 1757: 192; 1979: ix. 293). There was perfect balance and symmetry in all human relationships between humanity and God, between the human beings, and between humanity and creation, giving the concept of original righteousness an understanding of the original 'rightness' of all human relationships. This rightness of relations meant Adam's pleasure was uninterrupted by evil of any kind. Neither his body nor his mind knew sorrow or pain of any kind. He was incapable of suffering. 'To crown all, he was immortal' (Wesley 1985: 438–40).

EMPIRICAL ANTHROPOLOGY

The fall of humanity is where speculative anthropology ended for Wesley, and empirical anthropology began (Runyon 1998: 21). To Wesley it was obvious that something has always been wrong with humanity. As far, and as far back as he could see, the world was filled with wickedness, hatred, and perversion. This was his opening argument in Part I of his *Doctrine of Original Sin*. He was convinced that simple empirical observation would easily establish the universality of sin, and this was confirmed by Scripture. Sin could be seen everywhere. 'Look out of your own Doors: *Is there any evil in the city, and sin hath not done it?*... Sin in One or a few Cases, does not prove a sinful Nature: But Sin overspreading the Earth, does' (Wesley 1757: 84–5, 252; 1979: ix. 236, 324). It was Wesley's conviction that the universal human experience testifies unequivocally to original sin.

Because of the image of God, speculative anthropology said as much about the doctrine of God as it did the doctrine of humanity. Empirical anthropology, on the other hand, says more about the doctrine of humanity than the doctrine of God. In the same respect, in speculative anthropology, Wesley's Adam was created in God's image. His empirical anthropology tended to create fallen Adam in our image. Without the fall the entire image of God, 'in which Adam was first created, now remains in all his posterity' (Wesley 1757: 188; 1979: ix. 291). To Wesley it was clearly evident that the entire image of God did not remain. What the next section will attempt to do is outline Wesley's understanding of the nature and consequences of Adam's fall.

The Fall and Its Consequences

When Wesley spoke of 'the fall', he referred to a series of events that began with Eve believing the serpent and not God, and ended with the eating of the fruit, and the breaking of the moral law (Wesley 1985: 189). Belief means thinking God to be true. Sin begins with unbelief as a failure to believe God and God's word (ibid. 402–3). If living under a covenant of works meant Eve knew nothing of faith, more specifically 'saving faith', she could still 'believe' God. When she stopped believing God, she no longer thought God to be true. This is what brought about the actual sin. Unbelief led to sin, just as faith led to obedience (Wesley 1984: 441; 1985: 8–11; 214–17). Faithlessness is the original sin on Eve's part.

With Adam, however, it was a different matter. His sin was the result of yielding to temptation (Wesley 1757: 290; 1979: ix. 345). This temptation was not because he was deceived by Eve, but because he was persuaded by her (Wesley 1755: 560–1; 1985: 403). When Adam sinned he did so with eyes wide open, 'by inward idolatry, by loving the creature more than the Creator' (Wesley 1985: 403; 1986: 103–14). Through his action he exemplified the human propensity to worship creature rather than Creator. While all individuals might be born 'atheists in the world', this 'does not screen us from *idolatry*. In his natural state every man born into the world is rank idolater', the meanest forms of which are pride and self-will (Wesley 1985: 179). Ultimately, selfishness is the extreme form of idolatry.

Wesley believed Adam and Eve sinned in their hearts before eating the fruit (Wesley 1985: 403). Eve was deceived and no longer believed, and Adam was persuaded and no longer loved, resulting in idolatry. Wesley seeing original sin as idolatry is an important theological development (Leclerc 2001). For Wesley, unbelief and inward idolatry were the spiritual dynamics precipitating the fall, making faith and love, trust and relationships, the crux of the issue of original sin (Wesley 1984: 239–40, 245–6). It was the inward sin that preceded and gave rise to the outer, resulting in the fall.

When Adam and Eve did sin, they did so freely. This single act of wilful disobedience was for Wesley what accounts for the presence of evil, sin, pain, and suffering in the world. Original sin was a moral issue. It all happened because the moral law was violated and the Adamic covenant was broken. This was 'the fall'. What followed was God's punishment and the consequences of human faithlessness and idolatry. All of this suggests Wesley was moving away from explaining original sin through concupiscence, as set forth in Article IX, and an emphasis that would be lacking in Article VII.

THE LOSS OF THE MORAL IMAGE

With the loss of the moral image of God, Adam lost original righteousness and true holiness, that is, the image of perfect love, righteousness, and liberty. Without the image of love there is no human liberty, only slavery to sin. Without knowing and loving God, the image of God would not survive intact (Wesley 1985: 189). The first, and most profound consequence of breaking the moral law and losing the moral image was relational, as Adam and Eve experienced existential estrangement from, and broken communion with, God (Wesley 1757: 173–4: 1979: ix. 283–4). They no longer loved God with their hearts, souls, minds, and strength because they no longer trusted God, or believed God to be true. The disintegration of their relationship with the Divine quickly resulted in the experiences of fear, guilt, shame, sorrow, and despair (Wesley 1985: 403). The estranged relationship between the human and Divine eventually resulted in dysfunctional human relationships. Concerns for oneself overrode concerns for one's neighbour. The cause of this dysfunction was they no longer loved their neighbour as themselves. Love of self without love for neighbour is the fundamental expression of selfishness. More than anything else, the loss of the moral image meant the loss of communion with God, and the beginning of a dysfunctional relationship between Adam and Eve demonstrated through selfishness, mutual suspicion, and blame. It is particularly this relational aspect of original sin Wesley's doctrine of entire sanctification will seek to restore through love of God and love of one's neighbour as oneself. The moral image as a part of original righteousness represented the perfection of this relational aspect.

The loss of the moral image of God from the soul and the loss of relationality was equated with spiritual death. This spiritual death was eventually followed by physical death, and the eternal loss of relationality with God (Wesley 1984: 185). Taylor objected to such an all-encompassing notion of death, saying, 'no evil but temporal death came upon men in consequence of Adam's sin' (Wesley 1757: 92; 1979: ix. 240). Wesley's counter-argument was that God made Adam a living soul in an immortal body, that is, a duality. As a consequence of his eating the forbidden fruit, God took from him the lives given to Adam, soul and body— temporal, spiritual, and eternal

(Wesley 1757: 102–3; 1979: ix. 245). Although a duality, the body and soul were actually a unity: what affected one affected the other (Wesley 1987: 165, 296).

If the moral image of God was the chief way in which Adam was created in the image of God, then the loss of the moral image (resulting in the loss of original righteousness), and its relational aspects should be the primary way in which one thinks about Wesley on original sin, thus correcting distortions and deficiencies of many traditional post-Wesley views of sin. When looked at in this way it can be said that Wesley's underlying cause of original sin was unbelief and idolatry. The understanding of original sin as the depravation of the moral image of God and original righteousness provided a relational and ethical understanding of original sin. Entire sanctification then becomes the restoration of right relationships with oneself, God, and neighbour.

THE MARRING OF THE NATURAL AND POLITICAL IMAGES

But Wesley's view of original sin was not exclusively understood in terms of depravation. The depravation of the moral image and the consequence of relational estrangement inevitably resulted in the marring, and the depravation of the natural and political images. All human personhood was corrupted by the fall.

The natural image (Adam's rationality and understanding) was not lost as much as it was marred (Wesley 1985: 474–5). Adam did not become an arational creature, but an irrational one. The evidence of this could be seen in the 'absurdity' of Adam attempting to hide himself among the trees of the garden from the eye of God's omniscience (Wesley 1757: 96; 1979: ix. 242). His understanding was marred by error and ignorance, confusion and mental slowness (Wesley 1987: 298). Original sin was what placed limits upon human understanding. One might very well see the correlation between this and the place of reason in Wesley's 'scale of assent' discussed previously. Humankind's mental capacity decreased and the human mind had no freedom left. Consequently, there was neither liberty nor virtue.

Indeed, freedom had been exchanged for slavery, benevolence for tyranny, and virtue for vice (Wesley 1987: 298–9). Even the inner-personal relationship and the harmony between body and soul were critically affected. 'For all this we may thank Adam' (Wesley 1985: 423).

The political image was marred as well, influencing humanity's relationship with their surrounding environment and all creation. Adam ceased to mediate blessing to the remainder of the creation with which he started to be in conflict. Disorder and chaos became a way of life. All were subject to 'vanity', and became victims to that barbarous and ravenous 'monster, death, the conqueror of all that breathe' (ibid. 508–9). Animal suffering is even an indication of original sin. 'If beasts suffer, then man is fallen' (Wesley 1757: 377; 1979: ix. 389). To top it all off weeds grew from the soil and Adam consequently had to toil (Wesley 1985: 405). In general, Adam was responsible for the corruption of all the world around him (Wesley 1984: 225).

ORIGINAL SIN AND TOTAL DEPRAVITY

In this respect, Wesley was not optimistic in describing humanity apart from the grace of God. We are conceived in sin, shaped in wickedness, so that in our natural state there is 'no good thing' (Wesley 1985: 183). There were several metaphors used by Wesley to describe this depravity. Using the strongest language possible, Wesley said that instead of the image of God, Adam became stamped with the image of Satan, the personification of pride, self-will, and self-love (Wesley 1984: 351; 1985: 179). He also used medical metaphors of sin as a disease and sickness, more than he used legal or forensic ones, which had dominated the Western doctrine of salvation since the time of Anselm (Wesley 1984: 79; Maddox 1994: 73–4). When the image of God was lost sin overspread the entire human soul, like a 'loathsome leprosy' until it corrupted the soul's every power and faculty (Wesley 1984: 477). It is not just that a part of humanity is missing. Because of self-love's perversity the part of our humanity that remains is sick. Wesley exclaimed, 'Know your disease!' But he continued to say just as insistently, 'Know your cure! Ye were born in sin; therefore "ye must be born again", "born of God". By nature ye are wholly corrupted; by grace ye shall be wholly renewed. "In Adam ye all died"; in the second Adam, "in Christ, ye all are made alive"' (Wesley 1985: 185).

Salvation was seen as 'therapy of the soul' (Wesley 1757: p. vi). This genre of medical analogies provided an alternative way of looking at the problem of sin, and a fresh way of looking at salvation as sin's solution. It is a view that sees original sin as a sickness resulting from the lost image of righteousness, holiness, and love, marring the character of humanity, i.e. body, soul, and spirit, and that sees salvation as healing, resulting in wholeness, holiness, and love.

Where total depravity was concerned Wesley certainly stood with the Reformers. The reason for Wesley having such a strong doctrine of total depravity was somewhat simple. Original sin was the doctrinal presupposition to personal sin and, more significantly, the new birth (Wesley 1985: 190). Hence the logicality of the sermon, 'Original Sin' preceding the sermon, 'The New Birth' in volume iv of *Sermons on Several Occasions* (1760). But by using the strongest language possible Taylor accused Wesley of having a depravity that was so total it seemed to despise humanity. When this charge was made by Taylor, Wesley argued, the cross was sufficient reason to deny God's despising depraved humanity, and cause enough for the children of God to love as they have been loved (Wesley 1757: 257; 1979: ix. 327).

In a well-known letter to John Newton dated 14 May 1765, Wesley indicated there was not a 'hair's breadth' separating him from Calvin (Wesley 1931: iv. 298). The hair's breadth was prevenient grace and was the constitutive nature of Wesley's theology that made it 'responsible' (Maddox 1994). In that respect, there was no such thing as a 'natural man', as everyone had a certain measure of prevenient grace. There are five benefits that a fallen humanity has from prevenient grace (Collins 1997: 40–5; 2007: 77–82). First, God restores a certain measure of free will to a fallen humanity to guarantee that a decision for good or evil, obedience or disobedience could be made (Wesley 1979: x. 229–30, 392). Secondly, the moral law as knowledge of God, God's will, and God's law, was reinscribed in order that all humankind may discern good from evil and right from wrong (Wesley 1985: 2, 6, 8, 9, 10, 13). Thirdly, implicit to this was a sense of 'natural conscience' which is not actually 'natural' but a supernatural gift from God (Wesley 1986: 482). Since the moral law is given as 'conscience' no one sins because one has no grace, but because one does not use the grace one has (ibid. 207). Fourthly, prevenient grace enables a universal human ability to know God that does not depend on special revelation, or natural theology. This enables humanity to know something of the attributes of God (Wesley 1985: 571). However, all the lights of natural theology and conscience combined produce only a faint twilight (Wesley 1987: 52–3). Finally, because prevenient grace entails a knowledge of good and evil, it is possible for one to do good works without them being considered 'splendid sins' on the one hand, or works with saving merit on the other (Wesley 1986: 400–14). It is not by one's inherent goodness that one acts in kindness, Christian or not. It is only by God's grace than any acts of mercy are done at all (Wesley 1987: 174–5). Prevenient grace is what enables a check on human perversity (Collins 1997: 43; 2007: 80).

The Fall and Christology, or Adam and Christ

As seen above, in knowing our disease we should also know our cure. Wesley saw a biblical and theological link between Adam and Christ, between original sin and Christology (Deschner 1960: 96–100). At one point Wesley stated in the *Doctrine of Original Sin*, 'Christianity lies properly in the knowledge of what concerns Adam and Christ' (Wesley 1757: 455; 1979: ix. 429). Wesley saw several connections between Christ and Adam. Two of them were Adam as a 'federal head' and the *felix culpa* tradition. These links served as connections between creation and redemption, the fall of Adam and the death of Christ, consequently creating an essential relationship between original sin and the 'scripture way of salvation'.

'THE HEAD OF ALL MANKIND'

To Wesley, Adam was the 'representative of mankind', or a 'federal head' (Wesley 1757: 266–70; 1979: ix. 332–4). His reasoning started with Christ as a representative of mankind and went back to Adam, who was seen as the prefiguration of Christ. In this link it was reckoned that if we were not ruined by the first Adam, who was the representative of humankind, neither can we be restored by the second Adam, who is Christ. Likewise, if we do not derive our corruption from Adam, neither do we derive our new nature from Christ (Wesley 1757: 453; 1979: ix. 428–9). Because Adam was a public person, or a federal head, his sin was imputed to all his posterity. But how is this sin imputed?

The image of God was created in Adam's soul. But it is also the soul that reproduces and replicates the image of a fallen humanity, void of the moral image and marred in the natural and political images. Wesley extracted Henry Woolnor's work (1641) as *The True Origin of the Soul* for publication in the *Arminian Magazine* (Woolnor 1783: 41–3 etc.). Here Wesley used traducianism as a way of explaining how humanity shares in the corruption of Adam without focusing on the guilt. He hypothesized that when Adam sinned he lost the moral image of God, while marring the political and natural image. Since like begets like, when he begot a son, the son was in the image of fallen Adam. The traduction of the soul is the traduction of a soul sick with original sin, marred and devoid of God's image. The soul became not just a constitutive part of personhood, but an essential way to account for the universality of original sin as well. The traduction of the soul was for Wesley a metaphysical explanation of an empirical observation. We are the way Adam became after the fall because we participated in body and soul, in both the guilt and consequences of Adam's sin (Wesley 1757: 266; 1979: ix. 332).

Here is the irony. Because of the cross, this fall was a 'happy fault'.

O FELIX CULPA

If God is all knowing, did God not see the fall? Wesley's reply was yes, God saw the fall. If God saw it, could God not have stopped it? Wesley's response was yes, it was in God's power to prevent it (Wesley 1985: 424). Why, then, did God permit evil? Wesley's answer—God saw that by allowing the fall it would be better for humankind in general. More good would come out of the fall than evil (ibid. 411). Because of Adam's sin, 'We may now attain both higher degrees of holiness and higher degrees of glory than it would have been possible for us to attain if Adam had not sinned. For if Adam had not sinned, the Son of God had not died' (ibid. 411). Wesley quite clearly, and rather adamantly, believed the fall of Adam produced the death of Christ. 'If God had prevented the fall of man, "the Word" had never been "made flesh"; nor had we ever "seen his glory, the glory as of the only-begotten of the Father". Those mysteries never had been displayed "which the very angels desire to look into"' (ibid. 433).

In short, *felix culpa* means God is to be praised for the fall, because as a result of the fall there was incarnation. Incarnation was the driving force behind what was almost a doxology for original sin. *Felix culpa* saw in the fall not just what humanity lost through Adam, but what humanity might gain through Christ. God alone could see the fall from the perspective of the cross. Regardless of the cause, whether Divine or human, *felix culpa* bound sin, incarnation, and salvation together for Wesley in an intra-doctrinal relationship, with incarnation as the consequence of sin, and salvation the consequence of incarnation. Salvation culminated in the renovation of the image of God in humankind.

SUMMARY

Wesley saw the doctrine of original sin as a biblical doctrine that found authentic and accurate expression through credal forms, Anglican and eventually Methodist. As a biblical doctrine, original sin was an essential part of the foundation of the Christian system, and he defended it through reason and experience. Among other things this doctrine meant human beings were originally created in the image of the triune God and consisted of political, natural, and moral aspects. Through disbelief and idolatry the first sin was committed resulting in the fall. As a result of the fall the political image was marred and the relationship between humanity and creation became dysfunctional. Through the marring of the natural image, understanding, will, and liberty were severely limited and curtailed while the relationship between body and soul also became dysfunctional. Through the lost moral image, the relationship between God and humanity became estranged, while relationships between humans became self-serving and dysfunctional. The spreading of original sin to all persons in all times was accounted for through Adam being a 'federal head' and the traduction of human souls. But for all this we should not blame the first humans, but give them our thanks, because if Adam had not sinned, Christ had not died. One may conclude that original sin was significantly relational for Wesley. It was concerned with the divine and human relationship, the inner-personal relationship, and inter-personal relationships. The moral, natural, and political images also provided Wesley with a doctrine of original sin that allowed him to talk about the attainability of Christian perfection in this lifetime as the renewal of the moral image of God. All this illustrated how Wesley tried to rethink the association of original sin with concupiscence, and how he came to see original sin as a way of explaining the corruption of original sin without focusing on its guilt.

METHODISTS AFTER WESLEY

Wesley identified the importance of original sin to the Christian system. Many other doctrines converge in original sin—the doctrines of God, creation, humanity, Christology, to name just a few. Consequently the doctrine of original sin may be seen as a barometer in Wesleyan and Methodist theology. It is particularly sensitive to the doctrinal pressures exerted on it from a variety of sources. For example, theologians since Wesley have had to deal with the pressure exerted by the connection between original sin and epistemology. Wesley's epistemology consisted of a 'sin-tainted reason' that placed limits on human understanding, something denied by the logical positivism of most rationalists (Long 2005: pp. xiv–xvi). Wesley's construction and defence of the doctrine was essentially based on a pre-Enlightenment epistemology making use of a theological methodology that was different. Theologians since Wesley have emphasized the role of reason differently (Chiles 1965: 39). Consequently, the same methodology often yields different theological results and original sin often becomes its casualty. The second pressure point exists between an Augustinian view of human corruption and an Arminian/Wesleyan emphasis on prevenient grace. If original sin is a casualty of epistemology and methodology, then the doctrine of grace can neither make nor need a reference to it. 'Methodism must perennially resist the inviting temptation prematurely to cover the scourge of sin with the solace of grace and, further, to attribute to (humankind) a capacity which properly belongs to grace' (ibid. 29). A third point arises when Methodist theology shifts the discussion from free grace to free will. Without original sin, what meaning does prevenient grace have? It sets out to solve a problem that no longer exists theologically. Without original sin and without prevenient grace, the theological conversation is moved along to a discussion of free will. The result of a doctrine of grace without original sin results in an understanding of free will and liberty that is essentially Pelagian. Fundamentally, what these points suggest is that original sin bears the pressure created by the relationship between nature and grace. When a Methodist theology of original sin yields to grace without first acknowledging fallen human nature it becomes the theology Wesley sought to oppose. Between these two there is a creative tension that does not demand that we sacrifice one doctrine for the other.

Suggested Reading

Collins (2007).

De Rosa, Peter (1967). *Christ and Original Sin.* Milwaukee: Bruce.

Domning, Daryl P., and Hellwig, Monika K. (2006). *Original Selfishness: Original Sin and Evil in the Light of Evolution.* Aldershot: Ashgate.

Dunning, H. Ray (1998). *Reflecting the Divine Image: Christian Ethics in a Wesleyan Perspective.* Downers Grove, Ill.: Intervarsity Press.

Jones, Scott J. (2002). *United Methodist Doctrine: The Extreme Center.* Nashville: Abingdon.

Leclerc (2001).

Long (2005).

References

Benezet, Anthony (1781). *Notes on the Slave Trade.* Philadelphia: s.n.

Campbell, Ted A. (1991). *John Wesley and Christian Antiquity.* Nashville: Kingswood.

Chiles, Robert E. (1965). *Theological Transitions in American Methodism: 1790–1935.* Lanham, Md.: University Press of America.

Church of England (1676). *Certain sermons, or homilies, to be read in churches in the time of Queen Elizabeth of famous memory.* London: Printed by T.R. for Samuel Mearne and for Robert Powlet.

—— (1767). *Certain sermons or homilies appointed to be read in churches in the time of Queen Elizabeth of famous memory. Together with the Thirty-nine Articles of Religion.* Dublin: William Whitestone.

Collins, Kenneth J. (1997). *The Scripture Way of Salvation: The Heart of John Wesley's Theology.* Nashville: Abingdon.

—— (2007). *The Theology of John Wesley: Holy Love and the Shape of Grace.* Nashville: Abingdon.

Deschner, John (1960). *Wesley's Christology: An Interpretation.* Grand Rapids: Francis Asbury Press.

Gunter, W. Stephen, and Jones, Scott J., et al. (1997). *Wesley and the Quadrilateral: Renewing the Conversation.* Nashville: Abingdon.

Leclerc, Diane (2001). *Singleness of Heart: Gender, Sin, and Holiness in Historical Perspective.* Lanham, Md.: Scarecrow.

Long, D. Stephen (2005). *John Wesley's Moral Theology: The Quest for God and Goodness.* Nashville: Kingswood.

Maddox, Randy (1994). *Responsible Grace: John Wesley's Practical Theology.* Nashville: Kingswood.

Runyon, Theodore (1998). *The New Creation: John Wesley's Theology Today.* Nashville: Abingdon.

Smith, Warren T. (1986). *John Wesley and Slavery.* Nashville: Abingdon.

Taylor, John (1740). *The Scripture-Doctrine of Original Sin Proposed to Free and Candid Examination. In three parts.* London: J. Wilson.

Weber, Theodore R. (2001). *Politics in the Order of Salvation: Transforming Wesleyan Political Ethics.* Nashville: Kingswood.

Wesley, John (1755). *Explanatory Notes upon the New Testament.* London: William Boyer.

—— (1756). *A Compendium of Logic.* 2nd edn. London: s.n.

—— (1757). *The Doctrine of Original Sin According to Scripture, Reason, and Experience.* Bristol: Farley.

—— (1760). *Sermons on Several Occasions.* London: The Foundery; Bristol: J. Grabham & W. Pine.

—— (1772a). *Thoughts Concerning the Origin of Power.* Bristol: Pine.

—— (1772b). *Thoughts upon Liberty.* Bristol: s.n.

—— (1774). *Thoughts upon Slavery.* London: Hawes.

—— (1776). *Some Observations on Liberty: Occasioned by a Late Tract.* London: Hawes.

—— (1777). *A Survey of the Wisdom of God in the Creation, or, A Compendium of Natural Philosophy.* 3rd edn. 5 vols. London: J. Fry.

—— (1784). *The Sunday Service of the Methodists in North America: With Other Occasional Services.* London: s.n.

—— (1931). *The Letters of the Rev. John Wesley, A.M.*, ed. John Telford. 8 vols. London: Epworth.

—— (1975). *Works*, xi. *The Appeals to Men of Reason and Religion and Certain Related Open Letters*, ed. Gerald R. Crag. Oxford: Clarendon.

—— (1979). *Works*, ed. Thomas Jackson. 3rd edn. 14 vols. Grand Rapids: Baker Book House.

—— (1984). *Works*, i. *Sermons I*, ed. Albert C. Outler. Nashville: Abingdon.

—— (1985). *Works*, ii. *Sermons II*, ed. Albert C. Outler. Nashville: Abingdon.

—— (1986). *Works*, iii. *Sermons III*, ed. Albert C. Outler. Nashville: Abingdon.

—— (1987). *Works*, iv. *Sermons IV*, ed. Albert C. Outler. Nashville: Abingdon.

Woolnor, Henry (1641). *The True Originall of the Soule: Proving by both divine and naturall reason, that the production of mans soule is neither by creation nor propagation, but a certain meane way between both: wherein the doctrine of originall sinne, and the purity of Christs incarnation, is also more fully cleared then hath been heretofore published*, ed. Elias Palmer. London: T. Paine & M. Symmons.

—— (1783). 'The True Original of the Soul', *Arminian Magazine* 6: 41–3, 96–8, 149–51, 208–10, 265–7, 321–3, 375–7, 431–5, 492–4, 544–7, 603–6, 664–7.

CHAPTER 31

WESLEYAN GRACE

MARJORIE SUCHOCKI

In John Wesley, as in most of the Christian tradition, grace refers primarily to that which God freely does for us in God's redemptive work. Wesley thought of God's redemptive grace as operating under three categories: prevenient, justifying, and sanctifying grace. The theme to be explored in this chapter is the necessity in the twenty-first century of broadening a Wesleyan understanding of grace to include the whole of God's activity, so that God's redemptive grace is seen to be but one form of God's all-encompassing creative grace. While Wesley himself felt no need to expand the notion of grace, his work gives ground for such a move. Indeed, in so far as Wesley reckoned with his own context in his theological development, so must we. As we do so, I am suggesting the necessity of considering grace as synonymous with all God's work, including creative as well as redemptive acts.

A supposition of this exploration is that the task of theology is not simply to repeat the past in contemporary language, but to incorporate into the tradition as much current knowledge of the world as is feasible. In every age such incorporation results in theological adaptation, whether through accretion, change, or simply nuance. Perhaps the strongest illustration of this would be Anselm of Canterbury's reworking of the 'how' of God's redemptive activity by adapting it to the feudal honour system, yielding what became known as the 'satisfaction theory of the atonement'. Surely Anselm depended upon prior understandings such as 'ransom from the devil' theories, but his own rephrasing of atonement changed soteriology for all subsequent history. He adapted the tradition he had received to his contemporary knowledge of the world, giving new power to the church. In time, of course, theologians responding to the tradition as shaped by Anselm and adapted his insights to accommodate their own perceptions, shaped in turn by their own time.

By no means do I mean to indicate with this brief illustration from soteriological history that the tradition is simple, yielding relatively uniform interpretations in every age; that would be foolish. And indeed, every Wesleyan scholar knows well that John Wesley's theology finds strands from many aspects of the tradition, eastern as well as western, Anglican as well as Moravian, pietistic as well as moralistic. Wesley, as much as Anselm, shaped his received tradition according to the way he understood his contemporary world. It falls to us who are Wesleyan in the twenty-first century to be thoroughly Wesleyan by following his example, and adapting the tradition we now receive through him to what we know of our world. Our own contributions will hardly be definitive—they will merely be grist for the mill of the continuously shaping theological work done by those who succeed us. My suggestion here is that major work must be done particularly in the area of grace. This requires first, a clear understanding of Wesley's way of developing grace; second, the contextual world-view in which Wesley put forth his doctrines; third, highlighting several major changes in the centuries since Wesley and recontextualizing a Wesleyan understanding of grace so that it describes the whole of God's work within the universe, including, but not limited to, that part of God's work that relates to salvation.

Summary: Redemptive Grace in Wesley

Wesley's theology is hardly static; it is dynamically shaped through his constant attention to the needs of the people who came to be called Methodist. Randy Maddox, in his excellent *Responsible Grace* (1994), explores the way Wesley's theology developed over his long career. But while nuances changed relative to grace, several things remain constant in Wesley. First, he understood grace to be enabling, but not enforcing. That is, grace makes human response to God possible, but grace does not determine that response. Second, he describes grace in its threefold application to the earthly experience of salvation, with a fourth application denoting glorification beyond our earthly death.

In many respects Wesley's understanding of the enabling function of grace owes much to his reading of the Greek fathers, but he goes beyond them in his understanding of prevenient grace. In broad strokes, the Greeks held that humans are free to choose the good, but require divine aid in order to actualize this choice. For example, Chrysostom writes: 'For it is necessary that we first choose the good, and when we have chosen it, then [God] also brings his part. He does not anticipate our wishes in order that our freedom may not be destroyed. But when we have chosen, then he brings great help to us...it is ours to choose beforehand and to will, but it is God's to accomplish, and lead to the result' (Seeberg 1966: 329). This contrasts with western modes of thought, epitomized by Augustine, who argued that because humanity is thoroughly corrupted in and through Adam's fall, we are no longer capable of choosing the good that makes for salvation. Doing so (e.g. turning to God) is at the same time the evidence of grace given to make that choice possible. Augustine's qualifier, of course, is that because grace is the action of God it must affect that which it offers. Grace, for Augustine, is determinative; it not only makes the choice of the good possible, it accomplishes that choice. God's grace cannot be ineffective; it must accomplish that which it offers. Ultimately, this view leads to the notion of God's predestination of some individuals for salvation, and others for damnation. If God's grace always accomplishes its object, and if some do not appear to participate in salvation, it must be because they have not received divine grace. Response as well as offer is the work of God, not humans.

Wesley is, in a sense, a via media between the eastern and western conceptions of grace. With the Augustinian, western conception, he holds that God must initiate the act of salvation for each individual, but with the Greeks he holds to the efficacy of human response. Grace makes a response to God's offer possible, but it does not force that response. There is an essential freedom to the creature; for Wesley, this freedom is itself God-given—he calls it 'supernatural' in his writings to the Calvinists (Wesley 1872: x. 230). But it means that how the creature responds to God's grace is up to the creature. A positive response is possible, because it is enabled by grace, but a negative response is also possible, because of the creature's capacity to reject that enablement. What results in a positive response, of course, is a synergism of divine initiative and human freedom.

Wesley differs here from the eastern tradition as represented by Chrysostom, in so far as that tradition in effect made human choice the initiating factor, with God's grace enabling the results of that choice. And he differs from the western tradition as represented by Augustine in so far as that tradition viewed grace as determining human response. For Augustine, this was a necessary move, since he considered the human capacity to turn towards God and the things of God to be totally lost in Adam's fall. While Wesley, too, thought that the origin of human sin was occasioned by the corruption of human nature through the fall of a first parent, God's grace can penetrate this corruption, enabling a genuine human assent to grace: 'although I have not an absolute power over my own mind, because of the corruption of my own nature; yet, through the grace of God assisting me, I have a power to choose and do good, as well as evil' (ibid. vii. 228–9). Freedom is thus embraced, not annihilated, by grace.

The purpose of grace is to restore the image of God that was lost through the corruption of human nature consequent upon Adam's fall. Restoration of God's image, in turn, involves repentance of sin through prevenient grace, pardon for sin through justifying grace, and growth in love through sanctifying grace. These three modes are not different 'graces'—each is the adaptation of God's grace to the particular need of the human creature. Grace connotes the bending of God to meet our need, and our deepest need is restoration to God's image. The ground of grace is the very nature of God as unbounded love, manifested in the work of God through incarnation, crucifixion, and resurrection.

All grace leading up to the moment of acceptance of salvation is prevenient, taking place as God stirs the waters of one's soul through the gradual or sudden conviction of one's need for God's pardon. Prevenient grace makes possible not only a knowledge of one's sinful condition, but also repentance. This grace is both mediated and direct, for God's gracious activity takes place through the community and through ordinances of grace, as well as directly upon the soul. Preaching, conversation, holy example, prayer, sacraments, and the community itself become means through which God leads persons to recognize their embroilment in sin and their need for God's pardon. Their need is both corporate and individual—corporately, they participate in fallen human nature; individually, they have actualized evil through intentional and unintentional sin. And sin itself is always the violation of love to God and neighbour.

Awakened by grace to acknowledgment and repentance, the sinner is led to accept God's pardon based on God's own incarnate act in Christ. Grace now becomes justifying grace, the communication of God's pardon and its cleansing effects in the soul. The repentant sinner opens him- or herself to receive God's pardoning grace, which is at the same time justification. Here Wesley differs from the sixteenth-century Reformers by rejecting any sense of an 'alien righteousness' whereby the sinner is seen by God as covered by Christ's righteousness. 'Least of all does justification imply, that God is deceived in those whom he justifies; that he thinks them to be what, in fact, they are not; that he accounts them to be otherwise than they are. . . . The judgment of the all-wise God is always according to truth . . . he can no more . . . confound me with Christ, than with David or Abraham' (Wesley 1975–: i. 188). Rather, justification is God's pardon granted to the sinner, which is a cleansing that prepares the way for the sinner to be renewed in God's image. This renewal is participation in the love of God, which is at the same time an enabling call to righteousness. Luther also, of course, expected those who were clothed in Christ's 'alien righteousness' to grow in conformation to righteousness, but Luther depicts God as seeing Christ's righteousness covering the sinner. Wesley depicts God as seeing the repentant and cleansed sinner as precisely that—not covered with an imputed righteousness, but prepared for the sanctifying grace through which renewal in God's image can now happen. Just as in prevenient grace, the Christian is called to cooperate with grace—it is no automatic process, but a practice of loving that itself is enabled by God, and enacted by the Christian. In and through this work and response to sanctifying grace, God's end in creation—conforming the person to the love of God—is constantly in the process of fulfilment.

Sanctifying grace follows from justifying grace. Wesley termed the results of our positive response to sanctifying grace 'Christian perfection', by which he meant no more and no less than participating in the love of God. There are two senses to this: on the one hand, we are embraced by God's love, and in that embrace our own love for God is evoked. Second, since God's love is towards all creation, our participating in the love of and for God necessarily involves us in loving that which God loves. This, of course, is not simply oneself or those like oneself, but all creation. Hence, Christian perfection involves love of God and neighbour. Wesley puts it most succinctly towards the close of his 'A Plain Account of Christian Perfection': 'One of the principal rules of religion is, to lose no occasion of serving God. And, since he is invisible to our eyes, we are to serve him in our neighbour; which he receives as if done to himself in person, standing visibly before us' (Wesley 1872: xi. 440).

It is precisely because salvation involves participation in the love of and for God that Wesley insists upon works of love as essential to a living faith. He totally rejects the dichotomy between faith and works developed in Reformation thinking. For Wesley these are inseparable without, in any way, entailing the 'works righteousness' so feared by the Reformers. For Wesley grace brings about the possibility of a saving faith that trusts in God's pardon for sin, which then clears the way for the renewal in God's image that salvation is all about. And the renewal in God's image is, precisely, a participation in the love of God that is exercised in works of piety and mercy. It is a contradiction in terms, then, to imagine a faith without works of love. Since it is grace that enables the whole process—repentance, justification, sanctification—the whole of Christian life is a work of grace. It is foolishness to quibble about who gets credit for which part of salvation, since it is always God's grace that enables human response in each and every stage of the process of salvation.

Justifying and sanctifying grace, fully as much as prevenient grace, involve both God's direct action on the soul and means given through the community. With regard to God's direct action, Wesley held that in addition to our five physical senses of sight, sound, smell, taste, and touch, we are endowed by God with a spiritual sense, which is the capacity to experience God's direct influence upon us: 'there is a whole system of things which are not seen, which cannot be discerned by any of our outward senses, I mean, the spiritual world, understanding thereby the kingdom of God in the soul of man' (Wesley 1975– : iv. 34). Such spiritual sense is the means whereby we have the 'witness of the Spirit' convincing us directly of God's pardoning and sanctifying grace applied to our own soul. We are by virtue of God's gracious creation capable of experiencing God's love for us; hence God's grace can work directly on the soul.

Because God's grace flows from God's nature, and because God's nature is love, grace is also mediated through the community of God's people. This is entirely fitting, since the grace of God is the communication of the love of God, and love is no solitary thing. Hence the means God uses to arouse and enable human response include the Christian community's own living out of God's love, as well as those ordained sacraments that directly pull the believer into participation in God's supreme act of love, the atoning work of Christ.

The communal means of grace are first of all the sacraments, which pull the person and the community into participation in God's act of redemption in Christ. Baptism, like circumcision, incorporates the baptized one into the community of faith through identity with Christ; holy communion becomes participation in the crucifixion of Christ in and with the body of Christ, which is the church. The preached word and words of holy conversation illumine, convict, and encourage the Christian on the journey; prayer opens the soul directly to the gracious guidance of God, and also provides the means to participate directly in God's love through intercession; studying the Scriptures instructs and guides in the ways of God; class meetings provide the communal discipline of experiencing and participating in holy love.

In so far as Wesley extends the means of grace beyond the sacraments, he conveys the sense that God is constantly working with us towards our reflection of the divine image. In a sense, God leaves no stone unturned that will increase our capacity to love. The very provision of multiple means of grace is a call through the whole of Christian life to respond to grace, to act out our faith in the works that clothe our faith, and indeed ourselves, in the stuff of love. We are called and enabled by grace to become loving creatures. This loving is both a participation in the love that flows from God towards us and all creatures, and the generation of love in us, mingling in its own small way with the love of God towards extending the image of God through all creation.

The whole of this process is gracious, culminating finally in glorifying grace, the eschatological fulfilment of participation in God. Growth in our capacity to love is not a thing that ends with our death; rather, it is a process that turns our finite participation in God's love into everlasting participation in God's love. Throughout Christian life, our works of love are offered to God, received by God, purified by God. Following this life, we ourselves are received by God, there to participate everlastingly in God's infinite love.

Wesley gives a precursor towards our own eschatological glorification in the final pages of 'A Plain Account of Christian Perfection'. He has been discussing the paradox of works: by grace we do works of piety and mercy, and these works reflect the power of sanctification. They follow from our integrated response to God's enablement. Because grace calls us to an actual transformation of character, these works stem from the process of our renewal in God's image. Hence these works are our grace-enabled own. Since Wesley recognizes the need for our continual assent to grace, he also recognizes our capacity to veer from this assent. Thus a real temptation within the process of sanctification is to take pride in the actual works of love that we do—which of course is to taint these works of love. The antidote to such a sin is continually to offer all our works to God, so that works themselves become a prayer of thanksgiving to God for the enabling grace that allows our works in every moment. It is in imagining the flight of these works to God that Wesley gives a foretaste of glorifying grace. The passage is thus:

> Good works do not receive their last perfection, till they, as it were, lose themselves in God. This is a kind of death to them, resembling that of our bodies, which will not attain their highest life, their immortality, till they lose themselves in the glory of our souls, or rather of God, wherewith they shall be filled. And it is only what they had of earthly and mortal, which good works lose by this spiritual death.
>
> Fire is the symbol of love; and the love of God is the principle and the end of all our good works. But truth surpasses figure; and the fire of divine love has this advantage over material fire, that it can re-ascend to its source, and raise thither with it all the good works which it produces. And by this means it prevents their being corrupted by pride, vanity, or any evil mixture. But this cannot be done otherwise than by making these good works in a spiritual manner die in God, by a deep gratitude, which plunges the soul in him as in an abyss, with all that it is, and all the grace and works for which it is indebted to him; a gratitude, whereby the soul seems to empty itself of them, that they may return to their source, as rivers seem willing to empty themselves, when they pour themselves with all their waters into the sea.
>
> (Wesley 1872: xi. 441)

While this passage deals particularly with works rising like incense to God, it intimates the finality of salvation in sanctifying grace. By grace we are renewed in the image of God throughout Christian life; death is hardly the end of the process. To participate in the love of God is to participate in God's eternity, for God's essential nature is love. It is unthinkable, then, that God's love has a terminus in our death. To the contrary, death becomes our own 'plunging of the soul in him as in an abyss'. Glorifying grace effects the Christian's transition from perfecting the image of God in life to participation in the fullness of God in eternity: image becomes reality. Thus the process of salvation can be said to 'begin' in the eternal nature of God; to be experienced in the call to repentance from and pardon for sin; to be progressively realized in our conformation to the image of God; and, finally, to culminate in our unmediated incorporation into the eternity of God. Temporality is transformed into everlastingness. The whole is a work of grace, beginning, continuing, and everlastingly expressing the nature of God in interaction with God's creatures.

WESLEY'S SUPPOSITIONS

Original Sin

Basic to Wesley's development of grace is his understanding of precisely why we need grace. Here he follows the basic assumption of the Christian tradition that to be human is to participate in a corruption generated by Adam's fall. Unlike much of the tradition, he does not consider humans guilty of Adam's sin—that actually is unnecessary. It is enough that the nature inherited through Adam no longer reflects the image of God. Adam is the natural head of the human race, so that in his fall, human nature itself becomes corrupted. The clear understanding belonging originally to Adam before the fall gave way to minds that are weak and fallible, so that 'it is as natural to mistake as to breathe; and [we] can no more live without the one than the other' (ibid. 415). In place of the right ordering of affections, governed by love to God and all creatures, our affections are disordered, tending toward self-interest. In place of a body that works perfectly as the vehicle of right thinking and right affections, we are subject to misery and death. Wesley also assumes that death enters into all earthly existence through Adam's sin, spreading like a disease infecting all aspects of creaturely life. Because of Adam's corruption, all things die.

Already in Wesley's day questions were raised about the historicity of Adam: 'the whole body of Christians in all ages, did suppose this, till after seventeen hundred years a sweet-tongued orator arose, not only more enlightened than silly Adam, but than any of his wise posterity, and declared that the whole supposition was folly, nonsense, inconsistence, and blasphemy' (ibid. ix. 291). The value of Adam historically was not only to offer an account for why humans are so given to evil, but also to protect a view of God that requires an original goodness to that which God creates. If humans are flawed in their original creation, are they still accountable for their sins? And if God creates that which is flawed, how is creation still pronounced 'good'? Later philosophers and theologians, such as Immanuel Kant and Freidrich Schleiermacher, work with such questions, but for Wesley they were still marginal. Contemporary Wesleyans must work answers to the questions into their theologies. It remains to be considered how different assumptions concerning the origin of evil affect the understanding of prevenient, justifying, and sanctifying grace.

World-View

As are we all, Wesley was a person of his own time, reflecting dominant perceptions of the nature of the world and its place in the universe. His curiosity was unbounded, evidenced in his fascination with the nature of electricity, the healing or harming properties of plants, and the span of creation from inorganic to organic (Haas 1995: 234). He read extensively in the available sciences, and while he was initially sceptical of Isaac Newton's work, he came to acknowledge and appreciate its importance. In all of this, he is deeply convinced that whatever might be found in nature will conform to that which we know through biblical revelation, and he read the first chapters of Genesis as genuine accounts of the origin of earth and the creation of human beings.

There is a curious tension in Wesley's works between his acknowledgement of the immensity of the universe and the fallibility of human knowledge, and his certainty concerning applying biblical apocalyptic images to the universe. With regard to the immensity of the universe, he writes:

What is the magnitude of the earth itself, compared to that of the solar system? Including, beside that vast body, the sun, so immensely larger than the earth, the whole train of primary and secondary planets; several of which (I mean, of the secondary planets, suppose the satellites or moons of Jupiter and Saturn) are abundantly larger than the whole earth?

And yet, what is the whole quantity of matter contained in the sun, and all those primary and secondary planets, with all the spaces comprised in the solar system, in comparison of that which is pervaded by those amazing bodies, the comets? Who but the Creator himself can 'tell the number of these, and call them all by their names'?

. . . if, then, we add to the littleness of man the inexpressible shortness of his duration, is it any wonder that a man of reflection should sometimes feel a kind of fear, lest the great, eternal, infinite Governor of the universe should disregard so diminutive a creature as man?

(Wesley 1872: vii. 168–70)

In this same article he refers to the works of Newton and Huygens, considering their discoveries and judgements as expansions of that which we know of God's works through Scripture. In another, but similar vein, he writes a treatise in which he considers the reasons why moisture forms on the inside of carriage windows (ibid. xi. 526)! But if Wesley can refer to what was current scientific knowledge with regard to the growing understanding of the universe, he can also blatantly contradict that knowledge. In 'The Cause and Cure of Earthquakes' he unequivocally argues that sin is the moral cause of earthquakes. 'Sin is the cause, earthquakes the effect, of [God's] anger' (ibid. vii. 387). Likewise, when musing on 'The New Creation', he speaks of comets as 'those horrid, eccentric orbs . . . half-formed planets in a chaotic state' (ibid. vi. 290). These will certainly have no place in a new heaven, where all such disorder will be replaced with order and harmony.

But he also plainly holds to the fallibility of human knowledge. Repeatedly in 'A Plain Account of Christian Perfection' as well as in other writings (ibid. 337–50) he insists that our intellectual capacities are damaged by the corruption of our nature, and that Christian perfection does not eliminate this damage (ibid. and 350–60). Christian perfection has to do with the perfection of love, not knowledge. In 'The Imperfection of Human Knowledge' he writes, 'But although our desire of knowledge has no bounds, yet our knowledge itself has. It is, indeed, confined within very narrow bounds; abundantly narrower than common people imagine, or men of learning are willing to acknowledge' (ibid. 337). While Wesley writes, therefore, in relative confidence about the nature of the earth and its place in the universe, he is emendable in so far as our knowledge of earth becomes more accurate. His own certainty concerning the compatibility of Scripture and science would undoubtedly tend towards his resistance should he consider a contradiction entailed. The hermeneutical findings since his time might leaven that resistance.

The Omnipresence of God

Wesley holds to the three traditional attributes of omnipotence, omniscience, and omnipresence of God, but of these three, omnipresence is particularly important with regard to grace. Omnipresence is allied to the eternity of God; 'as he exists through infinite duration, so he cannot but exist through infinite space' (Wesley 1975– : iv. 61). God's omnipresence is active, not passive, so that '[God] is the only agent in the material world, all matter being essentially dull and inactive, and moving only as it is moved by the finger of God. And he is the spring of action in every creature, visible and invisible, which could neither act nor exist, without the continual influx and agency of his almighty power' (ibid. i. 581).

In discussing creation, Wesley does not specifically refer to the omnipresence of God. Rather, he frames the notion of God as creator and as governor. But there is a strong correlation between his suggestion that God is 'the spring of action in every creature' (ibid. 581) and his understanding of the creative and governing power of God. As creator, God brings the world into existence, according to God's pleasure. As governor, God exercises providential justice both in the present and the eschatological world. Both creating and governing assume God's omnipresence, God's intimate knowledge of all that is. Omniscience follows from omnipresence, and omnipotence expresses God's omnipresence.

WESLEYAN CREATIVE GRACE

Genetic and biological probings into the stuff of creaturely existence suggest that in many respects we have gone far beyond Darwin's initial evidence for evolution. We have supplemented his 'natural selection' argument with chemical data concerning the teeming interrelational aspects of all existence, and the emergence of new forms from old (Ackerman 2001). Everything that lives has emerged from predecessor beings, with remarkable structural similarities pervading all earthly life. Human beings are indeed specialized and highly complex forms of life, but we are hardly alien to all other forms. All of life is interrelated.

Exploring the past history of life through its genetic traces yields fascinating data relative to the emergence of human beings. As in the story of Genesis, all human life descends from an original human being, but that original being was female, not male, and emergent from earlier forms, not singular. Genetic studies suggest that human replication first occurred parthogenetically, and later through sexual differentiation, eventually leading to the complexity of the human species as we know it today (ibid. 113–14).

The theological import of such studies forces a reconceptualization of the origins of sin, evil, and the corruption of human nature, which of course entails further consideration of how we understand the grace of God. The notion of Adam and his fall from grace no longer accounts for evil. As was noted above, the historicity of Adam was already becoming problematic in the eighteenth century, and in the nineteenth century Schleiermacher responded by positing something similar to God's creation through evolution. He suggested that humans evolved physiologic-ally prior to their attaining the capacity for spiritual existence. Physiological survival depended upon self and kin protection, which in turn depended upon modes of violence. But, suggested Schleiermacher, in the long process of evolution God influences humankind to the point where spiritual existence is possible, and spiritual existence is defined as going beyond self and kin protection, to acting according to the interdependence of all humankind and the absolute dependence of all upon God. The paradox is that as soon as humans become capable of spiritual existence, they know their previous forms of self-oriented existence as sin. But physiological existence has a 'head start' as it were, entangling habits of action and intent that must be turned completely around in order to achieve the spirituality to which God calls us. Humanity is caught in sin and corruption in the very moment that it is capable of sensing its call to transformation into spiritual existence. Spiritual existence, in its turn, is not the repudiation of physiological existence, but the taking up of the physiological into the spiritual, so that spirituality governs all thought and action. The parallel here with Wesley's understanding of Christian perfection is clear, and I am suggesting that a resolution akin to Schleiermacher's is possible within the principles of Wesley's understanding of grace, adapted to the complexity of creation as we now know it.

The issue requires a deeper consideration of how the omnipresence of God is related to grace. When Wesley discusses God as creator, he has the sovereign will of God in view, which accounts for the detailed existence of all things in the universe. He differentiates that sovereignty from God's governance, which involves justice. This differentiation lies behind Wesley's view of the atonement, associating it primarily with God's governance. God's action in Christ satisfies the justice of God, making the way for pardon and the renewal of creation. It is here that prevenient grace takes hold, operating to urge humankind towards readiness for this renewal. The renewal itself, then, connects again with God as sovereign creator, for it is the correction of creation, the coalescence of sovereignty and governance in the righting of wrong. And this process is the application of grace to creation.

If sovereignty and governance be considered in the light of Wesley's view of God's omnipresence, then the distinction between them is muted. It is God's pervasive presence to every creature throughout the universe that is also at the same time God's omniscience, God's knowledge of everything that is exactly as it is. This conforms to Wesley's insistence that in justifying the sinner, God sees the sinner precisely as he or she is; there is no covering of the sinner as if God sees

Christ instead of the sinner. God is omnipresent; knowing all things as they are with a perfect knowledge, knowing things even more thoroughly than they know themselves.

But this omnipresent knowing is not something that happens after creation is launched in some God-determined past. On the contrary, creation itself comes into being in response to the call of God. We must conclude that God creates by calling existence into being bit by bit, moment by moment, calling it or driving it through emergent processes into ever more complex forms of being, according to the parameters of the whole as well as the parameters of each creature's locality. The universe, greater even than was possible to imagine in Wesley's day, is an immeasurably vast network of dynamic motion. And the omnipresent God pervades the whole, creatively guiding its becoming. The process would be similar to what Wesley says of God's redemptive grace: the omnipresent God is present to the creature, enabling a response that will allow the creature to act in accordance with God's gracious touch. But this is how creation itself happens. God brings a responsive universe into being; God creates by calling into existence creatures who can—acting on that call—create themselves. God always acts graciously because it is the nature of God so to act.

If creative grace encompasses the sovereignty of God in creation, it also entails the justice that obtains in the governance of God, and in the justifying and sanctifying modes of grace. Wesley writes a version of the *o felix culpa* of earlier Christian history when he says:

If Adam had not sinned, the Son of God had not died; Consequently that amazing instance of the love of God to man had never existed, which has, in all ages, excited the highest joy, and love, and gratitude from his children. We might have loved God the Creator, God the Preserver, God the Governor; but there would have been no place for love to God the Redeemer.   (Wesley 1975– : ii. 411–12)

But if God creates through emergent evolution, then something akin to Schleiermacher's understanding of the need for redemption holds. Scientist Robert M. Hazen (2005: 17) says, 'Our emergence most likely occurred through a sequence of steps: the synthesis of simple organic molecules, then the assembly of macromolecules. Eventually, an evolving, self-replicating collection of macromolecules emerged. Each of these stages added some degree of chemical and structural complexity.' Such an astonishing mode of creation is fraught with challenges. If God always acts with enabling grace, evoking responses from each becoming existent reality, and then working with what those responses actually are, then there is need enough for redemptive grace, need enough for justice as well as sovereignty. Schleiermacher's intuition that the physiological precedes the spiritual, and that the physiological is driven primarily by the need for survival of oneself and one's kind, appears to be congruent with current understandings of the emergence of life on earth. In this case, creative grace must also include redemptive grace if

God's will for creation to mirror the divine image is to occur in any measure at all, and redemptive grace must be a specialized mode of creative grace. If God is omnipresent, adapting grace to the needs of the creature, then grace must be creative and redemptive.

What Wesley calls prevenient grace is creative grace, specially considered. It refers to the fullness through which God knows the creature, and therefore the specificity with which God can guide the creature. This includes the creative emergence into complex modes of existence such as ourselves, and the capacity to recognize the requirements of love. This in turn requires the capacity to recognize when love is not served, when sin mars and marks one's being. For Wesley, justifying grace is pardon for sins, the freeing from the chains of bondage to restricted arenas of love. In Schleiermacher's version of this grace, God not only interacts with existence, but enters incarnationally into existence in order to enact the creaturely fulfilment of the divine image. Because this divine action occurs in a totally interdependent world, it influences all things in the world. For Wesley as well, it is God's own self present in Christ; God participating directly in our plight, remedying it not only through example, but also through justice: experiencing the deadly effects of evil in crucifixion, overcoming evil in resurrection. For Schleiermacher, God's action in Christ, in an interdependent world, reverberates throughout creation, making the transformation into spiritual existence possible. In Wesley, God's act in Christ is necessarily universal, since it is the act of the omnipresent God, who is active throughout the universe. Justice exposes the deathliness of all that is contrary to the love of God, overcoming it in resurrection. Since this is an action of God, it becomes a universal basis for pardoning grace.

Wesley teeters on the edges of making this grace available to those beyond Christianity. 'The Imperfection of Human Knowledge' offers an extended question concerning the effect of God's providence in those vast portions of the earth that do not have access to the holiness available through Christ. 'We know', he writes, 'the Lord is loving unto every man, and his mercy is over all his works. But we know not how to reconcile this with the present dispensations of his providence' (Wesley 1975– : ii. 344). If everything God does for creaturely existence is a work of grace, and if God's omnipresence suggests that every localized action of God has universal implications, then God's redemptive work anywhere is of import everywhere. This may in fact intimate the reconciliation Wesley requires. By understanding grace to be basic to all God's actions, so that God everlastingly offers good to every aspect of creation whatever its condition, then the tension is eased.

We are a part of a world that is constantly in the process of emergence. The drive towards complexity that marks our existence is itself the gracious work of God, ever calling us into being, ever calling us to repentance from our sin, ever calling us to accept God's pardon, ever calling us to deeper forms of living according to the love of God. Everything that God does is a work of grace, expressing the divine nature, adapting divine love to the circumstances and capacities of the creature. Because every adaptation reflects the love of God, and because the love of God always contains judgement against that which violates love, justice is included in this adaptation. Thus the creative grace of God that calls us—and all things—into existence includes the dimensions of redemptive grace within it. The ground of pardon, the call to repentance, the possibility of conformity to God's call in the particularity of place and circumstance, is embraced within the creative grace of God. Creative grace enfolds redemptive grace, manifesting and expressing the omnipresent God.

SUGGESTED READING

COBB, JOHN B., JR. (1995). *Grace and Responsibility.* Nashville: Abingdon.

MADDOX, RANDY (1994). *Responsible Grace.* Nashville: Abingdon.

MANSKAR, STEVE (2004). *A Perfect Love: Understanding John Wesley's A Plain Account of Christian Perfection.* Nashville: Discipleship Resources.

SCHLEIERMACHER, FREIDRICH (1963). *The Christian Faith.* 2 vols. New York: Harper.

STONE, BRYAN P., and OORD, THOMAS JAY (eds.) (2001). *Thy Nature and Thy Name is Love: Wesleyan and Process Theologies in Dialogue.* Nashville: Abingdon.

REFERENCES

ACKERMAN, JENNIFER (2001). *Chance in the House of Fate: A Natural History of Heredity.* Boston: Houghton Mifflin.

HAAS, J. W., JR. (1995). 'John Wesley's Vision of Science in the Service of Christ'. *Perspectives on Science and Christian Faith* 47 (December).

HAZEN, ROBERT M. (2005). *Origins of Life.* Chantilly, Va.: The Teaching Company.

MADDOX, RANDY (1994). *Responsible Grace.* Nashville: Abingdon.

SEEBERG, R. (1966). *Textbook of the History of Doctrines.* Ann Arbor: Baker.

WESLEY, JOHN (1872). *The Works of John Wesley, A.M.; with the last Corrections of the Author,* ed. Thomas Jackson. 3rd edn. 14 vols. London: Wesleyan Conference Office.

—— (1975–). *The Bicentennial Edition of the Works of John Wesley* 34 vols. Nashville: Abingdon.

CHAPTER 32

CHRISTOLOGY

JASON E. VICKERS

In classical and contemporary systematic theology, it is customary to subdivide Christology into four areas. These areas include the person of Christ, the work of Christ, the offices of Christ, and the states of Christ. While each of these areas is important in its own right, some areas clearly take precedence over others. Most notably, the person of Christ merits special consideration above and beyond the other areas of Christology.

There are at least two good reasons for giving priority to the person of Christ. First, the other areas of Christology supervene on prior judgements about the person of Christ. This is clearly the case, for example, with the work of Christ. How Christ makes atonement for the sins of the world depends on prior judgements about the person of Christ. Similarly, theological reflection on the states of Christ (humiliation and exaltation), obviously trades on prior commitments concerning the person of Christ.

The second reason the person of Christ merits priority over the other areas of Christology has to do with the ecumenical canon of doctrine. At no stage has the ecumenical church canonized specific doctrines of the atonement, the offices of Christ, or the states of Christ. By contrast, the ecumenical councils of Nicaea (AD 325) and Chalcedon (AD 451) did canonize doctrines related to the person of Christ, affirming the fullness of Christ's divinity, the fullness of Christ's humanity, and the unity of Christ's person. The resulting Christological dogmas were enshrined in the Nicene Creed and Chalcedonian Definition and have served across the centuries as a benchmark or touchstone for Christology.

Given its logical and canonical priority, the person of Christ will be the primary focus of enquiry in this chapter. What have Methodists said about the person of

Christ across the years? What have Methodists taught concerning the fullness of Christ's humanity, the fullness of Christ's divinity, and the unity of Christ's person? What role, if any, have the Nicene Creed and Chalcedonian Definition played in the history of Methodist Christology? How have Methodist theologians viewed the Christological dogmas embedded in the ecumenical creeds and endorsed repeatedly by the great ecumenical councils?

THE EIGHTEENTH CENTURY: DEFENDING THE DIVINITY OF CHRIST

By the standards of Nicaea and Chalcedon, early Methodist Christology can appear theologically suspect. The chief issue has to do with John Wesley's purported beliefs concerning the humanity of Christ. Not a few theologians question whether the founder of Methodism held heterodox views of Christ's humanity. For example, some theologians suggest that Wesley embraced *monophysitism*, a doctrine according to which Christ's human nature is entirely absorbed by Christ's divine nature. Others go so far as to suspect Wesley of *docetism*, a doctrine that says that Christ only appeared to have a human nature (Collins 2007: 92–5; Maddox 1994: 310 n. 123).

What evidence is there that John Wesley was either a monophysite or a docetist? The crucial evidence does not take the form of explicit assertions denying the humanity of Jesus. In fact, Wesley nowhere makes such assertions. Rather, the crucial evidence has to do with Wesley's work as an editor and as a biblical commentator (Maddox 1994: 115–16). As an editor, Wesley sometimes eliminated statements about Jesus' humanity (Campbell 1991: 81). As a biblical commentator, he often downplayed or explained away passages that attributed human emotions to Jesus. At the same time, Wesley persistently emphasized the divinity or deity of Jesus (Deschner 1985: 60). Some historians and theologians conclude that this evidence strongly suggests that Wesley at least had *monophysite* or *docetic* inclinations. For some reason, Wesley was reluctant to emphasize the humanity of Christ.

What might help to explain Wesley's reluctance openly to affirm the fullness of Christ's human nature? Eighteenth-century England was home to an entire range of Christological heterodoxies, including Arianism, Socinianism or Unitarianism, and Deism. These heterodoxies challenged, modified, or rejected the divinity of Christ. Few, if any, questioned whether Jesus was truly human. On the contrary, many theologians in Wesley's day stressed the humanity or created nature of Christ over against the notion of Christ's eternal sonship.

Given the growing popularity of these Christological heterodoxies in eighteenth-century England, it is not surprising that Wesley stressed the divinity of Christ. Nor is it especially perplexing that he sometimes downplayed Christ's human nature. There was, after all, no shortage of persons emphasizing Jesus' humanity. Thus it is reasonable to suppose that Wesley and other early Methodists were simply responding to what they perceived to be a major theological problem of their age. Conversely, speculation on the part of twentieth- and twenty-first-century Methodist theologians about John Wesley's supposed *monophysitism* may say more about their concerns and contexts than about his.

The foregoing explanation for Wesley's purported reservations about the humanity of Christ is not without evidence. In the latter third of the eighteenth century, Wesley was deeply concerned about the popularity of Joseph Priestley's publications opposing Christ's divinity. Lacking time to compose a response to Priestley, Wesley urged John Fletcher (d. 1785) to do so. Unfortunately, Fletcher died before he could complete the assignment. At the request of Wesley and Fletcher's widow, Joseph Benson (d. 1821) completed the work, publishing a two-part treatise addressed to Priestley and a series of letters to John Wesley in which he defended the divinity of Christ (Fletcher 1833).

Fletcher and Benson's joint defence of the divinity of Christ constitutes the first major prose work devoted exclusively to Christology in the Methodist tradition. Unfortunately, subsequent generations of Methodist theologians have rarely commented on this insightful work in Christology. Consequently, it deserves special consideration here.

Theologians in late seventeenth- and eighteenth-century England who set out to defend the Trinity and the divinity of Christ often did so by attempting to demonstrate the compatibility between these doctrines and varying accounts of reason. Some attempted to show that the divinity of Christ and the Trinity were compatible with an Aristotelian account of reason, while others preferred either Cartesian or Lockean accounts (Vickers 2008). Fletcher and Benson did not take this route. Instead, they appealed directly and unapologetically to the grammar or internal logic of Christianity itself. The notion of the grammar or internal logic of the Christian faith is today widely associated with the theology of Hans Frei, Paul Holmer, George Lindbeck, and Bruce D. Marshall. However, post-liberal theology does not invent a new way of doing theology so much as recover a way of doing theology rooted in the ante-Nicene and Nicene Fathers. Both this two-part treatise and the letters to Wesley consist almost entirely of grammatical or logical analyses of Scripture, baptism and the eucharist, and the church's prayers and worship.

For Fletcher and Benson, Christ's divinity is the essential hermeneutical presupposition that renders intelligible four vital components of Christian faith and practice. Apart from Christ's divinity, they argue, Scripture, baptism, worship, and the Christian understanding of salvation are all unintelligible. For example, Benson observes that, 'when opened with Dr. Priestley's key, and interpreted according to his doctrine', the Scriptures 'appear to be so absurd, that...no person pretending to common sense would have written them' (Fletcher 1833: iii. 605). From Benson's perspective, so many passages of Scripture are 'ridiculous' when read with Unitarian presuppositions that either 'the authors of them were not Unitarians', or they were lacking 'in *common sense*' (ibid.).

Fletcher and Benson clearly understood what was at stake in the debate with Priestley and the Unitarians. If Christians were wrong about Christ's divinity, then they were guilty of idolatry. If they were right, however, then Priestley and the Unitarians were guilty of impiety, which is to say, failing to worship one who is truly God. Fletcher writes,

Hence it appears that idolatry and impiety are the two precipices between which the Christian's road lies all the way to heaven. Dr. Priestley supposes that we are fallen into the former; and we fear that he and his admirers rush into the latter. Let us see who are mistaken. It is one of the most important questions that was ever debated. Either we are idolators in worshipping that which by nature is not God, or the Socinians are impious in refusing Divine worship to that which is really God; and what is more dreadful still, they worship a mangled notion of Deity, and not the God revealed to us in the sacred Scriptures.   (ibid. 447)

Finally, in a move that resembles the logic of the Nicene fathers in the fourth century, Benson argues that, if Christ is not divine, then Christians are not saved. He says,

If Jesus Christ . . . be but a mere man, it is certain his life must be of incomparably less value than this eternal salvation of all mankind, thus said to be procured by it. For however holy and excellent we may suppose him to be yet his life could not be worth the lives of all men—especially his temporal life could not be worth the eternal lives of all men.   (ibid.)

Wesley, Fletcher, and Benson were not the only Methodists in the eighteenth century to defend the divinity of Jesus. At the founding Conference of American Methodism in 1784, Thomas Coke (d. 1814) preached a sermon on 'the Godhead of Christ'. Like his counterparts in England, Coke was deeply concerned about the 'mere man' Christologies being popularized by Arians and Socinians. He concluded his sermon, saying,

And now, having such a flood of divine testimonies for the establishment of the important doctrine of Christ's Supreme Godhead, well may we confess with St. John, that, 'the Word was God'—God, not by office only, but by nature, not figuratively, but properly, not made or created, or (as some of the subtle *Arians* say) *derived*, but co-eternally existing with the Father.   (Coke 1785: 19–20)

Like Wesley, Fletcher, and Benson, Coke was so concerned about challenges to Christ's divinity that he was reluctant to speak of Christ's human nature. Thus Coke appears to have rejected the doctrine of the eternal *sonship* of Christ. There is even significant circumstantial evidence that Coke personally eliminated the phrase 'begotten from everlasting of the Father', from the Articles of Religion that Wesley sent over to the American Methodists in 1784 (Vickers 2006: 251–61). Ironically,

Arians and Unitarians were also opposed to the doctrine of the eternal sonship. The difference has to do with the rationale for opposition. Arians and Unitarians opposed the *eternality* of Christ's sonship. Coke affirmed Christ's eternality, hesitating over the term *sonship* or any other term that made Christ appear subordinate to the Father and therefore presumably less than fully divine.

Throughout the eighteenth century, British and American Methodist theologians defended the divinity of Christ in sermons, commentaries, and theological treatises. It is not the case, however, that no Methodist theologian in the eighteenth century emphasized the humanity of Christ. On the contrary, Charles Wesley affirmed Christ's human nature in the *Hymns for the Nativity of Our Lord* (1745), a collection that appeared in no less than thirty editions by century's end.

Two defining characteristics of Charles Wesley's nativity hymns are especially worth noting. First and foremost, the incarnation is an occasion for awe; it inspires worship, thanksgiving, and praise. The proper response to the incarnation is doxological celebration, not epistemological or metaphysical speculation. Throughout the hymns, the fact that the 'Eternal Son of God' (Charles does not scruple over the doctrine of Christ's eternal sonship) became a 'mortal son of man' is cause for the inhabitants of heaven and earth to 'stand amazed'.

Second, Charles stresses that the eternal Son took on human flesh and dwelled among human persons in order to restore them to fellowship with God. Here it is crucial to note that Charles consistently uses the intimate language of friendship and brotherhood to express the purpose of the incarnation. The incarnation is not simply a necessary step on the way to making the sacrifice needed to appease the divine wrath of God the Father. In taking on human flesh, the eternal Son of God befriends human persons, becoming their brother.

These two defining characteristics are represented magnificently in the fourth hymn of the collection. Charles says,

> 1. See the eternal Son of God,
>   A mortal son of man,
>   Dwelling in an earthly clod,
>   Whom heaven cannot contain!
>   Stand amazed, ye heavens, at this!
>   See the Lord of earth and skies!
>   Humbled to the dust he is,
>   And in a manger lies!
>
> 2. We the sons of men rejoice,
>   The Prince of peace proclaim,
>   With heaven's host lift up our voice,
>   And shout Immanuel's name:
>   Knees and hearts to him we bow;
>   Of our flesh, and of our bone
>   Jesus is our brother now,
>   And God is all our own!   (C. Wesley 1991: 8–11; Vickers 2007)

The Nineteenth Century: Confessing the Christ of the Ecumenical Creeds

In the early nineteenth century, Methodist theologians continued to stress the divinity of Christ. Nor was this merely a matter of abstract debate unrelated to the life of the church. On the contrary, Methodist theologians had good reason to be concerned, as the early nineteenth century witnessed the spread of Unitarianism within Methodist congregations. Indeed, Unitarianism infiltrated enough Methodist congregations that a Methodist Unitarian Movement soon emerged. By mid-century, congregations involved in this movement officially left Methodism, becoming independent Unitarian churches (Vickers 2006: 251–61).

As it had for Thomas Coke in the preceding century, concern to emphasize the fullness of Christ's divinity caused leading Methodist theologians in both England and America to reject the doctrine of the eternal sonship of Christ. For example, Adam Clarke (d. 1832), a well-known British Methodist biblical commentator, asserted that the doctrine of Christ's eternal sonship was 'destructive of the *eternal* and *essential Deity* of Jesus' (Clarke 1826: 16–17). Similarly, in rejecting the doctrine of Christ's eternal sonship, David Wasgatt Clark (d. 1871), an American Methodist bishop, asked, 'How should the Arian shoals be escaped but by steering close to the Sabellian rock?' (Clark 1851: 118).

In response to these objections, leading nineteenth-century Methodist theologians set out to defend the doctrine of the eternal sonship. Two of the most notable theologians to do so were Richard Watson (d. 1833) and Miner Raymond (d. 1897), from England and America respectively (Watson 1847: vii; Raymond 1873: 562–75). For Watson and Raymond alike, Sabellianism was no less a concern than Arianism. Thus Raymond wanted to bring an end to 'the controversy with all classes of anti-trinitarians', including 'Monarchians, Nominal Trinitarians, Sabellians, Arians, or Socinians' (Raymond 1877: i. 396–7). In Scripture, he argued, the Son is clearly distinct from God the Father not only by virtue of his human birth but from eternity. For example, in the Prologue of the Gospel of John, the word 'with' in the phrase 'the Word was with God' indicates a relation 'of some kind'. Moreover, said Raymond, 'relation requires plurality, and plurality necessitates characteristics by which one is distinguished from the other' (Raymond 1875: 567–8).

While the debates over the eternal sonship of Christ revolved primarily around the interpretation of Scripture, Watson and Raymond represent a wider trend in nineteenth-century Methodist Christology. Beginning with Watson, nineteenth-century Methodist theologians increasingly appealed to the great ecumenical creeds and councils, most notably the Nicene Creed and the Chalcedonian Definition, as authoritative for Christian theology. The culmination of this trend can be seen in the work of T. O. Summers (d. 1882), Professor of Systematic Theology and

Dean of the Theology Faculty at Vanderbilt University, and W. B. Pope (d. 1903), Theological Tutor at Didsbury College (Summers 1888; Pope 1875).

In America, T. O. Summers began his *Systematic Theology* with a lengthy discussion of the 'creeds and confessions of Christendom'. More importantly, the Nicene Creed and Chalcedonian definition are the touchstones that guide Summers's five chapters on Christology. Indeed, Summers went to great lengths to explain the language and logic of the ecumenical church fathers' responses to the Christological heresies of Arianism, Nestorianism, and Eutychianism.

In England, Pope left no doubt that the ecumenical church councils and creeds were authoritative in theology. He even suggested that the church fathers gathered at the great ecumenical councils were divinely inspired, saying, 'There can be no doubt that the Holy Spirit watched over these decisions' (Pope 1881: i. 277). Elsewhere, he argued that the Christological dogmas enshrined in the Nicene Creed and Chalcedonian Definition have 'never been absent from the mind of the Church'. According to Pope, even when these dogmas are not being considered directly, they 'silently [enter] into all other discussions', absorbing and occupying 'the thoughts of the whole Christian world'. The ecumenical creeds and councils were 'a deep and strong testimony to the truth' that could be heard and discerned through all the 'confusions of heresy' (Pope 1875: 183). Pope concluded his work on the person of Christ with a lengthy section on the 'History of the Dogma', and he provided similar lengthy discussions of the major Christological controversies in *A Compendium of Christian Theology*.

The 1870s–1880s constitute the high water mark of Methodist dogmatic Christology, of which three characteristics are especially worth noting. First, the emphasis on the great ecumenical creeds and councils led nineteenth-century Methodist theologians to give equal, if not more, stress to the person of Christ than to the work of Christ. To be sure, they were interested in theories of the atonement, but were equally if not more interested in the doctrine of Christ's two natures. Pope's work is especially illustrative of this trend. Not only did he write a lengthy treatise on the person of Christ, he also devoted more space to the person of Christ than to the atonement in his major theological works (Pope 1884).

Second, paying close attention to the Christological dogmas of the ecumenical creeds and councils enabled nineteenth-century Methodist theologians to bring a much-needed balance to Methodist theological reflection on the person of Christ. For example, they corrected earlier tendencies to overemphasize the divine nature of Christ to the detriment of his human nature. Likewise, they captured for Methodism the delicate symmetry between the unity of Christ's person and the distinction of Christ's two natures that had been painstakingly worked out by the Council of Chalcedon. Perhaps most importantly, careful reflection on the Nicene Creed enabled them to bring an end to the long-standing controversy within Methodism over the doctrine of the eternal sonship of Christ, simultaneously avoiding Arianism and Sabellianism.

Third, nineteenth-century Methodist dogmatic theologians picked up on and endorsed the *apophatic* language and logic of the ecumenical creeds and councils, insisting on the importance of mystery for theology and worship. Thus Miner Raymond was keen to acknowledge, '[The ancient creeds] originated mostly in efforts for defense against heresy; they therefore make known the truth more by informing us of what it is not, than by direct statement of what it is' (Raymond 1873: 573). Similarly, Pope asserted that the long history of Trinitarian and Christological heresies was the result of 'the struggles of speculation' to comprehend 'this adorable mystery' (Pope 1881: 277).

Before turning to the twentieth century, it is important to acknowledge one more aspect of Methodist Christology in the nineteenth century. In the spirit of Charles Wesley's *Hymns on the Nativity of Our Lord*, Methodist worship and spirituality emphasized and celebrated the two natures of Christ. With regard to his divinity, Methodists worshipped and feared Christ as Lord. With regard to his humanity, they celebrated and gave thanks for the friend they had found in Jesus. Lester Ruth (2005: 32–3) beautifully summarizes this vital aspect of Methodist Christology in the nineteenth century, saying,

> The sheer graciousness or largesse of the love they found in Christ...overwhelmed them....Christ represented both the transcendence and the immanence of God. God's vastness and the opportunity to be intimate with God were wrapped up in the same person, Jesus Christ, whose basic disposition was a love that exceeded human description. This dual quality sparked a range of spiritual response from intimidation to intimacy. Reflecting this complexity, they called Jesus Christ both 'Lord' and 'dearest friend', and they loved him for the full spectrum.

THE TWENTIETH CENTURY: CRITIQUING THE CHRIST OF THE ECUMENICAL CREEDS

As the twentieth century began, Methodist theology was undergoing a deep transition from dogmatic to philosophical and moral theology. Interest in what the church had taught about Jesus was giving way to worries about philosophical and ethical considerations. For twentieth-century Methodist theologians, the task would be to make Jesus philosophically credible, morally relevant, or both. As such, much of twentieth-century Methodist Christology amounts to a critique of the Christ of the ecumenical creeds.

One of the best places to see this transition is in the work of Henry C. Sheldon (d. 1928), a theologian and historian of Christian doctrine at Boston University. On the one hand, Sheldon's work reflects the nineteenth-century interest in the

Christological dogma of the ecumenical creeds and councils. On the other hand, Sheldon is clearly worried about an entire host of philosophical and ethical considerations.

In his major work in systematic theology, Sheldon's philosophical worries are evident from the start. Thus he begins not with Scripture or the creeds but with a lengthy discussion of 'the principles or conditions of rational certainty' (Sheldon 1903: 3). More importantly, after surveying the development of Christological and Trinitarian doctrine in the early church, Sheldon asks whether the resulting dogma is 'conformable' to the 'demand' of philosophy (ibid. 223). Sheldon was concerned that Christological dogma should not be something imposed by 'ecclesiastical authority' and thereby constraining of free critical inquiry. 'The dogmatic value' of the church's 'christological consensus', he argued, was strictly a matter of the 'free mental engagement . . . back of it' (ibid. 330). Sheldon affirmed the church's teachings on the divinity of Jesus, the doctrine of two natures in one person, the eternal sonship of Christ, and the doctrine of the virgin birth, but his affirmation was contingent upon the compatibility of these teachings with contemporary philosophy (ibid. 223).

If Sheldon insisted that the church's teaching about Christ be philosophically credible, then he also argued that it should be morally relevant. This second concern precipitated a shift in the centre of gravity of Sheldon's Christology. Despite his strong interest in the person of Christ, Sheldon maintained that the 'greater weight' in Christology belongs to 'the demands of the Redeemer's offices' as prophet, priest, and king (ibid. 330). He believed that the offices of Christ were morally relevant in a more immediate way than the person of Christ.

In his dual concern that Christological dogma be philosophically credible and morally relevant, Sheldon is rightly associated with Boston Personalism, an approach to theology made famous at Boston University by Borden Parker Bowne, Alfred Knudson, and Edgar Brightman (Bowne 1884: 642–65; 1899: 203–17). Deeply influential on at least two generations of Methodist theologians, clergy and laity, the appeal of Boston Personalism was its purported ability to address the philosophical and ethical concerns of the times. Among those influenced by the Boston personalists were Peter Bertocci, L. Haarold DeWolf, Nels F. S. Ferre, Georgia Harkness, Martin Luther King Jr., and Walter Muelder to name just a few. Boston Personalists were especially keen to reformulate Christology.

At the core of Boston Personalism is a theistic form of metaphysics in the Kantian idealist tradition. Like all metaphysics, the metaphysics of Boston Personalism begins with 'the facts of human experience', testing its first principles by 'application to human experience' (Brightman 1943: 43). Consequently, any appeal to the Christology of the ecumenical creeds and councils would have to be compatible with and applicable to human experience.

For Boston Personalists, the most important first principle is that all reality is personal and pluralistic, consisting of a society of persons with God as the personal source or ground. As Edgar Brightman puts it, personalists hold that 'persons and selves are the only reality, that is, the whole universe is a system or society of interacting selves and persons—one infinite person who is the creator, and many dependent created persons' (Brightman 1963: 330). That said, simply identifying personality or personhood as a first principle that applies to all reality does not make one a Boston Personalist. One additional step is necessary.

For Boston Personalists, personality must be understood in ethical terms, whether it is applied to created reality or to the creator (Brightman 1921: 25). All reality has purpose and will. Moreover, all reality is the result of the 'ceaseless' and 'Living Will' of God (Bowne 1895: 24). As Bowne puts it, 'the fundamental reality is not merely mind or understanding, it is also will or agent'. This means that the world 'is not merely an idea; it is also an act'. The world exists not only as 'a conception in the divine understanding, but also as a form of activity in the divine will' (Bowne 1889: 412).

What did all of this mean for Christology? More specifically, how did Boston Personalists account for the person of Christ? To their credit, Boston Personalists readily admitted that 'the traditional doctrines of the Trinity, Incarnation, and Atonement do not easily fit into the framework . . . [of] personal idealism' (Knudson 1927: 80). Indeed, Bowne and Knudson were quick to concede that the Christological dogmas of Nicaea and Chalcedon were not compatible with their personal idealist metaphysics. For example, concerning the incarnation, Bowne argued that the doctrine is 'impossible' unless 'we assume the subordination of the Son'. Moreover, from Bowne's point of view, 'the formula of Chalcedon' went beyond 'both Scripture and reason' and therefore should be rejected (Bowne 1909: 92). Knudson also took issue with the Chalcedonian doctrine of two natures in one person on the grounds that it regarded the relationship between divine and human action in Jesus in substantialist terms. 'Neither human nor divine nature', said Knudson, 'has any existence apart from personality' (Knudson 1950: 137).

Given the personalists' opposition to viewing the divine and human natures as substances somehow 'compressed' (Bowne's term) together, Knudson set out to reformulate the doctrine of the person of Christ in order to make it compatible with personal idealism.

We are to think of Christ as a man in whom God was present in a unique manner and to a unique degree. This presence consisted in a unique metaphysical dependence on God and in a unique reciprocal interaction with the divine Spirit. As a result of this twofold relation to God there emerged in Christ a unique and potent God-consciousness in which God was both causally and consciously present and which expressed itself in qualities of mind and heart that have made him in the faith of the church the ideal man and perfect organ of divine revelation.   (ibid. 148)

It is crucial to see what is going on here. There is a strong commitment to Jesus' human nature, but the commitment to the divine nature is clearly wobbling. Christ is 'a man in whom God was present', but there is no straightforward assertion of Christ's divinity. On the contrary, divinity or 'God-consciousness' has gradually to emerge. Presumably, it is not there all along. To be sure, Christ is metaphysically dependent on God, but it is not clear how, if at all, this distinguishes Christ from other human persons, all of whom are no less metaphysically dependent. Christ is 'the ideal man' and 'perfect organ of divine revelation', but it is not clear that he is in himself the revelation of God.

If Knudson equivocates on the divinity of Jesus, then John Lavely, a later interpreter of personalism, does not. In what amounts to the language and logic of Arianism, Lavely appears to reject the eternality of Christ, saying, 'Only a reality analogous to Christ could *bring Christ into being* and sustain him in being what he was.' Lavely (1986: 271–2) continues,

If we do not exchange the precious and mysterious meaning of personal existence and personal relations for the coinage of substances and essences, then the Incarnation makes sense.... When Jesus says, 'He who has seen me has seen the Father', *it is doubtful that he is asserting that he is ontologically identical with God.* He is rather saying something like: I cannot tell you anything more about God than by being my (best) self. That is, there is no other analogy for God than a person at his or her best and the best analogy is the best person.

(emphasis added)

Boston Personalism's chief objective was to make Christology compatible with personal idealist metaphysics and thereby both intellectually credible and morally relevant. For personalists, Jesus is simply 'the best analogy' for God. What makes Jesus the best is not that he is the eternally begotten Son of God. Rather, it is simply that in Jesus we meet someone whose life is completely in line with the divine will or purpose. It is not clear, however, that Christ is truly unique in this respect. Presumably, the same thing might be said about other persons.

Boston Personalism's shift from the fullness of Christ's divinity from eternity to Christ's emerging God-consciousness and embodiment of divine will and purpose is paralleled by a shift in perspective regarding the most appropriate human response to Jesus. For personalists, the most appropriate response to Jesus Christ is not worship, thanksgiving, and praise, but emulation. Jesus is first and foremost a moral exemplar. For Boston Personalists, morality and ethics finally take precedence over doxology as the true aim of religion. As Bowne (1899: 216) himself says, 'The forms of worship and practices of piety are important, but they are only instrumental. They are not the thing.... The thing, the central thing, is the recognition of the divine will in all life, and the loyal, loving effort to make that will prevail in all life.'

If Boston Personalism is the form of theology most closely associated with Methodism in the first half of the twentieth century, then process theology is most closely associated with Methodism in the second half of the twentieth century (cf. Oord 2001). To be sure, a growing number of late twentieth-century Methodist theologians self-identify as liberation theologians, but liberation theology is not directly associated with Methodism to the same degree as Boston Personalism and process theology. Like Boston Personalism, process theology has flourished to an unusual degree within Methodism, most notably in the work of John Cobb Jr., Schubert Ogden, and Marjorie Suchocki. A striking fact about process theology is the degree to which it has thrived among African-American Methodist theologians.

Process theology is highly similar to Boston Personalism in at least three ways. First, it seeks to make Christology intellectually respectable by replacing a substance-oriented metaphysics with a relationally oriented metaphysics. In this case, the metaphysics of choice is the process metaphysics of Alfred North Whitehead and Charles Hartshorne (Cf. Lowe 1962; Cobb 1965). Second, process theologians clearly believe that the appropriation of process metaphysics in Christology makes Christ more morally relevant than he would be otherwise. Third, like personalists, process theologians are often criticized for compromising the uniqueness, if not the divinity, of Christ.

Process theology appears to differ significantly from personalism in so far as it is prima facie more favourably disposed to the Christology enshrined in the Nicene Creed and the Chalcedonian definition. Thus John Cobb regards 'Nicea and Chalcedon as basically faithful to the New Testament witness'. Moreover, Cobb claims that he wants 'to think christologically in continuity' with Nicaea and Chalcedon (Cobb Jr. 1988: 64). Similarly, Delwin Brown affirms 'the judgments of the successive Christological councils to the effect that the divinity incarnate in Jesus' humanity is full divinity, that the humanity of Jesus in which divinity was incarnate is real humanity, and that this incarnation in Jesus is pertained to the whole of Jesus' person and vocation' (Pinnock and Brown 1990: 169).

Having pledged their allegiance to Nicaea and Chalcedon at the outset, however, process theologians are quick to qualify the extent of their commitment to the Christology of the ecumenical creeds. On the one hand, they are committed to the language of the creeds. On the other hand, they reject what they take to be the substance-oriented metaphysics 'behind' that language. From the point of view of most process theologians, the metaphysics of Nicaea and Chalcedon marks a substantial departure from the New Testament witness to Jesus. As Schubert Ogden so memorably put it, the Christologies of the New Testament are 'so far from making the same metaphysical claim later made by the councils of Nicaea and Chalcedon that they may as well mean that Jesus is a human being whom God has appointed as that he is a divine being who has become man' (Ogden 1982: 76; 1984: 18–33). Consequently, according to process theologians, orthodoxy requires a commitment only to the language of the creeds, not to the metaphysics of the creeds. Otherwise put, one only has to say *that* Jesus is fully human and fully divine. What this language means is up for negotiation.

What, then, do process theologians mean when they say that Jesus Christ is fully human and fully divine? To answer this question, one must begin with the concept of the Logos. According to Cobb and David Ray Griffin (1976: 100), the Logos is a transcendent, timeless, and infinite principle or power of 'creative transformation', the nature of which is best described as 'responsive love'. This principle or power is incarnate to a greater or lesser extent 'in all things', events, and processes. In its incarnate form, it is called Christ. Thus, in process theology, the term 'Christ' does not refer exclusively to Jesus, although the Logos was clearly incarnate (Christ) in a special way in Jesus.

What is so special about Jesus? Cobb and Griffin (ibid. 98–9) suggest that 'the extent of the effectiveness of the Logos' in living creatures 'is largely decided by the creature'. They continue, 'Christ is present to a greater or lesser extent as the creature decides for or against the Logos. Christ is most fully present in human beings when they are most fully open to that presence.' Extending the logic of this analysis, Jesus is special or unique precisely in so far as he is 'most fully open' to the presence of the Logos. If there is 'a distinctive incarnation' in Jesus, then it is because he is so open to the Logos that 'his very selfhood' is constituted by responsive love (ibid. 139).

Process theologians routinely criticize 'traditional Christologies' for denying the 'full humanity of Jesus'. By contrast, process theologians stress that 'Jesus' relation to God' must be understood in a way that affirms 'his full humanity' (ibid. 104). They believe that they have found a way to do this. If there is a fundamental compatibility between the Logos as principle or power of creative transformation and all creaturely reality, including Jesus, then to say that the Logos is incarnate (Christ) in Jesus in no way violates or diminishes his human nature.

As with Boston Personalists, the significance of Jesus for process theologians has primarily to do with his teachings and actions. Otherwise put, Jesus is morally relevant because he exhibits in a special way the principle and power of creative transformation that is responsive love. To be Christian therefore is 'genuinely to hear Jesus' teaching' and 'to be opened to Christ as creative transformation' (ibid. 103).

Five things must be said about process Christology. First, process theologians rarely, if ever, claim that Jesus is divine *tout court*. Rather, they emphasize that Jesus is a fully human person in whom it is possible to see 'what the divine reality *is like*' (ibid. 102)   (emphasis added).

Second, despite claims to continuity, process Christology reverses the direction of the logic of the Christology embedded in the ecumenical creeds. In the creeds the eternally begotten Son takes on flesh and dwells among us. The Christology of the creeds begins 'above' or from outside creaturely reality. In process Christology, the human Jesus chooses to be fully open to the divine Logos or principle of creative transformation. Thus Process Christology begins 'below' or, perhaps more accurately, from within creaturely reality.

Third, whereas the Christ of the ecumenical creeds and counsels has a relationship with God that it is of a different *kind* from the relationship enjoyed by human persons, the Jesus on offer in process theology has a relationship to God that differs only in *degree*. In principle, all creatures are capable of having the same relationship with the divine Logos that Jesus had.

Fourth, it is not altogether clear that the degree to which the Logos is incarnate (Christ) in Jesus is in actuality unique. Thus in Cobb's later work he appears to expand the definition of Logos in directions that enable him to say that the Logos is fully incarnate (Christ) in other world religions (Cobb Jr. 1982).

Fifth, to the degree that the first four observations hold, it must be said that process Christology's reputed 'continuity' with the Christology of the ecumenical creeds and councils is dubious at best. On this front, Boston Personalists were more forthcoming in that they made no pretence to any such continuity.

While personalism and process theology are the two forms of theology most closely identified with Methodism in the twentieth century, a strong number of Methodist theologians have played leading roles in various forms of liberation theology. Even more than personalists and process theologians, liberation theologians are especially concerned to develop a Christology that is morally relevant. Indeed, many liberation theologians have a deep sense that both the Christology of the ecumenical creeds and the liberal Christologies of personalist and process theology fail directly to address the most pressing moral issues of the day. For some liberation theologians, the problem runs even deeper. The Christology of the ecumenical creeds is morally suspect because it has served as an instrument of oppression across the centuries.

A good place to begin an analysis of Methodist liberation Christology is with Black theology. James Cone, a Methodist, is widely regarded as the founding father of Black theology. In his seminal text, *A Black Theology of Liberation*, Cone (2004: 113) follows Paul Tillich in saying that Christianity must 'answer to the existential character of the human condition'. Accordingly, says Cone (ibid. 110–11), the 'task of black theology' is to make theology 'relevant to the black reality, asking, "What does Jesus Christ mean for the oppressed blacks of the land?"' Cone (ibid. 119) reiterates, 'The meaning of Jesus is an existential question.'

For Cone, the way to make Christology morally relevant is to take seriously the historical Jesus. Cone clearly favours the Christology embedded in the Scriptures over the Christology of the ecumenical creeds and councils. The problem with the latter is clear. By emphasizing Christ's relationship to God the Father and the relationship between Christ's divine and human natures, the creeds mask the extent to which the Jesus of Scripture and of history is 'the Oppressed One whose earthly existence was bound up with the oppressed of the land' (ibid. 113).

Once one sees that the historical Jesus dwelled constantly among the poor and oppressed of the land, it is a short step to the conclusion that, if Jesus is present at all today, then he is surely to be found among the poor and the oppressed. Thus Cone (1975: 135) asks, 'If Jesus' presence is real and not *docetic*, is it not true that Christ must be black in order to remain faithful to the divine promise to bear the suffering of the poor?' Of course, to ask whether Cone means that Jesus was literally or physically black is to miss the point. As Cone puts it, 'The importance of the concept of the black Christ is that it expresses the *concreteness* of Jesus' continued presence today.... Like yesterday, he has taken upon himself the misery of his people, becoming for them what is needed for their liberation.' This means that, 'to be a disciple of the black Christ', persons must become 'black like him' (Cone 2004: 123).

Like Black theologians, Latin American liberation theologians emphasize the particularities of social location and context (cf. Míguez-Bonino 1975). Here, however, class rather than race is the organizing concern around which Christology revolves. If Christology is to be credible, then it must speak to the contemporary problems of class conflict and the plight of the poor. Also like black theologians, Latin American liberation theologians tend to focus on the teachings and actions of Christ in the New Testament, regarding the Christ of the ecumenical creeds and councils with suspicion. At a minimum, the Christ of the ecumenical creeds and councils fails directly to address the plight of the poor in the world.

Similar moves are made in forms of liberation theology that revolve around gender. As with black theology and Latin American liberation theology, feminist, womanist, and mujerista theologians often attempt to go behind the ecumenical creeds in order to recover earlier biblical Christologies (Cf. Ruether 1981; 1982; 1983). For these liberation theologians, however, the problem with the Christ of the ecumenical creeds and councils runs even deeper, for they do not simply fail to address issues of gender equality; they appear to deify maleness (Edwards 2003: 3–13; Grant 1989).

Throughout the twentieth century, Boston Personalists, process theologians, and Methodist liberation theologians argued repeatedly that the Christ of the ecumenical creeds and councils is either intellectually indefensible, morally suspect, or both. The collective results of their criticism of classical Christology are manifold, but three consequences are especially worth noting. First, their collective criticisms of classical Christology resulted in a shift of emphasis away from the person of Christ and towards either the work or the offices of Christ. For example, Methodist liberation theologians are prone to emphasize Christ's prophetic office. Second, as a collective result of Boston Personalism, process theology, and liberation theologies, Methodists tend to stress the need for moral or ethical emulation of Christ over the worship of Christ. To be sure, Methodist theologians influenced by process and liberation theology sometimes write new liturgies, but these new liturgies often studiously avoid directing worship to Jesus Christ, preferring instead to direct worship to God the creator, redeemer, and sustainer. The name of Jesus is often conspicuous by its absence. Third, with regard to the person of Christ, Boston Personalists, process, and liberation theologians often emphasize the humanity of Christ more than the divinity of Christ, effectively reversing the imbalance in eighteenth-century Methodist Christology noted above.

Despite the widespread influence of these theological movements within Methodism, a minority report began to take shape in the last quarter of the twentieth century when a few Methodist theologians set out to retrieve and to reappropriate the Christological vision embedded in the Nicene Creed and Chalcedonian Definition. This minority report is generally associated with the work of Albert C. Outler (1996), Thomas Oden (2006), and Geoffrey Wainwright (1990; 1984). To date, the legacy of their work can be seen in two areas, including (1) the gradual recovery within Methodism of the vital connection between classical Christology and the liturgy and sacraments of the church, and (2) a recovery of the balance and symmetry of the creeds between the divinity and humanity of Christ and the distinction of natures and unity of person—a balance and symmetry sorely lacking in both eighteenth- and twentieth-century Methodist theology. There are even occasional rumours of a small but growing interest in the recovery of the dogmatic theological tradition that flourished in nineteenth-century Methodism. Clearly Oden, Outler, and Wainwright made a start in this direction. Whether their work develops more fully will be up to the next generation of Methodist theologians.

THE TWENTY-FIRST CENTURY: RETRIEVING THE CHRIST OF THE ECUMENICAL CREEDS

If Methodist theologians in the twenty-first century are to retrieve and reappropriate the Christ of the ecumenical creeds and councils, then they will have to address the two dominant concerns bequeathed to them by their twentieth-century predecessors. First, they will need to address the concern raised by Boston Personalism and process theology that Nicene and Chalcedonian Christology are wedded to a metaphysics that is now indefensible. The good news here is that there are at least two ways to address this concern. On the one hand, Methodist theologians can follow the lead of Radical Orthodoxy, unapologetically embracing the metaphysical vision of Augustine. On the other hand, Methodist theologians can call into question whether Nicaea or Chalcedon actually canonized a particular metaphysics and whether it is necessary to do so now (Abraham et al. 2008).

Second, Methodist theologians will have to address the concerns of liberation theologians that Nicaea and Chalcedon are either morally irrelevant or morally objectionable. Here the good news comes from a somewhat surprising source, namely liberation theology itself. Many liberation theologians are now modifying their views on the moral relevance of classical Christology. For example, after a lengthy consideration of the ways in which the ecumenical creeds and councils were a means for maintaining unity, hierarchy, and power in the Roman Empire, United Methodist theologian Joerg Rieger suggests that the Christological vision of

Nicaea and Chalcedon may also have the potential to function as a means for resisting and criticizing empire today. Thus he writes, 'But there is some surplus here that, if explored, pushes against the status quo, provided that the humanity in question is similar to that of Christ as reported in the Gospels—a humanity under pressure, suffering, struggling against the powers of empire' (Rieger 2007: 98). Moreover, Rieger (2007: 100) concludes his discussion of Nicaea and Chalcedon on a positive note, suggesting that, over against the recent emphasis on the work of Christ construed in terms of sacrifice and submission, the focus of the ecumenical creeds and councils on the person of Christ can 'push us in new directions that emphasize what is life giving rather than death dealing'.

Whatever the future holds, one thing is certain. Methodist theologians are not finished wrestling with the Christological legacy of Nicaea and Chalcedon. After a century of attempts either to rid Methodism of classical Christology entirely or radically revise classical Christology, the dogmatic formulations of the fourth and fifth centuries continue to function as a benchmark for theological reflection. Surely this is a fitting testimony to the ongoing generative power of the Christ of the ecumenical creeds and councils within Methodism today.

SUGGESTED READING

COLLINS (2007: 87–120).
GRANT (1989).
MADDOX (1994: 94–118).
OGDEN (1982).
POPE (1875).
RIEGER (2007).
WAINWRIGHT (1984: 45–86).

REFERENCES

ABRAHAM, WILLIAM J., VICKERS, JASON E., and VAN KIRK, NATALIE B. (eds.) (2008). *Canonical Theism: A Proposal for Theology and the Church*. Grand Rapids: Eerdmans.
BOWNE, BORDEN PARKER (1884). 'The Logic of Religious Belief'. *Methodist Quarterly Review* 66.
—— (1889). 'Philosophical Idealism'. *Methodist Review* 71: 395–412.
—— (1895). 'Natural and Supernatural'. *Methodist Review* 77: 9–24.
—— (1899). 'Secularism and Christianity'. *Methodist Quarterly Review* 48: 203–17.
—— (1909). *Studies in Christianity*. Boston: Houghton Mifflin.
BRIGHTMAN, EDGAR SHEFFIELD (1921). 'The Unpopularity of Personalism'. *Methodist Review* 104: 9–28.

—— (1943). 'Personality as a Metaphysical Principle'. In Edgar Sheffield Brightman (ed.), *Personalism in Theology: A Symposium in Honor of Albert Conelius Knudson*. Boston: Boston University Press.

—— (1963). *An Introduction to Philosophy*. 3rd revised edn. New York: Holt, Rinehart, & Winston.

CAMPBELL, TED A. (1991). *John Wesley and Christian Antiquity: Religious Vision and Cultural Change*. Nashville: Kingswood.

CLARK, DAVID WASGATT (1851). 'The Incarnation'. *Methodist Review* 33: 114–35.

CLARKE, ADAM (1826). *Love of God to a Lost World, Demonstrated by the Incarnation and Death of Christ: A Discourse*. New York: Nathan Bangs & J. Emory.

COBB, JOHN (1965). *A Christian Natural Theology: Based on the Thought of Alfred North Whitehead*. Philadelphia: Westminster.

COBB, JOHN B. Jr. (1982). *Beyond Dialogue: Toward a Mutual Transformation of Christianity and Buddhism*. Philadelphia: Fortress.

—— (1988). 'Critique'. In Stephen Davis (ed.), *Encountering Jesus: A Debate on Christology*. Atlanta: John Knox, 158–68.

—— and David Ray Griffin (1976). *Process Theology: An Introductory Exposition*. Louisville, Ky.: Westminster John Knox.

COKE, THOMAS (1785). *The Substance of a Sermon on the Godhead of Christ, Preached at Baltimore, in the State of Maryland, on the 26th Day of December, 1784 before the General Conference of the Methodist Episcopal Church*. London: J. Paramore.

COLLINS, KENNETH J. (2007). *The Theology of John Wesley: Holy Love and the Shape of Grace*. Nashville: Abingdon.

CONE, JAMES (1975). *God of the Oppressed*. New York: Seabury.

—— (2004). *A Black Theology of Liberation*. Maryknoll, N.Y.: Orbis.

DESCHNER, JOHN (1985). *Wesley's Christology: An Interpretation*. Dallas: Southern Methodist University Press.

EDWARDS, WENDY J. DEICHMANN (2003). 'Why God Became Man: A Gender-Inclusive Christology'. *Journal of Theology* 107: 3–13.

FLETCHER, JOHN (1833). *The Works of the Reverend John Fletcher, Late Vicar of Madeley*. 4 vols. New York: B. Waugh & T. Mason.

GRANT, JACQUELYN (1989). *White Women's Christ and Black Women's Jesus: Feminist Christology and Womanist Response*. Atlanta: Scholars.

KNUDSON, ALBERT C. (1927). *The Philosophy of Personalism: A Study in the Metaphysics of Religion*. New York: Abingdon.

—— (1950). *Basic Issues in Christian Thought*. New York: Abingdon-Cokesbury.

LAVELY, JOHN H. (1986). 'Reflections on a Philosophical Heritage'. In Paul Deats and Carol Robb (eds.), *The Boston Personalist Tradition in Philosophy, Social Ethics, and Theology*. Macon, Ga.: Mercer University Press, 253–72.

LOWE, VICTOR (1962). *Understanding Whitehead*. Baltimore: Johns Hopkins University Press.

MADDOX, RANDY L. (1994). *Responsible Grace: John Wesley's Practical Theology*. Nashville: Kingswood.

MÍGUEZ-BONINO, JOSE (1975). *Doing Theology in a Revolutionary Situation*. Minneapolis: Fortress.

ODEN, THOMAS C. (2006). *Systematic Theology*. 3 vols. Peabody: Hendrickson.

OGDEN, SCHUBERT (1982). *The Point of Christology*. Dallas: Southern Methodist University Press.

OGDEN, SCHUBERT (1984). 'Process Theology and the Wesleyan Witness'. *Perkins School of Theology Journal* 37: 18–33.

OORD, THOMAS JAY (2001). 'Wesleyan Theology, Boston Personalism, and Process Thought'. In Bryan P. Stone and Thomas Jay Oord (eds.), *Thy Nature & Thy Name is Love: Wesleyan and Process Theologies in Dialogue*. Nashville: Kingswood, 379–92.

OUTLER, ALBERT C. (1996). *Christology*, ed. Thomas C. Oden. Anderson, Ind.: Bristol Books.

PINNOCK, CLARK, and BROWN, DELWIN (1990). *Theological Crossfire: An Evangelical/Liberal Dialogue*. Grand Rapids: Zondervan.

POPE, WILLIAM BURT (1875). *The Person of Christ: Dogmatic, Scriptural, Historical*. London: Wesleyan Conference Office.

—— (1881). *A Compendium of Christian Theology*. 2 vols. New York: Phillips & Hunt.

—— (1884). *A Higher Catechism of Theology*. New York: Phillips & Hunt.

RAYMOND, MINER (1873). 'The Sonship of Christ'. *Methodist Review* 55: 562–75.

—— (1877). *Systematic Theology*. 2 vols. Cincinnati: Hitchcock & Walden.

RIEGER, JOERG (2007). *Christ & Empire: From Paul to Postcolonial Times*. Minneapolis: Fortress.

RUETHER, ROSEMARY RADFORD (1981). *To Change the World: Christology and Cultural Criticism*. New York: Crossroads.

—— (1982). *Disputed Questions: On Being a Christian*. Nashville: Abingdon.

—— (1983). *Sexism and God-Talk: Toward a Feminist Theology*. Boston: Beacon.

RUTH, LESTER (2005). *Early Methodist Life and Spirituality: A Reader*. Nashville: Kingswood.

SHELDON, HENRY C. (1903). *System of Christian Doctrine*. New York: Eaton & Mains; Cincinnati: Jennings & Graham.

SUMMERS, T. O. (1888). *Systematic Theology: A Complete Body of Wesleyan Arminian Divinity consisting of Lectures on the Twenty-five Articles of Religion*. 2 vols. Nashville: Methodist Episcopal Church South.

VICKERS, JASON E. (2006). ' "Begotten from Everlasting of the Father": Inadvertent Omission or Sabellian Trajectory in Early Methodism?' *Methodist History* 44/4: 251–61.

—— (2008). 'And We the Life of God Shall Know: Incarnation and the Trinity in Charles Wesley's Hymns'. *Anglican Theological Review* 90/2: 329–44.

—— (2008). *Invocation and Assent: The Making and Remaking of Trinitarian Theology*. Grand Rapids: Eerdmans.

WAINWRIGHT, GEOFFREY (1984). *Doxology: The Praise of God in Worship, Doctrine and Life*. Oxford: Oxford University Press.

—— (1990). 'Methodism and the Apostolic Faith'. In M. Douglas Meeks (ed.), *What Should Methodists Teach? Wesleyan Tradition and Modern Diversity*. Nashville: Kingswood.

WATSON, RICHARD (1847). 'Remarks on the Eternal Sonship of Christ'. In *The Works of the Rev. Richard Watson*. 13 vols. London: John Mason, vii.

WESLEY, CHARLES (1991). *Hymns for the Nativity of Our Lord*. Reprint edn. Madison, N.J.: Charles Wesley Society.

CHAPTER 33

PNEUMATOLOGY IN THE METHODIST TRADITION

D. LYLE DABNEY

'DIVINITY', John Wesley writes near the end of the preface to his *Explanatory Notes on the New Testament*, 'is nothing but a grammar of the language of the Holy Ghost' (Wesley 1950: 9). That this was anything but a casual comment is demonstrated by his subsequent remarks. For he goes on to commend a reading of the New Testament that burrows deeply beneath the surface of those texts and gets at what we might now call the 'deep logic' of the words of the 'apostles and evangelists'. He describes the substance of the 'divinity' buried in those documents as having to do with 'the holy affections expressed thereby, and the tempers shown by every writer' (ibid.)—by which he means those fundamental dispositions of the human heart transformed by the Holy Spirit and the holy behaviours or forms of life that accompany such a change. Finally, complaining that those who have gone before have paid little attention to these 'affections' and their transformation, as well as to what brings such re-creation about, Wesley intimates that his own chief concern in the *Explanatory Notes* that follow will be to read the New Testament, whose witness is the 'language of the Holy Ghost', employing just such a 'grammar of the Spirit'.

A 'grammar', according to the *Oxford English Dictionary*, describes the inflectional forms of a language, or other means of indicating the relations of words in a sentence, as well as identifying the rules for employing these in accordance with established usage. Thus grammar deals with both the analysis and the practice of a language, demonstrating how the various parts of the language relate to one another and how they are to be used. In the following I want to suggest that Wesley's notion of 'divinity' as a 'grammar of the Spirit'—that which explicates how the elements of the 'language of the Holy Ghost' relate to one another and gain their meaning in concert together—represents not just the approach he used in commenting upon Scripture, but is rather the theological hermeneutic implicit in his 'reading' and 'enacting' of the entirety of the Christian faith. 'Divinity' became for him, I contend, the description of how the Christian community bespeaks the witness to God's transformation of human lives, individually and corporately, and the very affections that shape them through Christ and in the Spirit. Moreover, it is precisely this pneumatological orientation that constitutes his theological distinctive. To give an account of John Wesley's pneumatology, therefore, is not simply to enumerate and explain the many passages in his writings in which he mentions the Holy Spirit, whether in passing or at length; it is to render an account of the trajectory of his theologizing as a whole. Moreover, it is to begin to give an account of pneumatology in the Methodist tradition as a whole and to speak of how that might best be appropriated today.

To begin to demonstrate the distinctive character of Wesley's reading of Christian theology and the role played in it by pneumatology, Wesley's 'Methodist divinity' must be seen against the background of the Western theological tradition. The last century has been an era of theological reassessment, as Christianity has faced both the challenge of the passing of the cultural and legal privilege that the churches have long enjoyed in Western society as well as the developing crisis of modernity. Representatives of the various theological traditions of the West have struggled to recover and critically reclaim the basic insights that provided each with their own original and distinct dynamic in their contributions to the long conversation that is the Western theological tradition. Thus there has occurred a dramatic renewal and reinterpretation of the thought of—among others—Augustine and the early church fathers, of Aquinas and the Scholastics, as well as of the Reformers, Luther and Calvin, and not to mention Wesley himself. In the course of these developments we have been reminded anew that, as Peter Brown has observed, 'the quality of a religious system depends perhaps less on its specific doctrine, then on the choice of problems that it regards as important, the areas of human experience to which it directs attention' (Brown 1969: 393). For this movement of recovery of the Western traditions has made it abundantly clear once again that the Western theological tradition has been dominated by two fundamentally conflicting trajectories or tendencies of thought that have taken very different 'problems' and 'areas of human experience' as their points of departure.

The first trajectory is seen most clearly in medieval monastic and scholastic theology, forms that take God's creation, more specifically, the capacities of created human nature, as the starting point for their reading of the faith, and interpret salvation accordingly as the ascent of the soul to knowledge of God the creator through the assistance of grace. In its scholastic form, this type of theology can be said to begin, therefore, with a kind of syllogism: God is good in being and act; creation is an act of God; ergo, creation is essentially good and in search of its highest good. That is by no means to be understood as denying the presence and pervasiveness of sin in the world, nor as implying that the act of creation is somehow complete. Rather, according to this theology, despite the acknowledged imperfection and incompleteness in the world, it is ultimately the goodness of God's creating that defines the creation. That goodness expresses itself above all in an innate human capacity for God, a created openness for or a desire to ascend to the fulfilment of our nature in union with our creator, a yearning for that which human nature cannot of itself attain. Thus the point of departure for this tradition is expressed in the words of Augustine, monk and priest and bishop, in his *Confessions*: 'You have made us for yourself, and our heart is restless until it rests in you' (Augustine 1998: 3). Catholic theology of this sort, therefore, came to be cast as an appeal to the created nature of human beings to find the fulfilment of their being by ascending to God through a receipt of an infusion of the grace that the Father has provided in Christ through the church. The natural virtues, both moral and intellectual, it is claimed, lead to even as they are transcended and guided to fulfilment by the theological virtues of faith, hope, and love. Hence, while medieval scholasticism carefully differentiates between nature and grace, it does not contrast but rather orders them in an unbroken hierarchical relationship. Its clear tendency, then, is to posit a fundamental continuum between nature and grace, the creator and the created, creation and redemption; for it is a theology of nature fulfilled by grace. Thus its representative affirmation was and is that of Aquinas: 'Grace does not destroy, but rather presupposes and perfects nature' (Aquinas 1948: i. 6).

Over and against that sort of thought stands the theology of the sixteenth-century Reformation, the second dominant theological trajectory in the West. The fundamental logic of Reformation theology is protest, indeed, Reformation theology is protesting, or Protestant theology. What it protests against is above all the root affirmation of medieval monastic and scholastic theology: that human nature by virtue of being God's good creation possesses an innate capacity for God and is thus intrinsically open to and in search of its creator. Casting itself in the role of the bishop of Hippo confronting the teachings of Pelagius, this tradition declares that any teacher of such a theology of 'human nature verses the grace of God' (Augustine 1956: 116) was one who simply did not understand 'why he was a Christian', (ibid. 122) for such doctrine would 'render the cross of Christ of no effect' (ibid. 123). Thus, Luther argued in his *Disputation Against Scholastic Theology* of 1517 that, 'on the part of man however nothing precedes grace except ill will and even rebellion against grace' (Luther 1955: xxxi. 11). Not the goodness but the sin and consequent incapacity of the creature for the creator, not the yearning for but the flight from God is, therefore, this theology's point of departure; and that sin and incapacity and flight is seen as the defining reality in all creaturely existence. Now that is not to say that all is interpreted as simply evil. When Calvin, for instance, spoke of the 'depravity' of nature, he did not mean that there was no good in the world, what he meant was there was no unalloyed good, no part or capacity or desire untouched by the fall. For sin has spoiled all, according to this theology, and there is no untouched part of our essential humanity or residual image of God to which one can appeal as purely good, as open to and in search of its creator. Indeed, according to this reading of the faith, the claim that there is such a possibility, such a capacity for God, is the essence of sin itself, in that it constitutes the implicit claim that one can by one's own efforts be redeemed.

Reformation theology, therefore, is cast not in the form of an appeal to the good, but in the form of a dialectic, according to which the Redeemer Jesus Christ as the Divine Word stands over and against creation, 'outside of us', *extra nos*, confronting human beings in their sin and summoning them to faith in the free grace of God made manifest in his death on the cross, 'on our behalf', *pro nobis*. We come to right relationship with God, it is claimed, not through being enabled by infused grace to fulfil nature's law and so ascend to our creator, but rather by forswearing such reliance on law and placing our trust in Christ the Redeemer who by grace freely imputes his righteousness to us. This sort of theology, therefore, finds its point of departure not in creaturely good, but in creaturely sin, and takes the form not of creation's ascent to its God and Father, but of God's descent to creation in Jesus Christ the Son. Its clear tendency, then, is to assert utter contradiction between law and gospel, God and world, creation and redemption, redeemer and those in need of redemption. Not creation *and* anything, most certainly not nature *and* grace, but rather 'Christ alone' (*solus Christus*), 'faith alone' (*sola fide*), 'Scripture alone' (*sola scriptura*), and 'grace alone' (*sola gratia*) were the Reformation watchwords. Reformation theology is a theology, therefore, not of continuum but of contradiction. As the Anglo-Catholic John Burnaby expressed the issue in the midst of a conflict with such theology earlier in this century: 'Against the "Both-And" of the Catholic, Protestantism here as everywhere sets with . . . insistence its "Either-Or"' (Burnaby 1991: 4).

To place John Wesley on the horizon of Western theology as it is defined by the two trajectories I have just sketched is both to illustrate the central dilemma of the Western tradition and to illuminate Wesley's own unique theological trajectory. For in the England of the eighteenth century Wesley found himself facing the dilemma of the Western theological tradition in microcosm. That dilemma consists in the interaction of the conflicting 'logics' of the two theologies that have dominated the Western tradition as described above: on the one hand, the Catholic trajectory that can be characterized for heuristic purposes as *a* 'theology of the first article' of the creed stressing the fulfilment of creation and of the created human capacities for God, and, on the other, the Reformation trajectory that can be characterized for heuristic purposes as *a* 'theology of the second article' stressing redemption as the sovereign act of God in Christ on behalf of humanity. The struggle between the representatives of those two positions in the Anglican Church and in English Christianity at large had led them to the constant tendency to champion either human potentiality and act to the detriment of divine activity or the electing and saving grace of God to the detriment of the works of human beings. In Wesley's early modern England, as in the West in general, this took place most often in terms of the possibilities of human knowing versus divine revelation or God's grace versus the possibilities of human obedience. One side of the characteristic problematic which thereby arose was indicated by Adolph Harnack when he noted that despite all its good intentions, the Reformation in its emphasis on the act of God over and against the acts of human beings, 'neglected far too much the moral problem, the "Be ye holy, for I am holy"' (Harnack 1976: 267). It was in forms of English Reformed Orthodoxy that Wesley concretely faced that neglect of Christian holiness. And it was his response to such neglect that determined the distinctive trajectory that marked his own theological development.

Wesley's reading of the Christian faith manifests a readily identifiable tendency, and the work of the last two generations of Wesleyan scholars has made the broad outlines of the development of his trajectory of thought increasingly clear. It was driven by his own spiritual pilgrimage from the 'Holy Club' during his student days at Oxford to the missionary expedition to Georgia he undertook for the sake of his own salvation to his career as an evangelist travelling throughout England, Scotland, Wales, and Ireland. His development began with what was essentially a theology of the first article—clearly discernible in his earliest sermons and correspondence in which he moralistically sought to conform his own life and that of others to God's commands. He then moved to and through a kind of theology of the second article—expressed most emphatically in the sermon 'Salvation by Faith', preached in 1738 soon after his 'heart had been strangely warmed' at Aldersgate while listening to a reading of Luther's preface to his commentary on Romans—according to which he called upon the people of the British Isles to place their faith in the God who freely bestows forgiveness (Wesley 1975– : i. 197, esp. n. 93).

But the course of Wesley's theological development did not stop there. Rather, first challenged by the question of spiritual assurance pressed upon him by the Moravian Peter Böhler and inspired by news of the work of the Holy Spirit in the Great Awakening in North America reported by Jonathan Edwards, and then forced to give account of himself in debate with Reformed Orthodoxy both within and without the evangelical revival of his day, Wesley's contribution to the Western theological tradition consists in his striving towards what can perhaps best be termed a 'theology of the third article' of the creed. This was a theology of the transforming redemption of God's human creature and all creation in and through the Holy Spirit that begins in forgiveness and ends in holiness of life. His theology, therefore, takes as its central concern neither the fulfilment of creation nor the contradiction of sin and grace but the divine initiation of a process of 'Christian perfection' in human life that is implicit in creation, explicit in reconciliation and, eventually, fully actualized in redemption. Moreover, he understands that 'perfection' not as moral conformity to an external command, but as a living expression of God's perfect love in the lives of human beings individually and collectively—transformed 'affections' indeed! Thus the point of departure for Wesley's theology ultimately became neither created human capacity nor sinful human incapacity, but rather the faithful presence and activity of God through the Spirit in the midst of creation, striving to bring humanity to God's good and perfect ends. It is thus a theology of neither 'created continuum', as in a theology of the first article, nor of 'evangelical contradiction', as in a theology of the second article, but of the continuity of God's work of faithful grace by the Son and in the Holy Spirit through the discontinuity of the creature's faithless estrangement.

This is clearly his emphasis as early as 1742 when, in his tract *The Character of a Methodist*, he sought to provide a proper definition for Methodism and its central concern by declaring that 'a Methodist is one who has "the love of God shed abroad in his heart by the Holy Ghost given unto him" ' (Wesley 1975– : ix. 35). Thus, while the primary language of grace for medieval scholasticism was that of the sacraments, and that of the Protestant Reformers the 'Word', with the Spirit embedded within and beneath those conceptualities and practices, for Wesley the primary language of grace was from beginning to end the language of the Spirit, certainly in conjunction with but by no means in subordination to the practice of Word or sacrament. Indeed, it was in making precisely this point concerning Spirit and grace that Wesley explicitly differentiated his own theological concern from that of the Reformation, and implicitly from that of scholasticism. Commenting on 2 Corinthians 1: 12, the text for his sermonic essay *The Witness of Our Own Spirit* (1746), he writes: 'By "the grace of God" is sometimes to be understood that free love, that unmerited mercy, by which I, a sinner, through the merits of Christ am now reconciled to God.' But then he goes on to elucidate his understanding of grace in this text—and the central theme in his own theology:

But in this place [the grace of God] rather means that power of God the Holy Ghost which 'worketh in us both to will and to do of His good pleasure'. As soon as ever the grace of God (in the former sense, his pardoning love) is manifested to our soul, the grace of God (in the latter sense, the power of his Spirit) takes place therein. And now we can perform, through God, what to man was impossible. Now we can order our conversation aright. We can do all things in the light and power of that love, through Christ which strengtheneth us. We now have 'the testimony of our conscience', which we could never have by fleshly wisdom, 'that in simplicity and godly sincerity... we have our conversation in the world'.   (Wesley 1975– : i. 309)

Wesley preached grace, therefore, not simply in terms of justification as 'unmerited mercy', the 'righteousness of Christ imputed to the one who has been brought to faith' that was the central Reformation concern, any more than he proclaimed grace as the infusion of 'operative leading to habitual and then to co-operative grace' leading to the righteousness that is fit for the vision of God, which was the medieval emphasis. Rather he was concerned to demonstrate, as Outler comments, 'how the process of sanctification, begun with regeneration, is really aimed at "the recovery of the image of God" (an equivalent phrase for holiness)' (Wesley 1975– : i. 299). In other words, while on the one hand we must say that Wesley was concerned not just with salvation as that which delivered us from the penalty of sin, but also—and even more so—with salvation as that which delivered us to a life in God's perfect love (*contra* a theology of the second article), then on the other hand we must say that Wesley was centrally concerned with the realization of God's righteousness in human individual and corporate life, not however as the fulfilment of nature but as the transformation of nature through new creation in the Holy Spirit (*contra* a theology of the first article). For once again, the point of departure for Wesley's theology was ultimately neither human capacity nor incapacity, but rather the gracious presence and activity of God through the Son and by the Spirit. In Wesley's words: 'I believe that Christ by his Spirit works righteousness in all those to whom faith is imputed for righteousness' (Wesley 1996: x. 272). Thus Robert Cushman rightly maintained that 'The first principle of Wesley's experimental divinity is, surely, the present and immediate working of the Holy Spirit' (Cushman 1989: 35).

In the role played by pneumatology in his theology, then, we find what is distinctive in Wesley's theologizing. He refused to remain mired in the dilemma of the either/or of Western theology and so play off creation against redemption or redemption against creation, human works against divine grace or divine grace against human works. His fundamental and unique concern was, rather, to seek a way beyond that impasse and pursue a theology that encompassed both those moments of God's activity in a unified vision of divine grace, a reading of the Trinitarian work of God in creation and reconciliation from the perspective of eschatological redemption; from the perspective, that is to say, of a theology of God the Holy Spirit, the transformer and perfecter of all creation. For this reason the very first sermon in the first published collection of Wesley's *Sermons on Several Occasions* begins with the by no means incidental declaration: 'All the blessings which God hath bestowed upon man are of his mere grace, bounty or favor'; and goes on to specify that those 'blessings' include both creation and salvation, describing the relationship of those two works of God in a phrase drawn from the Gospel of John (1: 16): 'grace upon grace' (Wesley 1975– : i. 117–18). The grace of God's creating in the Spirit is taken up and made perfect in the grace of God's redeeming of creation in the Spirit. And it was from that perspective of the Spirit that he proceeded to interpret Christian discourse accordingly. John Wesley was, therefore, as Albert Outler has remarked, 'working with a distinctive Pneumatology that has no exact equivalent ... up to [his] time' (Outler 1981: pp. xv–xvi). It was unique for one simple reason: because for him, the doctrine of the Holy Spirit came to be not simply a category interpreted within other categories in the larger body of Christian theology—as it had been for medieval scholasticism and the Protestant

Reformers—but rather gradually developed towards the defining category from which all else in the faith was interpreted. Note carefully: *the perspective from which all else was to be interpreted*—neither subordinated, nor downplayed, nor denied. In taking the sanctifying work of the Spirit as his point of departure, Wesley did not play off pneumatology against the work of the Father in the first article nor against the work of the Son in the second. He interpreted the work of the Father in creation and the Son in reconciliation, rather, in the light of the perfecting work of the Spirit—just as medieval monasticism and scholasticism and the Protestant Reformation had interpreted the Spirit from their respective points of departure. Thus he could write that the 'inspiration of the Spirit', by which he meant the whole of the work of the Spirit with the Father and the Son in creation and redemption to consummation, is 'the main doctrine of the Methodists' (Wesley 1931: ii. 64).

This, therefore, is the heritage of Methodist theology. In the course of Wesley's proclamation and practice of the gospel, his struggle to bring the Methodist societies to Christian discipline, his exegesis of Scripture and his explication of the doctrines of the faith, he came over time to intuit rightly that it was precisely the perspective offered by the 'grammar of the Spirit' that opened up his distinctive reading of the faith as the 'language of the Holy Ghost'. It was in this sense, that when Wesley came to write of the 'office and operation of the Holy Spirit', he understood himself to be speaking of 'the whole of real religion' (Wesley 1975– : ix. 467). For beginning with the transforming work of the Spirit of God in his *ordo salutis* (see Davies 1985: 92–3) he went on to speak of both creation, i.e. 'prevenient grace' (Rogers 1967), and reconciliation, i.e. Christ as 'spiritual prophet, priest and king' (Wesley 1950: 16), as 'grace upon grace'; as one complex, eschatological event in the Holy Spirit and through the Son that would culminate in the perfection of our humanity as God's 'image and likeness' in the world—indeed, would culminate in the perfection of all things. This was Wesley's 'Methodist Divinity', his 'grammar of the Spirit', with the aid of which he sought to elucidate the entirety of Christianity. It is this trajectory, I maintain, that constituted the promise of Wesley's theology then, and still constitutes the promise of the tradition that yet bears his name.

But why should that Wesleyan theological trajectory still constitute a promise to Methodism today? Wesley lived at the beginning of Modernity, while we live at its end; and he pursued his labours in the world of European Christendom, but our world is a global community in an age clearly post-Christendom and suffering what may very well be the final crisis of modernity. What does that eighteenth-century theological trajectory forged in England have to do with a twenty-first-century multicultural Methodism that encircles the planet? The answer to that question, I suggest, is that reclaiming the heritage of Methodist theology today is precisely that which would enable Methodism to learn to 'act its age' again; and in learning that lesson, to become faithful to both God and God's world anew. In the following I will briefly touch on three elements in such a reclaimed theology of the third article that could help Methodists do so.

The first characteristic of a contemporary Methodist theology of the third article would be that it would represent an expressly ecumenical theology. From the beginning, Wesley was involved in ecumenical dialogue as a constitutive part of the Methodist mission of calling men and women of every class and nationality to discipleship to Jesus Christ. He was convinced that his concern for holiness of life and for the Holy Spirit as that which brought such 'perfection' to fruition was no new discovery or invention, but belonged rather to the Christian tradition from the very beginning. What he sought to do was to critically reclaim that heritage in the context of the rapid cultural and ecclesiastical changes of eighteenth-century England and bring it into conversation with the churches as a resource for the renewal of Christianity in his own age. For Wesley, therefore, ecumenical dialogue and recourse to the past were for the sake of the whole of the Christian mission in the present—and in the future as well.

True to that heritage, Methodists have been at the forefront of the ecumenical movement throughout the past century, from its beginnings as an optimistic expression of the Modern missionary movement down to its desultory present when it has fallen prey to forms of the 'liberal/conservative' divide that was the bane of modern theology. Many now realize that if the ecumenical movement is to make progress once again, it must do so by regaining its focus on the mission to which God has called us through Christ and in the Spirit. By reclaiming its own distinctive kind of ecumenical heritage, a renewed Methodist theology of the third article could now serve Christianity at large by helping the churches discover anew the *missio Dei* that represents what is truly common among us in all the diversity of our past and our present—and in rediscovering that, to engage anew in that mission in the midst of the profound cultural and ecclesiological changes in the age in which we now live. Stanley Hauerwas has remarked that, 'Methodist identity makes sense only as it entails a commitment to discovering the unity of God's church through our different histories' (Hauerwas 1985: 19). By taking up a renewed theology of the third article and pursuing the kind of ecumenical agenda that marked its mission in the beginning, Methodism would thus begin to 'make sense' once again—and could help other Christian communities 'make sense' as well.

Such a theology is uniquely equipped to affirm the root concerns of the dominant traditions in the West and to point them beyond their mutual differences to a common theological effort with all other Christian communities in the context of the mission to which God has called us. Thus, on the one hand, with the champions of a theology of the first article, such a theology of the third article insists that the God who is redeemer in Christ Jesus is the selfsame creator of the world; and that creation, therefore, as an expression of the gracious goodness of God, is itself good and stands in a positive relationship with redemption. Yet the goodness of creation and its positive relation to redemption, according to such a theology, is not an ontological or anthropological 'given' but rather an ongoing pneumatological 'giving', for just as creation's good is the ever-renewed gift of God's life-giving and life-sustaining 'breath', so new creation through Christ is a new, eschatological impartation of such a divine Spirit taking up and transforming creation as an intimation of God's good purposes for all things. On the other hand, with the representatives of the theology of the second article, such a theology of the third article insists that it is God alone who brings about right relationship with humanity and God alone who makes the divine self known in and through Jesus Christ. Yet the question as to how the witness of Scripture itself attests to the way God achieves such reconciliation and self-revelation is answered by a theology of the third article in pointing to the work of the Spirit. According to that witness it is the Spirit who enables the Word to take up a broken and estranged creation in incarnation, whose anointing marks that Incarnate One as Son and Christ, whose descent is reflected in the consent of that Son to go the way of suffering and death on the cross, and who then finally takes up in resurrection that One who has fully entered into the horror of human estrangement and death. A theology of the third article, therefore, urges the dominant theologies in the West to a theological vision that begins neither with created capacity nor incapacity for God, but rather with God's capacity in and with and for all creation, the possibility of the Spirit; and in that possibility a theology of the third article seeks to encompass concerns for both creation and redemption on the horizon of God's eschatological promise of new creation, the 'perfection' or 'making holy' of all things in the Holy Spirit. And that horizon is one of God's mission into which we have been called by Jesus Christ.

Championing such an ecumenical theology would be for Methodists an act of repentance—and, just possibly, of renewal. For the truth is that for a variety of reasons the Methodist tradition has failed to achieve the promise of its own theological beginnings. In pointing to a theology of the third article, therefore, it would not be indulging in a further round of triumphalism, asserting its own superiority over all other forms of theologizing. Rather, it would serve to illustrate that the time for polemics and party-spirit in Christian theology is over. For this has indeed been a century of the rediscovery and reclamation of the various theological traditions of the West in the face of the twofold challenge of the passing of Christendom and the crisis of modernity. But in the course of that we have spent far too much time and effort trying to justify the various versions of those conflicting traditions we have reclaimed. Christendom, however, is now over, and modernity may be as well; and what that means positively is that the struggle for dominance over Western society and the self-justification of our theologizing may at last be set aside. Wesley could help teach us again to take up our theological task together today. Richard Heitzenrater has written of Wesley, that, although he held the early church in highest esteem, 'his purpose was not to replicate the first century in eighteenth-century England, but rather to live in his own day a life that was faithful to the love that God had shown for humankind in Jesus Christ' (Heitzenrater 1995: 319). We must do now what Wesley did then. And in doing that, we must in the same way do today what the monks and the scholastics as well as what Luther and the Reformers did in their day: we must give account in word and deed of the 'love God [has] shown for humankind in Jesus Christ' in the circumstances of the age in which we now live. A theology of the third article could very well be a way we could begin to do that together, and thus could begin to learn to 'act our age' again. Ecumenical theology, in this sense, would thus be best understood not simply as the task of resolving our 'internal' disputes concerning faith and practice, but rather as the common task of faithful living and thinking as disciples of Christ in the face of the challenge of the new 'external' situation in which we find ourselves called to pursue God's redemptive mission today.

The second characteristic of such a contemporary Methodist theology of the third article would be that it would offer the possibility of moving beyond the either/or that has characterized the Western theological tradition both in its classical and modern forms, for it would hold talk about God and talk about the creature called to be the 'image and likeness' of God in the world together. As I noted above, the conflicts of the two theologies that have dominated the Western tradition have tended to result in the one emphasizing the capacities of human nature at the expense of divine grace and the other the sovereignty of divine grace to the detriment of any human capacity of will or act. But a theology of the third article is a theology of 'grace upon grace'. That is, it is a theology that neither assumes the continuity of a divinely ordained teleology through the events of creation and redemption that would allow us to start with talk of the human, as does a theology of the first article, nor in protest declares the utter discontinuity of God's sovereign act of election between those two moments resulting in the necessity of starting with talk of divine contradiction of the human, as in a theology of the second article. A theology of the third article is, rather, an expressly Trinitarian theology that speaks of God neither in terms of first cause nor final decree, but as the *creator* of a humanity that is of itself prone to sin and subject to death and yet again as the *reconciler* who enacts new creation in and through Jesus Christ that by the renewed grace of the *redeemer* Holy Spirit opens up a hitherto unforeseeable and unrealizable possibility for human life as the 'image and likeness' of God in the world, that is, as the perfect expression in word and deed of divine love in and for God and thus in and for God's world. Such a theology, therefore, is a discourse that bespeaks the continuity of God's faithful loving-kindness through the discontinuity of creation's estrangement and death that calls forth a renewed, 'redeemed' (i.e. 'regained', 'recovered') creation that is the echo of such faithfulness. Thus talk about God and talk about humanity go together in such a theology.

That is why, while *pneumatology* is the 'field of discourse' of a theology of the third article, *Christology* is its centre. Jesus the Christ, the Son of God, is in the discourse of such a theology the humanity of God in the world, that divine humanity through whom and in relation to whom we begin to become truly human as the image of God in creation by the grace of the Spirit. In an age post-Christendom and in the midst of the crisis of modernity, the Christian community must learn again that in Jesus Christ we speak not just of humanity's God, but of

God's humanity; and indeed, that it is only by speaking of God's humanity that we can rightly speak of our humanity at all. For we live in an age that no longer has any common account of human being and becoming, that can no longer speak coherently or cogently of what it means to be a human or what would constitute a good or worthy human life. A contemporary Methodist theology of the third article would be a discourse that bespeaks the discovery of God's humanity in and for God's world though and in Jesus the Christ, a humanity whose beginning, whose mission in word and deed in God's creation, and whose end and new beginning is marked by the grace of the Holy Spirit.

The third element in such a contemporary Methodist theology of the third article would be that as a theology of Christian mission it would hold together what the Methodist and other traditions have in the past century too often allowed to be separated and played off against one another: evangelism and social action, the formation of disciples and the reformation of our social and material world, proclaiming the Word of God to the world and doing the Word in service to God's world. Thus we could address ourselves to the entirety of the creation that God has acted to redeem and avoid that evil that Wesley called 'practical atheism', the inability or refusal to see that 'nothing [is] separate from God' (Wesley 1975– : i. 515–16). The Methodists, just as the church in general in North America today, still bear the Modern marks of the deep division between those who, on the one hand, would stress continuity between church and society and call for the priority of social engagement in a world of suffering and injustice, and, on the other hand, those who emphasize the discontinuity between church and society and place the priority upon evangelism and discipleship in the midst of a world of sin. Addressing this divide, a renewed Methodist theology of the third article, once again, would represent a theology of continuity of God's grace through the discontinuity of creaturely sin. As a theology of 'grace upon grace' which can speak of the real and profound discontinuity of estrangement and death between creation and redemption, it is able to speak of the difference between church and society, and in doing so, would be able to help the church come to a new understanding of itself as a community of discipleship to Jesus Christ, led by the Spirit in the mission to the world to which God has called us. But precisely as a theology that can speak of such discontinuity, a theology of the third article can also speak of the continuity that the Spirit works between creation and redemption: the Spirit that led the Son—and all the daughters and sons in that Son—in his mission through the cross is the selfsame Spirit that raises the dead to new and transformed life and promises the eschatological transformation of all creation. The redemption God achieves through the Son and in the Spirit is not 'of' the creature or 'of' the world as created, but is rather 'for' the world that God is yet in the midst of creating. Thus it is precisely as a community called 'out of' the world that we are directed to and into God's world in hope and faith in the emergent Holy Spirit in whom God will yet 'make all things new'. For such a community remembers that the One who calls men and women to 'repent and believe the gospel of God' is the same One who breaks the loaves and the fishes to feed the multitude and who points to the 'least of these' in our midst. Therefore, a renewed Methodist theology of the third article would insist that no one can point the Christian community to the poor who does not at the same time point us to Christ, and no one can point us to Christ who does not at the same time point us to a world of suffering and death that Christ came to feed and clothe and heal and redeem. Moreover, no one in the Christian community can point us to God who does not point us to God's creation.

In a renewed Methodist theology of the third article we glimpse a way of laying claim to the Wesleyan theological tradition anew; a possibility that there might yet be a future for Methodism's past. In an age post-Christendom and struggling with the crisis of modernity, the church as a community of mission could very well find that such a theology of the 'Spirit who makes holy', in whom God creates and redeems, and in whom God's creatures can discover their full humanity in Christ, could serve to lead this broken and abandoned age in the words spoken by Jacob so long ago (Genesis 28: 16): 'Surely the Lord is in this place—and I did not know it!' Such is the promise, I suggest, of learning to read the faith anew with John Wesley according to the grammar of the Spirit.

Suggested Reading

CLAPPER, GREGORY S. (1997). 'John Wesley's "Heart Religion" and the Righteousness of Christ'. *Methodist History* 35: 148–56.

DABNEY, LYLE (2000). '*Pneumatologia Crucis*: Reclaiming *Theologia Crucis* for a Theology of the Spirit Today'. *Scottish Journal of Theology* 53: 511–24.

LESSMANN, THOMAS (1987). *Rolle und Bedeutung des Heiligen Geistes in der Theologie John Wesley.* Stuttgart: Christliches Verlagshaus.

MADDOX, RANDY L. (1994). *Responsible Grace: John Wesley's Practical Theology.* Nashville: Kingswood.

MATTHEWS, REX (1986). 'Religion and Reason Joined: A Study in the Theology of John Wesley'. Th.D. dissertation, Harvard University.

STARKEY, LYCURGUS, JR. (1996). *The Work of the Holy Spirit: A Study in Wesleyan Theology.* Reprint of 1962 edn. Nashville: Parthenon.

References

AQUINAS, THOMAS (1948). *Summa Theologica. Complete English Edition in Five Volumes,* trans. Fathers of the English Dominican Province. Westminster: Christian Classics.

AUGUSTINE (1956). *Nicene and Post-Nicene Fathers of the Christian Church,* v. *Anti-Pelagian Writings,* ed. Philip Schaff. 1st series. Grand Rapids: Eerdmans.

AUGUSTINE (1998). *Confessions*, trans. Henry Chadwick. Oxford: Oxford University Press.

BROWN, PETER (1969). *Augustine of Hippo*. Berkeley and Los Angeles: University of California Press.

BURNABY, JOHN (1991). *Amor Dei. A Study of the Religion of St. Augustine*. Norwich: Canterbury Press.

CUSHMAN, ROBERT E. (1989). *John Wesley's Experimental Divinity. Studies in Methodist Doctrinal Standards*. Nashville: Kingswood.

DAVIES, RUPERT (1985). *Methodism*. London: Epworth.

HARNACK, ADOLPH (1976). *History of Dogma*, trans. Neil Buchanan. Gloucester, Mass.: Peter Smith, vii.

HAUERWAS, STANLEY (1985). *Against the Nations*. Minneapolis: Winston.

HEITZENRATER, RICHARD (1995). *Wesley and the People Called Methodists*. Nashville: Abingdon.

LUTHER, MARTIN (1955). *Works*, ed. Jaroslav Pelikan. 55 vols. St Louis: Concordia; Philadelphia: Fortress.

OUTLER, ALBERT (1981). 'Preface'. In Frank Whaling (ed.), *John and Charles Wesley*. New York: Paulist.

ROGERS, CHARLES (1967). 'The Concept of Prevenient Grace in the Theology of John Wesley'. Ph.D. dissertation, Duke University.

WESLEY, JOHN (1931). *The Letters of the Rev. John Welsey*, ed. John Telford. London: Epworth.

—— (1950). *Explanatory Notes Upon the New Testament*. London: Epworth.

—— (1975–). *Works* (Bicentennial edn.). 34 vols. Nashville: Abingdon.

—— (1996). *The Works of John Wesley*. Grand Rapids: Baker Books.

CHAPTER 34

CHRISTIAN PERFECTION

WILLIAM J. ABRAHAM

JOHN WESLEY's doctrine of Christian perfection is at best a dead letter and at worst a source of political delusion among contemporary Methodists. This is not to say that we lack a significant body of literature on the topic; there is no lack of materials. Nor is it to claim that some clergy in Methodism do not profess whether they are expecting to achieve perfection in this life; they still do, for example, in responding to the formal questions required for ordination in the United Methodist Church. It is to claim that beyond vague platitudes and rhetorical flourishes the doctrine of Christian perfection is no longer operative. If true, this is a serious matter. What is at issue is the unravelling of the very core of the tradition. On the one hand, the breakaway groups that came into existence a century ago to preserve it, most notably the Church of the Nazarene, are now in the process of abandoning it (Lowery 2008). On the other hand, one of the leading contemporary Methodist theologians has turned to the self-avowed terrorist, Vladimir Lenin, for updating the doctrine of Christian perfection as reworked in terms of political liberation (Jennings 2007). Something has gone seriously wrong at the very heart of Methodist doctrine; if the patient is not already dead, it will take strong medicine to effect a cure.

We are so far removed from the originating doctrine of Christian perfection that retrieving it for the purposes of exposition is a challenge. John Wesley's vision of Christian perfection is an exercise in ascetic theology, a vision of realized eschatology, and a psychology of spiritual development. The ascetic element in the doctrine insists that a robust form of perfection is the goal of Christian existence under grace; Christian believers do not have to live morally defeated lives. The eschatological element posits that this perfection is possible now; it is not something that should be postponed to the life to come. The psychological element proposes that the attainment of perfection involves a radical spiritual reorientation beyond conversion; it is not something that characteristically occurs in conversion. Whatever the origins of his views, John Wesley posited the Christian life as a journey of grace to an attainable perfection that characteristically revolved around two crises. The first centred on the justification and new birth; the second on Christian perfection or entire sanctification. Beyond this, the believer continued to grow in grace until death. Entire sanctification was pivotal in this journey to glory; it was so important that Wesley considered it the grand *depositum* of Methodism to the world.

We should not be fooled by the spiritual mathematics involved. Wesley was well aware of the complexities of his special doctrine. He could handle differences of emphasis between himself and his brother Charles; he was not defensive about verbal differences with John Fletcher; he thought long and hard about how best to cultivate the prudential means of grace that would mediate its riches. He had a wide range of concepts for unpacking the nuances involved. He could speak not only of Christian perfection but also of entire sanctification, holiness of heart and life, the mind of Christ, circumcision of the heart, and perfect love. Moreover, the overarching ascetic vision was set within the Christian narrative of creation, freedom, fall, and redemption that informed his Trinitarian theology as a whole. He also knitted his doctrine of perfection seamlessly into a robust vision of human happiness. So there is no need to call into question the orthodoxy or the humanity of Wesley's views.

There are several excavation sites available that reveal Wesley's original position. His splendid mid-career sermon, 'The Scripture Way of Salvation' (Wesley 1985: 153–69), would fit the bill admirably. However, while Wesley was naive to think that there were not twists and turns in the development of his position, his *A Plain Account of Christian Perfection* (Wesley 1952) is as good a source as any. As early as 1725 when he was 23 Wesley began to show a deep interest in the quest for holy living. Prompted by Bishop Taylor's *Rules and Exercises of Holy Living and Dying*, Thomas à Kempis's *Christian's Pattern*, and William Law's *Christian Perfection* and *Serious Call*, he saw the impossibility of being half a Christian, taking to heart the desire to live a life totally devoted to God. When he came to believe that an entire inward and outward conformity to the mind of Christ was the material content of the only standard of truth in religion—the Bible—the issue was settled.

In time his vision of sanctification was recast within an analysis of the life of faith, but the fundamental horizon of thought and devotion did not change. The obvious danger, of course, was that Wesley would be drawn into a doctrine of works righteousness. On this he wavered, as can be seen in his early Sermon, 'The Image of God' (Wesley 1987: 290–303), where he has not yet come to terms with the doctrine of justification by grace through faith in all of its radical simplicity. He was still relying on human effort and sincerity as the core element in salvation. However, as Wesley worked through his fear of death, his shipboard encounter with the self-confident Moravians, his failure as a missionary in Georgia, and his Aldersgate experience, he began to sort through both the psychological and theological content of the issues involved. Wesley had first to come to terms with the pivotal place of justification by grace through faith in gaining forgiveness and assurance en route to his quest for holiness. Yet it is important not to lose sight of the pivotal place sanctification held in his theology as a whole. Even when he reintroduces a critical role for works in his final view of salvation, it bespeaks a new twist in the matter rather than a rerun of his earlier semi-Pelagian proposals.

As already indicated, Wesley was not slavish about what concepts best suited his purposes. Given that Christ himself had called on his followers to be 'perfect as our Father in heaven is perfect' (Matthew 5: 48) he did not draw back from using the language of perfection. In part this was driven by his resolute biblicism and by his rootedness in the church fathers; in part perhaps also by a desire to stake out in an aggressive manner his own convictions in the teeth of concerted opposition. Even his most sympathetic readers have baulked at this decision (Flew 1934; Sangster 1943). When Wesley carefully distinguishes Christian perfection from sinless perfection, the distinction can look terribly artificial. He restricts the possibility to adult Christians rather than babes in Christ. He limits sin to voluntary transgressions to the known law of God. He introduces deep qualifiers by noting, for example, the way that inevitable failure of knowledge leads to failure of action. As a logician, Wesley is at home in these kinds of move; what others would dismiss as pedantic hair-splitting, he sees as the natural correlation of precision and clarity. He could with equal firmness dismiss worries about fanaticism, self-deception, delusion, and pride, vices that most critics immediately raised.

Yet Wesley cannot be boxed into any neat system in his thinking about Christian perfection. It is the substantive issues at stake that he will not abandon. There is more to salvation than forgiveness, for salvation principally involves both justification and sanctification; it is mistaken to set limits to what the grace of God can do this side of the grave; Christ is deadly serious in the call to perfection; the Scriptures portray a model of pure religion in which those who are born of God do not commit sin; it really is possible in this life to love God with all our heart, soul, and mind and to love our neighbours as ourselves. By the grace of God, human agents can come to purity and singleness of intention; they can perfectly love God; they can be cleansed and cured of their evil tempers and dispositions; they can have the mind of Christ here and now; they can be pure in heart; they can be delivered from the power as well as the guilt of sin. Thereby they can attain the happiness intended for them by a good, omnipotent creator; and they can find peace in whatever providence lays upon them. To omit these themes or to marginalize them is to miss the heart and soul of Christianity.

As with the conceptual resources he deployed, Wesley was both firm and flexible in his vision of the psychological dimensions of the journey to entire sanctification. The general picture follows naturally from his overall vision of the Christian life. Initially the believer has to come to terms with the problem of guilt. As prevenient grace makes one aware of the reality of sin and the wrath of God, the problem of how one can be reconciled to God is an acute one. Hence the beginning believer needs to come to terms with God's love made known in the atoning death of Christ, with the nature of living faith as the condition of justification, with repentance, and with assurance. This is a tall order; for the temptation to think that it is all too good to be true is real, and the challenge of grasping the relevant concepts and doctrines takes time and effort. Experiencing justification, new birth, and assurance of forgiveness requires profound self-examination, the readiness to stay the course, and the learning of crucial elements of Paul and of Reformation theology. Contrary to what later commentators have often superficially averred, it was not the case that most people already possessed a solid sense of separation and guilt from God. The ridicule and opposition to the Methodist message undercuts this pleasing generalization. So too do Wesley's varied attempts to depict the natural person as one who could not care less about spiritual matters, his thoroughly robust vision of original sin, and his repeated insistence that it was only by grace that we come to see the truth about ourselves before God. To come to terms with guilt in a deep and realistic way was a demanding psychological achievement that took time and effort. Hence Wesley rightly observed that this was an important development that can readily be isolated and distinguished by perceptive observers of spiritual renewal.

It would not have surprised Wesley if converts were tempted to think that after coming to terms with justification all would be well. The sense of liberation from guilt was often exhilarating, so much so that it would be easy to think that the problem of gaining victory over evil had now been resolved. Wesley insisted otherwise. The challenge of facing the power of sin was as deep as the problem of the guilt of sin; most folk needed to work their way through a second set of issues to make progress. In this respect coming to terms with sin is like getting married; it is only within the relationship that its deeper demands and rewards can be appreciated much less addressed. Thus Wesley insisted both that there was a new crisis that had to be faced and that the fundamental theological grammar of this crisis was the same as that involved in justification. The believer had to confront the depth of sin, recognize that God intended to deal with sin's power in this life, wait expectantly upon God in the means of grace, and bear witness to the work of God as and how it happened.

We can see why purity of intention in entire sanctification was central to Wesley at this point, for on the human side what was at issue was a metachoice, a choice governing all other everyday choices, namely, the choice to allow one's life to be governed normatively and operationally by the will and power of God. It was not enough to tackle this or that sin; the deeper problem of the whole orientation of one's existence in love to God and neighbour was at issue. This required time and effort. So too did the fresh application of the relevant conceptual moves. God had given a resounding 'yes' to victory over evil in Christ and made that victory available through the presence of the Holy Spirit for all time and space; the believer should gladly say 'yes' to this 'yes' of God, most especially so since sanctifying grace was available to make this response a reality. Yet coming to terms with these truths was a demanding spiritual challenge existentially and intellectually.

One must not be misled by the breezy and easy way Wesley sorted out this vision of justification and sanctification. Wesley was a born teacher; the drive to simplify is essential to successful pedagogy; this shows up in his exposition of Christian perfection again and again. However, his flexibility of expression, his readiness to insist on divine freedom in achieving the end of holiness, and his sensitivity to contingent cases underlie the complexity of the life of sanctification. So too does the battery of resources he made available to those who were spiritually under his care. His sermons, tracts, and other writings tackle the relevant conceptual and theological issues from varied angles. His conversations with the preachers in conference show the need for revisiting what is involved. The invention of a complex network of societies, classes, and bands highlights the crucial place of informal spiritual direction for those on the journey to holiness. The brilliant and varied articulation of this faith presented in his brother's hymns brings home both the attraction and diverse nuances at stake. The carefully selected testimonial materials that he published in the *Arminian Magazine* both made holiness appear as an attainable goal and underwrote the place of experience as a hermeneutical lens for understanding the truth of Scripture on the matter. Once we locate entire sanctification in the full panoply of biblical exegesis, theological articulation, experiential testimony, and inventive spiritual and ecclesial practices, we can begin to see the massive experiment in the spiritual life that was at the core of Methodism. There was here a fresh synthesis that needs to be seen in its own terms as something intimately related to but different from earlier vision of conspicuous sanctity. It is a measure of the success of this experiment that it was readily exported to the new world in North America and took sufficient root to become there a pivotal force in the nineteenth century.

Aside from the intrinsic difficulties in the understanding and appropriation of the doctrine, there was always the possibility that an accident was waiting to happen. Wesley's work was located among the masses of spiritual and theological illiterates, so there was plenty of room for wayward development. This occurred as early as 1762 in London when Thomas Maxwell and others advanced the claim that entire sanctification opened the way for foretelling the arrival of the eschaton. Perfection could readily find a bedmate in 'enthusiasm'. It took courage and persistence on Wesley's part to stare down the opposition and stay the course (Gunter 1989). It is a measure of his commitment to entire sanctification that he soldiered on unabated. His response also showed that Wesley clearly distinguished between the moral goal of the Christian life and the attainment of various gifts of the Spirit, such as prophesy.

Making holiness logically and experientially distinct from the reception of spiritual gifts is one way in which Wesley's position differs radically from various strands of Pentecostalism. Even then we can see in Wesley and in the history of Methodism the undercurrents that were later to bear fruit in that remarkable movement. Wesley's two-stage vision of the Christian life provided the temporal framework for the doctrine of the Christian life within Pentecostalism. His care for the poor and his missionary zeal also reappear. John Fletcher (perhaps exploiting Wesley's discursive flexibility) spoke of baptism in the Holy Spirit as equivalent to entire sanctification (Wood 2003). The Holiness tradition in North America picked up this language and developed its own spin on the Methodist legacy. The resourceful Irish Methodist theologian and evangelist William Arthur began to mine the Pentecost narrative of Acts 2 for insight and exegetical elaboration. It was not long before the various undercurrents became a mighty wave of energy and theological experiment in its own right across virtually every nook and cranny of Christianity in the third world. The life and work of John Sung in China provides a brilliant example of a twentieth-century leader within Christianity in China whose debt to the Wesleyan tradition is obvious at first sight (Sung 2008). We can only speculate on what Wesley would make of his children and grandchildren in the faith; but there is no denying the fecundity of appropriation and development. The doctrine of perfection has lived on in radically altered ways in a Protestant underworld that tends to embarrass mainstream forms of Christianity in the West. Secular scholars rarely have the historical background and theological sensitivity to name much less understand what has been spawned across the last two centuries. Most modern Methodists in the West remain deeply discomfited by their offspring.

That embarrassment began in earnest with the reaction to the Holiness tradition in the late nineteenth century. When the bishops of the Methodist Episcopal tradition formally repudiated the Holiness version of Wesley at the General Conference of 1894 (Peters 1956: 147–8), the schisms that were already in place because of the upward mobility of the mainstream Methodist tradition were hardened and multiplied. Disputes about ministry to the poor dovetailed with disputes about the doctrine of sanctification. Yet the unease with holiness in mainstream Methodism needs to be seen in the light of a network of wider crises that inevitably shook the whole tradition to its foundations and that have left it scurrying for identity and unity for over a century.

First, the Civil War in the United States, together with the sheer challenge of sustaining the ecclesial disciplines, like class meetings, that were essential to the experience of holiness, destroyed the infrastructure of the tradition. Even that critical medium of indoctrination and pedagogy, the deep hymnody of Methodism, began to be sidelined. Second, social challenges of the late nineteenth century called into question the relevance of the quest for personal sanctity. For such figures as Harry Ward, the social causes of poverty required a different analysis of sin and how to meet it; he turned to Marxism and Soviet communism as the appropriate reformulation of the goals of the tradition (Abraham 2002: 161–80). Third, the difficulties for robust forms of Christian theism thrown up by historical criticism, by new developments in philosophy and science, and by public forms of scepticism eroded the native confidence of Methodists in the faith of the church across the centuries. Taken together these rifts in the wider Christian tradition across the West left the vision of holiness bereft of the critical background theological resources that quietly nourished it. Without these resources the doctrine would wither and die, or it would be reduced at the popular level to pious legalism or to suffocating forms of social activism. In time, Wesley himself was set aside as a creature of his times; his work may have been fine for the eighteenth century, it was thought, but it was not sufficient for the troubles and challenges of a new day. So deep was the fissure in the tradition that it took two generations for his life and legacy to be revisited.

There was more at work in these developments than the changing context. While Wesley had tried valiantly to ensure that his hard-won insights about the Christian life would be available after he died, there were potential seeds of self-destruction in place from the beginning. At a very general level, his version of biblicism was an unstable epistemological experiment in its own right that would make it deeply vulnerable to the turn to Liberal Protestantism in the nineteenth century (Chiles 1965). Wesley never really integrated his bedrock commitment to perception of the divine in religious experience with his vision of special revelation in Scripture. Moreover, the privileging of the epistemology of theology over theology proper meant that the tradition could never take Wesley's own material claims on the heart of the faith as primary. His vision of holiness and its canonical expressions would have to be articulated and defended afresh in every generation. Equally his stalwart Protestantism left little or no room either for the classical faith of the church or for his own quasi-canonical proposals over time. These were strictly human traditions that were secondary to the life of the church; they could only be approached with a hermeneutic of suspicion.

More particularly, Wesley's insistence that holiness was the heart and soul of the faith paved the way for a radically anthropocentric turn that bedevils the tradition as a whole. We can surely see the virtue of Wesley's move to cast holiness as the heart of Christianity. The Scriptures, together with the faith and practices of the church, have a purpose; they are intended to bring us to the radical renewal of human existence. However, if this is said without due care, the purpose can readily be divorced from its antecedents and drift off into a life of its own. We can begin well by looking at God in the work of creation and redemption but all too easily end up looking at ourselves looking at God. The shift from a theocentric to an anthropocentric vision can happen in the twinkling of an eye. Once this happened, and it happened in Wesley's own canonical sermons, the development of narrow forms of legalism and social activism are not inevitable but they are more than likely to occur. The deep truths of creation and redemption fade quietly into the background and then disappear altogether. Any doctrine of the Christian life nested within the faith of the church and critically dependent upon it will not long survive once this happens. This is even more so when holiness is isolated as the essence of Christianity.

When the reduction of the faith to a doctrine of the Christian life is accompanied by wider developments in theology, culture, and society then retaining any serious commitment to entire sanctification will be doubly difficult. In this respect Wesley was exceptionally fortunate in that he lived at a time when the wider faith of the church had been defended with skill by intellectuals such as Bishop Butler. In fact Wesley lived in a world where there were not just confessional universities and a confessional church as represented by the Church of England; there was also a confessional state. Wesley's doctrine of perfection and his judgemental eye hid all this from sight; as did his focus on the Christian life; but it is hard to underestimate the critical significance of this background music for the development and sustaining of the grand *depositum* of Methodism. Once functional atheism and secularization become the order of the day in state and society, if not in theology itself, then it is hard to see how entire sanctification could survive as a living option. Looking back, we can now see that this process of radical challenge and erosion was well under way by the late nineteenth century. Precisely at the time when Methodist leaders triumphantly saw themselves as the wave of the future, their ship was being torpedoed below the waterline.

This way of shaping the narrative makes it clear that it is a mistake to treat the doctrine of Christian perfection merely as an appendage to the wider doctrines of Methodism. We can, if we will, rework it as a distinctive development that was initially poorly grafted into the wider faith of the church. I shall consider that possibility later. Yet it was more than this originally; as one element in a complex doctrine of the Christian life, Christian perfection was of the very essence of Christianity. Hence the loss of this doctrine was not just a bump in the road; it was the end of the road.

Once the doctrine of perfection was lost, Methodism did what it could to invent a new identity with materials and practices that were more peripheral to the tradition as a whole. Hence this way of reading the tradition explains the deep ambivalences and fissures that have shown up in Methodism over the last century and a half. It is tempting to believe that the tradition has never really recovered despite the sunny optimism and cheerful pragmatism with which it often presented itself. The optimism and pragmatism were theological afterbirth that was mystically produced to prove that the baby was still alive and well. The naked truth is that once the doctrine of entire sanctification was abandoned, dissolved, or transmuted, Methodism (or at least Wesleyan Methodism) died. Methodism lived on institutionally as a disparate and distinctive network of dispositions, insights, rhetoric, interest groups, and practices; but there was no deep coherence or consensus at the level of liturgy, doctrine, or experience. This could have been disastrous. However, the weight of Wesley's own writings and the brilliance of his connexionalism provided a ready way for the tradition to continue and to adjust to both its own internal disintegration and to the changed contexts in which Methodism had to survive across the world. Despite its theological indifferentism and confusion, Methodism somehow managed to survive by means of constant internal conversation and by seeking working consensus in its conferencing. In this respect Methodism has been institutionally in better shape that many other forms of mainline Protestantism.

One way to discern the current status of the doctrine of Christian perfection in contemporary Methodism is to consult the work of Albert Cook Outler, the most influential Methodist theologian of the twentieth century. Driven inwardly by the need to remake Methodism for a new day and outwardly by the challenge of the ecumenical movement to explain his tradition to curious outsiders, he bet the store on the retrieval and updating of Wesley. His historical labours were monumental and his theological efforts no less diligent. There is no doubting his sympathy for the whole drift of Wesley's theology, including its quest for holiness; his rhetorical skill in finding ways to make Wesley's legacy come alive are unsurpassed. Yet his central convictions about the enduring elements in Wesley lie outside the doctrine of perfection. They rest on the so-called Wesleyan Quadrilateral as a solution to the longstanding problem of authority and on Wesley's synergism of divine and human action in resolving the dispute about freedom and grace in the debate between East and West. When it came to the actual content of Wesley's doctrine of perfection, Outler systematically ignored the marrow of Wesley's own views. Holiness is reduced to the moral platitude to love God and neighbour (Outler 1996: 128–31). In the wake of Outler, entire sanctification in the work of Randy Maddox became a gradualism of grace-driven change that also misses the hard core of his theological and psychological proposals (Maddox 1994: 153–4). Kenneth Collins (1997: 157) has tried valiantly to redress the balance in his reiterated criticisms of Maddox by insisting on a more accurate reading of Wesley. The debate about entire sanctification has of late become a scholastic exercise.

The most serious rival interpretation of entire sanctification has surfaced in the efforts to infuse the insights of liberation theology into Methodism. Liberation theology took hold in Methodist circles in the 1970s when it became the default, go-to position at the Oxford Institute for Methodist Studies, the quadrennial global forum for Methodist theology. The connection with sanctification was a natural one in that sanctification can easily become a synonym for the more generic appeal of liberation (Runyon 1981). Given that the shift from personal transformation to social transformation had already been forged in the late nineteenth century, the move to liberation theology was standing waiting to be exploited. Yet liberation theology was not simply a repetition of the earlier tradition. It developed a radically different epistemological stance in which the poor became a privileged site of truth either in the interpretation of Scripture or in their own right. The former paralleled Wesley's appeal to the experience of sanctification as a hermeneutic of Scripture; the latter fitted with Wesley's moralism that made much of the plight of the poor and with Wesley's conviction that works of mercy are a genuine means of grace. Proponents of the new view set aside Wesley's political conservatism and deployed Wesley's scattered essays and *obiter dicta* to construct a 'Wesleyan' vision of economics (Jennings 1990). The exposition faltered when Wesley himself was seen as an apostate from the 'Wesleyan' tradition.

The deep intention in the liberationist appropriation of sanctification is to highlight the crucial place of economics, oppression, and political power in any genuine transformation. This correlates with the suspicion that personal piety can readily become a mechanism of escape, with a sense that genuine salvation is social and political in character, and with scepticism towards standard forms of rational inquiry as applied to economics and politics. Liberation of the poor and oppressed becomes both the site of sanctification and the benchmark of truth. Given that these groups are often illiterate, it is pragmatically self-contradictory for rich academics to speak on behalf of the poor. The temptation to turn to Marxist sources for help in understanding the present and mapping the future is acute at this point in part because versions of Marxism have been pervasive both politically and intellectually. Yielding to this temptation neatly explains the extraordinary appeal to Vladimir Lenin as a serious source for Methodist political theology (Jennings 2007). The advice appropriated can be neatly summarized: work in broad solidarity with all groups that resist military hegemony and capitalist domination; be guided by a clearly thought out and applied theory; look upon imperialism as the highest stage of capitalism; move beyond denunciation to a careful sifting of the good and evil in the status quo; train a cadre of propagandists and agitators to expose the evils of capitalism and organize resistance.

This explanation of the appeal to Lenin is complemented by those theories that see the disastrous effects of modern humanism and Marxism as intelligible but illusory transformations of earlier theological materials (Gray 2007). The transmutation of sanctification into liberation mirrors, for example, the similar transmutation of eschatology into political utopia with the concomitant intellectual and moral blindness that ensues. So the shift from sanctification to liberation involves not just a tenacious commitment to a favoured political orthodoxy; it also entails either the unwillingness or the incapacity to take seriously radically different accounts of the complex relation between the state and globalization. The same holds *mutatis mutandis* for those who see in pacifism an apt expression of sanctification for today.

The salient point to note at this stage is that the doctrine of Christian perfection has become either a dead letter or a source of political delusion. This dénouement of Methodism's central doctrine is clearly an extraordinary challenge for modern Methodists. The easy way forward would be to accept that this element in the tradition is now well and truly dead and move on. After all, the doctrine as originally developed did not even have the merit of theological beauty or depth; it was developed by a theologian whose work 'is not a good advertisement for reading on horse-back' (Knox 1950: 447). So we should confess the error of our ways and salvage what we can of the tradition as a whole.

Wesley himself showed initial signs of wavering about the future of the doctrine of perfection, lamely asking: 'But whatsoever this doctrine is, I pray you what harm is there in it?' (Wesley 1952: 109). It is hard to see how a harmless doctrine can inspire much hope of recovery. However, Wesley's answer is worth pondering afresh.

Look at it again; survey it on every side, and that with the closest attention. In one view, it is purity of intention, dedicating all the life to God. It is the giving to God of all our hearts: it is one desire and design ruling all our tempers. It is the devoting, not a part, but all our soul, body, and substance to God. In another view, it is all the mind which was in Christ, enabling us to walk as Christ walked. It is the circumcision of the heart from all filthiness, all inward as well as outward pollution. It is a renewal of the heart in the whole image of God, the full likeness of Him that created it. In yet another, it is the loving God with all our heart, and our neighbour as ourselves ... Now, let this perfection appear in native form, and who can speak a word against it?   (ibid.)

As noted earlier, the doctrine of perfection was an exercise in ascetic theology, which was also a form of realized eschatology that posited a distinctive phenomenology of the Christian life. Methodism preached a vision of perfection as a real possibility for all believers here and now; it offered entire sanctification for the masses rather than postpone it till death or limit it to the chosen few in the monastery. It also insisted that entire sanctification characteristically involved an intentional reorientation of the totality of human existence after justification and new birth. Taken in the round this was its distinctive contribution, its grand *depositum*. Methodism failed to sustain this vision for a host of reasons. Clearly, Wesley and his heirs were not really able to integrate it into sufficiently robust networks of theological reflection and ecclesial practice. Nor did they have the capacity or the resources to sustain this vision in the teeth of extended criticism. Even so, Methodism's doctrine of perfection was a noble experiment in spirituality that gave birth to a host of fresh expressions of the Christian faith that continue into the present. These have not always been a pretty sight and some are doomed to extinction, but the question to be asked is whether the core elements can be retrieved and updated.

Given that the doctrine of perfection is fundamentally a vision of Christian existence, the first order of business must surely be within the field of ascetic theology. In this arena Wesley's insistence on the possibility of real victory over evil in entire sanctification should be seen not as an aberrant minority report but as constitutive of the Christian tradition. Once we get beyond the shibboleths of the language of perfection and recognize the heart of the doctrine, we can see that the doctrine of Christian perfection is central to the faith of the church in the first millennium. Wesley has his own distinctive interpretation of what is at issue, but he is on the right track. Paul Bassett is right to press the case for continuity rather than discontinuity with the teaching of the church (Bassett 1997). It is those who in a show of false humility make much of the impossibility of perfection who are out of step with the great tradition of the church; Wesley stands firmly inside the circle of faith, not outside it. Moreover, Wesley's aggressive optimism of grace fits much more aptly with the witness of Scripture and the wider canonical heritage of the church than does the systematic pessimism of Luther or Calvin or the sombre moderation of Anglicanism. While Wesley's Protestantism has no formal place for the canon of saints, their very existence makes it clear that conspicuous sanctity really is possible in this life. The call to perfection is not an idle ideal; it is an attainable goal, made visible in the lives of the saints.

Second, it is hard to see how such a goal can be achieved without the kind of intentional and radical submission to God that Wesley carefully noted in his own observations of the spiritual life. It was this element of radical decision that was picked up by Phoebe Palmer in the Holiness Movement. Elaine Heath's ground-breaking discovery that Palmer reinvented the spiritual insights of Teresa of Avila right within the heart of Methodism shows that Palmer's psychological observations were not as crude as they look at first sight (Heath 2009). If Palmer's version of the Wesleyan tradition can be assimilated to the wider treasures of ascetic theology, then the argument is equally compelling in the case of Wesley. To be sure, Wesley's vision has little place for, say, the dark night of the soul, or for the complex form of conspicuous sanctity embodied recently in the life of Mother Teresa. Nor would Wesley be comfortable with the gift of tears or transfiguration, as it shows up in Eastern Orthodoxy. Wesley is clearly intoxicated by those elements in ascetic theology that caught his attention; he is blind to other elements. However, the way forward is to enrich the important discoveries of Wesley rather than to ditch them. This enrichment needs a look backward into the deep tradition of the church and a courageous step forward into developments within Pentecostalism. Only then can the psychological insights of Wesley's doctrine be properly identified and assimilated.

Such work needs to be aided and abetted with much more serious endeavours in historical and systematic theology. These can begin by giving attention to the wealth of work in Methodist dogmatics right across the history of the tradition but most especially in the first century after Wesley. I use the term 'dogmatics' deliberately, for it challenges the theological indifference and imprecision that set in when Methodist theologians lost their intellectual nerve and repudiated the work of their predecessors in the nineteenth century. The target of investigation in this arena will take us initially beyond the canonical sermons of Wesley to the canonical doctrines of the various Methodist traditions, as seen initially, say, in the Articles of Religion and Confession of Faith of United Methodism. In turn this work can lead to a more sympathetic reading of the first generation of systematic theologians who have all too readily been dismissed as scholastic betrayers of the tradition. Serious mistakes were indeed made, but the way to avoid them in the future is to map them carefully and think through the issues afresh. The guiding insight in play here is that the doctrine of the Christian life belongs in the deeper faith of the church; indeed the history of Methodism shows that the doctrine of perfection cannot survive if its anthropocentric tendencies are not healed by radical immersion in the great sweep of Christian thinking embodied in creation, freedom, fall, and redemption. Moreover, reading the tradition with an eye to spiritual nourishment will give life to material dismissed as archaic and irrelevant. It should inspire fresh proposals in systematic theology that go beyond the political delusions and sentimental moralism that can be such a marked feature of Methodism as a whole.

Happily, the division of labour that is emerging between the epistemology of theology and theology proper provides a significant opportunity for the retrieval of the ascetic and theological resources so sorely needed. We can now readily distinguish between knowing God and knowing how we know God. We can chart the differences between radical appropriation of the faith of the church and rationally defending the faith of the church, between the practices of ascetic theology and the practices of intellectually justifying those practices. Modern and postmodern theology tends to privilege debates about the epistemic status of faith over the actual living of the faith. In his own way, Wesley shared this tendency, even though he was driven first and foremost by a thirst for holiness. However, we can now insist on the importance both of epistemology and of theology proper without allowing epistemic considerations to elbow aside the quest for union with God. The revolutions in epistemology that have arrived with the demise of classical foundationalism and the emergence, say, of virtue epistemology, create the kind of space that Butler and his cohorts provided for Wesley in the eighteenth century. Indeed, we can now see that ascetic practices may be vital to the epistemic status of robust forms of faith (Alston 1991). However, whatever we decide in this arena, we should not allow such deliberations to cut short the articulation of forms of systematic theology that build on and extend the kind of radical immersion into the life of God that Methodism championed. Methodism as a movement of revival and renewal was also a fresh exercise in catechesis; new work in ascetic and systematic theology should make a virtue out of this, just as the early pioneers of these disciplines in the patristic period did so successfully in their day and generation.

It might be thought that the recent turn to liberation theology within mainstream Methodism calls this kind of agenda into question. Fresh work in ascetic and systematic theology of the kind proposed will appear to some as a form of escapism that diverts the tradition from its true calling in the future, that is, from fresh reflection on social transformation, inclusivism, and liberation. Clearly, we need high-quality political theology; we can be grateful for the labours of those who have pioneered work in this area. However, it is an open question how political theology is best pursued. Given Wesley's own Burkean sensibilities (Weber 2001), it would be odd in the extreme to bet the store on any one political ideology as the only way forward, much less to allow that ideology to suffocate the freedom of theological studies as a whole. In any case, deep political love of neighbour can benefit from radical love of God; aggressive political work will depend in any serious Christian vision of politics on robust immersion in the life of faith. Thus this worry can be set aside without undue distress. The safer bet is that future forms of Methodism will need a supply of much richer spiritual and theological resources than are available in any political theology, much less liberation theology. The challenges of militant atheism and hard secularism make that abundantly clear. So too does the spread of Islam. It would be ironic and tragic if a tradition that made radical submission to God constitutive of its vision of attainable perfection were to find itself bereft of this treasure when it confronts the challenge that all forms of Islam present in the political and theological world we now occupy.

SUGGESTED READING

ABRAHAM, WILLIAM J. (2005). *Wesley for Armchair Theologians*. Louisville, Ky.: Westminster John Knox.

JONES, MARGARET (2004). 'Growing in Grace and Holiness'. In Clive Marsh, Brian Beck, Angela Shier-Jones, and Helen Wareing (eds.), *Unmasking Methodist Theology*. New York: Continuum, 155–68.

LINDSTRÖM, HARALD (1946). *Wesley and Sanctification*. Stockholm: Nya Bokförlags Aktiebolget.

MANSKAR, STEVEN W. (2003). *A Perfect Love: Understanding John Wesley's A Plain Account of Christian Perfection*. Nashville: Discipleship Resources.

ORCIBAL, JEAN (1965). 'The Theological Originality of John Wesley and Continental Spirituality'. In Rupert Davies and Gordon Rupp (eds.), *A History of the Methodist Church in Great Britain*. London: Epworth, i. 81–111.

SCHLIMM, MATTHEW R. (2003). 'The Puzzle of Perfection: Growth in John Wesley's Doctrine of Perfection'. *The Wesleyan Theological Journal* 38: 124–42.

WESLEY, JOHN (1985). 'The Scripture Way of Salvation'. In Wesley (1985).

REFERENCES

ABRAHAM, WILLIAM J. (2002). 'From Revivalism to Socialism: The Impact of the Poor on Harry Ward'. In Richard P. Heitzenrater (ed.), *The Poor and the People Called Methodists 1729–1999*. Nashville: Abingdon.

ALSTON, WILLIAM P. (1991). *Perceiving God: The Epistemology of Religious Experience*. Ithaca, N.Y.: Cornell University Press.

Bassett, Paul M. (1997). *Great Holiness Classics, i. Holiness Teaching—New Testament Times to Wesley*, ed. Paul M. Bassett. Kansas City: Beacon Hill.

Collins, Kenneth J. (1997). *The Scripture Way of Salvation: The Heart of John Wesley's Theology*. Nashville: Abingdon.

Chiles, Robert E. (1965). *Theological Transition in American Methodism, 1790–1935*. New York: Abingdon.

Flew, R. Newton (1934). *The Idea of Christian Perfection in Christian Theology: An Historical Study of the Christian Ideal for the Present Life*. New York: Humanities Press.

Gray, John (2007). *Black Mass, Apocalyptic Religion and the Death of Utopia*. London: Penguin.

Gunter, W. Stephen (1989). *The Limits of Love Divine: John Wesley's Response to Antinomianism and Enthusiasm*. Nashville: Kingswood.

Heath, Elaine (2009). *Naked Faith: The Mystical Theology of Phoebe Palmer*. Eugene, Ore.: Pickwick.

Jennings, Theodore, Jr. (1990). *Good News to the Poor: John Wesley's Evangelical Economics*. Nashville: Abingdon.

—— (2007). 'Lessons from Lenin', http://www.oxford-institute.org/docs/2007papers/2007–6Jennings.pdf, accessed 9 August 2008.

Knox, R. A. (1950). *Enthusiasm: A Chapter in the History of Religion*. Oxford: Clarendon.

Lowery, Kevin Twain (2008). *Salvaging Wesley's Agenda: A New Paradigm for Wesleyan Virtue Ethics*. Eugene, Ore.: Pickwick.

Maddox, Randy L. (1994). *Responsible Grace: John Wesley's Practical Theology*. Nashville: Abingdon.

Outler, Albert C. (1996). *Evangelism and Theology in the Wesleyan Spirit*. Nashville: Discipleship Resources.

Peters, John Leland (1956). *Christian Perfection and American Methodism*. Nashville: Abingdon.

Runyon, Theodore (1981). *Sanctification and Liberation: Liberation Theologies in the Light of the Wesleyan Tradition*. Nashville: Abingdon.

Sangster, W. E. (1943). *The Path to Perfection: An Examination and Restatement of John Wesley's Doctrine of Christian Perfection*. Nashville: Abingdon.

Sung, Levi (ed.) (2008). *The Journal Once Lost—Extracts from the Diary of John Sung*. Singapore: Genesis.

Weber, Theodore R. (2001). *Politics in the Order of Salvation, Transforming Wesleyan Political Ethics*. Nashville: Kingswood Books.

Wesley, John (1952). *A Plain Account of Christian Perfection*. London: Epworth.

—— (1985). *Works, ii. Sermons II, 34–70*, ed. Albert C. Outler. Nashville: Abingdon.

—— (1987). *Works, iv. Sermons IV, 115–151*, ed. Albert C. Outler. Nashville: Abingdon.

Wood, Lawrence E. (2003). *The Meaning of Pentecost in Early Methodism: Rediscovering John Fletcher as John Wesley's Vindicator and Designated Successor*. Lanham, Md.: Scarecrow.

CHAPTER 35

ASSURANCE

KENNETH J. COLLINS

The knowledge that one is not only forgiven but also a child of God constitutes what the early church recognized as Christian assurance. The classic texts for this biblically based teaching are found in Romans 8: 15–16, Galatians 4: 5–8, and 1 John 2: 12–14. With the rise of Montanism in the second century, a rigorist charismatic movement that afforded women a leadership role with the ministries of Priscilla and Maximilla, the old catholic church (not to be confused with the later historical developments of Roman Catholicism and Eastern Orthodoxy) took a turn away from a functional, gift-infused conception of the ecclesia to a more institutional one in which office, ritual, sacraments, and objective authority played a larger role.

During the Middle Ages the doctrine of Christian assurance, with its direct connection with the Holy Spirit, was virtually muted as the eastern and western communions (which formally divided in 1054) underscored the role of a burgeoning tradition. According to Lycurgus Starkey (1962: 26) they subjected the Holy Spirit to a sacred time and place within the sacramental life of the church now overseen by an increasingly powerful priesthood. By the time of the Council of Trent during the sixteenth century (1545–63) the substance of the doctrine of assurance at its highest levels, in other words, that believers could know beyond doubt or fear that they were the children of God, was repudiated outright. Even today the Roman Catholic *New Dictionary of Theology* does not contain a single, separate entry on either the doctrine of assurance or the witness of the Spirit, an omission that speaks volumes. This same oversight characterizes the popular Eastern Orthodox catechism, *The Living God*.

Although the Church of England, as a vital part of the Reformation, viewed her own life and ministry as containing many of the major elements of reform necessary to revitalize the church through the inculcation of scriptural Christianity, nevertheless the Anglican doctrinal standards themselves did not explicitly recover the teaching of personal assurance (though some contended it was implied)—a task that was by and large left to the Methodists. Indeed, though Methodism is often associated with an emphasis on Christian perfection when viewed by other traditions, it is rarely discerned that the reforming impulse of this movement was actually much broader and far more extensive than this single doctrine can allow. That is, Methodist reform included not simply the correction of outright errors in the western church (the failure to recognize the Holy Scriptures as the highest authority; the issue of works and merit and their relation to justification; the doctrine of purgatory) but also the transformation of a formalized, orthodox Christianity that in some instances, oddly enough, stifled the gracious and free agency of the Holy Spirit.

John Wesley

John Wesley, erstwhile Oxford don, was born to Samuel and Susanna in 1703 and became widely known as the Father of Methodism. On one occasion he referred to the doctrine of Christian assurance as a grand part of the testimony that God has given the Methodists to bear to all humanity, both inside and outside the church. Again, it is the main doctrine of the Methodists, he insisted, and as such lies at the heart of reform on the way to a revitalized, Spirit-infused Christian faith. Indeed, Wesley's long and anguished spiritual struggles, from 1725 to 1738, can be understood in one sense as the desire for the knowledge that he was a child of God, adopted by the Most High and beloved of the Lord.

The Direct Witness

Ever careful in his practical theology, Wesley expressed his basic understanding of Christian assurance in two key ways: the direct witness of the Holy Spirit and the indirect witness of our own spirit. In terms of the former, Wesley considered this witness to be an inward impression on the souls of believers whereby the Holy Spirit directly testifies to their spirit that they are the children of God. By the terminology of 'inward impression' Wesley likely had in mind the intimate relation of the Spirit to the human soul such that the Spirit reveals to the believer a divine and human harmony in holiness and love. This testimony, again wrought by no one less than the Spirit of God, is in its earliest degrees not an assurance of what is to come; rather, it is a witness to a present reality of both forgiveness and initial holiness. This testimony of adoption, in its efficacy, can no more be doubted, Wesley taught, than the shining of the sun in its full strength.

As such the direct witness of the Spirit, according to Wesley, is best understood not as a species of co-operant grace, of divine and human acting, but of free grace through which the superintending role of the Holy Spirit, as the administrator of redemption, is clearly evident. Indeed, many in Wesley's own age, and some even in the class meetings, were not only personally moral and socially respectable, but they also evidenced the fruit of the Spirit in their lives; and yet they lacked, for various reasons, this direct witness of the Spirit. To be sure, the immediate nature of this witness, which proves to be so baffling to some and is a window on the issue of grace and works, underscores the liberty and graciousness of God as the Father sends forth the Spirit of the Son into believing hearts such that they cry, 'Abba, Father'.

This witness is direct or immediate in that it does not represent the conclusion of a logical argument such as, 'I have the fruit of the Spirit; therefore, I am a child of God.' In other words, it is not a human witness marked by a sequence of deliberation or ratiocination but a divine witness marked by a superintending agency. The immediate nature of this witness, however, does not preclude the means of grace as the normal channels through which this supernatural grace is most often communicated. Indeed, as Colin Williams pointed out, the Spirit often illumines believing hearts as they read the Scriptures and hear the Word of God preached (Williams 1960: 99).

Again, the term 'immediate' in this context, as Wesley employed it, refers largely to the temporal elements of this witness indicating the importance of instantiation and actualization in the warp and woof of life. Put another way, if believers are actually assured of their adoption, that is, if this no longer simply remains a possibility in an open and unending process, then such a direct witness by its very nature must be instantaneous—or else it has not yet been actualized. Here the element of knowledge is crucial simply because believers will know at a particular point in time that they are indeed the sons and daughters of God. So memorable and distinct is this transforming knowledge lavished upon the soul by the Holy Spirit that it is almost impossible to mistake this testimony for the voice of nature or for the normal course of human, moral development. To be sure, Wesley, himself, opined on one occasion that he knew of twelve or thirteen hundred people who clearly recognized the very day when the Spirit first witnessed with their spirits. In addition, due to the direct communication of knowledge that makes up this witness the usual objections to the instantaneous nature of this divine, not human, work now appear to be both unfounded and confused, for how could one not be aware of the time when a direct, supernatural testimony was so graciously given since this witness necessarily entails knowledge. In short, it is part and parcel of the essence of the direct witness that the Holy Spirit makes believers cognizant of the gracious work that is being done in them.

Moreover, though the direct witness can indeed arise in a communal setting such as in a church service, class meeting, or prayer group, Wesley nevertheless maintained that this is a private and personal witness, not a public one. In other words, just as no two consciences are the same, so the testimony of the Spirit to the soul must necessarily be private, personal, and appropriate. Indeed, the direct witness entails not the general knowledge that Christ died for the sins of the whole world, but the particular and personal realization that Christ died for me and that I, even I, am a child of God, one who is richly and satisfyingly loved in the Lord.

Though Wesley repeatedly affirmed the reality of the witness of the Spirit, he recognized that the manner of this assurance given to believers was beyond his comprehension, and he therefore referred to the agency of the Spirit along these lines as a strong, though inexplicable operation. Such knowledge, Wesley maintained, was too wonderful and excellent for him and he therefore could not attain to it. The inexplicable nature of the manner of this witness, that is precisely how the Spirit bears testimony to the believing heart, underscores once again the private nature of this work. That is, those who have this witness in themselves cannot explain it to those who, for what ever reason, lack it. Nor is it reasonable to expect that they should ever be able to communicate this in a corporate or public way. In other words, such a witness cannot be naturally comprehended and therefore cannot be readily shared from one to the other. On the contrary, the things of the Spirit of God must be spiritually discerned and realized in a participatory and personal way, an activity that bespeaks of ineffability, mystery, and wonder.

The witness of the Spirit must be antecedent to the witness of our own spirit, Wesley reasoned, since we must be holy in heart and life before we can be conscious that we are so. Though this witness is direct and immediate as indicated above, Wesley nevertheless outlined the soteriological sequence in terms of love, holiness, and assurance that plays out in the believer's life. Thus, for instance, he revealed that we must love God before we can be holy at all, this being the root or fount of all holiness. But we cannot love God until we know that the Most High loves us. Therefore Wesley's delineation of these basic truths of redemption indicates quite clearly that some of the thinking about the witness of the Spirit in his own age was often confused. That is, when the testimony of the Holy Spirit was even acknowledged it was often relegated to one of the last things that occur in the process of redemption rather than as one of the first. 'We love because He first loved us' (1 John 4: 19).

Though Wesley affirmed a sequence along the *ordo salutis* and taught that the love of God, holiness, and the consciousness thereof are related, and though he also contended that the witness of the Spirit is the common, not rare, privilege of a child of God, he nevertheless allowed for psychological diversity, in some sense, in terms of the realization of this grace. Accordingly, the realization of the witness of the Spirit may not be dramatic but it will be memorable. It is not a paradigm of human experience that charts the course here but the free agency of the Spirit. So important was this direct witness to Samuel Wesley that on his deathbed he breathed forth: 'The inward witness, son, the inward witness... that is the proof, the strongest proof, of Christianity' (Wesley 1982: 289). Put another way, the reality of a Spirit-infused life, for which there is no substitute, is at the heart of the proper Christian faith. This then constitutes part of the reform that eighteenth-century Methodism sought to bring to the Anglican mother church and to the broader catholic tradition.

The Indirect Witness

Wesley, of course, recognized as a careful pastor that a sole emphasis on the witness of the Holy Spirit, apart from the witness of our own spirit, could easily result in fanaticism in that one might mistake the voice of God for a sinful and perverted self-will. To prevent this malaise, Wesley articulated a number of elements that make up an indirect witness, a composite of checks and balances that helped to inform believers of the soundness of their assurance. One vital element in this area is conscience, which for Wesley is not a natural faculty but a supernatural one in the sense that its origin lies in the free grace of God who established this gift, as a species of prevenient grace, in the wake of the fall of humanity. Conscience as a restored faculty, however, entails more than mere consciousness, for not only does it bring to mind both the past and present but it also exercises judgement in accordance with a norm. For Wesley, the rule or standard that conscience brings to bear on the moral and spiritual lives of non-Christians is the law written in their hearts, a law that represents yet another salient aspect of prevenient grace. For Christians, however, this law is explicitly acknowledged as the moral law, the holy law of love, contained in both the Old and New testaments.

A good conscience, then, a faculty properly ordered, emerges when a number of items are brought into play. There must first of all be a proper understanding of the Word of God, the principal standard for the Christian. Secondly, true knowledge of ourselves, of our hearts and lives is required: that is, a good conscience must necessarily exclude self-deception, and be accurately informed concerning one's true moral and spiritual condition in a forthright and honest way. Furthermore, an essential agreement must exist between our lives, on the one hand, and the rule of Scripture on the other. And it is precisely this habitual perception of harmony between norm and life which Wesley deemed a 'good conscience'.

Another element that makes up the indirect witness, what Wesley on occasion referred to as the witness of our own spirit, is keeping the commandments of God. 'Now by this we may be sure that we know him, if we obey his commandments' (1 John 2: 3 NRSV). Both the obedience of faith, the hallmark of genuine disciple-ship, and the love of God and neighbour are evidenced in a clear and practical way by obeying the commandments of God, commandments that constitute nothing less than the express will of the Most High as revealed in the moral law, a copy of the divine mind, the form of God as humans are able to bear it. Indeed, for Wesley Christians express their joy precisely in obedience and in loving God by submitting to the divine will. And to define Christian liberty as freedom from the commandments, as some Protestants were wont to do, was according to Wesley not an instance of high grace but an example of antinomianism or lawlessness.

Such obedience is best understood within the broader context of the theological virtues of faith, hope, and love that themselves make up the marks or characteristics of the new birth. In this context the indirect nature of this witness is most evident in the line of reasoning that since one has the marks of the new birth, therefore one is a child of God. More to the point, Wesley underscored the indirect and publicly evident nature of this witness by maintaining that these characteristics are manifested to others in a way that the direct witness is not. In other words, the indications of faith, hope, and love should be revealed to others in a number of ways, particularly in words and actions, and in a manner that is marked by both simplicity and sincerity. This witness, then, in some sense constitutes public knowledge.

Beyond conscience, keeping the commandments of God, and the marks of the new birth, Wesley also appealed to the fruit of the Spirit (love, joy, peace, patience, kindness, gentleness, self-control) as elements that bespeak of adoption. The indirect nature of this witness is revealed in the logic of the following syllogism that Wesley affirmed: as many as are led by the Spirit of God into all holy tempers and actions (the fruit of the Spirit) are the children of God. I am thus led by the Spirit of God. Therefore, I am a child of God. Thus, those who have the fruit of the Spirit in their lives have a measure of assurance, through indirect evidence, that they are the sons and daughters of God.

The great value of the indirect witness beyond the public display of gifts and graces that can be acknowledged by the church, is that this constellation of evidences is a good indicator that one has not been deluded in affirming, for example, the reality of the supernatural evidence of the direct witness of the Holy Spirit. For one thing, the pages of church history are filled with accounts of those who claimed a special unction of the Spirit but whose actions and public fruit belied such an anointing. The indirect witness is therefore necessary for the sake of balance and perspective lest those who claimed the reality of the direct witness of the Holy Spirit be led into error, mistaken judgement, and fanaticism. On the other hand, if only the indirect witness were affirmed by those who considered rational evidences sufficient, then the spectre of works righteousness, self-justification, and even the form of religion without its power could easily arise. So then, to guard against mistakes from either side Wesley postulated a conjoint witness. In other words, Wesley's doctrine of assurance illustrates the conjunctive style of his overall practical theology. Here as elsewhere it is a matter of both/and not either/or.

John Wesley's Enlightened Critics

By placing Christian assurance in general and the direct witness of the Spirit in particular at the heart of his ministry, John Wesley opened himself up to ongoing criticism from several Anglicans who had drunk deeply from Enlightenment principles. Preferring the guidance of reason and the development of a moderate sensibility, George Lavington, bishop of Exeter, published an anonymous work, 'The Enthusiasm of Methodists and Papists Compared', that deemed Wesley's emphasis on the direct witness, among other things, as rank enthusiasm or what today would simply be called fanaticism. Josiah Tucker and Joseph Trapp likewise railed against the intemperance and heated imaginations of the Methodists, while Charles Wheatly accused them in the pulpit of St Paul's Cathedral of being rapturous enthusiasts. And even one of Wesley's preachers, a certain Mr Hampson, added his voice to these charges and argued that a direct, immediate testimony of the Spirit that one is a child of God does not exist; the Spirit testifies only by the fruits.

Wesley's pointed response to Bishop Lavington came in the form of a key sermon, 'The Nature of Enthusiasm', published in 1750. In it, Wesley revealed his own understanding of the substance of this spiritual malaise to consist in the following: (1) imputing to God something that ought not to be, (2) imagining that one has the grace that one does not in fact have, (3) believing that one has the gifts that one, on the contrary, lacks, and (4) expecting to attain the end of religion, holy love, without employing the means of grace. So then, by the end of this sermon, Wesley had in effect turned the tables, so to speak, on his enlightened critics, for he not only claimed that it was the height of enthusiasm to think that one has the gifts and graces that one actually lacks but he also directed his searing criticism towards nominal Christianity, a favorite foil, a faith that stifles or resists the gracious and liberating presence of the Holy Spirit.

Assurance and Real Christianity

In responding to his critics on the issue of the direct witness of the Spirit, Wesley made it clear that neither he nor the Methodists made any claim for extraordinary gifts of the Spirit but only for those gifts and graces that were common, as he put it, to all real Christians. Clearly, the witness of the Holy Spirit is an integral part of Wesley's practical theology and it is tied to the larger purpose of his ministry to reform the land and to spread scriptural holiness. In fact, so crucial was the direct witness to Wesley's estimation of the proper Christian faith that he employed the distinction between the faith of a servant and the faith of a child of God to highlight the direct witness as the common privilege of the children of God.

To illustrate this salient truth it must first of all be noted that Wesley defined the faith of a servant in two key ways: the first, which constitutes the broad sense, corresponds to those who are under the spirit of bondage (in contrast to the spirit of adoption) and the reason they do not have the witness of the Spirit, and the assurance it brings, is due to the ongoing practice of sin. Second, Wesley considered the faith of a servant in another way, what we are calling the narrow sense, to embrace those who, though lacking the direct witness (not because of sin but due to ignorance or bodily disorder), nevertheless are justified and born of God. In other words, Wesley considered those who have the faith of a servant in this second, narrow sense, to be exceptions or exempt cases in what should otherwise be the common privilege of a child of God. To fail to recognize this distinction that emerges in Wesley's writings, to conflate the one sense of the faith of a servant with the other, making room for ongoing sin and confusing it with a justified state, will invariably lower the standards and therefore the promises of what Wesley referred to as the proper Christian faith.

It is well known that Wesley strongly associated the direct witness of the Spirit with the privileges of the children of God during the early 1740s. What is less known, however, (although Wesley made some important adjustments to his teaching at the 1745 Conference and in a letter to his brother, Charles, in 1747 in terms of the exempt cases), is that he continued to affirm the strong association of the witness of the Spirit with redemptive faith, properly speaking, throughout the remainder of his career. In fact, in 1755 he not only claimed that the whole Christian church during the early centuries enjoyed this witness but he also maintained in 1775 that he could not fathom how anyone could be a Christian believer till he has ' "the witness in himself;" till "the Spirit of God witnesses with his spirit, that he is a child of God;" ' (Wesley 1984: ii. 385). Not surprisingly, then, the seasoned Wesley reserved his language of the real, true, proper, scriptural Christian faith for the theological complex of justification, regeneration, and the direct witness of the Spirit. If any of these elements were lacking on an ongoing basis, then he referred to such faith as that of a servant in accordance with the two ways already defined.

Degrees of Assurance

Beyond the postulation of exceptions or exempt cases Wesley had also made an important modification to his teaching on assurance in 1739 when he came to acknowledge, in the wake of some Moravian misunderstanding and confusion, degrees of assurance occasionally marked by doubt and fear—even for those who hold the proper Christian faith. In other words, the children of God, even in the flush of graces that mark justification and regeneration, will not evidence the full assurance of faith that excludes all doubt as well as fear and therefore properly pertains to entire sanctification. Instead the children of God, babes in the Lord, will have a measure of assurance in accordance with this early, though important, degree of faith.

The difficulty with Wesley's view at this point, suggesting possible problems with coherence, is that on the one hand he affirmed the strong association of the direct witness of the Spirit with being a son or daughter of God, a real Christian as he put it, throughout much of his ministry. And yet, on the other hand, as he became more pastorally sensitive, he acknowledged that the assurance that pertains to a genuine child of God is occasionally marked by doubt and fear. Add to this that Wesley affirmed the direct witness is like the shining of the sun in its clarity, as noted earlier, and the problem on this score becomes readily apparent. Two solutions have therefore been suggested: the first contends that the assurance of a child of God is occasionally marked by doubt and fear since the direct witness itself is temporarily interrupted, not due to sin of course, but due to human, existential concerns as reflected in Wesley's sermon, 'Heaviness through Manifold Temptations'. Such an approach holds that the direct witness does indeed bring both knowledge and clarity, and its presence therefore eliminates both doubt and fear. What doubt and fear do emerge in the lives of genuine believers then is a function of a temporal interruption of a witness that is recurrent and only in that specialized sense can be deemed abiding. The weakness of this view, however, is that if the direct witness to a child of God does eliminate doubt and fear (when it is not interrupted) then this seems to be an assurance that pertains not to the new birth or adoption but to entire sanctification.

The second solution maintains that the direct witness is continual and abiding and is not interrupted as in the first solution. In this view the witness of the Holy Spirit and doubt and fear, at least on this level of spiritual development, can indeed exist in the human heart at the same time. In other words, the direct witness, though it remains clear, does not always eliminate all doubt and fear in those children of God in whom the carnal nature yet remains. The weakness of this second view can be put in the form of the question: how can doubt and fear remain in a soul at the same time the clarity of the witness of the Holy Spirit is enjoyed, especially since this witness is direct? At its best this position is paradoxical; at its worst, contradictory. Unfortunately, Wesley never articulated precisely how his major affirmations on the whole matter of the new birth, adoption, the direct witness, and a measure of assurance could be harmonized, presented as part of a larger, coherent whole.

At any rate, Wesley employed the terminology of the 'full assurance of faith' to refer to the Spirit's direct witness to perfect love in which the parallelism between the witness to regeneration, on the one hand, and entire sanctification, on the other, is striking. However, this assurance, unlike its incremental predecessors, is qualitatively distinct in that it excludes all doubt and fear since the heart has now been perfected in love. As the apostle John explains: 'There is no fear in love; but perfect love casts out fear' (1 John 4: 18 NRSV). Wesley explored the different measures of assurance suggested in this passage in the following fashion: 'A natural man has neither fear nor love; one that is awakened, fear without love; a babe in Christ, love and fear; a father in Christ, love without fear' (Wesley 1755: 638). Moreover, though such an assurance, a fullness of faith, does indeed exclude doubt and fear Wesley notes that it is not properly an assurance of what is future, but only of what now is. That is, it depicts not a future possibility, but once again a present reality.

Interestingly enough, the full assurance of faith, though it is associated with Christian perfection in which holy love reigns in the heart without a rival, is not the highest measure of assurance in Wesley's practical theology. In reflecting on the full testimony of Scripture, Wesley also posited a different kind of witness, namely, the full assurance of hope. By way of contrast, the full assurance of faith relates to present pardon; the full assurance of hope to future glory. Again, the former is a full conviction of present pardon without doubt or fear; the latter is an assurance of having no doubt of reigning with Christ in glory.

In a real sense, Wesley's doctrine of assurance, constituted by both a direct and indirect witness, is an answer to the Calvinist doctrine of election and the perseverance of the saints. That is, as believers grow in grace and holy tempers so too does their measure of assurance. Fortified by the presence of the Holy Spirit in an abundance of grace, mature Christians hold the faith in serene holiness knowing not only that they are the adopted children of God but also that if they remain in such salvific graces they will be with God for all eternity. Wesley's doctrine of assurance, then, is full of grace and comfort—a comfort befitting the saints.

SUBSEQUENT METHODIST THEOLOGIANS

When the contributions of Methodist theologians after Wesley are considered it is immediately apparent that the doctrine of assurance, especially the direct witness of the Spirit, did not receive the same kind of attention as it had in the writings of the father of Methodism. In some cases this reveals a relative lack of interest since theological attention is generally directed elsewhere, preoccupied by other concerns. In other instances, however, it may simply be an indication that Wesley's own carefully articulated doctrine is presupposed, and little is then added.

Adam Clarke

Born in Ireland in either 1760 or 1763, Adam Clarke was converted under Methodist preaching in 1779. A few years later he was received in full connexion in the Methodist Conference and energetically proclaimed the faith that had captivated his heart.

Clarke's theological interests are reflected in his *Christian Theology* (1967) and in his *Commentary on the Whole Bible*. In these works, the doctrine of Christian assurance received a fair amount of attention. Like Wesley, Clarke underscored that the assurance wrought by the Holy Spirit was only given to true believers, that is, to those who no longer grieved the Spirit. Without this direct witness of the life-giving Spirit, Christianity would become a dead letter and believers would therefore be left in uncertainty and doubt. As such, the witness of the Holy Spirit is a supernatural work graciously given by God. No human power or cunning can acquire it.

Distinguishing the witness of the Spirit from the testimony of conscience and the fruit of the Spirit, Clarke maintained that the knowledge of salvation by induction or inference, which pertains to the indirect witness, can hardly give comfort to a troubled heart, to an awakened sinner. In fact, Clarke so emphasized an awareness of the direct witness in his writings that he claimed that even the best educated and enlightened will have a distinct knowledge of the time, place, and circumstances of the witness of the Holy Spirit since he reasoned to the effect how could one have the direct witness and not know it?

Clarke, however, did not develop, to any great extent, Wesley's understanding of the degrees of assurance from a babe in Christ to one who has the full assurance of hope. As such this Methodist theologian did not fully recognize, in a way that Wesley did in 1739, that even a child of God, a genuine son or daughter in the Lord, will have a witness and assurance that is occasionally marked by doubt and fear. Instead, Clarke simply claimed that the direct witness is continual and abiding so long as the Holy Spirit is not grieved—a teaching that apparently lacks Wesley's carefully developed pastoral sensitivity in terms of the children of God.

Richard Watson

Richard Watson was born in 1781 in Lincolnshire, England, and entered the Wesleyan ministry in 1796, withdrew in 1800, became an itinerant in the Methodist New Connexion in 1803, and finally returned to the Wesleyan ministry in 1812. A decade later, in 1823, he undertook a systematic presentation of Wesleyan theology in his *Theological Institutes* (1856).

Unlike Wesley's sermons, Watson's *Institutes* do not devote sufficient attention to the matter of assurance; that is, enough to answer some of the most basic questions that would emerge in the challenges of practical Christian discipleship in any age. With a systematic purpose in mind, Watson focused briefly on the specific issue of adoption in this work, but he then offered a number of reasons why the term 'assurance' must be used sparingly. He contended, for instance, that it could easily, though not necessarily, imply the absence of all doubt. But this consideration alone should not lead to employing the term rarely for even Wesley himself, as pointed out earlier maintained that the faith of a child of God, though assured, is occasionally marked by doubt and fear. The point, though, is that a rich and sustained treatment of the doctrine of assurance is not to be found in Watson's *Institutes*. For that one must look elsewhere.

William Burt Pope

Hailing from Horton, Nova Scotia, William Burt Pope was born on 19 February 1822 but was raised in Plymouth, England where his father was a missionary. As one who had demonstrated intellectual promise throughout his school years, Pope eventually became a theological tutor at Didsbury College, Manchester in 1867. The following decade he published his *Compendium of Christian Theology* (1875–6).

In his theological classic, Pope revealed significant interest in the doctrine of Christian assurance and carefully delineated the objective basis for this teaching. Focusing on the death and resurrection of Christ, he taught that these events were the external and everlasting ground of certainty for the Christian church. In particular, he argued that the covenant of grace is certain in the resurrection of its surety, which is not only declared historically but is also confirmed by the Holy Ghost in a subjective fashion. Thus, in this view, the death and resurrection of Christ ground assurance such that these truths must then be received and inwardly appropriated by believers through the Spirit.

Trading upon a distinction between the direct witness and what Wesley had called the witness of our own spirit, Pope contended that the witness of the Holy Spirit generally rests upon the indirect witness of external pledges. And though he asserted that the Word of God and prayer were invariably the channels, the instruments, for the impartation of assurance, Pope nevertheless was critical of any sacramental theory that refused to admit a state of present assurance as included in the provisions of the Christian covenant. Like Wesley, he declared that the testimony of God's Spirit was 'the experience of all real Christians' (Pope 1876: iii. 129).

John Miley

One of Drew University's outstanding professors of the nineteenth century was born in Ohio on Christmas Day in 1813. Eventually, John Miley became Professor of Systematic Theology at this institution in 1873 but it was not until 1892 that he published his *Systematic Theology* in two volumes.

Miley's chief contribution to the doctrine of assurance lies in two key areas: first, he underscored the psychological diversity that pertains to the reception of assurance. He noted, for example, that believers may be gradually assured in terms of a twofold witness. That is, though the direct witness of the Holy Spirit is immediate it may not be instantly full. Second, though assurance is composed of two basic testimonies, as Wesley himself had clearly taught, Miley insisted that as a mental state, as a form of human consciousness, they are perceived not as two but as one. That is, a single state of confidence springs from a joint witnessing.

A. M. Hills

Converted in a Baptist church in 1859, A. M. Hills eventually became a Nazarene minister and was appointed to Asbury College in 1898. Many years later, in 1932, he published his *Fundamental Christian Theology* (1980) in which he articulated his basic teaching on assurance. In some sense critical of the sacramental traditions, Hills contended that it was not consistent with the divine love revealed at Calvary that it should be permanently concealed from believers. Like Miley, Hills affirmed a single state of consciousness in the wake of a twofold witness, but he also noted that the body and the circumstances of life can unduly affect that consciousness such that the testimony of the Spirit can become less distinct. Indeed, taking into account what effect infirmities (slowness of understanding, confusedness of thought, mistaken judgement, bodily disorder, etc.) have upon believers in their reception of assurance is an important chord struck in the work of Hills.

Albert C. Knudson

This Boston University professor was born in Minnesota in 1873. In his work *The Validity of Religious Experience* (1937), Knudson developed some earlier themes addressed by William James. Knudson's approach, for the most part, was phenomenological focusing on human consciousness and what arises within it. And since he looked askance at the approach to certainty in Christian belief, contending that it was a theological will-o'-the-wisp, Knudson's doctrine of the witness of the Spirit is hardly developed, not even in his work, *The Doctrine of Redemption*. In fact, in his writings this salient doctrine of serious Christian discipleship is relegated almost to a historical curiosity in simply pointing out that it was widely held in early Methodism. Moreover Knudson's estimation of this heritage, in line with his earlier judgements, is revealed in his observation that the historic Methodist teaching 'likens the assurance of salvation characteristic of Christian experience to the certainty produced by an unimpeachable witness. In this case the witness is the infallible Spirit of God', a teaching he apparently thought was fraught with all manner of difficulties (Knudson 1937: 413).

Arthur S. Yates

Remarkably enough, it was not until the middle of the twentieth century that a major treatment of the doctrine of assurance beyond Wesley finally appeared in the

Methodist tradition. In covering some familiar ground, Arthur Yates in his work *The Doctrine of Assurance: With Special Reference to John Wesley* (1952), affirmed John Wesley's Aldersgate experience of 24 May 1738 as the time when he had finally gained assurance of his own personal salvation. Turning his attention to Charles Wesley, Yates argued that the teaching on assurance found in the hymns of the younger brother is essentially that of John as well. Little difference exists between the brothers—at least on this score.

A fair portion of the argument of Yates in his seminal book concerns the failure of the sacramental traditions, in this case Roman Catholicism and Anglicanism, to develop an adequate doctrine of assurance. In terms of the former tradition, Yates observed that the emphasis on the sacraments tended to push the need for inner assurance into the background. With respect to the latter communion, he noted that several Anglican leaders of the eighteenth century, Thomas Green and the bishop of Lichfield among them, concluded that assurance was an extraordinary gift of the Spirit and therefore had ceased when the canon of Scripture was closed. In contrast, Yates asserted that the teaching of assurance as the common privilege of a child of God in any age was at the heart of Methodist reform especially when it faced theologically orthodox, sacramental communions.

Thomas C. Oden

In his work *Life in the Spirit* (1994), Thomas C. Oden focused on the gift of adoption and pointed out, in a sensitive and realistic fashion, that the children of God sometimes go through periods of trial and temptation that may temporarily eclipse the experience of God. What's more, Christians may even experience intense doubt and inner division due to the ongoing presence of the carnal nature. It may therefore be appropriate even for those who have a measure of assurance to cry out, 'I believe, help my unbelief' (Mark 9: 24 NRSV).

ASSURANCE AND THE FUTURE OF METHODISM

In the light of the preceding, the doctrine of assurance, especially the direct witness of the Spirit, has played a significant role in the life and ministry of historic Methodism. In a real sense, this teaching lies at the very heart of Methodism's character as John Wesley understood it. That is, the people of God becoming the tabernacle of the Holy Spirit, being energized and assured through the realization of a love that can only be divine, was an ongoing emphasis in eighteenth-century Methodism. Without this accent on the active role of the Spirit, Christianity could easily descend into formalism, ideology, or simple moral reasoning.

Subsequent to Wesley, as Methodism no longer functioned as a reforming movement (*ecclesiolae in ecclesia*) but took on all the trappings of an established church, it began to mistake participating in the means of grace and being socialized into the faith as the very substance of the Wesleyan witness, whereby it now had, in many instances, the form of religion but lacked the power thereof. In other words, in sloughing off Wesley's own evangelical heritage in its emphasis on the immediate presence of the Holy Spirit, many Methodists, especially in the United States, charted a course that was indistinguishable from the programme of Christian nurture articulated by Horace Bushnell. In such a view nothing distinctly memorable occurs in the Christian life, certainly not something so uncanny and numinous as the knowledge of assurance, a knowledge that even today is for the most part neglected by the sacramental traditions. Instead what was offered to the faithful was the slow, gradual advance in grace that occurs through the ministrations of the clergy and through the broader means of grace. Accordingly, the Methodism of the late twentieth and early twenty-first century has on one level lost its identity and purpose. Ironically enough, it has more in common with the established and culturally accommodated eighteenth-century critics of John Wesley than it does with Wesley himself—at least on the issue of Christian assurance and the direct witness of the Spirit.

As a consequence contemporary Methodists, while grasping bells and robes, have by and large neglected what the free grace of God can do as the sheer gift that it is. Due to the liberty of the divine will, the grace of God is not so tidy as to be utterly channelled through the ways that human will and preferences have prescribed. On the contrary, the doctrine of Christian assurance, as Wesley taught it, became an important way to underscore the immediacy of a person's relation to God, an immediacy that settled clergy often found troubling, especially when it detracted from the power and prerogatives of their office. Here a necessary administrative understanding of the church was unfortunately in conflict with a charismatic, Spirit-animated one. Moreover, unswervingly emphasizing gradual, incremental growth in grace may yet be another way of not only neglecting the free grace of God but also the actualization of the direct witness of the Spirit itself. Indeed, though Wesley's theology is currently being read utterly in terms of a catholic, cooperative understanding of grace, Wesley himself, and in a very conjunctive way, also stressed the free grace of God, a grace through which so many poor Methodists of the eighteenth century, though they were neglected by the established church and broader society, were yet surprised by joy to learn that they were indeed the favoured ones, the beloved of the Lord.

REFERENCES

CLARKE, ADAM (1967). *Christian Theology.* Salem, Ohio: Convention Book Store.

HILLS, A. M. (1980). *Fundamental Christian Theology: A Systematic Theology.* Salem, Ohio: Schmul.

KNUDSON, ALBERT C. (1937). *The Validity of Religious Experience.* Nashville: Abingdon.

MILEY, JOHN (1892). *Systematic Theology.* Peabody, Mass.: Hendrickson.

ODEN, THOMAS C. (1994). *Life in the Spirit: Systematic Theology.* San Francisco: Harper, iii.

POPE, WILLIAM BURT (1876). *A Compendium of Christian Theology.* 3 vols. New York: Phillips & Hunt.

STARKEY, LYCURGUS M. (1962). *The Work of the Holy Spirit: A Study in Wesleyan Theology.* Nashville: Abingdon.

WATSON, RICHARD (1856). *Theological Institutes: Or a View of the Evidences, Doctrines, Morals, and Institutions of Christianity.* New York: Carlton & Phillips.

WESLEY, JOHN (1755). *Explanatory Notes upon the New Testament.* London: William Bowyer.

—— (1982). *Works,* xxvi. *Letters,* ed. F. Baker. Bicentennial Edition. Nashville: Abingdon.

—— (1984–7). *Works: Sermons,* ed. A. C. Outler. 4 vols. Nashville: Abingdon.

WILLIAMS, COLIN (1960). *John Wesley's Theology Today.* Nashville: Abingdon.

YATES, ARTHUR S. (1952). *The Doctrine of Assurance: With Special Reference to John Wesley.* London: Epworth.

CHAPTER 36

JOHN WESLEY ON PREDESTINATION AND ELECTION

JERRY L. WALLS

JOHN WESLEY's place in the history of the church is secure as an evangelist and leader in the eighteenth-century revival. While his primary concern was not 'speculative theology', his evangelistic work inevitably led him to take positions on certain controversial theological issues. Evangelism is not a theologically neutral enterprise. Both the message and the methods of evangelism require evangelists to take sides on questions that have been, and remain, hotly contested in the history of the church, whether they do so consciously and thoughtfully or implicitly and casually. Wesley's place in historical theology is due particularly to his engagement with issues involving the doctrine of salvation, issues obviously close to the heart of an evangelist (Bromiley 1978: 329–42).

The issues I shall focus on, namely, predestination and election, have to do with the existentially vital questions of whom God chooses to save and how and why he does so. Engaging these questions takes us straight to the perennially central issue of how we understand the nature and character of God, as we shall see. To dismiss the classic debate on predestination and election as a mere historical curiosity is to betray that one is oblivious to these larger implications.

Wesley defended an Arminian position over against the Calvinistic views of his fellow evangelist and good friend George Whitefield, and he did so with both vigour and impressive rigour. He devoted numerous polemical essays to defending his views as well as attacking his critics, and doing so required him to entertain some of the finer points of speculative theology that he normally preferred to leave to others. The tone of the controversy was often sharp, the rhetoric sometimes unrestrained, and each side accused the other of misunderstanding and in some cases caricature and outright misrepresentation. Such charges, however, are not confined to the eighteenth century. Today as then, Wesley's writings incite the animus of Calvinist theologians who accuse him of misunderstanding their view. A notable example of this is the popular Anglican theologian J. I. Packer, who has written dismissively of Wesley: 'In the eighteenth century a confused Calvinist named John Wesley (pardon me! but truth will out) muddled the discussion in a rather grievous way. He insisted that he was an Arminian because he wished to affirm the universal invitation of the gospel and the love of God expressed in the gospel. Well, Calvinists do that too!' (Packer 1999: iv. 215). Wesley was a 'confused Calvinist' according to Packer because much of his powerful preaching was Reformed in substance, though marred by glaring inconsistencies and irresponsible misrepresentations (Packer 1985: 141).

In this chapter I will explicate and critically assess Wesley's account of predestination, focusing on the most important issues that separate him from his *Calvinist* critics. Does he present a coherent view that is theologically defensible, or is he a confused Calvinist, whose thinking on these issues was deeply muddled?

The Issues that Divide

Before getting to the issues that divided Wesley from the Calvinists, it is important to emphasize that the controversy was carried out against a background of broad agreement about the human condition. He agreed with his critics in holding a strong view of original sin that disabled humanity and made it impossible for human beings to please God or be in a right relationship with him. He also agreed with them that not all persons would be saved in the end. At the heart of the difference between Wesley and the Calvinists was the question of why some persons among the mass of fallen humanity will never be restored to a right relationship with God and be saved.

Wesley saw that there were two broad options that could be held with consistency for those who were committed to a strong view of original sin and also rejected universal salvation. Here is how he stated the matter to his Reformed counterparts.

You may drive me, on the one hand, unless I will contradict myself, or retract my principles, to own a measure of free will in every man; (though not by nature, as the Assembly of

Divines) and, on the other hand, I can drive you, and every other assertor of unconditional election, unless you will contradict yourself, or retract your principles, to own unconditional reprobation.   (Wesley 1979: x. 232)

Now what is striking and revealing about this passage is the place Wesley understands freedom to have in the structure of his thought. Notice, Wesley says he must 'own a measure of freedom in every man' unless he will contradict himself or deny his own principles. What this means is that his view of human freedom follows from more fundamental convictions of his, and it is something he must own if he is to remain consistent with those convictions. Consequently, human freedom is far from being his primary concern or the heart of his position on these issues. Indeed, the fact that he says he must own it on pain of inconsistency almost implies a certain reluctance in doing so.

It is important to underline this point because Calvinist critics sometimes allege that the desire to maintain human freedom and autonomy is the heart and soul of Arminian theology. Reformed apologist R. C. Sproul makes this claim rather colourfully when he asserts that the main Arminian concern is protecting the tree of liberty in such a way that Patrick Henry would be proud. He accordingly depicts the Arminian perspective as follows: 'The specter of an all-powerful God making choices for us, and perhaps even against us, makes us scream, "Give me liberty or give me death"' (Sproul 1986: 9).

It is also worth emphasizing Wesley's claim that unconditional reprobation follows by logical implication from Calvinist principles. Again, the suggestion is that Calvinists may be reluctant to own this implication, but must do so on pain of inconsistency. The main thrust of Wesley's argument here then, is that the relative strength of Arminian and Calvinist principles can be evaluated by considering the implications that follow from those principles, respectively. Let us turn now to consider the issues related to freedom and unconditional reprobation in order to assess Wesley's argument.

THE NATURE OF FREEDOM
AND RESPONSIBILITY

A good place to begin to understand Wesley's estimate of the value of freedom is an early sermon from 1730 in which he dealt with the problem of evil and the difficult question of why God allows it in his creation. Wesley clearly believed that evil must be traced to the misuse of free will, a lifelong conviction. But what is interesting at this point of his career is his ambivalent attitude towards freedom itself, and his uncertainty over whether it might have been better for God to have created us without it.

But can we say it would have been contrary to [his attributes] to have acted in a different manner? To have determined man to God, to have tied him down to happiness, to have given him no choice of misery? It was perfectly consistent with his goodness and justice to set life and death before his creatures; but would it have been inconsistent with them to have let him know only life? (Wesley 1984: iv. 285–6)

Notice Wesley's assumption that if God were going to determine us, rather than give us freedom, he would determine us to himself, and tie us down to happiness. Note also his assumption that if God were to determine us, we would not be free, which implies that freedom and determinism are incompatible.

Now this brings us to one of the most important issues we need to be clear on if we are to discuss with real insight the differences that separated Wesley from his Calvinist opponents. The issue is the nature of true freedom, particularly the sort of freedom that is necessary for us to be responsible for our actions. While this is hardly the most important issue that divides these two theological traditions, it is crucial to have a firm grip on it in order to assess the deeper issues. Two very different views of freedom in particular need to be distinguished.

The first view, typically called the libertarian view of freedom, holds that a truly free act cannot be causally determined in the sense that it has a sufficient cause or condition prior to its occurrence. Faced with action A, if an agent is truly free, it is up to him whether he will choose A. He has the power to choose A as well as to refrain from A. While the agent may have reasons for his actions that explain why he chooses as he does, these reasons do not determine his action. Indeed, part of freedom so understood is the capacity to *weight* reasons as well as *weigh* them as a matter of rational deliberation. Such deliberation is open-ended to some extent in that reasons for acting are up to the agent to weigh, and the relevant reasons do not have a predetermined force for all persons.

The second view is called soft determinism or compatibilism because according to it, freedom and determinism are perfectly compatible. That is to say, an act can be perfectly free even though it is fully determined by prior causes or conditions. While this claim is counter-intuitive, and at odds with the commonsense understanding of the term, freedom can be coherently defined in these terms. The essence of this view is that a free act is one that is done willingly, in accordance with a person's own beliefs and desires. Those beliefs and desires are themselves caused as are the actions that flow from them but the important point is that a person who is so determined is still acting according to his own will rather than being compelled to act against it. It is also the case, counterfactually, that if he wanted to act differently, he could. That is, if he had been determined to have different beliefs and desires, he would then act according to those.

Now Calvinism is distinguished by a view of divine sovereignty as all-determining. The notion of all-embracing determinism raises numerous issues and difficulties that we cannot explore here, and it is worth noting that some Calvinists would deny that they are committed to comprehensive determinism. But what is essential to Calvinism as well as central to our concerns is the claim that God unconditionally determines who is saved and who is not. Before the foundation of the world, God unconditionally chooses who will receive saving grace and who will be passed over. Moreover, God determines means as well as ends. So those who are elect 'are effectually called unto faith in Christ by his Spirit working in due season; are justified, adopted, sanctified, and kept by his power through faith unto salvation' (*Westminster Confession of Faith* 1970: 3. 6). By contrast, those who are not elect are left in their fallen condition, a condition in which they cannot but continue to sin, and thereby accumulate guilt before God. Nor can they truly repent and come to saving faith, so damnation is their inevitable fate.

It is understandable that critics of Calvinism, particularly the philosophically innocent, may see it as a fatalistic system of thought that denies human freedom and responsibility. This reading is an overly hasty one, however, that does not appreciate the subtleties of the Reformed view. For it is clear that Calvinists strongly affirm freedom and responsibility on their own terms. Perhaps there is no better example to illustrate this point than this passage in the *Westminster Confession* describing the effectual call of the elect in which the action of God has the effect of

enlightening their minds spiritually and savingly, to understand the things of God; taking away their heart of stone, and giving them an heart of flesh; renewing their wills, and by his almighty power determining them to that which is good, and effectually drawing them to Jesus Christ, yet so as they come most freely, being made willing by his grace.

(ibid. 10. 1)

What is striking about this passage is the claim, embedded within strongly deterministic language, that the effectually called come to Christ 'most freely'. The effectually called are determined to the good by God's almighty power, and yet they remain free because they are 'made willing' to come to Christ. God exercises his almighty power in such a way that the effectually called are changed internally, in their thinking, in their hearts and in their willing. So they are not forced to come against their will, but rather, their will is changed in such a way that they act entirely in accordance with their own wishes when they come to Christ.

This is of course a compatibilist account of freedom. As we shall see, it poses serious theological problems, but it is an internally coherent position. So long as freedom is understood as essentially doing what one wants to do, one can be described as free even if one's will is entirely determined. The same point applies to sinners as well as those who come to Christ. They sin 'most freely' in the sense that they want to sin and do so quite willingly even though they cannot possibly do otherwise.

By sharp contrast, Wesley insisted on a libertarian view of freedom and this represents a crucial divide between him and his Calvinist opponents. His earlier ambivalence about the value of freedom gave way in his later thinking to a strong conviction that freedom was an essential means to goods of extreme worth. The passage below is a good summary of his mature thought on the nature and importance of freedom. In this passage he distinguishes what he calls 'liberty' from will. The latter he generally identifies with desires and affections, and he emphasizes that it is will that allows us to delight in and love that which is good. But liberty is the true locus of freedom and it is this faculty that makes it possible for us to make meaningful choices.

> Without this both the will and the understanding would have been utterly useless. Indeed, without liberty man had been so far from being a free agent that he could have been no agent at all.... And observe: 'liberty necessitated', or overruled, is really no liberty at all. It is a contradiction in terms.... It may be further observed (and it is an important observation) that where there is no liberty there can be no moral good or evil, no virtue or vice.
>
> (Wesley 1984: i. 474–5)

This passage shows that Wesley had a subtle, nuanced view of freedom but it is not altogether clear that he always clearly grasped the compatibilist view of freedom. It is clear, however, that he thinks there is an utter inconsistency in the notion of a determined free choice and that the only view of freedom that he thinks worthy of the name is that of the libertarian variety. It is worth underscoring in the passage cited earlier in which Wesley concedes that his opponents can drive him to own a measure of free will that he seems to be assuming that they themselves have no room in their view for any sort of free will. It is inconceivable to him that sinners who can do nothing but sin, even if they do so willingly, could be considered free in any meaningful sense, or that those who are 'made willing' to come to Christ could do so 'most freely'.

It was precisely the difficulty of affirming both total depravity and needing 'to own a measure of free will' that led Wesley to develop his doctrine of prevenient grace. He was in agreement with the Calvinists that in our fallen condition, we have no recourse but to sin, nor any desire to do otherwise. 'Natural free will, in the present state of mankind, I do not understand: I only assert, that there is a measure of free-will supernaturally restored to every man, together with that supernatural light which "enlightens every man that cometh into the world"' (Wesley 1979: x. 229–30). The purpose of prevenient grace is to restore a measure of what Wesley called liberty, the capacity to choose God as well as to reject him.

It is also worth emphasizing that Wesley not infrequently uses language of compulsion to describe the Calvinist account of predestination. He uses such verbs as 'force', 'compel', and 'override' in picturing the Calvinist view of God's work in the wills of the elect. Consider his description of how prevenient grace works in the lives of sinners and its implied contrast with Calvinism.

> To reclaim these, God uses all manner of ways; he tries every avenue of their souls. He applies sometimes to their understanding, showing them the folly of their sins; sometimes to their affections, tenderly expostulating with them for their ingratitude, and even condescending to ask, 'What could I have done for' you [sic] (consistent with my purpose, not to force you) 'which I have not done?'   (Wesley 1979: x. 233)

Wesley is even prepared to say that at times 'he gently moves their wills, he draws and woos them as it were, to walk in the light. He instills into their hearts good desires, though perhaps they know not from whence they come' (ibid.).

It is interesting and instructive to compare this passage with the one cited above from the *Westminster Confession of Faith* describing the effectual calling of the elect. Both depict God working internally in persons, addressing their understanding, their emotions, and their wills. The difference is that on the Calvinist account, God determines them to that which is good, whereas for Wesley, he woos, he draws, he tenderly expostulates in order to elicit an undetermined free response. In short, God does everything short of determining their choice in order to win them to himself, which he would see as forcing them and overriding their freedom. Again, it is crucial to recognize that for Wesley a determined choice is a contradiction in terms, whereas for the authors of the *Westminster Confession* such a choice can be made 'most freely' so long as the person making it does so willingly.

Although Wesley at times used tendentious language in criticizing his Reformed opponents, and perhaps did not always clearly grasp the compatibilist account of freedom, his distinction between will and liberty is very much to the point for bringing into focus the difference between his view of freedom and theirs. Wesley seems especially aware of this in one of his most technical essays, 'Thoughts upon Necessity', in which he surveys a wide range of writers who affirm determinism. In addition to his familiar point about vice and virtue, he also advances the argument in more pointed theological terms in contending that if all we do is determined, there is no ground for reward or punishment. For Wesley, this 'strikes at the foundation of Scripture' since the Bible clearly teaches the 'doctrines of future judgment, heaven and hell' (ibid. 467). With the stakes this high, involving heaven and hell, the whole issue of freedom and responsibility takes on enormous proportions.

Some of the writers Wesley surveys frankly deny human freedom and responsibility in the light of their deterministic views, while others, in a compatibilist vein, insist on human responsibility. Of particular interest for our concerns are Wesley's comments on Jonathan Edwards, the great American Calvinist. Wesley notes that Edwards defends human responsibility by emphasizing the voluntary nature of human actions. Because sinners sin voluntarily, even gladly, they can rightly be held accountable and punished for their actions. For Wesley, this is not nearly enough to establish responsibility.

For their will, on your supposition, is irresistibly impelled; so they cannot help willing thus and thus. If so, they are no more blamable for that will than the actions which follow it. There is no blame if they are under a necessity of willing. There can be no moral good or evil, unless they have liberty as well as will, which is entirely a different thing. And the not adverting to this seems to be the direct occasion of Mr. Edwards's whole mistake.   (ibid.)

In this passage, Wesley seems to have a good grasp of the compatibilist distinction between compulsion and necessity. He does not charge that on this view of freedom anyone is forced or compelled, but rather, that their actions are irresistibly necessitated. He recognizes that persons who are so necessitated may nonetheless be willing to act as they do, but he still registers the judgement that willingness is not sufficient for moral responsibility.

Now here is a fundamental philosophical judgement that is a major parting of the ways. And both sides, notice, are committed to a controversial philosophical judgement. On the one side are those who think that willingness is sufficient to ascribe moral responsibility, and on the other are those who think responsibility requires the ability to do otherwise. This controversy does not admit of easy resolution since it is a dispute involving basic philosophical and moral intuitions, but the point is that Wesley's judgement is widely shared, though there is hardly unanimity on the matter.

Before moving on to the next set of issues, it is worth highlighting an extremely interesting and significant implication of the compatibilist view of freedom, namely, that if freedom and determinism are indeed compatible, then God could save all persons with their freedom intact. He could call all persons effectually so that they would come to Christ 'most freely'. Indeed, he could have determined all persons freely to have loved and worshipped him from the beginning of the world so that none would have sinned or disobeyed him in any way, but only lived in loving harmony with their creator and with each other.

UNCONDITIONAL REPROBATION AND THE CHARACTER OF GOD

Let us turn now to issues raised by unconditional reprobation, to which Wesley said he could drive his opponents unless they were to be inconsistent or deny their own principles. Wesley pressed this point particularly against those Calvinists who wanted to hold unconditional election to salvation, but who shrunk back from affirming that the lost are unconditionally chosen for damnation. Such Calvinists typically claimed that the choice to save the elect is an active one, whereas the lost are simply not elected or passed over. Thus, God does not actively choose to damn them in the same sense that he chooses to save the elect.

For Wesley this was a hair that could not be split, a distinction without a difference, for unconditional election logically entailed unconditional reprobation. As he memorably put it, 'unconditional election cannot appear without the cloven foot of reprobation' (ibid. 209). Now what is striking here is Wesley's unshakeable conviction that the doctrine of unconditional reprobation is simply immoral and therefore cannot possibly be true. When such moral objections to the doctrine are raised, Calvinists typically retort that, whatever seems the case to us, the doctrine is clearly taught in Scripture and therefore it must be believed. We are fallen, moreover, so our moral judgements are hardly to be trusted.

The claim that the doctrine is clearly taught in Scripture is question-begging, and Wesley took sharp issue with that claim. 'Find out any election which does not imply reprobation, and I will gladly agree to it. But reprobation I can never agree to while I believe the Scripture to be of God; as being utterly irreconcilable to the whole scope and tenor both of the Old and New Testament' (ibid. 210–11). In support of this claim, Wesley spent several pages citing passages that show 'the whole tenor and scope' of the Bible to be very much at odds with the doctrine of unconditional predestination. Moreover, he offered his own interpretation of those relatively few texts that might seem to teach unconditional election. In short, it is clear that he takes the authority of Scripture fully as seriously as his Reformed opponents, and seeks to ground his theology in a proper interpretation of its teaching, one that requires a theologically sensitive reading of the overall biblical narrative of God's dealing with humanity.

What is utterly clear from the biblical narrative for Wesley is that the character of God is one of holy love. The nature of God's love and mercy is moreover clearly such that it is simply unthinkable that he would unconditionally damn any of his beloved children that he has created. Consequently, it is impossible that any biblical text, rightly interpreted, could teach that doctrine. Wesley put this point quite emphatically in one of most rhetorically strident sermons, 'Free Grace', an early sermon that marked a rift between him and Whitefield that would last for years. In this sermon, Wesley went so far as to label the Calvinist doctrine of predestination a blasphemy that made God worse than the devil. So whatever Scripture may teach, it could not possibly teach this. If it appears on the surface to do so, it would be better to acknowledge that we do not know what the text means, since some texts may not be clear to us until eternity, than to interpret it in a way that so utterly impugns the character of God.

But this I know, better it were to say it had no sense at all than to say it had such a sense as this. It cannot mean, whatever it mean besides, that the God of truth is a liar. Let it mean what it will, it cannot mean that the Judge of all the world is unjust. No Scripture can mean that God is not love or that his mercy is not over all his works.   (Wesley 1984: iii. 556)

Notice what is rock-solid certain for Wesley, what he is confident he *knows*. He knows that God is truthful, that he is just, that he is loving and merciful. And he has a clear enough sense of what these terms mean that he can be certain that there are some things such a God could not do. God's sovereignty, in other words, must be understood in the light of his clearly revealed character of holy love. 'Much less does [Scripture] anywhere speak of the sovereignty of God as singly disposing the eternal states of men. No, no; in this awful work, God proceeds according to the known rules of his justice and mercy; but never assigns his sovereignty as the cause why any man is punished with everlasting destruction' (Wesley 1979: x. 220).

Now the issue of the relationship between God's sovereignty and his moral attributes is a variation on one of the most famous and difficult questions in moral philosophy, namely, the *Euthyphro* dilemma. Simply put, the question is whether something is good because God commands it, or does he command it because it is good? If one takes the first horn of the dilemma, it seems God could command anything, even things that seem utterly wicked, and they would become good by virtue of God's command. If one takes the second horn of the dilemma, it appears that what is good and bad is true independently of God, which would seem to compromise his sovereignty. Not surprisingly, Calvinists have been inclined to grasp the first horn of the dilemma.

And what is particularly interesting for our purposes is that they have done so in the context of defending their view of predestination. Consider, for instance, the following words of Calvin in response to his critics.

It therefore seems to them that men have reason to expostulate with God if they are predestined to eternal death solely by his decision, apart from their merit. If thoughts of this sort ever occur to pious men, they will be sufficiently armed to break their force by the one consideration that it is very wicked merely to investigate the causes of God's will.... For God's will is so much the rule of righteousness that whatever he wills, by the very fact that he wills it, must be considered righteous.   (Calvin 1960: ii. 23)

Wesley addressed the *Euthyphro* dilemma quite directly, but unlike Calvin, he rejected both horns of the dilemma and looked for a solution that avoided both sets of difficulties. Here is the essence of his view of the matter. 'It seems then, that the whole difficulty arises from considering God's will as distinct from God: otherwise it vanishes away. For none can doubt but God is the cause of the law of God. But the will of God is God himself. It is God considered as willing thus or thus' (Wesley 1984: ii. 13). Wesley agrees with Calvin that the will of God is the standard of good, as is evident from his claim that 'God is the cause of the law of God'. But whereas Calvin appeals to the will of God as sufficient to justify unconditional reprobation, Wesley is confident that what we know of the nature of 'God himself' is sufficient to preclude the very possibility of such a doctrine being true. For the will of God is simply 'God considered as willing thus or thus'. And what Wesley thinks we can be most sure of is that God is love, and that his rules of justice and mercy are 'known', that is, revealed to us in a way that is rationally accessible to us. They accord with our best moral intuitions and thinking since these are a reflection of the image of God within us. God's rules of justice and mercy are not claims that clash fundamentally with our best moral judgements and must therefore simply be accepted by faith (Walls 1989: 261–76).

CRYSTALLIZING THE ISSUES

To bring these points further into focus and to crystallize where Wesley differs from his Calvinist opponents, consider the following logical argument. As we do so, recall Packer's claim, cited earlier, that Wesley was confused in thinking that what divided him from Calvinism was his convictions about the universal invitation of the gospel and love of God. That is, Packer wants to claim that Calvinists also affirm that God loves all persons and makes a genuine offer to save all. If so, it appears that he and his fellow Calvinists should be prepared to accept most, if not all, of the premises of this argument.

1. God truly loves all persons and invites them to accept the gospel.
2. Truly to love someone is to desire their well-being and to promote their true flourishing as much as you can.
3. The true well-being and flourishing of all persons is to be found in a right relationship with God, a saving relationship in which we accept the invitation of the gospel and come to love and obey him.
4. God could determine all persons freely to accept the invitation of the gospel and come to a right relationship with himself and be saved.

Now what follows from these premises, however, is a conclusion that Calvinists typically do not accept, nor did Wesley.

5. Therefore, all will be saved.

To the contrary, both would affirm:

6. Not all will be saved.

But if 6 replaces 5, the set of claims is obviously inconsistent. In order to deny 5 and affirm 6, at least one of the previous premises must be rejected.

Now it is clear which of these premises Wesley would reject in order to maintain consistency, namely, 4. This illumines his earlier claim that he can be driven, on pain of inconsistency, to own a measure of (libertarian) freedom if he is to be true to his principles. His conviction that God truly loves all persons and does everything he can to save them short of overriding freedom, along with his belief that despite this not all will be saved, led him inexorably to the conclusion that we must be free in the libertarian sense.

It is much less obvious which of the premises Calvinists could reject to maintain consistency. As we have noted, 4 is a straightforward implication of a compatibilist view of freedom; 3, moreover, is an obvious component of any Christian anthropology and essential to the claim that human beings are created in the image of God. Presumably, given Packer's claim, Calvinists also want to affirm 1. This leaves as the only remaining option premise 2. That is, to maintain any sort of consistency, Calvinists will have to have an idiosyncratic if not a radically equivocal definition of love. And once this is recognized, it is difficult for Calvinists to maintain premise 1.

Let us consider this in light of how Calvinists must understand Wesley's two claims that Packer insists Calvinists also affirm: the universal invitation of the gospel and the love of God for all persons. First, with respect to the call of the gospel, it is important to recognize that Calvinists have traditionally distinguished between the general call that goes out to all persons and the effectual call, discussed above, that goes out only to the elect. Now given this distinction, along with their understanding of freedom, Calvinists can sincerely say, 'whosoever will may come and accept the gospel'. In this sense, Calvinists can truly affirm the universal invitation and call of the gospel.

On closer inspection, however, this universal call is not what it appears to be, and it is certainly a far cry from what Wesley wanted to affirm. The uninitiated who lacks a clear grasp of the subtleties of compatibilist freedom will probably assume that all the invited can actually come, and that God truly wishes them to come, and consequently, they are to blame if they do not. But of course, this is not the case. While it is true that they do not want to come, if they are not elect they cannot possibly truly want to come. And to make matters worse, God could extend to them the effectual call so that they would come 'most freely' but has chosen not to do so.

Now when the smoke clears and all this is seen with full clarity, the claim that Calvinists affirm the universal call of the gospel in anything remotely like the sense Wesley insisted upon evaporates into thin air. Indeed, as Wesley recognized, such a call is altogether hollow, an invitation that is an empty farce that depicts the God of love and truth as utterly insincere (Wesley 1979: x. 227).

Now at this point, Calvinists may point out that Wesley has a problem that is at least somewhat parallel, for on his own view, God offers grace to persons he knows will not respond, persons that from all eternity he knew would not be saved. While there is something to this point, the problem simply is not nearly of the same magnitude as the one faced by Calvinism. For on Wesley's view, what God knows from all eternity is who will and who will not respond to his offer of grace, an offer that all really could receive, and indeed that he prefers that they receive. In this sense, the elect are known before the foundation of the world, but they are conditionally elect, depending on their response to the grace that God sincerely offers to all. Wesley insisted that the sincerity of God's love and mercy for fallen humanity is demonstrated 'in offering salvation to every creature, actually saving all that consent thereto, and doing for the rest all that infinite wisdom, almighty power, and boundless love can do, without forcing them to be saved, which would be to destroy the very nature that he had given them' (ibid. 235).

Calvinists can make no similar claims about God's desire to save all. And again, the problem is only exacerbated if one recognizes that God could determine all persons freely to respond, but has chosen to withhold the grace that would have this effect. If this is clearly spelled out, it is quite clear that Calvinists do not affirm the universal call of the gospel in anything like the sense Wesley did, and only the equivocal use of language that the philosophically unsophisticated cannot decipher keeps the claim from being recognized as disingenuous.

For similar reasons, the claim that God truly loves the non-elect loses all meaning on Calvinist premises. Consider the approach taken to this issue by the contemporary Calvinist biblical scholar D. A. Carson, who informs us that he is often asked by young Reformed pastors if they should tell the unconverted that God loves them. His answer to them is: '*Of course* I tell the unconverted that God loves them' (Carson 2000: 78). Now what is interesting is how he justifies this emphatic, positive answer. He distinguishes different senses in which God loves people. First, there is the love of God shown in providential blessings that come to all people generally, such as the rain that falls on the just and the unjust. Second, there is the love of God in the invitation of the gospel that goes out to all people, to which 'whosoever will' may respond. Third, there is the 'particular, effective, selecting love toward the elect' (ibid. 18) that is given to them alone.

It is with these distinctions in hand that Carson can emphatically assure the unconverted that God loves them. While he cannot be in a position to know which ones among the unconverted are the fortunate elect for whom Christ died effectually, he can know that all receive rain on their gardens and are invited to believe the gospel. On this basis he assures the unconverted that God loves them. But this too seems more than a little disingenuous. For all he knows, after their appointed years of receiving temporal blessings (for which they cannot be properly grateful in their fallen condition), and hearing an invitation to believe the gospel they cannot possibly accept, they will be damned forever because they are not the recipients of electing love. If Carson were forthright about all this, would not his claim that of course God loves the unconverted be exposed as an empty piece of pious rhetoric?

CONCLUSION

In conclusion, Wesley is vindicated of the charge of being a confused Calvinist, and indeed, his position is sharply at odds with his Reformed opponents on the issues of God's love for all persons and his genuine desire to save all. It is important to be clear on this for it makes apparent that Wesley offers a distinctively different account of God and his saving activity from the Reformed tradition, despite important agreement with them on the disabling nature of sin and the necessity of grace for salvation.

While theologians in old-line denominations may have little interest in or concern with issues of predestination, the debate is alive and well in many of the more populous quarters of the church. Indeed, Calvinism is resurgent in the

Southern Baptist Convention, and has garnered considerable appeal with the current younger generation (Hansen 2008). How we shall understand the character of God, how we shall preach the gospel, and how we shall interpret crucial matters of practical Christian experience are all at stake.

Wesley continues to be an important historical source as well as a dialogue partner in the current discussion of these issues (Nettles 1995: 297–322; Peterson and Williams 2006). It is important that the true substance and logic of his position is understood for his views to get the hearing they deserve. We have seen that he was not always a fair critic of Calvinism and at times apparently misunderstood its claims, particularly with respect to how freedom is understood. But to be fair to Wesley, we have seen that Calvinists themselves are not always clear and forthright about their view of freedom and its implications, and indeed, that this sort of confusion may well lend Calvinism a credibility with the philosophically unin-formed that it would not otherwise enjoy (Walls and Dongell 2004: 153–215). Clarity about the nature of freedom and its implications is what brings into the light of day the most profound difference that divides Wesley from Calvinism, namely, an unambiguous and forthright conviction that the God of holy love truly desires the well-being of all his creatures and does all he can to secure it, short of overriding their freedom.

SUGGESTED READING

COLLINS, KENNETH J. (2007). *The Theology of John Wesley: Holy Love and the Shape of Grace.* Nashville: Abingdon.

OLSON, ROGER (2006). *Arminian Theology: Myths and Realities.* Downers Grove, Ill.: Intervarsity Press.

PETERSON, ROBERT A., and WILLIAMS, MICHAEL D. (2006). *Why I Am Not an Arminian.* Downers Grove, Ill.: Intervarsity Press.

TRINKAUS, LINDA (2004). 'Recent Work on Divine Foreknowledge and Free Will'. In Robert Kane (ed.), *The Oxford Handbook of Free Will.* New York: Oxford University Press, 45–64.

REFERENCES

BROMILEY, GEOFFREY, W. (1978). *Historical Theology: An Introduction.* Grand Rapids: Eerdmans.

CALVIN, JOHN (1960). *Institutes of the Christian Religion,* ed. John T. McNeil, trans. Ford Lewis Battles. 2 vols. Philadelphia: Westminster.

CARSON, D. A. (2000). *The Difficult Doctrine of the Love of God.* Wheaton, Ill.: Crossway.

HANSEN, COLLIN (2008). *Young, Restless, Reformed: A Journalist's Journey with the New Calvinists*. Wheaton, Ill.: Crossway.

NETTLES, THOMAS J. (1995). 'John Wesley's Contentions with Calvinism: Interactions Then and Now'. In Thomas Schreiner, and Bruce Ware (eds.), *The Grace of God: The Bondage of the Will*. Grand Rapids: Baker Book House, ii.

PACKER, J. I. (1999). 'Predestination in Church History'. In *Honouring the People of God: The Collected Shorter Writings of J. I. Packer*. Carlisle: Paternoster.

—— (1985). 'Arminianism'. In W. Robert Godfrey and Jesse L. Boyd III (eds.), *Through Christ's Word*. Phillipsburg, N.J.: Presbyterian and Reformed.

SPROUL, R. C. (1986). *Chosen by God*. Wheaton, Ill.: Tyndale House.

WALLS, JERRY L. (1989). 'Divine Commands, Predestination, and Moral Intuition'. In Clark Pinnock (ed.), *The Grace of God and the Will of Man*. Minneapolis: Bethany.

—— and DONGELL, JOSEPH R. (2004). *Why I Am Not a Calvinist*. Downers Grove, Ill.: Intervarsity Press.

WESLEY, JOHN (1979). *The Works of John Wesley*. Grand Rapids: Baker Book House.

—— (1984). *Works*, ed. Albert C. Outler. Nashville: Abingdon.

Westminster Confession of Faith (1970). 'The Constitution of The United Presbyterian Church in the United States of America, Book of Confessions'. 2nd edn. Part I.

PART VI

ETHICS AND POLITICS

THEOLOGICAL ETHICS

D. STEPHEN LONG
STANLEY HAUERWAS

WHY METHODISTS CANNOT DISTINGUISH BETWEEN THEOLOGY AND ETHICS

IN *Practical Divinity: Theology in the Wesleyan Tradition*, Tommy Langford suggests that an essential clue for appreciating Wesley's theological vision is the selection of materials he put in the *Christian Library*. The *Christian Library* was the fifty-volume theological resource Wesley published from 1749 to 1755. He described the books as 'Extracts from the Abridgements of the Choicest Pieces of Practical Divinity'. Langford observes that this is a perfect description of Wesley's understanding of theology; that is, theology is never an end in itself but should serve the interests of transformed living. Accordingly theology is in service to essential Christian practices, which means that theology is first and foremost to be preached, sung, and lived (Langford 1983: 20–1). Wesleyan theology is not abstract speculation but joyful contemplation and obedience, manifest in the conjoining of happiness and holiness.

Perhaps one of the most striking implications of Wesley's theology is his insistence that there is an essential connection between happiness and holiness. Methodism defied the modern presumption that you must choose between being happy or being sanctified. Wesley was well aware that his refusal to separate happiness and holiness would put him at odds with much of his society, but one of the reasons he was so successful was his ability to describe how empty lives could be in which the desire to be happy was separated from holiness.

For example in his 'An Earnest Appeal to Men of Reason and Religion', Wesley observed one of the most important questions you can ask anyone is 'Are you happy?' He then describes the kind of life many lead, which they think confirms they are happy—but it leads only to boredom:

> You eat, and drink, and sleep, and dress, and dance, and sit down to play. You are carried abroad. You are at the masquerade, the theatre, the opera house, the park, the levee, the drawing-room. What do you do there? Why, sometimes you talk; sometimes you look, at one another. And what are you to do tomorrow, the next day, the next week, the next year? You are to eat, drink, and sleep, and dance, and play again. Are you, can you, or any reasonable man be satisfied with this? You are not. It is not possible you should. But what else can you do? You would have something better to employ your time; but you know not where to find it on earth. And, indeed, it is obvious that the earth, as it is now constituted, even with the help of all European arts, does not afford sufficient employment to take up half the waking hours of its inhabitants. What then can you do? How can you employ the time that lies so heavy upon your hands? This very thing which you seek declare we unto you. The thing you want is the religion we preach. That alone leaves no time upon our hands. It fills up all the blank spaces of life.   (Wesley 1978: viii. 18–19)

Holiness makes us happy because it gives us something to do. Accordingly for Wesley there can be no separation between theology and ethics. For such a separation suggests a Christianity that has accommodated itself to the world in 'beliefs' separated from how we live. It is, therefore, not surprising that many theologians in the Methodist tradition do their theology as 'ethics' or, perhaps more accurately, as 'theological ethics'. But, as Langford suggests, perhaps the best description we have for the way Methodists do theology is what Wesley called, 'practical divinity'.

That Methodism is so constituted does not mean it is unique when compared with other ecclesial bodies. In fact, the question—'are you happy?'—is a common question in much of the Christian and philosophical tradition. Methodists also share with other Christians common resources that enable the ethical life: Scripture, sacraments, the moral theological tradition, conciliar doctrinal commitments, as well as the communion of saints ancient and contemporary. Yet, within this larger common treasury, it is not surprising that the sermons of John Wesley have proven to be a crucial resource for ensuring that no strong distinction can be made between theology and ethics. Wesley's sermons, like most theology prior to modernity, are traditioned reflections on Scripture. For the refusal to divorce holiness and happiness is a refusal required by Scripture.

If Methodists have a distinct charism to contribute to the church, it is less the content of its theological ethic and more the form by which Methodists pursue this common end of happiness and holiness, as well as the expectation of its embodiment in the time between the times. In order to develop this understanding of a Methodist theological ethics we will present three interrelated characteristics. First, we will display Wesley's understanding of the content of a good life, that is, the relation between happiness and holiness, by directing attention to what the Methodist tradition calls this life of beatitude. Such a life is often identified as 'the religion of the heart', but that phrase, so often used to separate theology from ethics, we hope to show must be understood in the light of the Sermon on the Mount.

Secondly, we will spell out the ecclesial presumption necessarily implied by the refusal to separate happiness and holiness. Every ethic, as MacIntyre has argued, entails a sociology. For Methodists the sociology that makes holiness inseparable from happiness is the church: a church, moreover, that must be separated from the world so that the world might be served. Finally, we will explore why Methodists have rightly refused to turn holiness into an ideal never to be realized. Wesley's understanding of perfect love, we believe, offers the means to help all Christians understand why growth is ongoing for Christians who would be holy and happy.

RELIGION OF THE HEART

Mr Wesley stated, 'The sum of all true religion is laid down in eight particulars.' Those eight particulars he identifies with the beatitudes Jesus annunciated in the Sermon on the Mount in the Gospel of Matthew. Wesley referred to the first six of these—poverty of spirit, mournfulness, meekness, righteousness, mercy, and purity of heart—as 'the religion of the heart' (Wesley 1978: i. 517). The seventh, 'peacemaking', expresses the Christian's outward embodiment of the six. Those who best exemplify the religion of the heart and its external witness will embody the eighth, 'persecution for righteousness' sake'. These eight particulars define the 'sum of true religion' for Wesley and for the Methodist tradition.

Wesley's focus on the beatitudes for the depiction of the Christian life is, of course, not unique. Saints Augustine and Aquinas developed a very similar understanding of the Christian life in their reflections on the Sermon. Dietrich Bonhoeffer, Martin Luther King Jr., Dorothy Day, Oscar Romero not only reflected on the Beatitudes in a similar fashion, they actually embodied this religion of the heart—which entailed that three of them received the eighth beatitude as well.

Methodist theological ethics, therefore, has no monopoly nor does it have any stake in claiming to be alone the 'religion of the heart'. Servais Pinckaers, a contemporary Roman Catholic moral theologian, traces this kind of theological ethics through much of Christian tradition. He claims that Thomas Aquinas's monumental *Summa Theologiae*, which was vastly influential for the moral life from the Middle Ages on, was primarily a 'listening to the Lord teaching on the mountain' in the company of the church fathers, doctors, and philosophers. For in this teaching we find 'the answer to the question of happiness' (Pinckaers 2002: 24, 28).

We are not suggesting that Wesley drew directly on Aquinas to inform his account of the Christian life, but rather that Wesley stood in the central stream of the Christian tradition refusing to separate happiness from holiness. Wesley rightly thought that all great philosophers and theologians maintained that the end of the moral life is happiness. For example Aristotle claimed that happiness is our true end which is rightly sought for its own sake rather than a means to something else.

The Christian tradition built on and radically converted this basic Aristotelian notion. Such a conversion was necessary because only God is rightly sought for no other end than himself. Aristotle presumed everything was given an end that it naturally had the means to achieve. The virtues were the natural excellences one could achieve by rightly ordering the passions towards that end, which would bring happiness.

Yet for the Christian tradition, the end that would bring happiness was friendship with God, something Aristotle would have found impossible. This end could not be an achievement for we do not have the means intrinsic to attain it. Something more is needed. For this reason, the Christian tradition found that the virtues were not only important for the moral life, but that the virtues themselves come to us as gifts. These gifts, the beatitudes and theological virtues, are given to us through the work of the Holy Spirit mediated through word and sacrament. For Wesley this meant happiness and holiness were inseparable through the one work of the Spirit.

Wesley's account of the beatitudes, therefore, locates him in the great catholic tradition of the virtues as crucial for the formation of a holy people. The virtues are habits that form our passions and direct our desires and actions towards their true end: the goodness of God. Christian tradition does not dispense with the natural virtues for the human ethical life, but it does resituate them. We cultivate virtues within the context of communities that form our character. Because only the church participates in Christ's divinity as one of the threefold forms of his body (along with his historical body and the eucharist), it is necessary for the perfection of the ethical life. The church takes up the natural, everyday, ordinary passions associated with family, economics, and politics, and converts and perfects them by ordering them to their true end in God. The result is a holiness that bears witness to God's renewal of creation.

It is not surprising that this understanding of the role of the virtues in the Christian life has found resonance in Methodism. Wesley founded the Methodist societies that offered the resources necessary for people to acquire the virtues necessary for a happy and holy life. Originally they were small ecumenical communities within the church held together by three general rules: do good, avoid harm, and attend upon the ordinances of God. The first two rules are the primary precepts of the natural law tradition. The third shows how Wesley read that tradition in terms of word and sacrament, which are the primary ordinances of God. They give us the resources necessary to live out this law. By themselves, the precepts to do good and avoid evil are so purely formal that they are of little or no help. The word and sacraments specify the good to be achieved and any evil to be avoided. For this reason, the law is not an end in itself. It directs our actions to virtuous ends. The purpose of the law is the religion of the heart. The sacraments are the means that assist us in the journey.

'The religion of the heart' is Wesley's phrase to describe the life made possible by Jesus' death and resurrection. So there can be no separation of doctrine and life. As we suggested at the beginning, Methodist theological ethics brings those two modes of discourse—'theology' and 'ethics'—into such a close identity that one cannot be decisively distinguished from the other. To understand and embody the good, we must know God. Ethics cannot be known or done well without theology. Theology cannot be done or known well without its performance in everyday life.

As a result Methodist theological ethics has never developed elaborate accounts of natural law or common grace that seek to explain ethics outside of specific theological doctrines. Nor does it fit well the modern political and moral theology that rejected revelatory doctrinal claims for a morality grounded in reason alone (Lilla 2007: 118–62; Taylor 2007). These developments were just coming into focus when Wesley came to the end of his life. But he recognized what was at stake—the notion that the first and second tables of the Law (Ten Commandments), the love of God, and the love of neighbour could be divided. In 1789, towards the end of his life, Wesley wrote,

Thus almost all men of letters, both in England, France and Germany, yea, and all the civilized countries of Europe, extol 'humanity' to the skies as the very essence of religion. To this great triumvirate, Rousseau, Voltaire and David Hume, have contributed all their labours, sparing no pains to establish a religion which should stand on its own foundation, independent of any revelation whatever, yea, not supposing even the being of a God. So leaving him, if he has any being, to himself, they have found out both a religion and a happiness which have no relation at all to God, nor any dependence upon him. It is no wonder that this religion should grow fashionable, and spread far and wide in the world. But call it 'humanity', 'virtue', 'morality' or what you please, it is neither better nor worse than atheism. Men hereby willfully and designedly put asunder what God has joined, the duties of the first and the second table. It is separating the love of our neighbour from the love of God. It is a plausible way of thrusting God out of the world he has made.

(Wesley 1978: iv. 69)

It is not surprising, given Wesley's critique of this modern development, that Methodist theological ethics found resonances with two twentieth-century theological movements from vastly different ecclesial homes: the Reformed theology of

Karl Barth and the Catholic theology of Henri de Lubac. Both can help us identify what Wesley and the Methodist tradition recognized. The virtue of 'liberality', which could also be understood as a genuine humanism or a generosity towards others seems consistently to be abandoned when shorn of its theological particularity in Christological and Trinitarian claims, as it inevitably does in procedural liberalism. Barth saw this in his former teacher Adolf von Harnack's politics where 'culture' became a source of its own independent of Christology. De Lubac saw it in the politics of neoscholastic Garigou-Lagrange's defence of Vichy France based on 'nature' as an autonomous source. It may seem counter-intuitive for those of us taught that morality and theology should be divorced for the sake of humanism, but a Methodist ethics at its best recognizes the inextricable link between its particular doctrines of God and the shape of the moral life.

Methodist theological ethics, in conformity with previous moral theologies in the Christian tradition, bring together the two great mountains in the biblical narrative in order to give shape to the moral life. First the law is given to Moses on Mount Sinai as he gazes upon the glory of God. Then, without abrogating that law, Jesus looks down from the mountain and pronounces blessedness upon all who embody its meaning. In so doing, he radiates the glory of God (a glory he also demonstrated on a mountain in his transfiguration). These two mountains merge into one as Jesus' beatitudes 'fulfil', that is, complete or perfect, the law. The law is not an end in itself, but rather it points forward to its figural fulfilment in Christ who alone recognizes its meaning and offers the eschatological judgement: 'blessed are you when...' Gazing upon the vision directs our will and intellect to the knowledge and desires of God. Theology and morality are united. This is the religion of the heart.

MEANS FOR THE PURSUIT OF THE RELIGION OF THE HEART

This 'religion of the heart' should not be misunderstood to be only an inward, pious disposition, as it can be—and has been—so misunderstood by Methodists. The blessed life Jesus announces in the beatitudes is not a private, interior possession of individuals but a communal form of life that will be displayed socially and politically. In the Sermon on the Mount, Jesus shows us the goal of the Christian life. This is the form of life he will bless on the Last Day. But between the times it is of great joy that Christ has made it possible for some to become the earnest of the coming kingdom.

The life of such a people will include three elements. First, they will recognize that only one Person ever lived this blessed way of life by his own agency. Jesus is the only one who embodied the fullness of righteousness found in the beatitudes. As often happens in a world in rebellion against God and God's goodness, such a perfect performance ended in his persecution even to death. Thus, as we suggested above some who fully embody the first seven beatitudes will often receive the 'gift' of the eighth. The church is built on the blood of the martyrs.

Second, we must seek to embody his righteousness in our own lives. This is what it means to confess 'the Lord is our righteousness'. It means more than a purely external imputation of righteousness; it also entails an inherent sanctifying righteousness. Third, we should honour those who embody these ways of life and hold them up as examples to be emulated, recognizing that such a righteousness must be socially enacted. Holiness is not a heroic ethic for individuals. To be made holy is difficult and demanding because our lives are made vulnerable to others. Such a people become witnesses so that the world might see the kind of life God would have all people live.

Just as the doctrines of the church are the communal norms for how we should think and teach, so the beatitudes and gifts are the communal norms for how we should live. Whenever and wherever we find the fruits of peaceableness, righteousness, mercy, etc. we should recognize a proper performance of the grace of the Holy Spirit. We should not be surprised then, or dismiss it as the politicization of our doctrinal standards, when we discover that our Methodist doctrines speak about matters of war and economics.

For instance, Article XVI of the United Methodist Church states that we believe war and bloodshed are contrary to the gospel and spirit of Jesus. This is not a private judgement, it is a public confession that reminds us that the religion of the heart requires a political embodiment in how we think about such matters as participation in war, economics, family life, and the government. We cannot assess how we should live in these important social institutions without keeping our vision on the way of life Christ announces as blessed. This vision must be the focus of the Christian life and the source of our evangelistic witness to the world.

This is why Wesley said, 'Christianity is essentially a social religion.' By that he did not mean that we should be involved in some vague thing called 'social justice'. Much good may be done in the name of justice, but too often calls for justice do not capture the rich character of the Methodist tradition's understanding of Christianity's essential social character. For Methodists to live out the beatitudes means we must live in a community in which people have learned to be accountable to one another in their daily life. Such accountability means that we will also have to learn, as Matthew 18 indicates, what it means to live as a reconciled people. Only a justice shaped by the practice of reconciliation makes it possible for Christians to be a people of peace in a world of violence. We are called to witness to this peaceableness even while we wait upon it.

For instance, in reference to the beatitude of peacemaking, John Wesley 'bemoaned' the violence Christians perpetrated on other Christians. He wrote,

Yea, what is most dreadful, most to be lamented of all, these Christian churches!—churches ('Tell it not in Gath' but alas, how can we hide it, either from Jews, Turks, or pagans?) that hear the name of Christ, 'the Prince of Peace', and wage continual war with each other.... O God! How long? Shall thy promise fail? Fear it not, ye little flock. Against hope believe in hope. It is your Father's good pleasure yet to renew the face of the earth. Surely all these things shall come to an end, and the inhabitants of the earth shall learn righteousness. 'Nation shall not lift up sword against nation, neither shall they know war any more'... They shall all be without spot or blemish, loving one another, even as Christ hath loved us. Be thou part of the first-fruits if the harvest is not yet.   (Wesley 1978: i. 507–9)

Methodist ethics takes to heart this call to be 'first-fruits'. Even though the face of the earth is not yet renewed, we are called to witness to its reality. This makes Christianity 'social'. This emphasis on a holiness that witnesses to the renewed creation gives Methodist ethics resonances with the work of the Anabaptist tradition. As Albert Outler noted, Wesley's ecclesiology is a potentially unstable blend of Anabaptist and Anglican or catholic doctrines of the church. Like the Anabaptists, 'holiness' and witness characterizes the church more so than its offices. Like the catholics, Wesley still 'unselfconsciously' assumed the sacraments, and to some extent an episcopal order, gave the church its common identity across time and space.

It is not surprising, given this understanding of the beatitudes, that some theologians in the Methodist tradition have been influenced by the Anabaptist theologian John Howard Yoder. For Yoder emphasized the relationship between eschatology, ethics, and holiness. Christians engage in politics and ethics based not on the desire to find the right 'handle' on history to ensure it goes in the direction they think it should. Rather Yoder argues we are called to faithfulness and patience in the Lamb who was slain and yet was victorious. Yoder commenting on John's visions in *Revelation* says,

'The lamb that was slain is worthy to receive power!' John is here saying, not as an inscrutable paradox but as a meaningful affirmation, that the cross and not the sword, suffering and not brute power determines the meaning of history. The key to the obedience of God's people is not their effectiveness but their patience. The triumph of the right is assured not by the might that comes to the aid of the right, which is of course the justification of the use of violence and other kinds of power in every human conflict. The triumph of the right, although it is assured, is sure because of the power of the resurrection and not because of any calculation of causes and effects, nor because of the inherently greater strength of the good guys. The relationship between the obedience of God's people and the triumph of God's cause is not a relationship between cause and effect but one of cross and resurrection.   (Yoder 1994: 232)

Yoder's understanding of the relationship between ethics and eschatology nicely frames Wesley's understanding of the kind of life we must live as a holy people. It is no surprise that so many Methodists draw on Yoder's work to help make sense of our calling as Christians in the Methodist tradition. For example, Yoder wrote an important essay originally titled, 'Peace without Eschatology?' Much of Christian ethics from early to mid-twentieth century assumed that ethics replaced eschatology. Yoder challenged this displacement arguing that only if we have a robust eschatology can Christian ethics make sense.

According to Yoder to live eschatologically is to live in the light of 'a hope which, defying present frustration, defines a present position in terms of the yet unseen goal which gives it meaning' (Yoder 1971: 53). This is why 'witness' is so important both to the Holiness and Anabaptist traditions, that is, we believe we can take the time to be faithful to what Jesus gives us in the Sermon on the Mount because we know that the present age does not constrain and define all our ethical options. We witness to what is coming because it already came: 'Christ has died, Christ is risen, Christ will come again.' Eschatological earnestness defines Methodist ethics. For this reason our ethics need not be reactive. It does not begin with evil and ask how we avoid it. It begins with the fullness of the gift received in word and sacrament and asks how we embody and bear witness to it.

THE EMBODIMENT OF SANCTIFICATION AND PERFECTION

While Methodism was still a movement and not yet a church, the only requirement for admission was 'a desire to flee from the wrath to come and to be saved from sins'. To flee eschatological judgement acknowledges God intends to restore creation consistent with Jesus' work in Scripture. The greatest ethical failure would be to reject or neglect that restoration. The role of the Methodist movement was to assist persons in living the life God intended, which was to flee from eschatological judgement by avoiding evil, doing good, and being attentive to what God gave us for this purpose.

The 'General Rules' of the United Methodist Church were developed to help Methodists lead lives of accountability to one another. Membership vows assume these rules to this day. Under each of these general rules were a number of other rules Methodists were expected to live by. This could appear to be a contradiction. If the only requirement for membership in Methodism was a desire to flee from eschatological judgement and be saved from sin, why were the Methodists given so many rules to which they were held accountable? The answer is found in the understanding of what it means to 'be saved from sin'. As the United Methodist Discipline still states, 'wherever this is really fixed in the soul, it will be shown by its fruits'. This is why the 'religion of the heart' cannot be understood as a private, interior disposition about which no one can discern or make judgements. A Methodist theological ethic assumes that the good to be done and the evil to be avoided will always have an external shape. It can be indicated by the manner of life of the Methodist people.

That Methodists expect the Christian life will of necessity be given an external shape provides its tradition with both its temptation and its promise. Its temptation is the tendency towards a moralistic legalism. For instance, Methodists for long periods of their history did not drink alcohol. To do so violated one of the general rules which stated that Methodists should do no harm through 'drunkenness: buying or selling spirituous liquors, or drinking them, unless in cases of extreme necessity'. Drunkenness is not, of course, a vice Methodists alone oppose. It has made the list of the 'seven deadly vices' throughout Christian tradition, usually under the larger vice of gluttony, something that the early Methodists particularly eschewed. It is also a social matter. Alcohol and drug abuse have grave social consequences. Methodist clergy were required to take vows against all consumption of alcohol throughout much of the twentieth century. But the Methodist opposition to alcohol was so strident and moralistic that they were even responsible for breaking the common Christian tradition of using wine for the eucharist in favour of grape juice. (Dr Charles Welch, pioneer of pasteurized grape juice, was a Methodist.) Methodists turned an important social issue into a personal code of conduct that lost its social significance. Eucharists with Wonder Bread and grape juice saw Methodism succumb to the temptation to be moralistic. The fact that in many Methodist churches and seminaries one can proclaim just about any kind of Christology available, but the use of wine for the eucharist is impermissible, shows Methodism still falls prey to legalism.

During the same time that we Methodists were convinced that a necessary external fruit of salvation would be prohibition from alcohol, we did not feel the same moral compunction in overturning another one of our General Rules: the prohibition against slaveholding. As we look back on our history we can see that our attempts to identify the necessary fruit of salvation fell far short. Methodist theological ethics boldly asks and answers, 'what does the religion of the heart look like in ordinary life?' We often got, and surely still get, those answers wrong. When we do we quickly become moralistic and legalistic. This occurs on the one hand when Methodists turn the shape of the Christian life into a private piety. It happens on the other hand when we turn it into a proceduralism that will supposedly ensure fairness through rigorous laws of interest group representation. Methodist theological ethics are tempted by epistemological 'methodism' (cf. Abraham 2006: 33).

Perhaps it would be easier and safer for a Methodist theological ethics to avoid altogether the effort to identify the shape of the Christian moral life? We could follow some Christian traditions that are much more sober about the ability either to identify or embody the shape of a blessed, happy, good life in the time between the times. Who could know what it looks like? We could emphasize the importance of the Christian as *simul justus et peccator* and develop a theological ethics based on a dialectic where every account of a righteous life must also stand under its negation by its inevitable participation in evil.

Yet Methodists have rightly refused this option. We have done so because, as we have emphasized, Methodism stands in the great catholic tradition that refuses to separate holiness and happiness. We pray and sing: 'Finish, then, thy new creation; pure and spotless let us be. Let us see thy great salvation perfectly restored in thee; changed from glory into glory, till in heaven we take our place, till we cast our crowns before thee, lost in wonder, love, and praise'. Notice that the prayer to finish and perfect the new creation comes before we take our place in heaven.

Charles Wesley's hymn significantly suggests the eschatological position we iden- tified above that is at the heart of Wesley's (and Yoder's) understanding of the Christian life. The new creation is not something that simply takes place in heaven at the end of time; it begins with Jesus' victory. His is the perfect performance of what it means to be human in time. Because we can now participate in his life, we do not know what is possible or impossible. Perfection of the new creation even in a small way is open because of Christ's work. The creation is not something inevitably marred with sin such that it must be destroyed. Christ vindicates it and in that vindication new possibilities emerge, even the possibility of perfection. This is why Methodists are asked at ordination, 'do you expect to be made perfect in love in this lifetime?' Forensic notions of justification that only emphasize imputation cannot sustain this theological ethic. As Wesley put it, we cannot claim the Lord is our righteousness if he, through the Holy Spirit, cannot then produce in us our own righteousness.

The Methodist understanding of sanctification and the call to holiness must refuse to forgo the identification and embodiment of the Christian life in this lifetime because of its call to perfection. We do not expect to see it completely until Christ's return. Nor can we assume we have arrived. As Wesley put it,

Yea, and when we have attained a measure of perfect love, when God has circumcised our heart, and enabled you to love him with all your heart and with all your soul, think not of resting there. That is impossible. You cannot stand still; you must either rise or fall; rise higher or fall lower. Therefore the voice of God to the children of Israel, to the children of God, is, 'Go forward'.   (cited in Hauerwas 1998: 124)

If Wesley had any weakness in his conception of perfection, which has carried over into the Methodist tradition, it was his view that perfection consists of easily identifiable stages.

But we have anticipations of the life we will share with God. The Christian, therefore, can bear witness to God's gift that sanctifies us into God's own perfec- tion. Wesley saw this clearly exemplified in the beatitudes. Yet what is crucial to sustain his understanding of Christian holiness is that the call to perfection is never separated from its Christological home which makes it intelligible. When such a separation occurs, as has sometimes happened, the call to perfection and holiness can degenerate into various versions of humanistic and sentimental progressivism.

We believe that Wesley has been and can continue to be a resource to help Methodists and all Christians recognize that any time a strong distinction between theology and ethics occurs something has gone wrong. Wesley's insistence that holiness and happiness were but two sides of the same coin rightly indicates that Christian theology is an exercise in practical divinity. Whether a discipline called theological ethics exists or does not exist is not of great importance. What is important is that Christians at this time and in this place discover—a discovery Wesley makes possible—that to be a Christian is to be made a participant in the very life of God.

REFERENCES

ABRAHAM, WILLIAM J. (2006). *Crossing the Threshold of Divine Revelation*. Grand Rapids: Eerdmans.

HAUERWAS, STANLEY (1998). *Sanctify Them in Truth*. Nashville: Abingdon.

LANGFORD, THOMAS (1983). *Practical Divinity: Theology in the Wesleyan Tradition*. Nashville: Abingdon.

LILLA, MARK (2007). *The Stillborn God: Religion, Politics and the Modern West*. New York: Knopf.

PINCKAERS, SERVAIS (2002). 'The Sources of the Ethics of St. Thomas Aquinas'. In Stephen J. Pope (ed.), *Ethics of Aquinas*. Moral Traditions Series. Washington, D.C.: Georgetown University Press.

TAYLOR, CHARLES (2007). *The Secular Age*. Belknap.

WESLEY, JOHN (1978). *The Works of Wesley*. Baker Book House.

YODER, JOHN HOWARD (1971). *The Original Revolution*. Scottdale, Pa.: Herald.

—— (1994). *The Politics of Jesus: Vicit Agnus Noster*. Grand Rapids: Eerdmans.

CHAPTER 38

MORAL THEOLOGY

ROBIN W. LOVIN

MORAL theology is a field of theological inquiry in which questions of ethics are systematically related to God. The good human life is understood in relation to God's goodness, God's ordering of creation, and God's commandments. Although the knowledge, will, and perseverance required to live this life may depend in important ways on faith, all persons are part of God's creation, so that the conclusions of moral theology about how we ought to live apply to everyone. Moral theology thus aims at an understanding of human life as part of the created order and an evaluation of human choice and action in the context of the history of salvation. It may be contrasted to practical theology, understood as specifically concerned with the formation of Christian lives and Christian communities, and to Christian social ethics, concerned with a theological understanding of the political, economic, and social forces that shape a particular society. In Methodism, where theology generally has a strong social and practical orientation, these distinctions are not always sharply drawn, but we may take moral theology as the comprehensive term for studies that seek to relate human goods to God's purposes and to direct human action in accordance with God's ordering of nature and history.

BACKGROUND

Christians understood from an early point that their moral lives were both connected to and distinct from the social context in which they lived. Following

Jesus set them free from the constraints of legalism and the pursuit of riches, pleasure, and honours. The result, however, was not supposed to be ungoverned and unpredictable conduct, but a sober and honest life that would commend itself even to those who did not share the Christian faith (1 Peter 2: 11). Augustine (d. 430) sharply divided humanity into the heavenly city united by love for God and the earthly city fragmented by love of self, but he also incorporated the chief virtues of Greek and Roman ethics into his account of the Christian life, and he recognized that Christians had a stake in the peace of whatever earthly city they find themselves in for the present. Augustine's realistic assessment of the social context helped the western church survive the end of the Roman Empire and the emergence of a new feudal order in Europe.

Some seven centuries later, a revival of learning and the rediscovery of Greek philosophy elicited a more comprehensive understanding of Christian society as part of a cosmic order. At the height of medieval Christianity, Thomas Aquinas (d. 1274) organized his moral theology around the idea that God is the beginning and end of all things. Individual conscience and human law are formed in accordance with natural law which is shaped, in turn, by the eternal law by which God orders all reality. Individual and social choices guided by reason are able to discern God's purposes in nature, and the goods all people seek bind them to God, whether or not they understand this relationship. Grace and nature work together as God completes what cannot be fully accomplished by conscientious human action.

For some, the Protestant Reformation marked a radical break with this medieval unity of the moral life and created order. Anabaptists and later Pietists associated the Christian life with an inward relationship to God nurtured by strong communal disciplines, rather than objective requirements of reason that might be known by anyone. Lutheran and Calvinist theologians emphasized the importance of moral law as the foundation of social order, but they saw this law as a restraint on evil, rather than a way of knowing the good, and they stressed that Christian people and their rulers must often rely on Scripture to provide guidance when unaided reason ends in uncertainty. Anglicans characteristically retained much of the medieval emphasis on reason and natural law, with Richard Hooker (d. 1600) adapting the Thomistic framework to the demands of a more modern civil and ecclesiastical polity. This produced an emphasis on order, uniformity, and authority that was congenial to the established church, but it also gave rise to an independent rational inquiry into social purposes that would develop in quite different directions in the hands of enlightened Scottish Presbyterians, English Congregationalists, and secular social reformers.

At the beginning of the eighteenth century, the Anglican version of Aquinas' theological unification of the moral life was still dominant in Britain, but the century that produced the Methodist movement would test the Anglican consensus in many ways. Methodism would be both part of the tradition and part of the test, taking direction from John Wesley's Anglican theology, his experiences with Moravian piety, and his political conservativism. Wesley drew upon piety, reason, and order as he needed them, without worrying too much about where he found them. If nothing like a fully developed moral theology emerged from the early Methodist movement, that was in part because the broad Anglican tradition encompassed Wesley's concern for practical choices, his openness to reasoned argument, and his trust in the accumulated wisdom of generations of Christian life. But Methodism could not easily be held to traditional patterns of moral thinking. It grew from the immediacy of personal experience, and those who are focused on their own experience are often ready to leave tradition behind and move in new directions.

WESLEY'S MORAL THEOLOGY

Like many theologians and philosophers of his time, Wesley emphasized the role of conscience in his accounts of the moral life. It was a concept that resonated with growing demands for individual responsibility and political freedom in eighteenth-century England, but the common use of the term concealed a range of meanings. For example, the moral philosopher Francis Hutcheson (d. 1746) called attention to a 'moral sense' shared by all persons, so that some actions have an 'immediate goodness' that pleases us when we think about them and leads us to think highly of those who perform them (Hutcheson 2004: 88). For Wesley, conscience was less this intuitive sense of right and wrong than it was a faculty of reasoned judgement, making the connection between a general moral rule and its application to a specific case. Like most English thinkers since the time of John Locke (d. 1704), Wesley understood that all knowledge was derived from the senses, and he denied that the human mind holds innate ideas of God and goodness by which we could judge choices and actions. Wesley even spoke of the knowledge of God that comes through religious experience in terms of the awakening of a 'spiritual sense', but there is little to suggest that he acknowledged anything like Hutcheson's moral sense (Long 2005: 117).

In fact, Wesley attacked Hutcheson's views in a sermon on conscience published in 1788. Stating his own case, he succinctly describes conscience as 'that faculty of the soul which, by the assistance of the grace of God, sees at one and the same time, (1) our own tempers and lives, the real nature and quality of our thoughts, words and action; (2) the rule whereby we are to be directed, and (3) the agreement or disagreement therewith' (Wesley 1986: 485). The empirical element is evident in the accurate apprehension of our own situation, but nothing can be determined from that knowledge alone. The moral conclusion follows when the actual situation is measured against a rule. Conscience is the name for the faculty that enables us to make that comparison and draw the appropriate conclusions. It is a faculty of reason, not perception. In those ways, Wesley's understanding of conscience parallels that of Thomas Aquinas, five centuries earlier (Long 2005: 62–6).

Differences from the medieval view must nonetheless be noted. Wesley emphasizes that 'the assistance of the grace of God' is essential to this act of judgement, suggesting that natural reason alone is inadequate to the task. Nor, for that matter, can natural benevolence motivate us to that disinterested love of right actions and good persons Hutcheson's moral sense requires (Wesley 1985: 598). The judgements of conscience and the feelings of moral approval may be universal, in the sense that no one completely lacks these internal witnesses to God's purposes, but for Wesley, they are not 'natural' in the way that Hutcheson thought the moral sense was part of human nature or that Aquinas spoke of a 'natural law' knowable by human reason. An honest conscience and genuine benevolence are the results of prevenient grace (Wesley 1986: 484).

This understanding of prevenient grace has important implications for Wesley's moral theology. He can appeal to his hearers' shared understanding of right and wrong and draw on their moral feelings with as much confidence as any Thomist or moral sense theorist. Unlike some Calvinists, he does not have to suppose that some of their understandings are so darkened that they cannot hear. Neither, however, can he follow the lead of some of the moral philosophers of his time, who built on this universal moral experience by encouraging people to follow their own reason or their moral sentiments independently of their relationship to God. For Wesley, these moral stirrings are God's own work. There can be no question of a point or purpose to the moral life apart from a relationship with God.

Perhaps more important, Wesley thinks of the general moral truth from which conscience frames its conclusion as a rule, and not as a goal. If Wesley has an idea of human good towards which all our actions should be directed, it is here very much in the background. It would seem not only that reason requires divine assistance in the task of judgement, but also that it is incapable of full understanding of the normative goal. Even a sincere desire to see God's will done is bound to fail for want of full understanding of what God's purposes are (Wesley 1985b: 582–6). Like his sometime adversary, Bishop Joseph Butler (d. 1752), Wesley appears to think that while God may order all things towards an ultimate good, our moral task is to follow the rules that God has given us. 'Though the good of the creation be the only end of the Author of it, yet He may have laid us under particular obligations, which we may discern and feel ourselves under, quite distinct from a perception, that the observance or violation of them is for the happiness or misery of our fellow-creatures. And this is in fact the case' (Butler 2006: 126).

In this, Wesley and Butler stand together on one side of a question that was being answered very differently by Hutcheson, Adam Smith (d. 1790), and William Paley (d. 1805). Hutcheson, Smith, and Paley look forward to an emerging idea of the greatest good for the greatest number, and they justify particular moral choices in relation to this underlying principle of utility that explains why the moral sense approves what it approves (Schneewind 1998: 408–13). Wesley and Butler look backward to a tradition of casuistry in which moral rules are applied to particular cases by a conscience trained in the use of moral reason. For Wesley, this was a tradition to which he was immediately connected through his maternal grandfather, Samuel Annesley (d. 1696), and he concludes the sermon in which he denounces Hutcheson's moral sense with a lengthy extract from a treatise by Annesley. It is an understanding of conscience that is steeped in Puritan self-discipline and traditional virtues. It stresses honest application of established rules to the details of the immediate situation, but leaves little room for reinterpreting the rules in the light of a greater good.

In many ways, then, Wesley's moral theology has more in common with the medieval theory of Thomas Aquinas than with the moral philosophy of his contemporaries in England and Scotland. In theology, as in politics, Wesley was a conservative who preferred to bend established systems to his evangelical purposes, rather than to abandon them. Nevertheless, evangelical purpose and Lockean epistemology have wrought their changes here. In place of the great system of ordered goods known to reason in Aquinas' theology, Wesley works with a sense of right and wrong supplied by prevenient grace and a system of rules applied to cases with divine assistance. The comprehensive understanding of human goods in relation to God's purposes has become a system of theological ethics.

MORAL PHILOSOPHY AND SOCIAL ETHICS

If Wesley and Butler relied on a system of rules as the starting point for moral judgement, others, as we have seen, sought to identify the features of social life that a disinterested benevolence would approve as just and suited to an increase in general happiness. While these developments culminated in Utilitarianism, which sometimes seems to dispense with fixed moral rules altogether, the aims of most moral philosophers were less radical. Since the principle behind feelings of moral approval seemed to be that we approve the things that make for an increase in general human happiness, they sought to refine the rules in the light of that purpose and, more importantly, to identify the social arrangements that would actually achieve that result. The key to this, according to Adam Smith, was to create systems that would serve the public good as a result of persons pursuing their private interests. Markets in which persons exchange goods and services are the best example of such a system, according to Smith, who pointed out that we have abundant material goods not because butchers, bakers, and candlestick makers are benevolent to us, but because the market rewards them for meeting our needs (Smith 1976: 27).

Wesley rejected this turn from moral rules to human goods, seeing it as tantamount to atheism (Wesley 1986: 484). It is perhaps good for Methodism that he did. Imagine the history of a Methodist movement committed by its founder to Adam Smith's enthusiasm for the workings of the market! Given Wesley's conviction that our feelings of conscience are the work of prevenient grace, the effort to explain moral sentiments in natural terms as human feelings that could be more accurately guided to their goal by a principle of utility had to seem to him like casting God aside. For Hutcheson, Smith, and Paley, the moral sense was part of God's creation, and anything that made it more effective and efficient in reaching its goal also served God's purposes.

Wesley was in some ways resisting the dominant intellectual trend of his time. However, he probably shared more of this empiricism in moral thought than he acknowledged. Like many others in the eighteenth century, he had an interest in the complex workings both of new machines and new social mechanisms, and his occasional writings are full of his own efforts to explain social, economic, and scientific developments. His understanding of how conscience works relies on moral rules and reason, but it begins with an account of 'our own tempers and lives, the real nature and quality of our thoughts, words, and actions'. Without an accurate understanding of the facts of the case, Wesley recognized, applications of the rules are apt to be mistaken, even if the good intentions are assisted by grace.

The combination of a Lockean philosophy that drew all knowledge from experience and a rapidly changing social environment drew moral thinking into more concrete and practical channels. Frances Hutcheson studied for the ministry and turned to moral philosophy. Adam Smith left his post as professor of moral philosophy to found the modern study of economics. This movement from moral theology, through empiricist ethics, to social science is an easily understandable path for an eighteenth-century intellect, and there were many who followed it.

It would take another century to reconnect the scientific understanding of society to moral theology, as the social gospel movement began to put scientific foundations under its programme of religiously motivated social reform. Accurate knowledge of social systems was the necessary starting point for efforts to change society in ways that would relieve the misery of immigrants crowded into urban tenements, former slaves living in rural poverty, and factory workers labouring long hours for low wages in unsafe conditions. Compassionate people had to know what would work, if their social conscience was to make a real difference in people's lives.

That was not to say that social science alone was sufficient. By the beginning of the twentieth century, religious reformers had seen too much of the effects of *laissez-faire* capitalism and the claims of Social Darwinism to suppose that this knowledge supplied its own moral compass. But scientific understanding combined with moral purpose could be the key to a millennial change in the human condition, as Walter Rauschenbusch (d. 1918) argued: 'For the first time in religious history we have the possibility of so directing religious energy by scientific knowledge that a comprehensive and continuous reconstruction of social life in the name of God is within the bounds of human possibility' (Rauschenbusch 1907: 209).

Methodists were important participants in the social gospel and in the subsequent development of what came to be called Christian 'social ethics'. World war and global economic depression muted the enthusiastic expectations of social transformation that marked the beginning of the twentieth century, but the effort to understand the concrete realities of social problems persisted, and so did the sense that the transformation of these realities is part of God's work in history. In some ways, this was a recovery of the eschatological theme of the 'new creation' that always had a place in Wesley's theology, though it remains quite distinct from his rule-oriented discussions of conscience and moral judgement and became part of his thinking about social realities only late in his career (Maddox 2004: 33–43).

The general human happiness that was the goal of eighteenth-century moral philosophy was too focused on material well-being and personal satisfaction to sustain much theological reflection. It was perhaps also too relativistic, since the formula of the greatest good for the greatest number could be used to justify a quasi-Darwinian programme of social selection that weeded out those less likely to contribute to the sum of happiness as well as a compassionate system of general benevolence that took care of the less fortunate. Normative direction needed something more than what was immanent in the social processes themselves, and that could be provided by returning to the ancient theme that the goodness of anything in the created order must be understood in relation to its ultimate destiny in God's plan. What sustained the teleology of Christian social ethics was the conviction that even complex social realities are part of that created order. It is therefore possible to participate in God's purposes through these institutions, just as it is necessary to repent for our misuse of them for our own ends and our idolatrous elevation of them as objects of devotion in their own right. This eschatology frames the successive statements of 'Social Principles' affirmed by many American Methodists down to the present day:

We believe in God, Creator of the world; and in Jesus Christ, the Redeemer of creation. We believe in the Holy Spirit, through whom we acknowledge God's gifts, and we repent of our sin in misusing these gifts to idolatrous ends ...

We believe in the present and final triumph of God's Word in human affairs and gladly accept our commission to manifest the life of the gospel in the world.

(*Book of Discipline* 2004: §166. 124–5)

Methodists have from the beginning understood in practice that to 'manifest the life of the gospel in the world' requires knowledge of both the gospel's eschatological hope and the realities of the world. The empiricist, goal-oriented moral philosophy of the eighteenth century sought to leave much of the heritage of moral theology behind, but it contributed in important ways to the development of the social sciences by which later Christian social ethics would guide its efforts to participate in the redemptive and transformative work by which creation is directed towards the end that God intends.

DUTY AND RESPONSIBILITY

The work of Hutcheson, Smith, and Paley culminated in the programmes of moral and political reform suggested by the utilitarians Jeremy Bentham (d. 1832) and John Stuart Mill (d. 1873). The aim of utilitarian politics and legislation is to increase human happiness, and proposals to do this are, they argued, best tested by our moral approval of the results, rather than by moral or religious principles that declare choices right or wrong prior to experience. A central democratic theme running through utilitarian ethics was the universality of moral feeling, the 'moral sense' that Hutcheson saw at work in every person's conscience. To respect the dignity of ordinary people in politics meant precisely to consider their feelings, with 'everybody to count for one, nobody for more than one' (Mill 1998: 105).

Not all moral philosophers, however, followed this line of thinking. The dramatic break with previous moral thinking that alarmed John Wesley, in fact, soon produced a reaction that turned from results back to rules, and from moral feelings and intuitions back to reason. Some asked how it is that respect for feelings comes to be taken as a measure of human dignity. What distinguishes human beings, moralists had insisted from Aristotle's time onward, is their ability to make choices guided by reason. Perhaps we acknowledge humanity best when we call upon a person to do what reason requires, especially when this duty runs counter to inclination. Immanuel Kant (d. 1804) developed this position systematically. Arguing specifically against Hutcheson and the moral sense theorists, Kant holds that actions done because we approve the results have no more moral value than actions done under compulsion, or good deeds performed in hope of a reward (Sullivan 1989: 40). Only a universal rule that applies to all rational beings, precisely because it is dictated by the impartial requirements of reason, provides a 'categorical imperative', a moral guide that cannot be set aside for any other consideration.

Wesley probably knew nothing of Kant's work, but he would certainly have agreed with Kant's rejection of Hutcheson. No doubt Wesley would have amplified the theological presuppositions to this account of duty and insisted that the relation between God and duty is more than a 'postulate' of pure reason, as Kant had it, but the capacity of reason to determine duty without reference to the hypothetical results of an action was essential to Wesley's account of conscience, and Kant's account of how moral reason works may provide a systematic under-standing of moral cognition that reinforces Wesley's rejection of a straightforward reliance on feelings of moral approval (Lowery 2008: 237–43). This emphasis on moral reason was already present in the Anglican moral theology on which Wesley relied (ibid. 252), and there is, in fact, a certain parallel between Kant's categorical imperative and advice that Wesley's grandfather offers in the treatise that Wesley appended to his own sermon on conscience. Kant says that the categorical impera-tive is to 'act only in accordance with that maxim through which you can at the same time will that it become a universal law' (Kant 1997: 31). Samuel Annesley concludes his discourse with a kind of reverse formulation of the principle, urging his hearers to remember that 'what is the duty of another in your case is your own' (Wesley 1986: 489).

This emphasis on duty continued in Methodist preaching and piety, despite the consequentialist tendencies in British and American philosophy. It returned to Methodist moral theology as Methodists expanded their educational institutions and their leading thinkers gained more exposure to German philosophy and theology that had been influenced by Kant's ethics and Hegel's understanding of the human person. Respect for the human person as a unique part of God's creation, distinguished by a capacity for moral choice and for a relationship with God and other people, was a central theme of 'Boston Personalism', the influential school of thought that developed at Boston University and was a major influence on Methodist theology and preaching in the early twentieth century (Dorrien 2003: 352–5). This idealist account of human personality provided an important coun-terweight to social ethics' reliance on social scientific analysis that could sometimes reduce human identity and action to highly predictable outcomes of observed social forces.

Moral theology influenced by this renewed appreciation of reason and duty also challenged the goal-oriented emphasis on social transformation in Christian social ethics. The questions arose in part from disagreement over specific responses to the problems of race and war in the late twentieth century. Paul Ramsey spoke for many Methodists who were alienated from the radical demands of Christian social ethics when he asked, 'Who speaks for the church?' (Ramsey 1967b). But he also raised a theological objection to the eschatological argument by which social ethics identified the pursuit of social goals as the way to manifest the presence of the gospel in the world. Eschatology, as Ramsey understood it, had always meant a response to the reign of God in the present moment, regardless of consequences. Eschatology does not authorize social transformation so much as it demands responsibility in relation to existing options. These choices cannot be made on the basis of projected consequences. They have to rely on moral principles. 'A teleological calculus (no matter how *ideal*) can be included in Christian ethics only in the service of its definition of righteousness, and subordinate to its view of obedient love. Whether this means that Christian ethics is a form of deontology, or is a third type of normative theory that is neither deontology nor teleology, remains unresolved. But the reduction of Christian ethics to teleology is nearly the same thing as abandoning it' (Ramsey 1967*a*: 109).

The reassertion of the importance of duty and principle did not signal a retreat from the church's involvement in social issues. Ramsey and others who shared this deontological critique of social ethics understood their moral judgements in universal terms, as articulating the will of God for all persons and situations, not just for those who accepted it. They understood their reasons as public reasons, even when they were expressed in theological terms. But a deontological approach to moral theology did change the way in which public issues were addressed. 'Obedient love' could be formulated in principles, but not in policies. The identification of Christian moral obligation with specific goals had to be tentative and subject to reassessment. Individual Christians would have to risk it in their responsible choices, but strong claims to provide theological direction for social transformation might best be avoided in the official statements of church bodies. Considerable latitude had to be allowed to secular authorities to set policy within the framework of principles. Social ethics, of course, responded that this severed the connection between Christian life and the new creation and reduced moral theology to a collection of rules and principles. Towards the end of Methodism's second century, the tension that Randy Maddox (2004) noted in Wesley's social thought between eschatology and authority would be played out between competing understandings of goals and rules in moral theology.

VIRTUE AND COMMUNITY

One reason why deontological moral theology emphasized universal, rational moral principles was to avoid the relativist teleology that seemed to result when ethics was guided by social science. Social science provided an explanation of how particular societies work, and the plans it suggested could claim no more than that they were the sort of arrangements that might be expected to work in a given context. A moral theology based on reason would not be so easily reduced to the practical requirements of a social system.

The emphasis on reason made another important claim, too: the Christian account of moral order and human duties was not for Christians alone. In so far as it was rational, it should be intelligible to everyone, and its moral claims would demand consideration by the whole society. An increasingly secular society might ignore the authority of its Christian past, but it would have to listen to the arguments of reasonable Christians.

This claim was not new, nor were the questions about it. What is perhaps surprising in the longer view of history is how many of those questions have come from within the Christian tradition. For Thomas Aquinas, writing in the thirteenth century, reality was a unified moral and metaphysical order, knowable by reason and mirrored in legal and ecclesial institutions shaped by human intelligence according to the rational patterns given in natural and divine law. In that framework, the authority and intelligibility of moral theology could be taken for granted, and there would be no reason to think of its requirements as peculiarly Christian. Questions were raised, however, about whether this order exists and whether it can be known. The questions began almost as soon as the system was formulated. They were themselves theological questions, not the result of modern sceptical criticism, and they have remained part of the theological argument ever since.

At issue was the relationship between divine will and moral order. For Aquinas, the duties that structure a moral life can be seen both as God's will and as requirements of a created, rational order. Later medieval theologians increasingly argued, however, that God's freedom requires us to ground the moral law in God's commands, rather than in God's creation. The intelligible moral order is replaced by a sovereign God whose commands deserve obedience simply because they are God's commands. This theological move provided a convenient model for rulers in a fragmented post-Reformation Europe who wanted to claim a similar authority for their own sovereignty (Elshtain 2008).

The Anglican moral theology that shaped John Wesley's understanding of moral reason was deeply influenced by these late-medieval and Reformation-era developments, despite its many connections to the work of Thomas Aquinas. One reason why both Butler and Wesley emphasized God's commands rather than moral goals was their shared conviction that we cannot see very far into whatever moral order might lie behind the commandments. For both of them, too, the authority of divine command extended to the authority of the king's law, so that even in this more voluntaristic way of thinking, there was unity between the religious, moral, and legal orders.

There was, however, another way of thinking that emerged from the Reformation that connected the law of love to a gathered church completely distinct from the coercive order of religious and civil authority. The leaders of this 'Radical Reformation' saw it as a return to early Christianity, before the church had acquired a share in the power of government. This was when Christians understood themselves as a people set apart, without responsibility for the world and its authorities.

Wesley was drawn to the piety of these groups that had survived to his day outside the religious establishment, and he and the members of his Methodist movement could identify with their suspect position as outsiders on the margins of society. He was not sure that real devotion and authentic Christian community could be sustained in a church that enjoyed the favour of the authorities, and he spoke of 'that evil hour when Constantine the Great called himself "a Christian"' (Wesley 1987: 77). Just as there were elements of his eschatology that were in conflict with his Anglican emphasis on duty apart from consequences, he had an understanding of Christian piety that also sat uneasily with the idea of moral rules that everyone could understand and should obey. The tensions in Wesley's thought have been reflected in the subsequent history of Methodist moral theology.

Sociologists have tended to see Methodism as a sect that became a church over time. This may be more accurate as an external view of the standing Methodists in society than as a report of how Methodists see themselves, but the sectarian ideal has remained present in the thinking of those who see themselves as a 'peculiar people', not only set apart for mission, but differentiated from other Christians by character and self-understanding. Today, when most people have a view of Christian ethics that is undistinguishable from ordinary good behaviour, the desire for a clearer statement of what it means to be a Christian and a clearer differentiation of the Christian community from the rest of society has once again emerged as a strong theme in Methodist theology, preaching, and practice.

The result is a moral theology that is critical of both deontological moral principles and teleological social ethics. It draws explicitly on Anabaptist understandings of church and society, including the conviction that all government rests on coercion, which Christians must reject by a pacifist refusal to cooperate with its organized violence. The 'quandary ethics' that reduces the moral life to a set of problems to be resolved by the application of abstract principles is replaced by an ethics of virtue that concentrates on how lives are shaped by the Christian narrative and by participation in Christian community. Christians should also recognize that the ordinary understanding of social ethics comes from a 'Constantinian' theology that mistakenly assumes that the church has responsibility for the ordering of society. The social task of the church is to be the church, 'and thus help the world understand itself as world' (Hauerwas 1983: 100).

A church formed in this way will no longer speak a reasonable language that makes a claim on everyone's understanding. Indeed, it will expect that the way it speaks of God will be unintelligible to anyone who does not share its convictions (Hauerwas 2001: 15). Its task cannot be to make moral arguments, or to propose solutions to social problems, or even to make a public case for its own beliefs. It can only serve as a witness that some other way of life is possible over against the ways that make sense to the world.

This articulation of a moral theology centred on virtue, the Christian narrative, and the Christian community focuses attention on its connection to the Radical Reformation, and like those movements of the sixteenth century, it claims to restore to the church its original, pre-Constantinian self-understanding. That is a matter for historical debate, but however the history of the church is narrated, it is important to see that this contemporary version also draws on a rejection of reason and nature and an assertion of divine sovereignty. Well before the Reformation began, this theology had begun to draw moral theology away from its most comprehensive claims about the relation between human action and God's order. An anti-Constantinian moral theology will, of course, be particularly vigilant against any attempt to extend this model of divine sovereignty to human rulers in the way that early modern political thought did. The idea that God's sovereignty must be set against human understanding is a more comprehensive claim, and one that has earlier roots.

Conclusion

Moral theology is the ambitious project of understanding human choice and action in relation to a comprehensive account of God's creative, redemptive, and reconciling work. Moral theology makes large claims, and it is not surprising that sceptical thinkers have said that it is impossible, or that Protestants have sometimes suggested that it is unfaithful (Bonhoeffer 2005: 378). The term 'moral theology' is in fact most often used in Catholic writing, where Thomistic metaphysics and an authoritative tradition of teaching help hold together the large and diverse body of claims that a comprehensive moral theology must make.

As human knowledge expands and ways of speaking of God become more diverse, moral theology tends to disintegrate. Social ethics, moral principles, and Christian virtues are spun off from the same source, but each tends to regard the others as a betrayal of their common origin, or to portray itself as the only authentic representative of the Christian past. This is not a new phenomenon, as we have seen. Wesley was alarmed by moral sense theories that limited their moral inquiries to the conditions that make for human happiness. In Francis Hutcheson's way of thinking, Wesley exclaimed, Jesus himself would have no share in virtue (Wesley 1986: 484). But what would Thomas Aquinas have made of John Wesley and Joseph Butler, who seem to agree that we should confine our moral explorations to reasoned judgements about what God has commanded us to do, and not inquire too closely into what God's purposes behind those duties might be?

The fragmentation of moral theology is not a new phenomenon, though it is reflected in the contemporary textbook division of ethics into deontology, teleology, and virtue ethics, just as we have seen it worked out in recent Methodist versions of social ethics, moral principles, and Christian witness. The process was underway centuries before John Wesley and the Methodist movement appeared on the scene, and Wesley himself participates in it. He aligns himself with the Anglican casuistry that limits moral reason to working out the implications of duty, but he cannot completely avoid the sense that what we ought to do has some relation to the goal of God's work in the new creation, and he admires the piety of those who have nothing to say about authority in society, but understand everything through love in the Christian community.

One lesson we might draw from this history is the sceptical conclusion that moral theology is impossible. The order that God has created is so vast and what we can know of it is so limited that the comprehensive understanding of human choice and action at which moral theology aims is simply beyond our grasp. Thomas Aquinas could sketch a neat hierarchy of eternal law, natural law, and human law, but who among us can really expect to explain our moral choices in relation to an order that includes God's love, quantum physics, and international terrorism? No wonder it was theologians who first warned that Aquinas' system was overreaching itself, long before physicists and political realists called it into question.

Or perhaps the lesson is that moral theology is not a system, but a task. Moral theology is the Christian's refusal to settle for reductive explanations that strip history and human action of meaning. It is the continuous effort to assert ultimate meaning and the continuous correction of each successive assertion as its incompleteness and partiality becomes apparent. Moral theology can only be done by the whole church, working together through history. This is not a work to be done apart from the world, the church telling its own story to itself. It happens as Christians work with others on evolutionary biology and astrophysics, on international law and ending poverty, and on understanding their own story in relation to a reality that is reported in each of these other languages, too. Christians cannot expect others to take responsibility for the theological integrity that is rightly their own task, but they should not confuse integrity with isolation. Moral theology understood in this way may never again be wrapped up in a unified moral, metaphysical, and theological system, but if this way of thinking about human choice and action is a continuous task of the church, we may say, paraphrasing Stanley Hauerwas, that the church does not *have* a moral theology. The church *is* moral theology.

SUGGESTED READING

LONG (2005).

LOWERY (2008).

RUNYON, THEODORE (1998). *The New Creation: John Wesley's Theology Today.* Nashville: Abingdon.

WOGAMAN, J. PHILIP (1993). *Christian Ethics: A Historical Introduction.* Louisville, Ky.: Westminster John Knox.

References

BONHOEFFER, DIETRICH (2005). *Ethics*, ed. Clifford J. Green. Minneapolis: Fortress.

The Book of Discipline of the United Methodist Church (2004). Nashville: United Methodist Publishing House.

BUTLER, JOSEPH (2006). 'Sermon XII: Upon the Love of Our Neighbor'. In David E. White (ed.), *The Works of Bishop Butler*. Rochester, N.Y.: University of Rochester Press.

DORRIEN, GARY (2003). *The Making of American Liberal Theology: Idealism, Realism, and Modernity, 1900–1950*. Louisville, Ky.: Westminster John Knox.

ELSHTAIN, JEAN BETHKE (2008). *Sovereignty: God, State, and Self*. New York: Basic Books.

HAUERWAS, STANLEY (1983). *The Peaceable Kingdom*. Notre Dame, Ind.: University of Notre Dame Press.

—— (2001). *With the Grain of the Universe*. Grand Rapids: Brazos.

HUTCHESON, FRANCIS (2004). *An Inquiry into the Original of Our Ideas of Beauty and Virtue*. Indianapolis: Liberty Fund.

KANT, IMMANUEL (1997). *Groundwork of the Metaphysics of Morals*. Cambridge: Cambridge University Press.

LONG, D. STEPHEN (2005). *John Wesley's Moral Theology: The Quest for God and Goodness*. Nashville: Kingswood.

LOWERY, KEVIN TWAIN (2008). *Salvaging Wesley's Agenda: A New Paradigm for Wesleyan Virtue Ethics*. Princeton Theological Monograph Series 86. Eugene, Ore.: Pickwick.

MADDOX, RANDY (2004). 'Nurturing the New Creation: Reflections on a Wesleyan Trajectory'. In M. Douglas Meeks (ed.), *Wesleyan Perspectives on the New Creation*. Nashville: Kingswood.

MILL, JOHN STUART (1998). *Utilitarianism*, ed. Roger Crisp. Oxford: Oxford University Press.

RAMSEY, PAUL (1967a). *Deeds and Rules in Christian Ethics*. New York: Charles Scribner's Sons.

—— (1967b). *Who Speaks for the Church?* Nashville: Abingdon.

RAUSCHENBUSCH, WALTER (1907). *Christianity and the Social Crisis*. New York: Macmillan.

SCHNEEWIND, J. B. (1998). *The Invention of Autonomy*. Cambridge: Cambridge University Press.

SMITH, ADAM (1976). *An Inquiry into the Nature and Causes of the Wealth of Nations*. Oxford: Oxford University Press, i.

SULLIVAN, ROGER (1989). *Immanuel Kant's Moral Theory*. Cambridge: Cambridge University Press.

WESLEY, JOHN (1985a). 'The Case of Reason Impartially Considered'. In *Works*, ed. Albert C. Outler. Nashville: Abingdon, ii.

—— (1985b). 'The Imperfection of Human Knowledge'. In *Works*, ed. Albert C. Outler. Nashville: Abingdon, ii.

—— (1986). 'On Conscience'. In *Works*, ed. Albert C. Outler. Nashville: Abingdon, iii.

—— (1987). 'Prophets and Priests'. In *Works*, ed. Albert C. Outler. Nashville: Abingdon, iv.

CHAPTER 39

METHODISM AND FEMINISM

JANE CRASKE

INTRODUCTION

'FEMINISM' is a contentious word. It induces strong reactions, many of them negative. These gut reactions often obscure attempts to define or explain more clearly what feminism has been, is, and might be in the future. In fact to write of 'feminism' in the singular is no longer accurate or helpful. 'Feminism' is now a range of feminisms, a complex, fascinating multiplicity of perspectives through which to examine and analyse the lives of women and men in the twenty-first century, in many and varied contexts across the world.

What, though, might this have to do with Methodism? Feminisms are not necessarily theological and where they are theological, they are certainly not specific to particular Christian denominations. For a handbook of Methodist studies, I will focus on feminist *theologies*, though taking some space to locate them in the history of twentieth- and twenty-first-century feminisms.

This chapter, then, chiefly examines some instances of Methodist engagement with feminist theologies. It proceeds through snapshot examples rather than attempting to summarize and systematize more broadly, since this is the way to tackle such a broad subject within the limits of a single chapter. But this way of proceeding also echoes the emphasis on particularity among feminist theologies. In this chapter, I discuss the work of some Methodist scholars who have contributed to thinking and action with and on behalf of women in various situations of oppression around the world. There are examples of scholars tackling what can be seen as characteristically Methodist or Wesleyan themes. The question has been asked at least informally whether there is anything in Methodism's ethos or theologies that supports or encourages the work of liberation, black, and feminist/womanist scholars, and that will be a question to which I return. There are also in this chapter examples of how particular Methodist churches have debated, fought against, or engaged with feminist ideas. But to limit the chapter entirely to a discussion of Methodist distinctives would be a distortion of feminist theological work which does not run on denominational lines. This chapter cannot just be about what goes on in Methodist churches, or even in the Christian church as a whole. To be true to feminisms of any and all kinds, it must connect with the whole of life. Theologians who may call themselves feminist, womanist, *mujerista*, African or Asian women interact with the agenda of the churches but also with so-called 'secular' agendas particularly if those secular agendas appear at times to be better for women than the church's teaching or general practice.

Therefore there may be questions about how 'Methodist' some of this material is. The question is part of a more general debate about what makes something Methodist (or Wesleyan). Does material have to engage with Wesley to be Methodist, or with other explicit aspects of Methodist theology? Does it simply have to come from a Methodist background to be Methodist? There are examples in this chapter of both these ways of answering the question and I set them alongside each other. I cannot push too far a narrow question about Methodist distinctives. The boundaries and limits of the discussion, particularly when the subject is feminist theologies, are not so clear, so in this chapter I point to aspects of convergence where they are to be found and I point to contextual factors which situate material, or the scholars who produce it, within Methodism. But I do not believe trying to establish the strongest and most exclusive of definitions of what is 'Methodist' or not is possible or fruitful.

Within work that comes from some kind of feminist perspective, it is important to define the point of view from which the analysis proceeds. I am a white, well-educated Western woman. I am ordained as a presbyter in the British Methodist Church and I undertake theological study and writing with feminist commitment. All those aspects of my background open particular perspectives, and not others. They are limits to be observed and a place from which conversation may begin with those who live and work with other perspectives.

DEFINING FEMINISMS

There have been various analyses of the history of feminist thought. One of the earlier, influential ones was Rosemarie Tong's *Feminist Thought* (1989). Tong traced developments in 'second-wave' feminism—from the 1960s on, initially focused in the Western world. She noted the different theoretical frameworks that resulted in feminisms that could be variously labelled liberal, Marxist, radical, psychoanalytic, socialist, and existentialist. Although, in the late 1980s, her work drew attention to the differences among women, Tong's book strikes the reader now as highly abstract in its discussion of concepts of race and class, with a lack of attention to the actual voices of women of colour or women in the developing world. The critique that feminism of the 1970s and early 1980s did not take sufficient account of other aspects of identity, particularly ethnicity, precipitated controversies and divisions within feminism. Some saw what resulted as fragmentation, but it is better described as a rich diversification of feminism into a multiplicity of perspectives.

Feminism/s are a series of ideas and movements in the social, political, and cultural spheres of human life which focus on an analysis of women's oppression and seek to alleviate it. Feminist work of any kind begins from the belief that women have been devalued and oppressed in all cultures throughout history, though always in culturally specific ways. Building from description and analysis of the specifics of women's lives—at best carefully focused on particular women or groups of women rather than generalized about 'women's experience'—feminisms will also have a concern for justice, seeking remedies for specific instances where women are oppressed. Feminist analysis also focuses on the production of knowledge, particularly understandings of what it is to be human, or to be male or female, which are implicated in the devaluing and oppression of women, when women are seen and treated as second-class citizens. Mercy Amba Oduyoye's definition of feminism emphasizes this: 'Feminism calls for the incorporation of the woman into the community of interpretation of what it means to be human' (1986: 121). Feminist theorists ask questions about the construction of gendered identity and its relationship to status based on biological categories, and even how biological categories are defined and by whom. Feminist insights are those that raise questions about power specifically, though not necessarily only, in relation to gender. They ask about whether women's voices are heard or not, or which women's voices are heard.

FEMINIST THEOLOGIES

Feminism is not necessarily theological, but there are a considerable number and variety of feminist theologies. They have at least a dual background. They emerge from the feminist critiques of societies in general, from the belief that in all cultures women have been discriminated against in relation to men and from a commitment to do something about it where such discrimination still exists. Feminist theologies also, however, emerge from liberation theologies. As such they are a way of doing theology. 'We know that Liberation Theology is not a theology subject. It is a Method of doing theology. Its starting point is reality, concrete life, where the people experience oppression and discrimination and at the same time they have an encounter with the God of life and solidarity' (Tamez 2001). The key methodological point for liberation theologies is the way in which people's experiences are used, analysed, and developed within theological praxis. In feminist theologies, women's experiences need to be taken seriously as a starting point for theological reflection.

However, as with non-theological feminism, the earliest feminist theologians made too many assumptions that the experiences of other women and the concerns of women about churches or about Christian theology were all like their own. This universalizing fallacy was exposed crucially in such works as Jacquelyn Grant's *White Women's Christ, Black Women's Jesus* (1989). From these critiques emerged a number of theologies for which their proponents needed labels other than 'feminist', where 'feminist' had come to be seen as the preserve of white, middle-class, Western women. Thus, such terms as 'womanist' (African-American), *mujerista* (Latina/Hispanic), or African women's or Asian women's theologies have emerged, to define further the standpoint from which particular theologies are being written. Though the label 'feminist theology' may no longer be helpful, it may be possible to use the term 'feminist theologies' in an overarching sense, if the variety of perspectives from which theology is being done can be more explicitly acknowledged.

When feminist theology emerged in the 1960s, it was as a critique of how the churches discriminated against women through theological ideas, and of women's lack of participation in some spheres of church life throughout Christian history. The work of Mary Daly was key. While her first book, *The Church and the Second Sex* (1968), now reads as a trenchant but familiar critique of the Roman Catholic Church's practice, it was *Beyond God the Father* (1973) that signalled a much more radical break with the Christian tradition. Daly's fierce and angry analysis that Christianity's imagery and practice were male-centred through and through, and therefore bound to discriminate against women, has been hugely influential. Her position is summed up in her much-quoted dictum, 'if God is male, then the male is God' (ibid. 19). For Daly Christianity was *irredeemably* patriarchal and the ideas for reform proposed in her earlier book were pointless. Her exodus from Christianity and her development of, first, a post-Christian philosophy, then a radical feminist philosophy have been subject to much critique, but have also inspired many others to leave Christianity behind. Subsequent developments into thealogy/ feminist work focusing on the Goddess—owe much to Daly, even if thealogians have not necessarily followed Daly's own intellectual and spiritual journey.

Two major journals of feminist work in theology and religious studies highlight how feminist theologies have evolved, at least in the Western academy, under the influence of varied voices within and beyond the West. In an edition of the US-based *Journal of Feminist Studies in Religion* celebrating the journal's twentieth anniversary, Emilie Townes noted that *JFSR* had been intended to address the theological academy, women's movements, and the women's studies arena. Her assessment was that its strongest contribution had been in the theological academy and its weakest in persuading the women's studies arena to take the subject of religion more seriously (Townes 2005: 111–12). *Feminist Theology*, published in Britain, has in recent years highlighted debates between theologians and thealogians. It suggests there is somewhat less tension between Christian feminist theologians and thealogians than in the US (Isherwood 2005: 133). But these debates appear amidst a wide range of issues discussed from feminist theological perspectives. Both journals try to give space for constructive dialogue between proponents of different feminist theologies.

The basic question in Christian feminist theologies remains the extent that Christian traditions can be used by theologians seeking to work with and on behalf of women who are oppressed, when some of those traditions are clearly patriarchal (emerging from dominantly male perspectives and discriminating against women, but which women can also support and perpetuate). There can, though, be a temptation in denominational studies to give insufficient attention to the ways in which the denomination must take account of that with which all Christian theology struggles. Thus, when Beverley Clack (1999) wrote about her Methodist background and then about her journey out of Christianity, under the influence both of non-realist theology and of feminist theology, it was suggested to the editors of the book in which her chapter appeared that this was not really about Methodism.

Feminist theologies intersect with Christian theologies; they are not contained within them. For those doing feminist, womanist, *mujerista*, etc. theologies who remain in churches, there is always some degree, often a marked degree, of struggle with Christian theologies and Christian churches. Such theologians will see possibilities for reforming the churches rather than giving up on them entirely. There is no easy relationship between Methodism and feminist theologies, inasmuch as there is no easy relationship between feminist theologies/thealogies and Christian churches and philosophies in general. Yet out of feminist theologies has emerged a rediscovery of women in Christian history; campaigning for women's full participation in churches; considerable critique of what Christian churches have done to women, through specific Christian teaching about women, as well as through theology formulated and taught without reference to women's experiences. Feminist theologies/thealogies have generated change.

FEMINISMS AND WOMEN'S ORGANIZATIONS

One of the tensions about feminisms within churches arises from the tendency of early second-wave feminism to generalize about 'women' and to claim to speak for and about all women, only to discover that not all women agreed with feminist analysis or with one another. This became most obvious in church organizations for women formed since the nineteenth century, which were often strong and influential (at least in limited ways). Without taking the historical perspective at this juncture, a simple example of the different aims and focus of organizations may make the point. In the British Methodist Church, Women's Network was formed in 1987, bringing together two previous women's organizations. It was to represent all Methodist women, to encourage, enable, and equip them. A considerable proportion of British Methodist women are in groups affiliated in some way, or open to the support of Network. It is a grassroots movement and certainly not explicitly feminist. At a national, organizational level, though, there is evidence of influence by feminist concerns, not least in Network's representation on the church's Gender Justice Committee, concerned with monitoring questions of gender discrimination within the British Methodist Church. Its strong interest in social justice issues that are women-focused (though not exclusively about or for women) has led Network to campaign on the kind of issues that have been highlighted over recent decades often through the work of feminists, particularly domestic abuse and the trafficking of women and children to work in the sex industry. This is echoed in and linked to the World Federation of Methodist and Uniting Church Women's encouragement to the whole Methodist family to take part in action towards the Millennium Development Goals, particularly as they affect women and children.

Over a similar period of time in Britain, a less formal, specifically feminist organization emerged, mainly among women ministers—the Methodist Women's Forum. Its agenda was radical and sought to be campaigning as well as personally supportive to its membership and others. This group always remained small and has recently ceased to exist. Though passionately supported by some, it could not generate wider interest; yet it had an impact beyond its small membership numbers.

Though this example is recent and anecdotal, there are patterns in it that are repeated in other cultural contexts: women's organizations that split on lines of feminist/non-feminist, the impact of a small interest group or a mass movement, associations with professionals or non-professionals, the radical or the mainstream. There are distinctions to be made between feminisms, women's issues, and women's organizations and all these exist within Methodism.

In the next sections of this chapter, I explore some examples of feminist theological work. This is work by Methodist scholars who engage from a perspective for which the label 'feminist' may or may not be used, but which specifically includes a commitment to women's lives, from a starting point that acknowledges discrimination and injustice on the basis of gender (though rarely as the only factor of oppression) and seeks change. By using examples, much work and many names are left out. A look at websites from Methodist theological seminaries in the United States, for instance, shows many scholars working from feminist perspectives, which argues for a considerable amount of theological reflection emerging from the engagement of Methodist traditions and feminist and womanist perspectives in particular. However, the scope of space here imposes the limits I shall follow.

I have also discussed personalized examples because feminist, womanist, or women-identified theologians find their way in the theological field as scholars and theologians, not first and foremost as Methodists. If such theologians have roles in Methodist churches it is often not first and foremost as feminist theologians, but may be in spite of that self-designation.

MERCY ODUYOYE

In a special issue of the *Journal of Feminist Studies in Religion*, Elisabeth Schussler Fiorenza describes Mercy Amba Oduyoye as 'the foremost African feminist theologian and outstanding leader in the ecumenical movement' (2004: 1). That particular issue of *JFSR* honoured Oduyoye's seventieth birthday and was devoted to feminist cultural hermeneutics, naming this as the field to which Oduyoye has especially contributed. She was a Deputy General Secretary of the World Council of Churches from 1987 to 1994 and involved from the beginnings of the Ecumenical Association of Third World Theologians (EATWOT) and the Ecumenical Association of African Theologians. She was also a key figure in the founding of the Circle of Concerned African Women Theologians, formally set up in 1989. In her work she sometimes highlights elements of her Methodist background. But she has always worked beyond that denominational background and develops connections with many others in a number of fields.

Oduyoye writes on the interpretation and development of African Christianity and African Christian theology. In *Hearing and Knowing* (1986), she analyses the various phases of Christianity in Africa over the centuries of Christian history. Like many African theologians, she is critical of the way that the missionary movement separated Christianity and African Christians from African cultures, imposing Western culture on Africa. But she always also writes with the lives of women, and particularly the oppression of women, in view. She is critical of Western *and* African cultures for their narrowing of women's opportunities for participation and leadership and for the devaluing of women's lives and experiences:

much as I would like to join the chorus of voices that points out women's prominence in traditional cults, experience prevents me from doing so. Traditional Africa has many cults from which women, sometimes even girls, are excluded, and some whose practices women may not even see... In addition the supposed ritual impurity of the menstruating woman places her outside full involvement in religious ritual for almost half her life.

(Oduyoye 1986: 121)

Out of her work at the World Council of Churches, Oduyoye wrote *Who Will Roll the Stone Away?*, a mid-term account of the development of the WCC's Ecumenical Decade of the Churches in Solidarity with Women. She notes that some churches found the WCC's work on the community of women and men in the church much less threatening when it started to tackle global issues of sexism rather than concentrating on the theological stumbling blocks to women's ordination (Oduyoye 1990: 3). Churches wanted to focus on the world beyond the church in dealing with sexist oppression. However, it is a fallacy to imagine that the churches stand somehow apart from the sexism of the world.

Oduyoye's constructive theological work is particularly demonstrated in *Daughters of Anowa*. There she draws on African cultures through 'folk-talk'—proverbs, songs, and mythical stories—examining how they reflect and shape women's lives. In this book in particular, she demonstrates how an African woman's perspective does not have to be that of a Western feminist. Though refuting the notion that there is no need for feminism in Africa (Oduyoye 1995: 13), she also demonstrates that the issues that arise from the situations of women in Africa are not necessarily the same as the debates that exercise Western feminists. For example: 'For me...the grammar of the gender of God is not the heart of the matter' (ibid. 194). Her work demonstrates that it is right for issues to be tackled differently in a range of feminist theologies since they are *contextual* theologies, yet she can affirm similar aims: 'Western approaches to feminism may differ, but the goal—an end to the marginalization of women—is sound' (ibid. 214). An insight into her own experience comes in an autobiographical reflection towards the end of Oduyoye's contribution to the Sheffield Academic Press series introducing feminist theologies, *Introducing African Women's Theology*:

Nigeria is my second home and the place that jolted me from a naïve asexual approach to human relations...When I woke up, I became a 'feminist', a person who takes women's lives, women's words, women's experience, women's writings and women's wisdom as a cardinal part of a heritage to be appropriated, one who sought out other women so that together we might be strong enough to make our contributions as women to a world that has been hijacked by men.   (Oduyoye 2001: 122)

ELSA TAMEZ

Elsa Tamez is a Methodist scholar from Mexico, working in biblical hermeneutics at the Biblical University of Costa Rica. Her scholarship emerges from Latin American liberation theology. In a volume of women's theological work from Africa, Asia, and Latin America, Tamez situates women's rereading of the Bible as emerging out of the rereading of the Bible in the context of daily life and suffering by the poor of Latin

America. Historically she notes how women (including herself) found questions about the Bible and what it had to say about women had to be addressed in the light of their participation in the base communities. With her Protestant background, she notes that theologies of biblical authority often particularly hampered Protestant women in their rereading of the Bible. 'Women are called, therefore, to deny the authority of those readings of the Bible that harm them', she argues (Tamez 1988: 176). At the same time, she sees the essential message of the Bible as one about a liberating God, and therefore cannot go along with first-world feminists who reject the Bible.

Two books edited by Tamez demonstrate a commitment to facilitate dialogue and broaden the availability of Latin American women's theological work. Like Oduyoye, she exemplifies the different style of making known women's theological work from the standard, Western, single-authored publication. Collaboration and symposia have become characteristic of the theological work of women in Africa, Asia, and Latin America. Both from the 1980s, *Through Her Eyes* (1989) allows emerging women's voices to be heard while *Against Machismo* (1987) is the record of a series of interviews with male Latin American liberation theologians about their interaction with emerging women's perspectives. In her introduction to *Against Machismo*, she explains the importance of including men in the struggle against the ideology of machismo in Latin America (Tamez 1987: p. vii). Her interviews with men who share her Methodist background are particularly interesting. Bonino argues that, even in a church as relatively liberal over women's participation in leadership as the Methodist Church, still there were areas of exclusion for women. Women's societies, he suggests (as does Mortimer Arias), were a sign that women needed a church within a church. 'Women created, they had to create, a place where they could really be subjects' (ibid. 51).

In her interview with Bonino, Tamez asks what he thinks might be a woman's perspective on the doctrine of justification by faith. Bonino's reply suggests that a perspective he identifies as inclined more to synthesis than to sharp dichotomies might help with the problematic dichotomizing of God's initiative and human action in the traditional interpretation of justification by faith (ibid. 53–4). This is the area that Tamez explores in *The Amnesty of Grace* (1993). As a central theme in Protestant Christianity, the doctrine of justification has also been given specific attention in the Methodist tradition, not least because of its crucial role in John Wesley's theology. Tamez can be seen as part of a recent strand of exploration that opens up new readings of this doctrine, some specifically in a Wesleyan vein (e.g. Maddox 1994). She situates herself, however, in her Latin American context, where she describes the negative consequences of a traditional understanding of justification for those excluded from the good things of society. When justification is expounded solely as a transaction between the individual and God, in which the individual can do nothing and is simply identified as the helpless sinner, 'God saves by faith' is used to question the call to social change of the liberation movement, since action for change is labelled 'works', as opposed to 'faith'. In the face of such teaching, Tamez argues for a reconnection of the notion of justification to its roots in justice and thus a much stronger linking to notions of liberation. *Amnesty of Grace* (1993) is an important example of doctrinal theology developed out of a deep hermeneutical engagement with biblical texts. In this case, Tamez rereads the letters of Paul, with socio-political questions in mind. From that emerges Tamez's proposed rereading of justification: 'God makes it possible for human beings to do justice' (1993: 110). Though this book does not apparently foreground a feminist perspective, she specifically gives examples of the varieties of women's oppression within the situation of the oppressed to which her theological work responds.

Feminist Theological Reflection in Engagement with Wesleyan Traditions

If a theologian approaches Christian theological traditions from a feminist or womanist perspective, or with the experiences of a particular group of women and their social context in mind, there may be many theological themes and doctrines to be re-examined—if the theologian thinks such re-examination and reinterpretation worthwhile. God-language at its broadest, the significance of Jesus Christ, the place of women in the church might all be examined. In addition to the example in *The Amnesty of Grace*, discussed above, three further examples show how such theological reflection goes on in practice. Would some Wesleyan themes either call for reinterpretation or be particularly conducive to feminist approaches? The prominence of soteriological themes in Wesleyan traditions would be hard to deny and the examples I give all fall within that broad area of Christian reflection, following on from Tamez's re-examination of justification by faith. These examples are again all from theologians from Methodist or Wesleyan (in one case Nazarene) backgrounds.

Marjorie Hewitt Suchocki

Marjorie Hewitt Suchocki is a theologian who works from the insights of process philosophy. Process philosophy remains considerably more influential in the United States than in other parts of the world and is one indication of the specific context within which this theology is written. There might, then, be questions to ask about whether Suchocki's work takes sufficient notice of that limitation of perspective. She clearly also engages with feminist perspectives. In *God–Christ–Church* (1989), her guide to process theology, she articulates how these fit together for her: 'for if the scientists have highlighted the relativity of experience, African-American, feminist and third world proponents have insisted upon the social consequences of relativity' (ibid. 3). Feminist influence on her work is demonstrated in the women-centred examples she uses and in the highlighting of issues raised in feminist theologies (though not only those), as for instance the question of Christian discipleship characterized as a self-denial so total as to be destructive.

In *The Fall to Violence* (1994), Suchocki engages with traditional interpretations of original sin. Doctrines of sin have been one target of many different feminist theologies which have analysed the ways in which women (black women in particular in some social contexts, as Delores Williams (1993) demonstrates), have been disproportionately blamed for the origins of sin or for temptation to sin, or have been described as the weakest in the face of temptation. Many feminist theologians, at least in the Western world, have wrestled with Augustine's theology of sin. Suchocki terms her theology a 'relational theology' and thereby signals both the process philosophy background and also a key theme of many feminist and womanist scholars and ethicists. Her reconstructed definition of sin is 'rebellion against creation through unnecessary violence'. In doing so, she critiques twentieth-century reconstructions of sin by such as Tillich or Niebuhr, as feminist theologians have done before her. 'To a woman, it seems a strange understanding of God that roots sin as violence, whether against women or others, in the desire to be like God, even if that desire is judged as doomed to failure. Likewise, pride and/or existential anxiety seem stretched to address the scope and intensity of such violence' (Suchocki 1994: 29).

She argues that the idea of sin as primarily against God should be replaced by a notion of sin as primarily against the well-being of creation, but her process perspective means that sin is rebellion against God in the (secondary) sense that God 'feels' all that happens in creation, being internally as well as externally related to creation. Violence—further specified as unnecessary violence—is the key form of sin for Suchocki and she tries to relate her discussion, as many feminist theologians would do, to some of the hardest examples of violence/sin, to check any tendency to abstraction which would not deal with actual violence. The soteriological picture is completed with her account of forgiveness in relation to this definition of sin: 'Forgiveness is an alternative response to violence that has the capacity to break this cycle' (ibid. 144).

Diane LeClerc

Diana LeClerc also writes on potential reconstructions of the notion of sin (2001). She describes her perspective and context as Wesleyan-Holiness-feminist, and hers is a study in historical theology. In fact she states one of her aims as looking for the historical precursors of such reconstructions as Suchocki undertakes in *The Fall to Violence* (2001: 3). She examines the theology of Augustine, Jerome, and John Chrysostom from early Christian history, analysing their practice in relation to women as well as their writings. She examines the contradictions she finds between misogynist rhetoric and evidence about actual relationships. What emerges for her from this examination is the notion of sin as not simply idolatry of the self or pride—i.e. the primary exposition of sin in the Western Christian tradition as putting the self before God—but additionally a form of sin she describes as relational idolatry that puts relationships before a 'singleness of heart' that is as possible for women as for men. She notes that, in practice, autonomy for women is put forward by some early church teachers both as a good and as a possibility, in contrast to rhetoric throughout Christian history that confines women to being defined through other people. Her hope is that her study will contribute to women finding 'full, unhindered, empowered, authentic subjectivity' (LeClerc 2001: p. xiii).

LeClerc then goes on to trace her themes in the life and work of John Wesley. She looks at his hostility to traditional domestic roles for women, deeply ambivalent as that could be for women. She examines his practical regard for women's spiritual equality with men, alongside a rhetorical misogyny which assumed women's 'natural weaknesses'. She notes his demanding and often intrusive letters to his women friends; yet 'Wesley's repeated charge to submit *only* to God and not to any creature allowed many women to defy convention and centuries of suppression. Put simply: Methodist women preached. Their single devotion to God freed them to do so' (ibid. 92). In the Holiness tradition, LeClerc takes her historical study a further step into the work of Phoebe Palmer, finding there a model of someone who rejected the idolatry of relationships without having to reject the relationships themselves.

ELAINE CRAWFORD

Elaine Crawford also offers a study of early Wesleyan theology, this time in explicit relationship to womanist theology in North America, in an article published in *Black Theology: An International Journal* (Crawford 2004: 213–20). She outlines her starting point in womanist theology in this way: 'Womanist theology critiques the multidimensional oppression of African-American women's lives, with respect to sexism, racism, classism and heterosexism.... As I study Wesleyan theology, I see some convergence with the basic tenets of Womanist theology' (ibid. 214). She names as specific points of convergence Methodism's beginning 'as a grassroots movement with concerns for the poor and marginalized of society' and a strand of theology that is inclusive, yet attends to the various voices of particular communities, that she can see worked out in United Methodist practice.

Crawford, in this article, engages with the questions asked by the womanist theologian Delores Williams (1993: 167–70) about theologies of the cross that can or cannot be appropriated in the face of the abuse and suffering of black women across many years. Where abuse has seemed to deny the presence of God in the bodies of black women, Crawford (2004: 218) highlights a Wesleyan theology of 'God's sanctifying grace, available to all', alongside Wesley's own opposition to slavery and his support of women's ministry. In interpretation for today, she implies that these strands can be placed alongside each other (whether or not Wesley specifically did that) to support black women in their resistance to abuse. Her key argument about the cross is expressed thus: 'the cross does not sacralize abuse but is an example of it. The cross represents what God was willing to sacrifice so that no others would be sacrificed' (ibid. 219).

These examples of both scholars and particular pieces of scholarly work show interaction between Methodism and feminism, not in abstract but in particular and concrete terms. In the introduction I highlighted the question of whether there is anything in Methodism's ethos or theologies that particularly supports or encourages the work of liberation, black, and feminist/womanist scholars. We might point, as Crawford does, to an early history in Methodism of concern and action for the weakest in society, or support for women's participation in some leadership roles; we might point to a 'grace for all' mission theology that potentially affirms the value and worth of each individual in God's sight. Bonino's question in his interview with Elsa Tamez about whether feminist insights could challenge the dichotomizing of God's initiative and human action might be matched with a claim that Wesleyan theology adopts a both/and approach to that particular dualism. There are strands in Wesleyan theologies that have emphasized experience, even if that now tends to be reinterpreted to mean something much broader than the religious experience that Wesley would have meant by it; those strands offer space for the experiential and praxis approach of all liberation theologies. Wesleyan theology has offered hope of sanctification—whole-life transformation—which is conducive to the transformation-seeking of many radical theologies.

However, there are also strands in Methodist history and Wesleyan theologies that do not tend in these directions at all. Women's participation, especially in public preaching, was also criticized, challenged, and repressed in nineteenth-century Methodisms. Strands of a much more conservative and much more individualized theological vision, which would not emphasize work for social justice, are also to be found in Methodism. As with the traditions of many denominations—as with Christianity itself—there are aspects that can support and energize action to empower women and other aspects which would keep women under-represented and confined to the most traditional and narrow of roles. Methodism, historically and today, is an ambiguous environment for feminisms.

THE CONTROVERSIES

I have given a number of examples of the valuable work of Methodist scholars in various feminist-inspired or engaged theologies. Although those theologians seek to respond in their work to the realities of many women's lives and to the lives of men also oppressed by patriarchal systems, their work can often be dismissed as 'academic theology', remote from the concerns of 'ordinary' Christians. That is one of the ways in which churches in the Methodist tradition as well as in any other tradition contrive to ignore contemporary theological debate. However, with feminist theologies in particular, there can be moments of eye-opening clarity about what some theologians (or thealogians) are doing that provoke controversy on a huge scale. Such controversies arise in many fields of theological work (biblical studies would be another example), but they certainly hit the headlines when related in some way to feminism or specifically woman-identified. Two instances can illustrate this, one from the United States and one from Britain.

In November 1993, the Re-imagining Conference was held in Minnesota in the United States. The *New York Times* reported on the controversy that followed in May 1994, which itself gives some indication of both how long the controversy had gone on for and how vitriolic it had been. Groups opposed to the feminist theological ideas and rituals that had been aired (and debated) at the conference publicized what they saw as dangerous heresy and denounced the denominations they believed had supported the conference, implicitly or explicitly, including the United Methodist Church. In March 1994, the Administrative Committee of the Women's Division of the UMC issued a statement in response to representations made to them following the Re-imagining Conference. Much of the controversy centred on the use of images of wisdom and whether what had been promoted by some at the conference amounted to goddess worship. In November 1994, following the work of a task group, the bishops of the United Methodist Church published teaching guidance on the biblical image of wisdom, modelling appropriate theological exploration. Language about God and ritual based on women's experiences as well as hostility to some aspects of 'traditional' Christianity were at the heart of the dispute. The controversy is still fresh for some, more than fifteen years later.

In Britain, the report *Inclusive Language and Imagery About God* was adopted by the Conference in 1992. It was preceded by some years of debate and work: a response of the Faith and Order Committee to a memorial on 'Masculine Terms in the Methodist Service Book' was offered to Conference in 1984, though the issue had first been raised in the early 1970s. While the debate centred at first on language about people, the Faith and Order Committee asked Conference for permission to engage in a wider piece of theological work, also examining language about God (*Statements and Reports* 2000: 457–90). When the report became public, however, and again around the time of the decision of Conference to adopt it, considerable hostility was expressed, for instance in the letters pages of the *Methodist Recorder*. The debate, as reported by the *Methodist Recorder*, included reference to a headline in *The Times* newspaper: 'Methodists put their faith in a female God.' Similar headlines greeted the one instance in the *Methodist Worship Book* (1999) of the use of 'God our Father and our Mother' as an address to God and similar controversy had surrounded the liturgical phrasing since it was first published in a draft order for consultation in 1992 (Dixon 2003: 12–13). Though the controversy was not so divisive as that over the Re-imagining Conference in the US, there did seem to be a tendency to trivialize the issues. In both cases serious theological dialogue over the issues raised by a so-called 'feminist minority' was minimal, not assisted by the temperature of the rhetoric on any side. In the British context, though Conference made decisions and recommendations over liturgical and theological language that were read by some as 'giving in' to feminist concerns, strong encouragement to preachers to use inclusive language about people and varied imagery for God is still regularly ignored.

WHERE NOW?

In the late 1990s, when I was invited to write a book about preaching, I was asked because I was a woman and I was asked to write from my perspective as a woman. The book became *A Woman's Perspective on Preaching* (Craske 2001). What I was told it could not be was a *feminist* perspective on preaching—at least not signalled as such in the title (though the feminist perspective is signalled within the content of the book). Targeted at a church readership, such a title would have put off too many readers. It was a further illustration of hostility in the church to the word 'feminism'. Yet many Christian churches, not least the Methodist churches that I experience, have been influenced by feminisms of many kinds. They have also been influenced by the greater visibility of women in leadership roles. Changes in theological and liturgical language, greater attention to stories of women in the

Bible, as well as campaigning on issues that affect women but which were often hidden or ignored in past eras, all bear the imprint of feminist theological concern. It would be good to see this acknowledged.

Certain of the justice-seeking perspectives of feminist theologies are still received more positively in the church than discussions of symbolism, language, and identity. Non-feminist women's organizations have taken on board many issues that were first raised by feminists, without accepting the feminist analysis of why these issues of discrimination and harm arise in the first place. This may be a case of tackling the symptoms while not investigating the cause sufficiently. However, if there is room for different explanations of cause, any of which can energize people to take action, then there can be common effort, with respect for different starting points, so that life is better for many who have previously been shut out and oppressed on grounds of gender, class, race, sexuality, and many other factors.

Feminisms, however, still seem to be fair game for trivialization and marginalization. The critique offered by theologians writing under the broadest umbrella of 'feminist/womanist theologies' is often met by ridicule. Marginalization in the churches has been matched by marginalization and suspicion in the academy. Feminists have been seen as simply too confrontational. There is space for the phenomenological approach of women's studies or gender studies, but not for the campaigning and confrontational radicalism of some feminists. This is true beyond the disciplines of theology and religious studies. Some feminists, particularly in the West, have responded by continuing the dialogue among the like-minded, engaging less and less with 'mainstream' churches or theological disciplines. That can be an unfortunate narrowing of debates that need to continue in the widest possible contexts. Combating marginalization, a continuing, interdisciplinary conversation that celebrates the diversity of women's voices and debates is what is needed.

Around issues of gender, it seems the wheel always has to be reinvented. It is clear that specific roles seen as 'appropriate', or not, for women have been discussed since the beginnings of the church—or there would not be biblical references to such issues! Yet however often biblical texts are explored, and argued over, still the same discussions surface in many guises, in different parts of the world, when women are told they should not teach or have authority over men, that God does not call them to leadership, that their primary roles (as their cultures have always said) are to serve men, bear children, and be subservient in all things. Many of us will continue to deny that such a perspective has anything to do with God's will.

There remains a need to continue monitoring and combating issues of discrimination in Methodist churches and in societies across the world, on the basis of gender as well as on the basis of other characteristics. It is sometimes alleged that the emphases of feminist theologies simply follow non-theological social trends in many cultures to be more 'liberal' in their attitudes to women's rights. However, the

insistence on real possibilities of participation for all emerges from deep theological conviction. It is an essential component of a Wesleyan tradition that
preaches grace for all.

REFERENCES

CLACK, BEVERLEY (1999). 'On Leaving the Church'. In Jane Craske and Clive Marsh (eds.),
Methodism and the Future. London: Cassell.

CRASKE, JANE (2001). *A Woman's Perspective on Preaching*. Peterborough: Foundery.

CRAWFORD, A. ELAINE (2004). 'Womanist Christology and the Wesleyan Tradition'. *Black
Theology: An International Journal* 2: 2.

DALY, MARY (1968). *The Church and the Second Sex*. New York: Harper & Row.

—— (1973). *Beyond God the Father*. Boston: Beacon.

DIXON, NEIL (2003). *Wonder, Love and Praise*. Peterborough: Epworth.

FIORENZA, ELISABETH (ed.) (2004). 'Introduction'. *Journal of Feminist Studies in Religion* 20: 1.

GRANT, JACQUELYN (1989). *White Women's Christ, Black Women's Jesus: Feminist Christology
and Womanist Response*. Atlanta: Scholars.

ISHERWOOD, LISA (2005). 'Editorial'. *Feminist Theology* 13: 2: *Creative Conversations: Theal-
ogy and Theology in Dialogue*.

LECLERC, DIANE (2001). *Singleness of Heart: Gender, Sin and Holiness in Historical Perspective*. Lanham, Md.: Scarecrow.

MADDOX, RANDY (1994). *Responsible Grace: John Wesley's Practical Theology*. Nashville:
Kingswood.

New York Times (1994). 'Cries of Heresy After Feminists Meet'. 14 May. http://query.nytimes.
com/gst.html, accessed 20 October 2007.

ODUYOYE, MERCY AMBA (1986). *Hearing and Knowing: Theological Reflections*. New York:
Orbis.

—— (1990). *Who Will Roll The Stone Away? The Ecumenical Decade of the Churches in
Solidarity with Women*. Geneva: WCC.

—— (1995). *Daughters of Anowa*. New York: Orbis.

—— (2001). *Introducing African Women's Theology*. Sheffield: Sheffield Academic Press.

Statements and Reports of the Methodist Church on Faith and Order, ii. *1984–2000* (2000).
Peterborough: Methodist Publishing House.

SUCHOCKI, MARJORIE HEWITT (1989). *God–Christ–Church: A Practical Guide to Process
Theology*. Rev. edn. New York: Crossroad.

—— (1994). *The Fall to Violence: Original Sin in Relational Theology*. New York: Continuum.

TAMEZ, ELSA (1987). *Against Machismo*, trans. John Eagleson. New York: Meyer Stone.

—— (1988). 'Women's Re-reading of the Bible'. In Mercy Oduyoye and Virginia Fabella
(eds.), *With Passion and Compassion: Third World Women Doing Theology*. New York:
Orbis.

—— (ed.) (1989). *Through Her Eyes, Women's Theology from Latin America*. New York: Orbis.

—— (1993). *The Amnesty of Grace: Justification by Faith from a Latin American Perspective*,
trans. Sharon H. Ringe. Nashville: Abingdon.

—— (2001). Address to Call to Action Conference, http://www.cta-usa.org/conf2001talks. html, accessed 5 April 2007.

TONG, ROSEMARIE (1989). *Feminist Thought.* Boulder: Westview.

TOWNES, EMILIE M. (2005). 'The Contribution of *JFSR* to Shaping the Field'. *Journal of Feminist Studies in Religion* 21: 2.

WILLIAMS, DELORES (1993). *Sisters in the Wilderness: The Challenge of Womanist God-Talk.* New York: Orbis.

CHAPTER 40

IN A DIVIDED WORLD, METHODISM MATTERS

HAROLD J. RECINOS

HOME Street—the South Bronx. A tough place. A crucified place. The kind of place where one continually asks what is the meaning of the good news of Jesus of Nazareth. I grew up on Home Street. It was on the bitter streets of the South Bronx that I learned to believe the mystery of God's word made flesh in the world of the poor and crucified (Matthew 25: 31–46). My immigrant Latino parents, beaten down by poverty and racial intolerance, abandoned me at age 12 to the streets. During several years of living on them, the streets of New York City, Los Angeles and San Juan, Puerto Rico, I discovered the God who offers hope and restores dignity to persons pushed to the edge of society.

Life in abandoned tenements, city parks, and parked Greyhound buses enabled me to understand that Christian faith means discovering the God who is always hidden in the drama of the powerless. For me the experience of utter abandonment resulted in a deeper awareness of the God who comes looking for us in Christ to make a common cause with the repentant, excluded, degraded, and rejected. I grew up hearing the church answer the question of Jesus' identity by saying this Galilean Jew is the Saviour, the Son of God, the lamb of God, brother, prophet, superstar, teacher, mystic Christ, Almighty God, Prince of Peace, and Consoler; however, with those who lived with me on the streets, people whose lives reflected nothing better than a clash with death-dealing economic and social conditions, I met Jesus as an unemployed labourer, an indigent, One who died before his time.

One cold night in a windowless abandoned tenement, I read these words from a pocket Bible: 'Fear not, for I have redeemed you; I have called you by name, you are mine' (Isaiah 43: 1). As I lay awake that night—a junior high school dropout, abandoned, criminalized by society's politics of representation—I could tell God was leading me out of death into a world where I was not simply a social problem, a world where individual despair would be examined in the light of the massive inequalities of a social order that denied a full life to the poor and racially despised. Living close to those who suffer, I became aware that following the One who was born in the stench of a stable required confessing God in the company of persons who have a special place in the good news of God—the racially unwelcome, the oppressed, the poor, the sick, foreigners, and outcasts.

I find myself a long way now from the street life, but the tide of racial and ethnic violence darkening our world brings to mind those bitter lanes. In our post-9/11 context, far too many American Christians go away from the cross eager to harmonize the gospel with the darkest impulses of national security thinking and the most terrible expressions of unthinking patriotism. In the wake of the September 11th terrorist attacks, few persons can hold on to the conventional understanding that religion is always a force for peace and good in the world. Pious people motivated by religious belief can favour the use of violence and murder to promote their cause. *Islamophobia* has overtaken many in the United States, but it is not only crazed Islamic terrorists who reconcile piety with murder today. As we listen to the incessant beat of the US war drums, Christ invites us not to surrender to the power of darkness and death.

The coming of God is not only good news for shared creation, but a call to stay close to those who suffer in the world. As I think about the message of Jesus in a diverse world, it occurs to me that one of the greatest challenges of the twenty-first century is both learning how to live with human diversity and admitting that God is intolerant of our fatal divisions (Hall 1993). As we stand in the early years of the twenty-first century, the global rise of social groups whose thinking espouses anti-immigrant, racist, and violent politics gives us a reason to consider the meaning of race as a socio-political and cultural phenomenon. Church witness in a racially divided world must proclaim today that Jesus came into the world to comfort the despised, love his enemies, reject exclusionary practices, defend the poor, heal the sick, feed the hungry, feast with sinners, disclose the God of radical welcome, and die in order to save us.

I want to imagine Methodists will not be so untouched by the ministry, death, and resurrection of Jesus as to walk away from the Lord disobedient servants. The constructive task before us is to promote a theological anthropology that celebrates Jesus' coming by changing cultural rules of exclusion in favour of the least among us, practising forgiveness without exception, feeding the hungry, healing the sick, sheltering the homeless, clothing the naked, defending the exploited, naming the voiceless, seeing the forgotten, and changing crucifying structures in the name of the life God promises to all in shared creation. Because theology itself has played a role in racist violence and dehumanization, hurtful theological constructions need to be deconstructed before swords can ever be beaten into ploughshares in our racially divided world.

As theologians in this world so alienated by difference ponder Christian identity and witness, people in the pew should consider deeply the miracle of God's imagination that sends a saviour into the world by way of a homeless family; a truth-teller who shatters the cultural system of lies that enclose people with injustice, hate, violence, and exclusion; a child of colour that grows up to live for others all the way to the cross. The tortuous histories of dehumanization and exploitation linking the world in a common time as well as unequal experiences of power encourage Christians to discover Jesus' cry from the cross is nothing less than a call to move beyond all divisions to embody the reconciling union of God.

In what follows, I will address the politics of race and racist nationalism in the context of the United States. First, I will examine salient features of the politics of race in North Atlantic and American society and its impact on persons of colour. Second, I will suggest that John Wesley's practical Christianity provides Methodism with the resources for denouncing the social injustices legitimated by oppositional neo-nationalist and neo-racist ideology that aims to take away the rights of the undeserving and excludable other. Wesley would reject distorted theologies that construe God as unwelcoming to the trampled poor and having Christians act antagonistically to 'foreigners'. Third, I will conclude the chapter by offering a Christian narrative framework for building life together drawn from the story of the Good Samaritan.

THE POLITICS OF RACE IN A NEW CENTURY

Although the Americas were unknown to the ancient Mediterranean world that had influenced European humanity with Aristotelian terms for understanding the difference between civilized and barbarian people, by the time of European colonial expansionism new ranking schemes were devised by theorists of the day to locate people on a scale of civilization. In time, the inferiority attributed to subjugated non-white humanity came to be associated with not having white skin (Sampson 2005: 14). European colonialism resulted in confrontations with different people in the new world and created a transnational network of forced labour that consolidated racist beliefs and practices (Wood 1995: 29). To be sure, the process of nation-building and capital formation that unfolded with the rise of the West used racial thinking as a powerful motive for overseas expansion. Howard Winant writes,

The subjugation of the Americas and the enslavement of Africa financed the rise of the European empires... Vast flows of treasure were shipped to Europe; millions came under the lash of planters and mine-owners.... The transition to an integrated, global society with an increasingly complex division of labor demanded the creation of a worldwide racial division between Europe and the 'others'.   (Winant 2001: 24–5)

Christianity was introduced to Europeans by dark-skinned missionaries from North Africa and the Eastern Mediterranean world (Sampson 2005: 13), but that did not prevent the development of white racial thinking. Among the many varieties of colonialism, the power dynamics that issued forth from European imperialism and the encounters with non-Europeans caused white humanity to come up with racialized hierarchies that explained physical and cultural differences. Europeans alienated indigenous populations from land control in the Americas, for instance, and they questioned whether or not indigenous groups were human beings worthy of Christian baptism, or bothersome animal elements worthy of exploitation or elimination like wild animals. 'Indians' were believed more like animals and whites were associated with the culture of rationality.

Racial beliefs and practices vary according to particular time, place and the ethnic groups involved, but it is 'evident that European cultures have played a special role in the evolution, dissemination, and exploitation of [the idea of race] over the last six centuries' (Wood 1995: 27). Racism probably began at the end of the Middle Ages, especially rehearsed by the anti-Islamic and anti-Jewish crusades and the Inquisition. New world conquest, colonization, violent evangelization, capitalist development, near genocide of Native Americans, and African enslavement are linked with the rise of the West. European notions of racial supremacy became a global reality with the expansion and establishment of colonial empires.

Racism is a deeply distorted way to view human unity contained within the theological idea of the parenthood of God and the kinship of all people. As a cultural invention, racism is a belief and practice that attributes status to individuals and groups in reference to differences in physical appearance. The modern-day belief in a global racial hierarchy with Europeans at the top justified the violent dispossession of indigenous people, African enslavement, and ethnic genocide. Racial thinking led some white Christians to ignore that God had made 'of one blood all nations' (Acts 17: 26). European racial thinking created the world in a white image, but that did not mean that Europeans understood the world of their creation.

The Enlightenment period introduced faith in progress, the myth of cumulative development underwriting Western culture; however, the philosophical justifications of this system of life were based on racist interpretations of 'the hierarchical division of humanity into superior and inferior races' (Winant 2001: 28). The scientific thought of the enlightenment reflected in the ethnological work of Carl Linnaeus (1735) and Johan Friedrich Blumenbach (1776), for instance, opened a door on scientific racism, which included a system of classification that placed white humanity at the top. When they considered human beings part of the natural world, these two ethnologists moved away from the older theological anthropology that viewed human beings as children of God endowed with a spirit unmatched in the natural world.

At the time W. E. B. Du Bois, an African-American sociologist and rights activist, observed the problem of the 'colour line', the idea of race was reflected in an elaborate system of social philosophy and historical interpretation that promoted White Supremacy; indeed, the inequality of conditions between white and non-white humanity was understood by many intellectuals as a sign of the innate superiority of whites and the natural inferiority of non-Europeans. The American anthropologist Daniel Brinton, the English historian Herbert Spencer, German philosophers G. W. Hegel and Immanuel Kant, and the social gospel American expansionist Josiah Strong reflect how history, science, philosophy, and religion legitimated White Supremacy (Eze 1997; Goldberg 1993; Griffin 1999). The racist pride of the age of reason is evident in words written by the English philosopher David Hume:

I am apt to suspect the Negroes and in general all other species of men (for there are four or five different kinds) to be inferior to whites. There never was a civilized nation of any other complexion than white, nor even any individual eminent either in action or speculation.

(cited in Eze 1997: 33)

Racism reached its most virulent form in the Nazi government under Adolf Hitler, which perpetrated the genocide of six million Jews, among others. In Nazi Germany Nordic people were imagined not only as the most superior, but most threatened especially by assimilated Jews and other so-called inferior races. The genocidal programme of the Third Reich was to provide a final solution to the whites' threatened existence (Arnold 2006). In the 1930s, Ruth Benedict (1940) had Hitler's racist regime on her mind when she noted that racism is

the dogma that one ethnic group is condemned by nature to hereditary inferiority and another group is destined to hereditary superiority. It is the dogma that the hope of civilization depends upon eliminating some races and keeping others pure. It is the dogma that one race has carried progress through human history and can alone ensure future progress.

As a modern theory and practice of whiteness, the brutality against indigenous peoples, the moral degradation of slavery, and, more recently, the extreme racist Nazi regime that aimed to annihilate Jews have not produced the moral revulsion needed to wipe out racist beliefs and practices. The racist ideologies that legitimated colonialism, the slave trade, Jim Crow in the Southern United States, South African apartheid, and Hitler's genocidal treatment of Jews invoked a logic that dehumanized those placed beneath white humanity on the so-called scale of civilization. In many societies today, racism persists in social institutions, cultural views, and the plight of individuals without state and legal support.

Race, power, and national identity are elements of the cultural process that shape the relationships between people (Goldschmidt and McAllister 2004; Spickard 2005). The racially despised who live at the edge of society epitomize our crucified God, who himself would be a rejected immigrant of colour in the United States and many European societies and who calls Christians to seek a future where diverse cultural voices can speak and be heard: voices that critique established ideologies; voices that promote a hermeneutics of justice and diversity; voices that opt to build a world that struggles for a more just life in less crucifying structures. What is most necessary today is a publicly engaged theology that restores the self-worth of the marginalized, offers a reason for hope, and empowers struggles for justice and peace in a racially divided world.

New Forms of Racism

Michel Foucault writes,

in any society there are manifold relations of power which permeate, characterize, and constitute the social body and these relations of power cannot themselves be established, consolidated, nor implemented without the production, accumulation and functioning of a discourse. There can be no possible exercise of power without a certain economy of discourses of truth which operates through and on the basis of this association.

(Foucault 1980: 93)

Racism is not only a system of classification for perceived differences between human beings, but it reflects a discourse regime through which relations of unequal power are exercised. In the United States and parts of European society today, racist discourse provides significant advantages for white humanity at the expense of communities of colour.

In thinking about racist culture, I am reminded of the words of W. E. B. Du Bois who said, in 1900, 'the problem of the twentieth century is the problem of the color line' (Du Bois 1996). Du Bois's statement shaped a great deal of the discussion about race and racism in the twentieth century, but that discussion unfolded exclusive of his reference to more than black and white humanity. Since Du Bois penned these words all around the world you find people taking up residence in places other than where they were born and adding a new racial mix to their host society. Both in the United States and Europe a mixed, hybrid, or multicultural age has emerged that appears to have led to increased racism and xenophobia rather than an enriching intercultural exchange.

Today, the new forms of racism that are issuing forth in a number of European societies and the United States are best understood by the term 'cultural racism'. Cultural racism legitimates hostility and discrimination towards those considered different by promoting the idea that inferior cultural groups cannot be allowed to threaten superior white society. Cultural racist thinking holds that certain third world and non-Western newcomers to European and US society have such deep-seated cultural differences they are inassimilable. The clash of culture is the problem, not alleged biological differences among human beings. In the US, for instance, the anti-immigrant climate discourse of many white citizens, politicians, and public intellectuals suggests Latino newcomers are culturally incompatible with the American way of life.

The discourse that produces difference and identity is embedded in particular cultural histories, which include the 'us versus them' ideology, views of a feared Other, and the power to inferiorize. In the US, the drama of racial conflict and xenophobia was uniquely heightened by the events of 9/11 resulting in resurgent racial thinking and practices focused on controlling access to labour, education, housing, media, political and legal rights, and symbolic resources (Herik 2004: 153). Racist and xenophobic public speech keeps on equating whiteness with worthiness and belonging, at the same time as Latinos/as, Arabs, Asians, and Africans are turned into suspect classes. In other words, those considered 'the Other' are imagined inferior, culturally incompatible, and a threat to the unity of an ostensible white nation. As noted by:

In order to provide security for their population, nations develop traditions...systems of justice and rights, ensure the security and stability of a nation. Through the disruption of existing traditions, immigrants, who bring with them different cultures, imbalance the nation. The principle, or position, which links immigrants and the demise of the nation, is that cultural differences threaten the existing way of life. It is thus seen as rational to preserve one's culture through the exclusion of other groups. This negative attitude toward migrants should be understood as racism.   (Ibrahim 2005: 166)

In my country, a new white nationalist movement is influencing conventional thinking about non-white humanity and foreign newcomers, which is working against already fragile US race relations. White racist nationalists have expanded their influence in the US mainly through a public discourse targeted at white Americans who are already troubled and resentful of race-based affirmative action policies, high crime rates that they blame on persons of colour, racial identity politics, and the immigration policies that opened the door wide for persons from Asia, Africa, and Latin America. In her book, *The New White Nationalism in America: Its Challenge to Integration*, Carol M. Swain (2002: pp. xv–xvi) observes,

White nationalism thrives by its willingness to address many contemporary issues and developments that mainstream politicians and media sources either ignore entirely or fail to address with any degree of openness or candor. These developments include the continuing influx into the country of nonwhite immigrants and the prospect that America in the not-too-distant future will cease to be a white majority nation; the decline in high-paying, low-skill-requisite, industrial jobs as a result of globalization and other structural changes in the American economy; continuing white resentment over affirmative action policies that favor officially designated minority groups over native whites in education and employment; continued white fear of black crime; the continued emphasis on racial identity politics and the fostering of an ethnic group pride on the part of nonwhite minority groups; and the expanding influence and reach of the Internet. When these conditions combine with the rising expectations on the part of racial and ethnic minorities for a larger share of power and influence in American society, the stage is set for increased political conflict and turmoil.

With respect to the complexion of the new immigration, white nationalism reflects four cultural themes: first, a strong feeling among many Americans of European descent that persons from Latin America, Asia, and Africa are racially and culturally inferior. Second, these inferior races are simply unable to assimilate to the dominant Anglo culture. Third, persons from these 'inferior races' take jobs away from native-born Americans and cause national economic decline. Lastly, these undesirable races stress the welfare and school system and may someday politically threaten white racial hegemony (Feagin 1997: 13–14). As a form of cultural racism, white racist nationalist ideology influences many US citizens of European ancestry to accept the idea that the way to preserve society is to assure a white future.

European immigrants were welcomed with food, medicine, showers, and beds on Ellis Island a century ago, but now not a few Americans prefer to greet today's mostly non-white newcomers with military aircraft, border agents, and vigilantes to keep them out. In the United States, white racist nationalists resent the growing visibility of Spanish-speakers in society, Muslims erecting mosques in their neighbourhoods, and Koreans, Arabs, Indians, and persons from other ethnic-communities owning businesses with signs in languages other than English. Europe's non-Western immigrants share a great deal with America's communities of colour and non-European newcomers, especially in that both are similarly vilified, marginalized, and told they don't belong.

Although the United States is a nation of immigrants, hate and violence towards the culturally unlike is regularly conjured up by many politicians, talk-show radio hosts, private militiamen, and racist grassroots organizations. Every weekday evening Lou Dobbs of CNN warns of the 'illegal alien invasion', spouting the kind of racist and anti-immigrant sentiment that legitimates the view that Latinos/as are a source of social breakdown in America. The cultural difference imagined by Lou Dobbs envisions a bounded America that differentiates itself from outsiders and makes use of fear of the Other to justify the promotion of mistreatment and regressive public policy. In post-9/11 America, the increasingly strident racist and anti-immigrant message of political leaders, academics, and anti-immigrant media darlings such as Dobbs results in heightened anxiety for immigrants of colour and their US-born children.

In his book *Alien Nation*, Peter Brimelow speaks for Americans who are dismayed that their country is already one-seventh Hispanic. He uses racist nationalist rhetoric and fear to win support for his proposed race-based immigration policy, which aims to secure a white future for the United States. Brimelow believes the Immigration Act (1965) sponsored by then freshman Senator Ted Kennedy is to blame for a demographic shift that will result in white Americans being outnumbered by persons of colour in the not too distant future. According to Brimelow, the Immigration Act sparked an ethnic and racial transformation of America that threatens what he refers to as the 'white ethnic core' of the nation. In other words, 'The racial and ethnic balance of America', Brimlow writes, 'is being radically altered through public policy' (Brimelow 1995: p. xvii).

Brimelow claims he is only preaching 'common sense' about the 'third world' immigration problem demographically changing the United States. He is disturbed that in less than a hundred years Americans of African, Asian, and Latin-American ancestry will outnumber Euro-Americans, which will include Latinos as the largest community of colour. Not only is his message that immigrants are a cultural threat, but his book of factual flaws outlandishly begins with this extraordinary statement:

There is a sense in which current immigration policy is Adolf Hitler's posthumous revenge on America. The U.S. political elite emerged from the war passionately concerned to cleanse itself from all taints of racism or xenophobia. Eventually, it enacted the epochal Immigration Act... of 1965. And this, quite accidentally, triggered a renewed mass immigration, so huge and so systematically different from anything that had gone before as to transform— and ultimately, perhaps, even to destroy—the one unquestioned victor of World War II: the American nation.   (ibid. p. xvii)

The issue of immigrants' rights is subordinate to the defence of white American culture in Brimelow's thinking; however, he does not define American culture nor bother to describe the contributions of people of colour to the formation of American national identity.

Brimelow's exclusionary discourse and abhorrence for diversity is particularly directed towards the Latino community which he names a 'strange anti-nation in the United States' who refuse to Americanize (ibid. 218). His solution to the Latino problem includes improving enforcement efforts; building a US–Mexico border barrier; sealing the border by instituting national identity cards as well as imprisoning and deporting all 'illegal immigrants'; eliminating all public benefits to illegal immigrants and reducing them for legal immigrants; having an English-language requirement and a stand against bilingualism; devising a system to interdict money transfers by illegal aliens to their home country; temporarily stopping or reducing all legal immigration; eliminating humanitarian categories altogether (refugees and asylees); eliminating family reunification; excluding legal immigrants from affirmative action benefits; and repealing the birthright citizenship clause in the Fourteenth Amendment.

Preposterously, Brimelow's immigration agenda is based on the idea that national identity depends for the most part on white racial unity. Apart from not spending any time reading the vast body of literature on race and ethnicity that human beings cannot be categorized into discrete racial groups with identifiable cultural characteristics, Brimelow fails to understand the power of American society to acculturate newcomers. Linguistic and cultural fragmentation is not the outcome of the new immigration, since children who grow up in the United States undergo a language shift to English as well as an identity change over time. What ought to concern the US citizenry about persons coming from Asia, Africa, and Latin America is that immigrant newcomers are entering a society of growing income inequality and labour market segmentation that offers fewer opportunities for upward mobility and assures growth in ethno-linguistic enclave communities, which slows integration into the American mainstream.

In *Who Are We? The Challenges to America's National Identity* Samuel Huntington also expresses fear about the complexion of immigration, arguing that America is cracking apart, owing especially to the growing numbers and geographic concentration of Latinos. According to Huntington, American national identity and unity is threatened by Mexican newcomers who both refuse to assimilate and act in very un-American ways. Huntington says Latinos bring a self-understanding to American society that challenges the core Anglo-Protestant values of US society, which are foundational to American national identity. Because most immigrants now come from Mexico and speak Spanish, Huntington (2004: 221) contends the United States is becoming a culturally bifurcated Anglo-Hispanic society with two national languages.

In *Who Are We?* Huntington does not engage in disciplined social science, rather his personal insecurities about the character of a changing American society guide him to write a rather emotional polemical text that inflates the Anglo-Protestant roots of American culture; misreads the relationship between culture and society; misrepresents past immigrant assimilation; and minimizes how new Latino immigrants are being positively incorporated into American society (Massey 2004: 543–8). He believes the changing complexion of immigration to the United States has issued forth in the threat of multiculturalism and bilingualism. He thinks the problems associated with illegal immigration, bilingual education, and assimilation of newcomers will disappear by the dramatic reduction of Mexican immigration. Huntington may be surprised to learn that the majority of Latinos in the United States who were born here are more American than Peter Brimelow!

Huntington's message to Latinos in American society is that, 'there is no Americano dream. There is only the American dream created by an Anglo-Protestant society. Mexican-Americans will share in that dream and in that society only if they dream in English' (Huntington 2004: 256). His vision of American culture suggests that only White Anglo-Protestants have made any worthy contribution to the formation of American national identity; indeed, the historic contributions of African Americans, Asian Americans, Hispanic Americans, and Native Americans have deeply enriched the understanding of what it means to be an American. Clearly, the American dream was made vastly richer the moment it dared to dream in various languages and cultural styles. Huntington forgets that America cannot accept anything less than its luxurious diversity in order to continue to build on the fullness of its history and the achievements of its past.

Huntington writes, he says, 'as a patriot and a scholar', but blaming Latino immigrants for problems in American society, turning Hispanics into a suspect class, and arguing that Latinos will destroy American unity evidences a lack of analytical skills and deeply flawed scholarship. When he argues that immigrants become citizens less out of a concern for the American social creed and largely to qualify for social welfare and affirmative action programmes, he outruns the evidentiary base. If he had consulted the great American institution—the Smithsonian Institute—on the matter of Latinos and American society, he would have learned that from the American Revolution to the war on terrorism, the documented evidence shows patriotism, American culture, and Latinos are also at the core of American national unity (Rochin and Fernandez 2005). Racial discrimination against Latinos will persist so long as credible intellectuals use questionable scholarship to assure a lack of recognition for Latinos in the American project of nation building.

Demonizing, dehumanizing, and criminalizing the cultural Other in either the American context or European societies will give rise only to relational systems of exclusion and racial hate that are unworthy of any just society. What does the Wesleyan tradition contribute to guide the social discourse about how to engage human differences? How can American Methodists use their voice to say that the nation's multiracial transition offers hope, not trouble? What is the good news of the church for our bad news of a divided world? The good news is that God-in-Christ aims to overcome disunity in the world. There is no place in God's reign for racist and xenophobic rhetoric, forces, institutions, and structures. The church must not only denounce dehumanizing discourse and practices, but proclaim the good news of a God of welcome who proclaims all outsiders radical insiders.

GOD DISCLOSED IN THE RACIALLY DESPISED

John Wesley, founder of the Methodist movement in eighteenth-century England, was deeply concerned about the poor and enslaved. Wesley gleaned much from his social interaction and study, but his understanding of race and class relations issued forth fundamentally from his biblical and theological insight. Wesley's concern for the poor and enslaved led him to attack the causes of poverty and denounce the social practices oppressing the racially despised. Wesley's attack on slavery is well known and reflected in the General Rules of 1743, which forbade 'the buying and selling of the bodies and souls of men, women, or children, with the intention to enslave them' (Matlack 1881: 58). Days before dying, in a letter written to William Wilberforce, John Wesley envisioned the abolition of slavery in America, which he judged to be a most vile institution and one that went against God.

John Wesley was motivated by a sense of divine calling to proclaim the grace that motivates Christian life for the sake of the world. Wesley's combination of piety and social witness reflected a theology that insisted that the gospel leads Christians to see the world of the poor, the racially despised, and disinherited as the ultimate context of Christian revelation. Wesley's concern for the poor and enslaved speaks to us now of the importance of following Christ motivated by the concern to bring good news to the bad news situations of the racially and ethnically excluded. In national contexts where racial and ethnic minorities are increasingly perceived as a problem and threat to white societies, Methodists must confront distorted theological views of an exclusionary God supportive of systems of unequal power and imagined homogenous nationhood.

The ministry of John Wesley should inspire Methodists to find in Jesus a reason to resist suffering caused by oppression, a discipleship concerned with shaping cultures of justice, and a spirituality opposed to models of society that crucify the vulnerable. Methodist Scripture reading should now empower Christians to understand that Jesus Christ committed himself to bring good news to the poor and justice to a broken world. Wesley believed the practical outcome of faith is 'love which the Lord requires of all His followers . . . the love of God and man; of God, for His own, and of man for God's sake' (Wesley 1987: iv. 383). Wesley's following of Christ led him to a ministry of compassion that served the needs of those adversely affected by social conditions and cultural rules in English society.

The parable of the Good Samaritan may help Methodists imagine Wesley's compassionate ministry and spirituality for an alternative future for society. The parable offers good news by telling us that a sure way to overcome a divided and dehumanizing social world is to act with compassion to others. The principle of compassion so carefully laid out in the parable describes how to restore a sense of hope and transformation to human beings disconnected by cultural rules and practices. As Wesley demonstrated in his time, the story of the Good Samaritan makes plain that human beings are to love those whom God places before them. What also cannot be missed in the narrative is the one disclosing the compassion of God for the wounded human being was himself a member of a suspect class in established society.

The parable of the Good Samaritan is about human beings defined as outsiders by the cultural rules. The story is also about not drawing the line on who deserves to be loved and the importance of exercising justice towards all others. In Luke's narrative, Jesus speaks to us with considerable power when he suggests the ideal human being acts in the world against ideologies that divide people and social conventions that say 'neighbours' are the people tied to us by race, ethnicity, language, or membership in the same group. Jesus tells us here that in a world of social divisions one sees a neighbour even in despised others and feared outcasts. In the light of the murderous social divisions at work in the modern world, the parable's message is that human beings find their unequalled depth when love draws them near to the excluded, where God is found in plain truth.

The self-satisfied theologian to whom the parable was directed, and who was concerned about where to draw the line on the question of loving others, discovered the importance of linking God's self-disclosure with the existential reality of a hurt person. In practising compassion towards a beaten-down human being one enters into a serious conversation about what is needed to end the affliction and promote human action that transforms society in the direction of life. The God who enters into solidarity by looking after trampled human beings invites us from the ditches of the dying to make a preferential option for strangers by expanding our circle of genuine community.

Although Jesus tells the self-justifying theologian (Luke 10: 29) to engage in God-talk from the edges of society, the challenge did not end there. This religious leader was going to learn a lesson about justice and the love of God (Luke 10: 27) from hearing about the right action of a Samaritan. For the theologian a neighbour could be a Levite, a priest, someone from his own class, race, or group, but never a racially impure and religiously heretical Samaritan. Nonetheless, Jesus invites him to face without denial the fact that a Samaritan, a representative of the one group that all in established society considered worthy of exclusion, would instruct him about being a neighbour. In other words, this theologian was to learn from a Samaritan how to set aside a restrictive world-view in order to evolve a more complete vision of God and human community.

What did the Samaritan do? The Samaritan was willing to stop on the side of the road to help the victim of robbers. The Levite and the priest did not stop, because of the requirements of the law. These religious officials who kept the cultural rules failed fully to grasp God's perfection. God refuses to make persecuted people invisible. God does not allow persons to remain outcast on the basis of race, culture, laws, gender, or religion. It took a member of a despised racial group to name the basic contradiction between faith in God and avoidance of brutalized humanity. For the Samaritan real knowledge of God means acting in the world God aims to save and loving those whom God asks us to love.

The parable proposes to a theologian of mainline piety what truly matters to God. What finally counts is not religious orthodoxy—the basis of the reasonableness

of the religious officials' response to the victim of robbers on the side of the road—
but right action. In other words, our actions correspond to the reality of God;
when moved by compassion one goes forth to serve the needs of those disfavoured
by the social and religious order. How did the Samaritan act rightly? The Samaritan
'had compassion...bound up the victims wounds...set him on his own beast
and brought him to an inn...took care of him...took out two denarii [the
equivalent of two days' wages for a labourer] and gave them to the innkeeper'
(Luke 10: 33–5).

The socially divisive values and practices of established culture are overcome by
engaging the needs of ignored persons experiencing the weight of a crucifying
reality. What does this all finally mean? First, it means the instant we go to the side
of the road and attend to needs of vilified people we confess God did not make
human beings for unjust suffering. Second, it means that compassionate action
restores the dignity of despised human beings and contributes to the process of
overcoming oppressed conditions of existence. Third, it means a willingness to
engage in extraordinary measures to take care of the stranger or outcast God puts
before us to love. Fourth, it means trusting the God who gets trampled with us in
order to save.

In the parable of the Good Samaritan, it is the excluded of this world—either in
the form of the assaulted person or the racially despised—that make God historically present in the bad news of the real world. The theologian who listened to the
story was expected to grasp that God was finally not like his image of God; instead,
God was truly all in all; a God for him and for all those his thinking and acting
rejected. Faith in a God who gets trampled and killed by murderous human beings
demands that we become aware of ourselves through the suffering and hope of
peoples injured and discriminated against. The Samaritan went out of his way to
step into society's conflict running the personal risk of coming under attack
himself. He acted with mercy. We are all called to act in a similar way, especially
towards those who are violently deprived of their quality of life.

One obvious conclusion to draw from the parable of the Good Samaritan is that
the church betrays the redemptive action of God in the world when it denies that
God offers a radical welcome to all. In a world of crucifying divisions, churches are
relevant to the extent that Christians challenge an unjust society and perform
works of mercy that humanize the death-dealing systems that condemn some
people rather than others. Our trampled God cannot be named a partner of unjust
decisions that are based on the wicked strategy of avoidance. The ministry of the
church needs to focus on the God who crosses all boundaries and points to the
gracious love that makes the first last and outsiders welcome. Jesus invites us to go
out of our way to be a neighbour to the oppressed Other and to reject strategies of
self-preservation.

One can hardly mistake the message of the Good Samaritan, which reflects Jesus
inviting us to live beyond ethnic divisions and embrace difference as a sign of the

God who is always more than our comprehension of God. The evangelist has Jesus tell us the story of the Good Samaritan to communicate clearly that 'believing in Jesus is also at the same time reconciliation between those who are estranged, the creation of an inclusive fellowship' (Gundry-Volf 1995). Many walls divide people in the church and society, such as class, education, race, ethnicity, immigration status, gender, age, language, or sexual orientation; yet, the mark of a good news community consists of the commitment to overcome distrust and misunderstanding by living the miracle of coming together in Christ and helping others walk in unity toward God's reign.

The messianic age is with us when we set out to overcome a divided world with love and justice, especially struggling primarily for all those persons who hold onto hope in the midst of despair in a world that takes it away. By walking the Samaritan road and acting compassionately in the world we become signs of the approaching reign of God. The compassionate action of the Samaritan suggests that the church in its truest sense is mission, mercy, and life-giving community. There is no message here of withdrawing from the world or acquiescing to divisive ideologies; instead, the idea of 'doing likewise' signifies entering a broken world and setting it right. On the Samaritan road, understanding the teaching of Jesus means entering into relationship with those persons who are hated, accused, and rejected. The church is good news when it crosses every boundary to become a neighbour to the battered, excluded, and set aside. The church fulfils the promise of God by acting mercifully in the world, defending human rights, and seeking peace and justice for those who suffer at the hands of unjust others.

CONCLUSION

The racism, xenophobia, and ethnic violence of the modern world leave us crying out with Jeremiah, 'We look for peace, but find no good; for a time of healing but there is terror instead' (14: 19). Crossing the racial and ethnic divide is what allows human beings to build the alliances that lead towards a fuller and more just life together. Although the United States and much of Europe is multiethnic, the concern to impose stricter controls on immigration reflects the idea that persons of colour do not belong to fundamentally white nation-state societies; indeed, the promise and certainty of belonging is not attached to those that in popular discourse are considered racialized national others. In the post-9/11 world, it is clear that in the United States and Europe Islamophobia is premised on the racialization of Muslims and the fear that they threaten so-called white Christian societies. Muslims have been among the racially suspect in Europe for years, but in the United States they now join in that status the ranks of black, Asian, Native American, and Latino/Latina humanity.

Today, all around the globe race matters in more than black and white, as evidenced by immigration being a site for racist discourse. Americans should not move too rapidly to build the fence along the Mexico–US border, because the white imagined sameness of national identity so well articulated by Huntington and Brimelow reflects one that already exists in the popular mind. Ethnic diversity is well represented in the United States and Europe, which suggests that the way white humanity in these societies envision who belongs in them requires at the very least recognition of the complex ethnic composition of the societies in which individuals live. Finally, the parable of the Good Samaritan invites Methodists to engage in practices that overcome divisions in society, while suggesting to members of mainstream society how racially despised and beaten-down persons can finally reveal the meaning of the promise of life offered by God.

References

ARNOLD, BETTINA (2006). 'Arierdammerung: Race and Archaeology in Nazi Germany'. In *World Archaeology* 38/1: 8–31.

BENEDICT, RUTH (1940). *Race: Science and Politics*. New York: Viking.

BRIMELOW, PETER (1995). *Alien Nation: Common Sense About America's Immigration Disaster*. New York: Harper Perennial.

DU BOIS, W. E. B. (1996). *The Souls of Black Folk*. New York: Penguin.

EZE, EMMANUEL CHUKWUDE (ed.) (1997). *Race and the Enlightenment: A Reader*. Cambridge: Blackwell.

FEAGIN, JOE R. (1997). 'Old Poison in New Bottles'. In Juan F. Perea (ed.), *Immigrants Out*. New York: New York University Press.

FOUCAULT, MICHEL (1980). *Power/Knowledge: Selected Interview and Other Writings. Michel Foucault, 1972–1977*. Brighton: Harvester.

GOLDBERG, DAVID THEO (1993). *Racist Culture: Philosophy and the Politics of Meaning*. Cambridge: Blackwell.

GOLDSCHMIDT, HENRY, and MCALLISTER, ELIZABETH (eds.) (2004). *Race, Nation, and Religion in the Americas*. New York: Oxford University Press.

GRIFFIN, PAUL R. (1999). *Seeds of Racism in the Soul of America*. Cleveland: Pilgrim.

GUNDRY-VOLF, JUDITH (1995). 'Spirit, Mercy and the Other'. *Theology Today* 51: 508–24.

HALL, STUART (1993). 'Culture, Community, Nation'. *Cultural Studies* 7/3: 349–63.

HERIK, PETER (2004). 'Anthropological Perspectives on the New Racism in Europe'. *Ethnos* 69/2: 149–55.

HUNTINGTON, SAMUEL (2004). *Who Are We? The Challenges to America's National Identity*. New York: Simon & Schuster.

IBRAHIM, MAGIE (2005). 'The Securitization of Migration: A Racial Discourse'. *International Migration* 43/5: 147–63.

MASSEY, DOUGLASS (2004). 'Who Are We? The Challenges to America's National Identity by Samuel P. Huntington'. *Population and Development Review* 30/3: 543–8.

MATLACK, LUCIOUS (1881). *The Antislavery Struggle and Triumph in the Methodist Episcopal Church.* New York: Phillips Hunt.

ROCHIN, REFUGIO, and FERNANDEZ, LIONEL (2005). *U.S. Latino Patriots: From the American Revolution to the War in Afghanistan: An Overview.* Michigan: Julian Zamora Research Institute.

SAMPSON, JANE (2005). *Race and Empire.* Harlow: Pearson/Longman.

SPICKARD, PAUL (ed.) (2005). *Race and Nation: Ethnic Systems in the Modern World.* New York: Routledge.

SWAIN, CAROL (2002). *The New White Nationalism in America: Its Challenge to Integration.* Cambridge: Cambridge University Press.

WESLEY, JOHN (1987). *The Works of John Wesley,* iii. *Sermons IV, 114–151,* ed. Albert C. Outler. Nashville: Abingdon.

WINANT, HOWARD (2001). *The World is A Ghetto.* New York: Basic Books.

WOOD, PETER (1995). 'If Toads Could Speak: How the Myth of Race Took Hold and Flourished in the Minds of Europe's Renaissance Colonizers'. In Benjamin Bowser (ed.), *Racism and Anti-Racism in the World Perspective.* London: Sage.

CHAPTER 41

METHODISM AND POLITICS IN AFRICA

SIMEON O. ILESANMI

INTRODUCTION

No other relationship in history has been more vetted and fraught with controversy as that between religion and politics. The controversy is less about sociological determinations than normative judgement. Given their common competition for people's loyalty and their historical propensity to provide regulatory frameworks by which issues of order and justice, freedom and responsibility, as well as of personal identity and social meaning are resolved, it is not surprising that religion and politics engage each other the way they do. From societies as ancient as the Graeco-Roman world to the contemporary and relatively stable democratic societies, the role that religion and theology can and should play in shaping public lives has been contested and continually negotiated. Africa has experienced its fair share of this debate. Muslims, Christians, and adherents of the traditional religions are divided over the limits, if any, that should be imposed on their freedom and the scope of responsibility they should have in shaping political life, broadly construed. Their disagreement has spanned the long stretch of Africa's political history, and is rendered more complex by other streams of pluralism that are latent in Africa, including ethnicity, class, and region. In addition, the absence of common symbols of discourse deriving from the indigenous traditions with which to think and speak as Africans about the meaning of political reality and responsibility, coupled with the frequent destabilization of the various political systems with which Africans have experimented, complicate the task of explaining the nature of the relationship between politics and any particular religious institution. Nonetheless, it is against this backdrop of complex cultural and ideological pluralism that I will examine the relationship between Methodism and African politics.

METHODISM AND POLITICS IN PRE-COLONIAL AFRICA

Africa's involvement with Christianity dates back to the origin of the religion. However, the immediate impetus for the implantation of Methodism on African soil must be traced to certain developments that began in the seventeenth century in the Atlantic world, among which were exploration, steam-power, medical advances, and the Maxim gun. These products of the industrial revolution power-fully assisted the penetration, survival, and reinforcement of the pioneer mission-aries, and in part the Christian gospel floated in on the rising tide of European influence. But these facts, obvious and widely recognized, are not the whole story; for, at the end of the eighteenth century, the missionary movement itself was revolutionized by the far-reaching changes in the ideology and organization of its home-base, and these in turn dramatically increased its distinctive impact on Africa. There were two aspects to the emerging ideological changes—religious and politico-economic, notably the ethical reorientation that was instantiated in the movement for the abolition of the slave trade. A key figure behind the change in the religious sphere was John Wesley, whose challenge to the established Anglican Church gave rise to evangelicalism that demanded a renewed zeal and commitment on the part of the individual Christian and a deep concern for a personal act of conversion.

As with German pietism which had produced the Moravian missions, Wesley's emphasis greatly strengthened the deepest motives for missionary work, creating an impelling sense of gratitude for the gift of the gospel and a desire to extend its sway. But the imperative to extend what Wesley believed to be 'true Christianity' beyond England was articulated by his partners in faith Thomas Coke and Francis Asbury, whose efforts gave birth to two forms of Methodism—British and American—with corresponding missionary wings that were instrumental to the global spread of the Methodist revolution. Coke's vision to take the gospel to the whole world led to the founding in London of the Methodist Missionary Society in 1819 (Hogg 1971: 380–1). As one of the mission outposts touched by these territorial expressions of the Wesleyan spirit, Africa quickly proved to be a fertile ground for Christianity, rivalling Islam in terms of numerical strength and co-opting the indigenous world-views into its orbit in the name of a deftly conceived theological project of inculturation (cf. Idowu 1965; Dickson 1984; Shorter 1997). One cannot but agree with John Peel (2003: 1), a long-time student of African Christianity, that 'the large-scale adoption of Christianity has been one of the master themes of modern African history', and with the onset of a new century, 'it may well prove to be of world historical significance too, contributing to a decisive shift in Christianity's geopolitical placement, from North to South'.

This sanguine view of Christianity's odyssey in Africa challenges the often polemical and squint-eyed accounts that not only credit European missionaries exclusively with the success of the faith in Africa, but also deride Africans for betraying their traditions and embracing what is stigmatized as a culturally alienating world-view. Although this is not the occasion to evaluate the various theories of conversion (cf. Ikenga-Metuh 1987: 11–27) that sought to explain why so many Africans had, over the past century or so, turned to Christianity, it must be insisted that any credible account has to recognize what Lamin Sanneh aptly refers to as the 'African factor' in mission (Sanneh 1983: p. xii). The real origins of African Christianity, Sanneh argues, lie in the perception and experience of compatibility between the basic forms of indigenous cosmology and Christian ideas, as well as in 'the preponderance of African agents' (catechists and evangelists) who presented this fusion of cultural horizons as not only a sign of theological maturity but also a *sine qua non* to evangelical success (ibid.). 'Western missionaries for their part', Sanneh argues further, 'squeezed Christianity into a conformist pattern that was largely in accord with the imperialist tradition, paying more attention to creating an acquiescent African population than to issues of religious assimilation' (ibid.). It will be more accurate to say, however, that Christianity has taken root in Africa as a result of the combined efforts of expatriate missionaries and indigenous responses and initiatives than to assign its success exclusively to one party.

Methodism is a good example of this partnership in mission, but its story in Africa is not just *religious* but also political. Telling this story, however, will inevitably take us beyond the African shore, and even with that it is not clear how we should proceed. One way is to investigate whether Methodism had, from its time and place of inception, a political philosophy which was propagated alongside its theological doctrines at home and abroad. If this is the case, we can then examine how that understanding of political life has fared in Africa. As one scholar rightly notes,

a Wesleyan political language is both necessary and possible. It is necessary for purposes of communication among Wesleyans on matters of political ethics, of guiding the translation of Wesleyan spirit and theology into political and social action, of completing the Wesleyan theological project, and of bringing something distinctively Wesleyan to the ecumenical debate. It is possible because there are resources in John Wesley's theology—largely unnoticed by Wesley himself—that allow and enable the transcending of the limits of his eighteenth-century politics in the formulation of a political ethic and method dependent mainly on Wesleyan theology itself and not on the contingencies of political currents and conditions.   (Weber 2001: 27)

Another approach is to take an empirical route, which would require us to enquire into the various concrete political conditions in which Methodism—as both a theological principle and an organizational structure—has found itself. The focus here will be on, inter alia, official state policies about religion, religion's responses to those policies or their articulation of the normative functions of the state that might be influenced by their own consciousness of a divine mission within history, and the degrees of accommodation or resistance that might exist between the state and religious institutions as they struggle to maintain their respective boundaries or negotiate the terms by which they will interact with each other (cf. Niebuhr 1951; Sanders 1964).

Does Methodism have a political theory? From available evidence, the answer is resoundingly 'yes', but historians are divided on what the content of Methodist political thought is. One view identifies Methodism with a pro-establishment political temperament whose members 'were conspicuously more mindful of tradition, and readier to assert a national character. Its leaders, lay and ministerial, were ... exponents of the imperial doctrines espoused by British public opinion in the closing decade of the century' (Koss 1975: 105). John Wesley was seen as the main inspiration for this conservative political position. His 'firm defense of the crown and doggedly determined belief that England was the world's freest state, whose citizens enjoyed the utmost in religious and civil liberties' (Raymond 1976: 317) led him to espouse an arguably extreme political ethic, one in which passive obedience to governing authority is the hallmark of civic virtue. Bernard Semmel challenges this political portrait of Methodism, instead associating it, on the basis of Wesley's Arminianism, with a liberal reformist and modernizing movement. According to him, Wesley's evangelical theology of universal grace and individual responsibility showed affinities with liberal Enlightenment notions of individual rights and contractarian constitutionalism. The coincidence of theological and political lines of development contributed to what he calls the 'Methodist Revolution' (Semmel 1973; Hynson 1983: 57–85).

These two political tendencies—conservative and progressive—have found expressions in the African incarnation of Methodism, but theological differences cannot be invoked as the reason why African Methodists have espoused them. We have to seek explanations within what I referred to above as the empirical sphere. It is in fact difficult to identify what can remotely be called a 'Methodist theology of politics' in Africa. This is not to suggest that African Methodists, as individual members or churches, do not participate in politics or *do* politics in various and sundry contexts, such as running for elective offices or proposing some theologically grounded visions of political life. Rather, such participations are often dictated by pragmatic and contextual considerations than by any common clarifying vision rooted in a collective identity or understanding of what it means to be *Methodists*. The diversity within Methodism presents a further obstacle to the effort to investigate its perspectives on politics. It is not enough to refer to oneself as a Methodist in Africa; one has to further specify whether one is of British Wesleyan Methodist or United Methodist Church (with its roots in American Methodism) or African Methodist Episcopal (Zion), all of whom consider themselves heirs of the Wesleyan heritage. Unless otherwise explained, I will use the term 'African Methodists' to refer to all three. More significant, it is the character of the state and the policies it has promulgated or endorsed that have provided occasions on which Methodists have spoken or acted *politically*, thus establishing the basis for postulating what may count as a Methodist theory of politics. Whatever the character of the regime, African politics has continually had to work with or around religious realities rather than against them. This much is clear from the attempts by successive regimes in the continent to translate power into authority, in other words to seek legitimation or justification for that authority not only from those directly involved in the politics itself but from religious collectivities.

The state in Africa is a Janus-faced phenomenon. There is a sense in which it has changed over time—from pre-colonial to colonial and to post-colonial period, each historical phase representing different political and policy agendas, triggering appropriate responses from the religious communities. But there is also a sense in which the state has remained essentially the same—as 'a rapacious *structure* of interlinked interests (involving the creation and perpetuation of clientelistic relationships), where public institutions are colonized and emasculated; and . . . as the location of a hegemonic *process* whereby political figures engage in a pursuit of power' (Haynes 1996: 9). Both dimensions of the state—its protean historical character and its persistent predatory and oppressive behaviour—have shaped how Methodists engage with politics in rhetoric and conduct.

The first occasion on which African Methodists articulated a theory of church–state relations took place a century before the official imposition of colonial rule on Africa. These Methodists were among the first group of ex-slaves from London and Nova Scotia resettled in Freetown, Sierra Leone. Following the formal establishment in 1787 of the Committee for the abolition of the slave trade, a number of its members, and notably Granville Sharp, was persuaded that it would be a real step forward if some of the black people in London, many of whom were penniless and in trouble, could be resettled on the coast of Africa. The 'Black Poor' of London could be transformed into a flourishing, free agricultural community, an example of the way things could be without the slave trade. There was, in Sharp's vision, to be no governor. They would rule themselves according to the ancient Anglo-Saxon principles of the Frankpledge, as understood in eighteenth-century England. The government embraced the idea, and the first settlement arrived in the then known 'Province of Freedom' in late 1787. Around the same time, some of the black

Americans who had fought on the British side in the American Revolutionary War and had been resettled in Nova Scotia after the war, expressed interest to relocate to Sierra Leone. In January 1792 they sailed; six weeks later they arrived in Freetown and, according to Adrian Hastings (1994: 180), 'the real history of Sierra Leone began'.

In the ensuing tensions that inevitably arose between this ostensibly Christian settlement, whose core element consisted of 'services, sermons and hymns' and in which 'a multitude of congregations and preachers' provided it 'a viable minimum of social structure' (ibid. 181), and the administrators and governors of the slaving forts established by the various European trading companies—the Dutch, English, and Danish, among others—the Methodists played a crucial role. Protesting against the destruction unleashed by the French (who were then at war with Britain) on the new colony, about 128 Methodists sent a signed 'Remonstrance' to the Governor in which they declared 'we cannot persuade ourselves that politics and religion have any connection, and therefore think it not for a Governor to be meddling with the other' (Knutsford 1901: 145). Twenty years later, when a British Methodist missionary, William Davies, had quarrelled irrevocably with the Nova Scotian Methodists he had come to serve, he complained, 'As far as I can judge, most of our leaders are of the American Republican spirit and are strongly averse to Government. I am a loyal subject to my King, and wish to do the little I can for the support of that Government especially in a foreign part' (Walls 1970: 126). Here we have expressed in early colonial Sierra Leone two contrary views of the relationship between Methodism and colonial power that would come back again and again in one form or another over the next several years: the separation of church and state, the missionary desire to support and be supported by government, especially in foreign parts.

The ambivalence towards the secular state that seems to be displayed by Methodism in pre-colonial Africa undoubtedly reflects the same sentiments that one finds among the first generation of Methodists, especially John Wesley himself, the only theological resource common to all branches of the Methodist family. But it would be a stretch to imply that this early community of African Methodists was consciously borrowing its ideas about normative church–state relations from its English spiritual progenitor. As is clear from the dismissive comment made by William Davies about the Nova Scotian Methodists, there was no consensus within the community on this issue. That the division was a result of the differing political traditions of the two societies—America/Canada and England—from which the members of this settler community emigrated might be a good guess. Davies, however, gave the impression that the blacks who emigrated from England had been influenced by and did retain a uniquely *English Methodist* ideology characterized by an organicist view of society, one in which the king, church, and people are united in a common purpose. Wesley seems to have held such a view of political community. In a tract addressed to members of his movement, he explained why they should vote for the man who loves God, the king, the country's interest, and the church. Ultimately, he draws all these loves together into a combined relationship:

Above all, mark that man who talks of loving the Church, and does not love the King. If he does not love the King, he cannot love God. And if he does not love God, he cannot love the Church. He loves the Church and the King just alike. For indeed he loves neither one nor the other.

O beware, you who truly love the Church, and therefore cannot but love the King; beware of dividing the King and the Church, any more than the King and country. Let others do as they will, what is that to you? Act you as an honest man, a loyal subject, a true Englishman, a lover of the country, a lover of the Church; in one word, a Christian!   (quoted in Weber 2001: 31)

The Nova Scotians, in contrast, displayed an anti-establishmentarian religious temper, even though they too could not quite disconnect politics and religion for long. They knew perfectly well that they needed and benefited from British rule and a general British patronage of Christianity. They had fought against the American Republicans under the British flag precisely because they shared with the Republicans a concern for freedom that now they were able to express most emphatically in the sphere of religion. And in Sierra Leone they were constitutionally free to do so, however much their governors might personally prefer a more Anglican face for the church.

It is also clear that both sides involved in this intra-family Methodist debate— the Nova Scotian and their British emigrant counterparts—paid little or no regard to the indigenous African political institutions. Perceiving their newly established Christian community as something of a cultural, linguistic, and religious bridge between the Euro-American world and Africa, the new immigrants ironically replicated in Africa the same kind of cultural hubris and elitist attitude that had been shown towards them in the societies from which they came. They thus prepared the ground for the close association that would later exist between Christianity and imperialism after the formal imposition of colonial rule on Africa in the closing decades of the nineteenth century. Nowhere is this irony more striking and fully embodied than in Liberia, a country with its founding in the repatriation of ex-slaves from the United States and where power remained concentrated until recently in a few families, all of American origin.

METHODISM AND POLITICS IN COLONIAL AND POST-COLONIAL AFRICA

To gauge the full extent of Methodism's contributions to African political culture, we have to fast forward, spatially and temporally, looking beyond Sierra Leone and more closely at the dynamics of church–state relations during the heyday of colonial rule. To be sure, it was the successful establishment of Christianity in Sierra Leone that acted as a powerful stimulus for its extension to other parts of Africa. For over the next hundred years after the establishment of Sierra Leone and Liberia, Africa became the widest possible laboratory for the experimentation and implementation of the Great Commission, playing host to a stream of missionaries from Europe and America, all fired by the zeal to save Africans from their 'heathenism'. The aim of any mission is to insert itself into the ongoing history of the evangelized people, and so to transform it. With successful missions a complex mutual adaptation nearly always occurs, in which Christianity is seen as fulfilling or conforming with key elements of local culture, even as it challenges or rejects others. To appropriate and rework local versions of the past and to use them to legitimate the new religion is a critical aspect of this process. Elizabeth Isichei rightly observed that the missionaries were 'distinguished less by their doctrines than by characteristic emphasis, such as the necessity of conversion, the Atonement and the vital operation of Christian doctrines upon the heart and conduct' (Isichei 1995: 81). Reflecting the ethos of Victorian England, all the missionaries, regardless of their denominational traditions, shared these general aims, but they considered it neither necessary nor desirable to negotiate with Africans on the terms of the envisioned transformation of their society. From the missionaries' perspective, the conversion of Africans would entail more than a personal surrendering of life to Christ or membership of the church, but also require the adoption of a new paradigm of civilization serving as a template for overhauling 'moribund' traditions, redefining social relations, and incorporating the continent into the emerging global capitalist system shaped and largely dominated by the West.

The parent missionary bodies, including the Wesleyan Methodist Missionary Society, realized that accomplishing this task would require more than European hands. In fact, given their conviction that the whole of Africa, not just a section of it, needed to be transformed, it became clear from the start that 'there was no substitute for partnership with Africans in missionary work, for, more than outsiders, they knew what motivated their people' (Sanneh 1983: 106). The majority of the local partners were recruited from among the so-called recaptives, that is, Africans sold into slavery but recaptured on the sea by the British preventive squadron, often within a few days of their being shipped, and set free in Sierra Leone two or three months after that (cf. Ayandele 1966; Isichei 1995). To many of these liberated Africans, their return had a significance of Biblical proportions—the return of the exiles from Babylon—and they needed no convincing when presented with the opportunity to be involved in the *missio Dei*. Through their efforts, many prominent centres of Methodism emerged, including Ghana, Nigeria, and the Republic of Benin in West Africa; Kenya, Zimbabwe, and the Congo in East and Central Africa; and in southern Africa, Angola and the Republic of South Africa.

It was the combination of local interests and the nature of political structure in each of these jurisdictions rather than a uniform theological blueprint that determined how the church related to the secular establishments. Outside the sphere of education on which the Church's policy was nearly uniform across Africa, Methodism was inextricably bound up with politics for much of the period under consideration. Unlike the earlier era, however, the political stakeholders belonged to two sides: African kings and chiefs representing local interests and traditional institutions, and the newly established colonial administrations whose charge was to further the agenda of their respective home governments. The inevitable conflict between both entities often created an unenviable dilemma for the church. It was the manner in which instances of such dilemma were handled that show how Methodism remains a living tradition, in that the elements of Wesley's political thought previously identified—conservatism and hermeneutical suspicion—are immune to spatio-temporal variations.

Methodism arrived in Nigeria, for example, at a time when many of its southern kingdoms, especially the Yoruba, were involved in civil wars. What is important for our purpose in this chapter is not the fact that the missionaries chose to intervene in the crises, but the manner of their intervention. They deployed the ethical insights of the religion they represented to forge a new understanding of the issues in controversy, and in the process were able to reconfigure the political terrain in radically different directions. The Christian tradition contains a rich deposit of moral wisdom to guide its adherents on how to think about the quandary of war, and the three moral stances on the use of lethal force identified by Roland Bainton (1960) in his classic study of this problem—the Crusade (holy war), pacifism, and just war—still provide the normative framework by which most Christians evaluate different concrete situations of conflict. No single perspective has dominated the theological scene; rather, the Christian story on the issue of war has been 'a story of shifting combinations among these three essentially irreconcilable attitudes' (Little 1991: 135). Nowhere is this observation truer than in nineteenth-century Nigerian Christianity when 'the missionaries tended to identify themselves with the communities among whom they lived and worked, and they saw issues mostly from the point of view of those particular communities' (J. Ajayi 1965: 60). Thomas Birch Freeman, a Wesleyan missionary widely recognized as the 'father of West African Methodism', was representative of this general pragmatic predilection of the missionaries. In his support of the community where he was working, Abeokuta in south-western Nigeria, one of the warring parties, he justified the appeal made to the British consul in Lagos for military assistance on behalf of the town on the grounds that its people 'represent progress and advancing civilization and it is to be feared if they should be conquered our cause or rather that of God would suffer at least for a time immensely' (Biobaku 1957: 37). A fellow missionary from the Church Missionary Society (CMS), Henry Townsend, agreed that the political stabilization of Abeokuta was a moral imperative, for it was from there that 'commerce and Christian civilization would radiate into the dark but fertile interior' (ibid.). In their separate memos to their respective Mission Boards in London, which had cautioned against entanglement in local politics, they defended their participation in the war, as Christians, on the grounds that 'Christianity does not remove from converts civil duties and the obligation to obey their rulers in the things that are not contrary to the law of God' (W. Ajayi 1967: 231).

The rulers intended here were not the colonial administrators, but the local chiefs and kings, whose goodwill must be courted for permission to establish stations, move from place to place, and evangelize. For their loyalty, the missionaries were bountifully rewarded with free access to the palaces and the hearts of their occupants, occasionally serving as political and economic advisers to the kings, and as intermediaries between the kings and the colonial administrators. Yet, on some important issues of conscience, especially in the realm of family relations, the missionaries were willing to jeopardize this ecclesio-royal friendship in order to affirm and uphold human dignity as they understood it. Well aware of what unrestrained patriarchy could do to women, given the nature of gender relations in their own societies, they determinedly challenged African forms of patriarchy on such controversial subjects as polygamy, the payment of bridewealth, clitoridectomy, the killing of twins, and the pursuit of alleged witches. Anticipating what over a century later would be appropriately called liberation theology with its preferential option for the poor, the missionaries articulated, albeit unsystematically, a theological–ethical stance that gave priority to society's dropouts—'people who in one way or another no longer belonged to a society either because that society was actually disintegrating or because it had driven them out or wished to kill them and they had fled' (Hastings 1989: 39; Oduyoye 1977).

While the relationship between Methodism and the local African political institutions was fraught with ambiguity, its interaction with the colonial regime and its successor African governments was no less contentious. On the one hand, the missionaries helped both to create and to represent the colonial and post-colonial worlds of Africa. Perhaps it was a role they could not have escaped, partly because of the political environment in which they found themselves, partly because of their patriotic instincts, and partly because it was the logical outcome of their activity. Whatever the reasons may be, the association between them and imperialism rested on the same postulate: the superiority of one's own culture to that of the other. In the judgement of one African scholar, the missionary programme was so much 'more complex than the simple transmission of the Christian faith' that it was difficult 'not to identify it with cultural propaganda, patriotic motivations and commercial interests', and that more than other kinds of colonialists, the missionary was 'the best symbol of the colonial enterprise' (Mudimbe 1988: 45–7). As such, 'the study of Christianity in Africa is more than just an exercise in the analysis of religious change' (Comaroff and Comaroff 1991: 11).

The precise manner in which the missionaries, and as such the church, aided the colonial enterprise remains a subject of intense debate among African and Africanist scholars. The Comaroffs argue that evangelical missions serve to sustain modern capitalist colonialism mainly through a myriad of mundane, material practices:

The impact of Protestant evangelists as harbingers of industrial capitalism lay in the fact that their civilizing mission was simultaneously symbolic and practical, theological and temporal. The goods and messages they brought with them to Africa presupposed the messages and meanings they proclaimed in the pulpit and vice versa. Both were vehicles of a moral economy that celebrated the global spirit of commerce, the commodity, and the imperial marketplace.   (ibid. 8–9)

For Mudimbe, the colonial character of missionary activity is more general, intrinsic, and connected with their *religious* objective: to refashion inwardly people whom they define as pagans and savages, to work whole cultures according to divine law. Conversion is control at its most complete, and it is this that makes mission colonialist to the core: 'missionary speech is always predetermined, pre-regulated, let us say *colonized*... The missionary does not enter into dialogue with "pagans" and "savages" but must impose the law of God that he incarnates... Consequently "African conversion", rather than being the outcome of a dialogue—unthinkable *per se*—came to be the sole position the African could take in order to survive' (Mudimbe 1988: 47–8). A Primitive Methodist missionary, Robert Fairley, captured the essence of this relationship of mutuality between the missionaries and the colonial project in Africa. In his private papers, he recorded the following humorous statement ascribed to a schoolboy in England:

Africa is a British Colony. For this England is much indebted to her missionaries. When the missionary arrives in a hitherto unknown part, he calls all the natives to him. When they have gathered around him, he makes them kneel down and close their eyes. This done, he hoists the British flag and proclaims the country British territory.   (Ayandele 1966: 30)

But the missionaries did not always do the bidding of the colonial administration; the relationship between the two was far more complex. An endemic source of friction between them was the extent to which Africans should be educated. The different Christian denominations became involved in the education of Africans for a variety of reasons, including the belief that schoolchildren would be good recruits for proselytization or that education could be an effective 'means of social control, to instill in the African a proper attitude of subservience towards the white man, usually in connection with tilling the land and producing the raw materials needed to feed western industries' (Sanneh 1983: 127). Although there is evidence in the literature to support these assertions, they present an incomplete truth about the philosophy of education that governed the social action of the various missions, especially the Wesleyan Mission and CMS, the two leading providers of Western education in sub-Saharan Africa (Ayandele 1966: 287). Surely, their extensive investment in the construction of schools, both primary and secondary, was a continuation of their religious theme, their overarching desire was to 'create an African middle class' (J. Ajayi 1965: 17), not just because it would be the most expedient way to build up personnel for the church but as an aim worthy of being pursued for its own sake. Believing that education is an indispensable instrument by which Africans can be assisted to enjoy 'the temporal blessings' of 'the true religion', they mounted an arguably unassailable defence of their commitment to education:

In the history of man, there has been no civilization which has not been cemented and sustained in existence by a division of the people into higher, lower, and middle classes. We may affirm, indeed, that this constant attendant upon society—gradation of classes—is indispensable to civilization in any form, however low or high. . . . In Africa there was no class of eminent men whose attainments may give unity, force and direction to Society; no middle class who are prepared by their attainments to receive impulses of knowledge and wisdom and power from their superiors and communicate it to the millions of the common people. With the single exception of political chiefs, themselves barbarians, the whole society of Sudan rests and stagnates on a dead level, and the people remain poor, ignorant and wretched, because they have no superiors.   (J. Ajayi 1965: 17–18)

Terence Ranger (1995) has argued that the Wesleyan Methodist Church pursued this objective to a fault in Zimbabwe (formerly Rhodesia). He credits Methodism with the cultivation of a distinctive orientation to life among the African Christian elite, one in which family life, educational strategies, and economic advance and political aspirations are intricately linked together. The 'Wesleyan evangelists' were the first to mobilize citizens and natives for political awareness by organizing ecumenical and community meetings at which issues relevant to local interests and human rights were discussed, and strategies for dealing with the colonial government were mapped out. The mission house was not only a symbol of advancing civilization but also a centre of African political life. It is on record that the Methodist Church was the first to appoint a black circuit superintendent in Zimbabwe, a development described by the local newspaper, the *Bantu Mirror*, as history-making and 'a proof of the alertness of the Methodist Church to the aspirations of Africans and their possibilities' (*Bantu Mirror* 15 February 1936). The development stirred a similar aspiration from the members of other denominations. For example, the delegates to the Presbyterian Native Women Christians' Association, members of a church that as yet had no black clergy, petitioned the church authorities thus:

We pray to God Almighty, Our Father, and in Christ His only Begotten Son to bless this work and that through His power a Moses or Joshua may be raised among our native men, to lead the tribes of Africa from Egypt to Canaan. But how can it be done? As Presbyterians, we mothers, on looking about, we see in other churches a Moses or a Joshua: one of their own leading them. We have not.   (Ranger 1995: 8)

It was a development such as this that the colonial officials had feared and explains why they tended to condemn missionaries who pushed secondary education 'for "spoiling" Africans and turning black men into white' (Hastings 1994: 542). Officials and settlers worried that mission education would inculcate ideas about equality, thereby exposing the myth upon which the idea of racial superiority and its political expression had been based. The fear was not unjustified, especially in the context of Zimbabwe whose experience of colonialism, maintained by a minority white settler community, was far more oppressive and exploitative than obtained in many parts of West Africa where the European powers, especially the British, operated what was euphemistically designated as an Indirect Rule system. Kenya, Uganda, Zambia, and South Africa also had minority white settler populations. Hastings observed that across much of southern, central, and eastern Africa, 'settler communities were establishing themselves, acquiring large stretches of land which required for their cultivation a cheap black labor force and erecting around themselves the sharpest of color bars' (ibid. 542–3). Churches believed that literacy was the only way out of this situation of oppression, and they backed up their tradition of criticism of the colonial order and white settlers with the proliferation of schools in villages and towns. Their investment paid off. What Coleman said about its impact in Nigeria is also true of Zimbabwe and other similarly colonized societies:

Western education did not merely facilitate the emergence of a separate class; it endowed the individuals in that class with the knowledge and skills, the ambitions and aspirations, that enabled them to challenge the Nigerian colonial government and ultimately to wrest control over the central political power from it. By the latter achievement the Western-educated elements placed themselves above the traditional African authorities in the new Nigerian political system. Thus, within the short span of two generations, Western education made possible a nearly complete reversal in the status of Nigerian political leaders. The rapidity of upward mobility in this revolutionary transformation is possibly unparalleled in history.   (Coleman 1965: 115)

Nearly all African nationalist leaders were Christians, notably Anglican and Methodist, although as independence loomed, neither church could be said to have had any corporate significance for pro-independence politics. In fact, the Methodist Church allegedly maintained a stupefying, lukewarm attitude during the liberation struggle in Zimbabwe and during a similar critical period in Kenya (Kurewa 1997: 143–76). Thus, while Methodism remains a visible religious and cultural presence in post-colonial Africa, its political impact is less direct now than it was in the preceding eras. The reasons have as much to do with the character of the post-colonial state as with the status of Methodism itself in Africa. Following independence, a number of African governments avowed a secular constitutional principle that denied any privileged or preferential treatment to any religion, citing increasing religious pluralism as a justification. One immediate consequence of this was the abolition of mission schools, a move that stripped the churches of the main artery they had to social engineering. But it has also succeeded in excluding appeals to religion or religiously based values in determining public laws and policies.

In consequence, the integrating moral vision that is necessary both to legitimate and to act as a check upon governmental excesses has decayed. Ironically, the present Zimbabwe under Robert Mugabe exemplifies the dormancy and power-lessness of Christianity in Africa today, notwithstanding the bourgeoning success of Pentecostalism in the same continent—a fact that accentuates the internal contradictions within African societies.

It appears that the church—Methodist and others—is now so preoccupied with the mundane and clientelistic concerns about how to survive in an environment of resource shortages that they too have embraced the 'Big Man model' (Gifford 1993: 310) of politics that also characterizes the behaviour of temporal leaders. This is a type of politics that thrives on the assumption that 'public office *can* bring about private profit and influence' and fuels the perception of many ordinary Africans that 'the "success" of a religion is reflected at least in part in the ability of its leaders to exhibit a high level of material wealth' (Haynes 1996: 9). The result has been bad for both church and state. Neither is trusted or taken seriously by the people. The challenge for Methodism in contemporary Africa lies in finding creative ways to retrieve its strong social and humane commitments rising out of its founder's concern for the poor and society's drop-outs, and enacting a vision of political community that gives priority to human rights, social justice, and the defence of human dignity.

References

AJAYI, J. F. ADE, and SMITH, R. S. (1965). *Yoruba Warfare in the Nineteenth Century.* Cambridge: Cambridge University Press.

AJAYI, W. O. (1967). 'Christian Involvement in the Ijaye War'. *The Bulletin of the Society for African Church History* 2/3.

AYANDELE, E. A. (1966). *The Missionary Impact on Modern Nigeria 1842–1914: A Political and Social Analysis.* New York: Humanities Press.

BAINTON, ROLAND H. (1960). *Christian Attitudes Toward War and Peace: A Historical Survey and Critical Re-Evaluation.* Nashville: Abingdon.

BIOBAKU, S. O. (1957). *The Egba and their Neighbours 1842–1872.* Oxford: Clarendon.

COLEMAN, JAMES S. (1965). *Nigeria: Background to Nationalism.* Berkeley and Los Angeles: University of California Press.

COMAROFF, JEAN, and COMAROFF, JOHN (1991). *Of Revelation and Revolution: Christianity, Colonialism and Consciousness in South Africa.* Chicago: University of Chicago Press.

DICKSON, KWESI A. (1984). *Theology in Africa.* Maryknoll: Orbis.

GIFFORD, PAUL (1993). *Christianity and Politics in Doe's Liberia.* Cambridge: Cambridge University Press.

HASTINGS, ADRIAN (1989). *African Catholicism: Essays in Discovery.* London: SCM.

—— (1994). *Church in Africa, 1450–1950.* Oxford: Clarendon.

HAYNES, JEFFREY (1996). *Religion and Politics in Africa.* London: Zed Books.

HOGG, W. RICHIE (1971). 'Methodist Missions'. In Stephen Neill, Gerald H. Anderson, and John Goodwin (eds.), *Concise Dictionary of the Christian World Mission*. Nashville: Abingdon.

HYNSON, LEON O. (1983). 'Human Liberty as Divine Right: A Study in the Political Maturation of John Wesley'. *Journal of Church and State* 25.

IDOWU, E. BOLAJI (1965). *Towards an Indigenous Church*. Ibadan: Oxford University Press.

IKENGA-METUH, E. (1987). 'The Shattered Microcosm: A Critical Survey of Explanations of Conversion in Africa'. In Kristen Holst Peterson (ed.), *Religion, Development and African Identity*. Uppsala: Scandinavian Institute of African Studies.

ISICHEI, ELIZABETH (1995). *A History of Christianity in Africa*. Grand Rapids: Eerdmans.

KOSS, STEPHEN (1975). 'Wesleyanism and Empire'. *Historical Journal* 17/1.

KNUTSFORD, M. (1901). *Life and Letters of Zachary Macaulay*. London: Edward Arnold.

KUREWA, JOHN WESLEY Z. (1997). *The Church in Mission: A Short History of the United Methodist Church in Zimbabwe, 1897–1997*. Nashville: Abingdon.

LITTLE, DAVID (1991). 'Holy War Appeals and Western Christianity: A Reconsideration of Bainton's Aproach'. In John Kelsay and James Turner Johnson (eds.), *Just War and Jihad: Historical and Theoretical Perspectives on War and Peace in Western and Islamic Traditions*. Westport, Conn.: Greenwood.

MUDIMBE, V. Y. (1988). *The Invention of Africa*. Bloomington: Indiana University Press.

NIEBUHR, H. RICHARD (1951). *Christ and Culture*. New York: Harper & Row.

ODUYOYE, MERCY AMBA (1977). *And Women, Where Do They Come In?* Lagos: Methodist Church Nigeria Literature Bureau.

PEEL, J. D. Y. (2003). *Religious Encounter and the Making of the Yoruba*. Bloomington: Indiana University Press.

RANGER, TERENCE (1995). *Are We Not Also Men? The Samkange Family and African Politics in Zimbabwe 1920–1964*. London: James Currey.

RAYMOND, ALLAN (1976). 'I Fear God and Honour the King: John Wesley and the American Revolution'. *Church History* 45/3.

SANDERS, THOMAS G. (1964). *Protestant Concepts of Church and State: Historical Backgrounds and Approaches for the Future*. New York: Holt, Rinehart, & Winston.

SANNEH, LAMIN (1983). *West African Christianity: The Religious Impact*. London: Hurst & Co.

SEMMEL, BERNARD (1973). *The Methodist Revolution*. New York: Basic Books.

SHORTER, AYLWARD (1997). *Toward a Theology of Inculturation*. Maryknoll: Orbis.

WALLS, ANDREW F. (1970). 'A Christian Experiment: The Early Sierra Leone'. In G. J. Cumming (ed.), *The Mission of the Church and the Propagation of the Faith*. Studies in Church History 6. Cambridge: Cambridge University Press.

WEBER, THEODORE R. (2001). *Politics in the Order of Salvation: Transforming Wesleyan Political Ethics*. Nashville: Kingswood.

CHAPTER 42

....

METHODISM AND CULTURE

....

DAVID W. BEBBINGTON

THE gospel, according to Andrew Walls, is the 'prisoner and liberator of culture'. Walls, perhaps the pre-eminent Methodist missiologist of the last half-century, is suggesting by this dictum that expressions of the Christian religion are both heavily conditioned by their circumstances and powerfully capable of transforming their settings. Believers are simultaneously subject to what Walls calls the 'indigenizing' principle, the desire to live as Christians in their own societies, and the 'pilgrim' principle, the willingness to identify with members of the family of faith in other times and places. They therefore accept a great deal of the way of life around them, blending it into their religious practice, and yet are likely to break with part of the accustomed lifestyle because of allegiance to distinctive Christian principles (Walls 1996: 7–9).

For historical purposes, however, this twofold model can usefully be adapted to a threefold pattern of how Methodism has interacted with culture. In the first place, the adherents of the movement have regularly been moulded by their context, a process corresponding to part of Walls's indigenizing principle. Methodists have adapted to their surrounding culture, merging their attitudes with the common assumptions of their societies, as when, during the nineteenth century, they gradually dropped their objections to reading fiction. Secondly, they have frequently challenged the stance of their contemporaries, criticizing rather than accommodating themselves to prevailing habits. This dimension of their practice, closely related to Walls's pilgrim principle, is well illustrated by the commitment of twentieth-century Methodists to the temperance movement. Thirdly, they have repeatedly proved a creative element in the societies they have inhabited, adapting existing forms of behaviour and establishing entirely novel ones. This aspect of the Methodist role, partly indigenizing (because they forged fresh bonds with the host culture) but also partly pilgrim (because they helped to Christianize it), can easily be overlooked, but it was historically important, not least in the evolution of the peoples receiving missionaries during the nineteenth and twentieth centuries. Methodism was responsive to its setting and often willing to challenge custom, but it was also an innovative force in many lands.

This chapter attempts to analyse the relations between gospel and culture in these three respects. It takes for granted the way in which Walls, as a missiologist, uses the word 'culture', as a term for the mixture of patterns of behaviour and perceptions of reality that constitute the human as opposed to the natural environment. This usage, normal in anthropology, is very broad, including the full range of expressions of social life. It therefore encompasses other and narrower applications of the word. On the one hand it takes in popular culture, whether the traditional forms encountered by John Wesley in the eighteenth century or the modern types generated by the mass media in the twenty-first. Methodism sometimes showed an affinity for the customs of the people, often proved capable of denouncing them unsparingly and at times itself generated fresh folkways. On the other hand, the broad anthropological approach incorporates high culture, whether art or architecture, music or literature. Currents of fashion in these areas affected Methodism more than has usually been recognized. So, while addressing questions arising from the widest interpretation of the phenomenon of culture, this chapter explores aspects of both the popular and the high varieties. Its central concern is with Methodism in Britain and the United States, but it also considers case-studies of other lands where the denominational family's missionaries ventured. It tries to discover how the gospel in its Methodist form interacted with culture in this diverse sense.

It may begin with the popular culture that E. P. Thompson depicted as under threat from Methodism in England. Thompson celebrated what he called 'plebeian culture', the inherited customs of the common people of the eighteenth century with their respect for fairness, their strain of neighbourliness, and their rough but vibrant ways. Methodism, according to Thompson, was its inveterate enemy, trying to impose a form of psychological warping that would turn the masses into the disciplined workforce of industrial capitalism (Thompson 1963). In reality, however, there was far more of a bond between early Methodism, whether in England or America, and popular culture than Thompson allows. Early modern England had possessed a deeply ingrained sense of the supernatural (Walsham 1999), and it survived into the eighteenth century to mesh readily with the message of Wesley's helpers. Thus in west Cornwall, where Methodism enjoyed huge success, it was widely believed that there existed a shadowy local spirit called Bucca who had to be propitiated if fisherman were to expect success (Bottrell 1873: 246). This openness to the supernatural smoothed the path for the reception of a gospel involving divine intervention in human life. The early preachers frequently saw visions, discerned portents, and marked providences. Thus Lorenzo Dow, an eccentric but charismatic American who took camp meetings to Britain, once accurately foretold the death of a giddy girl who laughed during one of his sermons (Woolsey 1852: 123–4). The travelling preachers who shared a cosmology of signs and wonders with their public were not set apart by social distance. They relied for hospitality on the homes of the poor. When they moved on to other preaching stations, evangelistic work was sustained in the same cottages. In many the woman of the household took the lead in providing a haven from the troubling social changes of the era (Valenze 1985). Methodism displayed a definite affinity for much of the popular culture of early industrial England and early national America.

Nevertheless Methodists showed a fierce antagonism towards much of the value system of the times. Card playing, gambling, horse racing, and cock fighting—some of the chief foci of male sociability—came under their censure. Dancing was condemned, especially because it exposed women and men alike to the risk of sexual immorality. Likewise the denominational magazine in England presumed in 1799 that 'no Methodist attends a theatre' (Rosman 1984: 76). In the early years dress was also subject to close scrutiny. 'Give no tickets', the *Discipline* of 1784 instructed the American preachers, 'to any that wear High-Heads, enormous Bonnets, Ruffles or Rings.' The countercultural stance extended to opposing slavery outright: 'we all agreed', wrote Francis Asbury about the 1783 annual conference, 'in the spirit of African liberty' (Wigger 1998: 101, 139). The decay of that conviction in American Methodism during the early nineteenth century formed one of the most striking instances of accommodation to prevailing norms (Heyrman 1997). Yet a willingness to resist customary practice persisted as a powerful feature of Methodist witness long afterwards. In the area of strong drink, in particular, there were stern attitudes. As soon as the first American state, Maine, adopted prohibition, the Methodist Episcopal Church issued tracts describing the new measure as 'a Christian law' (*Christian Advocate*, 27 January 1853: 14). The Primitive Methodists of England turned early to teetotalism, but during the 1850s beer was still the normal drink at Wesleyan quarterly meetings (Penman 1916: 26). In the 1870s, however, Wesleyan opinion veered in favour of total abstinence and entrenched Methodist policy became hostile to all forms of alcohol for much of the twentieth century. There were annual temperance sermons; Bands of Hope encouraged the young to take the pledge; and on both sides of the Atlantic the struggle against the saloon bar turned into a formidable political campaign (Brake 1974). A gulf opened between the poor who liked a drink, and the Methodists who abominated hard liquor. Gospel and culture in its popular dimension were in constant collision.

Yet Methodism also played a creative role in the life of the people. The watch night service on Christmas Eve, partly designed to replace noisy revelling in the street, gained a secure place in the hearts of the community at large. The class meeting and love feast, two institutions borrowed from the Moravians, became treasured possessions. 'Where else', asked the American Edmund S. Janes, 'is found such Christian intimacy, such stated seasons of fellowship, such familiar conversation on religious experience, such spiritual sympathy, so much helping of each others [sic] faith, and such watching over one another in love?' (Wigger 1998: 88). So entrenched in popular mores did the class meeting become that the Chartists of England, working-class political activists of the 1830s and 1840s, copied it as a means of fostering cohesion and raising money. Perhaps the most striking instance of Methodist creativity, however, was in music. The hymns of Charles Wesley formed a major contribution to the life of the English-speaking nations. His brother was keen to ensure that singing was done properly. 'Do not bawl', John Wesley urged his followers in the introduction to *Sacred Melody* (1761), 'so as to be heard above or distinct from the rest of the congregation' (Seed 1907: 191). The Methodist people heeded their founder in paying particular attention to song. At a Sheffield Wesleyan chapel, for instance, there was a choir from its opening, and the leading singers originally received a stipend. The music was accompanied down to 1860 by nothing but a cello, which was solemnly transferred when the congregation moved premises. Some of the chief early members, it was said, were attracted by the excellent singing (ibid. 183, 196). The major musical events of several northern English towns, such as annual performances of Handel's *Messiah*, owed their origins to the musical enthusiasts of the Methodist chapels. In such ways as this the movement played a part in the enrichment of popular culture.

Nor was Methodism divorced from developments in high culture. John Wesley, it is increasingly appreciated, should be seen as an Enlightenment thinker. It is true that he showed a credulous side; but so did most of the other illuminati of the eighteenth century. Wesley had no sense that reason was the enemy of faith. 'We ... earnestly exhort', he wrote in 1743, 'all who seek after true religion to use all the reason which God hath given them in searching out the things of God' (Wesley 1975: 56). Wesley displayed many of the most characteristic views of the age of reason. He disdained metaphysics as a species of obscurantism, insisting on the need for simplicity in philosophy. Equally he held a high estimate of experience, contending that faith was analogous to one of the five senses (Dreyer 1983). Empiricism, in fact, was his lodestar, inducing him to pursue the experiments in the therapeutic uses of electricity that he recommended in *Primitive Physic*. Wesley, like other progressive thinkers of his day, was pragmatic on a variety of issues, adopting field preaching, allowing female ministry, and in 1784, though only a priest, ordaining men for service in America. The moral emphasis of the age was echoed in his constant summons to go on to perfection. And the high expectations of the future evident in the idea of progress emerging in the later eighteenth century were paralleled in his postmillennial confidence that the evangelical revival would usher in 'the latter day glory'. The intellectual stance of John Wesley was to a remarkable extent that of his enlightened contemporaries.

Methodism became a vehicle for the dissemination of Enlightenment attitudes. Richard Watson, whose teaching moulded the minds of generations of Methodist preachers, appealed to John Locke on the first page of his *Theological Institutes* (Watson 1836: 1). Although the early preachers received no institutional theological training, one of Wesley's men in England claimed to have read every one of the evangelist's more than four hundred works and some of the American itinerants wrote of their 'thirst for knowledge' that was slaked by intense reading (Telford n.d.: vi. 148; Wigger 1998: 72). Methodism was engaged not only in the propagation of the gospel but also in a civilizing mission. In England humble society members would meet on weekday evenings to instruct their unlettered friends in how to sing the Sunday hymns, and by such means literacy spread (Church 1949: 49, 46). In America preachers were allowed a discount on their sales of Methodist literature, sometimes earning twice as much from books as from their regular salary (Nall 1964: 143). In the single year of 1817 on the Limestone circuit of the Ohio Conference, Benjamin Lakin sold 57 catechisms, 39 hymn books, 18 abridgements of Thomas à Kempis, 14 lives of Hester A. Rogers, 14 copies of the *Discipline*, 14 volumes of John Nelson's journal, and a great deal more (Richey 1999: 117). The absorption of such a deluge of literature made Methodists notable in many a region for their devotion to self-culture. They were in the forefront of founding Sunday schools and soon played a prominent part in promoting common schools. In Canada, for example, a Methodist minister, Egerton Ryerson, became superintendent of schools for the whole of Ontario between 1844 and 1876, putting its public education system on a firm basis (Sissons 1937–47). For all its early exuberance, Methodism was a movement that, in the spirit of the Enlightenment, was devoted to spreading an appreciation of learning.

The legacy of the Enlightenment coloured the missionary enterprise of Methodism. The cosmopolitan thinkers of the eighteenth century and those they swayed were notably lacking in a sense of cultural relativism. One of their most cherished axioms was the constancy of human nature, so that, in their view, people in different lands were fundamentally the same. The instructions issued to Wesleyan missionaries in 1825 and their subsequent amplifications were based on this assumption. While insisting on the missionaries' duty to advance in piety and 'to increase your stock of useful knowledge', the guidelines offered no advice on how to understand the customs of other lands. In the same spirit Jabez Bunting, the senior secretary of the Wesleyan Methodist Missionary Society, insisted that every missionary must be prepared to go anywhere. John Hunt possessed a strong sense of call to Africa, but Bunting, telling him that in their day God gave nobody a call to a particular locality, dispatched him to the South Seas (Gunson 1978: 339, 101). Likewise in America preachers were transferred frequently between white and Indian circuits so that they had little chance of developing an affinity for the culture of any particular tribe (Forbes 1993: 219). Once Hunt reached his destination, he rejoiced in the utility of love feasts and class meetings. 'We find', he reported in 1844, 'these means are as applicable to Feejee as to England. "Methodism for ever!" ' (Gunson 1978: 128). If their own distinctive institutions were universally valid, Methodists also supposed that the Western packaging of the gospel possessed merits on an absolute scale. Like other evangelical missionaries during the early and middle years of the nineteenth century, Wesleyans believed that the delivery of the gospel must not be delayed until 'savages' were civilized, but equally they held that the gospel would inevitably bring the advantages of civilization in its train (Stanley 2001). Hoping to rescue those whom they evangelized from barbarism, Methodists often lacked the sensitivity ideally required in cross-cultural mission.

Nevertheless it would be mistaken to conclude that Methodist missions were primarily a destructive force. It is widely believed that indigenous cultures, existing from time immemorial, were demeaned, truncated, or even eradicated by the missionary movement. Stephen S. Kim, for example, has written of the 'iconoclasm of "heathen" culture' displayed by early Methodist missionaries to Korea. The customary Korean veneration of ancestors, he argues, was unnecessarily attacked because of an 'identification of Christianity with American civilization' (Kim 1998: 220, 224). The premise of such critiques is frequently that traditional cultures embodied timeless values and so had previously been immune to alteration. That supposition, however, is open to question, because in reality most societies throughout the world were subject to constant flux, being remodelled from inside and modified from outside over the centuries. At any point in time the issue was not whether there should be change but what form change should take. The modifications ushered in by Methodist missions, because of the attachment to a single scale of values derived from the Enlightenment that has just been considered, were sometimes ill-judged and unnecessarily drastic. Yet equally they could be beneficial, introducing innovations that were warmly welcomed and rooting the gospel in local folkways. Two case-studies, of Ghana and Fiji, both lands where Methodism made a large impact, can be used to illustrate the point.

Wesleyan missionaries arrived on the Gold Coast of west Africa, the modern Ghana, in the 1830s. In preaching the gospel they directly denounced beliefs associated with fetishism and they condemned the dancing that they would have censured at home. But, with a certain insensitivity, they went beyond these unavoidable challenges to raise objections to other practices. It was the custom on the Gold Coast to contribute to the cost of non-Christian funeral rites for fellow members of a clan, a useful way of spreading the expenses over more than the immediate family. George Wrigley, who served as the second Wesleyan missionary from his arrival in 1836 until his early death the following year, was asked how believers should behave when called upon to pay their share. His unequivocal reply was that church members could not contribute and remain Christians. Ignoring the latitude on such matters suggested by the New Testament's discussion of food sacrificed to idols, he attacked such 'vain and foolish customs' (Bartels 1965: 26).

As in most parts of Africa, there was also tension over marriage. Polygamy was normal on the Gold Coast, but the missionaries required converts to put away all but one of their wives. What further rules should be enforced in this minefield of relationships was a matter of debate. Eventually the local synod determined in 1885 that no member should marry a non-Christian; that no woman should marry a man already a husband; and that no polygamist was to be accepted into membership. It was left to superintendents to consider on its merits each case of a wife of a polygamist applying for membership (ibid. 135–6). Once more, although some missionaries were concerned to respect what was called 'native marriage', the more rigorous were inclined to ride roughshod over deeply entrenched local custom. In the case of funerals, and sometimes in the case of marriage, there was a failure to give indigenous culture its due.

Yet Ghana also provides evidence of some of the ways in which Methodism could contribute to local culture. Western practices were perceived by the people of the region as hugely beneficial. Church plantations near chapels showed the value of cultivating cotton, arrowroot, olives, vines, cinnamon, black pepper, mango, and ginger. The techniques of the carpenters and bricklayers introduced from the coast to erect chapels in the interior were copied by the builders of private houses. Agriculture and architecture, in the eyes of the locals, were transformed for the better (ibid. 69, 54). Perhaps the greatest revolution was in education. Schools sprang up beside the chapels, training children in literacy skills and sometimes in elementary accounting and translation from the local language of Fante into English. Wrigley learned Fante as soon as he arrived, being able to preach in the language within a year. He translated the catechism, the Ten Commandments, and portions of the New Testament into Fante before his untimely death; the first Fante primer was printed in 1863; and by the 1880s several titles were available in the tongue of the people. The effect, as in many other lands, was to generate a written literature where none had previously existed and so to preserve some of the riches of Fante culture (ibid. 62, 66, 22, 79, 96). Methodism inspired equally important developments in music. Singing bands from the Sunday schools accompanied preachers to outlying villages. The children's Band of Hope generated vernacular singing that was taken up by skilled choirs. The traditional African 'lyric', a type of solo and chorus in free rhythm including improvisation, counterpoint, and conclusion in a minor key, was retained and elaborated in the church (ibid. 135, 82, 234). As in the English-speaking countries, Methodism's creativity was specially marked in song.

The second case-study, the Fiji archipelago in the South Seas, was also reached by Wesleyan missionaries in the 1830s. By 1874, the year the islands were transferred to British rule, there were over 25,000 members and five times as many in attendance. Methodism had become the Fijian folk church, closely identified with land, chief, and people. Even though the substance of the social fabric was Christianized intact, various customs came under the censure of the missionaries. Polygamy was challenged: one prominent chief put away seventy-eight wives on conversion. The semi-naked appearance of the people was superseded by wrap-around clothes. So closely was the apparel identified with the new faith that pagan tribesmen demanded that converts should return to the old ways by calling upon them to 'strip or die' (Thornley 2002: 508, 176, 350). Missionaries successfully opposed boxing and wrestling but found it impossible to extinguish dancing, which persisted in church life (Gunson 1978: 182; Forman 1996: 9). They also found the Fijian addiction to *kava*, a mild stimulant, a persistent problem. 'What opium is to China', wrote one of them, '*kava* is to Fiji.' In the 1870s expulsions for intoxication equalled those for every other cause put together (Thornley 2002: 187–8, 484). Work on Sunday was banned, though the strict sabbatarian practice seems to have owed more to the zeal of the Fijians than to the sternness of the missionaries (Forman 1996: 7). The pagan custom of amputating the fingers of the dead was abandoned, probably largely spontaneously, and so was cannibalism. John Hunt, a leading missionary in the islands, noted in his journal in 1844 that a recent victim of the internecine wars was brought to his island 'to be eaten' (Thornley 2002: 83; Kanailagi 1996: 68). Ten years later, by contrast, pagans were astonished when a newly converted chief returned bodies to his enemies rather than consuming them (Thornley 2002: 73). It is not surprising, in the light of the various practices under assault, that the unconverted peoples saw the new religion as an agent of destruction. In a broader perspective, however, it might be thought that some of this transformation was a welcome change.

Methodism also acted creatively in Fiji. Missionaries encouraged the production of coconut oil, which was transported to Sydney in a vessel called the *John Wesley* and sold to defray some of the costs of the mission. Elaborate churches were erected in stone (ibid. 228, 359). So, as in Ghana, there were developments in agriculture and architecture that the inhabitants greeted with delight. Some of the novelties were patterned on Western models: that was true, for example, of the annual missionary meetings, when the Fijian women gleefully wore new clothes, ribbons, and hats. Other fresh practices, however, had the authentic flavour of the South Seas. That was true, for instance, of the feasts that normally followed morning service (ibid. 489; Forman 1996: 8). The language was turned into script for the first time by the early missionaries, with the New Testament being issued in Fijian in 1847 and the Old Testament following in 1865. The mission promoted education in the vernacular to enable the rising generation to read their Bibles. By 1874 nearly 50,000 children were in school (Thornley 2002: 192–3, 191, 508). And there was inventiveness in the area of music. Traditional Fijian chants were associated with the calling of spirits and so discouraged, but a visitor to the islands in 1849 observed that Methodist services were partly chanted in the old manner, sometimes inducing pagans to come in (Jakes 1996: 116; Thornley 2002: 24). Although one missionary spoke disparagingly of schools teaching 'unnecessary songs and ridiculous dances', instruction in singing became a regular feature of education. Another missionary commented that 'Singing is peculiarly a happy employment to the Fijian, in fact at certain times it seems to take the form of meditation with them' (ibid. 353, 191, 241). In Fiji, as in Ghana, music was a dimension of life in which Methodism successfully promoted the merger of gospel and culture.

Cultural innovation, however, was not confined to the mission field. Another powerful current in Western civilization impinged on religion during the nineteenth century. The new mood, Romanticism, developed in pioneering literary circles, especially in Germany, from the last years of the eighteenth century. In Britain its most celebrated exponents were the Lake Poets, William Wordsworth and S. T. Coleridge, and the historical novelist Sir Walter Scott. In America its early champions were the transcendentalists around R. W. Emerson. The term 'Romantic', however, is used here not in a sense restricted to those generations of authors, but rather it encompasses the whole cultural wave that spread out from them, enveloping first some of the highly educated and then a slowly increasing proportion of the population as the nineteenth century wore on. The preferences of the era of Enlightenment were gradually—but by no means entirely—supplanted over the decades. Instead of the Enlightenment exaltation of reason there was an emphasis on will, emotion, and intuition. Simplicity was replaced by mystery, the artificial by the natural, and the novel by the traditional. The new taste underlay the appeal to history of the Oxford Movement in the Church of England and the ornate display of Ultramontane ritual in the Roman Catholic Church. Coleridge was a major inspiration for other Anglicans such as F. D. Maurice who shaped subsequent Broad Church theology. By mid-century members of other denominations such as the American Congregationalist Horace Bushnell began to be deeply swayed. So Romanticism exerted a powerful influence over the direction of Christian thought in the Victorian age (Bebbington 2005: 139–72).

What was initially most striking about Methodism was its stout resistance to the trends of thought associated with Romanticism. Daniel Whedon, editor in America of the *Methodist Quarterly Review* from 1856 until his death in 1885, took the stemming of the Romantic tide as his mission. The notion that human beings grow organically like flowers or trees, a commonplace of the novel body of ideas, had been turned by Bushnell, in his *Discourses on Christian Nurture* (1847), into the notion that families should enable their children to develop Christian character without any sudden change of direction. In 1861 Whedon denounced the second edition of Bushnell's work for ignoring the cruciality of radical conversion. Whedon's continuing allegiance to the older way of looking at the world, derived from the Enlightenment, is plain in a diatribe that was published after his death. He wanted to uphold the appeal to 'Christian FACTS' for which William Paley, the Anglican apologist of the late eighteenth century, had been celebrated: 'we would not give one ounce of Paley's evidential sense for the entire volume of transcendental gas that exhilarates the brains of . . . glowing intuitionalists' (Scott 1993: 283 n., 284). Likewise in England W. B. Pope, the author of the most authoritative systematic exposition of Methodist theology of the century, took pains to rebut both Coleridge and Maurice (Langford 1998: 63). The refusal to draw on the theological currents flowing from the Romantic fountainhead is particularly evident in eschatological attitudes. Romanticism had revived the premillennial teaching that the second coming of Jesus was imminent, but Methodists adhered to the postmillennial doctrine that there would be a steady improvement of earthly conditions before the return of the Lord. Thus Mark Guy Pearse, a prominent English Methodist preacher, had 'a firm belief that the world was getting better' (Unwin and Telford 1930: 233). Still in 1914 at a representative premillennialist conference in Chicago only 8 out of 269 delegates were Methodists (Spann 2005: 206 n.). For many years few Methodists were willing to modify the fusion of theology with Enlightenment assumptions that had marked their founder.

Only a few isolated individuals found it possible to combine strong Romantic traits with Methodist commitment. One was James Smetham, a painter in the high Victorian years who was at the heart of Methodism. His father was a minister; his brother, two uncles, three cousins, two brothers-in-law, and a nephew were either travelling or local preachers. He himself was a class leader and a Sunday school teacher. But he was also an artist, producing sketches, oils, and watercolours in a variety of genres, his atmospheric pastoral landscapes being considered his greatest achievement. He aimed to blend his Methodism with his talent, holding, as he put it in 1853, that 'the business of art should be to create spiritual perceptions'. Like most contributors to the visual arts of his generation, Smetham's œuvre was moulded by Romantic influences. He was deeply swayed by Nathaniel Hawthorne and Edgar Allan Poe; he loved the poetry of Shelley, Keats, and Tennyson; he praised George Eliot's writing because it was 'all NATURE'. Admiring J. M. W. Turner's artistic accomplishments, he was on close terms with John Ruskin, the greatest of Victorian art critics, and closer terms with Dante Gabriel Rossetti, the Pre-Raphaelite painter. Smetham shared the medieval enthusiasms of so many creative artists, taking particular pleasure in illuminated manuscripts. His feeling for medieval themes was not necessarily reciprocated by his Methodist patrons. A painting of the Saxon poet Caedmon singing to an abbess and nuns, though sold to a prosperous layman, was dismembered by the purchaser, Caedmon being retained but the popish figures being discarded. Altogether Smetham possessed a love for what he once called 'the ROMANTIC mood'. He was therefore prepared to break with some of Wesley's more rational recommendations such as the preacher's discountenancing of play for children. But Smetham, who suffered from an obsessional personality disorder, found it acutely difficult to adjust his profession as a painter to his allegiance as a Christian. In 1863 he wrote that 'to be at once Artist and Methodist is a puzzling position in the universe'. He refused to court art critics and potential buyers, considering their circles 'worldly', and so never achieved the breakthrough to celebrity that he craved. Becoming chronically depressed, he was ultimately classed as insane. If Smetham illustrates that Methodism could be combined with avant-garde creativity in the Victorian years, it also confirms that the task was fraught with tension (Casteras 1995: 71, 65, 120, 49).

Social change in Western lands was drastically transforming Methodism at the same epoch. The growing wealth of Britain, the first industrial nation, and the rising prosperity of America, by the later nineteenth century overtaking Britain in many fields of enterprise, meant that Methodism soon contained a wealthy commercial elite. Men such as Samuel Budgett, a Bristol grocer, could amass huge fortunes and, remembering the advice of Wesley, give much of it away in philanthropy. Budgett's achievement was celebrated in an oft-reprinted biography by William Arthur, a prominent Wesleyan minister, called *The Successful Merchant* (1852). Likewise the American *Cyclopedia of Methodism* (1878) included 148 lay members of the Methodist Episcopal Church (North) who had made fortunes in business (Marti 1993: 267). The managerial style of the movement, allowing immense scope for lay initiative, made it attractive to men keen to imitate the successful. The Methodist artisans of Philadelphia in the early nineteenth century were notably inclined to upward social mobility and their equivalents in Stoke-on-Trent Primitive Methodism often bettered themselves in life later in the century (Wigger 1998: 175; Field 1977: 209). The result of these processes was what historians have summed up as the rise of respectability. In the 1820s the Sunday-school publications of American Methodism confined themselves to religious matters, making no mention of questions of gentility, but by the 1850s they were endorsing refined behaviour. Little girls in one Sunday school now received a penny every time they remembered to wear a bonnet (Bushman 1992: 321; Long 2001: 283). The *Ladies' Repository*, published by the Methodists of New York from 1841, announced in 1850 that, alongside 'pure religion', it aimed to promote 'good sense, sound knowledge, correct taste' (Gillespie 1993: 257). Methodists were rising in the social scale and increasingly keen to advertise their superior standing.

This steady *embourgeoisement* powerfully reinforced the appreciation of newer cultural values associated with Romantic sensibility. Samuel Budgett's oldest son, James, was a leading patron of James Smetham, encouraging and purchasing his art. A Wesleyan minister who was a close friend of Smetham's, Frederick Jobson, was the author of a book on chapel and Sunday-school architecture that commended the Gothic style (Casteras 1995: 143, 73–4). In 1855 the first Gothic Revival structure erected by American Methodists was built as Christ Church, Pittsburgh (Marti 1993: 266). By 1858, even in Australia, the editor of the Methodist newspaper expressed a strong admiration for Gothic (*Christian Advocate and Wesleyan Record*, 21 September 1858: 43). In America the Gothic phase was superseded before the end of the century by a general preference for the Romanesque style, with solid masonry and theatrical auditoriums, so that when, in 1891, Christ Church, Pittsburgh, was replaced after a fire, it was rebuilt in the new fashion. Although the fresh idiom still had the medieval inspiration so characteristic of those swayed by Romanticism, it possessed the monumentality of commercial and public buildings

(Rowe 1997: 118; Kilde 2002: 107). In the grand churches of the cities, whether Gothic or Romanesque, the pattern of worship became much more elaborate and liturgically structured. Thus at Trinity Methodist Episcopal Church, Denver, in 1888 the service might contain an organ voluntary, a duet, a tenor solo with chorus, a choral arrangement, a male quartet, a responsive reading, a recitation of the Apostles' Creed, and a unison prayer. It is no surprise that a woman social worker visiting the church felt herself out of place because she wore no kid gloves (Kilde 2002: 137–8, 144). The spontaneous cries of old-time Methodist worship had been abandoned, in deference, it was said, to 'the opinions and tastes of so-called refined and cultivated society' (*Christian Advocate*, 14 January 1892: 17). The worship of Methodism, in content and setting, had been transformed.

Theology followed suit around the opening of the twentieth century, abandoning Daniel Whedon's resistance to Romantic trends. In England, John Scott Lidgett, deeply influenced by F. D. Maurice, published *The Spiritual Principle of the Atonement* (1897). Despite the title, Lidgett's book subordinated the cross to the incarnation in a way previously customary among Anglicans swayed by Romantic feeling; earlier Methodist discussion of the atonement as an exercise of divine sovereignty was dismissed as mechanical; and the stress was now on the personal role of God as Father (Turberfield 2003: 46–55). In a very similar way in America, Borden Parker Bowne, whose thought was moulded by the idealist school of philosophy bound up with Romanticism, treated the cross as an episode of the incarnation; he constantly criticized previous coverage of the theme as tainted by 'the mechanical'; and he rejoiced in a new and stronger grasp of the Fatherhood of God. Bowne might have been speaking for Lidgett in celebrating 'a language of poetry, of conscience, of emotion, of aspiration, of religion, as well as a language of logical understanding' (Bowne 1909: 65). Both Lidgett and Bowne were accused of heresy, an indication of the revolutionary nature of their views, but an approximation to their stance soon became popular in their denominations. Nine of the leading bishops of the Methodist Episcopal Church (North) in the 1920s had been students of Bowne (Spann 2005: 201 n.). In that decade there was a flowering of concern for the aesthetic in American Methodism, with a writer published by the denominational press arguing for high ideals in music and liturgy and recommending that each church should appoint a 'Minister of Fine Arts in Religion' (Harper 1924: 64). In England the Fellowship of the Kingdom promoted a broader and higher version of Methodist teaching than had previously been current. Robert Newton Flew, one of its leading lights, urged in 1918 that, by contrast with the early Methodist preachers, their modern successors should see 'a vision of God affirming the world as good, as delighting in the colour and gaiety and many-sidedness of human life, ceaselessly operative as in Nature so among men . . . and strengthening all impulses after the pure and true and beautiful' (Wakefield 1971: 44). Much of the denominational leadership on both sides of the Atlantic in the twentieth century possessed a world-view that was as Romantic as it was Methodist.

From that matrix there emerged some remarkable creative achievements catering for a mass market. In the arts, where there was less resistance than in theology, Romantic assumptions had made headway at an earlier date. In the field of literature, once shunned as worldly, Methodists already played a significant part before the nineteenth century was over. Although there was still much denunciation of popular novels ('Fetid fiction ruins girls', declared the *Michigan Christian Advocate* in 1907), some Methodist writers had determined to expel the bad by means of the good. Edward Eggleston's *The Circuit Rider* (1874) drew on its author's experience of the Methodist ministry to produce a memorable heroic tale (Herbst 2006: 242, 247). In England, two Cornish brothers who began in the ministry, Silas and Joseph Hocking, together with their sister Salome, composed altogether over two hundred novels between the 1870s and the 1930s. If they often lapsed into sentiment and the melodramatic, that formula appealed to the Romantic taste that was permeating a broad public (Kent 2002). In the visual arts there was Frank O. Salisbury, a specialist in portraits, book illustrations, and the recording of scenes of historic pageantry. Salisbury enjoyed a friendship with the British royal family and his portrait of F. D. Roosevelt was selected to hang in the White House after the president's death. A devout Methodist, Salisbury cast his thought into a religio-aesthetic mould: 'what is beauty', he asked in 1937, 'but the assurance that we might approach the precincts of God?' (McMurray 2003: 216). In film, the potent new art form of the twentieth century, perhaps the most enterprising pioneer in Britain was J. Arthur Rank, who was also treasurer of the Methodist Home Mission Department from 1933 to his death in 1972. His early promotion of films was said to have been the result of hearing a bad sermon and looking for a more effective evangelistic medium. By the end of the Second World War he dominated the British cinema industry (Wakelin 1996: 215, 42). These British Methodists helped to form the popular culture of the twentieth century.

The Methodism of the United States played a similar role, but in certain instances was closer to the cutting edge of cultural innovation. Among the fine church buildings erected during the inter-war years, none is more striking than the Boston Avenue Church in Tulsa, Oklahoma, of 1927–9. Tulsa's novel oil wealth allowed the church's minister, John A. Rice, to encourage his building committee to be adventurous. Discarding the original architect's plans, the committee selected Adah Robinson, a Tulsa art professor, and Bruce Goff of the architects Rush, Endicott, & Rush for the commission. The result, costing the huge sum of $1 1/2 million, was a steel and concrete structure clad in limestone. The massive building occupies the whole of a large city block, contains 125 rooms and boasts a tower rising 280 feet into the sky. It is truly Methodist, for among the equestrian statues over the south porch Jesus is flanked by John Wesley and Francis Asbury, but it is also wholly modern, for its design, consistently carried through exterior and interior, is the art deco style of the radio age (Brodrick 1958: 202–6; Howe 2003: 302–5). Equally novel was the earliest phase of gospel music. Charles Albert Tindley, the African-American pastor of East Calvary Methodist Episcopal Church, Philadelphia, for thirty-three years from 1900, was an able preacher who catered for his largely middle-class black congregation by preparing songs for church concerts. Taking up traditional themes of black oppression as well as Christian imagery, the songs included 'I shall overcome some day', the anthem of the civil rights movement. Published as a collection, *New Songs of Paradise* (1916), his compositions were to inspire others to launch the career of gospel music as a distinct popular genre (Lincoln and Mamiya 1990: 360–1; Southern 1997: 457–8). In their different ways, Boston Avenue Church and Tindley's songs marked the opening of a new cultural epoch.

The novel cultural currents of the twentieth century, in some measure displacing the legacy of the Enlightenment and Romanticism, have been summed up as 'Expressivism'. In a variety of fields, starting with art and literature around the opening of the century, it became fashionable to express whatever was in the mind, including the newly discovered subconscious. The fresh temper affected bodies such as Methodism first through the Oxford Group movement led by Frank Buchman, an American Lutheran minister who specialized in youth evangelism. The Group encouraged adherents to be totally frank with each other about their failings. Although Methodists were sometimes put off by the Group's dropping of hymns for the sake of appearing modern, in the 1930s a number of younger leaders in English congregations were attracted by its insistence on the need for conversion (Wakefield 1966: 14). For a while there was a Methodist version of the movement called the 'Cambridge Group' (Raynor 1934). By the 1960s the attitudes associated with Expressivism spread to a mass audience, transmitted particularly by popular music. The counter-culture born in that decade became dominant among members of a new generation of young people. The religious equivalent was charismatic renewal, the injection into the historic denominations of an openness to the work of the Holy Spirit previously confined to Pentecostalists. Two English Methodists considered the glossolalia typical of the early phases of the movement to be a form of self-expression comparable to abstract art. Arthur Rank was among those drawn in, but by 1976 the magazine representing renewal enthusiasts in British Methodism had attained a circulation of only 6,000 (Bebbington 1993: 248, 246; Wakelin 1996: 207–8). In America the transfer of Oral Roberts, the most prominent evangelist identified with spiritual renewal, to the United Methodist Church in 1968 was a great boost to the charismatic movement in the denomination, but a decade later the American magazine for Methodist charismatics had no more than 12,000 subscribers (Girolimon 1995: 94, 100). In the relatively few Methodist congregations where renewal put down permanent roots on either side of the Atlantic, the most striking characteristic by the end of the century was upbeat music. Churches adopting this style had discovered a formula for appealing to young people formed by the culture of the late twentieth century.

In summary, it is clear that the interaction of Methodism with its surrounding culture has passed through many phases. Early Methodists had far tighter bonds with popular patterns of life than has been suggested, and, although they were forward in criticizing folkways that fell short of gospel standards, they also made original contributions to their communities, especially through song. The Enlightenment attitudes learned from John Wesley were disseminated through the movement, promoting a devotion to learning but fostering a blindness to cultural relativism. Hence the missionaries could display insensitivity to local traditions, and yet Methodism brought enduring benefits to lands such as Ghana and Fiji. When during the nineteenth century Enlightenment assumptions started to be undermined by Romanticism, Methodists, except in unusual cases, initially proved resistant. The rise of respectability, however, reinforced the appeal of the new taste, which made headway in architecture, worship, and eventually in theology. Methodists contributed in significant ways to fiction, art, and film and also, in America, to innovative architecture and music. The Expressivist idiom of the twentieth century did exert an appeal, but only to limited numbers. So Methodism was moulded by the successive waves of influence shaping Western civilization. In addition it mounted sustained criticism of what it considered wrong with its host culture, whether at home or abroad. But it also proved a creative force, helping to generate new cultural forms with a distinctly Christian aspect. Methodism, we may conclude, was the liberator as well as the prisoner of culture.

Suggested Reading

BEBBINGTON (1993).

CASTERAS (1995).

HEMPTON, DAVID (2005). *Methodism: Empire of the Spirit.* Yale: Yale University Press.

RICHEY, RUSSELL E., ROWE, KENNETH E., and SCHMIDT, JEAN MILLER (eds.) (1993). *Perspectives on American Methodism: Interpretive Essays.* Nashville: Kingswood.

ROSMAN, DOREEN (1984). *Evangelicals and Culture.* Aldershot: Ashgate.

THORNLEY (2002).

WALLS (1996).

WIGGER, JOHN H. (1998).

—— and HATCH, NATHAN O. (eds.) (2001). *Methodism and the Shaping of American Culture.* Nashville: Abingdon.

References

BARTELS, FRANCIS L. (1965). *The Roots of Ghana Methodism.* Cambridge: Cambridge University Press.

BEBBINGTON, DAVID W. (1993). *Evangelicalism in Modern Britain: A History from the 1730s to the 1980s.* London: Routledge.

—— (2005). *The Dominance of Evangelicalism: The Age of Spurgeon and Moody*. Leicester: Inter-Varsity Press.

BOTTRELL, WILLIAM (1873). *Traditions and Hearthside Stories of West Cornwall*. 2nd series. Penzance: For the author, by Beare & Son.

BOWNE, BORDEN PARKER (1909). *Studies in Christianity*. Boston: Houghton Mifflin.

BRAKE, GEORGE THOMPSON (1974). *Drink: Ups and Downs of Methodist Attitudes to Temperance*. London: Oliphants.

BRODRICK, ROBERT C. (1958). *Historic Churches of the United States*. New York: Wilfred, Funk.

BUSHMAN, RICHARD L. (1992). *The Refinement of America: Persons, Houses, Cities*. New York: Alfred A. Knopf.

CASTERAS, SUSAN P. (1995). *James Smetham: Artist, Author, Pre-Raphaelite Associate*. Aldershot: Scholars.

Christian Advocate. New York: T. Carlton & Z. Phillips.

Christian Advocate and Wesleyan Record. Sydney: Wesleyan Methodist Book Depot.

CHURCH, LESLIE F. (1949). *More about the Early Methodist People*. London: Epworth.

DREYER, FREDERICK (1983). 'Faith and Experience in the Thought of John Wesley'. *American Historical Review* 88: 12–30.

FIELD, C. D. (1977). 'The Social Structure of English Methodism: Eighteenth–Twentieth Centuries'. *British Journal of Sociology* 28: 199–225.

FORBES, BRUCE DAVID (1993). ' "And Obey God, etc.": Methodism and American Indians'. In Russell E. Richey, Kenneth E. Rowe, and Jean Miller Schmidt (eds.), *Perspectives in American Methodism: Interpretive Essays*. Nashville: Kingswood.

FORMAN, CHARLES W. (1996). 'Methodism in the Pacific and Fiji Context'. In Andrew Thornley and Tauga Vulaono (eds.), *Mai Kea Ki Vei? Stories of Methodism in Fiji and Rotuma, 1835–1995*. Suva: Fiji Methodist Church.

GILLESPIE, JOANNA BOWEN (1993). 'The Emerging Voice of Methodist Women: *The Ladies' Repository*, 1841–61'. In Russell E. Richey, Kenneth E. Rowe, and Jean Miller Schmidt (eds.), *Perspectives on American Methodism*. Nashville: Kingswood.

GIROLIMON, MICHAEL T. (1995). ' "The Charismatic Wiggle": United Methodism's Twentieth-Century Neo-Pentecostal Impulses'. *Pneuma: The Journal of the Society for Pentecostal Studies* 17: 89–103.

GUNSON, NIEL (1978). *Messengers of Grace: Evangelical Missionaries in the South Seas, 1797–1860*. Melbourne: Oxford University Press.

HARPER, EARL ENYEART (1924). *Church Music and Worship*. New York: Abingdon.

HERBST, MATTHEW T. (2006). ' "The Moral Hurt of Novel Reading": Methodism and American Fiction, 1865–1914'. *Methodist History* 44: 239–50.

HEYRMAN, CHRISTINE LEIGH (1997). *Southern Cross: The Beginnings of the Bible Belt*. New York: Alfred A. Knopf.

HOWE, JEFFERY (2003). *Houses of Worship: An Identification Guide to the History and Styles of American Religious Architecture*. San Diego: Thunder Bay.

JAKES, ROBERT L. (1996). 'Surrounded as We Are ... Heb. 12:1–2: Reflections on the Contribution of Fijian Missionaries on Papua New Guinea and the Solomon Islands'. In Andrew Thornley and Tauga Vulaono (eds.), *Mai Kea Ki Vei? Stories of Methodism in Fiji and Rotuma, 1835–1995*. Suva: Fiji Methodist Church.

KANAILAGI, TOMASI (1996). 'The Life and Work of Rev. John Hunt'. In Andrew Thornley and Tauga Vulaono (eds.), *Mai Kea Ki Vei? Stories of Methodism in Fiji and Rotuma, 1835–1995*. Suva: Fiji Methodist Church.

KENT, ALAN (2002). *Pulp Methodism: The Lives & Literature of Silas, Joseph & Salome Hocking: Three Cornish Novelists*. St Austell: Cornish Hillside.

KILDE, JEANNE HALGREN (2002). *When Church Became Theatre: The Transformation of Evangelical Architecture and Worship in Nineteenth-Century America*. New York: Oxford University Press.

KIM, STEPHEN S. (1998). 'Methodist Missions to Korea: A Case Study in Methodist Theology of Mission and Culture'. In William B. Lawrence, Dennis M. Campbell, and Russell E. Richey (eds.), *The People(s) Called Methodist: Forms and Reforms of their Life*. Nashville: Abingdon.

LANGFORD, THOMAS A. (1998). *Practical Divinity*, i. *Theology in the Wesleyan Tradition*. Nashville: Abingdon.

LINCOLN, C. ERIC, and MAMIYA, LAWRENCE H. (1990). *The Black Church in the African American Experience*. Durham, N.C.: Duke University Press.

LONG, KATHRYN T. (2001). 'Consecrated Respectability: Phoebe Palmer and the Refinement of American Methodism'. In Nathan O. Hatch and John H. Wigger (eds.), *Methodism and the Shaping of American Culture*. Nashville: Kingswood.

MCMURRAY, NIGEL (2003). *Frank O. Salisbury: 'Painter Laureate'*. n.p.: n.pub.

MARTI, DONALD B. (1993). 'Rich Methodists: The Rise and Consequences of Lay Philanthropy in the Mid-Nineteenth Century'. In Russell E. Richey, Kenneth E. Rowe, and Jean Miller Schmidt (eds.), *Perspectives on American Methodism*. Nashville: Kingswood.

NALL, T. OTTO (1964). 'Methodist Publishing in Historical Perspective, 1865–1939'. In Emory Stevens Bucke (ed.), *The History of American Methodism*, iii. New York: Abingdon.

PENMAN, GEORGE (1916). *'I Remember'*. London: C. H. Kelly.

RAYNOR, FRANK C. (1934). *The Finger of God: A Book about the Group Movements*. London: Group Publications.

RICHEY, RUSSELL E. (1999). 'Early American Methodism'. In Peter W. Williams (ed.), *Perspectives on American Religion and Culture*. Malden, Mass.: Blackwell.

ROSMAN, DOREEN (1984). *Evangelicals and Culture*. London: Croom Helm.

ROWE, KENNETH E. (1997). 'Redesigning Methodist Churches: Auditorium-Style Sanctuaries and Akron-Plan Sunday Schools in Romanesque Costume, 1875–1925'. In Russell E. Richey, Dennis M. Campbell, and William B. Lawrence (eds.), *Connectionalism: Ecclesiology, Mission and Identity*. Nashville: Abingdon.

SCOTT, LELAND (1993). 'The Concern for Systematic Theology, 1840–70'. In Russell E. Richey, Kenneth E. Rowe, and Jean Miller Schmidt (eds.), *Perspectives on American Methodism: Interpretive Essays*. Nashville: Kingswood.

SEED, T. ALEXANDER (1907). *Norfolk Street Wesleyan Chapel, Sheffield*. London: Jarrold & Sons.

SISSONS, CHARLES BRUCE (1937–47). *Egerton Ryerson: His Life and Letters*. 2 vols. Toronto: Clarke, Irwin.

SOUTHERN, EILEEN (1997). *The Music of Black Americans*, 3rd edn. New York: W. W. Norton.

SPANN, GLENN (2005). 'Theological Transition within Methodism: The Rise of Liberalism and the Conservative Response'. *Methodist History* 43: 198–225.

STANLEY, BRIAN (2001). 'Christianity and Civilization in English Evangelical Mission Thought'. In Brian Stanley (ed.), *Christian Missions and the Enlightenment*. Grand Rapids: Eerdmans.

TELFORD, JOHN (ed.) (n.d.). *Wesley's Veterans*. London: Robert Culley.

THOMPSON, E. P. (1963). *The Making of the English Working Class.* London: Gollancz.

THORNLEY, ANDREW (2002). *Exodus of the I Taukei: The Wesleyan Church in Fiji, 1848–74.* Suva, Fiji: Institute of Pacific Studies, University of the South Pacific.

TURBERFIELD, ALAN (2003). *John Scott Lidgett: Archbishop of British Methodism?* Peterborough: Epworth.

UNWIN, Mrs GEORGE, and TELFORD, JOHN (1930). *Mark Guy Pearse: Preacher, Author, Artist.* London: Epworth.

VALENZE, DEBORAH M. (1985). *Prophetic Sons and Daughters: Female Preaching and Popular Religion in Industrial England.* Princeton: Princeton University Press.

WAKEFIELD, GORDON S. (1966). *Methodist Devotion: Spiritual Life in the Methodist Tradition.* London: Epworth.

—— (1971). *Robert Newton Flew, 1886–1962.* London: Epworth.

WAKELIN, MICHAEL (1996). *J. Arthur Rank: The Man Behind the Gong.* Oxford: Lion.

WALLS, ANDREW (1996). *The Missionary Movement in Christian History: Studies in the Transmission of Faith.* New York: Orbis.

WALSHAM, ALEXANDRA (1999). *Providence in Early Modern England.* Oxford: Oxford University Press.

WATSON, RICHARD (1836). *The Works of the Rev. Richard Watson,* ix. London: John Mason.

WESLEY, JOHN (1975). *The Works of John Wesley,* xi. *The Appeals to Men of Reason and Religion and Certain Related Open Letters,* ed. G. R. Cragg. Oxford: Clarendon.

WIGGER, JOHN H. (1998). *Taking Heaven by Storm: Methodism and the Rise of Popular Christianity in America.* New York: Oxford University Press.

WOOLSEY, ELIJAH (1852). *The Supernumerary: Or Lights and Shadows of Itinerancy.* New York: Lane & Scott.

Index